Social Structure Theory	Social Process Theory	Critical Theory	Developmental Theory	
				Life Course	Latent Trait
	Sociological Theory		Marxist/Conflict Theory	Multifactor Theory	
	Clifford R. Shaw & Henry D. McKay; Walter Miller; Albert Cohen; Richard Cloward & Lloyd Ohlin	Edwin Sutherland; Travis H[illegible] Edwin [illegible] Howard [illegible]	Willem Bonger; Ralf Dahrendorf; [illegible]	Sheldon & Eleanor Glueck; John Laub & Robert Sampson	James Q. Wilson & Richard Herrnstein; Travis Hirschi & Michael Gottfredson
	1920s to Present	1930[illegible]	[illegible]	[illegible]930s to Present	1980s to Present
	Social and economic forces are the key determinants of criminal behavior patterns. Crime is the result of an individual's location within the structure of society.	Crimin[illegible] of the [illegible] individ[illegible] crimin[illegible] of grou[illegible] sociali[illegible]	[illegible]	[illegible] people go through the life [illegible]urse, social and personal [illegible]its undergo change and [illegible]luence behavior.	A master trait that controls human development interacts with criminal opportunity.
	Social Disorganization Theory; Strain Theory; Anomie Theory; Institutional Anomie; General Strain Theory (GST); Cultural Deviance Theory; Theory of Delinquent Subcultures; Theory of Differential Opportunity	Social [illegible] Differe[illegible] Differe[illegible] Theory[illegible] Social [illegible] Theory[illegible]	[illegible]	[illegible]cial Development Model; [illegible]teractional Theory; General [illegible]eory of Crime and Delin[illegible]ency; Age-Graded Theory	General Theory of Crime (GTC); Integrated Cognitive Antisocial Potential (ICAP) Theory; Differential Coercion Theory; Control Balance Theory
	Poverty; transitional neighborhoods; concentric zones; subculture; cultural transmission; social ecology; collective efficacy; relative deprivation; anomie; conduct norms; focal concerns; differential opportunity	Sociali[illegible] family relations; differential association; techniques of neutralization; self-concept; social bond; stigma; retrospective reading; primary and secondary deviance	[illegible] marginalization; capitalism; social class; globalization; left realism; exploitation; patriarchy; restorative justice; social justice; reintegrative shaming; restoration	[illegible]oblem behavior syndrome; pathways to crime; turning points; social capital	Impulsive personality; low self-control; latent traits

© AP/Harry Cabluck

Resources that help you excel in your criminology course!

The resource-packed Book Companion Website: www.thomsonedu.com/criminaljustice/siegel

Interactive *Pre-Tests* for every chapter help you identify areas where you need to focus your study time. Specific page references direct you to places in the text where you'll find the answers to questions you answered incorrectly. *Post-Tests* help you monitor your progress. The site also includes Internet and InfoTrac® College Edition exercises, links to criminology and other criminal justice sites, flash cards, and glossary—all organized by textbook chapter.

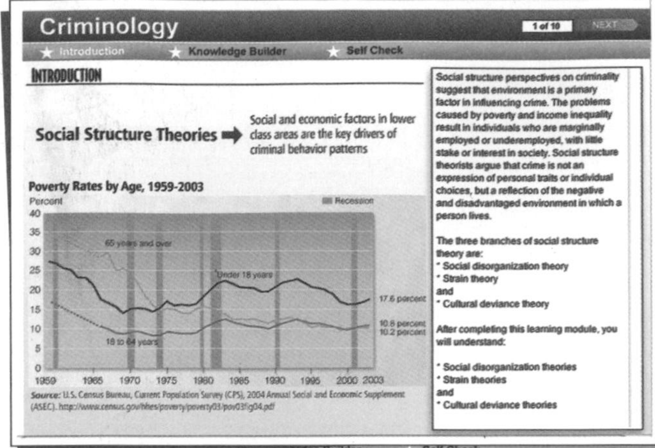

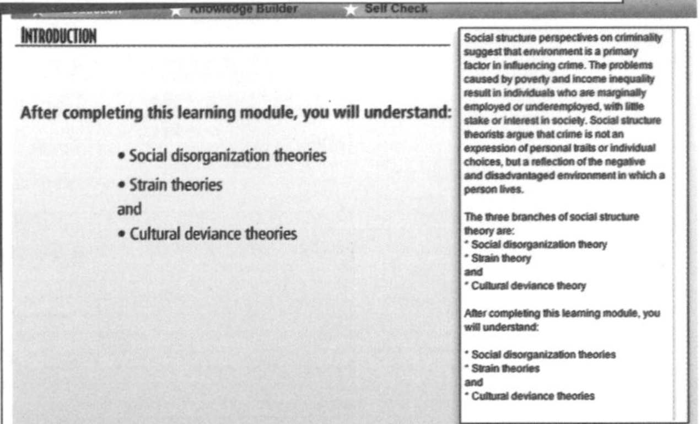

NEW! Thomson Audio Study Products for Siegel's *Criminology: The Core*

Simply load these files into your digital music player and you can review course material while walking to class, driving, working out—whenever it's impossible or inconvenient to read! The audio files for each chapter of this textbook include chapter summaries, key concept reviews, quizzing, and glossary materials. For more information, go to www.thomsonedu.com.

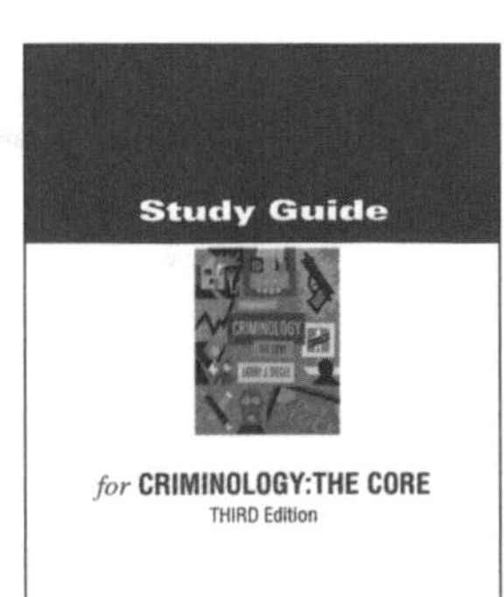

Study Guide

Helping you study efficiently

The *Study Guide* includes a variety of pedagogical aids that help you do your best on exams, as well art and figures from the main text. Each text chapter is outlined and summarized, major terms and figures are defined, and self-tests are provided for review. **0-495-10001-3**

CRIMINOLOGY

THE CORE

THIRD EDITION

CRIMINOLOGY

THE CORE

Larry J. Siegel

University of Massachusetts, Lowell

Australia • Brazil • Canada • Mexico • Singapore • Spain
United Kingdom • United States

Criminology: The Core, Third Edition
Larry J. Siegel

Acquisitions Editor, Criminal Justice: Chris Caldeira
Development Editor: Shelley Murphy
Assistant Editor: Christina Ho
Editorial Assistant: Tali Beesley
Technology Project Manager: Amanda Kaufmann
Marketing Manager: Terra Schultz
Marketing Assistant: Emily Elrod
Marketing Communications Manager: Tami Strang
Project Manager, Editorial Production: Jennie Redwitz
Creative Director: Rob Hugel
Art Director: Vernon Boes
Print Buyer: Becky Cross
Permissions Editor: Bob Kauser
Production Service: Linda Jupiter, Jupiter Productions
Text Designer: Diane Beasley
Photo Researcher: Linda Rill
Copy Editor: Judith Brown
Proofreader: Mary Kanable
Illustrators: John and Judy Waller
Indexer: Medea Minnich
Cover Designer: Hatty Lee, Yvo Riezebos Design
Cover Image: Noah Woods
Compositor: Pre-Press Company
Text and Cover Printer: Courier Corporation/Kendallville

Printed in the United States of America

1 2 3 4 5 6 7 11 10 09 08 07

Library of Congress Control Number: 2006929282

ISBN-13: 978-0-495-09477-7
ISBN-10: 0-495-09477-3

Thomson Higher Education
10 Davis Drive
Belmont, CA 94002–3098
USA

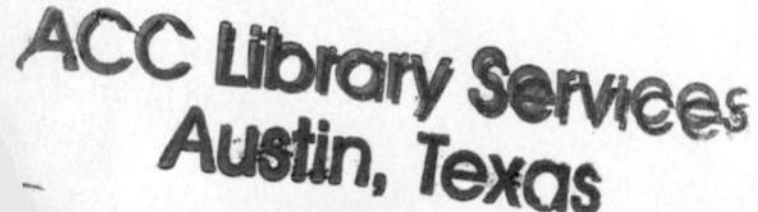

This book is dedicated to my kids, Eric, Andrew, Julie, and Rachel, and to my grandkids, Jack, Kayla, and Brooke

About the Author

LARRY J. SIEGEL was born in the Bronx in 1947. While living on Jerome Avenue and attending City College of New York in the 1960s, he was swept up in the social and political currents of the time. He became intrigued with the influence contemporary culture had on individual behavior: Did people shape society or did society shape people? He applied his interest in social forces and human behavior to the study of crime and justice. After graduating CCNY, he attended the newly opened program in criminal justice at the State University of New York at Albany, earning both his M.A. and Ph.D. degrees there. After completing his graduate work, Dr. Siegel began his teaching career at Northeastern University, where he was a faculty member for nine years. After leaving Northeastern, he held teaching positions at the University of Nebraska–Omaha and Saint Anselm College in New Hampshire. He is currently a professor at the University of Massachusetts–Lowell. Dr. Siegel has written extensively in the area of crime and justice, including books on juvenile law, delinquency, criminology, criminal justice, and criminal procedure. He is a court certified expert on police conduct and has testified in numerous legal cases. The father of four and grandfather of three, Larry Siegel and his wife, Terry, now reside in Bedford, New Hampshire, with their two dogs, Watson and Cody.

Brief Contents

PART 1 CONCEPTS OF CRIME, LAW, AND CRIMINOLOGY

PART 2 THEORIES OF CRIME CAUSATION

PART 3 CRIME TYPOLOGIES

PART 4 THE CRIMINAL JUSTICE SYSTEM

Contents

PART 1 CONCEPTS OF CRIME, LAW, AND CRIMINOLOGY

CHAPTER 3

Victims and Victimization 52

PART 2 THEORIES OF CRIME CAUSATION

CHAPTER 4

Choice Theory: Because They Want To 71

CHAPTER 5

Trait Theory: It's in Their Blood 92

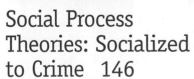

CHAPTER 9

Developmental Theories: Things Change . . . or Do They? 197

PART 3 CRIME TYPOLOGIES

CHAPTER 10

Violent Crime 223

CHAPTER 11

Property Crimes 257

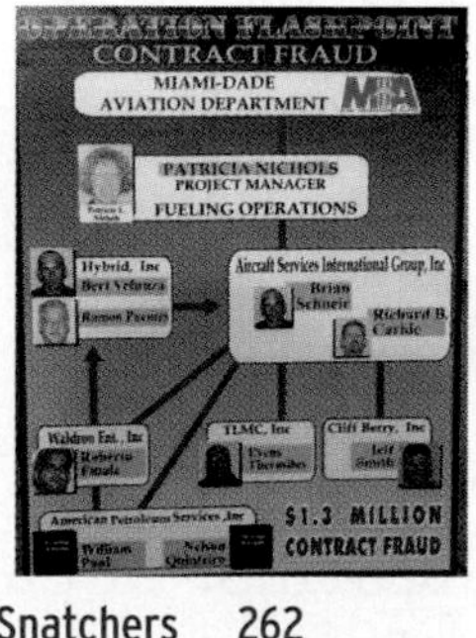

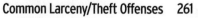

CHAPTER 12

Enterprise Crime: White-Collar Crime, Cyber Crime, and Organized Crime 279

CHAPTER 13

Public Order Crimes 310

PART 4 THE CRIMINAL JUSTICE SYSTEM

Preface

On May 26, 2006, James Paul Lewis, Jr., the former director of Orange County, California–based Financial Advisory Consultants (FAC), was sentenced to 30 years in federal prison for running a massive Ponzi scheme that raised more than $300 million and caused more than 1,600 victims to lose more than $156 million of their hard-earned money. What exactly did James Lewis do to earn a 30-year prison sentence? He offered investors opportunities to invest in two mutual funds. Through false and fraudulent brochures and other promotional material issued by FAC, he told investors that they would earn annual rates of return of up to 18 percent in an Income Fund, which claimed to generate revenue from the leasing of medical equipment, commercial lending and financing of insurance premiums, and 40 percent annual returns in a Growth Fund, which claimed to generate revenue through the purchase and sale of distressed businesses. Instead of using the investors' money as promised, Lewis used the funds to purchase several homes in California and Connecticut. He also used investors' money to purchase luxury automobiles for himself, his wife, and his girlfriend. Among other schemes, he used investors' money to trade currency futures, managing to lose at least $22 million. To conceal the scheme at FAC, Lewis used what is known as a Ponzi scheme: He took the money of new investors (and new purchases of those who had already bought into the funds) to pay the rates of return promised to investors. In other words, he used the principal to pay the interest! That is, until the money ran out. At one point, nearly 3,300 investors had a total balance of $813,932,080 in the funds, but FAC and Lewis's bank accounts held only slightly more than $2 million. At his sentencing hearing, U.S. District Judge Cormac J. Carney ordered Lewis to pay $156 million in restitution. Because many of his victims were elderly, Judge Carney described the scheme as a "crime against humanity." Several victims told the court about their losses, which included life savings and college funds. Many victims described being forced to go back to work after losing their retirement savings in the scheme.*

It is not surprising, considering the magnitude of criminal enterprises such as James Lewis's Ponzi scheme, that many Americans are concerned about crime and are worried about becoming the victims of fraud, violent crime, and theft. We alter our behavior to limit the risk of victimization and question whether legal punishment alone can control criminal offenders. We watch movies about law firms, clients, fugitives, and stone-cold killers. We are shocked by the graphic accounts of school shootings, police brutality, and sexual assaults that we see in the news media.

I, too, have had a life-long interest in crime, law, and justice. Why do people behave the way they do? What causes a person such as James Lewis to cheat people out of their life savings, while another channels his or her energy into work, school, and family? Why are some adolescents able to resist the "temptation of the streets" and become law-abiding citizens, while others join gangs and enter into a criminal career? Conversely, what accounts for the behavior of the multimillionaire who cheats on his or her taxes or engages in fraudulent schemes? If Lewis had the ability to raise hundreds of millions of dollars, why couldn't he have run a legitimate financial enterprise? And what should be done with convicted criminals? Should we put Lewis into prison for 30 years? He is not a danger to anyone (except investors). Does his severe punishment deter others who might be contemplating a get-rich-quick fraudulent investment scheme?

GOALS OF THIS BOOK

For the past 35 years I have been able to channel this interest into a career as a teacher of criminology. My goal in writing this book is to help students generate the same enthusiasm for criminology that has sustained me during my teaching career. What could be more important or fascinating than a field of study that deals with such wide-ranging topics as the motivation for mass murder, the effects of violent media on young people, drug abuse, and organized crime? Criminology is a dynamic field, changing constantly with the release of major research studies, Supreme Court rulings, and governmental policy. Its dynamism and diversity make it an important and engrossing area of study. It all comes down to this: Why do people do the things they do? How can we explain the intricacies and diversity of human behavior?

Because interest in crime and justice is so great and so timely, this book is designed to review these ongoing issues and cover the field of criminology in an organized and comprehensive manner. It is meant as a broad overview of the field, designed to whet the reader's appetite and encourage further and more in-depth exploration. Several major themes recur throughout the book.

Competing Viewpoints

One reason that the study of criminology is so important is that debates continue over the nature and extent of crime and the causes and prevention of criminality. Some view criminals as society's victims who are forced to violate the law because of poverty and lack of opportunity. Others view aggressive, antisocial behavior as a product of mental and physical abnormalities, present at birth or soon after, which are stable over the life course. Still another view is that crime is a function of the rational choice of greedy, selfish people who can only be deterred through the threat of harsh punishments. The chapters in this book explore how different theoretical frameworks cover different aspects of criminology. Students are helped in this regard by concept summary boxes that compare different viewpoints, showing both their main points and their strengths.

Critical Thinking

It is important for students to think critically about law and justice and to develop a critical perspective toward the social institutions and legal institutions entrusted with crime control. Throughout the book, students are asked to critique research highlighted in boxed material and to think outside the box. To aid in this task, each chapter ends with a feature called Thinking Like a Criminologist, which presents a scenario that can be analyzed with the help of material found in the chapter. There are also critical thinking questions to guide classroom interaction.

Diversity and Cross-Cultural Comparisons

Because diversity is a key issue in the field of criminology, issues of racial, ethnic, gender, and cultural diversity are integrated throughout the book and are highlighted in several *Race, Culture, Gender, & Criminology* boxed features. I discuss gender issues such as the rising rate of female criminality, cross-cultural comparisons on global and international issues such as the use of the death penalty around the world, and racial issues such as how race influences sentencing in criminal courts (covered in depth in Chapter 14).

Current Theory and Research

Throughout the book, every attempt is made to use the most current research to show students major trends in criminological research and policy. Most people who use the book have told me that this is one of its strongest features. I have attempted to present current research in a balanced fashion, though this sometimes can be frustrating to students. Although it is comforting to reach an unequivocal conclusion about an important topic, sometimes that is simply not possible. In an effort to be objective and fair, each side of significant criminological debates is presented in full. Throughout the book, *Current Issues in Crime* boxes review research in criminology. For example, in Chapter 2, a box called "Explaining Crime Trends" discusses research that helps explain why crime rates rise and fall.

Social Policy

There is a focus on social policy throughout the book so that students can see how criminological theory has been translated into crime prevention programs. Because of this theme, *Policy & Practice in Criminology* boxes are included to show how criminological ideas and research can be put into action. For example, a *Policy & Practice in Criminology* box called "The Legacy of Reentry" in Chapter 14 discusses the long-term effects of an increasing prison population. It presents the rather provocative view that rather than deterring or preventing crime, imprisoning large numbers of offenders has an opposing effect: It causes the crime rate to increase. What is the cause of this unexpected phenomenon?

In sum, the primary goals in writing this book are as follows:

- To provide students with a thorough knowledge of criminology and show its diversity and intellectual content
- To be as thorough and up-to-date as possible
- To be objective and unbiased
- To describe current theories, crime types, and methods of social control, and analyze their strengths and weaknesses
- To show how criminological thought has influenced social policy

TOPIC AREAS

Criminology: The Core is a thorough introduction to this fascinating field and intended for students in introductory courses in criminology. It is divided into four main sections or topic areas.

Section 1 provides a framework for studying criminology. The first chapter defines the field and discusses its most basic concepts: the definition of crime, the component areas of criminology, the history of criminology, the concept of criminal law, and the ethical issues that confront the field. Chapter 2 covers criminological research methods and the nature, extent, and patterns of crime. Chapter 3 is devoted to the concept of victimization, including the nature of victims, theories of victimization, and programs designed to help crime victims.

Section 2 contains six chapters that cover criminological theory: Why do people behave the way they do? Why do they commit crimes? These views focus on choice (Chapter 4); biological and psychological traits (Chapter 5); social structure and culture (Chapter 6); social process and socialization (Chapter 7); social conflict (Chapter 8); and human development (Chapter 9).

Section 3 is devoted to the major forms of criminal behavior. The chapters in this section cover violent crime (Chapter 10); common theft offenses (Chapter 11); white-collar crime, cyber crime, and organized crime (Chapter 12); and public order crimes, including sex offenses and substance abuse (Chapter 13).

Section 4 contains one chapter that covers the criminal justice system. It provides an overview of the entire justice system, including the process of justice, the major organizations that make up the justice system, and concepts and perspectives of justice.

Goals and Objectives

The book has been carefully structured to cover relevant material in a comprehensive, balanced, and objective fashion and to make the presentation of material interesting and contemporary. No single political or theoretical position dominates the book; instead, the many diverse views that are contained within criminology and characterize its interdisciplinary nature are presented. The book not only includes analysis of the most important scholarly works and scientific research reports, but also includes a great deal of topical information on recent cases and events, such as the Mumia Abu-Jamal case and the conviction of style guru Martha Stewart for securities-related crimes.

WHAT IS NEW IN THIS EDITION

Chapter One, *Crime and Criminology,* now begins with a vignette describing how one man used the Internet to engage in sex with children and how he was apprehended by the FBI. There is a new *Profiles in Crime* feature entitled "The Mother of All Snakeheads" that tells the story of Cheng Chui Ping, one of the most powerful underworld figures in New York. A new section on ethics in criminology has also been added to Chapter 1 for this edition.

Chapter Two, *The Nature and Extent of Crime,* has a new *Profiles in Crime* feature entitled "FEMA Fraud," about an effort to take advantage of the Hurricane Katrina tragedy. The latest data have been added from the Monitoring the Future study, the National Crime Victimization Survey, and the Uniform Crime Report. These are the focus of a new *Concept Summary* on data collection methods. The *Policy & Practice in Criminology* box on gun control has been updated.

Chapter Three, *Victims and Victimization,* starts with the story of Imette St. Guillen, a young graduate student brutally murdered in New York City. A *Profiles in Crime* feature, "Jesse Timmendequas and Megan's Law" (Megan Kanka story), discusses how the death of a young New Jersey girl led to the development of laws for registration of sex offenders. A new *Policy & Practice in Criminology* box discusses victims' rights in Europe.

Chapter Four, *Choice Theory: Because They Want To,* now opens with the story of Johnny Ray Gasca, "Prince of Pirates," who made a career out of pirating new videos in order to sell them on the Internet. A new *Profiles in Crime* box, "Copping the Cappers," discusses an intricate case of Medicare fraud. The chapter includes another new *Current Issues in Crime* feature on the deterrent effect of the death penalty.

Chapter Five, Trait Theory: *It's in Their Blood,* discusses the latest findings from the Minnesota Study of Twins Reared Apart. A new *Profiles in Crime* feature focuses on Andrea Yates, the young mother who drowned her children. There are also updated sections on diet and crime and mental illness and crime. A review of oppositional defiant disorder (ODD) and its effect on criminality is included in this chapter.

Chapter Six, *Social Structure Theory: Because They're Poor,* begins with a new vignette discussing how Los Angeles gangs are moving to El Salvador and causing unrest in that country. Expanded coverage of community cohesion shows how it influences crime rates, and the concept of collective efficacy is also explored in greater depth. There is new information on the neighborhood context of policing, as well as the association of neighborhood structure and parenting processes. A section exploring neighborhood ecology and victimization is new to this edition. And a *Race, Culture, Gender, & Criminology* feature, "The Code of the Streets," is new to Chapter 6.

Chapter Seven, *Social Process Theories: Socialized to Crime,* begins with a new vignette on the Littleton, Colorado, school shootings. A *Current Issues in Crime* boxed feature called "When Being Good Is Bad" provides a new and provocative take on neutralization theory. The chapter reviews a number of new research studies examining the effects of socialization on criminality. The importance of family and school in shaping adolescent deviance is discussed, including the effects of being bullied in school and being a social outcast. A *Profiles in Crime* feature has been added to this chapter telling the strange case of Jesse James

Hollywood ("Alpha Dog"), soon to be the subject of a major motion picture. The sections on stigma, labeling, and delinquency have all been updated for this edition.

Chapter Eight, *Critical Criminology: It's a Class Thing,* opens with a new vignette on the Paris riots that rocked the nation in November 2005. It now includes a major section on the effects of globalization on crime and well-being. Research on a wide variety of conflict theory topics, including the effects of racial profiling and whether human empathy can transform the justice system, is included in Chapter 8. There is a fascinating new *Profiles in Crime* feature on Mumia Abu-Jamal, the former radical who has been incarcerated on charges that his supporters believe were racially and politically motivated.

Chapter Nine, *Developmental Theories: Things Change . . . or Do They?,* now begins with the shocking Xbox murder case. New material on how marriage helps reduce the likelihood of chronic offending is included. And new research covering such topics as childhood predictors of offense trajectories; stability and change in antisocial behavior; the relationship of childhood and adolescent factors to offending trajectories; the intergenerational transmission of antisocial behavior; and the relationship between race, life circumstances, and criminal activity is also included in Chapter 9.

Chapter Ten, *Violent Crime,* has expanded coverage on the causes of violence. It opens with a new vignette on the well-known case of Natalee Holloway, the young student who disappeared while on a trip to Aruba. There are new *Profiles in Crime* boxes on Osama Bin Laden and the serial killer known as the "Angel of Death." A new *Current Issues in Crime* box looks at modern forms of terrorism. "Spree killers" is the topic of a new section in Chapter 10, and there is new coverage of the psychological and social learning views of rape causation. Rape law change has been updated with a new section on consent. The sections on murder and homicide have been expanded, including new material on who is at risk to become a school shooter. There is also new coverage of the causes of child abuse and parental abuse, a new section on acquaintance robbery, and expanded material on hate crimes and stalking, including cyber stalking. Cyber terrorism is now covered in Chapter 10, as well.

Chapter Eleven, *Property Crimes,* now begins with a vignette on a couple who lived a life of luxury financed at the expense of thousands of victims through credit card fraud. There is a new *Profiles in Crime* box on body snatchers—people who sell organs taken from dead bodies—and the havoc they cause. New material on shoplifting, including its estimated costs, has been added. The section on auto theft now lists the cars and car parts crooks love best, and why, according to the National Insurance Crime Bureau. There is expanded coverage of credit card theft and what is being done to control the problem. New material on burglary, including repeat burglary, has been added, and a new *Current Issues in Crime* box, "Confessions of a Dying Thief," describes the memoirs of a long-time fence.

Chapter Twelve, *Enterprise Crime: White-Collar Crime, Cyber Crime, and Organized Crime,* reflects the growing importance of cyber crimes and cyber criminals. Cyber crimes involve people using the instruments of modern technology for criminal purposes. Among the topics now covered are Internet securities fraud and identity theft, file sharing and warez. There are new sections on cyber crime enforcement issues and a new *Current Issues in Crime* feature on controlling cyber vandalism that covers efforts now being made to control computer- and Internet-based criminal activities. A new *Profiles in Crime* box on the Enron, Tyco, and WorldCom cases has been added to Chapter 12, as well as a new *Race, Culture, Gender, & Criminology* feature on Russian organized crime.

Chapter Thirteen, *Public Order Crimes,* begins with the recent story of a successful Dallas businessman, Tom Malin, whose ill-fated campaign for public office derailed when the news got out that he had been involved in a gay escort service, illustrating the concerns the public and the media have with issues of morality and values. More information concerning moral crusades and moral crusaders has been added to the chapter, with examples of recent moral crusades being mounted in this country and internationally. New material has been added regarding changes in the distribution of pornography via the Internet. Chapter 13 has expanded coverage of the international trade in prostitution, cyber prostitution, child prostitution, and new information about the problems faced daily in the lives of prostitutes. The latest data are also included on drug use and the association between substance abuse and crime, as well as a new *Profiles in Crime* feature on the life of a New York City drug trafficker.

Chapter Fourteen, *The Criminal Justice System*, has the latest material on important criminal justice issues within policing, courts, and corrections. Data have been updated on the number of people behind bars, and recent trends in the correctional population are discussed. New material on race and justice has been added, including the influence of race in sentencing decisions. And there is a new *Profiles in Crime* box, "Mafia Cops," about two police detectives who worked as hit men for the mob.

FEATURES

This book contains different kinds of pedagogy that help students analyze material in greater depth and also link it to other material in the book:

- ***Current Issues in Crime*** boxed inserts review important issues in criminology. For example, in Chapter 2, the feature "Explaining Crime Trends" discusses the social and political factors that cause crime rates to rise and fall. And in Chapter 4, a new *Current Issues in Crime* box explores the question, "Does Capital Punishment Deter Murder?"
- ***Policy & Practice in Criminology*** boxes show how criminological ideas and research can be put into action. A *Policy & Practice in Criminology* box in Chapter 2, "Should Guns Be Controlled?" examines the pros and cons of the gun control debate, and a new *Policy & Practice in Criminology* feature in Chapter 3 explores victims' rights in Europe.
- ***Race, Culture, Gender, & Criminology*** boxes cover issues of racial, sexual, and cultural diversity. For example, in Chapter 6, a *Race, Culture, Gender, & Criminology* box, "Bridging the Racial Divide," discusses the work and thoughts of William Julius Wilson, one of the nation's leading sociologists, on racial problems and racial politics in American society. A new feature in Chapter 6, "The Code of the Streets," explores the interrelationship between culture and behavior and the cultural forces that run through neighborhoods to shape reactions to risk of crime and deviant behavior.

Each of these boxes is accompanied by critical thinking questions and links to articles in the InfoTrac College Edition Research online database. In addition to these boxes, there are several other recurring features:

- ***Profiles in Crime*** (**NEW** in this edition) are designed to present students with case studies of actual criminals and crimes to help illustrate the position or views within the chapter. For example, in the chapter on victimization, Chapter 3, a *Profiles in Crime* box entitled "Jesse Timmendequas and Megan's Law" discusses the horrendous murder of young Megan Kanka and the effect it had on protecting victims from sex offenders.
- ***Connections*** are brief inserts that help link the material to other areas covered in the book. For example, a *Connections* box in Chapter 11 shows how efforts to control theft offenses are linked to the choice theory of crime discussed in Chapter 4.
- ***Checkpoints*** appear at the end of each major section throughout each chapter of the book and review the key concepts of the section to reinforce the chapter's learning objectives.

- ***Chapter Outlines*** provide a roadmap to coverage and serve as a useful review tool.
- ***Chapter Objectives*** help students get the most out of the chapter coverage.
- A ***running glossary*** in the margins ensures that students understand words and concepts as they are introduced.
- ***Thinking Like a Criminologist*** sections near the end of each chapter present challenging questions or issues in a hypothetical scenario-based activity that students must use their criminological knowledge to answer or confront. Applying the information learned in the book will help students begin to "think like criminologists." For example, the scenario in Chapter 6 challenges students to imagine they have a position as an assistant to the undersecretary of urban affairs in Washington, and propose an urban redevelopment plan and recommend programs to revitalize an inner-city neighborhood and bring down the crime rate.
- Each chapter ends with ***Critical Thinking Questions***, to help develop students' analytical abilities, and a list of ***Key Terms***.

ANCILLARIES

The most extensive package of supplemental aids available for a criminal justice textbook accompanies this edition. Many separate items have been developed to enhance the course and to assist instructors and students. They are available to qualified adopters. Please consult your local sales representative for details.

For the Instructor

Instructor's Edition Designed just for instructors, the Instructor's Edition includes a visual walkthrough that illustrates the key pedagogical features of the book, as well as the media and supplements that accompany it. Use this handy tool to quickly learn about the many options this book provides to help you keep your instruction engaging and informative.

Instructor's Resource Manual with Test Bank An improved and completely updated *Instructor's Resource Manual with Test Bank* has been developed by Anthony LaRose of the University of Tampa. The manual includes learning objectives, detailed chapter outlines, key terms, discussion topics and student activities, distance learning activities, Internet connections, film suggestions and assignments, and a test bank. Each chapter's test bank contains questions in multiple choice, true-false, fill-in-the-blank, and essay format, with a full answer key, including the page numbers in the main textbook where the answers can be found. All test bank questions were peer-reviewed by an editorial board to ensure the highest quality. The Resource Integration Guide within the manual will help you to maximize your use of the rich supplements package that comes with the book through integrating media, Internet, video, and other resources. The *Instructor's Resource Manual* is backed up by ExamView, a computerized test bank available for Windows and Macintosh computers.

ExamView® Computerized Testing Create, deliver, and customize tests and study guides (both print and online) in minutes with this easy-to-use assessment and tutorial system. ExamView offers both a Quick Test Wizard and an Online Test Wizard that guide you step-by-step through the process of creating tests. You can build tests of up to 250 questions using up to 12 question types. Using ExamView's complete word processing capabilities, you can enter an unlimited number of new questions or edit existing questions.

Instructor's PowerLecture CD This instructor resource includes Microsoft® PowerPoint® lecture slides with graphics from the textbook, making it easy for you to assemble, edit, publish, and present custom lectures for your course. The PowerLecture

CD also includes video-based polling and quiz questions that can be used with the JoinIn on TurningPoint personal response system, and integrates ExamView testing software for customizing tests of up to 250 items that can be delivered in print or online. Finally—all of your media teaching resources in one place!

WebTutor™ ToolBox on Blackboard® and WebCT® A powerful combination: easy-to-use course management tools with content from this book's rich companion website all in one place. You can use ToolBox as is, from the moment you log on, or, if you prefer, customize the program with Web links, images, and other resources.

JoinIn™ on TurningPoint Enhance the way your students interact with you, your lecture, and each other. This exciting new response system supplement allows you to transform your classroom and assess student progress with instant in-class quizzes and polls. The TurningPoint software lets you pose book-specific questions and display students' answers seamlessly within the Microsoft® PowerPoint® slides of your own lecture, in conjunction with the "clicker" hardware of your choice.

The Wadsworth Criminal Justice Video Library So many exciting, new videos—so many great ways to enrich your lectures and spark discussion of the material in this book. View our full video offerings and download clip lists with running times at www.cj.wadsworth.com/videos. Your Thomson Wadsworth representative will be happy to provide details on our video policy by adoption size. The library includes these selections and many others:

- *ABC® Videos*: These brief, high-interest clips from current news events as well as historic raw footage going back 40 years are perfect for discussion starters or to enrich your lectures and spark interest in the material in the book. The videos provide students with a new lens through which to view the past and present, one that will greatly enhance their knowledge and understanding of significant events and open new dimensions in learning. Clips are drawn from such programs as *World News Tonight*, *Good Morning America*, *This Week*, *PrimeTime Live*, *20/20*, and *Nightline*, as well as numerous ABC News specials and material from the Associated Press Television News and British Movietone News collections. Your Thomson Wadsworth representative will be happy to provide a complete listing of videos and policies.
- *60 Minutes DVD*: Featuring 12-minute clips from CBS's *60 Minutes* news program, this DVD lets you explore a topic in more depth with your students without taking up a full class session. Topics include the Green River Killer, the reliability of DNA testing, and California's Three Strikes Law. (Produced by Wadsworth, CBS, and Films for the Humanities.)
- *The Wadsworth Custom Videos for Criminal Justice*: Produced by Wadsworth and Films for the Humanities, these videos include five- to ten-minute segments that encourage classroom discussion. Topics include white-collar crime, domestic violence, forensics, suicide and the police officer, the court process, the history of corrections, prison society, and juvenile justice.
- *Oral History Project*: Developed in association with the American Society of Criminology, the Academy of Criminal Justice Society, and the National Institute of Justice, these videos will help you introduce your students to the scholars who have developed the criminal justice discipline. Compiled over the last several years, each video features a set of Guest Lecturers—scholars whose thinking has helped to build the foundation of present ideas in the discipline. Vol. 1: Moments in Time; Vol. 2: Great Moments in Criminological Theory; Vol. 3: Research Methods.
- *Court TV Videos*: One-hour videos presenting seminal and high-profile cases, such as the interrogation of Michael Crowe and serial killer Ted Bundy, as well as crucial and current issues such as cyber crime, double jeopardy, and the management of the prison on Riker's Island.

- *A&E American Justice*: Forty videos to choose from, on topics such as deadly force, women on death row, juvenile justice, strange defenses, and Alcatraz.
- *Films for the Humanities*: Nearly 200 videos to choose from on a variety of topics such as elder abuse, supermax prisons, suicide and the police officer, the making of an FBI agent, domestic violence, and more . . .

For the Student

Pre- and Post-Tests on the Web This personalized plan focuses students' study time on the concepts they need to master. Students will have access to our pre- and post-tests on the free companion website. These tests allow students to determine where they still need help in order to perform well on exams. Students take a pretest, and the diagnostic tool tells them exactly where to go in the book to get help in areas where they are not performing well.

Study Guide An extensive student guide has been developed and updated for this edition by Anthony LaRose of the University of Tampa. Because students learn in different ways, the guide includes a variety of pedagogical aids to help them, as well as integrated art and figures from the main textbook. Each chapter is outlined and summarized, major terms and figures are defined, and self-tests are provided.

Companion Website www.thomsonedu.com/criminaljustice/siegel This book-specific website provides many chapter-specific resources, such as outlines and summaries, glossary, flash cards, Internet activities, and tutorial quizzing. The site also features multistep learning modules (concept builders) that present key concepts with animations and activities followed by multiple-choice questions for students to apply their knowledge and critical thinking skills.

The Wadsworth Criminal Justice Resource Center www.thomsonedu.com/criminaljustice Designed with the instructor in mind, this website features information about Thomson Wadsworth's technology and teaching solutions, as well as several features created specifically for today's criminal justice student. Supreme Court updates, timelines, and hot-topic polling can all be used to supplement in-class assignments and discussions. You'll also find a wealth of links to careers and news in criminal justice, book-specific sites, and much more.

Careers in Criminal Justice Website www.thomsonedu.com This website helps students investigate and focus on the criminal justice career choices that are right for them through several outstanding features.

- Career Profiles feature video testimonials from a variety of practicing professionals in the field and information on many criminal justice careers, including job descriptions, requirements, training, salary and benefits, and the application process.
- Interest Assessment helps students decide which careers suit their personalities and interests.
- Career Planner features résumé writing tips and worksheets, interviewing techniques, and successful job search strategies.
- Links for Reference offer direct links to federal, state, and local agencies where students can get contact information and learn more about current job opportunities.

Wadsworth's Guide to Careers in Criminal Justice, Third Edition This handy guide, compiled by Caridad Sanchez-Leguelinel, of John Jay College of Criminal Justice, gives students information on a wide variety of career paths, including requirements, salaries, training, contact information for key agencies, and employment outlooks.

Handbook of Selected Supreme Court Cases, Third Edition This supplementary book provides briefs of key cases that have defined the administration of justice in this country, along with citations and commentary.

Current Perspectives: Readings from InfoTrac College Edition These readers, designed to give students deeper insight into special topics in criminal justice, include free access to InfoTrac College Edition. Experts in each topic select the timely articles from within InfoTrac. They are available free when bundled with the textbook.

- *Terrorism and Homeland Security*
- *Juvenile Justice*
- *Public Policy*

Terrorism: An Interdisciplinary Perspective Available for bundling with each copy of *Criminology: The Core*, Third Edition, this 80-page booklet (with companion website) discusses terrorism in general and the issues surrounding the events of September 11, 2001. This information-packed booklet examines the origins of terrorism in the Middle East, focusing on Osama bin Laden in particular, as well as issues involving bioterrorism, the specific role played by religion in Middle Eastern terrorism, globalization as it relates to terrorism, and the reactions and repercussions of terrorist attacks.

Crime Scenes 2.0: An Interactive Criminal Justice CD-ROM Recipient of several *New Media Magazine* Invision Awards, this interactive CD-ROM allows students to take on the roles of investigating officer, lawyer, parole officer, and judge in excitingly realistic scenarios. Available FREE when bundled with every copy of *Criminology: The Core*, Third Edition. An online instructor's manual is also available for the CD-ROM.

Mind of a Killer CD-ROM *(bundle version)* Voted one of the top 100 CD-ROMs by an annual *PC Magazine* survey, *Mind of a Killer* gives students a chilling glimpse into the realm of serial killers, with over 80 minutes of video and 3D simulations, and extensive mapping system, a library, and much more.

Internet Guide for Criminal Justice, Second Edition Internet beginners will appreciate this helpful booklet. With explanations and the vocabulary necessary for navigating the Web, it features customized information on criminal justice–related websites and presents Internet project ideas.

Internet Activities for Criminal Justice, Second Edition This completely revised 96-page booklet shows how to best use the Internet for research through searches and activities.

Criminal Justice Internet Explorer, Third Edition This colorful brochure lists the most popular Internet addresses for criminal justice–related websites. It includes URLs for corrections, victimization, crime prevention, high-tech crime, policing, courts, investigations, juvenile justice, research, and sites just for fun.

Criminology: An Introduction Using MicroCase© ExplorIt, Fifth Edition This brief book, written by Steven F. Messner (State University of New York, Albany), introduces students to the real world of criminological research and data. In tandem with Messner's discussion of major criminological theories and the data supporting them, students work with the unique software that accompanies the book to assess those theories by means of review worksheets and data analysis exercises. This can be packaged with the textbook at a substantial discount—contact your Thomson Wadsworth representative for ordering information.

ACKNOWLEDGMENTS

The preparation of this book would not have been possible without the aid of my colleagues who helped by reviewing the previous editions and gave me important suggestions for improvement.

Reviewers for the Third Edition

Doris Chu, *Arkansas State University*
Dorinda L. Dowis, *Columbus State University*
Heather Melton, *University of Utah*
Adam Rafalovich, *Texas Technology University*

Reviewers of Previous Editions include

John Broderick, *Stonehill College*
Stephen J. Brodt, *Ball State University*
Dana C. De Witt, *Chadron State College*
Yvonne Downs, *Hibert College*
Sandra Emory, *University of New Mexico*
Dorothy M. Goldsborough, *Chaminade University*
Robert G. Hewitt, *Edison Community College*
Catherine F. Lavery, *Sacred Heart University*
Danielle Liautaud-Watkins, *William Paterson University*
Larry A. Long, *Pioneer Pacific College*
Ronald Sopenoff, *Brookdale Community College*
Mark A. Stelter, *Montgomery College*
Tom Tomlinson, *Western Illinois University*
Matt Vetter, *Saint Mary's University*
Scott Wagner, *Columbus State Community College*
Jay R. Williams, *Duke University*

My colleagues at Wadsworth Publishing did their typically outstanding job of aiding me in the preparation of the book and putting up with my seasonal angst. Chris Caldeira is my new criminology editor, and she helped guide this project from start to finish. The fabulous Shelley Murphy is a terrific development editor whom I cannot live without. Linda Rill did her usual fantastic job on photo research. I have worked with Linda Jupiter, the book's production editor, many times, and she is always there to hold my hand as well as produce the book. The sensational Jennie Redwitz somehow pulls everything together as production manager, and Terra Schulz serves as marketing manager extraordinaire.

Larry Siegel
Bedford, New Hampshire

* FBI Press Release, "Operator of Orange County-Based Ponzi Scheme That Caused More Than $150 Million in Losses Sentenced to 30 Years in Federal Prison," May 30, 2006, http://losangeles.fbi.gov/dojpressrel/pressrel06/la053006 usa.htm.

Crime and Criminology

CHAPTER 1

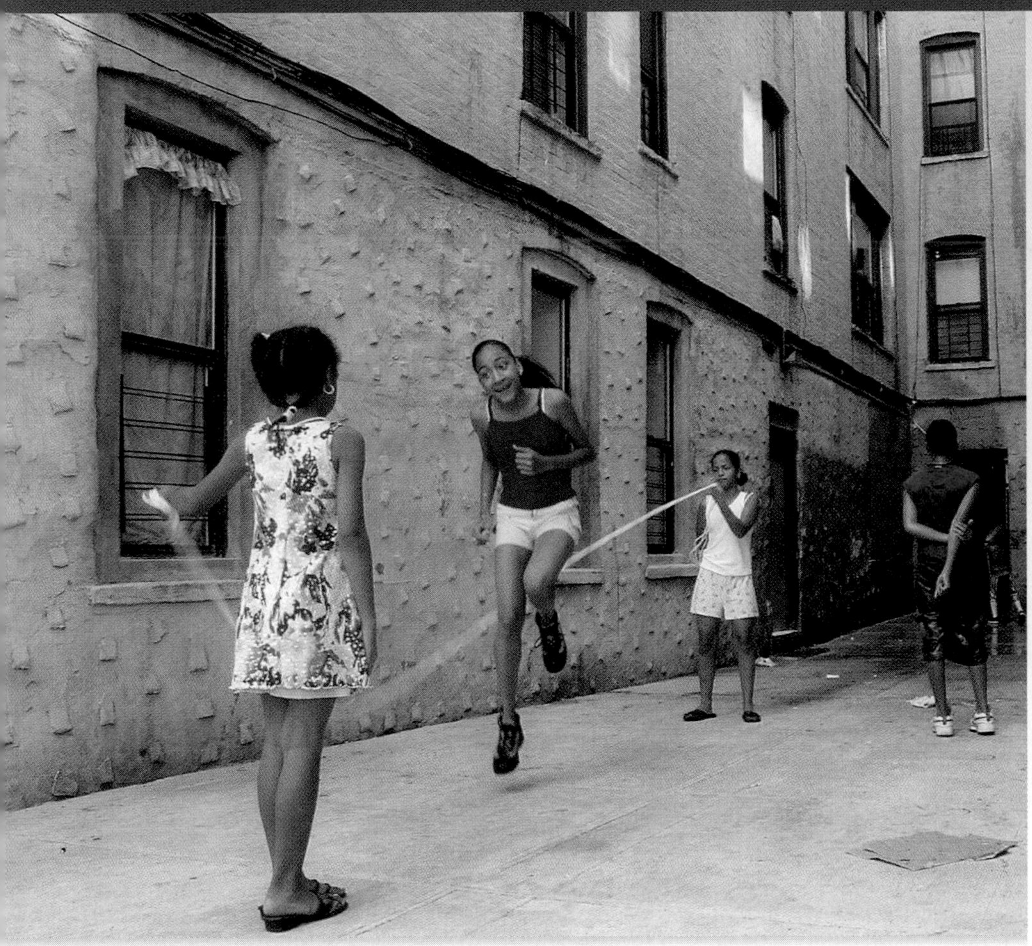

© AP

ON DECEMBER 7, 2005, DOUGLAS RICHARD STEVENS, 53, OF ONTARIO, CANADA, BEGAN COMMUNICATING ONLINE WITH "JANE," whom he believed had a 10-year-old daughter named "Mary." Using the screen name "ontm4momand-daughter," Stevens told "Jane" that he wanted to engage in sexual acts with "Mary" and bragged about previous conquests of girls he met online. He arranged to meet "Jane" and "Mary" in Atlanta so that he could sexually molest "Mary." When he arrived, federal law enforcement agents arrested Stevens in a restaurant parking lot. "Jane" and "Mary" never existed and were in fact identities created and used by an undercover FBI agent working as part of the FBI's Safe Child Task Force designed to lure predators such as Stevens. He was indicted by a federal grand jury in January

2006 on charges that included using a computer to entice a minor to engage in sexual activity and traveling across state lines to engage in sexual acts with the minor. On March 15, 2006, Stevens pleaded guilty to both counts, charges that could net him up to life in prison.[1]

CHAPTER OBJECTIVES

1. Understand what is meant by the "field of criminology."
2. Know the historical context of criminology.
3. Recognize the differences between the various schools of criminological thought.
4. Discuss the concept of "positivism."
5. Be familiar with the various elements of the criminological enterprise.
6. Be able to discuss how criminologists define crime.
7. Recognize the concepts of criminal law.
8. Describe the various defenses to crime.
9. Show how the criminal law is undergoing change.
10. Be able to discuss ethical issues in criminology.

Take a Pre-Test. Visit www.thomsonedu.com/criminaljustice/siegel and take a Pre-Test to determine what you already know and identify the areas where you'll need to focus your study. The program will direct you to specific pages within the text where you can find further information on the correct answers to the questions you've missed.

The Stevens case illustrates the evolution of criminal behavior in contemporary society. The computer and Internet have enabled people to engage in criminal activities unknown a decade ago. Besides crimes like the one Stevens committed, these range from identity theft to online securities fraud.

CONNECTIONS
Crime in cyberspace, including online stalking, identity theft, and securities fraud, is covered in Chapter 12.

The reach of crime has become truly international, creating new challenges for law enforcement authorities. The questions about crime and its control raised by the Stevens case and others have spurred interest in **criminology,** an academic discipline that uses scientific methods to study the nature, extent, cause, and control of criminal behavior. Unlike political figures and media commentators, whose opinions about crime may be colored by personal experiences, biases, and election concerns, criminologists remain objective as they study crime and its consequences.[2]

CONNECTIONS
For the criminological view on the relationship between media and violence, see Chapter 5. For more on acquaintance rape, go to Chapter 10.

Criminology is an **interdisciplinary science.** Criminologists hold degrees in a variety of diverse fields, most commonly sociology, but also **criminal justice,** political science, psychology, economics, and the natural sciences. For most of the twentieth century, criminology's primary orientation was sociological, but today it can be viewed as an integrated approach to the study of criminal behavior. How this field developed, its major components, and its relationship to crime law and deviance are some of the topics discussed in this chapter.

A BRIEF HISTORY OF CRIMINOLOGY

The scientific study of crime and criminality is a relatively recent development. During the Middle Ages (1200–1600), people who violated social norms or religious practices were believed to be witches or possessed by demons.[3] The use of cruel torture to extract confessions was common practice. Those convicted of violent or theft crimes suffered extremely harsh penalties, including whipping, branding, maiming, and execution.

criminology
The scientific study of the nature, extent, cause, and control of criminal behavior.

interdisciplinary science
Involving two or more academic fields.

criminal justice
Referring to the agencies of social control, such as police departments, the courts, and correctional institutions that handle criminal offenders.

Classical Criminology

By the mid-eighteenth century, social philosophers began to argue for a more rational approach to punishment. They sought to eliminate cruel public executions, which were designed to frighten people into obedience. Reformers stressed that the relationship between crime and punishment should be balanced and fair. This more moderate view of criminal sanctions can be traced to the writings of an Italian scholar, Cesare Beccaria (1738–1794), who was one of the first scholars to develop a systematic understanding of why people committed crime.

Beccaria believed in the concept of **utilitarianism:** In their behavior choices, people want to achieve pleasure and avoid pain. Crimes occur when the potential pleasure and reward from illegal acts outweigh the likely pains of punishment. To deter crime, punishment must be sufficient—no more, no less—to counterbalance criminal gain. Beccaria's famous theorem was that in order for punishment to be effective it must be public, prompt, necessary, the least possible in the given circumstances, proportionate, and dictated by law.[4]

The writings of Beccaria and his followers form the core of what today is referred to as **classical criminology.** As originally conceived in the eighteenth century, classical criminology theory had several basic elements:

- In every society, people have free will to choose criminal or lawful solutions to meet their needs or settle their problems.
- Criminal solutions may be more attractive than lawful ones because they usually require less work for a greater payoff.
- A person's choice of criminal solutions may be controlled by his or her fear of punishment.
- The more severe, certain, and swift the punishment, the better able it is to control criminal behavior.

This classical perspective influenced judicial philosophy, and sentences were geared to be proportionate to the seriousness of the crime. Executions were still widely used but gradually came to be employed for only the most serious crimes. The catch phrase was "let the punishment fit the crime."

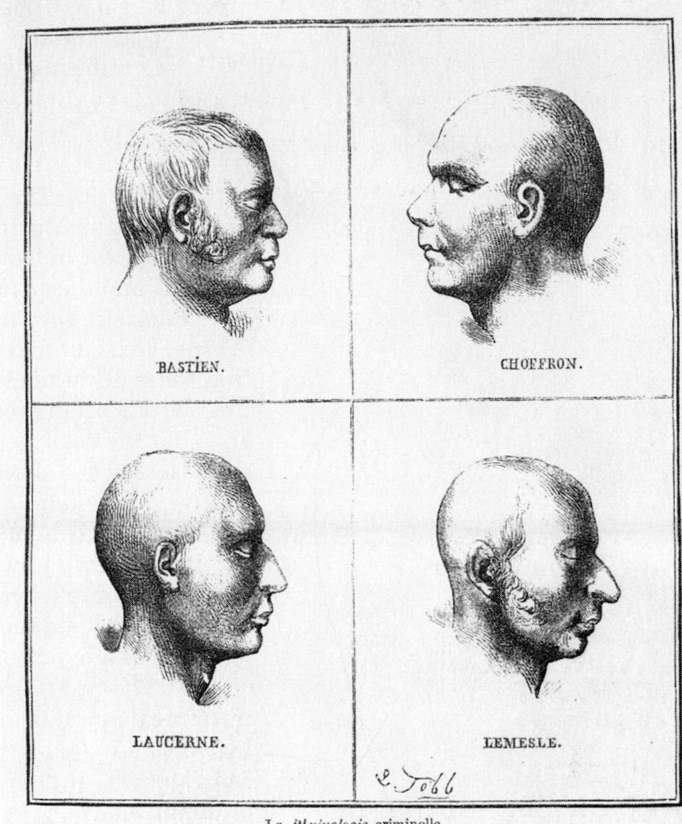

Early positivists believed the shape of the skull was a key determinant of behavior. These drawings from the nineteenth century illustrate "typical" criminally shaped heads.

Positivist Criminology

During the nineteenth century, a new vision of the world challenged the validity of classical theory and presented an innovative way of looking at the causes of crime. The scientific method was beginning to take hold in Europe and North America. Scientists were using careful observation and analysis of natural phenomena to explain how the world worked. New discoveries were being made in biology, astronomy, and chemistry. If the scientific method could be applied to the study of nature, then why not use it to study human behavior?

Auguste Comte (1798–1857), considered the founder of sociology, argued that societies pass through stages that can be grouped on the basis of how people try to understand the world in which they live. People in primitive societies believe that inanimate objects have life (for example, the sun is a god); in later social stages, people embrace a rational, scientific view of the world. Comte called this the positive stage, and those who followed his writings became known as positivists.

Positivism has a number of elements:

- Positivists use the **scientific method** to conduct research. The scientific method is universal and remains constant in all cultural and social boundaries.
- Positivists maintain the goal of predicting and explaining social phenomena in a logical manner. This means identifying necessary and sufficient conditions for any phenomenon to occur.

utilitarianism
The view that people's behavior is motivated by the pursuit of pleasure and the avoidance of pain.

classical criminology
The theoretical perspective suggesting that (1) people have free will to choose criminal or conventional behaviors; (2) people choose to commit crime for reasons of greed or personal need; and (3) crime can be controlled only by the fear of criminal sanctions.

positivism
The branch of social science that uses the scientific method of the natural sciences and suggests that human behavior is a product of social, biological, psychological, or economic forces.

scientific method
Using verifiable principles and procedures for the systematic acquisition of knowledge; typically involves formulating a problem, creating a hypothesis, and collecting data through observation and experiment, to verify the hypothesis.

- Only real and observed phenomena can be tested scientifically. Such concepts as "God" and the "soul" cannot be measured and therefore are not the subject of scientific inquiry; they remain a matter of faith.
- Science should be value free and not influenced by a person's biases or political point of view.

Early Positivism The earliest "scientific" studies examining human behavior now seem quaint and primitive. Physiognomists, such as J. K. Lavater (1741–1801), studied the facial features of criminals and found that the shape of the ears, nose, and eyes and the distances between them were associated with antisocial behavior. Phrenologists, such as Franz Joseph Gall (1758–1828) and Johann K. Spurzheim (1776–1832), studied the shape of the skull and bumps on the head and concluded that these physical attributes were linked to criminal behavior. They believed that the size of a brain area could be determined by inspecting the contours of the skull, and that the relative size of brain areas could be increased or decreased through exercise and self-discipline.[5] Though their techniques and methods are no longer practiced or taken seriously, these efforts were an early attempt to use a scientific method to study human behaviors.

By the early nineteenth century, abnormality in the human mind was being linked to criminal behavior patterns. Phillipe Pinel, one of the founders of French psychiatry, coined the phrase *manie sans delire* to denote what eventually was referred to as a psychopathic personality.

CONNECTIONS

Many of us have grown up with movies showing criminals as "homicidal maniacs." Some may laugh, but *Freddie vs. Jason* was a big hit in 2003. For more on psychosis as a cause of crime, go to Chapter 5.

In 1812 an American, Benjamin Rush, described patients with an "innate preternatural moral depravity."[6] English physician Henry Maudsley (1835–1918) believed that insanity and criminal behavior were strongly linked.[7] These early research efforts shifted attention to brain functioning and personality as the keys to criminal behavior.

Biological Determinism In Italy, Cesare Lombroso (1835–1909), known as the "father of criminology," began to study the cadavers of executed criminals in an effort to determine scientifically how criminals differed from noncriminals. Lombroso was soon convinced that serious and violent offenders had inherited criminal traits. These "born criminals" suffered from "atavistic anomalies"; physically, they were throwbacks to more primitive times when people were savages and were believed to have the enormous jaws and strong canine teeth common to carnivores and savages who devour raw flesh. Lombroso's version of criminal anthropology was brought to the United States via articles and textbooks that adopted his ideas.[8] By the beginning of the twentieth century, American authors were discussing "the science of penology" and "the science of criminology."[9]

Although Lombroso's version of strict biological determinism is no longer taken seriously, some criminologists have recently linked crime and biological traits. Because they believe that social and environmental conditions also influence human behavior, the term **biosocial theory** has been coined to reflect the assumed link between physical and social traits and their influence on behavior.

Sociological Criminology

At the same time that biological views were dominating criminology, another group of positivists were developing the field of sociology to study scientifically the major social changes taking place in nineteenth-century society. The foundations of **sociological criminology** can be traced to the work of pioneering sociologists L. A. J. (Adolphe) Quetelet (1796–1874) and (David) Émile Durkheim (1858–1917).[10]

Quetelet was a Belgian mathematician who (along with a Frenchman, Andre-Michel Guerry) used social statistics that were just being developed in Europe to investigate the influence of social factors on the propensity to commit crime. In addition to finding a strong influence of age and sex on crime, Quetelet uncovered evidence that season, climate, population composition, and poverty were also related to criminality.[11] He was one of the first criminologists to link crime rates to alcohol consumption.[12]

biosocial theory
Approach to criminology that focuses on the interaction between biological and social factors as they relate to crime.

sociological criminology
Approach to criminology, based on the work of Quetelet and Durkheim, that focuses on the relationship between social factors and crime.

According to Durkheim's vision of social positivism, crime is normal because it is virtually impossible to imagine a society in which criminal behavior is totally absent.[13] Durkheim believed that crime is inevitable because people are so different from one another and use such a variety of methods and forms of behavior to meet their needs. Even if "real" crimes were eliminated, human weaknesses and petty vices would be elevated to the status of crimes. Durkheim suggested that crime can be useful and occasionally even healthful for society because it paves the way for social change. To illustrate this concept, Durkheim offered the example of the Greek philosopher Socrates, who was considered a criminal and put to death for corrupting the morals of youth simply because he expressed ideas that were different from what people believed at that time.

In his famous book *The Division of Labor in Society,* Durkheim described the consequences of the shift from a small, rural society, which he labeled "mechanical," to the more modern "organic" society with a large urban population, division of labor, and personal isolation.[14] From the resulting structural changes flowed **anomie,** or norm and role confusion. An anomic society is in chaos, experiencing moral uncertainty and an accompanying loss of traditional values. People who suffer anomie may become confused and rebellious. Might the dawning of the "Internet age" create anomie in our own culture?

The Chicago School The primacy of sociological positivism was secured by research begun in the early twentieth century by Robert Ezra Park (1864–1944), Ernest W. Burgess (1886–1966), Louis Wirth (1897–1952), and their colleagues in the sociology department at the University of Chicago. The scholars who taught at this program created what is still referred to as the **Chicago School** in honor of their unique style of doing research.

These urban sociologists examined how neighborhood conditions, such as poverty levels, influenced crime rates. They found that social forces operating in urban areas created a crime-promoting environment; some neighborhoods were "natural areas" for crime.[15] In urban neighborhoods with high levels of poverty, the fabric of critical social institutions, such as the school and the family, came undone. Their traditional ability to control behavior was undermined, and the outcome was a high crime rate.

Chicago School sociologists argued that crime was not a function of personal traits or characteristics but rather a reaction to an environment that was inadequate for proper human relations and development. Thus, they challenged the widely held belief that criminals were biologically or psychologically impaired or morally inferior. Instead, crime was a social phenomenon and could be eradicated by improving social and economic conditions.

Socialization Views During the 1930s and 1940s, another group of sociologists began conducting research that linked criminal behavior to the quality of an individual's relationship to important social processes, such as education, family life, and peer relations. They found that children who grew up in homes wracked by conflict, attended inadequate schools, or associated with deviant peers became exposed to pro-crime forces. One position, championed by the preeminent American criminologist Edwin Sutherland, was that people learn criminal attitudes from older, more experienced law violators. Another view, developed by Chicago School sociologist Walter Reckless, was that crime occurs when children develop an inadequate self-image, which renders them incapable of controlling their own misbehavior. Both of these views linked criminality to the failure of **socialization**—the interactions people have with the various individuals, organizations, institutions, and processes of society that help them mature and develop.

Critical Criminology

While most criminologists of the late nineteenth and early twentieth centuries embraced either the ecological view (stemming from Durkheim's theory) or the socialization view of crime, the writings of another social thinker, Karl Marx (1818–1883), had sown the seeds for a new approach in criminology, referred to as **conflict theory**.[16]

CONNECTIONS

Did your mother ever warn you about staying away from "bad neighborhoods" in the city? If she did, how valid were her concerns? To find out, go to Chapter 6 for a discussion of the structural conditions that cause crime.

anomie
A lack of norms or clear social standards. Because of rapidly shifting moral values, the individual has few guides to what is socially acceptable.

Chicago School
Group of urban sociologists who studied the relationship between environmental conditions and crime.

socialization
Process of human development and enculturation. Socialization is influenced by key social processes and institutions.

conflict theory
The view that human behavior is shaped by interpersonal conflict and that those who maintain social power will use it to further their own ends.

In his *Communist Manifesto* and other writings, Marx described the oppressive labor conditions prevalent during the rise of industrial capitalism. Marx was convinced that the character of every civilization is determined by its mode of production—the way its people develop and produce material goods. The most important relationship in industrial culture is between the owners of the means of production, the capitalist bourgeoisie, and the people who do the labor, the proletariat. The economic system controls all facets of human life; consequently, people's lives revolve around the means of production. The exploitation of the working class, Marx believed, would eventually lead to class conflict and the end of the capitalist system.

Although these writings laid the foundation for a Marxist-based criminology, it was not until the social and political upheaval of the 1960s, fueled by the Vietnam War, the development of an antiestablishment counterculture movement, the civil rights movement, and the women's movement, that criminologists began to analyze the social conditions in the United States that promoted class conflict and crime. What emerged from this intellectual ferment was a Marxist-based **critical criminology** that indicted the economic system as producing the conditions that support a high crime rate. Critical criminologists have played a significant role in the field ever since.

Developmental Criminology

During the twentieth century some criminologists began to integrate sociological, psychological, and economic elements into more complex developmental views of crime causation. Sheldon and Eleanor Glueck, who conducted research on delinquent careers while at Harvard University in the 1930s, are today considered founders of this branch of criminological theory. They followed the careers of known delinquents to determine the factors that predicted persistent offending and made extensive use of interviews and records in their elaborate comparisons of delinquents and nondelinquents.

The Glueck's research focused on early onset of delinquency as a harbinger of a criminal career: "[T]he deeper the roots of childhood maladjustment, the smaller the chance of adult adjustment."[17] They also noted the stability of offending careers: Children who are antisocial early in life are the most likely to continue their offending careers into adulthood.

The Gluecks identified a number of personal and social factors related to persistent offending, the most important of which was family relations. This factor was considered in terms of quality of discipline and emotional ties with parents. The adolescent raised in a large, single-parent family of limited economic means and educational achievement was the most vulnerable to delinquency.

The Gluecks did not restrict their analysis to social variables. When they measured such biological and psychological traits as body type, intelligence, and personality, they found that physical and mental factors also played a role in determining behavior. Children with low intelligence, who had a background of mental disease, and who had a powerful ("mesomorph") physique were the most likely to become persistent offenders.

The Glueck's vision then integrated biological, social, and psychological elements. It suggested that the initiation and continuity of a criminal career was a developmental process influenced by both internal and external situations, conditions, and circumstances. Their **developmental theory** model is still influential in the field today.

Contemporary Criminology

These various schools of criminology, developed over 200 years, have been constantly evolving. Classical theory has evolved into modern **rational choice theory,** which argues that criminals are rational decision makers: They use available information to choose criminal or conventional behaviors, and their choice is structured by the fear of punishment. Lombrosian theory has evolved into contemporary biosocial and psychological **trait theory** views. Criminologists no longer believe that a

critical criminology
The view that crime is a product of the capitalist system.

developmental theory
The view that criminality is a dynamic process, influenced by social experiences as well as individual characteristics.

rational choice theory
The view that crime is a function of a decision-making process in which the potential offender weighs the potential costs and benefits of an illegal act.

trait theory
The view that criminality is a product of abnormal biological or psychological traits.

CONCEPT SUMMARY 1.1 Criminological Perspectives

The major perspectives of criminology focus on individual (biological, psychological, and choice theories); social (structural and process theories); political and economic (conflict theory); and multiple (developmental theory) factors.

CLASSICAL/CHOICE PERSPECTIVE
Situational forces. Crime is a function of free will and personal choice. Punishment is a deterrent to crime.

BIOLOGICAL/PSYCHOLOGICAL PERSPECTIVE
Internal forces. Crime is a function of chemical, neurological, genetic, personality, intelligence, or mental traits.

STRUCTURAL PERSPECTIVE
Ecological forces. Crime rates are a function of neighborhood conditions, cultural forces, and norm conflict.

PROCESS PERSPECTIVE
Socialization forces. Crime is a function of upbringing, learning, and control. Peers, parents, and teachers influence behavior.

CRICTICAL PERSPECTIVE
Economic and political forces. Crime is a function of competition for limited resources and power. Class conflict produces crime.

DEVELOPMENTAL PERSPECTIVE
Multiple forces. Biological, social-psychological, economic, and political forces may combine to produce crime.

single trait or inherited characteristic can explain crime, but some are convinced that biological and psychological traits interact with environmental factors to influence all human behavior, including criminality. Biological and psychological theorists study the association between criminal behavior and such factors as diet, hormonal makeup, personality, and intelligence.

The original Chicago School vision has been updated in **social structure theory,** which maintains that the social environment directly controls criminal behavior. According to this view, people at the bottom of the social hierarchy, who cannot achieve success through conventional means, experience anomie, strain, failure, and frustration; they are the most likely to turn to criminal solutions to their problems.

In contrast, some criminologists focus their attention on socialization. As a group, they are referred to as **social process theorists.** Some believe that children learn to commit crime by interacting with and modeling their behavior after others they admire. Other theorists in this group find that criminal offenders are people whose life experiences have shattered their social bonds to society.

The writings of Marx and his followers continue to be influential. Many criminologists still view social and political conflict as the root cause of crime. They believe that the inherently unfair economic structure of the United States and other advanced capitalist countries is the engine that drives the high crime rate.

Another group of contemporary criminologists have continued to integrate social, biological, and psychological concepts in a manner influenced by the Gluecks' pioneering research. They are now creating complex developmental theories of criminal careers. Each of the major perspectives is summarized in Concept Summary 1.1. ✔ CHECKPOINTS

✔ CHECKPOINTS

✔ The first criminologists believed that crime was a matter of free will. This is referred to as classical criminology.

✔ In the nineteenth century, positivist criminologists began to use the scientific method to study crime. They were convinced that the cause of crime could be found in the individual offender.

✔ During the early twentieth century, sociological criminology was developed to explain the effect of the social environment on individual behavior.

✔ Critical criminologists attempted to explain how economic forces create crime.

✔ Developmental criminologists trace criminal careers over the life course.

✔ Contemporary criminology carries on and refines these traditions.

WHAT CRIMINOLOGISTS DO

Regardless of their background or training, criminologists are primarily interested in studying crime and criminal behavior. Their professional training, occupational role, and income are derived from a scientific approach to the study and analysis of crime and criminal behavior.[18]

Several subareas exist within the broader arena of criminology. Taken together, these subareas make up the field of criminology. Criminologists may specialize in a subarea in the same way that psychologists might specialize in a subfield of psychology, such as child development, perception, personality, psychopathology, or sexuality. Some of the more important criminological specialties are described in the following sections and summarized in Concept Summary 1.2.

social structure theory
The view that disadvantaged economic class position is a primary cause of crime.

social process theory
The view that criminality is a function of people's interactions with various organizations, institutions, and processes in society.

CONCEPT SUMMARY 1.2 The Criminological Enterprise

These subareas constitute the discipline of criminology.

CRIMINAL STATISTICS
Gathering valid crime data: devising new research methods; measuring crime patterns and trends.

THE SOCIOLOGY OF LAW
Determining the origin of law: measuring the forces that can change laws and society.

THEORY CONSTRUCTION
Predicting individual behavior: understanding the cause of crime rates and trends.

CRIMINAL BEHAVIOR SYSTEMS
Determining the nature and cause of specific crime patterns: studying violence, theft, organized, white-collar, and public order crimes.

PENOLOGY
Studying the correction and control of criminal behavior: using scientific methods to assess the effectiveness of crime control and offender treatment programs.

VICTIMOLOGY
Studying the nature and cause of victimization: aiding crime victims; understanding the nature and extent of victimization; developing theories of victimization risk.

Criminal Statistics/Crime Measurements

The subarea of criminal statistics/crime measurement involves calculating the amount and trends of criminal activity: How much crime occurs annually? Who commits it? When and where does it occur? Which crimes are the most serious?

Criminologists interested in computing criminal statistics try to create **valid** and **reliable** measurements of criminal behavior. For example, to analyze the activities of police and court agencies, they formulate techniques for collecting and analyzing institutional records and activities. To measure criminal activity not reported to the police, they develop survey instruments that estimate the percentage of people who commit crimes but escape detection by the justice system. They also develop measures that identify the victims of crime, especially those who have not reported their victimization to the police.

The study of criminal statistics is a crucial aspect of the criminological enterprise. Without valid and reliable data sources, efforts to conduct research on crime and create criminological theories would be futile. One of the more challenging aspects of developing criminal statistics is devising methods to compare international crime rates, the topic of the Race, Culture, Gender, & Criminology feature on pages 10–11.

Sociology of Law

The sociology of law is a subarea of criminology concerned with the role social forces play in shaping criminal law and the role of criminal law in shaping society. Criminologists study the history of legal thought in an effort to understand how criminal acts, such as theft, rape, and murder, evolved into their present form.

Often criminologists are asked to join the debate when a new law is proposed to outlaw or control a particular behavior. For example, across the United States a debate has been raging over the legality of artworks, films, photographs, and even music that some people find offensive and lewd and others consider harmless. Criminologists help determine the role that the law will play in curbing public access to controversial media. They may be called upon to help answer relevant questions: Do children exposed to pornography experience psychological harm? Will they later go on to commit violent crime? The answers to these questions may one day shape the direction of legislation controlling the sexual content of the Internet.

Criminologists also help lawmakers alter the content of the criminal law in response to changing times and conditions. For example, computer fraud, theft from

valid
Actually measuring what one intends to measure; relevant.

reliable
Producing consistent results from one measurement to another.

automatic teller machines, Internet scams, and illegal tapping of television cable lines are behaviors that did not exist when criminal law was originally conceived. The law must be constantly revised to reflect cultural, societal, and technological adaptations of common acts. For example, in a 2003 case, *Smith v. Doe,* the U.S. Supreme Court ruled that the Alaska Sex Offender Registration Act, which requires an incarcerated sex offender or child kidnapper to register with the Department of Corrections within 30 days before his or her release, is legal and may be required even for inmates convicted before the act's passage and that this is not a violation of the Constitution's ban on **ex post facto laws.**[19] The Court reasoned that the registration act was nonpunitive and designed to protect the public from sex offenders rather than to punish those who had committed the act. The Court's ruling reflects the public's concern about sexual predators and the desire to create and maintain sex offender registries. Could the Court have just as easily ruled that making people register as sex offenders was a violation of their basic civil rights? After all, we do not make robbers and burglars register, even though they present a danger to society! Was the Court's legal interpretation influenced by public opinion?

© Reuters/DOD/HO/Landov

Abu Musab al-Zarqawi, the mastermind behind hundreds of bombings, kidnappings and beheadings in Iraq, was killed on June 8, 2006 by an air strike north of Baghdad. The terrorist activities of Zarqawi and others like him convince criminologists that antisocial behavior, in any culture, may be caused by social, psychological, economic, and/or political factors.

Developing Theories of Crime Causation

Criminologists also explore the cause of crime. Some who have a psychological orientation view crime as a function of personality, development, social learning, or cognition. Others investigate the biological correlates of antisocial behavior and study the biochemical, genetic, and neurological linkages to crime. Sociologists look at the social forces producing criminal behavior, including neighborhood conditions, poverty, socialization, and group interaction.

Sometimes criminologists investigate crime causation by conducting research on common behavioral practices in order to understand how they may influence crime. Criminologists may use innovative methods to test theory: Consider the two examples in Exhibit 1.1. Understanding one true cause of crime remains a difficult

ex post facto law
A law applied retroactively to punish acts that were not crimes before its passage, or one that raises the grade of an offense, or that renders an act punishable in a more severe manner than it was when committed.

Exhibit 1.1
Innovative Research Used to Test Criminological Theories

- In order to investigate the theory that adding police would deter crime, Dennis Wilson used data from the National Hockey League to test the hypothesis that adding an enforcement agent (in this case, an additional referee) would deter law violations (penalties). Because his analysis of game data supported the theory that adding monitors (referees) reduces the number of rule violations (penalties), his research gave support to the premise that adding police would bring the crime rate down.
- Ronald Simons and his colleagues employed a sample of young adults in order to test the theory that romantic mating choices have a strong influence on criminal behavior. They discovered that people who engaged in delinquent behaviors when they were adolescents were the ones most likely to choose antisocial romantic partners as young adults, a choice which reinforced their criminal activities. Simons also found a gender effect: Females were quite likely to be influenced by criminal boyfriends; males were less likely to be influenced by criminal girlfriends. For females, then, the choice of a romantic partner may be a key element in a criminal career; males are less likely to be influenced by their choice of mates. Their male friends are actually more influential.

SOURCES: Dennis Wilson, "Additional Law Enforcement as a Deterrent to Criminal Behavior: Empirical Evidence from the National Hockey League," *Journal of Socio-Economics* 34 (2005): 319–330. Ronald Simons, Eric Stewart, Leslie Gordon, Rand Conger, and Glen Elder Jr., "Test of Life-Course Explanations for Stability and Change in Antisocial Bebopper from Adolescence to Young Adulthood," *Criminology* 40 (2002): 401–434.

Race, Culture, Gender, & Criminology

International Crime Trends

India has experienced a shocking form of violence against women known as bride burning: A woman may be burned to death if her family fails to provide the expected dowry to the groom's family or if she is suspected of premarital infidelity. Many Indian women commit suicide to escape the brutality of their situation.

The danger from various forms of violent behavior, such as bride burning in India, has become a worldwide epidemic. Although crime rates are trending downward in the United States, they seem to be increasing abroad. The United States in 1980 clearly led the Western world in overall crime, but there has been a marked decline in U.S. crime rates, a trend which has now placed crime rates in the United States below those of other industrial nations, including England and Wales, Denmark, and Finland. And, contrary to the common assumption that the United States is the most heavily armed nation on earth, there is new evidence that people around the world are arming themselves in record numbers: Residents in the 15 countries of the European Union have an estimated 84 million firearms. Of that, 67 million (80 percent) are in civilian hands. With a total population of 375 million people, this amounts to 17.4 guns for every 100 people.

Though these trends are alarming, making international comparisons is often difficult because the legal definitions of crime vary from country to country. There are also differences in the way crime is measured. For example, in the United States, crime may be measured by counting criminal acts reported to the police or by using victim surveys, while in many European countries the number of cases solved by the police measures crime. Despite these problems, valid comparisons can still be made about crime across different countries using a number of reliable data sources. For example, the United Nations Survey of Crime Trends and Operations of Criminal Justice Systems (UNCJS) is the most well known source of information on cross-national data. The International Crime Victims Survey (ICVS) is conducted in 60 countries and managed by the Ministry of Justice of the Netherlands, the Home Office of the United Kingdom, and the United Nations Interregional Crime and Justice Research Institute. There is also the United Nations International Study on the Regulation of Firearms. INTERPOL, an international police agency, collects data from police agencies in 179 countries. The World Health Organization (WHO) has conducted surveys on global violence. The *European Sourcebook of Crime and Criminal Justice Statistics* provides data from police agencies in 36 European nations.

What do these various sources tell us about international crime rates?

Homicide

Many nations, especially those experiencing social or economic upheaval, have murder rates much higher than the United States. Colombia has about 63 homicides per 100,000 people and South Africa, 51, compared to less than 6 in the United States. During the 1990s, there were more homicides in Brazil than in the United States, Canada, Italy, Japan, Australia, Portugal, Britain, Austria, and Germany taken together. Why are murder rates so high in Brazil? Law enforcement officials link the upsurge in violence to drug trafficking, gang feuds, vigilantism, and disputes over trivial matters, in which young, unmarried, uneducated males are involved.

Rape

Until 1990, U.S. rape rates were higher than those of any Western nation, but by 2000, Canada took the lead. Violence against women is related to economic hardship and the social status of women. Rates are high in poor nations in which women are oppressed. Where women are more emancipated, the rates of violence against women are lower.

For many women, sexual violence starts in childhood and adolescence and may occur in the home, school, and community. Studies conducted in a wide variety of nations ranging from Cameroon to New Zealand found high rates of reported forced sexual initiation. In some nations, as many as 46 percent of adolescent women and 20 percent of adolescent men report sexual coercion at the hands of family members, teachers, boyfriends, or strangers.

Sexual violence has significant health consequences, including suicide, stress, mental illnesses, unwanted

CONNECTIONS

Criminologists have sought to reconcile the differences among various visions of crime by combining or integrating them into unified but complex theories of criminality. At their core, these integrated theories suggest that as people develop over the life course, a variety of factors—some social, others personal—shape their behavior patterns. What these factors are and the influence they have on human behavior is discussed in Chapter 9.

white-collar crime
Illegal acts that capitalize on a person's status in the marketplace. White-collar crimes may include theft, embezzlement, fraud, market manipulation, restraint of trade, and false advertising.

problem. Criminologists are still unsure why, given similar conditions, some people choose criminal solutions to their problems while others conform to accepted social rules of behavior.

Understanding and Describing Criminal Behavior

Another subarea of criminology involves research on specific criminal types and patterns: violent crime, theft crime, public order crime, organized crime, and so on. Numerous attempts have been made to describe and understand particular crime types. Marvin Wolfgang's 1958 study, *Patterns in Criminal Homicide,* is considered a landmark analysis of the nature of homicide and the relationship between victim and offender.[20] Edwin Sutherland's analysis of business-related offenses helped coin a new phrase, **white-collar crime,** to describe economic crime activities of the affluent.[21]

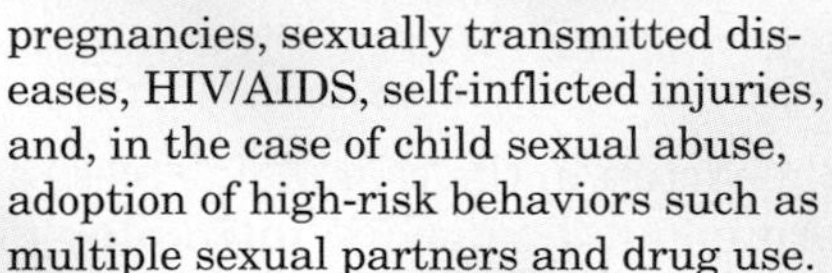

pregnancies, sexually transmitted diseases, HIV/AIDS, self-inflicted injuries, and, in the case of child sexual abuse, adoption of high-risk behaviors such as multiple sexual partners and drug use.

Robbery

Countries with more reported robberies than the United States include England and Wales, Portugal, and Spain. Countries with fewer reported robberies include Germany, Italy, and France, as well as Middle Eastern and Asian nations.

Burglary

The United States has lower burglary rates than Australia, Denmark, Finland, England and Wales, and Canada. It has higher reported burglary rates than Spain, Korea, and Saudi Arabia.

Vehicle Theft

Australia, England and Wales, Denmark, Norway, Canada, France, and Italy now have higher rates of vehicle theft than the United States.

Child Abuse

A World Health Organization report found that child physical and sexual abuse takes a significant toll around the world. In a single year, about 57,000 children under 15 years are murdered. The homicide rates for children aged 0 to 4 years were over twice as high as rates among children aged 5 to 14 years. Many more children are subjected to nonfatal abuse and neglect; 8 percent of male and 25 percent of female children up to age 18 experience sexual abuse of some kind.

Why the Change?

Why are crime rates increasing around the world while leveling off in the United States? In some developing nations, crime rates may be spiraling upward because of rapid changes in social and economic makeup. In Eastern Europe, the fall of Communism has brought about a transformation of the family, religion, education, and economy. These changes increase social pressures and result in crime rate increases. Some Asian societies, such as China, are undergoing rapid industrialization, urbanization, and social change. The shift from an agricultural to an industrial and service economy has produced political turmoil and a surge in their crime rates. For example, the island of Hong Kong, long a British possession but now part of the People's Republic of China, is experiencing an upsurge in club drugs. Tied to the local dance scene, the use of ecstasy and ketamine has skyrocketed and is in synch with the traditional drug of choice, heroin. The problems we experience at home are not unique to the United States.

Critical Thinking

1. Although risk factors at all levels of social and personal life contribute to youth violence, young people in all nations who experience change in societal-level factors—such as economic inequalities; rapid social change; and the availability of firearms, alcohol, and drugs—seem the most likely to get involved in violence. Can anything be done to help alleviate these social problems?
2. The United States is notorious for employing much tougher penal measures than Europe. Do you believe our tougher measures explain why crime is declining in the United States while increasing abroad?

InfoTrac College Edition Research

To find out more about violence around the world, use "violence Europe," "violence Asia," and "violence Africa" as key words in InfoTrac College Edition.

SOURCES: Karen Joe Laidler, "The Rise of Club Drugs in a Heroin Society: The Case of Hong Kong," *Substance Use & Misuse* 40 (2005): 1257–1279; Virendra Kumar and Sarita Kanth, "Bride Burning," *Lancet* 364 (2004): 18–19; Etienne Krug, Linda Dahlberg, James Mercy, Anthony Zwi, and Rafael Lozano, *World Report on Violence and Health.* (Geneva: World Health Organization, 2002); Gene Stephens, "Global Trends in Crime: Crime varies greatly around the world, statistics show, but new tactics have proved effective in the United States. To keep crime in check in the twenty-first century, we'll all need to get smarter, not just tougher," *The Futurist* 37 (2003): 40–47; Graeme Newman, *Global Report on Crime and Justice* (New York: Oxford University Press, 1999); Gary Lafree and Kriss Drass, "Counting Crime Booms among Nations: Evidence for Homicide Victimization Rates, 1956–1998," *Criminology* 40 (2002): 769–801; The Small Arms Survey, 2004, www.smallarmssurvey.org/publications/yb_2004.htm (accessed July 10, 2005); Pedro Scuro, *World Factbook of Criminal Justice Systems: Brazil* (Washington, DC: Bureau of Justice Statistics, 2003).

Penology

The study of **penology** involves the correction and control of known criminal offenders. Some criminologists are advocates of **rehabilitation;** they direct their efforts at identifying effective treatment strategies for individuals convicted of law violations. Others argue that crime can be prevented only through a strict policy of social control; they advocate such measures as **capital punishment** and **mandatory sentences.**

Criminologists interested in penology may help evaluate crime control programs in order to determine whether they are effective and how they will impact people's lives. When Samuel Gross and his colleagues sought to appraise the effect of the death penalty, they found that between 1989 and 2003, 340 people (327 men and 13 women) were exonerated after having served an average of more than 10 years each in prison. Almost half (144 people) were cleared by

penology
Subarea of criminology that focuses on the correction and control of criminal offenders.

rehabilitation
Treatment of criminal offenders that is aimed at preventing future criminal behavior.

capital punishment
The execution of criminal offenders; the death penalty.

mandatory sentences
A statutory requirement that a certain penalty shall be carried out in all cases of conviction for a specified offense or series of offenses.

DNA evidence. Gross and his colleagues found that death row prisoners were more than 100 times more likely to be exonerated than the average imprisoned felons.[22] The Gross research illustrates how important it is to evaluate penal measures such as capital punishment in order to determine their effectiveness and reliability.

CONNECTIONS

Though the terms "criminology" and "criminal justice" may seem similar, and people often confuse the two or lump them together, there are major differences between these fields of study. "Criminology" explains the etiology (origin), extent, and nature of crime in society, whereas "criminal justice" refers to the study of the agencies of social control–police, courts, and corrections. Criminologists are mainly concerned with identifying the suspected causes of crime, while criminal justice scholars strive to identify effective methods of crime control. There is a great deal of overlap in the fields, however, and many criminologists, especially those interested in penology, find themselves teaching in criminal justice departments at colleges and universities. The criminal justice system will be discussed in detail in Chapter 14.

Victimology

Criminologists recognize the critical role of the victim in the criminal process and that the victim's behavior is often a key determinant of crime.[23] **Victimology** includes the following areas of interest:

- Using victim surveys to measure the nature and extent of criminal behavior and to calculate the actual costs of crime to victims
- Calculating probabilities of victimization risk
- Studying victim culpability in the precipitation of crime
- Designing services for crime victims, such as counseling and compensation programs

Criminologists who study victimization have uncovered some startling results. For one thing, criminals have been found to be at greater risk for victimization than noncriminals.[24] This finding indicates that rather than being passive targets who are in the "wrong place at the wrong time," victims may themselves be engaging in a high-risk behavior, such as crime, that increases their victimization risk and renders them vulnerable to crime.

DEVIANT OR CRIMINAL? HOW CRIMINOLOGISTS DEFINE CRIME

Criminologists devote themselves to measuring, understanding, and controlling crime and deviance. How are these behaviors defined, and how do we distinguish between them?

Criminologists view deviant behavior as any action that departs from the social norms of society.[25] **Deviance** thus includes a broad spectrum of behaviors, ranging from the most socially harmful, such as rape and murder, to the relatively inoffensive, such as joining a religious cult or cross-dressing. A deviant act becomes a **crime** when it is deemed socially harmful or dangerous; it then will be specifically defined, prohibited, and punished under the criminal law.

Crime and deviance are often confused because not all crimes are deviant and not all deviant acts are illegal or criminal. For example, recreational drug use such as smoking marijuana may be a crime, but is it deviant? A significant percentage of the population (including some well-known politicians) has used recreational drugs.[26] To argue that all crimes are behaviors that depart from the norms of society is probably erroneous. Similarly, many deviant acts are not criminal, even though they may be shocking or depraved. If a passerby who observes a person drowning does not jump in or render aid in some way, the general public would probably condemn the person's behavior as callous, immoral, and deviant. But no legal action could be taken, because citizens are not required by law to effect rescues. In sum, many criminal acts, but not all, fall within the concept of deviance. Similarly, some deviant acts, but not all, are considered crimes.

Criminologists are often concerned with the concept of deviance and its relationship to criminality. For example, when does sexually oriented material stop being merely erotic and suggestive (deviant) and become obscene and pornographic (criminal)? Can a clear line be drawn separating sexually oriented materials into two groups, one that is legally acceptable and a second that is considered depraved or obscene? And if such a line can be drawn, who gets to draw it? If an illegal act, such as viewing Internet pornography, becomes a norm, should society reevaluate its criminal status and let it become merely an unusual or deviant act? The shifting definition of deviant behavior is closely associated with

victimology
The study of the victim's role in criminal events.

deviance
Behavior that departs from the social norm but is not necessarily criminal.

crime
An act, deemed socially harmful or dangerous, that is specifically defined, prohibited, and punished under the criminal law.

our concepts of crime: Where should society draw the line between behavior that is merely considered deviant and unusual and behavior that is considered dangerous and criminal?

Becoming Criminal

To understand the nature and purpose of law, criminologists study both the process by which deviant acts are criminalized (become crimes) and, conversely, how criminal acts are **decriminalized** and/or legalized.

In some instances, individuals, institutions, or government agencies mount a campaign aimed at convincing both the public and lawmakers that what was considered merely deviant behavior is actually dangerous and must be outlawed. During the 1930s, Harry Anslinger, then head of the Federal Bureau of Narcotics, used magazine articles, public appearances, and public testimony to sway public opinion about the dangers of marijuana, which up until that time had been legal to use and possess.[27] In testimony before the House Ways and Means Committee considering passage of the Marijuana Tax Act of 1938, Anslinger stated:

> In Florida a 21-year-old boy under the influence of this drug killed his parents and his brothers and sisters. The evidence showed that he had smoked marihuana. In Chicago recently two boys murdered a policeman while under the influence of marihuana. Not long ago we found a 15-year-old boy going insane because, the doctor told the enforcement officers, he thought the boy was smoking marihuana cigarettes. They traced the sale to some man who had been growing marihuana and selling it to these boys all under 15 years of age, on a playground there.[28]

As a result of Anslinger's efforts, a deviant behavior, marijuana use, became a criminal behavior, and previously law-abiding citizens were defined as criminal offenders. Today, some national organizations, such as the Drug Policy Alliance, are committed to repealing draconian drug laws and undoing Anslinger's "moral crusade." They call for an end to the "war against drugs," which they believe has become overzealous in its effort to punish drug traffickers. In 2004, the alliance issued this statement:

> Many of the problems the drug war purports to resolve are in fact caused by the drug war itself. So-called "drug-related" crime is a direct result of drug prohibition's distortion of immutable laws of supply and demand. Public health problems like HIV and Hepatitis C are all exacerbated by zero tolerance laws that restrict access to clean needles. The drug war is not the promoter of family values that some would have us believe. Children of inmates are at risk of educational failure, joblessness, addiction and delinquency. Drug abuse is bad, but the drug war is worse.[29]

Moral crusades designed to draw a clear line between behavior that is deviant but legal and behavior that is outlawed and criminal did not end in the 1930s. In 2004, "shock jock" radio host Howard Stern was fined by the Federal Communications Commission (FCC) for "repeated, graphic and explicit sexual descriptions that were pandering, titillating or used to shock the audience."[30] The government action prompted Clear Channel Communications to drop Stern's show from their stations. In retaliation, Stern posted on his website transcripts from the *Oprah* TV show that used very similar language but were deemed nonoffensive by government regulators.[31] Stern was so outraged by the campaign to censor his program that he left public broadcasting for unregulated satellite radio.

In sum, criminologists are concerned with the concept of deviance and its relationship to criminality. The shifting definition of deviant behavior is closely associated with our concept of crime. The relationship among criminology, criminal justice, and deviance is illustrated in Concept Summary 1.3.

CONNECTIONS

Some of the drugs considered highly dangerous today were once sold openly and considered medically beneficial. For example, the narcotic drug heroin, now considered extremely addicting and dangerous, was originally given its name in the mistaken belief that its pain-killing properties would prove "heroic" to medical patients. The history of drug and alcohol abuse and legalization efforts will be discussed further in Chapter 13.

The Concept of Crime

Professional criminologists usually align themselves with one of several schools of thought, or perspectives. Each of these perspectives maintains its own view of what constitutes criminal behavior and what causes people to engage in criminality. A

decriminalized
Having criminal penalties reduced rather than eliminated.

CONCEPT SUMMARY 1.3 Criminology: Criminal Justice and Deviance

CRIMINOLOGY

Criminology explores the etiology (origin), extent, and nature of crime in society. Criminologists are concerned with identifying the nature, extent, and cause of crime.

CRIMINAL JUSTICE

Criminal justice refers to the agencies of social control that handle criminal offenders. Criminal justice scholars engage in describing, analyzing, and explaining operations of the agencies of justice, specifically the police departments, courts, and correctional facilities. They seek more effective methods of crime control and offender rehabilitation.

OVERLAPPING AREAS OF CONCERN

Criminal justice experts cannot begin to design effective programs of crime prevention or rehabilitation without understanding the nature and cause of crime. They require accurate criminal statistics and data to test the effectiveness of crime control and prevention programs.

DEVIANCE

Deviance refers to the study of behavior that departs from social norms. Included within the broad spectrum of deviant acts are behaviors ranging from violent crimes to joining a nudist colony. Not all crimes are deviant or unusual acts, and not all deviant acts are illegal.

OVERLAPPING AREAS OF CONCERN

Under what circumstances do deviant behaviors become crimes? When does sexually oriented material cross the line from merely suggestive to obscene and therefore illegal? If an illegal act becomes a norm, should society reevaluate its criminal status? There is still debate over the legalization and/or decriminalization of abortion, recreational drug use, possession of handguns, and assisted suicide.

criminologist's choice of orientation or perspective depends, in part, on his or her definition of crime. The three most common concepts of crime used by criminologists are the consensus view, the conflict view, and the interactionist view.

Consensus View of Crime

According to the **consensus view**, crimes are behaviors that all elements of society consider to be repugnant. The rich and powerful as well as the poor and indigent are believed to agree on which behaviors are so repugnant that they should be outlawed and criminalized. Therefore, the **criminal law**—the written code that defines crimes and their punishments—reflects the values, beliefs, and opinions of society's mainstream. The term "consensus" implies general agreement among a majority of citizens on what behaviors should be prohibited by criminal law and hence be viewed as crimes.[32]

This approach to crime implies that it is a function of the beliefs, morality, and rules inherent in Western civilization. Ideally, the laws apply equally to all members of society, and their effects are not restricted to any single element of society.

Conflict View of Crime

Although most practicing criminologists accept the consensus model of crime, others take a more political orientation toward its content. The **conflict view** depicts society as a collection of diverse groups—such as owners, workers, professionals, and students—who are in constant and continuing conflict. Groups able to assert their political power use the law and the criminal justice system to advance their economic and social position. Criminal laws, therefore, are viewed as acts created to protect the haves from the have-nots. Conflict criminologists often contrast the harsh penalties exacted on the poor for their "street crimes" (burglary, robbery, and larceny) with the minor penalties the wealthy receive for their white-collar crimes (securities violations and other illegal business practices). Whereas the poor go to prison for minor law violations, the wealthy are given lenient sentences for even the most serious breaches of law.

consensus view
The belief that the majority of citizens in a society share common values and agree on what behaviors should be defined as criminal.

criminal law
The written code that defines crimes and their punishments.

conflict view
The belief that criminal behavior is defined by those in a position of power to protect and advance their own self-interest.

Interactionist View of Crime

According to the **interactionist view,** the definition of crime reflects the preferences and opinions of people who hold social power in a particular legal jurisdiction. These people use their influence to impose their definition of right and wrong on the rest of the population. They maintain their power by stigmatizing or labeling people who fall outside their definition of right and wrong. Criminals therefore are individuals that society labels as outcasts or deviants because they have violated social rules. In a classic statement, sociologist Howard Becker argued, "The deviant is one to whom that label has successfully been applied; deviant behavior is behavior people so label."[33] Crimes are outlawed behaviors because society defines them that way, not because they are inherently evil or immoral acts.

Interactionists see criminal law as conforming to the beliefs of "moral crusaders," or moral entrepreneurs, who use their influence to shape the legal process as they see fit.[34] Laws against pornography, prostitution, and drugs are believed to be motivated more by moral crusades than by capitalist sensibilities. Consequently, interactionists are concerned with shifting moral and legal standards.

A Definition of Crime

Because of their diverse perspectives, criminologists have taken a variety of approaches in explaining crime's causes and suggesting methods for its control (see Concept Summary 1.4). Considering these differences, we can take elements from each school of thought to formulate an integrated definition of crime such as the following:

> "Crime" is a violation of societal rules of behavior as interpreted and expressed by the criminal law, which reflects public opinion, traditional values, and the viewpoint of people currently holding social and political power. Individuals who violate these rules are subject to sanctions by state authority, social stigma, and loss of status.

This definition combines the consensus view that the criminal law defines crimes, the conflict perspective's emphasis on political power and control, and the interactionist concept of stigma. Thus, crime as defined here is a political, social, and economic function of modern life.

No matter which definition of crime we embrace, criminal behavior is tied to the criminal law. It is therefore important for all criminologists to have some understanding of the development of criminal law, its objectives, its elements, and how it evolves. ✔ CHECKPOINTS

✔ CHECKPOINTS

✔ Criminal statistics calculation involves creating accurate measurements of crime trends and patterns.

✔ Some criminologists study the origins and sociology of law.

✔ Theorists search for the origins of crime causations.

✔ Some criminologists try to understand and describe patterns and trends in particular criminal behaviors such as serial murder or rape.

✔ Penologists study the correctional system and the control of criminals.

✔ Victimologists try to understand why some people become crime victims.

✔ There are a number of views of what crime entails. The three major views are consensus, conflict, and interactionist.

CONCEPT SUMMARY 1.4 The Definition of Crime

The definition of crime affects how criminologists view the cause and control of illegal behavior and shapes their research orientation.

CONSENSUS VIEW

- The law defines crime.
- Agreement exists on outlawed behavior.
- Laws apply to all citizens equally.

CONFLICT VIEW

- The law is a tool of the ruling class.
- Crime is a politically defined concept.
- "Real crimes," such as racism, sexism, and classism, are not outlawed.
- The law is used to control the underclass.

INTERACTIONIST VIEW

- Moral entrepreneurs define crime.
- Acts become crimes because society defines them that way.
- Criminal labels are life-transforming events.

interactionist view
The belief that those with social power are able to impose their values on society as a whole, and these values then define criminal behavior.

CRIME AND THE CRIMINAL LAW

● Common law was created by English judges during the Middle Ages. It unified local legal practices into a national system of laws and punishments. Common law serves as the basis for the American legal system.

The concept of criminal law has been recognized for more than 3,000 years. Hammurabi (1792–1750 BCE), the sixth king of Babylon, created the most famous set of written laws of the ancient world, known today as the **Code of Hammurabi.**

Preserved on basalt rock columns, the code established a system of crime and punishment based on physical retaliation ("an eye for an eye"). The severity of punishment depended on class standing: If convicted of an unprovoked assault, a slave would be killed, whereas a freeman might lose a limb.

More familiar is the **Mosaic Code** of the Israelites (1200 BCE). According to tradition, God entered into a covenant, or contract, with the tribes of Israel in which they agreed to obey his law (the 613 laws of the Old Testament, including the Ten Commandments), as presented to them by Moses, in return for God's special care and protection. The Mosaic Code is not only the foundation of Judeo-Christian moral teachings but also a basis for the U.S. legal system. Prohibitions against murder, theft, perjury, and adultery preceded, by several thousand years, the same laws found in the modern United States.

Common Law

After the Norman conquest of England in 1066, royal judges began to travel throughout the land, holding court in each county several times a year. When court was in session, the royal administrator, or judge, would summon a number of citizens who would, on their oath, tell of the crimes and serious breaches of the peace that had occurred since the judge's last visit. The royal judge would then decide what to do in each case, using local custom and rules of conduct as his guide. Courts were bound to follow the law established in previous cases unless a higher authority, such as the king or the pope, overruled the law.

The present English system of law came into existence during the reign of Henry II (1154–1189), when royal judges began to publish their decisions in local cases. Judges began to use these written decisions as a basis for their decision making, and eventually a fixed body of legal rules and principles was established. If a new rule was successfully applied in a number of different cases, it would become a **precedent.** These precedents would then be commonly applied in all similar cases—hence the term **common law.** Crimes such as murder, burglary, arson, and rape are common-law crimes whose elements were initially defined by judges. They are referred to as *mala in se,* or inherently evil and depraved. When the situation required, the English Parliament enacted legislation to supplement the judge-made common law. Crimes defined by Parliament, which reflected existing social conditions, were referred to as *mala prohibitum,* or **statutory crimes.**

Before the American Revolution, the colonies, then under British rule, were subject to the common law. After the colonies acquired their independence, state legislatures standardized common-law crimes such as murder, burglary, arson, and rape by putting them into statutory form in criminal codes. As in England, whenever common law proved inadequate to deal with changing social and moral issues, the states and Congress supplemented it with legislative statutes, creating new elements in the various state and federal legal codes.

Code of Hammurabi
The first written criminal code, developed in Babylonia about 2000 BCE.

Mosaic Code
The laws of the ancient Israelites, found in the Old Testament of the Judeo-Christian Bible.

precedent
A rule derived from previous judicial decisions and applied to future cases; the basis of common law.

common law
Early English law, developed by judges, which became the standardized law of the land in England and eventually formed the basis of the criminal law in the United States.

statutory crimes
Crimes defined by legislative bodies in response to changing social conditions, public opinion, and custom.

Contemporary Criminal Law

Criminal laws are now divided into felonies and misdemeanors. The distinction is based on seriousness: A **felony** is a serious offense; a **misdemeanor** is a minor or petty crime. Crimes such as murder, rape, and burglary are felonies; they are punished with long prison sentences or even death. Crimes such as unarmed assault and battery, petty larceny, and disturbing the peace are misdemeanors; they are punished with a fine or a period of incarceration in a county jail.

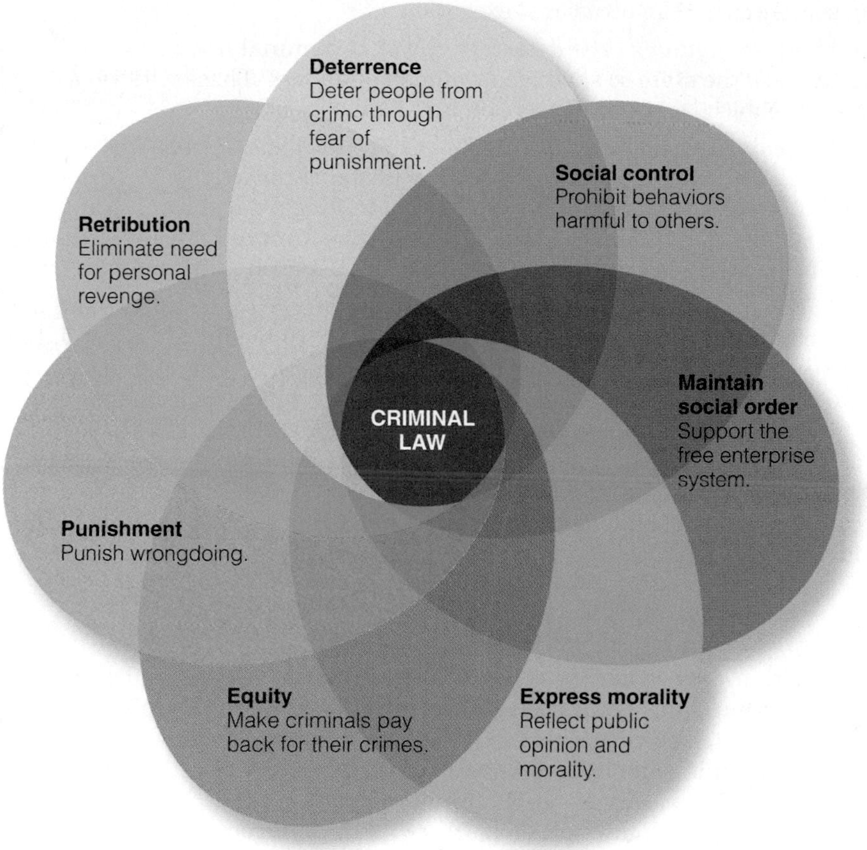

Figure 1.1
Purposes of the Criminal Law

Deterrence Deter people from crime through fear of punishment.

Social control Prohibit behaviors harmful to others.

Retribution Eliminate need for personal revenge.

CRIMINAL LAW

Maintain social order Support the free enterprise system.

Punishment Punish wrongdoing.

Equity Make criminals pay back for their crimes.

Express morality Reflect public opinion and morality.

Regardless of their classification, acts prohibited by the criminal law constitute behaviors considered unacceptable and impermissible by those in power. People who engage in these acts are eligible for severe sanctions. By outlawing these behaviors, the government expects to achieve a number of social goals (see Figure 1.1).

- *Enforcing social control.* Those who hold political power rely on criminal law to formally prohibit behaviors believed to threaten societal well-being or to challenge their authority. For example, U.S. criminal law incorporates centuries-old prohibitions against the following behaviors harmful to others: taking another person's possessions, physically harming another person, damaging another person's property, and cheating another person out of his or her possessions. Similarly, the law prevents actions that challenge the legitimacy of the government, such as planning its overthrow, collaborating with its enemies, and so on.
- *Discouraging revenge.* By punishing people who infringe on the rights, property, and freedom of others, the law shifts the burden of revenge from the individual to the state. As Oliver Wendell Holmes stated, this prevents "the greater evil of private retribution."[35] Although state retaliation may offend the sensibilities of many citizens, it is greatly preferable to a system in which people would have to seek justice for themselves.
- *Expressing public opinion and morality.* Criminal law reflects constantly changing public opinions and moral values. *Mala in se* crimes, such as murder and forcible rape, are almost universally prohibited; however, the prohibition of legislatively created *mala prohibitum* crimes, such as traffic offenses and gambling violations, changes according to social conditions and attitudes. Criminal law is used to codify these changes.
- *Deterring criminal behavior.* Criminal law has a social control function. It can control, restrain, and direct human behavior through its sanctioning power. The threat of punishment associated with violating the law is designed to prevent crimes before they occur. During the Middle Ages, public executions drove this

felony
A serious offense that carries a penalty of imprisonment, usually for one year or more, and may entail loss of political rights.

misdemeanor
A minor crime usually punished by a short jail term and/or a fine.

point home. Today criminal law's impact is felt through news accounts of long prison sentences and an occasional execution.

- *Punishing wrongdoing.* The deterrent power of criminal law is tied to the authority it gives the state to sanction or punish offenders. Those who violate criminal law are subject to physical coercion and punishment.
- *Creating equity.* Criminals benefit from their misdeeds. People who violate business laws make huge profits from their illegal transactions; the drug dealer accumulates wealth because of his trafficking in illegal substances. Through fines, forfeiture, and other economic sanctions, the criminal law redistributes illegal gains back to society, thereby negating the criminal's unfair advantage.
- *Maintaining social order.* All legal systems are designed to support and maintain the boundaries of the social system they serve. In medieval England, the law protected the feudal system by defining an orderly system of property transfer and ownership. Laws in some socialist nations protect the primacy of the state by strictly curtailing profiteering and individual enterprise. Our own free enterprise system is also supported and sustained by criminal law. In a sense, the content of criminal law is more a reflection of the needs of those who control the existing economic and political system than a representation of some idealized moral code.

The Evolution of Criminal Law

The criminal law is constantly evolving in an effort to reflect social and economic conditions. Sometimes legal changes are prompted by highly publicized cases that generate fear and concern. For example, a number of highly publicized cases of celebrity stalking, including Robert John Bardo's fatal shooting of actress Rebecca Schaeffer on July 18, 1989, prompted more than 25 U.S. states to enact stalking statutes. Such laws prohibit "the willful, malicious, and repeated following and harassing of another person."[36] Similarly, after 7-year-old Megan Kanka of Hamilton Township, New Jersey, was killed in 1994 by a repeat sexual offender who had moved into her neighborhood, the federal government passed legislation requiring that the general public be notified of local pedophiles (sexual offenders who target children).[37] California's sexual predator law, which took effect on January 1, 1996, allows people convicted of sexually violent crimes against two or more victims to be committed to a mental institution after their prison terms have been served. This law has already been upheld by **appellate court** judges in the state.[38]

The criminal law may also change because of shifts in culture and social conventions and reflect a newfound tolerance for behavior condemned only a few years before. In an important 2003 case, *Lawrence v. Texas,* the Supreme Court declared that laws banning sodomy were unconstitutional because they violated the due process rights of citizens because of their sexual orientation.[39] The Profiles in Crime feature discusses one such emerging form of criminal behavior. The future direction of U.S. criminal law remains unclear. Certain actions, such as crimes by corporations and political corruption, will be labeled as criminal and given more attention. Other offenses, such as recreational drug use, may be reduced in importance or removed entirely from the criminal law system. In addition, changing technology and its ever-increasing global and local roles in our lives will require modifications in criminal law. ✔ CHECKPOINTS

✔ CHECKPOINTS

✔ The American legal system is a direct descendant of the British common law.

✔ The criminal law has a number of different goals, including social control, punishment, retribution, deterrence, equity, and the representation of morality.

✔ Each crime has both a physical and a mental element.

✔ Persons accused of crimes can defend themselves either by denying the criminal act or by presenting an excuse or justification for their actions.

✔ The criminal law is constantly changing in an effort to reflect social values and contemporary issues and problems.

ETHICAL ISSUES IN CRIMINOLOGY

A critical issue facing criminology students involves recognizing the field's political and social consequences. All too often criminologists forget the social responsibility they bear as experts in the area of crime and justice. When government agencies request their views of issues, their pronouncements and opinions may become the basis for sweeping social policy.

appellate court
Court that reviews trial court procedures to determine whether they have complied with accepted rules and constitutional doctrines.

Profiles in Crime

The Mother of All Snakeheads

Cheng Chui Ping was one of the most powerful underworld figures in New York. Known by the slang term "the Mother of all Snakeheads," this meant that she was top dog in the human smuggling trade; to her friends in Chinatown she was "Sister Ping."

Cheng was an illegal immigrant herself. Born in 1949 in the poor farming village of Shengmei in Fujian province, she left her husband and family behind and set out for the West, traveling via Hong Kong and Canada before ending up in New York in 1981. She opened a grocery store and started on other ventures that became fronts for her people trafficking business. For more than a decade, Cheng smuggled as many as 3,000 illegal immigrants from her native China into the United States—charging upwards of $40,000 per person. To ensure her clients paid their smuggling fees, Sister Ping hired members of the Fuk Ching, Chinatown's most feared gang, to transport and guard them in the United States.

In addition to running her own operation, Sister Ping helped other smugglers by financing large cargo vessels designed for human cargo. She also ran a money transmitting business out of her Chinatown variety store. She used this business to collect smuggling fees from family members of her own "customers," and also collected ransom money on behalf of other alien smugglers.

Conditions aboard the smuggling vessels were often inhumane. The voyages were dangerous, and at least once, one of the boats capsized while off-loading people to a larger vessel, and 14 of her "customers" drowned. The *Golden Venture,* a smuggling ship Sister Ping helped finance for others, was intentionally grounded off the coast of Rockaway, Queens, in early June 1993 when the off-loading vessel failed to meet it in the open sea. Many of the passengers could not swim; ten drowned.

Cheng Chui Ping was indicted in 1994 when members of the Fuk Ching gang cooperated with federal agents. After her indictment, Cheng fled to China, where she continued to run a smuggling operation. In April 2000, Hong Kong police arrested her at the airport. Cheng fought extradition but was eventually delivered to the United States in July 2003. She was convicted in New York less than two years later on multiple counts, including money laundering, conspiracy to commit alien smuggling, and other smuggling-related offenses, and was sentenced to 35 years in prison.

© AP

The activities of Sister Ping illustrate how the law must evolve to confront newly emerging social problems such as illegal immigration. Other areas include cyber crime, drug importation, and terrorism. Unfortunately, the law is sometimes slow to change, and change comes only after conditions have reached a crisis. How might laws be changed to reduce illegal immigration? Should people caught entering the country illegally be charged with a felony and imprisoned?

SOURCES: FBI news release, "Sister Ping Sentenced to 35 Years in Prison for Alien Smuggling, Hostage Taking, Money Laundering, and Ransom Proceeds Conspiracy," March 16, 2006; http://newyork.fbi.gov/dojpressrel/pressrel06/sister_ping031606.htm; BBC news, Cheng Chui Ping: 'Mother of snakeheads' http://news.bbc.co.uk/2/hi/americas/4816354.stm.

The lives of millions of people can be influenced by criminological research data. Debates over gun control, capital punishment, and mandatory sentences are ongoing and contentious. Some criminologists have argued successfully for social service, treatment, and rehabilitation programs to reduce the crime rate; others consider these a waste of time, suggesting instead that a massive prison construction program coupled with tough criminal sentences can bring the crime rate down. By accepting their roles as experts on law-violating behavior, criminologists place themselves in a position of power. The potential consequences of their actions are enormous. Therefore, they must be both aware of the ethics of their profession and prepared to defend their work in the light of public scrutiny. Major ethical issues include what to study, whom to study, and how to conduct those studies.

- *What to study.* Criminologists must be concerned about the topics they study. Their research must not be directed by the sources of funding on which research projects rely. The objectivity of research may be questioned if studies are funded by organizations that have a vested interest in the outcome of the research. A study on the effectiveness of the defensive use of handguns to stop crime may be tainted if the funding for the project comes from a gun manufacturer whose sales may be affected by the research findings. It has been shown over the past decades that criminological research has been influenced by government funding linked to the topics the government wants research on and those it wishes to avoid. Recently, funding by political agencies has increased the likelihood that criminologists will address drug issues while spending less time on topics such as incapacitation and white-collar crime.[40] Should the nature and extent of scientific research be shaped by the hand of government, or should it remain independent of outside interference?

- *Whom to study.* Another ethical issue in criminology concerns selection of research subjects. Too often, criminologists focus their attention on the poor and minorities while ignoring middle-class white-collar crime, organized crime, and government crime. For example, a few social scientists have suggested that criminals have lower intelligence quotients than the average citizen and that because the average IQ score is lower among some minority groups, their crime rates are high.[41] This was the conclusion reached in *The Bell Curve,* a popular but highly controversial book written by Richard Herrnstein and Charles Murray.[42] Although such research is often methodologically unsound, it brings to light the tendency of criminologists to focus on one element of the community while ignoring others.
- *How to study.* A third area of concern involves the methods used in conducting research. One issue is whether subjects are fully informed about the purpose of research. When European American and African American youngsters are asked to participate in a survey of their behavior or to take an IQ test, are they told in advance that the data they provide may later be used to demonstrate racial differences in their self-reported crime rates? Criminologists must also be careful to keep records and information confidential in order to maintain the privacy of research participants. But ethical questions still linger: Should a criminologist who is told in confidence by a research subject about a future crime report her knowledge to the police? How far should a criminologist go to protect her sources of information; should stated intentions to commit offenses be disclosed?[43]

In studies that involve experimentation and treatment, care must be taken to protect those subjects who have been chosen for experimental and control groups. For example, is it ethical to provide a special program for one group while depriving others of the same opportunity just so they can later be compared? Conversely, criminologists must be careful to protect subjects from experiments that may actually cause harm. An examination of the highly publicized "Scared Straight" program, which brings youngsters into contact with hard-core felons in a prison setting, found that participants may have been harmed by their experience. Rather than being frightened into conformity, subjects actually increased their criminal behavior.[44] Finally, criminologists must take extreme care to ensure that research subjects are selected in a random and unbiased manner.[45]

THINKING Like a Criminologist

You have been experimenting with various techniques in order to identify a surefire method for predicting violent behavior in delinquents. Your procedure involves brain scans, DNA testing, and blood analysis. Used with samples of incarcerated adolescents, your procedure has been able to distinguish with 75 percent accuracy between youths with a history of violence and those who are exclusively property offenders. Your research indicates that if all youths were tested with your techniques, potentially violence-prone career criminals could be easily identified for special treatment. For example, children in the local school system could be tested, and those identified as violence-prone could be carefully monitored by teachers. Those at risk for future violence could be put into special programs as a precaution.

Some of your colleagues argue that this type of testing is unconstitutional because it violates the subjects' Fifth Amendment right against self-incrimination. There is also the problem of error: Some children may be falsely labeled as violence-prone.

How would you answer your critics? Is it fair or ethical to label people as potentially criminal and violent, even though they have not yet exhibited any antisocial behavior? Do the risks of such a procedure outweigh its benefits?

Summary

- Criminology is the scientific approach to the study of criminal behavior and society's reaction to law violations and violators. It is essentially an interdisciplinary field; many of its practitioners were originally trained as sociologists, psychologists, economists, political scientists, historians, and natural scientists.
- Criminology has a rich history, with roots in the utilitarian philosophy of Beccaria, the biological positivism of Lombroso, the social theory of Durkheim, and the political philosophy of Marx.
- The criminological enterprise includes subareas such as criminal statistics, the sociology of law, theory construction, criminal behavior systems, penology, and victimology.
- When they define crime, criminologists typically hold one of three perspectives: the consensus view, the conflict view, or the interactionist view.
- The consensus view holds that criminal behavior is defined by laws that reflect the values and morals of a majority of citizens.
- The conflict view states that criminal behavior is defined in such a way that economically powerful groups can retain their control over society.
- The interactionist view portrays criminal behavior as a relativistic, constantly changing concept that reflects society's current moral values. According to the interactionist view, behavior is labeled as criminal by those in power; criminals are people whom society chooses to label as outsiders or deviants.
- The criminal law is a set of rules that specify the behaviors society has outlawed.
- The criminal law serves several important purposes: It represents public opinion and moral values, it enforces social controls, it deters criminal behavior and wrongdoing, it punishes transgressors, it creates equity, and it banishes private retribution.
- The criminal law used in U.S. jurisdictions traces its origin to the English common law. In the U.S. legal system, lawmakers have codified common-law crimes into state and federal penal codes.
- The criminal law is undergoing constant reform. Some acts are being decriminalized—their penalties are being reduced—while penalties for others are becoming more severe.
- Ethical issues arise when information-gathering methods appear biased or exclusionary. These issues may cause serious consequences because research findings can significantly impact individuals and groups.

Take a Post-Test. Visit www.thomsonedu.com/criminaljustice/siegel and take the chapter Post-Test to monitor your progress and identify areas for further improvement. In addition to discovering what you've mastered, you'll learn which concepts need your added attention and get specific page references that direct you to the places in the text where you can find more information on them.

Key Terms

Critical Thinking Questions

1. What are the specific aims and purposes of the criminal law? To what extent does the criminal law control behavior? Do you believe that the law is too restrictive? Not restrictive enough?

2. If you ran the world, which acts, now legal, would you make criminal? Which criminal acts would you legalize? What would be the likely consequences of your actions?

3. Beccaria argued that the threat of punishment controls crime. Are there other forms of social control? Aside from the threat of legal punishment, what else controls your own behavior?

4. Would it be ethical for a criminologist to observe a teenage gang by hanging with them, drinking, and watching as they steal cars? Should the criminologist report that behavior to the police?

The Nature and Extent of Crime

CHAPTER 2

© Erik S. Lesser/Getty Images

ON MAY 31, 2003, ERIC RUDOLPH WAS ARRESTED BEHIND A GROCERY STORE in rural western North Carolina after five years on the run. Rudolph had detonated a bomb that exploded outside a Birmingham abortion clinic on January 29, 1998, killing a police officer and critically injuring a clinic nurse. He also set off a bomb that killed one person and injured 150 others in a park in downtown Atlanta during the 1996

Olympics and was involved in the 1997 bombings of a gay nightclub and a building that housed an abortion clinic.

Rudolph's crime spree is believed to have been motivated by his extreme political beliefs. He was a member of a white supremacist group called the Army of God. Rudolph was also an ardent anti-Semite who claimed that the Holocaust never happened and that the Jews now control the media and the government. Ironically, soon after he was arrested, the court appointed Richard S. Jaffe, a practicing Jew, to lead Rudolph's defense team.[1] On April 8, 2005, Rudolph agreed to plead guilty in all the attacks he was accused of executing in order to avoid the death penalty; he was sentenced to four consecutive life terms.[2]

CHAPTER OBJECTIVES

1. Be familiar with the various forms of crime data.
2. Know the problems associated with collecting data.
3. Be able to discuss the recent trends in the crime rate.
4. Be familiar with the factors that influence crime rates.
5. Be able to discuss the patterns in the crime rate.
6. Be able to discuss the association between social class and crime.
7. Recognize that there are age, gender, and racial patterns in crime.
8. Describe the various positions on gun control.
9. Be familiar with Wolfgang's pioneering research on chronic offending.
10. Be able to discuss the influence that the discovery of the chronic offender has had on criminology.

Take a Pre-Test. Visit www.thomsonedu.com/criminaljustice/siegel and take a Pre-Test to determine what you already know and identify the areas where you'll need to focus your study. The program will direct you to specific pages within the text where you can find further information on the correct answers to the questions you've missed.

Stories such as Rudolph's help convince most Americans that we live in a violent society. Are Americans justified in their fear of violent crime? Should they barricade themselves behind armed guards? Are crime rates actually rising or falling? And where do most crimes occur and who commits them? To answer these and similar questions, criminologists have devised elaborate methods of crime data collection and analysis. Without accurate data on the nature and extent of crime, it would not be possible to formulate theories that explain the onset of crime or to devise social policies that facilitate its control or elimination. Accurate data collection is also critical in order to assess the nature and extent of crime, track changes in the crime rate, and measure the individual and social factors that may influence criminality.

In this chapter, we review how crime data are collected on criminal offenders and offenses and what this information tells us about crime patterns and trends. We also examine the concept of criminal careers and discover what available crime data can tell us about the onset, continuation, and termination of criminality. We begin with a discussion of the most important sources of crime data that criminologists use to measure the nature and extent of crime.

PRIMARY SOURCES OF CRIME DATA

The primary sources of crime data are surveys and official records. Criminologists use these techniques to measure the nature and extent of criminal behavior and the personality, attitudes, and background of criminal offenders. Understanding how these data are collected provides insight into how professional criminologists approach various problems and questions in their field.

Official Records: The Uniform Crime Report

In order to understand more about the nature and extent of crime, criminologists use the records of government agencies such as police departments, prisons, and courts. The Federal Bureau of Investigation collects the most important crime record data from local law enforcement agencies and publishes them yearly in their **Uniform Crime Report (UCR)**. The UCR includes crimes reported to local law enforcement departments and the number of arrests made by police agencies.[3] The FBI receives and compiles records from more than 17,000 police departments

Uniform Crime Report (UCR)
Large database, compiled by the FBI, of crimes reported and arrests made each year throughout the United States.

Exhibit 2.1
Part I Crime Offenses

Criminal Homicide

Murder and Nonnegligent Manslaughter The willful (nonnegligent) killing of one human being by another. Deaths caused by negligence, attempts to kill, assaults to kill, suicides, accidental deaths, and justifiable homicides are excluded. Justifiable homicides are limited to (1) the killing of a felon by a law enforcement officer in the line of duty and (2) the killing of a felon, during the commission of a felony, by a private citizen.

Manslaughter by Negligence The killing of another person through gross negligence. Traffic fatalities are excluded. Although manslaughter by negligence is a Part I crime, it is not included in the crime index.

Forcible Rape

The carnal knowledge of a female forcibly and against her will. Included are rapes by force and attempts or assaults to rape. Statutory offenses (no force used—victim under age of consent) are excluded.

Robbery

The taking or attempting to take anything of value from the care, custody, or control of a person or persons by force or threat of force or violence and/or by putting the victim in fear.

Aggravated Assault

An unlawful attack by one person upon another for the purpose of inflicting severe or aggravated bodily injury. This type of assault is usually accompanied by the use of a weapon or by means likely to produce death or great bodily harm. Simple assaults are excluded.

Burglary/Breaking or Entering

The unlawful entry of a structure to commit a felony or a theft. Attempted forcible entry is included.

Larceny/Theft (except motor vehicle theft)

The unlawful taking, carrying, leading, or riding away of property from the possession or constructive possession of another. Examples are thefts of bicycles or automobile accessories, shoplifting, pocket picking, or the stealing of any property or article that is not taken by force and violence or by fraud. Attempted larcenies are included. Embezzlement, con games, forgery, worthless checks, and so on are excluded.

Motor Vehicle Theft

The theft or attempted theft of a motor vehicle. A motor vehicle is self-propelled and runs on the surface and not on rails. Specifically excluded from this category are motorboats, construction equipment, airplanes, and farming equipment.

Arson

Any willful or malicious burning or attempt to burn, with or without intent to defraud, a dwelling house, public building, motor vehicle, or aircraft, personal property of another, or the like.

SOURCE: FBI, *Uniform Crime Report*, 2004.

serving a majority of the U.S. population. The FBI tallies and annually publishes the number of reported offenses by city, county, standard metropolitan statistical area, and geographical divisions of the United States for the most serious crimes, referred to as **Part I crimes**: murder and nonnegligent manslaughter, forcible rape, robbery, aggravated assault, burglary, larceny, arson, and motor vehicle theft. Exhibit 2.1 defines these crimes.

In addition to these statistics, the UCR contains data on the number and characteristics (age, race, and gender) of individuals who have been arrested for these and all other crimes, referred to as non-index, or **Part II crimes**.

Compiling the Uniform Crime Report The methods used to compile the UCR are quite complex. Each month, law enforcement agencies report the number of Part I crimes known to them. These data are collected from records of all crime complaints that victims, officers who discovered the infractions, or other sources reported to these agencies.

Whenever criminal complaints are found through investigation to be unfounded or false, they are eliminated from the actual count. However, the number of actual offenses known is reported to the FBI whether or not anyone is arrested for the crime, the stolen property is recovered, or prosecution ensues.

In addition, each month, law enforcement agencies also report how many crimes were **cleared**. Crimes are cleared in two ways: (1) when at least one person is arrested, charged, and turned over to the court for prosecution; or (2) by exceptional means, when some element beyond police control precludes the physical arrest of an offender (such as the offender leaving the country). Data on the

Part I crimes
The eight most serious offenses included in the UCR: murder, rape, assault, robbery, burglary, arson, larceny, and motor vehicle theft.

Part II crimes
All crimes, including Part I crimes.

cleared crimes
Crimes are considered cleared when at least one person is arrested, charged, and turned over to the court for prosecution, or when some element beyond police control, such as the offender leaving the country, precludes the physical arrest of an offender.

Figure 2.1
Percentage of Part I Crimes Cleared by Arrest
SOURCE: www.fbi.gov/ucr/05cius/offenses/clearances/index.html#figure

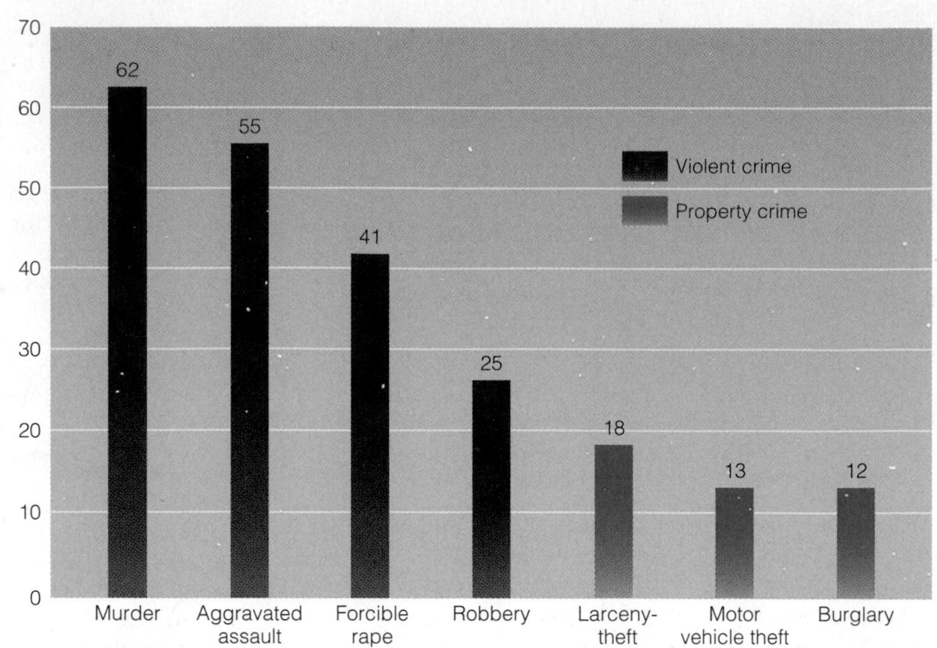

number of clearances involving the arrest of only juvenile offenders, data on the value of property stolen and recovered in connection with Part I offenses, and detailed information pertaining to criminal homicide are also reported. Traditionally, slightly more than 20 percent of all reported Part I crimes are cleared by arrest each year (Figure 2.1).

Violent crimes are more likely to be solved than property crimes because police devote more resources to these more serious acts. For these types of crime, witnesses (including the victim) are frequently available to identify offenders, and in many instances the victim and offender were previously acquainted.

The UCR uses three methods to express crime data. First, the number of crimes reported to the police and arrests made are expressed as raw figures (for instance, 16,692 murders occurred in 2005). Second, crime rates per 100,000 people are computed. That is, when the UCR indicates that the murder rate was 5.6 in 2005, it means that almost 6 people in every 100,000 were murdered between January 1 and December 31, 2005. This is the equation used:

$$\frac{\text{Number of Reported Crimes}}{\text{Total U.S. Population}} \times 100{,}000 = \text{Rate per } 100{,}000$$

Third, the FBI computes changes in the number and rate of crime over time. Murder rates declined 3.3 percent between 2003 and 2004, and the number of murders decreased 2.4 percent.

Validity of the UCR The accuracy of the UCR is somewhat suspect. Surveys indicate that fewer than half of all crime victims report incidents to police. Those who don't report may believe that the victimization was "a private matter," that "nothing could be done," or that the victimization was "not important enough."[4] Some victims do not trust the police or have confidence in their ability to solve crimes. Others do not have property insurance and therefore believe it is useless to report theft. In other cases, victims fear reprisals from an offender's friends or family, or in the case of family violence, from their spouse, boyfriend, or girlfriend.[5] Or they may believe that they are themselves somehow responsible for the crime: for example, the date rape victim who was drinking or had taken drugs before the attack.[6]

There is also evidence that local law enforcement agencies make errors in their reporting practices. Some departments may define crimes loosely—for example, reporting an assault on a woman as an attempted rape—whereas others pay strict

Profiles in Crime

FEMA Fraud

The UCR is a helpful method of assessing crime patterns and trends, but it fails to record many crimes, including violations of federal law. Take for instance the rather callous efforts of people such as Henry Edwards and Dwight Thomas, who hoped to criminally profit from tragedies such as the devastation caused by Hurricane Katrina.

On March 15, 2006, Henry Edwards of Atlanta, Georgia, and Dwight Thomas of Doraville, Georgia, pleaded guilty in federal district court to stealing federal relief funds intended for Hurricane Katrina victims. According to the U.S. attorney, on September 3, 2005, Edwards had filed a false claim for emergency assistance with FEMA, the federal relief agency, claiming he was a victim of Hurricane Katrina. He told authorities he lived at 701 Loyola Avenue, New Orleans, when Hurricane Katrina made landfall and that he had sustained losses. He received, cashed, and spent the $2,000 check FEMA sent to him for emergency assistance. FEMA later discovered that Edwards never lived in New Orleans and was a resident of Atlanta when the hurricane made landfall. In fact, 701 Loyola Avenue, New Orleans, is not an address for a residence, but the address for a U.S. post office building.

Thomas made his false claim on September 12, 2005, when he applied for emergency assistance and rental assistance from FEMA, claiming that he was residing at 2700 Whitney Avenue, in Harvey, Louisiana, when Hurricane Katrina made landfall. Thomas received and spent both the $2,000 emergency assistance check and the $2,358 rental assistance check, even though he was not a victim of Hurricane Katrina and was in fact living with his girlfriend and her family in Doraville at the time Hurricane Katrina made landfall.

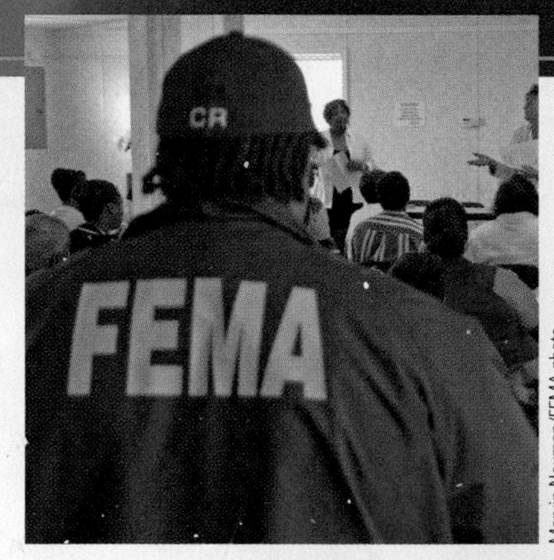

Marvin Nauman/FEMA photo

Edwards and Thomas were charged with a variety of crimes, including mail fraud, filing false claims, and theft of FEMA funds, and both could receive up to 20 years in prison. Even though their crimes were quite serious, they would not have shown up in the UCR.

SOURCE: Department of Justice news release, "Two Plead Guilty to Stealing Hurricane Katrina Funds," March 15, 2006, http://atlanta.fbi.gov/dojpressrel/pressrel06/katrina_fraud031506.htm.

attention to FBI guidelines.[7] Ironically, what appears to be a rising crime rate may simply be an artifact of improved police record-keeping ability.[8]

Methodological issues also contribute to questions regarding the UCR's validity. The complex scoring procedure used by the FBI means that many serious crimes are not counted. For example, during an armed bank robbery, the offender strikes a teller with the butt of a handgun. The robber runs from the bank and steals an automobile at the curb. Although the offender has technically committed robbery, aggravated assault, and motor vehicle theft, because robbery is the most serious offense, it is the only one recorded in the UCR.[9] Clearly, a more reliable source for crime statistics is needed. The most common issues affecting the validity of the UCR are summarized in Exhibit 2.2.

NIBRS: The Future of the Uniform Crime Report

Clearly there must be a more reliable source for crime statistics than the UCR as it stands today. Beginning in 1982, a five-year redesign effort was undertaken to provide more comprehensive and detailed crime statistics. The effort resulted in the **National Incident-Based Reporting System (NIBRS)**, a program that collects data on each reported crime incident. Instead of submitting statements of the kinds of crime that individual citizens report to the police and summary statements of resulting arrests, the new program requires local police agencies to provide at least a brief account of each incident and arrest, including the incident, victim, and offender information.

Under NIBRS, law enforcement authorities provide information to the FBI on each criminal incident involving 46 specific offenses, including the eight Part I crimes, that occur in their jurisdiction; arrest information on the 46 offenses plus 11 lesser offenses is also provided in NIBRS. These expanded crime categories

National Incident-Based Reporting System (NIBRS)
Program that requires local police agencies to provide a brief account of each incident and arrest within 22 crime patterns, including incident, victim, and offender information.

Exhibit 2.2

Factors Affecting the Validity of the Uniform Crime Report

1. No federal crimes are reported. (See Profiles in Crime.)
2. Reports are voluntary and vary in accuracy and completeness.
3. Not all police departments submit reports.
4. The FBI uses estimates in its total crime projections.
5. If an offender commits multiple crimes, only the most serious is recorded. Thus, if a narcotics addict rapes, robs, and murders a victim, only the murder is recorded. Consequently, many lesser crimes go unreported.
6. Each act is listed as a single offense for some crimes but not for others. If a man robbed six people in a bar, the offense would be listed as one robbery; but if he assaulted or murdered them, it would be listed as six assaults or six murders.
7. Incomplete acts are lumped together with completed ones.
8. Important differences exist between the FBI's definition of certain crimes and those used in a number of states.
9. Victimless crimes often go undetected.
10. Many cases of child abuse and family violence are unreported.

SOURCE: Leonard Savitz, "Official Statistics," in *Contemporary Criminology,* ed. Leonard Savitz and Norman Johnston (New York: John Wiley, 1982), pp. 3–15; updated 2006.

include numerous additional crimes, such as blackmail, embezzlement, drug offenses, and bribery; this allows a national database on the nature of crime, victims, and criminals to be developed. Other collected information includes statistics gathered by federal law enforcement agencies, as well as data on hate or bias crimes. Thus far, more than 20 states have implemented their NIBRS programs, and 12 others are in the process of finalizing their data collections. When this program is fully implemented and adopted across the nation, it should bring about greater uniformity in cross-jurisdictional reporting and improve the accuracy of official crime data.[10]

Survey Research

Another important method of collecting crime data is through surveys in which people are asked about their attitudes, beliefs, values, and characteristics, as well as their experiences with crime and victimization. Surveys typically involve **sampling**, the process of selecting for study a limited number of subjects who are representative of entire groups sharing similar characteristics, called the **population**. To understand the social forces that produce crime, a criminologist might interview a sample of 3,000 prison inmates drawn from the population of more than 2 million inmates in the United States; in this case, the sample represents the entire population of U.S. inmates. It is assumed that the characteristics of people or events in a carefully selected sample will be similar to those of the population at large. If the sampling is done correctly, the responses of the 3,000 inmates should represent the entire population of inmates.

sampling
Selecting a limited number of people for study as representative of a larger group.

population
All people who share a particular characteristic, such as all high school students or all police officers.

National Crime Victimization Survey (NCVS)
The ongoing victimization study conducted jointly by the Justice Department and the U.S. Census Bureau that surveys victims about their experiences with law violation.

The National Crime Victimization Survey (NCVS)

Because many victims do not report their experiences to the police, the UCR cannot measure all the annual criminal activity. To address the nonreporting issue, the federal government sponsors the **National Crime Victimization Survey (NCVS)**, a comprehensive, nationwide survey of victimization in the United States.

Each year data are obtained from a large nationally representative sample; in 2005, more than 77,000 households with more than 134,000 people age 12 or older were interviewed.[11] People are asked to report their experiences with such crimes as rape, sexual assault, robbery, assault, theft, household burglary, and motor vehicle theft. Due to the care with which the samples are drawn and the high completion rate, NCVS data are considered a relatively unbiased, valid estimate of all victimizations for the target crimes included in the survey.

The NCVS finds that many crimes go unreported to police. The UCR shows that slightly more than 90,000 rapes or attempted rapes occur each year, but the NCVS estimates that more than 200,000 actually occur. The reason for such discrepancies is that fewer than half of violent crimes, fewer than one-third of personal theft crimes (such as pocket picking), and fewer than half of household thefts are reported to police. Victims seem to report to the police only crimes that involve considerable loss or injury. If we are to believe NCVS findings, the official UCR statistics do not provide an accurate picture of the crime problem because many crimes go unreported to the police.

CONNECTIONS

Victim surveys provide information not only about criminal incidents that have occurred but also about the individuals who are most at risk of falling victim to crime and where and when they are most likely to become victimized. Data from recent NCVS surveys are used in Chapter 3 to draw a portrait of the nature and extent of victimization in the United States.

Validity of the NCVS The NCVS may also suffer from some methodological problems. As a result, its findings must be interpreted with caution. Among the potential problems are the following:

- Overreporting due to victims' misinterpretation of events. A lost wallet may be reported as stolen, or an open door may be viewed as a burglary attempt.
- Underreporting due to the embarrassment of reporting crime to interviewers, fear of getting in trouble, or simply forgetting an incident.
- Inability to record the personal criminal activity of those interviewed, such as drug use or gambling; murder is also not included, for obvious reasons.
- Sampling errors, which produce a group of respondents who do not represent the nation as a whole.
- Inadequate question format that invalidates responses. Some groups, such as adolescents, may be particularly susceptible to error because of question format and wording.[12]

Self-Report Surveys

Another common tool used to measure crime is the **self-report survey** that asks people to describe, in detail, their recent and lifetime participation in criminal activity. Self-reports are given in groups, and the respondents are promised anonymity in order to ensure the validity and honesty of the responses. Most self-report studies have focused on juvenile delinquency and youth crime.[13] However, self-reports can also be used to examine the offense histories of prison inmates, drug users, and other segments of the population.[14]

Most self-report surveys also contain questions about attitudes, values, and behaviors. There may be questions about a participant's substance abuse history (for instance, How many times have you used marijuana?) and the participant's family history (Did your parents ever strike you with a stick or a belt?). By correlating the responses, criminologists can analyze the relationship between personal factors and criminal behaviors. Statistical analysis of the responses can be used to determine such issues as (1) are people who report being abused as children also more likely to use drugs as adults, and (2) does school failure lead to delinquency?[15] Figure 2.2 illustrates some typical self-report items.

Validity of Self-Reports Critics of self-report studies frequently suggest that expecting people to candidly admit illegal acts is unreasonable. This is especially true of those with official records, who may be engaging in the most criminality. At the same time, some people may exaggerate their criminal acts, forget some of them, or be confused about what is being asked. Some surveys contain an overabundance of trivial offenses, such as shoplifting small items or using false identification to obtain alcohol, often lumped together with serious crimes to form a total crime index. Consequently, comparisons between groups can be highly misleading.

The "missing cases" phenomenon is also a concern. Even if 90 percent of a school population voluntarily participate in a self-report study, researchers can never be sure whether the few who refuse to participate or are absent that day constitute a significant portion of the school's population of persistent high-rate

self-report survey
A research approach that requires subjects to reveal their own participation in delinquent or criminal acts.

Please indicate how often in the past 12 months you did each act (check the best answer).

	Never did act	One time	2–5 times	6–9 times	10+ times
Stole something worth less than $50					
Stole something worth more than $50					
Used cocaine					
Participated in a fistfight					
Carried a weapon such as a gun or knife					
Fought someone using a weapon					

Figure 2.2
Self-Report Survey Questions

CONNECTIONS

Criminologists suspect that a few high-rate offenders are responsible for a disproportionate share of all serious crime. Results would be badly skewed if even a few of these chronic offenders were absent or refused to participate in schoolwide self-report surveys. For more on chronic offenders, see the section that begins on page 48.

offenders. Research indicates that offenders with the most extensive prior criminality are also the most likely "to be poor historians of their own crime commission rates."[16] It is also unlikely that the most serious chronic offenders in the teenage population are willing to cooperate with criminologists administering self-report tests.[17] Institutionalized youths, who are not generally represented in the self-report surveys, are not only more delinquent than the general youth population but are also considerably more misbehaving than the most delinquent youths identified in the typical self-report survey.[18] Consequently, self-reports may measure only nonserious, occasional delinquents while ignoring hard-core chronic offenders who may be institutionalized and unavailable for self-reports.

To address these criticisms, various techniques have been used to verify self-report data.[19] The "known group" method compares youths known to be offenders with those who are not, to see whether the former report more delinquency. Research shows that when kids are asked if they have ever been arrested or sent to court, their responses accurately reflect their true life experiences.[20]

One way to improve the reliability of self-reports is to use them in a consistent way with different groups of subjects over time. That way, trends in self-reported crime and drug abuse can be measured to see if changes have occurred. One source of longitudinal self-report data is the Monitoring the Future study, which researchers at the University of Michigan Institute for Social Research (ISR) have been collecting yearly since 1978. This national survey, which typically involves more than 2,500 high school seniors, is one of the most important sources of self-report data.[21] You can reach the Monitoring the Future website at http://monitoringthefuture.org.

Like victimization surveys, the MTF data indicate that the number of people who break the law is far greater than the number projected by official statistics. Almost everyone questioned is found to have violated some law at some time, including truancy, alcohol abuse, use of a false ID, shoplifting or larceny under $50, fighting, marijuana use, and damage to the property of others. Furthermore, self-reports dispute the notion that criminals and delinquents specialize in one type of crime or another; offenders seem to engage in a "mixed bag" of crime and deviance.

Although these studies are supportive, self-report data must be interpreted with some caution. Asking subjects about their past behavior may capture more serious crimes but miss minor criminal acts; that is, people remember armed robberies and rapes better than they do minor assaults and altercations.[22] In addition, some classes of offenders (for example, substance abusers) may have a tough time accounting for their prior misbehavior.[23]

Evaluating Crime Data

Each source of crime data has strengths and weaknesses. The FBI survey contains data on the number and characteristics of people arrested, information that the other data sources lack. Some recent research indicates that for serious crimes, such as drug trafficking, arrest data can provide a meaningful measure of the level of criminal activity in a particular neighborhood environment that other data sources cannot provide. It is also the source of information on particular crimes such as murder, which no other data source can provide.[24] The UCR remains the standard unit of analysis upon which most criminological research is based. However, this survey omits the many crimes that victims choose not to report to police, and it is subject to the reporting caprices of individual police departments.

The NCVS includes unreported crime and important information on the personal characteristics of victims. However, the data consist of estimates made from relatively limited samples of the total U.S. population, so that even narrow fluctuations in the rates of some crimes can have a major impact on findings. It also relies on personal recollections that may be inaccurate. The NCVS does not include data on important crime patterns, including murder and drug abuse.

Self-report surveys can provide information on the personal characteristics of offenders, such as their attitudes, values, beliefs, and psychological profiles, that is unavailable from any other source. Yet, at their core, self-reports rely on the honesty of criminal offenders and drug abusers, a population not generally known for accuracy and integrity.

Although their tallies of crimes are certainly not in synch, the crime patterns and trends that all three sources record are often quite similar.[25] For example, they all generally agree about the personal characteristics of serious criminals (such as age and gender) and where and when crime occurs (such as urban areas, nighttime, and summer months). In addition, the problems inherent in each source are consistent over time. Therefore, even if the data sources are incapable of providing a precise and valid count of crime at any given time, they are reliable indicators of changes and fluctuations in yearly crime rates. In addition to these primary sources of crime data, criminologists use other data in their studies. These are discussed in Exhibit 2.3.

CRIME TRENDS

Crime is not new.[26] Studies have indicated that a gradual increase in the crime rate, especially in violent crime, occurred from 1830 to 1860. Following the Civil War, this rate increased significantly for about 15 years. Then, from 1880 up to the time of the First World War, with the possible exception of the years immediately preceding and following the war, the number of reported crimes decreased. After a period of readjustment, the crime rate steadily declined until the Depression (about 1930), when another crime wave was recorded. As measured by the UCR, crime rates increased gradually following the 1930s until the 1960s, when the growth rate became much greater. The homicide rate, which had actually declined from the 1930s to the 1960s, also began a sharp increase that continued through the 1970s.

In 1981 the number of Part I crimes rose to about 13.4 million and then began a gradual upward trend until 1991 when police recorded almost 15 million crimes. Since then, the number of crimes has been in decline. Figure 2.3 illustrates crime rate trends between 1960 and 2005, the last data available.

As the figure shows, there has been a significant downward trend in the rate of crime for more than a decade. Even teenage criminality, a source of national concern, has been in decline during this period, decreasing by about one-third over the past 20 years. The factors that help explain the upward and downward movement in crime rates are discussed in the Current Issues in Crime feature "Explaining Crime Trends on pages 34–35.

Trends in Violent Crime

The violent crimes reported by the FBI include murder, rape, assault, and robbery. In 2005, the last data available, violent crime increased from the year before. About 1.4 million violent crimes were reported to police, a rate of around 466 per

Exhibit 2.3
Alternative Crime Measures

In addition to the primary sources of crime data—UCR, NCVS, and self-report surveys—criminologists use several other methods to acquire data. Although not exhaustive, the methods described here are routinely used in criminological research and data collection.

Cohort Research Data

Collecting cohort data involves observing over time a group of people who share a like characteristic. Researchers might select all girls born in Boston in 1970 and then follow their behavior patterns for 20 years. The research data might include their school experiences, arrests, hospitalizations, and information about their family life (marriages, divorces, parental relations, for example). Data may also be collected directly from the subjects during interviews and meetings with family members. If the cohort is carefully drawn, it may be possible to accumulate a complex array of data that can be used to determine which life experiences produce criminal careers. Another approach is to take a contemporary cohort, such as men in prison in New York in 2006, and then look back into their past and collect data from educational, family, police, and hospital records—a format known as a retrospective cohort study. If criminologists wanted to identify childhood and adolescent risk factors for criminality, they might acquire the inmates' prior police and court records, school records, and so on.

Experimental Data

Sometimes criminologists conduct controlled experiments to collect data on the cause of crime. To conduct experimental research, criminologists manipulate or intervene in the lives of their subjects to see the outcome or the effect of the intervention. True experiments usually have three elements: (1) random selection of subjects, (2) a control or comparison group, and (3) an experimental condition. For example, to determine whether viewing violent media content is a cause of violence, a criminologist might randomly select one group of subjects and have them watch an extremely violent and gory film (such as *Kill Bill*) and then compare their behavior to a second randomly selected group who watch something mellow (such as *Princess Diaries*). The behavior of both groups would be monitored; if the subjects who had watched the violent film were significantly more aggressive than those who had watched the nonviolent film, an association between media content and behavior would be supported. The fact that both groups were randomly selected would prevent some preexisting condition from invalidating the results of the experiment.

Criminological experiments are relatively rare because they are difficult and expensive to conduct. They involve manipulating subjects' lives, which can cause ethical and legal roadblocks; and they require long follow-up periods to verify results. Nonetheless, they have been an important source of criminological data.

Observational and Interview Research

Sometimes criminologists focus their research on relatively few subjects, interviewing them in depth or observing them as they go about their activities. This research often results in the kind of in-depth data absent in large-scale surveys. In one such effort, Claire Sterk-Elifson focused on the lives of middle-class female drug abusers. The 34 interviews she conducted provide insight into a group whose behavior might not be captured in a large-scale survey. Sterk-Elifson found that these women were introduced to cocaine at first "just for fun": "I do drugs," one 34-year-old lawyer told her, "because I like the feeling. I would never let drugs take over my life." Unfortunately, many of these subjects succumbed to the power of drugs and suffered both emotional and financial stress.

Another common criminological method is to observe criminals firsthand to gain insight into their motives and

Figure 2.3
Crime Rate Trends
SOURCE: FBI, *Crime in the United States,* 2005.

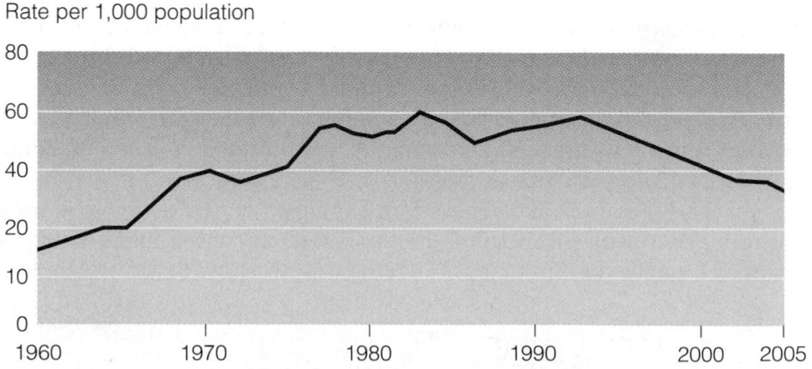

activities. This may involve going into the field and participating in group activities; this was done in sociologist William Whyte's famous study of a Boston gang, *Street Corner Society.* Other observers conduct field studies but remain in the background, observing but not being part of the ongoing activity.

Meta-Analysis and Systematic Review

Meta-analysis involves gathering data from a number of previous studies. Compatible information and data are extracted and pooled together. When analyzed, the grouped data from several different studies provide a more powerful and valid indicator of relationships than the results provided from a single study. A systematic review is another widely accepted means of evaluating the effectiveness of public policy interventions. It involves collecting the findings from previously conducted scientific studies that address a particular problem, appraising and synthesizing the evidence, and using the collective evidence to address a particular scientific question.

Data Mining

A relatively new criminological technique, data mining uses multiple advanced computational methods, including artificial intelligence (the use of computers to perform logical functions), to analyze large data sets usually involving one or more data sources. The goal is to identify significant and recognizable patterns, trends, and relationships that are not easily detected through traditional analytical techniques. Data mining might be employed to help a police department determine whether burglaries in their jurisdiction have a particular pattern. To determine whether such a pattern exists, a criminologist might employ data mining techniques with a variety of sources, including calls for service data, crime or incident reports, witness statements, suspect interviews, tip information, telephone toll analysis, or Internet activity. The data mining might uncover a strong relationship between the time of day and place of occurrence. The police could use the findings to plan an effective burglary elimination strategy.

Crime Mapping

Criminologists now use crime mapping to create graphic representations of the spatial geography of crime. Computerized crime maps allow criminologists to analyze and correlate a wide array of data to create immediate, detailed visuals of crime patterns. Crime mapping is a research technique that employs computerized crime maps and other graphic representations of crime data patterns. The simplest maps display crime locations or concentrations and can be used, for example, to help law enforcement agencies increase the effectiveness of their patrol efforts. More complex maps can be used to chart trends in criminal activity. For example, criminologists might be able to determine whether certain neighborhoods in a city have significantly higher crime rates than others—whether they are so-called hot spots of crime.

SOURCES: David Farrington, Lloyd Ohlin, and James Q. Wilson, *Understanding and Controlling Crime* (New York: Springer-Verlag, 1986), pp. 11–18; Claire Sterk-Elifson, "Just for Fun? Cocaine Use among Middle-Class Women," *Journal of Drug Issues* 26 (1996): 63–76; William F. Whyte, *Street Corner Society* (Chicago: University of Chicago Press, 1955) 38; Herman Schwendinger and Julia Schwendinger, *Adolescent Subcultures and Delinquency* (New York: Praeger, 1985); David Farrington and Brandon Welsh, "Improved Street Lighting and Crime Prevention," *Justice Quarterly* 19 (2002): 313–343; Colleen McCue, Emily Stone, and Teresa Gooch, "Data Mining and Value-Added Analysis," *FBI Law Enforcement Bulletin* 72 (2003): 1–6; Jerry Ratcliffe, "Aoristic Signatures and the Spatio-Temporal Analysis of High Volume Crime Patterns," *Journal of Quantitative Criminology* 18 (2002): 23–43.

100,000 Americans. Most disturbingly, the number of murders and nonnegligent manslaughters rose 4.8 percent. In addition, robberies increased 4.5 percent, and aggravated assaults were up 1.9 percent. Forcible rape was the only offense among the violent crimes that decreased in volume in 2005, down 1.9 percent from the 2004 figure. Interestingly, this recent increase occurred in all types of metropolitan areas (small towns, suburban counties, and so on) in all regions of the countries *except* in large cities.

Although the 2005 data is disturbing, at the time of this writing it is too soon to tell whether it is the beginning of a new long-term trend or a single-year aberration. Remember that violence in the United States decreased more than 20 percent between 1995 and 2005; in 1995 the violence rate was 684 per 100,000, and about 1.8 million violent crimes took place; today the violence rate is under 500. And even though the murder rate increased dramatically in 2005, it is still much lower than it was in the past.

Explaining Crime Trends

Crime experts have identified a variety of social, economic, personal, and demographic factors that influence crime rate trends. Although crime experts are still uncertain about how these factors impact these trends, directional change in the factor—for example, an economic downturn or upturn—seems to be associated with changes in crime rates.

Age

Because teenagers have extremely high crime rates, crime experts view change in the population age distribution as having the greatest influence on crime trends: As a general rule, the crime rate follows the proportion of young males in the population. Kids who commit a lot of crime early in childhood are also likely to continue to commit crime in their adolescence and into adulthood. The more teens in the population, the higher the crime rate. The number of juveniles should be increasing over the next decade, and some crime experts fear that this will signal a return to escalating crime rates. On the other hand, the number of senior citizens is also expanding, and their presence in the population may have a moderating effect on crime rates (seniors do not commit much crime), offsetting the effect of teens.

Economy/Jobs

There is debate over the effect the economy has on crime rates. It seems logical that when the economy turns down, people (especially those who are unemployed) will become more motivated to commit theft crimes. As the economy heats up, crime rates should decline because people can secure high-paying jobs; why risk crime when there are legitimate opportunities? Recent (2006) research by Thomas Arvanites and Robert Defina found that the crime rate drop in the 1990s could be linked to the strong economy's effect on criminal motivation.

Some criminologists believe that a poor economy may actually help to lower crime rates because it limits the opportunity to commit crime: (1) Unemployed parents are at home to supervise children and guard their possessions; (2) with less money to spend, people have fewer valuables worth stealing. Moreover, law-abiding, middle-aged workers do not turn to a life of crime when they lose their jobs during an economic downturn.

Although the effect of the economy on crime rates seems insignificant, it is possible that over the long haul, a strong economy will help lower crime rates, while long periods of sustained economic weakness and unemployment may eventually lead to increased rates: Crime skyrocketed in the 1930s during the Great Depression; crime rates fell when the economy surged for almost a decade during the 1990s. Also, economic effects may be very localized: While people in one area of the city are doing well, their neighbors living in another part of town may be suffering unemployment. The economic effect on the crime rates may vary by neighborhood or even by street.

Social Malaise

As the level of social problems increases—such as single-parent families, dropout rates, racial conflict, and teen pregnancies—so too do crime rates. Crime rates are correlated with the number of unwed mothers in the population. It is possible that children of unwed mothers need more social services than children in two-parent families. As the number of kids born to single mothers increases, the child welfare system will be taxed and services depleted. The teenage birthrate has trended downward in recent years, and so too have crime rates.

Racial conflict may also increase crime rates. Areas undergoing racial change, especially those experiencing an in-migration of minorities into predominantly white neighborhoods, seem prone to significant increases in their crime rate. Whites in these areas may be using violence to protect what they view as their home turf. Racially motivated crimes diminish as neighborhoods become more integrated and power struggles are resolved.

Abortion

In a controversial work, John J. Donohue III and Steven D. Levitt found empirical evidence that the recent drop in the crime rate can be attributed to the availability of legalized abortion. In 1973, *Roe v. Wade* legalized abortion nationwide. Within a few years of *Roe v. Wade*, more than 1 million abortions were being performed annually, or roughly one abortion for every three live births. Donohue and Levitt suggest that the crime rate drop, which began approximately 18 years later in 1991, can be tied to the fact that at that point the first groups of potential offenders affected by the abortion decision began reaching the peak age of criminal activity. They find that states that legalized abortion before the rest of the nation were the first to experience decreasing crime rates and that states with high abortion rates have seen a greater fall in crime since 1985. According to Donohue and Levitt, if abortion were illegal, crime rates might increase by 10 to 20 percent. If these estimates are correct, legalized abortion can explain about half of the recent fall in crime.

Guns

The availability of firearms may influence the crime rate, especially the proliferation of weapons in the hands of teens. Surveys of high school students indicate

Figure 2.4 illustrates homicide rate trends since 1900. Note that the rate peaked around 1930, then held relatively steady at about 4 to 5 per 100,000 population from 1950 through the mid-1960s, at which point it started rising to a peak of 10.2 per 100,000 population in 1980. From 1980 to 1991, the homicide rate fluctuated between 8 to 10 per 100,000 population; in 1991 the number of murders topped 24,000 for the first time in the nation's history. Between 1991 and 2005, homicide rates dropped more than 40 percent; about 16,000 murders now occur each year.

that between 6 and 10 percent carry guns at least some of the time. Guns also cause escalation in the seriousness of crime. As the number of gun-toting students increases, so too does the seriousness of violent crime as a schoolyard fight turns into murder.

Gangs

Another factor that affects crime rates is the explosive growth in teenage gangs. Surveys indicate that there are about 750,000 gang members in the United States. Boys who are members of gangs are far more likely to possess guns than non-gang members; criminal activity increases when kids join gangs.

Drug Use

Some experts tie increases in the violent crime rate between 1980 and 1990 to the crack epidemic, which swept the nation's largest cities, and to drug-trafficking gangs that fought over drug turf. These well-armed gangs did not hesitate to use violence to control territory, intimidate rivals, and increase market share. As the crack epidemic has subsided, so too has the violence in New York City and other metropolitan areas where crack use was rampant. A sudden increase in drug use, on the other hand, may be a harbinger of future increases in the crime rate.

Media

Some experts argue that violent media can influence the direction of crime rates. As the availability of media with a violent theme skyrocketed with the introduction of home video players, DVDs, cable TV, computer and video games, and so on, so too did teen violence rates. Watching violence on TV is correlated to aggressive behaviors, especially when people have a preexisting tendency toward crime and violence. Research shows that the more kids watch TV, the more often they get into violent encounters.

Justice Policy

Some law enforcement experts have suggested that a reduction in crime rates may be attributed to adding large numbers of police officers and using them in aggressive police practices that target "quality of life" crimes such as panhandling, graffiti, petty drug dealing, and loitering. By showing that even the smallest infractions will be dealt with seriously, aggressive police departments may be able to discourage potential criminals from committing more serious crimes. Michael White and his associates have recently shown that cities employing aggressive, focused police work may be able to lower homicide rates in the area.

It is also possible that tough laws imposing lengthy prison terms on drug dealers and repeat offenders can affect crime rates. The fear of punishment may inhibit some would-be criminals and place a significant number of potentially high-rate offenders behind bars, lowering crime rates. As the nation's prison population expanded, the crime rate has fallen.

Critical Thinking

Although crime rates have been declining in the United States, they have been increasing in Europe. Is it possible that factors that correlate with crime-rate changes in the United States have little utility in predicting changes in other cultures? What other factors may increase or reduce crime rates?

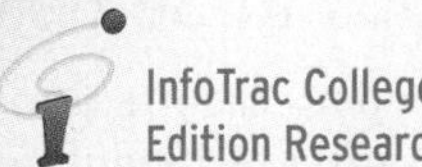

Gang activity may have a big impact on crime rates. To read about the effect, see the following articles: John M. Hagedorn, Jose Torres, and Greg Giglio, "Cocaine, Kicks, and Strain: Patterns of Substance Use in Milwaukee Gangs," *Contemporary Drug Problems* 25 (spring 1998): 113–145; Mary E. Pattillo, "Sweet Mothers and Gangbangers: Managing Crime in a Black Middle-Class Neighborhood," *Social Forces* 76 (March 1998): 747.

SOURCES: Thomas Arvanites and Robert Defina, "Business Cycles and Street Crime," *Criminology* 44 (2006): 139–164; David Fergusson, L. John Horwood, and Elizabeth Ridder, "Show Me the Child at Seven: The Consequences of Conduct Problems in Childhood for Psychosocial Functioning in Adulthood," *Journal of Child Psychology & Psychiatry & Allied Disciplines* 46 (2005): 837–849; Fahui Wang, "Job Access and Homicide Patterns in Chicago: An Analysis at Multiple Geographic Levels Based on Scale-Space Theory," *Journal of Quantitative Criminology* 21 (2005): 195–217; Gary Kleck and Ted Chiricos, "Unemployment and Property Crime: A Target-Specific Assessment of Opportunity and Motivation as Mediating Factors," *Criminology* 40 (2002): 649–680; Steven Levitt, "Understanding Why Crime Fell in the 1990s: Four Factors that Explain the Decline and Six that Do Not," *Journal of Economic Perspectives* 18 (2004): 163–190; Michael White, James Fyfe, Suzanne Campbell, and John Goldkamp, "The Police Role in Preventing Homicide: Considering the Impact of Problem-Oriented Policing on the Prevalence of Murder," *Journal of Research in Crime and Delinquency* 40 (2003): 194–226; Jeffrey Johnson, Patricia Cohen, Elizabeth Smailes, Stephanie Kasen, and Judith Brook, "Television Viewing and Aggressive Behavior during Adolescence and Adulthood," *Science* 295 (2002): 2,468–2,471; Brad Bushman and Craig Anderson, "Media Violence and the American Public," *American Psychologist* 56 (2001): 477–489; Steven Messner, Lawrence Raffalovich, and Richard McMillan, "Economic Deprivation and Changes in Homicide Arrest Rates for White and Black Youths, 1967–1998: A National Time-Series Analysis," *Criminology* 39 (2001): 591–614; John Laub, "Review of the Crime Drop in America," *American Journal of Sociology* 106 (2001): 1,820–1,822; John J. Donohue and Steven D. Levitt,. "The Impact of Legalized Abortion on Crime," *Quarterly Journal of Economics* 116 (2001): 379–420; Robert O'Brien, Jean Stockard, and Lynne Isaacson, "The Enduring Effects of Cohort Characteristics on Age-Specific Homicide Rates, 1960–1995," *American Journal of Sociology* 104 (1999): 1,061–1,095.

Trends in Property Crime

The property crimes reported in the UCR include larceny, motor vehicle theft, and arson. In 2005, about 10 million property crimes were reported, a rate of about 3,500 per 100,000 population. Property crime rates have declined in recent years, though the drop has not been as dramatic as that experienced by the violent crime rate. And, unlike the violent crime rate, the property crime rate has continued to fall. In 2005, property crimes were down almost 2 percent from the year before. Between

Figure 2.4

Homicide Rate Trends

SOURCES: Bureau of Justice Statistics, *Violent Crime in the United States* (Washington, DC: 1992); updated with data from FBI, *Crime in the United States*, 2005.

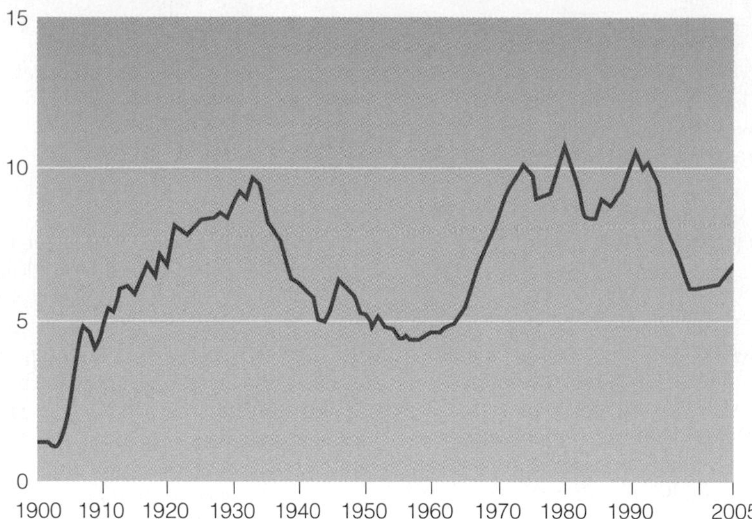

1995 and 2005, the total number of property crimes declined about 15 percent, and the property crime rate declined almost 25 percent.

● Although property crime rates have trended downward, valuable new commodities such as the iPod may encourage more theft activity. Thefts on New York City subway trains have risen as thieves target music-playing devices such as the iPod, game-playing cell phones, and other popular mobile electronic devices.

© Simon Taplin/Corbis

Trends in Victimization Data (NCVS Findings)

According to the latest NCVS survey, at last count (2005) residents age 12 or older experienced about 23 million violent and property victimizations. In 2005, about 17 million households experienced one or more property crimes or had a member age 12 or older who experienced one or more violent crimes.

Reported victimizations have declined significantly during the past 30 years when an estimated 44 million victimizations were recorded (1973). Between 1993 and 2005 the violent crime rate decreased more than 50 percent, from 50 to 21 victimizations per 1,000 persons age 12 or older, and the property crime rate declined at about the same rate (from 319 to 154 crimes per 1,000 households). Figure 2.5 shows the recent trends in violent crime, and Figure 2.6 tracks property victimizations.

Trends in Self-Reporting

Self-report results appear to be more stable than the UCR. When the results of recent self-report surveys are compared with various studies conducted over a 20-year period, a uniform pattern emerges: The use of drugs and alcohol increased markedly in the 1970s, leveled off in the 1980s, and then began to increase in the mid-1990s until 1997, when the use of most drugs began to decline. Theft, violence, and damage-related crimes seem more stable. Although a self-reported crime wave has not occurred, neither has there been any visible reduction in self-reported criminality. Table 2.1 contains data from the most recent (2005) Monitoring the Future (MTF) survey. A surprising number of these *typical* teenagers reported involvement in serious criminal behavior: About 12 percent reported hurting someone badly enough that the victim needed medical care (7 percent said they did it more than once); about 27 percent reported stealing something worth less than $50, and another 9 percent stole something worth more than $50; 28 percent reported shoplifting; 12 percent damaged school property.

Figure 2.5

Violent Crime Trends

Violent victimization rates have declined significantly between 1993 and 2005.

SOURCE: www.ojp.usdoj/gov/bjs/pub/pdf/cv04.pdf.

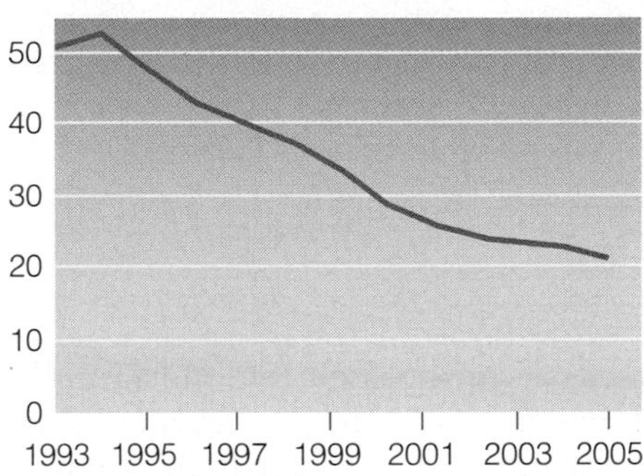

Figure 2.6

Property Crime Trends

Property victimization rates have declined between 1993 and 2005.

SOURCE: www.ojp.usdoj/gov/bjs/pub/pdf/cv04.pdf.

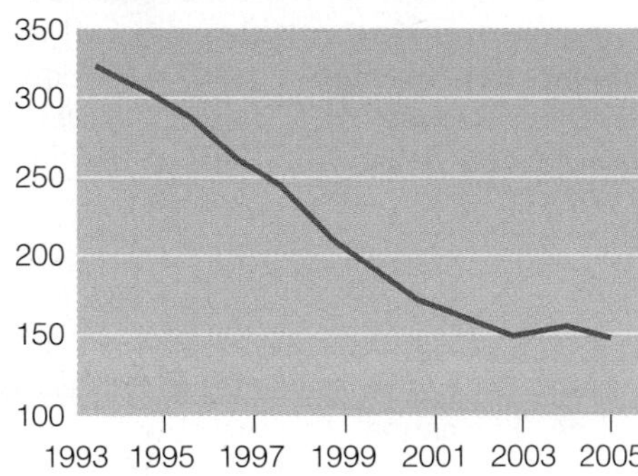

Table 2.1

Survey of Criminal Activity of High School Seniors

	PERCENTAGE ENGAGING IN OFFENSES	
CRIME	TOTAL	COMMITTED MORE THAN ONCE
Set fire on purpose	4	2
Damaged school property	12	6
Damaged work property	7	4
Auto theft	5	3
Auto part theft	4	2
Break and enter	26	13
Theft, less than $50	27	15
Theft, more than $50	9	5
Shoplift	25	13
Gang fight	19	8
Hurt someone badly enough to require medical care	12	5
Used force to steal	4	2
Hit teacher or supervisor	3	2
Participated in serious fight	12	5

SOURCE: *Monitoring the Future, 2005* (Ann Arbor, MI: Institute for Social Research, 2005).

What the Future Holds

Speculating about the future of crime trends is risky because current conditions can change rapidly, but some criminologists have tried to predict future patterns. There are approximately 50 million school-age children in the United States, and many are under age 10; this is a greater number than we have had for decades. Many come from stable homes, but some lack stable families and adequate supervision. These children will soon enter their prime crime years, and as a result, crime rates may increase in the future.[27] The recent uptick in the murder rate may reflect the growing influence on the crime rate by this large cohort of teens and young adults. However, while kids increase crime rates, seniors depress them. Even if teens commit more crime in the future, their contribution may be offset by the aging of the population, which will produce a large number of senior citizens and elderly, a group with a relatively low crime rate.[28]

✔ CHECKPOINTS

- ✔ The FBI's Uniform Crime Report is an annual tally of crime reported to local police departments. It is the nation's official crime database.
- ✔ The National Crime Victimization Survey (NCVS) samples more than 50,000 people annually to estimate the total number of criminal incidents, including those not reported to police.
- ✔ Self-report surveys ask respondents about their own criminal activity. They are useful in measuring crimes rarely reported to police, such as drug usage.
- ✔ Crime rates peaked in the early 1990s and have been in sharp decline ever since. The murder rate underwent a particularly steep decline until 2004 but upticked in 2005.
- ✔ A number of factors are believed to influence the crime rate, including the economy, drug use, gun availability, and crime control policies that include adding police and putting more criminals in prison.
- ✔ Gauging future trends is difficult. Some experts forecast an increase in crime, whereas others foresee a long-term decline in the crime rate.

Although population trends are important, the economy, technological change, and social factors may shape the direction of the crime rate.[29] The narcissistic youth culture that stresses materialism is being replaced by more moralistic cultural values.[30] Positive social values have a "contagion effect"; those held by the baby boomers will influence the behavior of all citizens, even crime-prone teens. The result may be a moderation in the potential growth of the crime rate.

Such prognostication is reassuring, but there is, of course, no telling what changes are in store that may influence crime rates either up or down. Technological developments such as e-commerce on the Internet have created new classes of crime. Although crime rates have trended downward, it is too early to predict that this trend will continue into the foreseeable future. ✔ CHECKPOINTS

CRIME PATTERNS

Criminologists look for stable crime-rate patterns to gain insight into the nature of crime. The cause of crime may be better understood by examining the rate. If, for example, criminal statistics consistently show that crime rates are higher in poor neighborhoods in large urban areas, the cause of crime may be related to poverty and neighborhood decline. If, in contrast, crime rates are spread evenly across society, and rates are equal in poor and affluent neighborhoods, this would provide little evidence that crime has an economic basis. Instead, crime might be linked to socialization, personality, intelligence, or some other trait unrelated to class position or income. In this section we examine traits and patterns that may influence the crime rate.

The Ecology of Crime

Patterns in the crime rate seem to be linked to temporal and ecological factors. Some of the most important of these are discussed here.

Day, Season, and Climate Most reported crimes occur during the warm summer months of July and August. During the summer, teenagers, who usually have the highest crime levels, are out of school and have greater opportunity to commit crime. People spend more time outdoors during warm weather, making themselves easier targets. Similarly, homes are left vacant more often during the summer, making them more vulnerable to property crimes. Two exceptions to this trend are murders and robberies, which occur frequently in December and January (although rates are also high during the summer).

Crime rates also may be higher on the first day of the month than at any other time. Government welfare and Social Security checks arrive at this time, and with them come increases in such activities as breaking into mailboxes and accosting recipients on the streets. Also, people may have more disposable income at this time, and the availability of extra money may relate to behaviors associated with crime such as drinking, partying, gambling, and so on.[31]

Temperature Weather effects (such as temperature swings) may have an impact on violent crime rates. Traditionally, the association between temperature and crime was thought to resemble an inverted U-shaped curve: Crime rates increase with rising temperatures and then begin to decline at some point (85 degrees) when it may be too hot for any physical exertion[32] (Figure 2.7). However, criminologists continue to debate this issue:

- Some believe that crime rates rise with temperature (the hotter the day, the higher the crime rate).[33]
- Others have found evidence that the curvilinear model is correct.[34]
- Some research shows that a rising temperature will cause some crimes (such as domestic assault) to continually increase, while others (such as rape) will decline after temperatures rise to an extremely high level.[35]

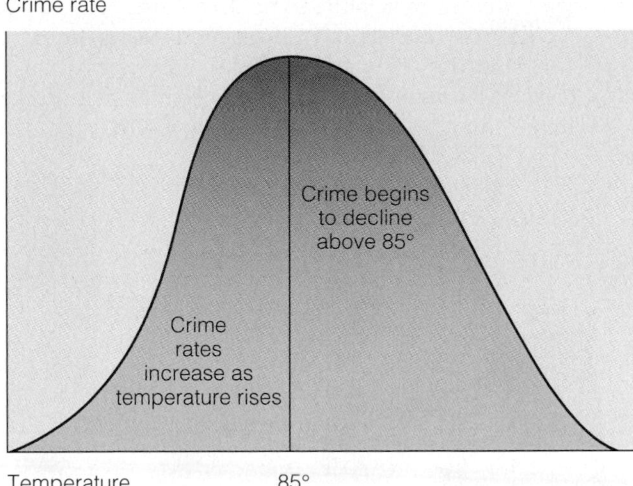

Figure 2.7
Relationship between Temperature and Crime

If, in fact, there is an association between temperature and crime, can it be explained? The relationship may be due to the stress and tension caused by extreme temperature. The human body generates stress hormones (adrenaline and testosterone) in response to excessive heat; hormonal activity has been linked to aggression.[36]

Regional Differences Large urban areas have by far the highest violence rates; rural areas have the lowest per capita crime rates. Exceptions to this trend are low population resort areas with large transient or seasonal populations—such as Atlantic City, New Jersey. Typically, the western and southern states have had consistently higher crime rates than the Midwest and Northeast (Figure 2.8). This pattern has convinced some criminologists that regional cultural values influence crime rates; others believe that regional differences can be explained by economic differences.

Use of Firearms

Firearms play a dominant role in criminal activity. According to the NCVS, firearms are typically involved in about 20 percent of robberies, 10 percent of assaults, and more than 5 percent of rapes. According to the UCR, about two-thirds of all murders involve firearms; most of these weapons are handguns. Criminals of all races and ethnic backgrounds are equally likely to use guns in violent attacks, and the presence of a weapon increases the likelihood that a violent incident will result in serious injury and/or death.[37]

Because of these findings, there is an ongoing debate over gun control. Some criminologists staunchly favor gun control. Franklin Zimring and Gordon Hawkins believe the proliferation of handguns and the high rate of lethal violence they cause is the single most significant factor separating the crime problem in the United States from the rest of the developed world.[38] Differences between the United States and Europe in nonlethal crimes are modest at best and getting smaller over time.[39]

In contrast, some criminologists believe that personal gun use can actually be a deterrent to crime. Gary Kleck and Marc Gertz have found that as many as 400,000 people per year use guns in situations in which they later claim that the guns almost "certainly" saved lives. Even if these estimates are off by a factor of 10, it means that armed citizens may save 40,000 lives annually. Although Kleck and Gertz recognize that guns are involved in murders, suicides, and accidents, which claim more than 30,000 lives per year, they believe their benefit as a crime prevention device should not be overlooked.[40] Because this is so important, the Policy & Practice in Criminology feature "Should Guns Be Controlled?" discusses this issue in some detail on pages 42–43.

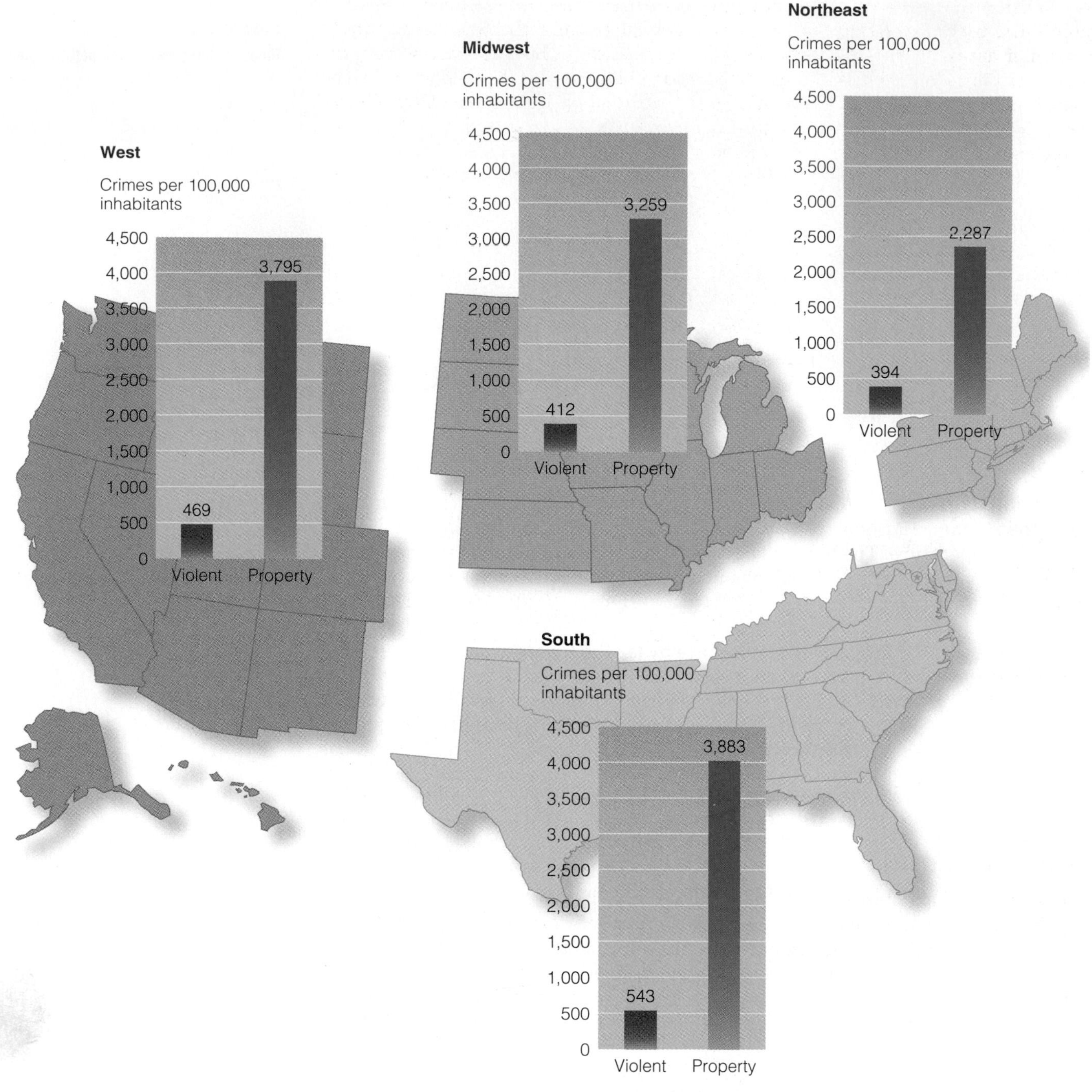

Figure 2.8
Regional Crime Rates: Violent and Property Crimes per 100,000 Inhabitants

instrumental crimes
Offenses designed to improve the financial or social position of the criminal.

expressive crimes
Offenses committed not for profit or gain but to vent rage, anger, or frustration.

Social Class, Socioeconomic Conditions, and Crime

It makes logical sense that crime is a lower-class phenomenon. After all, people at the lowest rungs of the social structure have the greatest incentive to commit crimes. Those unable to obtain desired goods and services through conventional means may consequently resort to theft and other illegal activities—such as selling narcotics—to obtain them. These activities are referred to as **instrumental crimes**. Those living in poverty are also believed to engage in disproportionate amounts of **expressive crimes**, such as rape and assault, as a result of their rage, frustration, and anger against society. Alcohol and drug abuse, common in impoverished areas, help fuel violent episodes.[41]

When measured with UCR data, official statistics indicate that crime rates in inner-city, high-poverty areas are generally higher than those in suburban or wealthier areas.[42] Surveys of prison inmates consistently show that prisoners were members of the lower class and unemployed or underemployed in the years before their incarceration. Nor is this relationship restricted to the United States. Cross-national comparisons show that wealthier nations, as measured by GNP, have lower violence rates than less economically developed nations.[43]

An alternative explanation for these findings is that the relationship between official crime and social class is a function of law enforcement practices, not actual criminal behavior patterns. Police may devote more resources to poor areas, and consequently apprehension rates may be higher there. Similarly, police may be more likely to formally arrest and prosecute lower-class citizens than those in the middle and upper classes, which may account for the lower class's overrepresentation in official statistics and the prison population.

Social Class and Self-Reports Self-report data have been used extensively to test the class–crime relationship. If people in all social classes self-report similar crime patterns, but only those in the lower class are formally arrested, that would explain higher crime rates in lower-class neighborhoods. However, if lower-class people report greater criminal activity than their middle- and upper-class peers, this would indicate that official statistics accurately represent the crime problem.

Surprisingly, early self-report studies conducted in the 1950s, specifically those conducted by James Short and F. Ivan Nye, did not find a direct relationship between social class and youth crime.[44] They found that socioeconomic class was related to official processing by police, courts, and correctional agencies but not to the actual commission of crimes. In other words, although lower- and middle-class youth self-reported equal amounts of crime, the lower-class youths had a greater chance of being arrested, convicted, and incarcerated and becoming official delinquents. In addition, factors generally associated with lower-class membership, such as broken homes, were found to be related to institutionalization but not to admissions of delinquency. Other studies of this period reached similar conclusions.[45]

For more than 20 years after the use of self-reports became widespread, a majority of self-report studies concluded that a class–crime relationship did not exist: If the poor possessed more extensive criminal records than the wealthy, this difference was attributable to differential law enforcement and not to class-based behavior differences. That is, police may be more likely to arrest lower-class offenders and treat the affluent more leniently.

Almost 30 years ago, Charles Tittle, Wayne Villemez, and Douglas Smith published what is still considered the definitive review of the relationship between class and crime.[46] They concluded that little if any support exists for the contention that crime is primarily a lower-class phenomenon. Consequently, Tittle and his associates argued that official statistics probably reflect class bias in processing lower-class offenders. In a subsequent article written with Robert Meier, Tittle once again reviewed existing data on the class–crime relationship and found little evidence of a consistent association between class and crime.[47] More recent self-report studies generally support Tittle's conclusions: There is no direct relationship between social class and crime.[48]

Tittle's findings have sparked significant debate in the criminological community. Many self-report instruments include trivial offenses such as using a false ID or drinking alcohol, which may invalidate findings. It is possible that affluent youths frequently engage in trivial offenses such as petty larceny, drug use, and simple assault but rarely escalate their criminal involvement. Those who support a class–crime relationship suggest that if only serious felony offenses are considered, a significant association can be observed.[49] Some studies find that when only serious crimes, such as burglary and assault, are considered, lower-class youths are significantly more delinquent than their more affluent peers.[50]

Like so many other criminological controversies, the debate over the true relationship between class and crime will most likely persist. The weight of recent evidence seems to suggest that serious, official crime is more prevalent among the lower classes, whereas less serious and self-reported crime is spread more evenly

Policy & Practice in Criminology

Should Guns Be Controlled?

The association between guns and crime has spurred many Americans to advocate controlling the sale of handguns and banning the cheap mass-produced handguns known as Saturday night specials. In contrast, gun advocates view control as a threat to personal liberty and call for severe punishment of criminals rather than control of handguns. They argue that the Second Amendment of the Constitution protects the right to bear arms.

Efforts to control handguns have come from many different sources. States and many local jurisdictions have laws banning or restricting sales or possession of guns; some regulate dealers who sell guns. The Federal Gun Control Act of 1968, which is still in effect, requires that all dealers be licensed, fill out forms detailing each trade, and avoid selling to people prohibited from owning guns, such as minors, ex-felons, and drug users. Dealers must record the source and properties of all guns they sell and carefully account for their purchase. Gun buyers must provide identification and sign waivers attesting to their ability to possess guns. Unfortunately, the resources available to enforce this law are meager.

On November 30, 1993, the Brady Handgun Violence Prevention Act was enacted, amending the Gun Control Act of 1968. The bill was named after former Press Secretary James Brady, who was severely wounded in the attempted assassination of President Ronald Reagan by John Hinckley in 1981. The Brady Law imposes a waiting period of five days before a licensed importer, manufacturer, or dealer may sell, deliver, or transfer a handgun to an unlicensed individual. The waiting period applies only in states without an acceptable alternate system of conducting background checks on handgun purchasers. Beginning November 30, 1998, the Brady Law changed, providing an instant check on whether a prospective buyer is prohibited from purchasing a weapon. Federal law bans gun purchases by people convicted of or under indictment for felony charges, fugitives, the mentally ill, those with dishonorable military discharges, those who have renounced U.S. citizenship, illegal aliens, illegal drug users, and those convicted of domestic violence misdemeanors or who are under domestic violence restraining orders. (Individual state laws may create other restrictions.) The Brady Law now requires background approval not just for handgun buyers but also for those who buy long guns and shotguns. In addition, the Federal Violent Crime Control and Law Enforcement Act of 1994 banned a group of military-style semiautomatic firearms (assault weapons). This ban on assault weapons was allowed to lapse in 2004.

Although gun control advocates see this legislation as a good first step, some question whether such measures will ultimately curb gun violence. When Jens Ludwig and Philip Cook compared two sets of states—32 that installed the Brady Law in 1994 and 18 states plus the District of Columbia, which already had similar types of laws before 1994—they found that there was no evidence that implementing the Brady Law contributed to a reduction in homicide.

Another approach is to severely punish people caught with unregistered handguns. The most famous attempt to regulate handguns using this method is the Massachusetts Bartley-Fox Law, which provides a mandatory one-year prison term for possessing a handgun (outside the home) without a permit. A detailed analysis of violent crime in Boston after the law's passage found that the use of handguns in robberies and murders did decline substantially (in robberies by 35 percent and in murders by 55 percent in a two-year period). However, these optimistic results must be tempered by two facts: Rates for similar crimes dropped significantly in comparable cities that did not have gun control laws, and the use of other weapons, such as knives, increased in Boston.

Some jurisdictions have tried to reduce gun violence by adding extra punishment, such as a mandatory prison sentence for any crime involving a handgun. California's "10–20-life" law requires an additional 10 years in prison for carrying a gun while committing a violent felony, 20 years if the gun is fired, and from 25 years to life in prison if someone is injured.

Can Guns Be Outlawed?

Even if outlawed or severely restricted, the government's ability to control guns is problematic. If legitimate gun stores were strictly regulated, private citizens could still sell, barter, or trade handguns. Unregulated gun fairs and auctions are common throughout the United States; many gun deals are made at gun shows with few questions asked. People obtain firearms illegally through a multitude of unauthorized sources, including unlicensed dealers, corrupt licensed dealers, and "straw" purchasers (people who buy guns for those who cannot purchase them legally).

If handguns were banned or outlawed, they would become more valuable; illegal importation of guns might increase as it has for other controlled substances (for instance, narcotics). Increasing penalties for gun-related crimes has also met with limited success because judges may be reluctant to alter their sentencing policies to accommodate legislators. Regulating dealers is difficult, and tighter controls on them would only encourage private sales and bartering. Relatively few guns are stolen in burglaries, but many are sold to licensed gun dealers who circumvent the law by ignoring state registration requirements or making unrecorded or misrecorded sales to individuals and

throughout the social structure.[51] Income inequality, poverty, and resource deprivation are all associated with the most serious violent crimes, including homicide and assault.[52] Members of the lower class are more likely to suffer psychological abnormality, including high rates of anxiety and conduct disorders, conditions that may promote criminality.[53]

unlicensed dealers. Even a few corrupt dealers can supply tens of thousands of illegal handguns.

Is There a Benefit to Having Guns?

Not all experts are convinced that strict gun control is a good thing. Gary Kleck, a leading advocate of gun ownership, argues that guns may actually inhibit violence. Along with Marc Gertz, Kleck conducted a national survey that indicates that Americans use guns for defensive purposes up to 2.5 million times a year. This figure seems huge, but it must be viewed in the context of gun ownership: About 47.6 million households own a gun; more than 90 million, or 49 percent of the adult U.S. population, live in households with guns; and about 59 million adults personally own guns. Considering these numbers, it is not implausible that 3 percent of the people (or 2.5 million people) with access to guns could have used one defensively in a given year.

Guns have other uses. In many assaults, Kleck reasons, the aggressor does not wish to kill but only scare the victim. Possessing a gun gives aggressors enough killing power so that they may actually be inhibited from attacking. Research by Kleck and Karen McElrath found that during a robbery, guns can control the situation without the need for illegal force. Guns may also enable victims to escape serious injury. Victims may be inhibited from fighting back without losing face; it is socially acceptable to back down from a challenge if the opponent is armed with a gun. In this way, guns can de-escalate a potentially violent situation. Kleck, along with Michael Hogan, finds that people who own guns are only slightly more likely to commit homicide than nonowners. The benefits of gun ownership, he concludes, outweigh the costs.

John Lott has evaluated the passage of right-to-carry laws across the United States. He, along with David Mustard, found that jurisdictions that allow citizens to carry concealed weapons also have lower violent crime rates. If all states allowed citizens to carry concealed weapons, Lott's and Mustard's analysis indicates that 1,500 murders, 4,000 rapes, 11,000 robberies, and 60,000 aggravated assaults would be avoided yearly. The annual social benefit from each additional concealed handgun permit is as high as $5,000, saving society more than $6 billion per year. Lott's research has been the subject of numerous reviews that find its methodology seriously flawed.

Does Defensive Gun Use Really Work?

Although this research is persuasive, many criminologists remain skeptical about the benefits of carrying a handgun. Tomislav Kovandzic and his colleagues used data for all large (population over 100,000) U.S. cities to examine the impact of "right to carry" concealed handgun laws on violent crime rates from 1980 to 2000 and found that carry laws have little effect on local crime rates. And while Kleck's research shows that carrying a gun can thwart crimes, other research shows that defensive gun use may be more limited than he believes. Even people with a history of violence and mental disease are less likely to kill when they use a knife or other weapon than when they employ a gun. Do guns kill people, or do people kill people? Research indicates that even the most dangerous people are less likely to resort to lethal violence if the gun is taken out of their hands.

Critical Thinking

1. Should the sale and possession of handguns be banned?
2. Which of the gun control methods discussed do you feel would be most effective in deterring crime?

InfoTrac College Edition Research

One method of reducing gun violence may be to make guns safer. Read more about this plan in Krista D. Robinson, Stephen P. Teret, Susan DeFrancesco, and Stephen W. Hargarten, "Making Guns Safer," *Issues in Science and Technology* 14 (1998): 37–41.

SOURCES: Robert Martin and Richard Legault, "Systematic Measurement Error with State-Level Crime Data: Evidence from the 'More Guns, Less Crime Debate,'" *Journal of Research in Crime & Delinquency* 42 (2005): 187–210; Tomislav Kovandzic, Thomas Marvell, and Lynne Vieraitis, "The Impact of 'Shall-Issue' Concealed Handgun Laws on Violent Crime Rates: Evidence From Panel Data for Large Urban Cities," *Homicide Studies* 9 (2005): 292–323; Donald Kennedy, "Research Fraud and Public Policy," *Science* 300 (April 18, 2003): 393; Tomislav Kovandzic and Thomas Marvell, "Right-to-Carry Concealed Handguns and Violent Crime: Crime Control through Gun Control?" *Criminology & Public Policy* 2 (2003): 363–396; Lisa Hepburn and David Hemenway, "Firearm Availability and Homicide: A Review of the Literature," *Aggression & Violent Behavior* 9 (2004): 417–440; "The Small Arms Survey, 2003," www.smallarmssurvey.org (accessed July 5, 2006); Matthew Miller, Deborah Azrael, and David Hemenway, "Rates of Household Firearm Ownership and Homicide across U.S. Regions and States, 1988–1997," *American Journal of Public Health* 92 (2002): 1,988–1,993; Stephen Schnebly, "An Examination of the Impact of Victim, Offender, and Situational Attributes on the Deterrent Effect of Gun Use: A Research Note," *Justice Quarterly* 19 (2002): 377–399; John Lott, *More Guns, Less Crime: Understanding Crime and Gun-Control Laws*, 2nd ed. (Chicago: University of Chicago Press, 2000); John Lott, Jr., and David Mustard, "Crime, Deterrence, and Right-to-Carry Concealed Handguns," *Journal of Legal Studies* 26 (1997): 1–68; Anthony A. Braga and David M. Kennedy, "The Illicit Acquisition of Firearms by Youth and Juveniles," *Journal of Criminal Justice* 29 (2001): 379–388; Anthony Hoskin, "Armed Americans: The Impact of Firearm Availability on National Homicide Rates," *Justice Quarterly* 18 (2001): 569–592; Gary Kleck and Marc Gertz, "Armed Resistance to Crime: The Prevalence and Nature of Self-Defense with a Gun," *Journal of Criminal Law and Criminology* 86 (1995): 150–187.

Age and Crime

There is general agreement that age is inversely related to criminality. Criminologists Travis Hirschi and Michael Gottfredson state, "Age is everywhere correlated with crime. Its effects on crime do not depend on other demographic correlates of crime."[54]

Regardless of economic status, marital status, race, sex, and other factors, younger people commit crime more often than older people do; research indicates this relationship has been stable across time periods ranging from 1935 to the present.[55] Official statistics tell us that young people are arrested at a disproportionate rate to their numbers in the population; victim surveys generate similar findings for crimes in which assailant age can be determined. Whereas youths ages 13 to 17 collectively make up about 6 percent of the total U.S. population, they account for about 25 percent of index crime arrests and 17 percent of arrests for all crimes. As a general rule, the peak age for property crime is believed to be 16, and for violence, 18 (Figure 2.9). In contrast, adults 45 and over, who make up 32 percent of the population, account for only 7 percent of index crime arrests. The elderly are particularly resistant to the temptations of crime; they make up more than 12 percent of the population and less than 1 percent of arrests. Elderly males 65 and over are predominantly arrested for alcohol-related matters (such as public drunkenness and drunk driving) and elderly females for larceny (for example, shoplifting). The elderly crime rate has remained stable for the past 20 years.[56]

CONNECTIONS

Hirschi and Gottfredson have used their views on the age-crime relationship as a basis for their General Theory of Crime. This important theory holds that the factors that produce crime change little after birth and that the association between crime and age is constant. For more on this view, see the section on the General Theory of Crime in Chapter 9.

Aging Out of Crime Most criminologists agree that people commit less crime as they age.[57] Crime peaks in adolescence and then declines rapidly thereafter. According to criminologist Robert Agnew, this peak in criminal activity can be linked to essential features of adolescence in modern, industrial societies. Because adolescents are given most of the privileges and responsibilities of adults in these cultures, they also experience:

- A reduction in supervision
- An increase in social and academic demands
- Participation in a larger, more diverse, peer-oriented social world
- An increased desire for adult privileges
- A reduced ability to cope in a legitimate manner and increased incentive to solve problems in a criminal manner[58]

Adding to these incentives is the fact that young people, especially the indigent and antisocial, tend to discount the future.[59] They are impatient, and because their future is uncertain, they are unwilling or unable to delay gratification. As they mature, troubled youths are able to develop a long-term life view and resist the need for immediate gratification.[60] **Aging out** of crime may be a function of the natural history of the human life cycle.[61] Deviance in adolescence is fueled by the need for money and sex and reinforced by close relationships with peers who defy conventional morality. At the same time, teenagers are becoming independent from parents and other adults who enforce conventional standards

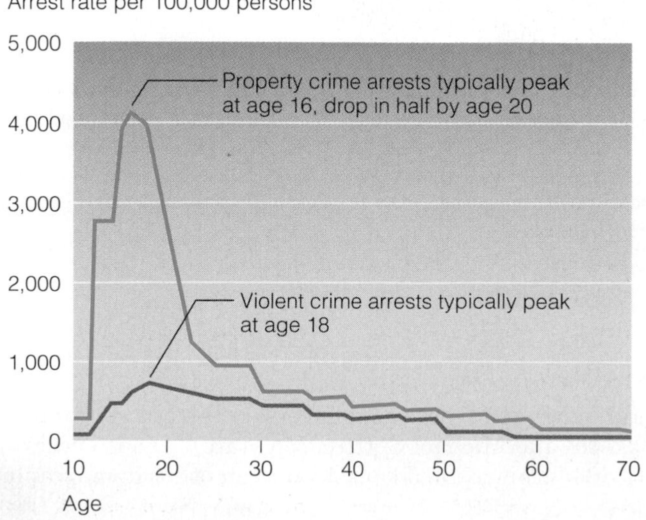

Figure 2.9
Relationship between Age and Serious Crime Arrests
SOURCE: FBI, *Uniform Crime Report*, 2003, p. 280.

of morality and behavior. They have a new sense of energy and strength and are involved with peers who are similarly vigorous and frustrated. Adults, on the other hand, develop the ability to delay gratification and forgo the immediate gains that law violations bring. They also start wanting to take responsibility for their behavior and to adhere to conventional mores, such as establishing long-term relationships and starting a family.[62] Research does show that people who maintain successful marriages are more likely to desist from antisocial behaviors than those whose marriages fail.[63]

Gender and Crime

Male crime rates are much higher than those of females. Victims report that their assailant was male in more than 80 percent of all violent personal crimes. The Uniform Crime Report arrest statistics indicate that the overall male–female arrest ratio is almost 4 male offenders to 1 female offender; for serious violent crimes, the ratio is almost 5 males to 1 female; murder arrests are 8 males to 1 female. MTF data also show that males commit more serious crimes, such as robbery, assault, and burglary, than females. However, although the patterns in self-reports parallel official data, the ratios are smaller. In other words, males self-report more criminal behavior than females—but not to the degree suggested by official data (Table 2.2). How can these differences be explained?

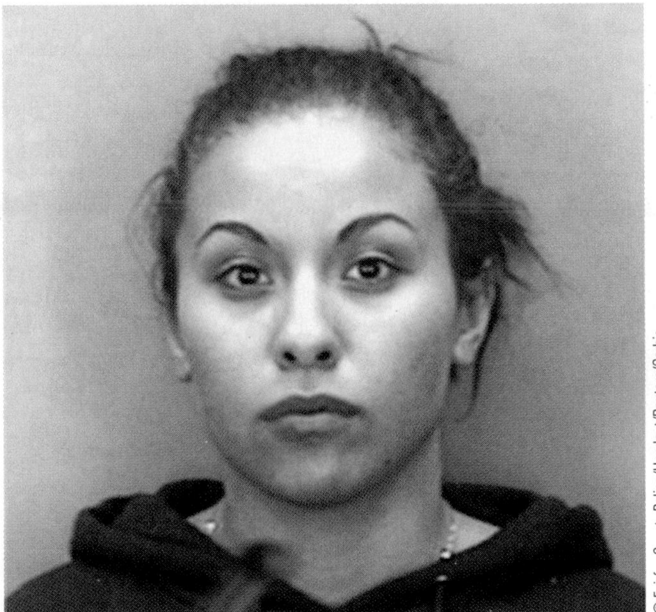

● Woman are now committing serious violent crimes at a faster pace than before. Candice Rose Martinez is shown in this Fairfax County, Virginia, booking photo November 15, 2005. Martinez became known as the "cell phone bandit" after surveillance photos showed her talking on her cell phone throughout each of the four bank robberies she committed in 2005. She pleaded guilty to two felony charges and on March 3, 2006 was sentenced to 12 years in prison.

Trait Differences Why are there gender differences in the crime rate? Early criminologists pointed to emotional, physical, and psychological differences between males and females to explain the differences in crime rates. They maintained that because females were weaker and more passive, they were less likely to commit crimes. Cesare Lombroso argued that a small group of female criminals lacked "typical" female traits of "piety, maternity, undeveloped intelligence, and weakness."[64] Lombroso's theory became known as the **masculinity hypothesis**; in essence, a few "masculine" females were responsible for the handful of crimes that women commit.[65]

Although these early writings are no longer taken seriously, some criminologists still consider trait differences a key determinant of crime rate differences. Some criminologists link antisocial behavior to hormonal influences by arguing that male sex hormones (androgens) account for more aggressive male behavior;

Table 2.2
Percentage of High School Seniors Admitting to at Least One Offense during the Past 12 Months, by Gender

DELINQUENT ACTS	MALES	FEMALES
Serious fight	13	9
Gang fight	22	16
Hurt someone badly	18	6
Used a weapon to steal	5	1
Stole less than $50	33	22
Stole more than $50	16	7
Shoplift	35	22
Breaking and entering	30	22
Arson	5	1
Damaged school property	17	7

SOURCE: *Monitoring the Future, 2005* (Ann Arbor, MI: Institute for Social Research, 2005).

aging out
The fact that people commit less crime as they mature.

masculinity hypothesis
The view that women who commit crimes have biological and psychological traits similar to those of men.

thus, gender-related hormonal differences can explain the gender gap in the crime rate.[66]

Socialization Differences Although there are few gender-based differences in aggression during the first few years of life, girls are socialized to be less aggressive than boys and are supervised more closely by parents. Males are taught to be more aggressive and assertive and are less likely to form attachments to others. They may seek approval by knocking down or running through peers on the playing field, while females literally cheer them on.[67] Male perceptions of power, their ability to have freedom and hang with their friends, help to explain the gender differences in crime and delinquency.

Cognitive Differences Psychologists note significant cognitive differences between boys and girls that may affect their antisocial behaviors. Girls have been found to be superior to boys in verbal ability, while boys test higher in visual-spatial performance. Girls acquire language faster, learning to speak earlier and with better pronunciation. Girls are far less likely to have reading problems than boys, while boys do much better on standardized math tests. (This difference is attributed by some experts to boys receiving more attention from math teachers.) In most cases these cognitive differences are small, and getting smaller, and usually attributed to cultural expectations. Their superior verbal skills may allow girls to talk rather than fight. When faced with conflict, women might be more likely to attempt to negotiate, rather than to respond passively or resist physically, especially when they perceive increased threat of harm or death.[68]

Social/Political Differences In the 1970s **liberal feminist theory** focused attention on the social and economic role of women in society and its relationship to female crime rates.[69] This view suggested that the traditionally lower crime rate for women could be explained by their "second-class" economic and social position. As women's social roles changed and their lifestyles became more like men's, it was believed that their crime rates would converge.

Criminologists, responding to this research, began to refer to the "new female criminal." The rapid increase in the female crime rate, especially in what had traditionally been male-oriented crimes (such as burglary and larceny), supports the feminist view. In addition, self-report studies seem to indicate that (1) the pattern of female criminality, if not its frequency, is similar to that of male criminality; and (2) the factors that predispose male criminals to crime have an equal impact on female criminals.[70]

Recent trends seem to support the feminist view of crime rate differences. Although male arrest rates are still considerably higher than female rates, female arrest rates seem to be increasing while male rates are in decline; it is possible that they may eventually converge.[71] Young girls are joining gangs in record numbers.[72]

Although these trends indicate that gender differences in the crime rate may be eroding, some criminologists remain skeptical about the data. According to Darrell Steffensmeier and his associates, these arrest trends may be explained more by changes in police activity than in criminal activity: Police today may be more willing to arrest girls for crimes.[73] Police may be abandoning their traditional deference toward women in an effort to be gender neutral. In addition, changing laws, such as dual arrest laws in domestic cases, which mandate both parties be taken into custody, result in more women suffering arrest in domestic incidents.[74]

CONNECTIONS

Critical criminologists view gender inequality as stemming from the unequal power of men and women in a capitalist society and the exploitation of females by fathers and husbands. This perspective is considered more fully in Chapter 8.

Race and Crime

Official crime data indicate that minority group members are involved in a disproportionate share of criminal activity. African Americans make up about 12 percent of the general population, yet they account for about 39 percent of Part I violent crime arrests and 29 percent of property crime arrests. They also are responsible for a disproportionate number of Part II arrests (except for alcohol-related arrests, which detain primarily white offenders).

It is possible that these data reflect true racial differences in the crime rate, but it is also likely that they reflect bias in the justice process. We can evaluate this

liberal feminist theory
A view of crime that suggests that the social and economic role of women in society controls their crime rates.

issue by comparing racial differences in self-report data with those found in official delinquency records. Charges of racial discrimination in the justice process would be substantiated if whites and blacks self-reported equal numbers of crimes, but minorities were arrested and prosecuted far more often.

Early efforts by noted criminologists Leroy Gould in Seattle, Harwin Voss in Honolulu, and Ronald Akers in seven midwestern states found virtually no relationship between race and self-reported delinquency.[75] These research efforts supported a case for police bias in the arrest decision. Other, more recent self-report studies that use large national samples of youths have also found little evidence of racial disparity in crimes committed.[76] These and other self-report studies seem to indicate that the delinquent behavior rates of black and white teenagers are generally similar and that differences in arrest statistics may indicate a differential selection policy by police.[77] Suspects who are poor, minority, and male are more likely to be formally arrested than suspects who are white, affluent, and female.[78]

Racial differences in the crime rate remain an extremely sensitive issue. Although official arrest records indicate that African Americans are arrested at a higher rate than members of other racial groups, self-report data suggest that these differences are an artifact of justice system bias.[79] Some critics charge that police officers routinely use racial profiling to stop African Americans and search their cars without probable cause or reasonable suspicion. Findings from a national survey of driving practices show that young black and Latino males are more likely to be stopped by police and suffer citations, searches, and arrests, as well as be the target of force, even though they are no more likely to be in possession of illegal contraband than white drivers.[80]

Although the official statistics, such as UCR arrest data, may reflect discriminatory justice system practices, African Americans are arrested for a disproportionate amount of serious violent crime, such as robbery and murder. It is improbable that police discretion and/or bias alone could account for these proportions. It is doubtful that police routinely release white killers, robbers, and rapists while arresting violent black offenders who commit the same offenses.[81] How can these racial differences in serious crimes be explained?

Racism and Discrimination Some criminologists view black crime as a function of socialization in a society where the black family was torn apart and black culture destroyed in such a way that recovery has proven impossible. Early experiences, beginning with slavery, have left a wound that has been deepened by racism and lack of opportunity.[82] Children of the slave society were thrust into a system of forced dependency and ambivalence and antagonism toward one's self and group.

Racism is still an element of daily life in the African American community, a factor that undermines faith in social and political institutions and weakens confidence in the justice system. Such fears are supported by empirical evidence that, at least in some jurisdictions, young African American males are treated more harshly by the criminal and juvenile justice systems than are members of any other group.[83] According to the **racial threat theory**, as the percentage of African Americans in the population increases, so does the amount of social control that police direct at blacks.[84]

The racial threat theory has received only mixed support, but a significant body of research shows that the justice system may be racially biased.[85] Research shows that black and Latino adults are less likely to receive bail in violent crime cases than whites, and that minority juveniles are more likely to be kept in detention pending trial in juvenile court.[86]

There is also evidence that African Americans, especially those who are indigent or unemployed, receive longer prison sentences than whites with the same employment status. It is possible that judges impose harsher punishments on unemployed African Americans because they view them as "social dynamite," considering them more dangerous and more likely to recidivate than white offenders.[87] Yet when African Americans are victims of crime, their predicaments receive less public concern and media attention than that afforded white victims.[88] Murders involving whites (and females) are much more likely to be punished with death than those whose victims are black males, a fact not lost on the minority population.[89]

racial threat theory
As the size of the black population increases, the perceived threat to the white population increases, resulting in a greater amount of social control imposed against blacks.

✔ CHECKPOINTS

✔ There are stable and enduring patterns in the crime rate.

✔ Crime is more common during the summer and in urban areas.

✔ Although the true association between class and crime is still unknown, the official data tell us that crime rates are highest in areas with high rates of poverty.

✔ Young people have the highest crime rates; people commit less crime as they mature.

✔ Males have a higher crime rate than females, but the female crime rate appears to be rising.

✔ Some criminologists suggest that institutional racism, such as police profiling, accounts for the racial differences in the crime rate. Others believe that African American crime rates are a function of living in a racially segregated society.

Economic and Social Disparity Racial and ethnic differentials in crime rates may also be tied to economic and social disparity. Racial and ethnic minorities are often forced to live in high crime areas, where the risk of victimization is significant and social support, such as government programs, is lacking.[90]

Racial and ethnic minorities face a greater degree of social isolation and economic deprivation than the white majority, a condition that has been linked by empirical research to high violence rates.[91] Many black youth are forced to attend essentially segregated schools that are underfunded and deteriorated, a condition that elevates the likelihood of their being incarcerated in adulthood.[92]

Family Dissolution In the minority community, family dissolution may be tied to low employment rates among African American males, which places a strain on marriages. The relatively large number of single, female-headed households in these communities may be tied to the high mortality rate among African American males due in part to their increased risk of early death by disease and violence.[93] When families are weakened or disrupted, their social control is compromised. It is not surprising, then, that divorce and separation rates are significantly associated with homicide rates in the African American community.[94]

In sum, the weight of the evidence shows that although there is little difference in the self-reported crime rates of racial groups, Latinos and African Americans are more likely to be arrested for serious violent crimes. The causes of minority crime have been linked to poverty, racism, hopelessness, lack of opportunity, and urban problems experienced by all too many nonwhite citizens. Research indicates that if racial and ethnic disparity in social and economic resources were to end and minority group members enjoyed the same social and educational benefits as do whites, crime rates would be significantly reduced.[95] ✔ CHECKPOINTS

CHRONIC OFFENDERS/CRIMINAL CAREERS

Crime data show that most offenders commit a single criminal act and upon arrest discontinue their antisocial activity. Others commit a few less serious crimes. A small group of criminal offenders, however, account for a majority of all criminal offenses. These persistent offenders are referred to as **career criminals**, or **chronic offenders**. The concept of the chronic, or career, offender is most closely associated with the research efforts of Marvin Wolfgang, Robert Figlio, and Thorsten Sellin.[96] In their landmark 1972 study, *Delinquency in a Birth Cohort*, they used official records to follow the criminal careers of a cohort of 9,945 boys born in Philadelphia in 1945 from the time of their birth until they reached 18 years of age in 1963. Official police records were used to identify delinquents. About one-third of the boys (3,475) had some police contact. The remaining two-thirds (6,470) had none. Each delinquent was given a seriousness weight score for every delinquent act.[97] The weighting of delinquent acts allowed the researchers to differentiate between a simple assault requiring no medical attention for the victim and serious battery in which the victim needed hospitalization. The best-known discovery of Wolfgang and his associates was that of the so-called chronic offender. The cohort data indicated that 54 percent (1,862) of the sample's delinquent youths were repeat offenders, whereas the remaining 46 percent (1,613) were one-time offenders. The repeaters could be further categorized as nonchronic recidivists and chronic recidivists. The former consisted of 1,235 youths who had been arrested more than once but fewer than five times and who made up 35.6 percent of all delinquents. The latter were a group of 627 boys arrested five times or more, who accounted for 18 percent of the delinquents and 6 percent of the total sample of 9,945.

The chronic offenders (known today as "the chronic 6 percent") were involved in the most dramatic amounts of delinquent behavior: They were responsible for 5,305 offenses, or 51.9 percent of all the offenses committed by the cohort. Even more striking was the involvement of chronic offenders in serious criminal acts. Of the entire sample, the chronic 6 percent committed 71 percent of the homicides, 73 percent of the rapes, 82 percent of the robberies, and 69 percent of the aggravated assaults.

chronic offenders (career criminals)
Small group of persistent offenders who account for a majority of all criminal offenses.

Wolfgang and his associates found that arrests and court experience did little to deter the chronic offender. In fact, punishment was inversely related to chronic offending: The more stringent the sanction chronic offenders received, the more likely they would be to engage in repeated criminal behavior.

In a second cohort study, Wolfgang and his associates selected a new, larger birth cohort, born in Philadelphia in 1958, which contained both male and female subjects.[98] Although the proportion of delinquent youths was about the same as that in the 1945 cohort, the researchers again found a similar pattern of chronic offending. Chronic female delinquency was relatively rare—only 1 percent of the females in the survey were chronic offenders. Wolfgang's pioneering effort to identify the chronic career offender has been replicated by a number of other researchers in a variety of locations in the United States.[99] The chronic offender has also been found abroad.[100]

© AP

● Flanked by court officers, Thomas A. Desautels, 45, of Oxford, Massachusetts, stands during his arraignment on drunk driving charges in Dudley, Massachusetts, District Court, on November 14, 2005. Desautels was arrested for allegedly driving while intoxicated and driving with a revoked license. A background check revealed that Desautels had nine prior convictions for driving under the influence. He pleaded not guilty. Would you consider Desaultels a chronic offender?

What Causes Chronicity?

As might be expected, kids who have been exposed to a variety of personal and social problems at an early age are the most at risk to repeat offending; a concept referred to as **early onset**. One important study of delinquent offenders in Orange County, California, conducted by Michael Schumacher and Gwen Kurz, found several factors (see Exhibit 2.4) that characterized the chronic offender, including problems in the home and at school.[101] Other research studies have found that involvement in criminal activity (getting arrested before age 15), relatively low intellectual development, and parental drug involvement were key predictive factors for chronicity.[102]

Implications of the Chronic Offender Concept

The findings of the cohort studies and the discovery of the chronic offender have revitalized criminological theory. If relatively few offenders become chronic criminals, perhaps they possess some individual trait that is responsible for their behavior. Most people exposed to troublesome social conditions, such as poverty, do not become chronic offenders, so it is unlikely that social conditions alone can cause chronic offending. Traditional theories of criminal behavior have failed to distinguish between chronic and occasional offenders. They concentrate more on explaining why people begin to commit crime and pay scant attention to why people stop offending. The

early onset
The view that repeat offenders begin their criminal careers at a very young age.

Exhibit 2.4
Characteristics That Predict Chronic Offending

School Behavior/Performance Factor
- Attendance problems (truancy or a pattern of skipping school)
- Behavior problems (recent suspensions or expulsion)
- Poor grades (failing two or more classes)

Family Problem Factor
- Poor parental supervision and control
- Significant family problems (illness, substance abuse, discord)
- Criminal family members
- Documented child abuse, neglect, or family violence

Substance Abuse Factor
- Alcohol or drug use (by minors in any way but experimentation)

Delinquency Factor
- Stealing pattern of behavior
- Runaway pattern of behavior
- Gang member or associate

SOURCE: Michael Schumacher and Gwen Kurz, *The 8% Solution: Preventing Serious Repeat Juvenile Crime* (Thousand Oaks, CA: Sage, 1999).

discovery of the chronic offender 30 years ago forced criminologists to consider such issues as **persistence** and desistance in their explanations of crime; more recent theories account for not only the onset of criminality but also its termination.

The chronic offender has become a central focus of crime control policy. Apprehension and punishment seem to have little effect on the offending behavior of chronic offenders, and most repeat their criminal acts after their correctional release.[103] Because chronic offenders rarely learn from their mistakes, sentencing policies designed to incapacitate chronic offenders for long periods without hope of probation or parole have been established. Incapacitation rather than rehabilitation is the goal. Among the policies spurred by the chronic offender concept are mandatory sentences for violent or drug-related crimes; **"three strikes"** policies, which require people convicted of a third felony offense to serve a mandatory life sentence; and "truth in sentencing" policies, which require that convicted felons spend a significant portion of their sentence behind bars. Whether such policies can reduce crime rates or are merely "get tough" measures designed to placate conservative voters remains to be seen.

persistence
The idea that those who started their delinquent careers early and who committed serious violent crimes throughout adolescence were the most likely to persist as adults.

"three strikes"
Laws that require an offender to serve life in prison after being convicted of a third felony.

THINKING Like a Criminologist

The planning director for the State Department of Juvenile Justice has asked for your advice on how to reduce the threat of chronic offenders. Some of the more conservative members of her staff seem to believe that these kids need a strict dose of rough justice if they are to be turned away from a life of crime. They believe juvenile delinquents who are punished harshly are less likely to recidivate than youths who receive lesser punishments, such as community corrections or probation. In addition, they believe that hard-core, violent offenders deserve to be punished; excessive concern for offenders and not their acts ignores the rights of victims and society in general.

The planning director is unsure whether such an approach can reduce the threat of chronic offending. Can tough punishment produce deviant identities that lock kids into a criminal way of life? She is concerned that a strategy stressing punishment will have relatively little impact on chronic offenders and, if anything, may cause escalation in serious criminal behaviors.

She has asked you for your professional advice. On one hand, the system must be sensitive to the adverse effects of stigma and labeling. On the other hand, the need for control and deterrence must not be ignored. Is it possible to reconcile these two opposing views?

Summary

- Criminologists use various research methods to gather information that will shed light on criminal behavior. These include official record studies, surveys, cohort studies, experiments, observations, meta-analysis and systematic reviews.
- The FBI's Uniform Crime Report (UCR) is an annual tally of crime reported to local police departments. It is the nation's official crime database.
- The National Crime Victimization Survey (NCVS) samples more than 50,000 people annually in order to estimate the total number of criminal incidents, including those not reported to police.
- Self-report surveys, which ask respondents about their own criminal activity, are useful in measuring crimes rarely reported to police, such as drug use.
- Each data source has its strengths and weaknesses, and although different from one another, they actually agree on the nature of criminal behavior.
- Crime rates peaked in the early 1990s and have been in sharp decline ever since. The murder rate has undergone a particularly steep decline.
- A number of factors are believed to influence the crime rate, including the economy, drug use, gun availability, and crime control policies like adding police and putting more criminals in prison.
- Gauging future trends is difficult, but experts try nonetheless. Some experts forecast an increase in crime, while others foresee a long-term decline in the crime rate.
- Data sources show stable patterns in the crime rate.
- Ecological patterns show that some areas of the country are more crime prone than others, that there are seasons and times for crime, and that these patterns are quite stable.
- There is also evidence of gender and age gaps in the crime rate: Men commit more crime than women, and

young people commit more crime than the elderly. Crime data show that people commit less crime as they age, but the significance and cause of this pattern is not completely understood.

- Similarly, racial and class patterns appear in the crime rate, but whether these are true differences or a function of discriminatory law enforcement is unclear. Some criminologists suggest that institutional racism, such as police profiling, accounts for the racial differences in the crime rate. Others believe that high African American crime rates are a function of living in a racially segregated society.
- One of the most important findings in the crime statistics is the existence of the chronic offender, a repeat criminal responsible for a significant amount of all law violations. Chronic offenders begin their careers early in life and, rather than aging out of crime, persistently offend into adulthood. The discovery of the chronic offender has led to the study of developmental criminology—why people persist, desist, terminate, or escalate their deviant behavior.

Take a Post-Test. Visit www.thomsonedu.com/criminaljustice/siegel and take the chapter Post-Test to monitor your progress and identify areas for further improvement. In addition to discovering what you've mastered, you'll learn which concepts need your added attention and get specific page references that direct you to the places in the text where you can find more information on them.

Key Terms

Uniform Crime Report (UCR) 24
Part I crimes 25
Part II crimes 25
cleared crimes 25
National Incident-Based Reporting System (NIBRS) 27
sampling 28
population 28
National Crime Victimization Survey (NCVS) 28
self-report survey 29
instrumental crimes 40
expressive crimes 40
aging out 44
masculinity hypothesis 45
liberal feminist theory 46
racial threat theory 47
chronic offenders (career criminals) 48
early onset 49
persistence 50
"three strikes" 50

Critical Thinking Questions

1. Would you answer honestly if a national crime survey asked you about your criminal behavior, including drinking and drug use? If not, why not? If you would not answer honestly, do you question the accuracy of self-report surveys?

2. How would you explain gender differences in the crime rate? Why do you think males are more violent than females?

3. Assuming that males are more violent than females, does that mean crime has a biological rather than a social basis (because males and females share a similar environment)?

4. The UCR reports that crime rates are higher in large cities than in small towns. What does that tell us about the effects of TV, films, and music on teenage behavior?

5. What social and environmental factors do you believe influence the crime rate?

6. Do you think a national emergency would increase or decrease crime rates?

CHAPTER 3

Victims and Victimization

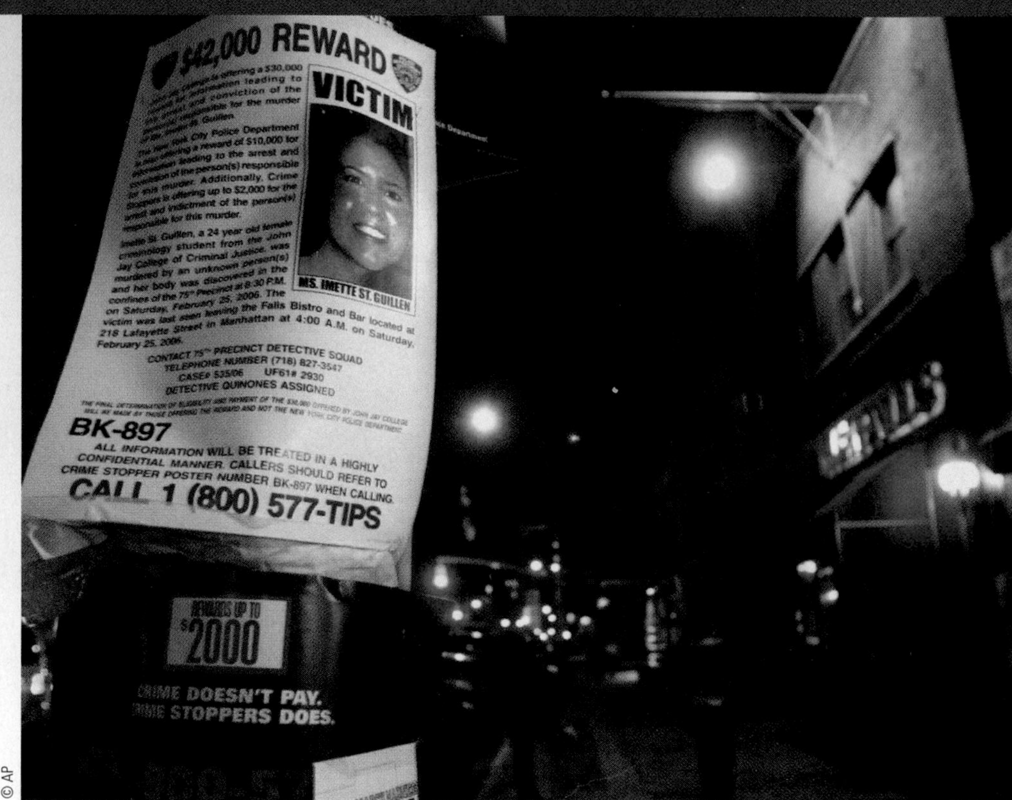

© AP

ON FEBRUARY 25, 2006, IMETTE ST. GUILLEN STOPPED IN FOR A LATE NIGHT DRINK IN THE FALLS BAR, A POPULAR NEW YORK CITY NIGHTSPOT. Later that evening, the bar's manager asked the bouncer Darryl Littlejohn to escort St. Guillen out after she stayed past the 4:00 AM closing time.[1] He recalled hearing the pair argue before they disappeared through a side door. Sometime during the next 17 hours, St. Guillen was raped and killed and her bound body left on the side of a desolate Brooklyn roadway. Police investigators soon set their sights on Littlejohn, a felon with prior convictions for robbery, drugs, and gun possession. He was indicted for murder, when blood found on plastic ties that were used to bind St. Guillen's hands behind her back matched Littlejohn's DNA.

Imette St. Guillen was a brilliant and beautiful young woman loved by her family and friends. She attended Farragut Elementary School, the Boston Latin School in Massachusetts, and graduated magna cum laude from George Washington University in 2003 as a member of Phi Beta Kappa. At the time of her death, she was a graduate student at John Jay College of Criminal Justice in New York City, where she would have completed her master's degree in

May 2006. "New York was Imette's home," her sister Alejandra St. Guillen later told reporters. "She loved the city and its people . . . Imette was a good person, a kind person. Her heart was full of love. With Imette's death, the world lost someone very special too soon."[2]

CHAPTER OBJECTIVES

1. Understand the concept of victimization.
2. Describe the nature of victimization.
3. Be able to discuss the problems of crime victims.
4. Be familiar with the costs of victimization.
5. Be able to discuss the relationship between victimization and antisocial behavior.
6. Recognize the age, gender, and racial patterns in victimization data.
7. Be able to discuss the association between lifestyle and victimization.
8. Understand the term "victim precipitation."
9. List the routine activities associated with victimization risk.
10. Be able to discuss the various victim assistance programs.

Take a Pre-Test. Visit www.thomsonedu.com/criminaljustice/siegel and take a Pre-Test to determine what you already know and identify the areas where you'll need to focus your study. The program will direct you to specific pages within the text where you can find further information on the correct answers to the questions you've missed.

The St. Guillen murder case illustrates the importance of understanding the victim's role in the crime process. Why do people become targets of predatory criminals? Do some become victims because of their lifestyle and environment? Did St. Guillen contribute to her attack by staying out late at night, drinking, and being alone? Her friends, who were with her earlier in the evening, left her in the early morning hours because they considered the neighborhood around The Falls bar safe. If St. Guillen had been with friends to guard her, would she be alive today? And is this a matter of unfairly "blaming the victim" for risky behavior? Can someone deflect or avoid criminal behavior, or is it a matter of fate and chance? What can be done to protect victims; should convicted criminals be prohibited from working in clubs where they might take advantage of patrons? And, failing that, what can be done to help victims in the aftermath of crime?

THE VICTIM'S ROLE

For many years, crime victims were viewed by criminologists as merely the passive recipients of a criminal's anger, greed, or frustration; they were considered to be people "in the wrong place at the wrong time." In the late 1960s, a number of pioneering studies found that, contrary to popular belief, the victim's own behavior is important in the crime process. Victims were found to influence criminal behavior by playing an active role in a criminal incident, as when an assault victim initially provokes an eventual attacker. Victims can also play an indirect role in a criminal incident, as when a woman adopts a lifestyle that continually brings her into high-crime areas.

The discovery that victims play an important role in the crime process has prompted the scientific study of victims, or **victimology**. Criminologists who focus their attention on crime victims refer to themselves as **victimologists**.

In this chapter, we examine victims and their relationship to the criminal process. First, using available victim data, we analyze the nature and extent of victimization. We then discuss the relationship between victims and criminal offenders. In this context, we look at various theories of victimization that attempt to explain the victim's role in the crime problem. Finally, we examine how society has responded to the needs of victims and consider what special problems they still face.

victimology
The study of the victim's role in criminal events.

victimologists
Criminologists who focus on the victims of crime.

VICTIMIZATION'S TOLL ON SOCIETY

The National Crime Victimization Survey (NCVS) indicates that the annual number of victimizations in the United States is about 24 million incidents. Being the target or victim of a rape, robbery, or assault is a terrible burden that can have considerable long-term consequences. The costs of victimization can include such things as damaged property, pain and suffering to victims, and the involvement of the police and other agencies of the justice system. The pain and suffering inflicted on an individual from an assault or robbery can result in medical care, lost wages from not being able to go to work, as well as reduced quality of life from debilitating injuries and/or fear of being repeatedly victimized. These consequences can result in long-term unemployment and the need for medical care and counseling.

Economic Loss

When the costs of goods taken during property crimes is added to productivity losses caused by injury, pain, and emotional trauma, the cost of victimization is estimated to be in the hundreds of billions of dollars.

System Costs Part of the economic loss due to victimization is the cost to American taxpayers of maintaining the justice system. Violent crime by juveniles alone costs the United States $158 billion each year.[3] This estimate includes some of the costs incurred by federal, state, and local governments to assist victims of juvenile violence, such as medical treatment for injuries and services for victims, which amounts to about $30 billion. The remaining $128 billion is due to losses suffered by victims, such as lost wages, pain, suffering, and reduced quality of life. Not included in these figures are the costs incurred trying to reduce juvenile violence, which include early prevention programs, services for juveniles, and the juvenile justice system.

Juvenile violence is only one part of the crime picture. If the cost of the justice system, legal costs, treatment costs, and so on, are included, the total loss due to crime amounts to $450 billion annually, or about $1,800 per U.S. citizen.[4]

Individual Costs In addition to these societal costs, victims may suffer long-term losses in earnings and occupational attainment. Victim costs resulting from an assault are as high as $9,400, and costs are even higher for rape and arson; the average murder costs around $3 million.[5] Research by Ross Macmillan shows that Americans who suffer a violent victimization during adolescence earn about $82,000 less than nonvictims; Canadian victims earn $237,000 less. Macmillan reasons that victims bear psychological and physical ills that inhibit first their academic achievement and later their economic and professional success.[6]

Some victims are physically disabled as a result of serious wounds sustained during episodes of random violence, including a growing number that suffer paralyzing spinal cord injuries. And if victims have no insurance, the long-term effects of the crime may have devastating financial as well as emotional and physical consequences.[7]

Abuse by the System

The suffering endured by crime victims does not end when their attacker leaves the scene of the crime. They may suffer more victimization by the justice system.

While the crime is still fresh in their minds, victims may find that the police interrogation following the crime is handled callously, with innuendos or insinuations that they were somehow at fault. Victims have difficulty learning what is going on in the case; property is often kept for a long time as evidence and may never be returned. Some rape victims report that the treatment they receive from legal, medical, and mental health services is so destructive that they can't help feeling "re-raped."[8] Victims may also suffer economic hardship because of wages lost while they testify in court, and they may find that authorities are indifferent to their fear of retaliation if they cooperate in the offender's prosecution.[9]

Long-Term Stress

Victims may suffer stress and anxiety long after the incident is over and the justice process has been completed. **Post-traumatic stress disorder (PTSD)**—a condition whose symptoms include depression, anxiety, and self-destructive behavior—is a common problem, especially when the victim does not receive adequate support from family and friends.[10]

Adolescent Stress Adolescent victims are particularly at risk to PTSD.[11] Kids who have undergone traumatic sexual experiences later suffer psychological deficits.[12] Many run away to escape their environment, which puts them at risk for juvenile arrest and involvement with the justice system.[13] Others suffer post-traumatic mental problems, including acute stress disorders, depression, eating disorders, nightmares, anxiety, suicidal ideation, and other psychological problems.[14] Stress however does not end in childhood. Children who are psychologically, sexually, or physically abused are more likely to suffer low self-esteem and be more suicidal as adults.[15] They are also placed at greater risk to be reabused as adults than those who escaped childhood victimization.[16] The reabused carry higher risks for psychological and physical problems, ranging from sexual promiscuity to increased HIV infection rates.[17] Abuse as a child may lead to despair, depression, and even homelessness as adults. One study of homeless women found that they were much more likely than other women to report childhood physical abuse, childhood sexual abuse, adult physical assault, previous sexual assault in adulthood, and a history of mental health problems.[18]

Relationship Stress Spouse abuse takes a particularly heavy toll on victims. Numerous research efforts show that victims of spousal abuse suffer an extremely high prevalence of psychological problems, including but not limited to depression, generalized anxiety disorder (GAD), panic disorder, substance use disorders, borderline personality disorder, antisocial personality disorder, post-traumatic stress disorder (an emotional disturbance following exposure to stresses outside the range of normal human experience), anxiety disorder, and obsessive-compulsive disorder (an extreme preoccupation with certain thoughts and compulsive performance of certain behaviors).[19] One reason for the prevalence of psychological disorders may be that abusive spouses are as likely to abuse their victims psychologically with threats and intimidation as they are to use physical force; psychological abuse can lead to depression and other long-term disabilities.[20]

Fear

Some victims, especially the elderly, the poor, and minority group members, develop a persistent and paralyzing fear that they will again become victimized; they remain fearful long after their wounds have healed.[21] And even those who have escaped attack themselves may develop fears and become timid and cautious after hearing about another's victimization.[22]

Victims of violent crime are the most deeply affected, fearing a repeat of their attack. There may be a spillover effect in which victims become fearful of other forms of crime they have not yet experienced; people who have been assaulted develop fears that their house will be burglarized.[23] In a moving book, *Aftermath: Violence and the Remaking of a Self*, rape victim Susan Brison recounts the difficult time she had recovering from her ordeal. The trauma of rape disrupted her memory, cut off events that happened before the rape from those that occurred afterward, and eliminated her ability to conceive of a happy or productive future. Although sympathizers encouraged her to forget the past, she found that confronting it can have healing power.[24]

✔ CHECKPOINTS

- ✔ Victimology is the branch of criminology that examines the nature and extent of crime victimization.
- ✔ The total economic loss from crime victimization amounts to hundreds of billions of dollars annually.
- ✔ Victims may suffer long-term trauma, including post-traumatic stress disorder.
- ✔ Many victims become fearful and go through a fundamental life change.
- ✔ People who are victims may be more likely to engage in antisocial acts themselves.

post-traumatic stress disorder (PTSD)
Psychological reaction to a highly stressful event; symptoms may include depression, anxiety, flashbacks, and recurring nightmares.

Antisocial Behavior

There is evidence that crime victims themselves are more likely than nonvictims to commit crimes. Being abused or neglected as a child increases the odds of being arrested, both as a juvenile and as an adult.[25] People who were physically or sexually abused, especially young males, are much more likely to smoke, drink, and take drugs than nonabused youth. Incarcerated offenders report significant amounts of post-traumatic stress disorder as a result of prior victimization, which may in part explain their violent and criminal behaviors.[26] Some may seek revenge against the people who harmed them, and sometimes these feelings are generalized to others who share the same characteristics of their attackers.[27] The abuse–crime phenomenon is referred to as the **cycle of violence**.[28] ✓ CHECKPOINTS

THE NATURE OF VICTIMIZATION

How many crime victims are there in the United States, and what are the trends and patterns in victimization? As you may recall from Chapter 2, according to the National Crime Victimization Survey:

- U.S. residents age 12 or older experienced approximately 23 million crimes:
  - 77% (18 million) were property crimes
  - 22% (5.2 million) were crimes of violence
  - 1% were personal thefts
- For every 1,000 persons age 12 or older, there occurred
  - 1 rape or sexual assault
  - 1 assault with injury
  - 3 robberies
- Murders were the least frequent violent victimization—about 6 murder victims per 100,000 persons.[29]

Patterns in the victimization survey findings are stable and repetitive, suggesting that victimization is not random but is a function of personal and ecological factors. The stability of these patterns allows judgments to be made about the nature of victimization; policies can then be created in an effort to reduce the victimization rate. Who are victims? Where does victimization take place? What is the relationship between victims and criminals? The following sections discuss some of the most important victimization patterns and trends.

The Social Ecology of Victimization

The NCVS shows that violent crimes are slightly more likely to take place in an open, public area, such as a street, a park, or a field, or at a commercial establishment such as a tavern, during the daytime or early evening hours than in a private home during the morning or late evening hours. Schools unfortunately are the locale of a great deal of victimization because they are populated by one of the most dangerous segments of society, teenage males. The most recent surveys show that although victim rates are declining, about 5 percent of students experienced a crime at school—about 4 percent reported a crime of theft and 1 percent reported having been a violence victim at school. This equals an estimated 1.2 million crimes of theft against students and about 740,000 violent crimes, including an estimated 150,000 of the most serious violent victimizations (rape, sexual assault, robbery, aggravated assault). Students also reported that about two-thirds of the serious violent crimes they experienced did not occur at school.[30]

The more serious violent crimes, such as rape and aggravated assault, typically take place after 6:00 PM. Approximately two-thirds of rapes and sexual assaults

cycle of violence
Victims of crime, especially childhood abuse, are more likely to commit crimes themselves.

occur at night—6:00 PM to 6:00 AM. Less serious forms of violence, such as unarmed robberies and personal larcenies like purse snatching, are more likely to occur during the daytime.

Neighborhood characteristics affect the chances of victimization. Those living in the central city have significantly higher rates of theft and violence than suburbanites; people living in rural areas have a victimization rate almost half that of city dwellers. The risk of murder for both men and women is significantly higher in disorganized inner-city areas where gangs flourish and drug trafficking is commonplace.

CONNECTIONS

As we saw in Chapter 2, the NCVS is currently the leading source of information on the nature and extent of victimization. It uses a sophisticated sampling methodology to collect data; statistical techniques then estimate victimization rates, trends, and patterns for the entire U.S. population.

The Victim's Household

The NCVS tells us that within the United States, larger, African American, western, and urban homes are the most vulnerable to crime. In contrast, rural, European American homes in the Northeast are the least likely to contain crime victims or be the target of theft offenses, such as burglary or larceny. People who own their homes are less vulnerable than renters.

Recent population movement and changes may account for recent decreases in crime victimization. U.S. residents have become extremely mobile, moving from urban areas to suburban and rural areas. In addition, family size has been reduced; more people than ever before are living in single-person homes (about 25 percent of households). The fact that smaller households in less populated areas have a lower victimization risk is a possible explanation for the decline in household victimization rates during the past 15 years.

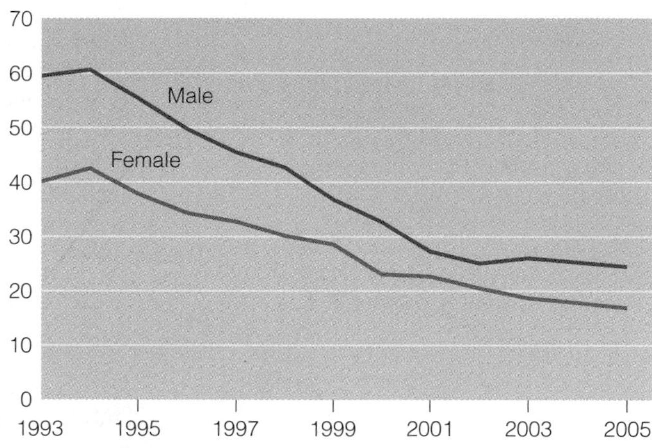

Figure 3.1
Violent Victimization by Gender
SOURCE: Bureau of Justice Statistics, Criminal Victimization, www.ojp.usdoj.gov/bjs/pub/pdf/cv05.pdf, 2005, p. 6.

Victim Characteristics

Social and demographic characteristics also distinguish victims and nonvictims. The most important of these factors are gender, age, social status, race, marital status, and repeat victimization.

Gender As Figure 3.1 shows, gender affects victimization risk. Except for the crimes of rape and sexual assault, males are more likely than females to be the victims of violent crime. Men are almost twice as likely as women to experience robbery. Women, however, are six times more likely than men to be victims of rape or sexual assault. Although males are more likely to be victimized than females, gender differences in victimization seem to have narrowed.

One significant gender difference in victimization is that women are much more likely to be victimized by someone they know. Of those offenders victimizing females, about two-thirds were described as someone the victim knew or to whom they were related. In contrast, only about half of male victims were

© AP

● Both personal characteristics and environmental factors influence victimization risk. Males, minority group members, and city dwellers have a greater chance of becoming victims than women, European Americans, and people living in rural areas. Living in a high-crime area also increases the likelihood of becoming a crime victim. Here Kokomo, Indiana, police assist a victim of an attempted robbery on April 10, 2006. One man was wounded by police and another was arrested following a four-hour standoff at a local residence.

Table 3.1
Violent Crime by Age of Victim

	AVERAGE ANNUAL RATE OF VIOLENT CRIMES PER 1,000 PERSONS		
	2002–03	2004–05	PERCENTAGE CHANGE
12–15 years	48.1	46.9	–2.5
16–19 years	55.6	45.0	–19.0
20–24 years	45.4	45.0	–0.9
25–34 years	26.3	23.7	–10.0
35–49 years	18.3	17.7	–3.5
50–64 years	10.5	11.2	6.8
65+ years	2.7	2.3	–15.1

SOURCE: Bureau of Justice Statistics, Criminal Victimization, www.ojp.usdoj.gov/bjs/pub/pdf/cv05.pdf, 2005, p. 4.

attacked by a friend, relative, or acquaintance. However, intimate partner violence seems to be declining. One reason may be an increasing amount of economic and political opportunities for women: Research shows that economic inequality is significantly related to female victimization rates. As more laws or acts favorable to women are passed and more economic opportunities become available, the lower their rates of violent victimization.[31]

Age Victim data reveal that young people face a much greater victimization risk than do older persons. As Table 3.1 shows, victim risk diminishes rapidly after age 25. The elderly, who are thought of as the helpless targets of predatory criminals, are actually much safer than their grandchildren. People over 65, who make up about 15 percent of the population, account for only 1 percent of violent victimizations; teens 12 to 19, who also make up 15 percent of the population, typically account for more than 30 percent of victimizations. For example, teens 16 to 19 suffer 50 violent crimes per 1,000, whereas people over 65 experience only 2.

> **CONNECTIONS**
> The association between age and victimization is undoubtedly tied to lifestyle: Adolescents often stay out late at night, go to public places, and hang out with other young people who have a high risk of criminal involvement. Teens also face a high victimization risk because they spend a great deal of time in the most dangerous building in the community: the local school!

Although the elderly are less likely to become crime victims than the young, they are most often the victims of a narrow band of criminal activities from which the young are more immune. Frauds and scams, purse snatching, pocket picking, stealing checks from the mail, and committing crimes in long-term care settings claim more older than younger victims. The elderly are especially susceptible to fraud schemes because they have insurance, pension plans, proceeds from the sale of homes, and money from Social Security and savings that make them attractive financial targets. Because many elderly live by themselves and are lonely, they remain more susceptible to telephone and mail fraud. Unfortunately, once victimized, the elderly have more limited opportunities either to recover their lost money or to earn enough to replace what they have lost.[32]

Social Status The poorest Americans are also the most likely victims of violent and property crime. This association occurs across all gender, age, and racial groups.

The homeless, who are among the poorest individuals in America, suffer very high rates of assault.[33] In contrast, the wealthy are more likely targets of personal theft crimes such as pocket picking and purse snatching. Perhaps the affluent, who sport more expensive attire and drive better cars, attract the attention of thieves.

Race and Ethnicity As Table 3.2 shows, African Americans are more likely than European Americans to be victims of violent crime: For every 1,000 persons in their own racial group, 26 blacks, 21 whites, and 13 persons of other races sustained a violent crime.

Why do these discrepancies exist? Because of income inequality, racial and minority group members are often forced to live in deteriorated urban areas beset by alcohol and drug abuse, poverty, racial discrimination, and violence. Consequently, their lifestyle places them in the most "at-risk" population group.

Marital Status Victimization risk is also influenced by marital status: Never-married males and females are victimized more often than married people.

Widows and widowers have the lowest victimization risk. This association between marital status and victimization is probably influenced by age, gender, and lifestyle:

- Many young people, who have the highest victim risk, are actually too young to have been married.
- Young single people also go out in public more often and sometimes interact with high-risk peers, increasing their exposure to victimization.

Table 3.2
Victimization Rates by Race

CHARACTERISTIC OF VICTIM	POPULATION	VICTIMIZATIONS PER 1,000 PERSONS AGE 12 OR OLDER						
		VIOLENT CRIMES						
					ASSAULT			
		ALL	RAPE/SEXUAL ASSAULT	ROBBERY	TOTAL	AGGRAVATED	SIMPLE	PERSONAL THEFT
Race								
European American	200,263,410	20.1	0.6	2.2	17.2	3.8	13.4	0.9
African American	29,477,880	27.0	1.8	4.6	20.6	7.6	13.0	1.7
Other race	12,522,090	13.9	0.5*	3.0	10.4	2.5*	7.9	0.2*
Two or more	2,230,050	83.6	3.8*	1.8*	78.0	16.6	61.5	0.0*

Note: The National Crime Victimization Survey includes as violent crime rape, sexual assault, robbery, and assault. Because the NCVS interviews persons about their victimizations, murder and manslaughter cannot be included. Racial and ethnic categories in 2005 are not comparable to categories used prior to 2003.

*Based on 10 or fewer sample cases.

SOURCE: Bureau of Justice Statistics, Criminal Victimization, www.ojp.usdoj.gov/bjs/cvictgen.htm, 2005.

- Widows and widowers suffer much lower victimization rates because they are older, interact with older people, and are more likely to stay home at night and to avoid public places.

Repeat Victimization Does prior victimization enhance or reduce the chances of future victimization? Individuals who have been crime victims have a significantly higher chance of future victimization than people who have remained nonvictims.[34] Households that have experienced victimization in the past are the ones most likely to experience it again in the future.[35]

What factors predict chronic victimization? Most repeat victimizations occur soon after a previous crime has occurred, suggesting that repeat victims share some personal characteristic that makes them a magnet for predators.[36] For example, children who are shy, physically weak, or socially isolated may be prone to being bullied in the schoolyard.[37] David Finkelhor and Nancy Asigian have found that three specific types of characteristics increase the potential for victimization:

- *Target vulnerability*. The victims' physical weakness or psychological distress renders them incapable of resisting or deterring crime and makes them easy targets.
- *Target gratifiability*. Some victims have some quality, possession, skill, or attribute that an offender wants to obtain, use, have access to, or manipulate. Having attractive possessions, such as a leather coat, may make one vulnerable to predatory crime.
- *Target antagonism*. Some characteristics increase risk because they arouse anger, jealousy, or destructive impulses in potential offenders. Being gay or effeminate, for example, may bring on undeserved attacks in the street; being argumentative and alcoholic may provoke barroom assaults.[38]

Repeat victimization may occur when the victim does not take defensive action. If an abusive husband finds out that his battered wife will not call police, he repeatedly victimizes her; or if a hate crime is committed and the police do not respond to reported offenses, the perpetrators learn they have little to fear from the law.[39]

Victims and Their Criminals

The victim data also tell us something about the relationship between victims and criminals. As stated earlier, males are more likely to be violently victimized by a stranger, and females to be victimized by a friend, an acquaintance, or an intimate.

✔ CHECKPOINTS

✔ Males are more often the victims of crime than females; women are more likely than men to be attacked by a relative.

✔ The indigent are much more likely than the affluent to be the victims of violent crime; the wealthy are more likely to be the targets of personal theft.

✔ Younger, single people are more often targets than older, married people.

✔ Rates of violent victimization are much higher for African Americans than for European Americans. Crime victimization tends to be intraracial.

✔ Some people and places are targets of repeat victimization.

Victims report that most crimes were committed by a single offender over age 20. Crime tends to be intraracial: African American offenders victimize blacks, and European Americans victimize whites. Because the country's population is predominantly white, however, it stands to reason that criminals of all races will be more likely to target white victims. Victims report that substance abuse was involved in about one-third of violent crime incidents.[40]

Although many violent crimes are committed by strangers, a surprising number of violent crimes are committed by relatives or acquaintances of the victims. In fact, more than half of all nonfatal personal crimes are committed by people who are described as being known to the victim. Women are especially vulnerable to people they know. More than 6 in 10 rape or sexual assault victims stated the offender was an intimate, a relative, a friend, or an acquaintance. Women were more likely than men to be robbed by a friend or acquaintance. ✔ CHECKPOINTS

THEORIES OF VICTIMIZATION

For many years criminological theory focused on the actions of the criminal offender; the role of the victim was virtually ignored. More than 50 years ago scholars began to realize that the victim was not simply a passive target in crime but someone whose behavior can influence his or her own fate, who "shapes and molds the criminal."[41] These early works helped focus attention on the role of the victim in the crime problem and led to further research efforts that have sharpened the image of the crime victim. Today a number of different theories attempt to explain the causes of victimization.

Victim Precipitation Theory

According to **victim precipitation theory**, some people may actually initiate the confrontation that eventually leads to their injury or death. Victim precipitation can be either active or passive.

Active precipitation occurs when victims act provocatively, use threats or fighting words, or even attack first.[42] In 1971, Menachem Amir suggested that female rape victims often contribute to their attack by dressing provocatively or pursuing a relationship with the rapist.[43] Although Amir's findings are controversial, courts have continued to return not guilty verdicts in rape cases if a victim's actions can in any way be construed as consenting to sexual intimacy.[44]

In contrast, **passive precipitation** occurs when the victim exhibits some personal characteristic that unknowingly either threatens or encourages the attacker. The crime can occur because of personal conflict, such as when two people compete over a job, promotion, love interest, or some other scarce and coveted commodity. A woman may become the target of intimate violence when she improves her job status and her success results in a backlash from a jealous spouse or partner.[45] In other situations, although the victim may never have met the attacker or even known of his or her existence, the attacker feels menaced and acts accordingly.[46]

victim precipitation theory
The view that victims may initiate, either actively or passively, the confrontation that leads to their victimization.

active precipitation
Aggressive or provocative behavior of victims that results in their victimization.

passive precipitation
Personal or social characteristics of victims that make them attractive targets for criminals; such victims may unknowingly either threaten or encourage their attackers.

lifestyle theories
Views on how people become crime victims because of lifestyles that increase their exposure to criminal offenders.

Lifestyle Theories

Some criminologists believe that people may become crime victims because their lifestyle increases their exposure to criminal offenders. Victimization risk is increased by such behaviors as associating with young men, going out in public places late at night, and living in an urban area. Conversely, one's chances of victimization can be reduced by staying home at night, moving to a rural area, staying out of public places, earning more money, and getting married. The basis of such **lifestyle theories** is that crime is not a random occurrence; rather, it is a function of the victim's lifestyle.

High-Risk Lifestyles People who have high-risk lifestyles—drinking, taking drugs, getting involved in crime—have a much greater chance of victimization.[47] Take for example young runaways: The more time they are exposed to street life, the greater their risk of becoming crime victims.[48]

Teenage males have an extremely high victimization risk because their lifestyle places them at risk both at school and once they leave the school grounds.[49] They spend a great deal of time hanging out with their friends and pursuing recreational fun.[50] Their friends may give them a false ID so they can drink in the neighborhood bar. They may hang out in taverns at night, which places them at risk because many fights and assaults occur in places that serve liquor. Exposure to violence and associating with violent peers enmeshes young men in a violent lifestyle that increases their own risk of violent offending. One way for young males to avoid victimization: limit their male friends and hang out with girls! The greater the number of girls in their peer group, the lower their chances of victimization.[51] Those who have a history of engaging in serious delinquency, getting involved in gangs, carrying guns, and selling drugs have an increased chance of being shot and killed.[52] Lifestyle risks continue into young adulthood. As adults, those who commit crimes increase their chances of becoming the victims of homicide.[53]

College Lifestyle College students maintain a lifestyle—partying, taking recreational drugs—that makes them victimization prone.[54] One research effort by Bonnie Fisher and her colleagues surveyed thousands of college students and found that coeds face the risk of sexual assault at a higher rate than women in the general population.[55] Fisher and her colleagues found that 90 percent of the victims knew the person who sexually victimized them. Most often this was a boyfriend, ex-boyfriend, classmate, friend, acquaintance, or coworker; college professors were not identified as committing any rapes or sexual coercions. The vast majority of sexual victimizations occurred in the evening (after 6:00 PM), typically (60 percent) in the students' living quarters; many were connected to drinking. Other common crime scenes were other living quarters on campus and fraternity houses (about 10 percent). Off-campus sexual victimizations, especially rapes, also occurred in residences. Incidents where women were threatened or touched also took place in settings such as bars, dance clubs or nightclubs, and work settings.

Criminal Lifestyle One element of lifestyle that may place some people at risk for victimization is an ongoing involvement in a criminal career. Both convicted and self-reported criminals are much more likely to suffer victimization than are noncriminals.[56]

The association between criminal lifestyle and victimization risk can be assessed with data from the Rochester and Pittsburgh Youth Studies, two ongoing surveys tracking thousands of at-risk youth. Researchers discovered that kids who get involved in gangs and carry a weapon are up to four times more likely than non-gang members to become victims of serious crime. About 40 percent of males involved in gang/group fights had been seriously injured themselves; among females, 27 percent of those involved in gang/group fights had been seriously injured. Carrying a weapon was another surefire way to become a crime victim. Males who carried weapons were approximately three times more likely to be victimized than those who did not carry weapons—33 percent of the weapons carriers became victims as opposed to 10 percent who did not carry weapons.[57] These data indicate that criminals and victims may not be two separate and distinct groups. Rather, the risk of victimization is directly linked to the high-risk lifestyle of young, weapon-toting male gang members.

© AP

● Irvington, New Jersey, Mayor Sara Bost looks up at a bullet hole in a door to her home. Nine gunshots were fired into Bost's home about a week after Bost stopped someone marking graffiti on a stop sign near her home. Bost says she believes she was targeted because of a crackdown on crime and drug dealers in Irvington.

Deviant Place Theory

According to **deviant place theory**, the greater their exposure to dangerous places, the more likely people will become victims of crime and violence.[58] Victims do not encourage crime but are victim prone because they reside in socially disorganized high-crime areas where they have the greatest risk of coming into contact with criminal

deviant place theory
The view that victimization is primarily a function of where people live.

Profiles in Crime

Jesse Timmendequas and Megan's Law

Richard and Maureen Kanka thought that their daughter Megan was safe in their quiet, suburban neighborhood in Hamilton Township, New Jersey. Then on July 29, 1994, their lives were shattered when their 7-year-old daughter Megan went missing. Maureen Kanka soon began to search the neighborhood and met 33-year-old Jesse Timmendequas, who lived across the street. Timmendequas told her that he had seen Megan earlier that evening while he was working on his car. The police were called in and soon focused their attention on Timmendequas's house when they learned that he along with two other residents were convicted sex offenders who had met at a treatment center and decided to live together upon their release. Timmendequas, who appeared extremely nervous when questioned, was asked to accompany police to their headquarters, where he confessed to luring Megan into his home by telling her she could see his puppy and then raping and strangling her to death.

Timmendequas had served six years in prison for aggravated assault and attempted sexual assault on another child. The fact that a known sex offender was living anonymously in the Kanka's neighborhood turned Megan's death into a national crusade to develop laws that (1) require sex offenders to register with local police when they move into a neighborhood and (2) require local authorities to provide community notification of the sex offender's presence. New York State's Sex Offender Registration Act is typical of these efforts commonly known as "Megan's Laws." The statute, which became effective on January 21, 1996, requires that sex offenders in New York be classified by the risk of reoffense. A court determines whether an offender is a level 1 (low risk), 2 (moderate risk), or 3 (high risk). The court also determines whether an offender should be given the designation of a sexual predator, sexually violent offender, or predicate (repeat) sex offender. Offenders are required to register for 20 years or life. Level 1 offenders with no designation must register for 20 years. Level 1 offenders with a designation, as well as level 2 and level 3 offenders regardless of whether they have a designation, must register for life.

Local law enforcement agencies are notified whenever a sex offender moves into their jurisdiction. That agency may notify schools and other "entities with vulnerable populations" about the presence of a level 2 or level 3 offender if the offender poses a threat to public safety. The act established a free 1–800 number information line that citizens can call to inquire whether a person is listed in the registry and to access information on sex offenders living in their neighborhoods. On the federal level, the Jacob Wetterling Crimes Against Children Law, passed in May 1996, requires states to pass some version of "Megan's Law" or lose federal aid. At least 47 states plus the District of Columbia have complied. Jesse Timmendequas was sentenced to death on June 20, 1997.

© AP

● Jesse Timmendequas, the accused killer of Megan Kanka.

The case of Megan Kanka illustrates both the risk children face from sexual predators and the efforts being made by the justice system to limit that risk. To some civil liberty groups, such as the American Civil Liberties Union, registration laws go too far because they will not prevent sex offenders from committing crimes and because they victimize rehabilitated ex-offenders and their families. Should the rights of the victim take precedent over the privacy of the offender?

SOURCES: New York State Sex Offender Registry and the Sex Offender Registration Act (SORA), http://criminaljustice.state.ny.us/nsor/; New York State Correction Law Article 6-C (Section 168 et seq.); CourtTV Library, *New Jersey v. Timmendequas*, www.courttv.com/archive/casefiles/verdicts/kanka.html (accessed March 28, 2006).

offenders, irrespective of their own behavior or lifestyle.[59] Neighborhood crime levels may be more significant than individual characteristics or lifestyle for determining the chances of victimization. Consequently, there may be little reason for residents in lower-class areas to alter their lifestyle or take safety precautions, because personal behavior choices do not influence the likelihood of victimization.[60]

So-called deviant places are poor, densely populated, highly transient neighborhoods in which commercial and residential properties exist side by side.[61] The commercial establishments provide criminals with easy targets for theft crimes, such as shoplifting and larceny. Successful people stay out of these stigmatized areas. They are home to "demoralized kinds of people," who are easy targets for crime: the homeless, the addicted, the retarded, and the elderly poor.[62]

People who live in more affluent areas and take safety precautions significantly lower their chances of becoming crime victims; the effect of safety precautions is less pronounced in poor areas. Residents of poor areas have a much greater risk of becoming victims because they live in areas with many motivated offenders; to protect themselves, they have to try harder to be safe than do the more affluent.[63] But even in affluent areas, victimization risk may be increased if motivated, dangerous offenders move into the neighborhood, a condition described in this chapter's Profiles in Crime feature.

Routine Activities Theory

A series of papers by Lawrence Cohen and Marcus Felson first articulated **routine activities theory**.[64] Cohen and Felson assume that both the motivation to commit crime and the supply of offenders are constant.[65] Every society will always have some people willing to break the law for revenge, greed, or some other motive. Therefore, the volume and distribution of predatory crime (violent crimes against a person and crimes in which an offender attempts to steal an object directly) are closely related to the interaction of three variables that reflect the routine activities of the typical American lifestyle:

- The availability of **suitable targets**, such as homes containing easily salable goods.
- The absence of **capable guardians**, such as police, homeowners, neighbors, friends, and relatives.
- The presence of **motivated offenders**, such as a large number of teenagers.

The presence of these components increases the likelihood that a predatory crime will take place. Targets are more likely to be victimized if they are poorly guarded and exposed to a large group of motivated offenders such as teenage boys.[66] Increasing the number of motivated offenders and placing them in close proximity to valuable goods will increase property victimizations. Even after-school programs, designed to reduce criminal activity, may produce higher crime rates because they lump together motivated offenders, such as teen boys, with vulnerable victims, such as teen boys.[67] Figure 3.2 illustrates the interacting components of routine activities theory.

Research supports many facets of routine activities theory. Cohen and Felson themselves found that crime rates increased between 1960 and 1980

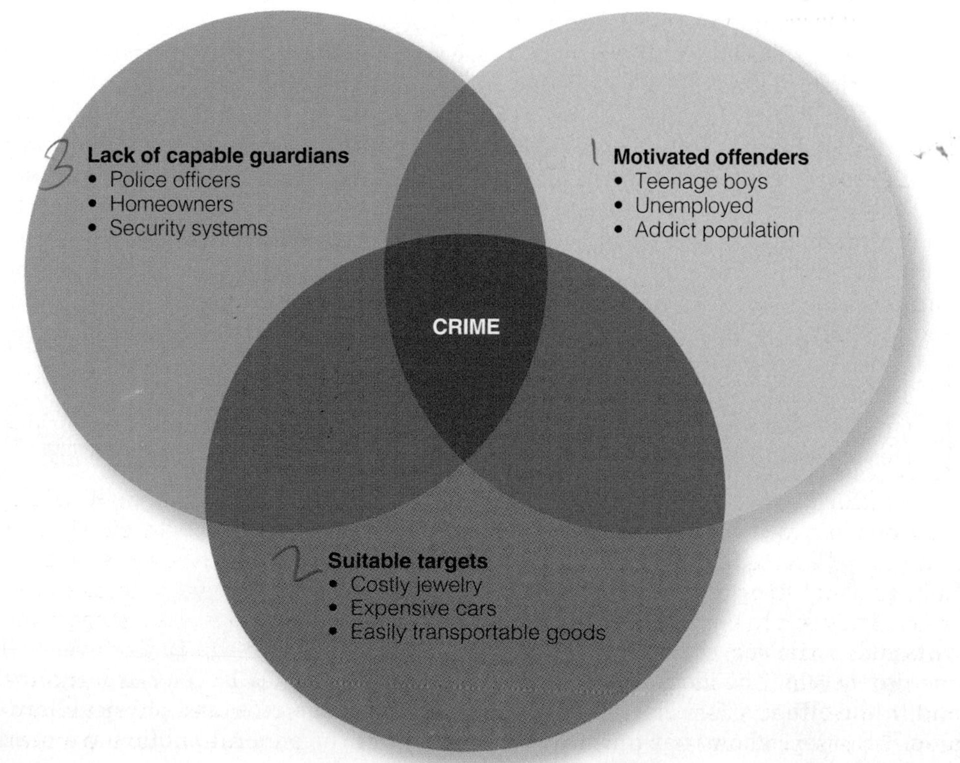

Figure 3.2
Routine Activities Theory
Crime and victimization involve the interaction of three factors.

routine activities theory
The view that victimization results from the interaction of three everyday factors: the availability of suitable targets, the absence of capable guardians, and the presence of motivated offenders.

suitable targets
Objects of crime (persons or property) that are attractive and readily available.

capable guardians
Effective deterrents to crime, such as police or watchful neighbors.

motivated offenders
People willing and able to commit crimes.

CONCEPT SUMMARY 3.1 Victimization Theories

THEORY	MAJOR PREMISE
Victim precipitation	Victims provoke criminals.
Lifestyle	Victims put themselves in danger by engaging in high-risk activities, such as going out late at night, living in a high-crime area, and associating with high-risk peers.
Deviant place	Victimization risk is related to neighborhood crime rates.
Routine activities	A pool of motivated offenders exists and these offenders will take advantage of unguarded, suitable targets.

because the number of adult caretakers at home during the day (guardians) decreased as a result of increased female participation in the workforce. While mothers are at work and children in day care, homes are left unguarded. Similarly, with the growth of suburbia and the decline of the traditional neighborhood, the number of such familiar guardians as family, neighbors, and friends diminished.[68] Supporting research by Steven Messner and his associates found that between the years of 1967 and 1998, as adult unemployment rates *increased*, juvenile homicide arrest rates *decreased*. It is possible that juvenile arrests decreased because unemployed adults were at home to supervise their children and make sure they did not get in trouble or join gangs.[69] The availability and cost of easily transportable goods has also been shown to influence victimization rates: As the costs of goods such as mobile phones and camcorders declined, so too did burglary rates.[70]

Routine Activities and Lifestyle Routine activities theory and the lifestyle approach have a number of similarities. They both assume that a person's living arrangements can affect victim risk and that people who live in unguarded areas are at the mercy of motivated offenders. These two theories both rely on four basic concepts: (1) proximity to criminals, (2) time of exposure to criminals, (3) target attractiveness, and (4) guardianship.[71]

Based on the same basic concepts, these theories share five predictions: People increase their victimization risk if they (1) live in high-crime areas, (2) go out late at night, (3) carry valuables such as an expensive watch, (4) engage in risky behavior such as drinking alcohol, and (5) are without friends or family to watch or help them.[72] Young women who drink to excess in bars and fraternity houses may elevate their risk of date rape because (1) they are easy targets, and (2) their attackers can rationalize raping them because they are intoxicated. ("She's loose and immoral, so I didn't think she'd care.") Intoxication is sometimes seen as making the victim culpable for the crime.[73] Conversely, people can reduce their chances of repeat victimization if they change their lifestyle and adopt crime-suppressing routines such as getting married, having children, or moving to a small town.[74]

The Current Issues in Crime feature "Crime and Everyday Life" shows how these relationships can be influenced by cultural and structural change. The various theories of victimization are summarized in Concept Summary 3.1. ✔ CHECKPOINTS

✔ CHECKPOINTS

- ✔ Victim precipitation theory suggests that crime victims may trigger attacks by acting provocatively.
- ✔ Some experts link victimization to high-risk lifestyles.
- ✔ Some people live in places that are magnets for criminals.
- ✔ The routine activities approach suggests that the risk of victimization may be an interaction among suitable targets, effective guardians, and motivated criminals. Victims present attractive targets with insufficient protection to motivated criminals.

CARING FOR THE VICTIM

National victim surveys indicate that almost every American age 12 and over will one day become the victim of a common-law crime, such as larceny or burglary, and in the aftermath suffer financial problems, mental stress, and physical hardship.[75] Surveys show that upward of 75 percent of the general public have been

Crime and Everyday Life

A core premise of routine activities theory is that, all things being equal, the greater the *opportunity* to commit crime, the higher the crime and victimization rates. Marcus Felson elaborates on this thesis in his classic book, *Crime and Everyday Life*. Using a routine activities perspective, Felson shows why he believes American crime rates are so high and why U.S. citizens suffer such high rates of victimization.

According to Felson, there are always impulsive, motivated offenders willing to take the chance, if conditions are right, of committing crime for profit. Therefore, crime rates are a function of changing social conditions. Crime increased in the United States as the country changed from a nation of small villages and towns to one of large urban environments. In a village, not only could a thief easily be recognized, but the items that were stolen could be identified long after the crime occurred. Cities provided a critical population mass, enabling predatory criminals to hide and evade apprehension. After the crime, criminals could blend into the crowd, disperse their loot, and make a quick escape using the public transportation system.

The modern-day equivalent of the urban center is the shopping mall. Here, strangers converge in large numbers and youths "hang out." The interior is filled with people, so drug deals can be concealed in the pedestrian flow. Stores have attractively displayed goods, encouraging shoplifting and employee pilferage. Substantial numbers of cars are parked in areas that make larceny and car theft virtually undetectable. Cars that carry away stolen merchandise have an undistinguished appearance: Who notices people placing items in a car in a shopping mall lot? Also, shoppers can be attacked in parking lots as they walk in isolation to and from their cars.

As American suburbs grew in importance, labor and family life began to scatter away from the household, decreasing guardianship. Microwave ovens, automatic dishwashers, and fast-food meals have freed adolescents from common household chores. Rather than help prepare the family dinner and wash dishes afterward, adolescents are free to meet with their peers and avoid parental control. As car ownership increases, teens have greater access to transportation outside parental control. Greater mobility and access to transportation makes it impossible for neighbors to know if a teen belongs in an area or is an intruder planning to commit a crime. As schools become larger and more complex, they provide ideal sites for crime. The many hallways and corridors prevent teachers from knowing who belongs where; spacious school grounds reduce teacher supervision.

Felson finds that these changes in the structure and function of society have been responsible for changes in the crime rates. He concludes that, rather than trying to change people, crime prevention strategies must reduce the opportunity to commit crime.

Critical Thinking

1. What recent technological changes have influenced crime rates? The Internet? Video and computer games? Paging systems? Fax machines? Automatic teller systems?
2. Would increased family contact decrease adolescent crime rates, or would it increase the opportunity for child abuse?

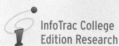

InfoTrac College Edition Research

To see how the routine activities approach is used to explain violent victimizations, read Thoroddur Bjarnason, Thordis J. Sigurdardottir, and Thorolfur Thorlindsson, "Human Agency, Capable Guardians, and Structural Constraints: A Lifestyle Approach to the Study of Violent Victimization," *Journal of Youth and Adolescence* 28 (1999): 105.

SOURCE: Marcus Felson, *Crime and Everyday Life: Insights and Implications for Society*, 3rd ed. (Thousand Oaks, CA: Sage, 2002).

victimized by crime at least once in their lives. As many as 25 percent of the victims develop post-traumatic stress syndrome, with symptoms that last for more than a decade after the crime occurred.[76]

Helping the victim to cope is the responsibility of all of society. Law enforcement agencies, courts, and correctional and human service systems have come to realize that due process and human rights exist not only for the criminal defendant but also for the victim of criminal behavior.

Because of public concern over violent personal crime, President Ronald Reagan created a Task Force on Victims of Crime in 1982.[77] This group suggested that a balance be achieved between recognizing the victim's rights and providing the defendant with due process. Recommendations included providing witnesses and victims with protection from intimidation, requiring restitution in criminal cases, developing guidelines for fair treatment of crime victims and witnesses, and expanding programs of victim compensation.[78]

As a result, Congress passed the Omnibus Victim and Witness Protection Act, requiring the use of victim impact statements at sentencing in federal criminal cases, greater protection for witnesses, more stringent bail laws, and the use of restitution in criminal cases. In 1984, the Comprehensive Crime Control Act and the Victims of Crime Act authorized federal funding for state victim compensation and assistance projects.[79] With these acts, the federal government recognized the

plight of the victim and made victim assistance an even greater concern of the public and the justice system.

Victim Service Programs

An estimated 2,000 **victim–witness assistance programs** have been developed throughout the United States. These programs are organized on a variety of government levels and serve a variety of clients. We will look briefly at some prominent forms of victim assistance operating in the United States.[80]

Victim Compensation

A primary goal of victim advocates has been to lobby for legislation creating crime victim **compensation** programs.[81] As a result of such legislation, the victim ordinarily receives compensation from the state to pay for damages associated with the crime. Rarely are two compensation schemes alike, however, and many state programs suffer from a lack of both adequate funding and proper organization within the criminal justice system. Compensation may be provided for medical bills, loss of wages, loss of future earnings, and counseling. In the case of death, the victim's survivors may receive burial expenses and aid for loss of support.[82] Awards typically range from $100 to $15,000. Occasionally, programs will provide emergency assistance to indigent victims until compensation is available. Emergency assistance may come in the form of food vouchers or replacement of prescription medicines.

In 1984, the federal government created the Victim of Crime Act (VOCA), which grants money derived from fines and penalties imposed on federal offenders to state compensation boards. The money is distributed each year to the states to fund both their crime victim compensation programs and their victim assistance programs, such as rape crisis centers and domestic violence shelters. VOCA payments have increased by more than $200 million (or 82.5 percent) in the past five years! Victims of child abuse made up 23 percent of the recipients of crime victim compensation, while domestic violence victims were 26 percent of all adult victims compensated. What did the payments go for? Medical expenses were 41 percent of all payments; economic support for lost wages and lost support in homicides made up 26 percent of the total; and 15 percent went toward mental health counseling for crime victims. Estimates are that $625 million was paid to victims of violent crime in fiscal year 2004.[83]

Victim Advocates

Some programs assign counselors to victims to serve as advocates to help them understand the operations of the justice system and guide them through the process. Victims of sexual assault may be assigned the assistance of a rape victim advocate to stand by their side as they negotiate the legal and medical systems that must process their case. Research shows that rape survivors who had the assistance of an advocate were significantly more likely to have police reports taken, less likely to be treated negatively by police officers, and reported less distress from their medical contact experiences.[84]

Court advocates prepare victims and witnesses by explaining court procedures: how to be a witness, how bail works, and what to do if the defendant makes a threat. Lack of such knowledge can cause confusion and fear, making some victims reluctant to testify in court procedures.

Many victim programs also provide transportation to and from court and counselors who remain in the courtroom during hearings to explain procedures and provide support. Court escorts are particularly important for elderly and disabled victims, victims of child abuse and assault, and victims who have been intimidated by friends or relatives of the defendant. These types of services may be having a positive effect: Recent research shows that victims may now be less traumatized by a court hearing than previously believed.[85]

Victim Impact Statements

Most jurisdictions allow victims to make an impact statement before the sentencing judge. This gives the victim an opportunity to tell of his or her experiences and describe the ordeal; in the case of a murder

victim–witness assistance programs
Government programs that help crime victims and witnesses; may include compensation, court services, and/or crisis intervention.

compensation
Financial aid awarded to crime victims to repay them for their loss and injuries; may cover medical bills, loss of wages, loss of future earnings, and/or counseling.

trial, the surviving family can recount the effect the crime has had on their lives and well-being.[86] The effect of victim/witness statements on sentencing has been the topic of some debate. Some research finds that victim statements result in a higher rate of incarceration, but others find that victim/witness statements are insignificant.[87] Those who favor the use of impact statements argue that because the victim is harmed by the crime she or he has a right to influence the outcome of the case. After all, the public prosecutor is allowed to make sentencing recommendations because the public has been harmed by the crime. Logically, the harm suffered by the victim legitimizes her or his right to make sentencing recommendations.[88]

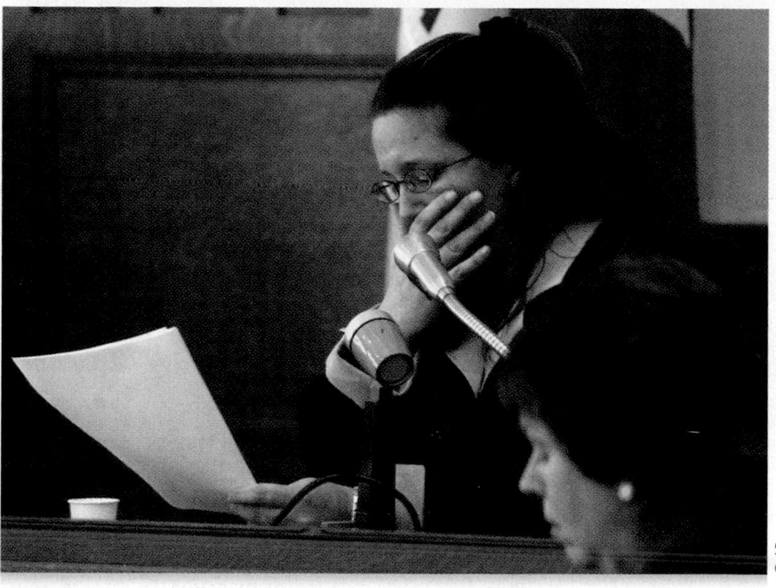
© AP

● Trena Gage, tries to compose herself while reading her victim impact statement during the sentencing of Roger Paul Bentley, February 24, 2006, at the Johnson County Courthouse in Iowa City. Bentley, who kidnapped, raped, and murdered Gage's 10-year-old daughter Jetseta, was convicted of first-degree murder and first-degree kidnapping and sentenced to two consecutive terms of life in prison.

Public Education More than half of all victim programs include public education to help familiarize the general public with their services and with other agencies that help crime victims. In some instances, these are primary prevention programs, which teach methods of dealing with conflict without resorting to violence. School-based programs present information on spousal and dating abuse, followed by discussions of how to reduce violent incidents.[89]

Crisis Intervention Most victim programs refer victims to specific services to help them recover from their ordeal. Clients are commonly referred to the local network of public and private social service agencies that provide emergency and long-term assistance with transportation, medical care, shelter, food, and clothing. In addition, more than half of all victim programs provide **crisis intervention** for victims who feel isolated, vulnerable, and in need of immediate services. Some programs counsel at their offices; others visit victims in their homes, at the crime scene, or in the hospital.

Victim-Offender Reconciliation Programs Mediators facilitate face-to-face encounters between victims and their attackers in **victim–offender reconciliation programs (VORPs)**. The aim is to engage in direct negotiations that lead to restitution agreements and, possibly, reconciliation between the two parties involved.[90] More than 120 reconciliation programs currently in operation handle an estimated 16,000 cases per year. Designed at first to handle routine misdemeanors such as petty theft and vandalism, programs now commonly hammer out restitution agreements in more serious incidents such as residential burglary and even attempted murder.

CONNECTIONS

Reconciliation programs are based on the concept of restorative justice, which rejects punitive correctional measures and instead suggests that crimes of violence and theft should be viewed as interpersonal conflicts that need to be settled in the community through noncoercive means. See Chapter 8 for more on this approach.

Victims' Rights

Because of the influence of victims' rights advocates, every state now has a set of legal rights for crime victims in its code of laws, often called a Victims' Bill of Rights.[91] These generally include the right:

- To be notified of proceedings and the status of the defendant
- To be present at criminal justice proceedings
- To make a statement at sentencing and to receive restitution from a convicted offender
- To be consulted before a case is dismissed or a plea agreement entered
- To a speedy trial
- To keep the victim's contact information confidential

crisis intervention
Emergency counseling for crime victims.

victim–offender reconciliation programs (VORPs)
Mediated face-to-face encounters between victims and their attackers, designed to produce restitution agreements and, if possible, reconciliation.

Policy & Practice in Criminology

Victims' Rights in Europe

While the United States has taken steps to improve the rights of victims, the European Union has also moved toward increasing the role of victims in the justice process. The Council of the European Union—the main decision-making body of the European Union—has been at the forefront of this effort.

Recently, the council agreed to implement the Framework Decision on the standing of victims in criminal proceedings. The Framework Decision is groundbreaking in that it sets out minimum standards for the treatment of victims of crime (and their families) that apply throughout the European Union. European states are expected to modify their laws to conform to the Framework.

Principles of the Framework Decision

The Framework Decision stipulates that minimum standards must be drawn up for the protection of victims of crime, in particular to secure access to justice and rights to compensation for damages, including legal costs. A series of principles underpinning these entitlements state that:

- Victims of crime are entitled to a high level of protection.
- The laws and regulations of Member States should be approximated [brought closer] to achieve the main rights set out in the Framework Decision.
- The needs of crime victims should be addressed in a comprehensive and coordinated manner to avoid secondary victimization; thus provisions are not confined to criminal proceedings.
- Cooperation between Member States should be strengthened through networks of victims' organizations.
- Suitable and adequate training should be given to people who come into contact with victims of crime.

Provisions—Minimum Standards of Treatment

All victims of crime should be provided these minimum standards of treatment:

- Be treated with respect
- Have their entitlement to a real and appropriate role in criminal proceedings recognized
- Have the right to be heard during proceedings, and to supply evidence, safeguarded
- Receive information on the type of support available; where and how to report an offense; criminal proceedings and their role in them; access to protection and advice; entitlement to compensation; and, if they wish, the outcomes of their complaints, including sentencing and release of the offender
- Have communication safeguards: Member States should take measures to minimize communication difficulties in criminal proceedings
- Have access to free legal advice concerning their role in the proceedings and where to receive appropriate legal aid
- Receive payment of expenses incurred as a result of participation in criminal proceedings
- Receive reasonable protection, including protection of privacy
- Receive compensation in the course of criminal proceedings
- Receive penal mediation in the course of criminal proceedings where appropriate
- Benefit from various measures to minimize the difficulties faced when victims are resident in another Member State, especially when organizing criminal proceedings

In addition, cooperation between Member States is to be encouraged; specialist services and victims' organizations should be promoted; training for personnel who come into contact with victims should be encouraged; and steps should be taken to prevent secondary victimization and to avoid placing victims under unnecessary pressure. Therefore, each Member State must consider its facilities within courts, police stations, public services, and victims' organizations.

SOURCES: Council Framework Decision of 15 March 2001 on the standing of victims in criminal proceedings, http://europa.eu.int/eurlex/pri/en/oj/dat/2001/l_082/l_08220010322en00010004.pdf (accessed May 30, 2006); Proposal for a Council Directive on compensation to crime victims, http://europa.eu.int/eur-lex/en/com/pdf/2002/com2002_0562en01.pdf (accessed May 30, 2006).

There is also an international movement to establish victims' rights, a phenomenon discussed in the Policy & Practice in Criminology feature, "Victims' Rights in Europe."

Assuring victims' rights may involve an eclectic mix of advocacy groups—some independent, others government sponsored, and some self-help. Advocates can be especially helpful when victims need to interact with the agencies of justice. For example, advocates can lobby police departments to keep investigations open as well as request the return of recovered stolen property. They can demand that prosecutors and judges provide protection from harassment and reprisals by, for example, making "no contact" a condition of bail. They can help victims make statements during sentencing hearings and probation and parole revocation procedures. Victim advocates can also interact with news media, making sure that reporting is accurate and that victims' privacy is not violated. Victim advocates can be part of an independent agency similar to a legal aid society. If successful, top-notch advocates may eventually open private offices, similar to attorneys, private investigators, or jury consultants.[92]

A final, albeit controversial, element of the victims' rights movement is the development of offender registration laws that require that the name and sometimes addresses of known sex offenders be posted by law enforcement agencies. Today almost every state has adopted sex offender laws, and the federal government runs a National Sex Offender Public Registry with links to every state.[93]

CONNECTIONS

Sex offender registration is indelibly linked to the death of Megan Kanka, an incident described in the Profiles in Crime feature earlier in this chapter.

THINKING Like a Criminologist

The director of the state's department of human services has asked you to evaluate a self-report survey of adolescents ages 10 to 18. She has provided you with the following information on physical abuse.

Adolescents experiencing abuse or violence are at high risk of immediate and lasting negative effects on health and well-being. Of the high school students surveyed, an alarming one in five (21 percent) said they had been physically abused. Of the older students, ages 15 to 18, 29 percent said they had been physically abused. Younger students also reported significant rates of abuse: 17 percent responded "yes" when asked whether they had been physically abused. Although girls were far less likely to report abuse than boys, 12 percent said they had been physically abused. Most abuse occurs at home; it occurs more than once; and the abuser is usually a family member. More than half of those physically abused had tried alcohol and drugs, and 60 percent had admitted to a violent act. Nonabused children were significantly less likely to abuse substances, and only 30 percent indicated they had committed a violent act.

How would you interpret these data? What factors might influence their validity? What is your interpretation of the association between abuse and delinquency?

Summary

- Criminologists now consider victims and victimization a major focus of study.
- About 24 million U.S. citizens are victims of crime each year.
- Like the crime rate, the victimization rate has been in sharp decline.
- The social and economic costs of crime are in the billions of dollars annually.
- Victims suffer long-term consequences such as experiencing fear and post-traumatic stress disorder.
- Research shows that victims are more likely than nonvictims to engage in antisocial behavior.
- Like crime, victimization has stable patterns and trends.
- Violent crime victims tend to be young, poor, single males living in large cities, although victims come in all ages, sizes, races, and genders.
- Females are more likely than males to be victimized by somebody they know.
- Adolescents maintain a high risk of being physically and sexually victimized. Their victimization has been linked to a multitude of subsequent social problems.
- Many victimizations occur in the home, and many victims are the target of relatives and loved ones.
- One view of the cause of victimization, called victim precipitation, is that victims provoke criminals.
- Lifestyle theories suggest that victims put themselves in danger by engaging in high-risk activities, such as going out late at night, living in a high-crime area, and associating with high-risk peers.
- Deviant place theory argues that victimization risk is related to neighborhood crime rates.
- The routine activities theory maintains that a pool of motivated offenders exists and that these offenders will take advantage of unguarded, suitable targets.
- Numerous programs help victims by providing court services, economic compensation, public education, and crisis intervention.
- Most states have created a Victims' Bill of Rights.

Take a Post-Test. Visit www.thomsonedu.com/criminaljustice/siegel and take the chapter Post-Test to monitor your progress and identify areas for further improvement. In addition to discovering what you've mastered, you'll learn which concepts need your added attention and get specific page references that direct you to the places in the text where you can find more information on them.

Key Terms

victimology 53
victimologists 53
post-traumatic stress disorder (PTSD) 55
cycle of violence 56
victim precipitation theory 60
active precipitation 60
passive precipitation 60
lifestyle theories 60
deviant place theory 61
routine activities theory 63
suitable targets 63
capable guardians 63
motivated offenders 63
victim–witness assistance programs 66
compensation 66
crisis intervention 67
victim–offender reconciliation programs (VORPs) 67

Critical Thinking Questions

1. Considering what you have learned in this chapter about crime victimization, what measures can you take to better protect yourself from crime?

2. Do you agree with the assessment that a school is one of the most dangerous locations in the community? Did you find your high school to be a dangerous environment?

3. Do people bear some of the responsibility for their victimization if they maintain a lifestyle that contributes to the chances of becoming a crime victim? That is, should we "blame the victim"?

4. Have you ever experienced someone "precipitating" crime? If so, did you do anything to help the situation?

5. What would you advise freshman girls to do to lower the risk of being sexually assaulted?

Choice Theory: Because They Want To

CHAPTER 4

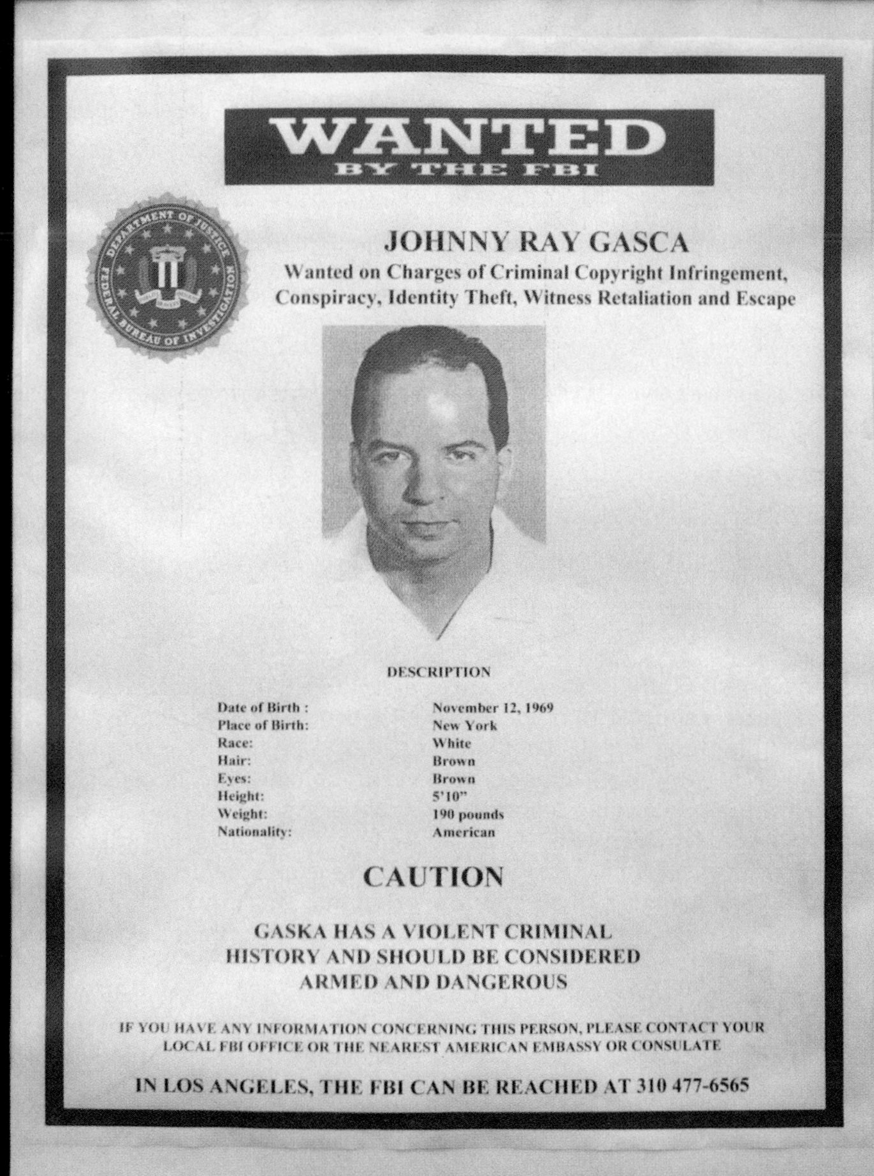
WANTED
BY THE FBI
DEPARTMENT OF JUSTICE
FEDERAL BUREAU OF INVESTIGATION
JOHNNY RAY GASCA
Wanted on Charges of Criminal Copyright Infringement, Conspiracy, Identity Theft, Witness Retaliation and Escape
DESCRIPTION
Date of Birth : November 12, 1969
Place of Birth: New York
Race: White
Hair: Brown
Eyes: Brown
Height: 5'10"
Weight: 190 pounds
Nationality: American
CAUTION
GASKA HAS A VIOLENT CRIMINAL HISTORY AND SHOULD BE CONSIDERED ARMED AND DANGEROUS
IF YOU HAVE ANY INFORMATION CONCERNING THIS PERSON, PLEASE CONTACT YOUR LOCAL FBI OFFICE OR THE NEAREST AMERICAN EMBASSY OR CONSULATE
IN LOS ANGELES, THE FBI CAN BE REACHED AT 310 477-6565

JOHNNY RAY GASCA WAS A NATIVE NEW YORKER WITH A TRACK RECORD OF PETTY CRIME when he moved to Hollywood in 2002 to seek his fortune in the movie business.[1] Given his criminal leanings, Gasca was less interested in making movies than in stealing them!

Refer to the front endpapers for a study tool that summarizes each of the major theories discussed in this book.

CHAPTER OBJECTIVES

1. Understand the concept of rational choice.
2. Know the work of Beccaria.
3. Be able to discuss the concepts of offense- and offender-specific crime.
4. Be able to discuss why violent and drug crimes are rational.
5. Summarize the various techniques of situational crime prevention.
6. Be able to discuss the association between punishment and crime.
7. Be familiar with the concepts of certainty, severity, and speed of punishment.
8. Understand what is meant by specific deterrence.
9. Be able to discuss the issues involving the use of incapacitation.
10. Understand the concept of "three strikes and you're out."

Take a Pre-Test. Visit www.thomsonedu.com/criminaljustice/siegel and take a Pre-Test to determine what you already know and identify the areas where you'll need to focus your study. The program will direct you to specific pages within the text where you can find further information on the correct answers to the questions you've missed.

Gasca began to pose as a movie industry insider and would hang around theaters where advance screenings of feature films were scheduled. Once inside the theater, he would rig his camera to an armrest for stability and start filming when the lights went down. He used high-end sound and recording equipment that produced extraordinarily good quality master recordings. He would then mass produce the recordings on 11 interlinked VCRs and sell them over the Internet. By beating the public release of blockbuster films, he cleared as much as $4,500 a week from his illegal pirating scheme.

Though he was known as the "Prince of Pirates," Gasca had a bad habit of getting caught in the act. Police in Burbank, California, arrested him when he was filming the science fiction film *The Core*. He was also arrested when he began filming *Anger Management* and *8 Mile*. When Gasca's apartment was searched, federal agents found 2 video cameras, a microcamera built onto a trouser belt, 2 DVD recorders, the 11 linked VCRs, a stolen Social Security card, and his 2 diaries, which chronicled his exploits. While he was out on bail, Gasca threatened to sell up to 20 more unreleased movies online unless the Motion Picture Association of America (MPAA) helped him get his equipment back. In 2003, Gasca became the first person ever indicted on federal charges of movie piracy. Placed in his lawyer's custody, he disappeared without a trace until he was located two years later in Kissimmee, Florida, where, not surprisingly, he was supporting himself by illegally copying movies. On June 29, 2005, Gasca was found guilty of eight federal criminal charges, including three counts of copyright infringement.

Criminals such as Johnny Ray Gasca carefully plan their criminal activities. Their calculated actions suggest that the decision to commit crime can involve rational and detailed planning and decision making, designed to maximize personal gain and avoid capture and punishment. Some criminologists go as far as suggesting that any criminal violation—committing a robbery, selling drugs, attacking a rival, or filing a false tax return—is based upon *rational decision making*. Such a decision may be based on a variety of personal reasons, including greed, revenge, need, anger, lust, jealousy, thrill-seeking, or vanity. But if it is made after weighing the potential benefits and consequences, then the illegal act is a rational choice. This view of crime is referred to here as choice theory.

In this chapter, we review the philosophical underpinnings of choice theory—the view that criminals rationally choose crime. We then turn to theories of crime prevention and control that flow from the concept of choice: situational crime control, general deterrence theory, specific deterrence theory, and incapacitation. Finally, we take a brief look at how choice theory has influenced criminal justice policy.

DEVELOPMENT OF RATIONAL CHOICE THEORY

CONNECTIONS

In Chapter 1 we traced the history of classical theory. As you may recall, Beccaria believed that criminals weighed the benefits and consequences of crime before choosing to violate the law. They would be unlikely to choose crime if punishment was swift, certain, and severe.

As you may recall from Chapter 1, rational choice theory has its roots in the *classical school of criminology* developed by the Italian social thinker Cesare Beccaria, whose utilitarian approach powerfully influenced the criminal justice system and was widely accepted throughout Europe and the United States.[2] Though influential for more than 100 years, by the end of the nineteenth century, the popularity of the classical approach began to decline. During this period, positivist criminologists focused on internal and external factors—poverty, IQ, education—rather than personal choice and decision making.

Beginning in the late 1960s, criminologists once again began to embrace classical ideas, producing books and monographs expounding the theme that criminals are rational actors who plan their crimes, could be controlled by the fear of punishment, and deserve to be penalized for their misdeeds. In the 1960s, Nobel Prize–winning economist Gary Becker applied his views on rational behavior and human capital (that is, human competence and the consequences of investments in human competence) to criminal activity. He argued that with the exception of a few mentally ill people, criminals behave in a predictable or rational way when deciding to commit crime. They engage in a cost-benefit analysis of crime, weighing what they expect to gain against the risks they must undergo and the costs they may incur, such as going to prison.[3] Instead of regarding criminal activity as irrational behavior, Becker viewed criminality as rational behavior that might be controlled by increasing the costs and reducing the potential for gain.

In *Thinking About Crime*, political scientist James Q. Wilson observed that people who are likely to commit crime are unafraid of breaking the law because they value the excitement and thrills of crime, have a low stake in conformity, and are willing to take greater chances than the average person. If they could be convinced that their actions would bring severe punishment, only the totally irrational would be willing to engage in crime.[4]

From these roots has evolved a more contemporary version of classical theory, based on intelligent thought processes and criminal decision making; today this is referred to as the rational choice approach to crime causation.[5]

CONCEPTS OF RATIONAL CHOICE

According to contemporary rational choice theory, law-violating behavior is the product of careful thought and planning. Offenders choose crime after considering both personal—money, revenge, thrills, entertainment—and situational factors, such as target availability, security measures, and police presence. Before deciding to commit a crime, the reasoning criminal evaluates the risk of apprehension, the seriousness of expected punishment, the potential value or benefit of the criminal enterprise, his or her ability to succeed, and the need for criminal gain.

The decision to commit a specific type of crime, then, is a matter of personal choice made after weighing and evaluating available information. Conversely, the decision to forgo crime may be based on the criminal's perception that the potential rewards of the criminal act are not worth the risk of apprehension. A burglar, for instance, may choose *not* to commit crime if he believes a neighborhood is well patrolled by police, that neighbors are vigilant, and that many people in the neighborhood have installed security devices.[6]

Offense- and Offender-Specific Crime

Rational choice theorists view crime as both offense- and offender-specific.[7] Crime is said to be **offense-specific** because offenders react selectively to the characteristics of particular crimes. Deciding to commit a particular burglary might involve evaluating the target's likely cash yield, the availability of resources such as a getaway car, and the probability of capture by police.[8]

Crime is **offender-specific** because criminals are not simply driven people who, for one reason or another, engage in random antisocial acts. Before deciding to commit crime, they analyze whether they have what it takes to be successful; they carefully evaluate their skills, motives, needs, and fears. A criminal act might be ruled out if potential offenders perceive that they can reach a desired personal goal through legitimate means, such as a part-time job or borrowing money from a relative.

Note the distinction made here between "crime" and "criminality."[9] "Crime" is an event; "criminality" is a personal trait. Criminals do not commit crime all the time; conversely, even the most honest citizens may, on occasion, violate the law. On one hand, some high-risk people lacking opportunity may never commit crime;

offense-specific
The idea that offenders react selectively to the characteristics of particular crimes.

offender-specific
The idea that offenders evaluate their skills, motives, needs, and fears before deciding to commit crime.

on the other hand, given enough provocation or opportunity, a low-risk, law-abiding person may commit crime. What are the factors that structure criminality and the decision to commit crime?

Structuring Criminality

A number of personal factors condition people to choose criminality.

Economic Need/Opportunity In a recent issue of *Boston Magazine*, a university lecturer with an Ivy League education, including a PhD in cultural anthropology, wrote a first-person account of how she became a call girl to help pay her bills.[10] Rather than living on the meager teaching salary she was offered, she *chose* to take the tax free $140 per hour for her services (she charged $200, handing over $60 to the "escort service" that arranged her "dates"). She left the "business" when she became financially self-sufficient. The "Ivy League Hooker's" illegal activity was shaped by her economic needs. She is not alone. Drug users report that they will increase their criminal involvement proportionate to the costs of their habit. Once they become cocaine and heroin users, the benefits of criminal enterprise become overwhelmingly attractive and their crime rates increase.[11]

False Expectations People may also choose to commit crime because they believe they have little chance of becoming successful in the conventional world. They view criminality as their ticket to a better life. Unfortunately, many overestimate the value of criminal rewards. They may know people who have made "big scores" and are quite successful at crime and assume erroneously that anyone can be a successful crook.[12] In reality, the rewards of crime are often quite meager. When Steven Levitt and Sudhir Alladi Venkatesh studied the financial rewards of being in a drug gang, they found that despite enormous risks to their health, life, and freedom, average gang members earned slightly more than what they could in the legitimate labor market (about $6 to $11 per hour).[13] Why then did they stay in the gang? Members believed that there was a strong potential for future riches if they stayed in the drug business and earned a "management" position (gang leaders earned a lot more). In this case, the rational choice is structured by the person's perception of the potential for future criminal gain versus the reality of conventional alternatives and opportunities.[14]

Personal Traits and Experience Personal experience may be an important element in structuring criminality.[15] Career criminals may learn the limitations of their powers; they know when to take a chance and when to be cautious. Experienced criminals may turn from a life of crime when they develop a belief that the risk of crime is greater than its potential profit.[16] Personality and lifestyle also affect criminal choices. Criminals appear to be more impulsive and have less self-control than other people; they seem unaffected by fear of criminal punishment.[17] They are typically under stress or facing some serious personal problem or condition that forces them to choose risky behavior.[18]

Learning Criminal Techniques Criminals report learning techniques of crime to help them avoid detection. Female crack dealers learn how to camouflage their activities within the bustle of their daily lives. They sell crack while hanging out in a park or shooting hoops in a playground. They meet their customers in a lounge and try to act normal, having a good time, anything not to draw attention to themselves and their business. They use props to disguise drug deals.[19] Research conducted by Leanne Fiftal Alarid and her partners found that women drawn into dealing drugs learn the trade in a businesslike manner. One young dealer told Alarid how she learned the techniques of the trade from an older male partner:

> He taught me how to "recon" [reconstitute] cocaine, cutting and repacking a brick from 91 proof to 50 proof, just like a business. He treats me like an equal partner, and many of the friends are business associates. I am a catalyst. . . . I even get guys turned on to drugs.[20]

Note the business terminology used. This coke dealer could be talking about taking a computer training course at a major corporation. If criminal acts are treated as business decisions, in which profit and loss potential must be carefully calculated, then crime must indeed be a rational event.

CONNECTIONS

Rational choice theory dovetails with routine activities theory, which you learned about in Chapter 3. Although not identical, these approaches both claim that crime rates are a product of criminal opportunity. They suggest that increasing the number of guardians, decreasing the suitability of targets, or reducing the offender population should lower crime rates. Conversely, increased opportunity and reduced guardianship will increase crime rates.

Structuring Crime

According to the rational choice approach, the decision to commit crime, regardless of its substance, is structured by (1) where it occurs, and (2) the characteristics of the target.

Choosing the Place of Crime Criminals carefully choose where they will commit their crime. Criminologist Bruce Jacobs's interviews with 40 active crack cocaine street dealers in a midwestern city showed that dealers carefully evaluate the desirability of their sales area before setting up shop.[21] Dealers consider the middle of a long block the best choice because they can see everything in both directions; police raids can be spotted before they occur.[22] Another tactic is to entice new buyers into spaces between apartment buildings or into back lots. Although the dealers may lose the tactical edge of being on a public street, they gain a measure of protection because their colleagues can watch over the operation and come to the rescue if the buyer tries to "pull something."[23]

Choosing Targets Evidence of rational choice may also be found in the way criminals locate their targets. Burglars check to make sure that no one is home before they enter a residence. Some call ahead; others ring the doorbell, preparing to claim they had the wrong address if someone answers. Some find out which families have star high school athletes because those that do are sure to be at the weekend football game, leaving their houses unguarded.[24] Others seek unlocked doors and avoid the ones with deadbolts; houses with dogs are usually considered off-limits.[25] Burglars also report being sensitive to the activities of their victims. They note that homemakers often develop predictable behavior patterns, which helps them plan their crimes.[26] Burglars seem to prefer "working" between 9:00 AM and 11:00 AM and in midafternoon, when parents are either working or dropping off or picking up children at school. Burglars appear to monitor car and pedestrian traffic and avoid selecting targets on heavily traveled streets.[27] It does not seem surprising that well-organized communities that restrict traffic and limit neighborhood entrance and exit routes have experienced significant declines in property crime.[28]

In sum, rational choice involves both shaping criminality and structuring crime. Personality, age, status, risk, and opportunity seem to influence the decision to become a criminal; place, target, and techniques help to structure crime.[29]

✔ CHECKPOINTS

✔ CHECKPOINTS

✔ Choice theory can be traced to Beccaria's view that crime is rational and can be prevented by punishment that is swift, severe, and certain.

✔ Crime is said to be offense-specific because criminals evaluate the characteristics of targets to determine their suitability.

✔ Crime is offender-specific because criminals evaluate their skills, motivations, and needs before committing a specific crime.

✔ Criminal choice involves such actions as choosing the place of crime, selecting targets, and learning criminal techniques.

IS CRIME RATIONAL?

It is relatively easy to show that some crimes are the product of rational, objective thought, especially when they involve an ongoing criminal conspiracy centered on economic gain. When prominent bankers in the savings and loan industry were indicted for criminal fraud, their elaborate financial schemes not only showed signs of rationality but exhibited brilliant, though flawed, financial expertise.[30] Similarly, the drug dealings of organized crime bosses demonstrate a reasoned analysis of market conditions, interests, and risks. But what about crimes that are immediate rather than ongoing? Do they show signs of rationality?

Is Theft Rational?

There is evidence that theft-related crimes are the product of careful risk assessment, including environmental, social, and structural factors. Target selection seems highly rational. Ronald Clarke and Patricia Harris found that auto thieves are very selective in their choice of targets. Vehicle selection seems to be based on attractiveness and suitability for a particular purpose: German cars are selected

Profiles in Crime

Copping the Cappers

On March 21, 2006, Konstantin Grigoryan, his wife, Mayya Leonidovna Grigoryan, and Eduard Gersheli, Aleksandr Treynker, and Haroutyun Gulderyan were all arrested on charges related to a long-running Medicare fraud scheme that federal authorities believe netted them at least $20 million. The scheme involved defrauding the federal health care program that paid for tests that either were unnecessary or were never performed.

According to the Justice Department, the group paid kickbacks to recruit patients and to submit fraudulent billings to Medicare on behalf of medical service providers, such as medical clinics and diagnostic testing centers. The scheme, commonly referred to as "beneficiary-sharing" or "patient-rotating," involves "marketers" who obtain data about Medicare beneficiaries and sell the information to Medicare providers who engage in fraudulent billings. Some marketers, known as "cappers," recruit patients with Medicare coverage to travel to clinics and receive services that are medically unnecessary, and sometimes they receive no medical services at all.

The alleged plot began in 1997, when Konstantin Grigoryan conducted fraudulent activity through 12 Los Angeles–area medical providers. The providers were controlled by the defendants and purportedly conducted diagnostic tests, such as ultrasound examinations and blood tests. The medical providers allegedly generated revenue by using cappers who brought in Medicare beneficiaries by car, van, and bus from across California in exchange for kickbacks. Once the patients came into a physician's office, the medical providers allegedly billed the patients' Medicare numbers on the dates of their visits and on many other dates—whether or not any services were in fact provided to the beneficiaries. In many cases where diagnostic testing services were billed to Medicare, no test was actually performed on the patient on the purported date of service. The conspirators would fabricate the tests so that the patients' files could withstand an audit by Medicare. The criminal scheme caused Medicare to pay out at least $20 million in fraudulent claims from 2000 until 2005. Much of the money was deposited into a maze of bank accounts of "management" and "consulting" companies, including a Panamanian shell corporation with a Swiss account.

Schemes such as this convince advocates of rational choice theory that crime is not an impulsive random event, but a carefully thought out and planned action designed to provide the greatest benefit at the lowest cost. Of course, even the best-laid schemes may go astray, leading to arrest, conviction, and punishment.

SOURCE: Department of Justice press release, "Five Arrested in Health Care Fraud Scheme That Collected at Least $20 Million from Medicare Program," March 21, 2006, http://losangeles.fbi.gov/dojpressrel/pressrel06/la032106usa.htm (accessed March 31, 2006).

for stripping, for example, because they usually have high-quality audio equipment that has good value on the second-hand market.[31]

Burglars seem to choose targets based on their value, freshness and resale potential. A relatively new piece of electronic gear, such as Ipod, may be a prime target because it has not yet saturated the market and still retains high value.[32] While they may seek out easily salable goods, burglars also report that they like to work close to home; perhaps a familiar location allows them to blend in, not look out of place, and not get lost when returning home with their loot.[33] As the Profiles in Crime feature shows, some theft schemes are so complex that they cannot be anything but a "rational choice."

Is Drug Use Rational?

Did actor Robert Downey, Jr., make an objective, rational choice to abuse drugs and potentially sabotage his career? Did comedians John Belushi and Chris Farley make a rational choice when they abused drugs to the point that it killed them? Is it possible that drug users and dealers, a group not usually associated with clear thinking, make rational choices? Research does in fact show that at its onset drug use is controlled by rational decision making. Users report that they begin taking drugs when they believe the benefits of substance abuse outweigh its costs: They believe drugs will provide a fun, exciting, thrilling experience. They choose what they consider safe sites to buy and sell drugs.[34] Their entry into substance abuse is facilitated by their perception that valued friends and family members endorse and encourage drug use and abuse substances themselves.[35]

Drug dealers approach their profession in a businesslike fashion. Traffickers and dealers face many of the same problems as legitimate retailers. If they are too successful in one location, rivals will be attracted to the area, and stiff competition may drive down prices and cut profits. The dealer can fight back against competitors by discounting the price of drugs or increasing quality, as long as it doesn't reduce profit margins.[36] If these "business tactics" are not working, dealers can always turn to violence. They may start drug wars on their rivals' turf, convincing customers to stay away from such a dangerous area; in retaliation, rivals may cut prices to lure customers back. In other words, drug dealers face many of the same problems as legitimate businesspeople; they differ in the tactics they use to help settle disputes.[37]

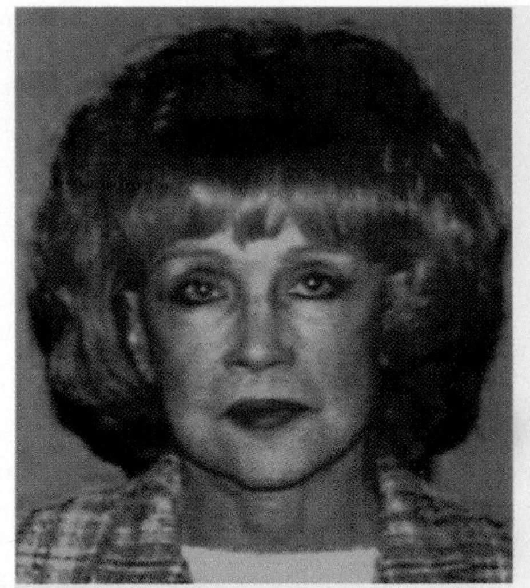

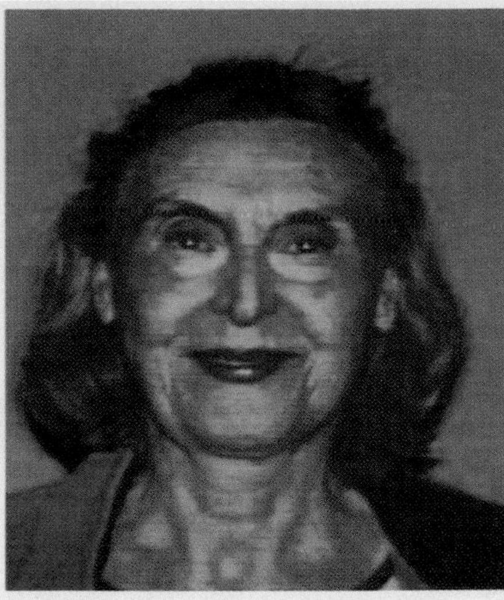

Golay Rutterschmidt

© AP

● Is violence rational, or spontaneous and unplanned? It is hard to imagine that violence can be a "rational" choice, but the evidence proves otherwise. Many violent criminals are cold and calculating, not impulsive and impetuous. Here are photos of suspects Helen Golay and Olga Rutterschmidt, accused of befriending, insuring, then killing two homeless men. The two elderly women, both in their mid-70s, are alleged to have hatched a scheme to collect $2.5 million from the life insurance policies of the two indigent men.

Can Violence Be Rational?

Is it possible that violent acts, through which the offender gains little material benefit, are the product of reasoned decision making? Evidence confirms that even violent criminals select suitable targets by picking people who are vulnerable and lack adequate defenses.[38] Richard Wright and Scott Decker interviewed active street robbers in St. Louis, Missouri. Their subjects expressed a considerable amount of rational thought before choosing a robbery, which may involve violence, over a burglary, which involves stealth and cunning.[39] One told them why he chose to be a robber:

> I feel more safer doing a robbery because doing a burglary, I got a fear of breaking into somebody's house not knowing who might be up in there. . . . On robbery I can select my victims, I can select my place of business. I can watch and see who all work in there, or I can rob a person and pull them around in the alley or push them up in a doorway and rob them.[40]

Robbers generally choose targets close to their homes or in areas to which they routinely travel. Familiarity with the area gives them ready knowledge of escape routes; this is referred to as their "awareness space."[41] Robbers may be wary of people who are watching the community for signs of trouble; robbery levels are relatively low in neighborhoods where residents keep a watchful eye on their neighbors' property.[42] Many robbers avoid freestanding buildings because they can more easily be surrounded by police; others select targets that are known to do a primarily cash business, such as bars, supermarkets, and restaurants.[43] Robbers also tend to shy away from victims who are perceived to be armed and potentially dangerous.[44] However, some actually target fellow criminals, for example, drug dealers.[45] Though these fellow criminals may be dangerous, robbers recognize that people with "dirty hands" are unlikely to call police and get entangled with the law. When Bruce Jacobs interviewed armed robbers he found that some specialize in targeting drug dealers because they believe that even though their work is hazardous, the rewards outweigh the risks. In some ways, drug dealers represent the perfect victim. They are plentiful, visible, accessible, and carry plenty of cash. Their merchandise is valuable, easily transportable, and can be used by the robber or sold to another. Drug dealers are not particularly popular, so they cannot rely on bystanders to come to their aid. Nor can they call the police and ask them to recover their stolen goods! Of course, drug dealers may be able to "take care of business" themselves, but, surprisingly, Jacobs finds that many choose not to carry a pistol. Drug dealers may be tough and bad, the robbers claim, but they are tougher and badder![46]

CONNECTIONS

As you may recall from earlier discussion in this chapter, criminals may find that despite its risks crime can provide economic rewards that are far higher than they could hope to achieve in conventional employment. Many overestimate the profits from crime, though most seem to realize that the chances of a big payoff are remote.

What about Airplane Hijackers? Certainly the activities of people who hijack airplanes can't be called rational. Or can they? In a recent study, Laura Dugan, Gary Lafree, and Alex Piquero found that even airplane hijackers, a rather unique sort of violent criminal, may be rational decision makers. Hijacking rates declined when airlines employed measures to make it more difficult to commit crime (for example, using metal detectors in airports) or to increase the cost of crime (for example, boosting the punishments for hijacking). Dugan and her associates found that

CONNECTIONS

Dugan found that people who hijacked planes for terrorist purposes were not deterred by countermeasures. Terrorists may not be using the same rational processes as other criminals and/or hijackers. For more on the mind-set of terrorists, see Chapter 10's discussion on the making of a terrorist.

hijacking rates significantly increased soon after a spate of successful hijackings and decreased when antihijacking policies were implemented. The fact that hijackers were deterred by the threat of apprehension and punishment and encouraged by others' success is surely a sign of rational decision making.[47]

WHY DO PEOPLE COMMIT CRIME?

Assuming that crime is rational, why—knowing its often unpleasant consequences—do people choose to commit crime? Rational choice theorists believe that crime is a natural choice people make after weighing such issues as their personal needs, mental state, legitimate alternatives such as a job, the risks of getting caught, and the threat of punishment. All these factors are considered before the decision is made to commit crime. Consequently, even the most desperate criminal might hesitate to attack a well-defended target, whereas a group of teens might choose to rip off an unoccupied home on the spur of the moment.[48]

For many people, crime is a more attractive alternative than law-abiding behavior. It brings rewards, excitement, prestige, or other desirable outcomes without lengthy work or effort. Whether it is violent or profit-oriented, crime has an allure that some people cannot resist. Crime may produce a natural "high" and other positive sensations that are instrumental in maintaining and reinforcing criminal behavior.[49] Some law violators describe the "adrenaline rush" that comes from successfully executing illegal activities in dangerous situations. This has been termed **edgework** the "exhilarating, momentary integration of danger, risk, and skill" that motivates people to try a variety of dangerous criminal and noncriminal behaviors.[50]

Sociologist Jack Katz argues that there are, in fact, immediate benefits to criminality. These situational inducements, which he labels the **seductions of crime**, directly precede the commission of crime and draw offenders into law violations. For example, someone challenges their authority or moral position, and they vanquish their opponent with a beating; or they want to do something exciting, so they break into and vandalize a school building.[51] According to Katz, choosing crime can help satisfy personal needs. For some people, shoplifting and vandalism are attractive because getting away with crime is a thrilling demonstration of personal competence (Katz calls this "sneaky thrills"). Even murder can have an emotional payoff: Killers behave like the avenging gods of mythology, choosing to have life-or-death control over their victims.[52]

The criminal lifestyle fits well with people who organize their life around risk taking and partying. Criminal events provide money for drugs and are ideal for displaying courage and fearlessness to one's peers. Rather than create overwhelming social problems, a criminal way of life may be beneficial to some people, helping them overcome the problems and stress they face in their daily lives. Antisocial behavior gives adolescents the opportunity to exert control over their own lives and destinies by helping them avoid situations they find uncomfortable or repellant (e.g., by cutting school or running away from an abusive home) or to obtain resources for desired activities and commodities (e.g., by stealing or selling drugs to buy stylish outfits).[53] ✔ CHECKPOINTS

✔ CHECKPOINTS

✔ Theft crimes appear to be rational because thieves and burglars typically choose targets that present little risk, and they plan their attacks carefully.

✔ Robbers report that they select vulnerable targets who are unlikely to fight back. Some like to attack drug dealers who have lots of cash and cannot call the police when it is taken.

✔ Drug users and dealers use elaborate ploys to avoid detection.

✔ They employ businesslike practices in their commercial enterprises.

✔ Even serial killers use cunning and thought to avoid detection.

✔ Crime is seductive. People may rationally choose crime because it provides them with psychological and social benefits. It helps them solve problems.

CONTROLLING CRIME

If committing crime is a rational choice, it follows that crime can be controlled or eradicated by convincing potential offenders that crime is a poor choice—that it will not bring them rewards but bring pain, hardship, and deprivation. According to rational choice theory, street-smart offenders (1) calculate the potential success of committing crime; (2) select their targets on the basis of risk assessment; and (3) will choose not to commit a crime if the disadvantages, such as getting caught and punished, outweigh the benefits, such as making lots of money. A number of potential strategies for controlling crime flow from this premise. Among the most important of these are situational crime prevention strategies, general deterrence strategies, specific deterrence strategies, and incapacitation strategies.

edgework
The excitement or exhilaration of successfully executing illegal activities in dangerous situations.

seductions of crime
The situational inducements or immediate benefits that draw offenders into law violations.

SITUATIONAL CRIME PREVENTION

According to the concept of **situational crime prevention**, in order to reduce criminal activity, planners must be aware of the characteristics of sites and situations that are at risk to crime; the things that draw or push toward these sites and situations; what equips such people to take advantage of the criminal opportunities offered by these sites and situations; and what constitutes the immediate triggers for actual criminal actions.[54] Criminal acts will be avoided if (1) potential targets are carefully guarded, (2) the means to commit crime are controlled, and (3) potential offenders are carefully monitored. Desperate people may contemplate crime, but only the truly irrational will attack a well-defended, inaccessible target and risk strict punishment.

One way of preventing crime, then, is to reduce the opportunities people have to commit particular crimes. This approach was first popularized in the United States in the early 1970s by Oscar Newman, who coined the term **defensible space**. The idea is that crime can be prevented or displaced through the use of residential designs that reduce criminal opportunity, such as well-lit housing projects that maximize surveillance.[55]

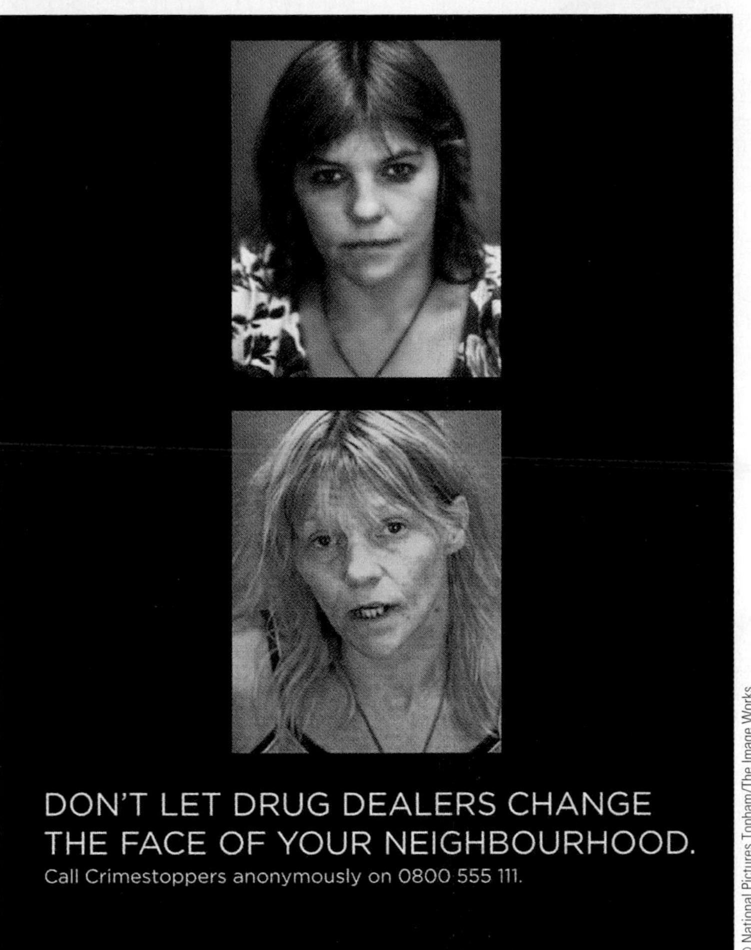

DON'T LET DRUG DEALERS CHANGE THE FACE OF YOUR NEIGHBOURHOOD.
Call Crimestoppers anonymously on 0800 555 111.

● According to rational choice theory, potential criminals calculate the possible benefits of committing crime and choose not to commit a crime if the disadvantages outweigh the benefits. Crime can therefore be prevented if people are convinced that it is not in their best interest to violate the law. This image from an advertising campaign uses photos that show the degenerative effects of drug addiction. This woman was addicted to methamphetamine, and her decline is depicted over a four-year period, ages 36 to 40. Would you be afraid of using speed after seeing these results? (Correct answer: Yes!)

Crime Prevention Strategies

Situational crime prevention involves developing tactics to reduce or eliminate a specific crime problem (such as shoplifting in an urban mall or street-level drug dealing). According to Derek Cornish and Ronald Clarke, situational crime prevention efforts may be divided into five different strategies, as described next.[56]

Increase the Effort Needed to Commit Crime

Tactics to increase effort include target-hardening techniques such as putting unbreakable glass on storefronts, locking gates, and fencing yards. Removing signs from store windows, installing brighter lights, and instituting a pay-first policy have helped reduce thefts from gas stations and convenience stores.[57] Technological advances can also make it more difficult for would-be offenders to commit crimes; having an owner's photo on credit cards should reduce the use of stolen cards; security products such as steering locks on cars have reduced the incidence of theft.[58] Installing a locking device on cars that prevents drunken drivers from starting the vehicle (Breath Analyzed Ignition Interlock Device) significantly reduces drunk-driving rates among people with a history of driving while intoxicated.[59]

Increase the Risk of Committing Crime

If the risk of getting caught can be increased, rational offenders will most likely choose not to commit crime. Marcus Felson argues that the risk of crime may be increased by improving the effectiveness of **crime discouragers**: people who serve as guardians of property or people.[60] Discouragers can be grouped into three categories: "guardians," who monitor potential targets (such as store security guards); "handlers," who monitor potential offenders (such as parole officers and parents); and "managers," who monitor places (such as homeowners and garage attendants). If the discouragers do their jobs correctly, the potential criminal will be convinced that the risk of crime outweighs any potential gains.[61] Police are invaluable crime discouragers, and their effectiveness has been linked to reductions in the crime rate in cities such as New York and Boston.[62]

situational crime prevention
A method of crime prevention that seeks to eliminate or reduce particular crimes in narrow settings.

defensible space
The principle that crime can be prevented or displaced by modifying the physical environment to reduce the opportunity individuals have to commit crime.

crime discouragers
People who serve as guardians of property or people.

Policy & Practice in Criminology

CCTV or Not CCTV? Comparing Situational Crime Prevention Efforts in Britain and the United States

International criminologists Brandon Welsh and David Farrington have been using systematic review and meta-analysis as a technique to assess the comparative effectiveness of situational crime prevention techniques. In one recent study they evaluated the effectiveness of closed-circuit television (CCTV) surveillance cameras and improved street lighting, techniques currently being used in both England and the United States.

Welsh and Farrington found significant differences in the use of these methods in the United States and Great Britain. CCTV is quite popular in Britain, where it is the single most heavily funded crime prevention measure. Between 1999 and 2001, the British government spent approximately $320 million for CCTV schemes in town and city centers, parking lots, crime hot spots and residential areas; CCTV accounted for more than three-quarters of total spending on crime prevention by the British Home Office; there are more than 40,000 surveillance cameras currently in use! In contrast, CCTV is less popular in America, perhaps because it raises the specter of a "Big Brother" society that is constantly watching (and recording) every person's behavior and activities.

There are also cross-national differences in the use of street lighting to prevent criminal activity. Improving street lighting to reduce crime is not a popular crime control mechanism in Britain. In contrast, many American towns and cities have embarked upon major street lighting programs as a means of reducing crime.

After an exhaustive search of the existing research, Welsh and Farrington found 32 relevant studies that met their standards for inclusion (19 for CCTV and 13 for street lighting). Of the 19 CCTV studies, 14 were from Britain and the other 5 were from North America (4 from the United States and 1 from Canada). Of the 13 improved street lighting evaluations, 8 were from the United States and the other 5 were from Britain. All of these evaluations were carried out in one of four settings: city center, residential or public housing, parking lots, or public transportation.

Based on their analysis of the existing data, Welsh and Farrington concluded that CCTV and street lighting are equally effective in reducing crime. Improved street lighting seemed to be a more effective method of reducing crime in city centers, both techniques were more effective in reducing property crimes than violent crimes, and there were additional benefits when both techniques were used together.

Welsh and Farrington also found that both measures were far more effective in reducing crime in Britain than in America. Though there may be a number of possible reasons for this puzzling cross-national difference, Welsh and Farrington suspect there may be a cultural explanation: In Britain, there is a high level of public support for the use of CCTV cameras in public settings to prevent crime, while the American public seems more wary of sophisticated surveillance technology. Public resistance can sometimes take a legal form resulting in lawsuits charging that surveillance undermines the U.S. Constitution's Fourth Amendment prohibition against unreasonable searches and seizures. Although the British Home Office embraces CCTV, American caution has resulted in cuts in program funding, the police assigning lower priority to the schemes, and attempts to discourage desirable media coverage. In contrast, improving street lighting has engendered little public enmity in the United States. Nonetheless, while Americans may be cautious about the installation of CCTV, the terrorist attack of September 11, 2001, has resulted in increased use of CCTV surveillance cameras around the nation.

Critical Thinking

Would you be willing to have a surveillance camera set up in your home/dorm in order to prevent crime, knowing that your every move was being watched and recorded?

InfoTrac College Edition Research

Use "situational crime prevention" in a key word search on InfoTrac College Edition.

SOURCE: Brandon Welsh and David Farrington, "Surveillance for Crime Prevention in Public Space: Results and Policy Choices in Britain and America," *Criminology and Public Policy* 3 (2004): 701–730.

Some crime discouragers are mechanical rather than human. Efforts have been made to create and install mechanical devices, such as closed-circuit TV cameras, that may discourage crime while reducing the need for higher-cost security personnel.[63] The Policy & Practice in Criminology feature discusses a recent evaluation of such methods in the United States and Britain.

Reduce Rewards of Crime Target reduction strategies are designed to reduce the value of crime to the potential criminal. These include making car radios removable so they can be kept in the home at night, marking property so that it is more difficult to sell when stolen, and having gender-neutral phone listings to discourage obscene phone calls. Tracking systems, such as those made by the Lojack Corporation, help police locate and return stolen vehicles.

Induce Guilt Inducing guilt or shame might include such techniques as setting strict rules to embarrass offenders. For example, publishing "John lists" in the newspaper punishes those arrested for soliciting prostitutes. Facilitating compliance by providing trash bins might shame chronic litterers into using them. Ronald Clarke found that caller ID in New Jersey resulted in significant reductions in the number of obscene phone calls, presumably because of the shame presented by the threat of exposure.[64]

Reduce Provocation Some crimes are the result of extreme provocation, for example, road rage. It might be possible to reduce provocation by creating programs that reduce conflict. Creating an early closing time in local bars and pubs might limit assaults that are the result of late-night drinking and conflicts in pubs at closing time. Posting guards outside schools at closing time might prevent childish taunts from escalating into full-blown brawls. Antibullying programs that have been implemented in schools are another method of reducing provocation.

Remove Excuses Crime may be reduced by making it difficult for people to excuse their criminal behavior by saying things like "I didn't know that was illegal" or "I had no choice." For example, municipalities have set up roadside displays that electronically flash a car's speed as it passes, eliminating the driver's excuse that she did not know how fast she was going when stopped by police. Litter boxes, brightly displayed, can eliminate the claim that "I just didn't know where to throw my trash." Reducing or eliminating excuses in this way also makes it physically easy for people to comply with laws and regulations, thereby reducing the likelihood they will choose crime.

Costs and Benefits of Situational Crime Prevention

Situational crime prevention efforts bring with them certain hidden costs and benefits that can either increase their effectiveness or undermine their success. Before the overall success of this approach can be evaluated, these costs and benefits must be considered.

Hidden Benefits When efforts to prevent one crime unintentionally prevent another, it is known as **diffusion**.[65] Video cameras set up in a mall to reduce shoplifting can also reduce property damage because would-be vandals fear they are being caught on camera. Police surveillance set up to reduce drug trafficking may unintentionally reduce the incidence of prostitution and other public morals crimes by scaring off would-be clients.[66] **Discouragement** occurs when crime control efforts targeting a particular locale help reduce crime in surrounding areas and populations. In her study of the effects of the SMART program (a drug enforcement program in Oakland, California, that enforces municipal codes and nuisance abatement laws), criminologist Lorraine Green found that drug dealing decreased not only in targeted areas but also in adjacent areas. The drug control program most likely discouraged buyers and sellers who saw familiar hangouts closed. This sign that drug dealing would not be tolerated probably decreased the total number of people involved in drug activity, even though they did not operate in the targeted areas.[67]

Hidden Costs Situational crime prevention efforts may also contain hidden costs that may limit their effectiveness. **Displacement** occurs when crime control efforts simply move or redirect offenders to less heavily guarded alternative targets.[68] For example, beefed-up police patrols in one area may shift crimes to a more vulnerable neighborhood lacking in police.[69] **Extinction** refers to the phenomenon in which crime reduction programs may produce a short-term positive effect, but benefits dissipate as criminals adjust to new conditions. They learn to dismantle alarms or avoid patrols. **Replacement** occurs when criminals try new offenses they had previously avoided because situational crime prevention programs neutralized their crime of choice. If every residence in a neighborhood installs a foolproof burglar alarm system, motivated offenders may turn to armed robbery, a riskier and more violent crime, to replace the income they lost from burglaries. Before the effectiveness of situational crime prevention can be accepted, these hidden costs and benefits must be weighed and balanced.

diffusion
An effect that occurs when efforts to prevent one crime unintentionally prevent another.

discouragement
An effect that occurs when crime control efforts targeting a particular locale help reduce crime in surrounding areas and populations.

displacement
An effect that occurs when crime control efforts simply move or redirect offenders to less heavily guarded alternative targets.

extinction
An effect that occurs when crime reduction programs produce a short-term positive effect, but benefits dissipate as criminals adjust to new conditions.

replacement
An effect that occurs when criminals try new offenses they had previously avoided because situational crime prevention programs neutralized their crime of choice.

GENERAL DETERRENCE

According to the rational choice view, motivated people will violate the law if they do not fear the consequences of their crimes. It stands to reason then that crime can be controlled by increasing the real or perceived threat of criminal punishment; this is the concept of **general deterrence**. Based on Beccaria's famous equation, general deterrence theory holds that the greater the severity, certainty, and speed of legal sanctions, the lower the crime rate. Is the general deterrence theory valid? Does the certainty, severity, and speed of punishment affect the decision to commit crime?

Certainty of Punishment

According to general deterrence theory, if the certainty of arrest, conviction, and sanctioning increases, crime rates should decline. If certainty increases, rational offenders will soon realize that the increased likelihood of punishment outweighs any benefit they perceive from committing crimes. Crime will persist, however, when people believe that even if caught they have a good chance of escaping punishment.[70] If people believe that their criminal transgressions will almost certainly result in punishment, then only the truly irrational would commit crime.[71]

A number of research efforts do show a direct relationship between crime rates and the certainty of punishment. And while the issue is far from settled, the weight of the evidence seems to be on the side of deterrence: People who believe that they will get caught if they commit crime are the ones most likely to be deterred from committing criminal acts.[72] What happens to them after apprehension seems to have a lesser impact on their decision-making process.[73]

Police and Certainty of Punishment If certainty of apprehension and punishment deters criminal behavior, then increasing the number of police officers on the street should cut the crime rate. Moreover, if these police officers are active, aggressive crime fighters, would-be criminals should become convinced that the risk of apprehension outweighs the benefits they can gain from crime.[74]

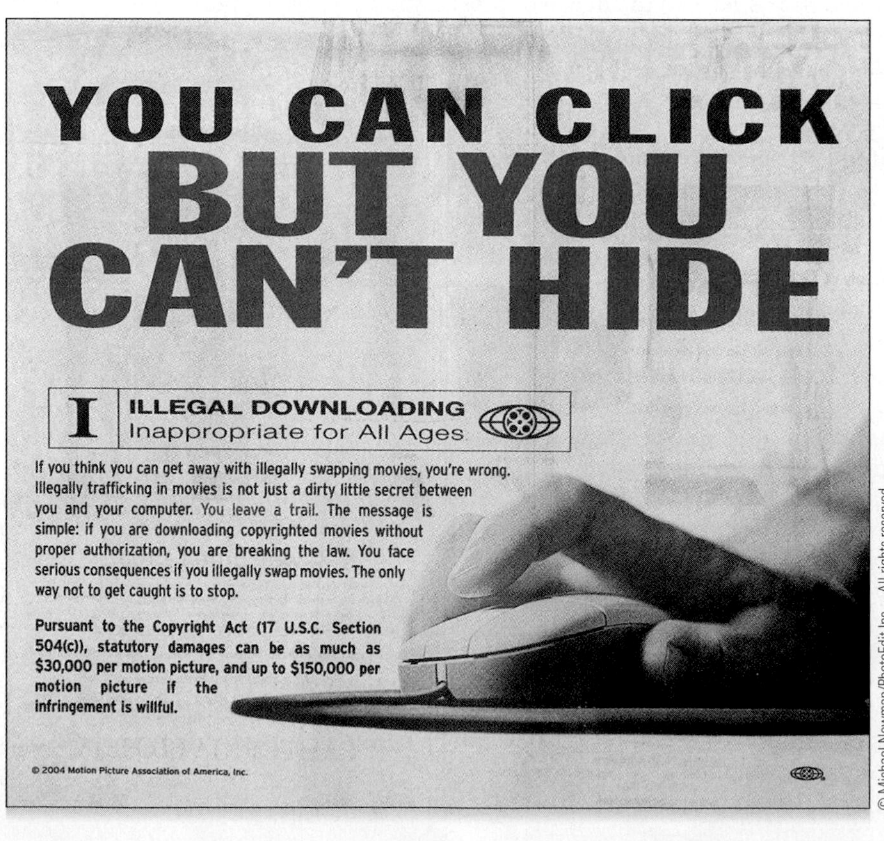

YOU CAN CLICK
BUT YOU CAN'T HIDE
I
ILLEGAL DOWNLOADING
Inappropriate for All Ages
If you think you can get away with illegally swapping movies, you're wrong. Illegally trafficking in movies is not just a dirty little secret between you and your computer. You leave a trail. The message is simple: if you are downloading copyrighted movies without proper authorization, you are breaking the law. You face serious consequences if you illegally swap movies. The only way not to get caught is to stop.
Pursuant to the Copyright Act (17 U.S.C. Section 504(c)), statutory damages can be as much as $30,000 per motion picture, and up to $150,000 per motion picture if the infringement is willful.
© 2004 Motion Picture Association of America, Inc.

● A newspaper ad sponsored by the Motion Picture Association of America gives a chilling reminder of the consequences for illegally downloading copyrighted material such as films or music. According to deterrence theory, severe punishments should convince would-be law violators to think twice before committing crimes. Would you download copyrighted music after viewing this ad? I didn't think so!

general deterrence
A crime control policy that depends on the fear of criminal penalties, convincing the potential law violator that the pains associated with crime outweigh its benefits.

The deterrent effect of police has been supported by a number of recent studies that have found that police presence does in fact reduce crime levels.[75] Evidence shows that cities with larger police departments that have more officers per capita than the norm also experience lower levels of violent crimes.[76] The mere presence of added police, however, may not be sufficient to deter crime; the manner in which they approach their task may make more of a difference. Proactive, aggressive law enforcement seems more effective than routine patrol. Improving response time and increasing the number of patrol cars that respond per crime may be one way of increasing police efficiency and deterring crime.[77]

Severity of Punishment

According to deterrence theory, the threat of severe punishment should also bring the crime rate down. Some studies have found that people who believe that they will be punished severely for a crime will forgo committing criminal acts.[78] Nonetheless, there is little consensus that strict punishments alone can reduce criminal activities.[79] Certainty rather than severity of punishment seems to have a greater deterrent effect.

It stands to reason that if severity of punishment can deter crime, then fear of the death penalty, the ultimate legal deterrent, should significantly reduce murder rates. Because no one denies its emotional impact, if the death penalty failed to deter violent crime, the validity of the entire deterrence concept would be jeopardized. Because this topic is so important, it is discussed in the Current Issues in Crime feature.

Swiftness of Punishment

A core element of general deterrence theory is that people who believe they will be swiftly punished if they break the law will abstain from crime.[80] Again, the evidence on the association between perceived punishment risk and crime has been mixed. Some research efforts have found a relationship;[81] others have not.[82]

The threat of swift retaliation seems to work best when would-be criminals believe they will be subjected to very harsh punishments.[83] But even this fear may be negated or overcome by the belief that a crime gives them a significant chance for large profit—greed overcomes fear![84]

Critique of General Deterrence

Some experts believe that the purpose of the law and justice system is to create a "threat system."[85] The threat of legal punishment should, on the face of it, deter lawbreakers through fear. Nonetheless, the relationship between crime rates and deterrent measures is far less than choice theorists might expect. Despite efforts to punish criminals and make them fear crime, there is little evidence that the fear of apprehension and punishment alone can reduce crime rates. How can this discrepancy be explained?

Rationality Deterrence theory assumes a rational offender who weighs the costs and benefits of a criminal act before deciding on a course of action. Criminals may be desperate people who choose crime because they believe there is no reasonable alternative. Some may suffer from personality disorders that impair their judgment and render them incapable of making truly rational decisions. Psychologists believe that chronic offenders suffer from an emotional state that renders them both incapable of fearing punishment and less likely to appreciate the consequences of crime.[86] Research on repeat sex offenders finds that they suffer from an elevated emotional state that negates the deterrent effect of the law.[87] There is also evidence that drinking alcohol may impede a person's ability to reasonably assess the costs and benefits of crime.[88] If the benefits of crime are exaggerated, the law's deterrent effect may be deflated.

Certainty, Severity, and Speed As Beccaria's famous equation tells us, the threat of punishment involves not only its severity but its certainty and speed. The American legal system is not very effective. Only 10 percent of all serious offenses result in apprehension. Half of these crimes go unreported, and police make arrests in only

Does Capital Punishment Deter Murder?

According to deterrence theory, the death penalty—the ultimate deterrent—should deter murder—the ultimate crime. Most Americans approve of the death penalty; including, as Norma Wilcox and Tracey Steele found, convicted criminals who are currently behind bars. But is the public's approval warranted? Does the death penalty actually deter murder?

Empirical research on the association between capital punishment and murder can be divided into three types: immediate impact studies, comparative research, and time-series analysis.

- *Immediate impact*. If capital punishment is a deterrent, the reasoning goes, its impact should be greatest after a well-publicized execution. Robert Dann began testing this assumption in 1935 when he chose five highly publicized executions of convicted murderers in different years and determined the number of homicides in the 60 days before and after each execution. Each 120-day period had approximately the same number of homicides, as well as the same number of days on which homicides occurred. Dann's study revealed that an average of 4.4 more homicides occurred during the 60 days following an execution than during those preceding it, suggesting that the overall impact of executions might actually be an increase in the incidence of homicide. Recently (2004) Lisa Stolzenberg and Stewart D'Alessio examined the effect of the death penalty on the murder rate in Houston, Texas. They found that even when executions were highly publicized in the local press, an execution had little influence on the murder rate.
- *Comparative research*. Another type of research compares the murder rates in jurisdictions that have abolished the death penalty with the rates of those that employ the death penalty. Studies using this approach have found little difference in the murder rates of adjacent states, regardless of their use of the death penalty; capital punishment did not appear to influence the reported rate of homicide. Research conducted in 14 nations around the world found little evidence that countries with a death penalty have lower violence rates than those without; homicide rates actually decline after capital punishment is abolished, a direct contradiction to its supposed deterrent effect.
- *Time-series studies*. These studies look at the long-term association between capital sentencing and murder. If capital punishment is a deterrent, then periods that have an upswing in executions should also experience a downturn in violent crime and murder. Most research efforts have failed to show such a relationship. For example, a recent test of the deterrent effect of the death penalty in Texas by Jon Sorenson and his colleagues found no association between the frequency of execution during the years 1984 to 1997 and murder rates.

These findings seem to indicate that the threat and/or reality of execution has relatively little influence on murder rates. Why the threat of capital punishment fails as a deterrent is uncertain, but the cause may lie in the nature of homicide itself. Murder is often an expressive "crime of passion" involving people who know each other and who may be under the influence of drugs and alcohol. Those who choose to take a life may be less influenced by the threat of punishment, even death, than those who commit crime for economic gain

Rethinking the Deterrent Effect of Capital Punishment

Despite this lack of empirical verification, some recent studies have concluded that executing criminals may in fact bring the murder rate down. Those who still maintain that an association exists

about 20 percent of reported crimes. Even when offenders are detected, police officers may choose to warn rather than arrest.[89] The odds of receiving a prison term are less than 20 per 1,000 crimes committed. As a result, some offenders believe that they will not be severely punished for their acts and consequently have little regard for the law's deterrent power. Even those accused of murder are often convicted of lesser offenses and spend relatively short amounts of time behind bars.[90] In making their "rational choice," offenders may be aware that the deterrent effect of the law is minimal.

Some Offenders Are More "Deterrable" Than Others Research by Greg Pogarsky indicates that deterrent measures may have greater impact on some people while having a lesser effect on others: "Acute conformists" obey the law because of their own moral beliefs and values; the "deterrable" are those people influenced by the threat of legal sanctions; the "incorrigible" are immune to the threat of legal sanctions. Of the three groups identified by Pogarsky, only the deterrable will respond to the threat of legal sanctions.[91]

Are there people who cannot be deterred? Among some groups of high-risk offenders, such as teens living in economically depressed neighborhoods, the threat of formal sanctions is irrelevant. Young people in these areas have little to lose if arrested; their opportunities are few, and they have little attachment to social institutions such as school or family. Even if they truly fear the consequences of the law, they must commit crime to survive in a hostile environment. Similarly, some people may be suffering from personality disorders and mental infirmity, which make them immune to the deterrent power of the law.[92]

between capital punishment and murder rates believe that the relationship has been masked or obscured by faulty research methods. Newer studies, using sophisticated data analysis, have been able to uncover a more significant association. For example, criminologist Steven Stack has conducted a number of research studies showing that the immediate impact of a well-publicized execution can lower the murder rate during the following month. James Yunker, using a national data set, has found evidence that there is a deterrent effect of capital punishment now that the pace of executions has accelerated. Economists Hashem Dezhbakhsh, Paul H. Rubin, and Joanna M. Shepherd performed an advanced statistical analysis on county-level homicide data in order to calculate the effect of each execution on the number of homicides that would otherwise have occurred. Using a variety of models (for example, what effect an execution conducted today has on homicides in five years), they found that each execution leads to an average of 18 fewer murders.

These efforts contradict findings that capital punishment fails as a deterrent. They suggest instead that now that the death penalty is being used more frequently it is possible that the "tipping point" has been reached, after which it may become an effective deterrent measure. All this contradictory data and conclusions highlight the national debate over the death penalty. After years of study, it is still uncertain whether the ultimate deterrent actually has a deterrent effect!

Critical Thinking

Even if effective, there is no question the death penalty still carries with it tremendous baggage. For example, when Geoffrey Rapp studied the effect of the death penalty on the safety of police officers, he found that the introduction of capital punishment actually created an extremely dangerous environment for law enforcement officers. Because the death penalty does not have a deterrent effect, criminals are more likely to kill police officers when the death penalty is in place. Tragically, the death penalty may lull officers into a false sense of security, causing them to let down their guard, killing fewer citizens but getting killed more often themselves. Given Rapp's findings should we still maintain the death penalty?

Info Trac College Edition Research

Use "capital punishment" and the "death penalty" as subject searches on InfoTrac College Edition.

SOURCES: Lisa Stolzenberg and Stewart D'Alessio, "Capital Punishment, Execution Publicity, and Murder in Houston, Texas," *Journal of Criminal Law & Criminology* 94 (2004): 351–380; Geoffrey Rapp, "The Economics of Shootouts: Does the Passage of Capital Punishment Laws Protect or Endanger Police Officers?" *Albany Law Review* 65 (2002) 1,051–1,084; Robert Dann, "The Deterrent Effect of Capital Punishment," *Friends Social Service Series* 29 (1935); Thorsten Sellin, *The Death Penalty* (Philadelphia: American Law Institute, 1959); Walter Reckless, "Use of the Death Penalty," *Crime and Delinquency* 15 (1969): 43–51; Dane Archer, Rosemary Gartner, and Marc Beittel, "Homicide and the Death Penalty: A Cross-National Test of a Deterrence Hypothesis," *Journal of Criminal Law and Criminology* 74 (1983): 991–1,014; Jon Sorenson, Robert Wrinkle, Victoria Brewer, and James Marquart, "Capital Punishment and Deterrence: Examining the Effect of Executions on Murder in Texas," *Crime and Delinquency* 45 (1999): 481–493; Norma Wilcox and Tracey Steele, "Just the Facts: A Descriptive Analysis of Inmate Attitudes Toward Capital Punishment," *Prison Journal*, 83 (2003): 464–483; Zhiqiang Liu, "Capital Punishment and the Deterrence Hypothesis: Some New Insights and Empirical Evidence," *Eastern Economic Journal* (2004); Steven Stack, "The Effect of Well-Publicized Executions on Homicide in California," *Journal of Crime and Justice* 21 (1998): 1–12; James Yunker, "A New Statistical Analysis of Capital Punishment Incorporating U.S. Postmoratorium Data," *Social Science Quarterly* 82 (2001): 297–312; Hashem Dezhbakhsh, Paul H. Rubin, and Joanna M. Shepherd, "Does Capital Punishment Have a Deterrent Effect? New Evidence from Postmoratorium Panel Data," *American Law and Economics Review* 5 (2003): 344–376.

SPECIFIC DETERRENCE

The theory of **specific deterrence** (also called special or particular deterrence) holds that criminal sanctions should be so powerful that known criminals will never repeat their criminal acts. According to this view, the drunk driver whose sentence is a substantial fine and a week in the county jail should be convinced that the price to be paid for drinking and driving is too great to consider future violations. Similarly, burglars who spend five years in a tough, maximum-security prison should find their enthusiasm for theft dampened.[93] In principle, punishment works if a connection can be established between the planned action and memories of its consequence; if these recollections are adequately intense, the action will be unlikely to occur again.[94]

Research on specific deterrence does not provide any clear-cut evidence that punishing criminals is an effective means of stopping them from committing future crimes. In a famous study conducted in Minneapolis, Lawrence Sherman and Richard Berk evaluated the effect of police action on repeat domestic violence. They found clear evidence that when police take formal action (arrest), offenders are less likely to recidivate than when less severe methods are used (a warning or a cooling-off period).[95] Subsequent to this study, a number of states adopted legislation mandating that police either take formal action in domestic abuse cases or explain in writing their failure to act. However, when the Minneapolis experiment was repeated in other locales, evaluations failed to duplicate the original results.[96]

specific deterrence
The view that criminal sanctions should be so powerful that offenders will never repeat their criminal acts.

In these locales, formal arrest was not a greater specific deterrent to domestic abuse than warning or advising the assailant.

Sherman and his associates later found that the effect of arrest quickly decays and, in the long run, may actually escalate the frequency of repeat domestic violence.[97] A possible explanation is that offenders who are arrested fear punishment initially, but eventually replace fear with anger and violent intent toward their mates when their cases do not result in severe punishment.

Research on chronic offenders indicates that arrest and punishment also seem to have little effect on experienced criminals and may even increase the likelihood that first-time offenders will commit new crimes.[98] About two-thirds of all convicted felons are rearrested within three years of their release from prison, and those who have been punished in the past are the most likely to commit a new offense.[99] **Incarceration** may sometimes slow down or delay **recidivism** in the short term, but the overall probability of rearrest is not reduced, and may even be increased, by serving a prison sentence.[100] Rather than reduce recidivism, harsher punishments may increase the likelihood of reoffending.[101] It is possible that punishment may bring defiance rather than deterrence, and the stigma of apprehension may help lock offenders into a criminal career. Criminals who are punished may also believe that the likelihood of getting caught twice for the same type of crime is remote: "Lightning never strikes twice in the same spot," they may reason. "No one is that unlucky."[102]

Although these results are not encouraging, some studies show that arrest and conviction may, under some circumstances, lower the frequency of reoffending, a finding that supports specific deterrence.[103] These contradictory findings suggest that further research is needed to clarify the impact of formal sanctions on individual decision making.

INCAPACITATION

It stands to reason that if more criminals are sent to prison, the crime rate should go down. Because most people age out of crime, the duration of a criminal career is limited. Placing offenders behind bars during their prime crime years should reduce their lifetime opportunity to commit crime. The shorter the span of opportunity, the fewer offenses they can commit during their lives; hence, crime is reduced. This theory, known as the **incapacitation effect**, seems logical, but does it work?

In the past 20 years we have witnessed significant growth in the number and percentage of the population held in prisons and jails. Today more than 2 million Americans are incarcerated. Advocates of incapacitation suggest that this effort has been responsible for the decade-long decline in crime rates. Critics counter that what appears to be an incapacitation effect may actually reflect the effect of some other legal or social phenomenon. The economy has improved, police may be more effective, and the crack cocaine epidemic has waned. Crime rates may be dropping simply because potential criminals now recognize and fear the tough new sentencing laws that provide long mandatory prison sentences for drug and violent crimes. What appears to be an incapacitation effect may actually be an effect of general deterrence.[104]

Can Incapacitation Reduce Crime?

There has long been debate among criminologists over the effect of incarceration on the crime rate.[105] Some experts question the effect of incarceration.[106] Others find that it can reduce crime.[107]

Considering that criminals are unable to continue their illegal activities while housed in a prison or jail, incapacitation should be an excellent crime control strategy. One study of 201 heroin abusers in New York City found that if given a one-year jail sentence, they would not have been able to commit their yearly haul of crimes: 1,000 robberies, 4,000 burglaries, 10,000 shopliftings, and more than 3,000 other property crimes.[108]

There are also those who question whether incapacitation really controls crime rates. For one thing, there is little evidence that incapacitating criminals will deter them from future criminality and even more reason to believe that they

incarceration
Confinement in jail or prison.

recidivism
Repetition of criminal behavior.

incapacitation effect
The idea that keeping offenders in confinement will eliminate the risk of their committing further offenses.

may be more inclined to commit crimes upon release. Prison has few specific deterrent effects: The more prior incarceration experiences inmates have, the more likely they are to recidivate (and return to prison) within 12 months of their release.[109] The short-term crime reduction effect of incapacitating criminals is negated if the prison experience has the long-term effect of escalating the frequency of criminal behavior upon release. By its nature, the prison experience exposes young, first-time offenders to higher-risk, more experienced inmates who can influence their lifestyle and help shape their attitudes. Novice inmates also run an increased risk of becoming infected with AIDS and other health hazards, and that exposure reduces their life chances after release.[110]

Furthermore, the economics of crime suggest that if money can be made from criminal activity, there will always be someone to take the place of the incarcerated offender. New criminals will be recruited and trained, offsetting any benefit accrued by incarceration. Imprisoning established offenders opens new opportunities for competitors who were suppressed by the more experienced criminals. For example, incarcerating organized crime members may open drug markets to new gangs. The flow of narcotics into the country may actually increase after the more experienced organized crime leaders are imprisoned because newcomers are willing to take greater risks.

Another reason incarceration may not work is that most criminal offenses are committed by teens and very young adult offenders, and it is unlikely that they will be sent to prison for a single felony conviction. At the same time, many incarcerated criminals, aging behind bars, are already past the age when they are likely to commit crime. As a result, a strict incarceration policy may keep people in prison beyond the time they are a threat to society while a new cohort of high-risk adolescents is on the street. It is possible that the most serious criminals are already behind bars and that adding less dangerous offenders to the population will have little appreciable effect while adding tremendous costs to the correctional system.[111]

An incapacitation strategy is terribly expensive. The prison system costs billions of dollars each year. Even if incarceration could reduce the crime rate, the costs would be enormous. Are U.S. taxpayers willing to spend billions more on new prison construction and annual maintenance fees? A strict incarceration policy would result in a growing number of elderly inmates whose maintenance costs, estimated at $69,000 per year, are three times higher than those of younger inmates. Today more than 15 percent of the prison population is over age 50.[112]

Concept Summary 4.1 outlines the various methods of crime control and their effects. ✔ CHECKPOINTS

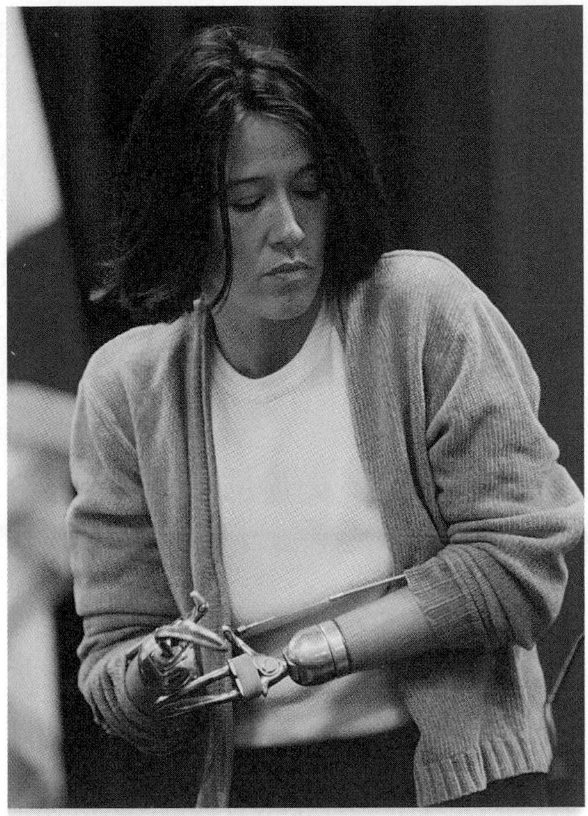

© AP

● Simply put, if dangerous criminals were incapacitated, they would never have the opportunity to prey upon others. One of the most dramatic examples of the utility of incapacitation is the case of Lawrence Singleton, who in 1978 raped a young California girl, Mary Vincent, and then chopped off her arms with an axe. He served eight years in prison for this vile crime. Upon his release, he moved to Florida, where in 1997 he killed a woman, Roxanne Hayes. Vincent is shown here as she testifies at the penalty phase of Singleton's trial; he was sentenced to death. Should a dangerous predator such as Singleton ever be released from incapacitation? Is rehabilitation even a remote possibility?

CONCEPT SUMMARY 4.1 Crime Control Methods

CRIME CONTROL METHOD	CORE CONCEPT	IS IT SUCCESSFUL?
Situational crime control	Reduce the payoff of crime.	Some methods seem to reduce particular crimes.
General deterrence	Scare would-be criminals.	Certainty of punishment more effective than severity.
Specific deterrence	Scare known criminals.	Limited effectiveness underscored by high recidivism rates.
Incapacitation	Reduce criminal opportunity.	As prison rates have increased, the crime rate has declined.

✔ CHECKPOINTS

✔ Situational crime prevention efforts are designed to reduce or redirect crime by making it more difficult to profit from illegal acts.

✔ General deterrence models are based on the fear of punishment that is severe, swift, and certain.

✔ Specific deterrence aims at reducing crime through the application of severe punishments. Once offenders experience these punishments, they will be unwilling to repeat their criminal activities.

✔ Incapacitation strategies are designed to reduce crime by taking known criminals out of circulation, preventing them from having the opportunity to commit further offenses. The effectiveness of incapacitation strategies is hotly debated.

POLICY IMPLICATIONS OF CHOICE THEORY

From the origins of classical theory to the development of modern rational choice views, the belief that criminals choose to commit crime has influenced justice policy. Although research on the core principles of choice theory and deterrence theories has produced mixed results, these models have had a significant impact on contemporary crime prevention strategies.

When police patrol in well-marked cars, it is assumed that their presence will deter would-be criminals by increasing the certainty that their criminal acts will be punished. And when tough mandatory criminal sentences are created to control violent crime and drug trafficking, the underlying vision is that the severity of punishment can control crime. These measures assume criminals are rational decision makers who will choose not to commit crime if they believe that they will be caught and severely punished for their crimes. Two current, albeit controversial, justice policies represent the influence of choice on justice policy: three strikes laws and the death penalty.

The "three strikes and you're out" sentencing policy, which provides a mandatory life sentence for people convicted on their third felony offense, has received widespread publicity. The rationale for its use relies on both general deterrence—scaring off would-be criminals—and incapacitation—keeping repeat offenders off the streets. Can such hard-line policies work? The results are mixed. Some criminologists, using highly sophisticated research techniques, have found a significant association between the increased use of incarceration and reductions in the crime rate.[113] A strict incarceration policy may also have residual benefits. Ilyana Kuziemko and Steven Levitt found that as the number of prisoners incarcerated on drug-related offenses rose dramatically (1500 percent) between 1980 and 2000, crime rates dropped. One reason was that the incarceration policy had an unforeseen impact on drug markets: Putting dealers in prison increased the cost of cocaine by 10 to 15 percent, and the higher prices resulted in a drop of cocaine usage by as much as 20 percent.[114]

Although get-tough policies have political appeal in our conservative society, some criminologists conclude that it is premature to embrace a three strikes policy:

- Most three-time losers are on the verge of aging out of crime anyway.
- Current sentences for violent crimes are already quite severe.
- An expanding prison population will drive up already high prison costs.
- There would be racial disparity in sentencing.
- The police would be in danger because two-time offenders would violently resist a third arrest, knowing they face a life sentence.[115]
- The prison population probably already contains the highest-frequency criminals.

Concept Summary 4.2 summarizes the main features of choice theories.

Nowhere can the influence of choice theory be felt more dramatically than in the use of the death penalty as a deterrent to murder. Despite its questionable effect, advocates argue that the death penalty can effectively restrict criminality; at least it ensures that convicted criminals never again get the opportunity to kill. Many observers are dismayed because people who are convicted of murder sometimes kill again when released on parole. One study of 52,000 incarcerated murderers found that 810 had been previously convicted of murder and had killed 821 people following their previous release from prison.[116] About 9 percent of all inmates on death row have had prior convictions for homicide. Death penalty advocates argue that if these criminals had been executed for their first offenses, hundreds of people would be alive today.[117] While critics bemoan the use of capital punishment, advocates retort that the murder rate has been in dramatic decline now that it is in frequent use and the general public approves of its use as a deterrent to murder.

CONCEPT SUMMARY 4.2 Choice Theories of Crime

THEORY	MAJOR PREMISE	STRENGTHS	RESEARCH FOCUS
Rational choice	Law-violating behavior occurs after offenders weigh information on their personal needs and the situational factors involved in the difficulty and risk of committing a crime.	Explains why high-risk youths do not constantly engage in delinquency. Relates theory to delinquency control policy. It is not limited by class or other social variables.	Offense patterns—where, when, and how crime takes place.
General deterrence	People will commit crime and delinquency if they perceive that the benefits outweigh the risks. Crime is a function of the severity, certainty, and speed of punishment.	Shows the relationship between crime and punishment. Suggests a real solution to crime.	Perception of punishment, effect of legal sanctions, probability of punishment and crime rates.
Specific deterrence	If punishment is severe enough, criminals will not repeat their illegal acts.	Provides a strategy to reduce crime.	Recidivism, repeat offending, punishment type and crime.
Incapacitation	Keeping known criminals out of circulation will reduce crime rates.	Recognizes the role that opportunity plays in criminal behavior. Provides a solution to chronic offending.	Prison population and crime rates, sentence length and crime.

THINKING Like a Criminologist

A Justice Department official contacts you and asks your opinion on crime control. She is concerned about the following data acquired by the Bureau of Justice Statistics:

- In 2002, state and federal courts convicted a combined total of nearly 1,114,000 adults of felonies: State courts convicted an estimated 1,051,000 adults, and federal courts convicted 63,217 adults (accounting for 6 percent of the national total).
- In 2002, 69 percent of all felons convicted in state courts were sentenced to a period of confinement—41 percent to state prisons and 28 percent to local jails. Jail sentences are for short-term confinement (usually for a year or less) in a county or city facility, while prison sentences are for long-term confinement (usually for over a year) in a state facility.
- State courts sentenced 31 percent of convicted felons to straight probation with no jail or prison time to serve.
- Felons sentenced to a state prison in 2002 had an average sentence of 4 1/2 years but were likely to serve 51 percent of that sentence—or just 2 1/4 years—before release, assuming that 2002 release policies continue in effect.
- The average sentence to local jail was seven months. The average probation sentence was about three years.
- Besides being sentenced to incarceration or probation, 36 percent or more of convicted felons also were ordered to pay a fine, pay victim restitution, receive treatment, perform community service, or comply with some other additional penalty. A fine was imposed on at least 25 percent of convicted felons.

(continued)

Lengths of Felony Sentences Imposed by State Courts, 2002

AVERAGE MAXIMUM SENTENCE LENGTH (IN MONTHS) FOR FELONS SENTENCED TO:

	INCARCERATION			
MOST SERIOUS CONVICTION OFFENSE	TOTAL	PRISON	JAIL	PROBATION
All offenses	36 mo	53 mo	7 mo	38 mo
Violent offenses	62 mo	84 mo	8 mo	43 mo
Property offenses	28 mo	41 mo	7 mo	37 mo
Drug offenses	32 mo	48 mo	6 mo	36 mo
Weapons offenses	28 mo	38 mo	7 mo	35 mo
Other offenses	23 mo	38 mo	6 mo	37 mo

SOURCE: www.ojp.usdoj.gov/bjs/sent.htm.

She asks you, "Could these sentencing practices be responsible for U.S. crime rates that, though off their peaks, are still relatively high?" What would you recommend doing to alter sentencing policies in order to have a significant impact on crime rates? What might the unforeseen consequences be of radical sentencing changes?

Summary

- Choice theories assume that criminals carefully choose whether to commit criminal acts. These theories are summarized in Concept Summary 4.2.
- People are influenced by their fear of the criminal penalties associated with being caught and convicted for law violations.
- The choice approach is rooted in the classical criminology of Cesare Beccaria, who argued that punishment should be certain, swift, and severe enough to deter crime.
- Today, choice theorists view crime as offense- and offender-specific.
- Offense-specific means that the characteristics of the crime control whether it occurs. For example, carefully protecting a home makes it less likely to be a target of crime.
- Offender-specific refers to the personal characteristics of potential criminals. People with specific skills and needs may be more likely to commit crime than others.
- Research shows that offenders consider their targets carefully before deciding on a course of action. Even violent criminals and drug addicts show signs of rationality.
- By implication, crime can be prevented or displaced by convincing potential criminals that the risks of violating the law exceed the benefits.
- Situational crime prevention is the application of security and protective devices that make it more difficult to commit crime or that reduce criminal rewards.
- Deterrence theory holds that if criminals are indeed rational, an inverse relationship should exist between punishment and crime.
- The certainty of punishment seems to deter crime. If people do not believe they will be caught, even harsh punishment may not deter crime.
- Deterrence theory has been criticized on the grounds that it wrongly assumes that criminals make a rational choice before committing crimes, that it ignores the intricacies of the criminal justice system, and that it does not take into account the social and psychological factors that may influence criminality.
- A big disappointment for deterrence theory is the fact that the death penalty does not seem to reduce murders.
- Specific deterrence theory holds that the crime rate can be reduced if known offenders are punished so severely that they never commit crimes again.
- There is little evidence that harsh punishment actually reduces the crime rate. Most prison inmates recidivate.
- Incapacitation theory maintains that if deterrence does not work, the best course of action is to incarcerate known offenders for long periods so that they lack criminal opportunity.
- Research efforts have not proved that increasing the number of people in prison—and increasing prison sentences—will reduce crime rates.

Take a Post-Test. Visit www.thomsonedu.com/criminaljustice/siegel and take the chapter Post-Test to monitor your progress and identify areas for further improvement. In addition to discovering what you've mastered, you'll learn which concepts need your added attention and get specific page references that direct you to the places in the text where you can find more information on them.

Key Terms

offense-specific 73
offender-specific 73
edgework 78
seductions of crime 78
situational crime prevention 79
defensible space 79
crime discouragers 79
diffusion 81
discouragement 81
displacement 81
extinction 81
replacement 81
general deterrence 82
specific deterrence 85
incarceration 86
recidivism 86
incapacitation effect 86

Critical Thinking Questions

1. Are criminals rational decision makers, or are most motivated by noncontrollable psychological and emotional drives or social forces such as poverty and despair?

2. Would you want to live in a society where crime rates are quite low because they are controlled by extremely harsh punishments, such as flogging for vandalism?

3. Which would you be more afraid of if you were caught by the police while shoplifting: receiving criminal punishment or having to face the contempt of your friends or relatives?

4. Is it possible to create a method of capital punishment that would actually deter murder—for example, by televising executions? What might be some of the negative consequences of such a policy?

CHAPTER 5

Trait Theory: It's in Their Blood

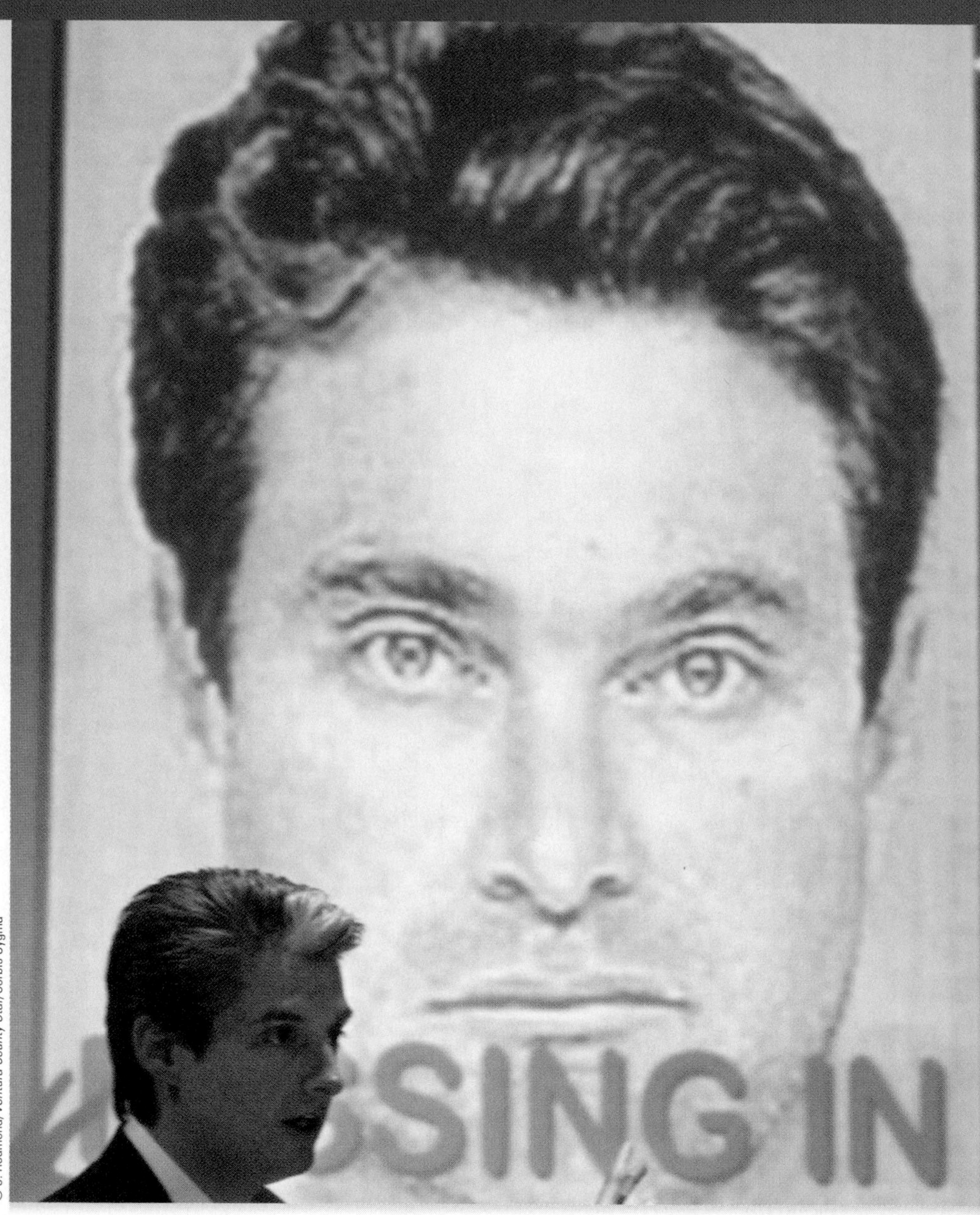

© J. Redmond/*Ventura County Star*/Corbis Sygma

Refer to the front endpapers for a study tool that summarizes each of the major theories discussed in this book.

ANDREW LUSTER, AN HEIR TO THE MAX FACTOR COSMETIC FORTUNE, lived a privileged life of sun and fun in a beach house in an exclusive community near Santa Barbara. However, Andrew has a darker side, which came to light on July 17, 2000, when he was arrested after a young woman accused him of drugging her with the "date rape" drug GHB and then having sex with her while she was unconscious. When police served a warrant on his home, they found tapes indicating Luster had a habit of drugging women and raping them while they were comatose. Halfway through the trial, Luster jumped bail, disappeared, and was declared a fugitive from justice. In his absence, the jury found him guilty on 86 of the 87 counts, and he was eventually sentenced to more than 100 years in prison. Five months later, he was captured in the resort town of Puerto Vallarta, Mexico, by bounty hunter Duane "Dog" Chapman. On July 3, 2003, an appellate court denied Luster's appeal of his guilty verdicts because he had jumped bail.

CHAPTER OBJECTIVES

1. Be familiar with the concept of sociobiology.
2. Know what is meant when biosocial theorists use the term "equipotentiality."
3. Be able to discuss the relationship between diet and crime.
4. Be familiar with the association between hormones and crime.
5. Be able to discuss why violent offenders may suffer from neurological problems.
6. Know the factors that make up the ADHD syndrome.
7. Be able to discuss the role genetics plays in violent behavior.
8. Be familiar with the concepts of evolutionary theory.
9. Be able to discuss the psychodynamics of criminality.
10. Understand the association between media and crime.
11. Discuss the role of personality and intelligence in antisocial behaviors.

Take a Pre-Test. Visit www.thomsonedu.com/criminaljustice/siegel and take a Pre-Test to determine what you already know and identify the areas where you'll need to focus your study. The program will direct you to specific pages within the text where you can find further information on the correct answers to the questions you've missed.

How can we explain the bizarre behavior of Andrew Luster? Why would a wealthy, handsome man drug and rape unsuspecting women? Could his acts possibly be the result of calculation and planning, or are they the product of some mental aberration or personality disturbance? The image of a disturbed, mentally ill offender seems plausible because a generation of Americans has grown up on films and TV shows that portray violent criminals as mentally deranged and physically abnormal. Beginning with Alfred Hitchcock's film *Psycho*, producers have made millions depicting the ghoulish acts of people who at first seem normal and even friendly but turn out to be demented and dangerous. Lurking out there are deranged roommates (*Single White Female*), abnormal girlfriends (*Fatal Attraction*) and boyfriends (*Fear*), and lunatic high school friends (*Scream*), who evolve into even crazier college classmates (*Scream II*) and then grow up to become nutty young adults (*Scream III*). Some of these psychos do not act alone but are part of extended demented families (*Texas Chainsaw Massacre*). No one is safe when the psychologists and psychiatrists who are hired to treat these disturbed people turn out to be demonic murderers themselves (*Silence of the Lambs, Hannibal, Red Dragon*). Is it any wonder that we respond to a particularly horrible crime by saying of the perpetrator, "That guy must be crazy" or "She is a monster"?

This chapter reviews the theories that suggest that criminality is a matter of abnormal human traits. These **trait theories** can be subdivided into two major categories: one stressing biological makeup and the other stressing psychological functioning. Although these views often overlap (for example, brain function may have a biological basis), each branch has its unique characteristics and will be discussed separately.

DEVELOPMENT OF TRAIT THEORY

The view that criminals have physical or mental traits that make them different and abnormal is not restricted to movie viewers but began with the Italian physician and criminologist Cesare Lombroso. The early research of Lombroso and his contemporaries is today regarded as historical curiosity, not scientific fact. The research methodology they used was slipshod, and many of the traits they assumed to be

trait theory
The view that criminality is a product of abnormal biological or psychological traits.

inherited are not really genetically determined but are caused by environment and diet. As criticism of this early work mounted, biological explanations of crime fell out of favor and were abandoned in the early twentieth century.[1]

In the early 1970s, spurred by the publication of *Sociobiology* by Edmund O. Wilson, biological explanations of crime once again emerged.[2] **Sociobiology** differs from earlier theories of behavior in that it stresses that biological and genetic conditions affect how social behaviors are learned and perceived. It suggests that both animal and human behavior is determined in part by the need to ensure survival of offspring and replenishment of the gene pool. These perceptions, in turn, are linked to existing environmental structures.

Sociobiologists view biology, environment, and learning as mutually interdependent factors. These views revived interest in finding a biological or psychological basis for crime and delinquency. It prompted some criminologists to conclude that personal traits must be what separates the deviant members of society from the nondeviant. Possessing these traits may help explain why, when faced with the same life situation, one person commits crime whereas another obeys the law. Put another way, living in a disadvantaged neighborhood will not cause a well-adjusted person to commit crime; living in an affluent area will not stop a maladapted person from offending.[3] All people may be aware of and even fear the sanctioning power of the law, but some are unable to control their urges and passions.

CONTEMPORARY TRAIT THEORY

Contemporary trait theorists do not suggest that a single biological or psychological attribute adequately explains all criminality. Rather, each offender is considered physically and mentally unique; consequently, there must be different explanations for each person's behavior. Some may have inherited criminal tendencies; others may be suffering from neurological problems; still others may have blood chemistry disorders that heighten their antisocial activity. Criminologists who focus on the individual see many explanations for crime because, in fact, there are many differences among criminal offenders.

Contemporary trait theorists focus on basic human behavior and drives that are linked to antisocial behavior patterns. Because humans are not all born with equal potential to learn and achieve (**equipotentiality**), the combination of physical traits and the environment produces individual behavior patterns. There is a significant link between behavior patterns and physical or chemical changes in the brain, autonomic nervous system, and central nervous system.[4]

Trait theorists today recognize that having a particular physical characteristic does not, in itself, produce criminality. Crime-producing interactions involve both personal traits (such as defective intelligence, impulsive personality, and abnormal brain chemistry) and environmental factors (such as family life, educational attainment, socioeconomic status, and neighborhood conditions). People may develop physical or mental traits at birth or soon after that affect their social functioning over the life course and influence their behavior choices; they suffer some biological or psychological condition or trait that renders them incapable of resisting social pressures and problems.[5] For example, low birth weight babies have been found to suffer poor educational achievement later in life; academic deficiency, in turn, has been linked to delinquency and drug abuse.[6] A condition present at birth or soon after can thus affect behavior across the life span. Although some people may have a predisposition toward aggression, that does not mean they will necessarily or automatically engage in violent behaviors; environmental stimuli can either suppress or trigger antisocial acts.[7]

Trait theories have gained prominence recently because of what is now known about chronic recidivism and the development of criminal careers. If only a few offenders become persistent repeaters, what sets them apart from the rest of the criminal population may be an abnormal biochemical makeup, brain structure, genetic constitution, or some other human trait.[8] Even if crime is a choice, the fact that some people make that choice repeatedly could be linked to their physical and mental makeup. According to this view, biological makeup contributes significantly to human behavior. ✔ CHECKPOINTS

CONNECTIONS

As you may recall (Chapter 1), Lombroso's work on the born criminal was a direct offshoot of applying the scientific method to the study of crime. His identification of primitive, atavistic anomalies was based on what he believed to be sound empirical research using established scientific methods.

✔ CHECKPOINTS

✔ Early criminologists, such as Cesare Lombroso, suggested that some people had crime-producing biological traits.

✔ Some contemporary criminologists believe that human traits interact with environmental factors to produce criminal behaviors.

✔ No single trait is responsible for all crime. Suspected crime-producing traits include neurological problems, blood chemistry disorders, and personality disorders.

✔ People are not all born physically and psychologically equal; if they were, all people living in the same environment would act in a similar way.

sociobiology
The view that human behavior is motivated by inborn biological urges to survive and preserve the species.

equipotentiality
The view that all humans are born with equal potential to learn and achieve.

BIOLOGICAL TRAIT THEORIES

One branch of contemporary trait theory focuses on the biological conditions that control human behavior. Criminologists who work in this area typically refer to themselves as biocriminologists, biosocial criminologists, or biologically oriented criminologists; the terms are used here interchangeably.

The following sections examine some important subareas within biological criminology (Figure 5.1). First we review the biochemical factors that are believed to affect how proper behavior patterns are learned. Then we consider the relationship between brain function and crime. Next we analyze current ideas about the association between genetic factors and crime. Finally, we evaluate evolutionary views of crime causation.

CONNECTIONS

Biosocial theory focuses on the violent crimes of the lower classes while ignoring the white-collar crimes of the upper and middle classes. That is, although it may seem logical to believe there is a biological basis to aggression and violence, it is more difficult to explain how insider trading and fraud are biologically related. The causes of white-collar crime are discussed in Chapter 12.

Biochemical Conditions and Crime

Some trait theorists believe that biochemical conditions, including both those that are genetically predetermined and those that are acquired through diet and environment, influence antisocial behavior. This view of crime received national attention in 1979 when Dan White, who confessed to killing San Francisco Mayor George Moscone and City Councilman Harvey Milk, claimed that his behavior was precipitated by an addiction to sugar-laden junk foods.[9] White's successful "Twinkie defense" prompted a California jury to find him guilty of the lesser offense of diminished-capacity manslaughter rather than first-degree murder. (White committed suicide after serving his prison sentence.) Some of the biochemical factors that have been linked to criminality are set out in detail here.

Diet Biocriminologists maintain that a healthy diet can provide minimal levels of minerals and chemicals needed for normal brain functioning and growth, especially in the early years of life. An improper diet can cause chemical and mineral imbalance and lead to cognitive and learning deficits and problems, and these factors in turn are associated with antisocial behaviors.[10]

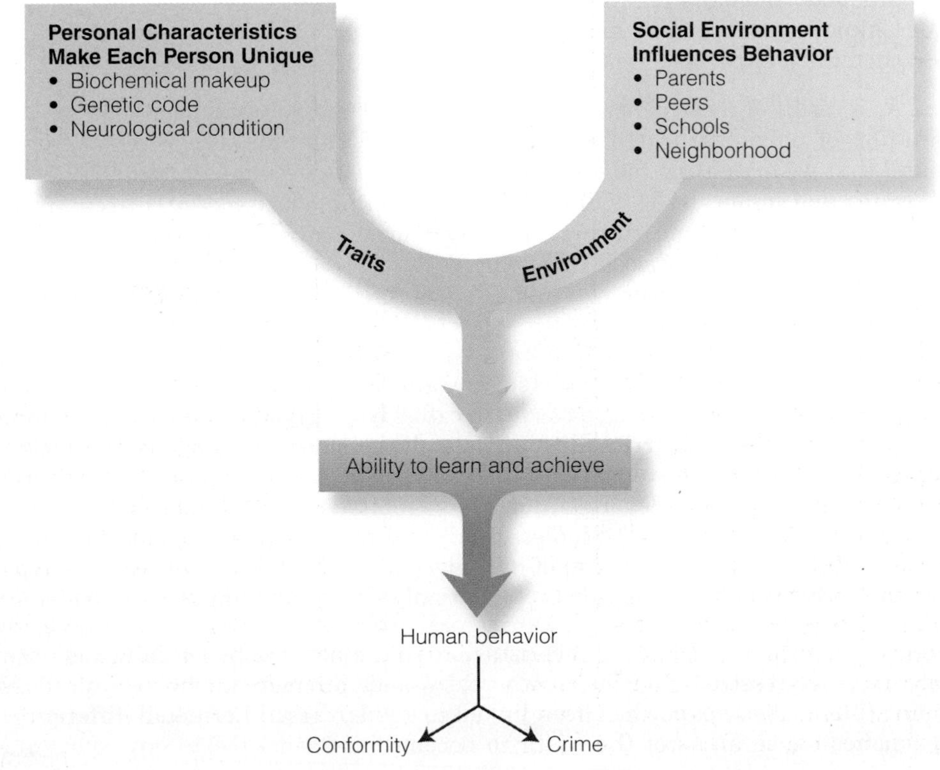

Figure 5.1
Biosocial Perspectives on Criminality

Research conducted over the past decade shows that an over- or undersupply of certain chemicals and minerals, including sodium, mercury, potassium, calcium, amino acids, and/or iron, can lead to depression, hyperactivity, cognitive problems, memory loss, or abnormal sexual activity.[11] Either eliminating harmful substances or introducing beneficial ones into the diet can reduce the threat of antisocial behaviors.[12]

A recent (2005) review of existing research on the association between diet and crime was recently released in Great Britain.[13] The report found that the combination of nutrients most commonly associated with good mental health and well-being is as follows:

- Polyunsaturated fatty acids (particularly the omega-3 types found in oily fish and some plants)
- Minerals, such as zinc (in whole grains, legumes, meat and milk); magnesium (in green leafy vegetables, nuts, and whole grains); and iron (in red meat, green leafy vegetables, eggs, and some fruit)
- Vitamins, such as folate (in green leafy vegetables and fortified cereals); a range of B vitamins (whole grain products, yeast, and dairy products); and antioxidant vitamins such as C and E (in a wide range of fruits and vegetables)

People eating diets that lack one or more of this combination of polyunsaturated fats, minerals, and vitamins, and/or contain too much saturated fat (or other elements, including sugar and a range of food and agricultural chemicals) seem to be at higher risk of developing the following conditions:

- Attention-deficit/hyperactivity disorder (ADHD)
- A range of depressive conditions
- Schizophrenia
- Dementia, including Alzheimer's disease

According to this thorough review, the agricultural and industrial revolutions, followed by the globalization of world food trade, mean that the diets of most people in rich countries (and growing proportions in poor countries) consist of:

- Small amounts of a few types of vegetables and fruit
- Very few whole-grain products and a very narrow range of cereals
- Very little oily fish, but large quantities of intensively produced meat, meat products, and dairy products
- Unknown (and possibly unknowable) combinations of food and agricultural chemicals, either as intentional additives or accidental residues

As a result of these deficiencies, instead of our diets providing a healthy combination of polyunsaturated fats, minerals, and vitamins, the English survey found that we are eating too much saturated fat, sugar, and salt and not enough vitamins and minerals. This diet is not only fueling obesity, cardiovascular disease, diabetes, and some cancers, but may also be contributing to rising rates of mental ill-health and antisocial behavior.

The association between diet and crime is further reviewed in the Current Issues in Crime feature.

Hypoglycemia When blood glucose (sugar) falls below levels necessary for normal and efficient brain functioning, a condition called **hypoglycemia** occurs. Symptoms of hypoglycemia include irritability, anxiety, depression, crying spells, headaches, and confusion. Research studies have linked hypoglycemia to outbursts of antisocial behavior and violence.[14] Several studies have related assaults and sexual offenses to hypoglycemic reactions.[15] Studies of jail and prison inmate populations have found a higher than normal level of hypoglycemia.[16] High levels of reactive hypoglycemia have been found in groups of habitually violent and impulsive offenders.[17]

hypoglycemia
A condition that occurs when glucose (sugar) in the blood falls below levels necessary for normal and efficient brain functioning.

Hormonal Influences Biosocial theorists note that males are biologically and naturally more aggressive than females, whereas women are more nurturing toward the young.[18] This discrepancy has been linked to gender-based hormonal differences. Hormones cause areas of the brain to become less sensitive to environmental stimuli. Abnormally high hormone levels require people to seek excess stimulation and to be willing to tolerate pain in their quest for thrills. Hormones are linked to brain seizures that, under stressful conditions, can result in emotional volatility. They also affect the brain structure itself: They influence the left hemisphere of the neocortex, the part of the brain that controls sympathetic feelings toward others.[19] These effects promote violence and other serious crimes by causing people to seek greater levels of environmental stimulation and to tolerate more punishment, and by increasing impulsivity, emotional volatility, and antisocial emotions.[20]

Biosocial research has found that abnormal levels of male sex hormones (**androgens**) do in fact produce aggressive behavior.[21] Other androgen-related male traits include sensation seeking, impulsivity, dominance, and reduced verbal skills; all of these androgen-related traits are also related to antisocial behavior.[22] A growing body of evidence suggests that hormonal changes are also related to mood and behavior. Adolescents experience more intense mood swings, anxiety, and restlessness than their elders, explaining in part the high violence rates found among teenage males.[23]

Testosterone, the most abundant androgen, which controls secondary sex characteristics such as facial hair and voice timbre, has been linked to criminality.[24] Research conducted on both human and animal subjects has found that prenatal exposure to unnaturally high levels of testosterone permanently alters behavior. Girls who were unintentionally exposed to elevated amounts of testosterone during their fetal development display an unusually high, long-term tendency toward aggression. Conversely, boys who were prenatally exposed to steroids that decrease testosterone levels display decreased aggressiveness.[25] Gender differences in the crime rate, therefore, may be explained by the relative difference in testosterone and other androgens between the two sexes. Females may be biologically protected from deviant behavior in the same way they are immune from some diseases that strike males.[26] Girls who have high levels of testosterone or are exposed to testosterone in utero may become more aggressive in adolescence.[27]

Hormone levels also help explain the aging-out process: Levels of testosterone decline during the life cycle, and so too do violence rates.[28]

Premenstrual Syndrome The suspicion has long existed that the onset of the menstrual cycle triggers excessive amounts of the female sex hormones, which stimulate antisocial, aggressive behavior. This condition is commonly referred to as **premenstrual syndrome (PMS)**.[29] The link between PMS and delinquency was first popularized more than 30 years ago by Katharina Dalton, whose studies of English women indicated that females are more likely to commit suicide and to be aggressive and otherwise antisocial just before or during menstruation.[30]

Although the Dalton research is often cited as evidence of the link between PMS and crime, methodological problems make it impossible to accept her findings at face value. There is still significant debate over any link between PMS and aggression. Some doubters argue that the relationship is spurious; it is equally likely that the psychological and physical stress of aggression brings on menstruation and not vice versa.[31] However, Diana Fishbein, a noted expert on biosocial theory, concludes that there is in fact an association between elevated levels of female aggression and menstruation. Research efforts, she argues, show that (1) a significant number of incarcerated females committed their crimes during the premenstrual phase, and (2) at least a small percentage of women appear vulnerable to cyclical hormonal changes that make them more prone to anxiety and hostility.[32]

The debate is ongoing, but the overwhelming majority of females who suffer anxiety and hostility before and during menstruation do not engage in violent criminal behavior. Thus, any link between PMS and crime is tenuous at best.[33]

Environmental Contaminants Dangerous amounts of copper, cadmium, mercury, and inorganic gases, such as chlorine and nitrogen dioxide, are found in the ecosystem.[34] Of critical importance is lead contamination. At high levels, lead exposure can cause severe illness or death; at more moderate levels, it has been linked to emotional and behavioral disorders.[35] There is also evidence linking lead exposure to mental illnesses, such as schizophrenia, which have been linked to antisocial behaviors.[36] Delinquents have been found to have much higher bone lead levels than children in

CONNECTIONS

Should a person be excused from crime if he or she suffers from a disease that impairs judgment? If eating junk foods can excuse crime, what about drinking alcohol? Go to Chapter 1 for more on criminal defenses.

androgens
Male sex hormones.

testosterone
The principal male hormone.

premenstrual syndrome (PMS)
A condition that involves symptoms including depression, anxiety, fatigue, irritability, headaches, abdominal swelling, and inability to concentrate, which occur in relation to the menstrual cycle and may interfere with a woman's life.

Current Issues in Crime

Diet and Crime

Can what you eat control your behavior? Some recent experimental studies conducted in the United States and abroad have shown that diet and crime may have a significant association. Research done in the United States, Britain, Canada, Australia, and Argentina seems to link homicide rates and omega-6 fats found in corn, safflower, soybean, cottonseed, and sunflower oils. Research by the National Institutes of Health scientists found that murder rates were 20 times higher in countries with the highest omega-6 intake, compared with those with the lowest; within countries, homicide rates rose over time in direct proportion to increasing omega-6 consumption. Experts think Western diets' excess omega-6 fats may overwhelm omega-3.

In Great Britain, Bernard Gesch and his associates studied the behavior of 231 inmates at a maximum-security prison. Half of the group received daily capsules containing vitamins, minerals, and essential fatty acids, such as omega-3 and omega-6, while the other half took a placebo. Antisocial behavior among inmates was recorded before and during distribution of the dietary supplements. Gesch found that the supplement group broke prison rules 25 percent less than those on the placebo. The greatest reduction was for serious offenses—instances of fighting, assaulting guards, or taking hostages dropped 37 percent. There was, however, no significant change in the control group. A recent (2003) Finnish study of 115 depressed outpatients being treated with antidepressants found that those who responded fully to treatment had higher levels of vitamin B_{12} in their blood at the beginning of treatment and six months later. Depression has been linked to antisocial activities. The researchers speculated that vitamin B_{12} deficiency leads to the accumulation of the amino acid homocysteine, which has been linked to depression.

In the United States, Carlos Iribarren and colleagues recently (2004) examined the relationship between omega-3 intake and hostility. Using a sample of 3,600 young adults living in urban environments, the researchers controlled for a wide range of factors and found that a higher consumption of the omega-3 fatty acid docosahexaenoic acid (DHA), or of omega-3-rich fish in general, was related to significantly lower levels of hostility.

Stephen Schoenthaler, a well-known biocriminologist, has conducted a number of studies that indicate a significant association between diet and aggressive behavior patterns. In some cases, the relationship is direct; in others, a poor diet may compromise individual functioning, which in turn produces aggressive behavior responses. For example, a poor diet may inhibit school performance, and children who fail at school are at risk for delinquent behavior and criminality.

In one study of 803 New York City public schools, Schoenthaler found that the academic performance of 1.1 million schoolchildren rose 16 percent after their diets were modified. The number of "learning disabled" children fell from 125,000 to 74,000 in one year. No other changes in school programs for the learning disabled were initiated that year. In a similar experiment conducted in a correctional institution, violent and nonviolent antisocial behavior fell an average of 48 percent among 8,047 offenders after dietary changes were implemented. In both these studies, the improvements in behavior and academic performance were attributed to diets containing more vitamins and minerals as compared with the old diets. The greater amounts of these essential nutrients in the new diets were believed to have corrected impaired brain function caused by poor nutrition.

More recently, Schoenthaler conducted three randomized controlled studies in which 66 elementary school children, 62 confined teenage delinquents, and 402 confined adult felons received dietary supplements—the equivalent of a diet providing more fruits, vegetables, and whole grains. In order to remove experimental bias, neither subjects nor researchers knew who received the supplement and who received a placebo. In each study, the subjects receiving the dietary supplement demonstrated significantly less violent

the general population.[37] Criminologist Deborah Denno investigated the behavior of more than 900 African American youths and found that lead poisoning was one of the most significant predictors of male delinquency and persistent adult criminality.[38]

Lead is not the only environmental contaminant linked to social and psychological problems. Exposure to the now banned PCB (polychlorinated biphenyls), a chemical once used in insulation materials, has been shown to influence brain functioning and intelligence levels.[39]

Neurophysiological Conditions and Crime

Some researchers focus their attention on **neurophysiology**, or the study of brain activity.[40] They believe that inherited or acquired neurological and physical abnormalities control behavior throughout the life span.[41] Studies conducted in the United States and elsewhere have shown a significant relationship between impairment in executive brain functions (such as abstract reasoning, problem solving, and motor skills) and aggressive behavior.[42] Research using memorization and visual awareness tests, short-term auditory memory tests, and verbal IQ tests indicate that this relationship can be detected quite early and that children who suffer measurable neurological deficits at birth or in adolescence are more likely to become antisocial later in life.[43] Neurological deficits have been linked to a full

neurophysiology
The study of brain activity.

and nonviolent antisocial behavior when compared to the control subjects who received placebos. The carefully collected data verified that a very good diet, as defined by the World Health Organization, has significant behavioral benefits beyond its health effects.

Schoenthaler and his associates have also evaluated the relationship between nutrition and intelligence. These studies involved 1,753 children and young adults in California, Arizona, Oklahoma, Missouri, England, Wales, Scotland, and Belgium. In each study, subjects who were poorly nourished and who were given dietary supplements showed a greater increase in IQ—an average of 16 points—than did those in the placebo group. (Overall, IQ rose more than 3 points.) The differences in IQ could be attributed to about 20 percent of the children who were presumably inadequately nourished before supplementation.

The IQ research was expanded to include academic performance in two studies of more than 300 schoolchildren ages 6 to 14 years in Arizona and California. In both studies, children who received daily supplements at school for three months achieved significantly higher gains in grade level compared to the matched control group taking placebos. The children taking a supplement improved academically at twice the rate of the children who took placebos.

Schoenthaler concludes that parents with a child who behaves badly, or does poorly in school, may benefit from having the child take a blood test to determine whether concentrations of certain nutrients are below the reference norms; if so, a dietary supplement may correct the child's conduct and performance. There is evidence that 19 nutrients may be critical; low levels appear to adversely affect brain function, academic performance, intelligence, and conduct. When attempting to improve IQ or conduct, it is critical to assess all these nutrients and correct deficiencies as needed. If blood nutrient concentrations are consistently in the normal range, physicians and parents should consider looking elsewhere for the cause of a child's difficulties.

Though more research is needed before the scientific community reaches a consensus on how low is "too low," Schoenthaler finds evidence that vitamins, minerals, chemicals, and other nutrients from a diet rich in fruits, vegetables, and whole grains can improve brain function, basic intelligence, and academic performance. These are all variables that have been linked to antisocial behavior.

Critical Thinking

1. If Schoenthaler is correct in his assumptions, should schools be required to provide a proper lunch for all children?
2. How would Schoenthaler explain the "aging out" process? *Hint*: Do people eat better as they mature? What about after they get married?

InfoTrac College Edition Research

To read more about the relationship between nutrition and behavior, use "nutrition and behavior" as key terms in InfoTrac College Edition.

SOURCES: Gloria McVeigh, "Calming Foods," *Prevention* 77 (2005); Jukka Hintikka Tommi Tolmunen, Antti Tanskanen, and Heimo Viinamäki, "High Vitamin B_{12} Level and Good Treatment Outcome May Be Associated in Major Depressive Disorder," *BMC Psychiatry* 3 (2003): 17–18; C. Iribarren, J. H. Markovitz, D. R. Jacobs, Jr., P. J. Schreiner, M. Daviglus, and J. R. Hibbeln, "Dietary Intake of Omega-3, Omega-6 Fatty Acids and Fish: Relationship with Hostility in Young Adults—the CARDIA study," *European Journal of Clinical Nutrition* 58 (2004): 24–31; C. Bernard Gesch, Sean M. Hammond, Sarah E. Hampson, Anita Eves, and Martin J. Crowder, "Influence of Supplementary Vitamins, Minerals and Essential Fatty Acids on the Antisocial Behaviour of Young Adult Prisoners: Randomized, Placebo-Controlled Trial," *British Journal of Psychiatry* 181 (2002): 22–28; Stephen Schoenthaler, "Intelligence, Academic Performance, and Brain Function," California State University, Stanislaus, 2000. See also S. Schoenthaler and I. Bier, "The Effect of Vitamin–Mineral Supplementation on Juvenile Delinquency among American Schoolchildren: A Randomized Double-Blind Placebo-Controlled Trial," *Journal of Alternative and Complementary Medicine: Research on Paradigm, Practice, and Policy* 6 (2000): 7–18.

range of criminal activity. Recent research by J. Arturo Silva and colleagues found that serial killers exhibit evidence of Asperger's disorder (AD), a neurological impairment that severely affects communication, social skills, behavior, and learning.[44]

Brain-scanning techniques using electronic imaging, such as magnetic resonance imaging (MRI), positron emission tomography (PET), brain electrical activity mapping (BEAM), and the superconducting interference device (SQUID), have made it possible to assess which areas of the brain are directly linked to antisocial behavior.[45] Findings from recent brain research include the following:

- Both violent criminals and substance abusers have impairment in the prefrontal lobes, thalamus, medial temporal lobe, and superior parietal and left angular gyrus areas of the brain.[46]
- PET studies of repetitively violent offenders reveal decreased cortical blood flow and hypometabolism in their nondominant frontal and temporal lobes, compared to control subjects. Some even show involvement into the prefrontal region, which affects cognitive understanding.[47]
- Domestic violence offenders have lower metabolism in the right hypothalamus and decreased correlations between cortical and subcortical brain structures than a group of control subjects.[48]

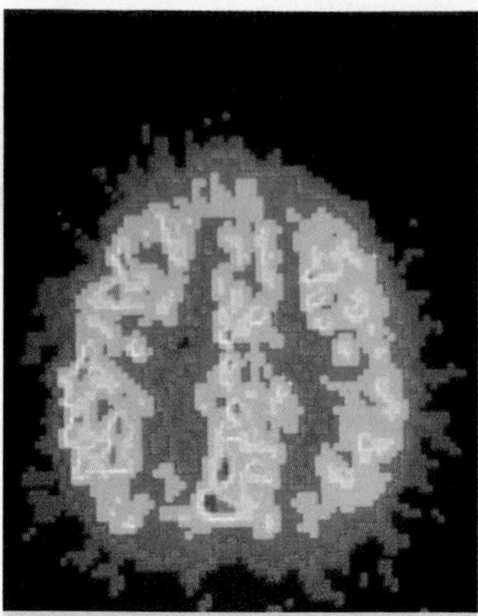

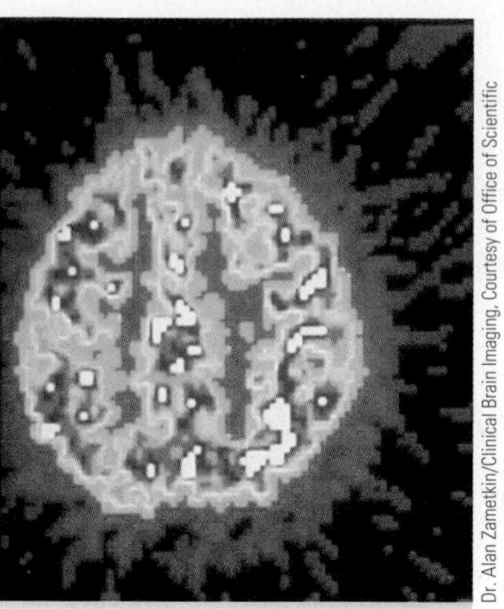

Dr. Alan Zametkin/Clinical Brain Imaging, Courtesy of Office of Scientific Information/NIMH

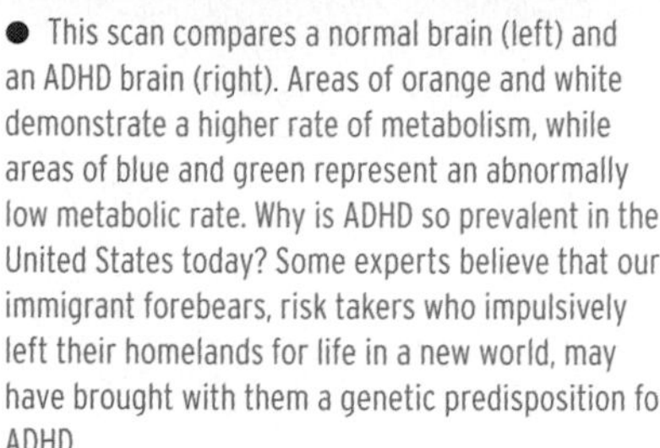

● This scan compares a normal brain (left) and an ADHD brain (right). Areas of orange and white demonstrate a higher rate of metabolism, while areas of blue and green represent an abnormally low metabolic rate. Why is ADHD so prevalent in the United States today? Some experts believe that our immigrant forebears, risk takers who impulsively left their homelands for life in a new world, may have brought with them a genetic predisposition for ADHD.

- People who are habitual liars maintain a 22 to 26 percent increase in prefrontal white matter and a 36 to 42 percent reduction in prefrontal gray/white ratios, and a 14.2 percent decrease in prefrontal gray matter compared to control group subjects.[49]
- Antisocial behavior is influenced by prefrontal dysfunction, a condition that occurs when demands on brain activity overload the prefrontal cortex and result in a lack of control over antisocial behaviors. Because the prefrontal lobes have not fully developed in adolescence, they may become overwhelmed.[50]

Attention Deficit Hyperactivity Disorder Many parents have noticed that their children do not pay attention to them—they run around and do things in their own way. Sometimes this inattention is a function of age; in other instances it is a symptom of **attention deficit hyperactivity disorder (ADHD)**, in which a child shows a developmentally inappropriate lack of attention, along with impulsivity and hyperactivity. Exhibit 5.1 lists the various symptoms of ADHD. About 3 percent of U.S. children, most often boys, are believed to suffer from this disorder, and it is the most common reason children are referred to mental health clinics. The condition has been associated with poor school performance, grade retention, placement in special needs classes, bullying, stubbornness, and lack of response to discipline.[51]

Although the origin of ADHD is still unknown, suspected causes include neurological damage, prenatal stress, and even reactions to food additives and chemical allergies. Recent research has suggested a genetic link.[52] There are also links to family turmoil: Mothers of ADHD children are more likely to be divorced

attention deficit hyperactivity disorder (ADHD)
A developmentally inappropriate lack of attention, along with impulsivity and hyperactivity.

Exhibit 5.1
Symptoms of Attention Deficit Hyperactivity Disorder

Lack of Attention

Frequently fails to finish projects
Does not seem to pay attention
Does not sustain interest in play activities
Cannot sustain concentration on schoolwork or related tasks
Is easily distracted

Impulsivity

Frequently acts without thinking
Often "calls out" in class
Does not want to wait his or her turn in lines or games
Shifts from activity to activity
Cannot organize tasks or work
Requires constant supervision

Hyperactivity

Constantly runs around and climbs on things
Shows excessive motor activity while asleep
Cannot sit still; is constantly fidgeting
Does not remain in his or her seat in class
Is constantly on the go like a "motor"

SOURCE: Adapted from American Psychiatric Association, *Diagnostic and Statistical Manual of Mental Disorders*, 4th ed. (Washington, DC: American Psychiatric Press, 1994).

or separated, and ADHD children are much more likely to move to new locales than non-ADHD children.[53] It may be possible that emotional turmoil either produces symptoms of ADHD or, if they already exist, causes them to intensify.

A series of research studies now link ADHD to the onset and sustenance of a delinquent career.[54] Children with ADHD are more likely to use illicit drugs, alcohol, and cigarettes in adolescence, are more likely to be arrested, to be charged with a felony, and to have multiple arrests than non-ADHD youths. Many ADHD children also suffer from **conduct disorder (CD)** and continually engage in aggressive and antisocial behavior in early childhood.[55] Children diagnosed as ADHD are more likely to be suspended from school and engage in criminal behavior as adults. This ADHD–crime association is important because symptoms of ADHD seem stable through adolescence into adulthood.[56] Hyperactive/ADHD children are at greater risk for adolescent antisocial activity and drug use/abuse that persists into adulthood.[57]

Early diagnosis and treatment of children with ADHD may enhance their life chances. Today the most typical treatment is doses of stimulants, such as Ritalin, which, ironically, help control emotional and behavioral outbursts. The relationship between chronic delinquency and attention disorders may also be mediated by school performance. Children who are poor readers are the most prone to antisocial behavior; many poor readers also have attention problems.[58] Early school-based intervention programs may thus benefit children with ADHD.

Brain Chemistry Chemical compounds called **neurotransmitters** influence or activate brain functions. Those studied in relation to aggression include dopamine, norepinephrine, serotonin, monoamine oxidase (MOMA), and gamma-aminobutryic acid (GABA). Evidence exists that indicates abnormally low levels of these chemicals are associated with aggression.[59] Avshalom Caspi and his colleagues examined groups of people who had been abused during adolescence, and found that people endowed with an abundance of MOMA were significantly more likely to cope with the effects of an unhappy or abusive childhood and lead a normal adult life than those born with lower levels of the enzyme. Male victims of child abuse in the study were nine times as likely to engage in antisocial activity if they maintained low levels of MOMA when compared to a group of equally abused children who had above-normal levels.[60] Other research efforts have linked low levels of MOMA to high levels of violence and property crime, including defiance of punishment, impulsivity, hyperactivity, poor academic performance, sensation seeking and risk taking, and recreational drug use.[61] Abnormal MOMA levels may explain both individual and group differences in the crime rate. Females naturally have higher MOMA levels than males, which may explain gender differences in the crime rate.[62] MOMA is not the only neurochemical linked to crime. Studies of habitually violent criminals show that low serotonin levels are associated with poor impulse control and hyperactivity, increased irritability, and sensation seeking.[63]

What is the link between brain chemistry and crime? Prenatal exposure of the brain to high levels of androgens can result in a brain structure that is less sensitive to environmental inputs. Affected individuals seek more intense and varied stimulation and are willing to tolerate more adverse consequences than individuals not so affected.[64] Because this linkage has been found, it is not uncommon for violence-prone people to be treated with antipsychotic drugs such as Haldol, Stelazine, Prolixin, and Risperdal. These drugs, which help control levels of neurotransmitters (such as serotonin or dopamine), are sometimes referred to as chemical restraints or chemical straitjackets.

Arousal Theory According to **arousal theory**, for a variety of genetic and environmental reasons, people's brains function differently in response to environmental stimuli. All of us seek to maintain a preferred or optimal level of arousal: Too much stimulation leaves us anxious and stressed, whereas too little makes us feel bored and weary. However, people vary in the way their brains process sensory input. Some nearly always feel comfortable with little stimulation, whereas others require a high degree of environmental input to feel comfortable. The latter group of "sensation seekers" looks for stimulating activities, which may include aggressive, violent behavior patterns.[65]

conduct disorder (CD)
A pattern of repetitive behavior in which the rights of others or the social norms are violated.

neurotransmitters
Chemical compounds that influence or activate brain functions.

arousal theory
The view that people seek to maintain a preferred level of arousal but vary in how they process sensory input. A need for high levels of environmental stimulation may lead to aggressive, violent behavior patterns.

● There is a link between parental deviance and a child's criminality, but whether it is a function of learning, environment, or genetics is a matter of debate. Here, Judy and William Gould, both of Jackson, Michigan, are arraigned before District Judge Carlene Walz in Jackson County District Court on three counts of contributing to the delinquency of a minor and one count of receiving stolen property valued at more than $100. Police say the couple kept three of their six children, ages 8, 10, and 12, padlocked in the basement of their home at night without access to a bathroom, and forced the children to steal thousands of dollars in collectible items by day. Between $30,000 and $50,000 worth of stolen items were recovered from the couple's home.

© AP

Although the factors that determine a person's level of arousal are not fully understood, suspected sources include brain chemistry (such as serotonin levels) and brain structure. Some brains have many more nerve cells with receptor sites for neurotransmitters than others. Another view is that people with low heart rates are more likely to commit crime because they seek stimulation to increase their arousal to normal levels.[66]

Genetics and Crime

Another biosocial theme is that the human traits associated with criminality have a genetic basis.[67] According to this view, (1) antisocial behavior is inherited, (2) the genetic makeup of parents is passed on to children, and (3) genetic abnormality is linked to a variety of antisocial behaviors.[68] The association between genetic makeup and antisocial behavior is often hard to validate. Even if a child's behavior is similar to his or her parents, proving whether the influence is genetic or a product of learning and socialization is difficult. How have criminologists tried to test the effects of inheritance on crime?

Parental Deviance If criminal tendencies are inherited, children of criminal parents should be more likely to become law violators than the offspring of conventional parents. A number of studies have found that parental criminality and deviance do, in fact, powerfully influence delinquent behavior.[69] The Cambridge Youth Survey, a longitudinal cohort study conducted in England, indicates that a significant number of delinquent youths have criminal fathers.[70] Whereas 8 percent of the sons of noncriminal fathers eventually became chronic offenders, about 37 percent of youths with criminal fathers were multiple offenders.[71] In another important analysis, David Farrington found that one type of parental deviance—schoolyard aggression, or bullying—may be both inter- and intragenerational. Bullies have children who bully others, and these second-generation bullies grow up to father children who are also bullies, in a never-ending cycle.[72]

Farrington's findings are supported by some recent research data from the Rochester Youth Development Study (RYDS), a longitudinal analysis that has been monitoring the behavior of 1,000 area youths since 1988. RYDS researchers have also found an intergenerational continuity in antisocial behavior, though their data do not allow them to definitively determine whether it is a result of genetics or socialization.[73]

In sum, there is growing evidence that crime is intergenerational: Criminal fathers produce criminal sons who then produce criminal grandchildren. Although there is no certainty about the relationship between parental and child deviance, it is possible that at least part of the association is genetic.[74] How can this relationship be more definitively tested?

Adoption Studies It seems logical that if the behavior of adopted children is more closely aligned to that of their biological parents than to that of their adoptive parents, the idea of a genetic basis for criminality would be supported. If, on the other hand, adoptees' behavior is more closely aligned to the behavior of their adoptive parents than of their biological parents, an environmental basis for crime would seem more valid.

Several studies indicate that some relationship exists between biological parents' behavior and the behavior of their children, even when they have had no contact.[75] In what is considered the most significant study in this area, Barry Hutchings and Sarnoff Mednick analyzed 1,145 male adoptees born in Copenhagen, Denmark, between 1927 and 1941. Of these, 185 had criminal records.[76] After following up on 143 of the criminal adoptees and matching them with a control group of 143 noncriminal adoptees, Hutchings and Mednick found that the biological father's criminality strongly predicted the child's criminal behavior. When both the biological and the adoptive fathers were criminal, the probability that the youth would engage in criminal behavior greatly increased. Of the boys whose adoptive and biological fathers were both criminals, 24.5 percent had been convicted of a criminal law violation. Only 13.5 percent of those whose biological and adoptive fathers were not criminals had similar conviction records.[77]

Twin Behavior If, in fact, inherited traits cause criminal behavior, we might expect that twins would be quite similar in their antisocial activities. And as predicted, research efforts confirm a significant correspondence of twin behavior in activities ranging from frequency of sexual activity to crime.[78] However, because twins are usually brought up in the same household and exposed to the same social conditions, determining whether their behavior is a result of biological, sociological, or psychological conditions is difficult. To control for environmental factors, criminologists have compared identical, **monozygotic (MZ) twins** with fraternal, **dizygotic (DZ) twins**.[79] MZ twins are genetically identical, whereas DZ twins have only half their genes in common. If heredity determines criminal behavior, we should expect that MZ twins would be much more similar in their antisocial activities than DZ twins.

Studies conducted on twin behavior have detected a significant relationship between the criminal activities of MZ twins and a much lower association between those of DZ twins; these genetic effects can be seen in children as young as 3 years old.[80] Among relevant findings:

- There is a significantly higher risk for suicidal behavior among monozygotic twin pairs than dizygotic twin pairs.[81]
- Differences in concordance between MZ and DZ twins have been found in tests measuring psychological dysfunctions such as conduct disorders, impulsivity, and antisocial behavior.[82]
- MZ twins are closer than DZ twins in such crime relevant measures as level of aggression and verbal skills.[83]
- Both members of MZ twin pairs who suffer child abuse are more likely to engage in later antisocial activity more often than DZ pairs. Because the association is stronger among MZ twins, the link between abuse and delinquency may be an inherited genetic component.[84]
- Callous, unemotional traits in very young children can be a warning sign for future psychopathy and antisocial behavior. Using samples of same-sex twin pairs, psychiatrist Essi Viding and colleagues found a powerful hereditary influence on levels of callous, unemotional behavior in children.[85]

Although this evidence is persuasive, many questions still need to be answered about the association between genetics and crime. (Exhibit 5.2 describes a current, ongoing study of MZ and DZ twins.) Even if the behavior similarities between MZ twins is greater than that between DZ twins, the association may be explained by environmental factors. MZ twins are more likely to look alike and to share physical traits than DZ twins, and they are more likely to be treated similarly. Similarities in their shared behavior patterns may therefore be a function of socialization and/or environment and not heredity.[86] It is also possible that what appears to be a genetic effect picked up by the twin research is actually the effect of sibling influence on criminality, referred to as the **contagion effect**: Genetic predispositions and early experiences make some people, including twins, susceptible to deviant behavior, which is transmitted by the presence of antisocial siblings in the household.[87] Twin influence is everlasting: If one twin is antisocial, it legitimizes and supports the criminal behavior in his or her co-twin. This effect may grow even stronger in adulthood because twin relations are more enduring than any other. What seems to be a genetic effect may actually be the result of sibling interaction with a brother or sister who engages in antisocial activity.

Evolutionary Views of Crime

Some criminologists believe that the human traits that produce violence and aggression have been advanced by the long process of human evolution.[88] According

monozygotic (MZ) twins
Identical twins.

dizygotic (DZ) twins
Fraternal (nonidentical) twins.

contagion effect
People become deviant when they are influenced by others with whom they are in close contact.

Exhibit 5.2
Findings from the Minnesota Study of Twins Reared Apart

One famous study of twin behavior still under way is the Minnesota Study of Twins Reared Apart. This research compares the behavior of MZ and DZ twin pairs who were raised together with others who were separated at birth and in some cases did not even know of each other's existence. The study shows some striking similarities in behavior and ability for twin pairs raised apart. An MZ twin reared away from a co-twin has about as good a chance of being similar to the co-twin in terms of personality, interests, and attitudes as one who has been reared with his or her co-twin. The conclusion: Similarities between twins are due to genes, not the environment. Because twins reared apart are so similar, if the environment contributes anything, it is to make them different! The study's findings include the following:

- MZ twins become *more* similar with respect to abilities such as vocabularies and arithmetic scores asthey age. As DZ (fraternal) twins get older they become less similar with respect to vocabularies and arithmetic scores.
- A P300 is a tiny electrical response (a few millionths of a volt) that occurs in the brain when a person detects something that is unusual or interesting. For example, if a person were shown nine circles and one square, a P300 brain response would appear after seeing the square because it's different. Identical (MZ) twin children have very similar looking P300s. By comparison, children who are fraternal (DZ) twins, do not show as much similarity in their P300s. These results indicate that the way the brain processes information may be greatly influenced by genes.
- An EEG is a measure of brain activity or brain waves that can be used to monitor a person's state of arousal. MZ twins tend to produce strikingly similar EEG spectra; DZ twins show far less similarity.
- MZ twins tend to have more similar ages at the time of death than DZ twins do. That is, MZ twins are more likely to die at about the same age, and DZ twins are more likely to die at different ages.

SOURCE: Minnesota Study of Twins Reared Apart, www.psych.umn.edu/psylabs/mtfs/special.htm (accessed January 16, 2006).

to this evolutionary view, the competition for scarce resources has influenced and shaped the human species.[89] Over the course of human existence, people whose personal characteristics allowed them to accumulate more than others were the most likely to breed and dominate the species. People have been shaped to engage in actions that promote their well-being and ensure the survival and reproduction of their genetic line. Males who are impulsive risk takers may be able to father more children because they are reckless in their social relationships and have sexual encounters with numerous partners. If, according to evolutionary theories, such behavior patterns are inherited, impulsive behavior becomes intergenerational, passed down from parents to children. It is therefore not surprising that human history has been marked by war, violence, and aggression.

The Evolution of Gender and Crime Evolutionary concepts that have been linked to gender differences in violence rates are based loosely on mammalian mating patterns. To ensure survival of the gene pool (and the species), it is beneficial for a male of any species to mate with as many suitable females as possible, because each can bear his offspring. In contrast, because of the long period of gestation, females require a secure home and a single, stable, nurturing partner to ensure their survival. Because of these differences in mating patterns, the most aggressive males mate most often and have the greatest number of offspring. Therefore, over the history of the human species, aggressive males have had the greatest impact on the gene pool. The descendants of these aggressive males now account for the disproportionate amount of male aggression and violence.[90]

Crime rate differences between the genders, then, may be less a matter of socialization than of inherent differences in mating patterns that have developed over time.[91] Among young men, reckless, life-threatening risk proneness is especially likely to evolve in cultures that force them to find suitable mates to ensure their ability to reproduce. Unless they are aggressive with potential mates and potential rivals for those suitable mates, they will remain childless.[92] Reproductive aggressiveness and similar evolutionary processes may explain why women of childbearing age are more attractive targets of rapists (and rapist-murderers) than women who are no longer able to bear children and therefore unlikely to serve as desirable mates.[93]

High rates of spouse abuse in modern society may be a function of aggressive men seeking to control and possess mates. Men who feel most threatened over the potential of losing mates to rivals are the most likely to engage in sexual violence. Research shows that women in common-law marriages, especially those who are much younger than their husbands, are at greater risk of abuse than older, married women. Abusive males may fear the potential loss of their younger mates, especially if they are not bound by a marriage contract, and may use force for purposes of control and possession.[94]

"Cheater" Theory According to **cheater theory**, a subpopulation of men has evolved with genes that incline them toward extremely low parental involvement. They are sexually aggressive and use cunning to achieve sexual conquest of as many females as possible. Because females would not willingly choose them as mates, they use stealth to gain sexual access, including such tactics as mimicking the behavior of more stable males. They use devious, illegal means to acquire resources they need for sexual domination. These deceptive reproductive tactics spill over into other endeavors, where their irresponsible, opportunistic behavior supports their antisocial activities. Deceptive reproductive strategies, then, are linked to a deceitful lifestyle.[95]

Psychologist Byron Roth notes that cheater-type males may be especially attractive to younger, less intelligent women who begin having children at a very early age. State-sponsored welfare, claims Roth, removes the need for potential mates to have the resources required of stable providers and family caretakers.[96] With the state meeting their financial needs, these women are drawn to men who are physically attractive and flamboyant. Their fleeting courtship produces children with low IQ scores, aggressive personalities, and little chance of proper socialization in father-absent families. Because the criminal justice system treats them leniently, argues Roth, sexually irresponsible men are free to prey upon young girls. Over time, their offspring will make up an ever-expanding supply of cheaters who are both antisocial and sexually aggressive.

CONNECTIONS

The relationship between evolutionary factors and crime has just begun to be studied. Criminologists are now exploring how social organizations and institutions interact with biological traits to influence personal decision making, including criminal strategies. See the discussion of latent trait theories in Chapter 9 for more about the integration of biological and environmental factors.

Evaluation of the Biological Branch of Trait Theory

Biosocial perspectives on crime have raised some challenging questions. Critics find some of these theories racist and dysfunctional. If there are biological explanations for street crimes such as assault, murder, or rape, the argument goes, and if, as official crime statistics suggest, the poor and minority-group members commit a disproportionate number of such acts, then by implication, biological theory says that members of these groups are biologically different, flawed, or inferior.

Biological explanations for the geographic, social, and temporal patterns in the crime rate are also problematic. Is it possible that more people are genetically predisposed to crime in the South and the West than in New England and the Midwest? Furthermore, biological theory seems to divide people into criminals and noncriminals on the basis of their genetic and physical makeup, ignoring self-reports that indicate that almost everyone has engaged in some type of illegal activity.

Biosocial theorists counter that their views should not be confused with Lombrosian, deterministic biology. Rather than suggesting that there are born criminals and noncriminals, they maintain that some people carry the potential to be violent or antisocial and that environmental conditions can sometimes trigger antisocial responses.[97] This would explain why some otherwise law-abiding citizens perform a single, seemingly unexplainable antisocial act and, conversely, why some people with long criminal careers often behave conventionally. It also explains geographic and temporal patterns in the crime rate: People who are predisposed to crime may simply have more opportunities to commit illegal acts in the summer in Los Angeles and Atlanta than in the winter in Bedford, New Hampshire, and Minot, North Dakota.

The most significant criticism of biosocial theory has been the lack of adequate empirical testing. Most research samples are relatively small and nonrepresentative. A great deal of biosocial research is conducted with samples of adjudicated offenders

✔ CHECKPOINTS

- ✔ Brain chemistry and hormonal differences are related to aggression and violence.
- ✔ Most evidence suggests that there is no relationship between sugar intake and crime.
- ✔ The male hormone testosterone is linked to criminality.
- ✔ Neurological impairments have been linked to crime.
- ✔ Genetic theory holds that violence-producing traits are passed on from generation to generation.
- ✔ According to evolutionary theory, instinctual drives control behavior. The urge to procreate influences male violence.
- ✔ Biological explanations fail to account for the geographic, social, and temporal patterns in the crime rate; critics question the methodology used.

cheater theory
A theory suggesting that a subpopulation of men has evolved with genes that incline them toward extremely low parental involvement. Sexually aggressive, they use deceit for sexual conquest of as many females as possible.

CONCEPT SUMMARY 5.1 Biosocial Theories of Crime

BIOCHEMICAL

- The major premise of the theory is that crime, especially violence, is a function of diet, vitamin intake, hormonal imbalance, or food allergies.
- The strengths of the theory are that it explains irrational violence; it shows how the environment interacts with personal traits to influence behavior.
- The research focuses of the theory are diet, hormones, enzymes, environmental contaminants, and lead intake.

NEUROLOGICAL

- The major premise of the theory is that criminals and delinquents often suffer brain impairment, as measured by the EEG. Attention deficit hyperactivity disorder and minimal brain dysfunction are related to antisocial behavior.
- The strengths of the theory are that it explains irrational violence; it shows how the environment interacts with personal traits to influence behavior.
- The research focuses of the theory are ODD, ADHD, learning disabilities, brain injuries, and brain chemistry.

GENETIC

- The major premise of the theory is that criminal traits and predispositions are inherited. The criminality of parents can predict the delinquency of children.
- The strengths of the theory are that it explains why only a small percentage of youth in high-crime areas become chronic offenders.
- The research focuses of the theory are twin behavior, sibling behavior, and parent–child similarities.

EVOLUTIONARY

- The major premise of the theory is that as the human race evolved, traits and characteristics have become ingrained. Some of these traits make people aggressive and predisposed to commit crime.
- The strengths of the theory are that it explains high violence rates and aggregate gender differences in the crime rate.
- The research focuses of the theory are gender differences and understanding human aggression.

who have been placed in clinical treatment settings. Methodological problems make it impossible to determine whether findings apply only to offenders who have been convicted of crimes and placed in treatment or to all criminals.[98] More research is needed to clarify the relationships proposed by biosocial researchers and to silence critics. Concept Summary 5.1 lists the major elements of biosocial theory. ✓ CHECKPOINTS

PSYCHOLOGICAL TRAIT THEORIES

The second branch of trait theory focuses on the psychological aspects of crime, including the associations among intelligence, personality, learning, and criminal behavior (Figure 5.2). This view has a long history, and psychologists, psychiatrists, and other mental health professionals have long played an active role in formulating criminological theory.

Among nineteenth-century pioneers in this area were Charles Goring (1870–1919) and Gabriel Tarde (1843–1904). Goring studied 3,000 English convicts and found little difference in the physical characteristics of criminals and noncriminals. However, he uncovered a significant relationship between crime and a condition he referred to as "defective intelligence," which involved such traits as feeblemindedness, epilepsy, insanity, and defective social instinct.[99] Tarde was the forerunner of modern learning theorists, who hold that people learn from one another through imitation.[100]

In their quest to understand and treat all varieties of abnormal mental conditions, psychologists have encountered clients whose behavior falls within the categories that society has labeled as criminal, deviant, violent, and antisocial. A number of different psychological views have been associated with criminal behavior causation. The most important of these perspectives are discussed in the following sections.

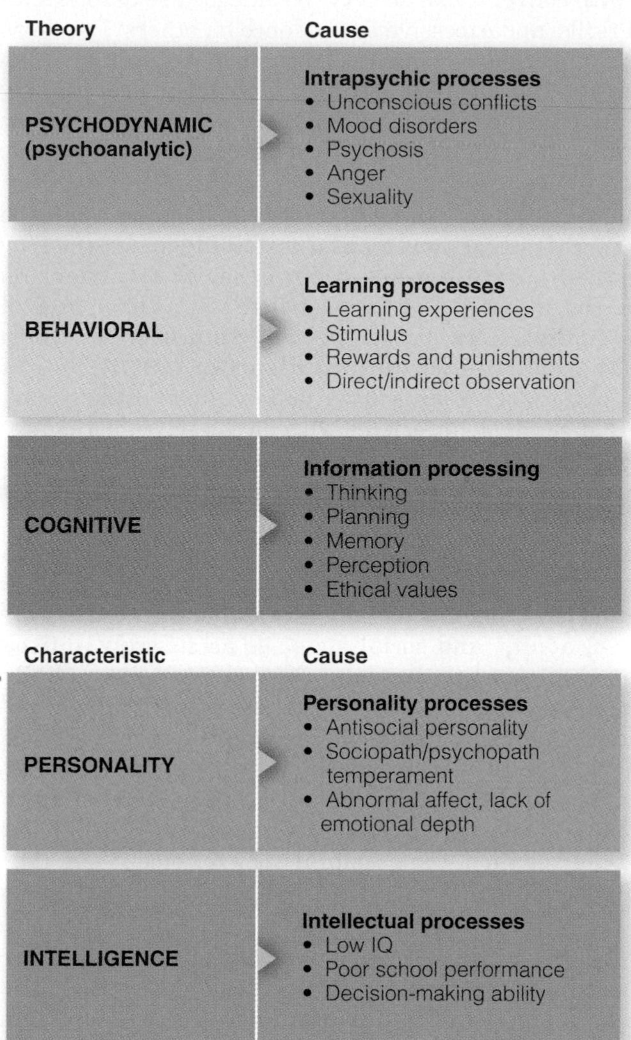

Theory
Cause
PSYCHODYNAMIC (psychoanalytic)
Intrapsychic processes
• Unconscious conflicts
• Mood disorders
• Psychosis
• Anger
• Sexuality
BEHAVIORAL
Learning processes
• Learning experiences
• Stimulus
• Rewards and punishments
• Direct/indirect observation
COGNITIVE
Information processing
• Thinking
• Planning
• Memory
• Perception
• Ethical values
Characteristic
Cause
PERSONALITY
Personality processes
• Antisocial personality
• Sociopath/psychopath temperament
• Abnormal affect, lack of emotional depth
INTELLIGENCE
Intellectual processes
• Low IQ
• Poor school performance
• Decision-making ability

Figure 5.2
Psychological Perspectives on Criminality

Psychodynamic Perspective

Psychodynamic (or **psychoanalytic**) psychology was originated by Viennese psychiatrist Sigmund Freud (1856–1939) and has remained a prominent segment of psychological theory ever since.[101] Freud believed that we all carry with us residue of the most significant emotional attachments of our childhood, which then guides our future interpersonal relationships.

According to psychodynamic theory, the human personality has a three-part structure. The **id** is the primitive part of people's mental makeup, present at birth, that represents unconscious biological drives for food, sex, and other life-sustaining necessities. The id seeks instant gratification without concern for the rights of others. The **ego** develops early in life, when a child begins to learn that his or her wishes cannot be instantly gratified. The ego is the part of the personality that compensates for the demands of the id by helping the individual guide his or her actions to remain within the boundaries of social convention. The **superego** develops as a result of incorporating within the personality the moral standards and values of parents, community, and significant others. It is the moral aspect of people's personalities; it judges their behavior.

The psychodynamic model of the criminal offender depicts an aggressive, frustrated person dominated by events that occurred early in childhood. Because they suffered unhappy experiences in childhood or had families that could not provide proper love and care, criminals suffer from weak or damaged egos that make them

psychodynamic (psychoanalytic) theory
Theory originated by Freud that the human personality is controlled by unconscious mental processes developed early in childhood, involving the interaction of id, ego, and superego.

id
The primitive part of people's mental makeup, present at birth, that represents unconscious biological drives for food, sex, and other life-sustaining necessities. The id seeks instant gratification without concern for the rights of others.

ego
The part of the personality developed in early childhood that helps control the id and keep people's actions within the boundaries of social convention.

superego
Incorporation within the personality of the moral standards and values of parents, community, and significant others.

unable to cope with conventional society. Weak egos are associated with immaturity, poor social skills, and excessive dependence on others. People with weak egos may be easily led into crime by antisocial peers and drug abuse. Some have underdeveloped superegos and consequently lack internalized representations of those behaviors that are punished in conventional society. They commit crimes because they have difficulty understanding the consequences of their actions.[102]

Mental Disorders and Crime

According to the psychodynamic approach, criminal behavior is a function of unconscious mental instability and turmoil. Offenders may suffer from a garden variety of mood and/or behavior **disorders** rendering them histrionic, depressed, antisocial, or narcissistic.[103] Some have been diagnosed with some form of **mood disorders** characterized by disturbance in expressed emotions.

Children with **oppositional defiant disorder (ODD)**, for example, experience an ongoing pattern of uncooperative, defiant, and hostile behavior toward authority figures that seriously interferes with day-to-day functioning. Symptoms of ODD may include frequent loss of temper, constant arguing with adults; defying adults or refusing adult requests or rules; deliberately annoying others; blaming others for mistakes or misbehavior; being angry and resentful; being spiteful or vindictive; swearing or using obscene language; or having a low opinion of yourself.[104]

Children who are diagnosed with conduct disorder (CD), have great difficulty following rules and behaving in a socially acceptable way.[105] They are often viewed by other children, adults, and social agencies as severely antisocial. Research shows that they are frequently involved in such activities as bullying, fighting, committing sexual assaults, and behaving cruelly toward animals.

According to the psychodynamic view, crime is a manifestation of feelings of oppression and the inability to develop the proper psychological defenses and rationales to keep these feelings under control. Criminality enables troubled people to survive by producing positive psychic results: It helps them to feel free and independent, and it gives them the possibility of excitement and the chance to use their skills and imagination.

Crime and Mental Illness

The most serious forms of personality disturbance will result in mental disorders referred to as psychosis, which include severe mental disorders, such as depression, **bipolar disorder** (manic-depression), and schizophrenia. These disorders are characterized by extreme impairment of a person's ability to understand reality, to think clearly, respond emotionally, communicate effectively, and behave appropriately. People with **schizophrenia** may hear nonexistent voices, hallucinate, and make inappropriate behavioral responses. Others exhibit illogical and incoherent thought processes and a lack of insight into their behavior. They may see themselves as agents of the devil, avenging angels, or the recipients of messages from animals and plants.

Some research efforts find that offenders who engage in serious, violent crimes suffer from some sort of mental disturbance, such as depression.[106] Female offenders seem to have more serious mental health symptoms, including schizophrenia, paranoia, and obsessive behaviors, than male offenders.[107] A recent (2003) review of the existing literature on the relationship between psychopathology and delinquent behavior concluded that delinquent adolescents have higher rates of clinical mental disorders when compared to adolescents in the general population.[108] In sum, people who suffer from severe mental illness and distress seem to be more violence-prone than members of the general population.[109]

Although these findings are persuasive, the association between crime and mental illness must be interpreted with some caution. It is possible that the link between mental illness and crime is spurious and caused by some other factor:

- People who suffer from prior social problems (for example, child abuse) may be more likely to commit violent acts and suffer mental illness. The original social problem is the cause of both crime and mental illness.[110]
- Mentally ill people may also be more likely to lack financial resources than the mentally sound. They are therefore forced to reside in deteriorated high-crime neighborhoods, a social factor that may increase criminal behavior.[111] Living in

disorder
Any type of psychological problem (formerly labeled neurotic or psychotic), such as anxiety disorders, mood disorders, and conduct disorders.

mood disorder
A condition in which the prevailing emotional mood is distorted or inappropriate to the circumstances.

oppositional defiant disorder (ODD)
A pattern of negativistic, hostile, and defiant behavior lasting at least six months, during which a child often loses temper, often argues with adults, often actively defies or refuses to comply with adults' requests or rules, often deliberately annoys people, often blames others for his or her mistakes or misbehavior, is often touchy or easily annoyed by others, is often angry and resentful, and is often spiteful or vindictive.

bipolar disorder
An emotional disturbance in which moods alternate between periods of wild elation and deep depression.

schizophrenia
A severe disorder marked by hearing nonexistent voices, seeing hallucinations, and exhibiting inappropriate responses.

Profiles in Crime

Andrea Yates

© David J. Phillip/Pool/Reuters/Corbis

Andrea (Kennedy) Yates was born on July 2, 1964, in Houston, Texas. She seemed to have a successful, normal life, being the class valedictorian, captain of the swim team and a member of the National Honor Society. She graduated from the University of Texas School of Nursing in Houston and worked as a nurse. She worked as a registered nurse at a facility run by the University of Texas. She met and married Rusty Yates, and the couple began to raise a family. Though money was tight and living conditions cramped, the couple had five children in the first eight years of their marriage. The pressure began to take a toll on Andrea, and her mental health deteriorated. On June 17, 1999, after attempting suicide by taking an overdose of pills, she was placed in Houston's Methodist Hospital psychiatric unit and diagnosed with a major depressive disorder. Even though she was medicated with powerful antipsychotics such as Haldol, Andrea continued to have psychotic episodes and was hospitalized for severe depression. Her losing battle with mental illness culminated in an act that shocked the nation: On June 20, 2001, she systematically drowned all five of her children, including her eldest, 7-year-old Noah, who tried to escape after seeing his siblings dead, but was dragged back into the bathroom by his mother and drowned also.

At trial, Yates's defense team attempted to show that she suffered from delusional depression and postpartum mood swings that can sometimes evoke psychosis. Though she drowned her children one by one, even chasing down 7-year-old Noah to drag him to the tub, did she really have any awareness that what she was doing was wrong? This disease affects about 40 percent of all mothers and in its mildest forms leaves new mothers feeling "blue" for a few weeks; more serious cases can last more than a year and involve fatigue, withdrawal, and eating disorders. The most serious form, which Andrea Yates is believed to have suffered, is a psychosis that produces hallucinations, delusions, feelings of worthlessness and inadequacy. Though very uncommon, postpartum psychosis increases the likelihood of both suicide and infanticide if left untreated. Despite her long history of mental illness and psychiatric testimony suggesting she lacked the capacity to understand her actions, the jury found her guilty of murder on March 12, 2002, ordering a life sentence instead of the death penalty sought by the prosecution.

Andrea's conviction was later overturned when a Texas appeals court ruled that an expert witness, Dr. Park Dietz, made a false statement during the trial. (He claimed she might have been influenced by an episode of *Law and Order*, though no such episode ever aired; it was actually *L.A. Law* that dealt with a case of a mother killing her children.) At the time of this writing Andrea remains in a psychiatric facility.

The Andrea Yates case illustrates the association between mental illness and crime. Who could claim that a woman as disturbed as Andrea *chose* to kill her own children? While the jury may have reached that verdict, it was constrained by the legal definition of insanity that relies on the immediate events that took place and not Andrea's long-term mental state that produced this horrible crime.

SOURCES: Andrea Yates, CourtTV Crime Library, www.crimelibrary.com/notorious_murders/women/andrea_yates/index.html (accessed April 3, 2006); CNN, "The Case of Andrea Yates," www.cnn.com/SPECIALS/2001/yates/ (accessed April 3, 2006).

a stress-filled urban environment may produce symptoms of both mental illness and crime.[112]

- The police may be more likely to arrest the mentally ill, giving the illusion that they are crime-prone.[113] The Profiles in Crime in this chapter discusses one of the better known of these cases.

CONNECTIONS

Chapter 1 discussed how some of the early founders of psychiatry tried to understand the criminal mind. Early theories suggested that mental illness and insanity were inherited and that deviants were inherently mentally damaged by their inferior genetic makeup.

Behavioral Perspective: Social Learning Theory

Behavior theory maintains that human actions are developed through learning experiences. The major premise of behavior theory is that people alter their behavior according to the reactions it receives from others: Behavior is supported by rewards and extinguished by negative reactions, or punishments. The behaviorist views crimes, especially violent acts, as learned responses to life situations, which do not necessarily represent abnormality or moral immaturity.

The branch of behavior theory most relevant to criminology is **social learning theory**.[114] Social learning theorists, most notably Albert Bandura, argue that people are not born with the ability to act violently; rather, they learn to be aggressive

behavior theory
The view that all human behavior is learned through a process of social reinforcement (rewards and punishment).

social learning theory
The view that people learn to be aggressive by observing others acting aggressively to achieve some goal or being rewarded for violent acts.

through their life experiences. These experiences include personally observing others acting aggressively to achieve some goal or watching people being rewarded for violent acts on television or in movies. People learn to act aggressively when, as children, they model their behavior after the violent acts of adults. Later in life, these violent behavior patterns persist in social relationships. For example, the boy who sees his father repeatedly strike his mother with impunity is likely to become a battering parent and husband.

Although social learning theorists agree that mental or physical traits may predispose a person toward violence, they believe a person's violent tendencies are activated by factors in the environment. The specific form of aggressive behavior, the frequency with which it is expressed, the situations in which it is displayed, and the specific targets selected for attack are largely determined by social learning. However, people are also self-aware and engage in purposeful learning. Their interpretations of behavior outcomes and situations influence the way they learn from experiences. One adolescent who spends a weekend in jail for drunk driving may find it the most awful experience of her life—one that teaches her never to drink and drive again. Another person, however, may find it an exciting experience about which he can brag to his friends.

Social learning theorists view violence as something learned through a process called **behavior modeling**. In modern society, aggressive acts are usually modeled after three principal sources:

- *Family interactions*. Studies of family life show that aggressive children have parents who use similar tactics when dealing with others. For example, the children of wife batterers are more likely to use aggressive tactics themselves than children in the general population, especially if the victims (their mothers) suffer psychological distress from the abuse.[115]
- *Environmental experiences*. People who reside in areas where violence occurs daily are more likely to act violently than those who dwell in low-crime areas whose norms stress conventional behavior.
- *Mass media*. Films, video games, and television shows commonly depict violence graphically. Moreover, violence is often portrayed as acceptable, especially for heroes who never have to face legal consequences for their actions.[116] Viewing violence is believed to influence behavior in a number of ways, which are summarized in Exhibit 5.3.

Social learning theorists have tried to determine what triggers violent acts. One position is that a direct, pain-producing, physical assault will usually trigger a violent response. Yet the relationship between painful attacks and aggressive responses has been found to be inconsistent. Whether people counterattack depends, in part, on their fighting skill and their perception of the strength of their attackers. Verbal taunts and insults have also been linked to aggressive responses. People who are predisposed to aggression by their learning experiences are likely to view insults from others as a challenge to their social status and to react violently.

In summary, social learning theorists suggest that the following factors may contribute to violent or aggressive behavior:

- *An event that heightens arousal*. For example, a person may frustrate or provoke another through physical assault or verbal abuse.
- *Aggressive skills*. Learned aggressive responses picked up from observing others, either personally or through the media.
- *Expected outcomes*. The belief that aggression will somehow be rewarded. Rewards can come in the form of reducing tension or anger, gaining some financial reward, building self-esteem, or gaining the praise of others.
- *Consistency of behavior with values*. The belief, gained from observing others, that aggression is justified and appropriate, given the circumstances of the current situation.

behavior modeling
The process of learning behavior (notably, aggression) by observing others. Aggressive models may be parents, criminals in the neighborhood, or characters on television or in movies.

Exhibit 5.3

How the Media Influence Violence

- Children learn from what they observe. In the same way they learn cognitive and social skills from their parents and friends, children learn to be violent by watching television.
- Media violence increases the arousal levels of viewers and makes them more prone to act aggressively. Studies measuring the galvanic skin response of subjects—a physical indication of arousal based on the amount of electricity conducted across the palm of the hand—show that viewing violent television increases arousal levels in young children.
- Media violence influences specific areas of the brain, including the precuneus, posterior cingulate, amygdala, inferior parietal, and prefrontal and premotor cortex of the right hemisphere region. These areas of the brain are involved in the regulation of emotion, arousal and attention, episodic memory encoding and retrieval, and motor programming. Extensive viewing may result in a large number of aggressive scripts stored in long-term memory in the posterior cingulate, which can then be used as a guide for social behavior.
- Observing media violence promotes negative attitudes such as suspiciousness and the expectation that the viewer will become involved in violence. Frequent television watchers view aggression and violence as common, socially acceptable behavior.
- Media violence allows aggressive youths to justify their behavior. Rather than causing violence, television may help violent youths rationalize their behavior as socially acceptable.
- Media violence may disinhibit aggressive behavior, which is normally controlled by other learning processes. Disinhibition takes place when adults are viewed as being rewarded for violence and when violence is seen as socially acceptable. This contradicts previous learning experiences in which violent behavior was viewed as wrong.

SOURCES: René Weber, Ute Ritterfeld, and Klaus Mathiak, "Does Playing Violent Video Games Induce Aggression? Empirical Evidence of a Functional Magnetic Resonance Imaging Study," *Media Psychology* 8 (2006): 39–60; John Murray, et al. "Children's Brain Activations While Viewing Televised Violence Revealed by fMRI," *Media Psychology* 8 (2006): 25–37; Dimitri Christakis, Frederick Zimmerman, David DiGiuseppe, and Carolyn McCarty, "Early Television Exposure and Subsequent Attentional Problems in Children," *Pediatrics* 113 (2004): 708–713; UCLA Center for Communication Policy, *Television Violence Monitoring Project* (Los Angeles, 1995); Jonathan Freedman, "Television Violence and Aggression: A Rejoinder," *Psychological Bulletin* 100 (1986): 372–378; Wendy Wood, Frank Wong, and J. Gregory Chachere, "Effects of Media Violence on Viewers' Aggression in Unconstrained Social Interaction," *Psychological Bulletin* 109 (1991): 371–383.

Cognitive Theory

One area of psychology that has received increasing recognition in recent years is **cognitive theory**. Psychologists with a cognitive perspective focus on mental processes—how people perceive and mentally represent the world around them and solve problems. The pioneers of this school were Wilhelm Wundt (1832–1920), Edward Titchener (1867–1927), and William James (1842–1920). Today the cognitive area includes several subdisciplines. The moral development branch is concerned with how people morally represent and reason about the world. Humanistic psychology stresses self-awareness and getting in touch with feelings. **Information-processing theory** focuses on how people process, store, encode, retrieve, and manipulate information to make decisions and solve problems.

When cognitive theorists who study information processing try to explain antisocial behavior, they do so in terms of mental perception and how people use information to understand their environment. When people make decisions, they engage in this sequence of cognitive thought processes: First, they encode information so that it can be interpreted; next, they search for a proper response and decide on the most appropriate action; and finally, they act on their decision.[117]

According to this cognitive approach, people who use information properly, who are better conditioned to make reasoned judgments, and who can make quick and reasoned decisions when facing emotion-laden events are best able to avoid antisocial behavior choices.[118] In contrast, crime-prone people may have cognitive deficits and use information incorrectly when they make decisions.[119] They view crime as an appropriate means to satisfy their immediate personal needs, which take precedence over more distant social needs such as obedience to the law.[120] They are not deterred by the threat of legal punishments because

cognitive theory
Psychological perspective that focuses on mental processes: how people perceive and mentally represent the world around them and solve problems.

information-processing theory
Theory that focuses on how people process, store, encode, retrieve, and manipulate information to make decisions and solve problems.

when they try to calculate the costs and consequences of an action—that is, deciding to commit a crime—they make mistakes because they are imperfect processors of information. As a result of their faulty calculations, they pursue behaviors that they perceive as beneficial and satisfying but which turn out to be harmful and detrimental.[121]

One reason for this faulty reasoning is that they may be relying on mental scripts learned in childhood that tell them how to interpret events, what to expect, how they should react, and what the outcome of the interaction should be.[122] Hostile children may have learned improper scripts by observing how others react to events; their own parents' aggressive, inappropriate behavior would have considerable impact. Some may have had early, prolonged exposure to violence (such as child abuse), which increases their sensitivity to slights and maltreatment. Oversensitivity to rejection by their peers is a continuation of sensitivity to rejection by their parents.[123] Violence becomes a stable behavior because the scripts that emphasize aggressive responses are repeatedly rehearsed as the child matures.

Errors in cognition and information processing have been used to explain the behavior of child abusers. Distorted thinking patterns abusers express include the following:

- *Child as a sexual being*. Children are perceived as being able to and wanting to engage in sexual activity with adults and also as not harmed by such sexual contact.[124]
- *Nature of harm*. The offender perceives that sexual activity does not cause harm (and may in fact be beneficial) to the child.
- *Entitlement*. The child abuser perceives that he is superior and more important than others and hence is able to have sex with whomever, and whenever, he wants.
- *Dangerous world*. An offender perceives that others are abusive and rejecting, and he must fight to regain control.
- *Uncontrollable*. The world is perceived as uncontrollable, and circumstances are outside of his control.

The various psychological theories of crime are set out in Concept Summary 5.2.

Personality and Crime

Personality can be defined as the reasonably stable patterns of behavior, including thoughts and emotions that distinguish one person from another.[125] One's personality reflects a characteristic way of adapting to life's demands and problems. The way we behave is a function of how our personality enables us to interpret life events and make appropriate behavioral choices. Can the cause of crime be linked to personality?

Several research efforts have attempted to identify criminal personality traits. Surveys show that traits such as impulsivity, hostility, narcissism, hedonism, and aggression are highly correlated with criminal and antisocial behaviors.[126] Personality defects have been linked not only to aggressive antisocial behaviors such as assault and rape, but also to white-collar and business crimes.[127] An important effort to categorize the dimensions of a criminal personality is Hans Eysenck's PEN model. He associates two personality traits, extroversion and introversion, with antisocial behavior:

- Extroverts are energetic, enthusiastic, action-oriented, chatty, glib, and self-confident.
- Introverts tend to be quiet, low-key, deliberate, and detached from others.

People who fall at the ends of either trait, either extremely extroverted or extremely introverted, are at risk for antisocial behaviors. For example, extroverts who are also unstable, a condition that Eysenck calls neuroticism, are anxious,

personality
The reasonably stable patterns of behavior, including thoughts and emotions, that distinguish one person from another.

CONCEPT SUMMARY 5.2 Psychological Theories of Crime

THEORY	MAJOR PREMISE	STRENGTHS	RESEARCH FOCUS
Psychodynamic	The development of the unconscious personality early in childhood influences behavior for the rest of a person's life. Criminals have weak egos and damaged personalities.	Explains the onset of crime and why crime and drug abuse cut across class lines.	Mental illness and crime personality
Behavioral	People commit crime when they model their behavior after others they see being rewarded for the same acts. Behavior is reinforced by rewards and extinguished by punishment.	Explains the role of significant others in the crime process. Shows how media can influence crime and violence.	Media and violence; effects of child abuse
Cognitive	Individual reasoning processes influence behavior. Reasoning is influenced by the way people perceive their environment.	Shows why criminal behavior patterns change over time as people mature and develop their reasoning powers. May explain the aging-out process.	Perception; environmental influences

tense, and emotionally unstable.[128] They may act self-destructively, for example, by abusing drugs and repeating their criminal activity over and over.[129]

Psychopathic Personality Some people lack affect, cannot empathize with others, and are short-sighted and hedonistic. These traits make them prone to problems ranging from psychopathology to drug abuse, sexual promiscuity, and violence.[130] As a group, people who share these traits are believed to have a character defect referred to as sociopathic, psychopathic, or **antisocial personality**. Although these terms are often used interchangeably, some psychologists distinguish between sociopaths and psychopaths by suggesting that the former are a product of a destructive home environment, whereas the latter are a product of a defect or aberration within themselves.[131]

Studies of the antisocial personality have been conducted worldwide.[132] There is evidence that offenders with an antisocial personality are crime-prone, respond to frustrating events with strong negative emotions, feel stressed and harassed, and are adversarial in their interpersonal relationships. They maintain "negative emotionality"—a tendency to experience aversive affective states such as anger, anxiety, and irritability. They are also predisposed to weak personal constraints and have difficulty controlling impulsive behavior urges. Because they are both impulsive and aggressive, crime-prone people are quick to act against perceived threats.

A number of factors are believed to contribute to the development of a criminal personality.[133] Some factors are related to improper socialization and include having a psychopathic parent, experiencing parental rejection and lack of love during childhood, and receiving inconsistent discipline. Some psychologists believe the cause is related to neurological or brain dysfunction.[134] They suspect that psychopaths suffer from a low level of arousal as measured by the activity of their autonomic nervous system. It is possible, therefore, that psychopaths are thrill seekers who engage in high-risk antisocial activities to raise their general neurological arousal level. Psychopaths may have brain-related physical anomalies that cause them to process emotional input differently from nonpsychopaths.[135]

Evidence that personality traits predict crime and violence suggests that the root cause of crime can be found in the forces that influence early human development.

antisocial personality
Combination of traits, such as hyperactivity, impulsivity, hedonism, and inability to empathize with others, that make a person prone to deviant behavior and violence; also referred to as sociopathic or psychopathic personality.

If these results are valid, rather than focus on job creation and neighborhood improvement, crime control efforts might be better focused on helping families raise reasoned, reflective children who enjoy a safe environment.

Intelligence and Crime

Early criminologists maintained that many delinquents and criminals have below-average intelligence and that low IQ causes their criminality. Criminals were believed to have inherently substandard intelligence and thus seemed naturally inclined to commit more crimes than more intelligent persons. Furthermore, it was thought that if authorities could determine which individuals had low IQs, they might identify potential criminals before they committed socially harmful acts. These ideas led to the nature versus nurture controversy that continues to rage today.

Nature Theory Proponents of **nature theory** argue that intelligence is largely determined genetically, that ancestry determines IQ, and that low intelligence, as demonstrated by low IQ, is linked to criminal behavior. When newly developed IQ tests were administered to inmates of prisons and juvenile training schools in the first decades of the twentieth century, the nature position gained support because most of the inmates scored low on the tests.[136] In 1926, William Healy and Augusta Bronner tested groups of delinquent boys in Chicago and Boston and found that 37 percent were subnormal in intelligence. They concluded that delinquents were 5 to 10 times more likely to be mentally deficient than normal boys.[137] These and other early studies were embraced as proof that low IQ scores indicated potentially delinquent children and that a correlation existed between innate low intelligence and deviant behavior. IQ tests were believed to measure the inborn genetic makeup of individuals, and many criminologists accepted the idea that individuals with substandard IQs were predisposed toward delinquency and adult criminality.

Nurture Theory Proponents of **nurture theory** argue that intelligence is not inherited and that low-IQ parents do not necessarily produce low-IQ children.[138] Intelligence must be viewed as partly biological but primarily sociological. Nurture theorists discredit the notion that persons commit crimes because they have low IQs. Instead, they postulate that environmental stimulation from parents, relatives, social contacts, schools, peer groups, and innumerable others account for a child's IQ level and that low IQs may result from an environment that also encourages delinquent and criminal behavior. Thus, if low IQ scores are recorded among criminals, these scores may reflect the criminals' cultural background, not their mental ability.

In 1931, Edwin Sutherland evaluated IQ studies of criminals and delinquents and questioned whether criminals in fact have low IQs.[139] Sutherland's research all but put an end to the belief that crime was caused by feeblemindedness; the IQ–crime link was almost forgotten in criminological literature.

IQ and Criminality Although the alleged IQ–crime link was dismissed by mainstream criminologists, it once again became an important area of study when respected criminologists Travis Hirschi and Michael Hindelang published a widely read 1977 article linking the two variables.[140] They proposed the idea that low IQ increases the likelihood of criminal behavior through its effect on school performance. That is, youths with low IQs do poorly in school, and school failure and academic incompetence are highly related to delinquency and later to adult criminality.

Hirschi and Hindelang's inferences have been supported by both U.S. and international research.[141] In their influential book *Crime and Human Nature*, James Q. Wilson and Richard Herrnstein concluded that the IQ–crime link is indirect: Low intelligence leads to poor school performance, which enhances the chances of criminality.[142] In the controversial 1994 book *The Bell Curve*, Herrnstein with Charles Murray confirmed that adolescents with low IQs are

nature theory
The view that intelligence is largely determined genetically and that low intelligence is linked to criminal behavior.

nurture theory
The view that intelligence is not inherited but is largely a product of environment. Low IQ scores do not cause crime but may result from the same environmental factors.

more likely to commit crime, get caught, and be sent to prison. Conversely, at-risk kids with higher IQs seem to be protected from becoming criminals by their superior ability to succeed in school and in social relationships. To those who suggest that the IQ–crime relationship can be explained by the fact that only low-IQ criminals get caught, Herrnstein and Murray counter with data showing little difference in IQ scores between self-reported and official criminals.[143] This means that even criminals whose activities go undetected have lower IQs than the general public; the IQ–crime relationship cannot be explained away by the fact that slow-witted criminals are the ones most likely to be apprehended.

Although these reviews supported an IQ–crime link, a number of studies have found that intelligence has negligible influence on criminal behavior.[144] An evaluation of research on intelligence conducted by the American Psychological Association concluded that the strength of an IQ–crime link is "very low."[145]

The IQ–criminality debate is unlikely to be settled soon. Measurement is beset by many methodological problems. The well-documented criticisms suggesting that IQ tests are race and class biased would certainly influence the testing of the criminal population, which is besieged with a multitude of social and economic problems. Even if it can be shown that known offenders have lower IQs than the general population, it is difficult to explain many patterns in the crime rate: Why are there more male than female criminals? Why do crime rates vary by region, time of year, and even weather patterns? Why does aging out occur? IQ does not increase with age, so why should crime rates fall? ✔ CHECKPOINTS

✔ CHECKPOINTS

✔ According to psychodynamic theory, unconscious motivations developed early in childhood propel some people into destructive or illegal behavior.

✔ Behaviorists view aggression as a learned behavior.

✔ Learning may be either direct and experiential or observational, such as watching TV and movies.

✔ Cognitive theory stresses knowing and perception. Some people have a warped view of the world.

✔ Some evidence suggests that people with abnormal or antisocial personalities are crime-prone.

✔ Although some criminologists find a link between intelligence and crime, others dispute any linkage between IQ level and law-violating behaviors.

SOCIAL POLICY AND TRAIT THEORY

For most of the twentieth century, biological and psychological views of criminality have influenced crime control and prevention policy. The result has been front-end or **primary prevention programs** that seek to treat personal problems before they manifest themselves as crime. To this end, thousands of family therapy organizations, substance abuse clinics, and mental health associations operate throughout the United States. Teachers, employers, courts, welfare agencies, and others make referrals to these facilities.

These services are based on the premise that if a person's problems can be treated before they become overwhelming, some future crimes will be prevented. **Secondary prevention programs** provide treatment such as psychological counseling to youths and adults after they have violated the law. Attendance at such programs may be a requirement of a probation order, part of a diversionary sentence, or aftercare at the end of a prison sentence.

Biologically oriented therapy is also being used in the criminal justice system. Programs have altered diets, changed lighting, compensated for learning disabilities, treated allergies, and so on.[146] More controversial has been the use of mood-altering chemicals, such as lithium, pemoline, imipramine, phenytoin, and benzodiazepines, to control behavior. Another practice that has elicited concern is the use of psychosurgery (brain surgery) to control antisocial behavior. Surgical procedures have been used to alter the brain structure of convicted sex offenders in an effort to eliminate or control their sex drives. Results are still preliminary, but some critics argue that these procedures are without scientific merit.[147]

Numerous psychologically based treatment methods range from individual counseling to behavior modification. Treatment based on how people process information takes into account that people are more likely to respond aggressively to provocation if thoughts intensify the insult or otherwise stir feelings of anger. Cognitive therapists attempt to teach explosive people to control aggressive impulses by viewing social provocations as problems demanding a solution rather than retaliation. Programs are aimed at teaching problem-solving skills that may include self-disclosure, role playing, listening, following instructions, joining in, and using

primary prevention programs
Programs, such as substance abuse clinics and mental health associations, that seek to treat personal problems before they manifest themselves as crime.

secondary prevention programs
Programs that provide treatment such as psychological counseling to youths and adults after they have violated the law.

● Prevention programs based on trait theory are aimed at treating the individual rather than improving the environment. A student identified only as Brandon leads workshop coordinator Silvia Dos Santos, left, during a class at the Judge Rotenberg Educational Center in Canton, Massachusetts, May 25, 2006. The center is a special needs school, teaching students with behavioral, psychiatric, and autistic-like problems ranging from moderate to lower functioning levels. The school is unique in that it uses a low-level electric shock program to control behavior.

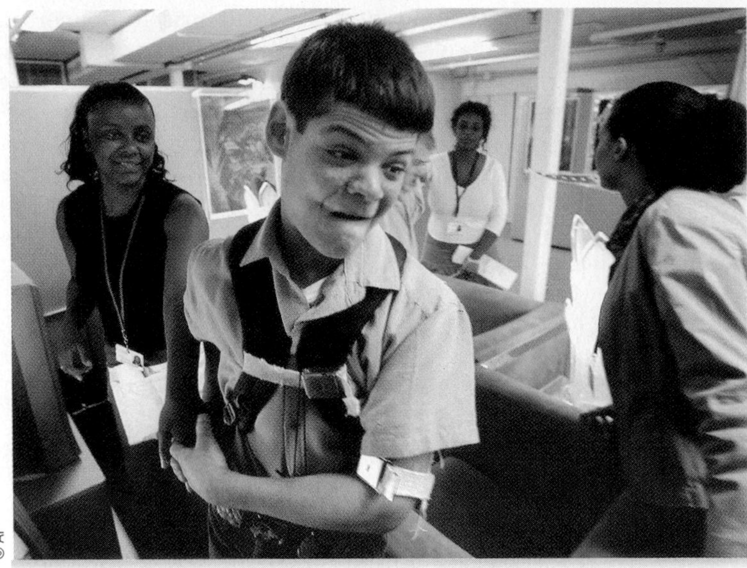

© AP

self-control.[148] Therapeutic interventions designed to make people better problem solvers may involve measures that enhance

- Coping and problem-solving skills
- Relationships with peers, parents, and other adults
- Conflict resolution and communication skills, and methods for resisting peer pressure related to drug use and violence
- Consequential thinking and decision-making abilities
- Prosocial behaviors, including cooperation with others, self-responsibility, respecting others, and public speaking efficacy
- Empathy[149]

THINKING Like a Criminologist

Fourteen-year-old Daphne A. is a product of Boston's best private schools; she lives with her wealthy family on Beacon Hill. Her father is an executive at a local financial services conglomerate and makes close to $1 million per year. Daphne, however, has a hidden, darker side. She is always in trouble at school, and teachers report that she is impulsive and has poor self-control. At times, she can be kind and warm, but on other occasions she is obnoxious, unpredictable, insecure, and craves attention. She is overly self-conscious about her body and has a drinking problem. Daphne attends AA meetings and is on the waiting list at High Cliff Village, a residential substance abuse treatment program. Her parents seem intimidated by her and confused by her complexities; her father even filed a harassment complaint against her once, saying she had slapped him.

Despite repeated promises to get her life together, Daphne likes to hang out most nights in the Public Gardens and drink with neighborhood kids. On more than one occasion she went to the park with her friend and confidant Christopher G., a quiet boy who had his own set of personal problems. His parents had separated and subsequently he began to suffer severe anxiety attacks. He stayed home from school and was diagnosed with depression for which he took two drugs—Zoloft, an antidepressant, and Lorazepam, a sedative.

One night Daphne and Chris met up with Michael M., a 44-year-old man with a long history of alcohol problems. After a night of drinking, a fight broke out and Michael was stabbed, his throat cut, and his body dumped in the pond. Daphne was quickly arrested when soon after the attack she placed a 911 call to police, telling them that a friend had "jumped in the lake and didn't come out." Police searched the area and found Michael's slashed and stabbed body in the water; he had been disemboweled by Chris and Daphne in an attempt to sink the body.

At a waiver hearing, Daphne admitted that she had participated in the killing but could not articulate what caused her to get involved. She had been drinking and remembers little of the events. She said she was flirting with Michael, and Chris stabbed him in a jealous rage. She speaks in a flat hollow voice and

(continued)

shows little remorse for her actions. It was a spur of the moment thing, she claims, and after all it was Chris who had the knife and not her. Later, Chris testifies, and claims that Daphne instigated the fight and egged him on, taunting him that he was too scared to kill someone. Chris says that Daphne, while drunk, often talked of killing an adult because she hated older people, especially her parents.

Daphne's parents claim that although she has been a burden with her mood swings and volatile behavior, she is still a child and can be helped with proper treatment. They are willing to supplement any state intervention with privately funded psychiatrists. Given that this is her first real offense and because of her age (14), the parents believe home confinement with intense treatment is the best course.

The district attorney wants Daphne treated as an adult and waived to adult court where, if she is found guilty, she can receive a 25-year sentence on second-degree murder; there is little question of her legal culpability.

As a criminologist, you are asked by a juvenile court judge to help her make a suitable disposition of this case. Would you conclude that Daphne's crime was a function of some abnormal trait or condition that is amenable to treatment? Or is she a calculating criminal who should be locked away in prison?

Summary

- The earliest positivist criminologists were biologists.
- Led by Cesare Lombroso, early researchers believed that some people manifested primitive traits that made them born criminals.
- Today the research by Lombroso and his followers is debunked because of poor methodology, testing, and logic.
- Biological views fell out of favor in the early twentieth century. In the 1970s, spurred by the publication of Edmund O. Wilson's *Sociobiology*, several criminologists again turned to study of the biological basis of criminality. For the most part, the effort has focused on the cause of violent crime.
- One area of interest is biochemical factors, such as diet, allergies, hormonal imbalances, and environmental contaminants (such as lead). The conclusion is that the propensity to commit crime, especially violence, may be influenced by diet, vitamin intake, or hormonal imbalance.
- Neurophysiological factors, such as brain disorders, ADHD, EEG abnormalities, tumors, and head injuries have been linked to crime. Criminals and delinquents often suffer brain impairment, as measured by the EEG. Attention deficit hyperactivity disorder and minimal brain dysfunction are related to antisocial behavior.
- Some biocriminologists believe that the tendency to commit violent acts is inherited. Research has been conducted with twin pairs and adopted children to determine whether genes are related to behaviors.
- A branch of biological theory takes an evolutionary view that holds that changes in the human condition, which have taken millions of years to evolve, may help explain crime rate differences. As the human race evolved, traits and characteristics have become ingrained.
- The psychodynamic view, developed by Sigmund Freud, links aggressive behavior to personality conflicts arising from childhood.
- The development of the unconscious personality early in childhood influences behavior for the rest of a person's life. Criminals have weak egos and damaged personalities.
- According to some psychoanalysts, psychotics are aggressive, unstable people who can easily become involved in crime.
- Cognitive psychology is concerned with human development and how people perceive the world. Criminality is viewed as a function of improper information processing. Individual reasoning processes influence behavior. Reasoning is influenced by the way people perceive their environment.
- Behavioral and social learning theorists see criminality as a learned behavior. Children who are exposed to violence and see it rewarded may become violent as adults. People commit crime when they model their behavior after others they see being rewarded for the same acts. Behavior is reinforced by rewards and extinguished by punishment.
- Psychological traits such as personality and intelligence have been linked to criminality. One important area of study has been the antisocial personality, a person who lacks emotion and concern for others.
- The controversial issue of the relationship of IQ to criminality has been resurrected once again with the publication of research studies purporting to show that criminals have lower IQs than noncriminals.

Take a Post-Test. Visit www.thomsonedu.com/criminaljustice/siegel and take the chapter Post-Test to monitor your progress and identify areas for further improvement. In addition to discovering what you've mastered, you'll learn which concepts need your added attention and get specific page references that direct you to the places in the text where you can find more information on them.

Key Terms

trait theory 93
sociobiology 94
equipotentiality 94
hypoglycemia 96
androgens 97
testosterone 97
premenstrual syndrome (PMS) 97
neurophysiology 98
attention deficit hyperactivity disorder (ADHD) 100
conduct disorder (CD) 101
neurotransmitters 101
arousal theory 101
monozygotic (MZ) twins 103
dizygotic (DZ) twins 103
contagion effect 103
cheater theory 105
psychodynamic (psychoanalytic) theory 107
id 107
ego 107
superego 107
disorder 108
mood disorder 108
oppositional defiant disorder (ODD) 108
bipolar disorder 108
schizophrenia 108
behavior theory 109
social learning theory 109
behavior modeling 110
cognitive theory 111
information-processing theory 111
personality 112
antisocial personality 113
nature theory 114
nurture theory 114
primary prevention programs 115
secondary prevention programs 115

Critical Thinking Questions

1. If research could show that the tendency to commit crime is inherited, what should be done with the young children of violence-prone criminals? Would it be unfair to monitor their behavior from an early age?

2. Considering the evidence on the association between media and crime, would you recommend that young children be forbidden to view films with violent content?

3. Knowing what you do about trends and patterns in crime, how would you counteract the assertion that people who commit crime are physically or mentally abnormal?

4. Aside from becoming a criminal, what other career paths are open to psychopaths?

5. Should sugar be banned from school lunches?

6. Can gender differences in the crime rate be explained by evolutionary factors? Do you agree that male aggression is linked to mating patterns developed millions of years ago?

Social Structure Theory: Because They're Poor

CHAPTER 6

© Elmer Martinez/AFP/Getty Images

THE TINY COUNTRY OF EL SALVADOR (POPULATION 6.6 MILLION) IS HOME TO MORE THAN 40,000 GANG MEMBERS. Rather than being a homegrown phenomenon, gangs are actually a U.S. import. How did this happen? In the early 1990s, hundreds of members of two of the largest gangs in Los Angeles, the 18th Street gang and the MS-13 gang, who had illegally made their home in the United States, were deported back to El Salvador. The deportees brought Los Angeles gang culture with them to a country already swamped with weapons from an ongoing civil war. Now on their home turf, gang boys recruited thousands of local teenagers into their reconstituted gangs. Joining a gang gives these poor, urban teenagers a powerful sense of identity and belonging. They were also free now to show their courage and manhood by engaging in a never-ending turf war with one another.

Ironically, both gangs were started in Los Angeles by Salvadorans fleeing a civil war. When they first arrived in Los Angeles, they were preyed upon by preexisting Mexican gangs. The MS-13 gang was formed as a means of self-protection. The name

Refer to the front endpapers for a study tool that summarizes each of the major theories discussed in this book.

CHAPTER OBJECTIVES

1. Be familiar with the concept of social structure.
2. Have knowledge of the socioeconomic structure of American society.
3. Be able to discuss the concept of social disorganization.
4. Be familiar with the works of Shaw and McKay.
5. Know what is meant by concentric zone theory.
6. Know the various elements of ecological theory.
7. Be able to discuss the association between collective efficacy and crime.
8. Be familiar with the concept of strain.
9. Know what is meant by the term "anomie."
10. Understand the concept of cultural deviance.

Take a Pre-Test. Visit www.thomsonedu.com/criminaljustice/siegel and take a Pre-Test to determine what you already know and identify the areas where you'll need to focus your study. The program will direct you to specific pages within the text where you can find further information on the correct answers to the questions you've missed.

refers to a *mara*, Spanish for "posse," or gang. *Salvatruchas* is local slang for being alert and ready to take action; the "13" is a reference to their beginnings on 13th street in Los Angeles.

Over time, both gangs' ranks grew, and members entered a variety of rackets, from extortion to drug trafficking. When law enforcement cracked down and deported members, the deportees quickly created outposts in El Salvador and throughout Central America. The Salvadoran government has responded by criminalizing gang membership and arresting thousands. But government efforts have not stemmed the tide of recruitment, and the gangs appear to be more popular than ever.[1] In the United States, gang membership has continued to grow, and, ironically, the Salavdoran gangs have returned to set up branches in the United States. Some experts believe that the 10,000-member MS-13 is now the nation's most dangerous gang, while others claim that the 18th street gang, with over 20,000 members, is the largest. Both are part of a significant national gang population, estimated to exceed 24,000 individual gangs, with 750,000 members, located in more than 2,000 cities; 90 percent of the largest cities (over 100,000 population) report gang activity.[2]

To criminologists it comes as no surprise that gangs develop in poor, deteriorated urban neighborhoods. Many kids in these areas grow up hopeless and alienated, believing that they have little chance of being part of the American Dream.[3] Joining a gang holds the promise of economic rewards and status enhancements that the conventional world simply cannot provide. Kids who become criminals are indigent and desperate people rather than abnormal, calculating, or evil. Raised in deteriorated parts of town, they lack the social support and economic resources available to more affluent members of society. To understand criminal behavior, we must analyze the influence of these destructive social forces on human behavior. According to this view, it is *social forces*—and not individual traits—that cause crime.

ECONOMIC STRUCTURE AND CRIME

According to some criminologists, the key to understanding the root cause of crime can be found in the nation's socioeconomic makeup. People in the United States live in a **stratified society**. Social strata are created by the unequal distribution of wealth, power, and prestige. **Social classes** are segments of the population whose members have a relatively similar portion of desirable things and who share attitudes, values, norms, and an identifiable lifestyle. In U.S. society, it is common to identify people as upper-, middle-, and lower-class citizens, with a broad range of economic variations existing within each group. The upper-upper class is reserved for a small number of exceptionally well-to-do families who maintain enormous financial and social resources. In contrast, as Figure 6.1 shows, there are now 37 million Americans living in poverty, defined as a family of four earning about $20,000 per year, who have scant, if any, resources and suffer socially and economically as a result. Today, the poorest fifth (20 percent) of all U.S. households receive 3.5 percent of the country's aggregate income, the smallest share ever. In contrast, the top fifth

stratified society
People grouped according to economic or social class; characterized by the unequal distribution of wealth, power, and prestige.

social class
Segment of the population whose members are at a relatively similar economic level and who share attitudes, values, norms, and an identifiable lifestyle.

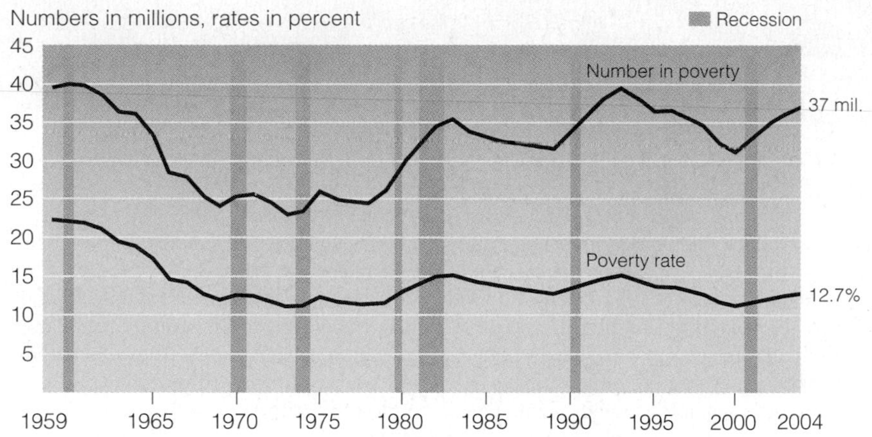

Figure 6.1
Number in Poverty and Poverty Rate
Note: The data points are placed at the midpoints of the respective years.
SOURCE: U.S. Census Bureau, Current Population Survey, 1960–2005 Annual Social and Economic Supplements.

(20 percent) of households receive more than 50 percent of all income, a record high; the top 5 percent collect more than 20 percent of all household income, the most in history.[4] Nor is the wealth concentration effect unique to the United States; it is a worldwide phenomenon: According to the most recent World Wealth Report, there are about 8 million high net worth individuals in the world today (people with more than $1 million in assets excluding their primary residence); they have a net worth of more than $30.8 trillion; and their numbers are steadily growing.[5]

Problems of the Lower Class

In 1966 sociologist Oscar Lewis argued that the crushing lifestyle of lower-class areas produces a **culture of poverty** that is passed from one generation to the next.[6] Apathy, cynicism, helplessness, and mistrust of social institutions, such as schools, government agencies, and the police, mark the culture of poverty. This mistrust prevents the inner-city poor from taking advantage of the meager opportunities available to them. Lewis's work was the first of a group of studies that described the plight of at-risk children and adults. In 1970 Swedish economist Gunnar Myrdal described a worldwide **underclass** that was cut off from society, its members lacking the education and skills needed to function successfully in modern society.[7]

Lower-class areas are scenes of inadequate housing and health care, disrupted family lives, underemployment, and despair. Members of the lower class also suffer in other ways. They are more prone to depression, less likely to have achievement motivation, and less likely to put off immediate gratification for future gain. Members of the lower classes may be less willing to stay in school because the rewards for educational achievement are in the distant future.

Child Poverty

Economic disadvantage and poverty can be especially devastating to younger children.[8] This is particularly important today because, as Figure 6.2 shows, children have a higher poverty rate than any other age group.

Children are hit especially hard by poverty. Children who grow up in low-income homes are less likely to achieve in school and are less likely to complete their schooling than children with more affluent parents.[9] Poor children are also more likely to suffer from health problems and to receive inadequate health care. The number of U.S. children covered by health insurance is declining and will continue to do so for the foreseeable future.[10] Without health benefits or the means to afford medical care, these children are likely to have health problems that impede their long-term development.

culture of poverty
A separate lower-class culture, characterized by apathy, cynicism, helplessness, and mistrust of social institutions such as schools, government agencies, and the police that is passed from one generation to the next.

underclass
The lowest social stratum in any country, whose members lack the education and skills needed to function successfully in modern society.

Race, Culture, Gender, & Criminology

Bridging the Racial Divide

William Julius Wilson, one of the nation's most prominent sociologists, has produced an impressive body of work detailing racial problems and racial politics in American society. In 1987 he described the plight of the lowest levels of the underclass, which he labeled the "truly disadvantaged." Wilson portrayed members of this group as socially isolated people who dwell in urban inner cities, occupy the bottom rung of the social ladder, and are the victims of discrimination. They live in areas in which the basic institutions of society—family, schools, housing—have long since declined. Their decline triggers similar breakdowns in the strengths of inner-city areas, including the loss of both community cohesion and the ability of people living in the area to control the flow of drugs and criminal activity. For example, in a more affluent area, neighbors might complain to parents that their children were acting out. In distressed areas, this element of informal social control may be absent because parents are under stress or, all too often, are absent. These effects magnify the isolation of the underclass from mainstream society and promote a ghetto culture and behavior.

Since the truly disadvantaged rarely come into contact with the actual source of their oppression, they direct their anger and aggression at those with whom they are in close and intimate contact, such as neighbors, businesspeople, and landlords. Members of this group, plagued by under- or unemployment, begin to lose self-confidence, a feeling supported by the plight of kin and friendship groups who also experience extreme economic marginality. Self-doubt is a neighborhood norm, overwhelming those forced to live in areas of concentrated poverty.

In his important book *When Work Disappears*, Wilson assesses the effect of joblessness and underemployment on residents in poor neighborhoods on Chicago's south side. He argues that for the first time in the twentieth century, most adults in inner-city ghetto neighborhoods are not working during a typical week. He finds that inner-city life is only marginally affected by the surge in the nation's economy, which has been brought about by new industrial growth connected with technological development. Poverty in these inner-city areas is eternal and unchanging and, if anything, worsening as residents are further shut out of the economic mainstream.

Wilson focuses on the plight of the African American community, which had enjoyed periods of relative prosperity in the 1950s and 1960s. He suggests that as difficult as life was for African Americans in the 1940s and 1950s, they at least had a reasonable hope of steady work. Now, because of the globalization of the economy, those opportunities have evaporated. Though in the past, opportunities had been limited by racial segregation, growth in the manufacturing sector fueled upward mobility and provided the foundation of today's African American middle class. Those opportunities no longer exist, as manufacturing plants have moved to inaccessible rural and overseas locations where the cost of doing business is lower. With manufacturing opportunities all but obsolete in the United States, service and retail establishments, which depended on blue-collar spending, have similarly disappeared, leaving behind an economy based on welfare and government supports. In less than 20 years, formerly active African American communities have become crime-infested slums.

The hardships faced by residents on Chicago's south side are not unique to that community. Beyond sustaining inner-city poverty, the absence of employment opportunities has torn at the social fabric of the nation's inner-city neighborhoods. Jobs help socialize young people into the wider society, instilling in them such desirable values as hard work, caring, and respect for others.

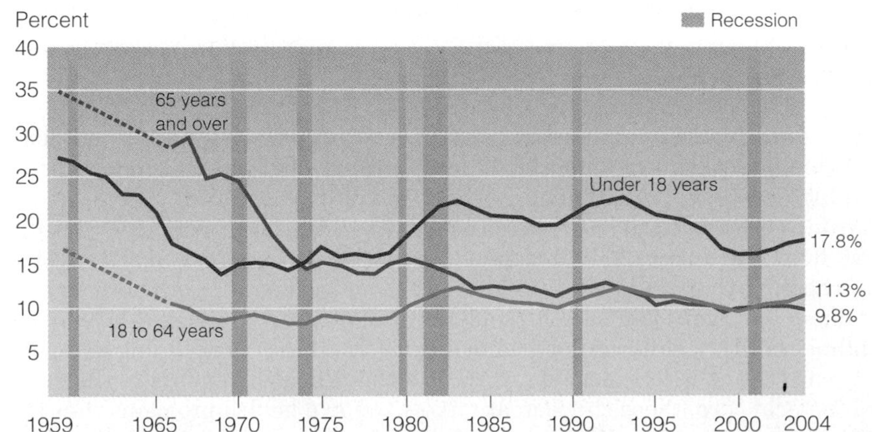

Figure 6.2

Poverty by Age

Children have a significantly higher poverty rate than adults.

Note: The data points represent the midpoints of the respective years. Data for people 18 to 64 and 65 and older are not available from 1960 to 1965.

SOURCE: U.S. Census Bureau, Current Population Survey, 1960–2003 Annual Social and Economic Supplements.

When work becomes scarce, however, the discipline and structure it provides are absent. Community-wide underemployment destroys social cohesion, increasing the presence of neighborhood social problems ranging from drug use to educational failure. Schools in these areas are unable to teach basic skills, and because desirable employment is lacking, there are few adults to serve as role models. In contrast to more affluent suburban households where daily life is organized around job and career demands, children in inner-city areas are not socialized in the workings of the mainstream economy.

In another book, *The Bridge over the Racial Divide: Rising Inequality and Coalition Politics*, Wilson expands further on his views of race in contemporary society. He argues that despite economic gains, inequality is growing in American society, and ordinary families, of all races and ethnic origins, are suffering. Whites, Latinos, African Americans, Asians, and Native Americans must therefore begin to put aside their differences and concentrate more on what they have in common—their aspirations, problems, and hopes. Mutual cooperation across racial lines is essential.

One reason for this set of mutual problems is that the government tends to aggravate rather than ease the financial stress being placed on ordinary families. Monetary policy, trade policy, and tax policy are harmful to working-class families. A multiracial citizens' coalition could pressure national public officials to focus on the interests of ordinary people. As long as middle- and working-class groups are fragmented along racial lines, such pressure is impossible.

Wilson finds that racism is becoming more subtle and harder to detect. Whites believe African Americans are responsible for their own inferior economic status because of their cultural traits. Because even affluent whites fear corporate downsizing, they are unwilling to vote for governmental assistance to the poor. Whites are continuing to be suburban dwellers, further isolating poor minorities in central cities and making their problems distant and unimportant. Wilson believes that the changing marketplace, with its reliance on sophisticated computer technologies, continually decreases demand for low-skilled workers, which has a larger negative impact on African Americans than on other, better educated and affluent groups.

Wilson argues for a cross-race, class-based alliance of working- and middle-class Americans to pursue policies that will benefit them rather than the affluent. These policies include full employment, programs to help families and workers in their private lives, and a reconstructed "affirmative opportunity" program that benefits African Americans without antagonizing whites.

Critical Thinking

1. Is it unrealistic to assume that a government-sponsored public works program can provide needed jobs in this era of budget cutbacks?
2. What are some hidden costs of unemployment in a community setting?
3. How would a biocriminologist explain Wilson's findings?

InfoTrac College Edition Research

For more on Wilson's view of poverty, unemployment, and crime, check out Gunnar Almgren, Avery Guest, George Immerwahr, and Michael Spittel, "Joblessness, Family Disruption, and Violent Death in Chicago, 1970–90," *Social Forces* 76 (June 1998): 1,465; William Julius Wilson, "Inner-City Dislocations," *Society* 35 (Jan–Feb 1998): 270.

SOURCES: William Julius Wilson, *The Truly Disadvantaged* (Chicago: University of Chicago Press, 1987); Wilson, *When Work Disappears, The World of the Urban Poor* (New York: Alfred Knopf, 1996); Wilson, *The Bridge over the Racial Divide: Rising Inequality and Coalition Politics*, (Berkeley: University of California Press, 1999).

Minority Group Poverty

The burdens of underclass life are most often felt most acutely by minority group members. While many whites use their economic, social, and political advantages to live in sheltered gated communities safeguarded by security guards and police, minorities are denied similar protections and privileges.[11] The issue of minority poverty is explored further in the Race, Culture, Gender, & Criminology feature above.

Although poverty has actually been declining faster among minorities than among whites, more than 20 percent of African Americans and Latino Americans still live in poverty, compared to less than 10 percent of whites. According to the U.S. Census Bureau, the median family income of Latinos and African Americans is two-thirds that of whites.[12]

Among recent findings about the plight suffered by young minority males are the following:

- The share of young black men without jobs has climbed relentlessly, with only a slight pause during the economic peak of the late 1990s. In 2000,

CONNECTIONS

Concern about the ecological distribution of crime, the effect of social change, and the interactive nature of crime itself has made sociology the foundation of modern criminology. This chapter reviews sociological theories that emphasize the relationship between social status and criminal behavior. In Chapter 7 the focus shifts to theories that emphasize socialization and its influence on crime and deviance; Chapter 8 covers theories based on the concept of social conflict.

65 percent of black male high school dropouts in their 20s were jobless—that is, unable to find work, not seeking it, or incarcerated. By 2004, the share had grown to 72 percent, compared with 34 percent of white and 19 percent of Hispanic dropouts. Even when high school graduates were included, half of black men in their 20s were jobless in 2004, up from 46 percent in 2000.

- Incarceration rates climbed in the 1990s and reached historic highs in the past few years. In 1995, 16 percent of black men in their 20s who did not attend college were in jail or prison; by 2004, 21 percent were incarcerated. By their mid-30s, 6 in 10 black men who had dropped out of school had spent time in prison.
- In the inner cities, more than half of all black males do not finish high school.[13]

These economic and social disparities continually haunt members of the minority underclass and their children. Even if they value education and other middle-class norms, their desperate life circumstances (including high unemployment and nontraditional family structures) may prevent them from developing the skills and habits that lead first to educational success and later to success in the workplace; these deficits have been linked to crime and drug abuse.[14]

Interracial differences in the crime rate could be significantly reduced by improving levels of education, lowering levels of poverty, and reducing the extent of male unemployment among minority populations.[15]

Poverty and Crime

According to this view, the root cause of crime can be traced directly to the socioeconomic disadvantages that have become embedded in American society. The social problems found in lower-class areas have been described as an "epidemic" that spreads like a contagious disease, destroying the inner workings that enable neighborhoods to survive; they become "hollowed out."[16] As neighborhood quality decreases, the probability that residents will develop problems sharply increases. Because they lack ties to the mainstream culture, some lower-class people are driven to desperate measures, such as crime and substance abuse, to cope with their economic plight.[17] Crime and violence may also take the form of a "slow epidemic," with a period, depending on the neighborhood, of onset, peak, and decline. Violence and crime have been found to spread and then contract in a pattern similar to a contagious disease epidemic.[18] When lower-class kids are exposed to a continual stream of violence, they are more likely to engage in violent acts themselves.[19]

Aggravating this dynamic is the constant media bombardment linking material possessions to self-worth. Because they are unable to attain desired goods and services through conventional means, members of the lower-class may turn to illegal solutions to their economic plight: They may deal drugs for profit, steal cars and sell them to "chop shops," or commit armed robberies for desperately needed funds. They may become so depressed that they take alcohol and drugs as a form of self-tranquilization, and because of their poverty, they may acquire the drugs and alcohol through illegal channels.

SOCIAL STRUCTURE THEORIES

Criminologists who view disadvantaged economic class position as a primary cause of crime are referred to as social structure theorists. As a group, **social structure theories** suggest that social and economic forces operating in deteriorated lower-class areas push many of their residents into criminal behavior patterns. These theories consider the existence of unsupervised teenage gangs, high crime rates, and social disorder in poor inner-city areas as major social problems. Because crime rates are higher in lower-class urban centers than in middle-class suburbs, social forces must influence or control behavior.[20]

social structure theory
The view that disadvantaged economic class position is a primary cause of crime.

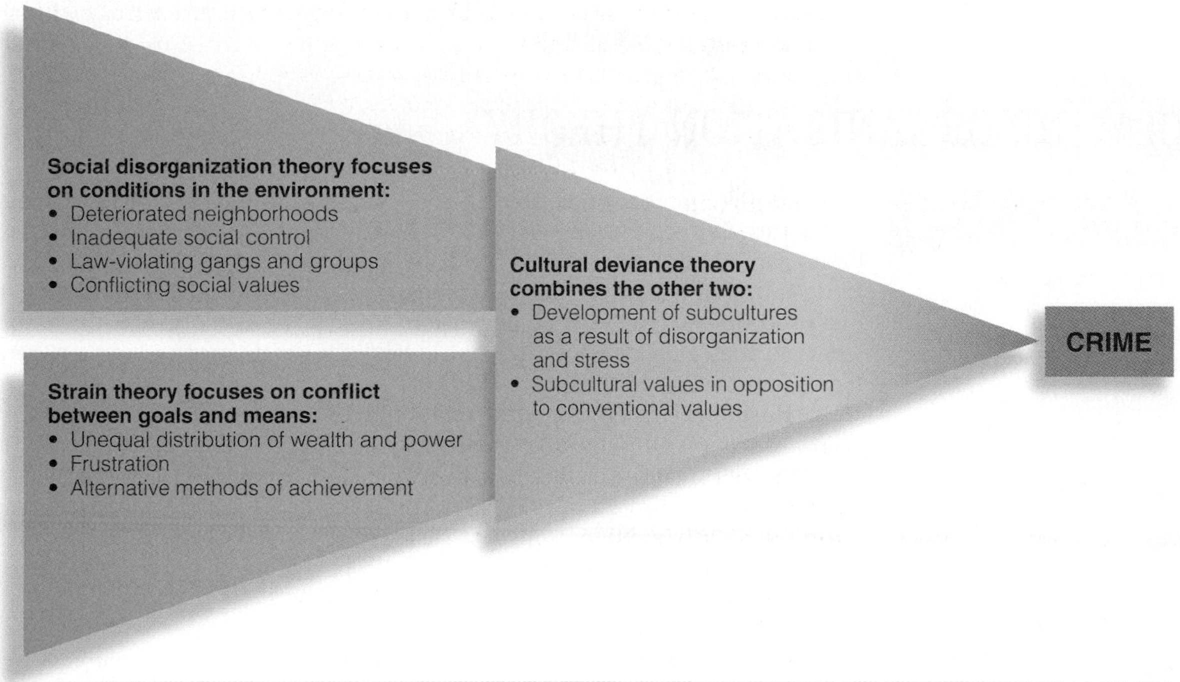

Social disorganization theory focuses on conditions in the environment:
- Deteriorated neighborhoods
- Inadequate social control
- Law-violating gangs and groups
- Conflicting social values

Strain theory focuses on conflict between goals and means:
- Unequal distribution of wealth and power
- Frustration
- Alternative methods of achievement

Cultural deviance theory combines the other two:
- Development of subcultures as a result of disorganization and stress
- Subcultural values in opposition to conventional values

CRIME

Figure 6.3
The Three Branches of Social Structure Theory

The social structure perspective encompasses three independent yet overlapping branches: social disorganization theory, strain theory, and cultural deviance theory. These three branches are summarized in Figure 6.3.

Social disorganization theory focuses on the urban conditions that affect crime rates. A disorganized area is one in which institutions of social control, such as the family, commercial establishments, and schools, have broken down and can no longer perform their expected or stated functions. Indicators of social disorganization include high unemployment and school dropout rates, deteriorated housing, low income levels, and large numbers of single-parent households. Residents in these areas experience conflict and despair, and, as a result, antisocial behavior flourishes.

Strain theory holds that crime is a function of the conflict between people's goals and the means they can use to obtain them. Strain theorists argue that although social and economic goals are common to people in all economic strata, the ability to obtain these goals is class dependent. Most people in the United States desire wealth, material possessions, power, prestige, and other life comforts. Members of the lower class are unable to achieve these symbols of success through conventional means. Consequently, they feel anger, frustration, and resentment, referred to collectively as **strain**. Lower-class citizens can either accept their conditions and live as socially responsible but unrewarded citizens, or they can choose an alternative means of achieving success, such as theft, violence, or drug trafficking.

Cultural deviance theory combines elements of both strain and social disorganization theories. According to this view, because of strain and social isolation, a unique lower-class culture develops in disorganized neighborhoods. These independent **subcultures** maintain unique values and beliefs that conflict with conventional social norms. Criminal behavior is an expression of conformity to lower-class subcultural values and traditions, not a rebellion from conventional society. Subcultural values are handed down from one generation to the next in a process called **cultural transmission**.

Although each of these theories is distinct in critical aspects, each approach has at its core the view that socially isolated people, living in disorganized neighborhoods, are likely to experience crime-producing social forces. In the

social disorganization theory
Branch of social structure theory that focuses on the breakdown of institutions such as the family, school, and employment in inner-city neighborhoods.

strain theory
Branch of social structure theory that sees crime as a function of the conflict between people's goals and the means available to obtain them.

strain
The anger, frustration, and resentment experienced by people who believe they cannot achieve their goals through legitimate means.

cultural deviance theory
Branch of social structure theory that sees strain and social disorganization together resulting in a unique lower-class culture that conflicts with conventional social norms.

subculture
A set of values, beliefs, and traditions unique to a particular social class or group within a larger society.

cultural transmission
Process whereby values, beliefs, and traditions are handed down from one generation to the next.

remainder of this chapter, each branch of social structure theory will be discussed in some detail. ✔ CHECKPOINTS

SOCIAL DISORGANIZATION THEORY

✔ CHECKPOINTS

✔ Because crime rates are higher in lower-class areas, many criminologists believe that the causes of crime are rooted in socioeconomic factors.

✔ Despite economic headway, there are still more than 37 million indigent Americans. Minority groups are more likely than the white majority to be poor.

✔ Some criminologists believe that destructive social forces in poverty areas are responsible for high crime rates.

✔ The strain and frustration caused by poverty are a suspected cause of crime.

✔ Indigents may become involved in a deviant subculture that sustains and supports criminality.

Social disorganization theory links crime rates to neighborhood ecological characteristics. Crime rates are elevated in highly transient, mixed-use (where residential and commercial property exist side by side), and changing neighborhoods in which the fabric of social life has become frayed. These localities are unable to provide essential services, such as education, health care, and proper housing, and as a result, they experience significant levels of unemployment, single-parent families, and families on welfare.

Residents in crime-ridden neighborhoods try to leave at the earliest opportunity. As a result they are uninterested in community matters; so the common sources of control—the family, school, business community, social service agencies—are weak and disorganized. Personal relationships are strained because neighbors are constantly moving. Constant resident turnover weakens communications and blocks attempts at solving neighborhood problems or establishing common goals (see Figure 6.4).[21]

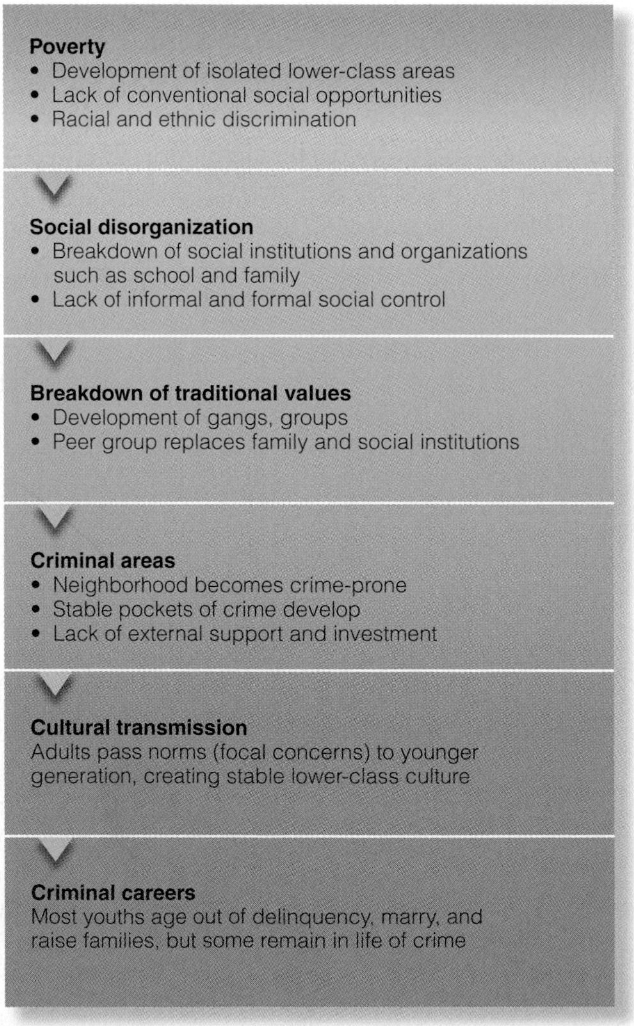

Poverty
- Development of isolated lower-class areas
- Lack of conventional social opportunities
- Racial and ethnic discrimination

Social disorganization
- Breakdown of social institutions and organizations such as school and family
- Lack of informal and formal social control

Breakdown of traditional values
- Development of gangs, groups
- Peer group replaces family and social institutions

Criminal areas
- Neighborhood becomes crime-prone
- Stable pockets of crime develop
- Lack of external support and investment

Cultural transmission
Adults pass norms (focal concerns) to younger generation, creating stable lower-class culture

Criminal careers
Most youths age out of delinquency, marry, and raise families, but some remain in life of crime

Figure 6.4
Social Disorganization Theory

The Work of Shaw and McKay

Social disorganization theory was popularized by the work of two Chicago sociologists, Clifford R. Shaw and Henry McKay, who linked life in transitional slum areas to the inclination to commit crime. Shaw and McKay began their pioneering work on Chicago crime during the early 1920s while working as researchers for a state-supported social service agency.[22]

Shaw and McKay explained crime and delinquency within the context of the changing urban environment and ecological development of the city. They saw that Chicago had developed into distinct neighborhoods (natural areas), some affluent and others wracked by extreme poverty. These poverty-ridden **transitional neighborhoods** suffered high rates of population turnover and were incapable of inducing residents to remain and defend the neighborhoods against criminal groups.

In transitional areas, successive changes in population composition, disintegration of traditional cultures, diffusion of divergent cultural standards, and gradual industrialization dissolve neighborhood culture and organization. The continuity of conventional neighborhood traditions and institutions is broken, leaving children feeling displaced and without a strong or definitive set of values.

Concentric Zones Shaw and McKay identified the areas in Chicago that had excessive crime rates. They noted that distinct ecological areas had developed in the city, forming a series of nine concentric circles, or zones, and that there were stable and significant interzone differences in crime rates (see Figure 6.5). The areas of heaviest crime concentration appeared to be the transitional inner-city zones, where large numbers of foreign-born citizens had recently settled.[23] The zones farthest from the city's center had correspondingly lower crime rates.

Analysis of these data indicated a surprisingly stable pattern of criminal activity in the nine ecological zones over a period of 65 years. Shaw and McKay concluded that multiple cultures and diverse values, both conventional and deviant, coexist in the transitional neighborhoods. Children growing up in the street culture often find that adults who have adopted a deviant lifestyle (gamblers, pimps, drug dealers) are the most financially successful people in the neighborhood. Forced to choose between conventional and deviant lifestyles, many slum kids opt for the latter. They join other like-minded youths and form law-violating gangs and cliques. The development of teenage law-violating groups is an essential element of youthful misbehavior in slum areas. The values that slum youths adopt often conflict with existing middle-class norms, which demand strict obedience to the legal code. Consequently, a value conflict further separates the delinquent youth and his or her peer group from conventional society; the result is a more solid embrace of deviant goals and behavior. To further justify their choice of goals, these youths seek support for their choice by recruiting new members and passing on the delinquent tradition.

Shaw and McKay's statistical analysis confirmed that even though crime rates changed, the highest rates were always in Zones I and II (the central city and a transitional area). The areas with the highest crime rates retained high rates even when their ethnic composition changed (the areas Shaw and McKay examined shifted from German and Irish to Italian and Polish).[24]

The Legacy of Shaw and McKay Social disorganization concepts articulated by Shaw and McKay have remained prominent within criminology for more than 75 years. Although cultural and social conditions have changed over time and today we live in a much more heterogeneous, mobile society, the most important of Shaw and McKay's findings—crime rates correspond to neighborhood structure—still holds up.[25]

Their research supported their belief that crime is a constant fixture in areas of poverty, regardless of residents' racial or ethnic identity. Because the basis of their theory was that neighborhood disintegration is the primary cause of criminal behavior, Shaw and McKay paved the way for many of the community action and treatment programs that have been developed in the last half-century.

CONNECTIONS

If social disorganization causes crime, why are most low-income people law abiding? To explain this anomaly, some sociologists have devised theoretical models suggesting that individual socialization experiences mediate environmental influences. These theories will be discussed in Chapter 7.

transitional neighborhood
An area undergoing a shift in population and structure, usually from middle-class residential to lower-class mixed use.

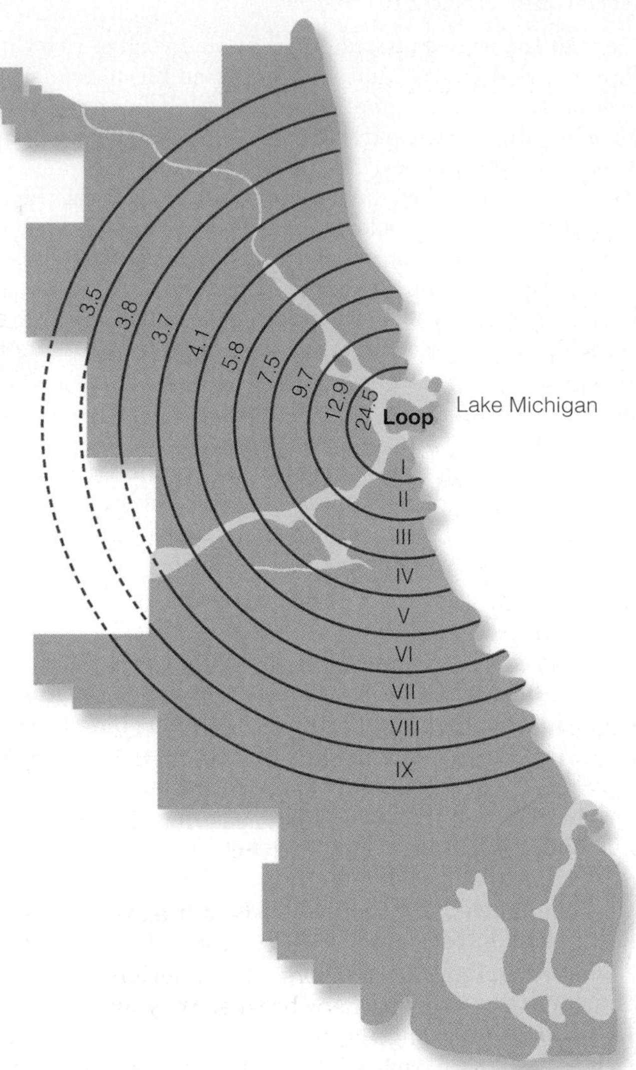

Figure 6.5

Shaw and McKay's Concentric Zones Map of Chicago

Note: Arabic numerals represent the rate of male delinquency.

SOURCE: Clifford R. Shaw et al., *Delinquency Areas* (Chicago: University of Chicago Press, 1929), p. 99. Reprinted with permission.

The Social Ecology School

During the 1970s, criminologists were influenced by several critical analyses of social disorganization theory that challenged its validity.[26] The criminological literature of the period was dominated by theories with a social-psychological orientation, stressing offender socialization within the family, school, and peer group.

In the 1980s, a group of criminologists continued studying ecological conditions, reviving concern about the effects of social disorganization.[27] These contemporary social ecologists developed a purer form of structural theory that emphasizes the association of community deterioration and economic decline with criminality but places less emphasis on value conflict. The following sections discuss some of the more recent social ecological research.

Community Disorder Crime rates and the need for police services are associated with community deterioration: disorder, poverty, alienation, disassociation, and fear of crime.[28] Even in rural areas, which normally have low crime rates, increased levels of crime and violence are associated with indicators of social disorganization such as residential instability (a large number of people moving in and out), family disruption, and changing ethnic composition.[29]

In larger cities, neighborhoods with a high percentage of deserted houses and apartments experience high crime rates; abandoned buildings serve as a "magnet for crime."[30] Areas in which houses are in poor repair, boarded up, and burned out, whose owners are best described as slumlords, are also the location of the highest violence rates and gun crime.[31] These neighborhoods, in which retail establishments often go bankrupt, are abandoned and deteriorate physically.[32]

Community Fear In neighborhoods where people help each other, residents are less likely to fear crime or to be afraid of becoming a crime victim.[33] In disorganized neighborhoods that suffer social and physical incivilities, residents experience rowdy youth, trash and litter, graffiti, abandoned storefronts, burned-out buildings, littered lots, strangers, drunks, vagabonds, loiterers, prostitutes, noise, congestion, angry words, dirt, and stench. Having parks and playgrounds where teens hang out and loiter may contribute to fear.[34] As fear increases, quality of life deteriorates.[35]

Fear is often based on experience. Residents who have already been victimized are more fearful of the future than those who have escaped crime.[36] People become afraid when they are approached by someone in the neighborhood selling drugs. They may fear that their children will also be approached and seduced into the drug life.[37] The presence of such incivilities, especially when accompanied by relatively high crime rates, convinces residents that their neighborhood is dangerous; becoming a crime victim seems inevitable.[38]

Fear can be contagious. People tell others when they have been victimized, thus spreading the word that the neighborhood is getting dangerous and that the chance of future victimization is high.[39] As a result, people dread leaving their homes at night and withdraw from community life.

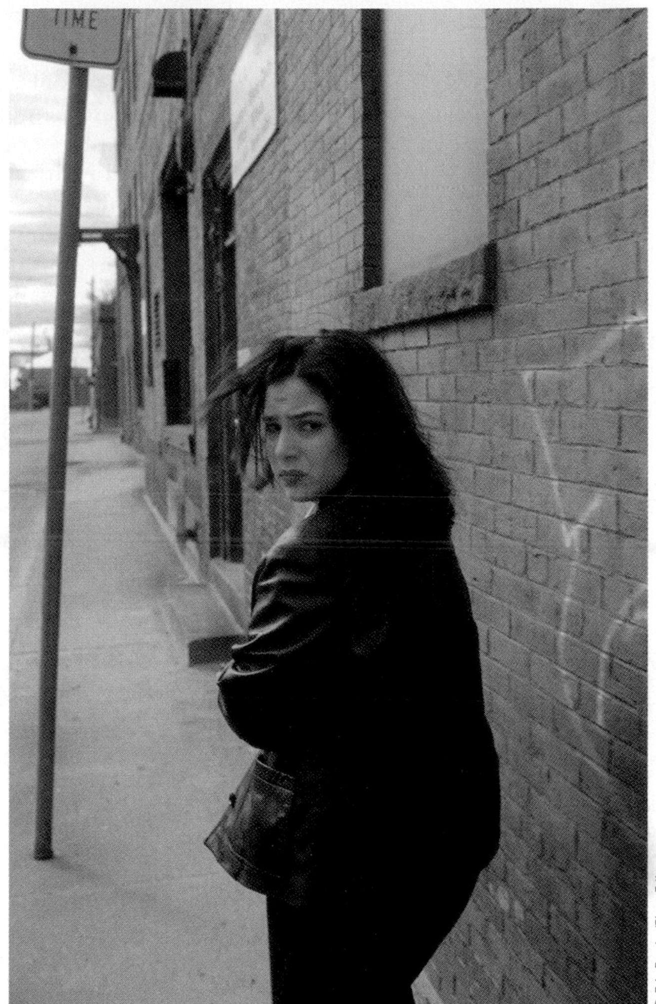

● Residents in disorganized neighborhoods suffer social and physical isolation and experience a great deal of fear. People dread leaving their homes at night and withdraw from community life. Those who have already been victimized are more fearful of the future than those who have escaped crime.

Siege Mentality People who live in neighborhoods that experience high levels of crime and civil disorder become suspicious and mistrusting.[40] Minority group members may experience greater levels of fear than whites, perhaps because they may have fewer resources to address ongoing social problems.[41] They develop a sense of powerlessness, which increases levels of mistrust. Some residents become so suspicious of authority that they develop a "siege mentality," in which the outside world is considered the enemy out to destroy the neighborhood.

Siege mentality often results in an expanding mistrust of social institutions, including business, government, and schools. Government officials seem arrogant and haughty. The police are believed to ignore crime and when they do take action to use excessive force.[42] Residents' fears may not be misplaced; research does show that police are more likely to use higher levels of force when suspects are encountered in high-crime, disadvantaged neighborhoods regardless of the suspects' behaviors or reactions.[43] When police ignore crime in poor areas or, conversely, when they are violent and corrupt, anger flares, and people take to the streets and react in violent ways.

Community Change Recent studies recognize that change, not stability, is the hallmark of inner-city areas. A neighborhood's residents, wealth, density, and purpose are constantly evolving. Even disorganized neighborhoods acquire new identifying features. Some may become multiracial and others racially homogeneous. Some areas become stable and family-oriented, whereas in others, mobile, never-married people predominate.[44] Urban areas undergoing rapid structural changes in racial and economic composition also seem to experience the greatest change in crime rates.[45] In contrast, stable neighborhoods, even those with a high rate of poverty, experience relatively low crime rates and have the strength to restrict substance abuse and criminal activity.[46]

As areas decline, residents flee to safer, more stable localities. Those who can move to more affluent neighborhoods find that their lifestyles and life chances improve immediately and continue to do so over their life span.[47] Those who cannot leave because they cannot afford to live in more affluent communities face an increased risk of victimization. Because of racial differences in economic well-being, those "left behind" are all too often minority citizens.[48] Whites may feel threatened as the number of minorities in the population increase and compete with them for jobs and political power.[49] As racial prejudice increases, the call for "law and order" aimed at controlling the minority population grows louder.[50]

CONNECTIONS

The racial threat theory, discussed in Chapter 2, hypothesizes that increases in the African American population will threaten the majority population and encourage more aggressive police tactics targeting minorities.

Those who cannot move find themselves surrounded by a constant influx of new residents. In response to this turnover, a culture may develop that dictates standards of dress, language, and behavior to neighborhood youth that are in opposition to those of conventional society. All these factors are likely to produce increased crime rates.

As communities change, neighborhood deterioration precedes increasing rates of crime and delinquency.[51] Neighborhoods most at risk for increased crime contain large numbers of single-parent families and unrelated people living together, have changed from owner-occupied to renter-occupied units, and have lost semiskilled and unskilled jobs (indicating a growing residue of discouraged workers who are no longer seeking employment).[52] These ecological disruptions strain existing social control mechanisms and inhibit their ability to control crime and delinquency.

Poverty Concentration One aspect of community change may be the concentration of poverty in deteriorated urban neighborhoods.[53] William Julius Wilson describes how working- and middle-class families flee inner-city poverty areas, resulting in a poverty **concentration effect** in which the most disadvantaged population is consolidated in the most disorganized urban neighborhoods. Poverty concentration has been associated with income and wealth disparities, nonexistent employment opportunities, inferior housing patterns, and unequal access to health care.[54] Urban areas marked by concentrated poverty become isolated and insulated from the social mainstream and more prone to criminal activity, violence, and homicide.[55]

CONNECTIONS

The concentration effect contradicts, in some measure, Shaw and McKay's position, discussed earlier in this chapter, that crime rates increase in transitional neighborhoods. Today the most crime-prone areas may be stable, homogeneous areas whose residents are trapped in public housing and urban ghettos.

How does neighborhood poverty concentration produce high crime rates? As the working and middle classes move out, they take with them their financial and institutional resources and support. Businesses are disinclined to locate in poverty areas; banks become reluctant to lend money for new housing or businesses.[56] Unemployment rates skyrocket, destabilizing households, and unstable families are likely to produce children who use violence and aggression to deal with limited opportunity. Large groups or cohorts of people of the same age are forced to compete for relatively scant resources.[57]

Limited employment opportunities reduce the stabilizing influence of parents and other adults, who may once have counteracted the allure of youth gangs. Sociologist Elijah Anderson's analysis of Philadelphia neighborhood life found that "old heads" (respected neighborhood residents), who at one time played an important role in socializing youth, have been displaced by younger street hustlers and drug dealers. Although the old heads may complain that these newcomers have not earned or worked for their fortunes in the old-fashioned way, the old heads admire and envy these young people whose gold chains and luxury cars advertise their wealth amid poverty[58] So the old heads admire the fruits of crime while they may disdain the violent manner in which they are acquired.

Collective Efficacy In contrast to areas plagued by poverty concentration, cohesive communities with high levels of social control and social integration, where people know one another and develop interpersonal ties, may also develop **collective efficacy**: mutual trust, a willingness to intervene in the supervision of children, and the maintenance of public order.[59] Cohesion among neighborhood residents, combined with shared expectations for informal social control of public space, promotes collective efficacy.[60] Residents in these areas enjoy a better life because the fruits of cohesiveness can be better education, health care, and housing opportunities.[61]

concentration effect
As working- and middle-class families flee inner-city poverty areas, the most disadvantaged population is consolidated in urban ghettos.

collective efficacy
Social control exerted by cohesive communities, based on mutual trust, including intervention in the supervision of children and maintenance of public order.

In contrast, socially disorganized neighborhoods find that efforts at social control are weak and attenuated. People living in economically disadvantaged areas are significantly more likely to perceive their immediate surroundings in more negative terms (with higher levels of incivilities) than those living in areas that maintain collective efficacy.[62] When community social control efforts are blunted, crime rates increase, further weakening neighborhood cohesiveness.[63] This suggests that there are spillover effects that extend beyond the geographic boundaries of a single neighborhood.

There are three forms of collective efficacy—informal social control, institutional social control, and public social control—and all three contribute to community stability.

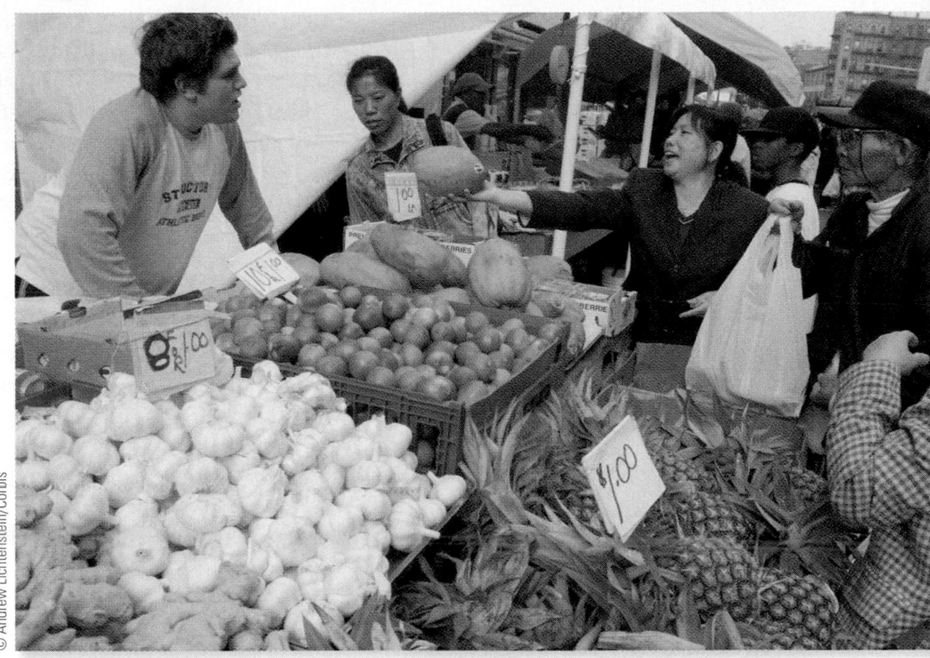

© Andrew Lichtenstein/Corbis

● Communities with high levels of social control and social integration, where people know one another and develop interpersonal ties, may also develop collective efficacy: mutual trust, a willingness to intervene in the supervision of children, and the maintenance of public order. It is the cohesion among neighborhood residents–despite their different backgrounds, races, religions, and ethnic origins–that promotes collective efficacy.

- *Informal social control.* Some elements of collective efficacy operate on the primary, or private, level and involve peers, families, and relatives. These sources exert informal control by either awarding or withholding approval, respect, and admiration. Informal control mechanisms include direct criticism, ridicule, ostracism, desertion, and physical punishment.[64]

  The most important wielder of informal social control is the family, which may keep at-risk kids in check through such mechanisms as corporal punishment, withholding privileges, or ridiculing lazy or disrespectful behavior. The informal social control provided by the family takes on greater importance in neighborhoods with few social ties among adults and limited collective efficacy. In these areas parents cannot call upon neighborhood resources to take up the burden of controlling children; family members face the burden of providing adequate supervision.[65] In neighborhoods with high levels of collective efficacy, parents are better able to function and effectively supervise their children. Confident and authoritative parents, who live in areas that enjoy collective efficacy, are able to effectively deter their children from affiliating with deviant peers and getting involved in delinquent behavior.[66]

  In some neighborhoods, even high-risk areas, people are willing to get involved in anticrime programs.[67] Neighbors may get involved in informal social control through surveillance practices, for example, by keeping an "eye out" for intruders when their neighbors go out of town. Informal surveillance has been found to reduce the levels of some crimes such as street robberies; however, if robbery rates remain high, surveillance may be terminated because people become fearful for their safety.[68]

- *Institutional social control.* Social institutions such as schools and churches cannot work effectively in a climate of alienation and mistrust. Unsupervised peer groups and gangs, which flourish in disorganized areas, disrupt the influence of those neighborhood control agents that do exist.[69] Children who reside in these neighborhoods find that involvement with conventional social institutions, such as schools and afternoon programs, is blocked; they are instead at risk for recruitment into gangs and law-violating groups.[70] As crime flourishes, neighborhood fear increases, which in turn decreases a community's cohesion and thwarts the ability of its institutions to exert social control over its residents.[71]

  To combat these influences, communities that have collective efficacy attempt to use their local institutions to control crime. Sources of institutional social control include businesses, stores, schools, churches, and social service and volunteer organizations.[72] When these institutions are effective, rates for some crimes such as burglary decline.[73] Some institutions, such as recreation centers for teens, have been found to lower crime rates because they exert a positive effect; others, such as taverns and bars, can help destabilize neighborhoods and increase the rate of violent crimes such as rape and robbery.[74]

- *Public social control.* Stable neighborhoods are also able to arrange for external sources of social control. If they can draw on outside help and secure external resources—a process referred to as public social control—they are better able to reduce the effects of disorganization and maintain lower levels of crime and victimization.[75]

  The level of policing, a primary source of public social control, may vary between neighborhoods. Police presence is typically greatest when community organizations and local leaders have sufficient political clout to get funding for additional law enforcement personnel.

  The presence of police sends a message that the area will not tolerate deviant behavior. Because they can respond vigorously to crime, police prevent criminal groups from gaining a toehold in the neighborhood.[76] Criminals and drug dealers avoid such areas and relocate to easier and more appealing "targets."[77] In contrast, crime rates are highest in areas where police are mistrusted because they engage in misconduct, such as use of excessive force, or because they are seemingly indifferent to neighborhood problems.[78]

  In more disorganized areas, the absence of political power brokers limits access to external funding and protection. Without money from the outside, the neighborhood lacks the ability to "get back on its feet."[79] In these areas there are fewer police, and those that do patrol the area are less motivated and their resources are stretched more tightly. These communities cannot mount an effective social control effort because as neighborhood disadvantage increases, the level of informal social control decreases.[80]

The government can also reduce crime by providing economic and social supports through publicly funded social support and welfare programs. Though welfare is often criticized by conservative politicians as being a government handout, there is evidence of a significant inverse association between the amount of welfare money people receive and crime rates.[81] Government assistance may help people improve their social status by providing the financial resources to clothe, feed, and educate their children while reducing stress, frustration, and anger. Using government subsidies to reduce crime is controversial, and not all research has found that it actually works as advertised.[82]

The ramifications of having adequate controls are critical. In areas where collective efficacy remains high, children are less likely to become involved with deviant peers and engage in problem behaviors.[83] In disorganized areas, remember, the population is transient, so interpersonal relationships remain superficial. And even when an attempt is made to revitalize a disorganized neighborhood by creating institutional support programs such as community centers and better schools, the effort may be countered by the ongoing drain of deep-rooted economic and social deprivation.[84]

Concept Summary 6.1 lists some of the basic concepts and theories of the social disorganization view. ✔ CHECKPOINTS

✔ CHECKPOINTS

✔ Social disorganization theory holds that destructive social forces present in inner-city areas control human behavior and promote crime.

✔ Shaw and McKay first identified the concepts central to social disorganization. They found stable patterns of crime in the central city.

✔ The social ecology school associates community deterioration and economic decline with crime rates.

✔ Ecological factors such as community deterioration, changing neighborhoods, fear, lack of employment opportunities, incivility, poverty, and deterioration produce high crime rates.

✔ Collective efficacy can reduce neighborhood crime rates by creating greater cohesiveness.

CONCEPT SUMMARY 6.1 Social Disorganization Theories

THEORY	MAJOR PREMISE	STRENGTHS	RESEARCH FOCUS
Shaw and McKay's concentric zones theory	Crime is a product of transitional neighborhoods that manifest social disorganization and value conflict.	Identifies why crime rates are highest in slum areas. Points out the factors that produce crime. Suggests programs to help reduce crime.	Poverty; disorganization
Social ecology theory	The conflicts and problems of urban social life and communities, including fear, unemployment, deterioration, and siege mentality, influence crime rates.	Accounts for urban crime rates and trends.	Social control; fear; collective efficacy; unemployment

STRAIN THEORIES

Inhabitants of a disorganized inner-city area feel isolated, frustrated, ostracized from the economic mainstream, hopeless, and eventually angry. How do these feelings affect criminal activities?

Strain theorists view crime as a direct result of lower-class frustration and anger. Although most people share similar values and goals, the ability to achieve personal goals is stratified by socioeconomic class. Strain is limited in affluent areas because educational and vocational opportunities are available. In disorganized areas, strain occurs because legitimate avenues for success are all but closed. To relieve strain, indigent people may achieve their goals through deviant methods, such as theft or drug trafficking, or they may reject socially accepted goals and substitute more deviant goals, such as being tough and aggressive (see Figure 6.6).

Theory of Anomie

Sociologist Robert Merton applied the sociological concepts first identified by Durkheim to criminology in his theory of anomie.[85] He found that two elements of culture interact to produce potentially anomic conditions: culturally defined goals and socially approved means for obtaining them. For example, U.S. society stresses the goals of acquiring wealth, success, and power. Socially permissible means include hard work, education, and thrift.

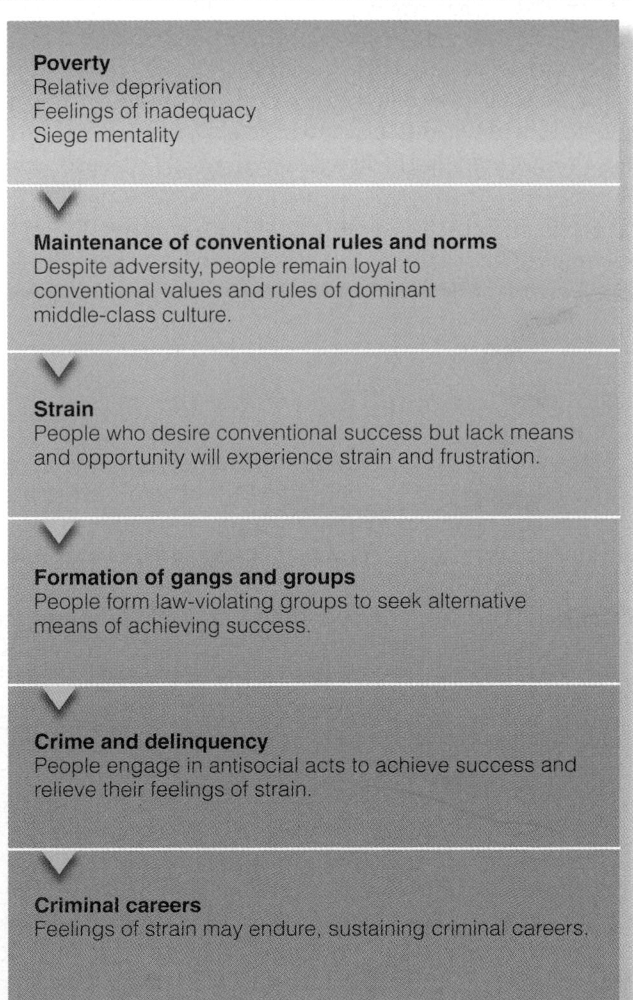

Poverty
Relative deprivation
Feelings of inadequacy
Siege mentality
Maintenance of conventional rules and norms
Despite adversity, people remain loyal to conventional values and rules of dominant middle-class culture.
Strain
People who desire conventional success but lack means and opportunity will experience strain and frustration.
Formation of gangs and groups
People form law-violating groups to seek alternative means of achieving success.
Crime and delinquency
People engage in antisocial acts to achieve success and relieve their feelings of strain.
Criminal careers
Feelings of strain may endure, sustaining criminal careers.

Figure 6.6
Basic Concepts of Strain Theory

Merton argues that in the United States legitimate means to acquire wealth are stratified across class and status lines. Those with little formal education and few economic resources soon find that they are denied the ability to legally acquire wealth—the preeminent success symbol. When socially mandated goals are uniform throughout society and access to legitimate means is bound by class and status, the resulting strain produces anomie among those who are locked out of the legitimate opportunity structure. Consequently, they may develop criminal or delinquent solutions to the problem of attaining goals.

Social Adaptations Merton suggests that each person has his or her own concept of society's goals and means to attain them. Some people have inadequate means of attaining success; others who have the means reject societal goals. The result is a variety of social adaptations:

- *Conformity*. When individuals embrace conventional social goals and also have the means to attain them, they can choose to conform. They remain law-abiding.
- *Innovation*. When individuals accept the goals of society but are unable or unwilling to attain them through legitimate means, the resulting conflict forces them to adopt innovative solutions to their dilemma: They steal, sell drugs, or extort money. Of the five adaptations, innovation is most closely associated with criminal behavior.
- *Ritualism*. Ritualists gain pleasure from practicing traditional ceremonies, regardless of whether they have a real purpose or goal. The strict customs in religious orders, feudal societies, clubs, and college fraternities encourage and appeal to ritualists.
- *Retreatism*. Retreatists reject both the goals and the means of society. They attempt to escape their lack of success by withdrawing, either mentally or physically, by taking drugs or becoming drifters.
- *Rebellion*. Some individuals substitute an alternative set of goals and means for conventional ones. Revolutionaries who wish to promote radical change in the existing social structure and who call for alternative lifestyles, goals, and beliefs are engaging in rebellion. Rebellion may be a reaction against a corrupt, hated government or an effort to create alternative opportunities and lifestyles within the existing system.

CONNECTIONS

As you may recall from Chapter 1, the roots of strain theories can be traced to Émile Durkheim's notion of anomie (from the Greek *a nomos*, "without norms"). According to Durkheim, an anomic society is one in which rules of behavior (the norms) have broken down or become inoperative during periods of rapid social change or social crisis such as war or famine.

Evaluation of Anomie Theory According to **anomie theory**, social inequality leads to perceptions of anomie. To resolve the goals–means conflict and relieve their sense of strain, some people innovate by stealing or extorting money; others retreat into drugs and alcohol; some rebel by joining revolutionary groups; and still others get involved in ritualistic behavior by joining a religious cult.

Merton's view of anomie has been one of the most enduring and influential sociological theories of criminality. By linking deviant behavior to the success goals that control social behavior, anomie theory attempts to pinpoint the cause of the conflict that produces personal frustration and consequent criminality. By acknowledging that society unfairly distributes the legitimate means to achieving success, anomie theory helps explain the existence of high-crime areas and the apparent predominance of delinquent and criminal behavior in the lower class. By suggesting that social conditions, not individual personalities, produce crime, Merton greatly influenced the directions taken to reduce and control criminality during the latter half of the twentieth century.

anomie theory
View that anomie results when socially defined goals (such as wealth and power) are universally mandated but access to legitimate means (such as education and job opportunities) is stratified by class and status.

A number of questions are left unanswered by anomie theory.[86] Merton does not explain why people choose to commit certain types of crime. For example, why does one anomic person become a mugger while another deals drugs? Anomie may explain differences in crime rates, but it cannot explain why most young criminals desist from crime as adults. Does this mean that perceptions of anomie dwindle with age? Is anomie short-lived?

Institutional Anomie Theory

Steven Messner and Richard Rosenfeld's **institutional anomie theory** is an updating of Merton's work.[87] Messner and Rosenfeld agree with Merton that the success goal is pervasive in American culture. For them, the **American Dream** refers to both a goal and a process. As a goal, the American Dream involves accumulating material goods and wealth via open individual competition. As a process, it involves both being socialized to pursue material success and believing that prosperity is achievable in American culture. Anomic conditions arise because the desire to succeed at any cost drives people apart, weakens the collective sense of community, fosters ambition, and restricts the desire to achieve anything other than material wealth. Achieving respect, for example, is not sufficient.

Why does anomie pervade American culture? According to Messner and Rosenfeld, it is because institutions that might otherwise control the exaggerated emphasis on financial success, such as religious or charitable institutions, have been rendered powerless or obsolete. These social institutions have been undermined in three ways:

- Noneconomic functions and roles have been devalued. Performance in other institutional settings—the family, school, or community—is assigned a lower priority than the goal of financial success.
- When conflicts emerge, noneconomic roles become subordinate to and must accommodate economic roles. The schedules, routines, and demands of the workplace take priority over those of the home, the school, the community, and other aspects of social life. People think nothing of leaving their neighborhood, city, or state for a better job, disrupting family relationships, and undermining informal social control.
- Economic language, standards, and norms penetrate noneconomic realms. Economic terms become part of the common vernacular: People want to get to the "bottom line." Spouses view themselves as "partners" who "manage" the household. Retired people say they want to "downsize" their household. We "outsource" home repairs instead of doing them ourselves. Corporate leaders run for public office promising to "run the country like a business."

According to Messner and Rosenfeld, the relatively high American crime rates can be explained by the interrelationship of culture and institutions. At the cultural level, the dominance of the American Dream mythology ensures that many people will develop desires for material goods that cannot be satisfied by legitimate means. Anomie becomes a norm, and extralegal means become a strategy for attaining material wealth. At the institutional level, the dominance of economic concerns weakens the informal social control exerted by family, church, and school. These institutions have lost their ability to regulate behavior and have instead become a conduit for promoting material success. Schools are evaluated not for imparting knowledge but for their ability to train students to get high-paying jobs. Social conditions reinforce each other: Culture determines institutions, and institutional change influences culture.[88] Crime rates may rise in a healthy economy because national prosperity heightens the attractiveness of monetary rewards, encouraging people to gain financial success by any means possible, including illegal ones. In this culture of competition, self-interest prevails and generates amorality, acceptance of inequality, and disdain for the less fortunate.[89]

Relative Deprivation Theory

There is ample evidence that neighborhood-level income inequality is a significant predictor of neighborhood crime rates.[90] Sharp divisions between the rich and the poor create an atmosphere of envy and mistrust. Criminal motivation is fueled both by perceived humiliation and the perceived right to humiliate a victim in return.[91] Psychologists warn that under these circumstances young males will begin to fear and envy "winners" who are doing very well at their expense. If they fail to use

institutional anomie theory
The view that anomie pervades U.S. culture because the drive for material wealth dominates and undermines social and community values.

American Dream
The goal of accumulating material goods and wealth through individual competition; the process of being socialized to pursue material success and to believe it is achievable.

risky aggressive tactics, they are surely going to lose out in social competition and have little chance of future success.[92] These generalized feelings of **relative deprivation** are precursors to high crime rates.[93]

The concept of relative deprivation was proposed by sociologists Judith Blau and Peter Blau, who combined concepts from anomie theory with those found in social disorganization models.[94] According to the Blaus, lower-class people may feel both deprived and embittered when they compare their life circumstances to those of the more affluent. People who feel deprived because of their race or economic class eventually develop a sense of injustice and discontent. The less fortunate begin to distrust the society that has nurtured social inequality and obstructed their chances of progressing by legitimate means. The constant frustration that results from these feelings of inadequacy produces pent-up aggression and hostility, eventually leading to violence and crime. The effect of inequality may be greatest when the impoverished believe that they are becoming less able to compete in a society whose balance of economic and social power is shifting further toward the already affluent. Under these conditions, the relatively poor are increasingly likely to choose illegitimate life-enhancing activities. Crime rates may then spiral upward even if the relative size of the poor population does not increase.[95]

Relative deprivation is felt most acutely by African American youths because they consistently suffer racial discrimination and economic deprivation that place them in a lower status than other urban residents.[96] Wage inequality may motivate young African American males to enter the drug trade, an enterprise that increases the likelihood that they will become involved in violent crimes.[97]

In sum, according to the relative deprivation concept, people who perceive themselves as economically deprived relative to people they know, as well as to society in general, may begin to form negative self-feelings and hostility, which motivate them to engage in deviant and criminal behaviors.[98]

CONNECTIONS

Can relative deprivation concepts be applied to white-collar crime? Perhaps some of the individuals involved in the savings and loan scandals or Wall Street stock fraud cases felt relatively deprived and socially frustrated when they compared the paltry few millions they had already accumulated with the hundreds of millions held by wealthier people whom they envied. For more on this issue, see discussions of the savings and loan scandal and the causes of white-collar crime in Chapter 12.

General Strain Theory (GST)

Sociologist Robert Agnew's **general strain theory (GST)** helps identify the micro- or individual-level influences of strain. Whereas Merton and Messner and Rosenfeld try to explain social class differences in the crime rate, Agnew tries to explain why individuals who feel stress and strain are likely to commit crimes. Agnew also offers a more general explanation of criminal activity among all elements of society rather than restricting his views to lower-class crime.[99]

Multiple Sources of Strain

Agnew suggests that criminality is the direct result of **negative affective states**—the anger, frustration, and adverse emotions that emerge in the wake of destructive social relationships. He finds that negative affective states are produced by a variety of sources of strain (see Figure 6.7):

- *Failure to achieve positively valued goals.* This cause of strain, similar to what Merton speaks of in his theory of anomie, is a result of the disjunction between aspirations and expectations. This type of strain occurs when a youth aspires to wealth and fame but, lacking financial and educational resources, assumes that such goals are impossible to achieve; he then turns to crime and drug dealing.
- *Disjunction of expectations and achievements.* Strain can also be produced by a disjunction between expectations and achievements. When people compare themselves to peers who seem to be doing a lot better financially or socially (such as making more money or getting better grades), even those doing relatively well feel strain. For example, when a high school senior is accepted at a good college but not a prestigious school, like some of her friends, she will feel strain. Perhaps she is not being treated fairly because the playing field is tilted against her: "Other kids have connections," she may say. Perceptions of inequity may result in many adverse reactions, ranging from running away from its source to lowering others' benefits through physical attacks or property vandalism.
- *Removal of positively valued stimuli.* Strain may occur because of the actual or anticipated loss of positively valued stimuli.[100] The sudden loss of a girl- or

relative deprivation
Envy, mistrust, and aggression resulting from perceptions of economic and social inequality.

general strain theory (GST)
The view that multiple sources of strain interact with an individual's emotional traits and responses to produce criminality.

negative affective states
Anger, frustration, and adverse emotions produced by a variety of sources of strain.

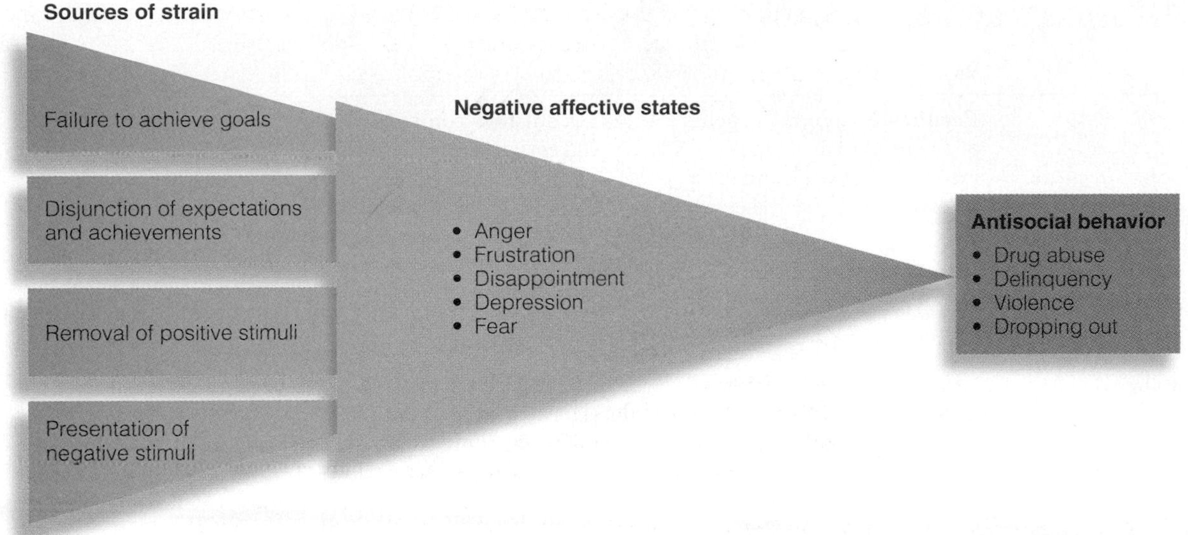

Figure 6.7
Elements of General Strain Theory (GST)

boyfriend can produce strain, as can the death of a loved one, or moving to a new neighborhood or school, or the divorce or separation of parents. The loss of positive stimuli may lead to delinquency as the adolescent tries to prevent the loss, retrieve what has been lost, obtain substitutes, or seek revenge against those responsible for the loss.

- *Presentation of negative stimuli*. Strain may also be caused by negative or noxious stimuli, such as child abuse or neglect, crime victimization, physical punishment, family or peer conflict, school failure, or stressful life events ranging from verbal threats to air pollution. Adolescent delinquency has been linked to maltreatment through the rage and anger it generates. Children who are abused at home may take out their rage on younger children at school or become involved in violent delinquency.[101]

Although these sources of strain are independent of one another, they may overlap. If a teacher insults a student, it may be viewed as an unfair application of negative stimuli that interferes with a student's academic aspirations. The greater the intensity and frequency of strain experiences, the greater their impact and the more likely they are to cause delinquency.

> **CONNECTIONS**
> The GST is not solely a cultural deviance theory because it recognizes non-class-related sources of strain. In this regard it is similar to the social process theories discussed in Chapter 7. It is included here because it incorporates the view that social class position can be an important source of strain, thus following in the tradition of Merton's theory of anomie.

Consequences of Strain According to Agnew, each type of strain increases the likelihood of experiencing negative emotions such as disappointment, depression, fear, and most importantly, anger. Anger increases perceptions of injury and of being wronged. It produces a desire for revenge, energizes individuals to take action, and lowers inhibitions. Violence and aggression seem justified if you have been wronged and are righteously angry. Because it produces these emotions, chronic, repetitive strain can be considered a predisposing factor for delinquency when it creates a hostile, suspicious, aggressive attitude. Individual strain episodes may trigger delinquency, such as when a particularly stressful event ignites a violent reaction.

Kids who report feelings of stress and anger are more likely to interact with delinquent peers and engage in criminal behaviors.[102] They may join deviant groups and gangs whose law-violating activities produce even more strain and pressure to commit even more crime. For example, the angry youngster who gets involved with substance abusing peers may feel forced to go on unwanted shoplifting sprees to pay for drugs.[103]

Coping with Strain Not all people who experience strain eventually resort to criminality. Some marshal their emotional, mental, and behavioral resources to cope with the anger and frustration produced by strain. Some individuals may be able

CONCEPT SUMMARY 6.2 Strain Theories

THEORY	MAJOR PREMISE	STRENGTHS	RESEARCH FOCUS
Anomie theory	People who adopt the goals of society but lack the means to attain them seek alternatives, such as crime.	Points out how competition for success creates conflict and crime. Suggests that social conditions and not personality can account for crime. Explains high lower-class crime rates.	Frustration; anomie; effects of failure to achieve goals
Institutional anomie theory	Material goods pervade all aspects of American life.	Explains why crime rates are so high in American culture.	Frustration; effects of materialism
Relative deprivation theory	Crime occurs when the wealthy and poor live close to one another.	Explains high crime rates in deteriorated inner-city areas located near more affluent neighborhoods.	Relative deprivation
General strain theory	Strain has a variety of sources. Strain causes crime in the absence of adequate coping mechanisms.	Identifies the complexities of strain in modern society. Expands on anomie theory. Shows the influence of social events on behavior over the life course. Explains middle-class crimes.	Strain; inequality; negative affective states; influence of negative and positive stimuli

to rationalize frustrating circumstances: Getting a good job is "just not that important"; they may be poor, but the "next guy is worse off"; if things didn't work out, they "got what they deserved." Others seek behavioral solutions, running away from adverse conditions or seeking revenge against those who caused the strain. Some try to regain emotional equilibrium with techniques ranging from physical exercise to drug abuse. Some people, especially those with an explosive temperament, low tolerance for adversity, poor problem-solving skills, and who are overly sensitive or emotional, are less likely to cope well with strain.[104] As their perception of strain increases so too does their involvement in antisocial behaviors.[105]

Although these traits, which are linked to aggressive, antisocial behavior, seem to be stable over the life cycle, they may peak during adolescence.[106] This is a period of social stress caused by weakening parental supervision and the development of relationships with a diverse peer group. Many adolescents going through the trauma of family breakup and frequent changes in family structure feel a high degree of strain. They may react by becoming involved in precocious sexuality or by turning to substance abuse to mask the strain.[107]

As children mature, their expectations increase. Some are unable to meet academic and social demands. Adolescents are very concerned about their standing with peers. Teenagers who are deficient in these areas may find they are social outcasts, another source of strain. In adulthood, crime rates may drop because these sources of strain are reduced. New sources of self-esteem emerge, and adults seem more likely to align their goals with reality.

Evaluating GST Agnew's important work both clarifies the concept of strain and directs future research agendas. It also adds to the body of literature describing how social and life history events influence offending patterns. Because sources of strain vary over the life course, so too do crime rates.

There is also empirical support for GST.[108] Some research efforts have shown that indicators of strain—family breakup, unemployment, moving, feelings of dissatisfaction with friends and school, dropping out of school—are positively related to criminality.[109] As predicted by GST, people who report feelings of stress and anger are more likely to interact with delinquent peers and to engage in criminal behaviors.[110] Lashing out at others may reduce feelings of strain, as may stealing or vandalizing property.[111] There is also evidence that, as predicted by GST, people

✔ CHECKPOINTS

✔ Strain theories hold that economic deprivation causes frustration, which leads to crime.

✔ According to Merton's anomie theory, many people who desire material goods and other forms of economic success lack the means to achieve their goals. Some may turn to crime.

✔ Messner and Rosenfeld's institutional anomie theory argues that the goal of success at all costs has invaded every aspect of American life.

✔ Agnew's general theory of strain suggests that there is more than one source of anomie.

who fail to meet success goals are more likely to engage in criminal activities.[112] Agnew himself has recently found evidence that experiencing violent victimization and anticipating future victimization are associated with antisocial behavior.[113] This finding indicates that not only is strain produced by actual experiences but it may result from anticipated ones as well.

Concept Summary 6.2 reviews major concepts and theories of the strain perspective. ✔ CHECKPOINTS

CULTURAL DEVIANCE THEORY

The third branch of social structure theory combines the effects of social disorganization and strain to explain how people living in deteriorated neighborhoods react to social isolation and economic deprivation. Because their lifestyle is draining, frustrating, and dispiriting, members of the lower class create an independent subculture with its own set of rules and values. Whereas middle-class culture stresses hard work, delayed gratification, formal education, and being cautious, the lower-class subculture stresses excitement, toughness, taking risks, fearlessness, immediate gratification, and street smarts.

The lower-class subculture is an attractive alternative because the urban poor find it impossible to meet the behavioral demands of middle-class society. However, subcultural norms often clash with conventional values. Urban dwellers are forced to violate the law because they obey the rules of the deviant culture with which they are in immediate contact (see Figure 6.8).

More than 40 years ago, sociologist Walter Miller identified the unique conduct norms that help define lower-class culture.[114] Miller referred to them as **focal concerns**, values that have evolved specifically to fit conditions in lower-class environments. The major lower-class focal concerns are set out in Exhibit 6.1.[115]

According to Miller, clinging to lower-class focal concerns promotes illegal or violent behavior. Toughness may mean displaying fighting prowess; street smarts may lead to drug deals; excitement may result in drinking, gambling, or drug abuse.[116] To illustrate, consider a recent study of violent young men in New York. Sociologist Jeffrey Fagan found that the most compelling function that violence served was to develop status as a "tough," an identity that helps young men acquire social power while insulating them from becoming victims. Violence was also seen as a means to acquire the trappings of wealth (such as nice clothes, flashy cars, or access to clubs), to control or humiliate another person, defy authority, settle drug-related disputes, attain retribution, satisfy the need for thrills or risk taking, and respond to challenges to one's manhood.[117]

To some criminologists, the influence of lower-class focal concerns and culture seem as relevant today as when first identified by Miller almost half a century ago. The Race, Culture, Gender, & Criminology feature, "The Code of the Streets," discusses conflict as a recent version of the concept of cultural deviance.

Theory of Delinquent Subcultures

Albert Cohen first articulated the theory of **delinquent subcultures** in his classic 1955 book, *Delinquent Boys*.[118] Cohen's central position was that delinquent behavior of lower-class youths is actually a protest against the norms and values of middle-class U.S. culture. Because social conditions prevent them from achieving success legitimately, lower-class youths experience a form of culture conflict that Cohen labels **status frustration**.[119] As a result, many of them join gangs and engage in behavior that is "non-utilitarian, malicious, and negativistic."[120]

Cohen viewed the delinquent gang as a separate subculture, possessing a value system directly opposed to that of the larger society. He described the subculture as one that "takes its norms from the larger culture, but turns them upside down. The delinquent's conduct is right by the standards of his subculture precisely because it is wrong by the norms of the larger culture."[121]

According to Cohen, the development of the delinquent subculture is a consequence of socialization practices in lower-class environments. Here children lack

focal concerns
Values, such as toughness and street smarts, that have evolved specifically to fit conditions in lower-class environments.

delinquent subculture
A value system adopted by lower-class youths that is directly opposed to that of the larger society.

status frustration
A form of culture conflict experienced by lower-class youths because social conditions prevent them from achieving success as defined by the larger society.

Figure 6.8
Elements of Cultural Deviance Theory

Poverty
Lack of opportunity
Anomie

Socialization
Lower-class youths are socialized to value middle-class goals and ideas. However, their environment inhibits future success.

Subculture
Blocked opportunities prompt formation of groups with alternative lifestyles and values.

Deviant values
The new subculture maintains values considered deviant by the normative culture.

Crime and delinquency
Obeying subcultural values involve youth in criminal behaviors such as drug use and violence.

Criminal careers
Some gang members can parlay their status into criminal careers; others become drug users or commit violent assault.

Exhibit 6.1
Miller's Lower-Class Focal Concerns

Trouble In lower-class communities, people are evaluated by their actual or potential involvement in making trouble. Getting into trouble includes such behaviors as fighting, drinking, and sexual misconduct. Dealing with trouble can confer prestige—for example, when a man establishes a reputation for being able to handle himself well in a fight. Not being able to handle trouble, and having to pay the consequences, can make a person look foolish and incompetent.

Toughness Lower-class males want local recognition of their physical and spiritual toughness. They refuse to be sentimental or soft and instead value physical strength, fighting ability, and athletic skill. Those who cannot meet these standards risk getting a reputation for being weak, inept, and effeminate.

Smartness Members of the lower-class culture want to maintain an image of being streetwise and savvy, using their street smarts, and having the ability to outfox and out-con the opponent. Although formal education is not admired, knowing essential survival techniques, such as gambling, conning, and outsmarting the law, is a requirement.

Excitement Members of the lower class search for fun and excitement to enliven an otherwise drab existence. The search for excitement may lead to gambling, fighting, getting drunk, and sexual adventures. In between, the lower-class citizen may simply "hang out" and "be cool."

Fate Lower-class citizens believe their lives are in the hands of strong spiritual forces that guide their destinies. Getting lucky, finding good fortune, and hitting the jackpot are all slum dwellers' daily dreams.

Autonomy Being independent of authority figures, such as the police, teachers, and parents, is required; losing control is an unacceptable weakness, incompatible with toughness.

SOURCE: Walter Miller, "Lower-Class Culture as a Generating Milieu of Gang Delinquency," *Journal of Social Issues* 14 (1958): 5–19.

Race, Culture, Gender, & Criminology

The Code of the Streets

A widely cited view of the interrelationship of culture and behavior is Elijah Anderson's concept of the "code of the streets." He sees that life circumstances are tough for the "ghetto poor"—lack of jobs that pay a living wage, stigma of race, fallout from rampant drug use and drug trafficking, and alienation and lack of hope for the future. Living in such an environment places young people at special risk of crime and deviant behavior.

There are two cultural forces running through the neighborhood that shape their reactions. "Decent values" are taught by families committed to middle-class values and representing mainstream goals and standards of behavior. Though they may be better off financially than some of their street-oriented neighbors, they are generally "working poor." They value hard work and self-reliance and are willing to sacrifice for their children; they harbor hopes that their sons and daughters will achieve a better future. Most go to church and take a strong interest in education. Some see their difficult situation as a test from God and derive great support from their faith and from the church community.

In opposition, "street values" are born in the despair of inner-city life and are in opposition to those of mainstream society. The street culture has developed what Anderson calls a code of the streets, a set of informal rules setting down both proper attitudes and ways to respond if challenged. If the rules are violated, there are penalties and sometimes violent retribution.

At the heart of the code is the issue of respect—loosely defined as being treated "right." The code demands that disrespect be punished or else hard-won respect be lost. With the right amount of respect, a person can avoid "being bothered" in public. If he is bothered, not only may he be in physical danger, but he has been disgraced or "dissed" (disrespected). Some forms of dissing, such as maintaining eye contact for too long, may seem pretty mild. But to street kids who live by the code, these actions become serious indications of the other person's intentions and a warning of imminent physical confrontation.

These two orientations—decent and street—socially organize the community. Their coexistence means that kids who are brought up in "decent" homes must be able to successfully navigate the demands of the "street" culture. Even in decent families, parents recognize that the code must be obeyed or at the very least "negotiated"; it cannot simply be ignored.

The Respect Game

Young men in poor inner-city neighborhoods build their self-image on the foundation of respect. Having "juice" (as "respect" is sometimes called on the street) means that they can take care of themselves even if it means resorting to violence. For street youth, losing respect on the street can be damaging and dangerous. Once they have demonstrated that they can be insulted, beaten up, or stolen from, they become an easy target. Kids from "decent" families may be able to keep their self-respect by getting good grades or a scholarship. Street kids do not have that luxury. With nothing to fall back on, they cannot walk away from an insult. They must retaliate with violence.

One method of preventing attacks is to go on the offensive. Aggressive, violence-prone people are not seen as "easy prey." Robbers do not get robbed, and street fighters are not the favorite targets of bullies. A youth who communicates an image of not being afraid to die and not being afraid to kill has given himself a sense of power on the street.

Anderson's work has been well received by the criminological community. A number of researchers, including Timothy Brezina and his colleagues, are doing analyses to determine whether Anderson's observations are in fact valid. Using data on violence, their assessment finds a link between violent behavior and the social processes uncovered by Anderson.

Critical Thinking

1. Does the code of the street, as described by Anderson, apply in the neighborhood in which you were raised? That is, is it universal?
2. Is there a form of "respect game" being played out on college campuses? If so, what is the substitute for violence?

Go to InfoTrac College Edition and use "street culture" in a key word search.

SOURCES: Elijah Anderson, *Code of the Street: Decency, Violence, and the Moral Life of the Inner City* (New York: Norton, 2000); Anderson, "Violence and the Inner-City Street Code," in *Violence and Children in the Inner City*, ed. Joan McCord (New York: Cambridge University Press, 1998), pp. 1–30; Anderson, "The Code of the Streets," *Atlantic Monthly* 273 (May 1994): 80–94; Timothy Brezina, Robert Agnew, Francis T. Cullen, and John Paul Wright, "The Code of the Street: A Quantitative Assessment of Elijah Anderson's Subculture of Violence Thesis and Its Contribution to Youth Violence Research," *Youth Violence and Juvenile Justice* 2 (2004): 303–328.

the basic skills necessary to achieve social and economic success, including a proper education, which renders them incapable of developing the skills to succeed in society. Lower-class parents are incapable of teaching children the necessary techniques for entering the dominant middle-class culture. The consequences of this deprivation include developmental handicaps, poor speech and communication skills, and inability to delay gratification.

Middle-Class Measuring Rods One significant handicap that lower-class children face is the inability to positively impress authority figures, such as teachers, employers, or supervisors. In U.S. society, these positions tend to be held by members of the middle class, who have difficulty relating to the lower-class youngster. Cohen calls the standards set by these authority figures **middle-class measuring rods**.

The conflict and frustration lower-class youths experience when they fail to meet these standards is a primary cause of delinquency. They may find themselves prejudged by others and not measuring up in the final analysis. Negative evaluations become part of a permanent file that follows an individual for the rest of his or her life. When the individual wants to improve, evidence of prior failures is used to discourage advancement.

Formation of Deviant Subcultures Cohen believes that lower-class boys rejected by middle-class decision makers usually join one of three existing subcultures: the corner boy, the college boy, or the delinquent boy.

The "corner boy" role is the most common response to middle-class rejection. The corner boy is not a chronic delinquent but may be a truant who engages in petty or status offenses, such as precocious sex and recreational drug abuse. His main loyalty is to his peer group, on which he depends for support, motivation, and interest. His values, therefore, are those of the group with which he is in close contact. The corner boy, well aware of his failure to achieve the standards of the American Dream, retreats into the comforting world of his lower-class peers and eventually becomes a stable member of his neighborhood, holding a menial job, marrying, and remaining in the community.

The "college boy" embraces the cultural and social values of the middle class. Rather than scorning middle-class measuring rods, he actively strives to succeed by those standards. Cohen views this type of youth as one who is embarking on an almost hopeless path because he is ill-equipped academically, socially, and linguistically to achieve the rewards of middle-class life.

The "delinquent boy" adopts a set of norms and principles that directly oppose middle-class values. He engages in short-run hedonism, living for today and letting "tomorrow take care of itself."[122] Delinquent boys strive for group autonomy. They resist efforts by family, school, or other sources of authority to control their behavior. Frustrated by their inability to succeed, these boys resort to a process Cohen calls **reaction formation**, including overly intense responses that seem disproportionate to the stimuli that trigger them. For the delinquent boy, this takes the form of irrational, malicious, and unaccountable hostility to the enemy, which in this case is "the norms of respectable middle-class society."[123]

Cohen's approach skillfully integrates strain and social disorganization theories and has become an enduring element of criminological literature.

Theory of Differential Opportunity

In their classic work *Delinquency and Opportunity*, written more than 40 years ago, Richard Cloward and Lloyd Ohlin combined strain and social disorganization principles to portray a gang-sustaining criminal subculture.[124]

The centerpiece of the Cloward and Ohlin theory is the concept of **differential opportunity**. According to this concept, people in all strata of society share the same success goals; however, those in the lower class have limited means of achieving them. People who perceive themselves as failures within conventional society will seek alternative or innovative ways to succeed. People who conclude that there is little hope for legitimate advancement may join like-minded peers to form a gang, which can provide them with emotional support. The youth who is considered a failure at school and is qualified for only a menial job at a minimum wage can earn thousands of dollars plus the respect of his or her peers by joining a gang and engaging in drug deals or armed robberies.

Cloward and Ohlin recognize that the opportunity for success in both conventional and criminal careers is limited. In stable areas, adolescents may be recruited by professional criminals, drug traffickers, or organized crime groups. Unstable areas, however, cannot support flourishing criminal opportunities. In these socially disorganized neighborhoods, adult role models are absent, and young criminals have few opportunities to join established gangs or learn the fine points of professional crime. Their most important finding, then, is that all opportunities for

middle-class measuring rods
The standards by which authority figures, such as teachers and employers, evaluate lower-class youngsters and often prejudge them negatively.

reaction formation
Irrational hostility evidenced by young delinquents, who adopt norms directly opposed to middle-class goals and standards that seem impossible to achieve.

differential opportunity
The view that lower-class youths, whose legitimate opportunities are limited, join gangs and pursue criminal careers as alternative means to achieve universal success goals.

success, both illegal and conventional, are closed for the most disadvantaged youths. Because of differential opportunity, young people are likely to join one of three types of gangs.

- *Criminal gangs*. These gangs exist in stable neighborhoods where close connections among adolescent, young adult, and adult offenders create an environment for successful criminal enterprise.[125] Youths are recruited into established criminal gangs that provide training for a successful criminal career. Gang membership is a learning experience in which the knowledge and skills needed for success in crime are acquired. During this apprenticeship, older, more experienced members of the criminal subculture hold youthful trainees on tight reins, limiting activities that might jeopardize the gang's profits (for example, engaging in nonfunctional, irrational violence).
- *Conflict gangs*. These gangs develop in communities unable to provide either legitimate or illegitimate opportunities.[126] They attract tough adolescents who fight with weapons to win respect from rivals and engage in unpredictable and destructive assaults on people and property. Conflict gang members must be ready to fight to protect their own and their gang's integrity and honor. By doing so, they acquire a "rep," which gains admiration from their peers and consequently helps them develop their self-image.
- *Retreatist gangs*. Retreatists are double failures, unable to gain success through legitimate means and unwilling to do so through illegal ones. Members of the retreatist subculture constantly search for ways of getting high—alcohol, pot, heroin, unusual sexual experiences, music. To feed their habits, retreatists develop a "hustle"—pimping, conning, selling drugs, or committing petty crimes. Personal status in the retreatist subculture is derived from peer approval.

Cloward and Ohlin's theory integrates cultural deviance and social disorganization variables and recognizes different modes of criminal adaptation. The fact that criminal cultures can be supportive, rational, and profitable seems to more realistically reflect the actual world of the delinquent than Cohen's original view of purely negativistic, destructive delinquent youths who oppose all social values.

Concept Summary 6.3 reviews the major concepts of cultural deviance theory.

✔ CHECKPOINTS

✔ CHECKPOINTS

✔ Cultural deviance theory shows how subcultures develop with norms in opposition to the general society.

✔ Walter Miller describes the focal concerns that shape this subculture.

✔ Albert Cohen analyzes the lifestyle of delinquent boys, revealing how they obey an independent social code with its own values.

✔ Cohen shows how members of the lower class fail when they are judged by "middle-class measuring rods."

✔ Richard Cloward and Lloyd Ohlin find that deviant subcultures form when people believe that their legitimate opportunities are blocked or impaired.

✔ Crime prevention efforts have been aimed at increasing the conventional options for success open to members of the lower class.

CONCEPT SUMMARY 6.3 Cultural Deviance Theories

THEORY	MAJOR PREMISE	STRENGTHS	RESEARCH FOCUS
Miller's focal concern theory	Citizens who obey the street rules of lower-class life (focal concerns) find themselves in conflict with the dominant culture.	Identifies the core values of lower-class culture and shows their association to crime.	Cultural norms; focal concerns
Cohen's theory of delinquent gangs	Status frustration of lower-class boys, created by their failure to achieve middle-class success, causes them to join gangs.	Shows how the conditions of lower-class life produce crime. Explains violence and destructive acts. Identifies conflict of lower class with middle class.	Gangs; culture conflict; middle-class measuring rods; reaction formation
Cloward and Ohlin's theory of opportunity	Blockage of conventional opportunities causes lower-class youths to join criminal, conflict, or retreatist gangs.	Shows that even illegal opportunities are structured in society. Indicates why people become involved in a particular type of criminal activity. Presents a way of preventing crime.	Gangs; cultural norms; culture conflict; effects of blocked opportunity

SOCIAL STRUCTURE THEORY AND PUBLIC POLICY

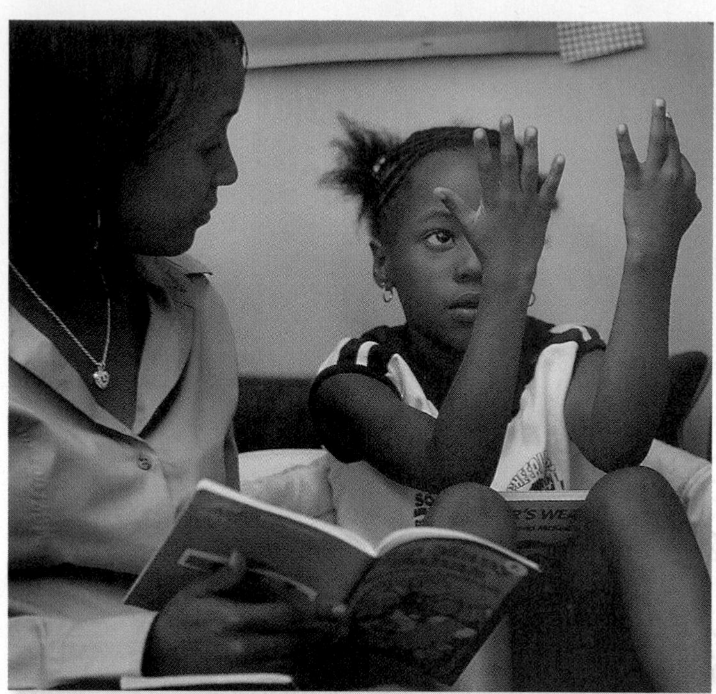

© AP

● Public policy based on social structure theories may emphasize opening opportunities to those who may not experience them in their current circumstances. Here, University of Missouri-Kansas City freshman Destiny Byers (left) watches first-grader Destiny Evans learning to count at the Santa Fe Accelerated Elementary School in Kansas City. Byers is one of 11 students in UMKC's Institute for Urban Education program, which trains inner-city students to become inner-city teachers.

Social structure theory has significantly influenced public policy. If the cause of criminality is viewed as a schism between lower-class individuals and conventional goals, norms, and rules, it seems logical that alternatives to criminal behavior can be provided by giving inner-city youth opportunities to share in the rewards of conventional society.

One approach is to give indigent people direct financial aid through public assistance or welfare. Although welfare has been curtailed under the Federal Welfare Reform Act of 1996, research shows that crime rates decrease when families receive supplemental income through public assistance payments.[127]

Efforts have also been made to reduce crime by improving the community structure in inner-city high-crime areas. Crime prevention efforts based on social structure precepts can be traced back to the Chicago Area Project supervised by Clifford Shaw. This program attempted to organize existing community structures to develop social stability in otherwise disorganized slums. The project sponsored recreation programs for neighborhood children, including summer camping. It campaigned for community improvements in such areas as education, sanitation, traffic safety, resource conservation, and law enforcement. Project members also worked with police and court agencies to supervise and treat gang youth and adult offenders.

Social structure concepts, especially Cloward and Ohlin's views, were a critical ingredient in the Kennedy and Johnson administrations' War on Poverty, begun in the early 1960s. War on Poverty programs—Head Start, Neighborhood Legal Services, and the Community Action Program—have continued to help people. Today the Weed and Seed program is a descendant of the social structure approach to crime prevention.

THINKING Like a Criminologist

You have accepted a position in Washington as an assistant to the undersecretary of urban affairs. The secretary informs you that he wants to initiate a demonstration project in a major city to show that government can reduce poverty, crime, and drug abuse.

The area he has chosen is a large inner-city neighborhood in a midwestern city of more than 3 million people. It suffers disorganized community structure, poverty, and hopelessness. Predatory delinquent gangs run free, terrorizing local merchants and citizens. The school system has failed to provide opportunities and educational experiences sufficient to dampen enthusiasm for gang recruitment. Stores, homes, and public buildings are deteriorated and decayed. Commercial enterprise has fled the area, and civil servants are reluctant to enter the neighborhood. There is an uneasy truce among the varied ethnic and racial groups that populate the area. Residents feel that little can be done to bring the neighborhood back to life. Merchants are afraid to open stores, and there is little outside development from major retailers or manufacturers. People who want to start their own businesses find that banks will not lend them money.

One of the biggest problems has been the large housing projects built in the 1960s. These are now overcrowded and deteriorated. Police are actually afraid to enter the buildings unless they arrive with a SWAT team. Each building is controlled by a gang whose members demand tribute from the residents.

You are asked to propose an urban redevelopment program to revitalize the area and eventually bring down the crime rate. You can bring any public or private element to bear on this overwhelming problem. You can also ask private industry to help in the struggle, promising them tax breaks for their participation. What programs would you recommend to break the cycle of urban poverty?

Summary

- Sociology has been the main orientation of criminologists because they know that crime rates vary among elements of the social structure, that society goes through changes that affect crime, and that social interaction relates to criminality.
- Social structure theories suggest that people's place in the socioeconomic structure influences their chances of becoming criminals.
- Poor people are more likely to commit crimes because they are unable to achieve monetary or social success in any other way.
- Social structure theory includes three schools of thought: social disorganization, strain, and cultural deviance theories.
- Social disorganization theory suggests that the urban poor violate the law because they live in areas in which social control has broken down. The origin of social disorganization theory can be traced to the work of Clifford Shaw and Henry McKay. Shaw and McKay concluded that disorganized areas, marked by divergent values and transitional populations, produce criminality. Modern social ecology theory looks at such issues as community fear, unemployment, and deterioration.
- Strain theories view crime as resulting from the anger people experience over their inability to achieve legitimate social and economic success.
- Strain theories hold that most people share common values and beliefs, but the ability to achieve them is differentiated by the social structure.
- The best-known strain theory is Robert Merton's theory of anomie, which describes what happens when people have inadequate means to satisfy their goals.
- Steven Messner and Richard Rosenfeld show that the core values of American culture produce strain.
- Robert Agnew suggests that strain has multiple sources and is linked to anger and frustration that people endure when their goals and aspirations are frustrated or when they lose something they value.
- Cultural deviance theories hold that a unique value system develops in lower-class areas. Lower-class values approve of behaviors such as being tough, never showing fear, and defying authority. People perceiving strain will bond together in their own groups or subcultures for support and recognition.
- Albert Cohen links the formation of subcultures to the failure of lower-class citizens to achieve recognition from middle-class decision makers, such as teachers, employers, and police officers.
- Richard Cloward and Lloyd Ohlin have argued that crime results from lower-class people's perception that their opportunity for success is limited. Consequently, youths in low-income areas may join criminal, conflict, or retreatist gangs.

Take a Post-Test. Visit www.thomsonedu.com/criminaljustice/siegel and take the chapter Post-Test to monitor your progress and identify areas for further improvement. In addition to discovering what you've mastered, you'll learn which concepts need your added attention and get specific page references that direct you to the places in the text where you can find more information on them.

Key Terms

stratified society 120
social class 120
culture of poverty 121
underclass 121
social structure theory 124
social disorganization theory 125
strain theory 125
strain 125
cultural deviance theory 125
subculture 125
cultural transmission 125
transitional neighborhood 127
concentration effect 130
collective efficacy 130
anomie theory 134
institutional anomie theory 135
American Dream 135
relative deprivation 136
general strain theory (GST) 136
negative affective states 136
focal concerns 139
delinquent subculture 139
status frustration 139
middle-class measuring rods 142
reaction formation 142
differential opportunity 142

Critical Thinking Questions

1. Is there a "transitional" area in your town or city? Does the crime rate remain constant there, regardless of who moves in or out?

2. Is it possible that a distinct lower-class culture exists? Do you know anyone who has the focal concerns Miller talks about? Were there "focal concerns" in your high school or college experience?

3. Have you ever perceived anomie? What causes anomie? Is there more than one cause of strain?

4. How would Merton explain middle-class crime? How would Agnew?

5. Could "relative deprivation" produce crime among college-educated white-collar workers?

CHAPTER 7 Social Process Theories: Socialized to Crime

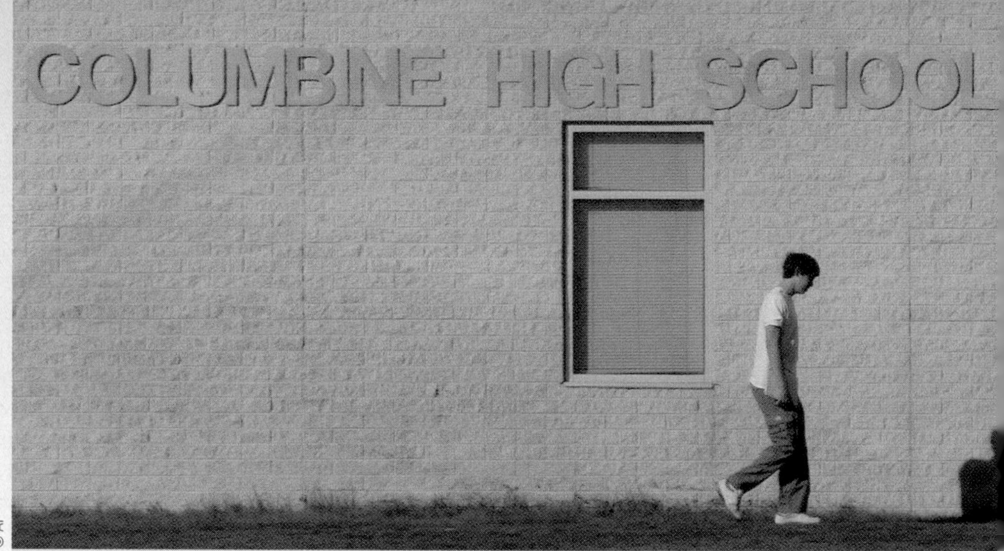

© AP

ON TUESDAY, APRIL 20, 1999, THE MOST SERIOUS SCHOOL SHOOTING IN THE NATION'S HISTORY occurred in the middle-class town of Littleton, Colorado. Two young men, Eric Harris, 18, and Dylan Klebold, 17, went on a rampage that left 13 dead, 25 injured. In the aftermath of the massacre, the cause of the shootings was linked to the boys' feelings of isolation and loneliness, their feelings of persecution, and their fascination with guns, violence, and Nazism. However, when it was reported that bombs, a shotgun barrel, a journal, and several handwritten notes had been found in clear view in Eric Harris's bedroom, the boys' parents became the target for blame. How could the Harrises and Klebolds not have been aware of their sons' violent tendencies? Or if they were aware of them, could they have chosen to ignore the problem? Friends said that the boys had kept their antisocial feelings carefully hidden from their parents until the day of the attack. Not surprisingly, the parents seemed to be as baffled and distressed as anyone else in the community. At no time had the school informed them of the dark poetry, antisocial behavior, or the video they had made. Nor were Eric Harris's parents aware that the police had been called about their son.[1]

Refer to the front endpapers for a study tool that summarizes each of the major theories discussed in this book.

Is it possible that Klebold's and Harris's shocking crime was the product of their strained relationship with their parents as well as their alienation from school and peers? Were they loners who had trouble forming social bonds? And were they the target of negative social labels because of their bizarre dress and behavior?

CHAPTER OBJECTIVES

1. Be familiar with the concept of socialization.
2. Discuss the effect of schools, family, and friends on crime.
3. Be able to discuss the differences between learning, control, and reaction.
4. Be familiar with the concept of differential association.
5. Be able to discuss what is meant by a definition toward criminality.
6. Understand the concept of neutralization.
7. Be able to discuss the relationship between self-concept and crime.
8. Know the elements of the social bond.
9. Describe the labeling process.
10. Be familiar with the concepts of primary and secondary deviance.
11. Show how the process of labeling leads to criminal careers.

Take a Pre-Test. Visit www.thomsonedu.com/criminaljustice/siegel and take a Pre-Test to determine what you already know and identify the areas where you'll need to focus your study. The program will direct you to specific pages within the text where you can find further information on the correct answers to the questions you've missed.

To some criminologists, an individual's relationship with critical elements of the social process is the key to understanding the onset and continuation of criminal behaviors. They believe that criminality is a function of individual **socialization** and the interactions people have with various organizations, institutions, and processes of society. Most people are influenced by their family relationships, peer group associations, educational experiences, and interactions with authority figures, including teachers, employers, and agents of the justice system.

SOCIALIZATION AND CRIME

Some criminologists focus their attention on the social processes and interactions that occur in all segments of society, not just the lower class. If the social relationships that most people rely on are positive and supportive, they can usually succeed within the rules of society; if these relationships are dysfunctional and destructive, conventional success may be impossible. Criminal solutions may become the only feasible alternative. This view of crime is referred to as **social process theory**.

Social process theories share one basic concept: All people, regardless of their race, class, or gender, have the potential to become delinquents or criminals. Although members of the lower class may have the added burdens of poverty, racism, poor schools, and disrupted family lives, these social forces can be counteracted by positive peer relations, a supportive family, and educational success. In contrast, even the most affluent members of society may turn to antisocial behavior if their life experiences are intolerable or destructive.

Social process theories have endured because the relationship between social class and crime is still uncertain. Most residents of inner-city areas refrain from criminal activity, and few of those that commit crimes persist into adulthood. If poverty were the sole cause of crime, indigent adults would be as criminal as indigent teenagers. But we know that, regardless of class position, most people age out of crime. The association between economic status and crime is problematic because class position alone cannot explain crime rates.[2] Simply living in a violent neighborhood does not produce violent children; research shows that family, peer, and individual characteristics play a large role in predicting violence in childhood.[3]

socialization
Process of human development and enculturation. Socialization is influenced by key social processes and institutions.

social process theory
The view that criminality is a function of people's interactions with various organizations, institutions, and processes in society.

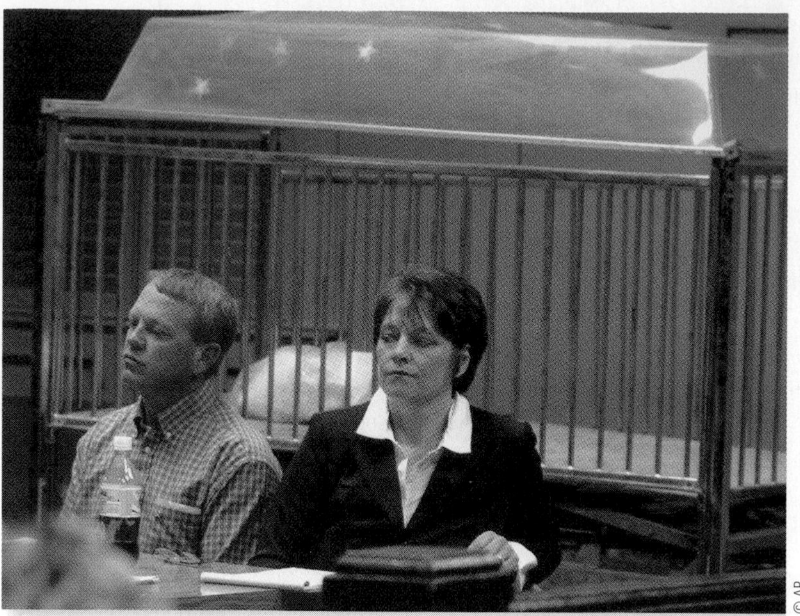

© AP

● Tom and Debra Schmitz, accused of child abuse, wait as lawyers have a sidebar with Judge Clayburn Peeples during the first day of their trial in Brownsville, Tennessee, January 30, 2006. The Schmitzes sit in front of what was called "the cage," a covered bed that was sometimes used for punishment according to one of the children living in their house at the time of the alleged incidents. Social process theorists would suggest that the abused victims of the Schmitzes would be more likely to get involved in criminality as adolescents and young adults.

Criminologists have long studied the critical elements of socialization to determine how they contribute to a burgeoning criminal career. Prominent among these elements are family, peer group, school, and church.

Family Relations

Family relationships are considered a major determinant of behavior.[4] In fact, parenting factors, such as the ability to communicate and provide proper discipline, may play a critical role in determining whether people misbehave as children and even later as adults. The family–crime relationship is significant across racial, ethnic, and gender lines and is one of the most replicated findings in the criminological literature.[5]

Parents who are supportive and effectively control their children in a noncoercive way are more likely to raise children who refrain from delinquency; this is referred to as **parental efficacy**.[6] Delinquency will be reduced if parents provide the type of structure that integrates children into families while giving them the ability to assert their individuality and regulate their own behavior.[7] Kids who report having troubled home lives also exhibit lower levels of self-esteem and are more prone to antisocial behaviors.[8] In contrast, children who have warm and affectionate ties to their parents report greater levels of self-esteem beginning in adolescence and extending into their adulthood; high self-esteem is inversely related to criminal behavior.[9]

Other family factors that have predictive value include the following:

- Inconsistent discipline, poor supervision, and lack of a warm, loving, supportive parent–child relationship are all associated with delinquency.[10]
- Adolescents who do not receive affection from their parents during childhood are more likely to use illicit drugs and be more aggressive as they mature.[11]
- Children growing up in homes where a parent suffers mental impairment are also at risk for delinquency.[12]
- Children whose parents abuse drugs are more likely to become persistent substance abusers than the children of nonabusers.[13]
- Children, both males and females, black or white, who experience abuse, neglect, or sexual abuse are believed to be more crime-prone and suffer from other social problems such as depression, suicide attempts, and self-injurious behaviors.[14] Mental health and delinquency experts have found that abused kids experience mental and social problems across their life span, ranging from substance abuse to possession of a damaged personality.[15]
- Children who grow up in homes where parents use severe discipline, yet the children lack warmth and involvement in their lives, are prone to antisocial behavior.[16] Links have been found among corporal punishment, delinquency, anger, spousal abuse, depression, and adult crime.[17]

CONNECTIONS

Chapter 2's analysis of the class-crime relationship showed why this relationship is still a hotly debated topic. Although serious criminals may be found disproportionately in lower-class areas, self-report studies show that criminality cuts across class lines. Middle-class use and abuse of recreational drugs, discussed in Chapter 13, suggests that law violators are not necessarily economically motivated.

Educational Experience

The educational process and adolescent school achievement have been linked to criminality. Children who do poorly in school, lack educational motivation, and feel alienated are the most likely to engage in criminal acts.[18] Children who fail in school offend more frequently than those who succeed. These children commit more serious and violent offenses and persist in crime into adulthood.[19]

Though national dropout rates are in decline, more than 10 percent of Americans ages 16 to 24 have left school permanently without a diploma; of these, more than 1 million withdrew before completing 10th grade. There are still

parental efficacy
Parents who are supportive and effectively control their children in a noncoercive way.

ethnic racial gaps in graduation rates. Students from historically disadvantaged minority groups (American Indian, Hispanic, African American) have little more than a fifty-fifty chance of finishing high school with a diploma.[20] Research findings over the past two decades indicate that many school dropouts, especially those who have been expelled, face a significant chance of entering a criminal career.[21]

Students are also subject to violence and intimidation on school grounds. Bullying is a sad but common occurrence in the U.S. educational system.[22] Research by Tonja Nansel found that more than 16 percent of U.S. schoolchildren say they have been bullied by other students during the current school term.[23] School crime surveys estimate that about 1.5 million violent incidents occur in public elementary and secondary schools each year.[24] The presence of weapons and violence is not lost on the average student. Data from a recent survey of high school students found that almost half report having seen other students carry knives at school, roughly 1 in 10 report having seen other students carry guns at school, and more than 1 in 5 report being fearful of weapon-associated victimization at school.[25]

Peer Relations

Psychologists have long recognized that peer groups have a powerful effect on human conduct and can dramatically influence decision making and behavior choices.[26] Children who are rejected by their peers are more likely to display aggressive behavior and to disrupt group activities through bickering, bullying, or other antisocial behavior.[27] Research shows that adolescents who report inadequate or strained peer relations, and who say they are not popular with the opposite sex, are most likely to become delinquent.[28]

Both in the United States and abroad, troubled kids find it tough to make friends; they choose delinquent peers out of necessity rather than desire. Recent research conducted in China shows that kids involved in delinquency are five times more likely than nonoffenders to associate with delinquent peers.[29] Being a social outcast causes them to hook up with friends who are dangerous and get them into trouble.[30] Those who acquire delinquent friends may find that peer influence is a powerful determinant of behavior. Once acquired, deviant peers may sustain or amplify antisocial behavior trends and amplify delinquent careers.[31]

Because delinquent friends tend to be, as criminologist Mark Warr puts it, "sticky" (once acquired, they are not easily lost), peer influence may continue through the life span.[32] The more antisocial the peer group, the more likely its members are to engage in delinquency. People who maintain close relations with antisocial peers will sustain their own criminal behavior into adulthood.[33] In contrast, nondelinquent friends help to moderate delinquency.[34] Having prosocial friends who are committed to conventional success may help shield kids from crime-producing inducements in their environment.[35]

CONNECTIONS

As you may recall from Chapter 2, most juveniles age out of crime and do not become adult offenders. Having delinquent friends may help to retard this process. According to the social process view, a chronic offender may have learned a delinquent way of life from his or her peer group members.

Religious Belief

Logic would dictate that people who hold high moral values and beliefs, who have learned to distinguish right from wrong, and who regularly attend religious services should also eschew crime and other antisocial behaviors. Religion binds people together and forces them to confront the consequences of their behavior. Committing crimes would violate the principles of all organized religions.

Recent research findings suggest that attending religious services does in fact have a significant negative impact on crime.[36] Kids living in disorganized, high-crime areas who attend religious services are better able to resist illegal drug use than nonreligious youth.[37] Interestingly, participation seems to be a more significant inhibitor of crime than merely having religious beliefs and values. That is, actually attending religious services has a more dramatic effect on behavior than merely holding religious beliefs.[38]

Effects of Socialization on Crime

According to the social process view, socialization is the key element in the formation of a criminal career. People living in even the most deteriorated urban areas can successfully resist inducements to crime if they have a positive self-image, strong moral values, and support from their parents, peers, teachers, and neighbors. The more social problems encountered during the socialization process, the greater the likelihood that youths will encounter difficulties and obstacles as they mature, such as being unemployed or becoming teenage parents.

The social process approach has several independent branches (see Figure 7.1). The first branch, **social learning theory**, suggests that people learn the techniques and attitudes of crime from close relationships with criminal peers: Crime is a learned behavior. The second branch, **social control theory**, maintains that everyone has the potential to become a criminal, but most people are controlled by their bonds to society. Crime occurs when the forces that bind people to society are weakened or broken. The third branch, **social reaction (labeling) theory**, says that people become criminals when significant members of society label them as such and they accept those labels as a personal identity.

Put another way, social learning theories assume that people are born good and learn to be bad; social control theory assumes that people are born bad and must be controlled in order to be good; and social reaction theory assumes that whether good or bad, people are controlled by the evaluations of others. Each of these independent branches will be discussed separately. ✔ CHECKPOINTS

✔ CHECKPOINTS

- ✔ Social process theories say that the way people are socialized controls their behavior choices.
- ✔ There is strong evidence that social relations influence behavior.
- ✔ Children growing up with conflict, abuse, and neglect are at risk for crime and delinquency.
- ✔ Educational failure has been linked to criminality.
- ✔ Adolescents who associate with deviant peers are more likely to engage in crime than those who maintain conventional peer group relations.
- ✔ Some criminologists maintain that crime is a learned behavior.
- ✔ Other criminologists view criminals as people whose behavior has not been controlled.
- ✔ Some view criminality as a function of labeling and stigma.

SOCIAL LEARNING THEORIES

Social learning theorists believe that crime is a product of learning the norms, values, and behaviors associated with criminal activity. Social learning can involve the actual techniques of crime (how to hot-wire a car or roll a joint) as well as the psychological aspects of criminality (how to deal with the guilt or shame associated with illegal activities). This section briefly reviews two of the most prominent forms of social learning theory: differential association theory and neutralization theory.

Differential Association Theory

One of the most prominent social learning theories is Edwin H. Sutherland's **differential association theory**. Often considered the preeminent U.S. criminologist, Sutherland first put forth his theory in 1939 in *Principles of Criminology*.[39] The final version of the theory appeared in 1947. When Sutherland died in 1950, his longtime associate Donald Cressey continued his work until his own death in 1987.

Sutherland's research on white-collar crime, professional theft, and intelligence led him to dispute the notion that crime was a function of the inadequacy of people in the lower classes.[40] He believed crime was a function of a learning process that could affect any individual in any culture. Acquiring a behavior is a socialization process, not a political or legal process. Skills and motives conducive to crime are learned as a result of contact with pro-crime values, attitudes, and definitions and other patterns of criminal behavior.

social learning theory
The view that people learn to be aggressive by observing others acting aggressively to achieve some goal or being rewarded for violent acts.

social control theory
The view that people commit crime when the forces binding them to society are weakened or broken.

social reaction (labeling) theory
The view that people become criminals when labeled as such and when they accept the label as a personal identity.

differential association theory
The view that people commit crime when their social learning leads them to perceive more definitions favoring crime than favoring conventional behavior.

Principles of Differential Association

Sutherland and Cressey explain the basic principles of differential association as follows:[41]

- *Criminal behavior is learned.* This statement differentiates Sutherland's theory from prior attempts to classify criminal behavior as an inherent characteristic of criminals. Sutherland implies that criminality is learned in the same manner as any other learned behavior, such as writing, painting, or reading.
- *Criminal behavior is learned as a by-product of interacting with others.* An individual does not start violating the law simply by living in a crimogenic

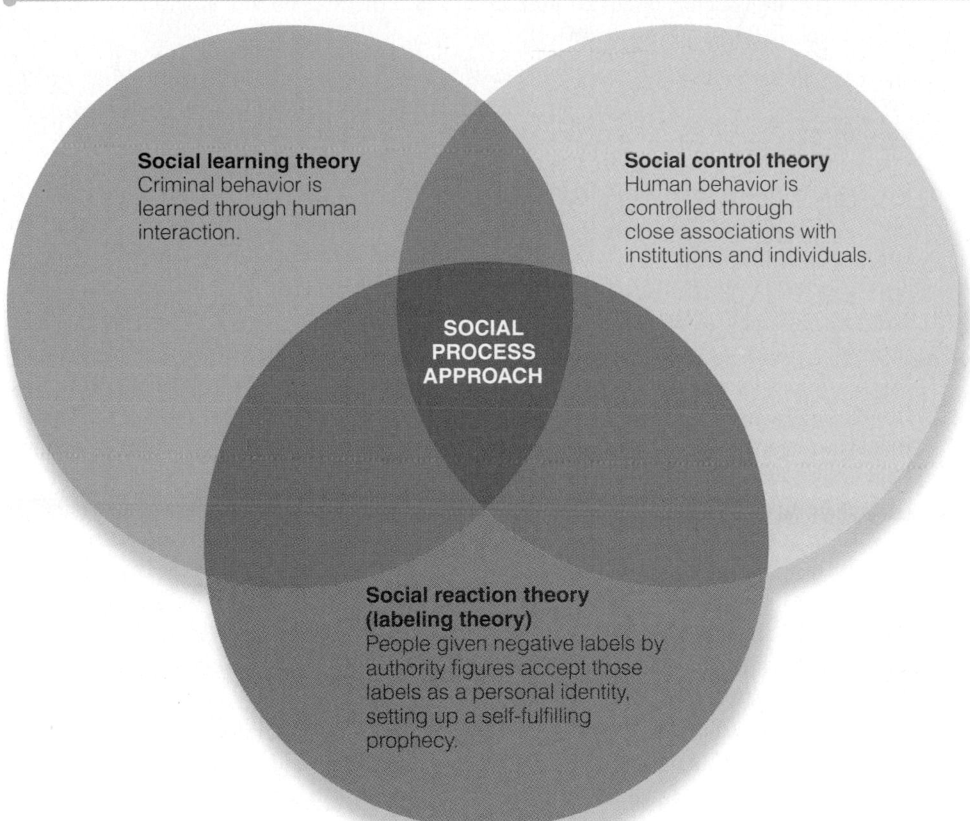
Social learning theory
Criminal behavior is learned through human interaction.
Social control theory
Human behavior is controlled through close associations with institutions and individuals.
SOCIAL PROCESS APPROACH
Social reaction theory (labeling theory)
People given negative labels by authority figures accept those labels as a personal identity, setting up a self-fulfilling prophecy.

Figure 7.1
The Complex Web of Social Processes That Controls Human Behavior

environment or by manifesting personal characteristics associated with criminality, such as low IQ or family problems. People actively learn as they are socialized and interact with other individuals who serve as teachers and guides to crime. Some kids may meet and associate with criminal "mentors" who teach them how to be successful criminals and gain the greatest benefits from their criminal activities.[42] Thus, criminality cannot occur without the aid of others.

- *Learning criminal behavior occurs within intimate personal groups*. People's contacts with their most intimate social companions—family, friends, and peers—have the greatest influence on their deviant behavior and attitude development. Relationships with these influential individuals color and control the way individuals interpret everyday events. For example, children who grow up in homes where parents abuse alcohol are more likely to view drinking as socially and physically beneficial.[43]
- *Learning criminal behavior involves assimilating the techniques of committing crime, including motives, drives, rationalizations, and attitudes*. Young delinquents learn from their associates the proper way to pick a lock, shoplift, and obtain and use narcotics. In addition, novice criminals learn the proper terminology for their acts and acquire approved reactions to law violations. Criminals must learn how to react properly to their illegal acts, such as when to defend them, rationalize them, or show remorse for them.
- *The specific direction of motives and drives is learned from perceptions of various aspects of the legal code as favorable or unfavorable*. Because the reaction to social rules and laws is not uniform across society, people constantly meet others who hold different views on the utility of obeying the legal code. Some people admire others who may openly disdain or flout the law or ignore its substance. People experience what Sutherland calls **culture conflict** when they are exposed to opposing attitudes toward right and wrong or moral and

culture conflict
Result of exposure to opposing norms, attitudes, and definitions of right and wrong, moral and immoral.

immoral. The conflict of social attitudes and cultural norms is the basis for the concept of differential association.

- *A person becomes a criminal when he or she perceives more favorable than unfavorable consequences to violating the law.* According to Sutherland's theory, individuals become law violators when they are in contact with persons, groups, or events that produce an excess of definitions favorable toward criminality and are isolated from counteracting forces (see Figure 7.2). A definition favorable toward criminality occurs, for example, when a person hears friends talking about the virtues of getting high on drugs. A definition unfavorable toward crime occurs when friends or parents demonstrate their disapproval of crime.
- *Differential associations may vary in frequency, duration, priority, and intensity.* Whether a person learns to obey the law or to disregard it is influenced by the quality of social interactions. Those of lasting duration have greater influence than those that are brief. Similarly, frequent contacts have greater effect than rare, haphazard contacts. "Priority" means the age of children when they first encounter definitions of criminality. Contacts made early in life probably have more influence than those developed later. Finally, "intensity" is generally interpreted to mean the importance and prestige attributed to the individual or groups from whom the definitions are learned. For example, the influence of a father, mother, or trusted friend far outweighs the effect of more socially distant figures.
- *The process of learning criminal behavior by association with criminal and anticriminal patterns involves all of the mechanisms that are involved in any other learning process.* Learning criminal behavior patterns is similar to learning nearly all other patterns and is not a matter of mere imitation.
- *Although criminal behavior expresses general needs and values, it is not excused by those general needs and values because noncriminal behavior also expresses the same needs and values.* This principle suggests that the motives for criminal behavior cannot logically be the same as those for conventional behavior. Sutherland rules out such motives as desire to accumulate money or social status, personal frustration, or low self-concept as causes of crime because they are just as likely to produce noncriminal behavior, such as getting a better education or working harder on a job. Only the learning of deviant norms through contact with an excess of definitions favorable toward criminality produces illegal behavior.

In sum, differential association theory holds that people learn criminal attitudes and behavior during their adolescence from close, trusted friends or relatives. A criminal career develops if learned antisocial values and behaviors are not matched or exceeded by conventional attitudes and behaviors. Criminal behavior, then, is learned in a process that is similar to learning any other human behavior.

Testing Differential Association Theory Despite the importance of differential association theory, research devoted to testing its assumptions has been relatively sparse. It has proven difficult to conceptualize the principles of the theory in a way that can be tested empirically. Social scientists find it difficult to evaluate such vague concepts as "definition favorable toward criminality." It is also difficult to follow people over time, establish precisely when definitions favorable toward criminality begin to outweigh prosocial definitions, and determine whether this imbalance produces criminal behavior.

Despite these limitations, several notable research efforts have supported the core principles of this theory:

- Crime appears to be intergenerational: Kids whose parents are deviant and criminal are more likely to become criminals themselves and eventually produce criminal children, a finding that supports the hypothesis that children learn criminal attitudes from deviant parents.[44]
- People who report having attitudes that support deviant behavior are also likely to engage in deviant behavior.[45]

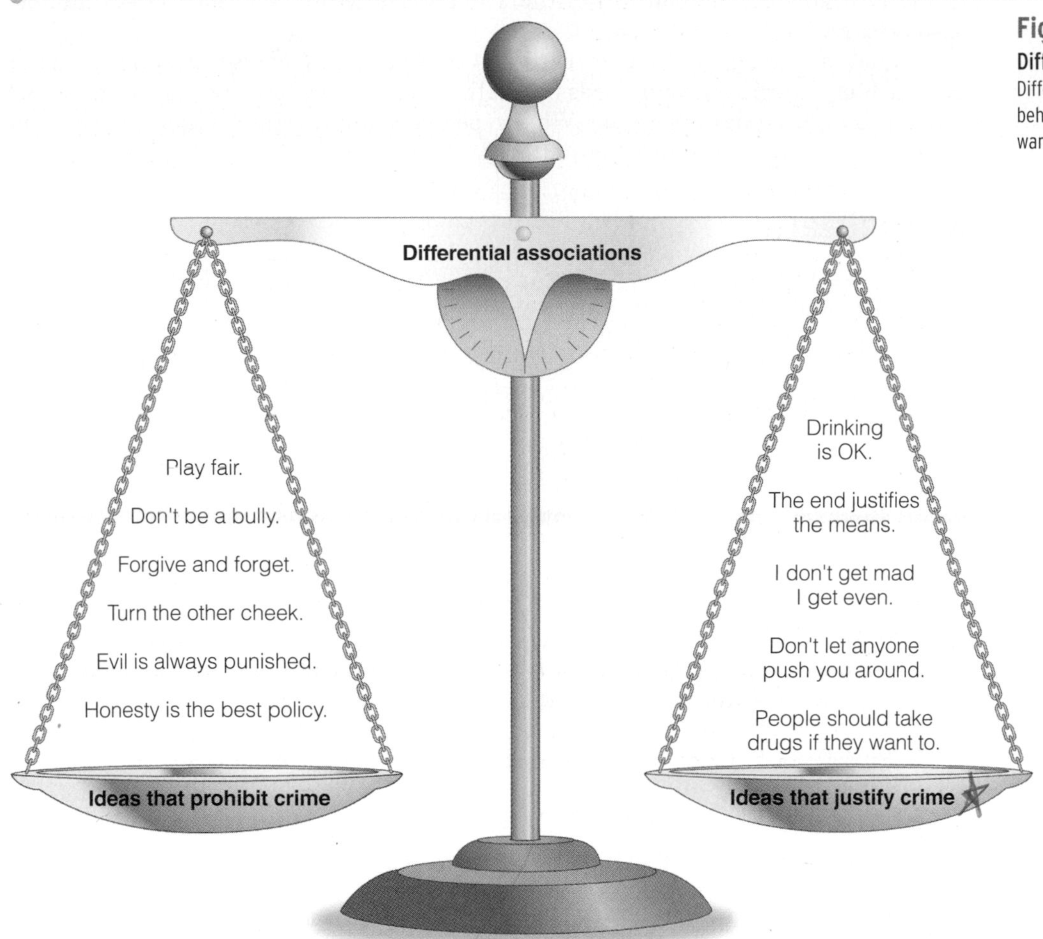

Figure 7.2

Differential Associations

Differential association theory suggests that criminal behavior will occur when the definitions favorable toward crime outweigh the unfavorable definitions.

- As people mature, having delinquent friends who support criminal attitudes and behavior is strongly related to developing criminal careers. Association with deviant peers has been found to sustain the deviant attitudes.[46]
- Romantic partners who engage in antisocial activities may influence their partner's behavior, suggesting that partner's "learn" from one another.[47]
- Kids who associate and presumably learn from aggressive peers are more likely to behave aggressively themselves.[48] Deviant peers interfere with the natural process of aging out of crime by helping provide the support that keeps kids in criminal careers.[49]
- Scales measuring differential association have been significantly correlated with criminal behaviors among samples taken in other nations and cultures.[50]

Analysis of Differential Association Theory Differential association theory is important because it does not specify that criminals come from a disorganized area or are members of the lower class. Outwardly law-abiding, middle-class parents can encourage delinquent behavior by their own drinking, drug use, or family violence. The influence of differential associations is affected by social class; deviant learning experiences can affect youths in all classes.[51]

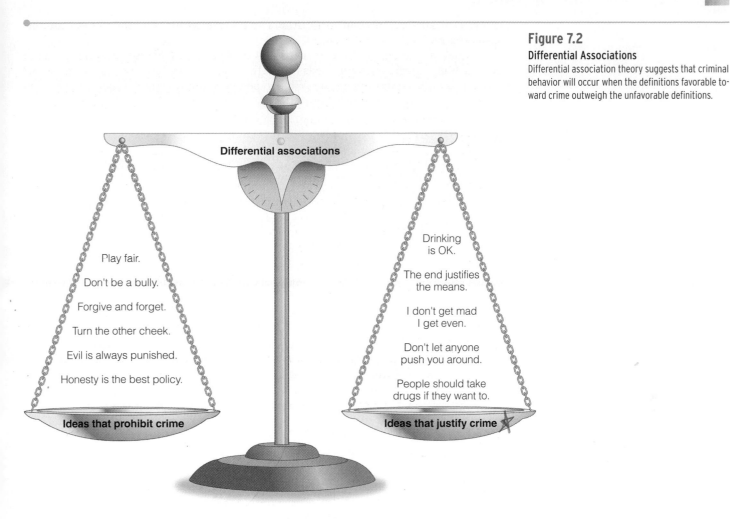

There are, however, a number of valid criticisms of Sutherland's work. It fails to account for the origin of criminal definitions. How did the first "teacher" learn criminal attitudes and definitions in order to pass them on? Another criticism of differential association theory is that it assumes criminal and delinquent acts to be rational and systematic. This ignores spontaneous, wanton acts of violence and damage that appear to have little utility or purpose, such as the isolated psychopathic killing that is virtually unsolvable because of the killer's anonymity and lack of delinquent associations.

Some critics suggest that the theory is tautological: How can we know when a person has experienced an excess of definitions favorable toward criminality? When he or she commits a crime! Why do people commit crime? When they are exposed to an excess of criminal definitions!

Neutralization Theory

Neutralization theory is identified with the writings of David Matza and his associate Gresham Sykes.[52] These criminologists also view the process of becoming a criminal as a learning experience. They theorize that law violators must learn and master techniques that enable them to neutralize conventional values and attitudes, thus allowing them to drift back and forth between illegitimate and conventional behavior.

Neutralization theory points out that even the most committed criminals and delinquents are not involved in criminality all the time; they also attend schools, family functions, and religious services. Thus, their behavior falls along a continuum between total freedom and total restraint. This process of **drift**, or movement from one extreme to another, produces behavior that is sometimes unconventional or deviant and at other times constrained and sober.[53] Learning **neutralization techniques** allows a person to temporarily drift away from conventional behavior and become involved in antisocial behaviors, including crime and drug abuse.[54]

Several observations form the basis of their theoretical model:[55]

- *Criminals sometimes voice guilt over their illegal acts.* If they truly embraced criminal or antisocial values, criminals would probably not exhibit remorse for their acts, other than regret at being apprehended.
- *Offenders frequently respect and admire honest, law-abiding persons.* Those admired may include entertainers, sports figures, priests and other clergy, parents, teachers, and neighbors.
- *Criminals define whom they can victimize.* Members of similar ethnic groups, churches, or neighborhoods are often off-limits. This practice implies that criminals are aware of the wrongfulness of their acts.
- *Criminals are not immune to the demands of conformity.* Most criminals frequently participate in the same social functions as law-abiding people—for example, school, church, and family activities.

Neutralization Techniques

Sykes and Matza suggest that people develop a distinct set of justifications for their law-violating behavior. They conclude that criminals must first neutralize accepted social values before they are free to commit crimes; they do so by learning a set of techniques that allow them to counteract the moral dilemmas posed by illegal behavior.[56]

Through their research, Sykes and Matza have identified the following techniques of neutralization:

- *Denial of responsibility.* Young offenders sometimes claim that their unlawful acts are not their fault—that they result from forces beyond their control or are accidents.
- *Denial of injury.* By denying the injury caused by their acts, criminals neutralize illegal behavior. For example, stealing is viewed as borrowing; vandalism is considered mischief that has gotten out of hand. Offenders may find that their parents and friends support their denial of injury. In fact, parents and friends may claim that the behavior was merely a prank, helping affirm the offender's perception that crime can be socially acceptable.
- *Denial of the victim.* Criminals sometimes neutralize wrongdoing by maintaining that the crime victim "had it coming." Vandalism may be directed against a disliked teacher or neighbor, or a gang may beat up homosexuals because they consider homosexual behavior offensive.

neutralization theory
The view that law violators learn to neutralize conventional values and attitudes, enabling them to drift back and forth between criminal and conventional behavior.

drift
Movement in and out of delinquency, shifting between conventional and deviant values.

neutralization techniques
Methods of rationalizing deviant behavior, such as denying responsibility or blaming the victim.

- *Condemnation of the condemners*. An offender views the world as a corrupt place with a dog-eat-dog code. Because police and judges are on the take, teachers show favoritism, and parents take out their frustrations on their children, offenders claim it is ironic and unfair for these authorities to condemn criminal misconduct. By shifting the blame to others, criminals repress the feeling that their own acts are wrong.
- *Appeal to higher loyalties*. Novice criminals often argue that they are caught in the dilemma of being loyal to their peer group while attempting to abide by the rules of society. The needs of the group take precedence because group demands are immediate and localized (see Figure 7.3).

In sum, neutralization theory states that people neutralize conventional norms and values by using excuses that allow them to drift into crime.

Testing Neutralization Theory Attempts have been made to verify neutralization theory empirically, but the results have been inconclusive.[57] One area of research has been directed at determining whether law violators really need to neutralize moral constraints. The thinking behind this research is that if criminals hold values in opposition to accepted social norms, there is really no need to neutralize. So far, the evidence is mixed. Some studies show that law violators approve of criminal behavior such as theft and violence, whereas others find evidence that even though they may be active participants themselves, criminals voice disapproval of illegal behavior.[58] Some studies indicate that law violators approve of social values such as honesty and fairness; other studies come to the opposite conclusion.[59]

Although the existing research findings are ambiguous, the weight of the evidence shows that most adolescents generally disapprove of deviant behaviors such as violence, and that neutralizations do in fact enable youths to engage in socially disapproved behavior.[60] And, as Matza predicted, people seem to drift in and out of antisocial behavior rather than being committed solely to a criminal way of life.[61]

CONNECTIONS

Denial of the victim may help explain hate crimes, in which people are victimized simply because they belong to the "wrong" race, religion, or ethnic group or because of their sexual orientation. Hate crimes are discussed in Chapter 10.

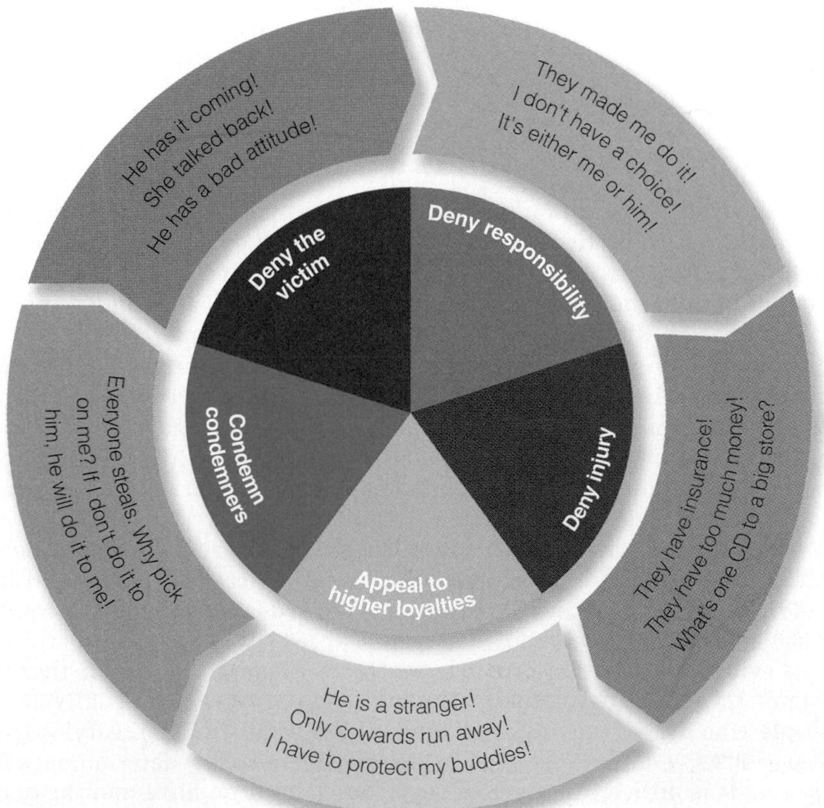

Figure 7.3
Techniques of Neutralization

Current Issues in Crime

When Being Good Is Bad

In their neutralization theory, Sykes and Matza claim that neutralizations provide offenders with a means of preserving a noncriminal self-concept even as they engage in crime and deviance. Sykes and Matza's vision assumes that most criminals believe in conventional norms and values and must use neutralizations in order to shield themselves from the shame attached to criminal activity. Recent research by criminologist Volkan Topalli finds that Sykes and Matza may have ignored the influential street culture that exists in highly disadvantaged neighborhoods. Using data gleaned from 191 in-depth interviews with active criminals in St. Louis, Missouri, Topalli finds that street criminals living in disorganized, gang-ridden neighborhoods "disrespect authority, lionize honor and violence, and place individual needs above those of all others." Rather than having to neutralize conventional values in order to engage in deviant ones, these offenders do not experience guilt that requires neutralizations; they are "guilt free." There is no need for them to "drift" into criminality, Topalli finds, because their allegiance to nonconventional values and lack of guilt perpetually leave them in a state of openness to crime.

Rather than being contrite or ashamed, the offenders Topalli interviewed took great pride in their criminal activities and abilities. Bacca, a street robber who attacked a long-time neighbor without provocation, exemplified such sentiments:

> *Actually I felt proud of myself just for robbing him, just for doing what I did I felt proud of myself. I didn't feel like I did anything wrong, I didn't feel like I lost a friend cause the friends I do have been there for me are lost, they're dead. I feel like I don't have anything to lose. I wanted to do just what I wanted to do.*

Topalli refers to streetwise offenders such as Bacca as "hardcores," who experience no guilt for their actions and operate with little or no regard for the law. They have little contact with agents of formal social control or conventional norms because their crimes are not directed toward conventional society—they rob drug dealers. Most hardcores maintain no permanent home, staying in various residences as their whim dictates. Their lifestyles are almost entirely dominated by the street ethics of violence, self-sufficiency, and opportunism. Obsessed with a constant need for cash, drugs, and alcohol in order to "keep the party going," on the one hand, and limited by self-defeating and reckless spending habits on the other, they often engage in violent crime to bankroll their street life activities. They do not have to neutralize conventional values because they have none.

Rather than neutralizing conventional values, hard-core criminals often have to neutralize deviant values: They are expected to be "bad" and have to explain good behavior. Even if they themselves are the victims of crime, they can never help police or even talk to them, a

Not all criminologists accept Matza's vision. In a recent reformulation of the theory, criminologist Volkan Topalli finds that Matza's vision may have been too narrow. Topalli's work is described in Current Issues in Crime.

Are Learning Theories Valid?

Learning theories contribute significantly to our understanding of the onset of criminal behavior. Nonetheless, the general learning model has been criticized. One complaint is that learning theorists fail to account for the origin of criminal definitions. How did the first criminal learn the necessary techniques and definitions? Who came up with the original neutralization technique?

Learning theories imply that people systematically learn techniques that allow them to be active, successful criminals. However, the theories fail to adequately explain spontaneous, wanton acts of violence, damage, and other expressive crimes that appear to have little utility or purpose. Although principles of differential association can easily explain shoplifting, is it possible that a random shooting is caused by excessive deviant definitions? It is estimated that about 70 percent of all arrestees were under the influence of drugs and alcohol when they committed their crime. Do "crackheads" pause to neutralize their moral inhibitions before mugging a victim? Do drug-involved kids stop to consider what they have learned about moral values?

Little evidence exists that people learn the techniques that enable them to become criminals before they actually commit criminal acts. It is equally plausible that people who are already deviant seek others with similar lifestyles to learn from. Early onset of deviant behavior is now considered a key determinant of criminal careers. It is difficult to see how very young children have had the opportunity to learn criminal behavior and attitudes within a peer group setting.

practice defined as snitching and universally despised and discouraged. Smokedog, a carjacker and drug dealer, described the anticipated guilt of colluding with the police in this way, "You know I ain't never told on nobody and I ain't never gonna tell on nobody 'cause I would feel funny in the world if I told on somebody. You know, I would feel funny, I would have regrets about what I did."

Street criminals are also expected to seek vengeance if they are the target of theft or violence. If they don't, their self-image is damaged and they look weak and ineffective. If they decide against vengeance, they must neutralize their decision by convincing themselves that they are being merciful, respecting direct appeals by their target's family and friends. T-dog, a young drug dealer and car thief, told Topalli how he neutralized the decision not to seek revenge by allowing his uncle to "calm him down." The older man, a robber and drug dealer himself, intervened before T-dog could leave his house armed with two 9 mm automatics: "That's basically what he told me, 'Calm down.' He took both my guns and gave me a little .22 to carry when I'm out to put me back on my feet. Gave me an ounce of crack and a pound of weed. That's what made me let it go." In other cases, offenders claimed the target was just not worth the effort, reserving their vengeance for those who were worthy opponents.

Do these findings indicate that neutralization theory is invalid? Topalli concludes that the strength of the theory is its emphasis on cognitive processes that occur prior to offending. These must be modified by abandoning the theory's current emphasis on a conventional cultural value orientation and expanding it to accommodate the values of the street culture.

Critical Thinking

1. Are there deviant norms and values that you have to neutralize in order to engage in conventional behaviors? What neutralizations have you come up with in order to save face when your friends wanted to engage in some forms of deviance but you decided not to take the risk?
2. Do you agree with Topalli that kids in disorganized neighborhoods shun conventional values? Or do you agree with Sykes and Matza that everyone shares conventional norms and values?

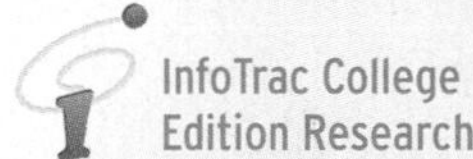

Can neutralization theory explain such minor crimes as deer poaching? To find out, go to Stephen Eliason and Richard Dodder, "Neutralization among Deer Poachers," *The Journal of Social Psychology* 140 (2000): 536.

SOURCE: Volkan Topalli, "When Being Good Is Bad: An Expansion of Neutralization Theory," *Criminology* 43 (2005): 797–836.

Despite these criticisms, learning theories have an important place in the study of delinquent and criminal behavior. They help explain the role that peers, family, and education play in shaping criminal and conventional behaviors. If crime were a matter of personal traits alone, these elements of socialization would not play as important a role in determining human behavior as they do. And unlike social structure theories, learning theories are not limited to explaining a single facet of antisocial activity; they explain criminality across all class structures. Even corporate executives may be exposed to pro-criminal definitions and learn to neutralize moral constraints. Learning theories can thus be applied to a wide assortment of criminal activity.

SOCIAL CONTROL THEORY

Social control theorists maintain that all people have the potential to violate the law and that modern society presents many opportunities for illegal activity. Criminal activities, such as drug abuse and car theft, are often exciting pastimes that hold the promise of immediate reward and gratification.

Considering the attractions of crime, social control theorists question why people obey the rules of society. They argue that people obey the law because behavior and passions are controlled by internal and external forces. Some individuals have **self-control**—a strong moral sense that renders them incapable of hurting others and violating social norms.

Other people have been socialized to have a **commitment to conformity**. They have developed a real, present, and logical reason to obey the rules of society, and they instinctively avoid behavior that will jeopardize their reputation and achievements.[62] The stronger people's commitment to conventional institutions,

self-control
A strong moral sense that renders a person incapable of hurting others or violating social norms.

commitment to conformity
A strong personal investment in conventional institutions, individuals, and processes that prevents people from engaging in behavior that might jeopardize their reputation and achievements.

individuals, and processes, the less likely they are to commit crime. If that commitment is absent, there is little to lose, and people are free to violate the law.[63]

Self-Concept and Crime

Early versions of control theory speculated that criminality was a product of weak self-concept and poor self-esteem. Youths who are socialized to feel good about themselves and who maintain a positive attitude are able to control their own behavior and resist the temptations of the streets.

As early as 1951, sociologist Albert Reiss described delinquents as having weak egos and lacking the self-control to produce conforming behavior.[64] Scott Briar and Irving Piliavin noted that youths who believe criminal activity will damage their self-image and their relationships with others are likely to conform to social rules; in contrast, those less concerned about their social standing are free to violate the law.[65] Pioneering control theorist Walter Reckless argued that a strong self-image insulates a youth from the pressures of crimogenic influences in the environment.[66] In studies conducted within the school setting, Reckless and his colleagues found that students who were able to maintain a positive self-image were insulated from delinquency.[67]

These early works suggested that people who have a weak self-image and damaged ego are crime-prone. They are immune from efforts to apply social control: Why obey the rules of society when you have no stake in the future and little to lose?

CONNECTIONS

The association of self-control and crime will be discussed more fully in Chapter 9 in the context of human development.

Contemporary Social Control Theory

The version of control theory articulated by Travis Hirschi in his influential 1969 book, *Causes of Delinquency*, is today the dominant version of control theories.[68] Hirschi links the onset of criminality to the weakening of the ties that bind people to society. He assumes that all individuals are potential law violators, but most are kept under control because they fear that illegal behavior will damage their relationships with friends, family, neighbors, teachers, and employers. Without these **social bonds**, or ties, a person is free to commit criminal acts. Among all ethnic, religious, racial, and social groups, people whose bond to society is weak may fall prey to crimogenic behavior patterns.

Hirschi argues that the social bond a person maintains with society is divided into four main elements: attachment, commitment, involvement, and belief (see Figure 7.4).

- Attachment refers to a person's sensitivity to and interest in others.[69] Hirschi views parents, peers, and schools as the important social institutions with which a person should maintain ties. Attachment to parents is the most important. Even if a family is shattered by divorce or separation, a child must retain a strong attachment to one or both parents. Without this attachment, it is unlikely that respect for other authorities will develop.
- Commitment involves the time, energy, and effort expended in conventional actions such as getting an education and saving money for the future. If people build a strong commitment to conventional society, they will be less likely to engage in acts that jeopardize their hard-won position. Conversely, the lack of commitment to conventional values may foreshadow a condition in which risk-taking behavior, such as crime, becomes a reasonable behavior alternative.
- Heavy involvement in conventional activities leaves little time for illegal behavior. Hirschi believes that involvement in school, recreation, and family insulates people from the potential lure of criminal behavior. Idleness, on the other hand, enhances that lure.
- People who live in the same social setting often share common moral beliefs; they may adhere to such values as sharing, sensitivity to the rights of others, and admiration for the legal code. If these beliefs are absent or weakened, individuals are more likely to participate in antisocial or illegal acts.

social bonds

The ties that bind people to society, including relationships with friends, family, neighbors, teachers, and employers. Elements of the social bond include commitment, attachment, involvement, and belief.

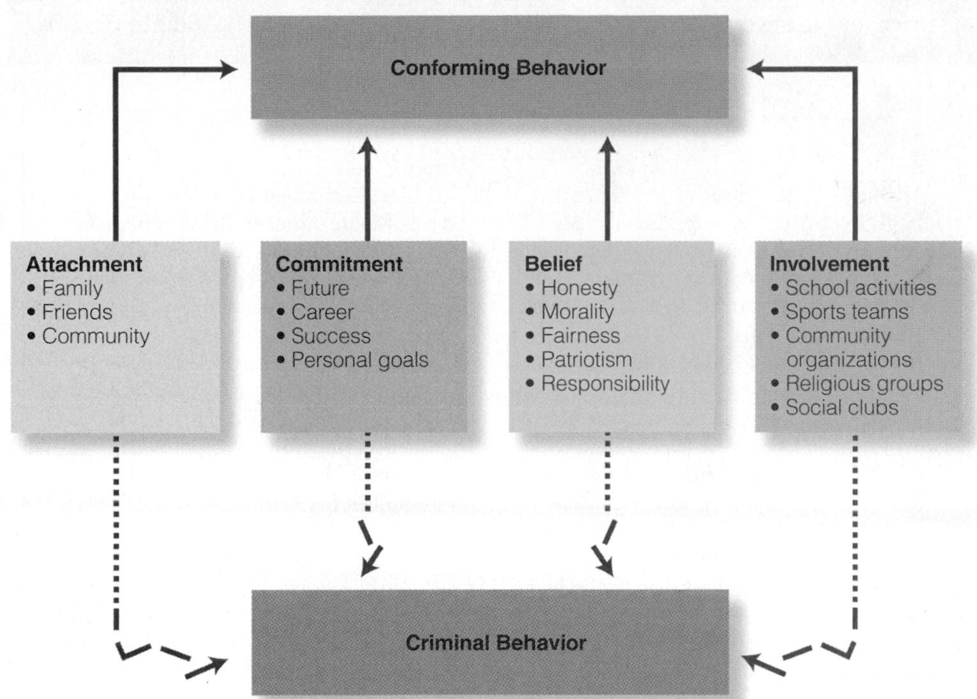

Figure 7.4
Elements of the Social Bond

Hirschi further suggests that the interrelationship of social bond elements controls subsequent behavior. For example, people who feel kinship and sensitivity to parents and friends should be more likely to adopt and work toward legitimate goals. A person who rejects such social relationships is more likely to lack commitment to conventional goals. Similarly, people who are highly committed to conventional acts and beliefs are more likely to be involved in conventional activities. The following Profiles in Crime feature describes a case that may rest on a frayed and tattered social bond.

CONNECTIONS

Travis Hirschi, along with Michael Gottfredson, has restructured his concept of control by integrating biosocial, psychological, and rational choice theory ideas into a General Theory of Crime. Because this new theory is essentially developmental, it will be discussed more fully in Chapter 9.

Testing Social Control Theory

One of Hirschi's most significant contributions to criminology was his attempt to test the principal hypotheses of social control theory. He administered a detailed self-report survey to a sample of more than 4,000 junior and senior high school students in Contra Costa County, California.[70] In a detailed analysis of the data, Hirschi found considerable evidence to support the control theory model. Among Hirschi's more important findings are the following:

- Youths who were strongly attached to their parents were less likely to commit criminal acts.
- Youths involved in conventional activity, such as homework, were less likely to engage in criminal behavior.
- Youths involved in unconventional behavior, such as smoking and drinking, were more prone to delinquency.
- Youths who maintained weak, distant relationships with people tended toward delinquency.
- Those who shunned unconventional acts were attached to their peers.
- Delinquents and nondelinquents shared similar beliefs about society.

Even when the statistical significance of Hirschi's findings was less than he expected, the direction of his research data was notably consistent. Only rarely did his findings contradict the theory's most critical assumptions.

Profiles in Crime

Alpha Dog

Twenty-five-year-old Jesse James Hollywood (his real name) was living a comfortable life in Brazil, teaching English and living in a fashionable neighborhood, when he was arrested in November 2005 and sent back to California, where he faces charges of kidnapping and killing a 15-year-old boy.

Though Hollywood never held a job, by age 19, he was able to purchase a $200,000 house in West Hills, California, and a Mercedes. His place became a popular spot for local kids who came and went at all hours of the day. Hollywood was a popular guy, an outgoing kid who, despite being short in stature, was an excellent athlete. How was he able to do all this? Unknown to many, Hollywood was a large-scale marijuana dealer.

Hollywood's world began to unravel when he came up with a scheme to get money owed to him by Benjamin Markowitz, 22, one of his customers. Hollywood went over to Markowitz's family home on August 6, 2000, to kidnap him and hold him for ransom. According to authorities, on the way there, Hollywood and his friends spotted Markowitz's 15 year-old stepbrother, Nicholas, and they forced him into a van and transported him to the home of another accomplice. After being held captive for a few days, Nick Markowitz was made to walk a mile into Los Padres National Forest before being shot nine times with a high-powered assault rifle and buried in a shallow grave. His body was discovered four days later by hikers. Four other kids were tried and convicted in the case, but Hollywood escaped and became the subject of an international manhunt, his mug shot plastered on the FBI's website. He wound up in Brazil, where he used fake papers that identified him as Michael Costa Giroux, a native of Rio de Janeiro. Brazilian authorities deported him as an illegal alien. A 2006 film *Alpha Dog*, starring Bruce Willis, Justin Timberlake, and Sharon Stone, is based on the case.

Jesse James Hollywood grew up in an affluent family and seemed to be popular and successful. How could he have become involved in an awful, violent crime? How would a control theorist explain his actions?

SOURCES: Jeremiah Marquez, "Longtime Fugitive Jesse James Hollywood Captured in Brazil Friday, March 11, 2005," http://sfgate.com/cgibin/article.cgi?file=/news/archive/2005/03/10/state/n085203S47.DTL; FBI press release, "Jesse James Hollywood, Fugitive in August 2000 Kidnap-Murder of Teenager, Arrested in Brazil, March 10, 2005," http://losangeles.fbi.gov/pressrel/2005/la031005.htm.

Supporting Research Hirschi's version of social control theory has been corroborated by numerous research studies showing that delinquent youths often feel detached from society.[71] What are some of the most important findings?

- *Attachment*. Kids who are attached to their families, friends, and school are less likely to get involved in a deviant peer group and consequently less likely to engage in criminal activities.[72] Teens who are attached to their parents are also able to develop the social skills that equip them both to maintain harmonious social ties and to escape life stresses such as school failure.[73] In contrast, family detachment, including intrafamily conflict, abuse of children, and lack of affection, supervision, and family pride, are predictive of delinquent conduct.[74]

  Attachment to education is equally important. Youths who are detached from the educational experience are at risk to criminality; those who are committed to school are less likely to engage in delinquent acts.[75]

  Attachment can come in many forms. In a recent study of adolescent motherhood, Trina Hope, Esther Wilder, and Toni-Terling Watt found that young girls who become pregnant are no more likely to engage in delinquent acts than their never-pregnant peers. The birth of a child serves as a mechanism of social control and reduces the likelihood of delinquent behavior. Attachment to a child, even during difficult circumstances, may produce the behavior change predicted by Hirschi.[76]

- *Belief*. Other research efforts have shown that holding positive beliefs are inversely related to criminality. Children who are involved in religious activities and hold conventional religious beliefs are less likely to become involved in substance abuse.[77] Kids who live in areas marked by strong religious values and who hold strong religious beliefs themselves are less likely to engage in delinquent activities than adolescents who do not hold such beliefs or who live in less devout communities.[78]

- *Commitment.* As predicted by Hirschi, kids who are committed to school and educational achievement are less likely to become involved in delinquent behaviors than those who lack such commitment.[79] The association may be reciprocal. Kids who drink and engage in deviant behavior are more likely to fail in school; kids who fail in school are more likely to later drink and engage in deviant behavior.[80]
- *Involvement.* Research shows that youths who are involved in conventional leisure activities, such as supervised social activities and non-competitive sports, are less likely to engage in delinquency than those who are involved in unconventional leisure activities and unsupervised, peer-oriented social pursuits.[81]

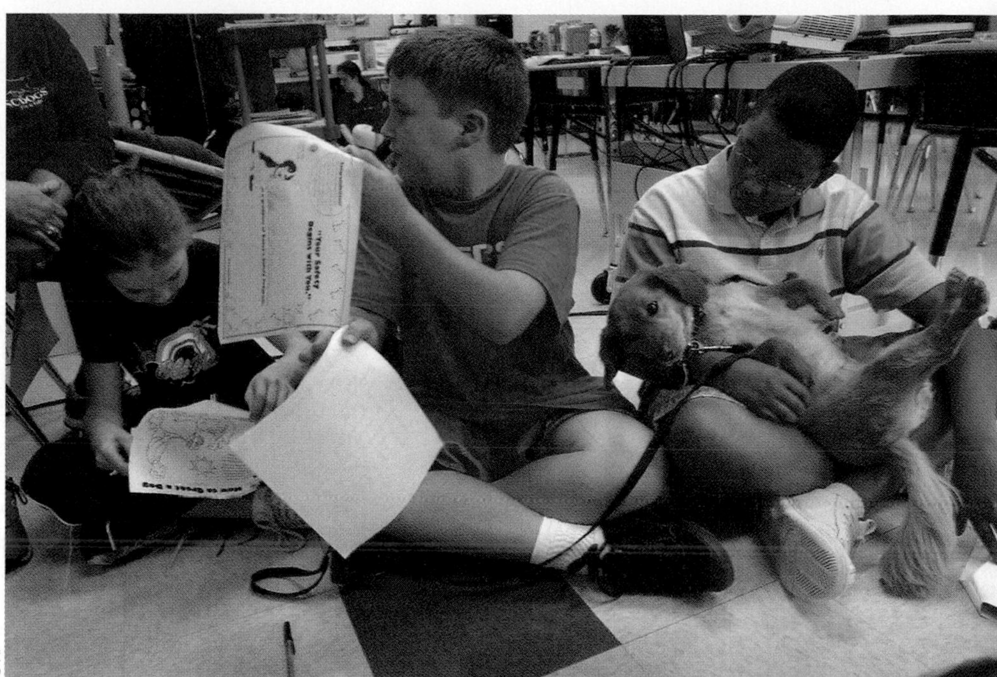

© AP

● According to Travis Hirschi, kids involved in productive activities are less likely to get involved in deviant activities. At La France Elementary School fifth-graders Taylor Davis (left) and Blake Duncan complete worksheets about how to be kind to animals and people, while Tracy Grate (right) holds Abby, an SCDogs Therapy Group dog. The "Fix It Fido" program, which aims to curb bullying, finished its pilot year during the 2005-2006 school year. The program may enhance children's bonds to society and promote prosocial behaviors.

Opposing Views Although there is a great deal of supportive research, a number of questions have been raised about the validity of control theory.

- *Friendship.* One significant criticism concerns Hirschi's contention that delinquents are detached loners whose bond to family and friends has been broken. In fact, delinquents seem not to be "lone wolves" whose only personal relationships are exploitative; their friendship patterns seem quite close to those of conventional youth.[82] Some types of offenders, such as drug abusers, may maintain even more intimate relations with their peers than nonabusers.[83] Hirschi would counter that what appears to be a close friendship is really a relationship of convenience.
- *Failure to achieve.* Hirschi argues that commitment to career and economic advancement reduces criminal involvement. However, research indicates that people who are committed to success but fail to achieve it may be crime-prone.[84]
- *Involvement negates supervision.* Adolescents who report high levels of involvement, which Hirschi suggests should reduce delinquency, actually report high levels of criminal behavior. Perhaps adolescents who are involved in activities outside the home have less contact with parental supervision and greater opportunity to commit crime.[85]
- *Deviant peers and parents.* Hirschi's conclusion that any form of social attachment is beneficial, even to deviant peers and parents, has also been disputed. Rather than deter delinquency, attachment to deviant peers may support and nurture antisocial behavior.[86] A number of research efforts have found that youths attached to drug-abusing parents are more likely to use drugs themselves.[87] Attachment to deviant family members, peers, and associates may help motivate youths to commit crime and facilitate their antisocial acts.[88]
- *Mistaken causal order.* Hirschi's theory proposes that a weakened bond leads to delinquency, but Robert Agnew suggests that the chain of events may flow in the opposite direction: Perhaps youngsters who break the law find that their bonds to parents, schools, and society eventually become weak. Other studies have also found that criminal behavior weakens social bonds and not vice versa.[89]

These criticisms are important, but Hirschi's views still constitute one of the preeminent theories in criminology.[90] Many criminologists consider social control theory the primary way of understanding the onset of youthful misbehavior. ✔ CHECKPOINTS

✔ CHECKPOINTS

✔ Social control theories maintain that behavior is a function of the attachment that people feel toward society. People who have a weak commitment to conformity are free to commit crime.

✔ A strong self-image may insulate people from crime.

✔ According to Travis Hirschi, social control is measured by a person's attachment, commitment, involvement, and belief.

✔ Significant research supports Hirschi's theory, but a number of criminologists question its validity.

SOCIAL REACTION (LABELING) THEORY

Social reaction theory, also called labeling theory (the two terms are used interchangeably), explains criminal careers in terms of destructive social interactions and stigma-producing encounters. Social reaction theory has a number of key points:

- *Behaviors that are considered criminal are highly subjective.* Even such crimes as murder, rape, and assault are only bad or evil because people label them as such. The difference between a forcible rape and a consensual sexual encounter often rests on whom a jury chooses to believe and how they interpret the events that took place. The difference between an excusable act and a criminal one is often subject to change and modification. Acts such as performing an abortion, using marijuana, possessing a handgun, and gambling have been legal at some times and places and illegal at others.
- *Crime is defined by those in power.* The content and shape of criminal law is defined by the values of those who rule and is not an objective standard of moral conduct. Howard Becker refers to people who create rules as **moral entrepreneurs**. An example of a moral entrepreneur is someone who campaigns against violence in the media and wants laws passed to restrict the content of television shows.
- *Not only are acts labeled, so too are people.* These symbolic labels help define not just one trait but the whole person. Valued labels, such as "smart," "honest," and "hardworking," suggest overall competence. Sometimes the labels are highly symbolic, such as being named "most likely to succeed" or class valedictorian. People who hold these titles are automatically assumed to be leaders who are well on their way to success. Without meeting them, we know that they are hardworking, industrious, and bright. These positive labels can improve self-image and social standing. Research shows that people who are labeled with one positive trait, such as being physically attractive, are assumed to have other positive traits, such as being intelligent and competent.[91] In contrast, people who run afoul of the law or other authorities, such as school officials, are given negative labels, including "troublemaker," "mentally ill," and "stupid," that **stigmatize** them and reduce their self-image. Negative labels also define the whole person. People labeled "insane" are also assumed to be dangerous, dishonest, unstable, violent, strange, and otherwise unsound.
- *Both positive and negative labels involve subjective interpretation of behavior.* A "troublemaker" is merely someone whom people label as "troublesome."

In a famous statement, Howard Becker sums up the importance of the audience's reaction:

> Social groups create deviance by making rules whose infractions constitute deviance, and by applying those rules to particular people and labeling them as outsiders. From this point of view, deviance is not a quality of the act a person commits, but rather a consequence of the application by others of rules and sanctions to an "offender." The deviant is one to whom the label has successfully been applied; deviant behavior is behavior that people so label.[92]

Even if some acts are labeled as bad or evil, those who participate in them can be spared a negative label. It is possible to take another person's life but not be considered a "murderer" because the killing was considered self-defense or even an accident. Acts have negative consequences only when labeled by others as being wrong or evil.

moral entrepreneur
A person who creates moral rules that reflect the values of those in power rather than any objective, universal standards of right and wrong.

stigmatize
To apply negative labeling with enduring effects on a person's self-image and social interactions.

Consequences of Labeling

Although a label may be a function of rumor, innuendo, or unfounded suspicion, its adverse impact can be immense. If a devalued status is conferred by a significant other—a teacher, police officer, parent, or valued peer—the negative label may permanently harm the target. The degree to which a person is perceived as a social deviant may affect his or her treatment at home, at work, at school, and in other social situations. Children may find that their parents consider them a bad influence on younger brothers and sisters. School officials may limit them to classes reserved for people with behavioral problems. Likewise, when adults are labeled as "criminal," "ex-con," or "drug addict," they may find their eligibility for employment severely restricted. If the label is bestowed as the result of conviction for a criminal offense, the labeled person may also be subjected to official sanctions ranging from a mild reprimand to incarceration. The simultaneous effects of labels and sanctions reinforce feelings of isolation and detachment.

Public denunciation plays an important part in the labeling process. Condemnation is often carried out in "ceremonies" in which the individual's identity is officially transformed. Examples of such reidentification ceremonies are a competency hearing in which a person is declared to be "mentally ill" or a public trial in which a person is found to be a "rapist" or "child molester." During the process, a permanent record is produced, such as an arrest or conviction record, so that the denounced person is ritually separated from a place in the legitimate order and placed outside the world occupied by citizens of good standing. Harold Garfinkle has called transactions that produce irreversible, permanent labels **successful degradation ceremonies**.[93]

Self-Labeling According to labeling theory, depending on the visibility of the label and the manner and severity with which it is applied, negatively labeled individuals will become increasingly committed to a deviant career. Labeled persons may find themselves turning to others similarly stigmatized for support and companionship.

Isolated from conventional society, labeled people may identify themselves as members of an outcast group and become locked into deviance. Kids who view themselves as delinquents after being labeled as such are giving an inner voice to their perceptions of how parents, teachers, peers, and neighbors view them. When they believe that others view them as antisocial or troublemakers, they take on attitudes and roles that reflect this assumption; they expect to become suspects and then to be rejected.[94]

Joining Deviant Cliques People labeled as deviant may join with similarly outcast peers who facilitate their behavior. Eventually, antisocial behavior becomes habitual and automatic.[95] The desire to join deviant cliques and groups may stem from self-rejecting attitudes ("At times, I think I am no good at all") that eventually weaken commitment to conventional values and behaviors. In turn, stigmatized individuals may acquire motives to deviate from social norms because they now share a common bond with similarly labeled social outcasts.[96] Eric Harris and Dylan Klebold formed the "Trenchcoat Mafia" whose members were also alienated and stigmatized, before the two committed the Columbine High School massacre. Membership in a deviant subculture often involves conforming to group norms that conflict with those of conventional society, further enhancing the effects of the labeling process.

Retrospective Reading Beyond any immediate results, labels tend to redefine the whole person. For example, the label "ex-con" may create in people's imaginations a whole series of behavior descriptions—tough, mean, dangerous, aggressive, dishonest, sneaky—that may or may not apply to a person who has been in prison. People react to the label description and what it signifies instead of reacting to the actual behavior of the person who bears it. The labeled person's past is reviewed and reevaluated to fit his or her current status—a process known as **retrospective reading**. When interviewed by the media, boyhood friends of an assassin or serial killer, report that the suspect was withdrawn, suspicious, and negativistic as a youth; they were always suspicious but never thought to report their concerns to the authorities. According to this retrospective reading, we can now understand what prompted his current behavior; therefore, the label must be accurate.[97]

successful degradation ceremony
A course of action or ritual in which someone's identity is publicly redefined and destroyed and they are thereafter viewed as socially unacceptable.

retrospective reading
The reassessment of a person's past to fit a current generalized label.

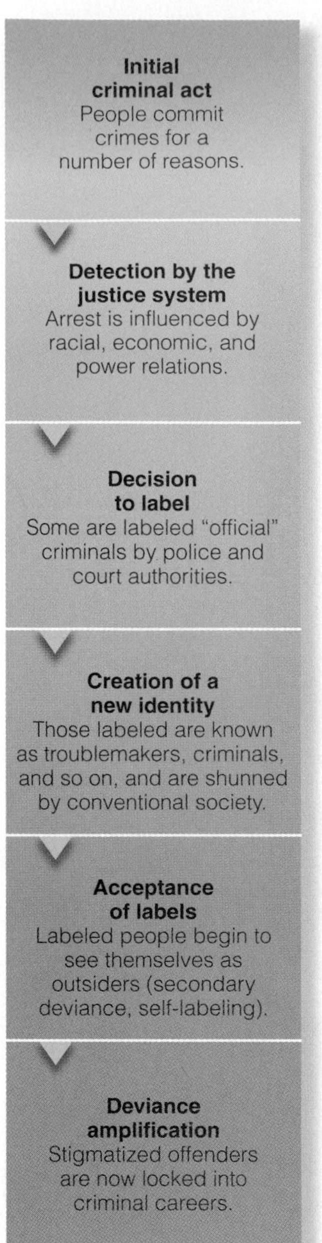

Initial criminal act
People commit crimes for a number of reasons.
Detection by the justice system
Arrest is influenced by racial, economic, and power relations.
Decision to label
Some are labeled "official" criminals by police and court authorities.
Creation of a new identity
Those labeled are known as troublemakers, criminals, and so on, and are shunned by conventional society.
Acceptance of labels
Labeled people begin to see themselves as outsiders (secondary deviance, self-labeling).
Deviance amplification
Stigmatized offenders are now locked into criminal careers.

Figure 7.5
The Labeling Process

Labels, then, become the basis of personal identity. As the negative feedback of law enforcement agencies, parents, friends, teachers, and other figures amplifies the force of the original label, stigmatized offenders may begin to reevaluate their own identities (see Figure 7.5). If they are not really evil or bad, they may ask themselves, "Why is everyone making such a fuss?" This process has been referred to as the "dramatization of evil."[98]

Primary and Secondary Deviance

One of the better-known views of the labeling process is Edwin Lemert's concept of primary deviance and secondary deviance.[99] According to Lemert, **primary deviance** involves norm violations or crimes that have little influence on the actor and can be quickly forgotten. For example, a college student successfully steals a textbook at the campus bookstore, gets an A in the course, graduates, is admitted to law school, and later becomes a famous judge. Because his shoplifting goes unnoticed, it is a relatively unimportant event that has little bearing on his future life.

In contrast, **secondary deviance** occurs when a deviant event comes to the attention of significant others or social control agents, who apply a negative label. The newly labeled offender then reorganizes his or her behavior and personality around the consequences of the deviant act. The shoplifting student is caught by a security guard and expelled from college. With his law school dreams dashed and his future cloudy, his options are limited; people say he lacks character, and he begins to share their opinion. He eventually becomes a drug dealer and winds up in prison (see Figure 7.6).

Secondary deviance involves resocialization into a deviant role. The labeled person is transformed into one who, according to Lemert, "employs his behavior or a role based upon it as a means of defense, attack, or adjustment to the overt and covert problems created by the consequent social reaction to him."[100] Secondary deviance produces a **deviance amplification** effect: Offenders feel isolated from the mainstream of society and become locked within their deviant role. They may seek others similarly labeled to form deviant groups. Ever more firmly enmeshed in their deviant role, they are trapped in an escalating cycle of deviance, apprehension, more powerful labels, and identity transformation. Lemert's concept of secondary deviance expresses the core of social reaction theory: Deviance is a process in which one's identity is transformed. Efforts to control offenders, whether by treatment or punishment, simply help to lock them in their deviant role.

primary deviance
A norm violation or crime with little or no long-term influence on the violator.

secondary deviance
A norm violation or crime that comes to the attention of significant others or social control agents, who apply a negative label with long-term consequences for the violator's self-identity and social interactions.

deviance amplification
Process whereby secondary deviance pushes offenders out of mainstream society and locks them into an escalating cycle of deviance, apprehension, labeling, and criminal self-identity.

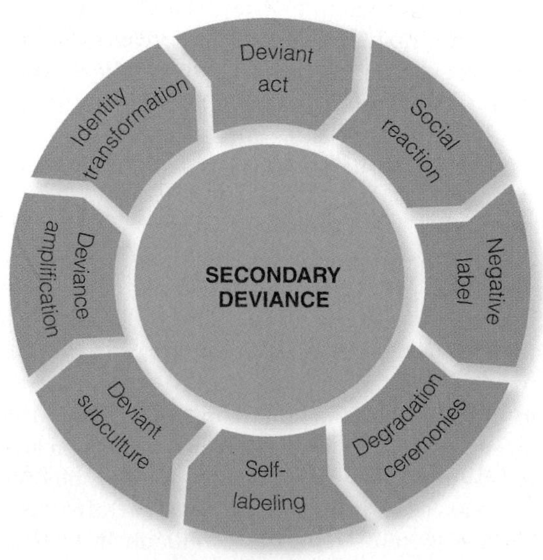

Figure 7.6
Secondary Deviance: The Labeling Process

Crime and Labeling

Because the process of becoming stigmatized is essentially interactive, labeling theorists blame the establishment of criminal careers on the social agencies originally designed for crime control, such as police, courts, and correctional agencies. It is these institutions, labeling theorists claim, that produce the stigma that harms the people they are trying to help, treat, or correct. As a result, they actually help to maintain and amplify criminal behavior.

Because crime and deviance are defined by the social audience's reaction to people and their behavior and the subsequent effects of that reaction, these institutions form the audience that helps define behavior as evil or wrong, locking people into deviant identities.

Differential Enforcement

An important principle of social reaction theory is that the law is differentially applied, benefiting those who hold economic and social power and penalizing the powerless. The probability of being brought under the control of legal authority is a function of a person's race, wealth, gender, and social standing. A core concept of social reaction theory is that police officers are more likely to formally arrest males, minority group members, and those in the lower class, and to use their discretionary powers to give beneficial treatment to more favored groups.[101] Minorities and the poor are more likely to be prosecuted for criminal offenses and to receive harsher punishments when convicted.[102] Judges may sympathize with white defendants and help them avoid criminal labels, especially if they seem to come from "good families," whereas minority youths are not afforded that luxury.[103] This helps to explain the significant racial and economic differences in the crime rate.

In sum, a major premise of social reaction theory is that the law is differentially constructed and applied, depending on the offender. It favors powerful members of society, who direct its content, and penalizes people whose actions threaten those in control, such as minority group members and the poor who demand equal rights.[104]

CONNECTIONS

Fear of stigma has prompted efforts to reduce the impact of criminal labels through such programs as pretrial diversion and community treatment. In addition, some criminologists have called for noncoercive "peacemaking" solutions to interpersonal conflict. This peacemaking or restorative justice movement is reviewed in Chapter 8.

Research on Social Reaction Theory

Research on social reaction theory can be classified into two distinct categories. The first focuses on the characteristics of those offenders who are chosen for labeling. The theory predicts that they will be relatively powerless people who are unable to defend themselves against the negative labeling. The second type of research attempts to discover the effects of being labeled. Labeling theorists predict that people who are negatively labeled will view themselves as deviant and commit increasing amounts of crime.

Targets of Labeling There is evidence that, as predicted by labeling theory, poor and powerless people are victimized by the law and justice system. Labels are not equally distributed across class and racial lines. From the police officer's decision on whom to arrest, to the prosecutor's decision on whom to charge and how many and what kinds of charges to bring, to the court's decision on whom to release or grant bail, to the grand jury's decision on indictment, to the judge's decision on sentence length, discretion works to the detriment of minorities.[105]

Effects of Labeling Empirical evidence shows that negative labels may dramatically influence the self-image of offenders. Considerable evidence indicates social sanctions lead to self-labeling and deviance amplification.[106] For example, children negatively labeled by their parents routinely suffer a variety of problems, including antisocial behavior and school failure.[107] This process has been observed in the United States and abroad, indicating that the labeling process is universal, especially in nations in which a brush with the law brings personal dishonor, such as China and Japan.[108]

● According to labeling theory, perceptions guide behavior. Would you want to invite this guy to lunch with your family? He is The Scary Guy (his real name) and he spends his time teaching students and adults about what they can do to change the world by taking responsibility for their own behavior. His mission is to eliminate hate, violence, and prejudice worldwide. He is shown here hammering home his message at Valencia Middle School in Tucson, Arizona. What do you think of him now?

This labeling process is important because once they are stigmatized as troublemakers, adolescents begin to reassess their self-image. Parents who label their children as troublemakers promote deviance amplification. Labeling alienates parents from their children, and negative labels reduce children's self-image and increase delinquency; this process is referred to as **reflected appraisals**.[109] Parental labeling is extremely damaging because it may cause adolescents to seek deviant peers whose behavior amplifies the effect of the labeling.[110]

As they mature, children are in danger of receiving repeated, intensive, official labeling, which has been shown to produce self-labeling and to damage identities.[111] Kids who perceive that they have been negatively labeled by significant others such as peers and teachers are also more likely to self-report delinquent behavior and to adopt a deviant self-concept.[112] They are likely to make deviant friends and join gangs, associations that escalate their involvement in criminal activities.[113] Youngsters labeled as troublemakers in school are the most likely to drop out; dropping out has been linked to delinquent behavior.[114]

Even in adults, the labeling process can take its toll. Male drug users labeled as addicts by social control agencies eventually become self-labeled and increase their drug use.[115] People arrested in domestic violence cases, especially those with a low stake in conformity (for example, those who are jobless and unmarried), increase offending after being given official labels.[116] And once in prison, inmates labeled high risk are more likely to have disciplinary problems than those who are spared such negative labels.[117]

Empirical evidence supports the view that labeling plays a significant role in persistent offending.[118] Although labels may not cause adolescents to initiate criminal behaviors, experienced delinquents are significantly more likely to continue offending if they believe their parents and peers view them in a negative light.[119] Labeling, then, may help sustain criminality over time.

Is Labeling Theory Valid?

Criminologists Raymond Paternoster and Leeann Iovanni have identified features of the labeling perspective that are important contributions to the study of criminality:[120]

- The labeling perspective identifies the role played by social control agents in crime causation. Criminal behavior cannot be fully understood if the agencies and individuals empowered to control and treat it are neglected.

reflected appraisal
When parents are alienated from their children, their negative labeling reduces their children's self-image and increases delinquency.

- Labeling theory recognizes that criminality is not a disease or pathological behavior. It focuses attention on the social interactions and reactions that shape individuals and their behavior.
- Labeling theory distinguishes between criminal acts (primary deviance) and criminal careers (secondary deviance) and shows that these concepts must be interpreted and treated differently.

Labeling theory also contributes to understanding crime because of its focus on interaction as well as the situation surrounding the crime. Rather than viewing the criminal as a robotlike creature whose actions are predetermined, it recognizes that crime often results from complex interactions and processes. The decision to commit crime involves actions of a variety of people, including peers, victim, police, and other key characters. Labels may foster crime by guiding the actions of all parties involved in these criminal interactions. Actions deemed innocent when performed by one person are considered provocative when engaged in by someone who has been labeled as deviant. Similarly, labeled people may be quick to judge, take offense, or misinterpret others' behavior because of past experience. ✔ CHECKPOINTS

✔ CHECKPOINTS

✔ According to labeling theory, stigma helps lock people into deviant careers.

✔ Labels amplify deviant behavior rather than deter future criminality.

✔ Primary deviants view themselves as good people who have done a bad thing; secondary deviants accept a negative label as an identity.

✔ Labels are bestowed in a biased way. The poor and minority group members are more likely to receive labels.

SOCIAL PROCESS THEORY AND PUBLIC POLICY

Social process theories have had a major influence on public policy since the 1950s. Learning theories have greatly influenced the way criminal offenders are treated. The effect of these theories has been felt mainly by young offenders, who are viewed as being more salvageable than hardened criminals. Advocates of the social learning approach argue that if people become criminal by learning definitions and attitudes favoring criminality, they can unlearn them by being exposed to definitions favoring conventional behavior.

This philosophy has been used in numerous treatment facilities based in part on two early, pioneering efforts: the Highfields Project in New Jersey and the Silverlake Program in Los Angeles. These residential treatment programs, geared toward young male offenders, used group interaction sessions to attack criminal behavior orientations while promoting conventional lines of behavior. It is common today for residential and nonresidential programs to offer similar treatment, teaching children and adolescents to refuse drugs, to forgo delinquent behavior, and to stay in school. It is even common for celebrities to return to their old neighborhoods to urge young people to stay in school or off drugs. If learning did not affect behavior, such exercises would be futile.

© AP

● According to social process theories, programs that aid children's socialization also help protect them from crime-producing influences in the environment. Here, as part of the ExCite/Head Start program, a retired professor spends time in the classroom with elementary students, teaching the colors of the rainbow, reading stories, tying dangling shoelaces, and giggling over games.

Policy & Practice in Criminology

Head Start

Head Start is probably the best-known effort to help lower-class youths achieve proper socialization and, in so doing, reduce their potential for future criminality. Head Start programs were instituted in the 1960s as part of President Johnson's War on Poverty. In the beginning, Head Start was a two-month summer program for children who were about to enter a school that was aimed at embracing the "whole child." In embracing the whole child, the school offered comprehensive programming that helped improve physical health, enhance mental processes, and improve social and emotional development, self-image, and interpersonal relationships. Preschoolers were provided with an enriched educational environment to develop their learning and cognitive skills. They were given the opportunity to use pegs and pegboards, puzzles, toy animals, dolls, letters and numbers, and other materials that middle-class children take for granted. These opportunities provided the children a leg up in the educational process. The program is divided into four segments:

- *Education*. Head Start's educational program is designed to meet the needs of each child, the community served, and its ethnic and cultural characteristics. Every child receives a variety of learning experiences to foster intellectual, social, and emotional growth.
- *Health*. Head Start emphasizes the importance of the early identification of health problems. Every child is involved in a comprehensive health program, which includes immunizations, medical, dental, and mental health, and nutritional services.
- *Parent involvement*. An essential part of Head Start is the involvement of parents in parent education, program planning, and operating activities.
- *Social services*. Specific services are geared to each family, including community outreach, referrals, family need assessments, recruitment and enrollment of children, and emergency assistance and/or crisis intervention.

Today, with annual funding of more than $6.5 billion, the Head Start program is administered by the Head Start Bureau, the Administration on Children, Youth, and Families (ACYF), the Administration for Children and Families (ACF), and the Department of Health and Human Services (DHHS). Head Start teachers strive to provide a variety of learning experiences appropriate to the child's age and development. These experiences encourage the child to read books, to understand cultural diversity, to express feelings, and to play with and relate to peers in an appropriate way. Students are guided in developing gross and fine motor skills, and self-confidence. Health care is also an issue, and most children enrolled in the program receive comprehensive health screening, physical and dental examinations, and appropriate follow-up. Many programs provide meals, and in so doing help children receive proper nourishment.

Head Start programs now serve parents in addition to their preschoolers. Some programs allow parents to enroll in classes, which cover parenting, literacy, nutrition/weight loss, domestic violence prevention, and other social issues. Social services, health, nutrition, and educational services are also available.

Considerable controversy has surrounded the success of the Head Start program. In 1970, the Westinghouse Learning Corporation issued an evaluation of the Head Start effort and concluded that there was no evidence of lasting cognitive gains by the participating children. Though disappointing, this evaluation focused on IQ levels and gave short shrift to improvement in social competence and other survival skills. More recent research has produced dramatically different results. One report found that, by age 5, children who experienced the enriched day care offered by Head Start averaged more than 10 points higher on their IQ scores than their peers who did not

Control theories have also influenced criminal justice and other social policies. Programs have been developed to increase people's commitment to conventional lines of action. Some work at creating and strengthening bonds early in life before the onset of criminality. The educational system has hosted numerous programs designed to improve basic skills and create an atmosphere in which youths will develop a bond to their schools. The Policy & Practice in Criminology feature discusses the Head Start program, perhaps the largest and most successful attempt to solidify social bonds.

Control theory's focus on the family has played a key role in programs designed to strengthen the bond between parent and child. Other programs attempt to repair bonds that have been broken and frayed. Examples of this approach are the career, work furlough, and educational opportunity programs being developed in the nation's prisons. These programs are designed to help inmates maintain a stake in society so they will be less willing to resort to criminal activity after their release.

Although labeling theorists caution that too much intervention can be harmful, programs aimed at reconfiguring an offender's self-image may help him or her develop revamped identities and desist from crime. With proper treatment, labeled offenders can cast off their damaged identities and develop new ones. As a result, they develop an improved self-concept that reflects the positive reinforcement they receive while in treatment.[121]

participate in the program. Other research that carefully compared Head Start children to similar youngsters who did not attend the program found that the former made significant intellectual gains. Head Start children were less likely to have been retained in a grade or placed in classes for slow learners; they outperformed peers on achievement tests; and they were more likely to graduate from high school.

Head Start kids also made strides in nonacademic areas: They appear to have better health, immunization rates, nutrition, and enhanced emotional characteristics after leaving the program. Research also shows that the Head Start program can have psychological benefits for the mothers of participants, such as decreasing depression and anxiety and increasing feelings of life satisfaction. The best available evidence suggests that

- Head Start is associated with short-term gains in cognitive skills as well as longer-term gains in school completion, and even greater gains are possible if children receive good follow-up in the early grades.
- Head Start may be focused too heavily on social supports at the expense of language and literacy training.
- Although Head Start centers vary in quality, on average they are better than privately run child care centers, have achieved short-term benefits, and would pay for themselves if they produced even a fraction of the long-term benefits associated with model programs. For this reason, they merit some expansion and greater attention paid to their quality.

If, as many experts believe, there is a close link between school performance, family life, and crime, programs such as Head Start can help some potentially criminal youths avoid problems with the law. By implication, their success indicates that programs that help socialize youngsters can be used to combat urban criminality. Although problems have been identified in individual centers, the government has shown its faith in Head Start as a socialization agent. Head Start's mission is to help low-income children start school ready to learn by providing early childhood education, child development, comprehensive health, and social services.

Since 1965, local Head Start programs across the country have served more than 21 million children and built strong partnerships with parents and families.

Critical Thinking

1. If crime was a matter of human traits, as some criminologists suggest, would a program such as Head Start help kids avoid criminal careers?
2. Can you suggest any other types of programs that might help parents or children avoid involvement in drugs or crime?
3. Were you in Head Start? If so, did it help you attain your current academic success?

InfoTrac College Edition Research

To learn more about the Head Start program and its current status, use "Head Start" as a subject guide on InfoTrac College Edition.

SOURCES: Head Start statistics can be accessed at the Head Start Bureau website, www.acf.hhs.gov/programs/hsb/research/2004.htm (accessed August 1, 2004); Janet Currie, *A Fresh Start for Head Start?* (Washington, DC: Brookings Institute, March 2001); statement by Wade F. Horn, Assistant Secretary for Children and Families on "Head Start and Child Care in the Context of Early Learning" before the House Committee on Appropriations, Subcommittee on Labor, Health, and Human Services, and Education, April 17, 2002; Edward Zigler and Sally Styfco, "Head Start, Criticisms in a Constructive Context," *American Psychologist* 49 (1994): 127–132; Nancy Kassebaum, "Head Start, Only the Best for America's Children," *American Psychologist* 49 (1994): 123–126; Faith Lamb Parker, Chaya Piorkowski, and Lenore Peay, "Head Start as Social Support for Mothers: The Psychological Benefits of Involvement," *American Journal of Orthopsychiatry* 57 (1987): 220–233.

The influence of labeling theory can also be seen in diversion and restitution programs. **Diversion programs** remove both juvenile and adult offenders from the normal channels of the criminal justice process by placing them in rehabilitation programs. For example, a college student whose drunken driving hurts a pedestrian may, before trial, be placed for six months in an alcohol treatment program. If he successfully completes the program, charges against him will be dismissed; thus he avoids the stigma of a criminal label. Such programs are common throughout the United States. Often they offer counseling, medical advice, and vocational, educational, and family services.

Another popular label-avoiding innovation is **restitution**. Rather than face the stigma of a formal trial, an offender is asked either to pay back the victim of the crime for any loss incurred or to do some useful work in the community in lieu of receiving a court-ordered sentence.

Despite their good intentions, stigma-reducing programs have not met with great success. Critics charge that they substitute one kind of stigma for another—for instance, attending a mental health program in lieu of a criminal trial. In addition, diversion and restitution programs usually screen out violent and repeat offenders. Finally, there is little hard evidence that these alternative programs improve recidivism rates. Concept Summary 7.1 outlines the major concepts of social process theories.

diversion programs
Programs of rehabilitation that remove offenders from the normal channels of the criminal justice process, thus avoiding the stigma of a criminal label.

restitution
Permitting an offender to repay the victim or do useful work in the community rather than face the stigma of a formal trial and a court-ordered sentence.

CONCEPT SUMMARY 7.1 Social Process Theories

THEORY	MAJOR PREMISE	STRENGTHS	RESEARCH FOCUS
Social Learning Theories			
Differential association theory	People learn to commit crime from exposure to antisocial definitions.	Explains onset of criminality. Explains the presence of crime in all elements of social structure. Explains why some people in high-crime areas refrain from criminality. Can apply to adults and juveniles.	Measuring definitions toward crime; influence of deviant peers and parents
Neutralization theory	Youths learn ways of neutralizing moral restraints and periodically drift in and out of criminal behavior patterns.	Explains why many delinquents do not become adult criminals. Explains why youthful law violators can participate in conventional behavior.	Do people who use neutralizations commit more crimes? Beliefs, values, and crime
Social Control Theory			
Hirschi's control theory	A person's bond to society prevents him or her from violating social rules. If the bond weakens, the person is free to commit crime.	Explains the onset of crime; can apply to both middle- and lower-class crime. Explains its theoretical constructs adequately so they can be measured. Has been empirically tested.	The association between commitment, attachment, involvement, belief, and crime
Social Reaction Theory			
Labeling theory	People enter into law-violating careers when they are labeled and organize their personalities around the labels.	Explains society's role in creating deviance. Explains why some juvenile offenders do not become adult criminals. Develops concepts of criminal careers.	Measuring the association between self-concept and crime; differential application of labels; the effect of stigma

THINKING Like a Criminologist

The state legislature is considering a bill that requires posting the names of people convicted of certain offenses, such as vandalism, soliciting a prostitute, or nonpayment of child support, in local newspapers under the heading "The Rogues Gallery." Those who favor the bill cite similar practices elsewhere: In Boston, men arrested for soliciting prostitutes are forced to clean streets. In Dallas, shoplifters are made to stand outside stores with signs stating their misdeeds.

Members of the state Civil Liberties Union have opposed the bill, stating, "It's simply needless humiliation of the individual." They argue that public shaming is inhumane and further alienates criminals who already have little stake in society, further ostracizing them from the mainstream. According to civil liberties attorneys, applying stigma helps criminals acquire a damaged reputation, which further locks them into criminal behavior patterns.

This "liberal" position is challenged by those who believe that convicted lawbreakers have no right to conceal their crimes from the public. Shaming penalties seem attractive as cost-effective

(continued)

alternatives to imprisonment. These critics ask what could be wrong with requiring a teenage vandal to personally apologize at the school he or she defaced and to wear a shirt with a big "V" on it while cleaning up the mess. If you do something wrong, they argue, you should have to face the consequences.

You have been asked to address a legislative committee on the issue of whether shaming could deter crime. What would you say?

Summary

- Social process theories view criminality as a function of people's interaction with various organizations, institutions, and processes in society.
- People in all walks of life have the potential to become criminals if they maintain destructive social relationships.
- Improper socialization is a key component of crime.
- Social process theory has three main branches. Social learning theory stresses that people learn how to commit crimes. Social control theory analyzes the failure of society to control criminal tendencies. Labeling theory maintains that negative labels produce criminal careers.
- Social learning theory suggests that people learn criminal behaviors much as they learn conventional behavior.
- Differential association theory, formulated by Edwin Sutherland, holds that criminality is a result of a person's perceiving an excess of definitions in favor of crime over definitions that uphold conventional values.
- Gresham Sykes and David Matza's theory of neutralization stresses that youths learn behavior rationalizations that enable them to overcome societal values and norms and break the law.
- Control theory maintains that all people have the potential to become criminals, but their bonds to conventional society prevent them from violating the law. This view suggests that a person's self-concept aids his or her commitment to conventional action.
- Travis Hirschi's social control theory describes the social bond as containing elements of attachment, commitment, involvement, and belief. Weakened bonds allow youths to behave antisocially.
- Social reaction or labeling theory holds that criminality is promoted by becoming negatively labeled by significant others. Such labels as "criminal," "ex-con," and "junkie" isolate people from society and lock them into lives of crime.
- Labels create expectations that the labeled person will act in a certain way; labeled people are always watched and suspected. Eventually these people begin to accept their labels as personal identities, locking them further into lives of crime and deviance.
- Edwin Lemert suggests that people who accept labels are involved in secondary deviance while primary deviants are able to maintain an undamaged identity.
- Research on labeling has not supported its major premises; consequently, critics have charged that it lacks credibility as a description of crime causation.
- Social process theories have greatly influenced social policy. They have been applied in treatment orientations as well as community action policies.

Take a Post-Test. Visit www.thomsonedu.com/criminaljustice/siegel and take the chapter Post-Test to monitor your progress and identify areas for further improvement. In addition to discovering what you've mastered, you'll learn which concepts need your added attention and get specific page references that direct you to the places in the text where you can find more information on them.

Key Terms

socialization 147
social process theory 147
parental efficacy 148
social learning theory 150
social control theory 150
social reaction (labeling) theory 150
differential association theory 150
culture conflict 151
neutralization theory 154
drift 154
neutralization techniques 154
self-control 157
commitment to conformity 157
social bonds 158
moral entrepreneur 162
stigmatize 162
successful degradation ceremony 163
retrospective reading 163
primary deviance 164
secondary deviance 164
deviance amplification 164
reflected appraisal 166
diversion programs 169
restitution 169

Critical Thinking Questions

1. If criminal behavior is learned, who taught the first criminal? Have you ever been exposed to pro-crime definitions? How did you handle them? Did they affect your behavior?

2. Children who do well in school are less likely to commit criminal acts than those who are school failures. Which element of Hirschi's theory is supported by the school failure–delinquency link?

3. Have you ever been given a negative label, and, if so, did it cause you social harm? How did you lose the label, or did it become a permanent marker that still troubles you today?

4. If negative labels are damaging, do positive ones help insulate children from crime-producing forces in their environment? Has a positive label ever changed your life?

5. How would a social process theorist explain the fact that many children begin offending at an early age and then desist from crime as they mature? Are you involved in fewer antisocial acts in college than you were in high school? If so, how do you explain your behavioral changes?

Critical Criminology: It's a Class Thing

© AP

IN NOVEMBER 2005, VIOLENCE WRACKED SOUTHERN AND WESTERN FRANCE AND THE SUBURBS OF PARIS. Youths burned buildings and torched vehicles. As the unrest spread, French Prime Minister Dominique de Villepin pledged to restore order and end the violence. Finally, before days of looting and burning, the rioting subsided, but not before thousands of vehicles were burned and buildings destroyed.

What sparked the rioting? The immediate cause was the accidental deaths of two Muslim teenagers who were electrocuted as they hid in a power substation to escape a police identity check. Hearing of the deaths, gangs of youths armed with bricks and sticks roamed the streets of housing estates torching cars and destroying property. Yet, the boys' deaths were only the tip of the iceberg. France has 751 neighborhoods officially classified as poverty areas, housing a total of 5 million people, around 8 percent of the population. Conditions in these areas are depressing, with high-rise projects, an unemployment rate (20 percent) that is twice the national average, and per capita income that is 40 percent below the

Refer to the front endpapers for a study tool that summarizes each of the major theories discussed in this book.

national average. A majority of France's Muslim population, estimated at 5 million, live in these poverty-stricken areas. Many residents are angry at the living conditions and believe they are the target of racial discrimination, police brutality, and governmental indifference. They only needed a spark, in this case the accidental deaths of two teens, to enrage them and set off a wave of violence and destruction.[1]

CHAPTER OBJECTIVES

1. Be familiar with the concept of social conflict and how it shapes behavior.
2. Be able to discuss elements of conflict in the justice system.
3. Be familiar with the idea of critical criminology.
4. Be able to discuss the difference between structural and instrumental theory.
5. Know the various techniques of critical research.
6. Be able to discuss the term "left realism."
7. Understand the concept of patriarchy.
8. Know what is meant by feminist criminology.
9. Be able to discuss peacemaking.
10. Understand the concept of restorative justice.

Take a Pre-Test. Visit www.thomsonedu.com/criminaljustice/siegel and take a Pre-Test to determine what you already know and identify the areas where you'll need to focus your study. The program will direct you to specific pages within the text where you can find further information on the correct answers to the questions you've missed.

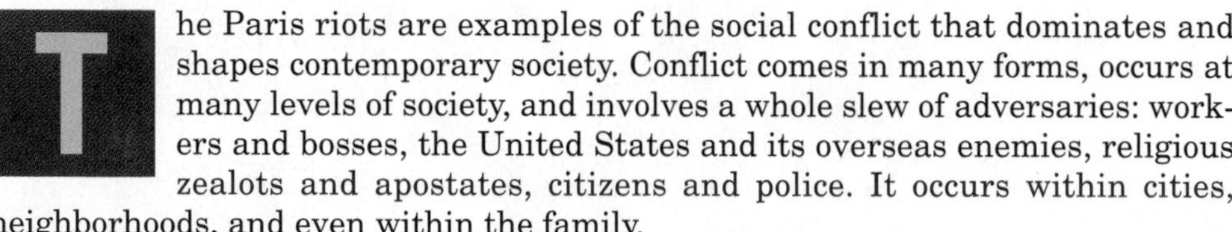

The Paris riots are examples of the social conflict that dominates and shapes contemporary society. Conflict comes in many forms, occurs at many levels of society, and involves a whole slew of adversaries: workers and bosses, the United States and its overseas enemies, religious zealots and apostates, citizens and police. It occurs within cities, neighborhoods, and even within the family.

Conflict can be destructive when it leads to war, violence, and death; it can be functional when it results in positive social change. Conflict promotes crime by creating a social atmosphere in which the law is a mechanism for controlling dissatisfied, have-not members of society while the wealthy maintain their power. This is why crimes that are the province of the wealthy, such as illegal corporate activities, are sanctioned much more leniently than those, such as burglary, that are considered lower-class activities.

Criminologists who view crime as a function of social conflict and economic rivalry have been known by a number of titles, including conflict, Marxist, or radical criminologists, but here we will refer to them as "critical criminologists" and their field of study as "critical criminology." Many, but not all, apply the type of socioeconomic analysis first used by Karl Marx to identify the economic structures in society that control all human relations. Critical criminologists reject the notion that law is designed to maintain a tranquil, fair society and that criminals are malevolent people who wish to trample the rights of others. Critical theorists consider acts of racism, sexism, imperialism, unsafe working conditions, inadequate child care, substandard housing, pollution of the environment, and war making as a tool of foreign policy to be "true crimes." The crimes of the helpless—burglary, robbery, and assault—are more expressions of rage over unjust economic conditions than actual crimes.[2] By focusing on how the capitalist state uses law to control the lower classes, Marxist thought serves as the basis for critical theory.

Contemporary critical criminologists try to explain crime within economic and social contexts and to express the connection between social class, crime, and social control.[3] They are concerned with issues such as these:

- The role government plays in creating a crimogenic environment
- The relationship between personal or group power and the shaping of criminal law

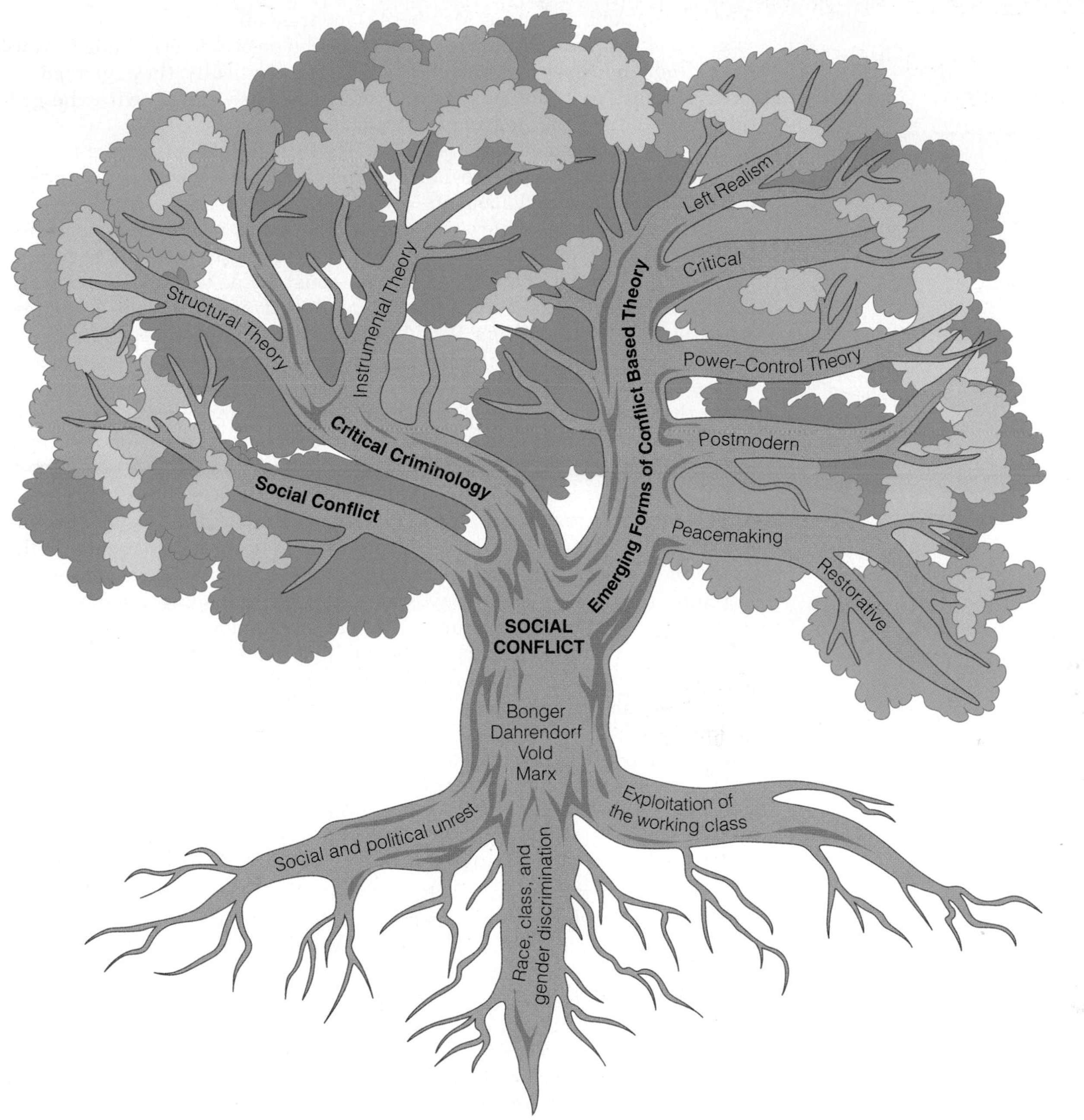

Figure 8.1
The Branches of Critical Criminology

- The prevalence of bias in justice system operations
- The relationship between a capitalistic, free enterprise economy and crime rates

Critical criminologists often take the broader view, opposing racism, sexism, and genocide, rather than focus on burglary, robbery, and rape.[4] This chapter reviews critical criminology—its development and principal ideas. Then it looks at policies that have been embraced by critical thinkers that focus on peace and restoration rather than punishment and exclusion.

ORIGINS OF CRITICAL CRIMINOLOGY

The social ferment of the 1960s gave birth to critical criminology (see Figure 8.1 above). In 1968, a group of British sociologists formed the National Deviancy Conference (NDC). With about 300 members, this organization sponsored several national symposiums and dialogues. Members came from all walks of life, but at its core was a group of academics who were critical of the positivist criminology being taught in British and American universities. More specifically, they rejected the conservative stance of criminologists and their close association with the government that funded many of their research projects.

The NDC called attention to ways in which social control might actually cause deviance rather than just respond to antisocial behavior. Many conference members became concerned about the political nature of social control.

In 1973, critical theory was given a powerful academic boost when British scholars Ian Taylor, Paul Walton, and Jock Young published *The New Criminology*.[5] This brilliant, thorough, and well-constructed critique of existing concepts in criminology called for the development of new methods of criminological analysis and critique. *The New Criminology* became the standard resource for scholars critical of both the field of criminology and the existing legal process. Since its publication there has been a tradition for critical criminologists to turn their attention to the field itself, questioning the role criminology plays in supporting the status quo and aiding in the oppression of the poor and powerless.[6]

U.S. scholars were also influenced during the late 1960s and early 1970s by the widespread unrest and social change that shook the world. The war in Vietnam, prison struggles, and the civil rights and feminist movements produced a climate in which criticism of the ruling class seemed a natural by-product. Mainstream, positivist criminology was criticized as being overtly conservative, pro-government, and antihuman. What emerged was a social conflict theory whose proponents scoffed when their fellow scholars used statistical analysis of computerized data to describe criminal and delinquent behavior. Several influential scholars embraced the idea that the social conflict produced by the unequal distribution of **power** and wealth was at the root cause of crime. William Chambliss and Robert Seidman wrote the well-respected treatise *Law, Order and Power,* which documented how the justice system protects the rich and powerful.[7] Chambliss and Seidman's work showed how control of the political and economic system affects the way criminal justice is administered and that the definitions of crime used in contemporary society favor those who control the justice system.

In another influential work, *The Social Reality of Crime*, Richard Quinney also proclaimed that in contemporary society criminal law represents the interests of those who hold power in society.[8] Where there is conflict between social groups—the wealthy and the poor—those who hold power will create laws that benefit themselves and hold rivals in check. Law is not an abstract body of rules that represents an absolute moral code; rather, law is an integral part of society, a force that represents a way of life and a method of doing things. Crime is a function of power relations and an inevitable result of social conflict. Criminals are not simply social misfits but people who have come up short in the struggle for success and are seeking alternative means of achieving wealth, status, or even survival.

As a group, these social conflict theorists began to show how in our postindustrial, capitalist society the economic system invariably produces haves and have-nots.[9] The mode of production shapes social life. Because economic competitiveness is the essence of capitalism, conflict increases and eventually destabilizes both social institutions and social groups.[10] From their work critical criminology emerged.

Contemporary Critical Criminology

From these early roots a robust critical criminology was formed. At first, these alternative forms of criminology were considered Marxist and radical. They have morphed into a critical criminology that is antiestablishment and questioning of the socioeconomic structures that produce crime and criminality.[11]

Today, critical criminologists devote their attention to a number of important themes and concepts. One is the use and misuse of power, or the ability of persons and groups to determine and control the behavior of others and to shape public opinion to meet their personal interests. Because those in power shape the content of the law, it comes as no surprise that their behavior is often exempt from legal

power
The ability of persons and groups to control behavior of others, to shape public opinion, and to define deviance.

sanctions. Those who deserve the most severe sanctions (wealthy white-collar criminals whose crimes cost society millions of dollars) usually receive lenient punishments, while those whose relatively minor crimes are committed out of economic necessity (petty thieves and drug dealers) receive stricter penalties, especially if they are minority group members who lack social and economic power.[12]

Critical criminologists also critique the field of criminology, questioning the role criminologists play in supporting the status quo and aiding in oppression of the poor and powerless.[13] After all, criminologists may spend their time creating effective crime control mechanisms, which swell the nation's prisons with indigent and desperate people while corporate executives make fat profits.

Critical criminologists are also deeply concerned about the current state of the American political system and the creation of what they consider to be an American Empire abroad. Ironically, recent events such as the war in Iraq and the efforts to penalize immigrants and close the borders, have energized critical thinkers; their vision seems as pertinent today as it was during its heyday in the 1960s and 1970s.[14] The conservative agenda, they believe, calls for the dismantling of welfare and health programs, lowering of labor costs through union busting, tax cuts that favor the wealthy, ending affirmative action, and reducing environmental control and regulation. Some critical criminologists try to show how racism still pervades the American system and manifests itself in a wide variety of social practices ranging from the administration of criminal justice to the "whitening" of the teaching force because selection rests upon a racially skewed selection process.[15]

While spending is being cut on social programs, it is being raised on military expansion. The rapid buildup of the prison system and passage of draconian criminal laws that threaten civil rights and liberties—the death penalty, three strikes laws, and the Patriot Act—are other elements of the conservative agenda. Critical criminologists believe that they are responsible for informing the public about the dangers of these developments.[16]

CONNECTIONS

The USA Patriot Act will be discussed further in Chapter 10 within the context of legal efforts to thwart terrorism. Some welcome its provisions, which make it easier for the government to monitor people considered dangerous, but critical thinkers fear loss of individual freedom at the expense of state power.

Critical criminologists have turned their attention to the threat competitive capitalism presents to the working class. They believe that in addition to perpetuating male supremacy and racialism, modern global capitalism helps destroy the lives of workers in less-developed countries. For example, capitalists hailed China's entry into the World Trade Organization in 2001 as a significant economic event. However, critical thinkers point out that the economic boom has significant costs: The average manufacturing wage in China is 20 to 25 cents per hour; in a single year (2001) more than 47,000 workers were killed at work, and 35.2 million Chinese workers were permanently or temporarily disabled.[17]

HOW CRITICAL CRIMINOLOGISTS DEFINE CRIME

According to critical theorists, crime is a political concept designed to protect the power and position of the upper classes at the expense of the poor. Some of these theorists, but not all, would include in a list of "real" crimes such acts as violations of human rights due to racism, sexism, and imperialism and other violations of human dignity and physical needs and necessities. Part of the critical agenda, argues criminologist Robert Bohm, is to make the public aware that these behaviors "are crimes just as much as burglary and robbery."[18]

The nature of a society controls the direction of its criminality; criminals are not social misfits but products of the society and its economic system. "Capitalism," claims Bohm, "as a mode of production, has always produced a relatively high level of crime and violence."[19] According to Michael Lynch and W. Byron Groves, three implications follow from this view:

1. Each society produces its own types and amounts of crime.
2. Each society has its own distinctive ways of dealing with criminal behavior.
3. Each society gets the amount and type of crime that it deserves.[20]

This analysis tells us that criminals are not a group of outsiders who can be controlled by increased law enforcement. Criminality, instead, is a function of social and economic organization. To control crime and reduce criminality, societies must remove the social conditions that promote crime.

In our advanced technological society, those with economic and political power control the definition of crime and the manner in which the criminal justice system enforces the law.[21] Consequently, the only crimes available to the poor are the severely sanctioned "street crimes": rape, murder, theft, and mugging. Members of the middle class cheat on their taxes and engage in petty corporate crime (employee theft), acts that generate social disapproval but are rarely punished severely. The wealthy are involved in acts that should be described as crimes but are not, such as racism, sexism, and profiteering. Although regulatory laws control illegal business activities, these are rarely enforced, and violations are lightly punished. One reason is that an essential feature of capitalism is the need to expand business and create new markets. This goal often conflicts with laws designed to protect the environment and creates clashes with those who seek their enforcement. In our postindustrial society, the need for expansion usually triumphs. For example, corporate spokespeople and their political allies will brand environmentalists as "tree huggers" who stand in the way of jobs and prosperity.[22]

The rich are insulated from street crimes because they live in areas far removed from crime. Those in power use the fear of crime as a tool to maintain their control over society. The poor are controlled through incarceration, and the middle class is diverted from caring about the crimes of the powerful by their fear of the crimes of the powerless.[23] Ironically, they may have more to lose from the economic crimes committed by the rich than the street crimes of the poor. Stock market swindles and savings and loan scams cost the public billions of dollars but are typically settled with fines and probationary sentences.

Because private ownership of property is the true measure of success in American society (as opposed to being, say, a worthy person), the state becomes an ally of the wealthy in protecting their property interests. As a result, theft-related crimes are often punished more severely than are acts of violence, because although the former may be interclass, the latter are typically intraclass. ✔ CHECKPOINTS

✔ CHECKPOINTS

✔ Critical criminology is aimed at identifying "real" crimes in U.S. society, such as profiteering, sexism, and racism.

✔ It seeks to evaluate how criminal law is used as a mechanism of social control.

✔ It describes how power relations create inequities in U.S. society.

✔ Critical criminologists are concerned with the conservative control over American domestic and foreign policy.

✔ According to critical theory, crime is defined by those who hold power.

✔ The wealthy shield themselves from crime through their control over law.

HOW CRITICAL CRIMINOLOGISTS VIEW THE CAUSE OF CRIME

Critical thinkers believe that the key crime-producing element of modern corporate capitalism is the effort to create **surplus value**—the profits produced by the laboring classes that are accrued by business owners. Once accumulated, surplus value can be either reinvested or used to enrich the owners. To increase the rate of surplus value, workers can be made to toil harder for less pay, be made more efficient, or be replaced by machines or technology. Therefore, economic growth does not benefit all elements of the population, and in the long run it may produce the same effect as a depression or recession.

As the rate of surplus value increases, more people are displaced from productive relationships, and the size of the marginal population swells. As corporations downsize to increase profits, high-paying labor and managerial jobs are lost to computer-driven machinery. Displaced workers are forced into service jobs at minimum wage. Many become temporary employees without benefits or a secure position.

As more people are thrust outside the economic mainstream—a condition referred to as **marginalization**—a larger portion of the population is forced to live in areas conducive to crime. Once people are marginalized, commitment to the system declines, producing another crimogenic force: a weakened bond to society.[24] This process is illustrated in Figure 8.2.

surplus value
The difference between what workers produce and what they are paid, which goes to business owners as profits.

marginalization
Displacement of workers, pushing them outside the economic and social mainstream.

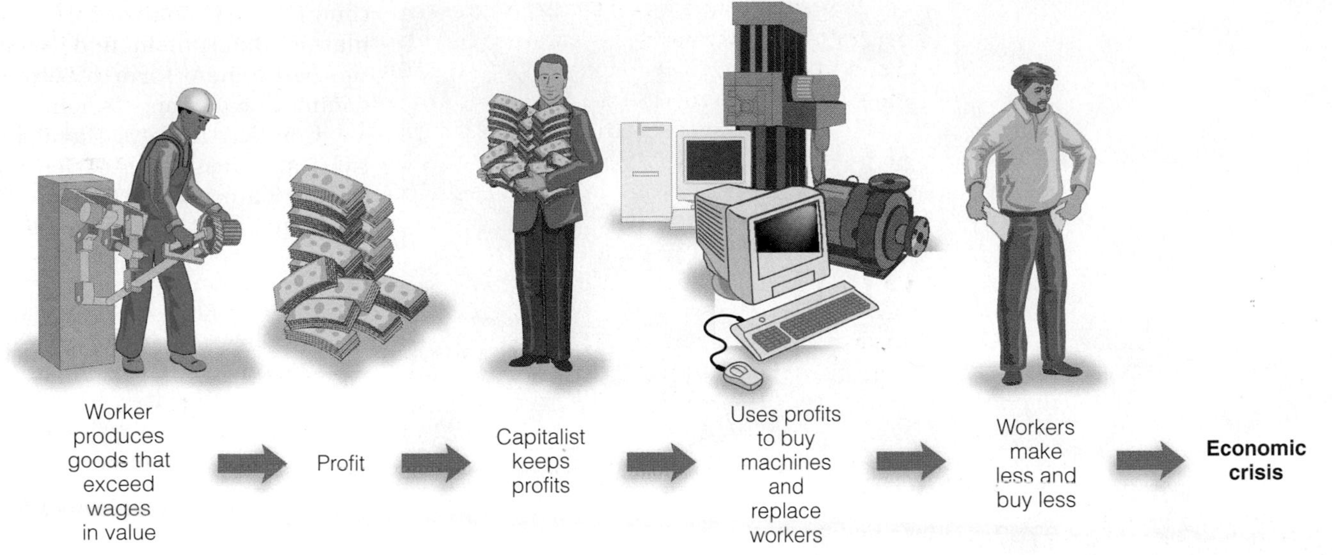
Worker produces goods that exceed wages in value
Profit
Capitalist keeps profits
Uses profits to buy machines and replace workers
Workers make less and buy less
Economic crisis

Figure 8.2
Surplus Value and Crime

The government may be quick to respond during periods of economic decline because those in power assume that poor economic conditions breed crime and social disorder. When unemployment is increasing, public officials assume the worst and devote greater attention to the criminal justice system, perhaps building new prisons to prepare for the coming "crime wave."[25] Empirical research confirms that economic downturns are indeed linked to both crime rate increases and government activities such as passing anticrime legislation.[26] As the level of surplus value increases, so too do police expenditures, most likely because of the perceived or real need for the state to control those on the economic margin.[27]

Globalization

The global economy is a particularly vexing development for critical theorists and their use of the concept of surplus value. **Globalization**, which usually refers to the process of creating transnational markets and political and legal systems, has shifted the focus of critical inquiry to a world perspective.

Globalization began when large companies decided to establish themselves in foreign markets by adapting their products or services to the local culture. The process took off with the fall of the Soviet Union, which opened new European markets. The development of China into an industrial superpower encouraged foreign investors to take advantage of China's huge supply of workers. As the Internet and communication revolution unfolded, companies established instant communications with their far-flung corporate empires, a technological breakthrough that further aided trade and foreign investments. A series of transnational corporate mergers (such as DaimlerChrysler) and takeovers (such as Ford and Volvo) produced ever-larger transnational corporations.

Some experts believe globalization can improve the standard of living in third world nations by providing jobs and training, but critical theorists question the altruism of multinational corporations. Their motives are exploiting natural resources, avoiding regulation, and taking advantage of desperate workers. When these giant corporations set up a factory in a developing nation, it is not to help the local population but to get around environmental laws and take advantage of needy workers who may be forced to labor in substandard

globalization
The process of creating a global economy through transnational markets and political and legal systems.

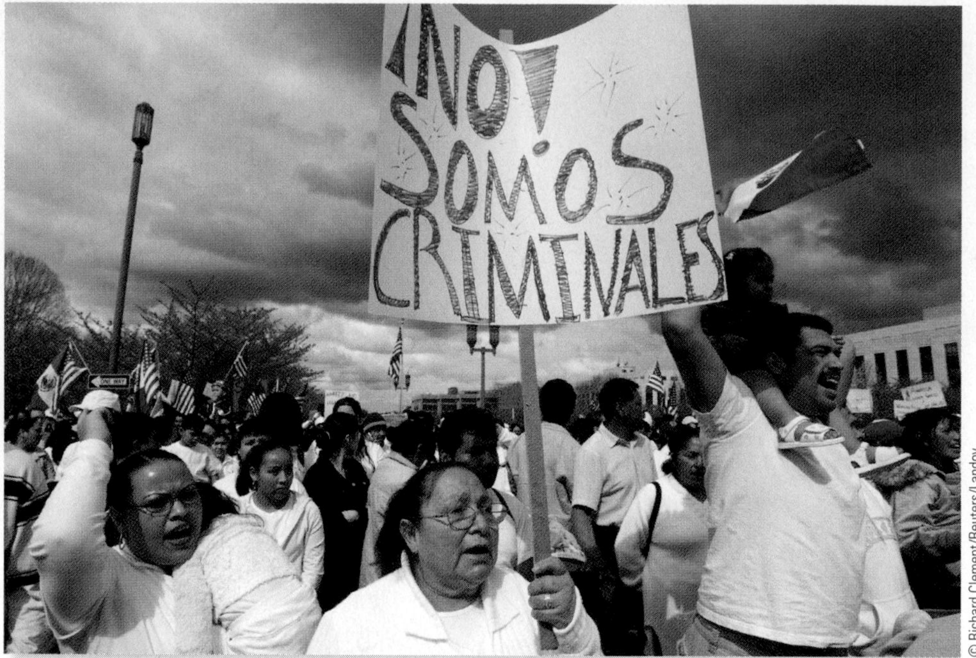

Globalization has changed the traditional ways of doing business, creating prosperity in some nations and chaos in others. People are now moving from nation to nation seeking jobs and a fresh start. Here, supporters of immigration reform rally for immigrants' rights at the state capitol in Salem, Oregon on April 9, 2006. Several thousand people gathered to support expanding immigrants' rights and to protest congressional bill HR 4437, which was designed to greatly tighten U.S. immigration. The sign reads "We are not criminals." Should immigration policies be tightened to protect American jobs, or should immigrants be allowed to enter the United States in order to take part in the "American Dream"?

conditions. Globalization has replaced imperialism and colonization as a new form of economic domination and oppression.

Conflict thinkers David Friedrichs and Jessica Friedrichs warn that globalization presents a four-pronged threat to the world economy:

1. Growing global dominance and the reach of the free-market capitalist system, which disproportionately benefits wealthy and powerful organizations and individuals
2. Increasing vulnerability of indigenous people with a traditional way of life to the forces of globalized capitalism
3. Growing influence and impact of international financial institutions (such as the World Bank) and the related relative decline of power of local or state-based institutions
4. Nondemocratic operation of international financial institutions[28]

Globalization may have a profound influence on the concept of surplus value. Workers in the United States may be replaced in high-paying manufacturing jobs not by machines but by foreign workers. Instant communication via the Internet and global communications, a development that Marx could not have foreseen, will speed the effect immeasurably. Globalization will have a significant effect on both the economy and eventually on crime rates.

INSTRUMENTAL VS. STRUCTURAL THEORY

Not all critical thinkers share a similar view of society and its control by the means of production. **Instrumental theorists** view criminal law and the criminal justice system solely as instruments for controlling the poor, have-not members of society. They view the state as the tool of capitalists. In contrast, **structural theorists** believe that the law is not the exclusive domain of the rich; rather, it is used to maintain the long-term interests of the capitalist system and to control members of any class who threaten its existence.

Instrumental Theory

According to the instrumental view, the law and justice system serves the powerful and rich and enables them to impose their morality and standards of behavior on the entire society. Those who wield economic power can extend their self-serving definition of illegal or criminal behavior to encompass those who might threaten the status quo or interfere with their quest for ever-increasing profits.[29] The concentration of economic assets in the nation's largest industrial firms translates into the political power needed to control tax laws to limit the firms' tax liabilities.[30] Some have the economic clout to hire top attorneys to defend them against antitrust actions, making them almost immune to regulation.

The poor, according to this branch of critical theory, may or may not commit more crimes than the rich, but they certainly are arrested and punished more often. Under the capitalist system, the poor are driven to crime because a natural

instrumental theory
Sees criminal law and the criminal justice system as capitalist instruments for controlling the lower class.

structural theory
Based on the belief that criminal law and the criminal justice system are means of defending and preserving the capitalist system.

frustration exists in a society in which affluence is well publicized but unattainable. When class conflict becomes unbearable, frustration can spill out in riots, such as the one that occurred in Los Angeles on April 29, 1992, which was described as a "class rebellion of the underprivileged against the privileged."[31] Because of class conflict, a deep-rooted hostility is generated among members of the lower class toward a social order they are not allowed to shape and whose benefits are unobtainable.[32]

Instrumental theorists consider it essential to **demystify** law and justice—that is, to unmask its true purpose. Criminological theories that focus on family structure, intelligence, peer relations, and school performance keep the lower classes servile by showing why they are more criminal, less intelligent, and more prone to school failure and family problems than the middle class. Demystification involves identifying the destructive intent of capitalist-inspired and funded criminology. Instrumental theory's goal for criminology is to show how capitalist law preserves ruling-class power.[33]

© AP

• Even the largest, most powerful corporations can be sanctioned if they violate the rules of the capitalist system. Microsoft Chairman Bill Gates speaks at the VSLive! technical conference of software developers at Moscone Center in San Francisco. On the same day, the European Union issued a $613 million fine against Microsoft for abusively wielding its Windows software monopoly. Does the case against Microsoft support the structural branch of critical criminology?

Structural Theory

Structural theorists disagree with the view that the relationship between law and capitalism is unidirectional, always working for the rich and against the poor.[34] If law and justice were purely instruments of the wealthy, why would laws controlling corporate crimes, such as price-fixing, false advertising, and illegal restraint of trade, have been created and enforced?

To a structuralist, the law is designed to keep the system operating efficiently, and anyone, worker or owner, who rocks the boat is targeted for sanction. For example, antitrust legislation is designed to prevent any single capitalist from dominating the system. If the free enterprise system is to function, no single person can become too powerful at the expense of the economic system as a whole. Structuralists would regard the efforts of the U.S. government to break up Microsoft as an example of a conservative government using its clout to keep the system on an even keel. The long prison sentences given to corporate executives who engage in insider trading is a warning to capitalists that they must play by the rules.

RESEARCH ON CRITICAL CRIMINOLOGY

Critical criminologists rarely use standard social science methodologies to test their views because many believe the traditional approach of measuring research subjects is antihuman and insensitive.[35] Critical thinkers believe that research conducted by mainstream liberal and positivist criminologists is often designed to unmask weak, powerless members of society so they can be better dealt with by the legal system. They are particularly offended by purely empirical studies, such as those designed to show that minority group members have lower IQs than whites or that the inner city is the site of the most serious crime whereas middle-class areas are relatively crime free. Critical scholars are more likely to examine historical trends and patterns than to do surveys and to crunch numbers. Historian Michael Rustigan examined changes in criminal law by analyzing historical records that revealed law reform in nineteenth-century England was largely a response to pressure from the business community to increase punishment for property law violations to protect their rapidly increasing wealth.[36] Other research has focused on topics such as how the relationship between convict work and capitalism evolved during the nineteenth century. During this period, prisons became a profitable method of centralized state control over lower-class criminals, whose labor was exploited by commercial concerns. These criminals were forced to labor to pay off wardens and correctional administrators.[37]

Empirical research is not considered totally incompatible with critical criminology, and there have been some important efforts to test its fundamental assumptions. One area of critical research involves examining the criminal justice system

CONNECTIONS

Enforcement of laws against illegal business activities such as price fixing, restraint of trade, environmental crimes, and false advertising is discussed in Chapter 12. Although some people are sent to prison for these white-collar offenses, many offenders are still punished with a fine or economic sanction.

demystify
To unmask the true purpose of law, justice, or other social institutions.

Profiles in Crime

Mumia Abu-Jamal

© AP

Mumia Abu-Jamal (born Wesley Cook, April 24, 1954) began his journalism career with the radical Black Panther Party in the 1960s. At 15, he was appointed Minister of Information for the Philadelphia chapter. After the party disbanded, he used his writing and speaking talent to become a local broadcaster, winning a Peabody Award for his coverage of the Pope's visit; he became president of the Philadelphia Association of Black Journalists.

Then Mumia Abu-Jamal's life was turned upside down when he was charged with first-degree murder in the killing of police officer Daniel Faulkner. According to authorities, on December 9, 1981, Faulkner, then a 25-year-old Philadelphia police officer, stopped a car for driving the wrong way down the street. Calling for backup, he approached the car and asked the driver, Mr. William Cook, to exit the vehicle. A struggle ensued. According to prosecutors, Mumia Abu-Jamal, Cook's older brother, was sitting in a taxicab across the street watching the events unfold. Abu-Jamal approached Officer Faulkner and shot him in the back. Faulkner was able to draw his gun and fire one return shot that struck Abu-Jamal in the upper abdomen. Having fired this shot, Officer Faulkner fell to the sidewalk. While Faulkner lay helpless, Abu-Jamal approached him and shot him numerous times at close range, killing him.

At trial, four eyewitnesses testified that they saw Abu-Jamal kill Faulkner, experts testified that the gun that killed Faulkner was Abu-Jamal's, and jurors heard that a wounded Abu-Jamal was found at the scene of the crime. He was convicted and sentenced to death. Despite the conviction, the case has become a *cause celebre* for many reasons. Supporters of Abu-Jamal claim that many procedural irregularities occurred during the trial and the conviction violated his constitutional rights to a fair trial. Among other things, Abu-Jamal was denied the right to represent himself at trial. Others claim that he was targeted and framed because of his radical political activities. The prosecution hid evidence, intimidated witnesses, and illegally excused potential African American jurors.

Abu-Jamal's death sentence was overturned in 2001 and the state is appealing that ruling. The case has attracted the attention of anti–death penalty activists from all over the world. Abu-Jamal has continued his political activism, published a book titled *Live from Death Row*, completed BA and MA degrees, and made frequent radio broadcasts. The French have made him an honorary citizen of Paris, and organizations including Amnesty International, Human Rights Watch, the European Parliament, and the Japanese Diet have demanded that he be awarded a new trial because of the problems in the original case.

Critical criminologists view the Mumia Abu-Jamal case as an indicator of the social conflict that infects the nation's social and political systems. People are targeted because of their political views, minorities cannot get a fair trial, and people who are viewed as a threat to the system may find themselves behind bars or even on death row. Conflict rather than consensus rules and shapes society.

SOURCES: Mumia Abu-Jamal's Freedom Journal, www.mumia.org/freedom.now/ (accessed June 4, 2006); Amnesty International, USA: Mumia Abu-Jamal, Amnesty International Calls for Retrial, February, 17, 2000, http://web.amnesty. org/library/Index/engAMR510202000 (accessed June 4, 2006); The Defense: Mumia Abu-Jamal's Legal Representation at Trial, www.amnestyusa .org/regions/americas/document.do?id=EB6C736A7369F3D78025686C00526C98 (accessed June 4, 2006).

to see if it operates as an instrument of class oppression or as a fair, even-handed social control agency. Research has found that jurisdictions with significant levels of economic disparity are also the most likely to have large numbers of people killed by police officers. Police may act more forcefully in areas where class conflict creates the perception that extreme forms of social control are needed to maintain order.[38]

Empirical research also shows, as predicted by critical theory, that a suspect's race is an important factor in shaping justice system decision making. Using data from a national survey, Ronald Weitzer and Steven Tuch found that about 40 percent of African American respondents claimed they were stopped by police because of their race as compared to 5 percent of whites; almost 75 percent of young African American men, ages 18 to 34, said they were victims of profiling.[39] Recent research by Albert Meehan and Michael Ponder found that police are more likely to use racial profiling to stop black motorists as they travel farther into the boundaries of predominantly white neighborhoods: Black motorists driving in an all-white neighborhood set up a red flag because they are "out of place."[40] It is not surprising to critical theorists that police brutality complaints are highest in minority neighborhoods, especially those that experience relative deprivation (African American residents earn significantly less money than the European American majority).[41] The conflict between police and the minority community can result in violence and charges of racism, a topic explored in the Profiles in Crime.

Criminal courts are also more likely to dole out harsh punishments to members of powerless, disenfranchised groups.[42] Both white and black offenders have been found to receive stricter sentences if their personal characteristics (single, young, urban, male) show them to be members of the "dangerous classes."[43] Unemployed racial minorities may be perceived as "social dynamite" who present a real threat to society and must be controlled and incapacitated.[44] Race also plays a role in prosecution and punishment. African American defendants are more likely to be prosecuted under habitual offender statutes if they commit crimes where there is a greater likelihood of a white victim, such as larceny and burglary, than if they commit violent crimes that are largely intraracial; where there is a perceived "racial threat," punishment is enhanced.[45] Critical analysis also shows that despite legal controls, use of the death penalty also seems to be skewed against racial minorities.[46]

Considering these examples of how conflict controls the justice process, it is not surprising when analysis of national population trends and imprisonment rates shows that as the percentage of minority group members increases in a population, the imprisonment rate does likewise.[47] Similarly, states with a substantial minority population have a much higher imprisonment rate than those with predominantly white populations.[48]

Some critical researchers have attempted to show how capitalism influences the distribution of punishment. Robert Weis found that the expansion of the prison population is linked to the need for capitalists to acquire a captive and low-paid labor force to compete with overseas laborers and domestic immigrant labor. Employing immigrants has its political downside because it displaces "American" workers and antagonizes their legal representatives. In contrast, using prison labor can be viewed as a humanitarian gesture. Weiss also observes that an ever-increasing prison population is politically attractive because it masks unemployment rates. Many inmates were chronically unemployed before their imprisonment; incarcerating the chronically unemployed allows politicians to claim they have lowered unemployment. When the millions of people who are on probation and parole and who must maintain jobs are added to the mix, the correctional system is now playing an ever-more important role in suppressing wages and maintaining the profitability of capitalism.[49]

✔ CHECKPOINTS

✔ Critical criminology tries to explain how the workings of the capitalist system produce inequality and crime.

✔ In this view, the state serves the interests of the ruling capitalist class.

✔ Criminal law is an instrument of economic oppression. Capitalism demands that the subordinate classes remain oppressed.

✔ The concept of surplus value means that capitalists exploit workers and keep the excess profits from workers' labors.

✔ Globalization has meant that capitalists can exploit foreign workers for labor and acquire foreign natural resources to maximize their profits.

✔ Instrumental theorists believe that the legal system supports the owners at the expense of the workers.

✔ Structural theorists believe that the law also ensures that no capitalist becomes too powerful. The law is used to maintain the long-term interests of the capitalist system.

✔ Critical research is designed to show how capitalism creates large groups of people who turn to crime for survival.

CRITIQUE OF CRITICAL CRIMINOLOGY

Critical criminology has been sharply criticized by some members of the criminological mainstream, who charge that its contribution has been "hot air, heat, but no real light."[50] In turn, critical thinkers have accused mainstream criminologists of being culprits in developing state control over individual lives and selling out their ideals for the chance to receive government funding.

Mainstream criminologists have also attacked the substance of critical thought. Some argue that critical theory simply rehashes the old tradition of helping the underdog, in which the poor steal from the rich to survive.[51] In reality, most theft is for luxury, not survival. While the wealthy do commit their share of illegal acts, these are nonviolent and leave no permanent injuries.[52] People do not live in fear of corrupt businessmen and stock traders; they fear muggers and rapists.

Other critics suggest that critical theorists unfairly neglect the capitalist system's efforts to regulate itself—for example, by instituting antitrust regulations and putting violators in jail. Similarly, they ignore efforts to institute social reforms aimed at helping the poor.[53] There seems to be no logic in condemning a system that helps the poor and empowers them to take on corporate interests in a court of law. Even inherently conservative institutions such as police departments have made attempts at self-regulation when they become aware of class- and race-based inequality such as the use of racial profiling in making traffic stops.[54]

Some argue that critical thinkers refuse to address the problems and conflicts that exist in socialist countries, such as the gulags and purges of the Soviet Union under Stalin. Similarly, they fail to explain why some highly capitalist countries, such as Japan, have extremely low crime rates. Critical criminologists are too quick to blame capitalism for every human vice without adequate explanation or regard for other social and environmental factors.[55] In so doing, they ignore objective reality and refuse to acknowledge that members of the lower classes tend to victimize one another. They ignore the plight of the lower classes, who must live in crime-ridden neighborhoods, while condemning the capitalist system from the security of the "ivory tower." ✔ CHECKPOINTS

EMERGING FORMS OF CRITICAL CRIMINOLOGY

Critical criminologists are now exploring new avenues of inquiry that fall outside the traditional models of conflict and critical theories. The following sections discuss in detail some recent developments in the conflict approach to crime.

Left Realism

Some critical scholars are now addressing the need for the left wing to respond to the increasing power of right-wing conservatives. They are troubled by the emergence of a strict "law and order" philosophy, which has as its centerpiece a policy of punishing juveniles severely in adult court. At the same time, these scholars find the focus of most left-wing scholarship—the abuse of power by the ruling elite—too narrow. It is wrong, they argue, to ignore inner-city gang crime and violence, which often target indigent people.[56] The approach of scholars who share these concerns is referred to as **left realism**.[57]

Left realism is most often connected to the writings of British scholars John Lea and Jock Young. In their well-respected 1984 work, *What Is to Be Done about Law and Order?* they reject the utopian views of idealists who portray street criminals as revolutionaries.[58] They take the more "realistic" approach that street criminals prey on the poor and disenfranchised, thus making the poor doubly abused, first by the capitalist system and then by members of their own class.

Lea and Young's view of crime causation borrows from conventional sociological theory and closely resembles the relative deprivation approach, which posits that experiencing poverty in the midst of plenty creates discontent and breeds crime. As they put it, "The equation is simple: relative deprivation equals discontent; discontent plus lack of political solution equals crime."[59]

In a more recent book, *Crime in Context: A Critical Criminology of Market Societies* (1999), Ian Taylor recognizes that anyone who expects an instant socialist revolution to take place is simply engaging in wishful thinking.[60] He uses data from both Europe and North America to show that the world is currently in the midst of multiple crises, which are shaping all human interaction including criminality. These crises include lack of job creation, social inequality, social fear, political incompetence and failure, gender conflict, and family and parenting issues. These crises have led to a society in which the government seems incapable of creating positive social change: People have become more fearful and isolated from one another and some are excluded from the mainstream because of racism and discrimination; manufacturing jobs have been exported overseas to nations that pay extremely low wages; and fiscal constraints inhibit the possibility of reform. These problems often fall squarely on the shoulders of young black men, who suffer from exclusion and poverty and who now feel the economic burden created by the erosion of manufacturing jobs due to the globalization of the economy. In response, they engage in a form of hypermasculinity, which helps increase their crime rates.[61]

Crime Protection Left realists argue that crime victims in all classes need and deserve protection; crime control reflects community needs. They do not view police and the courts as inherently evil tools of capitalism whose tough tactics alienate the lower classes. In fact, they recognize that these institutions offer life-saving public services. The left realists wish, however, that police would reduce their use of force and increase their sensitivity to the public.[62]

left realism
Approach that sees crime as a function of relative deprivation under capitalism and favors pragmatic, community-based crime prevention and control.

Preemptive deterrence is an approach in which community organization efforts eliminate or reduce crime before police involvement becomes necessary. The reasoning behind this approach is that if the number of marginalized youths (those who feel they are not part of society and have nothing to lose by committing crime) could be reduced, then delinquency rates would decline.[63]

Although implementing a socialist economy might help eliminate the crime problem, left realists recognize that something must be done to control crime under the existing capitalist system. To develop crime control policies, left realists not only welcome critical ideas but also build on the work of strain theorists, social ecologists, and other mainstream views. Community-based efforts seem to hold the greatest promise of crime control.

Left realism has been criticized by critical thinkers as legitimizing the existing power structure: By supporting existing definitions of law and justice, it suggests that the "deviants" and not the capitalist system cause society's problems. Critics question whether left realists advocate the very institutions that "currently imprison us and our patterns of thought and action."[64] In rebuttal, left realists say that to speak of a socialist state lacking a police force or a system of laws and justice is unrealistic. They believe the criminal code does, in fact, represent public opinion.

Critical Feminist Theory

Like so many theories in criminology, most of the efforts of critical theorists have been devoted to explaining male criminality.[65] To remedy this theoretical lapse, a number of feminist writers have attempted to explain the cause of crime, gender differences in crime rates, and the exploitation of female victims from a critical perspective.

Critical feminism views gender inequality as stemming from the unequal power of men and women in a capitalist society, which leads to the exploitation of women by fathers and husbands. Under this system, women are considered a commodity worth possessing, like land or money.[66]

The origin of gender differences can be traced to the development of private property and male domination of the laws of inheritance, which led to male control over property and power.[67] A **patriarchal** system developed in which men's work was valued and women's work was devalued. As capitalism prevailed, the division of labor by gender made women responsible for the unpaid maintenance and reproduction of the current and future labor force, which was derisively called "domestic work." Although this unpaid work done by women is crucial and profitable for capitalists, who reap these free benefits, such labor is exploitative and oppressive for women.[68] Even when women gained the right to work for pay, they were exploited as cheap labor. The dual exploitation of women within the household and in the labor market means that women produce far greater surplus value for capitalists than men.

Patriarchy, or male supremacy, has been and continues to be supported by capitalists. This system sustains female oppression at home and in the workplace.[69] Although the number of traditional patriarchal families is in steep decline, in those that still exist, a wife's economic dependence ties men more securely to wage-earning jobs, further serving the interests of capitalists by undermining potential rebellion against the system.

Patriarchy and Crime

Critical feminists link criminal behavior patterns to the gender conflict created by the economic and social struggles common in postindustrial societies. In *Capitalism, Patriarchy, and Crime*, James Messerschmidt argues that capitalist society is marked by both patriarchy and class conflict. Capitalists control the labor of workers, and men control women both economically and biologically.[70] This "double marginality" explains why females in a capitalist society commit fewer crimes than males. Because they are isolated in the family, they have fewer opportunities to engage in elite deviance (white-collar and economic crimes). Although powerful females as well as males will commit white-collar crimes, the female crime rate is restricted because of the patriarchal nature of the capitalist

preemptive deterrence
Efforts to prevent crime through community organization and youth involvement.

critical feminism
Approach that explains both victimization and criminality among women in terms of gender inequality, patriarchy, and the exploitation of women under capitalism.

patriarchal
Male-dominated.

© A. Ramey/PhotoEdit

● Critical feminists view gender inequality as a function of female exploitation by men. Women have become a "commodity" worth possessing, like land or money. The origin of gender differences can be traced to the development of private property and men's domination over the laws of inheritance, which led to their control over property and power. Are these teen prostitutes—shown here waiting to be booked at the Maricopa, Arizona, jail—a by-product of this view of women as commodities, which was engendered by the capitalist system?

system.[71] Women are also denied access to male-dominated street crimes. Because capitalism renders lower-class women powerless, they are forced to commit less serious, nonviolent, self-destructive crimes, such as abusing drugs.

Powerlessness also increases the likelihood that women will become targets of violent acts.[72] When lower-class males are shut out of the economic opportunity structure, they try to build their self-image through acts of machismo; such acts may involve violent abuse of women. This type of reaction accounts for a significant percentage of female victims who are attacked by a spouse or intimate partner. According to this view, female victimization should decline as women's place in society is elevated, and they obtain more power at home, in the workplace, and in government. Empirical research seems to support this view. A recent (2004) cross-national study of educational and occupational status of women shows that nations where the status of women is generally high, sexual violence rates are significantly lower than in nations where women do not enjoy similar educational and occupational opportunities.[73] Women's victimization rates decline as they are empowered socially, economically, and legally.[74]

In *Masculinities and Crime,* Messerschmidt expands on these themes.[75] He suggests that in every culture males try to emulate "ideal" masculine behaviors. In Western culture, this means being authoritative, in charge, combative, and controlling. Failure to adopt these roles leaves men feeling effeminate and unmanly. Their struggle to dominate women in order to prove their manliness is called "doing gender." Crime is a vehicle for men to "do gender" because it separates them from the weak and allows them to demonstrate physical bravery. Violence directed toward women is an especially economical way to demonstrate manhood. Would a weak, effeminate male ever attack a woman?

Feminist writers have supported this view by maintaining that in contemporary society men achieve masculinity at the expense of women. In the best-case scenario, men must convince others that in no way are they feminine or have female qualities. For example, they are sloppy and don't cook or do housework because these are "female" activities. More ominously, men may work at excluding, hurting, denigrating, exploiting, or otherwise abusing women. Even in all-male groups, men often prove their manhood by treating the weakest member of the group as "womanlike" and abusing him accordingly. Men need to defend themselves at all costs from being contaminated with femininity, and these efforts begin in children's play groups and continue into adulthood and marriage.[76]

Exploitation and Criminality Feminists also focus on the social forces that shape women's lives and experiences to explain female criminality.[77] For example, they attempt to show how the sexual victimization of girls is a function of male socialization because so many young males learn to be aggressive and to exploit women. Males seek same-sex peer groups for social support; these groups encourage members to exploit and sexually abuse women. On college campuses, peers encourage sexual violence against women who are considered "teasers," "bar pickups," or "loose women." These derogatory labels allow the males to justify their actions; a code of secrecy then protects the aggressors from retribution.[78]

According to the critical feminist view, exploitation triggers the onset of female delinquent and deviant behavior. When female victims run away and abuse substances, they may be reacting to abuse they have suffered at home or at school. Their attempts at survival are labeled as deviant or delinquent behavior.[79] In a sense, the female criminal is herself a victim.

Power-Control Theory John Hagan and his associates have created a critical feminist model that uses gender differences to explain the onset of criminality.[80] Hagan's view is that crime and delinquency rates are a function of two factors: (1) class position (power) and (2) family functions (control).[81] The link between these two variables is that, within the family, parents reproduce the power relationships they hold in the workplace; a position of dominance at work is equated with control in the household. As a result, parents' work experiences and class position influence the criminality of children.[82]

In **paternalistic families**, fathers assume the traditional role of breadwinners, while mothers tend to have menial jobs or remain at home to supervise domestic matters. Within the paternalistic home, mothers are expected to control the behavior of their daughters while granting greater freedom to sons. In such a home, the parent–daughter relationship can be viewed as a preparation for the "cult of domesticity," which makes girls' involvement in delinquency unlikely, whereas boys are freer to deviate because they are not subject to maternal control. Girls growing up in patriarchal families are socialized to fear legal sanctions more than are males; consequently, boys in these families exhibit more delinquent behavior than their sisters. The result is that boys not only engage in more antisocial behaviors but also have greater access to legitimate adult behaviors, such as working at part-time jobs or possessing their own transportation. In contrast, without these legitimate behavioral outlets, girls who are unhappy or dissatisfied with their status are forced to seek risky **role exit behaviors**, including such desperate measures as running away and contemplating suicide.

In **egalitarian families**—those in which the husband and wife share similar positions of power at home and in the workplace—daughters gain a kind of freedom that reflects reduced parental control. These families produce daughters whose law-violating behavior mirrors their brothers'. In an egalitarian family, girls may have greater opportunity to engage in legitimate adult status behaviors and less need to enact deviant role exits.[83]

Ironically, Hagan believes that these relationships also occur in female-headed households with absent fathers. Hagan and his associates found that when fathers and mothers hold equally valued managerial positions, the similarity between the rates of their daughters' and sons' delinquency is greatest. By implication, middle-class girls are the most likely to violate the law because they are less closely controlled than their lower-class counterparts. In homes in which both parents hold positions of power, girls are more likely to have the same expectations of career success as their brothers. Consequently, siblings of both sexes will be socialized to take risks and engage in other behavior related to delinquency.

Evaluating Power-Control This **power–control theory** has received a great deal of attention in the criminological community because it encourages a new approach to the study of criminality, one that includes gender differences, class position, and the structure of the family. Empirical analysis of its premises has generally been supportive. Brenda Sims Blackwell's research supports a key element of power–control theory: Females in paternalistic households have learned to fear legal sanctions more than have their brothers.[84]

Not all research is as supportive.[85] Some critics have questioned its core assumption that power and control variables can explain crime.[86] More specifically, critics fail to replicate the finding that upper-class girls are more likely to deviate than their lower-class peers or that class and power interact to produce delinquency.[87] Some researchers have found few gender-based supervision and behavior differences in worker-, manager-, or owner-dominated households.[88] Research indicates that single-mother families may be different from two-parent egalitarian families, though Hagan's theory equates the two.[89]

The concept of family employed by Hagan may have to be reconsidered. Power–control theorists should consider the multitude of power and control relationships emerging in postmodern society: blended families and families where mothers hold managerial positions and fathers are blue-collar workers, and so forth.[90]

Finally, power and control may interact with other personal traits, such as personality and self-control, to shape behavior.[91] Further research is needed to

paternalistic families
Father is breadwinner and rule maker; mother has menial job or is homemaker only. Sons are granted greater freedom than daughters.

role exit behaviors
Strategies such as running away or contemplating suicide used by young girls unhappy with their status in the family.

egalitarian families
Husband and wife share similar positions of power at home and in the workplace. Sons and daughters have equal freedom.

power-control theory
The view that gender differences in crime are a function of economic power (class position, one-versus two-earner families) and parental control (paternalistic versus egalitarian families).

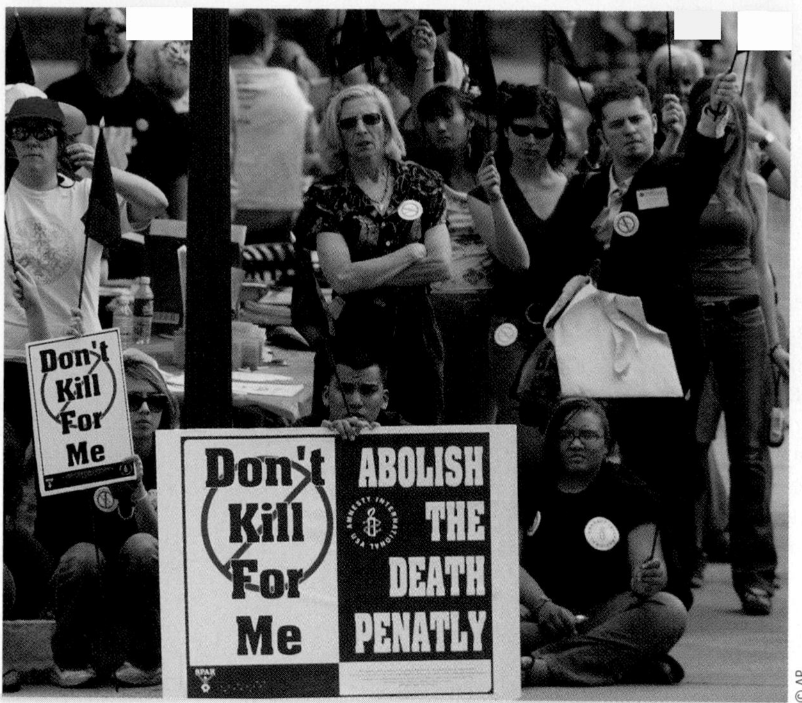

© AP

● Restorative justice advocates want to take coercion out of the justice process, and for that reason, they are opposed to the death penalty. At a rally kicking off Amnesty International USA's annual meeting in Austin, Texas, attendees raised black flags in protest and called on Republican Governor Rick Perry and Texas legislators to abolish the death penalty. Can restorative principles be applied to criminals who commit the most violent, heinous crimes, or are they only suitable for petty and first-time offenders?

determine whether power–control can have an independent influence on behavior and can explain gender differences in the crime rate.

Peacemaking Criminology

To members of the **peacemaking** movement, the main purpose of criminology is to promote a peaceful, just society. Rather than standing on empirical analysis of data, peacemaking draws its inspiration from religious and philosophical teachings ranging from Quakerism to Zen.[92]

Peacemakers view the efforts of the state to punish and control as crime encouraging rather than crime discouraging. These views were first articulated in a series of books with an anarchist theme written by criminologists Larry Tifft and Dennis Sullivan in 1980.[93] Tifft argues, "The violent punishing acts of the state and its controlling professions are of the same genre as the violent acts of individuals. In each instance these acts reflect an attempt to monopolize human interaction."[94]

Sullivan stresses the futility of correcting and punishing criminals in the context of our conflict-ridden society: "The reality we must grasp is that we live in a culture of severed relationships, where every available institution provides a form of banishment but no place or means for people to become connected, to be responsible to and for each other."[95] Sullivan suggests that mutual aid rather than coercive punishment is the key to a harmonious society. In their newest volume, *Restorative Justice* (2001), Sullivan and Tifft reaffirm their belief that society must seek humanitarian forms of justice without resorting to brutal punishments.

By allowing feelings of vengeance or retribution to narrow our focus on the harmful event and the person responsible for it—as others might focus solely on a sin committed and the "sinner"—we tell ourselves we are taking steps to free ourselves from the effects of the harm or the sin in question. But, in fact, we are putting ourselves in a servile position with respect to life, human growth, and the further enjoyment of relationships with others.[96] ✔ CHECKPOINTS

Concept Summary 8.1 summarizes the various emerging forms of critical criminology.

CRITICAL THEORY AND PUBLIC POLICY

At the core of all the varying branches of critical criminology is the fact that conflict causes crime. If conflict and competition in society could somehow be reduced, it is possible that crime rates would fall. Some critical theorists believe this goal can only be accomplished by thoroughly reordering society so that capitalism is destroyed and a socialist state is created. Others call for a more "practical" application of critical principles. Nowhere has this been more successful than in applying peacemaking principles in the criminal justice system.

There has been an ongoing effort to reduce the conflict created by the criminal justice system when it hands out harsh punishments to offenders, many of whom are powerless social outcasts. Critical theorists argue that the "old methods" of punishment are a failure and that upwards of two-thirds of all prison inmates recidivate soon after their release. They scoff at claims that the crime rate has dropped because the number of people in prison is at an all-time high, countering these claims with studies showing that imprisonment rates are not at all related to crime rates; there is no consistent finding that locking people up helps reduce crimes.[97]

peacemaking
Approach that considers punitive crime control strategies to be counterproductive and favors the use of humanistic conflict resolution to prevent and control crime.

CONCEPT SUMMARY 8.1 Emerging Forms of Critical Criminology

THEORY	MAJOR PREMISE	STRENGTHS	RESEARCH FOCUS
Left realism	Crime is a function of relative deprivation; criminals prey on the poor.	Represents a compromise between conflict and traditional criminology.	Deterrence; protection
Critical feminist theory	The capitalist system creates patriarchy, which oppresses women.	Explains gender bias, violence against women, and repression.	Gender inequality; oppression; patriarchy
Power-control theory	Girls are controlled more closely than boys in traditional male-dominated households. There is gender equity in contemporary egalitarian homes.	Explains gender differences in the crime rate as a function of class and gender conflict.	Power and control; gender differences; domesticity
Peacemaking criminology	Peace and humanism can reduce crime; conflict resolution strategies can work.	Offers a new approach to crime control through mediation.	Punishment; nonviolence; mediation

What can be done as an alternative? Rather than cast offenders aside, ways must be found bring offenders back into the community. This approach to offender rehabilitation is now known as **restorative justice**. Springing both from academia and reformers within the justice system itself, the restorative approach relies on nonpunitive strategies for crime prevention and control.[98] The next sections discuss the foundation and principles of restorative justice.

The Concept of Restorative Justice

The term "restorative justice" is often hard to define because it encompasses a variety of programs and practices. According to a leading restorative justice scholar, Howard Zehr, restorative justice requires that society address victims' harms and needs, hold offenders accountable to put right those harms, and involve victims, offenders, and communities in the process of healing. Zehr maintains that the core value of the restoration process can be translated into respect for all, even those who are different from us, even those who seem to be our enemies. At its core, Zehr argues, restorative justice is a set of principles, a philosophy, an alternate set of guiding questions that provide an alternative framework for thinking about wrongdoing.[99]

Restorative justice has grown out of a belief that the traditional justice system has done little to involve the community in the process of dealing with crime and wrongdoing. What has developed is a system of coercive punishments, administered by bureaucrats, that are inherently harmful to offenders and reduce the likelihood offenders will ever become productive members of society. This system relies on punishment, stigma, and disgrace. In his controversial book, *The Executed God: The Way of the Cross in Lockdown America*, theology professor Mark Lewis Taylor discusses the similarities between this contemporary, coercive justice system and that which existed in imperial Rome when Jesus and many of his followers were executed because they were an inspiration to the poor and slave populations. They represented a threat to the ruling Roman power structure. So,

✔ CHECKPOINTS

✔ Left realists are conflict scholars who believe the lower classes must be protected from predatory criminals until the social system changes and makes crime obsolete.

✔ Critical feminists study patriarchy and the oppression of women. They link female criminality to gender inequality.

✔ Power-control theory shows how family structure, women's economic status, and gender inequity interact to produce male/female differences in crime rates.

✔ Peacemaking criminologists seek nonviolent, humane alternatives to coercive punishment.

restorative justice
Using humanistic, nonpunitive strategies to right wrongs and restore social harmony.

Exhibit 8.1
Basic Principles of Restorative Justice

- Crime is an offense against human relationships.
- Victims and the community are central to justice processes.
- The first priority of justice processes is to assist victims.
- The second priority is to restore the community, to the degree possible.
- The offender has personal responsibility to victims and to the community for crimes committed.
- The offender will develop improved competency and understanding as a result of the restorative justice experience.
- Stakeholders share responsibilities for restorative justice through partnerships for action.

SOURCE: Anne Seymour, "Restorative Justice/Community Justice," in *National Victim Assistance Academy Textbook* (Washington, DC: National Victim Assistance Academy, 2001).

CONNECTIONS
Contrast the restorative justice approach with the crime control-deterrence policies advocated by rational choice theorists in Chapter 4.

too, is our modern justice system designed to keep the downtrodden in their place. Taylor suggests that there should be a movement to reduce such coercive elements of justice as police brutality and the death penalty before our "lockdown society" becomes the model used around the globe.[100]

Advocates of restorative justice argue that rather than today's "lockdown" mentality, what is needed is a justice policy that repairs the harm caused by crime and that includes all parties who have suffered from that harm: the victim, the community, and the offender. They have made an ongoing effort to reduce the conflict created by the criminal justice system when it hands out harsh punishments to offenders, many of whom are powerless social outcasts. Based on the principle of reducing social harm, restorative justice advocates argue that the old methods of punishment are a failure: After all, upwards of two-thirds of all prison inmates recidivate soon after their release. And tragically, not all inmates are ever released. Some are given life sentences for relatively minor crimes under so-called three strikes laws that mandate such a sentence for a third conviction; some are given "life no parole sentences," which are in actuality "death sentences."[101]

The principles of the restorative justice approach are set out in Exhibit 8.1.

The Process of Restoration

The restoration process begins by redefining crime in terms of a conflict among the offender, the victim, and affected constituencies (families, schools, workplaces, and so forth). Therefore, it is vitally important that the resolution take place within the context in which the conflict originally occurred rather than being transferred to a specialized institution that has no social connection to the community or group from which the conflict originated. In other words, most conflicts are better settled in the community than in a court.

By maintaining "ownership," or jurisdiction, over the conflict, the community can express its shared outrage about the offense. Shared community outrage is directly communicated to the offender. The victim is also given a chance to voice his or her story, and the offender can directly communicate his or her need for social reintegration and treatment. All restoration programs involve an understanding between the victim, the offender, and community. Although processes differ in structure and style, they generally include these elements:

- The offender is asked to recognize that he or she caused injury to personal and social relations along with a determination and acceptance of responsibility (ideally accompanied by a statement of remorse). Only then can the offender be restored as a productive member of the community.
- Restoration involves turning the justice system into a "healing" process rather than being a distributor of retribution and revenge.
- Reconciliation is a big part of the restorative approach. Most people involved in offender–victim relationships actually know one another or were related in some way before the criminal incident took place. Instead of treating one of

the involved parties as a victim deserving of sympathy and the other as a criminal deserving of punishment, it is more productive to address the issues that produced conflict between these people.[102]

- The effectiveness of justice ultimately depends on the stake a person has in the community (or a particular social group). If a person does not value his or her membership in the group, the person will be unlikely to accept responsibility, show remorse, or repair the injuries caused by his or her actions. In contrast, people who have a stake in the community and its principle institutions, such as work, home, and school, find that their involvement enhances their personal and familial well-being.[103]
- A commitment to both material (monetary) restitution and symbolic reparation (an apology) is expected.
- A determination of community support and assistance for both victim and offender is involved.

The intended result of the process is to repair injuries suffered by the victim and the community while assuring reintegration of the offender.

Restoration Programs

Negotiation, mediation, consensus building, and peacemaking have been part of the dispute resolution process in European and Asian communities for centuries.[104] Native American and Native Canadian people have long used the type of community participation in the adjudication process (some examples are sentencing circles, sentencing panels, elders panels) that restorative justice advocates are now embracing.[105]

In some Native American communities, people accused of breaking the law meet with community members, victims (if any), village elders, and agents of the justice system in a **sentencing circle**. Each member of the circle expresses his or her feelings about the act that was committed and raises questions or concerns. The accused can express regret about his or her actions and a desire to change the harmful behavior. People may suggest ways the offender can make things up to the community and those he or she harmed. A treatment program, such as Alcoholics Anonymous, can be suggested, if appropriate.

Restorative justice is now being embraced on many levels within our society and the justice system.

Community Communities that isolate people and have few mechanisms for interpersonal interaction encourage and sustain crime. Those that implement forms of community dialogue to identify problems and plan tactics for eliminating them, guided by restorative justice practices and principles, may create a climate in which violent crime is less likely to occur.[106]

Schools Some schools have embraced restorative justice practices to deal with students involved in drug and alcohol abuse without having to resort to more punitive measures such as expulsion. Schools in Minnesota, Colorado, and elsewhere are now trying to involve students in "relational rehabilitation" programs that strive to improve individuals' relationships with key figures in the community who may have been harmed by their actions.[107]

Police Restorative justice has also been implemented by police when crime is first encountered. The new community policing models that have been adapted around the country are an attempt to bring restorative concepts into law enforcement. Restorative justice relies on the fact that criminal justice policy makers need to listen and respond to the needs of those who are to be affected by their actions, and community policing relies on policies established with input and exchanges between officers and citizens.[108]

Courts Restorative programs in the courts typically involve diverting the formal court process. These programs encourage meeting and reconciling the

CONNECTIONS

Community policing will be discussed further in Chapter 14. This program relies on involving citizens in the policing process and using their input to improve neighborhoods. Community policing efforts are at the neighborhood level and are designed to improve the quality of life in formerly troubled areas.

sentencing circle
A peacemaking technique in which offenders, victims, and other community members are brought together in an effort to formulate a sanction that addresses the needs of all.

Practicing Restorative Justice Abroad

The restorative justice philosophy is catching on in the United States, but it is already widely practiced abroad. Below are just a few of the many programs found around the world.

South Africa

After 50 years of oppressive white rule in South Africa, the race-dividing apartheid policy was abolished in the early 1990s, and in 1994 Nelson Mandela, leader of the African National Congress (ANC), was elected president. Some black leaders wanted revenge for the political murders carried out during the apartheid era, but Mandela established the Truth and Reconciliation Commission. Rather than seeking vengeance for the crimes, this government agency investigated the atrocities with the mandate of granting amnesty to those individuals who confessed their roles in the violence and could prove that their actions served some political motive rather than being based on personal factors such as greed or jealousy.

Supporters of the commission believed that this approach would help heal the nation's wounds and prevent years of racial and ethnic strife. Mandela, who had been unjustly jailed for 27 years by the regime, had reason to desire vengeance. Yet, he wanted to move the country forward after the truth of what happened in the past had been established. Though many South Africans, including some ANC members, believe that the commission is too lenient, Mandela's attempts at reconciliation have prevailed. The commission is a model of restoration over revenge.

Australia

The justice system in Australia uses the conferencing process to divert offenders from the justice system. This offers offenders the opportunity to attend a conference to discuss and resolve their offense instead of being charged and appearing in court. (Those who deny guilt are not offered conferencing.) The conference, normally lasting one to two hours, is attended by the victims and their supporters, the defendant and his or her supporters, and other concerned parties. The conference coordinator focuses the discussion on condemning the act without condemning the character of the actor. Offenders are asked to tell their side of the story, what happened, how they have felt about the crime, and what they think should be done. The victims and others are asked to describe the physical, financial, and emotional consequences of the crime. This discussion may lead the offenders, their families, and their friends to experience the shame of the act, prompting an apology to the victim. A plan of action is developed and signed by key participants. The plan may include the offender's paying compensation to the victim, doing work for the victim or the community, or similar solutions. Conference participants are responsible for determining the outcomes that are most appropriate for these particular victims and these particular offenders.

All eight states and territories in Australia have used the conference model, but there are five in which conferencing is active. Of these five jurisdictions, all but one (the Australian Capital Territory or ACT) has legislatively established conferencing. South Australia began to use conferences routinely in 1994, Western Australia and the ACT in 1995, and New South Wales in 1998. Although Queensland is an active jurisdiction, it is experimenting with several formats of organizational placement and delivery, and conferencing is not available on a statewide basis. Tasmania passed legislation in 1997 that gave statutory authority to establish conferences, but a conferencing program has not yet started. The State of Victoria, like the ACT, is without a statutory scheme, but

conflicts between offenders and victims via victim advocacy, mediation programs, and sentencing circles, in which crime victims and their families are brought together with offenders and their families in an effort to formulate a sanction that addresses the needs of each party. Victims are given a chance to voice their stories, and offenders can help compensate them financially or provide some service (such as fixing damaged property).[109] The goal is to enable offenders to appreciate the damage they have caused, to make amends, and to be reintegrated into society.

Balanced and Restorative Justice (BARJ)

A number of restorative justice experts, including Gordon Bazemore and his associates, have suggested that restorative justice should be centered on the principle of balance.[110] According to this approach, the justice system should give equal weight to offender accountability, competency development, and community protection:

- *Holding offenders accountable to victims*. "Offender accountability" refers specifically to the requirement that offenders "make amends" for the harm resulting from their crimes by repaying or restoring losses to victims and the community.

a community organization, working in partnership with state agencies, uses the conference model in selected cases as a pre-sentencing option.

Ireland

The Nenagh Community Reparation Project is managed by a local committee representing different community interests in partnership with the Probation and Welfare Service. It began on the initiative of Judge Michael Reilly, who with the cooperation of the community and various agencies, has sought to use reparation in his court. In cases where an offender has admitted guilt, the judge can, at his or her discretion, offer the offender the choice of either the normal course of jail or participation in the community reparation project. At this point the court adjourns for approximately 30 minutes while the probation officer explains the project to the offender. If the offender decides to participate in the project, a meeting will be called in the near future.

This meeting is always attended by the offender, two panel members representing the community, the police officers who have been involved in the case, and the probation officer. If the crime involves victims, they are also invited to attend the meeting, although their participation is not mandatory.

At the meeting, offenders are asked to explain the circumstances of the offense, why it happened, how they felt about it then, and how they feel about their actions now. Together, the group decides how the offender might make reparation to the victim and/or the community for the damage caused by the offense.

Once agreement is reached about the form of the reparation, a contract is drawn up that sets out treatment courses the offender will be expected to take (treatment for alcoholism, substance abuse, anger management, and so on, as appropriate). Reparation may include letters of apology to the victim, monetary restitution, and other proportionate and appropriate activities. Contracts generally cover a period of approximately six months and are monitored by the probation officer. If the terms of the contract are successfully completed, the record of the offense will be dropped. If the terms are not met, the case will go back to court and proceed in the normal manner.

Critical Thinking

Restorative justice may be the model that best serves alternative sanctions. How can this essentially humanistic approach be sold to the general public that now supports more punitive sanctions? For example, would it be reasonable to expect that using restorative justice with nonviolent offenders frees resources for the relatively few dangerous people in the criminal population? Explain.

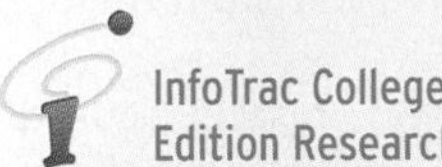

To learn more about the restorative justice approach, see Gordon Bazemore, "Restorative Justice and Earned Redemption: Communities, Victims, and Offender Reintegration," *American Behavioral Scientist* 41 (1998): 768; Tag Evers, "A Healing Approach to Crime," *The Progressive* 62 (1998): 30; Carol La Prairie, "The Impact of Aboriginal Justice Research on Policy: A Marginal Past and an Even More Uncertain Future," *Canadian Journal of Criminology* 41 (1999): 249.

SOURCES: Leena Kurki, *Incorporating Restorative and Community Justice into American Sentencing and Corrections* (Washington, DC: National Institute of Justice, 1999); Australian Government, Australian Institute of Criminology, "Restorative Justice: An Australian Perspective," www.aic.gov.au/rjustice/australia.html (accessed August 4, 2004); Restorative Justice in Ireland, Nenagh Community Reparation Project, Co. Tipperary, www.extern.org/restorative/ (accessed August 4, 2004); John W. De Gruchy, *Reconciliation: Restoring Justice* (Minneapolis, MN: Fortress, 2002).

- *Providing competency development for offenders in the system so they can pursue legitimate endeavors after release.* Competency development, the rehabilitative goal for intervention, requires that people who enter the justice system should exit the system more capable of being productive and responsible in the community.
- *Ensuring community safety.* The community protection goal explicitly acknowledges and endorses a longtime public expectation—a safe and secure community.

The balanced approach means that justice policies and priorities should seek to address each of the three goals in *each case* and that system balance should be pursued. The goal of achieving balance suggests that no single objective take precedence over any other without creating a system that is "out of balance" and implies that efforts to achieve one goal (such as offender accountability) should not hinder efforts to achieve other goals.

BARJ is founded on the belief that justice is best served when the victim, community, and offender are viewed as equal clients of the justice system who will receive fair and balanced attention, be actively involved in the justice process, and gain tangible benefits from their interactions with the justice system. Most BARJ programs are located today within the juvenile justice system.

The Policy & Practice in Criminology feature discusses some recent innovative community programs based on the principles of restorative justice.

Exhibit 8.2
Victim Concerns about Restorative Justice

- Restorative justice processes can cast victims as little more than props in a psychodrama focused on the offender, to restore him and thereby render him less likely to offend again.
- A victim, supported by family and intimates while engaged in restorative conferencing, and feeling genuinely free to speak directly to the offender, may press a blaming rather than restorative shaming agenda.
- The victims' movement has focused for years on a perceived imbalance of "rights." Criminal defendants enjoy the presumption of innocence, the right to proof beyond a reasonable doubt, the right not to have to testify, and lenient treatment when found guilty of crime. Victims were extended no rights at all in the legal process. Is restorative justice another legal giveaway to criminals?
- Victims' rights are threatened by some features of the restorative justice process, such as respectful listening to the offender's story and consensual dispositions. These features seem affronts to a victim's claim of the right to be seen as a victim, to insist on the offender being branded a criminal, to blame the offender, and not to be "victimized all over again by the process."
- Many victims do want an apology, if it is heartfelt and easy to get, but some want, even more, to put the traumatic incident behind them; to retrieve stolen property being held for use at trial; to be assured that the offender will receive treatment he is thought to need if he is not to victimize someone else. For victims such as these, restorative justice processes can seem unnecessary at best.
- Restorative processes depend, case by case, on victims' active participation in a role more emotionally demanding than that of complaining witness in a conventional criminal prosecution, which is itself a role avoided by many, perhaps most, victims.

SOURCE: Michael E. Smith, *What Future for "Public Safety" and "Restorative Justice" in Community Corrections?* (Washington, DC: National Institute of Justice, 2001).

The Challenge of Restorative Justice

Restorative justice holds great promise, but there are also some concerns:

- Is it a political movement or a treatment process? Restorative justice is viewed as an extremely liberal alternative, and its advocates often warn of the uneven exercise of state power. Some view it as a social movement rather than a method of rehabilitation.[111] Can it survive in a culture that is becoming increasingly conservative and focused on security rather than personal freedom?
- Restorative justice programs must be wary of the cultural and social differences that can be found throughout our heterogeneous society. What may be considered "restorative" in one subculture may be considered insulting and damaging in another.[112]
- There is still no single definition of what constitutes restorative justice.[113] Consequently, many diverse programs that call themselves "restorative" oriented pursue objectives that seem remote from the restorative ideal.
- Restorative justice programs face the difficult task of balancing the needs of offenders with those of their victims. If programs focus solely on victims' needs, they may risk ignoring the offenders' needs and increase the likelihood of reoffending. Declan Roche, a Lecturer in Law at the London School of Economics, makes the argument that the seductive promise of restorative justice may blind admirers to the benefits of traditional methods and prevent them from understanding or appreciating some of the pitfalls of restoration. There is danger, he warns, in a process that is essentially informal, without lawyers, and with little or no oversight on the outcome. The restoration process gives participants unchecked power without the benefit of procedural safeguards.[114]
- Benefits may only work in the short term while ignoring long-term treatment needs. Sharon Levrant and her colleagues suggest that restorative justice programs that feature short-term interactions with victims fail to help offenders learn prosocial ways of behaving. Restorative justice advocates may falsely assume that relatively brief interludes of public shaming will change deeply rooted criminal predispositions.[115]

- Restorative justice programs focus on offender needs at the expense of victims. Some victim advocates question this focus and argue that it creates a variety of problems set out in Exhibit 8.2.

These are a few of the obstacles that restorative justice programs must overcome to be successful and productive. Yet because the method holds so much promise, criminologists are now conducting numerous demonstration projects to find the most effective means of returning the ownership of justice to the people and the community.[116]

THINKING Like a Criminologist

An interim evaluation of Restoration House's New Hope for Families program, a community-based residential treatment program for women with dependent children, shows that 70 percent of women who complete follow-up interviews six months after treatment have maintained abstinence or reduced their drug use. The other 30 percent, however, lapse into their old habits.

The program relies on restorative justice techniques in which community people meet with the women to discuss the harm drug use can cause and how it can damage both them and their children. The community members show their support and help the women find a niche in the community.

Women who complete the Restoration House program improve their employment, reduce parenting stress, retain custody of their children, and restore their physical, mental, and emotional health. The program focuses not only on reducing drug and alcohol use but also on increasing health, safety, self-sufficiency, and positive attitudes.

As a criminologist, would you consider this program a success? What questions would have to be answered before it gets your approval? How do you think the program should handle women who do not succeed in the program? Are there any other approaches you would try with these women? If so, explain.

Summary

- Social conflict theorists view crime as a function of the conflict that exists in society.
- Conflict theorists suggest that crime in any society is caused by class conflict. Laws are created by those in power to protect their rights and interests.
- All criminal acts have political undertones. Richard Quinney has called this concept "the social reality of crime."
- One of critical criminology's most important premises is that the justice system is biased and designed to protect the wealthy.
- Critical criminology views the competitive nature of the capitalist system as a major cause of crime. The poor commit crimes because of their frustration, anger, and need. The wealthy engage in illegal acts because they are used to competition and because they must do so to keep their positions in society.
- Critical scholars have attempted to show that the law is designed to protect the wealthy and powerful and to control the poor, have-not members of society.
- Critical theorists can be divided into instrumental theorists and structural theorists. The former holds that those in power wield their authority to control society and keep the lower classes in check. The latter maintains that the justice system is designed to maintain the status quo and is also used to punish the wealthy if they bend the rules governing capitalism.
- Research on critical theory focuses on how the system of justice was designed and how it operates to further class interests. Quite often, this research uses historical analysis to show how the capitalist classes have exerted control over the police, courts, and correctional agencies.
- Both critical and conflict criminology have been heavily criticized by consensus criminologists, who suggest that social conflict theories make fundamental errors in their concepts of ownership and class interest.
- Critical feminist writers draw attention to the influence of patriarchal society on crime.
- According to power–control theory, gender differences in the crime rate can be explained by the structure of the family in a capitalist society.
- Left realism takes a centrist position on crime by showing its rational and destructive nature; the justice system is necessary to protect the lower classes until a socialist society can be developed, which will end crime.
- Peacemaking criminology brings a call for humanism to criminology.
- The restorative justice model holds that reconciliation rather than retribution should be used to prevent and control crime.

- Restoration programs are now being used around the United States in schools, justice agencies, and community programs. They employ mediation, sentencing circles, and other techniques.

Take a Post-Test. Visit www.thomsonedu.com/criminaljustice/siegel and take the chapter Post-Test to monitor your progress and identify areas for further improvement. In addition to discovering what you've mastered, you'll learn which concepts need your added attention and get specific page references that direct you to the places in the text where you can find more information on them.

Key Terms

power 176
surplus value 178
marginalization 178
globalization 179
instrumental theory 180
structural theory 180
demystify 181
left realism 184
preemptive deterrence 185
critical feminism 185
patriarchal 185
paternalistic families 187
role exit behaviors 187
egalitarian families 187
power–control theory 187
peacemaking 188
restorative justice 189
sentencing circle 191

Critical Thinking Questions

1. How would a conservative reply to a call for more restorative justice? How would a restorative justice advocate respond to a conservative call for more prisons?

2. Considering recent changes in American culture, how would a power–control theorist explain recent drops in the U.S. crime rate? Can it be linked to changes in the structure of the American family?

3. Is conflict inevitable in all cultures? If not, what can be done to reduce the level of conflict in our own society?

4. If Marx were alive today, what would he think about the prosperity enjoyed by the working class in industrial societies? Might he alter his vision of the capitalist system?

5. Has religious conflict replaced class conflict as the most important issue facing modern society? Can anything be done to heal the rifts between people of different faiths?

Developmental Theories: Things Change . . . or Do They?

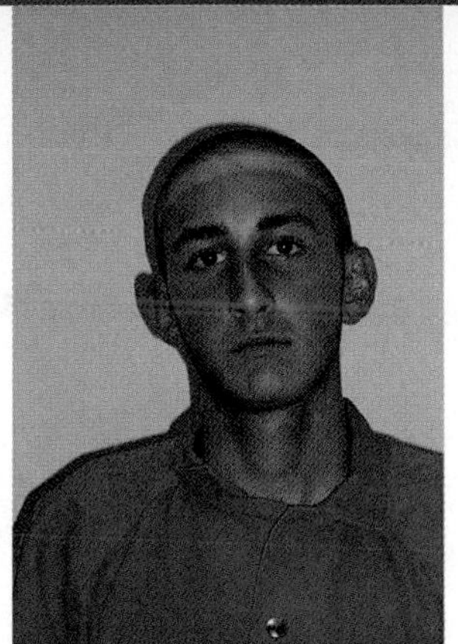
CANNON

HUNTER

SALAS

VICTORINO

IN JULY 2004 TROY VICTORINO AND SOME FRIENDS WERE ILLEGALLY SQUATTING IN A FLORIDA HOME whose owners were spending the summer in Maine. When their granddaughter and local resident Erin Belanger found them, she called the police and had them removed from the premises. The squatters were kicked out, but they left behind an Xbox and clothes, and the granddaughter took the items back to her home, which she was sharing with friends. Over the next few days, Victorino and his friends threatened Belanger and slashed the tires on her car. They warned her that they were going to come back there and beat her with a baseball bat when she was sleeping. Then on August 6, 2004, Victorino, accompanied by three accomplices armed with aluminum bats, kicked in the locked front door. The group, who wore black clothes

Refer to the front endpapers for a study tool that summarizes each of the major theories discussed in this book.

CHAPTER OBJECTIVES

1. Be familiar with the concept of developmental theory.
2. Know the factors that influence the life course.
3. Recognize that there are different pathways to crime.
4. Know what is meant by "problem behavior syndrome."
5. Differentiate between "adolescent-limited" and "life-course persistent" offenders.
6. Be familiar with the "turning points in crime."
7. Be able to discuss the influence of social capital on crime.
8. Know what is meant by a latent trait.
9. Be familiar with the concepts of impulsivity and self-control.
10. Be able to discuss Gottfredson and Hirschi's General Theory of Crime.

Take a Pre-Test. Visit www.thomsonedu.com/criminaljustice/siegel and take a Pre-Test to determine what you already know and identify the areas where you'll need to focus your study. The program will direct you to specific pages within the text where you can find further information on the correct answers to the questions you've missed.

and had scarves on their faces, grabbed knives inside and attacked victims in different rooms of the three-bedroom house as some of them slept. All six victims, including Erin Belanger, were beaten and stabbed beyond recognition.

Victorino was a career criminal. He had spent 8 of the last 11 years before the killing serving prison sentences for a variety of crimes, including auto theft, battery, arson, burglary, and theft. In 1996, he beat a man so severely that doctors needed 15 titanium plates to rebuild the victim's face. In 1997, a jury convicted him on a charge of aggravated battery, and he got a five-year sentence. His mother, Sharon Victorino, sent a letter to the judge before sentencing that said her son was sexually abused at age 2, an ordeal that "led to emotional scars that very few can fathom." Troy had been treated for depression since age 8 and had attempted suicide. "In a matter of a few days, you will be seeing before you my son. He will stand before you at 6-foot-6 tall, looking very much like a man," Sharon Victorino wrote. "In actuality, Troy is but a boy."[1]

The week before the attack in Florida, Troy Victorino was arrested for punching a 28-year-old man in the face and charged with felony battery; he was released after posting $2,500 bail. Victorino was arrested July 29 on a felony battery charge, accused of punching a man over a car debt. He was released on $2,500 bond and visited his probation officer for his regular check-in the day before the murders. He should have been arrested then for violating his probation, but his case supervisor failed to take action; in the aftermath of the crime, Victorino's probation officer and three of his supervisors were dismissed. On August 1, 2006, a Florida jury sentenced Victorino to death.

How can the violent and abusive actions of a Troy Victorino ever be explained? His history of antisocial acts began in his youth and persisted into his adulthood. Some experts believe that antisocial people like Victorino suffer from an abnormal personal trait, such as a low IQ or impulsive personality, which is present at birth or soon afterward. Yet, if the onset of crime is explained by abnormally low intelligence or a defective personality, why is it that most people **desist**, or age out of crime, as they mature? It seems unlikely that intelligence increases as young offenders mature or that personality flaws disappear. And why is it that most antisocial people start their criminal career with relatively minor crimes such as shoplifting or smoking marijuana and then commit progressively more serious crimes such as burglary and rape? Even if the onset of criminality can be explained by a single biological or personal trait, some other factor must explain its change, development, and continuance or termination.

Concern over these critical issues has prompted some criminologists to identify, describe, and understand the developmental factors that explain the onset and continuation of a criminal career. Rather than look at a single factor, such as poverty or low intelligence, and suggest that people who maintain this trait are predisposed to crime, **developmental theories** attempt to provide a more global vision of a criminal career encompassing its onset, continuation, and termination.

desist
To spontaneously stop committing crime.

developmental theory
The view that criminality is a dynamic process, influenced by social experiences as well as individual characteristics. Developmental factors include biological, social, and psychological structures and processes.

FOUNDATIONS OF DEVELOPMENTAL THEORY

As you may recall, the research efforts of Sheldon and Eleanor Glueck formed the basis of today's developmental approach. Soon after the publication of their work, the Glueck's methodology and their integration of biological, psychological, and social factors were heavily criticized, and for many years their work was ignored in criminology texts and overlooked in the academic curriculum.

During the 1990s, the Glueck legacy was rediscovered in a series of papers by criminologists Robert Sampson and John Laub, who used modern statistical techniques to reanalyze the Glueck's carefully drawn empirical measurements. Sampson and Laub's findings, published in a series of books and articles, fueled the current popularity of developmental type theories.[2]

A 1990 review paper by Rolf Loeber and Marc LeBlanc was another important event that helped establish interest in a developmental criminology. In this landmark work, Loeber and LeBlanc proposed that criminologists should devote time and effort to understanding basic questions about the evolution of criminal careers. Rather than view criminality as static and constant—a person is either a criminal or a noncriminal—they viewed criminality as a dynamic process, with a beginning, middle, and end and changes all along the way. Loeber and LeBlanc challenged criminologists to answer these questions: Why do people begin committing antisocial acts? Why do some stop while others continue? Why do some escalate the severity of their criminality (that is, go from shoplifting to drug dealing to armed robbery) while others deescalate and commit less serious crimes as they mature? If some terminate their criminal activity, what, if anything, causes them to begin again? Why do some criminals specialize in certain types of crime, whereas others are generalists engaging in a variety of antisocial behavior? According to Loeber and LeBlanc's developmental view, criminologists must pay attention to how a criminal career unfolds, how it begins, why it is sustained, and how it comes to an end.[3]

These scholarly advances created enormous excitement among criminologists and focused their attention on criminal career research. As research on criminal careers has evolved, two distinct developmental viewpoints have taken shape: the life-course view and the latent trait view. **Life-course theorists** view criminality as a dynamic process, influenced by a multitude of individual characteristics, traits, and social experiences. As people travel through the life course, they are constantly bombarded by changing perceptions and experiences, and as a result their behavior will change directions, sometimes for the better and sometimes for the worse. In contrast, **latent trait theorists** believe that human development is controlled by a "master trait," present at birth or soon after. Some criminologists believe that this master trait is inflexible, stable, and unchanging; others concede that under some circumstances a latent trait can be altered, influenced, or changed by experiences and interactions (Concept Summary 9.1). In either event, as people travel through their life course, this trait is always there, directing their behavior and shaping the course of their life. Because this master trait is enduring, the ebb and flow of criminal behavior is directed by the impact of external forces such as interpersonal interactions and criminal opportunity. In other words, people don't change their fundamental nature, but the world around them is constantly evolving. Each of these positions is discussed in detail in the following sections. ✔ CHECKPOINTS

✔ CHECKPOINTS

- ✔ Pioneering criminologists Sheldon and Eleanor Glueck tracked the onset and termination of criminal careers.
- ✔ The Glueck's work led to the creation of developmental theories.
- ✔ Developmental theories attempt to provide a global vision of a criminal career encompassing its onset, continuation, and termination.
- ✔ Developmental theories come in two different varieties.
- ✔ Life-course theories look at issues such as the onset of crime, escalation of offenses, continuity of crime, and desistance from crime.
- ✔ Latent trait theories project that a "master trait" exists that guides human development.

life-course theories
Theoretical views studying changes in criminal offending patterns over a person's entire life. Are there conditions or events that occur later in life that influence the way people behave, or is behavior predetermined by social or personal conditions at birth?

latent trait theories
Theoretical views that criminal behavior is controlled by a master trait, present at birth or soon after, that remains stable and unchanging throughout a person's lifetime.

LIFE-COURSE FUNDAMENTALS

According to the life-course view, even as toddlers, people begin relationships and behaviors that will determine their adult life course. At first they must learn to conform to social rules and function effectively in society. Later they are expected to begin to think about careers, leave their parental homes, find permanent relationships, and eventually marry and begin their own families.[4] These transitions are expected to take place in order—beginning with completing school, then entering the workforce, getting married, and having children.

CONCEPT SUMMARY 9.1 Two Types of Latent Traits

CONSTANT LATENT TRAIT	EVOLVING LATENT TRAIT
Inflexible	Flexible
Unchanging	Varying
Influenced by psychological/biological traits and conditions	Influenced by human interaction relationships, contact, and associations

CONNECTIONS

The Glueck research was reviewed in chapter 1. Chapter 2 addressed the issues of both chronic offending and aging out. These two issues are the cornerstones of contemporary criminological theories.

CONNECTIONS

The Philadelphia cohort research by Marvin Wolfgang and his associates was another milestone prompting interest in explaining criminal career development. Chapter 2 discussed how Wolfgang found that although many offenders commit a single criminal act and desist from crime, a small group of chronic offenders engage in frequent and repeated criminal activity and continue to do so across their life span. Wolfgang's research focused attention on criminal careers. His work prompted criminologists to ask this fundamental question: What prompts one person to engage in persistent criminal activity while another, who on the surface suffers the same life circumstances, finds a way to steer clear of crime and travel along a more conventional path?

Some individuals, however, are incapable of maturing in a reasonable and timely fashion because of family, environmental, or personal problems. In some cases, transitions can occur too early—an adolescent girl who engages in precocious sex gets pregnant and is forced to drop out of high school. In other cases, transitions may occur too late—a teenage male falls in with the wrong crowd, goes to prison, and finds it difficult to break into the job market; he puts off getting married because of his diminished economic circumstances. Sometimes interruption of one trajectory can harm another. A teenager who has family problems may find that her educational and career development is upset. Because a transition from one stage of life to another can be a bumpy ride, the propensity to commit crimes is neither stable nor constant: It is a developmental process. A positive life experience may help some criminals desist from crime for a while, whereas a negative one may cause them to resume their activities.[5]

Life-course theories also recognize that as people mature, the factors that influence their behavior change.[6] As people make important life transitions—from child to adolescent, from adolescent to adult, from unwed to married—the nature of social interactions also undergoes change.[7] At first, family relations may be most influential. It comes as no shock to life-course theorists when research shows that criminality runs in families and that having criminal relatives is a significant predictor of future misbehaviors.[8] In later adolescence, school and peer relations predominate; in adulthood, vocational achievement and marital relations may be the most critical influences. Some antisocial children who are in trouble throughout their adolescence may manage to find stable work and maintain intact marriages as adults; these life events help them desist from crime. In contrast, less fortunate adolescents who develop arrest records and get involved with the wrong crowd may find themselves limited to menial jobs and at risk for criminal careers.

From these and similar efforts, a view of crime has emerged that incorporates personal change and growth. The factors that produce crime and delinquency at one point in the life cycle may not be relevant at another; as people mature, the social, physical, and environmental influences on their behavior are transformed. People may show a propensity to offend early in their lives, but the nature and frequency of their activities are often affected by forces beyond their control, which elevate and sustain their criminal activity.[9]

The next sections review some of the more important concepts associated with the developmental perspective and discuss some prominent life-course theories.

Problem Behavior Syndrome

The life-course view is that criminality may best be understood as one of many social problems faced by at-risk youth, referred to here as **problem behavior syndrome (PBS)**. In this view, crime is one among a group of interrelated antisocial behaviors that cluster together and typically involve family dysfunction, sexual and physical abuse, substance abuse, smoking, precocious sexuality and early pregnancy, educational underachievement, suicide attempts, sensation seeking, and unemployment.[10] People who suffer from one of these conditions typically exhibit many symptoms of the rest.[11] Problem behaviors have a cumulative effect: The more risk factors a person suffers, the greater the likelihood that they will engage in antisocial behaviors.[12] All varieties of criminal behavior, including violence,

problem behavior syndrome (PBS)
A cluster of antisocial behaviors that may include family dysfunction, substance abuse, smoking, precocious sexuality and early pregnancy, educational underachievement, suicide attempts, sensation seeking, and unemployment, as well as crime.

Exhibit 9.1
Problem Behaviors

Social
- Family dysfunction
- Unemployment
- Educational underachievement
- School misconduct

Personal
- Substance abuse
- Suicide attempts
- Early sexuality
- Sensation seeking
- Early parenthood
- Accident-prone
- Medical problems
- Mental disease
- Anxiety
- Eating disorders (bulimia, anorexia)

Environmental
- High-crime area
- Disorganized area
- Racism
- Exposure to poverty

theft, and drug offenses, may be part of a generalized PBS, indicating that all forms of antisocial behavior have similar developmental patterns (Exhibit 9.1).[13]

Many examples support the existence of PBS:[14]

- Adolescents with a history of gang involvement are more likely to have been expelled from school, be a binge drinker, test positively for marijuana, have been in three or more fights in the past six months, have a non-monogamous partner, and test positive for sexually transmitted diseases.[15]
- Kids who gamble and take risks at an early age also take drugs and commit crimes.[16]
- People who exhibit one social problem typically exhibit many of the others.[17]

Those who suffer PBS are prone to more difficulties than the general population.[18] They find themselves with a range of personal dilemmas ranging from drug abuse to being accident prone, to requiring more health care and hospitalization, to becoming teenage parents, to having mental health problems.[19] PBS has been linked to individual-level personality problems (such as impulsiveness, rebelliousness, and low ego); family problems (such as intrafamily conflict and parental mental disorder); substance abuse; and educational failure.[20] Research shows that social problems such as drug abuse, low income, aggression, single parenthood, residence in isolated urban areas, lack of family support or resources, racism, and prolonged exposure to poverty are all interrelated.[21] According to this view, crime is a type of social problem rather than the product of other social problems.[22]

Pathways to Crime

Career criminals may travel more than a single road: Some may specialize in violence and extortion; some may be involved in theft and fraud; others may engage in a variety of criminal acts. Some offenders may begin their careers early in life, whereas others are late bloomers who begin committing crime when most people desist. Some are frequent offenders while others travel a more moderate path.[23]

Some of the most important research on delinquent paths, or trajectories, has been conducted by Rolf Loeber and his associates. Using data from a longitudinal study of Pittsburgh youth, Loeber has identified three distinct paths to a criminal career (Figure 9.1).[24]

1. The **authority conflict pathway** begins at an early age with stubborn behavior. This leads to defiance (doing things one's own way, disobedience) and then to authority avoidance (staying out late, truancy, running away).
2. The **covert pathway** begins with minor, underhanded behavior (lying, shoplifting) that leads to property damage (setting nuisance fires, damaging property). This behavior eventually escalates to more serious forms of crimi-

authority conflict pathway
Path to a criminal career that begins with early stubborn behavior and defiance of parents.

covert pathway
Path to a criminal career that begins with minor underhanded behavior and progresses to fire starting and theft.

Figure 9.1
Loeber's Pathways to Crime
SOURCE: "Serious and Violent Juvenile Offenders," *Juvenile Justice Bulletin*, May 1998.

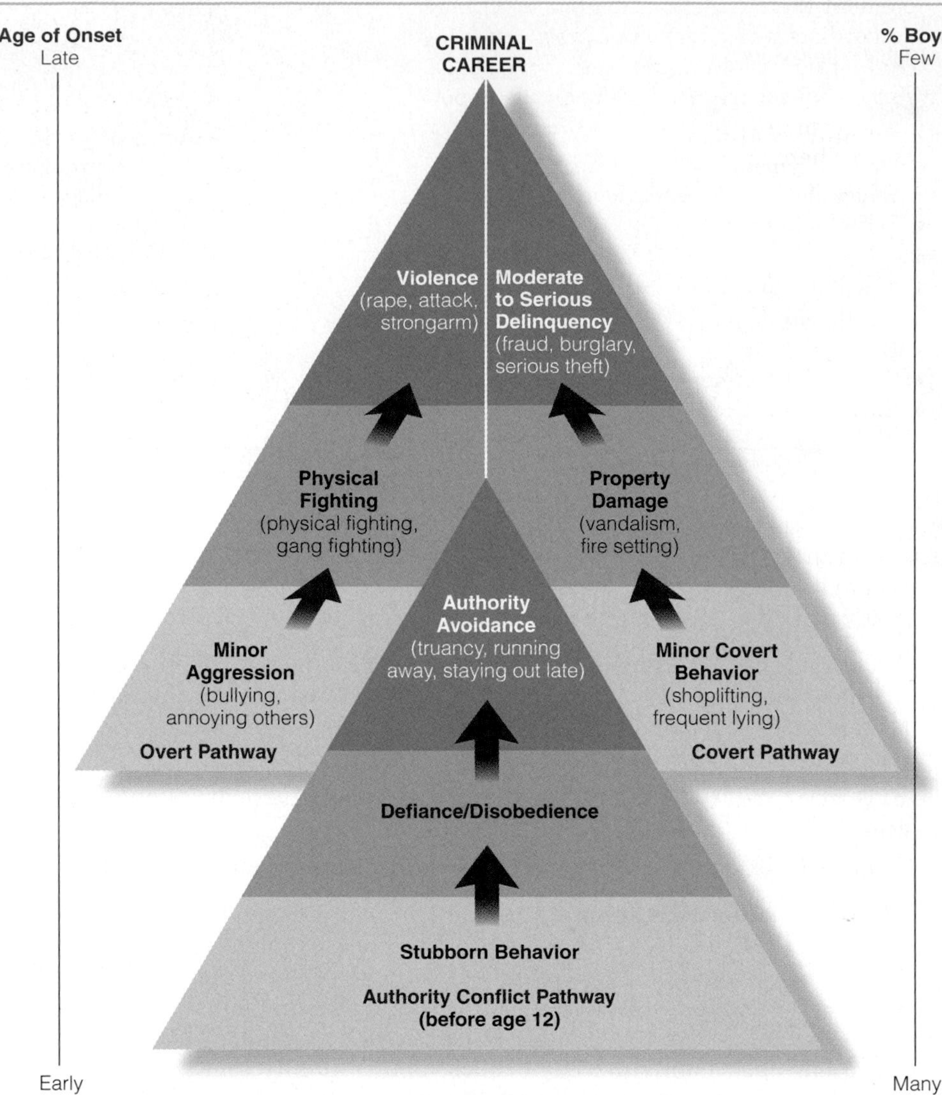

nality, ranging from joyriding, pocket picking, larceny, and fencing stolen goods, to passing bad checks, using stolen credit cards, stealing cars, dealing drugs, and breaking and entering.

3. The **overt pathway** escalates to aggressive acts, beginning with aggression (annoying others, bullying), leading to physical (and gang) fighting, and then to violence (attacking someone, forced theft).

The Loeber research indicates that each of these paths may lead to a sustained deviant career. Some kids enter two and even three paths simultaneously: They are stubborn, lie to teachers and parents, are bullies, and commit petty thefts. These adolescents are the most likely to become persistent offenders as they mature. As adolescents they cheat on tests, bully kids in the schoolyard, take drugs, commit burglary, steal a car, and then shoplift from a store. Later as adults, some specialize in a particular criminal activity such as drug trafficking, while others are involved in an assortment of deviant acts—selling drugs, committing robberies, and getting involved in break-ins—when the situation arises and the opportunities are present.[25]

overt pathway
Path to a criminal career that begins with minor aggression, leads to physical fighting, and eventually escalates to violent crime.

Offense Specialization/Generalization

Some offenders are specialists, limiting their criminal activities to a cluster of crime such as theft offenses, including burglary and larceny, or violent offenses such as assault and rape. Research shows, for example, that most burglars also shoplift to supplement their income from crime.[26] Others are generalists who engage in a garden variety of criminal activity ranging from drug abuse, burglary, and/or rape, depending on the opportunity to commit crime and the likelihood of success.[27] There is an ongoing debate over generalization/specialization: Some criminologists believe that most criminals are generalists, while others have found evidence that more serious offenders tend to specialize in a narrower range of antisocial activities.[28]

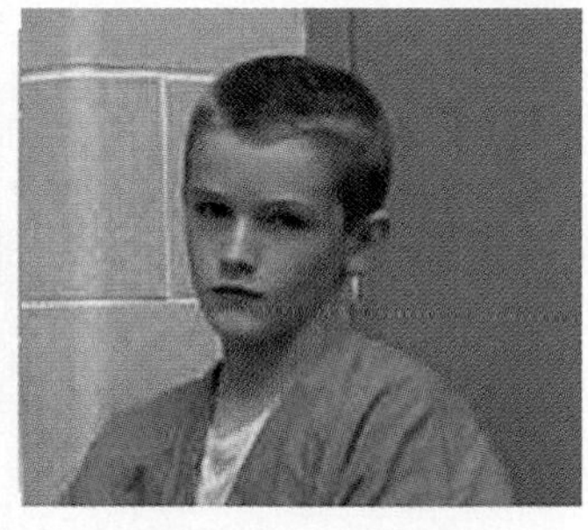

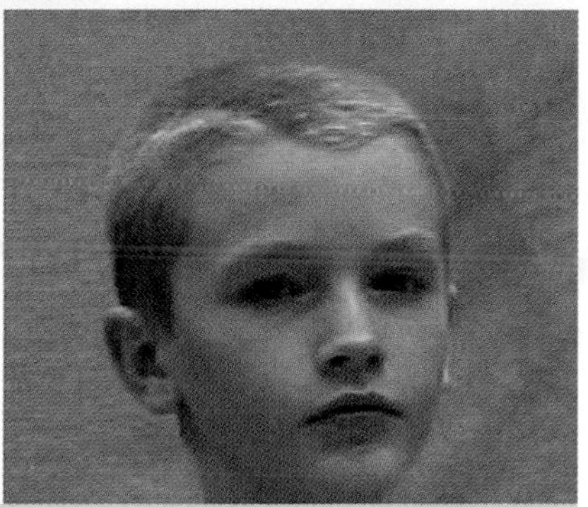

● According to the concept of early onset, the most serious offenders begin their offending careers at a very young age and then persist in their criminality. Twelve-year-old Alex King (upper-left inset) and his brother, 13-year-old Derek King, were indicted by a grand jury as adults on first-degree murder and arson charges for the bludgeoning death of their father Terry King, whose body was found in his burning home. Both boys were later found guilty of second-degree murder, but the judge overturned the conviction. They pleaded to a lesser charge and are currently serving seven- and eight-year sentences in a juvenile facility in Florida.

Age of Onset/Continuity of Crime

Most life-course theories assume that the seeds of a criminal career are planted early in life and that early onset of deviance strongly predicts later and more serious criminality.[29] Research supports this by showing that children who will later become the most serious delinquents begin their deviant careers at a very early (preschool) age and that the earlier the onset of criminality, the more frequent, varied, and sustained the criminal career.[30] Early-onset criminals are involved in such behaviors as truancy, cruelty to animals, lying, and theft and also appear to be more violent than their less precocious peers.[31] In contrast, late starters are more likely to be involved in nonviolent crimes such as theft.[32] Because symptoms appear early in life, it is not surprising that teachers' evaluations of children during their public school years have been found to be a significant predictor of troublesome and aggressive behavior in adulthood.[33]

The earlier the onset of crime, the longer its duration.[34] As they emerge into adulthood, persisters report less emotional support, lower job satisfaction, distant peer relationships, and more psychiatric problems than those who desist.[35]

What causes some kids to begin offending at an early age? Research shows that poor parental discipline and monitoring seem to be a key to the early onset of criminality and that these influences may follow kids into their adulthood. The psychic scars of childhood are hard to erase.[36]

Adolescent-Limiteds and Life-Course Persisters

Not all persistent offenders begin at an early age. Some begin their journey at different times: Some are precocious, beginning their criminal careers early and persist into adulthood.[37] Others stay out of trouble in adolescence and do not violate the law until their teenage years. Some offenders may peak at an early age, whereas others reach their peak in adulthood. Some youths maximize their offending rates at a relatively early age and then reduce their criminal activity; others persist into their 20s. Some non–early starters may "catch up" later in their adolescence. Some are high-rate offenders, whereas others offend at relatively low rates.[38]

According to psychologist Terrie Moffitt, most young offenders follow one of two paths: adolescent-limited offenders and life-course persisters. **Adolescent-limited offenders** may be considered "typical teenagers" who get into minor scrapes and engage in what might be considered rebellious teenage behavior with their friends.[39] As they reach their midteens, adolescent-limited delinquents begin to mimic the antisocial behavior of more troubled teens, only to reduce the frequency of their offending as they mature to around age 18.[40]

The second path is the one taken by a small group of **life-course persisters** who begin their offending career at a very early age and continue to offend well into adulthood.[41] Moffitt finds that life-course persisters combine family dysfunction with severe neurological problems that predispose them to antisocial behavior patterns. These afflictions can be the result of maternal drug abuse, poor nutrition, or

adolescent-limited offender
One who follows the most common criminal trajectory, in which antisocial behavior peaks in adolescence and then diminishes.

life-course persister
One of the small group of offenders whose criminal career continues well into adulthood.

exposure to toxic agents such as lead. It is not surprising then that life-course persisters display social and personal dysfunctions, including lower than average verbal ability, reasoning skills, learning ability, and school achievement.

Research shows that the persistence patterns predicted by Moffitt are valid and accurate.[42] Life-course persisters offend more frequently and engage in a greater variety of antisocial acts than other offenders; they also manifest significantly more mental health problems, including psychiatric pathologies, than adolescent-limited offenders.[43] Life-course persisters are more likely to manifest traits such as low verbal ability and hyperactivity, they display a negative or impulsive personality, and seem particularly impaired on spatial and memory functions.[44] Individual traits rather than environment seem to have the greatest influence on life-course persistence.[45]

THEORIES OF THE CRIMINAL LIFE COURSE

A number of systematic theories have been formulated that account for onset, continuance, and desistance from crime. As a group they integrate societal-level variables such as measures of social control, social learning, and social structure. It is not uncommon for life-course theories to interconnect *personal factors* such as personality and intelligence, *social factors* such as income and neighborhood, *socialization factors* such as marriage and military service, *cognitive factors* such as information processing and attention/perception, and *situational factors* such as criminal opportunity, effective guardianship, and apprehension risk into complex multifactor explanations of human behavior. In this sense they are **integrated theories** because they incorporate social, personal, and developmental factors into complex explanations of human behavior. They do not focus on the relatively simple question: Why do people commit crime? but on more complex issues: Why do some offenders persist in criminal careers while others desist from or alter their criminal activity as they mature?[46] Why do some people continually escalate their criminal involvement while others slow down and turn their lives around? Are all criminals similar in their offending patterns, or are there different types of offenders and paths to offending? Life-course theorists want to know not only why people enter a criminal way of life but why, once they do, they alter the trajectory of their criminal involvement. The next section covers one of the more important life-course theories, Sampson and Laub's age-graded theory, in detail. Exhibit 9.2 sets out the principles of three other life-course theories.

Sampson and Laub's Age-Graded Theory

If there are various pathways to crime and delinquency, are there trails back to conformity? In an important 1993 work, *Crime in the Making*, Robert Sampson and John Laub identify the **turning points** in a criminal career.[47] As devotees of the life-course perspective, Sampson and Laub find that the maintenance of a criminal career can be affected by events that occur later in life, even after a chronic delinquent career has been undertaken. They agree with other criminologists that formal and informal social controls restrict criminality and that crime begins early in life and continues over the life course; they disagree that once this course is set, nothing can impede its progress.

To conduct their research, Laub and Sampson reanalyzed the data originally collected by the Gluecks more than 40 years ago. Using modern statistical analysis, Laub and Sampson found evidence supporting their life-course view. They find that discrete factors influence people at different stages of their development, and, therefore, the propensity to commit crimes is neither stable nor unyielding. Children who enter delinquent careers are those who have trouble at home and at school; their parents and family life are the greatest influence on their behavior. As adolescents, peer relations becomes all important, and kids who maintain deviant friends are the ones most at risk for crime. In adulthood, marriage, family, and work influence behavior choices.

integrated theories
Models of crime causation that weave social and individual variables into a complex explanatory chain.

turning points
According to Laub and Sampson, the life events that alter the development of a criminal career.

Exhibit 9.2
Principal Life-Course Theories

Name Social Development Model (SDM)

Principal Theorists J. David Hawkins, Richard Catalano

Major Premise Community-level risk factors make some people susceptible to antisocial behaviors. Preexisting risk factors are either reinforced or neutralized by socialization. To control the risk of antisocial behavior, a child must maintain prosocial bonds. Over the life course, involvement in prosocial or antisocial behavior determines the quality of attachments. Commitment and attachment to conventional institutions, activities, and beliefs insulate youths from the crimogenic influences in their environment. The prosocial path inhibits deviance by strengthening bonds to prosocial others and activities. Without the proper level of bonding, adolescents can succumb to the influence of deviant others.

Name Interactional Theory

Principal Theorists Terence Thornberry and Marvin Krohn, Alan Lizotte, Margaret Farnworth

Major Premise The onset of crime can be traced to a deterioration of the social bond during adolescence, marked by weakening of attachment to parents, commitment to school, and belief in conventional values. The cause of crime and delinquency is bidirectional: Weak bonds lead kids to develop friendships with deviant peers and get involved in delinquency. Frequent delinquency involvement further weakens bonds and makes it difficult to reestablish conventional ones. Delinquency-promoting factors tend to reinforce one another and sustain a chronic criminal career. Kids who go through stressful life events, such as a family financial crisis, are more likely to get involved later in antisocial behaviors and vice versa. Criminality is a developmental process that takes on different meaning and form as a person matures. During early adolescence, attachment to the family is critical; by mid-adolescence, the influence of the family is replaced by friends, school, and youth culture; by adulthood, a person's behavioral choices are shaped by his or her place in conventional society and his or her own nuclear family. Although crime is influenced by these social forces, it also influences these processes and associations. Therefore, crime and social processes are interactional.

Name General Theory of Crime and Delinquency (GTCD)

Primary Theorist Robert Agnew

Major Premise Crime and social relations are reciprocal. Family relationships, work experiences, school performance, and peer relations influence crime. In turn, antisocial acts have a significant impact on family relationships, work experiences, school performance, and peer relations. Engaging in crime leads to a weakened bond with significant others and strengthened association with criminal peers. Close ties to criminal peers weakens bonds to conventional society. Crime is most likely to occur when the constraints against crime (fear of punishment, stake in conformity, self-control) are low and the motivations for crime (beliefs favorable to crime, exposure to criminals, criminal learning experiences) are high. The way an individual reacts to constraints and motivations is shaped by five key elements of human development called life domains:

1. *Self*: Irritability and/or low self-control
2. *Family*: Poor parenting and no marriage or a bad marriage
3. *School*: Negative school experiences and limited education
4. *Peers*: Delinquent friends
5. *Work*: Unemployment or having a bad job

The structure and impact of each of the life domains are continuously evolving; each has an influence over the other; they are mutually interdependent.

SOURCES: Robert Agnew, *Why Do Criminals Offend? A General Theory of Crime and Delinquency* (Los Angeles: Roxbury Publishing, 2005); Terence Thornberry, "Toward an Interactional Theory of Delinquency," *Criminology* 25 (1987): 863–891; Richard Catalano and J. David Hawkins, "The Social Development Model: A Theory of Antisocial Behavior," in *Delinquency & Crime: Current Theories*, ed. J. David Hawkins (New York: Cambridge University Press, 1996), pp. 149–197.

Social Capital Laub and Sampson recognize the role of **social capital** and its influence on the trajectory of a criminal career. Social scientists have long recognized that people build social capital—positive relations with individuals and institutions that are life sustaining. In the same manner that building financial capital improves the chances for personal success, building social capital supports conventional behavior and inhibits deviant behavior. Laub and Sampson find that at-risk kids who join the military and are honorably discharged significantly reduce the likelihood that they will become chronic offenders. A successful marriage, which creates social capital when it improves a person's stature, creates feelings of self-worth, and encourages people to trust the individual, also suppresses criminal activities. A successful career inhibits crime by creating a stake in conformity; why commit crime when you are doing well at your job? The relationship is reciprocal. If

social capital
Positive relations with individuals and institutions that are life sustaining.

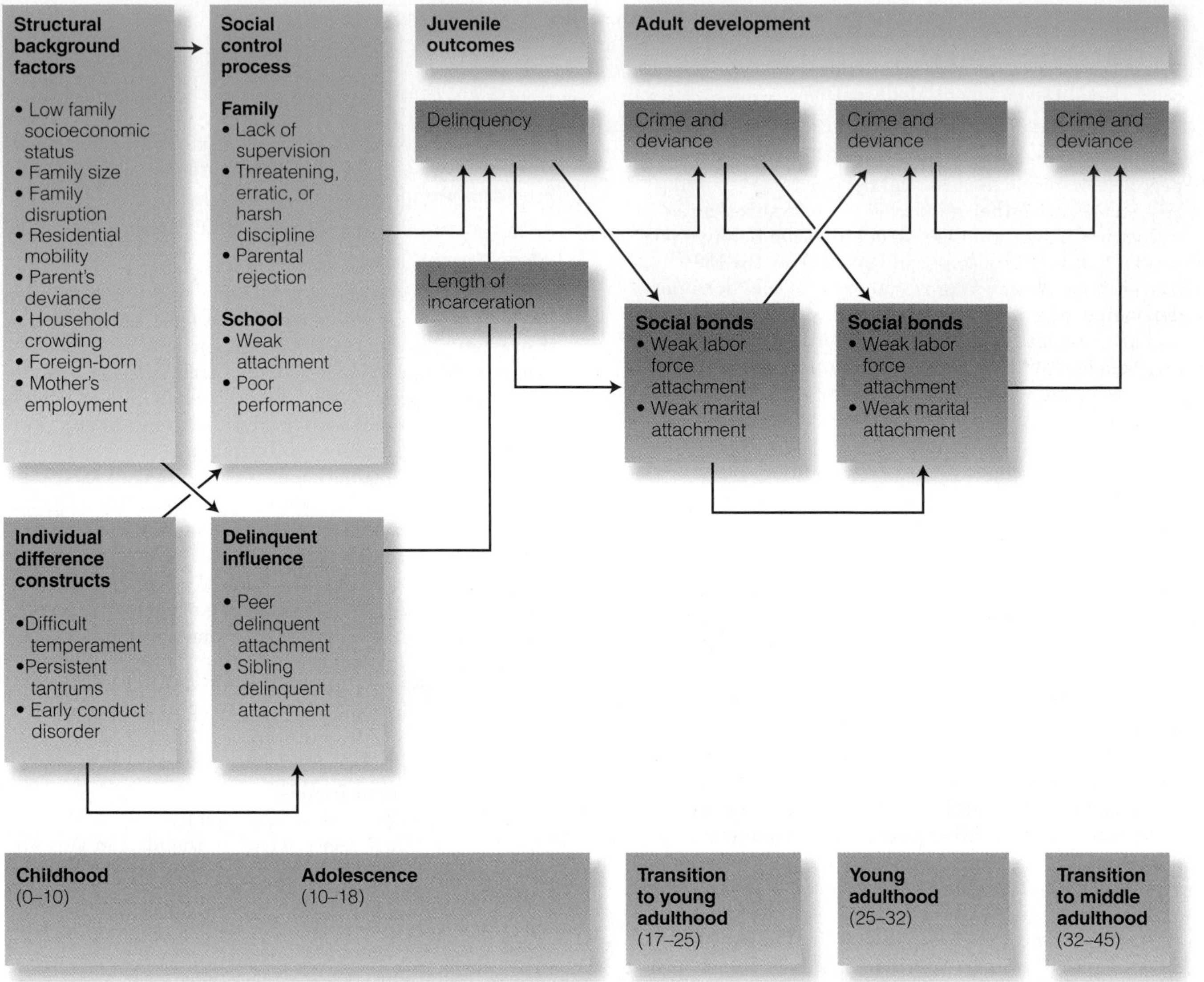

Figure 9.2

Sampson and Laub's Age-Graded Theory

SOURCE: Robert Sampson and John Laub, *Crime in the Making: Pathways and Turning Points through Life* (Cambridge, MA: Harvard University Press, 1993), pp. 244–245.

people are chosen to be employees, they return the favor by doing the best job possible; if they are chosen as spouses, they blossom into devoted partners. In contrast, people who fail to accumulate social capital are more prone to commit criminal acts.[48] When faced with personal crisis they lack the social supports that can help them reject criminal solutions and maintain a conventional behavior trajectory.

Turning Points One of Laub and Sampson's most important contributions is identifying the life events that enable adult offenders to desist from crime (Figure 9.2). Two critical turning points are marriage and career. Adolescents who are at risk for crime can live conventional lives if they can find good jobs or achieve successful careers. Their success may hinge on a lucky break. Even those who have been in trouble with the law may turn from crime if employers are willing to give them a chance despite their records.

When they achieve adulthood, adolescents who had significant problems with the law are able to desist from crime if they become attached to a spouse who supports and sustains them even when the spouse knows they had been in trouble when they were young. Happy marriages are life sustaining, and marital quality improves over time (as people work less and have fewer parental responsibilities).[49] Spending time in marital and family activities also reduces exposure to deviant peers, which in turn reduces the opportunity to become involved in delinquent activities.[50] People who cannot sustain secure marital relations are less likely to desist from crime.

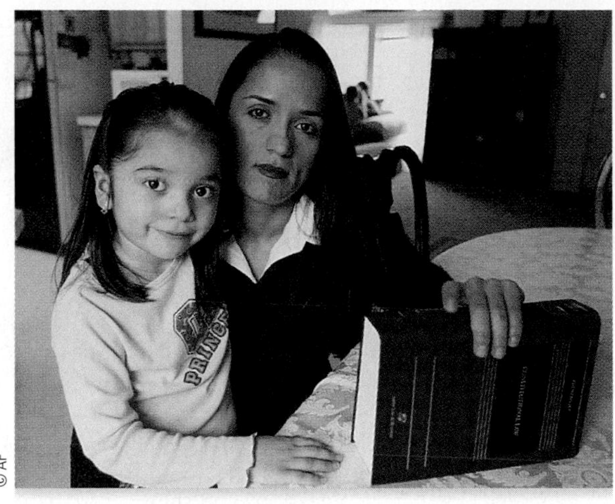

• According to age-graded theory, even people who have been at risk to become criminals can reach a turning point where they "knife off" from their path and enter a new, more productive life course. Ruth Esparza, 28, poses here with her daughter, Fancy Zaldivar, 5, in East Wenatchee, Washington. Esparza, who was a Wenatchee high school dropout, has gone back to school and is now a student at Gonzaga Law School in Spokane. She went back to school because, "I knew I didn't want my daughter to have an ignorant mom." How would Laub and Sampson explain Esparza's bold life-altering choice?

Testing Age-Graded Theory Empirical research now shows that, as predicted by Sampson and Laub, people change over the life course and that the factors that predict delinquency in adolescence, such as a weak social bond, may have less of an impact on adult crime.[51] Criminality appears to be dynamic and is affected by behaviors occurring over the life course, such as accumulating deviant peers: The more deviant friends one accumulates over time, the more likely the person is to get involved in crime.[52] Of critical importance is early labeling by the justice system: Adolescents who are convicted of crime at an early age are more likely to develop antisocial attitudes later in life. They later develop low educational achievement, declining occupational status, and unstable employment records.[53] People who get involved with the justice system as adolescents may find that their career paths are blocked well into adulthood.[54] The relationship is reciprocal: Men who are unemployed or underemployed report higher criminal participation rates than employed men.[55]

Evidence is also available that confirms Sampson and Laub's suspicion that criminal career trajectories can be reversed if life conditions improve.[56] For example, youths who have a positive high school experience, facilitated by occupationally oriented course work, small class size, and positive peer climates, are less likely to become incarcerated as adults than those who do not enjoy these social benefits.[57] Kids who have long-term exposure to poverty will find that their involvement in crime escalates. However, their involvement in crime will diminish if their life circumstances improve because their parents escape poverty and move to more attractive environments. Recent research by Ross Macmillan and his colleagues shows that children whose mothers were initially poor but escaped from poverty were no more likely to develop behavior problems than children whose mothers were never poor. Gaining social capital, then, may help erase some of the damage caused by its absence.[58]

A number of research efforts have supported Sampson and Laub's position that accumulating social capital reduces crime rates. Youths who accumulate social capital in childhood (for example, by doing well in school or having a tightly knit family) are also the most likely to maintain steady work as adults; employment may help insulate them from crime.[59] Delinquents who enter the military, serve overseas, and receive veterans' benefits enhance their occupational status (social capital) while reducing criminal involvement.[60] Similarly, high-risk adults who are fortunate enough to obtain high-quality jobs are likely to reduce their criminal activities even if they have a prior history of offending.[61]

The Marriage Factor People who maintain a successful marriage and become parents are the most likely to mature out of crime.[62] Marriage stabilizes people and helps them build social capital; it also may discourage crime by reducing contact with criminal peers. As Mark Warr states

> For many individuals, it seems, marriage marks a transition from heavy peer involvement to a preoccupation with one's spouse. That transition is likely to reduce interaction with former friends and accomplices and thereby reduce the opportunities as well as the motivation to engage in crime.[63]

Even people who have histories of criminal activity and have been convicted of serious offenses reduce the frequency of their offending if they live with spouses and maintain employment when they are in the community.[64] The marriage benefit may also be intergenerational: Children who grow up in two-parent families are more likely to have happier marriages themselves than children who are the product of divorced or never-married parents.[65] If people with marital problems are more crime-prone, their children will also suffer a greater long-term risk of marital failure and antisocial activity.

One recent research study (2002) further confirms the benefits of marriage as a crime-reducing social event. Researchers Alex Piquero, John MacDonald, and Karen Parker tracked each of 524 men in their late teens and early 20s for seven years after they were paroled from the California Youth Authority during the 1970s and 1980s.

Tracking Down the 500 Delinquent Boys in the New Millennium

Why are some delinquents destined to become persistent criminals as adults? John Laub and Robert Sampson have conducted a follow-up to their reanalysis of Sheldon and Eleanor Glueck's study that matched 500 delinquent boys with 500 nondelinquents. The individuals in the original sample were reinterviewed by the Gluecks at ages 25 and 32. Sampson and Laub have located the survivors of the delinquent sample, the oldest, 70 years old and the youngest, 62, and they have reinterviewed this cohort.

Persistence and Desistance

Laub and Sampson found that delinquency and other forms of antisocial conduct in childhood are strongly related to adult delinquency and drug and alcohol abuse. Former delinquents also suffer consequences in other areas of social life, such as school, work, and family life: They are far less likely to finish high school than are nondelinquents and subsequently are more likely to be unemployed, receive welfare, and experience separation or divorce as adults.

In their latest research, Laub and Sampson address a key question posed by life-course theories: Is it possible for former delinquents to turn their lives around as adults? The researchers found that most antisocial children do not remain antisocial as adults. Of men in the study cohort who survived to 50 years of age, 24 percent had no arrests for delinquent acts of violence and property (predatory delinquency) after age 17 (6 percent had no arrests for total delinquency); 48 percent had no arrests for predatory delinquency after age 25 (19 percent for total delinquency); 60 percent had no arrests for predatory delinquency after age 31 (33 percent for total delinquency); and 79 percent had no arrests for predatory delinquency after age 40 (57 percent for total delinquency). Laub and Sampson concluded that desistance from delinquency is the norm and that most, if not all, serious delinquents desist from delinquency.

Why Do Delinquents Desist?

Laub and Sampson's earlier research indicated that building social capital through marriage and jobs was the key component of desistance from delinquency. In this new round of research, however, Laub and Sampson found out more about long-term desistance by interviewing 52 men as they approached age 70. The follow-up showed a dramatic drop in criminal activity as the men aged: Between 17 and 24 years of age, 84 percent of the subjects had committed violent crimes; in their 30s and 40s, that number dropped to 14 percent; it fell to 3 percent as the men reached their 60s and 70s. Property crimes and alcohol- and drug-related crimes showed significant decreases. The researchers found that men who desisted from crime were rooted in structural routines and had strong social ties to family and community. Drawing on the men's own words, they found that one important element for "going straight" is the "knifing off" of individuals from their immediate environment, offering the men a new script for the future. Joining the military can provide this knifing-off effect, as does marriage or changing one's residence. One former delinquent (age 69) told them:

> *I'd say the turning point was, number one, the Army. You get into an outfit, you had a sense of belonging, you made your friends. I think I became a pretty good judge of character. In the Army, you met some good ones, you met some foul balls. Then I met the wife. I'd say probably that would be the turning point. Got married, then naturally, kids come. So now you got to get a better job, you got to make more money. And that's how I got to the Navy Yard and tried to improve myself.*

Former delinquents who "went straight" were able to put structure into their lives. Structure often led the men to disassociate from delinquent peers, reducing the opportunity to get into trouble. Getting married, for example, may limit the number of nights men can "hang with the guys." As one wife of a

The sample of men, who had been incarcerated for lengthy periods of time, was 48.5 percent white, 33 percent black, 16.6 percent Latino, and 1.9 percent other races.[66] The research team found former offenders were far less likely to return to crime if they settled down into the routines of a solid marriage. Common-law marriages or living with a partner did not have the same crime-reducing effect as did traditional marriages in which the knot is tied, the union is registered at the courthouse, and there is a general expectation to lead a steady life. Among non-Caucasians, parolees cohabiting without the benefit of marriage actually increased their recidivism rates. Piquero explains his findings by suggesting that people who are married often have schedules—they work nine-to-five jobs, come home for dinner, take care of children if they have them, watch television, go to bed, and repeat that cycle over and over again. People who are not married have a lot of free time to do a lot of what they want, especially if they are not employed. There's something about crossing the line of getting married that helps these men stay away from crime. If they don't cross that line, they can continue their lifestyles, which are pretty erratic.[67]

Although the Piquero research is persuasive, some questions still need to be answered: Why do some people enter strong marriages while others fail? Does the influence of marriage have an equal effect on men and women? Research by Ronald Simons and his associates found that while marriage significantly improves a woman's life chances, it has less impact on men.[68] For both males and females, former delinquent said, "It is not how many beers you have, it's who you drink with." Even multiple offenders who did time in prison were able to desist with the help of a stabilizing marriage.

Former delinquents who can turn their life around, who have acquired a degree of maturity by taking on family and work responsibilities, and who have forged new commitments are most likely to make a fresh start and find new direction and meaning in life. It seems that men who desisted changed their identity as well, and this, in turn, affected their outlook and sense of maturity and responsibility. The ability to change did not reflect delinquency "specialty": Violent offenders followed the same path as property offenders.

Although many former delinquents desisted from delinquency, they still faced the risk of an early and untimely death. Thirteen percent (N = 62) of the delinquent subjects as compared to 6 percent (N = 28) of the nondelinquent subjects died unnatural deaths, such as by violence, cirrhosis of the liver caused by alcoholism, poor self-care, and suicide. By 65 years of age, 29 percent (N = 139) of the delinquent and 21 percent (N = 95) of the nondelinquent subjects had died from natural causes. Frequent involvement in delinquency during adolescence and alcohol abuse were the strongest predictors of an early and unnatural death. So while many troubled youths are able to reform, their early excesses may haunt them across their life span.

Policy Implications

Laub and Sampson found that youth problems—delinquency, substance abuse, violence, dropping out, teen pregnancy—often share common risk characteristics. Intervention strategies, therefore, should consider a broad array of antisocial, criminal, and deviant behaviors and not limit the focus to one subgroup or delinquency type. Because criminality and other social problems are linked, early prevention efforts that reduce delinquency will probably also reduce alcohol abuse, drunk driving, drug abuse, sexual promiscuity, and family violence. The best way to achieve these goals is through four significant life-changing events: marriage, joining the military, getting a job, and changing one's environment or neighborhood. What appears to be important about these processes is that they all involve, to varying degrees, the following items: a knifing off of the past from the present; new situations that provide both supervision and monitoring as well as new opportunities of social support and growth; and new situations that provide the opportunity for transforming identity. Prevention of delinquency must be a policy at all times and at all stages of life.

Critical Thinking

1. Do you believe that the factors that influenced the men in the original Glueck sample are still relevant for change, for example, a military career?
2. Would it be possible for men such as these to join the military today?
3. Do you believe that some sort of universal service program might be beneficial and help people turn their lives around?

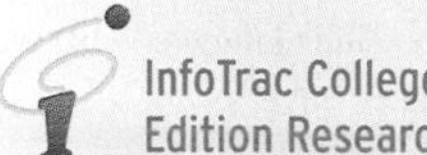
InfoTrac College Edition Research

Read a review of Laub and Sampson's *Crime in the Making* in Roland Chilton, "Crime in the Making: Pathways and Turning Points through Life," *Social Forces* 74 (September 1995): 357.

To learn more about the concept of "social capital," use it as a key word in InfoTrac College Edition.

SOURCES: John Laub and Robert Sampson, *Shared Beginnings, Divergent Lives: Delinquent Boys to Age 70* (Cambridge, MA: Harvard University Press, 2003); John Laub and Robert Sampson, "Understanding Desistance from Delinquency," in *Delinquency and Justice: An Annual Review of Research*, vol. 28, ed. Michael Tonry, (Chicago: University of Chicago Press, 2001), pp. 1–71; John Laub and George Vaillant, "Delinquency and Mortality: A 50-Year Follow-Up Study of 1,000 Delinquent and Nondelinquent Boys," *American Journal of Psychiatry* 157 (2000): 96–102.

however, having an antisocial romantic partner as a young adult increases the likelihood of later criminal behavior, a finding that supports Laub and Sampson.

Future Research Directions Age-graded theory has received enormous attention, but many research questions are still unanswered. Does a military career actually help reduce future criminality? Recent research (2005) by John Paul Wright and his colleagues found that Vietnam veterans significantly increased their involvement in substance abuse once they returned home. Considering the strong association between drug abuse and crime, their research casts doubt on whether all types of military service can be beneficial, as Laub and Sampson suggest. Future research may want to focus on individual experiences in the military and their effect on subsequent civilian behavior.[69]

Why are some troubled youths able to conform to the requirements of a job or career while others cannot? If acquiring social capital—family, friends, education, marriage, and employment—aids in the successful recovery from crime, does the effect produce an actual change in the propensity to commit crime or merely the reduction of criminal opportunity?[70] To answer some of these questions, Laub and Sampson contacted the surviving members of the Glueck cohort, and some of their findings are discussed in the Current Issues in Crime feature, "Tracking Down the 500 Delinquent Boys in the New Millennium." ✔ CHECKPOINTS

LATENT TRAIT THEORIES

✔ CHECKPOINTS

✔ Life-course theorists have identified a number of different concepts that influence human behavior.

✔ The concept of a problem behavior syndrome suggests that criminality may be just one of a cluster of social, psychological, and physical problems.

✔ There is more than one pathway to crime.

✔ Adolescent-limited offenders begin offending late and age out of crime. Life-course persisters exhibit early onset of crime that persists into adulthood.

✔ There are a number of theories based on life-course events.

✔ According to Laub and Sampson's age-graded theory, building social capital and strong social bonds reduces the likelihood of long-term deviance.

✔ Many criminals who desist from crime still face other risks such as an early and untimely death.

On August 7, 2005, police in Concord, New Hampshire, arrested Thaddeus Duprey aged 19 and three of his friends for driving around town and shooting at pedestrians with a BB gun.[71] The crime was rather unremarkable, and no one was seriously injured. But the incident made headlines in local newspapers because Duprey was a graduate of pricey Derryfield Academy, a local private school that caters to affluent students; he was a former member of Derryfield's crew team; and at the time of the incident, he was a student at the prestigious University of Pennsylvania. The police said the motive for the shootings appeared to have been "boredom."

What would motivate a privileged youth such as Thad Duprey to shoot at people he had never met? Certainly, his behavior was not a result of economic hardship or feelings of strain. Could some underlying trait, unknown and unseen to people who knew him well, be the catalyst for this inexplicable outburst of violence? Was this a singular incident or one in an ongoing pattern of antisocial activity? Had Duprey been involved in prior incidents of antisocial activity from early in his childhood that heretofore had gone undetected?

In a critical 1990 article, David Rowe, D. Wayne Osgood, and W. Alan Nicewander proposed the concept of latent traits to explain the flow of crime over the life cycle. Their model assumes that a number of people in the population have a personal attribute or characteristic that controls their inclination or propensity to commit crimes.[72] This disposition, or **latent trait**, may be either present at birth or established early in life, and it can remain stable over time. Suspected latent traits include defective intelligence, damaged or impulsive personality, genetic abnormalities, the physical-chemical functioning of the brain, and environmental influences on brain function, such as drugs, chemicals, and injuries.[73]

Regardless of gender or environment, those who maintain one of these suspect traits may be at risk to crime and in danger of becoming career criminals; those who lack the traits have a much lower risk.[74]

Because latent traits are stable, people who are antisocial during adolescence are the most likely to persist in crime. The positive association between past and future criminality detected in the cohort studies of career criminals reflects the presence of this underlying crimogenic trait. That is, if low IQ contributes to delinquency in childhood, it should also cause the same people to offend as adults because intelligence is usually stable over the life span.

Whereas the propensity to commit crime is stable, the opportunity to commit crime fluctuates over time. People age out of crime: As they mature and develop, there are simply fewer opportunities to commit crimes and greater inducements to remain "straight." As described earlier, they may marry, have children, and obtain jobs. The former delinquents' newfound adult responsibilities leave them little time to hang with their friends, abuse substances, and get into scrapes with the law.

To understand this concept better, assume that intelligence as measured by IQ tests is a stable latent trait associated with crime. Intelligence remains stable and unchanging over the life course, but crime rates decline with age. How can latent trait theory explain this phenomenon? Teenagers have more opportunity to commit crime than adults, so at every level of intelligence, adolescent crime rates will be higher. As they mature, however, teens with both high and low IQs will commit less crime because their adult responsibilities provide them with fewer criminal opportunities. They may get married and raise a family, get a job, and buy a home. And like most people, as they age they lose strength and vigor, qualities necessary to commit crime. Though their IQ remains stable and their propensity to commit crime unchanged, their living environment and biosocial condition has undergone radical change. Even if they wanted to engage in antisocial activities, former delinquents may lack the opportunity and the energy to engage in criminal activities.

latent trait
A stable feature, characteristic, property, or condition, present at birth or soon after, that makes some people crime-prone over the life course.

Crime and Human Nature

Latent trait theorists were encouraged when two prominent social scientists, James Q. Wilson and Richard Herrnstein, published *Crime and Human Nature* in 1985 and suggested that personal traits—such as genetic makeup, intelligence,

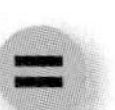

Figure 9.3
Gottfredson and Hirschi's General Theory of Crime

and body build—may outweigh the importance of social variables as predictors of criminal activity.[75]

According to Wilson and Herrnstein, all human behavior, including criminality, is determined by its perceived consequences. A criminal incident occurs when an individual chooses criminal over conventional behavior (referred to as "non-crime") after weighing the potential gains and losses of each: "The larger the ratio of net rewards of crime to the net rewards of non-crime, the greater the tendency to commit the crime."[76]

Wilson and Herrnstein's model assumes that both biological and psychological traits influence the crime–non-crime choice. They see a close link between a person's decision to choose crime and such biosocial factors as low intelligence, mesomorphic body type, genetic influences (parental criminality), and possessing an autonomic nervous system that responds too quickly to stimuli. Psychological traits, such as an impulsive or extroverted personality or generalized hostility, also determine the potential to commit crime.

In their focus on the association between these constitutional and psychological factors and crime, Wilson and Herrnstein seem to be suggesting the existence of an elusive latent trait that predisposes people to commit crime.[77] Their vision helped inspire other criminologists to identify the elusive latent trait that causes criminal behavior. The most prominent latent trait theory is Gottfredson and Hirschi's General Theory of Crime. Exhibit 9.3 discusses some other important contributions to the latent trait model.

General Theory of Crime

In their important work, *A General Theory of Crime,* Michael Gottfredson and Travis Hirschi modified and redefined some of the principles articulated in Hirschi's social control theory by integrating the concepts of control with those of biosocial, psychological, routine activities, and rational choice theories.[78]

CONNECTIONS

In his original version of control theory, discussed in Chapter 7, Hirschi focused on the social controls that attach people to conventional society and insulate them from criminality. In this newer work, he concentrates on self-control as a stabilizing force. The two views are connected, however, because both social control (or social bonds) and self-control are acquired through early experiences with effective parenting.

The Act and the Offender In their **General Theory of Crime (GTC)**, Gottfredson and Hirschi consider the criminal offender and the criminal act as separate concepts (Figure 9.3). On one hand, criminal acts, such as robberies or burglaries, are illegal events or deeds that offenders engage in when they perceive them to be advantageous. For example, burglaries are typically committed by young males looking for cash, liquor, and entertainment; the crime provides "easy, short-term gratification."[79] This aspect of the theory relies on concepts developed first as classical theory and later as rational choice and routine activities theories: Crime is rational and predictable; people commit crime when it promises rewards with minimal threat of pain; the threat of punishment can deter crime. If targets are well guarded, crime rates diminish. Only the truly irrational offender would dare to strike under those circumstances.

General Theory of Crime (GTC)
According to Gottfredson and Hirschi, a developmental theory that modifies social control theory by integrating concepts from biosocial, psychological, routine activities, and rational choice theories.

Although criminal offenders are people predisposed to commit crimes, they are not robots who violate the law without restraint; their days are also filled with conventional behaviors, such as going to school, parties, concerts, and church. But

Exhibit 9.3
Latent Trait Theories

Name Integrated Cognitive Antisocial Potential (ICAP) Theory

Principal Theorist David Farrington

Latent Trait Antisocial potential

Major Premise People maintain a range of "antisocial potential (AP)"—the potential to commit antisocial acts. AP can be viewed as both a long- and short-term phenomenon. Those with high levels of long-term AP are at risk for offending over the life course; those with low AP levels live more conventional lives. Though AP levels are fairly consistent over time, they peak in the teenage years because of the effects of maturational factors, such as increase in peer influence and decrease in family influence, that directly influence crime rates. Long-term AP can be reduced by life events such as marriage. Similarly, life events may increase a person's location on the AP continuum: A person with a relatively low long-term AP may suffer a temporary amplification if he is bored, angry, drunk, or frustrated. According to the ICAP theory, the commission of offenses and other types of antisocial acts depends on the interaction between the individual (with his or her immediate level of AP) and the social environment (especially criminal opportunities and victims).

Name Differential Coercion Theory

Principal Theorist Mark Colvin

Latent Trait Interpersonal/impersonal coercion

Major Premise Perceptions of coercion begin early in life when children experience punitive forms of discipline, including both physical attacks and psychological coercion such as negative commands, critical remarks, teasing, humiliation, whining, yelling, and threats. Through these destructive family interchanges, coercion becomes ingrained and guides reactions to adverse situations that arise in both family and nonfamily settings.

There are two sources of coercion: interpersonal and impersonal. Interpersonal coercion is direct, involving the use or threat of force and intimidation from parents, peers, and significant others. Impersonal coercion involves pressures beyond individual control, such as economic and social pressure caused by unemployment, poverty, or competition among businesses or other groups. High levels of coercion produce criminality, especially when the episodes of coercive behavior are inconsistent and random, because this teaches people that they cannot control their lives. Chronic offenders grew up in homes where parents used erratic control and applied it in an inconsistent way.

Name Control Balance Theory

Principal Theorist Charles Tittle

Latent Trait Control/balance

Major Premise The concept of control has two distinct elements: the amount of control one is subject to by others and the amount of control one can exercise over others. Conformity results when these two elements are in balance; control imbalances produce deviant and criminal behaviors.

People who sense a deficit of control turn to three types of behavior to restore balance: predation, defiance, or submission. Predation involves direct forms of physical violence, such as robbery, sexual assault, or other forms of physical violence. Defiance challenges control mechanisms but stops short of physical harm, for example, vandalism, curfew violations, and unconventional sex. Submission involves passive obedience to the demands of others, such as submitting to physical or sexual abuse without response.

An excess of control can result in crimes of exploitation, plunder, or decadence. Exploitation involves using others, such as contract killers or drug runners, to commit crimes; plunder involves using power without regard for others, such as committing a hate crime or polluting the environment; and decadence involves spur of the moment, irrational acts such as child molesting.

SOURCES: David P. Farrington, "Developmental and Life-Course Criminology: Key Theoretical and Empirical Issues." Sutherland Award Address at the American Society of Criminology meeting in Chicago, November 2002, revised March 2003; Charles Tittle, *Control Balance: Toward a General Theory of Deviance* (Boulder, CO: Westview Press, 1995); Mark Colvin, *Crime and Coercion: An Integrated Theory of Chronic Criminality* (New York: Palgrave Press, 2000).

given the same set of criminal opportunities, such as having a lot of free time for mischief and living in a neighborhood with unguarded homes containing valuable merchandise, crime-prone people have a much higher probability of violating the law than do noncriminals. The propensity to commit crimes remains stable throughout a person's life. Change in the frequency of criminal activity is purely a function of change in criminal opportunity.

By recognizing that there are stable differences in people's propensity to commit crime, the GTC adds a biosocial element to the concept of social control. Individual differences are stable over the life course, and so is the propensity to commit crime; only opportunity changes. The factors that make people impulsive and thereafter crime-prone may have physical or social roots, or perhaps both. Recent research shows that children who suffer anoxia (oxygen starvation) during the birthing process are persons most likely to lack self-control later in life, suggesting that impulsivity may have a biological basis.[80] There is also evidence that low self-control may develop through incompetent or absent parenting. If a child is not properly socialized, his or her neural pathways are physically affected. Once experiences are ingrained, the brain establishes a pattern of electrochemical activation that remains for life.[81]

Impulsivity and Crime? What, then, causes people to become excessively crime-prone? Gottfredson and Hirschi attribute the tendency to commit crimes to a person's level of self-control. People with limited self-control tend to be impulsive; they are insensitive to other people's feelings, physical (rather than mental), risk takers, shortsighted, and nonverbal.[82] They have a here-and-now orientation and refuse to work for distant goals; they lack diligence, tenacity, and persistence. People lacking self-control tend to be adventuresome, active, physical, and self-centered. As they mature, they often have unstable marriages, jobs, and friendships.[83] They are less likely to feel shame if they engage in deviant acts and are more likely to find them pleasurable.[84] They are also more likely to engage in dangerous behaviors such as drinking, smoking, and reckless driving; all of these behaviors are associated with criminality.[85]

Because those with low self-control enjoy risky, exciting, or thrilling behaviors with immediate gratification, they are more likely to enjoy criminal acts, which require stealth, agility, speed, and power, than conventional acts, which demand long-term study and cognitive and verbal skills. As Gottfredson and Hirschi put it, they derive satisfaction from "money without work, sex without courtship, revenge without court delays."[86] Many of these individuals who have a propensity for committing crime also engage in other behaviors such as smoking, drinking, gambling, and illicit sexuality.[87] Although these acts are not illegal, they too provide immediate, short-term gratification. Exhibit 9.4 lists the elements of impulsivity.

Gottfredson and Hirschi trace the root cause of poor self-control to inadequate child-rearing practices. Parents who refuse or are unable to monitor a child's behavior, to recognize deviant behavior when it occurs, and to punish that behavior will produce children who lack self-control. Children who are not attached to their parents, who are poorly supervised, and whose parents are criminal or deviant themselves are the most likely to develop poor self-control. In a sense, lack of self-control occurs naturally when steps are not taken to stop its development.[88]

Low self-control develops early in life and remains stable into and through adulthood.[89] Considering the continuity of criminal motivation, Hirschi and Gottfredson have questioned the utility of the juvenile justice system and of giving more lenient treatment to young delinquent offenders. Why separate youthful and adult offenders legally when the source of their criminality (for example, impulsivity) is essentially the same?[90]

Self-Control and Crime Gottfredson and Hirschi claim that the principles of **self-control theory** can explain all varieties of criminal behavior and all the social and behavioral correlates of crime. That is, such widely disparate crimes as burglary, robbery, embezzlement, drug dealing, murder, rape, and insider trading all stem from a deficiency of self-control. Likewise, gender, racial, and ecological differences in crime rates can be explained by discrepancies in self-control. Put another way, the male crime rate is higher than the female crime rate because males have lower levels of self-control.

Unlike other theoretical models that explain only narrow segments of criminal behavior (such as theories of teenage gang formation), Gottfredson and Hirschi argue that self-control applies equally to all crimes, ranging from murder to corporate theft. Gottfredson and Hirschi maintain that white-collar crime rates remain low because people who lack self-control rarely attain the positions necessary to commit those crimes. However, even though relatively few white-collar criminals

self-control theory
According to Gottfredson and Hirschi, the view that the cause of delinquent behavior is an impulsive personality. Kids who are impulsive may find that their bond to society is weak.

Exhibit 9.4
Elements of Impulsivity: Signs that a Person Has Low Self-Control

Insensitive	Lacks diligence
Physical	Lacks tenacity
Shortsighted	Adventuresome
Nonverbal	Self-centered
Here-and-now orientation	Shameless
Unstable social relations	Imprudent
Enjoys deviant behaviors	Lacks cognitive and verbal skills
Risk taker	Enjoys danger and excitement
Refuses to work for distant goals	

lack self-control to the same degree and in the same manner as criminals such as rapists and burglars. Although the criminal activity of individuals with low self-control also declines as those individuals mature, they maintain an offense rate that remains consistently higher than those with strong self-control.

Support for GTC Since the publication of *A General Theory of Crime*, numerous researchers have attempted to test the validity of Gottfredson and Hirschi's theoretical views. One approach involved identifying indicators of impulsiveness and self-control to determine whether scales measuring these factors correlate with measures of criminal activity. A number of studies conducted both in the United States and abroad have successfully showed this type of association.[91] Some of the most important findings are included in Exhibit 9.5. When Alexander Vazsonyi and his associates analyzed self-control and deviant behavior in samples drawn from a number of different countries (Hungary, Switzerland, the Netherlands, the United States, and Japan), they found that low self-control is significantly related to antisocial behavior and that the association can be seen regardless of culture or national settings.[92]

Analyzing the General Theory of Crime By integrating the concepts of socialization and criminality, Gottfredson and Hirschi help explain why some people who lack self-control can escape criminality and, conversely, why some people who have self-control might not escape criminality. People who are at risk because they have impulsive personalities may forgo criminal careers because there are no criminal opportunities that satisfy their impulsive needs; instead, they may find other outlets for their impulsive personalities. In contrast, if the opportunity is strong enough, even people with relatively strong self-control may be tempted to violate the law; the incentives to commit crime may overwhelm self-control.

Integrating criminal propensity and criminal opportunity can explain why some children enter into chronic offending while others living in similar environments are able to resist criminal activity. It can also help us understand why the corporate executive with a spotless record gets caught up in business fraud. Even a successful executive may find self-control inadequate if the potential for illegal gain is large. The driven executive, accustomed to both academic and financial success, may find that the fear of failure can overwhelm self-control. During tough economic times, the impulsive manager who fears dismissal may be tempted to circumvent the law to improve the bottom line.[93]

Although the General Theory of Crime seems persuasive, many questions and criticisms remain unanswered. Several of these are discussed next.

- *Tautological*. Some critics argue that the GTC is tautological, or involves circular reasoning: How do we know when people are impulsive? When they commit crimes! Are all criminals impulsive? Of course, or else they would not have broken the law![94]

Exhibit 9.5
Empirical Evidence Supporting the General Theory of Crime

1. Novice offenders, lacking in self-control, commit a garden variety of criminal acts.
2. More mature and experienced criminals become more specialized in their choice of crime (for example, robbers, burglars, drug dealers).
3. Male and female drunk drivers are impulsive individuals who manifest low self-control.
4. Repeat violent offenders are more impulsive than their less violent peers.
5. Incarcerated youth enjoy risk-taking behavior and hold values and attitudes that suggest impulsivity.
6. Kids who take drugs and commit crime are impulsive and enjoy engaging in risky behaviors.
7. Measures of self-control can predict deviant and antisocial behavior across age groups ranging from teens to adults age 50.
8. People who commit white-collar and workplace crime have lower levels of self-control than nonoffenders.
9. Gang members have lower levels of self-control than the general population; gang members report lower levels of parental management, a factor associated with lower self-control.
10. Low self-control shapes perceptions of criminal opportunity and consequently conditions the decision to commit crimes.
11. People who lack self-control expect to commit crime in the future.
12. Kids whose problems develop early in life are the most resistant to change in treatment and rehabilitation programs.
13. Gender differences in self-control are responsible for crime-rate differences. Females who lack self-control are as crime-prone as males with similar personalities.
14. Parents who manage their children's behavior increase their children's self-control, which in turn helps reduce delinquent activities.
15. Having parents (or guardians) available to control behavior may reduce the opportunity to commit crime.
16. Victims have lower self-control than nonvictims. Impulsivity predicts both the likelihood that a person will engage in criminal behavior and the likelihood that the person will become a victim of crime.
17. People with poor impulse control are the most likely to engage in serious violent crime.

SOURCES: 1. Xiaogang Deng and Lening Zhang, "Correlates of Self-Control: An Empirical Test of Self-Control Theory," *Journal of Crime and Justice* 21 (1998): 89–103; 2. Christopher Sullivan, Jean Marie McGloin, Travis Pratt, and Alex Piquero, "Rethinking the 'Norm' of Offender Generality: Investigating Specialization in the Short-Term," *Criminology* 44 (2006): 199–233; Alex Piquero, Raymond Paternoster, Paul Mazerolle, Robert Brame, and Charles Dean, "Onset Age and Offense Specialization," *Journal of Research in Crime and Delinquency* 36 (1999): 275–299; 3. Carl Keene, Paul Maxim, and James Teevan, "Drinking and Driving, Self-Control, and Gender: Testing a General Theory of Crime," *Journal of Research in Crime and Delinquency* 30 (1993): 30–46; 4. Judith DeJong, Matti Virkkunen, and Marku Linnoila, "Factors Associated with Recidivism in a Criminal Population," *Journal of Nervous and Mental Disease* 180 (1992): 543–550; 5. David Cantor, "Drug Involvement and Offending among Incarcerated Juveniles." Paper presented at the annual meeting of the American Society of Criminology, Boston, November 1995; 6. David Brownfield and Ann Marie Sorenson, "Self-Control and Juvenile Delinquency: Theoretical Issues and an Empirical Assessment of Selected Elements of a General Theory of Crime," *Deviant Behavior* 14 (1993): 243–264; John Cochran, Peter Wood, and Bruce Arneklev, "Is the Religiosity-Delinquency Relationship Spurious? A Test of Arousal and Social Control Theories," *Journal of Research in Crime and Delinquency* 31 (1994): 92–123; 7. Velmer Burton, T. David Evans, Francis Cullen, Kathleen Olivares, and R. Gregory Dunaway, "Age, Self-Control, and Adults' Offending Behaviors: A Research Note Assessing a General Theory of Crime," *Journal of Criminal Justice* 27 (1999): 45–54; John Gibbs and Dennis Giever, "Self-Control and Its Manifestations among University Students: An Empirical Test of Gottfredson and Hirschi's General Theory," *Justice Quarterly* 12 (1995): 231–255; 8. Carey Herbert, "The Implications of Self-Control Theory for Workplace Offending." Paper presented at the annual meeting of the American Society of Criminology, San Diego, 1997; 9. Dennis Giever, Dana Lynskey, and Danette Monnet, "Gottfredson and Hirschi's General Theory of Crime and Youth Gangs: An Empirical Test on a Sample of Middle School Youth." Paper presented at the annual meeting of the American Society of Criminology, San Diego, 1997; 10. Douglas Longshore, Susan Turner, and Judith Stein, "Self-Control in a Criminal Sample: An Examination of Construct Validity," *Criminology* 34 (1996): 209–228; 11. Deng and Zhang, "Correlates of Self-Control: An Empirical Test of Self-Control Theory"; 12. Linda Pagani, Richard Tremblay, Frank Vitaro, and Sophie Parent, "Does Preschool Help Prevent Delinquency in Boys with a History of Perinatal Complications?" *Criminology* 36 (1998): 245–268; 13. Velmer Burton, Francis Cullen, T. David Evans, Leanne Fiftal Alarid, and R. Gregory Dunaway, "Gender, Self-Control, and Crime," *Journal of Research in Crime and Delinquency* 35 (1998): 123–147; 14. John Gibbs, Dennis Giever, and Jamie Martin, "Parental Management and Self-Control: An Empirical Test of Gottfredson and Hirschi's General Theory," *Journal of Research in Crime and Delinquency* 35 (1998): 40–70; 15. Vic Bumphus and James Anderson, "Family Structure and Race in a Sample of Offenders," *Journal of Criminal Justice* 27 (1999): 309–320; 16. Christopher Schreck, "Criminal Victimization and Low Self-Control: An Extension and Test of a General Theory of Crime," *Justice Quarterly* 16 (1999): 633–654; 17. Daniel Nagin and Greg Pogarsky, "Time and Punishment: Delayed Consequences and Criminal Behavior," *Journal of Quantitative Criminology* 20 (2004): 295–317.

Gottfredson and Hirschi counter by saying that impulsivity is not itself a propensity to commit crime but a condition that inhibits people from appreciating the long-term consequences of their behavior. Consequently, if given the opportunity, they are more likely to indulge in criminal acts than their nonimpulsive counterparts.[95] According to Gottfredson and Hirschi, impulsivity and criminality are neither identical nor equivalent. Some impulsive people may channel their reckless energies into noncriminal activity, such as trading on the commodities markets or speculating in real estate, and make a legitimate fortune for their efforts.

- *Different classes of criminals*. As you may recall, Moffitt has identified two classes of criminals—adolescent-limited and life-course persistent.[96] Other researchers have found that there may be different criminal paths, or trajectories. People offend at a different pace, commit different kinds of crimes, and are influenced by different external forces.[97] For example, most criminals tend to be "generalists," who engage in a garden variety of criminal acts. However, people who commit violent crimes may be different from nonviolent offenders who have maintained a unique set of personality traits and problem behaviors.[98] This would contradict the GTC vision that a single factor causes crime and that there is a single class of offender.
- *Ecological differences*. The GTC also fails to address individual and ecological patterns in the crime rate. For example, if crime rates are higher in Los Angeles than in Albany, New York, can it be assumed that residents of Los Angeles are more impulsive than residents of Albany? There is little evidence of regional differences in impulsivity or self-control. Can these differences be explained solely by variation in criminal opportunity? Few researchers have tried to account for the influence of culture, ecology, economy, and so on. Gottfredson and Hirschi might counter that crime rate differences may reflect criminal opportunity: One area may have more effective law enforcement, more draconian laws, and higher levels of guardianship. In their view, opportunity is controlled by economy and culture.
- *Racial and gender differences*. Although distinct gender differences in the crime rate exist, there is little evidence that males are more impulsive than females (although females and males differ in many other personality traits).[99] Some research efforts have found gender differences in the association between self-control and crime; the theory predicts no such difference should occur.[100]

  Looking at this from another perspective, males who persist in crime exhibit different characteristics from those of female persisters. Women seem to be influenced by their place of residence, childhood and recent abuses, living with a criminal partner, selling drugs, stress, depression, fearfulness, their romantic relationships, their children, and whether they have suicidal thoughts. In contrast, men are more likely to persist because of their criminal peer associations, carrying weapons, alcohol abuse, and aggressive feelings. Impulsivity alone may not be able to explain why males and females persist or desist.[101]

  Similarly, Gottfredson and Hirschi explain racial differences in the crime rate as a failure of child-rearing practices in the African American community.[102] In so doing, they overlook issues of institutional racism, poverty, and relative deprivation, which have been shown to have a significant impact on crime rate differentials.
- *Moral beliefs*. The General Theory also ignores the moral concept of right and wrong, or "belief," which Hirschi considered a cornerstone in his earlier writings on the social bond.[103] Does this mean that learning and assimilating moral values has little effect on criminality? Belief may be the weakest of the bonds associated with crime, and the General Theory reflects this relationship.[104]
- *Peer influence*. A number of research efforts show that the quality of peer relations either enhances or controls criminal behavior and that these influences vary over time.[105] As children mature, peer influence continues to grow.[106] Research shows that kids who lack self-control also have trouble maintaining relationships with law-abiding peers. They may either choose (or be forced) to seek friends who are similarly limited in their ability to maintain self-control. Similarly, as they mature, they may seek romantic relationships with law-violating boyfriends and/or girlfriends, and these entanglements enhance the likelihood that they will get further involved in crime (girls seem more deeply influenced by their delinquent boyfriends than boys by their delinquent girlfriends).[107] This finding contradicts the GTC, which suggests the influence of friends should be stable and unchanging and that a relationship established later in life (for example, making friends) should not influence criminal propensity. Gottfredson and Hirschi might counter that it should come as

no surprise that impulsive kids, lacking in self-control, seek peers with similar personality characteristics.

- *People change.* One of the most important questions raised about the GTC concerns its assumption that criminal propensity (especially after age 10) does not change. Is it possible that human personality and behavior patterns remain unaltered over the life course? Research shows that changing life circumstances, such as starting and leaving school, abusing substances and then "getting straight," and starting or ending personal relationships, all influence the frequency of offending.[108] As people mature, they may be better able to control their impulsive behavior and reduce their criminal activities.[109] Although some people maintain the same level of self-control throughout their life span, others may find that it changes over time.[110]

  Ronald Simons found that boys who were involved in deviant and oppositional behavior during childhood were able to turn their lives around if they later experienced improved parenting, increased school commitment, and/or reduced involvement with deviant peers. So while early childhood antisocial behavior may increase the chances of later criminality, even the most difficult children are at no greater risk for delinquency than are their conventional counterparts if they later experience positive changes in their daily lives and increased ties with significant others and institutions.[111]

  Although the Simons research seems to contradict the GTC, Gottfredson and Hirschi acknowledge that external factors such as parenting and school involvement may indeed reduce crime because they limit the opportunity to commit illegal acts. The child's criminal propensity remains the same, and if these external supports were once again weakened or removed, they would still be at risk for criminality.

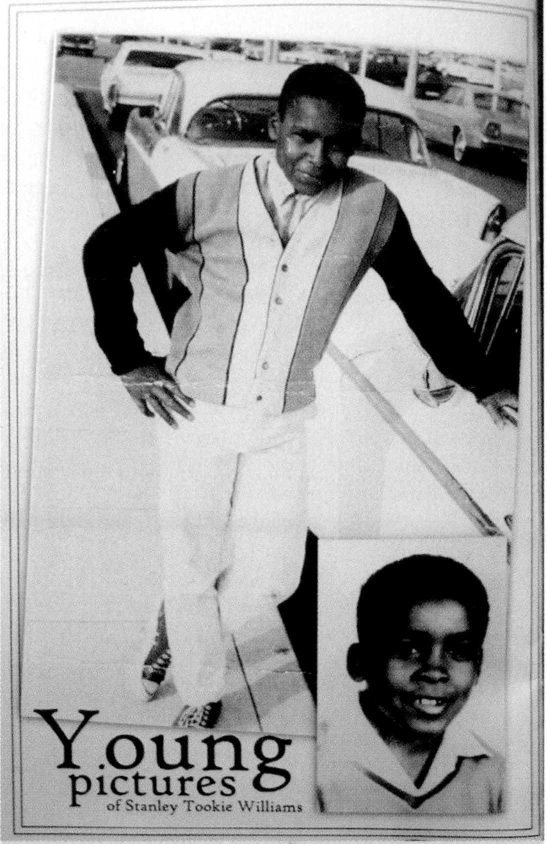

© David McNew/Getty Images

● One criticism of the General Theory of Crime is that people actually do change over their lifetime. Here, pictures in a memorial service program for executed cofounder of the Crips gang Stanley "Tookie" Williams show him at an early age. Sentenced to prison for the 1979 murders of four people, Williams spent several years involved with violent activities in prison, but around 1993 changed his behavior and become an anti-gang activist. Williams coauthored such books as *Life in Prison*, which encouraged kids to stay out of gangs, and his memoir *Blue Rage, Black Redemption*. Williams was nominated for the Nobel Peace Prize for his efforts. Do you believe that a gang leader like "Tookie" Williams can really change, or did his changing life circumstances (i.e., being incarcerated) simply prevent him from committing violent criminal acts?

- *Modest relationship.* Some research results support the proposition that self-control is a causal factor in criminal and other forms of deviant behavior but that the association is at best quite modest.[112] This would indicate that other forces influence criminal behavior and that low self-control alone cannot predict the onset of a criminal or deviant career. Perhaps antisocial behavior is best explained by a condition that either develops subsequent to the development of self-control or is independent of a person's level of impulsivity.[113] This alternative quality, which may be the real stable latent trait, is still unknown.
- *Cross-cultural differences.* There is some evidence that criminals in other countries do not lack self-control, indicating that the GTC may be culturally limited. For example, Otwin Marenin and Michael Resig found equal or higher levels of self-control in Nigerian criminals than in noncriminals.[114] Behavior that may be considered imprudent in one culture may be socially acceptable in another and therefore cannot be viewed as "lack of self-control."[115] There is, however, emerging evidence that the GTC may have validity in predicting criminality abroad.[116]
- *Misreads human nature.* According to Francis Cullen, John Paul Wright, and Mitchell Chamlin, the GTC makes flawed assumptions about human character.[117] It assumes that people are essentially selfish, self-serving, and hedonistic and must therefore be controlled lest they gratify themselves at the expense of others. A more plausible view is that humans are inherently generous and kind; selfish hedonists may be a rare exception.
- *One of many causes.* Research shows that even if lack of self-control is a prerequisite to crime, so are other social, neuropsychological, and physiological factors.[118] Sociocultural factors have been found to make an independent contribution to criminal offending patterns.[119] Among the many psychological characteristics that set criminals apart from the general population is their lack of self-direction—rather than aiming at providing long-term benefits, their behavior has a here-and-now orientation.[120] Law violators exhibit lower resting heart rate and perform poorly on tasks that trigger cognitive functions.[121]

Current Issues in Crime

Careers in the Drug Trade

According to Michael Gottfredson and Travis Hirschi's General Theory of Crime, criminals are impatient, or "present-oriented." They choose to commit crime because the rewards can be enjoyed immediately while the costs or punishments come later or may not come at all. As long as the gains from crime are immediate and the costs delayed, present-oriented individuals will commit crimes even if the crimes are not obviously lucrative.

In an important study, Steven Levitt and Sudhir Alladi Venkatesh detail the economics of a drug-selling criminal gang. Their data were compiled by the leader of a drug-dealing gang to facilitate the gang's operations. The data detail the wage and revenue structure of the gang over a four-year period. Using this rather unique data source, Levitt and Venkatesh found that the gang's compensation structure is highly skewed in favor of the leaders, who make most of the money. Younger or lower-ranking gang members must "rise through the ranks" before earning high wages.

Levitt and Venkatesh found that the gang's "foot soldiers" who are "street-level drug sellers" and are "typically 16–22 years of age" are paid at an "hourly wage that is below the federal minimum wage," ranging between $2.50 and $7.10 per hour in inflation-adjusted 1995 dollars. In order to survive on this pittance, these young men hold second jobs in the legitimate world and are forced to live with their families in order to save money. In contrast, a gang leader earns 10 to 20 times as much as a foot soldier (between $32.50 and $97.20 per hour over the four years). Other high-level gang members also make considerably more than those at the bottom of the hierarchy, so that overall, the average gang wage is four times higher than what a foot soldier makes. The gang leader's wages in particular are much higher than the wage that would be available to an individual with his level of human capital in the legitimate sector. Gang leaders make far more than they possibly could in the legitimate world; for them crime does pay.

Levitt and Venkatesh concluded that the economic aspects of the decision to join the gang are viewed as a tournament in which the participants vie for large awards that only a small fraction will eventually obtain. Members of the gang accept low wages in the present in the hope that they will advance in the gang and earn well above market wages in the future.

In his reanalysis of this data, Yair Listokin found that the tournament wage structure is strikingly inconsistent with the notion of present-oriented criminals. The supposedly

- *More than one kind of impulsivity*. Gottfredson and Hirschi assume that impulsivity is a singular construct: A person is either impulsive or not. There may be more than one kind of impulsive personality, however. Some people may be impulsive because they are sensation seekers constantly looking for novel experiences, while others lack deliberation and rarely think through problems. Some may give up easily, while others act without thinking when they get upset.[122]
- *Not all criminals are impulsive*. White-collar criminals, drug traffickers, and organized crime bosses seem more calculating than impulsive. As the criminological enterprise described in "Careers in the Drug Trade" shows, their career paths may contradict the GTC.

Although questions like these remain, the strength of the GTC lies in its scope and breadth: It attempts to explain all forms of crime and deviance, from lower-class gang delinquency to sexual harassment in the business community.[123] By integrating concepts of criminal choice, criminal opportunity, socialization, and personality, Gottfredson and Hirschi make a plausible argument that all deviant behaviors may originate at the same source. Continued efforts are needed to test the GTC and establish the validity of its core concepts. It remains one of the key developments of modern criminological theory.

A number of other theories suggesting that a master trait controls human development and the propensity to commit crime have been formulated. Concept Summary 9.2 summarizes the most prominent developmental theories. ✔ CHECKPOINTS

✔ CHECKPOINTS

✔ Latent trait theories assume a physical or psychological master trait makes some people crime-prone over the life course.

✔ Opportunity to commit crime varies; latent traits remain stable.

✔ Gottfredson and Hirschi's General Theory of Crime says an impulsive personality is key.

✔ Impulsive people have low self-control and a weak bond to society.

✔ Impulsive people often cannot resist criminal opportunities.

PUBLIC POLICY IMPLICATIONS OF DEVELOPMENTAL THEORY

Policies based on premises of developmental theory have inspired a number of initiatives. These typically feature multisystemic treatment efforts designed to provide at-risk youths with personal, social, educational, and family services. For example, one program found that an intervention promoting academic success, impulsive, present-oriented 16- to 22-year-old foot soldiers of the gang are sacrificing present wages for the hope of future gains. Listokin suggested that the gang is using the same compensation structure as one commonly used in law firms. The "foot soldiers," he concluded, are filling the role of law associates, a group not known for its impulsiveness. Moreover, foot soldiers seem acutely aware that they are making an investment in the future by foregoing present gains. As one foot soldier noted:

> *You think I want a be selling drugs on the street my whole life? No way, But I know these n— [above me] are making more money. . . . So you know, I figure I got a chance to move up. But if not, s—, I get me a job doin' something else.* (Levitt and Venkatesh 2000: 773)

This quotation does not comport with the notion of a super-impulsive young criminal.

Listokin believes that tournament-style compensation schemes are often used to ensure maximum effort by low-level employees. Executives (or gang leaders in this case) offer the new employee the promise of high future wages in the hierarchy to induce effort in the present. The prospect of high wages in the second period must suffice to induce effort in the first period. However, Listokin's analysis shows that few foot soldiers will ever become gang leaders and that the likelihood of their getting killed instead is quite high. Nonetheless, foot soldiers are willing to take the risk in order to earn a future benefit. This finding contradicts Gottfredson and Hirschi's vision of an impulsive criminal who lives for today without worrying about tomorrow.

Critical Thinking

1. What other professions use tournament-style competition for hiring and promotion? To get started, think about professors going up for tenure.
2. Would increasing the minimum wage reduce drug trafficking by offering adequate compensation in the legitimate world? Or does drug dealing have an allure that transcends wages?

InfoTrac College Edition Research

Use "drug gangs" and "drug dealing" in key word searches on InfoTrac College Edition.

SOURCES: Steven Levitt and Sudhir Alladi Venkatesh, "An Economic Analysis of a Drug-Selling Gang's Finances," *Quarterly Journal of Economics* 13 (2000): 755–789; Yair Listokin, "Future-Oriented Gang Members? Gang Finances and the Theory of Present-Oriented Criminals," *The American Journal of Economics and Sociology* 64 (2005): 1,073–1,083.

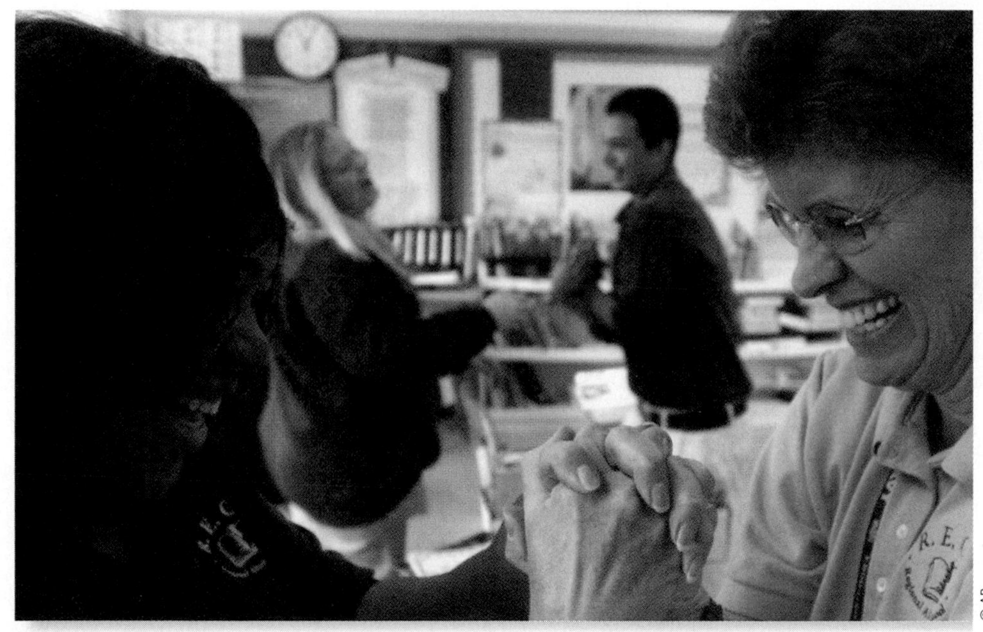

© AP

● Crime prevention programs based on developmental theory treat the whole person as well as her/his environment. Teacher Joan Chlan (right), of R. E. Cook Regional Alternative Education Center, in Vinton, Virginia, does brain-stimulating exercises with Kelly Jones and other students at the beginning of class. The students at the Center take part in various activities that get them up and moving and their minds working. In its past life, the hallways and classrooms of R. E. Cook were filled with young students–photos of them, neatly dressed, sitting primly at wooden desks, hang in the front office. Today the school is ghostly quiet, home to about 20 students from Roanoke and Bedford counties who were expelled from their home schools or sent by a superintendent. Repeated behavioral problems, drugs, assault and battery, or weapons often pave the way to Cook, as do problems at home, poor grades, and negative labels that have chipped away at the children's self-esteem. Can programs like this really help people change, or are the personal characteristics of antisocial people too firmly embedded in their psyche?

social competence, and educational enhancement during the elementary grades can reduce risky sexual practices and their accompanying health consequences in early adulthood.[124]

Other programs are now employing multidimensional strategies and are aimed at targeting children in preschool through the early elementary grades in order to alter the direction of their life course. Many of the most successful programs are aimed at strengthening children's social-emotional competence and positive coping skills and suppressing the development of antisocial, aggressive behavior.[125] Research evaluations indicate that the most promising multicomponent crime and substance abuse prevention programs for youths, especially those at high risk, are aimed at improving their developmental skills. They may include

CONCEPT SUMMARY 9.2 Developmental Theories

THEORY	MAJOR PREMISE	STRENGTHS	RESEARCH FOCUS
Life Course Theories	As people go through the life course, social and personal traits undergo change and influence behavior.	Explains why some at-risk children desist from crime.	Identify critical moments in a person's life course that produce crime.
Integrated Cognitive Antisocial Potential (ICAP) Theory	People with antisocial potential (AP) are at risk to commit antisocial acts. AP can be viewed as both a long- and short-term phenomenon.	Identifies different types of criminal propensity and shows how they may influence behavior in both the short and long term.	Identify the components of long- and short-term AP.
Interactional Theory	Criminals go through lifestyle changes during their offending career.	Combines sociological and psychological theories.	Identify crime-producing interpersonal interactions and their reciprocal effects.
General Theory of Crime and Delinquency (GTCD)	Five critical life domains shape criminal behavior and are shaped by criminal behavior.	Shows that crime and other aspects of social life are interactive and developmental.	Measure the relationship between life domains and crime.
Age-Graded Theory	As people mature, the factors that influence their propensity to commit crime change. In childhood, family factors are critical; in adulthood, marital and job factors are key.	Shows how crime is a developmental process that shifts in direction over the life course.	Identify critical points in the life course that produce crime. Analyze the association between social capital and crime.
Latent Trait Theories	A master trait controls human development.	Explains the continuity of crime and chronic offending.	Identify master trait that produces crime.
General Theory of Crime	Crime and criminality are separate concepts. People choose to commit crime when they lack self-control. People lacking self-control will seize criminal opportunities.	Integrates choice and social control concepts. Identifies the difference between crime and criminality.	Measure association among impulsivity, low self-control, and criminal behaviors.
Differential Coercion Theory	Individuals exposed to coercive environments develop social-psychological deficits that enhance their probability of engaging in criminal behavior.	Explains why feeling of coercion is a master trait that determines behavior.	Measuring the sources of coercion.
Control Balance Theory	A person's "control ratio" influences his or her behavior.	Explains how the ability to control one's environment is a master trait.	Measuring control balance and imbalance.

a school component, an after-school component, and a parent-involvement component. All of these components have the common goal of increasing protective factors and decreasing risk factors in the areas of the family, the community, the school, and the individual.[126] One example is the Boys and Girls Clubs and School Collaborations' Substance Abuse Prevention Program that includes a school component called SMART (skills mastery and resistance training) Teachers; an after-school component called SMART Kids; and a parent-involvement component called SMART Parents. Each component is designed to reduce specific risk factors in the children's school, family, community, and personal environments.[127]

THINKING Like a Criminologist

Gary L. Sampson, 41, addicted to alcohol and cocaine, was a deadbeat dad, a two-bit thief, and a bank robber with a long history of violence. On August 1, 2001, he turned himself in to the Vermont State Police after fleeing from a string of three murders he committed in Massachusetts and New Hampshire.

Those who knew Sampson speculated that his murders were a desperate finale to a troubled life. During his early life in New England, he once bound, gagged, and beat three elderly women in a candy store, hijacked cars at knifepoint, and had been medically diagnosed as schizophrenic. In 1977, he married a 17-year-old girl he had impregnated; two months later he was arrested and charged with rape for having "unnatural intercourse with a child under 16." Although he was acquitted of that charge, his wife noticed that Sampson had started developing a hair-trigger temper and had become increasingly violent; their marriage soon ended. As the years passed, Sampson had at least four failed marriages, was an absentee father to two children, and became an alcoholic and a drug user; he spent nearly half of his adult life behind bars.

Jumping bail after being arrested for theft from an antique store, he headed south to North Carolina and took on a new identity: Gary Johnson, a construction worker. He took up with Ricki Carter, a transvestite, but their relationship was anything but stable. Sampson once put a gun to Carter's head, broke his ribs, and threatened to kill his family. After his breakup with Carter, Sampson moved in with a new girlfriend, Karen Anderson, and began pulling bank jobs. When the police closed in, Sampson fled north. Needing transportation, he pulled three carjackings and killed the drivers, one a 19-year-old college freshman who had stopped to give Sampson a hand. In December 2003, Sampson received a sentence of death from a jury who was not swayed by his claim that he was mentally unfit.

The governor is unsettled by the verdict. She wants to grant clemency in the case and reduce Sampson's sentence to life in prison. She asks you to help her make the judgment: Were Sampson's crimes a product of his impaired development? Should he be spared death?

Summary

- Life-course theories argue that events that take place over the life course influence criminal choices.
- The cause of crime constantly changes as people mature. At first, the nuclear family influences behavior; during adolescence, the peer group dominates; in adulthood, marriage and career are critical.
- There are a variety of pathways to crime: Some kids are sneaky, others hostile, and still others, defiant.
- Crime may be part of a variety of social problems, including health, physical, and interpersonal troubles.
- Sampson and Laub's age-graded theory holds that the social sources of behavior change over the life course. People who develop social capital are best able to avoid antisocial entanglements. Certain life events or turning points enable adult offenders to desist from crime. Among the most important are getting married and serving in the military. Laub and Sampson have found that although many criminals desist from crime, they still face other risks, such as an untimely death.
- Latent trait theories hold that some underlying condition present at birth or soon after controls behavior. Suspect traits include low IQ, impulsivity, and personality structure. This underlying trait explains the continuity of offending because, once present, it remains with a person throughout his or her life. Opportunity to commit crime varies; latent traits remain stable.
- The General Theory of Crime, developed by Gottfredson and Hirschi, integrates choice theory concepts. People with latent traits choose crime over non-crime; the opportunity for crime mediates their choice.
- Impulsive people have low self-control and a weak bond to society; they often cannot resist criminal opportunities.
- Programs based on developmental theory are typically multidimensional and multifaceted.

Take a Post-Test. Visit www.thomsonedu.com/criminaljustice/siegel and take the chapter Post-Test to monitor your progress and identify areas for further improvement. In addition to discovering what you've mastered, you'll learn which concepts need your added attention and get specific page references that direct you to the places in the text where you can find more information on them.

Key Terms

desist 198
developmental theory 198
life-course theories 199
latent trait theories 199
problem behavior syndrome (PBS) 200
authority conflict pathway 201
covert pathway 201
overt pathway 202
adolescent-limited offender 203
life-course persister 203
integrated theories 204
turning points 204
social capital 205
latent trait 210
General Theory of Crime (GTC) 211
self-control theory 213

Critical Thinking Questions

1. Do you consider yourself to have social capital? If so, what form does it take?

2. Someone you know gets a perfect score on the SAT. What personal, family, and social characteristics do you think this individual has? Another person becomes a serial killer. Without knowing this person, what personal, family, and social characteristics do you think this individual has? If "bad behavior" is explained by multiple problems, is "good behavior" explained by multiple strengths?

3. Do you believe it is a latent trait that makes a person crime-prone, or is crime a function of environment and socialization?

4. Do you agree with Loeber's multiple pathways model? Do you know people who have traveled down those paths?

5. Do people really change, or do they stay the same but appear to be different because their life circumstances have changed?

CHAPTER 10

Violent Crime

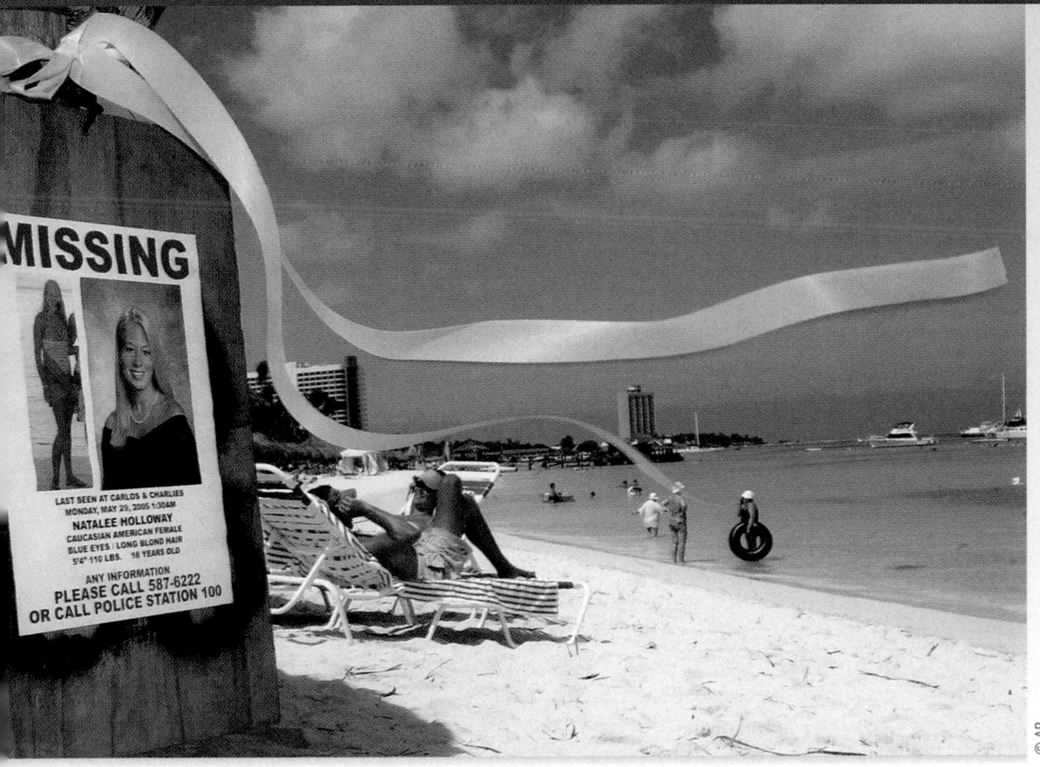

© AP

NATALEE HOLLOWAY, 18, FROM THE BIRMINGHAM, ALABAMA, SUBURB OF MOUNTAIN BROOK, celebrated her high school graduation by going on a holiday to the Caribbean island of Aruba with about 100 classmates and several parent chaperones. On the night of May 30, 2005, she went to a local bar and was later seen leaving with three men—two brothers from Surinam and a local boy, the son of a high-ranking Dutch judicial official. Holloway never returned to her hotel. The three young men told the police they took her to Arashi Beach, on Aruba's northern tip, and at 2:00 AM dropped her off at her hotel, where they saw her being approached by a security guard as they drove off. The young men, prime suspects in the case, were arrested, released, arrested again, and released again. Despite a massive hunt and investigation, at the time of this writing, the fate of the young woman, who wanted to become a doctor, remains unknown.[1]

The Holloway case grabbed national attention. Rumors of her fate abounded: Had the three young men raped and murdered Holloway? Was there a cover-up because one of the suspects was the son of a public official? Did they dispose of her body in a panic after she died from a drug or alcohol overdose? Had she been abducted into a sex slave ring?

CHAPTER OBJECTIVES

1. Be familiar with the various causes of violent crime.
2. Know the concept of the brutalization process.
3. Be able to discuss the history of rape.
4. Be familiar with the different types of rape.
5. Be able to discuss the legal issues in rape prosecution.
6. Recognize that there are different types of murder.
7. Be able to discuss the differences between serial killing, mass murder, and spree killing.
8. Be familiar with the nature of assault in the home.
9. Understand the careers of armed robbers.
10. Be able to discuss newly emerging forms of violence, such as stalking, hate crimes, and workplace violence.
11. Understand the different types of terrorism and what is being done today to combat terrorist activities.

Take a Pre-Test. Visit www.thomsonedu.com/criminaljustice/siegel and take a Pre-Test to determine what you already know and identify the areas where you'll need to focus your study. The program will direct you to specific pages within the text where you can find further information on the correct answers to the questions you've missed.

Whatever her fate, Holloway's case proved to the American public that violent crime could be encountered anywhere, even on a tranquil Caribbean island known for its beautiful beaches. No matter where they go, people may encounter violent acts. Some are expressive violence—acts that vent rage, anger, or frustration—and some are instrumental violence—acts designed to improve the financial or social position of the criminal, for example, through an armed robbery or murder for hire.

This chapter explores the concept of violence in some depth. First, it reviews the suggested causes of violent crime. Then it focuses on specific types of interpersonal violence—rape, homicide, assault, robbery, and newly recognized types of interpersonal violence such as stalking and workplace violence. Finally, it briefly examines political violence and terrorism.

CAUSES OF VIOLENCE

What sets off a violent person? Some experts suggest that a small number of inherently violence-prone individuals may themselves have been the victims of physical or psychological abnormalities. Another view is that violence and aggression are inherently human traits that can affect any person at any time. There may be violence-prone subcultures within society whose members value force, routinely carry weapons, and consider violence to have an acceptable place in social interaction.[2] A few of the most prominent factors discussed here are illustrated in Figure 10.1.

Personal Traits

Research has shown that a significant number of people involved in violent episodes may be suffering from severe mental abnormalities.[3] Psychologist Dorothy Otnow Lewis and her associates found that murderous youths suffer signs of major neurological impairment (such as abnormal EEGs, multiple psychomotor impairments, and severe seizures); low intelligence as measured on standard IQ tests; psychotic close relatives; and psychotic symptoms such as paranoia, illogical thinking, and hallucinations.[4] In her book *Guilty by Reason of Insanity*, Lewis finds that death row inmates have a history of mental impairment and intellectual dysfunction.[5]

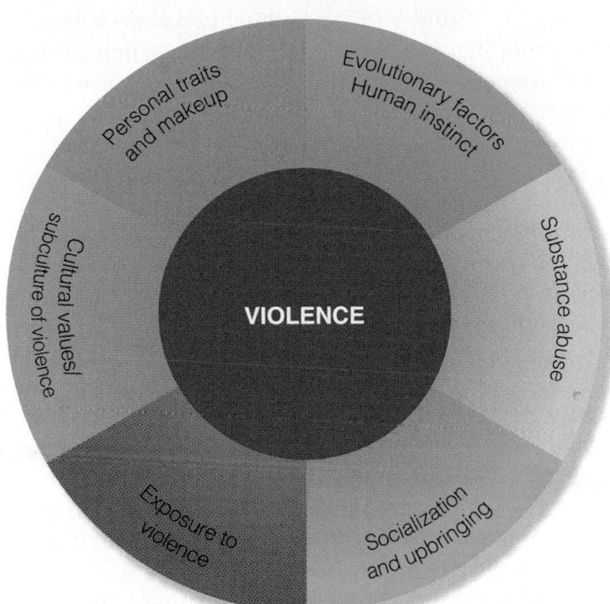

Figure 10.1
Sources of Violence

Abnormal personality structures, including such traits as depression, impulsivity, aggression, dishonesty, pathological lying, lack of remorse, borderline personality syndrome, and psychopathology, have been associated with various forms of violence.[6] Although this evidence indicates that violent offenders are more prone to psychosis than other people, no single clinical diagnosis can characterize their behavior.[7]

Ineffective Families

Absent or deviant parents, inconsistent discipline, physical abuse, and lack of supervision have all been linked to persistent violent offending.[8] Although infants demonstrate individual temperaments, who they become may have a lot to do with how they are treated during their early years. Some children are less easy to soothe than others; in some cases, difficult infant temperament has been associated with later aggression and behavioral problems.[9] Parents who fail to set adequate limits or to use proper, consistent discipline reinforce a child's coercive behavior.[10] The effects of inadequate parenting and early rejection may affect violent behavior throughout life.[11]

Some parents abuse their children sexually and physically. Those exposed to even minimal amounts of physical punishment may be more likely one day to use violence themselves; if the abuse is prolonged, so are the effects.[12] Abused kids suffer from long-term mental, cognitive, and social dysfunctions.[13] They are more likely to physically abuse a sibling and later engage in spouse abuse and other forms of criminal violence.[14] Abusive childhood experiences may be a key factor in the later development of relationship aggression.[15]

Evolutionary Factors/Human Instinct

Perhaps violent responses and emotions are actually inherent in all humans, and the right spark can trigger them. Sigmund Freud believed that human aggression and violence are produced by instinctual drives.[16] Freud maintained that humans possess two opposing instinctual drives that interact to control behavior: **eros**, the life instinct, which drives people toward self-fulfillment and enjoyment; and **thanatos**, the death instinct, which produces self-destruction. Thanatos can be expressed externally (as violence and sadism) or internally (as suicide, alcoholism, or other self-destructive habits). Because aggression is instinctual, Freud saw little hope for its treatment.

A number of biologists and anthropologists have also speculated that instinctual violence-promoting traits may be common in the human species. One view is

eros
The life instinct, which drives people toward self-fulfillment and enjoyment.

thanatos
The death instinct, which produces self-destruction.

CONNECTIONS

As you may recall from Chapter 5, biosocial theorists link violence to a number of biological irregularities, including but not limited to genetic influences and inheritance, the action of hormones, the functioning of neurotransmitters, brain structure, and diet. Psychologists link violent behavior to observational learning from violent TV shows, traumatic childhood experiences, low intelligence, mental illness, impaired cognitive processes, and abnormal (psychopathic) personality structure.

that aggression and violence are the result of instincts inborn in all animals, including human beings.[17] Unlike other animals, however, humans lack the inhibition against killing members of their own species, which protects animals from self-extinction, and are capable of killing their own kind in war or as a result of interpersonal conflicts.

Exposure to Violence

Kids who are constantly exposed to violence at home, at school, or in the environment may adopt violent methods themselves.[18] Exposure to violence can also occur at the neighborhood level when people are forced to live in violent, dangerous neighborhoods.[19] A 2005 report by Felton Earls and his associates finds that young teens who witness gun violence are more than twice as likely as nonwitnesses to commit violent crime.[20] Even a single exposure to firearm violence doubles the chance that a young person will later engage in violent behavior. Much of the differences in violent crime rates between whites and racial minorities can be explained by the fact that the latter are often forced to live in high-crime neighborhoods, which increases their risk of exposure to violence.[21] Children living in areas marked by extreme violence may eventually become desensitized to the persistent neighborhood brutality and conflict they witness, eventually succumbing to violent behaviors themselves.[22] And, not surprisingly, those children who are exposed to violence in the home and also live in neighborhoods with high violence rates are the ones most likely to engage in violent crime themselves.[23]

Substance Abuse

Substance abuse has been associated with violence on both the individual and social levels. Substance abusers have higher rates of violence than nonabusers. The most recent National Survey on Drug Use and Health found that young people ages 12 to 17 who used any illicit drug in the past year were almost twice as likely to have engaged in violent behavior as those who did not use any illicit drug (49.8 vs. 26.6 percent).[24]

Drug abuse rates are also associated with area violence rates: Neighborhoods with high levels of substance abuse also have higher violence.[25] Areas whose residents use drugs frequently also experience social disorganization, poverty, and unemployment, factors that further escalate violence rates.[26] Substance abuse influences violence in three ways:[27]

- A **psychopharmacological relationship** may be the direct consequence of ingesting mood-altering substances. Binge drinking, for example, has been closely associated with violent crime rates.[28] Heavy drinking reduces cognitive ability, information processing skills, and the ability to process and react to verbal and nonverbal behavior. As a result, miscommunication becomes more likely and the capacity for rational dialogue is compromised.[29] It is not surprising that males involved in sexual assaults often claim that they were drinking and misunderstood their victim's intentions.[30]
- Drug ingestion may also cause **economic compulsive behavior**, in which drug users resort to violence to support their habit. Studies conducted in the United States and Europe show that addicts commit hundreds of crimes each year.[31]
- A **systemic link** between drugs and violence occurs when drug dealers turn violent in their competition with rival gangs. Studies of drug gangs show that their attempts to gain and secure drug markets result in a significant proportion of all urban homicides.[32]

psychopharmacological relationship
When violence is the direct consequence of ingesting mood-altering substances.

economic compulsive behavior
Violence committed by drug users to support their habit.

systemic link
A link between drugs and violence that occurs when drug dealers turn violent in their competition with rival gangs.

Firearm Availability

Although firearm availability alone does not cause violence, it may be a facilitating factor. A petty argument can escalate into a fatal encounter if one party has a handgun. The nation has also been rocked by the use of firearms in schools and the resulting slew of well-publicized school shootings. Research indicates that a significant number of kids routinely carry guns to school; those who have been the victims of crime themselves and who hang with peers who carry weapons are most likely to bring guns to school.[33]

The Uniform Crime Report (UCR) indicates that two-thirds of all murders and about two-fifths of all robberies involve firearms.[34] Handguns kill two-thirds of all police who die in the line of duty. The presence of firearms in the home also significantly increases the risk of suicide among adolescents, regardless of how carefully the guns are secured or stored.[35]

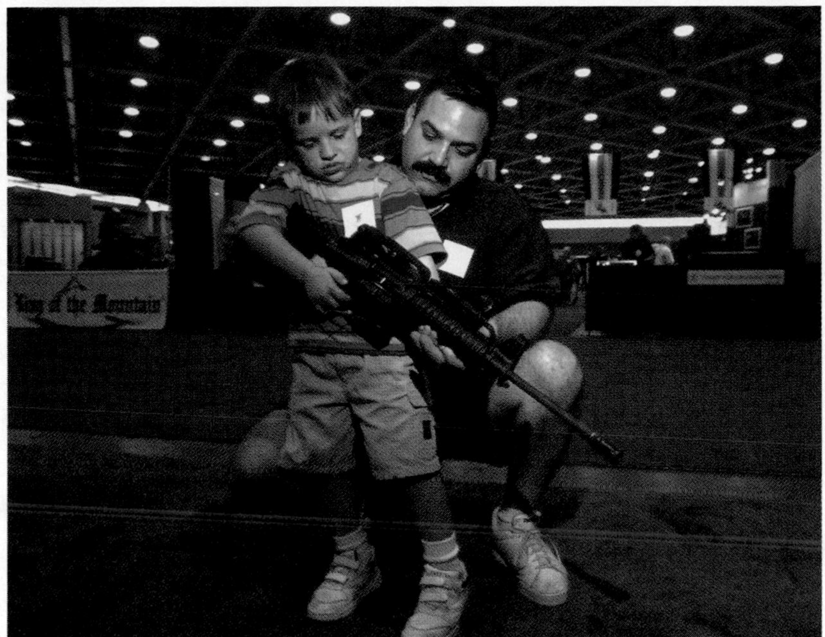

© Les Stone/Sygma/Corbis

● Socialization and upbringing have been linked to the onset of violent acts. Kids who are raised by deviant parents and subject to inconsistent discipline, physical abuse, and lack of supervision are more likely to engage in violent offending. Considering the link between socialization and crime, do you believe that parents who introduce their children to guns at an early age are leading them down the path toward violence?

Cultural Values

Areas that experience violence seem to cluster together.[36] To explain this phenomenon, criminologists Marvin Wolfgang and Franco Ferracuti formulated the famous concept that some areas contain an independent **subculture of violence**.[37]

The subculture's norms are separate from society's central, dominant value system. In this subculture, a potent theme of violence influences lifestyles, the socialization process, and interpersonal relationships. Even though the subculture's members share some of the dominant culture's values, they expect that violence will be used to solve social conflicts and dilemmas. In some cultural subgroups, then, violence has become legitimized by custom and norms. It is considered appropriate behavior within culturally defined conflict situations in which an individual who has been offended by a negative outcome in a dispute seeks reparations through violent means ("disputatiousness").[38]

Gangs are common in the subculture of violence. Gang boys routinely own guns and associate with violent peers who are also gun owners.[39] Violent gang friends support and sustain antisocial behavior.[40] The association between gang membership and violence has a number of roots. It can result from drug trafficking activities and turf protection but also stems from personal vendettas and a perceived need for self-protection.[41] Violence is a core value of gang membership, and once kids leave the gang, the frequency of their violent activities rapidly declines.[42]

Why a subculture of violence exists in a particular area may have historical roots. Historian Eric Monkkonen analyzed nearly two centuries of Los Angeles homicide data and found that regional cultural differences contributed to relatively high rates of homicide.[43] Since the city's Old West days, Los Angelinos accepted street justice, and the city has had high rates of "justifiable homicides." A considerable number of "executions" carried out by private citizens were initiated by individuals who "happened to be armed at the moment of need."[44] When Charis Kubrin and Ronald Weitzer studied homicide in St. Louis, Missouri, they discovered that in some neighborhoods residents resolve interpersonal conflicts informally—without calling the police—even if it means killing their opponent; neighbors understand and support their violent methods.[45] Because police and other agencies of formal social control are viewed as weak and devalued, understaffed, and/or corrupt, people are willing to take matters into their own hands and commit what they call "cultural retaliatory homicide."[46]

CONNECTIONS

Although it seems logical that banning the sale and ownership of firearms might help reduce violence, those in favor of gun ownership do not agree, as discussed in the Policy and Practice in Criminology feature on gun control in Chapter 2. Some experts believe taking guns away from citizens might endanger them when pitted against armed criminals.

CONNECTIONS

Delinquent subcultures were discussed in detail in Chapter 6. Recall that subculture theorists portray delinquents not as rebels from the normative culture but rather as people who are in accord with the informal rules and values of their immediate culture. By adhering to their own cultural norms, they violate the law.

National Values

Some nations—including the United States, Sri Lanka, Angola, Uganda, and the Philippines—have relatively high violence rates; others are much more peaceful. According to research by sociologist Jerome Neapolitan, a number of national characteristics are predictive of violence: a high level of social disorganization,

subculture of violence
A segment of society in which violence has become legitimized by the custom and norms of that group.

economic stress, high child abuse rates, approval of violence by the government, political corruption, and an inefficient justice system.[47] Children in high-violence nations are likely to be economically deprived and socially isolated, exposed to constant violence, and lacking in hope and respect for the law. Guns are common in these nations because, lacking an efficient justice system, people arm themselves or hire private security forces for protection.[48] In contrast, nations such as Japan have relatively low violence rates because of cultural and economic strengths. Japan boasts a system of exceptionally effective informal social controls that help reduce crime. It also has had a robust economy that may alleviate the stresses that produce violence.[49]

National values, as well as each of these factors just discussed, are believed to influence violent crime, including both traditional common-law crimes, such as rape, murder, assault, and robbery, and newly recognized problems, such as workplace violence, hate crimes, and political violence. Each of these forms of violent behavior is discussed in some detail in this chapter. ✔ CHECKPOINTS

FORCIBLE RAPE

✔ CHECKPOINTS

- ✔ There are a number of suspected causes of violence.
- ✔ Some violent criminals have personal traits that make them violence-prone, including mental impairment and intellectual dysfunction.
- ✔ Victims of severe child abuse and neglect may become violence-prone adults.
- ✔ Violence may have its roots in human evolution, being almost instinctual in some instances.
- ✔ Drug and alcohol abuse has been linked to violence through a psychopharmacological relationship, economic compulsive behavior, or systemic link.
- ✔ Although guns do not cause violence, their presence can escalate its severity.
- ✔ Subcultures of violence encourage people to use aggressive tactics to solve disputes.

The common-law definition of **rape** (from the Latin *rapere*, to take by force) is "the carnal knowledge of a female forcibly and against her will."[50] It is one of the most loathed, misunderstood, and frightening crimes. Under traditional common-law definitions, rape involves nonconsensual sexual intercourse with a female by a male. There are, of course, other forms of sexual assault, including male on male and female on male sexual assaults (some studies estimate that up to 25 percent of males have been the target of unwanted sexual advances by women), but these are not considered within the traditional concept of rape.[51] However, recognizing these other forms of sexual assault, all but three states have now revised their statutes to make them gender neutral.[52]

Rape was often viewed as a sexual offense in the traditional criminological literature. It was presented as a crime that involved overwhelming lust, driving a man to force his attentions on a woman. Criminologists now consider rape a violent, coercive act of aggression, not a forceful expression of sexuality. Take for instance the use of rape in war crimes, a practice that became routine during the war in Bosnia; human rights groups have estimated that more than 30,000 women and young girls were sexually abused in the Balkan fighting.[53] Though shocking, the war crimes discovered in Bosnia have not deterred conquering armies from using rape as a weapon. More recently, pro-government militias in the Darfur region of Sudan were accused of using rape and other forms of sexual violence "as a weapon of war" to humiliate African women and girls as well as the rebels fighting the Sudanese government in Khartoum.[54]

In the United States, there has been a national campaign to alert the public to the seriousness of rape, offer help to victims, and change legal definitions to facilitate the prosecution of rape offenders. Such efforts have been only marginally effective in reducing rape rates, but significant progress has been made in overhauling rape laws and developing a vast social service network to aid victims.

Incidence of Rape

According to the most recent UCR data, about 90,000 rapes or attempted rapes were reported to U.S. police in 2005, a rate of about 31 per 100,000 inhabitants or, more relevantly, 62 per 100,000 females.[55] Like other violent crimes, the rape rate has been in a decade-long decline, and the 2005 totals are significantly below 1992 levels, when 84 women per 100,000 were rape victims.

Population density influences the rape rate. Metropolitan areas today have rape rates significantly higher than rural areas; nonetheless, urban areas have experienced a much greater drop in rape reports than rural areas. The police make arrests in slightly more than half of all reported rape offenses. Of the offenders arrested, typically 45 percent were under 25 years of age, and more than 60 percent were white.

rape
The carnal knowledge of a female forcibly and against her will.

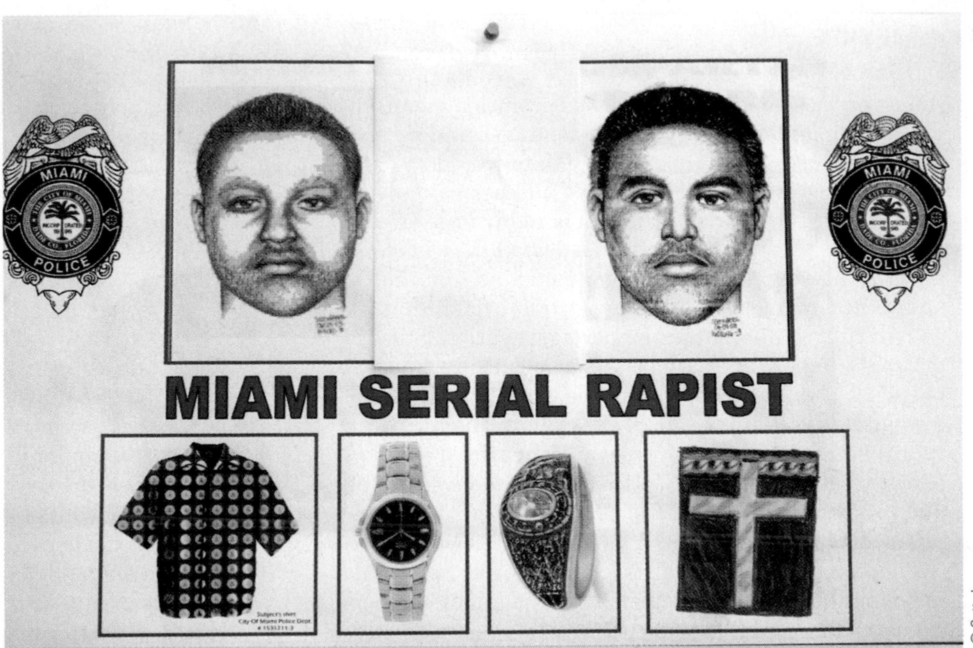

© Getty Images

● Some rapists are one-time offenders, but others engage in multiple or serial rapes over a long period of time. Research shows that serial rapists tend to be white males who are typically older than the norm for other rapists. A Miami police poster shows information relating to Reynaldo E. Rapalo, who was accused of at least seven rapes as well as four attempted rapes committed between September 2002 and September 2003. The victims ranged in age from 11 to 79. Rapalo was recently found guilty of one of the rapes he was charged with.

The racial and age pattern of rape arrests has been fairly consistent for some time. Rape is a warm-weather crime—most incidents occur during July and August, with the lowest rates occurring during December, January, and February.

These data must be interpreted with caution. According to the National Crime Victimization Survey (NCVS), rape is frequently underreported. The NCVS estimates that more than 200,000 rapes and attempted rapes take place each year, suggesting that almost two-thirds of rape incidents are not reported to police.[56] Many women fail to report rapes because they are embarrassed, believe nothing can be done, or blame themselves. Some victims of sexual assaults may even question whether they have really been "raped"; research indicates that when the assault involved a boyfriend, or if the woman was severely impaired by alcohol or drugs, or if the act involved oral or digital sex, the women were unlikely to label their situations as being a "real" rape.[57] Some victims refuse to report rape because they have histories of excessive drinking and prior sexuality, conditions which may convince them that their intemperate and/or immoderate behavior contributed to their own victimization.[58]

Because other victim surveys indicate that at least 20 percent of adult women, 15 percent of college-aged women, and 12 percent of adolescent girls have experienced sexual abuse or assault at some time during their lives, it is evident that both official and victimization statistics significantly undercount rape.[59] However, like the UCR, the NCVS indicates that the number of rapes has been in a sharp decline; the rape and attempted rape rate fell 75 percent between 1993 and 2005.

Types of Rapists

Some rapes are planned, others are spontaneous; some focus on a particular victim, whereas others occur almost as an afterthought during the commission of another crime, such as a burglary. Some rapists commit a single crime, whereas others are multiple offenders; some attack alone, and others engage in group or gang rapes.[60] Because there is no single type of rape or rapist, criminologists have attempted to define and categorize the vast variety of rape situations.

Criminologists now recognize that there are numerous motivations for rape and as a result various types of rapists. One of the best-known attempts to classify the personalities of rapists was made by psychologist A. Nicholas Groth, an expert on classifying and treating sex offenders. According to Groth, every rape encounter contains at least one of these three elements: anger, power, or sadism.[61] Consequently, rapists can be classified according to one of the three dimensions described in Exhibit 10.1. In treating rape offenders, Groth found that about 55 percent were of the power type; about 40 percent, the anger type; and about 5 percent, the sadistic type. Groth's major contribution has been his recognition that rape is generally a crime of violence, not a sexual act. In all of these circumstances, rape involves a violent criminal offense in which a predatory criminal chooses to attack a victim.[62]

Types of Rape

In addition to the variety of types of rapists, there are also different categories of rapes.

Exhibit 10.1

Varieties of Forcible Rape

Anger rape occurs when sexuality becomes a means of expressing and discharging pent-up anger and rage. The rapist uses far more brutality than would have been necessary if his real objective had been simply to have sex with his victim. His aim is to hurt his victim as much as possible; the sexual aspect of rape may be an afterthought. Often the anger rapist acts on the spur of the moment after an upsetting incident has caused him conflict, irritation, or aggravation. Surprisingly, anger rapes are less psychologically traumatic for the victim than might be expected. Because a woman is usually physically beaten during an anger rape, she is more likely to receive sympathy from her peers, relatives, and the justice system and consequently be immune from any suggestion that she complied with the attack.

Power rape involves an attacker who does not want to harm his victim as much as he wants to possess her sexually. His goal is sexual conquest, and he uses only the amount of force necessary to achieve his objective. The power rapist wants to be in control, to be able to dominate women and have them at his mercy. Yet it is not sexual gratification that drives the power rapist; in fact, he often has a consenting relationship with his wife or girlfriend. Rape is instead a way of putting personal insecurities to rest, asserting heterosexuality, and preserving a sense of manhood. The power rapist's victim is usually a woman equal in age to or younger than the rapist. The lack of physical violence may reduce the support given the victim by family and friends. Therefore, the victim's personal guilt over her rape experience is increased—perhaps, she thinks, she could have done something to get away.

Sadistic rape involves both sexuality and aggression. The sadistic rapist is bound up in ritual—he may torment his victim, bind her, or torture her. In the rapist's view, victims are usually related to a personal characteristic that he wants to harm or destroy. The rape experience is intensely exciting to the sadist; he gets satisfaction from abusing, degrading, or humiliating his captive. This type of rape is particularly traumatic for the victim. Victims of such crimes need psychiatric care long after their physical wounds have healed.

SOURCE: A. Nicholas Groth and Jean Birnbaum, *Men Who Rape* (New York: Plenum Press, 1979).

Date Rape One disturbing trend of rape involves people who are in some form of courting relationship—this is known as **date rape**. There is no single form of date rape. Some occur on first dates, others after a relationship has been developing, and still others occur after the couple has been involved for some time. In long-term or close relationships, the male partner may feel he has invested so much time and money in his partner that he is owed sexual relations or that sexual intimacy is an expression that the involvement is progressing.[63] Date rape is believed to occur frequently on college campuses; estimates are that 15 to 20 percent of all college women are victims of rape or attempted rape. Despite their seriousness and prevalence, fewer than 1 in 10 date rapes may be reported to police.[64] Some victims do not report because they do not view their experience as a "real" rape, which, they believe, involves a strange man "jumping out of the bushes." Other victims are embarrassed and frightened. Many tell their friends about their rape while refusing to let authorities know what happened. Reporting is most common in the most serious cases, for example, when a weapon is used; it is less common when drugs or alcohol are involved.[65]

Marital Rape Traditionally, a legally married husband could not be charged with raping his wife; this was referred to as the **marital exemption**. However, research indicates that many women are raped each year by their husbands as part of an overall pattern of spousal abuse, and these women deserve the protection of the law. Many spousal rapes are accompanied by brutal, sadistic beatings and have little to do with normal sexual interests.[66] Not surprisingly, the marital exemption has undergone significant revision. In 1980, only three states had laws against marital rape; today almost every state recognizes marital rape as a crime.[67]

Statutory Rape The term **statutory rape** refers to sexual relations between an underage minor female and an adult male. Although the sex is not forced or coerced, the law says that young girls are incapable of giving informed consent, so the act is legally considered nonconsensual. Typically a state's law will define an age of consent above which there can be no criminal prosecution for sexual relations.[68]

date rape
A rape that involves people who are in some form of courting relationship.

marital exemption
The formerly accepted tradition that a legally married husband could not be charged with raping his wife.

statutory rape
Sexual relations between an underage minor female and an adult male.

Causes of Rape

What factors predispose some men to commit rape? Criminologists' responses to this question are almost as varied as the crime itself. However, most explanations can be grouped into a few consistent categories.

Evolutionary, Biological Factors One explanation for rape focuses on the evolutionary, biological aspects of the male sexual drive. This perspective suggests that rape may be instinctual, developed over the ages as a means of perpetuating the species. In more primitive times, forcible sexual contact may have helped spread genes and maximize offspring. Some believe that these prehistoric drives remain: Males still have a natural sexual drive that encourages them to have intimate relations with as many women as possible.[69] The evolutionary view is that the sexual urge corresponds to the unconscious need to preserve the species by spreading one's genes as widely as possible. Men who are sexually aggressive will have a reproductive edge over their more passive peers.[70]

Male Socialization In contrast to the evolutionary biological view, some researchers argue that rape is a function of socialization. Some men have been socialized to be aggressive with women and believe that the use of violence or force is legitimate if their sexual advances are rebuffed ("women like to play hard to get and expect to be forced to have sex"). Those who have been socialized to believe that "no means yes" are more likely to be sexually aggressive.[71] The use of sexual violence is aggravated if pro-force socialization is reinforced by peers who share similar values.[72]

Diana Russell describes the **virility mystique**—the belief that males must separate their sexual feelings from needs for love, respect, and affection. She believes men are socialized to be the aggressors and expect to be sexually active with many women; consequently, male virginity and sexual inexperience are shameful. Similarly, sexually aggressive women frighten some men and cause them to doubt their own masculinity. Sexual insecurity may lead some men to commit rape to bolster their self-image and masculine identity.[73]

Psychological Abnormality Rapists may suffer from some type of personality disorder or mental illness. Research shows that a significant percentage of incarcerated rapists exhibit psychotic tendencies, and many others have hostile, sadistic feelings toward women.[74] A high proportion of serial rapists and repeat sexual offenders exhibit psychopathic personality structures.[75] There is evidence linking rape proclivity with **narcissistic personality disorder**, a pattern of traits and behaviors that indicate infatuation and fixation with one's self to the exclusion of all others and the egotistic and ruthless pursuit of one's gratification, dominance, and ambition.[76]

Social Learning This perspective submits that men learn to commit rapes much as they learn any other behavior. For example, sexual aggression may be learned through interaction with peers who articulate attitudes supportive of sexual violence.[77] Nicholas Groth found that 40 percent of the rapists he studied were sexually victimized as adolescents.[78] A growing body of literature links personal sexual trauma with the desire to inflict sexual trauma on others.[79] Watching violent or pornographic films featuring women who are beaten, raped, or tortured has been linked to sexually aggressive behavior in men.[80]

Sexual Motivation Most criminologists believe rape is a violent act that is not sexually motivated. Yet it might be premature to dismiss the sexual motive from all rapes.[81] NCVS data reveal that rape victims tend to be young and that rapists prefer younger, presumably more attractive, victims. Data show an association between the ages of rapists and their victims, indicating that men choose rape targets of approximately the same age as consensual sex partners. And, despite the fact that younger criminals are usually the most violent, older rapists tend to harm their victims more than younger rapists. This pattern indicates that older criminals may rape for motives of power and control, whereas younger offenders may be

CONNECTIONS

The social learning view will be explored further in Chapter 13 when the issue of pornography and violence is analyzed in greater detail. Most research does not show that watching pornography is directly linked to sexual violence, but there may be a link between sexual aggression and viewing movies with sexual violence as their theme.

virility mystique
The belief that males must separate their sexual feelings from needs for love, respect, and affection.

narcissistic personality disorder
A pattern of traits and behaviors that indicate infatuation and fixation with one's self to the exclusion of all others and the egotistic and ruthless pursuit of one's gratification, dominance, and ambition.

seeking sexual gratification. Victims may, therefore, suffer less harm from severe beatings and so forth from younger attackers.

Rape and the Law

Of all violent crimes, none has created such conflict in the legal system as rape. Even if women choose to report sexual assaults to police, they are often initially reluctant because of the sexist way in which rape victims are treated by police, prosecutors, and court personnel and the legal technicalities that authorize invasion of women's privacy when a rape case is tried in court.[82] Police officers may hesitate to make arrests and testify in court when the alleged assaults do not yield obvious signs of violence or struggle (presumably showing that the victim strenuously resisted the attack). Police are also loath to testify on the victim's behalf if she had previously known or dated her attacker.

Some state laws have made rape so difficult to prove that women believe the slim chance that their attacker will be convicted is not sufficient to warrant their participation in the legal process. However, police and courts are now becoming more sensitive to the plight of rape victims and are just as likely to investigate acquaintance rapes as they are **aggravated rapes** involving multiple offenders, weapons, and victim injuries. In some jurisdictions, the justice system takes all rape cases seriously and does not ignore those in which victim and attacker have had a prior relationship or those that did not involve serious injury.[83]

Proving Rape Proving guilt in a rape case is extremely challenging for prosecutors. Some judges also fear that women may charge men with rape because of jealousy, false marriage proposals, or pregnancy. There is also evidence that juries may consider the race of the victim and offender in their decision making, for example, believing victims and convicting in interracial rapes more often than they do in intrarace rapes.[84] Although the law does not recognize it, jurors are sometimes swayed by the insinuation that the rape was victim-precipitated; thus, the blame is shifted from rapist to victim. To get a conviction, prosecutors must establish that the act was forced and violent and that no question of voluntary compliance exists. They may be reluctant to prosecute cases where they have questions about the victim's moral character or if they believe the victim's demeanor and attitude will turn off the jury and undermine the chance of conviction.[85] And there is always fear that a frightened and traumatized victim may later identify the wrong man, which happened in the case of Dennis Maher, a Massachusetts man freed in 2003 after spending more than 19 years in prison for rapes he did not commit. Though three victims provided eyewitness identification at trial, DNA testing proved that Maher could not have been the rapist.[86]

Consent Rape represents a major legal challenge to the criminal justice system for a number of reasons.[87] One issue involves the concept of **consent**. It is essential to prove that the attack was forced and that the victim did not give voluntary consent to her attacker. In a sense, the burden of proof is on the victim to show that her character is beyond question and that she in no way encouraged, enticed, or misled the accused rapist. Proving victim dissent is not a requirement in any other violent crime. Robbery victims do not have to prove they did not entice their attackers by flaunting expensive jewelry; yet the defense counsel in a rape case can create reasonable doubt about the woman's credibility. A common defense tactic is to introduce suspicion in the minds of the jury that the woman may have consented to the sexual act and later regretted her decision. Conversely, it is difficult for a prosecuting attorney to establish that a woman's character is so impeccable that the absence of consent is a certainty. Research shows that even when a defendant is found guilty in a sexual assault case, his punishment is significantly reduced if the victim is believed to have negative personal characteristics such as being a transient, hitchhiker, alone in a bar, or a drug and alcohol abuser.[88]

Legal Reform Because of the difficulty rape victims have in obtaining justice, rape laws have been changing around the country. Reform efforts include changing the

aggravated rape
Rape involving multiple offenders, weapons, and victim injuries.

consent
The victim of rape must prove that she in no way encouraged, enticed, or misled the accused rapist.

language of statutes, dropping the condition of victim resistance, and changing the requirement of use of force to include the threat of force or injury.[89] Most states and the federal government have developed **shield laws**, which protect women from being questioned about their sexual history unless it directly bears on the case. In some instances these laws are quite restrictive, whereas in others they grant the trial judge considerable discretion to admit prior sexual conduct in evidence if it is deemed relevant for the defense. In an important 1991 case, *Michigan v. Lucas*, the U.S. Supreme Court upheld the validity of shield laws and ruled that excluding evidence of a prior sexual relationship between the parties did not violate the defendant's right to a fair trial.[90]

In addition to requiring evidence that consent was not given, the common law of rape required corroboration that the crime of rape actually took place. This involved the need for independent evidence from police officers, physicians, and witnesses that the accused was actually the person who committed the crime, that sexual penetration took place, and that force was present and consent absent. This requirement shielded rapists from prosecution in cases where the victim delayed reporting the crime or in which physical evidence had been compromised or lost. Corroboration is no longer required except under extraordinary circumstances, such as when the victim is too young to understand the crime, has had a previous sexual relationship with the defendant, or gives a version of events that is improbable and self-contradictory.[91]

The federal government may have given rape victims another source of redress when it passed the Violence Against Women Act in 1994. This statute allows rape victims to sue in federal court on the grounds that sexual violence violates their civil rights; so far, the provisions of this act have been upheld by appellate courts.[92] Despite these reform efforts, prosecutors may be influenced in their decision to bring charges by the circumstances of a crime.[93]

MURDER AND HOMICIDE

The common-law definition of **murder** is "the unlawful killing of a human being with malice aforethought."[94] It is the most serious of all common-law crimes and the only one that can still be punished by death. Western society's abhorrence of murderers is illustrated by the fact that there is no statute of limitations in murder cases. Whereas state laws limit prosecution of other crimes to a fixed period, usually 7 to 10 years, accused killers can be brought to justice at any time after their crimes were committed.

To legally prove that a murder has taken place, most state jurisdictions require prosecutors to show that the accused maliciously intended to kill the victim. "Express or actual malice" is the state of mind assumed to exist when someone kills another person in the absence of any apparent provocation. "Implied or constructive malice" is considered to exist when a death results from negligent or unthinking behavior. In these cases, even though the perpetrator did not wish to kill the victim, the killing resulted from an inherently dangerous act and therefore is considered murder. An unusual example of this concept is the case of Ignacio Perea, an AIDS-infected Miami man who kidnapped and raped an 11-year-old boy. Perea was convicted of attempted murder and sentenced to up to 25 years in prison when the jury agreed with the prosecutor's contention that the AIDS virus is a deadly weapon.[95]

Degrees of Murder

There are different levels, or degrees, of homicide.[96] **First-degree murder** occurs when a person kills another after premeditation and deliberation. **Premeditation** means that the killing was considered beforehand and suggests that it was motivated by more than a simple desire to engage in an act of violence. **Deliberation** means the killing was planned after careful thought rather than carried out on impulse: "To constitute a deliberate and premeditated killing, the slayer must weigh and consider the question of killing and the reasons for and against such

shield laws
Laws that protect women from being questioned about their sexual history unless it directly bears on the case.

murder
The unlawful killing of a human being with malice aforethought.

first-degree murder
Killing a person after premeditation and deliberation.

premeditation
Considering the criminal act beforehand, which suggests that it was motivated by more than a simple desire to engage in an act of violence.

deliberation
Planning a criminal act after careful thought rather than carrying it out on impulse.

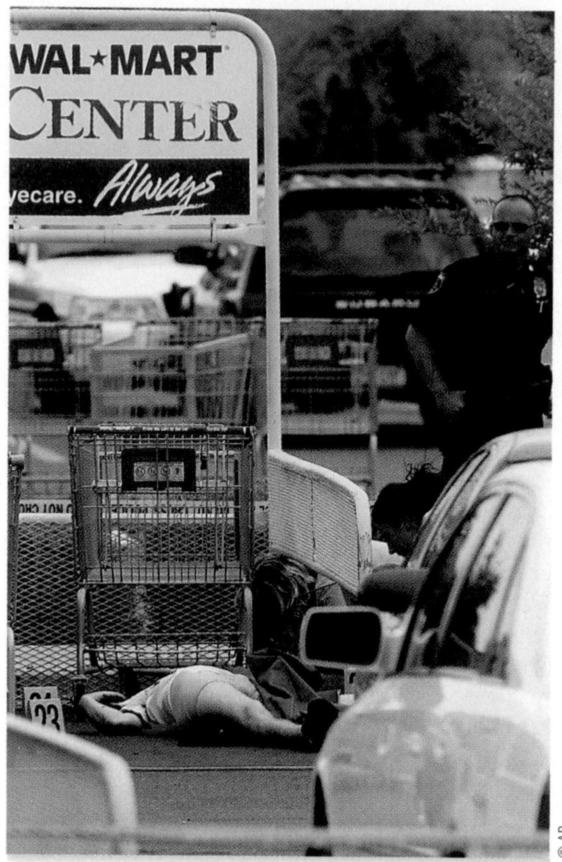

© AP

● Police officers gather evidence next to the body of one of two Wal-Mart employees who were shot to death while collecting shopping carts in the parking lot of a Wal-Mart Supercenter in Glendale, Arizona. Although the number of murders has been in decline, about 17,000 people are homicide victims each year. Most murder victims knew their attackers, but random killings by strangers, such as the Wal-Mart shootings, are on the rise. What motivates stranger homicides, and can they ever be controlled?

a choice; having in mind the consequences, he decides to and does kill."[97] The planning implied by this definition need not be a long process; it may be an almost instantaneous decision to take another's life. Also, a killing accompanying a felony, such as robbery or rape, usually constitutes first-degree murder (**felony murder**).

Second-degree murder requires the killer to have malice aforethought but not premeditation or deliberation. A second-degree murder occurs when a person's wanton disregard for the victim's life and his or her desire to inflict serious bodily harm on the victim result in the victim's death. Homicide without malice is called **manslaughter** and is usually punished by anywhere from 1 to 15 years in prison. **Voluntary or nonnegligent manslaughter** refers to a killing committed in the heat of passion or during a sudden quarrel that provoked violence. Although intent may be present, malice is not. **Involuntary or negligent manslaughter** refers to a killing that occurs when a person's acts are negligent and without regard for the harm they may cause others. Most involuntary manslaughter cases involve motor vehicle deaths—for example, when a drunk driver kills a pedestrian. However, one can be held criminally liable for the death of another in any instance where disregard of safety kills. One of the most famous cases illustrating the difference between murder and manslaughter occurred on January 26, 2001, when Diane Whipple, a San Francisco woman, died after two large dogs attacked her in the hallway of her apartment building. The dogs' owners/keepers, Marjorie Knoller and her husband, Robert Noel, were charged with second-degree murder and involuntary manslaughter, respectively. (Ms. Knoller faced the more severe charge of second-degree murder because she was present during the attack.) After the couple's conviction on March 21, 2002, Judge James Warren overturned the murder conviction of Marjorie Knoller and instituted one of manslaughter. He stated that Knoller could not have known that her two dogs would fatally attack Whipple and therefore the facts did not support the charge of second-degree murder.[98] Nonetheless, the case involved manslaughter because the couple knew the dogs were dangerous and did not exercise the proper precautions to ensure that they would not attack people.

felony murder
A killing accompanying a felony, such as robbery or rape.

second-degree murder
A person's wanton disregard for the victim's life and his or her desire to inflict serious bodily harm on the victim, which results in the victim's death.

manslaughter
Homicide without malice.

voluntary or nonnegligent manslaughter
A killing committed in the heat of passion or during a sudden quarrel that provoked violence.

involuntary or negligent manslaughter
A killing that occurs when a person's acts are negligent and without regard for the harm they may cause others.

The Nature and Extent of Murder

It is possible to track U.S. murder rate trends from 1900 to the present with the aid of coroners' reports and UCR data. The murder rate peaked in 1933, a time of high unemployment and lawlessness, and then fell until 1958. The homicide rate doubled from the mid-1960s to the late 1970s and then peaked at 10.2 per 100,000 population in 1980. After a brief decline, the murder rate rose again in the late 1980s and early 1990s to a peak in 1991 of 9.8 per 100,000 people. The murder rate has since been in a decline. In 2005, the number of murders rose to almost 17,000, a rate of more than 5.5 per 100,000 population. Yet, the murder rate remains significantly lower than its peak in the 1980s.

What else do official crime statistics tell us about murder today? Murder tends to be an urban crime. More than half of the homicides occur in cities with a population of 100,000 or more; almost one-quarter of homicides occur in cities with a population of more than 1 million.[99] Why is homicide an urban phenomenon? Large cities experience the greatest rates of structural disadvantage—poverty, joblessness, racial heterogeneity, residential mobility, family disruption, and income inequality—that are linked to high murder rates.[100] Not surprisingly, large cities are much more commonly the site of drug-related killings, gang-related murders, and relatively less likely to be the location of family-related homicides, including murders of intimates.

Murder victims and offenders tend to be males. Males represent 75 percent of homicide victims and nearly 90 percent of offenders. In terms of rates per 100,000, males are three times more likely to be killed and eight times more likely to commit homicide than are females. Approximately one-third of murder victims and almost half the offenders are under the age of 25. For both victims and offenders, the rate per 100,000 peaks in the 18- to 24-year-old age group.

About 49 percent of all victims are African Americans, and another 49 percent are white (including Hispanic and other races). Compared to their portion of the population, African Americans are disproportionately represented as both homicide victims and offenders.

Murder, like rape, tends to be an intraracial crime; about 90 percent of victims are slain by members of their own race. Similarly, people arrested for murder are generally young (under 35) and male, a pattern that has proved consistent over time.

Some murders involve very young children, a crime referred to as **infanticide** (killing older children is called **filicide**), and others involve senior citizens, referred to as **eldercide**.[101] The UCR indicates that about 500 children under 4 years of age are murdered each year. The younger the child, the greater the risk for infanticide. At the opposite end of the age spectrum, less than 5 percent of all homicides involve people age 65 or older. Males age 65 or older are more likely than females of the same age to be homicide victims. Although most of the offenders who committed eldercide were age 50 or younger, elderly females were more likely than elderly males to be killed by an elderly offender.[102]

Murderers typically have a long involvement in crime; few people begin a criminal career by killing someone. Research shows that people arrested for homicide are significantly more likely to have been in trouble with the law than the average citizen.[103]

Today few would deny that some relationship exists between social and ecological factors and murder. The following section explores some of the more important issues related to these factors.

Murderous Relations

Some murders are expressive, motivated by rage or anger; they typically involve friends, relatives, and acquaintances. Others are instrumental, the outcome of a botched robbery, rape, or drug deal where the perpetrator applied too much force to obtain his goals; these tend to be stranger homicides.[104]

Murderous relations are also shaped by gender: Males are more likely to kill others of similar social standing in more public contexts; women kill family members and intimate partners in private locations.[105] What other forms do murderous connections take?

CONNECTIONS

Recall from Chapter 3 the discussion of victim precipitation. The argument made by some criminologists is that murder victims help create the "transactions" that lead to their death.

Romantic Relations Many murders involve husbands and wives, boyfriends and girlfriends, and others involved in romantic relationships. Upwards of 40 percent of all murders in which the attacker can be identified involved an intimate partner, especially one who has young children.[106]

Research indicates that most females who kill their mates do so after suffering repeated violent attacks.[107] Perhaps the number of males killed by their partners has declined because alternatives to abusive relationships, such as shelters for battered women, are becoming more prevalent around the United States. Regions that provide greater social support for battered women and that have passed legislation to protect abuse victims also have lower rates of female-perpetrated homicide.[108]

Some people kill their mates because they find themselves involved in a *love triangle*.[109] Interestingly, women who kill out of jealousy aim their aggression at their partners; in contrast, men are more likely to kill their rival (their mates' suitors). Love triangles tend to become lethal when the offenders believe they have been lied to or betrayed. Lethal violence is more common when (1) the rival initiated the affair, (2) the killer knew the spouse was already in a steady relationship outside the marriage, and (3) the killer was repeatedly lied to or betrayed.[110]

CONNECTIONS

Men who perceive loss of face might aim their aggression at rivals who are competing with them for a suitable partner. Biosocial theory (Chapter 5) suggests that this behavior is motivated by the male's instinctual need to replenish the species and protect his place in the gene pool. Killing a rival would help a spouse maintain control over a potential mother for his children.

Personal Relations Most murders occur among people who are acquainted. Although on the surface the killing might seem senseless, it is often the result of a long-simmering dispute motivated by revenge, dispute resolution, jealousy, drug deals, racial bias, or threats to identity or status.[111] For example, a prior act of

infanticide
Murder of a very young child.

filicide
Murder of an older child.

eldercide
Murder of a senior citizen.

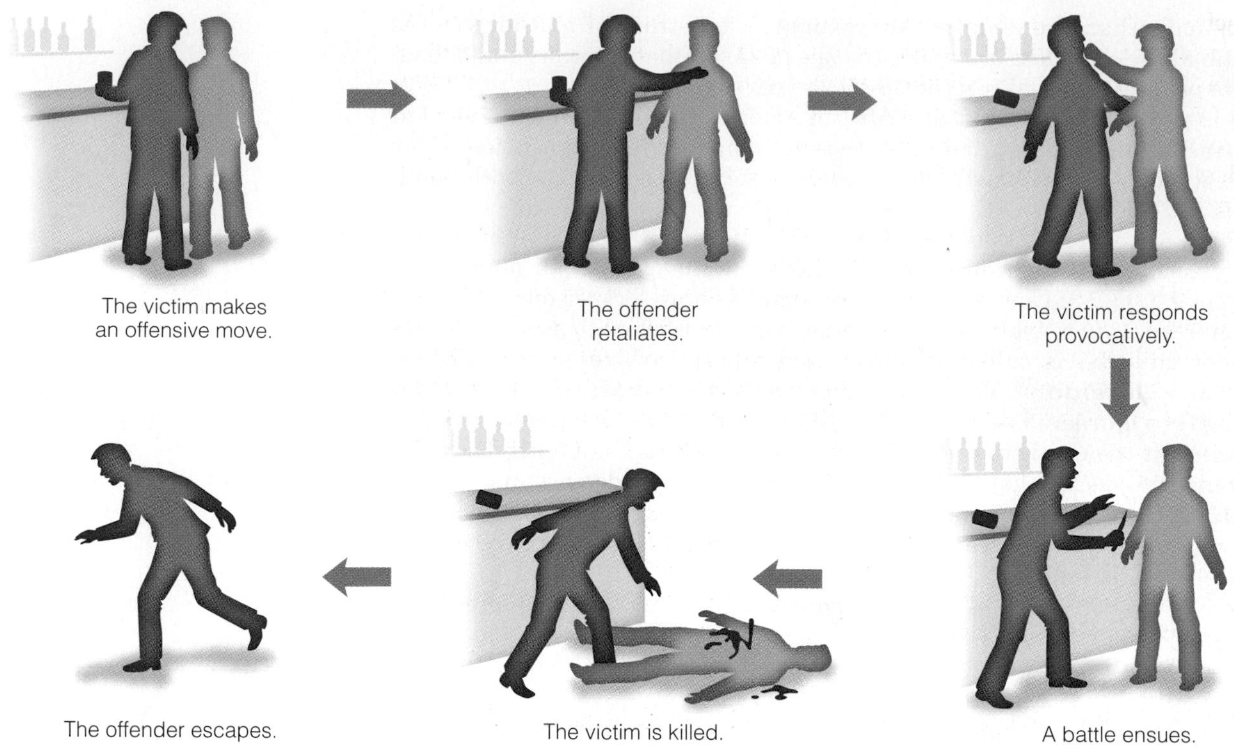
The victim makes an offensive move.
The offender retaliates.
The victim responds provocatively.
A battle ensues.
The victim is killed.
The offender escapes.

Figure 10.2
Murder Transactions

violence, motivated by profit or greed, may generate revenge killing, such as when a buyer robs his dealer during a drug transaction.

How do these murderous relations develop between two people who may have had little prior conflict? In a classic study, David Luckenbill studied murder transactions to determine whether particular patterns of behavior are common between the killer and the victim.[112] He found that many homicides follow a sequential pattern. First, the victim makes what the offender considers an offensive move. The offender typically retaliates verbally or physically. An agreement to end things violently is forged with the victim's provocative response. The battle ensues, leaving the victim dead or dying. The offender's escape is shaped by his or her relationship to the victim or the reaction of the audience, if any (Figure 10.2).

Stranger Relations In the past, people seemed to kill someone they knew or were related to, but over the last decade, the number of stranger homicides has increased. Today more than half of murderers are strangers to their victims, a significant increase from years past. Stranger homicides occur most often as felony murders during rapes, robberies, and burglaries. Others are random acts of urban violence that fuel public fear. For example, a homeowner tells a motorist to move his car because it is blocking the driveway, an argument ensues, and the owner gets a pistol and kills the motorist; or consider a young boy who kills a store manager because, he says, "Something came into my head to hurt the lady."[113]

Why do stranger killings now make up a greater percentage of all murders than in years past? Tough new sentencing laws, such as the three strikes laws used in California, and other habitual-criminal statutes could be responsible. These laws mandate that a "three-time loser" be given a life sentence if convicted of multiple felonies. It is possible, as Tomislav Kovandzic and his associates found, that these laws encourage criminals to kill while committing burglaries and robberies. Why hesitate to kill now, because if they are caught, they will receive a life sentence anyway.[114]

Student Relations Sadly, violence in schools has become commonplace. The most recent school surveys show that among students nationwide, an estimated 5 percent experienced a crime at school and at least 1 percent reported having been a violence victim at school. This means that an estimated 740,000 violent crimes, including 150,000 rapes, sexual assaults, robberies, and aggravated assaults, occurred on school grounds.[115] Violence and bullying have become routine; surveys indicate that more than 16 percent of U.S. schoolchildren have been bullied by other students during the current school term, and approximately 30 percent of 6th- through 10th-grade students reported being involved in some aspect of moderate to frequent bullying, either as a bully, the target of bullying, or both.[116] Sometimes violence and bullying can escalate into a school shooting, such as the Columbine High School massacre, which resulted in the deaths of 15 people.

While relatively rare, these incidents may be expected because up to 10 percent of students report bringing weapons to school on a regular basis.[117] Many of these kids have a history of being abused and bullied; many perceive a lack of support from peers, parents, and teachers.[118] Kids who have been the victims of crime themselves and who hang with peers who carry weapons are most likely to bring guns to school.[119] Troubled kids with little social support but carrying deadly weapons make for an explosive situation.

Research shows that most shooting incidents occur around the start of the school day, the lunch period, or the end of the school day.[120] In most of the shootings (55 percent), a note, threat, or other action indicating risk for violence occurred before the event. Shooters were also likely to have expressed some form of suicidal behavior and to have been bullied by their peers.[121]

Serial Killers, Mass Murderers, and Spree Killers

For 31 years, citizens of Wichita, Kansas, lived in fear of the serial killer known as BTK (for Bind, Torture, Kill). During his murder spree, BTK sent taunting letters and packages to the police and the media. Suddenly, after committing some gruesome killings in the 1970s, he went underground and disappeared from view. After 25 years of silence, he renewed his communications with a local news station. His last communication contained a computer disk, which was analyzed by the FBI and traced to 59-year-old Dennis Rader, who later confessed to 10 murders in an effort to escape the death penalty.

Serial Killers

Criminologists consider a **serial killer**, such as Rader, to be a person who kills three or more persons in three or more separate events. In between the murders, the serial killer reverts to his or her normal lifestyle.

Serial killers come from all walks of life. Two stereotypes surrounding serial killers are that they are almost always white males and that few African Americans are involved in serial killing. Research by Anthony Walsh found that in reality African Americans make up about 20 percent of all serial murderers and their involvement is masked because the media rarely focus on black multiple murderers (the Atlanta child killer and D.C. snipers being two exceptions).[122]

There are different types of serial killers.[123] Some are sadists who gain satisfaction from torturing and killing their victims. Dr. Michael Swango, who is suspected of killing between 35 and 60 patients, wrote in his diary of the "sweet, husky, close smell of indoor homicide" and how murders were "the only way I have of reminding myself that I'm still alive."[124] In contrast, some serial killers think they are helping people when they put them to death. Harold Frederick Shipman, Britain's most notorious serial killer, was a general practitioner convicted of 15 murders, most involving elderly patients. After he committed suicide in 2004, further investigation found that he actually killed at least 218 patients and perhaps even more.[125] As the Profiles in Crime shows, Swango's and Shipman's crimes are not unique.

Some experts have attempted to classify serial killers on their motivations and offense patterns.[126] According to James A. Fox and Jack Levin, there are at least three different types of serial killers:[127]

- "Thrill killers" strive for either sexual sadism or dominance. They enjoy the thrill, the sexual gratification, and the dominance they achieve over the lives of their victims. Serial killers rarely use a gun because this method is

serial killer
A person who kills three or more persons in three or more separate events.

Profiles in Crime

The Angel of Death

On March 2, 2006, Charles Cullen, a nurse who admitted to killing as many as 40 patients, was sentenced to life in prison. At the hearing, relatives of his victims confronted him, calling him "the monster" and blaming him for wrecking their lives. "You betrayed the ancient foundations of the healing professions," said Superior Court Judge Paul Armstrong, who sentenced him to life in prison.

A resident of Bethlehem, Pennsylvania, Cullen was the youngest of nine brothers and sisters. Both his father, a bus driver, and his mother, a homemaker, died when he was young. He enlisted in the Navy in 1978, and when he got out, he attended a nursing school. In 1997, divorced and bankrupt, Cullen was taken to a hospital in New Jersey because he suffered from depression. He refused to provide a blood sample and afterward filed a police report against the doctor. Just over two years later, he lit coals in a bathtub and sealed off his apartment in a suicide attempt. A neighbor called the police, and when they took him in, they learned that this was not his first attempt. He threatened a former girlfriend by breaking into her home to let her know how vulnerable she was.

Working as a nurse, Cullen moved from one hospital to another, and at St. Luke's in Bethlehem, he left rather than face an investigation into the deaths of 69 patients and a mysterious box of heart medication found in a disposal bin. Although the coroner determined at the time that there was no evidence of criminal conduct in any of the cases, many of those deaths will be reviewed again in light of Cullen's confession.

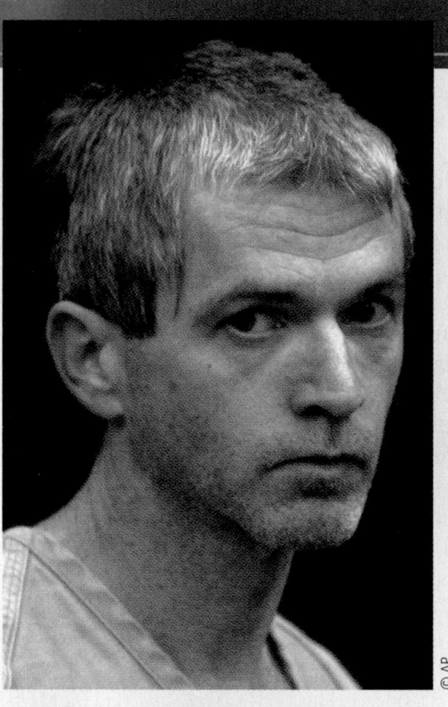
© AP

SOURCES: Charles Cullen, "Mercy or Death," CourtTV Crime Files, www.crimelibrary.com/notorious_murders/angels/male_nurses/index.html; Jeffrey Gettleman, "Nurse Who Killed 29 Is Sentenced to 11 Life Terms," *New York Times*, March 3, 2006, p. C1.

too quick and would deprive them of their greatest pleasure—exalting in the victim's suffering. Extending the time it takes the victim to die increases the pleasure they experience from killing and prolongs their ability to ignore or enjoy their victims' suffering. They typically have a propensity for basking in the media limelight when apprehended for their crimes. Killing provides a way to fill their emotional hunger and reduce their anxiety levels.[128]

- "Mission killers" want to reform the world or have a vision that drives them to kill.
- "Expedience killers" are out for profit or want to protect themselves from a perceived threat.

Female Serial Killers An estimated 10 to 15 percent of serial killers are women. Criminologists Belea Keeney and Kathleen Heide investigated the characteristics of a sample of 14 female serial killers and found some striking differences between the way male and female killers carried out their crimes.[129] Males were much more likely than females to use extreme violence and torture. Whereas males used a "hands-on" approach, including beating, bludgeoning, and strangling their victims, females were more likely to poison or smother their victims. Men tracked or stalked their victims, but women were more likely to lure victims to their death.

There are also gender-based personality and behavior characteristics. Female killers, somewhat older than their male counterparts, abused both alcohol and drugs; males were not likely to be substance abusers. Women were diagnosed as having histrionic, manic-depressive, borderline, dissociative, and antisocial personality disorders; men were more often diagnosed as having antisocial personalities. Aileen Wuornos, executed for killing seven men, was diagnosed with a severe psychopathic personality, a product most likely of her horrific childhood marred by beatings, alcoholism, rape, incest, and prostitution.[130]

The profile of the female serial killer that emerges is a person who smothers or poisons someone she knows. During childhood she suffered from an abusive relationship in a disrupted family. Female killers' education levels are below average, and if they hold jobs, they are in low-status positions.

Mass Murderers In contrast to serial killings, **mass murder** involves the killing of four or more victims by one or a few assailants within a single event.[131] The murderous incident can last but a few minutes or as long as several hours. In order to qualify as a mass murder, the incident must be carried out by one or a few offenders. Highly organized or institutionalized killings (e.g., war crimes and large-scale acts of political terrorism, as well as certain acts of highly organized crime rings), although atrocious, are not considered mass murder and are motivated by a totally different set of factors.

Fox and Levin define four types of mass murderers:

- "Revenge killers" want to get even with individuals or society at large. Their typical target is an estranged wife and "her" children or an employer and "his" employees.
- "Love killers" are motivated by a warped sense of devotion. They are often despondent people who commit suicide and take others, such as a wife and children, with them.
- "Profit killers" are usually trying to cover up a crime, eliminate witnesses, and carry out a criminal conspiracy.
- "Terrorist killers" are trying to send a message. Gang killings tell rivals to watch out; cult killers may actually leave a message behind to warn society about impending doom.[132]

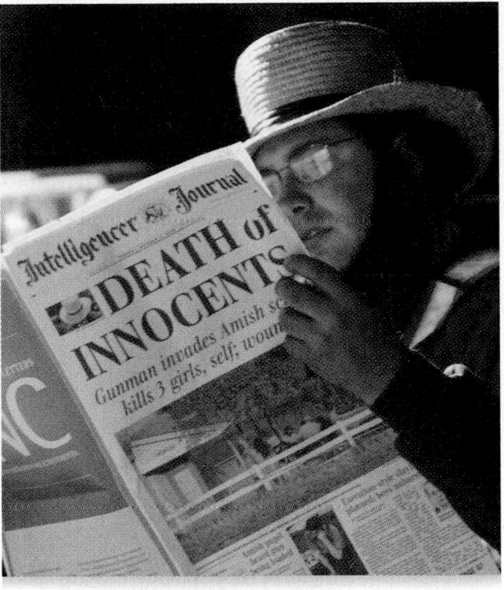

Though violence rates are in decline, horrific incidents of mass murder such as the October 2, 2006, killing of Amish schoolchildren by Charles Roberts kindle fear in the general public. A dairy truck driver who claimed he was nursing a 20-year-old grudge and "hated God," Roberts attacked a one-room schoolhouse in Lancaster County, Pennsylvania, about 55 miles west of Philadelphia. He ordered the 15 boys and adults to leave and then demanded that the 11 young girls in the room line up facing the blackboard. As he began tying the students' legs together with wire and plastic ties, a young teacher dashed from the room and called the police. Before he could be subdued, Roberts began shooting–killing six and wounding five before killing himself. What can be done to stop such murderous rampages? How can guns be taken out of the hands of potentially dangerous people like Roberts, who was armed with a 9 mm semiautomatic pistol, a 12-gauge shotgun and a rifle, 600 rounds of ammunition, two cans of smokeless powder, two knives, and a stun gun?

Spree Killers Unlike mass murders, spree killing is not confined to a single outburst, and unlike serial killers, spree killers do not return to their normal identities in between killings. **Spree killers** engage in a rampage of violence taking place over a period of days or weeks. The most notorious spree killing to date occurred in October 2002, in the Washington, D.C. area.[133] John Lee Malvo, 17, a Jamaican citizen, and his traveling companion John Allen Muhammad, 41, an Army veteran with an expert's rating in marksmanship, went on a rampage that left more than 10 people dead.

Some spree killers target a specific group or class. Joseph Paul Franklin targeted mixed-race couples (African Americans and Jews), committing over 20 murders in 12 states in an effort to instigate a race war. (Franklin also shot and paralyzed *Hustler* publisher Larry Flynt because he published pictures of interracial sex.)[134] Others, like the D.C. snipers Malvo and Muhammad, kill randomly and do not seek a specific class of victim; their targets included the young and old, African Americans and whites, men and women.[135]

ASSAULT AND BATTERY

Although many people mistakenly believe "assault and battery" refers to a single act, they are actually two separate crimes. **Battery** requires offensive touching, such as slapping, hitting, or punching a victim. **Assault** requires no actual touching but involves either attempted battery or intentionally frightening the victim by word or deed. Although common law originally intended these twin crimes to be misdemeanors, most jurisdictions now upgrade them to felonies either when a weapon is used or when they occur during the commission of a felony (for example, when a person is assaulted during a robbery).[136]

Under common law, battery required bodily injury, such as broken limbs or wounds. However, under modern law, an assault and battery occurs if the victim suffers a temporarily painful blow, even if no injury results. Battery can also involve offensive touching, such as if a man kisses a woman against her will or puts his hands on her body.

mass murder
The killing of four or more victims by one or a few assailants within a single event.

spree killer
A killer of multiple victims whose murders occur over a relatively short span of time and often follow no discernible pattern.

battery
Offensive touching, such as slapping, hitting, or punching a victim.

assault
Does not require actual touching but involves either attempted battery or intentionally frightening the victim by word or deed.

© AP

● What begins as an assault can sometimes get out of hand and escalate into homicide, especially when the conflict is a product of road rage. In an accident on Interstate 20 near Canton, Texas, two people died and two more were hospitalized as a result of road rage. One of the participants, Jason Youngblood, 32, of Fort Worth, was charged with two counts of criminal negligent homicide and one count of failure to stop and render aid at the scene of the accident.

Nature and Extent of Assault

The pattern of criminal assault is quite similar to that of homicide and rape; one could say that the only difference is that the victim survives.[137] Assaults may be common in our society simply because of common life stresses. Motorists who assault each other have become such a familiar occurrence that the term **road rage** has been coined. There have even been frequent incidents of violent assault among frustrated airline passengers who lose control while traveling.[138]

In 2005, the FBI recorded about 860,000 assaults, a rate of more than 290 per 100,000 inhabitants. Like other violent crimes, the number of assaults has been in decline, down about 25 percent in the past decade (though rates increased slightly between 2004 and 2005). People arrested for assault and those identified by victims are usually young, male (about 80 percent), and white, although the number of African Americans arrested for assault (33 percent) is disproportionate to their representation in the population. Assault victims tend to be male, but females also face a significant danger. Assault rates are highest in urban areas, during summer, and in southern and western regions. The most common weapons used in assaults are blunt instruments and hands and feet.

The NCVS indicates that only about half of all serious assaults are reported to the police. Victims report about 1 million aggravated assaults and 3.5 million simple or weaponless assaults annually. Like other violent victimizations the number of assaults has been in steep decline—down 52 percent since 1993, according to the NCVS.

Domestic Violence: Assault in the Home

road rage
Violent assault by a motorist who loses control while driving.

Violent attacks in the home are one of the most frightening types of assault. Criminologists recognize that intrafamily violence is an enduring social problem in the United States and abroad.

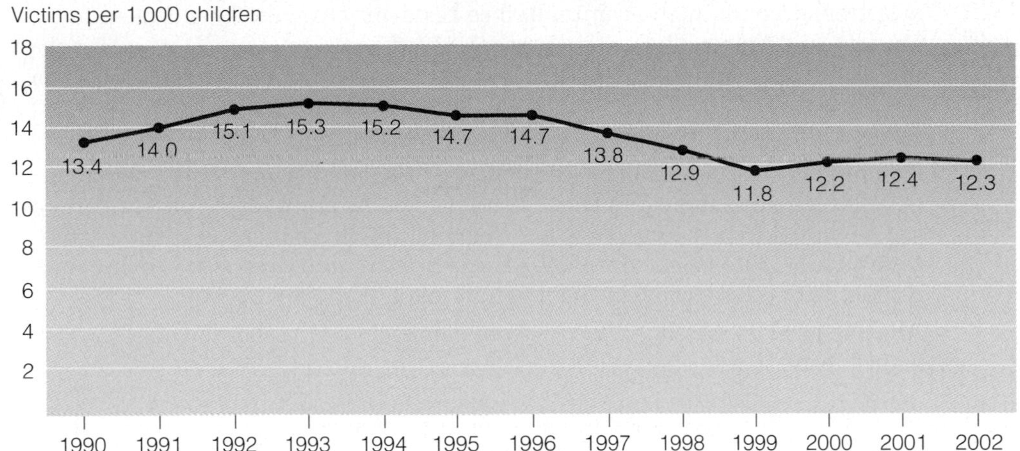

Figure 10.3
Child Maltreatment Rates
SOURCE: National Child Abuse and Neglect Data System (NCANDS), 2004, http://nccanch.acf.hhs.gov/pubs/factsheets/fatality.cfm.

Child Abuse One area of intrafamily violence that has received a great deal of media attention is **child abuse**. This term describes any physical or emotional trauma to a child for which no reasonable explanation, such as an accident or ordinary disciplinary practices, can be found.[139] Child abuse can result from physical beatings administered to a child by hands, feet, weapons, belts, sticks, burning, and so on. Another form of abuse results from **neglect**—not providing a child with the care and shelter to which he or she is entitled.

Estimating the actual number of child abuse cases is difficult because many incidents are never reported to the police. Child protective services (CPS) agencies throughout the United States receive nearly 2 million reports of suspected child abuse or neglect per year. Of these, about two-thirds are considered unfounded, which leaves an estimated 900,000 children across the country who are victims of abuse or neglect, or about 12.3 out of every 1,000 children.[140] The National Child Abuse and Neglect Data System (NCANDS) reported an estimated 1,400 child fatalities in 2002, or 1.98 children per 100,000 children in the general population.[141] However, as Figure 10.3 shows, maltreatment rates are lower today than they were a decade ago. The reason for the reduction in reported abuse is difficult to pinpoint, but it may be the result of better treatment strategies, lower substance abuse rates, reduced reliance on physical punishment, and availability of abortion (which reduces the number of unwanted children).

Child sexual abuse is the exploitation of children through rape, incest, and molestation by parents or other adults. Sexual abuse is of particular concern because children who have been abused experience a long list of symptoms, including fear, post-traumatic stress disorder, behavior problems, sexualized behavior, and poor self-esteem.[142] Women who were abused as children are also at greater risk to be reabused as adults than those who escaped childhood victimization.[143] The amount of force used during the abuse, its duration, and its frequency are all related to the extent of the long-term effects and the length of time needed for recovery.

Causes of Child Abuse Why do parents physically assault their children? Such maltreatment is a highly complex problem with neither a single cause nor a readily available solution. It cuts across ethnic, religious, and socioeconomic lines. Abusive parents cannot be categorized by sex, age, or educational level; they come from all walks of life.[144]

A number of factors have been commonly linked to abuse and neglect:

- Family violence seems to be perpetuated from one generation to another within families.
- The behavior of abusive parents can often be traced to negative experiences in their own childhood—physical abuse, lack of love, emotional neglect, incest, and so on.

child abuse
Any physical or emotional trauma to a child for which no reasonable explanation, such as an accident or ordinary disciplinary practices, can be found.

neglect
Not providing a child with the care and shelter to which he or she is entitled.

child sexual abuse
The exploitation of children through rape, incest, and molestation by parents or other adults.

- Blended families, which include children living with an unrelated adult such as a stepparent or another unrelated co-resident, have also been linked to abuse. Children who live with a mother's boyfriend are at much greater risk for abuse than children living with two genetic parents. Some stepparents do not have strong emotional ties to their nongenetic children, nor do they reap emotional benefits from the parent–child relationship.[145]
- Parents may also become abusive if they are isolated from friends, neighbors, or relatives who can help in times of crisis. Potentially abusive parents are often alienated from society; they have carried the concept of the shrinking nuclear family to its most extreme form and are cut off from ties of kinship and contact with other people in the neighborhood.[146]
- Abusive parents may be suffering from depression and other forms of psychological distress.[147]

Parental Abuse Parents are sometimes the target of abuse from their own children. Researchers Arina Ulman and Murray Straus found these factors in child-to-parent violence (CPV):

- The younger the child, the higher the rate of CPV.
- At all ages, more children were violent to mothers than to fathers.
- Both boys and girls hit mothers more than fathers.
- At all ages, slightly more boys than girls hit parents.

Ulman and Straus found that people who engage in child-to-parent violence were raised in homes with a history of violence, which could either be husband-to-wife, wife-to-husband, corporal punishment of children, or physical abuse. If the use of physical punishment could be eliminated or curtailed, these researchers suggest that child-to-parent violence would similarly decline.[148]

Spousal Abuse Spousal abuse has occurred throughout recorded history. By the mid-nineteenth century, severe wife beating fell into disfavor, and accused wife beaters were subject to public ridicule. Nonetheless, limited chastisement of abusers was still the rule. These ideas form the foundation of men's traditional physical control of women and have led to severe cases of spousal assault.

It is difficult to estimate how widespread spousal abuse is today; however, some statistics indicate the extent of the problem. In their classic study of family violence, Richard Gelles and Murray Straus found that 16 percent of surveyed families had experienced husband–wife assaults.[149] Nor is violence restricted to marriage: National surveys indicate that between 20 and 40 percent of females experience violence while dating.[150] According to a recently released survey conducted by researchers from the Harvard School of Public Health, one in five high school girls suffered sexual or physical abuse from a boyfriend. The study found that teen girls who had been abused by their boyfriends were also much more likely to use drugs or alcohol, to have unsafe sex, and to acquire eating disorders, among other social problems.[151]

In some instances spousal abuse tragically leads to the death of the intimate partner. Factors that predict a lethal conclusion to domestic violence include the perpetrator's access to a gun and previous threat with a weapon, having a stepchild living in the home, estrangement, especially from a controlling partner, and subsequent involvement with another partner[152] (see Exhibit 10.2).

ROBBERY

robbery
Taking or attempting to take anything of value from the care, custody, or control of a person or persons by force or threat of force or violence and/or by putting the victim in fear.

The common-law definition of **robbery** (and the one used by the FBI) is "the taking or attempting to take anything of value from the care, custody or control of a person or persons by force or threat of force or violence and/or by putting the victim in fear."[153] A robbery is considered a violent crime because it involves the use of force to obtain money or goods. Robbery is punished severely because

Exhibit 10.2
Factors That Predict Spousal Abuse

- *Presence of alcohol*: Excessive alcohol use may turn otherwise docile husbands into wife abusers.
- *Access to weapon*: The perpetrator's access to a gun and previous threat with a weapon may lead to abuse.
- *Stepchild in the home*: Having a stepchild living in the home may provoke abuse because a parent may have a more limited bond to the child.
- *Estrangement*: Alienation or separation from a controlling partner and subsequent involvement with another partner are contributing factors in abuse.
- *Hostility toward dependency*: Some husbands who appear docile and passive may resent their dependence on their wives and react with rage and violence; this reaction has been linked to sexual inadequacy.
- *Excessive brooding*: Obsession with a wife's behavior, however trivial, can result in violent assaults.
- *Social learning*: Some males believe society approves of spouse or mate abuse and may use these beliefs to justify their violent behavior. Peer support helps shape their attitudes and behaviors.
- *Socioeconomic factors*: Men who fail as providers and are under economic stress may take their frustrations out on their wives.
- *Flashes of anger*: Research shows that a significant amount of family violence results from a sudden burst of anger after a verbal dispute.
- *Military service*: Spouse abuse among men who have served in the military is extremely high. Similarly, those serving in the military are more likely to assault their wives than are civilian husbands. The reasons for this phenomenon may be the violence promoted by military training and the close proximity in which military families live to one another.
- *Having been battered as children*: Husbands who assault their wives were generally battered as children.
- *Unpredictability*: Batterers are unpredictable, unable to be influenced by their wives, and impossible to prevent from battering once an argument has begun.

SOURCES: Christine Sellers, John Cochran, and Kathryn Branch, "Social Learning Theory and Partner Violence: A Research Note," *Deviant Behavior* 26 (2005): 379–395; Jacquelyn Campbell, Daniel Webster, Jane Koziol-McLain, Carolyn Block, Doris Campbell, Mary Ann Curry, Faye Gary, et al., "Risk Factors for Femicide in Abusive Relationships: Results from a Multisite Case Control Study," *American Journal of Public Health* 93 (2003): 1,089–1,097; Neil Jacobson and John Mordechai Gottman, *When Men Batter Women: New Insights into Ending Abusive Relationships* (New York: Simon & Schuster, 1998); Kenneth Leonard and Brian Quigley, "Drinking and Marital Aggression in Newlyweds: An Event-Based Analysis of Drinking and the Occurrence of Husband Marital Aggression," *Journal of Studies on Alcohol* 60 (1999): 537–541.

the victim's life is put in jeopardy. In fact, the severity of punishment is based on the amount of force used during the crime, not the value of the items taken.

In 2005 the FBI recorded about 420,000 robberies, a rate of more than 140 per 100,000 population. As with most other violent crimes, there has been a significant reduction in the robbery rate during the past decade; the robbery rate is down more than 35 percent since 1994.

The ecological pattern for robbery is similar to that of other violent crimes, with one significant exception: Northeastern states have the highest robbery rates by far. According to the NCVS, about 500,000 robberies were committed or attempted each year. Like other violent crimes, there has been a decade-long drop in the robbery rate.

The Armed Robber

The typical armed robber is unlikely to be a professional who carefully studies targets while planning a crime. People walking along the street, convenience stores, and gas stations are much more likely robbery targets than banks or other highly secure environments. Robbers, therefore, seem to be diverted by modest defensive measures, such as having more than one clerk in a store or locating stores in strip malls; they are more likely to try an isolated store.[154]

Though most robbers may be opportunistic rather than professional, the patterns of robbery suggest that it is not merely a random act committed by an alcoholic or drug abuser. One indicator is the fact that even though most crime rates are higher in the summer, robberies seem to peak during the winter months. One reason may be that the cold weather allows for greater disguise; another reason is that robbers may be attracted to the high amounts of cash people and merchants carry during the Christmas shopping season.[155] Robbers

© Mark Peterson/Corbis

● An NYPD officer points his gun at a suspect as he makes an arrest in an armed robbery. Although there has been a significant reduction in the number of armed robberies, more than 400,000 occur each year in the United States.

may also be attracted to the winter because days are shorter, affording them greater concealment in the dark.

In an important book, *Armed Robbers in Action, Stickups and Street Culture*, Scott Decker and Richard Wright interviewed active robbers in St. Louis, Missouri, and found that robbers are rational decision makers. Wright and Decker found that most armed robberies are motivated by a pressing need for cash. Many robbers careen from one financial crisis to the next, prompted by their endless quest for stimulation and thrills. Interviewees told of how they partied, gambled, drank, and abused substances until they were broke. Their partying not only provided excitement, but it helped generate a street reputation as a "hip" guy who can "make things happen." Robbers had a "here and now" mentality, which required a constant supply of cash to fuel their appetites. Many choose victims who themselves are involved in illegal behavior, most often drug dealers. Ripping off a dealer kills three birds with one stone, providing both money and drugs while targeting a victim who is quite unlikely to call the police. Another ideal target is a married man who is looking for illicit sexual adventures. He also is disinclined to call the police and bring attention to himself. Because they realize that the risk of detection and punishment is the same whether the victim is carrying a load of cash or is penniless, experienced robbers use discretion in selecting targets. People whose clothing, jewelry, and demeanor mark them as carrying substantial amounts of cash make suitable targets; people who look like they can fight back are avoided. Some robbers station themselves at cash machines to spot targets who are flashing rolls of money.[156]

Wright and Decker are not the only researchers who found that robbers seek vulnerable victims. According to research by criminologist Jody Miller, female armed robbers are likely to choose female targets, reasoning that they will be more vulnerable and offer less resistance.[157] When robbing males, women "set them up" to catch them off guard; some feign sexual interest or prostitution to gain the upper hand.[158] As you may recall (Chapter 3), some robbers specialize in attacking drug dealers, recognizing that they have a lot of cash on hand and are unlikely to call the police. Of course, it is hard to view drug dealers as "vulnerable"; they are likely to seek vengeance, if they can, to repair their damaged reputation (not to mention recovering their drug money!).[159]

Acquaintance Robbery

One type of robber may focus on people they know, a phenomenon referred to as **acquaintance robbery**. This seems puzzling because victims can easily identify their attackers and report them to the police. However, despite this threat, acquaintance robbery may be attractive for a number of reasons:[160]

- Victims may be reluctant to report these crimes because they do not want to get involved with the police: They may be involved in crime themselves (drug dealers, for example), or they may fear retaliation if they report the crime. Some victims may be reluctant to gain the label of "rat" or "fink" if they go to the police.
- Some robberies are motivated by street justice. The robber has a grievance against the victim and settles the dispute by stealing the victim's property.

acquaintance robbery
Robbery in which the victim or victims are people the robber knows.

hate crimes (bias crimes)
Violent acts directed toward a particular person or members of a group merely because the targets share a discernible racial, ethnic, religious, or gender characteristic.

In this instance, robbery may be considered a substitute for an assault: the robber wants retribution and revenge rather than remuneration.[161]

- Because the robber knows the victim personally, the robber has inside information that there will be a "good take." Offenders may target people they know to be carrying a large amount of cash or who just purchased expensive jewelry.
- When a person in desperate need for immediate cash runs out of money, the individual may target people in close proximity simply because they are convenient targets.

When Richard Felson and his associates studied acquaintance robbery, they found that victims were more likely to be injured in acquaintance robberies than in stranger robberies, indicating that revenge rather than reward was the primary motive.[162] Similarly, robberies of family members were more likely to have a bigger pay-off than stranger robberies, an indication that the offender was aware that the target had a large amount of cash on hand. ✔ CHECKPOINTS

EMERGING FORMS OF INTERPERSONAL VIOLENCE

Assault, rape, robbery, and murder are traditional forms of interpersonal violence. As more data become available, criminologists have recognized relatively new subcategories within these crime types, such as serial murder and date rape. Additional new categories of interpersonal violence are now receiving attention in criminological literature; the next sections describe three of these forms of violent crime.

Hate Crimes

In the fall of 1998 Matthew Shepard, a gay college student, was kidnapped and severely beaten. He died five days after he was found unconscious on a Wyoming ranch, where he had been left tied to a fence for 18 hours in near freezing temperatures.[163] His two killers, Aaron J. McKinney and Russell A. Henderson, both 22, were sentenced to life in prison after the Shepard family granted them mercy.

Hate crimes, or **bias crimes**, are violent acts directed toward a particular person or members of a group merely because the targets share a discernible racial, ethnic, religious, or gender characteristic.[164] Hate crimes can include the desecration of a house of worship or cemetery, harassment of a minority group family that has moved into a previously all-white neighborhood, or a racially motivated murder.

Hate crimes usually involve convenient, vulnerable targets who are incapable of fighting back. For example, there have been numerous reported incidents of teenagers attacking vagrants and the homeless in an effort to rid their town or neighborhood of people they consider undesirable.[165] Another group targeted for hate crimes is gay men and women: Gay bashing has become common in U.S. cities.

Exhibit 10.3 lists the factors that precipitate hate crimes.

Roots of Hate Why do people commit bias crimes? In a series of research studies, Jack McDevitt, Jack Levin, and Susan Bennet identify four motivations for hate crimes:[166]

- *Thrill-seeking hate crimes*. In the same way some kids like to get together to shoot hoops, hate-mongers join forces to have fun by bashing minorities or destroying property. Inflicting pain on others gives them a sadistic thrill.
- *Reactive (defensive) hate crimes*. Perpetrators of these crimes rationalize their behavior as a defensive stand taken against outsiders whom they believe threaten their community or way of life. A gang of teens that attacks a new family in the neighborhood because they are the "wrong" race is committing a reactive hate crime.

✔ CHECKPOINTS

✔ Forcible rape has been known throughout history and is often linked with war and violence.

✔ Types of rape include date rape, marital rape, and statutory rape; types of rapists include serial rapists and sadists.

✔ Suspected causes of rape include male socialization, hypermasculinity, and biological determinism.

✔ Murder can involve either strangers or acquaintances. Typically, stranger murder occurs during a felony; whereas acquaintance murder involves an interaction or interpersonal transaction between people who may be related romantically or through business dealings, or in other ways.

✔ Mass murder refers to the killing of numerous victims in a single outburst; serial killing involves numerous victims over an extended period of time. Spree killers attack multiple victims over a short period of time.

✔ Patterns of assault are quite similar to those for homicide.

✔ Millions of cases of child abuse and spousal abuse occur each year. There are also numerous cases of parent abuse.

✔ Robbers use force to steal. Some are opportunists looking for ready cash; others are professionals who have a long-term commitment to crime. Both types pick their targets carefully, indicating that they are calculating rather than spontaneous.

Exhibit 10.3
Factors That Predict Hate Crimes

- Poor or uncertain economic conditions
- Racial stereotypes in films and on television
- Hate-filled discourse on talk shows or in political advertisements
- The use of racial code language, such as "welfare mothers" and "inner-city thugs"
- An individual's personal experiences with members of particular minority groups
- Scapegoating—blaming a minority group for the misfortunes of society as a whole

SOURCE: "A Policymaker's Guide to Hate Crimes," *Bureau of Justice Assistance Monograph* (Washington, DC: Bureau of Justice Assistance, 1997).

- *Mission hate crimes*. Some disturbed individuals see it as their duty to rid the world of evil. Those on a "mission," like skinheads, the Ku Klux Klan (KKK), and white supremacist groups, may seek to eliminate people who threaten their religious beliefs because they are members of a different faith, or threaten "racial purity" because they are of a different race.
- *Retaliatory hate crimes*. These offenses are committed in response to a hate crime, whether real or perceived; whether the original incident actually occurred is irrelevant. Sometimes a rumor of an incident may cause a group of offenders to take vengeance, even if the original information was unfounded or inaccurate; the hate crimes occur before anyone has had a chance to verify the accuracy of the original rumor. Attacks based on revenge tend to have the greatest potential for fueling and refueling additional hate offenses.

The research by McDevitt and his colleagues indicates that most hate crimes can be classified as thrill motivated (66 percent) followed by defensive (25 percent) and retaliation (8 percent); few, if any, cases had mission-oriented offenders.

Nature and Extent of Hate Crimes In its last annual count, the FBI recorded almost 7,700 hate crime incidents—motivated by a bias against a race, religion, disability, ethnicity, or sexual orientation—that involved 9,528 victims and 7,145 offenders.[167] Most incidents are motivated by race and to a lesser degree religion (most often anti-Semitism), sexual orientation, ethnicity, and about 1 percent by victim disability. Vandalism and property crimes were the products of hate crimes motivated by religion. However, criminals were more likely to turn to violent acts when race, ethnicity, and sexual orientation were the motivation. Most targets of hate crimes, especially the violent variety, were young white men. Similarly, the majority of known hate crime offenders were young white men.

In crimes where victims could identify the culprits, most victims reported that they were acquainted with their attackers or that their attackers were actually friends, coworkers, neighbors, or relatives.[168] Younger victims were more likely to be victimized by persons known to them. Hate crimes can occur in many settings, but most are perpetrated in public settings.

Controlling Hate Crimes Hate crime laws actually originated after the Civil War and were designed to protect the rights of freed slaves.[169] Today, almost every state jurisdiction has enacted some form of legislation designed to combat hate crimes: Thirty-nine states have enacted laws against bias-motivated violence and intimidation; 19 states have statutes that specifically mandate the collection of hate crime data.

Some critics argue that it is unfair to punish criminals motivated by hate any more severely than those who commit similar crimes whose motivation is revenge, greed, or anger. There is also the danger that what appears to be a hate crime, because the target is a minority group member, may actually be motivated by some other factor such as vengeance or monetary gain. In November 2004, Aaron McKinney, who is serving a life sentence for killing Matthew Shepard, told ABC

News correspondent Elizabeth Vargas that he was high on methamphetamine when he killed Shepard, and that his intent was robbery and not hate. His partner, Russell Henderson, who is appealing his sentence, also claims that the killing was simply a robbery gone bad: "It was not because me and Aaron had anything against gays."[170]

However, in his important book *Punishing Hate: Bias Crimes under American Law*, Frederick Lawrence argues that criminals motivated by bias deserve to be punished more severely than those who commit identical crimes for other motives.[171] He suggests that a society dedicated to the equality of all its people must treat bias crimes differently from other crimes for the following reasons:[172]

- Bias crimes are more likely to be violent and involve serious physical injury to the victim.
- Bias crimes will have significant emotional and psychological impact on the victim; they result in a "heightened sense of vulnerability," which causes depression, anxiety, and feelings of helplessness.
- Bias crimes harm not only the victim but also the "target community."
- Bias crimes violate the shared value of equality among citizens and racial and religious harmony in a heterogeneous society.

Free Speech? Should symbolic acts of hate, such as drawing a Swastika or burning a cross, be banned, or are they protected by the free speech clause of the First Amendment? The U.S. Supreme Court helped answer this question in the case of *Virginia v. Black* (2003) when it upheld a Virginia statute that makes it a felony "for any person . . . , with the intent of intimidating any person or group . . . , to burn . . . a cross on the property of another, a highway or other public place," and specifies that "[a]ny such burning . . . shall be prima facie evidence of an intent to intimidate a person or group." In its decision, the Court upheld Virginia's law, which criminalized cross burning. The Court ruled that cross burning was intertwined with the Ku Klux Klan and its reign of terror throughout the South. The Court has long held that statements in which the speaker intends to communicate intent to commit an act of unlawful violence to a particular individual or group of individuals are not protected free speech and can be criminalized; the speaker need not actually intend to carry out the threat.[173]

Workplace Violence

Workplace violence is now considered the third leading cause of occupational injury or death.[174] Who engages in workplace violence? The typical offender is a middle-aged white male who faces termination in a worsening economy. The fear of economic ruin is especially strong in agencies such as the U.S. Postal Service, where long-term employees fear job loss because of automation and reorganization. In contrast, younger workers usually kill while committing a robbery or another felony. A number of factors precipitate workplace violence. One suspected cause is a management style that appears cold and insensitive to workers. As corporations cut their staffs because of an economic downturn or workers are summarily replaced with cost-effective technology, long-term employees may become irate and irrational; their unexpected layoff can lead to violent reactions.[175]

Not all workplace violence is triggered by management-induced injustice. In some incidents coworkers have been killed because they refused romantic relationships with the assailants or reported them for sexual harassment. Others have been killed because they got a job the assailant coveted. Irate clients and customers have also killed because of poor service or perceived slights.[176] Hospital patients whose demands are not met may attack those people who are there to be caregivers: Health care and social services workers have the highest rate of nonfatal assault injuries. Nurses are three times more likely to experience workplace violence than any other professional group.[177]

These provocations have resulted in a significant number of violent incidents. Each year more than 2 million U.S. residents become victims of violent crime while they work. The most common type of victimization is assault, with an estimated

CONNECTIONS

Does the fact that salesclerks and police officers have the highest injury risk support routine activities theory? People in high-risk jobs who are out late at night and, in the case of salesclerks, do business in cash seem to have the greatest risk of injury on the job. See Chapter 3 for more on routine activities and crime.

workplace violence
Violence such as assault, rape, or murder committed at the workplace.

1.5 million simple assaults and about 400,000 aggravated assaults reported annually. Each year sees more than 80,000 robberies, about 50,000 rapes or sexual assaults, and more than 1,000 workplace homicides.[178]

Stalking

In Wes Craven's popular movies *Scream 1–3*, the heroine Sydney (played by Neve Campbell) is stalked by a mysterious adversary who scares her half to death while killing off most of her peer group. Although obviously extreme even by Hollywood standards, the *Scream* movies focus on a newly recognized form of long-term and repeat victimization: **stalking**.[179]

A complex phenomenon, stalking can be defined as a course of conduct directed at a specific person that involves repeated physical or visual proximity, nonconsensual communication, or verbal, written, or implied threats sufficient to cause fear in a reasonable person.[180]

According to a leading government survey, stalking affects an estimated 1.4 million victims annually.[181] Recent research by Bonnie Fisher and her associates suggests that even that substantial figure may undercount the actual problem. They found that about 13 percent of the women in a nationally drawn sample of more than 4,000 college women were victims of stalking. Considering that there are more than 6.5 million women attending college in the United States, about 700,000 women are being stalked each year on college campuses alone.[182] Though students are more likely to have a lifestyle that increases the risk of stalking compared to women in the general population, these data make it clear that stalking is a widespread phenomenon.

Although stalking usually stops within one to two years, victims experience its social and psychological consequences long afterward. About one-third seek psychological treatment, and about one-fifth lose time from work; some never return to work.

Though stalking is a serious problem, research indicates that many cases are dropped by the courts despite the fact that stalkers often have extensive criminal histories and are frequently the subject of protective orders. A lenient response may be misplaced considering that there is evidence that stalkers repeat their criminal activity within a short time after a stalking charge is lodged with police authorities.[183]

CONNECTIONS

The Fisher research found that the likelihood of being stalked may be related to the victim's lifestyle and routine activities. Female students who are the victims of stalking tend to date more, go out at night to bars and parties, and live alone. Their lifestyle both brings them into contact with potential stalkers and makes them vulnerable to stalking. For more on routine activities, go to Chapter 3.

TERRORISM

Despite its long history, terrorism is difficult to define precisely, and terrorist acts are not easily distinguished from interpersonal crimes of violence. Consider a group that robs a bank to obtain funds for its revolutionary struggles: Should the act be treated as terrorism or as a common bank robbery? In this instance, defining a crime as terrorism depends on the kind of legal response the act evokes from those in power. To be considered terrorism, which is a political crime, an act must carry with it the intent to disrupt and change the government and must not be merely a common-law crime committed for greed or egotism.

The complexities of terrorism make it difficult to formulate an all-encompassing definition, although most experts agree that it generally involves the illegal use of force against innocent people to achieve a political objective. According to the U.S. State Department, the term **terrorism** means premeditated, politically motivated violence perpetrated against noncombatant targets by subnational groups or clandestine agents, usually intended to influence an audience. The term **international terrorism** means terrorism involving citizens or the territory of more than one country. A **terrorist group** is any group practicing, or that has significant subgroups that practice, international terrorism.[184]

Terrorism usually involves a type of political crime that emphasizes violence as a mechanism to promote change. Whereas some political criminals may demonstrate, counterfeit, sell secrets, spy, and the like, terrorists systematically murder and destroy or threaten such violence to terrorize individuals, groups, communities, or governments into conceding to the terrorists' political demands.[185] However, it may be erroneous to equate terrorism with political goals because not all terrorist actions are aimed at political change. Some terrorists may try to bring about what

stalking
A course of conduct directed at a specific person that involves repeated physical or visual proximity, nonconsensual communication, or verbal, written, or implied threats sufficient to cause fear in a reasonable person.

terrorism
Premeditated, politically motivated violence perpetrated against noncombatant targets by subnational groups or clandestine agents, usually intended to influence an audience.

international terrorism
Terrorism involving citizens or the territory of more than one country.

terrorist group
Any group practicing, or that has significant subgroups that practice, international terrorism.

they consider to be economic or social reform—for example, by attacking women wearing fur coats or sabotaging property during a labor dispute. Terrorism must also be distinguished from conventional warfare because it requires secrecy and clandestine operations to exert social control over large populations.[186]

Contemporary Forms of Terrorism

Today the term "terrorism" encompasses many different behaviors and goals. Some of the more common forms are briefly described here.

Revolutionary Terrorists Revolutionary terrorists use violence to frighten those in power and their supporters in order to replace the existing government with a regime that holds acceptable political or religious views. Terrorist actions, such as kidnapping, assassination, and bombing, are designed to draw repressive responses from governments trying to defend themselves. These responses help revolutionaries to expose, through the skilled use of media coverage, the government's inhumane nature. The original reason for the government's harsh response may be lost as the effect of counterterrorist activities is felt by uninvolved people. For example, on October 12, 2002, a powerful bomb exploded in a nightclub on the Indonesian island of Bali, killing more than 180 foreign tourists. In the aftermath of the attack, the Indonesian government declared that the attack was the work of a fundamentalist Islamic group, Jemaah Islamiyah, which is a terrorist organization aligned with al-Qaeda. Jemaah Islamiyah is believed to be intent on driving away foreign tourists and ruining the nation's economy so that they can usurp the government and set up a pan-Islamic nation in Indonesia and neighboring Malaysia.[187]

Political Terrorists Political terrorism is directed at people or groups who oppose the terrorists' political ideology or whom the terrorists define as "outsiders" who must be destroyed. Political terrorists may not want to replace the existing government but to shape it so that it accepts its views.

U.S. political terrorists tend to be heavily armed groups organized around such themes as white supremacy, militant tax resistance, and religious revisionism. Over the nation's history, political terrorist groups have included the Aryan Republican Army, the Aryan Nation, the Posse Comitatus, and the Ku Klux Klan. Although unlikely to topple the government, individualistic acts of terror that characterize political terrorism are difficult to predict or control. On April 19, 1995, the Oklahoma City bombing killed 168 people. This is the most severe example of political terrorism in the United States.

Nationalist Terrorism Nationalist terrorism promotes the interests of a minority ethnic or religious group that believes it has been persecuted under majority rule and wishes to carve out its own independent homeland.

In the Middle East, terrorist activities have been linked to the Palestinians' desire to wrest their former homeland from Israel. For many years, the Palestine Liberation Organization (PLO), led by Yasser Arafat, directed terrorist activities against Israel. Another active group, Hamas, was created in 1987 by Shaikh Ahmed Yassin and is known chiefly for its suicide bombings and other attacks directed against Israeli civilians. Hamas's charter calls for the destruction of the State of Israel and its replacement with a Palestinian Islamic state. Currently, Hamas has political control over the West Bank and the Gaza Strip and has continued to conduct raids against Israel. Hamas and the Iranian-backed Hezbollah are perpetuating the conflict that Israel and the PLO sought to resolve and are behind a spate of suicide bombings and terrorist attacks designed to elicit a sharp response from Israel and set back any chance for peace in the region. In 2006, Hezbollah attacks prompted Israel to launch reprisal raids against their bases in Lebanon. The result: hundreds of deaths and billions in damage.

The Middle East is not the only source of nationalistic terrorism. The Chinese government has been trying to suppress separatist groups fighting for an independent state in the northwestern province of Xinjiang. The rebels are drawn from the region's Uyghur, most of whom practice Sufi Islam, speak a Turkic language,

Current Issues in Crime

Transnational Terrorism in the New Millennium

The traditional image of the armed professional terrorist group with a clear-cut goal, such as nationalism or independence, is giving way to a new breed of terrorists with diverse motives and sponsors. Rather than a unified central command, they are organized in far-flung nets. Not located in any particular nation or area, they have no identifiable address. They are capable of attacking anyone at any time with great destructive force. They may employ an arsenal of weapons of mass destruction—chemical, biological, nuclear—without fear of contaminating their own homelands, because in reality they may not actually have one.

Nor do contemporary transnational terrorists rely solely on violence to achieve their goals. They may use technology to attack their targets' economic infrastructure—such as through computers and the Internet—and actually profit from the resulting economic chaos by buying or selling securities in advance of their own attack. And they may use terror attacks to influence the economy of their target. Research by Sanjeev Gupta and his associates shows that terror attacks are associated with lower economic growth and higher inflation and also have adverse effects on government tax revenues and investment. They result in higher government spending on defense, which can slow growth in other areas of the economy. These outcomes can weaken the terrorists' targets and undermine their resolve to continue to resist.

The "postmodern terrorist" is becoming more lethal, and as a result, terrorism fatalities have been steadily increasing. Take for instance the coordinated bombing of railroad cars in Mumbai, India, which killed more than 200 and wounded an additional 700 people in a single attack on July 11, 2006. Terrorism expert Bruce Hoffman believes this may be attributed to the rise of religiously motivated terrorist groups such as al-Qaeda, which grew sixfold from 1980 to 1992 and has continued to increase steadily ever since. He suggests that religiously inspired terrorist attacks are more likely to result in higher casualties because they are motivated not by efforts to obtain political freedom or a national homeland but by culture conflict. Maintaining a differing value system allows the perpetrators to justify in their minds the deaths of large numbers of people: "For the religious terrorist, violence is a divine duty . . . executed in direct response to some theological demand . . . and justified by scripture" (p. 20).

The paradigm of the new value-oriented terrorist organization is al-Qaeda. Their masterminding of the 9/11 bombing was not designed to restore their homeland or bring about a new political state but to have their personal value structure adopted by Muslim nations. The attack may have been designed to create a military invasion of Afghanistan, which it did. According to Michael Scott Doran, members of al-Qaeda hoped their acts would reach the audience that concerned them the most: the *umma*, or universal Islamic community. The media would show Americans killing innocent civilians in Afghanistan, and the *umma* would find it shocking how Americans nonchalantly caused Muslims to suffer and die.

and wish to set up a Muslim state called Eastern Turkistan. During the past decade the Uyghur separatists have organized demonstrations, bombings, and political assassinations. The province has witnessed more than 200 attacks since 1990, causing more than 150 deaths.[188] In Russia, Chechen terrorists have been intent on creating a free Chechen homeland and have been battling the Russian government to achieve their goal. And in Spain the ETA (Euskadi Ta Askatasuna, which means "Basque Fatherland and Liberty") uses terror tactics, including bombings and assassinations, in hopes of forming an independent Basque state in parts of northern Spain and southwestern France.

Cause-Based Terrorism Some terrorists espouse a particular social or religious cause and use violence to attract followers to their standard. They do not wish to set up their own homeland or topple a government but rather want to impose their social and religious code on others. For example, antiabortion groups have demonstrated at abortion clinics, and some members have attacked clients, bombed offices, and killed doctors who perform abortions. On October 23, 1998, Dr. Barnett Slepian was shot by a sniper and killed in his Buffalo, New York, home; he was one of a growing number of abortion providers believed to be the victims of terrorists who ironically claim to be "pro-life."

The Current Issues in Crime feature further explores this relatively new form of terrorist activity.

Environmental Terrorism On August 22, 2003, members of the extremist environmental group Earth Liberation Front (ELF) claimed responsibility for fires that destroyed about a dozen sport utility vehicles at a Chevrolet dealership in West Covina, California.[189] This was neither the first nor the most costly of their attacks. On October 19, 1998, several suspicious fires were set atop Vail Mountain, a luxurious

The ensuing outrage would open a chasm between the Muslim population of the Middle East and the ruling governments in states such as Saudi Arabia, which were allied with the West. According to Doran, al-Qaeda's true aim was to cause an Islamic revolution within the Muslim world itself, in Saudi Arabia especially, and not to win a war with the United States. Their attacks are designed to force those governments to choose: You are either with the idol-worshipping enemies of God, or you are with the true believers. The attack on the United States was merely an instrument designed to help extremist Islam survive and flourish among the believers who could bring down these corrupt governments. Americans, in short, were drawn into somebody else's civil war.

This new generation of terrorists is especially frightening because they have no need to live to enjoy the fruits of victory. They do not hope to regain a homeland or a political voice; hence, they are willing to engage in suicide missions to achieve their goals. The devoted members of al-Qaeda are willing to martyr themselves because they believe they are locked in a life-or-death struggle with the forces of nonbelievers. They consider themselves true believers surrounded by blasphemers and conclude that the future of religion itself, and therefore the world, depends on them and their battle against idol worship. They believe that victory and salvation can be achieved in a martyr's death.

Critical Thinking

1. Are there parallels between an inner-city youth joining a gang in Los Angeles and a disaffected youth who joins an international terrorist group? Do they have the same goals? The same psychological needs?
2. Would you be willing to give up some of your civil rights, such as personal privacy, if it meant that the government could mount a more effective campaign against terrorist groups? For example, should government agents be allowed to search the homes of suspected terrorists without a warrant?

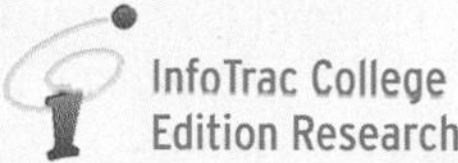

What can be done to prevent terrorism in the new millennium? Can technology hold the key? Find out by reading Richard K. Betts, "Fixing Intelligence," *Foreign Affairs* 81 (January–February 2002): 43.

SOURCES: Amelia Gentleman, "Mumbai Inquiry Focuses on Militants," *New York Times,* July 12, 2006, www.nytimes.com/2006/07/12/world/asia/12cnd-india.html?hp&ex=1152763200&en=1e6c72d31a08384a&ei=5094&partner=homepage; Sanjeev Gupta, Benedict Clements, Rina Bhattacharya, and Shamit Chakravarti, "Fiscal Consequences of Armed Conflict and Terrorism in Low- and Middle-Income Countries," *European Journal of Political Economy* 20 (2004): 403–421; Andrew Chen and Thomas Siems, "Effects of Terrorism on Global Capital Markets," *European Journal of Political Economy* 20 (2004): 349–356; Michael Scott Doran, "Somebody Else's Civil War," *Foreign Affairs* 81 (January–February 2002): 22–25; Bruce Hoffman, "Change and Continuity in Terrorism," *Studies in Conflict and Terrorism* 24 (2001); Harvey Kushner, *Terrorism in America, A Structured Approach to Understanding the Terrorist Threat* (Springfield, IL: Charles C Thomas, 1998); Ian Lesser, Bruce Hoffman, John Arquilla, David Ronfeldt, and Michele Zanini, *Countering the New Terrorism* (Washington, DC: Rand, 1999); Jessica Stern, *The Ultimate Terrorists* (Cambridge, MA: Harvard University Press, 1999).

ski resort in Colorado. Soon after, the Earth Liberation Front claimed that it set the fires to stop a ski operator from expanding into animal habitats (especially that of the mountain lynx). The fires, which caused an estimated $12 million in damages, are the most costly of the more than 1,500 terrorist acts committed by environmental terrorists during the past two decades. These groups commit terrorism in an effort to slow down developers who they believe are threatening the environment or harming animals. Fires have also been set in government labs where animal research is conducted. Spikes are driven into trees to prevent logging in fragile areas. Members of such groups as the Animal Liberation Front (ALF) and Earth First! take responsibility for these attacks; they have also raided turkey farms before Thanksgiving and rabbit farms before Easter. Their activities have had significant impact on the commercial aspects of scientific testing, driving up the price of products, such as drugs, which rely on animal experimentation.[190]

The Earth Liberation Front has been active for several years in the United States and abroad. In addition to its raid on Vail developers and car dealerships in California and Oregon, members have conducted arson attacks on property ranging from a Nike shop in a mall north of Minneapolis to new homes on Long Island, New York. One of their attacks, which took place on February 7, 2004, targeted construction equipment at a 30-acre development site in Charlottesville, Virginia. The FBI has determined that ELF merits investigating as a terrorist network.[191]

State-Sponsored Terrorism State-sponsored terrorism occurs when a repressive government regime forces its citizens into obedience, oppresses minorities, and stifles political dissent. **Death squads** and the use of government troops to destroy political opposition parties are often associated with Latin American political terrorism. Much of what we know about state-sponsored terrorism comes from the efforts of human rights groups. London-based Amnesty International maintains that tens of

death squads
Government-sanctioned covert military or paramilitary groups who carry out assassinations of political opponents and others whom government officials consider undesirable, such as ethnic minority group members.

thousands of people continue to become victims of security operations that result in disappearances and executions. Political prisoners are now being tortured in about 100 countries; people have disappeared or are being held in secret detention in about 20 countries; and government-sponsored death squads have been operating in more than 35 countries. Countries known for encouraging violent control of dissidents include Brazil, Colombia, Guatemala, Honduras, Peru, Iraq, and the Sudan.

Criminal Terrorism In December 2001, six men were arrested by Russian security forces as they were making a deal for weapons-grade uranium. Some of the men were members of the Balashikha criminal gang, and they were in possession of two pounds of top-grade radioactive material, which can be used to build weapons. They were asking $30,000 for the deadly merchandise.[192] Since 1990 there have been a half-dozen cases involving theft and transportation of nuclear material and other cases involving people who offered to sell material not yet in their possession. These are the known cases; it is impossible to know whether client states have already purchased enriched uranium or plutonium.

During the past decade, organized crime has become a major revenue source for terrorist groups worldwide. Criminal and terrorist groups appear to be learning from one another, and adapting to each other's successes and failures. Sometimes terrorist groups become involved in common-law crimes such as drug dealing and kidnapping, even selling nuclear materials. Others form partnerships with crime groups for their mutual benefit. The Revolutionary Armed Forces of Colombia (FARC) has reportedly entered into alliances with criminal groups outside of Colombia, including Mexican drug traffickers, sending cocaine to Mexico in return for arms shipments.[193]

According to terrorism expert Chris Dishman, these illegal activities may on occasion become so profitable that they replace the group's original focus. Burmese insurgents continue to actively cultivate, refine, and traffic opium and heroin out of the Golden Triangle (the border between Myanmar (Burma), Thailand, and Laos), and some have even moved into the methamphetamine market.

In some instances, the line between being a terrorist organization with political support and vast resources and being an organized criminal group engaging in illicit activities for profit becomes blurred. What appears to be a politically motivated action, such as the kidnapping of a government official for ransom, may turn out to be a for-profit crime.[194]

What Motivates Terrorists?

In the aftermath of the September 11, 2001, destruction of the World Trade Center in New York City, many Americans asked themselves the same simple question: Why? What could motivate someone like Osama bin Laden to order the deaths of thousands of innocent people? How could someone who had never been to the United States or suffered personally at its hands develop such lethal hatred?

One view is that terrorists are emotionally disturbed individuals who act out their psychosis within the confines of violent groups. According to this view, "terrorist" violence is not so much a political instrument as an end in itself; it is the result of compulsion or psychopathology. Terrorists do what they do because of a garden variety of emotional problems, including but not limited to self-destructive urges, disturbed emotions combined with problems with authority, and inconsistent and troubled parenting.[195]

Another view is that terrorists hold extreme ideological beliefs that prompt their behavior. At first they have heightened perceptions of oppressive conditions, believing that they are being victimized by some group or by the government. Once these potential terrorists recognize that these conditions can be changed by an active governmental reform effort that has not happened, they conclude that they must resort to violence to encourage change. Ironically, many terrorists appear to be educated members of the upper class. Osama bin Laden is a multimillionaire (see Profiles in Crime), and at least some of his followers are highly educated and trained. The acts of the modern terrorist—using the Internet, organizing logistically complex and expensive assaults, and writing and disseminating formal critiques, manifestos, and theories—require the training and education of the social elite, not the poor and the oppressed.

Responses to Terrorism

In the wake of the 9/11 attacks, Congress moved quickly to pass the **USA Patriot Act (USAPA)**,[196] giving law enforcement agencies a freer hand to investigate and apprehend suspected terrorists. The bill, more than 340 pages long, created new laws and made changes to more than 15 different existing statutes. Its aim was to give sweeping new powers to domestic law enforcement and international intelligence agencies in an effort to fight terrorism, to expand the definition of terrorist activities, and to alter sanctions for violent terrorism. Among its provisions, USAPA expands all four traditional tools of surveillance—wiretaps, search warrants, pen/trap orders (installing devices that record phone calls), and subpoenas. The Foreign Intelligence Surveillance Act (FISA), which allows domestic operations by intelligence agencies, was also expanded. USAPA gave greater power to the FBI to check and monitor phone, Internet, and computer records without first needing to demonstrate that they were being used by a suspect or were a target of a court order. Under USAPA, the government does not need to show a court that the information or communication is relevant to a criminal investigation, nor do they have to report where they served the order or what information they received.

Law Enforcement Responses The FBI is currently expanding its force of agents. In addition to recruiting candidates with the more traditional background of law enforcement, law, and accounting, the bureau is concentrating on hiring agents with scientific and technological skills as well as foreign language proficiency in priority areas, such as Arabic, Farsi, Pashtu, and Urdu, all dialects of Chinese, Japanese, Korean, Russian, Spanish, and Vietnamese, and other priority backgrounds such as foreign counterintelligence, counterterrorism, and military intelligence. In addition to helping in counterterrorism activities, these agents will help staff the new Cyber Division, which was created in 2001 to coordinate, oversee, and facilitate FBI investigations in which the Internet, online services, and computer systems and networks are the principal instruments or targets of terrorists.

In addition to the FBI, the Department of Homeland Security (DHS) has been assigned the following mission:

- Prevent terrorist attacks within the United States.
- Reduce America's vulnerability to terrorism.
- Minimize the damage and recovery from attacks that do occur.

The DHS now has five independent branches:

1. Border and Transportation Security (BTS) is responsible for maintaining the security of our nation's borders and transportation systems.
2. Emergency Preparedness and Response (EPR) ensures that our nation is prepared for, and able to recover from, terrorist attacks and natural disasters.
3. Science and Technology (S&T) coordinates efforts in research and development, including preparing for and responding to the full range of terrorist threats involving weapons of mass destruction.
4. Information Analysis and Infrastructure Protection (IAIP) merges the capability to identify and assess intelligence information concerning threats to the homeland under one roof, issue timely warnings, and take appropriate preventive and protective action.
5. Management is responsible for budget, management, and personnel issues in DHS.

The DHS task is formidable considering this country's large and porous border. In *Nuclear Terrorism*, Graham Allison, an expert on nuclear weapons and national security, describes the almost superhuman effort it would take to seal the nation's borders from nuclear attack. Every day, 30,000 trucks, 6,500 rail cars, and 140 ships deliver more than 50,000 cargo containers to the United States. And while fewer than 5 percent ever get screened, those that do are given nonphysical inspections that may not detect nuclear weapons or fissile material.[197] ✔ CHECKPOINTS

✔ CHECKPOINTS

✔ Hate crimes are violent acts against targets selected because of their religion, race, ethnic background, status, or sexual orientation.

✔ Some hate criminals are thrill seekers; others are motivated by hatred of outsiders; still others believe they are on a mission. More than 10,000 people are the targets of hate crimes each year in the United States.

✔ Workplace violence has become commonplace. It is believed to be related to a number of factors, including job stress and insensitive management style.

✔ Political crimes are committed when people believe that violence is the only means available to produce political change.

✔ Revolutionary terrorists seek to overthrow those in power; political terrorists oppose government policies; nationalist terrorists are minority group members who want to carve out a homeland; cause-based terrorists use violence to address their grievances; environmental terrorists aim at frightening off developers; state-sponsored terrorism is aimed at political dissenters or minority groups; criminal terrorists are more concerned with making profits from their cause than achieving some political purpose.

✔ The USA Patriot Act was passed to allow law enforcement agencies greater latitude in fighting terrorism.

USA Patriot Act (USAPA)
An act that gives sweeping new powers to domestic law enforcement and international intelligence agencies in an effort to fight terrorism, to expand the definition of terrorist activities, and to alter sanctions for violent terrorism.

Profiles in Crime

Osama bin Laden

© Mike Stewart/Corbis Sygma

Usamah bin Muhammad bin Awad bin Ladin was born in 1957 or 1958 in Riyadh, Saudi Arabia. He was the seventh son in a family of 52 children. His father, Sheik Mohammed Awad bin Laden, was a poor, uneducated laborer from Hadramout in South Yemen who worked as a lowly porter in Jeddah. In 1930, the elder bin Laden started his own construction business, which became so successful that his family grew to be known as "the wealthiest non-royal family in the kingdom." Despite his royal associations and great wealth, Mohammed bin Laden remained a humble and devoted Muslim who insisted that his children observe a strict religious and moral code. He went to great pains to teach his children to take charge of their own lives and maintain their independence. In 1968, this training came into play in a brutal way when Mohammed was killed in a plane crash near San Antonio, Texas, leaving his sons in charge, not only of the family business, but of their own destinies. Following his death, Mohammed bin Laden's eldest sons continued to expand their late father's company until it employed more than 40,000 people. The bin Laden group also expanded into Egypt, where it is now that country's largest foreign private group.

Osama bin Laden went on to complete his primary and secondary schooling and joined the Muslim Brotherhood. During this period he expanded his compulsory Islamic studies through a series of meetings that were conducted at the family home by his elder brothers. Among the contacts he made at these meetings were notable Islamic scholars and the leaders of various Muslim movements. Later, he attended King Abdul-Aziz University in Jeddah and completed degrees in public administration and economics. When he wasn't studying, the affluence of his family allowed him to broaden his knowledge through travel to other countries including Syria, Pakistan, Afghanistan, and Sudan.

In a 1995 interview with a French journalist, bin Laden explained why he chose to join the *mujahedeen* fight against the Russians at that time:

> *To counter these atheist Russians, the Saudis chose me as their representative in Afghanistan . . . I did not fight against the communist threat while forgetting the peril from the West. For us, the idea was not to get involved more than necessary in the fight against the Russians, which was the business of the Americans, but rather to show our solidarity with our Islamist brothers. I discovered that it was not enough to fight in Afghanistan, but that we had to fight on all fronts against communist or Western oppression. The urgent thing was communism, but the next target was America . . . This is an open war up to the end, until victory.*

The fortune bin Laden used to finance his terrorist activities was derived from an inheritance of more than $300 million from his family. It is also possible, however, that some deep-rooted psychological issues may have precipitated his murderous impulses. Some analysts note that bin Laden was the only son of his late father's least favorite wife, who was a Syrian and not a Saudi. Bin Laden may have been close to his mother, but he may have felt driven to achieve stature in the eyes of his father and the rest of the family. Bin Laden may have been willing to do anything to gain power and eclipse his father, who died when bin Laden was 10 years old.

The impulse for his murderous actions may have stemmed from bin Laden's unconscious efforts to gain his father's approval. He modeled his behavior after his father in many ways, including working with the Saudi royal family on construction deals. Bin Laden once told an interviewer of his desire to please his father: "My father was very keen that one of his sons should fight against the enemies of Islam. So I am the one son who is acting according to the wishes of his father." Perhaps this need for acceptance explains bin Laden's religious zeal, which was in excess of anyone else's in his large extended family.

After his father's death, bin Laden was mentored by a Jordanian named Abdullah Azzam whose motto was "Jihad and the rifle alone: no negotiations, no conferences and no dialogues." When Azzam was killed in 1989 by a car bomb in Pakistan, bin Laden vowed to carry on Azzam's "holy war" against the West. He threw himself into the Afghan conflict against the Soviet Union, and when the Russians withdrew, he was convinced that the West was vulnerable. "The myth of the superpower was destroyed not only in my mind, but also in the minds of all Muslims," bin Laden has told interviewers.

Bin Laden's motivations will probably never be fully understood, but is it possible that his violent urges stemmed from the same web of emotions that fuel the thousands of predatory criminals who prowl society looking for unwary victims? If so, his actions, although extreme, are certainly not unique. Many people have personally experienced violence or have a friend who has been victimized. Almost everyone has heard about someone being robbed, beaten, or killed. Riots and mass disturbances have ravaged urban areas; racial attacks plague schools and college campuses; assassination has claimed the lives of political, religious, and social leaders all over the world.

SOURCES: Peter L. Bergen, *Holy War, Inc.: Inside the Secret World of Osama bin Laden* (New York, Free Press, 2001), pp. 41–50; Yonah Alexander and Michael S. Swetnam, *Usama bin Laden's al-Qaida: Profile of a Terrorist Network* (New York: Transnational Publishers, 2001); Michael Kranish and Anthony Shadid, "Bin Laden Zeal for Stature Used Psychology, Religion," *Boston Globe*, November 19, 2001, p. 3; Frontline, "Osama bin Laden v. the U.S.: Edicts and Statements," www.pbs.org/wgbh/pages/frontline/shows/binladen/who/edicts.html.

THINKING Like a Criminologist

The state legislature has asked you to prepare a report on statutory rape because of the growing number of underage girls who have been impregnated by adult men. Studies reveal that many teenage pregnancies result from affairs that underage girls have with older men, with age gaps ranging from 7 to 10 years. For example, the typical relationship prosecuted in California involves a 13-year-old girl and a 22-year-old male partner. Some outraged parents adamantly support a law that provides state grants to counties to prosecute statutory rape. These grants would allow more vigorous enforcement of the law and could result in the conviction of more than 1,500 offenders annually.

However, some critics suggest that implementing statutory rape laws to punish males who have relationships with minor girls does not solve the problems of teenage pregnancies and out-of-wedlock births. Liberals dislike the idea of using criminal law to solve social problems because it does not provide for the girls and their young children and focuses only on punishing offenders. In contrast, conservatives fear that such laws give the state power to prosecute people for victimless crimes, thereby adding to the government's ability to control people's private lives. Not all cases involve much older men, and critics ask whether we should criminalize the behavior of 17-year-old boys and their 15-year-old girlfriends. As a criminologist with expertise on rape and its effects, what would you recommend regarding implementation of the law?

Summary

- Violence has become an all too common aspect of modern life.
- Among the various explanations for violent crimes are the availability of firearms, human traits, a subculture of violence that stresses violent solutions to interpersonal problems, and family conflict.
- Rape, the carnal knowledge of a female forcibly and against her will, has been known throughout history, but society's view of rape has evolved.
- At present, close to 100,000 rapes are reported to U.S. police each year; the actual number of rapes is probably much higher. However, like other violent crimes, the rape rate is in decline.
- There are numerous forms of rape, including statutory, acquaintance, and date rape.
- Rape is an extremely difficult charge to prove in court. The victim's lack of consent must be proven; therefore, it almost seems that the victim is on trial. Consequently, changes are being made in rape law and procedure.
- Rape shield laws have been developed to protect victims from having their personal life placed on trial.
- Murder is defined as killing a human being with malice aforethought. There are different degrees of murder, and punishments vary accordingly.
- Like rape, the murder rate and the number of annual murders is in decline.
- Murder can involve a single victim or be a serial killing, mass murder, or spree killing that involves multiple victims.
- One important characteristic of murder is that the victim and criminal often know each other.
- Murder often involves an interpersonal transaction in which a hostile action by the victim precipitates a murderous relationship.
- Assault, another serious interpersonal violent crime, often occurs in the home in the form of child abuse and spouse abuse. There also appears to be a trend toward violence between dating partners.
- Robbery involves theft by force, usually in a public place. Robbery is considered a violent crime because it can and often does involve violence.
- Newly emerging forms of violent crime include hate crimes, stalking, and workplace violence.
- Terrorism is a significant form of violence. Many terrorist groups exist at both the national and international levels.
- Terrorists have a variety of goals, including political change, nationalism, causes, criminality, and environmental protection.
- Terrorists may be motivated by criminal gain, psychosis, grievance against the state, or ideology.
- The FBI and the Department of Homeland Security have been assigned the task of protecting the nation from terrorist attacks. Congress passed the USA Patriot Act to provide them with greater powers.

Take a Post-Test. Visit www.thomsonedu.com/criminaljustice/siegel and take the chapter Post-Test to monitor your progress and identify areas for further improvement. In addition to discovering what you've mastered, you'll learn which concepts need your added attention and get specific page references that direct you to the places in the text where you can find more information on them.

Key Terms

eros 225
thanatos 225
psychopharmacological relationship 226
economic compulsive behavior 226
systemic link 226
subculture of violence 227
rape 228
date rape 230
marital exemption 230
statutory rape 230
virility mystique 231
narcissistic personality disorder 231
aggravated rape 232
consent 232
shield laws 233
murder 233
first-degree murder 233
premeditation 233
deliberation 233
felony murder 234
second-degree murder 234
manslaughter 234
voluntary or nonnegligent manslaughter 234
involuntary or negligent manslaughter 234
infanticide 235
filicide 235
eldercide 235
serial killer 237
mass murder 239
spree killer 239
battery 239
assault 239
road rage 240
child abuse 241
neglect 241
child sexual abuse 241
robbery 242
acquaintance robbery 244
hate crimes (bias crimes) 245
workplace violence 247
stalking 248
terrorism 248
international terrorism 248
terrorist group 248
death squads 251
USA Patriot Act (USAPA) 253

Critical Thinking Questions

1. Should different types of rape receive different legal sanctions? For example, should someone who rapes a stranger be punished more severely than someone who is convicted of marital rape or date rape? If your answer is yes, do you think someone who kills a stranger should be punished more severely than someone who kills a spouse or a friend?

2. Is there a subculture of violence in your home city or town? If so, how would you describe its environment and values?

3. There have been significant changes in rape law involving issues such as corroboration and shield laws. What other measures would you take to protect victims of rape when they are forced to testify in court?

4. Should hate crimes be punished more severely than crimes motivated by greed, anger, or revenge? Why should crimes be distinguished by the motivations of the perpetrator? Is hate a more heinous motivation than revenge?

5. In light of the 9/11 attacks, should acts of terrorism be treated differently from other common-law violent crimes? For example, should terrorists be executed for attempting to commit violence even if no one is killed during their attack?

CHAPTER 11

Property Crimes

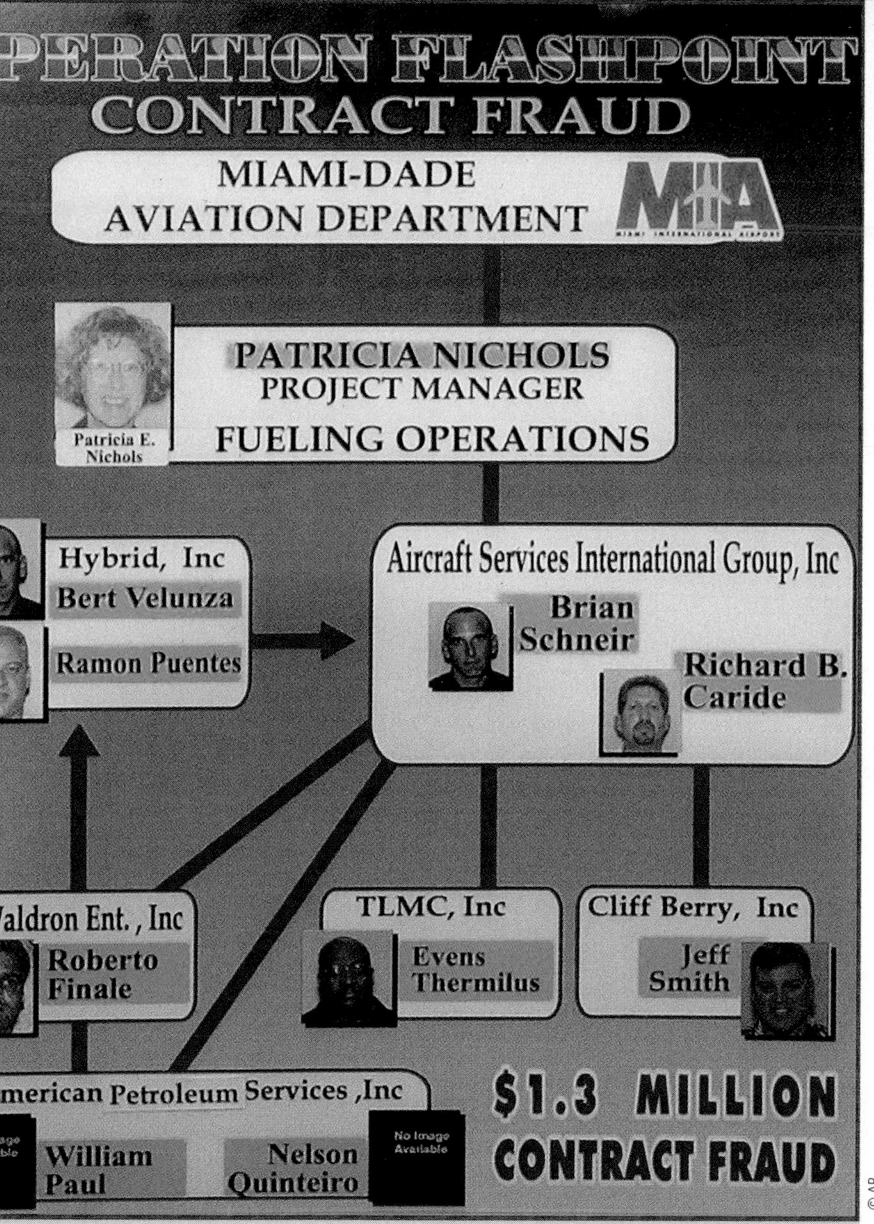

© AP

PHILIP ARCAND AND HIS WIFE, ROBERTA GALWAY, LIVED A LIFE OF LUXURY. They owned two homes, one in British Columbia and one in Las Vegas. They had a Mercedes, Corvette, and Ferrari in their driveways. They took frequent trips around the world. All this without having a job. How did they do it?

CHAPTER OBJECTIVES

1. Be familiar with the history of theft offenses.
2. Recognize the differences between professional and amateur thieves.
3. Know the similarities and differences between the different types of larceny.
4. Understand the different forms of shoplifting.
5. Be able to discuss the concept of fraud.
6. Know what is meant by a confidence game.
7. Understand what it means to burgle a home.
8. Know what it takes to be a "good burglar."
9. Understand the concept of arson.
10. Be able to discuss why people commit arson for profit.

Take a Pre-Test. Visit www.thomsonedu.com/criminaljustice/siegel and take a Pre-Test to determine what you already know and identify the areas where you'll need to focus your study. The program will direct you to specific pages within the text where you can find further information on the correct answers to the questions you've missed.

Through credit card fraud! Arcand wrote high-pressure scripts to lure victims, arranged for telemarketing companies to make the pitch, and set up businesses to process the illegal cash flow. The telemarketers claimed to be from a credit card company. They told victims how easy it is to steal a credit card number, especially over the Internet. They offered to sell "protection" policies, which would insure that the buyer wouldn't have to pay if thieves were to run up a huge tab on their account. The telemarketers told the victims that if they didn't get this protection, they would have to foot the bill for any "unauthorized charges" made if their credit cards were stolen. After making their pitch, the victims were asked, "May we have your credit card number, please?" Later, a charge of between $199 and $389 appeared on their account, even if they didn't sign up for the service.

The scheme was bogus, illegal, and entirely unnecessary because most major credit card companies protect you from fraudulent charges. Still, thousands of Americans were victimized by this scam, the overwhelming majority elderly. In all, they were defrauded out of more than $12 million. Arcand and Galway were ultimately caught when some of the victims reported their suspicions and complaints to authorities. Arcand was sentenced to 10 years in federal prison; his wife pleaded guilty and was sentenced to six months in jail.[1]

Each year, millions of people suffer billions in losses to thieves. As a group, these theft offenses can be defined as acts that violate criminal law and are designed to bring financial reward to an offender. The range and scope of U.S. criminal activity motivated by the desire for financial gain are tremendous. Self-report studies show that property crime is widespread among the young in every social class. National surveys of criminal behavior indicate that almost 30 million personal and household thefts occur annually; corporate and other white-collar crimes are accepted as commonplace; and political scandals, ranging from Watergate to Whitewater, indicate that even high government officials can be suspected of criminal acts.

This chapter begins with some background information on the history and nature of theft as a crime. It then discusses larceny/theft and related offenses, including shoplifting, check forgery, credit card theft, and auto theft. Then there is discussion of other common theft crimes, including fraud, confidence games, receiving stolen property, and embezzlement. Next the discussion turns to a more serious form of theft, burglary, which involves forcible entry into a person's home or workplace for the purpose of theft. Finally, the crime of arson is discussed briefly. Chapter 12 is devoted to white-collar crimes, cyber crimes, and economic crimes that involve criminal organizations.

HISTORY OF THEFT

Theft is not unique to modern times; the theft of personal property has been known throughout recorded history. The Crusades of the eleventh century inspired peasants and downtrodden noblemen to leave the shelter of their estates to prey upon passing pilgrims.[2] Crusaders felt it was within their rights to appropriate the possessions of any infidels—Greeks, Jews, or Muslims—they happened to encounter during their travels. By the thirteenth century, returning pilgrims, not content to live as serfs on feudal estates, gathered in the forests of England and the Continent to poach game that was the rightful property of their lord or king and, when possible, to steal from passing strangers. By the fourteenth century, many such highwaymen and poachers were full-time livestock thieves, stealing great numbers of cattle and sheep.[3]

Roy 20 CViif 41v British Library/Bridgeman Art Library

● Property crimes have a long history. This painting illustrates fourteenth-century thieves plundering a home in Paris.

The fifteenth and sixteenth centuries brought hostilities between England and France in the Hundred Years' War. Foreign mercenary troops fighting for both sides roamed the countryside; loot and pillage were viewed as a rightful part of their pay. As cities developed and a permanent class of propertyless urban poor[4] was established, theft became more professional. By the eighteenth century, three separate groups of property criminals were active:

- *Skilled thieves* typically worked in the larger cities, such as London and Paris. This group included pickpockets, forgers, and counterfeiters, who operated freely. They congregated in "flash houses"—public meeting places, often taverns, that served as headquarters for gangs. Here, deals were made, crimes were plotted, and the sale of stolen goods was negotiated.[5]
- *Smugglers* moved freely in sparsely populated areas and transported goods, such as spirits, gems, gold, and spices, without paying tax or duty.
- *Poachers* typically lived in the country and supplemented their diet and income with game that belonged to a landlord.

By the eighteenth century, professional thieves in the larger cities had banded together into gangs to protect themselves, increase the scope of their activities, and help dispose of stolen goods. Jack Wild, perhaps London's most famous thief, perfected the process of buying and selling stolen goods and gave himself the title "Thief Taker General of Great Britain and Ireland." Before he was hanged, Wild controlled numerous gangs and dealt harshly with any thief who violated his strict code of conduct.[6] During this period, individual theft-related crimes began to be defined by common law. The most important of these categories are still used today.

CONTEMPORARY THIEVES

Of the millions of property and theft-related crimes that occur each year, most are committed by **occasional criminals** who do not define themselves by a criminal role or view themselves as committed career criminals. Other thefts are committed by skilled professional criminals.

Criminologists suspect that most economic crimes are the work of amateur occasional criminals, whose decision to steal is spontaneous and whose acts are unskilled, unplanned, and haphazard. Millions of thefts occur each year, and most are not reported to police agencies. Many of these theft offenses are committed by school-age youths who are unlikely to enter criminal careers and who drift between conventional and criminal behavior. Added to the pool of amateur thieves are the millions of adults whose behavior may occasionally violate the law—shoplifters, pilferers, tax cheats—but whose main source of income is conventional and whose self-identity is noncriminal. Added together, their behaviors form the bulk of theft crimes.

Occasional property crime occurs when there is an opportunity or **situational inducement** to commit crime.[7] Members of the upper class have the opportunity to engage in lucrative business-related crimes such as price-fixing, bribery, and

occasional criminals
Offenders who do not define themselves by a criminal role or view themselves as committed career criminals.

situational inducement
Short-term influence on a person's behavior, such as financial problems or peer pressure, which increases risk taking.

embezzlement; lower-class individuals, lacking such opportunities, are overrepresented in street crime. Situational inducements are short-term influences on a person's behavior that increase risk taking. They include psychological factors, such as financial problems, and social factors, such as peer pressure.

Occasional criminals may deny their criminality and instead view their transgressions as out of character. For example, they were only "borrowing" the car the police caught them with; they were going to pay for the merchandise they stole from the store—eventually. Because of their lack of commitment to a criminal lifestyle, occasional offenders may be the most likely to respond to the general deterrent effect of the law.

In contrast to occasional criminals, **professional criminals** make a significant portion of their income from crime. Professionals do not delude themselves with the belief that their acts are impulsive, one-time efforts, nor do they use elaborate rationalizations to excuse the harmfulness of their actions ("shoplifting doesn't really hurt anyone"). Consequently, professionals pursue their craft with vigor, attempting to learn from older, experienced criminals the techniques that will earn the most money with the least risk. Although their numbers are relatively few, professionals engage in crimes that produce the greater losses to society and perhaps cause the more significant social harm.

Professional theft traditionally refers to nonviolent forms of criminal behavior that are undertaken with a high degree of skill for monetary gain and that maximize financial opportunities and minimize the possibilities of apprehension. The most typical forms include pocket picking, burglary, shoplifting, forgery, counterfeiting, extortion, sneak theft, and confidence swindling (see Exhibit 11.1).[8] The following sections discuss some of the more important contemporary theft categories in some detail. ✔ CHECKPOINTS

✔ CHECKPOINTS

✔ Theft offenses have been common throughout recorded history.

✔ During the Middle Ages, poachers stole game, smugglers avoided taxes, and thieves worked as pickpockets and forgers.

✔ Occasional thieves are opportunistic amateurs who steal because of situational inducements.

✔ Professional thieves learn their trade and develop skills that help them avoid capture.

LARCENY/THEFT

Theft, or **larceny** (from *latrocinium,* the Latin term for theft, and *latio*, robber), was one of the earliest common-law crimes created by English judges to define acts in which one person took for his or her own use the property of another.[9] According to common law, larceny was defined as "the trespassory taking and carrying away of the personal property of another with intent to steal."[10] Most U.S. states have incorporated the common-law crime of larceny in their legal codes. Contemporary definitions of larceny often include such familiar acts as shoplifting and car theft, which do not involve using force or threats on the victim or forcibly breaking into a person's home or workplace. (The former is robbery; the latter, burglary.)

As originally construed, larceny involved taking property that was in the possession of the rightful owner. It would have been considered larceny for someone to sneak into a farmer's field and steal a cow. Thus, the original common-law definition required a "trespass in the taking"; that is, for an act to be considered

professional criminals
Offenders who make a significant portion of their income from crime.

larceny
Taking for one's own use the property of another, by means other than force or threats on the victim or forcibly breaking into a person's home or workplace; theft.

Exhibit 11.1
Categories of Professional Theft

- Pickpocket (cannon)
- Thief in rackets related to confidence games
- Forger
- Extortionist from those engaging in illegal acts (shakedown artist)
- Confidence game artist (con artist)
- Thief who steals from hotel rooms (hotel prowl)
- Jewel thief who substitutes fake gems for real ones (pennyweighter)
- Shoplifter (booster)
- Sneak thief from stores, banks, and offices (heel)

SOURCE: Edwin Sutherland and Chic Conwell, *The Professional Thief* (Chicago: University of Chicago Press, 1937).

larceny, goods must have been taken from the physical possession of the rightful owner. In creating this definition of larceny, English judges were more concerned with disturbance of the peace than with theft itself. They reasoned that if someone tried to steal property from another's possession, the act could eventually lead to a physical confrontation and possibly the death of one party or the other. Consequently, the original definition of larceny did not include crimes in which the thief had taken the property by trickery or deceit. If someone entrusted with another person's property decided to keep it, it was not considered larceny.

The growth of manufacturing and the development of the free enterprise system required greater protection for private property. The pursuit of commercial enterprise often required that one person's legal property be entrusted to a second party; therefore, larceny evolved to include the theft of goods that had come into the thief's possession through legitimate means.

To get around the element of "trespass in the taking," English judges created the concept of **constructive possession**. This legal fiction applies to situations in which persons voluntarily, temporarily give up custody of their property but still believe that the property is legally theirs. If a person gives a jeweler her watch for repair, she still believes she owns the watch, although she has handed it over to the jeweler. Similarly, when a person misplaces his wallet and someone else finds it and keeps it (although identification of the owner can be plainly seen), the concept of constructive possession makes the person who has kept the wallet guilty of larceny.

Today, self-report studies indicate that a significant number of youths have engaged in theft. The FBI recorded about 7 million acts of larceny in 2005, a rate of almost 2,400 per 100,000 persons. Larceny rates declined more than 20 percent between 1995 and 2005.[11] According to the NCVS, more than 14 million thefts occur each year. And like the UCR, the victim survey indicates a steep decline has occurred in the number and rate of larcenies during the past decade.[12]

Common Larceny/Theft Offenses

Most U.S. state criminal codes separate larceny into **petit** (or **petty**) **larceny** and **grand larceny**. The former involves small amounts of money or property and is punished as a misdemeanor. Grand larceny, involving merchandise of greater value, is a felony punished by a sentence in the state prison. Each state sets its own boundary between grand larceny and petty larceny, but $50 to $100 is not unusual. In Virginia, if the value of the item stolen is $200 or more, the offense is grand larceny. If the value of the item stolen is less than $200, the offense is petit larceny. Grand larceny is punishable by 1–20 years in prison, or up to 12 months in jail and/or a fine up to $2,500. Petit larceny is a Class 1 misdemeanor punishable by up to 12 months in jail and/or a fine of up to $2,500.[13] The distinction between petit and grand larceny can be especially significant in states such as California that employ three strikes laws mandating that someone convicted of a third felony be given a life sentence. The difference may not be lost on potential criminals: Research by John Worrall shows that larceny rates in California have been significantly lowered since passage of the three strikes law.[14]

There are many different varieties of larceny. Some grand larceny schemes involve major conspiracies costing victims millions. The Profiles in Crime feature discusses one case, albeit unusual, of grand larceny, which sometimes makes the news. In contrast, petit larcenies involve items of relatively little value. Many of these go unreported, especially if the victims are business owners who do not want to take the time to get involved with police; they simply write off losses as a cost of doing business. Hotel owners estimate that each year guests filch $100 million worth of towels, bathrobes, ashtrays, bedspreads, showerheads, flatware, and even television sets and wall paintings.[15]

Under common law, larceny requires taking and carrying away the possessions of another. Today, numerous theft offenses may fall within the general category of larceny but represent slight variations where these elements are not present and therefore represent a somewhat different type of property crime. Note that in some jurisdictions common theft crimes are classified as a type of larceny, such as larceny-fraud, or larceny by trick, so that the line between larceny and theft is blurred.

constructive possession
A legal fiction that applies to situations in which persons voluntarily give up physical custody of their property but still retain legal ownership.

petit (petty) larceny
Theft of a small amount of money or property, punished as a misdemeanor.

grand larceny
Theft of money or property of substantial value, punished as a felony.

Profiles in Crime

Invasion of the Body Snatchers

In November 2004, New York Police investigated the Daniel George and Son Funeral Home in Brooklyn to check out what they considered to be a routine business dispute. But when they began looking around, they found a sealed room outfitted like an operating room, with a surgical table and overhead lights. They also found FedEx receipts made out to companies that purchase human tissue from cadavers for use in surgical procedures. The department's major case squad was called in, and they discovered that a former Manhattan dentist named Michael Mastromarino and three other men were running a multimillion-dollar body-snatching business that looted bones and tissue from more than a thousand corpses. The men then sold the body parts to legitimate companies that supplied hospitals around the United States. Hundreds of people in states as far away as Florida, Nebraska, and Texas received tissue and bone carved from looted corpses, including the cadaver of Alistair Cooke, the late host of PBS's *Masterpiece Theatre*. The tissue was used in such procedures as joint and heart-valve replacements, back surgery, dental implants, and skin grafts. Many people are now rushing to doctors to be tested for tainted tissue. Some have already filed civil lawsuits. (One New Jersey lawyer alone has signed up some 200 clients.) Mastromarino was charged with opening graves, body stealing, forgery, grand larceny, and racketeering.

Mastromarino had surrendered his dental license in 2000 because he was addicted to the painkiller Demerol. He started a career as a body harvester, opening Biomedical Tissue Services, an FDA-registered company that appeared completely legit. However, he got many of the corpses from Joseph Nicelli, an accomplice who had been hired by funeral directors in New York, New Jersey, and Philadelphia to embalm the bodies. A single harvested body yielded $7,000 in parts. After Nicelli sold the funeral home, he allegedly continued to help Mastromarino sneak into the secret operating room at night to dissect corpses. To hide their crimes, Mastromarino replaced looted bones with plumbing pipes, and they stuffed their surgical gloves and gowns into the bodies before stitching them back together.

Some of the recipients are being tested for diseases, including hepatitis. Although the FDA claims that the risk of serious infection is fairly remote, an agency advisory also mentions that the "actual infectious risk is unknown." A 41-year-old woman who underwent back surgery on Long Island and two patients in New Jersey say they contracted syphilis from stolen bone tissue.

The body snatchers case illustrates the wide variety of schemes that can involve taking the possessions of another. In this case, the possessions were bodily organs and the victims were dead!

SOURCES: Michael Powell and David Segal, "In New York, a Grisly Traffic in Body Parts, Illegal Sales Worry Dead's Kin, Tissue Recipients," *Washington Post*, January 28, 2006, p. A03; William Sherman, "Clients Flee Biz Eyed in Ghoul Probe," *New York Daily News*, October 13, 2005.

Shoplifting

Claude Allen, a top domestic-policy adviser to President George W. Bush, was regarded as someone on his way up in Republican politics. In March 2006, police in Montgomery County, Maryland, arrested him, charging him with stealing more than $5,000 worth of merchandise from Target and Hecht's department stores. According to authorities, Allen would buy expensive items and then shoplift identical ones only to return them for refunds on his credit cards.[16]

Shoplifting is a common form of larceny/theft involving the taking of goods from retail stores. Usually shoplifters try to snatch goods—such as jewelry, clothes, records, and appliances—when store personnel are otherwise occupied and hide the goods on their bodies. The "five-finger discount" is an extremely common crime, and retailers lose more than $10 billion annually to inventory shrinkage (see Exhibit 11.2).

Retail security measures add to the already high cost of this crime, all of which is passed on to the consumer. Shoplifting incidents have increased dramatically in the past 20 years, and retailers now expect an annual increase of from 10 to 15 percent. Some studies estimate that about one in every nine shoppers steals from department stores. Moreover, the increasingly popular discount stores, such as Lowes, Wal-Mart, and Target, have minimal sales help and depend on highly visible merchandise displays to attract purchasers, all of which makes them particularly vulnerable to shoplifters.

shoplifting
The taking of goods from retail stores.

Exhibit 11.2
Shoplifting Statistics

Hayes International provides asset protection and loss control to the retail industry. It also conducts an annual survey of retail theft. Its latest findings on shoplifting using a variety of sources, is contained below:

- Total retail losses are approximately $33 billion annually including employee theft
- Shoplifting is conservatively estimated to account for 30%–40% of total retail shrink/losses.
- Average shoplifting case is approximately $30.

TIME FRAME	DOLLARS	INCIDENTS
Annually	$10–$13 Billion ($9.963–$13.284 Billion)	330–440 Million (332.1–442.8 Million)
Daily (365 days)	$27–$36 Million ($27,295,890–$36,394,521)	900,000–1,200,000 (909,863–1,213,151)
Hours (24)	$1.1–$1.5 Million ($1,137,329–$1,516,438)	38,000–50,500 (37,911–50,548)
Minutes (60)	$19,000–$25,300 ($18,955–$25,274)	630–840 (631.85–842.47)

Shoplifting Apprehensions Survey

Based on over 750,000 shoplifting apprehensions taking place in 27 large retail companies representing 12,908 stores with combined annual sales in excess of $440 billion:

- About 700,000 shoplifters are apprehended each year by the 27 chains.
- Dollars recovered from shoplifting apprehensions totaled over $70 million.
- The average shoplifting case value is about one hundred dollars per incident.

SOURCE: Hayes International Shoplifting Survey, www.hayesinternational.com/thft_srvys.html (accessed April 15, 2006).

The Shoplifter In the early 1960s, Mary Owen Cameron conducted a classic study of shoplifting.[17] In her pioneering effort, Cameron found that about 10 percent of all shoplifters were professionals who derived the majority of their income from shoplifting. Sometimes called **boosters**, or heels, professional shoplifters steal with the intention of reselling stolen merchandise to pawnshops or fences, usually at half the original price.[18]

Cameron found that the majority of shoplifters are amateur pilferers, such as Claude Allen, called **snitches** in thieves' argot. Snitches are otherwise respectable persons who do not conceive of themselves as thieves but systematically steal merchandise for their own use. They are not simply overcome by an uncontrollable urge to snatch something that attracts them; they come equipped to steal. Snitches who are arrested usually have never been apprehended before. For the most part, they lack the kinds of criminal experience that suggest extensive association with a criminal subculture.

Criminologists view shoplifters as people who are likely to reform if apprehended. Cameron reasoned that because snitches are not part of a criminal subculture and do not think of themselves as criminals, they are deterred by initial contact with the law. Getting arrested traumatizes them, and they will not risk a second offense.[19] Although this argument seems plausible, some criminologists suggest that apprehension may in fact have a labeling effect that inhibits deterrence and results in repeated offending.[20]

Controlling Shoplifting Fewer than 10 percent of shoplifting incidents are detected by store employees; customers who notice boosters are unwilling to report even serious cases to managers.[21]

To encourage the arrest of shoplifters, a number of states have passed **merchant privilege laws** designed to protect retailers and their employees from

booster
Professional shoplifter who steals with the intention of reselling stolen merchandise.

snitch
Amateur shoplifter who does not self-identify as a thief but who systematically steals merchandise for personal use.

merchant privilege laws
Legislation that protects retailers and their employees from lawsuits if they arrest and detain a suspected shoplifter on reasonable grounds.

lawsuits stemming from improper or false arrests of suspected shoplifters.[22] These laws require that arrests be made on reasonable grounds or probable cause, that detention be short, and that store employees or security guards conduct themselves reasonably.

Retail stores are now initiating a number of strategies designed to reduce or eliminate shoplifting. **Target removal strategies** involve displaying dummy or disabled goods while the "real" merchandise is locked up. For example, audio equipment is displayed with parts missing, and only after items are purchased are the necessary components installed. Some stores sell from catalogs, keeping the merchandise in stockrooms.

Target hardening strategies involve locking goods into place or having them monitored by electronic systems. Clothing stores may use racks designed to prevent large quantities of garments from being slipped off easily. Store owners also rely on electronic article surveillance (EAS) systems, featuring tags with small electronic sensors that trip alarms if not removed by employees before the item leaves the store; these are used on highly desired yet small items such as Gillette's higher-priced razor blades.[23]

Security systems now feature source tagging, a process by which manufacturers embed the tag in the packaging or in the product itself. Thieves have trouble removing or defeating such tags, and retailers save on the time and labor needed to attach the tags at the store[24] (see Exhibit 11.3).

These methods may control shoplifting, but stores must be wary of becoming overzealous in their enforcement policies. Those falsely accused have won significant judgments when they filed civil actions. In one case, a woman accused of shoplifting at a J. C. Penney store in Media, Pennsylvania, was awarded $250,000, charging them with false confinement and malicious prosecution after she was mistakenly taken for a shoplifter.[25]

CONNECTIONS

Situational crime prevention measures, discussed in Chapter 4, are designed to make it more difficult to commit crimes. Some stores are now using these methods—for example, placing the most valuable goods in the least vulnerable places, posting warning signs to deter potential thieves, and using closed-circuit cameras.

Credit Card Theft

Use of stolen credit cards has become a major problem in the United States. Estimates are that about $1.8 billion per year is lost to stolen or faked credit cards.[26] Most credit card abuse is the work of amateurs who acquire stolen cards through theft or mugging and then use them for two or three days. However, professional credit card rings may be getting into the act. International credit card theft rings now buy cards from street thieves and pickpockets and offer stolen card numbers on the Internet. A card stolen in Amsterdam can be used to make bogus online purchases in Prague within hours. Largely run by former Soviet Union residents, these international cartels cost the world's financial system billions each year.[27]

target removal strategy
Displaying dummy or disabled goods as a means of preventing shoplifting.

target hardening strategy
Locking goods into place or using electronic tags and sensing devices as means of preventing shoplifting.

Exhibit 11.3

How to Stop Shoplifting: Recommendations of Retail Insurers

- Train employees to watch for suspicious behavior, such as a shopper loitering over a trivial item. Have them keep an eye out for shoppers wearing baggy clothes, carrying their own bag, or using some other method to conceal products taken from the shelf.
- Develop a call code. When employees suspect that a customer is shoplifting, they can use the call to bring store management or security to the area.
- Because products on lower floors face the greatest risk, relocate the most tempting targets to upper floors.
- Use smaller exits and avoid placing the most expensive merchandise near these exits.
- Design routes within stores to make theft less tempting and funnel customers toward cashiers.
- Place service departments (credit and packaging) near areas where shoplifters are likely to stash goods. Extra supervision reduces the problem.
- Avoid creating corners with no supervision sight lines in areas of stores favored by young males. Restrict and supervise areas where electronic tags can be removed.

SOURCES: Marcus Felson, "Preventing Retail Theft: An Application of Environmental Criminology," *Security Journal* 7 (1996): 71–75; Marc Brandeberry, "$15 Billion Lost to Shoplifting," *Today's Coverage,* A Newsletter of the Grocers Insurance Group (Portland, OR: Grocers Insurance Group, 1997).

To combat individual losses from credit card theft, in 1971 Congress limited a cardholder's liability to $50 per stolen card. Similarly, some states, such as California, have passed laws making it a misdemeanor to obtain property or services by means of cards that have been stolen, forged, canceled, or revoked, or whose use is unauthorized for any reason.[28] However, while the public is protected, merchants may have to foot the bill.

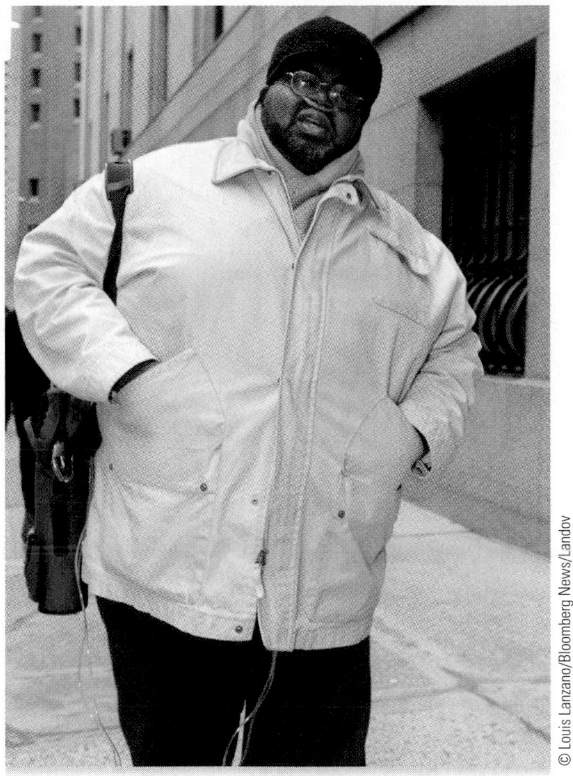
© Louis Lanzano/Bloomberg News/Landov

● Credit card theft is becoming a serious social problem. In one famous case, Philip Cummings, shown here going to a court appearance (and wearing an oxygen tank due to a heart ailment), victimized more than 30,000 people. He stole their credit data on file at Experian, Equifax, and TransUnion, and sold it to criminals who took out loans in the names of the victims. Are law enforcement agencies equipped to capture this new breed of cyber criminal, or should new agencies be created that specialize in Internet and computer crime?

Auto Theft

Motor vehicle theft is another common larceny offense. Because of its frequency and seriousness, it is treated as a separate category in the Uniform Crime Report (UCR). The FBI recorded slightly more than 1.2 million auto thefts in 2005, accounting for a total loss of $8 billion. UCR projections on auto theft are similar to the projections of the National Crime Victim Survey (NCVS), probably because almost every state requires owners to insure their vehicles, and auto theft is one of the most highly reported of all major crimes (75 percent of all auto thefts are reported to police).

Which Cars Are Taken Most? According to the National Insurance Crime Bureau (NICB), these are the most frequently stolen cars in order:[29]

1. 1995 Honda Civic
2. 1989 Toyota Camry
3. 1991 Honda Accord
4. 1994 Dodge Caravan
5. 1994 Chevrolet Full Size C/K 1500 Pickup
6. 1997 Ford F150 Series
7. 2003 Dodge Ram Pickup
8. 1990 Acura Integra
9. 1988 Toyota Pickup
10. 1991 Nissan Sentra

American cars were more attractive to thieves in cities such as Chicago, and pickups were more frequently stolen in Dallas. In the Los Angeles area, thieves preferred Japanese models. California cities and other Western towns seem to be the "hot spots of car theft" (see Figure 11.1).

According to the NICB, thieves typically choose these vehicles because of their high profit potential when the cars are stripped of their parts, which are then sold on the black market. These vehicles are popular overseas, and organized theft rings illegally export them to foreign destinations. Many of the highly desired cars are never recovered because they are immediately trans-shipped abroad where they command prices three times higher than U.S. sticker prices.[30]

Types of Auto Theft A number of attempts have been made to categorize the various forms of auto theft. Typically, distinctions are made between theft for temporary personal use, for resale, and for chopping or stripping cars for parts:[31]

- *Joyriding*. Many car thefts are motivated by teenagers' desire to acquire the power, prestige, sexual potency, and recognition associated with an automobile. Joyriders steal cars not for profit or gain but to experience, even briefly, the benefits associated with owning an automobile.
- *Short-term transportation*. Auto theft for short-term transportation is similar to joyriding. It involves the theft of a car simply to go from one place to another. In more serious cases, the thief may drive to another city or state and then steal another car to continue the journey.

Figure 11.1
National Hot Spots of Car Theft
SOURCE: National Insurance Crime Bureau, www.nicb.org/public/newsroom/hotwheels/index.cfm.

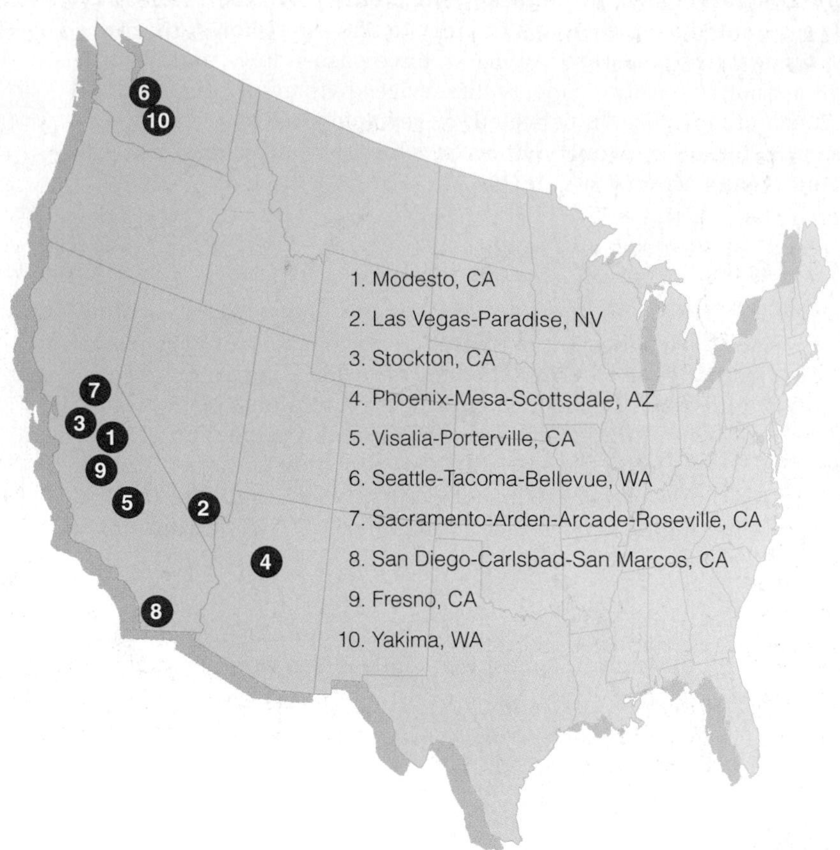

- *Long-term transportation*. Thieves who steal cars for long-term transportation intend to keep the cars for their personal use. Usually older than joyriders and from a lower-class background, these auto thieves may repaint and otherwise disguise cars to avoid detection.
- *Profit*. Auto theft for profit is motivated by the hope of monetary gain. At one extreme are highly organized professionals who resell expensive cars after altering their identification numbers and falsifying their registration papers. At the other end of the scale are amateur auto strippers who steal batteries, tires, and wheel covers to sell or to reequip their own cars.
- *Commission of another crime*. A few auto thieves steal cars to use in other crimes, such as robberies and thefts. This type of auto thief desires both mobility and anonymity.

At one time, joyriding was the predominant motive for auto theft, and most cars were taken by relatively affluent, white, middle-class teenagers looking for excitement.[32] There appears to be a change in this pattern: Fewer cars are being taken today, and fewer stolen cars are being recovered. Part of the reason is that there has been an increase in professional car thieves linked to chop shops, export rings, or both. Exporting stolen vehicles has become a global problem, and the emergence of capitalism in Eastern Europe has increased the demand for U.S. made cars.[33] Some cars are now stolen merely for spare parts that can be taken from stolen autos or simply ripped off parked cars on the street. Among the most attractive targets are these parts:

- *Headlights*. Blue-white, high-intensity discharge headlights. New ones go for $500 and up per light, sometimes $3,000 per car.
- *Air bags*. About 10 percent of all theft claims involve an air bag. The driver's side bag, mounted in the steering wheel, is the easiest to remove and costs $500 to $1,000 to replace.

- *Wheels*. Custom rims are attractive to thieves, especially the "spinners" that keep revolving when the car is stopped. They go from $100 each up to $15,000 for a set of super-deluxe models.[34]

Combating Auto Theft There has been an ongoing effort to reduce the number of auto thefts by using situational crime prevention techniques. One approach has been to increase the risks of apprehension. Information hot lines offer rewards for information leading to the arrest of car thieves. Another approach has been to place fluorescent decals on windows indicating that the car is never used between 1:00 AM and 5:00 AM; if police spot a car with the decal being operated during this period, they know it is stolen.

The Lojack system installs a hidden tracking device in cars; the device gives off a signal enabling the police to pinpoint its location. Research evaluating the effectiveness of this device finds that it significantly reduces crime.[35] Other prevention efforts involve publicity campaigns that have been directed at encouraging people to lock their cars. Parking lots have been equipped with theft-deterring closed-circuit TV cameras and barriers. Manufacturers have installed more sophisticated steering-column locking devices and other security systems that complicate theft.

A study by the Highway Loss Data Institute (HLDI) found that most car theft prevention methods, especially alarms, have little effect on theft rates. The most effective methods appear to be devices that immobilize a vehicle by cutting off the electrical power needed to start the engine when a theft is detected.[36] However, car thieves with modest resources—just a few hundred dollars' worth of off-the-shelf equipment—and some computer knowledge can crack the codes of millions of car keys and subvert their security systems.[37]

Bad Checks

Another form of larceny is cashing bad checks to obtain money or property. The checks are intentionally drawn on a nonexistent or underfunded bank account. In general, for a person to be guilty of passing a bad check, the bank the check is drawn on must refuse payment and the check casher must fail to make the check good within 10 days after finding out the check was not honored.

Edwin Lemert conducted the best-known study of check forgers more than 40 years ago.[38] Lemert found that the majority of check forgers—he calls them **naive check forgers**—are amateurs who do not believe their actions will hurt anyone. Most naive check forgers come from middle-class backgrounds and have little identification with a criminal subculture. They cash bad checks because of a financial crisis that demands an immediate resolution—perhaps they have lost money at the racetrack and have some pressing bills to pay. Naive check forgers are often socially isolated people who have been unsuccessful in their personal relationships. They are risk-prone when faced with a situation that is unusually stressful for them. The willingness of stores and other commercial establishments to cash checks with a minimum of fuss to promote business encourages the check forger to risk committing a criminal act.

Lemert found that a few professionals, whom he calls **systematic forgers**, make a substantial living passing bad checks. Estimating the number of such forgeries committed each year or the amounts involved is difficult. Stores and banks may choose not to press charges because the effort to collect the money due them is often not worth their while. It is also difficult to separate the true check forger from the neglectful shopper.

False Pretenses/Fraud

The crime of **false pretenses**, or **fraud**, involves misrepresenting a fact in a way that causes a victim to willingly give his or her property to the wrongdoer, who then keeps it.[39] In 1757, the English Parliament defined "false pretenses" to cover an area of law left untouched by larceny statutes. The first false pretenses law punished people who "knowingly and designedly by false pretense or pretenses,

naive check forgers
Amateurs who cash bad checks because of some financial crisis but have little identification with a criminal subculture.

systematic forgers
Professionals who make a living by passing bad checks.

false pretenses (fraud)
Misrepresenting a fact in a way that causes a deceived victim to give money or property to the offender.

CONNECTIONS

Similar frauds are conducted over the Internet. These are discussed in Chapter 12.

[obtained] from any person or persons, money, goods, wares or merchandise with intent to cheat or defraud any person or persons of the same."[40]

False pretense differs from traditional larceny because the victims willingly give their possessions to the offender, and the crime does not, as does larceny, involve a "trespass in the taking." An example of false pretenses would be an unscrupulous merchant selling someone a chair by claiming it was an antique, knowing all the while that it was a cheap copy. Another example would be a phony healer selling a victim a bottle of colored sugar water as an "elixir" that would cure a disease.

Confidence Games

Confidence games are run by swindlers who aspire to separate a victim from his or her hard-earned money. These con games often involve getting a mark (target) interested in some get-rich-quick scheme, which may have illegal overtones. The criminal's hope is that when victims lose their money, they will be either too embarrassed or too afraid to call the police. There are hundreds of varieties of con games.

Contemporary confidence games have gone high-tech. Corrupt telemarketers contact people, typically elderly victims, to bilk them out of their savings. The FBI estimates that illicit telephone pitches cost Americans some $40 billion a year.[41] In one scam, a salesman tried to get $500 out of a 78-year-old woman by telling her the money was needed as a deposit to make sure she would get $50,000 she had supposedly won in a contest. In another scheme, a Las Vegas–based telephone con game used the name Feed America Inc. to defraud people out of more than $1.3 million by soliciting donations for various causes, including families of those killed in the Oklahoma City bombing. With the growth of direct-mail marketing and "900" telephone numbers that charge callers more than $2.50 per minute for conversations with what are promised to be beautiful, willing sex partners, a flood of new confidence games may be about to descend on the U.S. public. Here are some common confidence games:

- Con artists read the obituary column and then send a surviving spouse bills supposedly owed by the person deceased. Or they deliver an item, such as a Bible, that they say the deceased relative ordered just before he died.
- A swindler, posing as a bank employee, stops a customer as he or she is about to enter the bank. The swindler claims to be an investigator who is trying to catch a dishonest teller. He asks the customer to withdraw cash to see if he or she gets the right amount. After the cash is withdrawn, the swindler asks that it be turned over to him so he can check the serial numbers.
- Pyramid schemes involve selling phony franchises. The investor buys a franchise to sell golf clubs or some other commodity, paying thousands of dollars. The investor is asked to recruit some friends to buy more franchises and is promised a percentage of the sales of every new franchisee he recruits. Eventually there are hundreds of distributors, few customers, and the merchandise is typically unavailable. Those at the top make a lot of money before the pyramid collapses, leaving individual investors without their cash.
- Shady contractors offer unusually low prices for expensive jobs such as driveway repair and then use old motor oil rather than asphalt to make the repairs. The first rain brings disaster. Some offer a low rate but conduct a "free" inspection that turns up several expensive repairs that are actually bogus.
- A business office receives an invoice in the mail with a self-addressed envelope that looks like it comes from the phone company (walking fingers on a yellow background). It appears to be a contract for an ad in the yellow pages. On the back, in small print, will be written, "By returning this confirmation, you're signing a contract to be an advertiser in the upcoming, and all subsequent, issues." If the invoice is returned, the business soon finds that it has agreed to a long-term contract to advertise in some private publication that is not widely distributed.

confidence game
A swindle set up to separate victims from their money, many involving a get-rich-quick scheme, often with illegal overtones so that the victim will be afraid or embarrassed to call the police.

Receiving and Fencing Stolen Property

The crime of receiving stolen goods is a type of larceny/theft that involves the buying or acquiring the possession of property by a person who knows (or should know) that the seller acquired it through theft, embezzlement, or some other illegal means. To constitute a crime, the receiver must know the goods were stolen at the time he receives them and have the intent to aid the thief. Depending on the value of the property received, receiving stolen property is either a misdemeanor or a felony. Fencing is a crime that involves an ongoing effort to be a middleman or distributor of illegally received goods.

Today, the professional **fence**, who earns his or her living solely by buying and reselling stolen merchandise, seems more like the "professional criminal" described by Sutherland earlier in the chapter than almost any other kind of criminal offender. Fences use stealth rather than violence, guile and knowledge rather than force or threat as they buy and sell stolen merchandise—ranging from diamonds to wheel rims.[42]

Carl Klockars examined the life and times of one successful fence who used the alias "Vincent Swaggi." Through 400 hours of listening to and observing Swaggi, Klockars found that this highly professional criminal had developed techniques that made him almost immune to prosecution. During the course of a long and profitable career in crime, Swaggi spent only four months in prison. He stayed in business, in part, because of his sophisticated knowledge of the law of stolen property. To convict someone of receiving stolen goods, the prosecution must prove that the accused was in possession of the goods and knew that they had been stolen. Swaggi had the skills to make sure that these elements could never be proved. Also helping Swaggi stay out of the law's grasp were the close working associations he maintained with society's upper classes, including influential members of the justice system. Swaggi helped them purchase stolen items at below-cost, bargain prices. He also helped authorities recover stolen goods and therefore remained in their good graces. Klockars's work strongly suggests that fences customarily cheat their thief-clients and at the same time cooperate with the law.

Sam Goodman, a fence interviewed by sociologist Darrell Steffensmeier, lived in a world similar to Vincent Swaggi's. He also purchased stolen goods from a wide variety of thieves and suppliers, including burglars, drug addicts, shoplifters, dockworkers, and truck drivers. According to Sam, to be successful, a fence must meet the following conditions:

- *Up-front cash.* All deals are cash transactions, so an adequate supply of ready cash must always be on hand.
- *Knowledge of dealing: learning the ropes.* The fence must be schooled in the knowledge of the trade, including developing a "larceny sense"; learning to "buy right" at acceptable prices; being able to "cover one's back" and not get caught; finding out how to make the right contacts; and knowing how to "wheel and deal" and how to create opportunities for profit.
- *Connections with suppliers of stolen goods.* The successful fence must be able to engage in long-term relationships with suppliers of high-value stolen goods who are relatively free of police interference. The warehouse worker who pilfers is a better supplier than the narcotics addict, who is more likely to be apprehended and talk to the police.
- *Connections with buyers.* The successful fence must have continuing access to buyers of stolen merchandise who are inaccessible to the common thief. For example, fences must make contacts with local pawnshops and other distributors of secondhand goods and be able to move their material without drawing attention from the authorities.[43]
- *Complicity with law enforcers.* The fence must work out a relationship with law enforcement officials who invariably find out about the fence's operations. Steffensmeier found that to stay in business the fence must either bribe officials with good deals on merchandise and cash payments or act as an informer who helps police recover particularly important merchandise and arrest thieves.

fence
A buyer and seller of stolen merchandise.

Confessions of a Dying Thief

In their new book *Confessions of a Dying Thief,* Darrell Steffensmeier and Jeffery Ulmer provide a close-up of the dynamics of the criminal career of Sam Goodman, a veteran thief and fence and quasi-legitimate businessman. Goodman's criminal career spanned 50 years, beginning in his midteens and ending with his death when he was in his 60s. Steffensmeier and Ulmer find that unlike amateur criminals who age out of crime, professional criminals such as Goodman, as well as skilled thieves, dealers in stolen goods, bookmakers, con artists, sex merchants, quasi-legitimate businessmen, local racketeers, and Mafiosi, frequently persist in their criminality until they are too old or feeble to do otherwise.

Their interviews with Goodman show that criminal opportunity is not merely passive: Professional criminals actively seek and create criminal opportunities that are attractive. They support their careers by gaining different types of criminal knowledge:

- *Civil knowledge*: widely accessible general knowledge that can be put to criminal use
- *Preparatory knowledge*: prior familiarity with criminal orientations, language, attitudes, and skills often gained by "hanging around" with criminal associates and observing their lifestyles
- *Technical knowledge*: more esoteric knowledge or skills that can only be obtained by access to specialized settings and experienced criminal practitioners

Goodman had a strong commitment to crime throughout the course of his life. The height of his personal commitment to crime was during the middle phase of his career when he was a "big, wide-open" fence. Nonetheless, his favorable attitudes toward crime and other criminals remained in the later, "moonlighting" phase of his career when he was less involved in crime. At that point, he also moved toward more positive attitudes toward legitimate people and associations (his employees, legitimate antique dealers). Furthermore, the moonlighting phase of his career also saw some changes in Goodman's self-definition, as reflected in this assessment in the final weeks of his life:

> *"I never cared how the cops saw me but I wanted the public to see me in a different light. Not as a guy who did time, not as a burglar, not even as a fence, but as a businessman. As a good joe. In that way I knew what I done was wrong. . . . If they saw me as a crook, that I could handle. But not a [expletive] bum. I wanted the people to respect me as me. As a businessman taking care of business in my shop." (p. 375)*

Deviants, even persistent criminals, are seldom deviant in all or even most aspects of their lives. Goodman comfortably rubbed shoulders with thieves, gamblers, and quasi-legitimate businessmen but also courted respectability and pledged allegiance to some major normative standards. However, his general lack of remorse for the crimes does not mean that he may have wished for a more legitimate, respectable life, as these deathbed comments illustrate:

> *"I do not feel sad about my life. I did what I thought I had to do at the time. But I would not wish my life on somebody else. I made that very god damn plain to your students—a life in crime can be a bitch. . . . I done wrong, pulled some very rank shit. But helped a whole lot of people, too. If somebody needed something, came into my shop, I more or less gave it away. Anyone that worked for me, I dealt with fairly. Got paid a good dollar and helped them out in little ways." (p. 373)*

The life of Sam Goodman shows that although most criminals age out of crime, many do not.

SOURCE: Darrell Steffensmeier and Jeffery Ulmer, *Confessions of a Dying Thief: Understanding Criminal Careers and Illegal Enterprise* (Chicago: Transaction-Aldine, 2005).

To learn more about the life of Sam Goodman, read the Current Issues in Crime feature above.

Fences handle a tremendous number of products—televisions, cigarettes, stereo equipment, watches, autos, and cameras.[44] In dealing their merchandise, they operate through many legitimate fronts, including art dealers, antique stores, furniture and appliance retailers, remodeling companies, salvage companies, trucking companies, and jewelry stores. When deciding what to pay the thief for goods, the fence uses a complex pricing policy: Professional thieves who steal high-priced items are usually given the highest amounts—about 30 to 50 percent of the wholesale price. For example, furs valued at $5,000 may be bought for $1,200. However, the amateur thief or drug addict who is not in a good bargaining position may receive only ten cents on the dollar.

Fencing seems to contain many elements of professional theft as described by Sutherland: Fences live by their wits, never engage in violence, depend on their skill in negotiating, maintain community standing based on connections and power, and share the sentiments and behaviors of their fellows. The only divergence between Sutherland's thief and the fence is the code of honor; it seems likely that the fence is much more willing to cooperate with authorities than most other professional criminals.

Embezzlement

© AP

● Even famous museums sometimes get caught in schemes involving stolen merchandise. In 2006, New York's Metropolitan Museum of Art was forced to return 21 looted artifacts to Italy in exchange for loans of other treasures in a deal that the Italians called a model for other museums with stolen goods in their collections. The deal, signed on February 21, 2006, calls for the Met to return the Euphronios Krater, a sixth-century BCE painted vase that is one of the Met's prized antiquities and widely regarded as one of the finest examples of its kind.

Embezzlement goes back at least to ancient Greece; the writings of Aristotle allude to theft by road commissioners and other government officials.[45] The crime of embezzlement was first codified into law by the English Parliament during the sixteenth century.[46] Until then, to be guilty of theft, a person had to take goods from the physical possession of another (trespass in the taking). In everyday commerce, store clerks, bank tellers, brokers, and merchants gain lawful possession but not legal ownership of other people's money. Embezzlement occurs when someone who is trusted with property fraudulently converts it—that is, keeps it for his or her own use or for the use of others. Most U.S. courts require a serious breach of trust before a person can be convicted of embezzlement. The mere act of moving property without the owner's consent, using it, or damaging it, is not considered embezzlement. However, using it up, selling it, pledging it, giving it away, and holding it against the owner's will are all considered embezzlement.[47]

Although it is impossible to know how many embezzlement incidents occur annually, about 12,000 people are arrested for embezzlement each year—probably an extremely small percentage of all embezzlers. The number of people arrested for embezzlement has increased in the past decade, indicating that (1) more employees are willing to steal from their employers, (2) more employers are willing to report instances of embezzlement, or (3) law enforcement officials are more willing to prosecute embezzlers. There has also been a rash of embezzlement-type crimes around the world, especially in Third World countries where poverty is all too common and the economy is poor and supported by foreign aid and loans. Government officials and businessmen who have their hands on this money are tempted to convert it for their own use, a scenario which is sure to increase the likelihood of embezzlement.[48] ✔ CHECKPOINTS

BURGLARY

Under common law the crime of **burglary** was defined as "the breaking and entering of a dwelling house of another in the nighttime with the intent to commit a felony within."[49] Burglary is considered a much more serious crime than larceny/theft because it involves entering another's home, which threatens occupants. Even though the home may be unoccupied at the time of the burglary, the potential for harm to the occupants is so significant that most state jurisdictions punish burglary as a felony.

The legal definition of burglary has undergone considerable change since its common-law origins. When first created by English judges during the late Middle Ages, laws against burglary were designed to protect people whose home might be set upon by wandering criminals. Including the phrase "breaking and entering" in the definition protected people from unwarranted intrusions; if an invited guest stole something, it would not be considered a burglary. Similarly, the requirement that the crime be committed at nighttime was added because evening was considered the time when honest people might fall prey to criminals.[50]

More recent U.S. state laws have changed the requirements of burglary, and most have discarded the necessity of forced entry. Entry through deceit (for example, by posing as a deliveryman), through threat, or through conspiracy with others such as guests or servants is deemed legally equivalent to breaking and is called "constructive breaking." Many states now protect all structures, not just dwelling houses. A majority of states have also removed the nighttime element from burglary

embezzlement
A type of larceny in which someone who is trusted with property fraudulently converts it to his or her own use or for the use of others.

burglary
Entering a home by force, threat, or deception with intent to commit a crime.

✔ CHECKPOINTS

✔ Larceny is the taking and carrying away of the constructive possessions of another.

✔ Shoplifting involves theft from a retail establishment by stealth and deception. Some shoplifters are impulsive; others are professionals who use elaborate means and devices.

✔ Passing bad checks without adequate funds is a form of larceny.

✔ Use of stolen credit cards and account numbers results in annual losses of almost $2 billion in the United States.

✔ Auto theft adds up to more than $8 billion in losses each year.

✔ Embezzlement occurs when trusted persons or employees take someone else's property for their own use.

definitions. States commonly enact laws creating different degrees of burglary. The more serious, heavily punished crimes involve nighttime forced entry into the home; the least serious involve daytime entry into a nonresidential structure by an unarmed offender. Several legal gradations may be found between these extremes.

The Nature and Extent of Burglary

The FBI's definition of burglary is not restricted to burglary from a person's home; it includes any unlawful entry of a structure to commit a theft or felony. Burglary is further categorized into three subclasses: forcible entry, unlawful entry where no force is used, and attempted forcible entry.

According to the UCR, more than 2 million burglaries occurred in 2005; the burglary rate has dropped by more than 35 percent since 1995. As in the past, burglars targeted homes more often than nonresidential structures. In 2005, most burglaries were of residences, while about one-third were of nonresidential structures. Most residential burglaries occur during the day, from 6:00 AM to 6:00 PM, when few people are home, while nonresidential structures are targeted in the evening, when businesses and shops are closed.

The average dollar loss per burglary offense is not more than $1,600. Burglaries cost victims more than $3 billion per year.

The NCVS reports that 3.4 million residential burglaries were either attempted or completed in 2004. Similar to the UCR, the NCVS indicates that the number of burglaries has declined significantly, dropping from almost 6 million in 1992.[51] According to the NCVS, those most likely to be burglarized are relatively poor Hispanic and African American families (annual income under $7,500). Owner-occupied and single-family residences had lower burglary rates than renter-occupied and multiple-family dwellings.

Types of Burglaries

Because it involves planning, risk, and skill, burglary has long been associated with professional thieves who carefully learn their craft.[52] Burglars must master the skills of their trade, learning to spot environmental cues that nonprofessionals fail to notice.[53] In an important book called *Burglars on the Job*, Richard Wright and Scott Decker describe the working conditions of active burglars (see Exhibit 11.4).[54] Most are motivated by the need for cash in order to get high; they want to enjoy the good life, "keep the party going," without having to work. They approach their job in a rational, businesslike fashion; still, their lives are controlled by their culture and environment. Unskilled and uneducated, urban burglars choose crime because they have few conventional opportunities for success.[55] Experienced burglars are more willing to travel to find rich targets. They have access to transportation, which enables them to select a wider variety of targets than younger, less experienced thieves.[56]

Residential Burglary Experienced burglars learn to avoid areas of the city in which most residents are renters and not home owners, reasoning that renters are less likely to be suitable targets than the homes of more affluent owners.[57] Most do not like to travel far from their residence, choosing neighborhoods with single-family homes close by.[58]

Francis Hoheimer, an experienced professional burglar, has described how he learned the "craft of burglary" from a fellow inmate, Oklahoma Smith, when the two were serving time in the Illinois State Penitentiary. Smith recommended the following:

> Never wear deodorant or shaving lotion; the strange scent might wake someone up. The more people there are in a house, the safer you are. If someone hears you moving around, they will think it's someone else. . . . If they call, answer in a muffled sleepy voice. . . . Never be afraid of dogs, they can sense fear. Most dogs are friendly, snap your finger, they come right to you.[59]

Despite his elaborate preparations, Hoheimer spent many years in confinement.

Exhibit 11.4
Burglars on the Job

According to active burglars:

- Most avoid occupied residences, considering them high-risk targets.
- Most are not deterred by alarms and elaborate locks; in fact, these devices tell them there is something inside worth stealing.
- Some call occupants from a pay phone, and if the phone is still ringing when they arrive, they know no one is home.
- Once entering a residence, anxiety turns to calm as they first turn to the master bedroom for money and drugs. They also search kitchens believing that some people keep money in the mayonnaise jar!
- Most work in groups, one serving as a lookout while the other(s) ransacks the place.
- Some dispose of goods through a professional fence; others try to pawn the goods. Some exchange goods for drugs; some sell them to friends and relatives; and a few keep the stolen items for themselves, especially guns and jewelry.
- Many approach a target masquerading as workmen such as carpenters or house painters.
- Some stake out residences to learn occupants' routine.
- Tipsters help them select attractive targets.
- Drug dealers are favored targets because they tend to have a lot of cash and drugs, and victims are not going to call police!
- Targets are often acquaintances.

SOURCE: Richard Wright and Scott Decker, *Burglars on the Job: Streetlife and Residential Break-Ins* (Boston: Northeastern University Press, 1994).

Burglars must "master" the skills of their "trade," learning to spot environmental cues "nonprofessionals" fail to notice.[60] They must learn which targets contain valuables worth stealing and which are most likely to prove to be dry holes. Research shows that burglary rates for student-occupied apartments are actually much lower than the rate for other residences in the same neighborhoods; burglars appear to have learned that student's apartments are ones to avoid![61] Burglars must learn to evaluate the value of the goods they take: what has good resale value and what should be avoided because the price is in decline. Obsolete audio equipment cannot be easily fenced; iPods have greater value.[62]

Commercial Burglars Some burglars prefer to victimize commercial property rather than private homes, and a growing amount of research indicates that business premises have a higher risk of experiencing crimes such as burglary than do households.[63]

Of all business establishments, retail stores are the favorite target. Because they display merchandise, burglars know exactly what to look for, where it can be found, and, because the prices are also displayed, how much they can hope to gain from resale to a fence. Burglars can legitimately enter a retail store during business hours and see what the store contains and where it is stored; they can also check for security alarms and devices. Commercial burglars perceive retail establishments as ready sources of merchandise that can be easily sold.[64]

Other commercial establishments, such as service centers, warehouses, and factories, are less attractive targets because gaining legitimate access to plan the theft is more difficult. The burglar must use guile to scope out these places, perhaps posing as a delivery person. In addition, the merchandise is more likely to be used or more difficult to fence at a premium price. If burglars choose to attack factories, warehouses, or service centers, the most vulnerable properties are those located far from major roads and away from pedestrian traffic. In remote areas, burglar alarms are less effective because it takes police longer to respond than on more heavily patrolled thoroughfares, and an alarm is less likely to be heard by a pedestrian who would be able to call for help. Even in the most remote areas, however, burglars are wary of alarms, though their presence suggests that there is something worth stealing.

CONNECTIONS

According to the rational choice approach discussed in Chapter 4, burglars make rational and calculating decisions before committing crimes. If circumstances and culture dictate their activities, their decisions must be considered a matter of choice.

Repeat Burglars Whether residential or commercial, some burglars strike the same victim more than once.[65] Graham Farrell, Coretta Phillips, and Ken Pease suggest some reasons burglars might want to hit the same target more than once:

- It takes less effort to burgle a home or apartment known to be a suitable target than an unknown or unsuitable one.
- The burglar is already aware of the target's layout.
- The ease of entry of the target has probably not changed, and escape routes are known.
- Lack of protective measures and the absence of nosy neighbors, which made the first burglary a success, have probably not changed.
- Goods have been observed that could not be taken out the first time.[66]

It is also likely that since burgled items are both indispensable (such as televisions and DVDs) and covered by insurance, burglars can safely assume they will be quickly replaced, encouraging a second round of burglary![67]

The repeat burglary phenomenon should mean that homes in close proximity to a burgled dwelling should have an increased burglary risk, especially if they are quite similar in structure to the initial target. When this hypothesis was recently tested by Michael Townsley and his colleagues in Brisbane, Australia, they found the opposite to be true: Little or no diversity in the physical construction and general appearance of dwellings serves to restrict the extent of repeat victimization. Townsley reasons that housing diversity allows offenders a choice of targets, and favored targets will be "revisited" by burglars. If houses are identical, there is no motive for an offender to favor one property over another, and therefore the risk of repeat victimization is limited.[68]

Careers in Burglary

Some criminals make burglary their career and continually develop new specialized skills. Neal Shover has studied the careers of professional burglars and uncovered the existence of a particularly successful type—the "good burglar."[69] Characteristics of the good burglar include technical competence, personal integrity, specialization in burglary, financial success, and the ability to avoid prison sentences. Shover found that to receive recognition as good burglars, novices must develop four key requirements of the trade:

- They must learn the many skills needed to commit lucrative burglaries. These skills may include gaining entry into homes and apartment houses; selecting targets with high potential payoffs; choosing items with a high resale value; opening safes properly without damaging their contents; and using the proper equipment, including cutting torches, electric saws, explosives, and metal bars.
- The good burglar must be able to team up to form a criminal gang. Choosing trustworthy companions is essential if the obstacles to completing a successful job—police, alarms, secure safes—are to be overcome.
- The good burglar must have inside information. Without knowledge of what awaits them inside, burglars can spend a tremendous amount of time and effort on empty safes and jewelry boxes.
- The good burglar must cultivate fences or buyers for stolen wares. Once the burglar gains access to people who buy and sell stolen goods, he or she must also learn how to successfully sell these goods for a reasonable profit.

CONNECTIONS

Shover finds that the process of becoming a professional burglar is similar to the process described in Sutherland's theory of differential association, discussed in Chapter 7.

Evidence of these skills was discovered in a recent study of more than 200 career burglars in Australia. Burglars reported that they had developed a number of relatively safe methods for disposing of their loot. Some traded stolen goods directly for drugs; others used fences, legitimate businesses, pawnbrokers, and secondhand dealers as trading partners. Surprisingly, many sold their illegal gains to family or friends. Burglars report that disposing of stolen goods was actually low risk and more efficient than expected. One reason was that in many cases fences and shady businesspeople put in a request for particular items and the ready-made market allowed the stolen merchandise to be disposed of quickly, often in less than one hour. Though the typical markdown was about 67 to 75 percent of the price of the goods, most burglars reported they could still earn a good living, averaging AUS$2,000 per week (about $1,000 in U.S. dollars). Those who benefit most from these transactions are the receivers of stolen property, who make considerable profits and are unlikely to get caught.[70]

According to Shover, an older burglar teaches the novice how to handle such requirements of the trade as dealing with defense attorneys, bail bond agents, and other agents of the justice system. Apprentices must be known to have the appropriate character before they are accepted for training. Usually the opportunity to learn burglary comes as a reward for being a highly respected juvenile gang member; from knowing someone in the neighborhood who has made a living at burglary; or, more often, from having built a reputation for being solid while serving time in prison. Consequently, the opportunity to become a good burglar is not open to everyone.

The "good burglar" concept is supported by the interviews Paul Cromwell, James Olson, and D'Aunn Wester Avary conducted with 30 active burglars in Texas. They found that burglars go through stages of career development, beginning as young novices who learn the trade from older, more experienced burglars—frequently, siblings or relatives. Novices continue to get this tutoring as long as they can develop their own markets (fences) for stolen goods. After their education is over, novices enter the journeyman stage, characterized by forays in search of lucrative targets and by careful planning. At this point they develop reputations as experienced, reliable criminals. They become professional burglars when they have developed advanced skills and organizational abilities that give them the highest esteem among their peers.[71] Cromwell, Olson, and Avary also found that many burglars had serious drug habits and that their criminal activity was, in part, aimed at supporting their substance abuse.

The Female Burglar Most people arrested for burglary are males, so it is not surprising that burglary is considered a "male profession." Because little is known about the female burglar, criminologists Scott Decker, Richard Wright, Allison Redfern Rooney, and Dietrich Smith interviewed 18 females, ranging in age from 15 to 51, who were active residential burglars. For comparison, 87 male burglars were also interviewed.[72]

Decker and his associates found that female burglars had offending patterns quite similar to those of males. In addition to burglary, both groups engaged in other thefts, such as shoplifting and assault. The major difference was that male burglars also stole cars, but females shunned this form of larceny.

Another difference was that whereas females always worked with a partner, about 39 percent of the males said they seldom worked with others. Males also began their offending careers at an earlier age than females and are more frequent offenders. Because the males started earlier and commit more crimes, it is not surprising that males had a much greater chance of getting caught and doing time (26 percent) than females (6 percent).

Decker and his associates found that the female burglars could be divided into two groups: "accomplices" and "partners." Accomplices committed burglaries because they were caught up in circumstances beyond their control. They felt compelled or pressured to commit crimes because of a relationship with another, more dominant person, typically a boyfriend or husband. Accomplices got into crime because they lacked legitimate employment, were drug dependent, or had alcohol problems. Accomplices exercised little control over their crimes and relied on others for planning and tactics. They commonly acted as lookouts or drivers.

In contrast, partners, who made up two-thirds of the sample, planned and carried out the crimes because they enjoyed both the reward and the excitement of burglary. In planning their crimes, partners displayed many characteristics of the rational criminal. They helped spot targets and planned entries. ✔ CHECKPOINTS

✔ CHECKPOINTS

✔ Burglary is the breaking and entering of a structure in order to commit a felony, typically theft.

✔ Some burglars specialize in residential theft; others steal from commercial establishments.

✔ Some burglars repeatedly attack the same target, mainly because they are familiar with the layout and protective measures.

✔ Professional burglars have careers in which they learn the tricks of the trade from older, more experienced pros.

ARSON

Arson is the willful, malicious burning of a home, public building, vehicle, or commercial building. The FBI reports that about 65,000 known arsons were recorded in 2005, with an average cost of about $12,000 each. Arson attacks are not unique to the United States. According to an English group that coordinates

arson
The willful, malicious burning of a home, building, or vehicle.

● Arson can have a devastating cost. More than 10,000 firefighters were needed to put out the huge Southern California wildfire set by arsonists in October 2003.

© AP

a national campaign to reduce arson, the Arson Prevention Bureau, every week in England:

- 2,100 arson attacks occur.
- 1 or 2 people die in arson attacks.
- 55 people are injured.
- 4 churches or places of worship are damaged or destroyed.
- 20 schools are damaged or destroyed.
- $60 million of damage and costs result from arson.[73]

There are several motives for arson. Adult arsonists may be motivated by severe emotional turmoil or a disturbed personality.[74] Research on the background characteristics of juvenile fire setters shows that their acts are often associated with antisocial behavior and psychopathology.[75] These findings support the claim that arson should be viewed as a mental health problem, not a criminal act, and should be treated with counseling and other therapeutic measures rather than with severe punishments.[76]

During the past decade, hundreds of jurisdictions across the nation have established programs to address the growing concern about juvenile fire setting. Housed primarily within the fire service, these programs are designed to identify, evaluate, and treat juvenile fire setters to prevent the recurrence of fire-setting behaviors. A promising approach is the FireSafe Families effort in Rhode Island, which combines a training curriculum for fire safety educators, a training program for community professionals to identify potential behavior that may lead to arson, and a cognitive behavioral therapy (CBT) program to treat not only children who are at risk to become juvenile fire starters but also their families.[77]

Not all fires are the work of emotionally disturbed youth; some are set by professionals who engage in arson for profit. People who want to collect insurance money but are afraid or unable to set the fires themselves hire professional arsonists who know how to set fires yet make the cause seem accidental (like an electrical short). Another form is arson fraud, which involves a business owner burning his or her property, or hiring someone to do it, to escape financial problems. Over the years, investigators have found that businesspeople are willing to become involved in arson to collect fire insurance or for these additional reasons:

- To obtain money during a period of financial crisis
- To get rid of outdated or slow-moving inventory

- To destroy outmoded machines and technology
- To pay off legal and illegal debts
- To relocate or remodel a business—for example, a theme restaurant that has not been accepted by customers
- To take advantage of government funds available for redevelopment
- To apply for government building money, pocket it without making repairs, and then claim that fire destroyed the "rehabilitated" building
- To plan bankruptcies to eliminate debts after the merchandise supposedly destroyed was secretly sold before the fire
- To eliminate business competition by burning out rivals
- To employ extortion schemes that demand that victims pay up or the rest of their holdings will be burned
- To solve labor–management problems (this type of arson may be committed by a disgruntled employee)
- To conceal another crime, such as embezzlement

THINKING Like a Criminologist

To reduce the risk of loss during the Christmas holidays, the Security Industry Association (SIA) suggests that you do not display presents where they can be seen from a window or doorway, and put gifts in a safe place before leaving the house or taking a trip. Closing drapes or blinds during even short trips away from home is a good habit.

It is important to trick burglars into believing someone is home. If you are away, the SIA suggests having lights on timers, stopping mail and newspaper delivery, and arranging, if possible, to have the walkways shoveled and have a car parked in the driveway as additional security measures. Other suggestions include installing a good-quality deadbolt lock with at least a one-inch throat into a solid wood or steel door that fits securely into a sturdy frame, keeping doors locked, putting a chain-link fence around a yard, getting a dog, and having police inspect the house for security. Also, buy a weighted safe deposit box to secure items that cannot be replaced, and engrave your driver's license number and state of residence on your property to give police a way to contact you if your home is burglarized and the stolen items are later found.

Con artists may take advantage of people's generosity during the holidays by making appeals for nonexistent charities. The SIA suggests that you always ask for identification from solicitors.

As a criminologist, can you come up with any new ideas that the Security Industry Association failed to cover?

Summary

- Economic crimes are designed to reap financial rewards for the offender.
- Opportunistic amateurs commit the majority of economic crimes.
- Economic crime has also attracted professional criminals. Professionals earn most of their income from crime, view themselves as criminals, and possess skills that aid them in their law-breaking behavior. An example of the professional criminal is the fence who buys and sells stolen merchandise.
- Common theft offenses include larceny, fraud, and embezzlement. These are common-law crimes, originally defined by English judges.
- Larceny involves taking the legal possessions of another. Petty larceny is typically theft of amounts under $100; grand larceny usually refers to amounts over $100. Larceny is the most common theft crime and involves such activities as shoplifting, passing bad checks, stealing, or illegally using credit cards.
- Some shoplifters are amateurs who steal on the spur of the moment, but others are professionals who use sophisticated techniques that help them avoid detection.
- The crime of false pretenses, or fraud, is similar to larceny in that it involves the theft of goods or money; it differs in that the criminal tricks victims into voluntarily giving up their possessions.

- Embezzlement involves people taking something that was temporarily entrusted to them, such as bank tellers taking money out of the cash drawer and keeping it for themselves.
- Auto theft usually involves amateur joyriders who "borrow" cars for short-term transportation and professional auto thieves who steal cars to sell the parts that are highly valuable.
- Burglary, a more serious theft offense, was defined in common law as the "breaking and entering of a dwelling house of another in the nighttime with the intent to commit a felony within."
- This definition has also evolved over time. Today most states have modified their definitions of burglary to include theft from any structure at any time of day.
- Because burglary involves planning and risk, it attracts professional thieves. The most competent have technical skill and personal integrity, specialize in burglary, are financially successful, and avoid prison sentences.
- Professional burglars size up the value of a particular crime and balance it against the perceived risks. Many have undergone training in the company of older, more experienced burglars. They have learned the techniques to make them "good burglars."
- Arson is another serious property crime. Although most arsonists are teenage vandals, others are professional arsonists who specialize in burning commercial buildings for profit.

Take a Post-Test. Visit www.thomsonedu.com/criminaljustice/siegel and take the chapter Post-Test to monitor your progress and identify areas for further improvement. In addition to discovering what you've mastered, you'll learn which concepts need your added attention and get specific page references that direct you to the places in the text where you can find more information on them.

Key Terms

occasional criminals 259
situational inducement 259
professional criminals 260
larceny 260
constructive possession 261
petit (petty) larceny 261
grand larceny 261
shoplifting 262
booster 263
snitch 263
merchant privilege laws 263
target removal strategy 264
target hardening strategy 264
naive check forgers 267
systematic forgers 267
false pretenses (fraud) 267
confidence game 268
fence 269
embezzlement 271
burglary 271
arson 275

Critical Thinking Questions

1. Differentiate between an occasional and a professional criminal. Which one would be more likely to resort to violence?

2. What crime occurs when a person who owns an antique store sells a client an "original" Tiffany lamp that she knows is a fake? Would it still be a crime if the seller was not aware that the lamp was a copy? Should antique dealers have a duty to determine the authenticity of the products they sell?

3. What is the difference between a booster and a snitch? If caught, should they receive different punishments? What about naive and systematic check forgers?

4. What are the characteristics of the "good burglar"? Can you compare them to any other professionals?

Enterprise Crime: White-Collar Crime, Cyber Crime, and Organized Crime

CHAPTER 12

© AP

ON OCTOBER 15, 2002, DR. SAMUEL WAKSAL, THE FOUNDER OF THE BIOTECH COMPANY IMCLONE SYSTEMS, pleaded guilty to charges of securities fraud, perjury, and obstruction of justice. The charges were a result of an investigation into the dumping of ImClone stock by Waksal and his friends and family shortly before the company announced that its application for approval of a cancer drug had been rejected by the Food and Drug Administration. "I have made terrible mistakes," Waksal, 55, told reporters after his courtroom appearance. "I deeply regret what has happened. I was wrong."[1] Ironically, in June 2003, clinical trials of ImClone's drug Erbitux proved positive, and the stock boomed at about the same time Waksal was sentenced to seven years in prison.

Another player in the ImClone case was domestic guru Martha Stewart, who dumped her shares just before the negative announcement. Stewart's suspicious stock sales quickly made her the target of a government probe. She was never actually accused of **insider trading**–the more serious charge of selling the ImClone stock based on privileged knowledge not available to the general public. Instead, Stewart was convicted of lying to the government when she claimed that she had a prior agreement with her stockbroker to sell ImClone stock at a certain price. Stewart was also convicted of altering a telephone log about a call from the broker before changing it back. People wondered how someone as wealthy and savvy as Stewart could get herself sent to prison for involvement in a legally questionable scheme. Stewart was released on March 4, 2005, from a federal women's prison in Alderson, West Virginia, after serving five months and returned to her estate in Katonah, New York, where she finished out the rest of her sentence–five months under house arrest.

CHAPTER OBJECTIVES

1. Understand the concept of enterprise crime.
2. Be familiar with the various types of white-collar crime.
3. Distinguish between various types of corporate crime.
4. Recognize the extent and various causes of white-collar crime.
5. Be able to discuss the different approaches to combating white-collar crime.
6. Recognize the forms taken by cyber crime.
7. Describe the methods being used to control cyber crime.
8. List the different types of illegal behavior engaged in by organized crime figures.
9. Describe the evolution of organized crime.
10. Explain how the government is fighting organized crime.

Take a Pre-Test. Visit www.thomsonedu.com/criminaljustice/siegel and take a Pre-Test to determine what you already know and identify the areas where you'll need to focus your study. The program will direct you to specific pages within the text where you can find further information on the correct answers to the questions you've missed.

It has become routine in our free enterprise, global economy for people such as Waksal and Stewart to use illegal tactics to make profit. We refer here to these crimes of the marketplace as **enterprise crime**. In this chapter, crimes of illicit entrepreneurship fall into three distinct categories: white-collar crime, cyber crime, and organized crime. **White-collar crime** involves illegal activities of people and institutions whose acknowledged purpose is profit through legitimate business transactions. **Cyber crime** involves people using the instruments of modern technology for criminal purposes. **Organized crime** involves illegal activities of people and organizations whose acknowledged purpose is profit through illegitimate business enterprise.

ENTERPRISE CRIME

insider trading
Illegal buying of stock in a company based on information provided by someone who has a fiduciary interest in the company, such as an employee or an attorney or accountant retained by the firm. Federal laws and the rules of the Securities and Exchange Commission require that all profits from such trading be returned and provide for both fines and a prison sentence.

enterprise crime
Use of illegal tactics to gain profit in the marketplace. Enterprise crimes can involve both the violation of law in the course of an otherwise legitimate occupation or the sale and distribution of illegal commodities.

White-collar crime, cyber crime, and organized crime are linked here because in each category offenders twist the legal rules of commercial enterprise for criminal purposes. The three types of crime often overlap. Organized criminals may use the Internet to conduct fraud schemes and then seek legitimate enterprises to launder money, diversify their sources of income, increase their power and influence, and gain and enhance respectability.[2] Otherwise legitimate businesspeople may turn to organized criminals to help them with economic problems (such as breaking up a strike or dumping hazardous waste products), stifle or threaten competition, and increase their influence.[3] Whereas some corporate executives cheat to improve their company's position in the business world, others are motivated purely for personal gain, acting more like organized criminals than indiscreet businesspeople.[4]

Enterprise crimes taint and corrupt the free market system. They mix and match illegal and legal methods and legal and illegal products in all phases of commercial activity. Organized criminals often use illegal marketing techniques (including threats, extortion, and smuggling) to distribute otherwise legal products and services (lending money, conducting union activities, selling securities). They also engage in the distribution of products and services, such as drugs, sex, gambling, and prostitution, that have been outlawed. White-collar criminals use illegal business practices (embezzlement, price fixing, bribery, and so on) to merchandise what are normally legitimate commercial products (securities, medical care, online auctions, for example).[5] ✔ CHECKPOINTS

WHITE-COLLAR CRIME

In the late 1930s, the distinguished criminologist Edwin Sutherland first used the phrase "white-collar crime" to describe the criminal activities of the rich and powerful. He defined white-collar crime as "a crime committed by a person of respectability and high social status in the course of his occupation."[6] As Sutherland saw it, white-collar crime involved conspiracies by members of the wealthy classes to use their positions in commerce and industry for personal gain without regard to the law. Most often these actions were handled by civil courts because injured parties were more concerned with recovering their losses than with seeing the offenders punished criminally. Consequently, Sutherland believed that the great majority of white-collar criminals avoided detection and those who were caught generally avoided punishment.[7]

Sutherland focused on corporate criminality and crimes committed by wealthy industrialists. Contemporary criminologists have continued to study corporate crimes committed by unscrupulous executives who craft elaborate criminal conspiracies designed to improve market share or simply to illegally siphon off corporate profits into their own pockets.[8] Contemporary definitions of white-collar crime are typically much broader than what Sutherland first envisioned. White-collar crime is now defined as any business-related act that uses deceit, deception, or dishonesty to carry out criminal enterprise. Included within the scope of white-collar crime are diverse acts that include income tax evasion, employee theft, soliciting bribes, accepting kickbacks, and embezzlement. Nor do criminologists restrict the definition to the wealthy and powerful; members of all social classes may engage in white-collar crimes.

Estimating the extent and influence of white-collar crime on victims is difficult because victims are often reluctant to report the crime to police, believing that nothing can be done and that getting further involved is pointless.[9] Experts place its total monetary value in the hundreds of billions of dollars, far outstripping the expense of any other type of crime. The National White Collar Crime Center, a nonprofit institute set up to provide a nationwide support system for agencies involved in the prevention, investigation, and prosecution of economic and high-tech crimes, conducts national surveys to track the incidence of white-collar victimization.[10] The most recent national survey (2005) found that:

- Nearly half of all households and more than one-third (36%) of individuals reported experiencing at least one form of white-collar victimizations within the previous year.
- About two-thirds of all people surveyed reported experiencing at least one form of white-collar crime victimization within their lifetimes.
- The most common white-collar crime victimizations were a result of product pricing fraud, credit card fraud, unnecessary object repairs, and being directly affected by national corporate scandals (such as Enron and WorldCom).
- Most crimes are not reported to police or legal authorities.
- The general public views white-collar crime seriously, calling for increased governmental resource allocations to combat these crimes.[11]

Figure 12.1 illustrates the percentage of individuals who experienced white-collar crimes during a single year.

✔ CHECKPOINTS

✔ Enterprise crimes involve illicit entrepreneurship and commerce.

✔ White-collar crime involves the illegal distribution of legal material.

✔ Cyber crime involves using technology to commit crime.

✔ Organized crime involves the illegal distribution of illegal material.

✔ White-collar crime and organized crime are linked because they involve entrepreneurship.

✔ Losses from enterprise crime may far outstrip those of any other type of crime.

✔ Enterprise crimes can cause deaths.

white-collar crime
Any business-related act that uses deceit, deception, or dishonesty to carry out criminal enterprise.

cyber crime
Use of the instruments of modern technology for criminal purposes.

organized crime
Illegal activities of people and organizations whose acknowledged purpose is profit through illegitimate business enterprise.

Figure 12.1
Individual White-Collar Crime Victimization Trends (12 months)
SOURCE: National White Collar Crime Center, 2006.

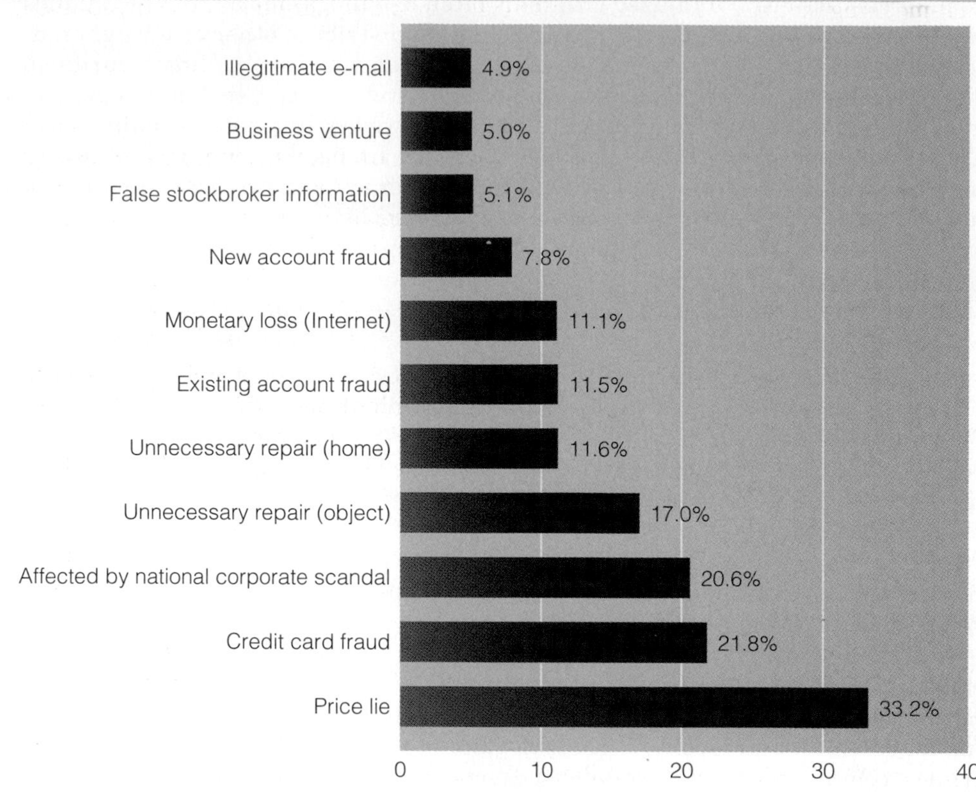

COMPONENTS OF WHITE-COLLAR CRIME

White-collar crime today represents a range of behaviors involving individuals acting alone and within the context of a business structure. The victims of white-collar crime can be the general public, the organization that employs the offender, or a competing organization. Numerous attempts have been made to create subcategories or typologies of white-collar criminality.[12] This book adapts a typology created by criminologist Mark Moore to organize the analysis of white-collar crime.[13] Moore's typology contains seven elements, ranging from an individual using a business enterprise to commit theft-related crimes, to an individual using his or her place within a business enterprise for illegal gain, to business enterprises collectively engaging in illegitimate activity.

Stings and Swindles

When oil prices skyrocketed, one enterprising swindler, Linda Stetler of Vision Oil Company in Albany, Kentucky, lured investors into risky schemes by claiming that God (not geologists) guided her company's oil exploration: "God gave me a vision of three oil wells," she said in a letter sent to potential investors. State regulators found that Stetler and her company engaged in illegal practices, including inadequate disclosures of risks and selling to unsuitable investors; Vision Oil and its agents were fined by the state and ordered to pay restitution to investors.[14]

It is estimated that fake religious organizations swindle thousands of people out of $100 million per year.[15] They are not alone. A **swindle**, or **sting**, involves people using their institutional or business position to trick others out of their money. Offenses in this category range from fraud involving the door-to-door sale of faulty merchandise to passing millions of dollars in counterfeit stock certificates to an established brokerage firm. Swindlers have little shame when defrauding people out of their money; they often target the elderly, sick, and infirm. In the aftermath of Hurricane Katrina, in 2005, the FBI felt it necessary to issue warnings about swindlers who used the tragedy to solicit relief funds from charitable and

CONNECTIONS

In Chapter 11 fraud was described as a common theft offense. Although common-law fraud and white-collar fraud are similar, common fraud involves a person using illegal methods to bilk another out of money, while white-collar fraud involves a person using his or her institutional or business position to reach the same goal. Common-law fraud is typically a short-term transaction, whereas white-collar fraud involves a long-term criminal conspiracy. Although the ends are similar, the means are somewhat different.

swindle (sting)
A white-collar crime in which people use their institutional or business position to trick others out of their money.

well-meaning victims.[16] If caught, white-collar swindlers are usually charged with common-law crimes such as embezzlement or fraud.

Chiseling

The second category of white-collar crime, **chiseling**, involves regularly cheating an organization, its consumers, or both. Chiselers may be individuals who want to make quick profits in their own businesses, or employees of large organizations who decide to cheat on obligations to their own company or its clients by doing something contrary to either the law or company policy. Chiseling can involve charging for bogus auto repairs, cheating customers on home repairs, or short-weighting (intentionally tampering with the accuracy of scales used to weigh products) in supermarkets or dairies. In 2005 the federal government announced the success of "Operation Bullpen," aimed at stopping chiseling in the sports memorabilia industry. Convicted in the investigation was the largest seller in the world of signed celebrity photos: Truly Unique Collectibles, who through their website, sold millions of dollars in forged and fraudulent posters, photos, and items. Their celebrity-signed pictures and posters were obtained by "runners," people who happen to catch a celebrity at an event and obtain a signed picture there. Though runners may have obtained one or two signatures from famous athletes, they simply forged many more, claiming all were genuine. The investigation found that the overwhelming number of celebrity-signed photographs and posters being sold throughout the world are sold under this pretense; they are almost all forged.[17]

Professional Chiseling It is not uncommon for professionals to use their positions to chisel clients. Pharmacists have been known to alter prescriptions or substitute low-cost generic drugs for more expensive name brands.[18] In one case that made national headlines in 2001, Kansas City pharmacist Robert R. Courtney was charged with fraud when it was discovered that he had been selling diluted mixtures of the cancer medications Taxol, Gemzar, Paraplatin, and Platinol, which are used to treat a variety of illnesses including pancreatic and lung cancer, advanced ovarian and breast cancer, and AIDS-related Kaposi's sarcoma. In one instance, Courtney provided a doctor with only 450 milligrams of Gemzar for a prescription that called for 1,900 mg, a transaction that netted him a profit of $779.[19] After he pleaded guilty, Courtney told authorities that his drug dilution activities were not limited to the conduct he admitted to at the time of his guilty plea. His criminal activities had actually begun in 1992 or even earlier, affected the patients of 400 doctors, involved 98,000 prescriptions, and harmed approximately 4,200 patients.[20] There is no telling how many people died or suffered serious medical complications because of Courtney's criminal conduct.

Securities Fraud A great deal of chiseling takes place on the commodities and stock markets, where individuals engage in deceptive practices that are prohibited by federal law.[21] Some investment counselors and insurance agents will use their positions to cheat individual clients by misleading them on the quality of their investments; financial organizations cheat their clients by promoting risky investments as being iron-clad safe. For example, stockbrokers violate accepted practices when they engage in **churning** the client's account by repeated, excessive, and unnecessary buying and selling of stock.[22] Other broker fraud includes **front running**, in which brokers place personal orders ahead of a customer's large order to profit from the market effects of the trade, and **bucketing**, which is skimming customer trading profits by falsifying trade information.[23]

Securities chiseling can also involve using one's position of trust to profit from inside business information, referred to as insider trading (mentioned earlier). The information can then be used to buy and sell securities, giving the trader an unfair advantage over the general public, which lacks this inside information.

Insider trading violations can occur in a variety of situations. As originally conceived, it was illegal for corporate employees with direct knowledge of market-sensitive information to use that information for their own benefit—for example, by buying stock in a company that they learn will be taken over by the larger

chiseling
Using illegal means to cheat an organization, its consumers, or both, on a regular basis.

churning
Repeated, excessive, and unnecessary buying and selling of a client's stock.

front running
Placing broker's personal orders ahead of a customer's large order to profit from the market effects of the trade.

bucketing
Skimming customer trading profits by falsifying trade information.

concern for which they work. In recent years, the definition of insider trading has been expanded by federal courts to include employees of financial institutions, such as law or banking firms, who misappropriate confidential information on pending corporate actions to purchase stock or give the information to a third party so that party may buy shares in the company. Courts have ruled that such actions are deceptive and violate security trading codes.[24]

Individual Exploitation of Institutional Position

In the oil-rich nation of Azerbaijan, prostitution is legal, but it is a crime to spread STDs. Police officers frequently threaten to take prostitutes to a high-security hospital to have them examined unless they pay them large sums of money in bribes. The hospital's "high-security" status means that it is guarded by security forces, creating an intimidating and frightening atmosphere for the women and making it easier for police to keep them there by force. To avoid complaints, police coerce prostitutes into signing a document stating that they came of their own will![25]

Both abroad and in the United States, **exploitation** is common. Some individuals exploit their power or position in organizations to take advantage of others who have an interest in how that power is used. A fire inspector who demands that the owner of a restaurant pay him to be granted an operating license is abusing his institutional position.

In most cases, this type of offense occurs when the victim has a clear right to expect a service, and the offender threatens to withhold the service unless an additional payment or bribe is forthcoming. The Azerbaijani prostitutes are being exploited by police because they are being forced to pay for a service they neither want nor need.

Exploitation can also occur in private industry. In this instance, a company employee might refuse to award a contract to a supplier unless the supplier gives them a "piece of the action." Purchasing agents in large companies often demand payment for awarding contracts to suppliers and distributors. Managing agents in some of New York City's most luxurious buildings have been convicted on charges that they routinely extorted millions of dollars from maintenance contractors and building suppliers in order to award them contracts that they deserved on the merits of their service.[26]

Influence Peddling and Bribery

Sometimes individuals holding important institutional positions sell power, influence, and information to outsiders who have an interest in influencing or predicting the activities of the institution. Offenses within this category include government employees taking kickbacks from contractors in return for awarding contracts they could not have won on merit, or outsiders bribing government officials, such as those in the Securities and Exchange Commission, who might sell information about future government activities. Political leaders have been convicted of accepting bribes to rig elections that enable their party to control state politics.[27]

One major difference distinguishes **influence peddling** from the previously discussed exploitation. While exploiters force victims to pay for services *to which they have a clear right*, influence peddlers take bribes in order to use their positions to grant favors and/or sell information to which their co-conspirators are not entitled. The victims in crimes of institutional exploitation are the people who are threatened and forced to pay, whereas the victims in crimes of influence peddling are the organization compromised by its employees for their own interests and the people who pay for those organizations and expect them to be run in a fair and legal manner.

Influence Peddling in Government It is unfortunately common for government workers and office holders to engage in official corruption, a circumstance that is particularly disturbing because society expects a higher standard of moral integrity from people empowered to uphold the law and judge their fellow citizens. In 2005, Rep. Randy "Duke" Cunningham (R-Calif.) resigned from Congress after confessing to accepting $2.4 million in bribes, including a Rolls-Royce, a yacht, and a 19th-century Louis-Philippe commode. As he entered his guilty plea at a federal

exploitation (of victims)
Forcing victims to pay for services to which they have a clear right.

influence peddling
Using one's institutional position to grant favors and sell information to which one's co-conspirators are not entitled.

courthouse in San Diego, he proclaimed: "In my life, I have known great joy and great sorrow. And now I know great shame."[28]

The Cunningham case is by no means unique. On April 17, 2006, former Governor George Ryan of Illinois was convicted of steering government contracts to people who were willing to give him kickbacks and bribes. The prosecution said Mr. Ryan and his family were given fancy vacations, money, and other items worth at least $167,000, and in return he offered special political favors and state business in the dozen years that he served in the state's top role.[29] On January 3, 2006, influential Washington lobbyist Jack Abramoff pleaded guilty to three felony counts: conspiracy, fraud, and tax evasion for bribing public officials, including Bob Ney, a Republican congressman from Ohio. Caught up in the Abramoff scandal was House Majority Leader Tom DeLay, who resigned his seat in Congress.[30]

● Tom DeLay was a major player in the House of Representatives until he was forced out of politics by his involvement with a bribery scandal involving influential Washington lobbyist Jack Abramoff. Before he decided not to run for reelection, DeLay was thought to be a target of a U.S. Department of Justice investigation focusing on Abramoff, who allegedly provided DeLay with trips, gifts, and political donations in exchange for favors to Abramoff's lobbying clients. (Clients included the government of the U.S. Commonwealth of the Northern Mariana Islands, Internet gambling services, and several Native American tribes.) Two of DeLay's former political aides, Tony Rudy and Michael Scanlon, as well as Abramoff himself, pleaded guilty in 2006 to charges relating to the investigation.

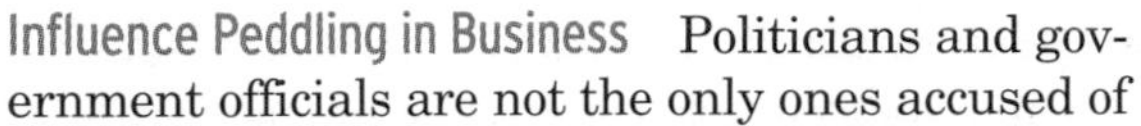

Influence Peddling in Business Politicians and government officials are not the only ones accused of bribery; business has had its share of scandals. One form, known as **payola**, involves the practice of record companies paying radio stations to play songs without making listeners aware of the bribes. Some large companies have been caught in payola scandals; Sony paid $10 million to the State of New York to settle a claim accusing its promoters of giving gifts to station managers to get songs played.[31]

In some foreign countries, soliciting bribes to do business is a common, even expected, practice. Not surprisingly, U.S. businesses have complained that stiff penalties in this country for bribery give foreign competitors an edge over them. In European countries, such as Italy and France, giving bribes to secure contracts is perfectly legal; and in West Germany, corporate bribes are actually tax deductible.[32] Some government officials solicit bribes to allow American firms to do business in their countries.[33]

To limit bribing of foreign officials, Congress passed the Foreign Corrupt Practices Act (FCPA) in 1977, which made it a criminal offense to bribe foreign officials or to make other questionable overseas payments. Violations of the FCPA draw strict penalties for both the defendant company and its officers.[34] Moreover, all fines imposed on corporate officers are paid by them, not absorbed by the company. For violations of the antibribery provisions of the FCPA, a domestic corporation can be fined up to $1 million. Company officers, employees, or stockholders who are convicted of bribery may have to serve a prison sentence of up to five years and pay a $10,000 fine. Congressional dissatisfaction with the harshness and ambiguity of the bill has caused numerous revisions to be proposed. Despite the penalties imposed by the FCPA, corporations that deal in foreign trade have continued to give bribes to secure favorable trade agreements.[35] On June 16, 2004, Schering-Plough Corporation agreed to pay a civil penalty of $500,000 for violating provisions of the FCPA. An employee of Schering-Plough's Polish subsidiary made a payment to a charitable foundation headed by a Polish government official. The government charged that these "charitable" payments were designed to influence the official to purchase Schering-Plough's pharmaceutical products for his region's health fund.[36]

Embezzlement and Employee Fraud

Another type of white-collar crime involves individuals' use of their positions to embezzle company funds or appropriate company property for themselves. Here, the company or organization that employs the criminal, rather than an outsider, is the victim of white-collar crime.

payola
The practice of record companies paying radio stations to play songs without making listeners aware of the bribes.

Blue-Collar Fraud In 2002, three employees and a friend allegedly stole moon rocks from a NASA laboratory in Houston, Texas. FBI agents arrested them after they tried to sell the contraband to an undercover agent in Orlando, Florida. The would-be seller reportedly asked $2,000 per gram for the rocks initially but later bumped the price to $8,000 per gram.[37] Although the theft of moon rocks does not happen very often, systematic theft of company property by employees, or **pilferage**, is common.[38]

Employee theft is most accurately explained by factors relevant to the work setting, such as job dissatisfaction and the workers' belief that they are being exploited by employers or supervisors; economic problems play a relatively small role in the decision to pilfer. So, although employers attribute employee fraud to economic conditions and declining personal values, workers themselves say they steal because of strain and conflict.

Though it is difficult to determine the value of goods taken by employees, some recent surveys indicate it is substantial and not confined to the United States. So-called shrinkage costs the European economy $29 billion—more than the losses due to car theft and/or domestic burglary.[39] Hayes International, a loss prevention firm, surveyed 27 retail clients and found that they had identified 60,000 people who were involved in $40 million of employee theft in a single year! The total amount of employee theft in the United States is probably staggering considering the number of apprehensions made in the relatively small number of companies (27) included in the Hayes sample.[40]

Management Fraud Blue-collar workers are not the only employees who commit corporate theft. Management-level fraud is also quite common. Such acts include converting company assets for personal benefit; fraudulently receiving increases in compensation (such as raises or bonuses); fraudulently increasing personal holdings of company stock; retaining one's present position within the company by manipulating accounts; and concealing unacceptable performance from stockholders.[41]

Management fraud has involved some of the nation's largest companies and richest people. The Profiles in Crime feature on pages 288–289 focuses on three of the most prominent cases of recent years.

Client Fraud

Another component of white-collar crime is theft by an economic client from an organization that advances credit to its clients or reimburses them for services rendered. These offenses are linked because they involve cheating an organization (such as a government agency or insurance company) with many individual clients that the organization supports financially (such as welfare clients), reimburses for services provided (such as health care providers), covers losses of (such as insurance policyholders), or extends credit to (such as bank clients or taxpayers). Included in this category are insurance fraud, credit card fraud, fraud related to welfare and Medicare programs, and tax evasion.

Health Care Fraud Some doctors violate their ethical vows and engage in fraud in obtaining patients and administering their treatment. Some extort or accept under-the-table payments for services that are supposed to be provided free of charge; others solicit payments in exchange for special privileges or treatment; and a few even extort or accept bribes to influence hiring decisions and decisions on licensing, accreditation, or certification of facilities.

Abusive and deceptive health care practices include such techniques as "ping-ponging" (referring patients to other physicians in the same office), "gang visits" (billing for multiple services), and "steering" (directing patients to particular pharmacies). Doctors who abuse their Medicaid or Medicare patients in this way are liable to civil suits and even criminal penalties.

In addition to individual physicians, some large health care providers have been accused of routinely violating the law to obtain millions in illegal payments. In 1998 the federal government filed suit against two of the nation's largest hospital chains, Columbia/HCA Healthcare Corporation (320 hospitals) and Quorum Health Group (250 hospitals), alleging that they routinely overstated expenses to

pilferage
Systematic theft of company property.

bilk Medicare.[42] It has been estimated that $100 billion spent annually on federal health care is lost to fraudulent practices.[43] Despite the magnitude of this abuse, state and federal governments have been reluctant to prosecute Medicaid fraud.[44]

The government has attempted to tighten control over the industry in order to restrict the opportunity for physicians to commit fraud. Health care companies providing services to federal health care programs are also regulated by federal laws that prohibit kickbacks and self-referrals. It is now a crime, punishable by up to five years in prison, to provide anything of value, money or otherwise, directly or indirectly, with the intent to induce a referral of a patient or a health care service. Liability attaches to both parties in the transaction—the entity or individual providing the kickbacks and the individual receiving payment of the referral.

Federal law also prohibits physicians and other health care providers from referring beneficiaries in federal health care programs to clinics or other facilities in which the physician or health care provider has a financial interest. It is illegal for a doctor to refer her patients to a blood-testing lab in which she has an ownership share. These practices—kickbacks and self-referrals—are prohibited under federal law because they would compromise a medical professional's independent judgment. Federal law prohibits arrangements that tend to corrupt medical judgment and put the provider's bottom line ahead of the patient's well-being.[45]

Tax Evasion Another important aspect of client fraud is tax evasion. Here, the victim is the government that is cheated by one of its clients, the errant taxpayer to whom it extended credit by allowing the taxpayer to delay paying taxes on money he or she had already earned. Tax fraud is a particularly challenging area for criminological study because so many U.S. citizens regularly underreport their income, and it is often difficult to separate honest error from deliberate tax evasion.

The basic law on tax evasion is contained in the U.S. Internal Revenue Code, section 7201, which states

> Any person who willfully attempts in any manner to evade or defeat any tax imposed by this title or the payment thereof shall, in addition to other penalties provided by law, be guilty of a felony and, upon conviction thereof, shall be fined not more than $100,000 or imprisoned not more than five years, or both, together with the costs of prosecution.

To prove tax fraud, the government must find that the taxpayer either underreported his or her income or did not report taxable income. No minimum dollar amount is stated before fraud exists, but the government can take legal action when there is a "substantial underpayment of tax." A second element of tax fraud is "willfulness" on the part of the tax evader. In the major case on this issue, willfulness was defined as a "voluntary, intentional violation of a known legal duty and not the careless disregard for the truth."[46] Finally, to prove tax fraud, the government must show that the taxpayer has purposely attempted to evade or defeat a tax payment. If the offender is guilty of passive neglect, the offense is a misdemeanor. "Passive neglect" means simply not paying taxes, not reporting income, or not paying taxes when due. On the other hand, "affirmative tax evasion," such as keeping double books, making false entries, destroying books or records, concealing assets, or covering up sources of income, constitutes a felony.

Corporate Crime

Yet another component of white-collar crime involves situations in which powerful institutions or their representatives willfully violate the laws that restrain these institutions from doing social harm or require them to do social good. This is also known as **corporate**, or **organizational, crime**.

Interest in corporate crime first emerged in the early 1900s, when a group of writers known as muckrakers targeted the monopolistic business practices of John D. Rockefeller and other corporate business leaders. In a 1907 article, sociologist E. A. Ross described the "criminaloid": a business leader who while enjoying immunity from the law victimized an unsuspecting public.[47] Edwin Sutherland

corporate (organizational) crime
Powerful institutions or their representatives willfully violate the laws that restrain these institutions from doing social harm or require them to do social good.

Tyco, Enron, and WorldCom: Enterprise Crime at the Highest Levels

The Tyco Case

Tyco International Ltd. is a gigantic corporate entity that today operates in all 50 U.S. states and over 100 countries and employs more than 250,000 people. Despite its great success, the U.S. government indicted Tyco's Chief Executive Officer L. Dennis Kozlowski and Chief Financial Officer Marc Swartz on a variety of fraud and larceny charges, including misappropriating $170 million in company funds by hiding unauthorized bonuses and secretly forgiving loans to themselves. Kozlowski and Swartz were also accused of making more than $430 million by lying about Tyco's financial condition in order to inflate the value of their stock.

During their 2004 trial, the government tried to establish a motive by showing jurors elements of the men's extravagant lifestyles. Kozlowski spent more than $2 million on a party for his wife on the Italian island of Sardinia that featured a performance by singer Jimmy Buffett; young men and women—dressed as Roman soldiers and maidens—danced and served the guests. He also spent $15 million to furnish an $18 million Tyco-owned apartment on Fifth Avenue in New York City; his expenses included a $15,000 umbrella holder, a $2,200 gilt metal trash basket, and a $6,000 shower curtain.

The defense claimed that the two men were merely highly paid executives and that everything they received was approved by Tyco's board of directors and their accounting firm, PricewaterhouseCoopers. Because there was no stealth, there could be no embezzlement. On September 19, 2005, both Swartz and Kozlowski were convicted of looting the company of $150 million and sentenced to 8-1/3 to 25 years in prison.

The Enron Case

Enron Corporation, an oil and gas trading firm, was one of the largest companies in the United States before it collapsed and cost thousands of employees their life savings and millions of investors their hard-earned money.

Enron was an aggressive energy company that sought to transform itself into the world's biggest energy trader. Enron's share price collapsed when word got out that the company had been setting up shell companies and limited partnerships to conceal debts so they did not show up in the company's accounts.

In one incident, six Enron executives negotiated complex deals in which they made at least $42 million on personal investments totaling $161,000, all the while knowing that the limited partnerships they sold to retirement plans and private foundations were collapsing in value. It is also suspected that Enron engaged in sham transactions in late 2000 that drove up electricity prices in California and helped worsen the energy crisis that plagued the West for more than a year.

Enron's auditors—Arthur Andersen, a prestigious accounting firm—shredded key documents to keep them out of the hands of the government. One man involved in the incident, David Duncan, a former Andersen partner who was head of the team that audited Enron, agreed to serve as a government witness after pleading guilty to obstruction of justice. Duncan admitted in court that he "knowingly, intentionally, and corruptly persuaded and attempted to persuade" Andersen employees to withhold records, documents, and other objects from an investigation by the Securities and Exchange Commission (SEC).

In the aftermath of the Enron collapse, Chairman Kenneth L. Lay was charged with conspiracy, securities fraud, wire fraud, bank fraud, and making false statements. Enron CEO Jeffrey K. Skilling and former Enron Chief Accounting Officer Richard Causey were also charged with money laundering and conspiracy. The government claimed that Lay, Skilling, Causey, and others oversaw a massive conspiracy to delude investors into believing that Enron was a growing company when, in fact, it was undergoing business setbacks.

The government charged that between 1999 and 2001, these executives used their position of trust to engage in a wide-ranging scheme to deceive the public and the SEC about the true performance of Enron's businesses. Their fraud helped inflate Enron's stock price from $30 per share in early 1998 to over $80 per share in January 2001. The three orchestrated a series of accounting frauds designed to make up the shortfall between what the company actually earned and what was expected by Wall Street analysts. Lay participated in management committee meetings at which he stated that Enron was doing great and was going to "hit its numbers," even though he knew the company was losing money.

focused theoretical attention on corporate crime when he began his research on the subject in the late 1930s and 1940s; as mentioned earlier, corporate crime was probably what he had in mind when he coined the phrase white-collar crime.[48]

Corporate crimes are socially injurious acts committed to further the business interests of people who control companies. The target of these crimes can be the general public, the environment, or even company workers. What makes these crimes unique is that the perpetrator is a legal fiction—a corporation—and not an individual. In reality, it is company employees or owners who commit corporate crimes and who ultimately benefit through career advancement or greater profits.

Some of the acts included within corporate crime are price fixing and illegal restraint of trade, false advertising, and the use of company practices that violate environmental protection statutes. The variety of crimes contained within this

What would motivate the head of one of the nation's largest companies to commit fraud? The government believes it was greed: Between 1998 and 2001, Lay received approximately $300 million from the sale of Enron stock options and restricted stock and made over $217 million in profit; he was also paid more than $19 million in salary and bonuses. In the end, many Enron executives were tried and punished. Andrew S. Fastow, the former chief financial officer of Enron, pleaded guilty to two counts of conspiracy to commit securities and wire fraud and is cooperating with an ongoing criminal investigation into Enron's collapse. On August 25, 2004, Mark Koenig, former director of investor relations and executive vice president at Enron, pleaded guilty to security charges and admitted that he was aware that Enron's publicly reported financial results and filings with the SEC did not truthfully present Enron's financial position. On May 25, 2006, Jeff Skilling, former CEO of Enron Corporation, was convicted of 19 out of 28 counts, including one count of conspiracy, one count of insider trading, five counts of making false statements to auditors, and 12 counts of securities fraud. Each conviction carries a maximum sentence of 5 to 10 years. Kenneth Lay himself was convicted on securities fraud charges but suffered a fatal heart attack on July 5, 2006 before he could be sentenced.

The WorldCom Case

WorldCom CEO Bernie Ebbers was found guilty and received a 25-year sentence for falsifying the company's financial statements by more than $9 billion; WorldCom was forced to file for the largest bankruptcy in U.S. history. One of the most important elements of the case was the more than $400 million that WorldCom loaned or guaranteed to loan Ebbers at an interest rate of 2.15 percent.

Ebbers began his career by creating the LDDS (Long Distance Discount Services), which gained many of America's largest corporations as customers for its voice and data network. He then bought IDB Company and renamed it WorldCom. Through a series of acquisitions, WorldCom became one of the largest Internet hookup and networking companies in the United States; its stock value increased 7,000 percent during the 1990s.

When the market collapsed in 2000, WorldCom was heavily in debt and hemorrhaging money. While people were being laid off, the company made its loans to Ebbers so he could hold onto his company stock, for which he had taken out loans to purchase. Then on June 25, 2002, WorldCom announced that it had illegally treated $3.8 billion in ordinary costs as capital expenditures. The bottom dropped out of the stock, creditors began to sue, and Ebbers was in no position to pay back the loans. The company admitted to overstating profits by a whopping $74.4 billion between 2000 and 2001, including at least $10.6 billion that the firm attributed to accounting "errors" as well as "improper" and "inappropriate" accounting. On May 15, 2005, a federal jury in New York convicted Ebbers on all nine counts on which he was charged, and Ebbers was sentenced to 25 years in prison.

© Peter Morgan/Reuters/Corbis

● A 24-foot representation of a screw is hoisted into position outside Federal Hall in New York's financial district as a protest against a settlement between WorldCom, the bankrupt long-distance telephone company, and securities regulators–U.S. District Judge Jed Rakoff later approved a $750 million settlement. The $11 billion accounting scandal originally drew a $1.5 billion fine. The fine, to be distributed among WorldComís victims, was reduced in light of the companyís bankruptcy proceeding, which is the largest filing in U.S. history, listing $107 billion of assets.

SOURCES: Krysten Crawford, CNN "Ex-WorldCom CEO Ebbers Guilty," March 15, 2006, http://money.cnn.com/2005/03/15/news/newsmakers/ebbers/index.htm; MSNBC, "Ebbers Sentenced to 25 Years in Prison, Ex-WorldCom CEO Guilty of Directing Biggest Accounting Fraud," July 13, 2005, www.msnbc.msn.com/id/8474930; Lynne W. Jeter, *Disconnected: Deceit and Betrayal at WorldCom* (New York: Wiley, 2003); Bethany McLean and Peter Elkind, *Smartest Guys in the Room: The Amazing Rise and Scandalous Fall of Enron* (New York: Penguin, 2003); Dan Ackman, "Bernie Ebbers Guilty," *Forbes*, March 15, 2005, www.forbes.com/home/management/2005/03/15/cx_da_0315ebbersguilty.html (accessed July 10, 2006); Kurt Eichenwald, "Ex-Andersen Partner Pleads Guilty in Record-Shredding," *New York Times*, 12 April 2002, p. C1; John A. Byrne, "At Enron, the Environment Was Ripe for Abuse," *BusinessWeek* (February 25, 2002): 12; Peter Behr and Carrie Johnson, "Govt. Expands Charges against Enron Execs," *Washington Post*, 1 May 2003, p.1.

category is great, and they cause vast damage. The following subsections examine some of the most important offenses.

Illegal Restraint of Trade and Price Fixing A restraint of trade involves a contract or conspiracy designed to stifle competition, create a monopoly, artificially maintain prices, or otherwise interfere with free market competition.[49] The control of restraint of trade violations has its legal basis in the **Sherman Antitrust Act**, which subjects to criminal or civil sanctions any person "who shall make any contract or engage in any combination or conspiracy" in restraint of interstate commerce.[50] For violations of its provisions, this federal law created criminal penalties of up to three years' imprisonment and $100,000 in fines for individuals and $10 million in fines for corporations.[51] The act outlaws conspiracies between corporations designed to control the marketplace.

Sherman Antitrust Act
Federal law that subjects to criminal or civil sanctions any person "who shall make any contract or engage in any combination or conspiracy" in restraint of interstate commerce.

In most instances, the act lets the presiding court judge decide whether corporations have conspired to "unreasonably restrain competition." However, through the Sherman Antitrust Act, four types of market conditions considered inherently anticompetitive have been defined by federal courts as illegal per se, without regard to the facts or circumstances of the case:

- *Division of markets*. Firms divide a region into territories, and each firm agrees not to compete in the others' territories.
- *Tying arrangement*. A corporation requires customers of one of its services to use other services it offers. For example, it would be an illegal restraint of trade if a railroad required that companies doing business with it or supplying it with materials ship all goods they produce on trains owned by the rail line.[52]
- *Group boycott*. An organization or company boycotts retail stores that do not comply with its rules or desires.
- *Price fixing*. A conspiracy to set and control the price of a necessary commodity is considered an absolute violation of the act.

Deceptive Pricing Even the largest U.S. corporations commonly use deceptive pricing schemes when they respond to contract solicitations. Deceptive pricing occurs when contractors provide the government or other corporations with incomplete or misleading information on how much it will actually cost to fulfill the contracts on which they are bidding, or use mischarges once the contracts are signed.[53] For example, defense contractors have been prosecuted for charging the government for costs incurred on work they are doing for private firms or for shifting the costs on fixed-price contracts to ones in which the government reimburses the contractor for all expenses ("cost-plus" contracts).

False Claims Advertising Executives in even the largest corporations sometimes face stockholders' expectations of ever-increasing company profits that seem to demand that sales be increased at any cost. At times they respond to this challenge by making claims about their products that cannot be justified by actual performance. However, there is a fine line between clever, aggressive sales techniques and fraudulent claims. It is traditional to show a product in its best light, even if that involves resorting to fantasy. Showing a delivery service vehicle taking off into outer space or implying that taking one sip of beer will make people feel they have just jumped into a freezer are not fraudulent. But it is illegal to knowingly and purposely advertise a product as possessing qualities that the manufacturer realizes it does not have, such as the ability to cure the common cold, grow hair, or turn senior citizens into rock stars (though some rock stars are senior citizens these days).

In 2003 the U.S. Supreme Court, in the case of *Illinois Ex Rel. Madigan v. Telemarketing Associates*, helped define the line separating illegal claims from those that are artistic hyperbole protected by free speech.[54] Telemarketing Associates, a for-profit fundraising corporation, was retained by a charity to solicit donations to aid Vietnam veterans in the state of Illinois. Though donors were told that a significant portion of the money would go to the vets, the telemarketers actually retained 85 percent of all the money collected. The Illinois attorney general filed a complaint in state court, alleging that such representations were knowingly deceptive and materially false. The telemarketers said they were exercising their First Amendment free speech rights when they made their pitch for money.

The Supreme Court disagreed and found that states may charge fraud when fundraisers make false or misleading representations designed to deceive donors about how their donations will be used. The Court held that it is false and misleading for a solicitor to fool potential donors into believing that a substantial portion of their contributions would fund specific programs or services, knowing full well that was not the case.

Worker Safety/Environmental Crimes Much attention has been paid to intentional or negligent environmental pollution caused by many large corporations. The numerous allegations in this area involve almost every aspect of U.S. business. There are many different types of environmental crimes. Some corporations have endangered the lives of their own workers by maintaining unsafe conditions in their plants and mines. It has been estimated that more than 20 million workers have been exposed to hazardous materials while on the job. Some industries have been hit particularly hard by complaints and allegations. The control of workers' safety in the United States has been the province of the Occupational Safety and Health Administration (OSHA), which sets industry standards for the proper use of such chemicals as benzene, arsenic, lead, and coke (from coal). Intentional violation of OSHA standards can result in criminal penalties.

The major enforcement arm against environmental crimes is the Environmental Protection Agency (EPA), which was given full law enforcement authority in 1988. The EPA has successfully prosecuted significant violations across all major environmental statutes, including data fraud cases (for instance, private laboratories submitting false environmental data to state and federal environmental agencies); indiscriminate hazardous waste dumping that resulted in serious injuries and death; industry-wide ocean dumping by cruise ships; oil spills that caused significant damage to waterways, wetlands, and beaches; international smuggling of CFC refrigerants that damage the ozone layer and increase skin cancer risk; and illegal handling of hazardous substances such as pesticides and asbestos that exposed children, the poor, and other especially vulnerable groups to potentially serious illness.[55] Its Criminal Investigation Division (EPA CID) investigates allegations of criminal wrongdoing prohibited by various environmental statutes. Such investigations involve, but are not limited to:

- Illegal disposal of hazardous waste
- Export of hazardous waste without the permission of the receiving country
- Illegal discharge of pollutants to a water of the United States
- Removal and disposal of regulated asbestos-containing materials in a manner inconsistent with the law and regulations
- Illegal importation of certain restricted or regulated chemicals into the United States
- Tampering with a drinking water supply
- Mail fraud
- Wire fraud
- Conspiracy and money laundering relating to environmental criminal activities[56] ✔ CHECKPOINTS

✔ CHECKPOINTS

- ✔ White-collar crime has a number of different subcategories.
- ✔ Stings and swindles involve long-term efforts to cheat people out of their money.
- ✔ Chiseling involves regular cheating of an organization or its customers.
- ✔ People who engage in exploitation demand payment for services to which victims are entitled by threatening consequences if their victims refuse. The victim here is the client.
- ✔ Influence peddling and bribery occur when a person in authority demands payment for a service to which the payer is clearly not entitled. The victim here is the organization.
- ✔ Embezzlement and employee fraud occur when a person uses a position of trust to steal from an organization.
- ✔ Client fraud involves theft from an organization that advances credit, covers losses, or reimburses for services.
- ✔ Organizational, or corporate, crime involves various illegal business practices such as price fixing, restraint of trade, and false advertising.

THEORIES OF WHITE-COLLAR CRIME

Why do they do it? Why do otherwise respectable people decide to break the law? As noted, most criminal offenders begin their offending careers when they are quite young. Yet by its very nature white-collar crime requires people to attain a position in the workplace before they can commit crime. Can the theories that predict common-law crime also apply to white-collar crime? There are a number of theories of white-collar crime. The next sections describe three of the most prominent.

Rationalization/Neutralization View

In his research on fraud, Donald Cressey found that the door to solving personal financial problems through criminal means is opened by the rationalizations people develop for white-collar crime: "Some of our most respectable citizens got their start in life by using other people's money temporarily"; "in the real estate business, there is nothing wrong about using deposits before the deal is closed"; "all people steal when they get in a tight spot."[57] Offenders use these and other rationalizations to resolve the conflict they experience over engaging in illegal behavior. Rationalizations allow offenders' financial needs to be met without compromising their values.

A recent study of Medicare/Medicaid fraud committed by speech, occupational, and physical therapists working in hospitals, nursing homes, and with home health agencies found that they frequently involved two fraudulent practices: cutting sessions short while charging for the entire session and charging individual session rates for group therapy sessions.[58] When interviewed, the workers described using three techniques of neutralization that enabled them to defuse guilt over what they recognized as deviant practices: (1) Everyone else does it, (2) it's not my fault or responsibility, and (3) no one is hurt except insurance companies, and they are wealthy.

Corporate Culture View

The corporate culture view is that some business organizations promote white-collar criminality in the same way that lower-class culture encourages the development of juvenile gangs and street crime. According to the corporate culture view, some business enterprises cause crime by placing excessive demands on employees while maintaining a business climate tolerant of employee deviance. New employees learn the attitudes and techniques needed to commit white-collar crime from their business peers.

The corporate culture theory can be used to explain the collapse of Enron. A new CEO had been brought in to revitalize the company, and he wanted to become part of the "new economy" based on the Internet. Layers of management were wiped out, and hundreds of outsiders were recruited. Huge cash bonuses and stock options were granted to top performers. Young managers were given authority to make $5 million decisions without higher approval. It became common for executives to change jobs two or three times in an effort to maximize bonuses and pay. Seminars were conducted showing executives how to hide profits and avoid taxes.[59]

CONNECTIONS

The view that white-collar crime is a learning process is reminiscent of Edwin Sutherland's description of how gang boys learn the techniques of drug dealing and burglary from older youths through differential association. See Chapter 7 for a description of this process.

Those holding the corporate culture view would point to the Enron scandal as a prime example of what happens when people work in organizations in which the cultural values stress profit over fair play, government scrutiny is limited and regulators are viewed as the enemy, and senior members encourage newcomers to believe that "greed is good."

Self-Control View

Not all criminologists agree with these two theories. Travis Hirschi and Michael Gottfredson take exception to the hypothesis that white-collar crime is a product of corporate culture.[60] If that were true, there would be much more white-collar crime than actually exists, and white-collar criminals would not be embarrassed by their misdeeds, as most seem to be. Instead, Hirschi and Gottfredson maintain that the motives that produce white-collar crimes—quick benefits with minimal effort—are the same as those that produce any other criminal behaviors.

CONNECTIONS

As you may recall from Chapter 9, Gottfredson and Hirschi's General Theory of Crime holds that criminals lack self-control. Because Gottfredson and Hirschi believe all crime has a similar basis, the motivation and pressure to commit white-collar crime is the same as for any other form of crime.

White-collar criminals have low self-control and are inclined to follow momentary impulses without considering the long-term costs of such behavior.[61] White-collar crime is relatively rare because, as a matter of course, business executives tend to hire people with self-control, thereby limiting the number of potential white-collar criminals. Hirschi and Gottfredson have collected data showing that the demographic distribution of white-collar crime is similar to other crimes. For example, gender, race, and age ratios are the same for crimes such as embezzlement and fraud as they are for street crimes such as burglary and robbery.

WHITE-COLLAR CRIME AND LAW ENFORCEMENT SYSTEMS

On the federal level, detection of white-collar crime is primarily in the hands of administrative departments and agencies.[62] The decision to pursue criminal rather than civil violations is usually based on the seriousness of the case and the perpetrator's intent, actions to conceal the violation, and prior record. Any evidence of criminal activity is then sent to the Department of Justice or the FBI for investigation. Some other federal agencies, such as the Securities and Exchange Commission and the U.S. Postal Service, have their own investigative arms. Enforcement is generally reactive (generated by complaints) rather than proactive (involving ongoing investigations or the monitoring of activities). Investigations are carried out by the various federal agencies and the FBI. If criminal prosecution is called for, the case will be handled by attorneys from the criminal, tax, antitrust, and civil rights divisions of the Justice Department. If insufficient evidence is available to warrant a criminal prosecution, the case will be handled civilly or administratively by some other federal agency. For example, the Federal Trade Commission can issue a cease and desist order in antitrust or merchandising fraud cases.

The number of state-funded technical assistance offices to help local prosecutors has increased significantly; more than 40 states offer such services. On the state and local levels, law enforcement officials have made progress in a number of areas, such as controlling consumer fraud. For example, the Environmental Crimes Strike Force in Los Angeles County, California, is considered a model for the control of illegal dumping and pollution.[63] Some of the more common environmental offenses investigated and prosecuted by the task force include

- Illegal transportation, treatment, storage or disposal of hazardous waste
- Oil spills
- Fraudulent certification of automobile smog tests[64]

Nonetheless, although local agencies recognize the seriousness of enterprise-type crimes, they rarely have the funds necessary for effective enforcement.[65]

Local prosecutors pursue white-collar criminals more vigorously if they are part of a team effort involving a network of law enforcement agencies.[66] National surveys of local prosecutors find that many do not consider white-collar crimes particularly serious problems. They are more willing to prosecute cases if the offense causes substantial harm and if other agencies fail to act. Relatively few prosecutors participate in interagency task forces designed to investigate white-collar criminal activity.[67]

Controlling White-Collar Crime

The prevailing wisdom is that unlike lower-class street criminals, white-collar criminals are rarely prosecuted and, when convicted, receive relatively light sentences. There have also been charges that efforts to control white-collar crime are biased against specific classes and races: Authorities seem to be less diligent when victims are poor or minority group members or the crimes take place in minority areas. When Michael Lynch and his associates studied whether petroleum refineries violating environmental laws in black, Latino, and low-income communities receive smaller fines than those refineries in white and affluent communities, they found that violations of the Clean Air Act, the Clean Water Act, and/or the Resource Conservation and Recovery Act in minority areas received much smaller fines than the same types of violations occuring in white areas ($108,563 vs. $341,590).[68]

What efforts have been made to bring violators of the public trust to justice? White-collar criminal enforcement typically involves two strategies designed to control organizational deviance: compliance and deterrence.[69]

Compliance Strategies One method of controlling white-collar crime is to give people and institutions a proactive reason to obey the law: It will cost them money and business if they do not obey the rules. These **compliance strategies** rely on the threat of economic sanctions or civil penalties to control potential violators. They attempt to create a marketplace incentive to obey the law—the more a company pollutes, the more costly and unprofitable that pollution becomes. Compliance strategies also avoid stigmatizing and shaming businesspeople by focusing on the act, rather than the actor, in white-collar crime.[70]

compliance strategies
Methods of controlling white-collar crime that rely on the threat of economic sanctions or civil penalties to control potential violators, creating a marketplace incentive to obey the law.

One method of compliance is to set up administrative agencies to oversee business activity. The Securities and Exchange Commission regulates Wall Street activities, and the Food and Drug Administration regulates drugs, cosmetics, medical devices, meats, and other foods. The legislation creating these agencies usually spells out the penalties for violating regulatory standards. This approach has been used to control environmental crimes by levying heavy fines based on the quantity and quality of pollution released into the environment.[71] It is easier and less costly to be in compliance, the theory goes, than to pay costly fines and risk criminal prosecution for repeat violations. Moreover, the federal government bars people and businesses from receiving government contracts if they have engaged in repeated business law violations.

It seems that enforcing compliance with civil penalties is on the upswing. The antitrust division of the U.S. Department of Justice reports that between 1997 and 2003, over $2 billion in criminal fines was levied on business violators, an amount equal to more than all the money collected during the prior 100 years! In the 10 years before 1997, on average, $29 million in criminal fines was levied annually; by 2001, fines amounted to over $280 million per year.[72]

Deterrence Strategies Another approach to white-collar crime control is reactive: Detect criminal violations, determine who is responsible, and penalize the offenders to deter future violations. Deterrence systems are oriented toward apprehending violators and punishing them rather than creating conditions that induce conformity to the law.

Deterrence strategies should work—and they have—because white-collar crime by its nature is a rational act whose perpetrators are extremely sensitive to the threat of criminal sanctions. Perceptions of detection and punishment for white-collar crimes appear to be powerful deterrents to future law violations. Although deterrence strategies may prove effective, federal agencies have traditionally been reluctant to throw corporate executives in jail. Federal courts have not hesitated to enforce the Sherman Antitrust Act in civil actions, but they have limited application of the criminal sanctions. Similarly, the government seeks criminal indictments in corporate violations only in "instances of outrageous conduct of undoubted illegality," such as price fixing.[73] The government has also been lenient with companies and individuals that cooperate voluntarily after an investigation has begun; leniency is not given as part of a confession or plea arrangement. Those who comply with the leniency policy are charged criminally for the activity reported.[74]

✔ CHECKPOINTS

- ✔ There are numerous explanations for white-collar crime.
- ✔ Some offenders are motivated by greed; others offend due to personal problems.
- ✔ The rationalization view is that white-collar crime allows offenders to meet their financial needs without compromising their values.
- ✔ Corporate culture theory suggests that some businesses actually encourage employees to cheat or cut corners.
- ✔ The self-control view is that white-collar criminals are like any other law violators: impulsive people who lack self-control.
- ✔ White-collar enforcement may encourage self-regulation. Organizations that violate the law are given civil fines.
- ✔ Deterrence systems punish individuals with prison sentences.

Is the Tide Turning?

On June, 20, 2005, Adelphia cable operator John Rigas was sentenced to 15 years in prison for bank and securities fraud, and his son Timothy Rigas was sentenced to 20 years after their conviction on charges that they used company funds to support their extravagant lifestyle. John Rigas took advantage of a shared line of credit with Adelphia, using the company's money—stockholder's money—for personal extravagances.[75]

The harsh prison sentences handed out to John and Timothy Rigas are not unique today, but they are a significant departure from years past when public humiliation at being caught was considered punishment enough for an upstanding businessperson. There is growing evidence that the days of shielding white-collar criminals from severe punishment are over. Although many people believe affluent corporate executives still avoid serious punishment, public displeasure with such highly publicized white-collar crimes may be producing a backlash that is resulting in more frequent use of prison sentences and more draconian fines.[76] With the Enron scandal depriving so many people of their life savings, the general public has become educated as to the damage caused by white-collar criminals and may now consider white-collar crimes as more serious offenses than common-law theft offenses.[77]

Some commentators now argue that the government may actually be going overboard in its efforts to punish white-collar criminals, especially for crimes that are the result of negligent business practices rather than intentional criminal conspiracy.[78] Both fines and penalties have been increasing, and in one case a food company executive was sentenced to serve more than five years in prison for his role in a bid-rigging scheme; it was the longest single prison sentence ever obtained for an antitrust violation.[79] The total collected from confiscated goods sold or auctioned off by the Justice and Treasury Departments rose to $926 million in 2005, from $627 million in 2001. Included in the 2005 figure was $595,000 for a Galveston, Texas, beach house that belonged to former Enron CFO Andrew S. Fastow.[80] ✓ CHECKPOINTS

CYBER CRIME

The widespread use of both computers and the Internet has ushered in the age of **information technology (IT)** and made it an intricate part of daily life in most industrialized societies.

IT can involve computer networking, the Internet, and/or advanced communications. It is the key to the economic system and will become more important as major industries shift their manufacturing plants to other areas of the world where production is much cheaper. IT is responsible for the **globalization** phenomenon or the process of creating transnational markets, politics, and legal systems—in other words, creating a global economy.

The cyber age has also generated an enormous amount of revenue. Spending on IT and telecommunications will grow by more than 6 percent each year, soon reaching about $2 trillion.[81] Today more than 1 billion people are using e-mail, and 240 million are mobile Internet users. Magnifying the importance of the Internet is the fact that many critical infrastructure functions, ranging from banking to control of shipping on the Mississippi River, are now being conducted online.[82]

This vast network has now become a tool for illegal activities and enterprise. As a group, these activities are referred to as cyber crime—any act of criminal enterprise that involves the use of communication, computer, and Internet networks. **Cyber theft** schemes range from illegal copying of copyrighted material, to using technology to commit traditional theft-based offenses such as larceny and fraud.

Cyber crime presents a compelling challenge for criminologists because (1) it is rapidly evolving, with new schemes being created daily, (2) it is difficult to detect through traditional law enforcement channels, and (3) its control demands that agents of the justice system develop technical skills that match those of the perpetrators.[83] The new computer-based technology allows criminals to operate in a more efficient and effective manner. Cyber thieves now have the luxury of remaining anonymous, living in any part of the planet, conducting their business during the day or in the evening, working alone or in a group, while reaching a much wider number of potential victims than ever before. No longer are con artists or criminal entrepreneurs limited to fleecing victims in a particular geographic locale; the whole world can be their target. And the technology revolution has opened novel methods for cyber theft—ranging from the unlawful distribution of computer software to Internet security fraud—that heretofore were nonexistent. Nor do all cyber criminals seek profit; some are intent on causing damage and destroying computer networks for malicious reasons (see the Current Issues in Crime entitled "Cyber Vandalism" on pages 298–299). But the rapid growth of cyber theft schemes now make them a serious new entry into the world of enterprise crime. Some of the most common forms of cyber crime are set out below.

Computer Fraud

Computer fraud is not in itself an offense but rather a common-law crime committed using contemporary technology. Consequently, many computer crimes are prosecuted under such traditional criminal statutes as larceny or fraud. However, not all computer crimes fall under common-law statutes because the property stolen may be intangible, for example, electronic and/or magnetic impulse. Some of these crimes are listed in Exhibit 12.1.

information technology (IT)
All forms of technology used to create, store, retrieve, and exchange data in all its various forms, including electronic, voice, and still image.

globalization
The process of creating transnational markets, politics, and legal systems and forming a global economy.

cyber theft
Use of computer networks for criminal profits. Illegal copyright infringement, identity theft, and Internet securities fraud are examples of cyber theft.

© Daniel Berehulak/Getty Images

● Some cyber criminals attack government installations. Gary McKinnon of North London enters the Bow Street Magistrates Court in London. McKinnon, 39, was wanted by the U.S. government for illegally accessing and making unauthorized modifications to 53 computers belonging to NASA, the Pentagon, the U.S. Army, Navy, and Air Force, and the Department of Defense, causing $1 million in damage. Is this a form of cyber terrorism or just cyber vandalism?

There are a number of recent trends in computer frauds. Internal attacks are now outgrowing external attacks at the world's largest financial institutions. According to a recent global security survey (2005) conducted by the international accounting firm Deloitte Touche Tohmatsu, 35 percent of financial institutions encountered attacks from inside their organization within the last 12 months (up from 14 percent in 2004) compared to 26 percent from external sources (up from 23 percent in 2004).[84] The shift from external to internal attacks may be explained by improved security technologies that make it more difficult for people unfamiliar with the system to misuse it for personal gain. It has become easier for disgruntled employees to attack computers today than for outsiders to breach a company's defenses.

Distributing Illegal Sexual Material

The IT revolution has revitalized the porn industry. The Internet is an ideal venue for selling and distributing obscene material; the computer is an ideal device for storing and viewing it. Because of their vast number it is difficult to estimate how many websites feature sexual content, including nude photos, videos, live sex acts, and webcam strip sessions, among other forms of "adult entertainment."[85] N2H2, a Seattle-based Web-filtering company, estimates that the number of pornography web pages has soared during the past six years, and there are now about 260 million pages of erotic content on more than 1.3 million

Exhibit 12.1

Examples of Computer Fraud

Theft of Information

The unauthorized obtaining of information from a computer (known as "hacking"), including software that is copied for profit, is a common form of computer fraud.

The "Salami Slice"

With this type of fraud the perpetrator carefully skims small sums from the balances of a large number of accounts in order to bypass internal controls and escape detection.

Software Theft

The comparative ease of making copies of computer software has led to a huge illegal market, depriving authors of very significant revenues.

Manipulation of Accounts/Banking Systems

Similar to a "salami slice," this is on a much larger and usually more complex scale.

Corporate Espionage

Trade secrets are stolen by a company's competitors, which can be either domestic or foreign. The goal is to increase the rival company's (or nation's) competitive edge in the global marketplace.

SOURCE: VoGon International, www.vogon-international.com/index.htm (accessed April 22, 2006).

sites, all hoping to cash in on the billions in revenue spent on Internet porn annually.[86] The number of visits to pornographic sites surpasses those made to Internet search engines; some individual sites report as many as 50 million hits per year.

How do adult sites operate today?[87]

- A large firm sells annual subscriptions in exchange for unlimited access to content.
- Password services charge an annual fee to deliver access to hundreds of small sites, which share the subscription revenues.
- Large firms provide free content to smaller "affiliate" sites. The affiliates post the free content and then try to channel visitors to the large sites, which give the smaller sites a percentage of the fees paid by those who sign up.
- Webmasters forward traffic to another porn site in return for a small per-consumer fee. In many cases, the consumer is sent to the other sites involuntarily, which is known in the industry as "mousetrapping." Web surfers who try to close out a window after visiting an adult site are sent to another web page automatically. This can repeat dozens of times, causing users to panic and restart their computers in order to escape.
- Adult sites cater to niche audiences looking for specific kinds of adult content.

CONNECTIONS

Pornography will be discussed more fully in Chapter 13.

Denial-of-Service Attack

A **denial-of-service attack** is characterized as an attempt to extort money from legitimate users of an Internet service by threatening to prevent them from accessing the service.[88] These attacks take different forms:

- Attempts to "flood" a computer network, thereby preventing legitimate network traffic
- Attempts to disrupt connections within a computer network, thereby preventing access to a service
- Attempts to prevent a particular individual from accessing a service
- Attempts to disrupt service to a specific system or person

A denial-of-service attack may involve threats of or actual flooding of an Internet site with millions of bogus messages or orders so that the services will be tied up and unable to perform as promised. Unless the site operator pays extortion, the attackers threaten to keep up the interference until consumers become frustrated and abandon the site.

Illegal Copyright Infringement

For the past decade, groups of individuals have been working together to obtain software illegally and then "crack" or "rip" its copyright protections, before posting it on the Internet for other members of the group to use; this is referred to as **warez**.

Frequently, these new pirated copies reach the Internet days or weeks before the legitimate product is commercially available. The government has actively pursued members of the warez community, and some have been charged and convicted under two acts passed in 1998. The Computer Fraud and Abuse Act (CFAA) criminalizes accessing computer systems without authorization to obtain information[89]; and the Digital Millennium Copyright Act (DMCA) makes it a crime to circumvent antipiracy measures built into most commercial software and also outlaws the manufacture, sale, or distribution of code-cracking devices used to illegally copy software.[90]

denial-of-service attack
Extorting money from Internet service users by threatening to prevent them from accessing the service.

warez
Refers to efforts of organized groups to download and sell copyrighted software in violation of its license.

File Sharing Another form of illegal copyright infringement involves file-sharing programs that allow Internet users to download music and other copyrighted material without paying the artists and record producers their rightful royalties. Theft

Current Issues in Crime

Cyber Vandalism: Cyber Crime with Malicious Intent

On September 8, 2005, a Massachusetts juvenile pleaded guilty in federal court and was sentenced to 11 months' detention in a juvenile facility, to be followed by 2 years of supervised release. During his periods of detention and supervised release, the juvenile was barred from possessing or using any computer, cell phone, or other electronic equipment capable of accessing the Internet. The basis for the charges was a course of criminal conduct that took place over a 15-month period beginning in March 2004, when the juvenile sent an e-mail to a Florida school with the caption, "this is URGENT!!!" The text of the e-mail read as follows:

> "your all going to perish and flourish...you will all die Tuesday, 12:00 p.m.
> we're going to have a "blast" hahahahahaha wonder where I'll be? youll all be destroyed.
> im sick of your [expletive deleted] school and piece of [expletive deleted] staff, your all gonna [expletive deleted] die you pieces of crap!!!!
> DIE MOTHER [expletive deleted] IM GONA BLOW ALL YOU UP AND MYSELF ALL YOU NAZI LOVING MEXICAN FAGGOT BITCHES ARE DEAD"

As a result of this bomb threat, the Florida school was closed for two days while a bomb squad, a canine team, the fire department, and emergency medical services were called in to protect the school.

Some cyber criminals, such as the young boy in Massachusetts, may not be motivated by greed or profit but by the desire for revenge, destruction, and to achieve a malicious intent. Their acts of cyber vandalism are motivated by a number of factors:

- Some seek revenge for some perceived wrong.
- Some desire to exhibit their technical prowess and superiority.
- Some wish to highlight the vulnerability of computer security systems.
- Some desire to spy on other people's private financial and personal information ("computer voyeurism").
- Some want to destroy computer security because they believe in a philosophy of open access to all systems and programs.

What forms does cyber vandalism take?

- *Virus*. A computer virus is a type of malicious software program (also called "malware") that disrupts or destroys existing programs and networks, causing them to perform the task for which the virus was designed. The virus is then spread from one computer to another when a user sends out an infected file through e-mail, a network, or a disk.
- *Worm*. Similar to viruses, worms use computer networks or the Internet to self-replicate and "send themselves" to other users, generally via e-mail without the aid of the operator. The damage caused by viruses and worms can be considerable. On March 26, 1999, the Melissa virus disrupted e-mail service around the world when it was posted to an Internet newsgroup, causing more than $80 million in damage.
- *Trojan horse*. A trojan horse looks like a benign application, but it contains illicit codes that can damage the system operations. Although trojan horses do not replicate themselves like viruses and worms, they can be just as destructive.
- *Logic bomb*. A logic bomb is a program that is secretly attached to a computer system, monitors the network's work output, and waits for a particular signal, such as a date, to appear. Also called a "slag code," it is a type of delayed-action virus that may be set off when a program user makes certain input that sets it in motion. A logic bomb can cause a variety of problems ranging from displaying or printing a spurious message to deleting or corrupting data.
- *Spam*. An unsolicited advertisement or promotional material, spam typically comes in the form of an unwanted e-mail message; spammers use electronic communications to send unsolicited messages in bulk. E-mail is the most common form of spam, but it

through the illegal reproduction and distribution of movies, software, games, and music is estimated to cost U.S. industries $19 billion worldwide each year. Although some students routinely share files and download music, criminal copyright infringement represents a serious economic threat. The U.S. Criminal Code provides penalties for a first-time offender of five years incarceration and a fine of $250,000.[91] Other provisions provide for the forfeiture and destruction of infringing copies and all equipment used to make the copies.[92]

Internet Securities Fraud

Internet securities fraud involves using the Internet to intentionally manipulate the securities marketplace for profit. There are actually three major types of Internet securities fraud today:

- *Market manipulation*. Stock market manipulation occurs when an individual tries to control the price of stock by interfering with the natural forces of supply and demand. There are two principal forms of this crime: the "pump and dump" and the "cyber smear." In a pump and dump scheme, erroneous and can also be sent via instant messaging, usenet newsgroups, and mobile phone messaging, among other mediums. Though most spam is benign, it can be damaging when it contains a Trojan horse disguised as an e-mail attachment advertising some commodity such as free software or electronic game. If the recipient downloads or opens the attachment, a virus may be launched that corrupts the victim's computer; the Trojan horse may also be designed to capture important data from the victim's hard drive and send it back to the hacker's e-mail address.

- *Web defacement*. Computer hackers sometimes damage or deface websites by inserting or substituting codes that expose visitors to misleading or provocative information. Defacement can range from installing humorous graffiti to sabotaging or corrupting the site. In some instances, defacement efforts are not easily apparent or noticeable, and may be subtly designed to give misinformation by substituting or replacing authorized text on a company's (or individual's) web page with false information. The intent is to mislead customers and frustrate their efforts to use the site, or make it difficult for people using search engines to find the site as they surf the net.

Symantec Corporation conducts an annual worldwide Internet Security Threat Report. The latest effort finds that hackers and malicious-software writers have made a significant increase in attack programs using malicious codes, hoping at least some will get past defenses. Personal computers are increasingly the target of attacks because they are considered the weak links in corporate network security and at the same time contain valuable consumer data, such as financial account numbers, passwords, and identifying information. Virus writers now routinely tweak old programs to create new variants in an effort to evade antivirus software. Attackers have been launching "bots," or programs that provide attackers with remote control of victim PCs at a record pace; more than 10,000 are now being launched daily. Symantec expects to see more diverse and sophisticated threats used for cyber crime as well as an increase in the theft of confidential, financial, and personal information for financial gain. Nor is cyber vandalism restricted to the United States. China experienced the largest increase of bot-infected computers, with 37 percent growth in a single year, putting China behind only the United States in this category. The increase is likely related to China's rapid growth in broadband Internet connections. So cyber vandalism has now become a worldwide problem.

Critical Thinking

1. Considering what you know about theories of crime, speculate on the motives of cyber vandals. What do they hope to achieve through malicious destruction of computer networks? What would Gottfredson and Hirschi say about their motivation?
2. If cyber vandalism was a matter of rational choice, what could be done to deter cyber vandals? Would you send them to prison for defacing a website?

InfoTrac College Edition Research

Use the terms "computer virus," "spam," and "logic bomb" in a key word search on InfoTrac College Edition.

SOURCES: Department of Justice, District of Massachusetts, press release, "Massachusetts Teen Convicted for Hacking into Internet and Telephone Service Providers and Making Bomb Threats to High Schools in Massachusetts and Florida," September 8, 2005, www.cybercrime.gov/juvenileSentboston.htm (accessed April 26, 2006); Anne Branscomb, "Rogue Computer Programs and Computer Rogues: Tailoring Punishment to Fit the Crime," *Rutgers Computer and Technology Law Journal* 16 (1990): 24–26; Heather Jacobson and Rebecca Green, "Computer Crimes," *American Criminal Law Review* 39 (2002): 272–326; Hyung-jin Woo, Yeora Kim, and Joseph Dominick, "Hackers: Militants or Merry Pranksters? A Content Analysis of Defaced Web Pages," *Media Psychology* 6 (2004): 63–82; Yona Hollander, "Prevent Web Page Defacement," *Internet Security Advisor* 2 (2000): 1–4; Symantec, Internet Security Threat Report, 2006, https://enterprise.symantec.com/enterprise/whitepaper.cfm ?id=2238.

deceptive information is posted online to interest unsuspecting investors in a stock while those spreading the information sell previously purchased stock at an inflated price. The cyber smear is a reverse pump and dump: Negative information is spread online about a stock, driving down its price and enabling people to buy it at an artificially low price before rebuttals by the company's officers reinflate the price.[93]

- *Fraudulent offerings of securities*. Some cyber criminals create websites specifically designed to fraudulently sell securities. To make the offerings look more attractive than they are, assets may be inflated, expected returns overstated, and risks understated. In these schemes, investors are promised abnormally high profits on their investments. No investment is actually made.
- *Illegal touting*. This crime occurs when individuals make securities recommendations and fail to disclose that they are being paid to disseminate their favorable opinions. Section 17(b) of the Securities Act of 1933 requires that paid touters disclose the nature, source, and amount of their compensation. If those who tout stocks fail to disclose their relationship with the company,

information misleads investors into believing that the speaker is objective and credible rather than bought and paid for.

E-tailing Fraud

New fraud schemes are evolving to reflect the fact that billions of dollars of goods are sold on the Internet each year. **E-tailing fraud** involves illegally buying or selling merchandise on the Net.

Some e-tailing scams involve failure to deliver on promised purchases or services, while others involve the substitution of cheaper or used material for higher-quality purchases. So, for example, a person buys expensive jewelry on an Internet site and receives a somewhat less valuable piece than they expected. eBay, the online auction site, is fertile ground for such fraud.[94]

Not only do e-tail frauds involve selling merchandise but they can also involve buyer fraud. One scam involves purchasing top-of-the-line electronic equipment over the Net and then purchasing a second, similar looking but cheaper model of the same brand. The cheaper item is then returned to the e-tailer after switching bar codes and boxes with the more expensive unit. Because e-tail return processing centers don't always check returned goods closely, they may send a refund for the value of the higher-priced model.

In another tactic called "shoplisting," a thief pays maybe $10 for an unexpired receipt covering $500 of legitimately bought electronics or clothing, shoplifts the listed items, and returns them for a refund or gift card. The cards are then sold over the Internet. Not surprisingly, the underground market for receipts has been growing, as stores have liberalized return policies.[95]

Identity Theft

Identity theft occurs when a person uses the Internet to steal someone's identity and/or impersonate the victim to open a new credit card account or conduct some other financial transaction. It is a type of cyber crime that has grown at surprising rates over the past few years.[96]

Identity thieves can seriously disrupt a person's life by manipulating credit records or stealing from the person's bank accounts. These thieves use a variety of techniques to steal information. They may fill out change of address cards at the post office and obtain people's credit card bills and bank statements. They may then call the credit card issuer and, pretending to be the victim, ask for a change in address on the account. They can then charge numerous items over the Internet and have the merchandise sent to the new address. It may take months for the victim to realize the fraud because the victim is not getting bills from the credit card company.

Phishing

Some identity thieves create false e-mails and/or websites that look legitimate but are designed to gain illegal access to a victim's personal information; this is known as **phishing** (also known as "carding" and "spoofing").

Some phishers send out e-mails that look like they come from a credit card company or online store telling victims that there is a problem with their account credit or balance. To fix the problem and update their account they are asked to submit their name, address, phone numbers, personal information, credit card account numbers, and Social Security number (SSN). Or the e-mail may direct them to a phony website that purports to be a legitimate company or business enterprise. Once a victim accesses the website, he or she is asked to provide personal information or financial account information to the website so that the problem can be fixed.

Once phishers have a victim's personal information, they can do three things with it: They can gain access to preexisting accounts, banking, credit cards, and buy things with those accounts. They can use the information to open brand-new banking accounts and credit cards without the victim's knowledge. Finally, the phishers can implant viruses into their software that forwards the phishing e-mail to other recipients once one person responds to the original e-mail, thereby luring more potential victims into their net.

e-tailing fraud
Using the Internet to illegally buy or sell merchandise on the Internet.

identity theft
Using the Internet to steal someone's identity and/or impersonate the victim in order to conduct illicit transactions such as committing fraud using the victim's name and identity.

phishing (carding, spoofing)
Illegally acquiring personal information, such as bank passwords and credit card numbers, by masquerading as a trustworthy person or business in what appears to be an official electronic communication, such as an e-mail or instant message. The term phishing is a play on "fishing" for financial information and passwords with increasingly sophisticated lures.

CONTROLLING CYBER CRIME

The proliferation of cyber crime and its cost to the economy has created the need for new laws and enforcement processes specifically aimed at controlling its new and emerging formulations. Because technology evolves so rapidly, the enforcement challenges are particularly vexing. Numerous organizations have been set up to provide training and support for law enforcement agents. In addition, new federal and state laws have been aimed at particular areas of high-tech crimes.

Congress has treated computer-related crime as a distinct federal offense since the passage of the Counterfeit Access Device and Computer Fraud and Abuse Law in 1984.[97] The 1984 act protects classified U.S. defense and foreign relations information, financial institution and consumer reporting agency files, and access to computers operated for the government. The act was supplemented in 1996 by the National Information Infrastructure Protection Act (NIIPA), which significantly broadens the scope of the law. Since then, legislation has evolved along with the scope of cyber crime in an ongoing effort to protect the public from this new breed of criminal. For example, before October 30, 1998, when the Identity Theft and Assumption Act of 1998 became law, there was no federal statute that made identity theft a crime. Today, federal prosecutors are making substantial use of the 1998 statute and are actively prosecuting cases of identity theft.[98] The states have followed suit and all states except Vermont have passed laws regulating identity theft.

In addition to these main acts, computer-related crimes can be charged under at least 40 different federal statutes. In additon to some of the statutes discussed earlier in the chapter, these include the Copyright Act and Digital Millennium Copyright Act, the National Stolen Property Act, the mail and wire fraud statutes, the Electronic Communications Privacy Act, the Communications Decency Act of 1996, the Child Online Protection Act, the Child Pornography Prevention Act of 1996, and the Internet False Identification Prevention Act of 2000.[99]

Cyber Crime and Law Enforcement Agencies

To enforce these laws the federal government is now operating a number of organizations to control cyber fraud. One approach is to create working groups that coordinate the activities of numerous agencies involved in investigating cyber crime. The Interagency Telemarketing and Internet Fraud Working Group brings together representatives of numerous U.S. attorneys' offices, the FBI, the Secret Service, the Postal Inspection Service, the Federal Trade Commission, the Securities and Exchange Commission, and other law enforcement and regulatory agencies to share information about trends and patterns in Internet fraud schemes.[100]

Specialized enforcement agencies have been created. The Internet Fraud Complaint Center, based in Fairmont, West Virginia, is run by the FBI and the National White Collar Crime Center. It brings together about 1,000 state and local law enforcement officials and regulators. Its goal is to analyze fraud-related complaints in order to find distinct patterns, to develop information on particular cases, and send investigative packages to law enforcement authorities in the jurisdiction that appears likely to have the greatest investigative interest in the matter. Today, the center receives more than 200,000 complaints per year.[101] Law enforcement has made remarkable strides in dealing with identity theft as a crime problem over the last several years.

One of the most successful federal efforts is the New York Electronic Crimes Task Force (NYECTF), a partnership between the U.S. Secret Service and a host of other public safety agencies and private corporations. The task force consists of over 250 individual members representing federal, state, and local law enforcement, the private sector, and computer science specialists from 18 different universities. Since 1995, the New York task force has charged over 1,000 individuals with electronic crime losses exceeding $1 billion. It has trained over 60,000 law enforcement personnel, prosecutors, and private industry representatives in cyber crime prevention. Its success has prompted similar task forces to be set up in Boston, Miami, Charlotte, Chicago, Las Vegas, San Francisco, Los Angeles, and Washington, D.C.[102]

ORGANIZED CRIME

The third branch of enterprise crime involves organized crime—ongoing criminal enterprise groups whose ultimate purpose is personal economic gain through illegitimate means. Here, a structured enterprise system is set up to continually supply consumers with merchandise and services banned by criminal law but for which a ready market exists: prostitution, pornography, gambling, and narcotics. The system may resemble a legitimate business run by an ambitious chief executive officer, his or her assistants, staff attorneys, and accountants, with thorough, efficient accounts receivable and complaint departments.[103]

Because of its secrecy, power, and fabulous wealth, a great mystique has grown up about organized crime. Its legendary leaders—Al Capone, Meyer Lansky, Lucky Luciano—have been the subjects of books and films. The famous *Godfather* films popularized and humanized organized crime figures; the media often glamorize organized crime figures.[104] Watching the exploits of Tony Soprano and his family life has become a national craze.

Most citizens believe organized criminals are capable of taking over legitimate business enterprises if given the opportunity. Almost everyone is familiar with such terms as mob, underworld, Mafia, wise guys, syndicate, or **La Cosa Nostra**, which refer to organized crime. Although most of us have neither met nor seen members of organized crime families, we feel sure that they exist, and we fear them. This section briefly defines organized crime, reviews its history, and discusses its economic effect and control.

Characteristics of Organized Crime

A precise description of the characteristics of organized crime is difficult to formulate, but here are some of its general traits:[105]

- Organized crime is a conspiratorial activity involving the coordination of numerous people in the planning and execution of illegal acts or in the pursuit of a legitimate objective by unlawful means (for example, threatening a legitimate business to get a stake in it). Organized crime involves continuous commitment by primary members, although individuals with specialized skills may be brought in as needed. Organized crime is usually structured along hierarchical lines—a chieftain supported by close advisers, lower subordinates, and so on.
- Organized crime has economic gain as its primary goal, although power and status may also be motivating factors. Economic gain is achieved through maintenance of a near-monopoly on illegal goods and services, including drugs, gambling, pornography, and prostitution.
- Organized crime activities are not limited to providing illicit services. They include such sophisticated activities as laundering illegal money through legitimate businesses, land fraud, and computer crime.
- Organized crime employs predatory tactics, such as intimidation, violence, and corruption. It appeals to greed to accomplish its objectives and preserve its gains.
- By experience, custom, and practice, organized crime's conspiratorial groups are usually very quick and effective in controlling and disciplining their members, associates, and victims. The individuals involved know that any deviation from the rules of the organization will evoke a prompt response from the other participants. This response may range from a reduction in rank and responsibility to a death sentence.
- Organized crime is not synonymous with the Mafia, which is really a common stereotype of organized crime. Although several families in the organization

La Cosa Nostra
A national syndicate of 25 or so Italian-dominated crime families who control crime in distinct geographic areas.

called the Mafia are important components of organized crime activities, they do not hold a monopoly on underworld activities.

- Organized crime does not include terrorists dedicated to political change. Although violent acts are a major tactic of organized crime, the use of violence does not mean that a group is part of a confederacy of organized criminals.

Activities of Organized Crime

What are the main activities of organized crime? The traditional sources of income are derived from providing illicit materials and using force to enter into and maximize profits in legitimate businesses.[106] Most organized crime income comes from narcotics distribution, loan sharking (lending money at illegal rates), and prostitution. However, additional billions come from gambling, theft rings, pornography, and other illegal enterprises. Organized criminals have infiltrated labor unions and taken control of their pension funds and dues.[107] Hijacking of shipments and cargo theft are other sources of income. Underworld figures fence high-value items and maintain international sales territories. In recent years they have branched into computer crime and other white-collar activities. Organized crime figures have also kept up with the information age by using computers and the Internet to sell illegal material such as pornography.

Organized crime figures are also involved in stock market manipulation. The FBI notes that organized crime groups target "small cap" or "micro cap" stocks, over-the-counter stocks, and other types of thinly traded stocks that can be easily manipulated and sold to elderly or inexperienced investors. The conspirators use offshore bank accounts to conceal their participation in the fraud scheme and to launder the illegal proceeds in order to avoid paying income tax.[108]

The Concept of Organized Crime

The term "organized crime" conjures up images of strong men in dark suits, machine gun–toting bodyguards, rituals of allegiance to secret organizations, professional "gangland" killings, and meetings of "family" leaders who chart the course of crime much as the board members at General Motors decide on the country's transportation needs. These images have become part of what criminologists refer to as the **alien conspiracy theory** concept of organized crime. This is the belief, adhered to by the federal government and many respected criminologists, that organized crime is a direct offshoot of a criminal society—the **Mafia**—that first originated in Italy and Sicily and now controls racketeering in major U.S. cities. A major premise of the alien conspiracy theory is that the Mafia is centrally coordinated by a national committee that settles disputes, dictates policy, and assigns territory.[109]

Not all criminologists believe in this narrow concept of organized crime, and many view the alien conspiracy theory as a figment of the media's imagination.[110] Their view depicts organized crime as a group of ethnically diverse gangs or groups who compete for profit in the sale of illegal goods and services or who use force and violence to extort money from legitimate enterprises. These groups are not bound by a central national organization but act independently on their own turf. We will now examine these perspectives in some detail.

Contemporary Organized Crime Groups

Even such devoted alien conspiracy advocates as the U.S. Justice Department now view organized crime as a loose confederation of ethnic and regional crime groups, bound together by a commonality of economic and political objectives.[111] Some of these groups are located in fixed geographical areas. Chicano crime families are found in areas with significant Latino populations, such as California and Arizona. White-ethnic crime organizations are found across the nation. Some Italian and Cuban groups operate internationally. Some have preserved their past identity, whereas others are constantly changing organizations.

alien conspiracy theory
The belief, adhered to by the federal government and many respected criminologists, that organized crime is a direct offshoot of a criminal society that was imported to the United States by Europeans who have a policy of restricting membership to people of their own ethnic background.

Mafia
A group that originated in Italy and Sicily and now controls racketeering in major U.S. cities.

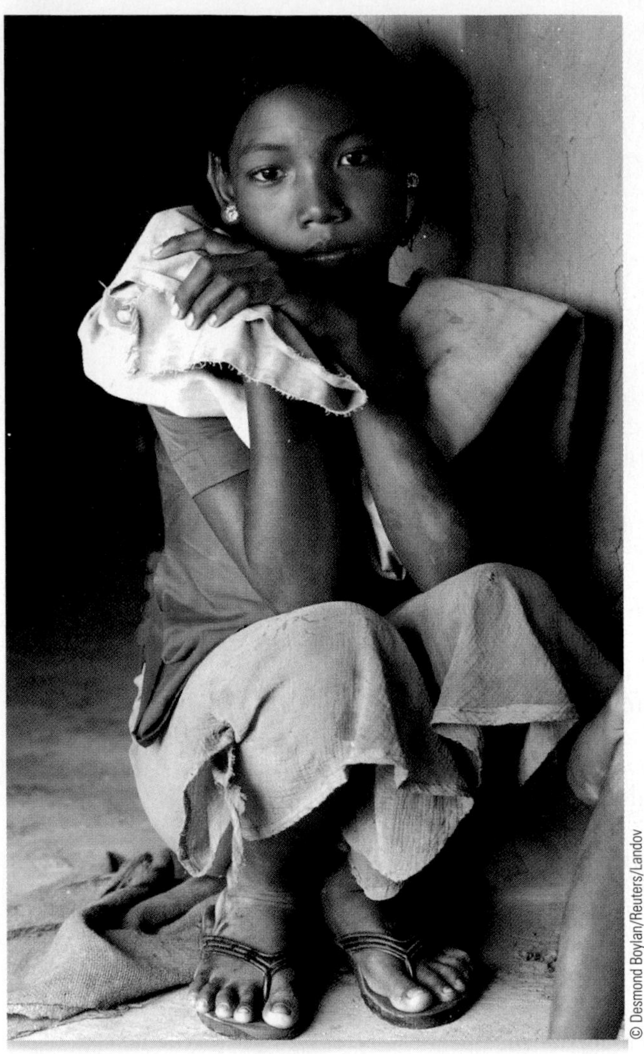

© Desmond Boylan/Reuters/Landov

● Young girls from the close-knit tribe known as the Dhimal, who live in eastern India near Nepal, have become the newest target of international organized crime figures who traffic in the international sex trade. Trafficking in people for forced labor is one of the most lucrative and fastest-growing criminal enterprises in the world, with an estimated 600,000-800,000 men, women, and children forced into slavery each year. There is evidence that criminal syndicates are switching from drugs to human trafficking, finding it easier to transport people than cocaine or heroin. Moreover, drugs can only be sold once; people can be resold again and again.

One important contemporary change in organized crime is the interweaving of ethnic groups into the traditional structure. African American, Latino, and Asian racketeers now compete with the more traditional groups, overseeing the distribution of drugs, prostitution, and gambling in a symbiotic relationship with old-line racketeers.

Eastern European Crime Groups Eastern Europe has been the scene of a massive buildup in organized crime since the fall of the Soviet Union. Trading in illegal arms, narcotics, pornography, and prostitution, they operate a multibillion-dollar transnational crime cartel. Organized groups prey upon women in the poorest areas of Europe—Romania, the Ukraine, Bosnia—and sell them into virtual sexual slavery. Many of these women are transported as prostitutes around the world, some finding themselves in the United States.

In September 2002, an intensive European enforcement operation conducted with American assistance to eliminate some of the major players in the international sex trade resulted in the arrest of 293 traffickers. However, this is the tip of the iceberg: It is estimated that 700,000 women are transported, mostly involuntarily, over international borders each year for the sex trade. One reason for the difficulty in creating effective enforcement is the complicity of local authorities with criminal organizations. For example, during the 2002 raids, the United Nations Mission in Sarajevo dismissed 11 Bosnian police officers, including members of the antitrafficking squad, after they were apprehended visiting brothels and abusing prostitutes.[112]

Since 1970, Russian and other eastern European groups have been operating on U.S. soil. Some groups are formed by immigrants from former satellites of the Soviet Union. In 1998 the FBI established the Yugoslavian/Albanian/Croatian/Serbian (YACS) Crime Group initiative as a response to the increasing threat of criminal activity by people originating from these areas. YACS gangs focus on highly organized and specialized thefts from ATM machines in the New York City area.[113]

In addition, thousands of Russian immigrants are believed to be involved in criminal activity, primarily in Russian enclaves in New York City. Beyond extortion from immigrants, Russian organized crime groups have cooperated with Mafia families in narcotics trafficking, fencing stolen property, money laundering, and other traditional organized crime schemes.[114]

Some of these gangs have engaged in wide-ranging multinational conspiracies. In 1999, after a two-year criminal investigation in Italy, investigators turned up evidence that alleged Russian organized crime operators had funneled millions of dollars through the Bank of New York in a massive money-laundering scheme.[115] Italian prosecutors found that the Russian criminal gangs were raising money in Italy through a mixture of legitimate business activities as well as extortion and tax fraud. Their targets were the Russian businessmen and immigrants who had flooded into Italy with the collapse of communism. The illegal funds were then routed to Moscow and New York, where they were transferred to accounts belonging to suspected organized crime operators. Between 1996 and 1999, the Russian mob is believed to have moved at least $7.5 billion from Russia into the Bank of New York.

Have these newly emerging groups achieved the same level of control as traditional crime families? Some experts argue that new ethnic gangs will have a tough time developing the network of organized corruption, which involves working with government officials and unions, that traditional crime families enjoyed.[116]

For more on the Russian mob, see the Race, Culture, Gender, and Criminology feature.

Controlling Organized Crime

Criminologist George Vold once argued that the development of organized crime parallels early capitalist enterprises. Organized crime employs ruthless monopolistic tactics to maximize profits; it is also secretive, protective of its operations, and defensive against any outside intrusion.[117] Consequently, controlling its activities is extremely difficult.

Federal and state governments actually did little to combat organized crime until fairly recently. One of the first measures aimed directly at organized crime was the Interstate and Foreign Travel or Transportation in Aid of Racketeering Enterprises Act (Travel Act).[118] The Travel Act prohibits travel in interstate commerce or use of interstate facilities with the intent to promote, manage, establish, carry on, or facilitate an unlawful activity; it also prohibits the actual or attempted engagement in these activities. In 1970, Congress passed the Organized Crime Control Act. Title IX of the act, probably its most effective measure, has been called the **Racketeer Influenced and Corrupt Organization Act (RICO)**.[119]

RICO did not create new categories of crimes but rather new categories of offenses in racketeering activity, which it defined as involvement in two or more acts prohibited by 24 existing federal and 8 state statutes. The offenses listed in RICO include state-defined crimes, such as murder, kidnapping, gambling, arson, robbery, bribery, extortion, and narcotic violations; and federally defined crimes, such as bribery, counterfeiting, transmission of gambling information, prostitution, and mail fraud. RICO is designed to limit patterns of organized criminal activity by prohibiting involvement in acts intended to do the following:

- Derive income from racketeering or the unlawful collection of debts and use or investment of such income
- Acquire through racketeering an interest in or control over any enterprise engaged in interstate or foreign commerce
- Conduct business through a pattern of racketeering
- Conspire to use racketeering as a means of making income, collecting loans, or conducting business

An individual convicted under RICO is subject to 20 years in prison and a $25,000 fine. Additionally, the accused must forfeit to the U.S. government any interest in a business in violation of RICO. These penalties are much more potent than simple conviction and imprisonment.

RICO's success has shaped the way the FBI attacks organized crime groups. They now use the **enterprise theory of investigation (ETI)** model as their standard investigative tool. Rather than investigate crimes after they are committed, under the ETI model, the focus is on criminal enterprise and investigation attacks on the structure of the criminal enterprise rather than on criminal acts viewed as isolated incidents.[120] For example, a drug trafficking organization must get involved in such processes as transportation and distribution of narcotics, finance such as money laundering, and communication with clients and dealers. The ETI identifies and then targets each of these areas simultaneously, focusing on the subsystems that are considered the most vulnerable. ✔ CHECKPOINTS

✔ CHECKPOINTS

✔ Organized crime is an ongoing criminal enterprise that employs illegal methods for personal gain.

✔ In some instances, organized crime involves the sale and distribution of illegal merchandise, such as drugs and pornography, while in other cases it uses illegitimate means to market legitimate services, such as lending money (loan sharking) or selling stocks (market manipulation).

✔ Traditional, organized crime families were Italian dominated and called La Cosa Nostra.

✔ Contemporary gangs are multicultural and multinational.

✔ Russian gangs are becoming more common.

✔ The government has used the Racketeer Influenced and Corrupt Organization Act (RICO) to go after gangs.

Racketeer Influenced and Corrupt Organization Act (RICO)
Federal legislation that enables prosecutors to bring additional criminal or civil charges against people engaged in two or more acts prohibited by 24 existing federal and 8 state laws. RICO features monetary penalties that allow the government to confiscate all profits derived from criminal activities. Originally intended to be used against organized criminals, RICO has also been used against white-collar criminals.

enterprise theory of investigation (ETI)
A standard investigation tool of the FBI that focuses on criminal enterprise and investigation attacks on the structure of the criminal enterprise rather than on criminal acts viewed as isolated incidents.

The Future of Organized Crime

Joseph Massino's nickname was "the Last Don." The name seemed quite apropos when in 2004 this boss of New York's Bonanno crime family was convicted on charges of murder and racketeering, ordered to pay fines of $9 million, and given two consecutive life sentences. Massino's greatest sin may, however, have been violating the Mafia's rule of *omerta*, the traditional "code of silence." While in prison, Massino cooperated with prosecutors, secretly taping a conversation with family *capo* Vincent "Vinnie Gorgeous" Basciano, who was outlining a plan to kill lead prosecutor Greg Andres. Massino's current circumstances are not unique. The heads of the four other New York Mafia families—Lucchese, Colombo, Gambino, and Genovese—have also been convicted and sentenced to prison terms.[121]

Russian Organized Crime

Since the collapse of the Soviet Union in 1991, criminal organizations in Russia and other former Soviet republics such as the Ukraine have engaged in a variety of crimes: drugs and arms trafficking, stolen automobiles, trafficking in women and children, and money laundering. No area of the world seems immune to this menace, especially not the United States. America is the land of opportunity for unloading criminal goods and laundering dirty money.

Unlike Colombian, Italian, Mexican, or other well-known forms of organized crime, Russian organized crime is not primarily based on ethnic or family structures. Instead, Russian organized crime is based on economic necessity that was nurtured by the oppressive Soviet regime. Here, a professional criminal class developed in Soviet prisons during the Stalinist period that began in 1924—the era of the gulag. These criminals adopted behaviors, rules, values, and sanctions that bound them together in what was called the thieves' world, led by the elite *vory v zakone*, criminals who lived according to the "thieves' law." This thieves' world, and particularly the *vory*, created and maintained the bonds and climate of trust necessary for carrying out organized crime.

The following are some specific characteristics of Russian organized crime in the post-Soviet era:

- Russian criminals make extensive use of the state governmental apparatus to protect and promote their criminal activities. For example, most businesses in Russia—legal, quasi-legal, and illegal—must operate with the protection of a *krysha* (roof). The protection is often provided by police or security officials employed outside their "official" capacities for this purpose. In other cases, officials are "silent partners" in criminal enterprises that they, in turn, protect.
- The criminalization of the privatization process has resulted in the massive use of state funds for criminal gain. Valuable properties are purchased through insider deals for much less than their true value and then resold for lucrative profits.
- Criminals have been able to directly influence the state's domestic and foreign policy to promote the interests of organized crime, either by attaining public office themselves or by buying public officials.

Beyond these particular features, organized crime in Russia shares other characteristics that are common to organized crime elsewhere in the world:

- Systematic use of violence, including both the threat and use of force
- Hierarchical structure
- Limited or exclusive membership
- Specialization in types of crime and a division of labor
- Military-style discipline, with strict rules and regulations for the organization as a whole
- Possession of high-tech equipment, including military weapons
- Use of threats, blackmail, and violence to penetrate business management and assume control of commercial enterprises or, in some instances, to

The successful prosecution of Massino and other high-ranking organized crime figures is an indication that the traditional organized crime syndicates are in decline. Law enforcement officials in Philadelphia, New Jersey, New England, New Orleans, Kansas City, Detroit, and Milwaukee all report that years of federal and state interventions have severely eroded the Mafia organizations in their areas.

What has caused this alleged erosion of Mafia power? First, a number of the reigning family heads are quite old, in their 80s and older, prompting some law enforcement officials to dub them "the Geritol gang."[122] A younger generation of mob leaders is stepping in to take control of the families, and they seem to lack the skill and leadership of the older bosses. In addition, active government enforcement policies have halved what the estimated mob membership was 25 years ago, and a number of the highest-ranking leaders have been imprisoned.

Additional pressure comes from newly emerging ethnic gangs that want to muscle in on traditional syndicate activities, such as drug sales and gambling. Chinese Triad gangs in New York and California have been active in the drug trade, loan sharking, and labor racketeering. Other ethnic crime groups include black and Colombian drug cartels and the Sicilian Mafia, which operates independently of U.S. groups.

found their own enterprises with money from their criminal activities

As a result of these activities:

- Russia has high rates of homicide that are now more than 20 times those in western Europe and approximately 3 times the rates recorded in the United States. The rates more closely resemble those of a country in civil war or in conflict than those of a country 15 years into a transition.
- Corruption and organized crime are globalized. Russian organized crime is active in Europe, Africa, Asia, and North and South America.
- Massive money laundering is now common. It allows Russian and foreign organized crime to flourish. In some cases, it is tied to terrorist funding.

The organized crime threat to Russia's national security is now becoming a global threat. Russian organized crime operates both on its own and in cooperation with foreign groups. The latter cooperation often comes in the form of joint money laundering ventures. Russian criminals have become involved in killings for hire in central and western Europe, Israel, Canada, and the United States.

In the United States, with the exception of extortion and money laundering, Russians have had little or no involvement in some of the more traditional types of organized crime, such as drug trafficking, gambling, and loan sharking. Instead, Russian criminal groups are extensively engaged in a broad array of frauds and scams, including health care fraud, insurance scams, stock frauds, antiquities swindles, forgery, and fuel tax evasion schemes. Recently, for example, Russians have become the main purveyors of credit card fraud in the United States. Legitimate businesses, such as the movie business and textile industry, have become targets of criminals from the former Soviet Union, and they are often used for money laundering.

Critical Thinking

The influence of new immigrant groups in organized crime seems to suggest that illegal enterprise is a common practice among "new" Americans. Do you believe that some aspect of American culture causes immigrants to choose a criminal lifestyle? Or does our open culture encourage criminal activities that may have been incubating in people's native lands?

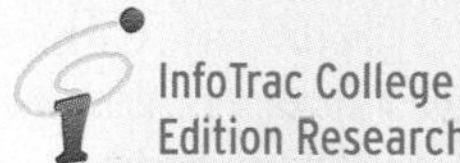

To read more about Russian organized crime, go to InfoTrac College Edition and access Scott O'Neal, "Russian Organized Crime," *FBI Law Enforcement Bulletin* 69 (May 2000): 1.

SOURCES: Louise I. Shelley, "Crime and Corruption: Enduring Problems of Post-Soviet Development," *Demokratizatsiya* 11 (2003): 110–114; James O. Finckenauer and Yuri A. Voronin, *The Threat of Russian Organized Crime* (Washington, DC: National Institute of Justice, 2001).

The Mafia has also been hurt by changing values in U.S. society. White, ethnic, inner-city neighborhoods, which were the locus of Mafia power, have been shrinking as families move to the suburbs. (It comes as no surprise that fictional character Tony Soprano lives in suburban New Jersey and his daughter went to Columbia.) Organized crime groups have consequently lost their political and social base of operations. In addition, the code of silence that protected Mafia leaders is now broken regularly by younger members who turn informer (and even older ones like Massino) rather than face prison terms. It is also possible that their success has hurt organized crime families: Younger members are better educated than their forebears and are equipped to seek their fortunes through legitimate enterprise.[123]

If traditional organized gangs are in decline, that does not mean the end of organized crime. Russian, Caribbean, and Asian gangs seem to be thriving, and there are always new opportunities for illegal practices. Law enforcement officials believe that Internet gambling sites are a tempting target for enterprise criminals. It is not surprising then that Illinois, Louisiana, Nevada, Oregon, and South Dakota have recently passed laws specifically banning Internet gambling.[124] It is unlikely, considering the demand for illegal goods and services and the emergence of newly constituted crime families, that organized criminal behavior will ever be eradicated.

THINKING Like a Criminologist

As a criminologist and expert on white-collar crime, you are asked to help his legal defense team prepare a sentencing statement in support of Anthony J. Facciabrutto, 33, recently convicted of numerous federal charges.

In 2003, Facciabrutto was charged with mail fraud, money laundering, telemarketing fraud against the elderly, and securities fraud. From 1994 through February 1999 Facciabrutto owned and operated Facciabrutto Holdings, Inc., a telemarketing company in the Los Angeles area. Facciabrutto Holdings, Inc., raised approximately $31 million from more than 800 victims across the United States. Facciabrutto's investors received only a fraction of their total investment in the company. One victim invested in excess of $400,000 and received less than $10,000 in return.

It is alleged that Facciabrutto and the telemarketers he employed sold investment in restaurants and what was marketed as luxury resorts, which never generated profits. The telemarketing operation was, according to the indictment, a scheme in which earlier investors were paid "dividend payments" derived from funds obtained from later investors.

Facciabrutto was the chief executive officer for Facciabrutto Holdings, Inc., and is alleged to have paid himself a 40 percent sales commission. Sales managers were paid 25 percent of total sales, and salespersons received a 25 percent commission. Facciabrutto allegedly misrepresented sales commissions and made false guarantees to customers. Facciabrutto misrepresented the company's imminent initial public offering, which never occurred. The SEC conducted a civil investigation into Facciabrutto during 1999 and as a result, Facciabrutto was ordered to pay a $3 million judgment. This is his first offense, and he claims that overwhelming personal problems drove him to commit crime. Facciabrutto had big personal debts and had borrowed heavily from organized crime figures.

Do you have any ideas on how to save your client from prison?

Summary

- Enterprise crime involves illicit entrepreneurship and commerce.
- White-collar crime and organized crime are linked because they involve entrepreneurship. Losses from enterprise crime may far outstrip any other type of crime.
- Embezzlement and employee fraud occur when a person uses a position of trust to steal from an organization.
- Client fraud involves theft from an organization that advances credit, covers losses, or reimburses for services.
- Corporate, or organizational, crime involves various illegal business practices such as price fixing, restraint of trade, and false advertising.
- There are numerous explanations for white-collar crime: Some offenders are motivated by greed; others offend due to personal problems. They use rationalizations to allow their financial needs to be met without compromising their values.
- Corporate culture theory suggests that some businesses actually encourage employees to cheat or cut corners.
- The self-control view is that white-collar criminals are like any other law violators: impulsive people who lack self-control.
- Little has been done in the past to combat white-collar crime. Most offenders do not view themselves as criminals and therefore do not seem to be deterred by criminal statutes.
- Although thousands of white-collar criminals are prosecuted each year, their numbers are insignificant compared with the magnitude of the problem.
- The government has used various law enforcement strategies to combat white-collar crime. Some involve deterrence, which uses punishment to frighten potential abusers. Others involve economic or compliance strategies, which create economic incentives to obey the law.
- Cyber crime is a new breed of offenses that involve the theft and/or destruction of information, resources, or funds using computers, computer networks, and the Internet.
- Cyber crime presents a challenge for the justice system because it is rapidly evolving, it is difficult to detect through traditional law enforcement channels, and its control demands that agents of the justice system develop technical skills that match those of the perpetrators.
- Cyber crime has grown because information technology (IT) has become part of daily life in most industrialized societies.
- Some cyber crimes use modern technology to accumulate goods and services; these are known as cyber theft.
- Computer fraud is not an offense in itself but rather a common-law crime committed using contemporary technology.

- The Internet has become a primary source of selling and distributing obscene material.
- Some sites cater to adult tastes, but others cross the legal border by peddling access to either obscene material or even kiddie porn. It is unlikely that any law enforcement efforts will put a dent in the Internet porn industry.
- A denial-of-service attack is an attempt to extort money from legitimate users of an Internet service by threatening to prevent them from accessing the service.
- Warez refers to activities of groups of individuals who work together to obtain professionally made software illegally and then "crack" or "rip" its copyright protections, before posting it on the Internet for other members of the group to use.
- Another type of illegal copyright infringement involves file-sharing programs that allow Internet users to download music and other copyrighted material without paying the artists and record producers their rightful royalties.
- Internet security fraud involves using the Internet to intentionally manipulate the securities marketplace for profit.
- Identity theft occurs when a person uses the Internet to steal someone's identity and/or impersonate the victim to open a new credit card account or conduct some other financial transaction.
- Identity thieves can seriously disrupt a person's life by manipulating credit records or stealing from the person's bank accounts.
- Phishing involves the creation of false e-mails and/or websites that look legitimate but are designed to gain illegal access to a victim's personal information.
- E-tailing scams involve either the failure to deliver on promised purchases or services, or the substitution of cheaper or used material for higher-quality purchases.
- Organized crime supplies alcohol, gambling, drugs, prostitutes, and pornography to the public.
- Organized criminals used to be white ethnics—Jews, Italians, and Irish—but today African Americans, Latinos, and other groups have become involved in organized crime activities. The old-line "families" are now more likely to use their criminal wealth and power to buy into legitimate businesses.
- Eastern European crime families are active abroad and in the United States. Russian organized crime has become a major problem for law enforcement agencies.
- There is debate over how to control organized crime. Some experts believe a national crime cartel controls all activities. Others view organized crime as a group of disorganized, competing gangs dedicated to extortion or to providing illegal goods and services. Efforts to control organized crime have been stepped up by the federal government, which has used antiracketeering statutes to arrest syndicate leaders. But as long as huge profits can be made, illegal enterprises will continue to flourish.

Take a Post-Test. Visit www.thomsonedu.com/criminaljustice/siegel and take the chapter Post-Test to monitor your progress and identify areas for further improvement. In addition to discovering what you've mastered, you'll learn which concepts need your added attention and get specific page references that direct you to the places in the text where you can find more information on them.

Key Terms

insider trading 280
enterprise crime 280
white-collar crime 281
cyber crime 281
organized crime 281
swindle (sting) 282
chiseling 283
churning 283
front running 283
bucketing 283
exploitation (of victims) 284
influence peddling 284
payola 285
pilferage 286
corporate (organizational) crime 287
Sherman Antitrust Act 289
compliance strategies 293
information technology (IT) 295
globalization 295
cyber theft 295
denial-of-service attack 297
warez 297
e-tailing fraud 300
identity theft 300
phishing (carding, spoofing) 300
La Cosa Nostra 302
alien conspiracy theory 303
Mafia 303
Racketeer Influenced and Corrupt Organization Act (RICO) 305
enterprise theory of investigation (ETI) 305

Critical Thinking Questions

1. How would you punish a corporate executive whose product killed people, if the executive had no knowledge that the product was potentially lethal? What if the executive did know?

2. Is organized crime inevitable as long as immigrant groups seek to become part of the American Dream?

3. Does the media glamorize organized crime? Does it paint an inaccurate picture of noble crime lords fighting to protect their families?

4. Apply traditional theories of criminal behavior to white-collar and organized crime. Which one seems to best predict why someone would engage in these behaviors?

CHAPTER

13

Public Order Crimes

© AP

ON FEBRUARY 17, 2006, THE FRONT PAGE OF THE *DALLAS MORNING NEWS* ANNOUNCED "CANDIDATE WORKED AS PROSTITUTE."[1] The story concerned Tom Malin's campaign for district 108 of the Texas House of Representatives. The 37-year-old Malin had been running as an openly gay candidate in the Democratic primary. A Dallas native, community activist, and successful businessman (sales director for Mary Kay cosmetics), Malin lived in a fashionable high-rise with his partner, a philanthropist and businessman.

Before the scandal made headlines, Malin seemed to have the race in hand. He had secured endorsements from the Dallas Stonewall Democrats, Dallas Tejano Democrats (a Latino political group), and the *Morning News*. His issues were school financing, crime, the economy, and tax and ethics reform. Then the story broke that he had been an escort on and off until 2001—mostly while a struggling actor in New York and Los Angeles.

He gave a statement to the *Morning News*: "I've made mistakes in my life, and I've stood before my creator and I've accepted responsibility for my behavior, I've also accepted his grace and his redemption and his love and his forgiveness, and that's what's important."[2] Nonetheless, Malin's campaign never recovered. On March 7, 2006, he lost the primary 55% to 45%. In the aftermath, *The Advocate,* a national gay and lesbian newsmagazine, issued the following statement:

> Even among many gays and lesbians—and certainly in mainstream culture—sex for pay remains the irredeemable sin. The president can be a recovering alcoholic with a DUI arrest; the vice president can accidentally shoot a man—all is forgiven. But if a person takes money for sex, the taint may be inescapable. Forget about running for office. Forget about a high-profile business career. Forget about acting, modeling, or MTV. It's over. Even many gays will prefer that you take a hike.

CHAPTER OBJECTIVES

1. Be able to discuss the legal cases that define the right to personal sexual relations between consenting adults.
2. Be familiar with the association between law and morality.
3. Know what is meant by the terms "moral crusade" and "moral entrepreneur."
4. Understand and be able to discuss some of the most common paraphilias.
5. Be able to discuss what is meant by "obscenity."
6. Know the various techniques being used to control pornography.
7. Be able to discuss the various types of prostitution.
8. Discuss the history of drug abuse.
9. Be able to discuss the cause of substance abuse.
10. Identify the various drug control strategies.

Take a Pre-Test. Visit www.thomsonedu.com/criminaljustice/siegel and take a Pre-Test to determine what you already know and identify the areas where you'll need to focus your study. The program will direct you to specific pages within the text where you can find further information on the correct answers to the questions you've missed.

Tom Malin's experience illustrates the concern the public and the media have with issues of morality and values. It is ironic that Malin could be a successful candidate for public office as an openly gay man, something that would have been unthinkable 50 years ago; yet his career was destroyed by his involvement in sex for hire. Although one act considered a violation of social norms only a few years ago is now accepted, another is still prohibited and shunned by "polite society." Who decides what is acceptable behavior, what is not, and how we distinguish between them are still matters of great concern to criminologists.

Societies have long banned or limited behaviors believed to run contrary to social norms, customs, and values. These behaviors are often referred to as **public order crimes** or victimless crimes, although the latter term can be misleading.[3] Public order crimes involve acts that interfere with the operations of society and the ability of people to function efficiently. Put another way, whereas such common-law crimes as rape or robbery are considered inherently wrong and damaging, other behaviors are outlawed because they conflict with social policy, prevailing moral rules, and current public opinion.

Statutes designed to uphold public order usually prohibit the manufacture and distribution of morally questionable goods and services such as erotic material, commercial sex, and mood-altering drugs. They may also ban acts that a few people holding political power consider morally tinged. Statutes like these are controversial in part because millions of otherwise law-abiding citizens often engage in these outlawed activities and consequently become criminals. These statutes are also controversial because they selectively prohibit desired goods, services, and behaviors; in other words, they outlaw sin and vice.

This chapter covers these public order crimes. It first briefly discusses the relationship between law and morality. Next, the chapter addresses public order crimes of a sexual nature: pornography, prostitution, and deviant sexual acts such as bondage. The chapter concludes by focusing on the abuse of drugs and alcohol.

public order crime
Behavior that is outlawed because it threatens the general well-being of society and challenges its accepted moral principles.

LAW AND MORALITY

Legislation of moral issues has continually frustrated lawmakers. There is little debate that the purpose of criminal law is to protect society and reduce social harm. When a store is robbed or a child assaulted, it is relatively easy to see and condemn the harm done the victim. It is, however, more difficult to sympathize with or even identify the victims of immoral acts, such as pornography or prostitution, in which the parties involved may be willing participants. If there is no victim, can there be a crime? Should acts be made illegal merely because they violate prevailing moral standards? If so, who defines morality?

To answer these questions, we might first consider whether there is actually a victim in so-called **victimless crimes**. Take the adult film industry for example. Are performers "victims" or highly paid and willing participants? Some participants may have been coerced into their acts; if so, they are victims. Opponents of pornography, such as Andrea Dworkin, charge that women involved in adult films, far from being highly paid stars, are "dehumanized—turned into objects and commodities."[4] Although taking drugs may be a matter of personal choice, it too has serious consequences. One study of 171 crack cocaine–using women found that since initiating crack use, 62 percent of the women reported suffering a physical attack and 32 percent suffered rape; more than half were forced to seek medical care for their injuries.[5]

Some scholars argue that pornography, prostitution, and drug use erode the moral fabric of society and therefore should be prohibited and punished. They are crimes, according to the great legal scholar Morris Cohen, because "it is one of the functions of the criminal law to give expression to the collective feeling of revulsion toward certain acts, even when they are not very dangerous."[6]

According to this view, so-called victimless crimes are prohibited because one function of criminal law is to express a shared sense of public morality.[7] However, basing criminal definitions on moral beliefs is often an impossible task. Who defines morality? Are we not punishing differences rather than social harm? As U.S. Supreme Court Justice William O. Douglas so succinctly put it, "What may be trash to me may be prized by others."[8] Would not any attempt to control or limit "objectionable" material eventually lead to the suppression of free speech and political dissent? Is this not a veiled form of censorship? Not so, according to social commentator Irving Kristol:

> If we start censoring pornography and obscenity, shall we not inevitably end up censoring political opinion? A lot of people seem to think this would be the case—which only shows the power of doctrinaire thinking over reality. We had censorship of pornography and obscenity for 150 years, until almost yesterday, and I am not aware that freedom of opinion in this country was in any way diminished as a consequence of this fact.[9]

Criminal or Immoral?

Many acts that most of us deem immoral are not criminal. There is no law against *superbia* (hubris/pride), *avaritia* (avarice/greed), *luxuria* (extravagance or lust), *invidia* (envy), *gula* (gluttony), *ira* (wrath), and *acedia* (sloth), even though they are considered the "seven deadly sins." Nor is it a crime in most jurisdictions to ignore the pleas of a drowning person, even though such callous behavior is surely immoral.

Some acts that seem both well intentioned and moral are nonetheless considered criminal. It is a crime (euthanasia) to kill a loved one suffering from an incurable disease to spare him or her further pain. Stealing a rich person's money to feed a poor family is considered larceny. Marrying more than one woman is considered a crime (bigamy), even though multiple marriages may conform to religious beliefs.[10] As legal experts Wayne LaFave and Austin Scott, Jr., state, "A good motive will not normally prevent what is otherwise criminal from being a crime."[11]

Generally, immoral acts can be distinguished from crimes on the basis of the social harm they cause: Acts that harm the public are usually outlawed. Yet this perspective does not always hold sway. Some acts that cause enormous amounts of social harm are perfectly legal. All of us are aware of the illness and death associated

victimless crime
Public order crime that violates the moral order but has no specific victim other than society as a whole.

with the consumption of tobacco and alcohol, but they remain legal to produce and sell. Manufacturers continue to sell sports cars and motorcycles that can accelerate to more than 100 miles per hour, although the legal speed limit is usually 65. More people die each year from alcohol-, tobacco-, and auto-related deaths than from all illegal drugs combined. Should drugs be legalized and fast cars outlawed?

And sometimes even "social harm" is hard to define. For example, the recent scandals involving the sexual activities of some Roman Catholic priests have been shocking. Most Americans would agree that sexuality and children never mix. It is not surprising then that Judith Levine caused a commotion with her book *Harmful to Minors: The Perils of Protecting Children from Sex.*[12] In this controversial book, Levine takes American culture to task for attempting to control, monitor, and suppress children's knowledge of sex and their sexual expression. Levine argues that children are more likely to be harmed by efforts to shield and protect them than they are in danger from information about sexuality. She hints that in some instances kids are not damaged by relations with older people and that some sexual relations between adults and minors can have a positive outcome. As a result, *Harmful to Minors* was rejected by many publishing houses and, when finally published by the University of Minnesota Press, became the target of a campaign by social conservatives to have it taken out of publication. Is Levine correct? Has American society become overly protective of adolescents and in denial that they may have sexual feelings?

Moral Crusades/Moral Crusaders

Public order crimes often trace their origin to moral crusaders who seek to shape the law toward their own way of thinking; Howard Becker calls them **moral entrepreneurs**. These rule creators, argues Becker, operate with an absolute certainty that their way is right and that any means are justified to get their way: "The crusader is fervent and righteous, often self-righteous."[13] Today's moral crusaders take on such issues as prayer in school, the right to legal abortions, and the distribution of sexually explicit books and magazines.

Moral crusades are often directed against people or institutions that crusaders consider evil, even though they may be admired by others who fail to share the crusaders' ideas and values. An antismut campaign may attempt to ban the books of a popular author from the school library or prevent a controversial figure from speaking at the local college, even though many people in the community admire their work. One way for moral crusaders to accomplish their goal is to prove to all who will listen that some unseen or hidden trait makes their target truly evil and unworthy of a public audience—they may claim the Bible condemns their behavior. This polarization of good and evil creates a climate in which those categorized as "good" are deified while the "bad" are demonized and become objects suitable for control.

Sometimes moral crusaders justify their actions by claiming that the very structure of our institutions and beliefs are in danger because of immorality that must be controlled. Andrea Friedman's analysis of antiobscenity campaigns during the Cold War era (post–World War II) found that the politics of the times led to an image of aggressive, even violent, males being used in comic books and pornography. At the time, antiobscenity advocates argued that this depiction threatened family values, a successful campaign that led to a ban on violent comics and porn magazines.[14]

Freedom vs. Control

Crusaders typically call upon political leaders to do something about the problem they find troubling; successful crusades result in some kind of policy change.[15] In some instances, moral crusades are aimed at controlling or limiting behavior considered immoral and/or harmful, while in others the crusaders want restrictions lifted so that people can engage in behavior previously outlawed.

An example of the first type of crusade is the one being mounted to protect young women from genital mutilation, a practice carried out in some Middle Eastern and African nations. Amnesty International estimates that 135 million of the world's girls and women have undergone genital mutilation, and 2 million girls a year are at risk of mutilation.[16]

CONNECTIONS

As you may recall from Chapter 10, gay men and women are still subject to thousands of incidents of violence and other hate crimes each year.

CONNECTIONS

Another similar effort is aimed at stamping out the worldwide sex trade that exploits young women in third world nations. This crusade is discussed later in the chapter.

moral entrepreneur
A person who creates moral rules, which thus reflect the values of those in power rather than any objective universal standards of right and wrong.

CONNECTIONS

Moral entrepreneurs are likely to use the interactionist definition of crime discussed in Chapter 1: Acts are illegal because they violate the moral standards of those in power and those who try to shape public opinion.

Some crusades are designed to secure rights and privileges that heretofore have been withheld. Gay activist groups have campaigned for same-sex marriage and to legalize same-sex relations that were previously criminalized under sodomy laws. In some instances their efforts have paid dividends: In 2003, Massachusetts' highest court ruled that same-sex couples are legally entitled to wed under the state constitution, ruling that the state of Massachusetts may not "deny the protections, benefits and obligations conferred by civil marriage to two individuals of the same sex who wish to marry."[17] Similarly, in 2003 the U.S. Supreme Court delivered a historic decision in *Lawrence v. Texas* that made it impermissible for states to criminalize oral and anal sex and all other forms of intercourse that are not heterosexual under statutes prohibiting sodomy, deviant sexuality, or buggery.[18] In so doing the Court overruled its 1986 decision in the *Bowers v. Hardwick* case, which had upheld a Georgia statute making it a crime to engage in consensual sodomy, even within one's own home.[19] The *Lawrence* case involved two gay men who had been arrested in 1998 for having sex in the privacy of their Houston home. In overturning their convictions, the Court said this:

> Although the laws involved . . . here . . . do not more than prohibit a particular sexual act, their penalties and purposes have more far-reaching consequences, touching upon the most private human conduct, sexual behavior, and in the most private of places, the home. They seek to control a personal relationship that, whether or not entitled to formal recognition in the law, is within the liberty of persons to choose without being punished as criminals. The liberty protected by the Constitution allows homosexual persons the right to choose to enter upon relationships in the confines of their homes and their own private lives and still retain their dignity as free persons.

As a result of the decision, sodomy laws in the United States that ban adult same sex contact are now unconstitutional and unenforceable. The *Lawrence* decision heralded a new era of legal and civil rights for homosexual men and women. A sign of a successful moral crusade is when the crusaders' views and ideology are incorporated in official government policy.

The public order crimes discussed in this chapter are divided into two broad areas. The first relates to what conventional society considers deviant sexual practices: paraphilias, prostitution, and pornography. The second area concerns the use of substances that have been outlawed or controlled because of the alleged harm they cause: drugs and alcohol. ✔ CHECKPOINTS

✔ CHECKPOINTS

- ✔ Societies can ban behaviors that lawmakers consider offensive. Critics question whether this amounts to censorship.
- ✔ The line between behaviors that are merely immoral and those that are criminal is often blurred.
- ✔ Immoral acts are considered crimes when they cause social harm.
- ✔ Though sometimes called victimless crimes, critics argue that seemingly voluntary crimes such as pornography or prostitution really do have victims.
- ✔ People who seek to control or criminalize deviant behaviors are called moral entrepreneurs. They often go on moral crusades.
- ✔ A successful moral crusade results in policy change that either prohibits a previously acceptable behavior or permits one that previously had been excluded.

PARAPHILIAS

During the past few years, the Catholic Church has been rocked by allegations that numerous priests had been involved in sexually molesting children. Nowhere did the scandal take on greater proportion than in Boston, where Cardinal Bernard Law was forced to step down as leader of the diocese. Among the most notorious offenders was Father James Porter, accused of molesting at least 125 children of both sexes over a 30-year period reaching back to the early 1960s. Porter was eventually sentenced to an 18- to 20-year prison term.

Porter's behavior is an extreme example of sexual abnormality referred to as **paraphilia**, from the Greek *para*, "to the side of," and *philos*, "loving." Paraphilias are bizarre or abnormal sexual practices involving recurrent sexual urges focused on (1) nonhuman objects (such as underwear, shoes, or leather), (2) humiliation or the experience of receiving or giving pain (as in sadomasochism or bondage), or (3) children or others who cannot grant consent.[20] Paraphilias have existed and been recorded for thousands of years. Buddhist texts more than 2,000 years old contain references to sexually deviant behaviors among monastic communities, including sexual activity with animals and sexual interest in corpses. Richard von Krafft-Ebing's *Psychopathia Sexualis,* first published in 1887, was the first text to discuss such paraphilias as sadism, bestiality, and incest.[21]

paraphilia
Bizarre or abnormal sexual practices that may involve nonhuman objects, humiliation, or children.

Some paraphilias, such as wearing clothes normally worn by the opposite sex (transvestite fetishism), can be engaged in by adults in the privacy of their homes and do not involve a third party; these relatively harmless escapades are outside

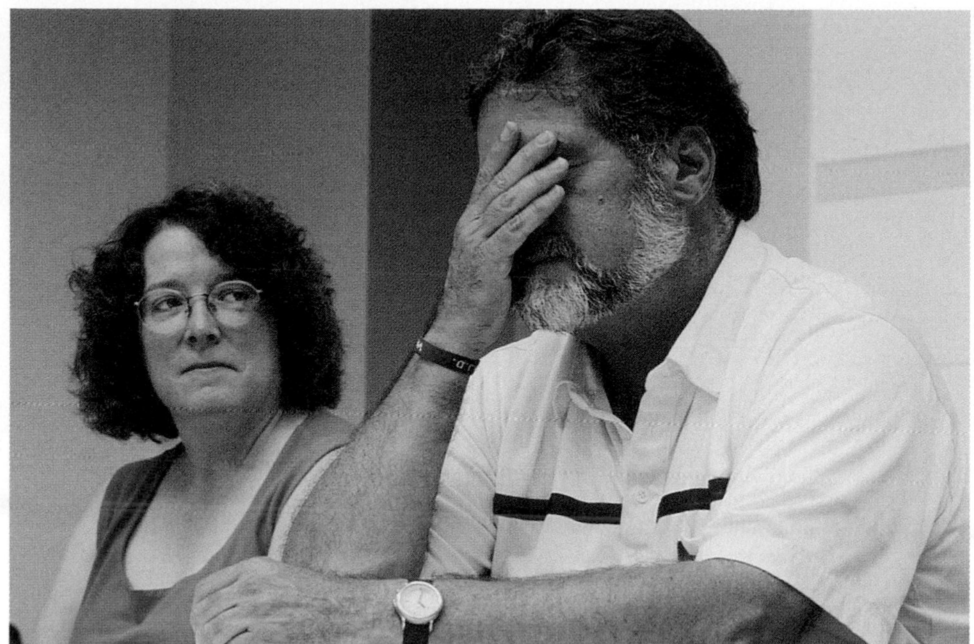

© AP

● Some of the most notorious cases of pedophilia concern Catholic priests who abused young children in their parishes. Here, Carol McCormick of Chelmsford, Massachusetts, looks on as Fred Paine of Warwick, Rhode Island, a victim of Rev. James Porter, pauses during a panel discussion on their experiences with settling civil suits against the Catholic Church.

the law's reach. Others, however, risk social harm and are subject to criminal penalties. This group of outlawed sexual behavior includes the following acts:

- *Frotteurism*: rubbing against or touching a nonconsenting person in a crowd, elevator, or other public area.
- *Voyeurism*: obtaining sexual pleasure from spying on a stranger while he or she disrobes or engages in sexual behavior with another.
- *Exhibitionism*: deriving sexual pleasure from exposing the genitals to surprise or shock a stranger.
- *Sadomasochism*: deriving pleasure from receiving pain or inflicting pain on another.
- *Pedophilia*: attaining sexual pleasure through sexual activity with prepubescent children.

PROSTITUTION

Known for thousands of years, the term prostitution derives from the Latin *prostituere*, which means "to cause to stand in front of." The prostitute is viewed as publicly offering his or her body for sale. The earliest record of prostitution appears in ancient Mesopotamia, where priests engaged in sex to promote fertility in the community. All women were required to do temple duty, and passing strangers were expected to make donations to the temple after enjoying their services.[22]

Modern commercial sex appears to have its roots in ancient Greece, where Solon established licensed brothels in 500 BCE. The earnings of Greek prostitutes helped pay for the temple of Aphrodite. Famous men openly went to prostitutes to enjoy intellectual, aesthetic, and sexual stimulation; prostitutes, however, were prevented from marrying.[23]

Today **prostitution** can be defined as granting nonmarital sexual access, established by mutual agreement of the prostitutes, their clients, and their employers, for remuneration. This definition is sexually neutral because prostitutes can be straight or gay and male or female. A recent analysis has amplified the definition of prostitution by describing the conditions usually present in a commercial sexual transaction:

- *Activity that has sexual significance for the customer*. This includes the entire range of sexual behavior, from sexual intercourse to exhibitionism, sadomasochism, oral sex, and so on.

prostitution
The granting of nonmarital sexual access for remuneration.

Race, Culture, Gender, & Criminology

International Trafficking in Prostitution

Trafficking in women and girls for the purpose of sexual exploitation is market-valued at $7 billion annually. Trafficking may be the result of force, coercion, manipulation, deception, abuse of authority, initial consent, family pressure, past and present family and community violence, economic deprivation, or other conditions of inequality for women and children. Women are trafficked to, from, and through every region in the world. Exact numbers are unknown, but international agencies and governmental bodies estimate that each year more than 1 million women and girls are trafficked for sexual exploitation in sex industries. Even fundamentalist nations such as Iran have joined the buying and selling of women and girls for prostitution. Exact numbers of victims are difficult to estimate, but according to an official source in Tehran, there has been a recent upsurge in the number of teenagers being sold into prostitution. In Tehran, Iran's capital city, there are an estimated 84,000 women and girls in prostitution, many of them on the streets, others in the 250 brothels that reportedly operate in the city. The trade is also international: Thousands of Iranian women and girls have been sold into sexual slavery abroad.

Studies conducted abroad, especially in third world countries, link prostitution to economic necessity. Prostitutes in Dakar, Senegal, report that they are in "the life" because it is a necessary means for survival even if it carries with it a high risk of HIV infection. Female sex workers in Tijuana, Mexico, mostly single mothers, report entering the sex trade as a means to support their children. While sex work has risks such as physical assault, diseases, and unwanted pregnancies, the women believe that sex work is a way to get off the streets and avoid homelessness.

Exporting Prostitution

The U.S. State Department estimates that 50,000 to 100,000 women and children are trafficked into the United States each year for labor or sexual exploitation. The moneymakers are transnational networks of traffickers and pimps who prey on women seeking employment and opportunities. These illegal activities and related crimes not only harm the women involved but also undermine the social, political, and economic fabric of the nations where they occur.

Countries with large sex industries create the demand for women; countries where traffickers easily recruit women provide the supply. For decades, the primary sending countries were in Asia, but the collapse of the Soviet Union opened a pool of millions of women from which traffickers can recruit. Former Soviet republics such as Belarus, Latvia, Moldova, Russia, and Ukraine have become major suppliers of women to sex industries all over the world.

In the sex industry today, the most popular and valuable women are from Russia and Ukraine. Authorities in the Ukraine estimate that more than 100,000 women were trafficked during the past 10 years. Popular destination countries include Canada, the Czech Republic, Germany, Greece, Hungary, the Netherlands, Turkey, the United Arab Emirates, the United States, and Yugoslavia. Large numbers of Ukrainian women are trafficked into Korea to be used as prostitutes near military bases.

Migration from the former Soviet republics has aided trafficking. Members of organized crime rings establish contacts with collaborators in overseas communities and work within migrating populations to build criminal networks. Increased migration also serves as a cover for traffickers transporting

- *Economic transaction*. Something of economic value, not necessarily money, is exchanged for the activity.
- *Emotional indifference*. The sexual exchange is simply for economic consideration. Although the participants may know one another, their interaction has nothing to do with affection for one another.[24] Men believe that the lack of involvement makes hiring a prostitute less of a hassle and less trouble than becoming involved in a romantic relationship.[25]

Incidence of Prostitution

Although it is difficult to assess the number of prostitutes operating in the United States, the Uniform Crime Report (UCR) indicates that about 90,000 prostitution arrests are made annually, with the gender ratio being about 2:1 female to male. The number of prostitution arrests has been trending downward for some time; 10 years ago more than 100,000 prostitution arrests were made each year. How can the decline in arrests be explained? It is possible that (1) fewer people are seeking the services of prostitutes, (2) police are reluctant to make arrests in prostitution cases, or (3) more sophisticated prostitutes using the Internet or other forms of technology to "make dates" are better able to avoid detection by police.

Fifty years ago, about two-thirds of non–college educated men and one-quarter of college educated men had visited a prostitute.[26] It is likely that the number of men who hire prostitutes has declined sharply since then. How can these changes be accounted for? Changing sexual mores, brought about by the so-called sexual women. Computer technologies have aided management of the growing volume and complexity of international financial transactions, increasing opportunities for transnational crime and decreasing the probability of detection.

Recruiting Women

Recruiters, traffickers, and pimps have developed common operating methods. One strategy is advertisements in newspapers offering lucrative job opportunities in foreign countries for low-skilled jobs, such as waitresses and nannies. Another method of recruitment is through "marriage agencies," sometimes called mail-order bride agencies or international introduction services. But the most common way for women to be recruited is through a friend or acquaintance who gains the woman's confidence. "Second wave" recruiting occurs when a trafficked woman returns home to draft other women. Once a woman has been trafficked and trapped in the sex industry, she has few options. One of the few means of escaping the brutality of being forced to have sex with multiple men each day is to move from being the victim to being the perpetrator.

Once women reach the destination country, travel documents are confiscated, and they are subjected to violence and threats to harm their family members. They are told they owe thousands in travel costs and must pay them off through prostitution. The women get to keep little, if any, of the money. Women must repay their purchase price and travel and other expenses before they are allowed to leave. They can expect little help from law enforcement authorities who are either ambivalent or working with the traffickers.

Combating Trafficking

Recently, the United States made stopping the trafficking of women a top priority. In 1998, a Memorandum on Steps to Combat Violence against Women and the Trafficking of Women and Girls was issued that directed the secretary of state, the attorney general, and the President's Interagency Council on Women to expand their work against violence against women to include work against the trafficking of women.

In the former Soviet Union, prevention education projects are aimed at potential victims of trafficking, and nongovernmental organizations have established hotlines for victims or women seeking information about the risks of accepting job offers abroad.

Critical Thinking

1. If put in charge, what would you do to slow or end the international trafficking in prostitution? Before you answer, remember the saying that prostitution is the "oldest profession," which implies that curbing it may prove quite difficult.
2. Should men who hire prostitutes be punished severely to deter them from getting involved in the exploitation of these vulnerable young women?

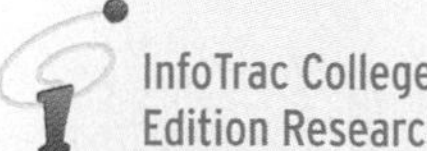

Brenda Platt, "Commercial Sexual Exploitation of Children: A Global Problem Requiring Global Action," *Sexual Health Exchange* (Summer 2002): 10.

SOURCES: Donna Hughes, "Sex Slave Jihad," FrontPageMagazine.com, January 27, 2004 www.uri.edu/artsci/wms/hughes/sex_slave_trade_iran.pdf (accessed April 18, 2006); "The 'Natasha' Trade: Transnational Sex Trafficking," *National Institute of Justice Journal* (January 2001); Maria Eugênia do Espirito Santo and Gina Etheredge, "And Then I Became a Prostitute . . . Some Aspects of Prostitution and Brothel Prostitutes in Dakar, Senegal," *Social Science Journal* 41 (2004): 137–146; Jesus Bucardo, Shirley Semple, Miguel Fraga-Vallejo, Wendy Davila, and Thomas Patterson, "A Qualitative Exploration of Female Sex Work in Tijuana, Mexico," *Archives of Sexual Behavior* 33 (2004): 343–352.

revolution, have liberalized sexuality. Men are less likely to use prostitutes because legitimate alternatives for sexuality are more open to them. In addition, the prevalence of sexually transmitted diseases has caused many men to avoid visiting prostitutes for fear of irreversible health hazards.[27] Why do men still employ prostitutes? Some are pressured by peers to try something different and exciting, others desire a sexual exchange free from obligations, while another group is just curious about the world of prostitution. Customers who become "regulars" may view prostitution as a service occupation not different from other service occupations.[28]

International Sex Trade

Although prostitution arrests are down in the United States, a troubling overseas trade called "sex tourism" is thriving. In this form of prostitution, men from wealthy countries frequent semiregulated sex areas in needy nations, such as Thailand, to procure young girls forced or sold into prostitution. There has also been a soaring demand for pornography, strip clubs, lap dancing, escorts, telephone sex, and "sex tours" in developing countries.[29] The international trade in prostitution is the subject of the Race, Culture, Gender, & Criminology feature.

In addition, every year, hundreds of thousands of women and children—primarily from Southeast Asia and Eastern Europe—are lured by the promise of good jobs and then end up forced into brothels or as circuit travelers in labor camps. It is believed that traffickers import up to 50,000 women and children

© AP

● Moonlite BunnyRanch prostitutes (from left) Nadia Ray, Alexis On Fire, Destiny, and Kandi sit at the bar at the brothel in Mound House, Nevada. Should prostitution be legalized and regulated as it is in Nevada? Why shouldn't adults be allowed to hire Destiny and Kandi in Boston and Cleveland as they do at the BunnyRanch in Nevada? Before you answer, consider that it is perfectly legal to be a doctor, chiropractor, massage therapist, and/or personal trainer, and people in these professions have physical contact with their clients. We allow liquor to be sold openly and for people to bet at casinos. Where should the line be drawn? Are these women being harmed by their profession, and does society have a duty to protect them from injury?

every year into the United States despite legal prohibitions (in addition to prostitution, some are brought in to work in sweatshops).[30] Several different types of prostitutes operate in the United States.

Types of Prostitutes

There are a variety of roles in the sex for hire trade. Some of the most common are discussed next.

Streetwalkers Prostitutes who work the streets in plain sight of police, citizens, and customers are referred to as hustlers, hookers, or streetwalkers. Although glamorized by the Julia Roberts character in the film *Pretty Woman* (who winds up with multimillionaire Richard Gere), streetwalkers are considered the least attractive, lowest paid, most vulnerable men and women in the profession. Streetwalkers wear bright clothing, makeup, and jewelry to attract customers; they take their customers to hotels. Commonly called "hookers," the term is not derived from the ability of streetwalkers to hook clients on their charms. It actually stems from the popular name given women who followed Union General "Fighting Joe" Hooker's army during the Civil War.[31] Studies indicate they are most likely to be impoverished members of ethnic or racial minorities. Many are young runaways who gravitate to major cities to find a new, exciting life and escape from sexual and physical abuse at home.[32] Of all prostitutes, streetwalkers have the highest incidence of drug abuse.[33]

The street life is very dangerous. Recent interviews conducted with 325 sex workers in Miami by Hilary Surratt and her colleagues found that over 40 percent experienced violence from clients in the prior year: 25 percent were beaten, 13 percent were raped, and 14 percent were threatened with weapons.[34] Research by Teela Sanders on the everyday life of British sex workers found that recognizing these dangers, street-level sex workers use rational decision making and learning experiences to reduce the risk of violent victimization. Experienced sex workers come up with protective strategies that help them manage the risk of the profession. Most do not randomly accept all clients, and they eliminate those they consider dangerous or threatening. They also develop methods to deal with the emotional strain of the work as well as techniques to maintain their privacy and keep their "occupation" hidden from family and neighbors.[35]

Bar Girls B-girls, as they are also called, spend their time in bars, drinking and waiting to be picked up by customers. Although alcoholism may be a problem, B-girls usually work out an arrangement with the bartender so they are served diluted drinks or water colored with dye or tea, for which the customer is charged an exorbitant price. In some bars, the B-girl is given a credit for each drink she gets the customer to buy. It is common to find B-girls in towns with military bases and large transient populations.[36]

Brothel Prostitutes Also called bordellos, cathouses, sporting houses, and houses of ill repute, brothels flourished in the nineteenth and early twentieth centuries. They were large establishments, usually run by madams, that housed several prostitutes. The madam employs the prostitutes, supervises their behavior, and receives a fee for her services; her cut is usually 40 to 60 percent of the prostitutes' earnings. The madam's role may include recruiting women into prostitution and socializing them in the trade.[37]

Brothels declined in importance following World War II. The closing of the last brothel in Texas is chronicled in the play and movie *The Best Little Whorehouse in*

Texas. Today the best-known brothels exist in Nevada, where prostitution is legal outside large population centers.

Call Girls The aristocrats of prostitution are call girls. They may charge customers thousands per night and may net more than $100,000 per year. Some gain clients through employment in escort services; others develop independent customer lists. Many call girls come from middle-class backgrounds and service upper-class customers. Attempting to dispel the notion that their service is simply sex for money, they concentrate on making their clients feel important and attractive. Working exclusively via telephone "dates," call girls get their clients by word of mouth or by making arrangements with bellhops, cab drivers, and so on. They either entertain clients in their own apartments or visit clients' hotels and apartments. Upon retiring, a call girl can sell her date book, listing client names and sexual preferences, for thousands of dollars. Despite the lucrative nature of their business, call girls suffer considerable risk by being alone and unprotected with strangers. They often request the business cards of their clients to make sure they are dealing with "upstanding citizens."

Escort Services/Call Houses Some escort services are fronts for prostitution rings. Both male and female sex workers can be sent out after the client calls an ad in the yellow pages. How common are adult sexual services? Las Vegas, Nevada, alone has more than 500 listings for adult services in the yellow pages; New York City has more than 100.

A relatively new phenomenon, the call house combines elements of the brothel and call girl rings. A madam receives a call from a prospective customer, and if she finds the client acceptable, she arranges a meeting between the caller and a prostitute in her service. The madam maintains a list of prostitutes who are on call rather than living together in a house. The call house insulates the madam from arrest because she never meets the client or receives direct payment.[38]

Circuit Travelers Prostitutes known as circuit travelers move around in groups of two or three to lumber, labor, and agricultural camps. They ask the foreman for permission to ply their trade, service the whole crew in an evening, and then move on. Some circuit travelers seek clients at truck stops and rest areas.

Sometimes young girls are forced to become circuit travelers by unscrupulous pimps who force them to work for months as prostitutes in agricultural migrant camps. The young women are lured from developing countries such as Mexico with offers of jobs in landscaping, health care, housecleaning, and restaurants. When they arrive in the United States they are told that they owe their captors thousands of dollars and must work as prostitutes to pay it off. The young women are raped and beaten if they complain or try to escape.[39]

Cyber Prostitute In 2004, nearly 70 men were arrested in Odessa, Texas, after a year-long prostitution sting that focused on a massage parlor run by a woman named Misty Lane. Ms. Lane had her own website, was known as Hot Fort Worth Girl, and contacted her clients via e-mail.[40] As Misty seemed to know, the technological revolution has altered the world of prostitution. "Cyber prostitutes" set up personal websites or put listings on web boards such as "Adult Friendfinder" that carry personals. They may use loaded phrases such as "looking for generous older man" in their self-descriptions. When contacted, they ask to exchange e-mails, chat online, or make voice calls with prospective clients. They may even exchange pictures. This allows them to be selective and avoid clients who may be threatening or dangerous. Some cyber prostitution rings offer customers the opportunity to choose women from their Internet page and then have them flown in from around the country.

Becoming a Prostitute

Why does someone turn to prostitution? In the United States, both male and female street-level sex workers often come from troubled homes marked by extreme conflict and hostility. One recent survey of street-level sex workers in Phoenix,

Arizona, found that women engaging in prostitution have limited educational backgrounds; most did not complete high school. They had experienced high rates of physical and sexual abuse in childhood, as well as parental substance abuse.[41]

Many prostitutes began their involvement in the sex trade while still children.[42] Many of these children had experienced sexual trauma at an early age.[43] Future prostitutes were initiated into sex by family members at ages as young as 10 to 12 years; they have long histories of sexual exploitation and abuse.[44]

Sexual abuse is not the only social problem that is a forerunner to prostitution. Girls who get into "the life" report conflict with school authorities, poor grades, and an overly regimented school experience; a significant portion have long histories of drug abuse.[45] Young girls who frequently use drugs and begin using at an early age are most at risk for prostitution to support their habits.[46]

Once they get into the life, personal danger begins to escalate. Girls who may be directed toward prostitution because of childhood sexual abuse are also likely to become revictimized as adults.[47] The threat of HIV and STDs is also a daily worry. While some take precautions, such as using or making their clients use condoms, many forego protection if their pimps and brothel owners forbid it or clients refuse to cooperate.[48] Their continuous exposure to danger and violence, both as victims and as witnesses, leads many to self-medication with illegal drugs. Prostitutes then find themselves in a vicious cycle of violence, substance abuse, and AIDS risk.[49]

While most research depicts prostitutes as troubled women who have lived troubled lives, there may be a trend for some young women to enter the sex trade as a rational choice based on economic need. Changing sexual mores help reduce or eliminate the stigma attached to prostitution. One recent research study conducted in Australia found that the sex industry has become attractive to college students as a way to supplement their income during a time of reduced government aid and increasing educational costs. They view sex work as a "normal" form of employment for students seeking to obtain a higher education.[50]

Controlling Prostitution

In the late nineteenth and early twentieth century, efforts were made to regulate prostitution in the United States through medical supervision and licensing and zoning brothels in districts outside residential neighborhoods.[51] After World War I, prostitution became associated with disease, and the desire to protect young servicemen from harm helped to end almost all experiments with legalization in the United States.[52] Some reformers attempted to paint pimps and procurers as immigrants who used their foreign ways to snare unsuspecting American girls into prostitution. Such fears prompted passage of the federal Mann Act (1925), which prohibited bringing women into the country or transporting them across state lines for the purposes of prostitution. Often called the "white slave act," it carried a $5,000 fine, five years in prison, or both.[53]

Today, prostitution is considered a misdemeanor, punishable by a fine or a short jail sentence. In practice, most law enforcement is uneven and aims at confining illegal activities to particular areas in the city.[54] Prostitution is illegal in all states except Nevada (except in the counties in which Las Vegas and Reno are located), where it is a highly regulated business enterprise.

Some local police agencies concerned about prostitution have used high-visibility patrols to discourage prostitutes and their customers, undercover work to arrest prostitutes and drug dealers, and collaboration with hotel and motel owners to identify and arrest pimps and drug dealers.[55] More efforts have been put into reducing child prostitution. One strategy is to punish people who travel abroad in order to procure child prostitutes; these are so-called "sex tourists." The Violent Crime Control and Law Enforcement Act of 1994 included a provision, referred to as the Child Sexual Abuse Prevention Act, that makes it a criminal offense to travel abroad for the purpose of engaging in sexual activity with a minor.[56] Some loopholes in the law were closed when President George W. Bush signed the Protect Act into law in 2003.[57] Despite these efforts, prosecuting sex tourists is often tricky due to the difficulty of gathering evidence of crimes committed in other countries that involve minors.[58]

In the United States, some local jurisdictions have made the control of child prostitution a priority.[59] In Georgia, the general assembly amended a law to make pimping of minors a felony offense. The U.S. Attorney's office for the Northern District of Georgia prosecuted 13 pimps under a variety of federal Racketeer Influenced and Corrupt Organizations (RICO) Act of 1970 statutes. This was the first time that the U.S. Attorney's office had used the RICO statutes to impose federal sentences for the crime of pimping. A local project called Angela's House was developed to treat minor girls and to provide a normalized environment for their nurture and care. Additionally, the Office of Juvenile Justice Delinquency Prevention instituted a five-year grant to create a multiagency database, with a model treatment and coordination plan.

Legalize Prostitution?

In some countries, especially in the Muslim world, prostitution carries the death penalty. In others, such as Holland, prostitutes pay taxes and belong to a union. Other countries, such as Australia, allow adults to engage in prostitution but regulate their activities—i.e., they must get timely health checkups. Still other countries, such as Sweden and Brazil, allow women to become prostitutes but criminalize earning money from the work of prostitutes (in other words, serving as a pimp). In the United States, prostitution is illegal in all states, though brothels are legal in a number of counties of Nevada (but not in Las Vegas or Reno). A loophole in the Rhode Island state law allows prostitution in the privacy of a home or business but criminalizes solicitation and operating a brothel.[60]

Should prostitution be legalized in the United States? Feminists have staked out conflicting views of prostitution. One position is that women must become emancipated from male oppression and reach sexual equality. The *sexual equality view* considers the prostitute a victim of male dominance. In patriarchal societies, male power is predicated on female subjugation, and prostitution is a clear example of this gender exploitation.[61] In contrast, for some feminists, the fight for equality depends on controlling all attempts by men or women to impose their will on women. The *free choice view* is that prostitution, if freely chosen, expresses women's equality and is not a symptom of subjugation.[62] Advocates of both positions argue that the penalties for prostitution should be reduced (decriminalized), but neither side advocates outright legalization. Decriminalization would relieve already desperate women of the additional burden of severe legal punishment. However, legalization might be coupled with regulation by male-dominated justice agencies. For example, required medical examinations would mean increased male control over women's bodies.

In her book *Brothel*, Alexa Albert, a Harvard-trained physician who interviewed young women working at a legal brothel in Nevada, makes a compelling case for legalization. She found that the women remained HIV-free and felt safer working in a secure environment than alone on city streets. Despite long hours and rules that gave too much profit to the owners, the women actually took "pride" in their work. Besides the security, most earn between $300 and $1,500 per day.[63]

PORNOGRAPHY

The term **pornography** derives from the Greek *porne*, meaning "prostitute," and *graphein*, meaning "to write." In the heart of many major cities are stores that display and sell books, magazines, and films explicitly depicting every imaginable sex act. Suburban video stores also rent and sell sexually explicit tapes, which make up 15 to 30 percent of the home rental market. The purpose of this material is to provide sexual titillation and excitement for paying customers. Although material depicting nudity and sex is typically legal, protected by the First Amendment's provision limiting government control of speech, most criminal codes prohibit the production, display, and sale of obscene material.

Obscenity, derived from the Latin *caenum* for "filth," is defined by Webster's dictionary as "deeply offensive to morality or decency . . . designed to incite to lust

pornography
Sexually explicit books, magazines, films, or tapes intended to provide sexual titillation and excitement for paying customers.

obscenity
Material that violates community standards of morality or decency and has no redeeming social value.

or depravity."[64] The problem of controlling pornography centers on this definition of obscenity. Police and law enforcement officials can legally seize only material that is judged obscene. "But who," critics ask, "is to judge what is obscene?" At one time, such novels as *Tropic of Cancer*, by Henry Miller, *Ulysses*, by James Joyce, and *Lady Chatterley's Lover*, by D. H. Lawrence, were prohibited because they were considered obscene; today they are considered works of great literary value. Thus, what is obscene today may be considered socially acceptable at a future time. After all, *Playboy* and other "men's magazines," sold openly in most bookstores, display nude models in all kinds of sexually explicit poses. The uncertainty surrounding this issue is illustrated by Supreme Court Justice Potter Stewart's famous 1964 statement on how he defined obscenity: "I know it when I see it." Because of this legal and moral ambiguity, the sex trade is booming around the United States.

Is Pornography Harmful?

Opponents of pornography argue that it degrades both the people who are photographed and members of the public who are sometimes forced to see obscene material. Pornographers exploit their models, who often include underage children. The Attorney General's Commission on Pornography, set up by the Reagan administration to review the sale and distribution of sexually explicit material, concluded that many performers and models are victims of physical and psychological coercion.[65]

One uncontested danger of pornography is "kiddie porn." Each year more than a million children are believed to be used in pornography or prostitution, many of them runaways whose plight is exploited by adults. Sexual exploitation by these rings can devastate the child victims. Exploited children are prone to such acting-out behavior as setting fires and becoming sexually focused in the use of language, dress, and mannerisms. They may also suffer physical problems ranging from headaches and loss of appetite to genital soreness, vomiting, and urinary tract infections and psychological problems including mood swings, withdrawal, edginess, and nervousness. In his book *Beyond Tolerance: Child Pornography on the Internet*, sociologist Philip Jenkins argues that activists focus on stamping out Internet pornography but not on kiddie porn, which is a bigger problem. Jenkins suggests that kiddie porn is best combated by more effective law enforcement; instead of focusing on users, enforcement should be directed against the suppliers. He also suggests that newsgroups and bulletin boards that advertise or discuss kiddie porn be criminalized.[66] Jenkins's warnings may have had an effect: Research indicates that the amount of Web-based kiddie porn is now in decline.[67]

Does Pornography Cause Violence?

An issue critical to the debate over pornography is whether viewing it produces sexual violence or assaultive behavior. This debate was given added interest when serial killer Ted Bundy claimed his murderous rampage was fueled by reading pornography.

The scientific evidence linking sexually explicit material to violence is mixed. National reviews have found little conclusive evidence of a causal relationship between watching pornography and crime.[68] Some research has found that viewing erotic material may actually reduce sex crimes: It may act as a safety valve for those whose impulses might otherwise lead them to violence.[69] When Neil Malamuth, Tamara Addison, and Mary Koss surveyed 2,972 male college students, they discovered that frequent use of pornography was not related to sexual aggression. There were only relatively minor differences in sexual aggression between men who reported using pornography very frequently and those who said they rarely used it.[70]

This issue is far from settled. Although there is little or no documentation of a causal relationship between pornography and violent crime, there is stronger evidence that people exposed to material that portrays violence, sadism, and women enjoying being raped and degraded are likely to be sexually aggressive toward female victims.[71] Laboratory experiments conducted by a number of leading authorities have found that men exposed to violent pornography are more likely to act aggressively toward women.[72] Pornography may trigger preexisting tendencies. Malamuth and his colleagues found that men who were both at high risk for sexual aggression and who were additionally very frequent users of pornography were also much more likely to engage in sexual aggression than their counterparts who consume pornography less frequently. Put simply, if a person is already sexually aggressive, pornography may activate and reinforce coercive tendencies and behaviors.[73]

Pornography and the Law

The First Amendment of the U.S. Constitution protects free speech and prohibits police agencies from limiting the public's right of free expression. However, the Supreme Court held in the twin cases of *Roth v. United States* and *Alberts v. California* that although the First Amendment protects all "ideas with even the slightest redeeming social importance—unorthodox ideas, controversial ideas, even ideas hateful to the prevailing climate of opinion . . . implicit in the history of the First Amendment is the rejection of obscenity as utterly without redeeming social importance."[74] These decisions left unclear how obscenity is defined. If a highly erotic movie tells a "moral tale," must it be judged legal even if 95 percent of its content is objectionable? A spate of movies made after the *Roth* decision claimed that they were educational or warned the viewer about sexual depravity, so they could not be said to lack redeeming social importance. Many state obscenity cases were appealed to federal courts so judges could decide whether the films totally lacked redeeming social importance. To rectify the situation, the Supreme Court redefined its concept of obscenity in the case of *Miller v. California*:

> The basic guidelines for the trier of fact must be (a) whether the average person applying contemporary community standards would find that the work taken as a whole appeals to the prurient interest; (b) whether the work depicts or describes, in a patently offensive way, sexual conduct specifically defined by the applicable state law, and (c) whether the work, taken as a whole, lacks serious literary, artistic, political or scientific value.[75]

To convict a person of obscenity under the *Miller* doctrine, the state or local jurisdiction must specifically define obscene conduct in its statute, and the pornographer must engage in that behavior. The Court gave some examples of what is considered obscene: "patently offensive representations or descriptions of masturbation, excretory functions and lewd exhibition of the genitals."[76] Obviously, a plebiscite cannot be held to determine the community's attitude for every trial concerning the sale of pornography. Works considered obscene in Omaha might be considered routine in New York, but how can we be sure? To resolve this dilemma, the Supreme Court in *Pope v. Illinois* articulated a reasonableness doctrine: A work is obscene if a reasonable person applying objective (national) standards would find the material lacking in any social value.[77]

Despite these cases, the First Amendment right to free speech makes legal control of pornography, even kiddie porn, quite difficult. Congress attempted to control the growth of Internet porn when it passed the Child Pornography Prevention Act of 1996 (CPPA). This act expanded the federal prohibition on child pornography to include not only pornographic images made using actual children but also "any visual depiction, including any photograph, film, video, picture, or computer or computer-generated image or picture" that "is, or appears to be, of a minor engaging in sexually explicit conduct," and any sexually explicit image that is "advertised, promoted, presented, described, or distributed in such a manner that conveys the impression" it depicts "a minor engaging in sexually explicit conduct." This language was used in order to ban "virtual child pornography," which appears to depict minors but is produced by means other than using real children, such as through the use of youthful-looking adults or computer-imaging technology. It also banned Web postings of material deemed "harmful to minors."[78] However, in 2002, the U.S. Supreme Court struck down some sections of the CPPA as being constitutionally deficient, especially those that ban "virtual porn":

> Finally, the First Amendment is turned upside down by the argument that, because it is difficult to distinguish between images made using real children and those produced by computer imaging, both kinds of images must be prohibited. The overbreadth doctrine prohibits the Government from banning unprotected speech if a substantial amount of protected speech is prohibited or chilled in the process.[79]

Since the Court's ruling, the act has not been enforced.

Can Pornography Be Controlled?

The legal difficulties encountered by the CPPA illustrate the difficulty society has controlling the distribution of sexually related materials. Recent reports indicate that the sex business is currently booming and now amounts to more than $10 billion per year.[80]

Although politically appealing, law enforcement crusades may not necessarily obtain the desired effect. A get-tough policy could make sex-related goods and services scarce, driving up prices and making their sale even more desirable and profitable. Going after national distributors may help decentralize the adult movie and photo business and encourage local rings to expand their activities, for example, by making and marketing videos as well as still photos or distributing them through computer networks.

An alternative approach has been for local efforts to restrict the sale of pornography within acceptable boundaries. New York City has enacted zoning that seeks to break up the concentration of peep shows, topless bars, and X-rated businesses in several neighborhoods, particularly in Times Square.[81] The law forbids sex-oriented businesses within 500 feet of residential zones, schools, churches, or day care centers. Sex shops cannot be located within 500 feet of each other; so concentrated "red light" districts must be dispersed. Rather than close their doors, sex shops got around the law by adding products such as luggage, cameras, T-shirts, and classic films. The courts have upheld the law, ruling that stores can stay in business if no more than 40 percent of their floor space and inventory are dedicated to adult entertainment.[82]

The biggest challenge to those seeking to control the sex-for-profit industry has been the technological change in the industry. Adult movie theaters are closing, as people are able to buy or rent tapes and DVDs in their local video stores and play them in the privacy of their homes. Adult CD-ROMs are now a staple of the computer industry. Internet sex services include live, interactive stripping and sexual activities.

To control the spread of Internet pornography, Congress passed the Communications Decency Act (CDA), which made all Internet service providers, commercial online services, bulletin board systems, and electronic mail providers criminally liable whenever their services are used to transmit any material considered "obscene, lewd, lascivious, filthy, or indecent" (S 314, 1996). However, in *Reno v. ACLU* (1997), the Supreme Court ruled that the CDA unconstitutionally restricted free speech, once again illustrating the difficulty law enforcement has when trying to balance the need to control obscenity with the First Amendment.[83]

✔ CHECKPOINTS

✔ CHECKPOINTS

- ✔ It is illegal to engage in homosexual acts in about half the U.S. states. Many organizations, including the Boy Scouts and the U.S. military, limit gay participation.
- ✔ Paraphilias are deviant sexual acts such as exhibitionism and voyeurism. Many are considered crimes.
- ✔ Prostitution has been common throughout recorded history. There are many kinds of prostitutes, including streetwalkers, bar girls, call girls, brothel prostitutes, and circuit travelers.
- ✔ It is feared that some girls are forced or tricked into prostitution against their will.
- ✔ A multibillion-dollar international sex trade involves tricking young girls from Eastern Europe and Asia into becoming prostitutes.
- ✔ Pornography is a billion-dollar industry that is growing through technological advances such as the Internet.
- ✔ There is great debate over whether or not obscene materials are harmful and are related to violence.
- ✔ The Supreme Court has ruled that material is obscene if it has prurient sexual content and is devoid of social value.
- ✔ Controlling obscene material is difficult because of the First Amendment's guarantee of free speech.

SUBSTANCE ABUSE

The problem of substance abuse stretches across the United States. Large urban areas are beset by drug-dealing gangs, drug users who engage in crime to support their habits, and alcohol-related violence. Rural areas are important staging centers for the shipment of drugs across the country and are often the production sites for synthetic drugs and marijuana farming.[84]

Another indication of the concern about drugs has been the increasing number of drug-related visits to hospital emergency rooms. Despite the scope of the drug problem, some still view it as another type of victimless public order crime. There is great debate over the legalization of drugs and the control of alcohol. Some consider drug use a private matter and drug control another example of government intrusion into people's private lives. Furthermore, legalization could reduce the profit of selling illegal substances and drive suppliers out of the market.[85] Others see these substances as dangerous, believing that the criminal activity of users makes the term "victimless" nonsensical. Still another position is that the possession and use of all drugs and alcohol should be legalized but that the sale and distribution of drugs should be heavily penalized. This would punish those profiting from drugs while enabling users to be helped without fear of criminal punishment.

When Did Drug Use Begin?

The use of chemical substances to escape reality and provide stimulation, relief, or relaxation has gone on for thousands of years. Mesopotamian writings indicate that opium was used 4,000 years ago—it was known as the "plant of joy."[86] The ancient Greeks knew and understood the problem of drug use. At the time of the Crusades, the Arabs were using marijuana. In the Western Hemisphere, natives of Mexico and South America chewed coca leaves and used "magic mushrooms" in their religious ceremonies.[87] Drug use was also accepted in Europe well into the twentieth century. Recently uncovered pharmacy records circa 1900 to 1920 show sales of cocaine and heroin solutions to members of the British royal family; records from 1912 show that Winston Churchill, then a member of Parliament, was sold a cocaine solution while staying in Scotland.[88]

In the early years of the United States, opium and its derivatives were easily obtained. Opium-based drugs were used in various patent medicine cure-alls. Morphine was used extensively to relieve the pain of wounded soldiers in the Civil War. By the turn of the century, an estimated 1 million U.S. citizens were opiate users.[89]

Alcohol and Its Prohibition

The history of alcohol and the law in the United States has also been controversial and dramatic. At the turn of the century, a drive was mustered to prohibit the sale of alcohol. This **temperance movement** was fueled by the belief that the purity of the U.S. agrarian culture was being destroyed by the growth of cities. Urbanism was viewed as a threat to the lifestyle of the majority of the nation's population, then living on farms and in villages. The forces behind the temperance movement were such lobbying groups as the Anti-Saloon League, led by Carrie Nation; the Women's Temperance Union; and the Protestant clergy of the Baptist, Methodist, and Congregationalist faiths.[90] They viewed the growing city, filled with newly arriving Irish, Italian, and Eastern European immigrants, as centers of degradation and wickedness. Ratification of the Eighteenth Amendment in 1919, prohibiting the sale of alcoholic beverages, was viewed as a triumph of the morality of middle- and upper-class Americans over the threat posed to their culture by the "new Americans."[91]

Prohibition failed. It was enforced by the Volstead Act, which defined intoxicating beverages as those containing one-half of 1 percent, or more, alcohol.[92] What doomed Prohibition? One factor was the continued supply of illicit liquor by organized crime. Also, the law made it illegal only to sell alcohol, not to purchase it, which reduced the deterrent effect. Finally, despite the work of Elliot Ness and his "Untouchables," law enforcement agencies were inadequate, and officials were likely to be corrupted by wealthy bootleggers.[93] In 1933, the Twenty-First Amendment to the Constitution repealed Prohibition, signaling the end of the "noble experiment."

Extent of Substance Abuse

Despite continuing efforts at control, the use of mood-altering substances persists in the United States. What is the extent of the substance abuse problem today?

A number of national surveys attempt to chart trends in drug abuse in the general population. One important source of information on drug use is the annual

temperance movement
The drive to prohibit the sale of alcohol in the United States, culminating in ratification of the Eighteenth Amendment in 1919.

Prohibition
The period from 1919 until 1933, when the Eighteenth Amendment to the U.S. Constitution outlawed the sale of alcohol; also known as the "noble experiment."

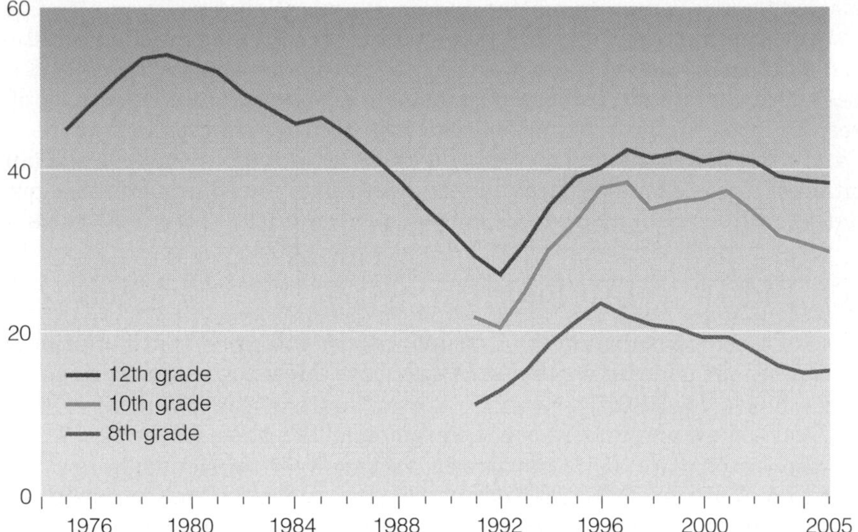

Figure 13.1
Trends in Annual Prevalence in Teenage Illicit Drug Use
SOURCE: Monitoring the Future, 2005, www.monitoringthefuture.org/pressreleases/05drugpr_complete.pdf.

Monitoring the Future (MTF) self-report survey of drug abuse among high school students conducted by the Institute of Social Research (ISR) at the University of Michigan.[94] This survey is based on the self-report responses of about 17,000 high school seniors, 15,500 tenth-graders, and 18,800 eighth-graders in hundreds of schools around the United States. As Figure 13.1 shows, drug use declined from a high point late in the 1970s until 1990, when it began to increase once again, and then has remained relatively stable since the mid-1990s. Nonetheless, the MTF finds that about 40 percent of all high school seniors report using an illicit substance during the past 12 months; other research surveys indicate that many students have no problem finding illegal drugs on campus.[95]

These data indicate that although drug use is still quite common and that a majority of all American teens have tried drugs before they graduate high school, general usage is lower than it was 20 years ago. Why has drug use declined? One reason may have been changing perceptions about the harmfulness of drugs such as cocaine and marijuana; as people come to view these drugs as harmful, they tend to use them less. Because of widespread publicity linking drug use, needle sharing, and the AIDS virus, people began to see drug taking as dangerous and risky.

In addition, declines in substance abuse may be tied to social disapproval. Today, a majority of youths report greater disapproval of drug use among their friends, and peer pressure may help account for lower use rates than those experienced by their parents.

Although the use of drugs such as cocaine and marijuana have been in decline, adolescent alcohol abuse has been a persistent problem. There appears to be a trend for alcohol abuse to begin at an early age and remain an extremely serious problem over the life course. According to research conducted at the National Center on Addiction and Substance Abuse at Columbia University, children under the age of 21 drink about 19 percent of the alcohol consumed in the United States. More than 5 million high school students (31.5 percent) admit to binge drinking at least once a month. The age at which children begin drinking is dropping: Since 1975, the proportion of children who begin drinking in the eighth grade or earlier has jumped by almost a third, from 27 percent to 36 percent.[96]

Causes of Substance Abuse

What causes people to abuse substances? Although there are many different views on the cause of drug use, most can be characterized as seeing the onset of an addictive career as either an environmental or a personal matter.

Subcultural View Those who view drug abuse as having an environmental basis concentrate on lower-class addiction. Because a disproportionate number of drug abusers are poor, the onset of drug use can be tied to such factors as racial prejudice, devalued identities, low self-esteem, poor socioeconomic status, and the high level of mistrust, negativism, and defiance found in impoverished areas.

Residing in a deteriorated inner-city area is often correlated with entry into a drug subculture. Youths living in these depressed areas, where feelings of alienation and hopelessness run high, often meet established drug users who teach them that narcotics provide an answer to their feelings of personal inadequacy and stress.[97] The youths may join peers to learn the techniques of drug use and receive social support for their habit. Research shows that peer influence is a significant predictor of drug careers that actually grows stronger as people mature.[98] Shared feelings and a sense of intimacy lead the youths to become fully enmeshed in what has been described as the "drug-use subculture."[99] Some join gangs and enter a career of using and distributing illegal substances while also committing property and violent crimes.[100]

Psychological View Not all drug abusers reside in lower-class areas; the problem of middle-class substance abuse is very real. Consequently, some experts have linked substance abuse to psychological deficits such as impaired cognitive functioning, personality disturbance, and emotional problems that can strike people in any economic class.[101] Personality traits such as high antisocial personality disorder and negative emotionality are associated with subsequent substance abuse.[102]

What is the connection between psychological disorder and drug abuse? Drugs may help people deal with unconscious needs and impulses and relieve dependence and depression. People may turn to drug abuse as a form of self-medication in order to reduce the emotional turmoil of adolescence, deal with troubling impulses, or cope with traumatic life experiences. Survivors of sexual assault and physical abuse have been known to turn to drug and alcohol abuse as a coping mechanism.[103] Depressed people may use drugs as an alternative to more radical solutions to their pain, such as suicide.[104]

Personality testing of known users suggests that a significant percentage suffer from psychotic disorders, including various levels of schizophrenia. Surveys show that youngsters with serious behavioral problems were more than seven times as likely as those with less serious problems to report that they were dependent on alcohol or illicit drugs. Youths with serious emotional problems were nearly four times more likely to report dependence on drugs than those without such issues.[105]

Genetic Factors Research shows that substance abuse may have a genetic basis.[106] The biological children of alcoholics reared by nonalcoholic adoptive parents develop alcohol problems more often than the biological children of the adoptive parents.[107] A number of studies comparing alcoholism among identical twins and fraternal twins have found that the degree of concordance (both siblings behaving identically) is twice as high among the identical twin groups. These inferences are still inconclusive because identical twins are more likely to be treated similarly than fraternal twins and are therefore more likely to be influenced by environmental conditions. Taken as a group, studies of the genetic basis of substance abuse suggest that people whose parents were alcoholic or drug dependent have a greater chance of developing a problem than the children of nonabusers, and this relationship occurs regardless of parenting style or the quality of the parent-child relationship.[108] Nonetheless, most children of abusing parents do not become drug dependent themselves, suggesting that even if drug abuse is heritable, environment and socialization must play some role in the onset of abuse.[109]

Social Learning Social psychologists suggest that drug abuse may also result from observing parental drug use. Parental drug abuse begins to have a damaging effect on children as young as 2 years old, especially when parents manifest drug-related personality problems such as depression or poor impulse control.[110] Children whose parents abuse drugs are more likely to have persistent abuse problems than the children of nonabusers.[111]

People who learn that drugs provide pleasurable sensations may be the most likely to experiment with illegal substances; a habit may develop if the user experiences lower anxiety, fear, and tension levels.[112] Having a history of family drug and alcohol abuse has been found to be a characteristic of violent teenage sexual abusers.[113] Heroin abusers report an unhappy childhood that included harsh physical punishment and parental neglect and rejection.[114]

According to the social learning view, drug involvement begins with using tobacco and drinking alcohol at an early age, which progresses to experimentation with marijuana and hashish and finally to cocaine and even heroin. Although most recreational users do not progress to "hard stuff," few addicts begin their involvement with narcotics without first experimenting with recreational drugs. By implication, if teen smoking and drinking could be reduced, the gateway to hard drugs would be narrowed. Research shows that a 50 percent reduction in the number of teens who smoke cigarettes can cut marijuana use by 16 to 28 percent.[115]

Problem Behavior Syndrome (PBS) For many people, substance abuse is just one of many problem behaviors. Longitudinal studies show that drug abusers are maladjusted, alienated, and emotionally distressed and that their drug use is one among many social problems.[116] Having a deviant lifestyle begins early in life and is punctuated with criminal relationships, family history of substance abuse, educational failure, and alienation. People who abuse drugs lack commitment to religious values, disdain education, spend most of their time in peer activities, engage in precocious sexual behavior, and experience school failure, family conflict, and other similar social problems.[117] There is robust support for the interconnection of problem drinking and drug abuse, delinquency, precocious sexual behavior, school failure, running away, homelessness, family conflict, and other similar social problems.[118]

Rational Choice Not all people who abuse drugs do so because of personal pathology. Some may use drugs and alcohol because they want to enjoy their effects: get high, relax, improve creativity, escape reality, and increase sexual responsiveness. Research indicates that adolescent alcohol abusers believe that getting high will make them powerful, increase their sexual performance, and facilitate their social behavior; they care little about negative future consequences.[119]

Substance abuse, then, may be a function of the rational but mistaken belief that drugs can benefit the user. The decision to use drugs involves evaluations of personal consequences (such as addiction, disease, and legal punishment) and the expected benefits of drug use (such as peer approval, positive affective states, heightened awareness, and relaxation). Adolescents may begin using drugs because they believe their peers expect them to do so.[120]

Is There a Single "Cause" of Drug Abuse? There are many different views of why people take drugs, and no theory has proved adequate to explain all forms of substance abuse. Recent research efforts show that drug users suffer a variety of family and socialization difficulties, have addiction-prone personalities, and are generally at risk for many other social problems.[121] One long-held assumption is that addicts progress along a continuum from using so-called gateway drugs such as alcohol and marijuana to using ever more potent substances, such as cocaine and heroin.[122] That view may also be misleading. Research by Andrew Golub and Bruce Johnson shows that many hard-core drug abusers have never smoked or used alcohol. And while many American youths have tried marijuana, few actually progress to crack or heroin abuse.[123] In sum, there may be no single cause of substance abuse.

Drugs and Crime

Research consistently indicates a significant association exists between drug abuse and criminality, beginning in adolescence and continuing into adulthood. A number of surveys have found that kids who use drugs are more likely than nonabusers to engage in violent behaviors.[124] The Department of Health and Human Services' annual survey on youth and violence found that about half of the adolescents who use marijuana in the past year also engage in violent behavior, as do those who used inhalants; more than two-thirds (69 percent) of the adolescents who use methamphetamine in the past year engage in violent behavior. The survey also found that the likelihood of having engaged in violent behavior increases with the number of drugs used. As Figure 13.2 shows, approximately 26 percent of adolescents who do not use any illicit drugs report violent behavior compared to 45 percent of those who use one illicit drug, 54 percent of those who use two illicit drugs, and 61 percent of those who use three or more illicit drugs.[125]

Nor does the association end in childhood. Substance abuse appears to be an important precipitating factor in domestic assault, armed robbery, and homicide cases.[126] Tests of arrestees show that a significant portion (two-thirds) of both females and males test positive for at least one illegal drug, including cocaine, opiates, marijuana, methamphetamine, and PCP.[127] Surveys of prison inmates disclose that many (80 percent) are lifelong substance abusers. More than one-third claim to have been under the influence of drugs when they committed their last offense.[128]

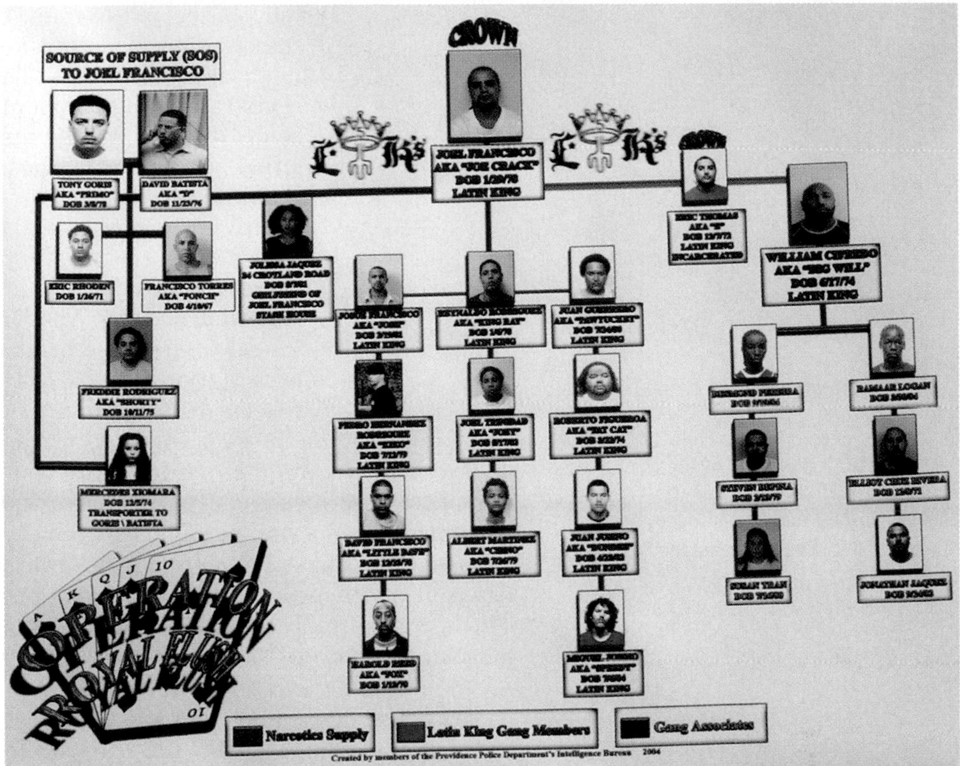

© AP

● An illustration put together by the Providence, Rhode Island, police department detailing the players in Operation Royal Flush, a 10-month investigation into a drug-trafficking ring, is seen prior to a news conference at the Providence Public Safety Building. Operation Royal Flush led to the arrest of 26 gang members and the seizure of marijuana, guns, five vehicles, over $200,000 in cash, and over $1 million worth of cocaine.

Although the drug–crime connection is powerful, the true relationship between them is still uncertain because many users have had a history of criminal activity before the onset of their substance abuse.[129] It is possible that:

- Chronic criminal offenders begin to abuse drugs and alcohol after they have engaged in crime; that is, crime causes drug abuse; or
- Substance abusers turn to a life of crime to support their habits; that is, drug abuse causes crime; or
- Drug use and crime co-occur in individuals; that is, both crime and drug abuse are caused by some other common factor (in other words, risk takers use drugs and also commit crime).[130]
- Drug users suffer social problems, such as heavy drinking, mental instability, that are linked to crime.[131]

Considering these possible scenarios, it is impossible to make a definitive statement such as "drugs cause crime." Although it is not certain whether drug use turns otherwise law-abiding citizens into criminals, it certainly amplifies the extent of criminal activities.[132] And, as addiction levels increase, so does the frequency and seriousness of criminality.[133] The link between drugs and crime is the basis of this chapter's Profiles in Crime.

Drugs and the Law

The federal government first initiated legal action to curtail the use of some drugs early in the twentieth century.[134] In 1906, the Pure Food and Drug Act required manufacturers to list the amounts of habit-forming drugs in products on the labels but did not restrict their use. However, the act prohibited the importation and sale of opiates except for medicinal purposes. In 1914, the Harrison Narcotics Act restricted the importation, manufacture, sale, and dispensing of narcotics. It defined **narcotic** as any drug that produces sleep and relieves pain, such as heroin,

narcotic
A drug that produces sleep and relieves pain, such as heroin, morphine, and opium; a habit-forming drug.

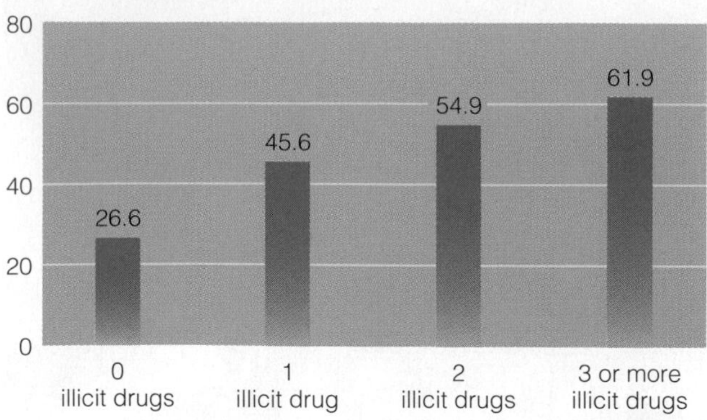

Figure 13.2

Percentages of Youths Aged 12 to 17 Engaging in Past Year Violent Behavior, by Number of Illicit Drugs Used in the Past Year

National Survey on Drug Use and Health, 2006, http://oas.samhsa.gov/2k6/youthViolence/youthViolence.htm.

morphine, and opium. The act was revised in 1922 to allow importation of opium and coca (cocaine) leaves for qualified medical practitioners. The Marijuana Tax Act of 1937 required registration and payment of a tax by all persons who imported, sold, or manufactured marijuana. Because marijuana was classified as a narcotic, those registering would also be subject to criminal penalty.

In later years, other federal laws were passed to clarify existing drug statutes and revise penalties. For example, the Boggs Act of 1951 provided mandatory sentences for violating federal drug laws. The Durham–Humphrey Act of 1951 made it illegal to dispense barbiturates and amphetamines without a prescription. The Narcotic Control Act of 1956 increased penalties for drug offenders. In 1965, the Drug Abuse Control Act set up stringent guidelines for the legal use and sale of mood-modifying drugs, such as barbiturates, amphetamines, LSD, and any other "dangerous drugs," except narcotics prescribed by doctors and pharmacists. Illegal possession was punished as a misdemeanor and manufacture or sale as a felony. And in 1970, the Comprehensive Drug Abuse Prevention and Control Act set up unified categories of illegal drugs and attached specific penalties to their sale, manufacture, or possession. The law gave the U.S. attorney general discretion to decide in which category to place any new drug.

Since then, various federal laws have attempted to increase penalties imposed on drug smugglers and limit the manufacture and sale of newly developed substances. For example, the 1984 Controlled Substances Act set new, stringent penalties for drug dealers and created five categories of narcotic and non-narcotic substances subject to federal laws.[135] The Anti–Drug Abuse Act of 1986 again set new standards for minimum and maximum sentences for drug offenders, increased penalties for most offenses, and created a new drug penalty classification for large-scale offenses (such as trafficking in more than one kilogram of heroin), for which the penalty for a first offense was 10 years to life in prison.[136] With then-President George H. W. Bush's endorsement, Congress passed the Anti–Drug Abuse Act of 1988, which created a coordinated national drug policy under a "drug czar," set treatment and prevention priorities, and, symbolizing the government's hard-line stance against drug dealing, imposed the death penalty for drug-related killings.[137]

For the most part, state laws mirror federal statutes. Some apply extremely heavy penalties for selling or distributing dangerous drugs, involving prison sentences of up to 25 years. ✔ CHECKPOINTS

✔ CHECKPOINTS

- ✔ Substance abuse is an ancient practice dating back more than 4,000 years.
- ✔ A wide variety of drugs are in use today; alcohol is a major problem.
- ✔ Drug use in the general population has increased during the past decade; about half of all high school seniors have tried illegal drugs at least once.
- ✔ There is no single cause of substance abuse. Some people may use drugs because they are predisposed to abuse.
- ✔ There is a strong link between drug abuse and crime. People who become addicts may increase their illegal activities to support their habits. However, there is no conclusive evidence that "drugs cause crime."
- ✔ Some people engage in violence as part of their drug-dealing activities.

Drug Control Strategies

Substance abuse remains a major social problem in the United States. Politicians looking for a safe campaign issue can take advantage of the public's fear of drug addiction by calling for a war on drugs. These wars have been declared even when drug usage is stable or in decline.[138] Can these efforts pay off? Can illegal drug use be eliminated or controlled?

A number of different drug control strategies have been tried, with varying degrees of success. Some aim to deter drug use by stopping the flow of drugs into the country, apprehending and punishing dealers, and cracking down on street-level drug deals. Others focus on preventing drug use by educating potential users to the dangers of substance abuse (convincing them to "say no to drugs") and by organizing community groups to work with the at-risk population in their area. Still another approach is to treat known users so they can control their addictions. Some of these efforts are discussed next.

Source Control One approach to drug control is to deter the sale and importation of drugs through the systematic apprehension of large-volume drug dealers, coupled with the enforcement of strict drug laws that carry heavy penalties. This approach is designed to capture and punish known international drug dealers and

Profiles in Crime

A Life in the Drug Trade

In the summer of 2004, a dramatic murder trial took place in New York City that aptly illustrates the link between drugs and crime. Two Bronx men, Alan Quiñones and Diego Rodriguez, were accused of heroin trafficking and killing a police informant. The trial hinged on the testimony of one of their confederates, Hector Vega, a key government witness who had previously pleaded guilty to taking part in the murder. He described in vivid detail how he watched the defendants beat the victim, Edwin Santiago, as he lay handcuffed on the floor of a Bronx apartment. He told the jury how the defendants Quiñones and Rodriguez spit in Santiago's face to show what they thought of police informants. Santiago's body was found mutilated and burned beyond recognition on June 28, 1999.

During the trial, Vega gave the jury a detailed lesson in retail drug operations. In the Bronx, beatings, slashings, and shootings are routinely used to enforce what he called "the drug law." "If people deserved it, I beat them up." He showed them a tattoo on his upper-right arm that meant "Money, Power, Respect." Vega, 31, also told the jury that he headed a group of heroin vendors who did business from his "spot," his sales area, between Daly and Honeywell Avenues in the Bronx. He said he had learned the trade from a stepfather, a building superintendent who he said had a second job as a narcotics entrepreneur: "I always knew about the drug business. I was raised around it."

As a midlevel drug dealer, Vega received heroin on consignment from big-time drug wholesalers and turned it over in $100 packages to people he called his "managers," who in turn found "runners" to sell it on the street. His job was to "make sure everybody is working, and I will make sure everything is running correctly." Vega received a "commission" of about 35 percent of all sales in his organization; he estimated that he made a total of at least $500,000 in the five years before his arrest.

Vega told how he used strict rules to run his organization. He did not sell between 1:00 PM and 3:00 PM, because of "school hours." He did not allow anyone to sell at his spot without his approval, or steal drugs from him, or pass him a counterfeit bill, or taint the quality of drugs sold under his name. If that happened, he said, "I'd be looking like a fool. The drug spot will go down." When one of his workers, named Manny, stole one package of heroin, Vega slashed his face with a box cutter. When the wound did not immediately bleed, "I didn't see nothing cut, I didn't see anything I did, so I did it a second time," he said, until he saw blood. Angered by a counterfeit bill he received from a crack addict, "I punched him in the face, I kicked him, I threw him on the floor and kicked him again." He disciplined one stranger who cheated him by hitting the man in the back of the head with a three-foot tree branch. Police informants were given special treatment: "In the drug world, in the drug law, we say that snitches get stitches," he said. "In jail you cut their face. In the street, you beat them. You kill them."

Vega testified that the defendants Quiñones and Rodriguez were heroin wholesalers and that he began buying drugs from them a few months before Santiago's death. After he learned that Quiñones suspected Santiago of working undercover for the police, Vega helped him lure Santiago to the apartment of a girlfriend where the beatings and murder took place. For his cooperation with the government, Vega faced a 15-year sentence rather than the death penalty.

You can see from this case how life in the drug trade is linked to crime. Drug dealing is a business with rules that have to be obeyed and roles that must be faithfully carried out. Drug deals are not spontaneous acts motivated by rage, mental disease, or economic desperation, but rational (albeit illegal) business enterprises engaged in by highly motivated players. Those who violate corporate policy are dealt with ruthlessly.

Critical Thinking

Do you agree that drug dealing is a "business" in the traditional sense, or are dealers forced into a life of crime by social forces beyond their control? Can an analogy be made between drug dealing and legitimate business enterprise?

Is drug dealing and smuggling a type of business enterprise? To find out read Terrance G. Lichtenwald, "Drug Smuggling Behavior: A Development Smuggling Model (Part 2)," *The Forensic Examiner* 13 (2004): 14–23.

SOURCE: Julia Preston, "Witness Gives Details of Life as Drug Dealer," *New York Times*, July 12, 2004.

deter those who are considering entering the drug trade. A major effort has been made to cut off supplies of drugs by destroying overseas crops and arresting members of drug cartels in Central and South America, Asia, and the Middle East, where many drugs are grown and manufactured. The federal government has been in the vanguard of encouraging exporting nations to step up efforts to destroy drug crops and prosecute dealers. Three South American nations, Peru, Bolivia, and Colombia, have agreed with the United States to coordinate control efforts. However, translating words into deeds is a formidable task. Drug lords are willing and able to fight back through intimidation, violence, and corruption when necessary. The Colombian drug cartels do not hesitate to use violence and assassination to protect their interests.

The amount of narcotics grown each year is so vast that even if three-quarters of the opium crop were destroyed, the U.S. market would still require only 10 percent of the remainder to sustain the drug trade. Adding to control problems is the fact that the drug trade is an important source of foreign revenue for third world nations, and destroying the drug trade undermines their economies. More than 1 million people in Peru, Bolivia, Colombia, Thailand, Laos, and other developing nations depend on the cultivating and processing of illegal substances. The federal government estimates that U.S. citizens spend more than $40 billion annually on illegal drugs, and much of this money is funneled overseas.

War and terrorism also may make source control strategies problematic. After the U.S. destroyed Afghanistan's Taliban government, local warlords seized power and resumed the drug trade; Afghanistan now supplies more than 90 percent of the world's opium.[139] Colombian guerillas finance their war against the government by aiding drug traffickers and taxing crops and sales.[140]

Interdiction Strategies Law enforcement efforts have also been directed at intercepting drug supplies as they enter the country. Border patrols and military personnel using sophisticated hardware have been involved in massive interdiction efforts; many impressive multimillion-dollar seizures have been made. Yet the U.S. borders are so vast and unprotected that meaningful interdiction is impossible. And even if all importation were shut down, homegrown marijuana and laboratory-made drugs, such as Ecstasy, LSD, and PCP, could become the drugs of choice. Even now, their easy availability and relatively low cost are increasing their popularity among the at-risk population.

Law Enforcement Strategies Local, state, and federal law enforcement agencies have been actively fighting drugs. One approach is to direct efforts at large-scale drug rings. The long-term consequence has been to decentralize drug dealing and encourage young independent dealers to become major suppliers. Ironically, it has proven easier for federal agents to infiltrate and prosecute traditional organized crime groups than to take on drug-dealing gangs. Consequently, some nontraditional groups have broken into the drug trade. Police can also target, intimidate, and arrest street-level dealers and users in an effort to make drug use so much of a hassle that consumption is cut back and the crime rate reduced. Approaches that have been tried include reverse stings, in which undercover agents pose as dealers to arrest users who approach them for a buy. Police have attacked fortified crack houses with heavy equipment to breach their defenses. They have used racketeering laws to seize the assets of known dealers. Special task forces of local and state police have used undercover operations and drug sweeps to discourage both dealers and users.[141]

Although some street-level enforcement efforts have succeeded, others are considered failures. Drug sweeps have clogged courts and correctional facilities with petty offenders while draining police resources. There are also suspicions that a displacement effect occurs; stepped-up efforts to curb drug dealing in one area or city simply encourage dealers to seek friendlier territory.[142]

Punishment Strategies Even if law enforcement efforts cannot produce a general deterrent effect, the courts may achieve the required result by severely punishing known drug dealers and traffickers. A number of initiatives have made the prosecution and punishment of drug offenders a top priority. State prosecutors have expanded their investigations into drug importation and distribution and created special prosecutors to focus on drug dealers. The fact that drugs such as crack are considered a serious problem may have convinced judges and prosecutors to expedite substance abuse cases.

However, these efforts often have their downside. Defense attorneys consider delay tactics sound legal maneuvering in drug-related cases. Courts are so backlogged that prosecutors are anxious to plea-bargain. The consequence of this legal maneuvering is that many people convicted on federal drug charges are granted probation or some other form of community release. Even so, prisons have become jammed with inmates, many of whom were involved in drug-related cases. Many drug offenders sent to prison do not serve their entire sentences because they are released in an effort to relieve prison overcrowding.[143]

Community Strategies Another type of drug control effort relies on the involvement of local community groups to lead the fight against drugs. Representatives of various local government agencies, churches, civic organizations, and similar institutions are being brought together to create drug prevention and awareness programs.

Citizen-sponsored programs attempt to restore a sense of community in drug-infested areas, reduce fear, and promote conventional norms and values.[144] These efforts can be classified into one of four distinct categories.[145] The first involves law enforcement aid–type efforts, which may include block watches, cooperative police–community efforts, and citizen patrols. These citizen groups are nonconfrontational: They simply observe or photograph dealers, write down their license plate numbers, and then notify police.

A second tactic is to use the civil justice system to harass offenders. Landlords have been sued for owning properties that house drug dealers; neighborhood groups have scrutinized drug houses for building code violations. Information acquired from these various sources is turned over to local authorities, such as police and housing agencies, for more formal action.

A third approach is through community-based treatment efforts in which citizen volunteers participate in self-help support programs, such as Narcotics Anonymous or Cocaine Anonymous, which have more than 1,000 chapters nationally. Other programs provide youths with martial arts training, dancing, and social events as alternatives to the drug life.

A fourth type of community-level drug prevention effort is designed to enhance the quality of life, improve interpersonal relationships, and upgrade the neighborhood's physical environment. Activities might include the creation of drug-free school zones (which encourage police to keep drug dealers away from the vicinity of schools). Consciousness-raising efforts include demonstrations and marches to publicize the drug problem and build solidarity among participants.

Drug Education and Prevention Strategies Prevention strategies are aimed at convincing youths not to get involved in drug abuse; heavy reliance is placed on educational programs that teach kids to say no to drugs. The most widely used program is Drug Abuse Resistance Education (DARE), an elementary school course designed to give students the skills for resisting peer pressure to experiment with tobacco, drugs, and alcohol. It is unique in that it employs uniformed police officers to carry the antidrug message to the students before they enter junior high school. The program focuses on five major areas:

- Providing accurate information about tobacco, alcohol, and drugs
- Teaching students techniques to resist peer pressure
- Teaching students respect for the law and law enforcers
- Giving students ideas for alternatives to drug use
- Building the self-esteem of students

DARE is based on the concept that young students need specific analytical and social skills to resist peer pressure and refuse drugs.[146] However, evaluations show that the program does little to reduce drug use or convince abusers that drugs are harmful.[147] Although there are indications that DARE may be effective with some subsets of the population, such as female and Hispanic students, overall success appears problematic at best.[148]

Drug-Testing Strategies Drug testing of private employees, government workers, and criminal offenders is believed to deter substance abuse. In the workplace, employees are tested to enhance on-the-job safety and productivity. In some industries, such as mining and transportation, drug testing is considered essential because abuse can pose a threat to the public.[149] Business leaders have been enlisted in the fight against drugs. Mandatory drug-testing programs in government and industry are common; more than 40 percent of the country's largest companies,

© AP

● Prevention and treatment rather than enforcement and punishment may be the key to tackling the problem of substance abuse. Grifyn Clay, 7 (foreground), gets sprinkled with water from a fire engine at Camp Hot Spot at Cascade View Elementary School in Snohomish, Washington. The camp is the work of the Snohomish Drug & Alcohol Committee and is part of an ongoing effort by local groups to tackle teen substance abuse. Sno-DAC, as it is called, came out of meetings with parents and community members in 1984 and became one of the first grassroots groups in the county to look at ways to combat local abuse.

including IBM and AT&T, have drug-testing programs. The federal government requires employee testing in regulated industries such as nuclear energy and defense contracting. About 4 million transportation workers are subject to testing.

Criminal defendants are now routinely tested at all stages of the justice system, from arrest to parole. The goal is to reduce criminal behavior by detecting current users and curbing their abuse. Can such programs reduce criminal activity? Two evaluations of pretrial drug-testing programs found little evidence that monitoring defendants' drug use influenced their behavior.[150]

Treatment Strategies A number of approaches are taken to treat known users, getting them clean of drugs and alcohol and thereby reducing the at-risk population. One approach rests on the assumption that users have low self-esteem and treatment efforts must focus on building a sense of self. For example, users have been placed in worthwhile programs of outdoor activities and wilderness training to create self-reliance and a sense of accomplishment.[151] More intensive efforts use group therapy approaches, relying on group leaders who have been substance abusers; through such sessions, users get the skills and support to help them reject social pressure to use drugs. These programs are based on the Alcoholics Anonymous approach, which holds that users must find within themselves the strength to stay clean and that peer support from those who understand their experiences can help them achieve a drug-free life.

There are also residential programs for the more heavily involved, and a large network of drug treatment centers has been developed. Some detoxification units use medical procedures to wean patients from the more addicting drugs and replace them with others, such as methadone, that can be more easily regulated. Methadone is a drug similar to heroin, and addicts can be treated at clinics where they receive methadone under controlled conditions. However, methadone programs have been undermined because some users sell their methadone on the black market, and others supplement their dosages with illegally obtained heroin. Other programs have used drugs such as Naxalone, which counters the effects of narcotics and eases the trauma of withdrawal, but results have not been conclusive.[152]

Another type of therapeutic program attempts to deal with the psychological causes of drug use in "therapeutic communities." Hypnosis, aversion therapy (getting users to associate drugs with unpleasant sensations, such as nausea), counseling, biofeedback, and other techniques are often used. Some programs report significant success with clients who are able to complete the full course of treatment.[153]

The long-term effects of treatment on drug abuse are still uncertain. Critics charge that a stay in a residential program can help stigmatize people as addicts even if they never used hard drugs; and in treatment they may be introduced to hard-core users with whom they will associate after release. Users do not often enter these programs voluntarily and have little motivation to change. Supporters of treatment argue that many addicts are helped by intensive inpatient and outpatient treatment, and the cost saving over criminal proceedings is considerable.[154] Moreover, it is estimated that less than half of the 5 million people who need drug treatment actually get it; so treatment strategies have not been given a fair trial.

Employment Strategies Research indicates that drug abusers who obtain and keep employment will end or reduce the incidence of their substance abuse.[155] Not surprisingly, then, there have been a number of efforts to provide vocational rehabilitation for drug abusers. One approach is the supported work program, which typically involves jobsite training, ongoing assessment, and jobsite intervention.

Rather than teach work skills in a classroom, support programs rely on helping drug abusers deal with real work settings. Other programs provide training to overcome barriers to employment, including help with motivation, education, experience, the job market, job-seeking skills, and personal issues. For example, female abusers may be unaware of child care resources that would enable them to seek employment opportunities. Another approach is to help addicts improve their interviewing skills so that once a job opportunity can be identified, they are equipped to convince potential employers of their commitment and reliability.[156]

Legalization of Drugs

Considering these problems, some commentators have called for the legalization or decriminalization of restricted drugs. The so-called war on drugs is expensive, costing more than $500 billion over the past 20 years—money that could have been spent on education and economic development. Drug enforcement and treatment now costs federal, state, and local governments about $100 billion per year. The National Center on Addiction and Substance Abuse at Columbia University claims states spent, conservatively, $81 billion dollars on substance abuse and addiction—13 percent of the $620 billion in total state spending.[157] The federal government plans to spend close to $12 billion more on drug control, up from $7 billion in 1995; this figure does not reflect treatment costs.[158]

And effectiveness is questionable. Two decades ago, a kilogram of cocaine sold for a wholesale price of $40,000; today it goes for $20,000 to $25,000. Translated into consumer prices, a gram of cocaine costs less than $50 today in larger cities, compared to $100 in 1990. Declining prices suggest that the supply of cocaine is rising despite the billions spent to prevent its importation.[159]

Legalization is warranted, according to drug expert Ethan Nadelmann, because the use of mood-altering substances is customary in almost all human societies; people have always wanted, and will find ways of obtaining, psychoactive drugs.[160] Banning drugs creates networks of manufacturers and distributors, many of whom use violence as part of their standard operating procedures. Although some believe that drug use is immoral, Nadelmann questions whether it is any worse than the unrestricted use of alcohol and cigarettes, both of which are addicting and unhealthful. Far more people die each year because they abuse these legal substances than are killed in drug wars or from abusing illegal substances.

Nadelmann also states that just as Prohibition failed to stop the flow of alcohol in the 1920s while it increased the power of organized crime, the policy of prohibiting drugs is similarly doomed to failure. When drugs were legal and freely available early in the twentieth century, the proportion of Americans using drugs was not much greater than today. Most users led normal lives, most likely because of the legal status of their drug use.

If drugs were legalized, the argument goes, price and distribution could be controlled by the government. This would reduce addicts' cash requirements so crime rates would drop because users would no longer need the same cash flow to support their habits. Drug-related deaths would decline because government control would reduce needle sharing and the spread of AIDS. Legalization would also destroy the drug-importing cartels and gangs. Because drugs would be bought and sold openly, the government would reap a tax windfall both from taxes on the sale of drugs and from income taxes paid by drug dealers on profits that have been part of the hidden economy. Of course, as with alcohol, drug distribution would be regulated, keeping drugs away from adolescents, public servants such as police and airline pilots, and known felons. Those who favor legalization point to the Netherlands as a country that has legalized drugs and remains relatively crime free.[161]

Critics reply that this approach might have short term benefits, but it might also have grave social consequences. Legalization might increase the nation's rate of drug usage, creating an even larger group of nonproductive, drug-dependent people who must be cared for by the rest of society.[162] In countries such as Iran and Thailand, where drugs are cheap and readily available, the rate of narcotics

CONCEPT SUMMARY 13.1 Drug-Control Strategies

CONTROL STRATEGY	MAIN FOCUS	PROBLEMS/ISSUES
Source control	Destroy overseas crops and drug labs	Drug profits hard to resist; drug crops in hostile nations are off limits
Interdiction	Seal borders; arrest drug couriers	Extensive U.S. borders hard to control
Law enforcement	Police investigation and arrest of dealers	New dealers are recruited to replace those in prison
Punishment	Deter dealers with harsh punishments	Crowded prisons promote bargain justice
Community development	Help community members deal with drug problems on the local level	Relies on community cohesion and efficacy
Drug education	Teach kids about the harm of taking drugs	Evaluations do not show programs are effective
Drug testing	Threaten employees with drug tests to deter use	Evaluations do not show effective; people cheat on tests
Treatment	Use of therapy to get people off drugs	Expensive, requires motivation; clients associate with other users
Employment	Provide jobs as an alternative to drugs	Requires that former addicts become steady employees
Legalization	Decriminalize or legalize drugs	Political hot potato; danger of creating more users

use is quite high. Historically, the availability of cheap narcotics has preceded drug use epidemics, as was the case when British and American merchants sold opium in nineteenth-century China. As drug use increases so too would collateral costs such as health care. The most recent survey by the federal government's DAWN program, which tracks drug- and alcohol-related emergency room visits, found that more than 620,000 cases are seen by ER doctors each year, including

- Cocaine, 125,000 cases
- Marijuana, 80,000 cases
- Heroin was involved in 48,000 cases
- Stimulants, including amphetamines and methamphetamine, were involved in 43,000 cases
- Alcohol, 141,000 cases
- Alcohol and drug combination were involved in 119,000 cases[163]

If drugs were legal, surely these numbers would skyrocket, taxing an already burdened health care system.

If juveniles, criminals, and members of other at-risk groups were forbidden to buy drugs, who would be the customers? Noncriminal, nonabusing, middle-aged adults? And would not those prohibited from legally buying drugs create an underground market almost as vast as the current one? If the government tried to raise money by taxing legal drugs, as it now does with liquor and cigarettes, that might encourage drug smuggling to avoid tax payments; these "illegal" drugs might then fall into the hands of adolescents.

Decriminalization or legalization of controlled substances is unlikely in the near term, but further study is warranted. What effect would a policy of partial decriminalization (for example, legalizing small amounts of marijuana) have on drug use rates? Would a get-tough policy help to "widen the net" of the justice system and actually deepen some youths' involvement in substance abuse? Can society provide alternatives to drugs that will reduce teenage drug dependency?[164] The answers to these questions have proven elusive. Concept Summary 13.1 summarizes the different types of drug control strategies.

THINKING Like a Criminologist

You have been called upon by the director of the Department of Health and Human Services to give your opinion on a recent national survey that found that serious mental illness is highly correlated with illicit drug use. Among adults who used an illicit drug in the past year, 17.1 percent had serious mental illness in that year, whereas the rate of serious mental illness was 6.9 percent among adults who did not use an illicit drug. Among adults with serious mental illness, 28.9 percent used an illicit drug in the past year, whereas the rate of illicit drug use was 12.7 percent among those without serious mental illness. The relationship is illustrated in Figure A.

Among adults with serious mental illness, 23.2 percent (4 million) were dependent on or abused alcohol or illicit drugs, whereas the rate among adults without serious mental illness was only 8.2 percent. Adults with serious mental illness were more likely than those without serious mental illness to be dependent on or to abuse illicit drugs (9.6 percent versus 2.1 percent) and more likely to be dependent on or to abuse alcohol (18 percent versus 7 percent). Among adults with substance dependence or abuse, 20.4 percent had serious mental illness. The rate of serious mental illness was 7 percent among adults who did not have substance abuse or dependence.

The director realizes that one possible explanation of these data is that drugs cause people to become mentally ill. He asks you to comment on other possible explanations. What will you tell her?

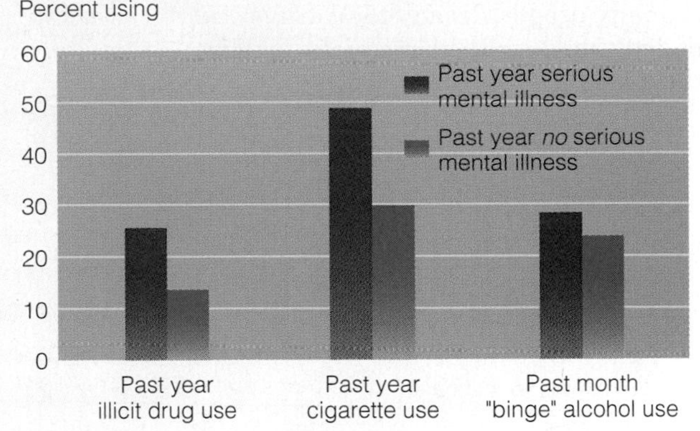

Figure A

Rates of Serious Mental Illness Correlated with Illicit Drug, Alcohol, and Cigarette Use among Adults Aged 18 or Older

SOURCE: *National Household Survey on Drug Abuse, 2002* (Washington, D.C.: U.S. Department of Health and Human Services, 2003).

Summary

- Public order crimes are acts considered illegal because they conflict with social policy, accepted moral rules, and public opinion.
- There is usually great debate over public order crimes. Some charge that they are not really crimes at all and that it is foolish to legislate morality. Others view such morally tinged acts as prostitution, gambling, and drug abuse as harmful and therefore subject to public control.
- Many public order crimes are sex related.
- In 2003 the Supreme Court ruled that sexual relations between gay people cannot be criminalized.
- Prostitution is another sex-related public order crime.
- Although prostitution has been practiced for thousands of years and is legal in some areas, most states outlaw commercial sex.
- There are a variety of prostitutes, including streetwalkers, B-girls, and call girls. A new type of prostitution is cyber prostitution, which is Internet based.
- Studies indicate that prostitutes come from poor, troubled families and have abusive parents. However, there is little evidence that prostitutes are emotionally disturbed, addicted to drugs, or sexually abnormal.
- Although prostitution is illegal, some cities have set up adult entertainment areas where commercial sex is tolerated by law enforcement agents.
- Pornography involves the sale of sexually explicit material intended to sexually excite paying customers. The depiction of sex and nudity is not illegal, but it does violate the law when it is judged obscene.
- Obscenity is a legal term that today is defined as material offensive to community standards. Thus, each local jurisdiction must decide what pornographic material is obscene. A growing problem is the exploitation of children in obscene materials (kiddie porn), which has been expanded through the Internet.
- The Supreme Court has ruled that local communities can pass statutes outlawing any sexually explicit material.
- There is no hard evidence that pornography is related to crime or aggression, but data suggest that sexual material with a violent theme is related to sexual violence by those who view it.
- Substance abuse is another type of public order crime. Most states and the federal government outlaw a wide variety of drugs they consider harmful, including narcotics, amphetamines, barbiturates, cocaine, hallucinogens, and marijuana.
- One of the main reasons for the continued ban on drugs is their relationship to crime. Numerous studies have found that drug addicts commit enormous amounts of property and violent crime.
- Alcohol is another commonly abused substance. Although alcohol is legal to possess, it too has been linked to crime. Drunk driving and deaths caused by drunk drivers are growing national problems.

- Strategies to control substance abuse range from source control to treatment. So far, no single method seems effective. Although legalization is debated, the fact that so many people already take drugs and the association of drug abuse with crime make legalization unlikely in the near term.

Take a Post-Test. Visit www.thomsonedu.com/criminaljustice/siegel and take the chapter Post-Test to monitor your progress and identify areas for further improvement. In addition to discovering what you've mastered, you'll learn which concepts need your added attention and get specific page references that direct you to the places in the text where you can find more information on them.

Key Terms

public order crime 311
victimless crime 312
moral entrepreneur 313
paraphilia 314
prostitution 315
pornography 321
obscenity 321
temperance movement 325
Prohibition 325
narcotic 329

Critical Thinking Questions

1. Why do you think people take drugs? Do you know anyone with an addiction-prone personality, or do you believe that is a myth?
2. What policy might be the best strategy to reduce teenage drug use: source control, reliance on treatment, national education efforts, or community-level enforcement?
3. Under what circumstances, if any, might the legalization or decriminalization of sexually related material be beneficial to society?
4. Do you consider alcohol a drug? Should greater control be placed on the sale of alcohol?
5. Is prostitution really a crime? Should men or women have the right to sell sexual favors if they so choose?

The Criminal Justice System

CHAPTER 14

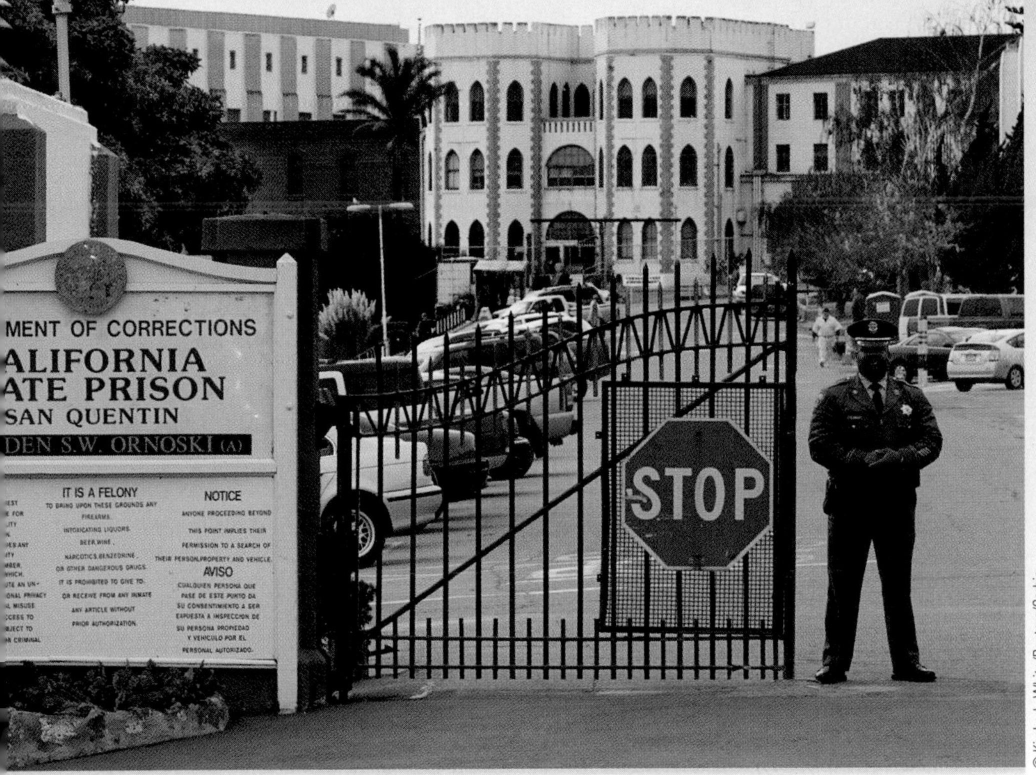

© Kimberly White/Reuters/Corbis

A NATIONWIDE SEARCH BEGAN WHEN LACI PETERSON, 27 YEARS OLD AND EIGHT MONTHS PREGNANT, disappeared from her home in Modesto, California, on Christmas Eve 2002. Her grieving husband, Scott, told her family and police that she had simply vanished from their home while he was on a fishing trip. She was going to take a walk in a nearby park, he said, and never came back. When her body and that of her unborn child were found four months later, Scott was charged with two counts of murder.

Though Laci's parents and relatives at first believed that Scott Peterson could not have harmed his wife, their trust was broken when detectives told them that he was having an affair with a massage therapist named Amber Frey and had also taken a $250,000 life insurance policy out on Laci.

Peterson pleaded not guilty to two counts of murder. During the trial, the defense first tried to blame the murder on transients who were in the park at the time Laci disappeared and then floated a theory of mistaken identity (saying that Laci looked like a prosecutor who lived in the neighborhood and it may have been a revenge killing). The prosecution presented evidence of Scott's infidelity and suspicious activity: He was seen carrying a large wrapped-up object out of his house the night Laci disappeared; his "fishing trip" was in the vicinity of where her body was recovered. At first the jury seemed hopelessly deadlocked. Then, on November 12, 2004, after two jurors were replaced, the reconstituted jury brought back a guilty verdict; Scott Peterson was sentenced to death soon after. He is currently incarcerated in California's San Quentin prison.

CHAPTER OBJECTIVES

1. Be familiar with the history of the criminal justice system.
2. Know the component agencies of criminal justice.
3. Be familiar with the various stages in the process of justice.
4. Understand how criminal justice is shaped by the rule of law.
5. Know the elements of the crime control model.
6. Be able to discuss the problem of prisoner reentry.
7. Know what is meant by the justice model.
8. Discuss the elements of due process.
9. Be able to argue the merits of the rehabilitation model.
10. Understand the concept of nonintervention.
11. Know the elements of the restorative justice model.

Take a Pre-Test. Visit www.thomsonedu.com/criminaljustice/siegel and take a Pre-Test to determine what you already know and identify the areas where you'll need to focus your study. The program will direct you to specific pages within the text where you can find further information on the correct answers to the questions you've missed.

The Peterson case garnered national headlines. It was a high-profile case that showcased the operations of the criminal justice system. It involved almost every element of justice, from police investigation, to prosecutorial decision making (including whether the death penalty should be invoked), to the trial process and sentencing. Such high-profile media cases have become routine ever since the O. J. Simpson trial was broadcast in 1994. Though they may sometimes seem like a media circus (the Michael Jackson trial comes to mind), these cases underscore the importance of the criminal justice system in contemporary society. The public relies on the agencies of the criminal justice system to provide solutions to the crime problem and to shape the direction of crime policy. This loosely coupled collection of agencies is charged with, among other matters, protecting the public, maintaining order, enforcing the law, identifying transgressors, bringing the guilty to justice, and treating criminal behavior.

Although firmly entrenched in our culture, common criminal justice agencies have existed for only 150 years or so. At first, these institutions operated independently, with little recognition that their functions could be coordinated or share common ground.

In 1931, President Herbert Hoover appointed the National Commission of Law Observance and Enforcement, commonly known as the Wickersham Commission. This national study group analyzed the American justice system in detail and helped usher in the era of treatment and rehabilitation. It showed the complex rules and regulations that govern the system and exposed how difficult it was for justice personnel to keep track of its legal and administrative complexity.

The modern era of criminal justice study began with a series of explorations of the criminal justice process conducted under the auspices of the American Bar Foundation.[1] As a group, the Bar Foundation studies brought to light some of the hidden or low-visibility processes at the heart of justice system operations. They showed how informal decision making and the use of personal discretion were essential ingredients of the justice process.

Another milestone occurred in 1967, when the President's Commission on Law Enforcement and the Administration of Justice (the Crime Commission), appointed by President Lyndon Johnson, published its final report, *The Challenge of Crime in a Free Society*.[2] This group of practitioners, educators, and attorneys had been charged with creating a comprehensive view of the criminal justice process and offering recommendations for its reform. Its efforts resulted in passage of the Safe Streets and Crime Control Act of 1968, which provided federal funds for state and local crime control efforts. This legislation helped launch a massive campaign to restructure the justice system by funding the Law Enforcement Assistance Administration (LEAA), an agency that provided hundreds of millions of dollars in aid to local and state justice agencies. Federal intervention through the LEAA ushered in a new era in research and development in criminal justice and established the concept that its component agencies actually make up a system.[3]

Though the LEAA is no longer in operation, its efforts helped identify the concept of a unified system of criminal justice. Rather than viewing police, courts, and correctional agencies as thousands of independent institutions, it has become common to see them as components of a large, integrated, people-processing system that manages law violators from the time of their arrest through trial, punishment, and release.

WHAT IS THE CRIMINAL JUSTICE SYSTEM?

The **criminal justice system** refers to the agencies of government charged with enforcing law, adjudicating crime, and correcting criminal conduct. The criminal justice system is essentially an instrument of social control: Society considers some behaviors so dangerous and destructive that it either strictly controls their occurrence or outlaws them outright. It is the job of the agencies of justice to prevent social harm by apprehending and punishing those who violate the law and in so doing deter those who may be contemplating future wrongdoing. Although society maintains other forms of social control, such as the family, school, and church, these are designed to deal with moral, not legal, misbehavior. Only the criminal justice system has the power to control crime and punish criminals.

The contemporary criminal justice system in the United States is monumental in size. It consists of more than 55,000 public agencies and now costs federal, state, and local governments about $150 billion per year for civil and criminal justice, increasing more than 300 percent since 1982.

One reason the justice system is so expensive to run is because it employs 2 million-plus people in more than 55,000 public agencies, including 17,000 police agencies, nearly 17,000 courts, more than 8,000 prosecutorial agencies, about 6,000 correctional institutions, and more than 3,500 probation and parole departments. There are also capital costs. State jurisdictions are now conducting a massive correctional building campaign, adding tens of thousands of prison cells.

The system is so big because it must process, treat, and care for millions of people each year. Although the crime rate has declined substantially, close to 14 million people are still being arrested each year, including more than 2 million for serious felony offenses.[4] In addition, about 1.5 million juveniles are handled by the juvenile courts. Today state and federal courts convict a combined total of more than 1 million adults on felony charges.[5]

Considering the enormous number of people processed each year, it comes as no surprise that the correctional system population is at an all-time high. More than 7 million people are now under the control of the correctional system, with more than 2 million men and women in the nation's jails and prisons. About 4 million adult men and women are being supervised in the community while on probation or parole, a number that has been increasing by more than 3 percent each year since 1990 (see Figure 14.1).

The major components of this immense system—the police, courts, and correctional agencies—are described in the sections that follow. What are their duties? What are the major stages in the formal criminal justice process, and how are decisions made at these critical junctures? What is the informal justice process, and how does it operate? These important questions are addressed next.

Police and Law Enforcement

Approximately 17,000 law enforcement agencies operate in the United States. State and local law enforcement agencies employ more than 1 million full-time personnel, including more than 700,000 sworn officers.[6] Most are municipal,

criminal justice system
The agencies of government—police, courts, and corrections—responsible for apprehending, adjudicating, sanctioning, and treating criminal offenders.

Figure 14.1
Adult Correctional Populations
SOURCE: Bureau of Justice Statistics Correctional Surveys (The Annual Probation Survey, National Prisoner Statistics, Survey of Jails, and the Annual Parole Survey) as presented in *Correctional Populations in the United States, Annual, Prisoners in 2004,* and *Probation and Parole in the United States, 2004.*

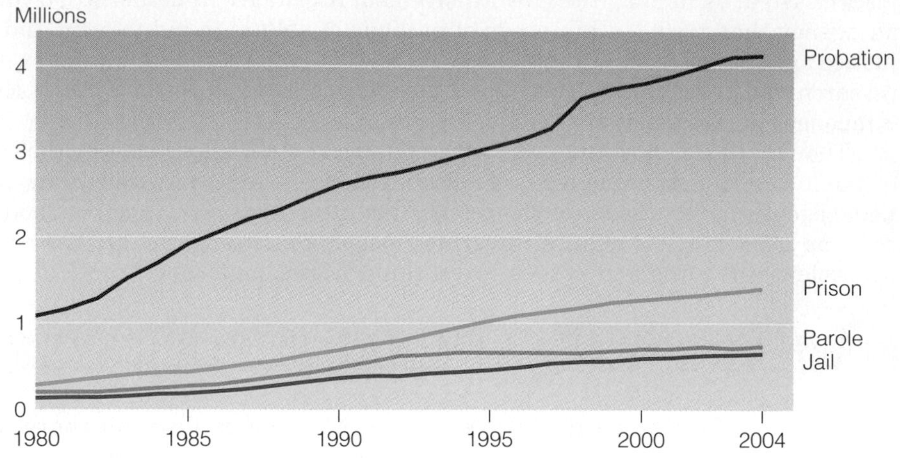

general-purpose police forces, numbering about 12,000 in all. In addition, local jurisdictions maintain more than 1,000 special police units, including park rangers, harbor police, transit police, and campus security agencies at local universities. At the county level, there are approximately 3,000 sheriff's departments, which, depending on the jurisdiction, provide police protection in unincorporated areas of a county, perform judicial functions such as serving subpoenas, and maintain the county jail and detention facilities. Every state except Hawaii maintains a state police force. The federal government has its own law enforcement agencies, including the FBI and Secret Service.

Law enforcement agencies have been charged with peacekeeping, deterring potential criminals, and apprehending law violators.[7] The traditional police role involved maintaining order through patrolling public streets and highways, responding to calls for assistance, investigating crimes, and identifying criminal suspects. The police role has gradually expanded to include a variety of human service functions, including preventing youth crime and diverting juvenile offenders from the criminal justice system, resolving family conflicts, facilitating the movement of people and vehicles, preserving civil order during emergencies, providing emergency medical care, and improving police–community relations.

Police are the most visible agents of the justice process. Their reactions to victims and offenders are carefully scrutinized in the news media. Police have been criticized for being too harsh or too lenient, too violent or too passive. Police response to minority groups, youths, political dissidents, protesters, and union workers has been publicly debated.

Compounding the problem is the tremendous **discretion** afforded police officers, who determine when a domestic dispute becomes disorderly conduct or criminal assault, whether it is appropriate to arrest juveniles or refer them to a social agency, and when to assume that probable cause exists to arrest a suspect for a crime. At the same time, police agencies have been criticized for such problems as internal corruption, inefficiency, lack of effectiveness, brutality, and discriminatory hiring.

Widely publicized cases of police brutality, such as the Rodney King beating in Los Angeles, and police corruption (see the Profiles in Crime feature) have prompted calls for the investigation and prosecution of police officers. Police departments have made noteworthy efforts to control both corruption and brutality, and the evidence suggests that significant progress has been made. The most recent national survey on police contacts with civilians found that in a single year about 45 million people report having face-to-face police contact and of these only 665,000 involved force or the threat of force (about 1.5%). When force was used, it typically involved the citizen being pushed or grabbed; only 8 percent of the force incidents involved the police kicking or hitting the resident, and less than 15 percent of those experiencing force reported an injury.[8] However, this is not to say

discretion
The use of personal decision making by those carrying out police, judicial, and sanctioning functions within the criminal justice system.

that a police officer's job is not dangerous or that violence is not a concern: At least 6,600 civilians have been killed by the police since 1976; about 600 law enforcement officers have been slain during the past decade.[9]

Community Policing Despite efforts to improve police–community relations, more citizens report having negative experiences than positive ones.[10] To remedy this situation while improving the quality of their services, police departments have experimented with new forms of law enforcement, referred to as **community policing** and **problem-oriented policing**. These models are proactive rather than reactive: Rather than responding to crime after it occurs, police departments are now shaping their forces into community change agents in order to prevent crimes before they occur.

Community programs involve police in such activities as citizen crime patrols and councils that identify crime problems. Community policing often involves decentralized units that operate on the neighborhood level in order to be more sensitive to the particular concerns of the public; community policing creates a sense of security in a neighborhood and improves residents' opinions of the police.[11] In neighborhoods that maintain collective efficacy, police work closely with existing neighborhood groups to implement crime reduction programs; programs in these areas seem quite successful.[12] In more disorganized areas, police use aggressive tactics to reduce crime and "take back the streets" before building relations with community leaders.[13]

CONNECTIONS

As you may recall, the concept of collective efficacy was discussed in Chapter 6. Neighborhoods with collective efficacy use community resources to exert informal social control over people who might otherwise disrupt the social order.

Community policing efforts have produced numerous benefits. There is empirical evidence that some community policing efforts can reduce disorder and lower crime rates.[14] The most successful programs give officers time to meet with local residents to talk about crime in the neighborhood and to use personal initiative to solve problems. Where it is used, citizens seem to like community policing initiatives, and those who volunteer and get involved in community crime prevention programs report higher confidence in local police agencies and their ability to create a secure environment.[15] They may find that officers are more respectful of citizens, a condition that helps lower the number of complaints and improves community relations.[16]

Despite success, police managers still face resistance from some experienced officers who hold traditional law-and-order values and question the utility of community policing models. It is unlikely that these innovative programs can enjoy long-term success unless veteran officers form a commitment to the values of community policing.[17]

The Criminal Court System

The criminal courts are considered by many to be the core element in the administration of criminal justice. The court is a complex social agency with many independent but interrelated subsystems—clerk, prosecutor, defense attorney, judge, and probation department—each having a role in the court's operation. It is also the scene of many important elements of criminal justice decision making—detention, jury selection, trial, and sentencing. Ideally, the judicatory process operates with absolute fairness and equality. The entire process—from filing the initial complaint to final sentencing of the defendant—is governed by precise rules of law designed to ensure fairness. No defendant tried before a U.S. court should suffer or benefit because of his or her personal characteristics, beliefs, or affiliations.

However, U.S. criminal justice can be selective. Discretion accompanies defendants through every step of the process, determining what will happen to them and how their cases will be resolved. Discretion means that two people committing similar crimes may receive highly dissimilar treatment. Almost one-third of all people convicted of serious felonies receive a probation sentence; only 40 percent go to prison. Probation is used even in the most serious felony cases: Although most people convicted on sexual assault and rape charges are incarcerated but about 20 percent get probation only; about 5 percent of people convicted on muder charges receive probation as a sole sentence compared to about 3 percent who were sentenced to death.[18]

community policing
A style of policing that requires departments to reshape their forces into community change agents in order to work with citizens to reduce crime at the neighborhood level.

problem-oriented policing
Proactive form of policing: Rather than responding to crime after it occurs, police identify and respond to potential problems before they occur.

Profiles in Crime

Mafia Cops

On November 7, 1990, the bullet-riddled corpse of Edward Lino was found on the front seat of an abandoned car in Brooklyn, New York. Lino, a member of the Gambino mob, was believed to have been responsible for killing Paul Castellano, the former mob boss. His death set the stage for John Gotti's ("The Dapper Don") rise to power. Although a mob killing was nothing new in New York City, investigators had little to go on until 1994 when a mob informer made the scandalous claim that two New York City detectives, Louis Eppolito and Stephen Caracappa, were the culprits. Still, it took investigators more than a decade to gather sufficient evidence to indict the pair.

Both detectives had interesting backgrounds. Louis Eppolito (bottom image) became a cop in 1969. His father, Ralph, was a Gambino family soldier known in the underworld as Fat the Gangster. His uncle James was a Gambino captain who went by Jimmy the Clam. Though Eppolito loved the force, he maintained his Mafia ties and associations, and would sometimes get in trouble when he showed up in FBI surveillance tapes associating with mobsters.

Caracappa (top image) also joined the force in 1969, and the pair met working at the Brooklyn robbery squad. Caracappa eventually moved on to the major case squad, where he helped form the organized crime homicide unit and had access to a flood of secret information on mob investigations.

By 1985, the two detectives had developed a business relationship with organized crime—chiefly with Anthony (Gaspipe) Casso, the Luchese family underboss. They helped him take control of the family after the leadership was decimated by federal investigations, indictments, and convictions on racketeering charges.

By 1986 the pair were on Casso's payroll to the tune of $4,000 per month. For this they supplied names of informants and the timing of arrests. For additional services, including the killing of rivals, they received extra money. They were paid $65,000 for the hit on Edward Lino. Among the other crimes they helped commit include the following:

January 1986 Eppolito and Caracappa accept contract from Gaspipe Casso to find and kill Gambino underboss Salvatore (Sammy Bull) Gravano. They track Sammy for a while, but do not carry out hit.

September 1986 James Hydell is abducted by Eppolito and Caracappa, who stuff him in the trunk of their sedan and deliver him to Luchese underboss Casso. Hydell is tortured and killed. His body has never been found.

December 1986 Nicholas Guido, a Brooklyn telephone installer, is murdered in a case of mistaken identity. Eppolito and Caracappa fingered the wrong Nicholas Guido, mistaking him for a mob associate with the same name.

October 1987 John Heidel, a member of a safecracking crew, is shot to death after Caracappa and Eppolito tell Casso he is cooperating with authorities.

February 1990 Anthony Dilapi, a Luchese soldier, is whacked after refusing to meet with Casso. Caracappa and Eppolito helped Casso locate him.

May 1990 James Bishop, an official in Painters Union Local 37, is slain

Court Structure The typical state court structure is illustrated in Figure 14.2. Most states employ a multitiered court structure. Lower courts try misdemeanors and conduct the preliminary processing of felony offenses. Superior trial courts try felony cases. Appellate courts review the criminal procedures of trial courts to determine whether offenders were treated fairly. Superior appellate courts or state supreme courts, used in about half the states, review lower appellate court decisions.

The independent federal court system has three tiers, as shown in Figure 14.3 on page 347. The U.S. district courts are the trial courts of the system; they have jurisdiction over cases involving violations of federal law, such as interstate transportation of stolen vehicles and racketeering. Appeals from the district court are heard in one of the intermediate federal courts of appeal. The highest federal appeals court, the U.S. Supreme Court, is the court of last resort for all cases tried in the various federal and state courts.

The Supreme Court The U.S. Supreme Court is composed of nine members, appointed for lifetime terms by the president with the approval of Congress. In general, the Court hears only cases it deems important and appropriate. When the Court decides to hear a case, it usually grants a writ of certiorari, requesting a transcript of the case proceedings for review.

The Supreme Court can word a decision so that it becomes a precedent that must be honored by all lower courts. If the Court grants a particular litigant the right to counsel at a police lineup, then all people in similar situations must be given the same right. This type of ruling is usually referred to as a **landmark decision**. The use of precedent in the legal system gives the Supreme Court

landmark decision
A ruling by the U.S. Supreme Court that serves as a precedent for similar legal issues; it often influences the everyday operating procedures of police agencies, trial courts, and corrections institutions.

after Caracappa and Eppolito disclose he is cooperating in a corruption investigation.

August 1990 Gambino soldier Bruno Facciola is slain after he is identified as an informant by Eppolito and Caracappa.

May 1991 Gambino soldier Bartolomeo (Bobby) Boriello is killed after Eppolito and Caracappa provide Casso with a possible address for him.

After they retired from the force, Eppolito had bit parts in movies like *Goodfellas* and worked on his book. The pair moved to Las Vegas to enjoy the sun and nightlife. Although they were suspects, the words of Casso, a known felon, was not enough for an indictment. Then, in 2003, investigators began gathering new leads that linked the pair to the mob killings. They found work schedules for particular days when hits were made and logs detailing corruption allegations against the detectives. A paper trail of computer records emerged that showed Caracappa had grossly abused his position in the organized crime homicide unit, and had given damaging information to his mob bosses that led to the deaths of informers.

On April 6, 2006, Eppolito and Caracappa were convicted on all charges. Assistant U.S. Attorney Daniel Wenner called the case "the bloodiest, most violent betrayal of the [police] badge this city has ever seen." Then on June 30, 2006, in an unforeseen twist, U.S. District Judge Jack Weinstein threw out the racketeering murder conviction against the two detectives, saying the statute of limitations had expired on the slayings. The judge also granted a new trial to the defendants on money laundering and drug charges, despite the fact that he believed the evidence of their guilt was overwhelming.

SOURCES: John Marzulli, "2 Cops Who Killed for Mafia: Feds Say Retired Detective Pals Are Linked to at Least 8 Murders," *Daily News*, March 10, 2005; Alan Feuer and William K. Rashbaum, "Blood Ties: 2 Officers' Long Path to Mob Murder Indictments," *New York Times*, March 12, 2005, p. A1; BBC News, "NY Police Guilty of Mafia Murders," http://news.bbc.co.uk/1/hi/world/americas/4885674.stm.

power to influence and mold the everyday operating procedures of police agencies, trial courts, and corrections institutions.

Prosecution and Defense

Within the structure of the court system, the prosecutor and defense attorney are opponents in what is known as the **adversary system**. These two parties oppose each other in a hotly disputed contest—the criminal trial—in accordance with rules of law and procedure. In every criminal case, the state acts against the defendant and the defense attorney acts for the defendant before an impartial judge or jury, with each side trying to bring forward evidence and arguments to advance its case. Theoretically, the ultimate objective of the adversary system is to seek the truth, determining the guilt or innocence of the defendant from the formal evidence presented at the trial. The adversary system is designed to ensure that the defendant is given a fair trial, that the relevant facts of a given case emerge, and that an impartial decision is reached.

adversary system
U.S. method of criminal adjudication in which prosecution (the state) and defense (the accused) each try to bring forward evidence and arguments, with guilt or innocence ultimately decided by an impartial judge or jury.

prosecutor
Public official who represents the government in criminal proceedings, presenting the case against the accused.

defendant
In criminal proceedings, the person accused of violating the law.

Criminal Prosecution

The **prosecutor** is the public official who represents the government and presents its case against the **defendant**, who is charged with a violation of the criminal law. Traditionally, the prosecutor is a local attorney whose area of jurisdictional responsibility is limited to a particular county or city. The prosecutor is known variously as a district attorney or a prosecuting attorney and is either an elected or an appointed official. On the state level, the prosecutor may be referred to as the attorney general; in the federal jurisdiction, the title is United States attorney.

The prosecutor is responsible not only for charging the defendant with the crime but also for bringing the case to trial and to a final conclusion. The prosecutor's

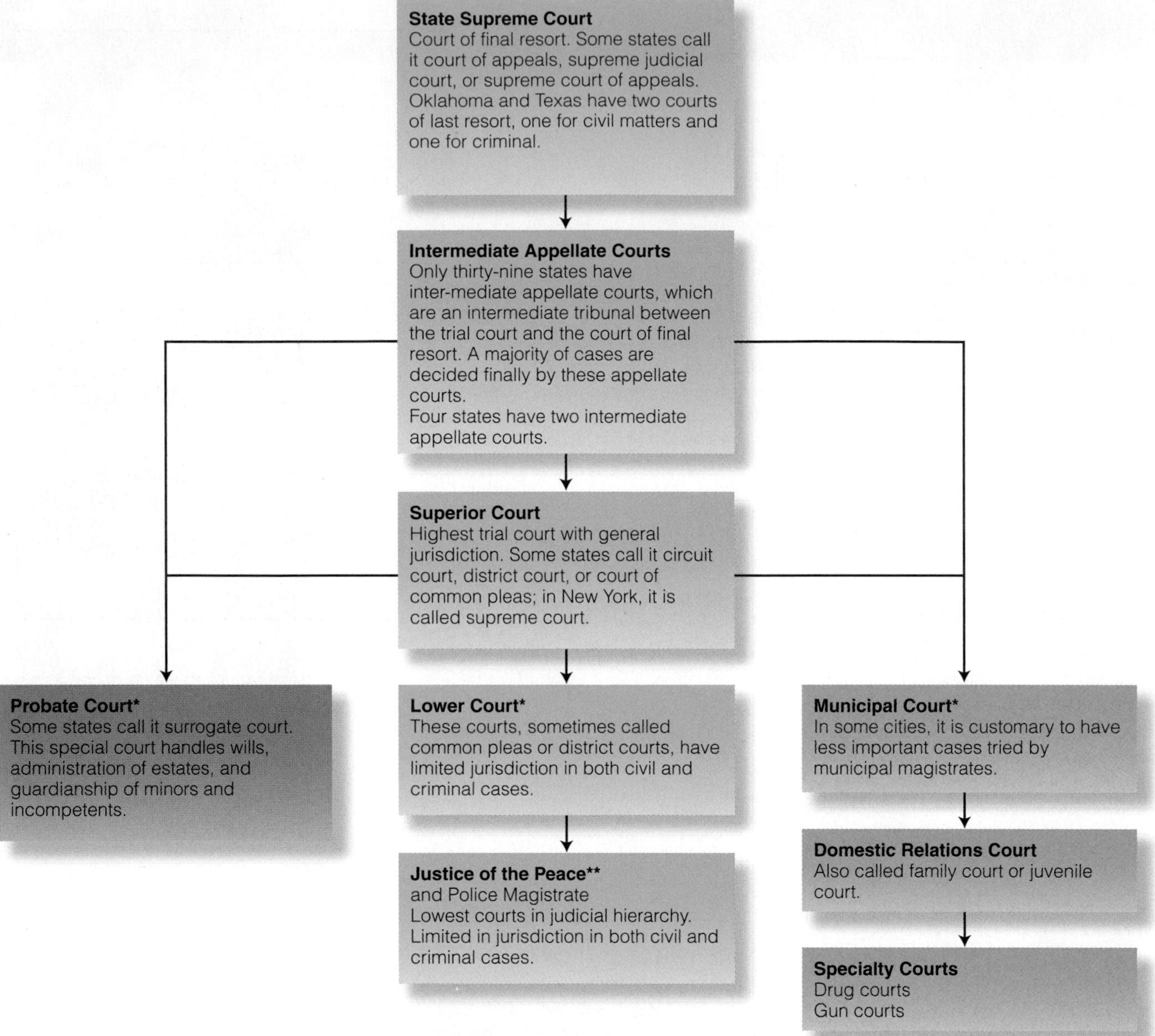

State Supreme Court
Court of final resort. Some states call it court of appeals, supreme judicial court, or supreme court of appeals. Oklahoma and Texas have two courts of last resort, one for civil matters and one for criminal.
Intermediate Appellate Courts
Only thirty-nine states have inter-mediate appellate courts, which are an intermediate tribunal between the trial court and the court of final resort. A majority of cases are decided finally by these appellate courts.
Four states have two intermediate appellate courts.
Superior Court
Highest trial court with general jurisdiction. Some states call it circuit court, district court, or court of common pleas; in New York, it is called supreme court.
Probate Court*
Some states call it surrogate court. This special court handles wills, administration of estates, and guardianship of minors and incompetents.
Lower Court*
These courts, sometimes called common pleas or district courts, have limited jurisdiction in both civil and criminal cases.
Municipal Court*
In some cities, it is customary to have less important cases tried by municipal magistrates.
Justice of the Peace**
and Police Magistrate
Lowest courts in judicial hierarchy. Limited in jurisdiction in both civil and criminal cases.
Domestic Relations Court
Also called family court or juvenile court.
Specialty Courts
Drug courts
Gun courts

Figure 14.2

Structure of a State Judicial System

Notes: *Courts of special jurisdiction, such as probate, family, or juvenile courts, and the so-called inferior courts, such as common pleas or municipal courts, may be separate courts or part of the trial court of general jurisdiction.

**Justices of the peace do not exist in all states. Where they do exist, their jurisdictions vary greatly from state to state.

SOURCE: American Bar Association, *Law and the Courts* (Chicago: ABA, 1974), p. 20. Updated information provided by West Publishing, Eagen, MN.

authority ranges from determining the nature of the charge to reducing the charge by negotiation or recommending that the complaint be dismissed. The prosecutor also participates in bail hearings, presents cases before a grand jury, and appears for the state at arraignments. In sum, the prosecutor is responsible for presenting the state's case from the time of the defendant's arrest through conviction and sentencing in the criminal court.

The prosecutor, like the police officer, exercises a great deal of discretion; he or she can decide initially whether to file a criminal charge, determine what charge to bring, or explore the availability of noncriminal dispositions.[19] Prosecutorial discretion would not be as important as it is, were it desirable to prosecute all violations of the law. However, full enforcement of every law is not practical because police officers and prosecutors ordinarily lack sufficient resources, staff, and support services to carry out that goal. Therefore, it makes sense to screen out cases where the accused is obviously innocent, where the evidence is negligible, or where criminal sanctions may seem inappropriate: The case must have **convictability**—it must stand a good chance for a conviction. Instead of total or automatic law enforcement, a process of selective or discretionary enforcement exists; as a result, the prosecutor must make many decisions that significantly

convictability
Existence of conditions surrounding a criminal case that indicate it has a good chance of a conviction.

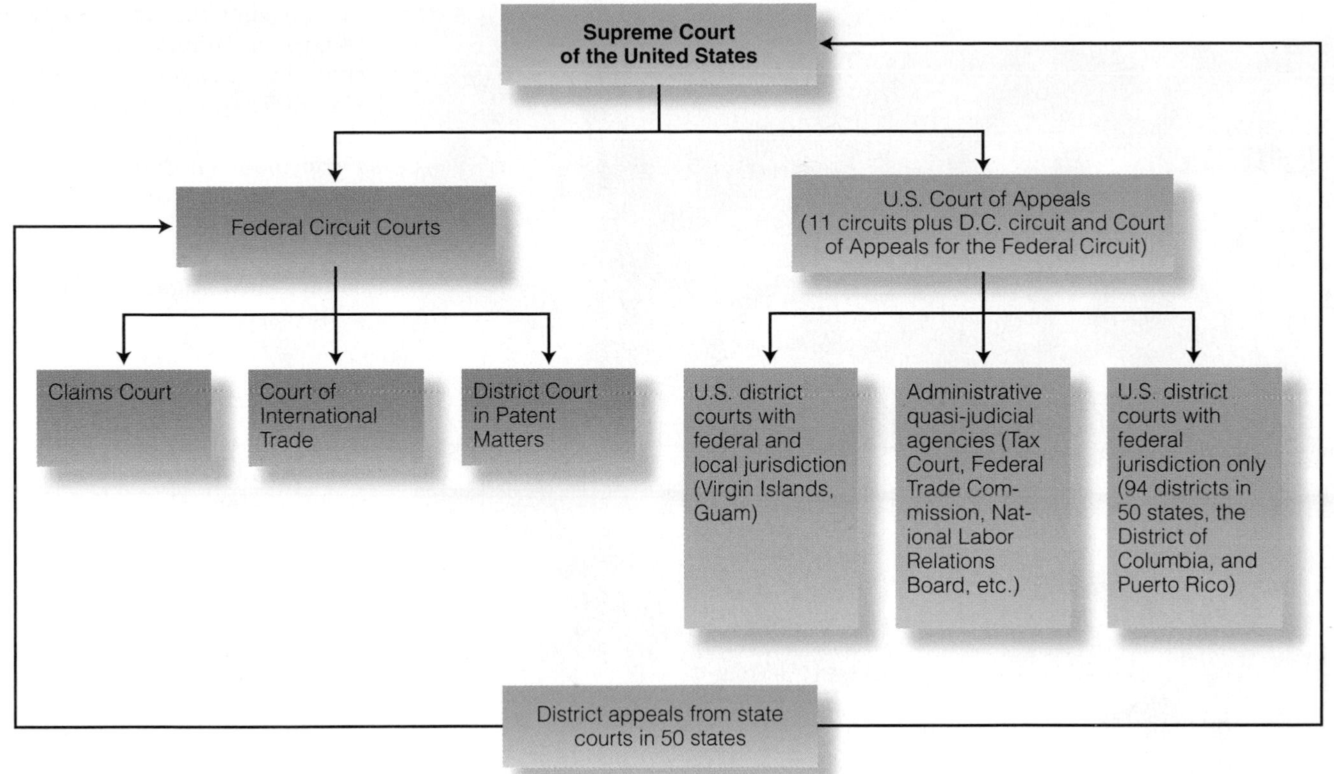

Figure 14.3
The Federal Judicial System
SOURCE: American Bar Association, *Law and the Courts* (Chicago: ABA, 1974), p. 20. Updated information provided by the Federal Courts Improvement Act of 1982 and West Publishing, Eagen, MN.

influence police operations and control the actual number of cases processed through the court and correctional systems.

Criminal Defense The **defense attorney** is responsible for providing legal representation of the defendant. This role involves two major functions: (1) protecting the constitutional rights of the accused and (2) presenting the best possible legal defense for the defendant.

The defense attorney represents a client from initial arrest through the trial stage, during the sentencing hearing, and, if needed, through the process of appeal. The defense attorney is also expected to enter into plea negotiations and obtain for the defendant the most suitable bargain regarding type and length of sentence.

Any person accused of a crime can obtain the services of a private attorney if he or she can afford to do so. One of the most critical questions in the criminal justice system has been whether an indigent (poor) defendant has a **right to counsel**. The federal court system has long provided counsel to the indigent on the basis of the Sixth Amendment of the U.S. Constitution, which gives the accused the right to have the assistance of defense counsel. Through a series of landmark U.S. Supreme Court decisions, beginning with *Powell v. Alabama* in 1932 and continuing with *Gideon v. Wainwright* in 1963 and *Argersinger v. Hamlin* in 1972, the right of a criminal defendant to have counsel has become fundamental to the U.S. system of criminal justice.[20] Today, state courts must provide counsel to indigent defendants charged with criminal offenses where the possibility of incarceration exists. Consequently, more than 1,000 **public defender** agencies have been set up around the United States to provide free legal counsel to indigent defendants. In other jurisdictions, defense lawyers volunteer their services, referred to as working **pro bono**, and are assigned to criminal defendants. A few rural counties have defense lawyers under contract who handle all criminal matters.

The Supreme Court has ruled that in addition to having an attorney, every defendant is entitled to a legally competent defense. A conviction can be overturned if it can be shown that an attorney did not meet this standard. To prove

defense attorney
Person responsible for protecting the constitutional rights of the accused and presenting the best possible legal defense; represents a defendant from initial arrest through trial, sentencing, and any appeal.

right to counsel
The right of a person accused of crime to the assistance of a defense attorney in all criminal prosecutions.

public defender
Attorney employed by the state whose job is to provide free legal counsel to indigent defendants.

pro bono
Free legal counsel provided to indigent defendants by private attorneys as a service to the profession and the community.

● In some jurisdictions, arraignments have gone high-tech and defendants do not have to be in court to be arraigned. Here, Tina Page (seated right) is arraigned for a misdemeanor by videoconference in front of Kanawha County Magistrate Jeanie Moore (left screen) without having to leave the South Central Regional Jail in Charleston, West Virginia. Assisting Page is Corrections Officer C. D. Fleming (left position on right screen) and First Sgt. R. E. Rogers (center of right screen).

legal assistance was legally ineffective, a defendant must show that her lawyer's performance was deficient, and that the deficiency prejudiced the defense. Performance is deficient if it falls below an objective standard of reasonableness, for instance, an attorney does not conduct a reasonable investigation of the facts of the case.[21]

Corrections

After conviction and sentencing, the offender enters the correctional system. Correctional agencies administer the postjudicatory care given to offenders, which can range from informal monitoring in the community to solitary confinement in a maximum-security prison, depending on the seriousness of the crime and the individual needs of the offender.

The most common correctional treatment, **probation**, is a legal disposition that allows the convicted offender to remain in the community, subject to conditions imposed by court order, under the supervision of a probation officer. This lets the offender continue working and avoids the crippling effects of **incarceration**.

A person given a sentence involving incarceration is ordinarily confined to a correctional institution for a specified period. Different types of institutions are used to hold offenders. **Jails**, or houses of correction, hold those convicted of misdemeanors and those awaiting trial or involved in other proceedings, such as grand jury deliberations, arraignments, or preliminary hearings. Many of these institutions for short-term detention are administered by county governments. Little is done to treat inmates because the personnel and institutions lack the qualifications, services, and resources.

State and federally operated facilities that receive felony offenders sentenced by the criminal courts are called **prisons** or **penitentiaries**. They may be minimum-, medium-, or maximum-security institutions. Prison facilities vary throughout the country. Some have high walls, cells, and large, heterogeneous inmate populations; others offer much freedom, progressive correctional programs, and small, homogeneous populations. Both the jail and prison populations have been steadily increasing despite a reduction in the crime rate. The increase is due to longer sentences for some crimes and the requirement that inmates serve a greater percentage of their time behind bars before they are eligible for early release mechanisms such as parole; this is referred to as **truth in sentencing**.

Most new inmates are first sent to a reception and classification center where they are given diagnostic evaluations and assigned to institutions that meet their individual needs as much as possible within the system's resources. The diagnostic process in the reception center may range from a physical examination and a single interview to an extensive series of psychiatric tests, orientation sessions, and numerous personal interviews. Classification is a way of evaluating inmates and assigning them to appropriate placements and activities within the state institutional system.

Because the gap between what correctional programs promise to deliver and their actual performance is often significant, many jurisdictions have instituted community-based correctional facilities. These programs emphasize the use of small neighborhood residential centers, halfway houses, prerelease centers, and work release and home furlough programs. Experts believe that only a small per-

probation
Conditional release of a convicted offender into the community under the supervision of a probation officer and subject to certain conditions.

incarceration
Confinement in jail or prison.

jail
Institution, usually run by the county, for short-term detention of those convicted of misdemeanors and those awaiting trial or other judicial proceedings.

prison (penitentiary)
State or federally operated facility for the incarceration of felony offenders sentenced by the criminal courts.

truth in sentencing
The requirement that inmates serve a greater percentage of their sentence behind bars before they are eligible for early release mechanisms such as parole.

centage of prison inmates require maximum security and that most can be more effectively rehabilitated in community-based facilities. Rather than totally confining offenders in an impersonal, harsh prison, such programs offer them the opportunity to maintain normal family and social relationships while providing rehabilitative services and resources at a lower cost to taxpayers.

The last segment of the corrections system, **parole**, is a process whereby an inmate is selected for early release and serves the remainder of the sentence in the community under the supervision of a parole officer. The main purpose of parole is to help the ex-inmate bridge the gap between institutional confinement and a positive adjustment within the community. All parolees must adhere to a set of rules of behavior while they are "on the outside." If these rules are violated, the parole privilege can be terminated (revoked), and the parolee will be sent back to the institution to serve the remainder of the sentence.

Other ways an offender may be released from an institution include mandatory release upon completion of the sentence and the pardon, a form of executive clemency. ✔ CHECKPOINTS

THE PROCESS OF JUSTICE

In addition to viewing the criminal justice system as a collection of agencies, it is possible to see it as a series of decision points through which offenders flow. This process, illustrated in Figure 14.4, begins with initial contact with police and ends with the offender's reentering society. At any point in the process, a decision may be made to drop further proceedings and allow the accused back into society without further penalty. In a classic statement, political scientist Herbert Packer described this process as follows:

> *The image that comes to mind is an assembly line conveyor belt down which moves an endless stream of cases, never stopping, carrying them to workers who stand at fixed stations and who perform on each case as it comes by the same small but essential operation that brings it one step closer to being a finished product, or to exchange the metaphor for the reality, a closed file. The criminal process is seen as a screening process in which each successive stage—pre-arrest investigation, arrest, post-arrest investigation, preparation for trial, or entry of plea, conviction, disposition—involves a series of routinized operations whose success is gauged primarily by their tendency to pass the case along to a successful conclusion.*[22]

Although each jurisdiction is somewhat different, a comprehensive view of the processing of a felony offender would probably contain the following decision points.

1. *Initial contact.* The initial contact an offender has with the justice system occurs when police officers observe a criminal act during patrol of city streets, parks, or highways. They may also find out about a crime through a citizen or victim complaint. Similarly, an informer may alert them about criminal activity in return for financial or other consideration. Sometimes political officials, such as the mayor or city council, ask police to look into ongoing criminal activity, such as gambling, and during their subsequent investigations police officers encounter an illegal act.
2. *Investigation.* Regardless of whether the police observe, hear of, or receive a complaint about a crime, they may investigate to gather sufficient facts, or evidence, to identify the perpetrator, justify an arrest, and bring the offender to trial. An investigation may take a few minutes, as when patrol officers see a burglary in progress and apprehend the burglar at the scene of the crime. An investigation may also take years to complete and involve numerous investigators. When federal agents tracked and captured Theodore Kaczinski (known as the Unabomber) in 1996, it completed an investigation that had lasted more than a decade.
3. *Arrest.* An **arrest** occurs when the police take a person into custody for allegedly committing a criminal act. An arrest is legal when all of the following conditions exist: (a) the officer believes there is sufficient evidence (**probable cause**) that

✔ CHECKPOINTS

✔ The concept of a criminal justice system is relatively new.

✔ The system is vast, costing taxpayers about $150 billion a year.

✔ The police are the largest component of the system. They identify law violators, keep the peace, and provide emergency services.

✔ The court system dispenses fair and even-handed justice.

✔ Prosecutors bring the criminal charge, and defense attorneys represent the accused.

✔ Correctional agencies incarcerate and treat millions of convicted offenders.

✔ Included within corrections are closed institutions, such as prisons and jails, and community correctional efforts, such as probation.

parole
Conditional early release from prison, with the offender serving the remainder of the sentence in the community under the supervision of a parole officer.

arrest
The taking into police custody of an individual suspected of a crime.

probable cause
Evidence of a crime, and of a suspect's involvement in it, sufficient to warrant an arrest.

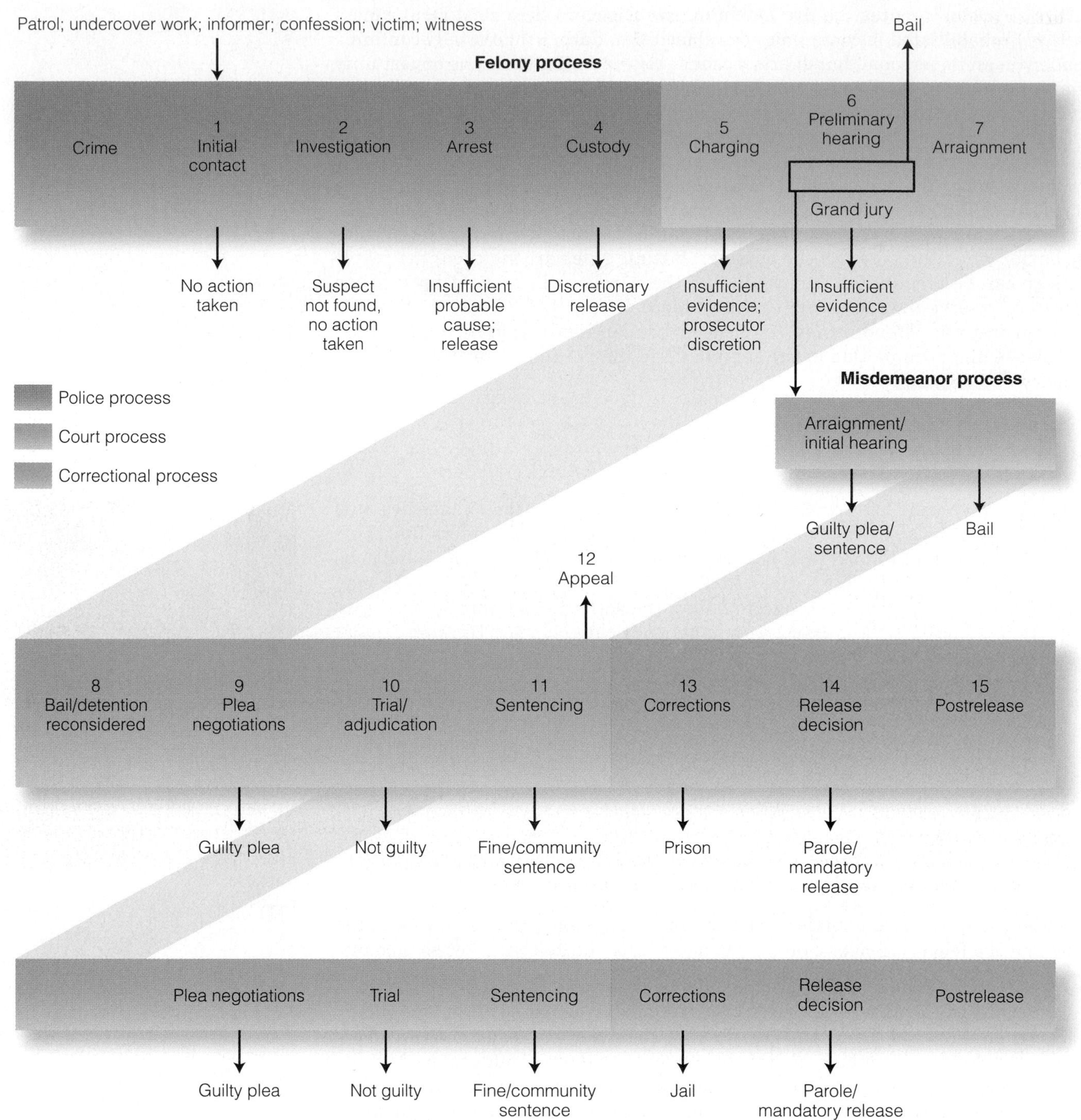

Figure 14.4
Critical Stages of the Justice Process

a crime is being or has been committed and that the suspect committed the crime; (b) the officer deprives the individual of freedom; and (c) the suspect believes that he or she is in the custody of a police officer and cannot voluntarily leave. The police officer is not required to use the word "arrest" or any similar word to initiate an arrest; nor does the officer first have to bring the suspect to the police station. For all practical purposes, a person who has been deprived of liberty is under arrest. Arrests can be made at the scene of a crime or after a warrant is issued by a magistrate.

> **booking**
> Fingerprinting, photographing, and recording personal information of a suspect in police custody.

4. *Custody*. After arrest, the suspect remains in police custody. The person may be taken to the police station to be fingerprinted and photographed and to have personal information recorded—a procedure popularly referred to as **booking**. Witnesses may be brought in to view the suspect (in a lineup), and

further evidence may be gathered on the case. Suspects may be interrogated by police officers to get their side of the story, they may be asked to sign a confession of guilt, or they may be asked to identify others involved in the crime. The law allows suspects to have their lawyer present when police conduct an in-custody **interrogation**.

5. *Complaint/charging*. After police turn the evidence in a case over to the prosecutor, who represents the state at any criminal proceedings, a decision will be made whether to file a complaint, information, or bill of indictment with the court having jurisdiction over the case. Complaints are used in misdemeanors; information and indictment are employed in felonies. Each is a charging document asking the court to bring a case forward to be tried.
6. *Preliminary hearing/grand jury*. Because it is a tremendous personal and financial burden to stand trial for a serious felony crime, the U.S. Constitution provides that the state must first prove to an impartial hearing board that there is probable cause that the accused committed the crime and, therefore, that there is sufficient reason to try the person as charged. In about half the states and in the federal system, the decision of whether to bring a suspect to trial (**indictment**) is made by a group of citizens brought together to form a **grand jury**. The grand jury considers the case in a closed hearing in which only the prosecutor presents evidence. In the remaining states, an **information** is filed before an impartial lower-court judge who decides whether the case should go forward. This is known as a **preliminary hearing** or probable cause hearing. The defendant may appear at a preliminary hearing and dispute the prosecutor's charges. During either procedure, if the prosecution's evidence is accepted as factual and sufficient, the suspect is called to stand trial for the crime. These procedures are not used for misdemeanors because of their lesser importance and seriousness.
7. *Arraignment*. An **arraignment** brings the accused before the court that will actually try the case. The formal charges are read, and defendants are informed of their constitutional rights (such as the right to legal counsel). Bail is considered, and a trial date is set.
8. *Bail or detention*. If the bail decision has not been considered previously, it is evaluated at arraignment. **Bail** is a money bond, the amount of which is set by judicial authority; it is intended to ensure the presence of suspects at trial while allowing them their freedom until that time. Suspects who do not show up for trial forfeit their bail. Suspects who cannot afford bail or whose cases are so serious that a judge refuses them bail (usually restricted to capital cases) must remain in detention until trial. In most instances, this means an extended stay in the county jail. Many jurisdictions allow defendants awaiting trial to be released on their own **recognizance**, without bail, if they are stable members of the community. As Figure 14.5 shows, most felony offenders receive bail.
9. *Plea bargaining*. After arraignment, it is common for the prosecutor to meet with the defendant and his or her attorney to discuss a possible **plea bargain**. If a bargain can be struck, the accused pleads guilty as charged, thus ending the criminal trial process. In return for the plea, the prosecutor may reduce charges, request a lenient sentence, or grant the defendant some other consideration. Pleas bargains end the trial process in upwards of 90 percent of all cases including serious felonies (see Exhibit 14.1).
10. *Adjudication*. If a plea bargain cannot be arranged, a criminal trial takes place. This involves a full-scale inquiry into the facts of the case before a judge, a jury, or both. The defendant can be found guilty or not guilty, or the jury can fail to reach a decision (**hung jury**), thereby leaving the case unresolved and open for a possible retrial. As Figure 14.6 shows, the number of adults convicted in state courts has been increasing despite the drop in the crime rate.
11. *Disposition*. After a criminal trial, a defendant who is found guilty as charged is sentenced by the presiding judge. **Disposition** usually involves a fine, a term of community supervision (probation), a period of incarceration in

● The initial contact an offender has with the justice system occurs when police officers observe a criminal act during their patrol of city streets, parks, or highways. Here, police attempt to capture Geraldo Sanchez outside the Freedom Tower in Miami, Florida, where mourners were paying their respects to Celia Cruz. Sanchez allegedly threw rocks, small pipes, and a cup of urine on police, and threatened to kill himself by jumping off the 25-foot pole. Officers used a taser and beanbag guns to subdue Sanchez.

interrogation
The questioning of a suspect in police custody.

indictment
A written accusation returned by a grand jury charging an individual with a specified crime, based on the prosecutor's presentation of probable cause.

grand jury
A group of citizens chosen to hear testimony in secret and to issue formal criminal accusations (indictments).

information
A filing before an impartial lower-court judge who decides whether the case should go forward (alternative to grand jury).

Figure 14.5
Pretrial Detention of Felony Defendants in the 75 Largest U.S. Counties, by Most Serious Arrest Charge

SOURCE: Thomas Cohen and Brian Reaves, *Felony Defendants in Large Urban Counties, 2002* (Washington, DC: Bureau of Justice Statistics, 2006), p. 16.

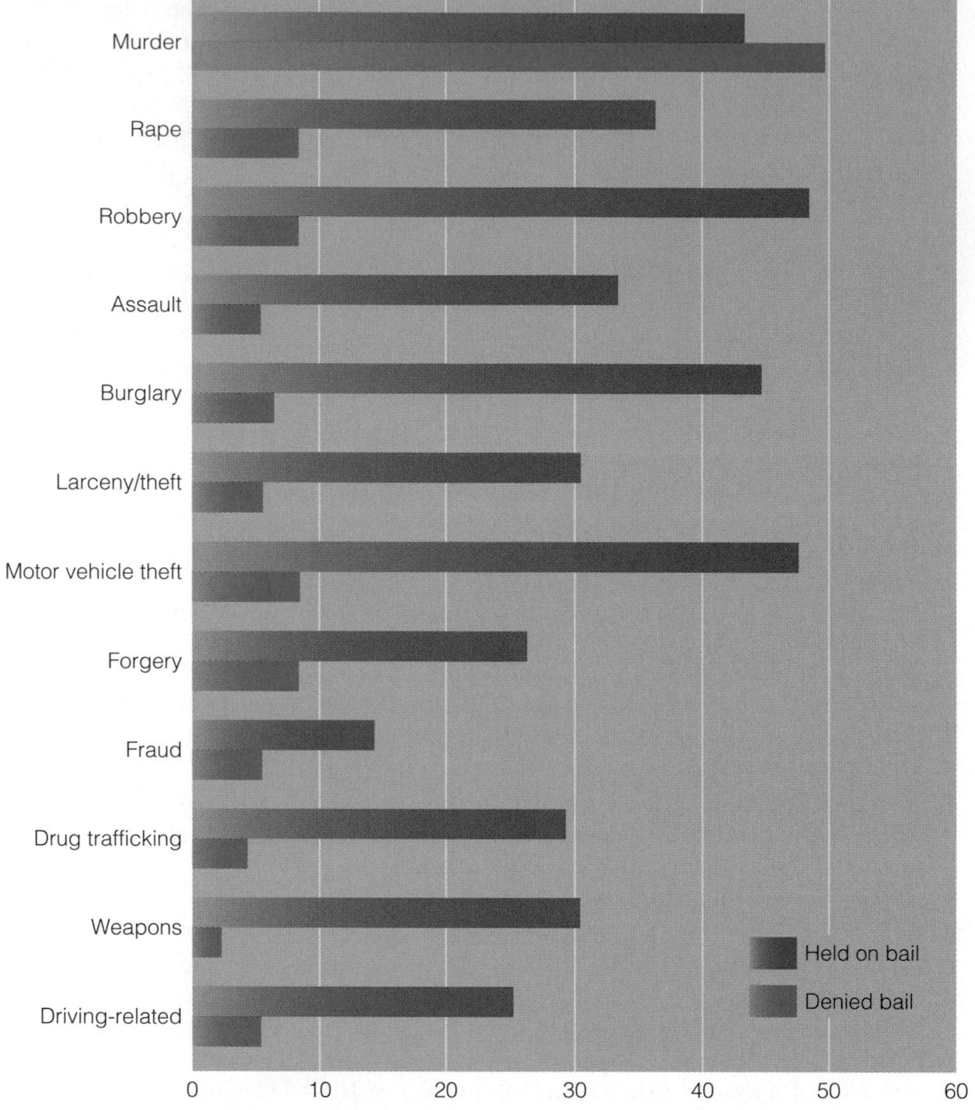

preliminary hearing
Alternative to a grand jury, in which an impartial lower-court judge decides whether there is probable cause sufficient for a trial.

arraignment
The step in the criminal justice process when the accused is brought before the trial judge, formal charges are read, defendants are informed of their rights, a plea is entered, bail is considered, and a trial date is set.

bail
A money bond intended to ensure that the accused will return for trial.

recognizance
Pledge by the accused to return for trial, which may be accepted in lieu of bail.

plea bargain
Agreement between prosecution and defense in which the accused pleads guilty in return for a reduction of charges, a more lenient sentence, or some other consideration.

hung jury
A jury that is unable to agree on a decision, thus leaving the case unresolved and open for a possible retrial.

disposition
Sentencing of a defendant who has been found guilty; usually involves a fine, probation, or incarceration.

appeal
Taking a criminal case to a higher court on the grounds that the defendant was found guilty because of legal error or violation of constitutional rights; a successful appeal may result in a new trial.

a penal institution, or some combination of these penalties. In the most serious capital cases, it is possible to sentence the offender to death. Dispositions are usually made after a presentencing investigation is conducted by the court's probation staff. After disposition, the defendant may appeal the conviction to a higher court. As Figure14.7 shows, as expected, those who commit the most serious crimes are the ones most likely to be convicted and sent to prison.

12. *Postconviction remedies*. After conviction, if the defendant believes he or she was not treated fairly by the justice system, the individual may **appeal** the conviction. An appellate court reviews trial procedures to determine whether an error was made. It considers such questions as whether evidence was used properly, whether the judge conducted the trial in an approved fashion, whether the jury was representative, and whether the attorneys in the case acted appropriately. If the court rules that the appeal has merit, it can hold that the defendant be given a new trial or, in some instances, order outright release of the defendant. Outright release can be ordered when the state prosecuted the case in violation of the double jeopardy clause of the U.S. Constitution or when it violated the defendant's right to a speedy trial.

Exhibit 14.1
To Plead or Not to Plead?

Although almost all cases are settled with a plea, a few proceed to a full-blown trial. What factors influence the decision to plead or not to plead?

- Court-appointed lawyers may want to gain trial experience. They convince their clients not to accept favorable bargains, fearing that the case will be settled out of court and they will lose the opportunity to try the case.
- Both the prosecution and defense may be overly optimistic about their abilities and skills. Overconfidence in their abilities may cloud their judgment, causing them either to refuse to offer a bargain in the case of the prosecution, or refuse to accept in the case of the defense.
- Some defendants falsely assume they are so charismatic and appealing that a jury will never reach a conviction.

SOURCE: Stephanos Bibas, "Plea Bargaining outside the Shadow of Trial," *Harvard Law Review* 117 (2004): 2,464–2,543.

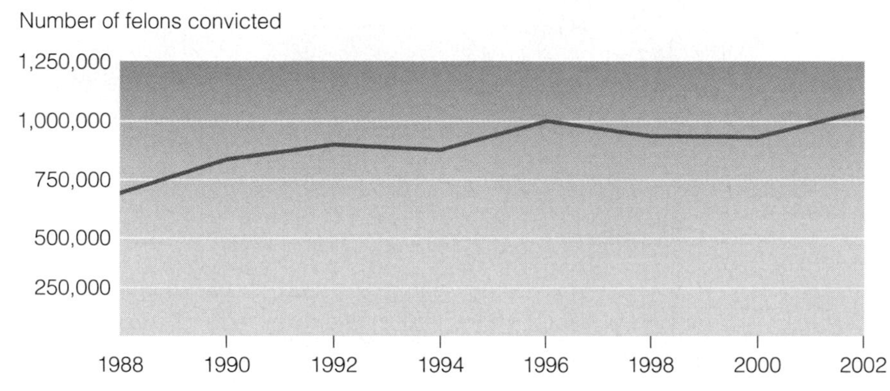

Figure 14.6
Number of Adults Convicted of a Felony in State Courts

SOURCE: Matthew Durose and Patrick Langan, *Felony Sentences in State Courts, 2002* (Washington, DC: Bureau of Justice Statistics, 2004).

13. *Correctional treatment*. Offenders who are found guilty and are formally sentenced come under the jurisdiction of correctional authorities. They may serve a term of community supervision under control of the county probation department; they may have a term in a community correctional center; or they may be incarcerated in a large penal institution.
14. *Release*. At the end of the correctional sentence, the offender is released into the community. Most incarcerated offenders are granted parole before the expiration of the maximum term given them by the court and therefore finish their prison sentences in the community under supervision of the parole department. Offenders sentenced to community supervision, if successful, simply finish their terms and resume their lives unsupervised by court authorities.
15. *Postrelease/aftercare*. After termination of correctional treatment, the offender must successfully return to the community. This adjustment is usually aided by corrections department staff members, who attempt to counsel the offender through the period of reentry into society. The offender may be asked to spend some time in a community correctional center, which acts as a bridge between a secure treatment facility and absolute freedom. Offenders may find that their conviction has cost them some personal privileges, such as the right to hold certain kinds of jobs. These privileges may be returned by court order once the offenders have proven their trustworthiness and willingness to adjust to society's rules. Successful completion of the postrelease period marks the end of the criminal justice process.

At every stage of the criminal justice process, a decision is made by an agency of criminal justice whether to send the case farther down the line or "kick it" from the system. An investigation may be pursued for a few days, and if a suspect is not identified, the case is dropped. A prosecutor decides not to charge a person in

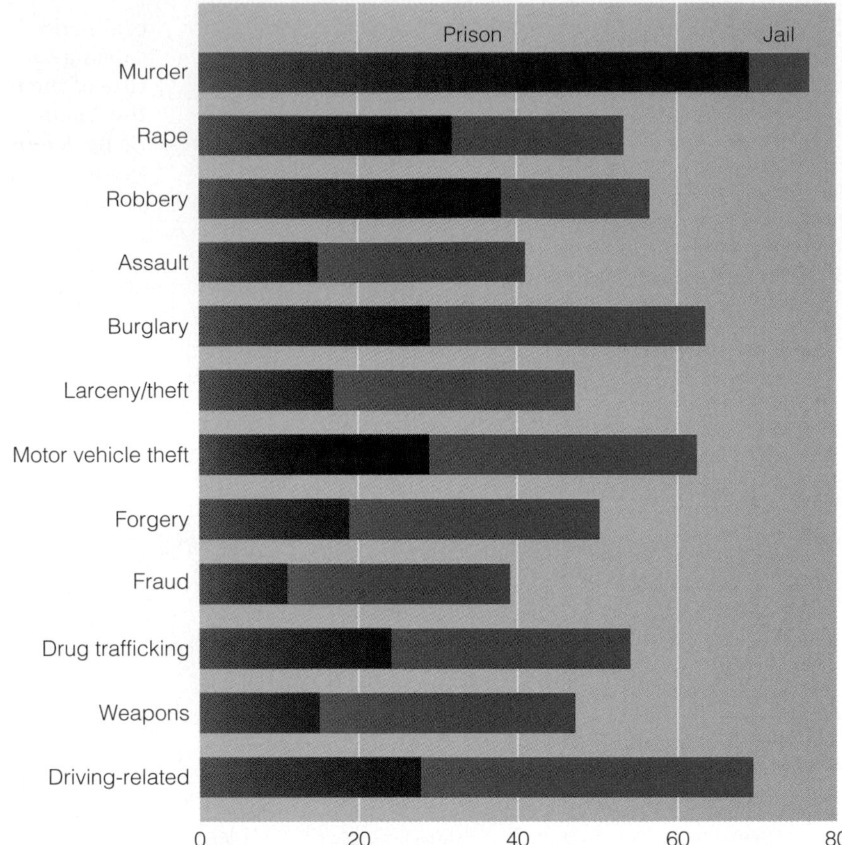

Figure 14.7

Probability of Being Convicted and Sentenced to Incarceration for Felony Defendants in the 75 Largest U.S. Counties

SOURCE: Thomas Cohen and Brian Reaves, *Felony Defendants in Large Urban Counties, 2002* (Washington, DC: Bureau of Justice Statistics, 2006), p. IV.

police custody because he or she believes there is insufficient evidence to sustain a finding of guilt. A grand jury fails to hand down an indictment because it finds that the prosecutor presented insufficient evidence. A jury fails to convict the accused because it doubts his or her guilt. A parole board decides to release one inmate but denies another's request for early release.

These decisions can help transform the identity of the individual passing through the system from an accused to a defendant, convicted criminal, inmate, and ex-con. Conversely, if decision makers take no action, people accused of crime can return to their daily lives with minimal interference in their lives or identities. Their friends and neighbors may not even know that they were once the subject of criminal investigation.

Because decision making and discretion mark each stage of the system, the criminal justice process serves as a funnel in which a great majority of cases are screened out before trial. As Figure 14.8 shows, cases are dismissed at each stage of the system, and relatively few actually reach trial. Those that do are more likely to be handled with a plea bargain than with a criminal trial. The funnel indicates that the justice system does not treat all felonies alike; only the relatively few serious cases make it through to the end of the formal process.[23]

Public perceptions about criminal justice are often formed on the basis of what happens in a few celebrated cases that receive widespread media attention. Some involve wealthy clients who can afford to be represented by high-powered attorneys who can hire the best experts to convince the jury that their client is innocent. The O. J. Simpson case is the best example of the celebrity defendant. Other defendants, such as Scott Peterson, become celebrities when they are accused of particularly heinous or notorious crimes and draw the attention of both the press and accomplished defense attorneys.

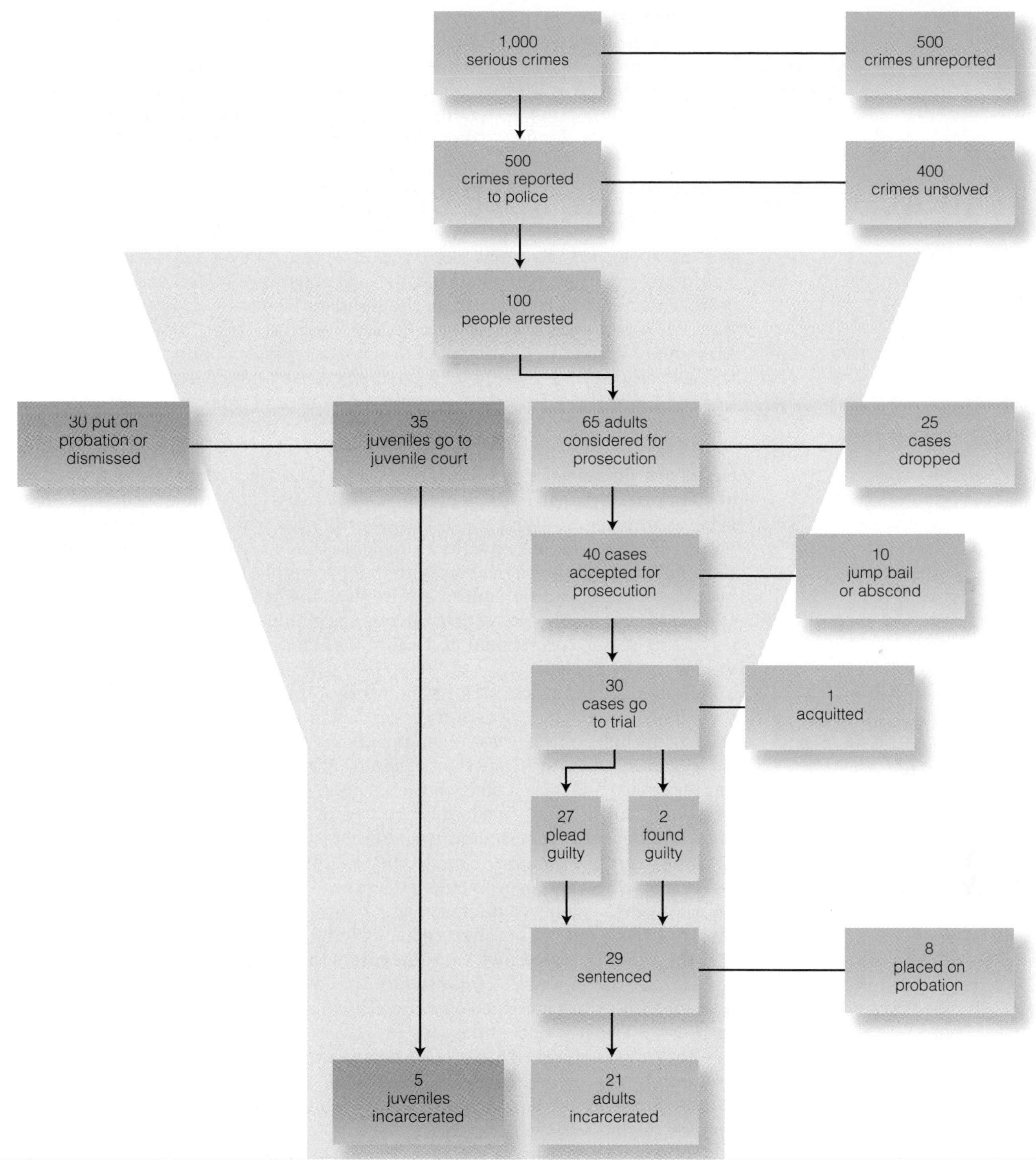

Figure 14.8

The Criminal Justice Funnel

SOURCES: Gerard Rainville and Brian Reaves, *Felony Defendants in Large Urban Counties, 2000* (Washington, DC: Bureau of Justice Statistics, 2003); Matthew Durose and Patrick Langan, *Felony Sentences in State Courts, 2002* (Washington, DC: Bureau of Justice Statistics, 2004).

In reality, these celebrity cases are few and far between. Most defendants are indigent people who cannot afford a comprehensive defense. The system is actually dominated by judges, prosecutors, and public defenders who work in concert to get cases processed quickly and efficiently. Trials are rare; most cases are handled with a quick plea bargain and sentencing. This pattern of cooperation is referred to as the **courtroom work group**. By working together cooperatively, the prosecution and defense make sure that the cases flowing through the justice system proceed in an orderly and effective manner. Such "bargain justice" is estimated to occur in

courtroom work group
Prosecution, defense, and judges working together to resolve criminal cases quickly and efficiently through plea bargaining.

more than 90 percent of all criminal cases. If each defendant were afforded the full measure of constitutional rights, including a jury trial, the system would quickly become overloaded. Court dockets are too crowded and funds too scarce to grant each defendant a full share of justice.[24] Although the criminal court system is founded on the concept of equality before the law, poor and wealthy citizens receive unquestionably different treatment when they are accused of crimes.

CRIMINAL JUSTICE AND THE RULE OF LAW

For many years, U.S. courts exercised little control over the operations of criminal justice agencies, believing that their actions were not an area of judicial concern. This policy is referred to as the hands-off doctrine. However, in the 1960s, under the guidance of Chief Justice Earl Warren, the U.S. Supreme Court became more active in the affairs of the justice system. Today, each component of the justice system is closely supervised by state and federal courts through the **law of criminal procedure**, which sets out and guarantees citizens certain rights and privileges when they are accused of crime.

Procedural laws control the actions of the agencies of justice and define the rights of criminal defendants. They first come into play when people are suspected of committing crimes and the police wish to investigate them, search their property, or interrogate them. Here the law dictates whether police can search the homes of or interrogate unwilling suspects. If a formal charge is filed, procedural laws guide pretrial and trial activities; for example, they determine when and if people can obtain state-financed attorneys and when they can be released on bail. If a person is found guilty of committing a criminal offense, procedural laws guide the posttrial and correctional processes; for example, they determine when a conviction can be appealed.

Procedural laws have several different sources. Most important are the first 10 amendments to the U.S. Constitution, ratified in 1791 and generally called the **Bill of Rights**. Included within these amendments are the right of the people to be secure in their homes from unwarranted intrusion by government agents, to be free from self-incrimination, and to be protected against cruel punishments, such as torture.

The guarantees of freedom contained in the Bill of Rights initially applied only to the federal government and did not affect the individual states. In 1868, the Fourteenth Amendment made the first 10 amendments to the Constitution binding on the state governments. However, it has remained the duty of state and federal court systems to interpret constitutional law and develop a body of case law that spells out the exact procedural rights to which a person is entitled. Thus, it is the U.S. Supreme Court that interprets the Constitution and sets out the procedural laws that must be followed by the lower federal and state courts. If the Supreme Court has not ruled on a procedural issue, the lower courts are free to interpret the Constitution as they see fit.

Today, procedural rights protect defendants from illegal searches and seizures and overly aggressive police interrogations. According to the exclusionary rule (covered in more detail in the next section), such illegally seized evidence cannot be used during a trial. ✔ CHECKPOINTS

✔ CHECKPOINTS

✔ The criminal justice process can be best understood as a series of decision points.

✔ At each stage of the system, a decision is reached whether to process an offender to the next stage or terminate the case.

✔ Although a few celebrity cases receive the full range of justice procedures, most cases are handled in a cursory fashion and are settled with a plea bargain.

✔ The justice system is bound by the rule of law, which ensures that criminal defendants are protected from violations of their civil rights.

CONCEPTS OF JUSTICE

law of criminal procedure
Judicial precedents that define and guarantee the rights of criminal defendants and control the various components of the criminal justice system.

Bill of Rights
The first 10 amendments to the U.S. Constitution, including guarantees against unreasonable search and seizure, self-incrimination, and cruel punishment.

Many justice system operations are controlled by the rule of law, but they are also influenced by the various philosophies or viewpoints held by its practitioners and policy makers. These, in turn, have been influenced by criminological theory and research. Knowledge about crime, its causes, and its control has significantly affected perceptions of how criminal justice should be managed.

Not surprisingly, many competing views of justice exist simultaneously in U.S. culture. Those in favor of one position or another try to win public opinion to their side, hoping to influence legislative, judicial, or administrative decision making. Over the years, different philosophical viewpoints tend to predominate, only to fall into disfavor as programs based on their principles fail to prove effective.

The remainder of this chapter briefly discusses the most important concepts of criminal justice.

Crime Control Model

Those who support the **crime control model** believe that the overriding purpose of the justice system is to protect the public, deter criminal behavior, and incapacitate known criminals. People want protection from dangerous criminals and expect the government to do what is necessary—punish criminals so that the public feels secure; crime control is part of the democratic process.[25]

Those who embrace its principles view the justice system as a barrier between destructive criminal elements and conventional society. Speedy, efficient justice, unencumbered by legal red tape and followed by punishment designed to fit the crime, is the goal of advocates of the crime control model. Its disciples promote such policies as increasing the size of police forces, maximizing the use of discretion, building more prisons, using the death penalty, and reducing legal controls on the justice system. Police departments, they would argue, would be more effective crime fighters if they employed a proactive, aggressive law enforcement style, improved their response time (the time it takes them to respond to a criminal incident), and increased the number of officers on patrol in the community.[26]

One impediment to effective crime control is the legal roadblocks set up by the courts to protect the due process rights of criminal defendants. Several hundred thousand criminals go free every year in cases dropped because police believe they have violated the suspects' ***Miranda* rights**.[27] Crime control advocates lobby for abolition of the **exclusionary rule**, which requires that illegally seized evidence be barred from criminal proceedings. Their voice has been heard: A more conservative Supreme Court has given police greater latitude to search for and seize evidence and has eased restrictions on how police operate. However, even in this permissive environment, research shows that police routinely violate suspects' rights when searching for evidence and that the majority of these incidents are never reviewed by the courts because the search was not followed up by arrest or citation.[28]

The crime control philosophy emphasizes protecting society and compensating victims. The criminal is responsible for his or her actions, has broken faith with society, and has chosen to violate the law for reasons such as anger, greed, or revenge. Therefore, money spent should be directed not at making criminals more comfortable but at increasing the efficiency of police in apprehending them and the courts in trying them effectively and the corrections system in meting out criminal punishment. This last element of justice is critical because punishment symbolizes the legitimate social order and the power societies have to regulate behavior and punish those who break social rules.[29]

The crime control philosophy has become a dominant force in U.S. justice. A number of important reviews claimed that treatment and rehabilitation efforts directed at known criminals just do not work.[30] There is more evidence that most criminals recidivate after their release from prison and that their reentry into society can destabilize the neighborhoods to which they return. Therefore a get-tough approach is the only way to control crime. The Policy & Practice in Criminology feature discusses this problem.

The lack of clear evidence that criminals can be successfully treated has produced a climate in which conservative, hard-line solutions to the crime problem are being sought. The results of this swing can be seen in such phenomena as the increasing use of the death penalty, erosion of the exclusionary rule, prison overcrowding, and attacks on the insanity defense. In the past few years, a number of states, including Tennessee, Utah, Iowa, Ohio, and West Virginia, have changed their juvenile codes, making it easier to try juveniles as adults. Other states have expanded their control over ex-offenders by requiring registration of sex offenders. New York has passed a death penalty statute, and other states, including

CONNECTIONS

The crime control model is rooted in choice theory, discussed in Chapter 4. Fear of criminal sanctions is viewed as the primary deterrent to crime. Because criminals are rational and choose to commit crime, it stands to reason that their activities can be controlled if the costs of crime become too high. Swift, sure, and efficient justice is considered an essential element of an orderly society.

crime control model
View that the overriding purpose of the justice system is to protect the public, deter criminal behavior, and incapacitate known criminals; favors speedy, efficient justice and punishment.

***Miranda* rights**
Rights of criminal defendants, including the right against self-incrimination and right to counsel, spelled out in the case of *Miranda v. Arizona*.

exclusionary rule
The rule that evidence against a defendant may not be presented in court if it was obtained in violation of the defendant's rights.

Policy & Practice in Criminology

The Legacy of Reentry

Because of America's two-decade-long imprisonment boom, more than 500,000 inmates are now being released back into the community each year. As criminologist Joan Petersilia warns, a number of unfortunate consequences will occur because many of those being released have not received adequate treatment and are unprepared for life in conventional society. The risks they present to the community include increases in child abuse, family violence, the spread of infectious diseases, homelessness, and community disorganization.

The increased reentry risks can be tied to legal changes in how people are released from prison. In the past, offenders were granted early release only if a parole board believed they were rehabilitated and had ties to the community—such as a family or a job. Inmates were encouraged to enter treatment programs to earn parole. Changes in sentencing law have resulted in the growth of mandatory release and limits on discretionary parole. People now serve a fixed sentence, and the discretion of parole boards has been blunted. Inmates may be discouraged from seeking involvement in rehabilitation programs (they do not influence the chance of parole), and the lack of incentive means that fewer inmates leaving prison have participated in programs to address work, education, and substance use deficiencies. Nor does the situation improve upon release. Many inmates are not assigned to supervision caseloads once back in the community. About 200,000 released inmates go unsupervised each year, three-quarters of whom have been released after completing their maximum sentence and therefore not obligated to be supervised.

Petersilia argues that most leave prison with no savings, no immediate entitlement to unemployment benefits, and few employment prospects. Upon release, some find that they are no longer welcome in subsidized public housing complexes due to the U.S. Department of Housing and Urban Development's "one strike and you're out" policy, where all members of the household are evicted if one member is involved in crime. One year after release, as many as 60 percent of former inmates are not employed in the regular labor market, and there is increasing reluctance among employers to hire ex-offenders. Ex-offenders are commonly barred from working in fields in which most jobs are being created, such as child care, education, security, nursing, and home heath care. More jobs are also now unionized, and many unions exclude ex-offenders.

Being barred from work opportunities produces chronic unemployment, a status closely related to drug and alcohol abuse. Losing a job can lead to substance abuse, which in turn is related to child and family violence. Mothers released from prison have difficulty finding services such as housing, employment, and child care, and this causes stress for them and their children. Children of incarcerated and released parents may suffer confusion, sadness, and social stigma, and these feelings often result in difficulties in school, low self-esteem, aggressive behavior, and general emotional dysfunction. If the parents are negative role models, children fail to develop positive attitudes about work and responsibility. Children of incarcerated parents are five times more likely to serve time in prison than are children whose parents are not incarcerated.

Prisoners have significantly more physical and mental health problems than the general population. More than three-fourths of the inmates leaving prison in the next year report a history of drug and/or alcohol abuse. Inmates with mental illness (about 16 percent of all inmates) also are increasingly being imprisoned—and then released. Even when public mental health services are available, many mentally ill individuals fail to use them because they fear insti-

© Shannon Stapleton/Reuters Newmedia Inc./Corbis

● The crime control philosophy emphasizes that criminals are responsible for their actions, and therefore the justice system should be willing to punish them for their misdeeds. The harsher the punishment, the less likely they will repeat their criminal acts, and others, observing the punishment, will be less willing to risk crime themselves.

tutionalization, deny they are mentally ill, or distrust the mental health system. The situation will become more serious as more and more parolees are released back into the disorganized communities whose deteriorated conditions may have motivated their original crimes.

Fear of a prison stay has less of an impact on behavior than ever before. As the prison population grows, the negative impact of incarceration may be lessening. In neighborhoods where "doing time" is more the rule than the exception, it becomes less of a stigma and more of a badge of acceptance. It also becomes a way of life from which some ex-convicts do rebound. Teens may encounter older men who have gone to prison and have returned to begin their lives again. With the proper skills and survival techniques, prison is considered "manageable." Although a prison stay is still unpleasant, it has lost its aura of shame and fear. By becoming commonplace and mundane, the "myth" of the prison experience has been exposed and its deterrent power reduced.

Effect on Communities

Parole expert Richard Seiter notes that when there were only a few hundred thousand prisoners, and a few thousand released per year, the issues surrounding the release of offenders did not overly challenge communities. Families could house ex-inmates, job-search organizations could find them jobs, and community social service agencies could respond to their individual needs for mental health or substance abuse treatment. Today, the sheer number of reentering inmates has taxed the communities to which they are returning. Charis Kubrin and Eric Stewart have found that communities that already face the greatest social and economic disadvantages are ones that produce the highest recidivism rates. Obviously, the influx of returning inmates can magnify their problems.

Research shows then that high rates of prison admissions produce high crime rates. Clearly, the national policy of relying on prison as a deterrent to crime may produce results that policy makers had not expected or wanted.

Critical Thinking

1. All too often, government leaders jump on the incarceration bandwagon as a panacea for the nation's crime problem. Is it a "quick fix" whose long-term consequences may be devastating for the nation's cities, or are these problems counterbalanced by the crime-reducing effect of putting large numbers of high-rate offenders behind bars?
2. If you agree that incarceration undermines neighborhoods, can you think of some other, indirect ways that high incarceration rates help increase crime rates?

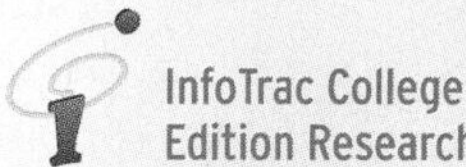

Alternatives to prison are now being sought because high incarceration may undermine a community's viability. What do you think? For some interesting developments, check out these articles on InfoTrac College Edition: Joe Loconte, "Making Criminals Pay: A New York County's Bold Experiment in Biblical Justice," *Policy Review* 87 (January–February 1998): 26, and Katarina Ivanko, "Shifting Gears to Rehabilitation," *Corrections Today* 59 (April 1997): 20.

SOURCES: Charis Kubrin and Eric Stewart, "Predicting Who Reoffends: The Neglected Role of Neighborhood Context in Recidivism Studies," *Criminology* 44 (2006): 165–197; Joan Petersilia, *When Prisoners Come Home: Parole and Prisoner Reentry* (New York: Oxford University Press, 2003); Petersilia, "Hard Time Ex-offenders Returning Home after Prison," *Corrections Today* 67 (2005): 66–72; Petersilia, "When Prisoners Return to Communities: Political, Economic, and Social Consequences," *Federal Probation* 65 (2001): 3–9; Richard Seiter, "Prisoner Reentry and the Role of Parole Officers," *Federal Probation* 66 (2002).

Delaware and South Dakota, have expanded the circumstances under which a person may be eligible for the death penalty.[31]

Can such measures deter crime? Crime control advocates point to one fact they claim is indisputable: As the number of people behind bars has increased, crime rates have decreased, proving that getting tough on crime can have an appreciable beneficial effect.

Justice Model

According to the **justice model**, it is futile to rehabilitate criminals, both because treatment programs are ineffective and because they deny people equal protection under the law.[32] It is unfair if two people commit the same crime but receive different sentences because only one is receptive to treatment. The consequence is a sense of injustice in the criminal justice system.

Beyond these problems, justice model advocates question the crime control perspective's reliance on deterrence. Is it fair to punish or incarcerate based on predictions of what offenders will do in the future or on whether others will be deterred from crime by their punishment? Justice model advocates are also

justice model
View that emphasizes fairness and equal treatment in criminal procedures and sentencing.

concerned with unfairness in the system, such as racism and discrimination, that causes sentencing disparity and unequal treatment before the law.[33]

As an alternative, the justice model calls for fairness in criminal procedure. This would require **determinate sentencing**, in which all offenders in a particular crime category would receive the same sentence. Prisons would be viewed as places of just, evenhanded punishment, not rehabilitation. Parole would be abolished to avoid the discretionary unfairness associated with that mechanism of early release.

The justice model has had an important influence on criminal justice policy. Some states have adopted flat sentencing statutes and have limited the use of parole. There is a trend toward giving prison sentences because people deserve punishment rather than because the sentences will rehabilitate them or deter others.

Due Process Model

In *The Limits of the Criminal Sanction*, Herbert Packer contrasted the crime control model with an opposing view that he refers to as the **due process model**.[34] According to Packer, the due process model combines elements of liberal/positivist criminology with the legal concept of procedural fairness for the accused. Those who adhere to due process principles believe in individualized justice, treatment, and rehabilitation of offenders. If discretion exists in the criminal justice system, it should be used to evaluate the treatment needs of offenders. Most important, the civil rights of the accused should be protected at all costs. This emphasis calls for strict scrutiny of police search and interrogation procedures, review of sentencing policies, and development of prisoners' rights.

Advocates of the due process model have demanded that competent defense counsel, jury trials, and other procedural safeguards be offered to every criminal defendant. They have also called for making public the operations of the justice system and placing controls over its discretionary power.

Due process advocates see themselves as protectors of civil rights. They view overzealous police as violators of basic constitutional rights. Similarly, they are skeptical about the intentions of meddling social workers, whose treatments often entail greater confinement and penalties than punishment does. Their concern is magnified by data showing that poor and minority group members are often maltreated in the criminal justice system. In some jurisdictions, such as Washington, D.C., almost half of all African American young men are under the control of the justice system. Is it possible that this reflects racism, discrimination, and a violation of their civil rights?[35] Research shows that in at least some states African Americans are more likely to be sent to prison than European Americans; these racial differences in the incarceration rate cannot be explained by the fact that blacks are arrested more often than whites.[36] The Race, Culture, Gender, & Criminology feature explores the issue of racial discrimination in the sentencing process.

Due process exists to protect citizens—both from those who wish to punish them and from those who wish to treat them without regard for their legal and civil rights. Due process model advocates worry about the government's expanding ability to use computers to intrude into people's private lives. In 1996, for example, the federal government announced plans for a computerized registry of sex offenders; there are plans for nationwide computer-based mug shot and fingerprint systems. These measures can harm privacy and civil liberties, although research shows that they may have relatively little impact on controlling crime.[37]

Advocates of the due process orientation are quick to point out that the justice system remains an adversary process that pits the forces of an all-powerful state against those of a solitary individual accused of crime. If an overriding concern for justice and fairness did not exist, the defendant who lacked resources could easily be overwhelmed. They point to miscarriages of justice such as the case of Jeffrey Blake, who went to prison for a double murder in 1991 and spent seven years behind bars before his conviction was overturned in 1998. The prosecution's star witness conceded that he had lied on the stand, forcing Blake to spend a quarter of his life in prison for a crime he did not commit.[38] His wrongful conviction would have been even more tragic if he had been executed for his alleged crime. Having

determinate sentencing
Principle that all offenders who commit the same crime should receive the same sentence.

due process model
View that focuses on protecting the civil rights of those accused of crime.

an attorney who puts on a spirited defense may mean the difference between life and death. Recent research (2005) by Talia Roitberg Harmon and William Lofquist that compared people who had been (1) falsely convicted of murder and later exonerated with those who were (2) most likely innocent but executed, found that the exonerated were defendants who employed private defense attorneys who were able to present a robust defense at trial.[39] Is it fair that a life versus death outcome may rest on the ability to afford private counsel?

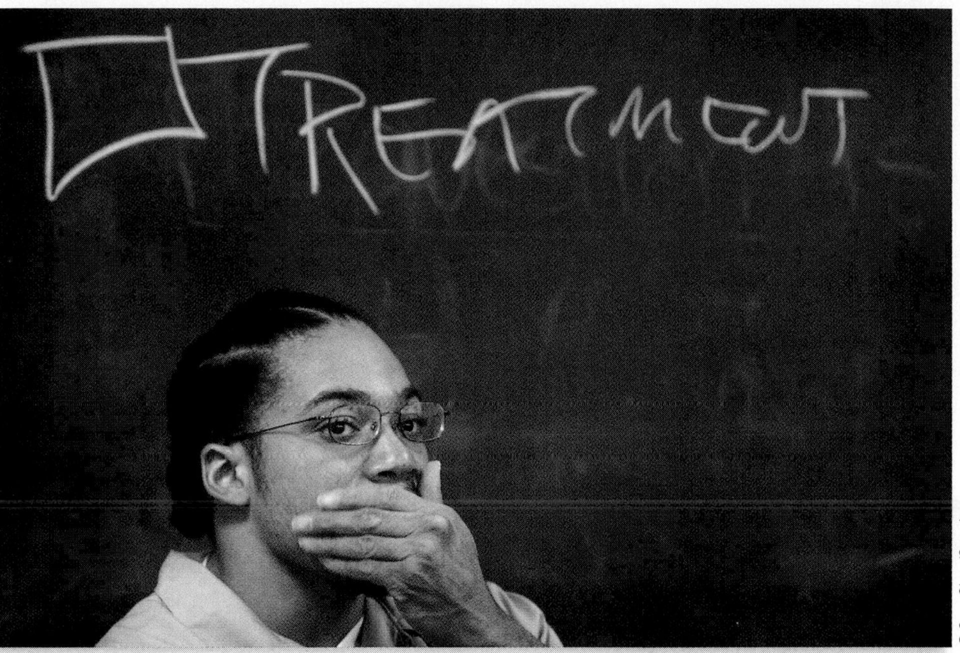

© Scott Olson/Getty Images

● Are prisons places for incapacitation and punishment or treatment and reform? Hasan Cunningham listens to speakers during a self-help group session focusing on life outside of prison at Sheridan Correctional Center in Sheridan, Illinois. A dedicated center for the treatment of inmates with drug and alcohol abuse problems, Sheridan was opened in January 2004 to combat a recidivism rate of 54 percent in the state's penal system. Nearly 69 percent of all inmates in Illinois are serving time for drug- or alcohol-related offenses. The recidivism rate for prisoners who have served time at Sheridan is 7.7 percent. Cunningham, whose drugs of choice were marijuana and alcohol, is nearing the end of a four-year sentence for drug conspiracy. It is his fourth time in prison. Can prison rehabilitation programs work?

Rehabilitation Model

The **rehabilitation model** embraces the notion that given the proper care and treatment, criminals can be changed into productive, law-abiding citizens. Influenced by positivist criminology, the rehabilitation school suggests that people commit crimes through no fault of their own. Instead, criminals themselves are the victims of social injustice, poverty, and racism; their acts are a response to a society that has betrayed them. And because of their disturbed and impoverished upbringing, they may be suffering psychological problems and personality disturbances that further enhance their crime-committing capabilities. Although the general public wants protection from crime, the argument goes, it also favors programs designed to help unfortunate people who commit crime because of emotional or social problems.[40]

Dealing effectively with crime requires attacking its root causes. Funds must be devoted to equalizing access to conventional means of success. This requires supporting such programs as public assistance, educational opportunity, and job training. If individuals run afoul of the law, efforts should be made to treat them, not punish them, by emphasizing counseling and psychological care in community-based treatment programs. Whenever possible, offenders should be placed on probation in halfway houses or in other rehabilitation-oriented programs.

This view of the justice system portrays it as a method for dispensing "treatment" to needy "patients." Also known as the "medical model," it portrays offenders as people who, because they have failed to exercise self-control, need the help of the state. The medical model rejects the crime control philosophy on the ground that it ignores the needs of offenders, who are people whom society has failed to help.

Research evidence suggests that some criminal justice–based treatment programs can have an important influence on offenders.[41] Given the proper treatment, offenders can significantly lower their rates of recidivism.[42] Community intervention programs have had significant success with drug offenders.[43] Within correctional settings, programs that teach interpersonal skills and use individual counseling and behavioral modification techniques have produced positive results both in the community and within correctional institutions.[44] And while some politicians call for a strict law-and-order approach, the general public is quite supportive of treatment programs such as early childhood intervention and services for at-risk children.[45]

CONNECTIONS

The rehabilitation model is linked to social structure and social process theories because it assumes that if lifestyle and socialization could be improved, crime rates would decline. See Chapters 6 and 7 for more on these theories.

Nonintervention Model

In the late 1960s and 1970s, both the rehabilitation ideal and the due process movement were viewed suspiciously by experts concerned by the stigmatization of offenders. Regardless of the purpose, the more the government intervenes in the lives of people, the greater the harm done to their future behavior patterns. Once arrested and labeled, the offender is placed at a disadvantage at home, at school,

rehabilitation model
View that sees criminals as victims of social injustice, poverty, and racism and suggests that appropriate treatment can change them into productive, law-abiding citizens.

Race, Culture, Gender, & Criminology

Does Racial Bias Exist in Criminal Sentencing?

Although critics of American race relations may think otherwise, research on sentencing has failed to show a definitive pattern of racial discrimination. Some research does indicate that a defendant's race has a direct impact on sentencing outcomes, but other efforts show that the influence of race on sentencing is less clear cut than anticipated. It is possible that the disproportionate number of minority group members in prison are a result of crime and arrest patterns and not racial bias by judges when they hand out criminal sentences; racial and ethnic minorities commit more crime, the argument goes, and therefore they are more likely to constitute a disproportionate share of the prison population.

Why does the critical issue of racial disparity remain so murky? One reason may be that if disparity is a factor in sentencing, its cause may lie outside of judicial sentencing practices. Research efforts show that minority defendants suffer discrimination in a variety of court actions that affect sentencing: They are more likely to be detained before trial than whites and, upon conviction, are more likely to receive jail sentences rather than fines. Prosecutors are less likely to divert minorities from the legal system than whites who commit the same crimes; minorities are less likely to win appeals than are white appellants. Pauline Brennan's research shows that minorities are more likely to receive harsher sentences than whites, not because of judicial bias, but because of social inequality: Minorities have less money for bail and attorneys, fewer ties to the community, and are more likely to have a prior record; each of these factors has an impact on sentencing.

It is also possible that some research efforts miss a racial effect because they use invalid measures of race. Some may combine Anglo and Hispanic cases into a single category of "white" defendants and then compare them with the sentencing of black defendants. Darrell Steffensmeier and Stephen Demuth's analysis of sentencing in Pennsylvania found that Hispanics are punished considerably more severely than non-Hispanic Anglos and that combining the two groups masks the ethnic differences in sentencing.

Where Race and Sentencing Collide

The relationship between race and sentencing may be difficult to establish because of external factors that shroud the association. Consider the following:

Nonlinear Association

Minority defendants may be punished more severely for some crimes, and under some circumstances, but they are treated more leniently for others. Sociologist Darnell Hawkins explains this phenomenon as a matter of "appropriateness": Certain crime types are considered less "appropriate" for blacks than for whites. Blacks who are charged with committing these offenses will be treated more severely than blacks who commit crimes that are considered more "appropriate." The inappropriate offense category includes white-collar offenses and crimes against political and social structures of authority. Race appropriate offenses would include various forms of victimless crimes associated with lower social status (such as prostitution, minor drug use, or drunkenness). This may also include various crimes against the person, especially those involving black victims.

Race may also have an impact on sentencing because some race-specific crimes are punished more harshly than others. African Americans receive longer sentences for drug crimes than Anglos because (1) they are more likely to be arrested for crack possession and sales and (2) crack dealing is more severely punished by state and federal laws than other drug crimes. Because whites are more likely to use marijuana and methamphetamines, prosecutors are more willing to plea-bargain and offer shorter jail terms.

The Victim's Race Is the Key

Racial bias has also been linked to victim–offender status. Minority defendants are sanctioned more severely if their victim is white than if their target is a fellow minority group member; minorities who kill whites are more likely to get the death penalty than those who kill other minorities. Judges may base sentencing decisions on the race of the victim and not the race of the defendant. Researchers Charles Crawford, Ted Chiricos, and Gary Kleck found that African American defendants are more likely to be prosecuted under habitual offender statutes if they commit crimes where there is a greater likelihood of a white victim (larceny and burglary) than if they commit violent crimes that are largely intraracial. Where there is a perceived "racial threat," punishments are enhanced.

Financial Effects

Tracy Nobiling, Cassia Spohn, and Miriam DeLone have found that racial

and in the job market.[46] Rather than deter crime, the stigma of a criminal label erodes social capital and jeopardizes future success and achievement.

The **noninterventionist model** calls for limiting government intrusion into the lives of people, especially minors, who run afoul of the law.[47] Noninterventionists advocate deinstitutionalization of nonserious offenders, diversion from formal court processes into informal treatment programs, and decriminalization of nonserious offenses, such as possessing small amounts of marijuana. Under this concept, the justice system should interact as little as possible with offenders. Police, courts, and correctional agencies would concentrate their efforts on diverting law violators out of the formal justice system, thereby helping them avoid the stigma of formal labels such as "delinquent" or "ex-con." Programs instituted under this

noninterventionist model
View that arresting and labeling offenders does more harm than good, that youthful offenders in particular should be diverted into informal treatment programs, and that minor offenses should be decriminalized.

status influences sentencing partially because minority group members have a lower income than whites and are more likely to be unemployed. Judges may possibly view their status as "social dynamite," considering them more dangerous and more likely to recidivate than white offenders.

Being poor also affects sentencing in other ways. Defendants who can afford bail receive more lenient sentences than those who remain in pretrial detention; minority defendants are less likely to make bail because they suffer a higher degree of income inequality. That is, minorities earn less on average and therefore are less likely to be able to make bail. Sentencing outcome is also affected by the defendant's ability to afford a private attorney and put on a vigorous legal defense that makes use of high-paid expert witnesses. These factors place minority group members at a disadvantage in the sentencing process and result in sentencing disparity.

The Persistent Problem of Race

Though efforts to limit racial disparity have been ongoing, research studies still find that minorities receive longer sentences and more punitive treatment than white defendants. When Shawn Bushway and Anne Morrison Piehl studied sentencing outcomes in Maryland, they found that, on average, African Americans have 20 percent longer sentences than whites, even when holding constant their age, gender, and recommended sentence length. Stephanie Bontrager, William Bales, and Ted Chiricos studied the effect of a Florida law that allows judges to withhold adjudication of guilt for persons who have either pleaded guilty or been found guilty of a felony in order to shield them from the stigma of a criminal conviction and enable them to retain all their civil rights; the law applies only to persons who will be sentenced to probation. They found that Hispanics and blacks, especially if they come from a disadvantaged background, are significantly less likely to have adjudication withheld than whites. So the nagging issue of racial disparity in sentencing still haunts the justice process.

Critical Thinking

Do you feel that sentences should be influenced by the fact that one ethnic or racial group is more likely to commit that crime? For example, critics have called for change in the way federal sentencing guidelines are designed, asking that the provisions that punish crack possession more heavily than powdered cocaine possession be repealed because African Americans are more likely to use crack and whites powdered cocaine. Do you approve of such a change? Because of the lingering problem of racial and class bias in the sentencing process, one primary goal of the criminal justice system in the 1990s was to reduce disparity by creating new forms of criminal sentences that limit judicial discretion and are aimed at uniformity and fairness.

Use the terms "race" and "sentencing" as key words to find out more about the relationship between these two factors.

SOURCES: Sara Steen, Rodney Engen, and Randy Gainey, "Images of Danger and Culpability: Racial Stereotyping, Case Processing, and Criminal Sentencing," *Criminology* 43 (2005): 435–468; Stephanie Bontrager, William Bales, and Ted Chiricos, "Race, Ethnicity, Threat, and the Labeling of Convicted Felons," *Criminology* 43 (2005): 589–622; Pauline Brennan, "Sentencing Female Misdemeanants: An Examination of the Direct and Indirect Effects of Race/Ethnicity," *Justice Quarterly* 23 (2006): 60–95; Mitchell Ojmarrh, "A Meta-Analysis of Race and Sentencing Research: Explaining the Inconsistencies," *Journal of Quantitative Criminology* 21 (2005): 439–466; Shawn Bushway and Anne Morrison Piehl, "Judging Judicial Discretion: Legal Factors and Racial Discrimination in Sentencing," *Law and Society Review* 35 (2001): 733–765; Barbara Koons-Witt, "The Effect of Gender on the Decision to Incarcerate before and after the Introduction of Sentencing Guidelines," *Criminology* 40 (2002): 97–129; Marian R. Williams and Jefferson E. Holcomb, "Racial Disparity and Death Sentences in Ohio," *Journal of Criminal Justice* 29 (2001): 207–218; Rodney Engen and Randy Gainey, "Modeling the Effects of Legally Relevant and Extra-legal Factors under Sentencing Guidelines: The Rules Have Changed," *Criminology* 38 (2000): 1207–1230; Darrell Steffensmeier and Stephen Demuth, "Ethnicity and Judges' Sentencing Decisions: Hispanic-Black-White Comparisons," *Criminology* 39 (2001): 145–178; Tracy Nobiling, Cassia Spohn, and Miriam DeLone, "A Tale of Two Counties: Unemployment and Sentence Severity," *Justice Quarterly* 15 (1998): 459–486; Travis Pratt, "Race and Sentencing: A Meta-Analysis of Conflicting Empirical Research Results," *Journal of Criminal Justice* 26 (1998): 513–525; Charles Crawford, Ted Chiricos, and Gary Kleck, "Race, Racial Threat, and Sentencing of Habitual Offenders," *Criminology* 36 (1998): 481–511; Jon'a Meyer and Tara Gray, "Drunk Drivers in the Courts: Legal and Extra-Legal Factors Affecting Pleas and Sentences," *Journal of Criminal Justice* 25 (1997): 155–163; Darnell Hawkins, "Race, Crime Type and Imprisonment," *Justice Quarterly* 3 (1986): 251–269.

model include mediation (instead of trial), diversion (instead of formal processing), and community-based corrections (instead of secure corrections).

Nonintervention advocates are also skeptical about the creation of laws that criminalize acts that were previously legal, thus expanding the reach of justice and creating new classes of offenders. An example is the growing popularity of expanding control over youthful offenders by passing local curfew laws that make it a crime for young people to be out at night after a certain hour, such as 11:00 PM. An adolescent who was formerly a night owl is now a criminal![48]

There are many examples of nonintervention ideas in practice. The juvenile justice system has made a major effort to remove youths from adult jails and to reduce the use of pretrial detention. Mediation programs have proven successful alternatives to the formal trial process. In the adult system, pretrial release programs (alternatives to bail) are now the norm instead of an experimental innovation. And, although the prison population is rising, probation and community treatment have become the most common forms of criminal sanction.

The noninterventionist philosophy also has its critics. There is little evidence that alternative programs reduce recidivism rates. Some critics charge that alternative programs actually result in "widening the net."[49] That is, efforts to remove people from the justice system enmesh them further within it by ordering them to spend more time in treatment than they would have had to spend in the formal legal process.

In the future, the nonintervention philosophy will be aided by the rising cost of justice. Although low-impact, nonintrusive programs may work no better than prison, they are certainly cheaper; program costs may receive greater consideration than program effectiveness.

Restorative Justice Model

Some justice scholars believe that the true purpose of the criminal justice system is to promote a peaceful, just society; they advocate peacemaking, not punishment.[50] This vision has become known as restorative justice.

The **restorative justice model** draws its inspiration from religious and philosophical teachings ranging from Quakerism to Zen. Advocates of restorative justice say that state efforts to punish and control encourage crime. The violent punishing acts of the state, they claim, are not dissimilar from the violent acts of individuals.[51] Whereas crime control advocates associate lower crime rates with increased punishment, restorative justice advocates counter that with studies showing punitive methods of correction (such as jail) are no more effective than more humanitarian efforts (such as probation with treatment).[52] Therefore, mutual aid rather than coercive punishment is the key to a harmonious society. Without the capacity to restore damaged social relations, society's response to crime has been almost exclusively punitive.

Restorative justice is guided by three essential principles: (1) community "ownership" of conflict (including crime), (2) material and symbolic reparation for crime victims, and (3) social reintegration of the offender.[53] Maintaining ownership, or jurisdiction, over the conflict means that the conflict between criminal and victim should be resolved in the community in which it originated, not in some faraway prison. The victim should be given a chance to voice his or her story, and the offender should help compensate the victim financially or by providing some service. The goal is to enable the offender to appreciate the damage caused, to make amends, and to be reintegrated into society.

Restorative justice programs are geared to these principles. The ability of police officers to mediate disputes rather than resort to formal arrest has long been recognized; it is an essential element of community policing.[54] Mediation and conflict resolution programs are now common in efforts to resolve harmful human interactions ranging from domestic violence to hate crimes.[55] Financial and community-service restitution programs as an alternative to imprisonment have been in operation for more than two decades.

Although restorative justice has become an important perspective in recent years, there are so many diverse programs calling themselves "restorative" that there is still no single definition of what constitutes restorative justice.[56] Restorative justice programs must also be wary of the cultural and social differences that can be found throughout our heterogeneous society; what may be considered "restorative" in one subculture may be considered insulting and damaging in another.[57]

CONNECTIONS

The basis of restorative justice was reviewed in Chapter 8, in the discussion of policy implications of critical criminology.

Trends in Justice Today

The various philosophies of justice compete today for dominance in the criminal justice system (see Figure 14.9). Each has supporters who lobby diligently for their positions. At the time of this writing, it seems that the crime control and justice models have captured the support of legislators and the general public.

restorative justice model
View that emphasizes the promotion of a peaceful, just society through reconciliation and reintegration of the offender into society.

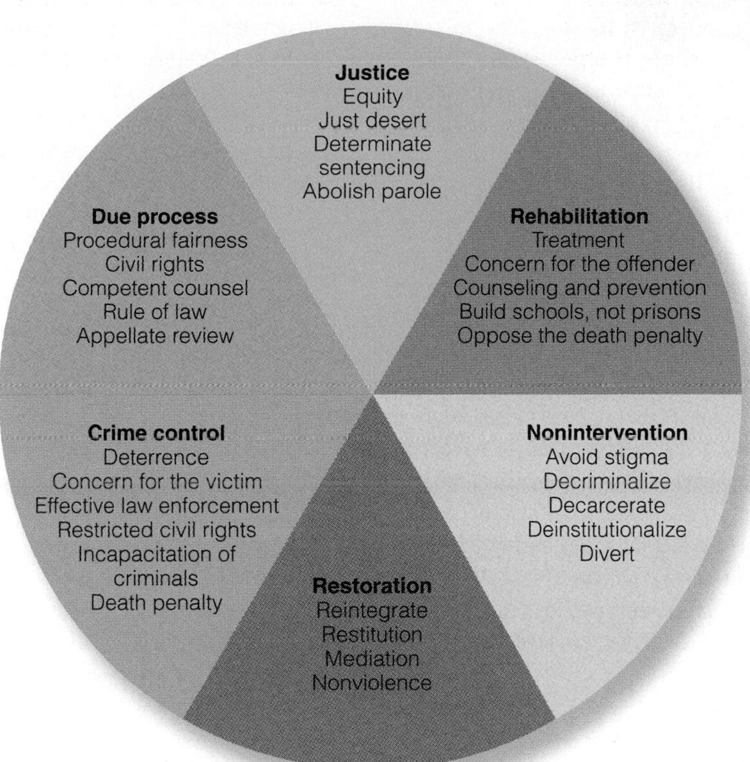

Figure 14.9
Perspectives on Justice: Key Concerns and Concepts

There is a growing emphasis on protecting the public by increasing criminal sentences and swelling prison populations.[58] Yet the association between adoption of crime control programs and reduction in the crime rate may be misleading. It is possible that the crime rate is merely undergoing a natural revision from the abnormally high, unprecedented increases brought about by the crack cocaine epidemic in the 1980s; the success of get-tough crime control programs may be illusory. Locking more and more people up may have a harmful effect in the long run: Most offenders eventually return to society, and most eventually reoffend. Their chances of success in the legitimate world may, if anything, be severely diminished by their prison experiences. As rehabilitation advocates suggest, punishment may produce short-term reductions in the crime rate, but only rehabilitation and treatment can produce long-term gains.

So, despite the demand for punishing serious, chronic offenders, the door to treatment for nonviolent, nonchronic offenders has not been closed. The number of noninterventionist and restorative justice programs featuring restitution and nonpunitive sanctions is growing. As the cost of justice skyrockets and the correctional system becomes increasingly overcrowded, alternatives such as house arrest, electronic monitoring, intensive probation supervision, and other cost-effective programs have come to the forefront. ✔ CHECKPOINTS

✔ CHECKPOINTS

✔ The U.S. Supreme Court maintains legal control over the justice system through its application of the Bill of Rights.

✔ There are a number of models of justice.

✔ The most conservative view is the crime control model, which holds that the justice system is designed to protect the public and deter criminal behavior.

✔ In contrast, the rehabilitation model holds that the justice system can help treat needy people and help them turn their lives around.

✔ Some justice experts believe that the system must be on the lookout for violations of due process.

✔ The restorative justice model holds that the system is an ideal venue for reconciliation and healing.

THINKING Like a Criminologist

You have been appointed assistant to the president's drug czar, who is in charge of coordinating the nation's drug control policy. She has asked you to develop a plan to reduce drug abuse by 25 percent within three years.

You realize that multiple perspectives of justice exist and that the agencies of the criminal justice system can use a number of strategies to reduce drug trafficking and the use of drugs. It might be possible to control the drug trade through a strict crime control effort, for example, using law enforcement officers to cut off supplies of drugs by destroying crops and arresting members of drug cartels in drug-producing countries. Border patrols and military personnel using sophisticated hardware could also help prevent drugs from entering the country. According to the justice model, if drug violations were punished with criminal sentences commensurate with their harm, then the rational drug trafficker might look for a new line of employment. The adoption of mandatory sentences for drug crimes to ensure that all offenders receive similar punishment for their acts might reduce crime. The rehabilitation model suggests that strategies should be aimed at reducing the desire to use drugs and increasing incentives for users to eliminate substance abuse. A noninterventionist strategy calls for the legalization of drugs so distribution could be controlled by the government. Crime rates would be cut because drug users would no longer need the same cash flow to support their habit.

Considering these different approaches, how would you shape drug control strategies?

Summary

- "Criminal justice" refers to the formal processes and institutions that have been established to apprehend, try, punish, and treat law violators.
- The major components of the criminal justice system are the police, the courts, and correctional agencies.
- Police maintain public order, deter crime, and apprehend law violators.
- Police departments are now experimenting with community and problem-oriented policing.
- The courts determine the criminal liability of accused offenders brought before them and dispense sanctions to those found guilty of crime.
- Corrections agencies provide postadjudicatory care to offenders who are sentenced by the courts to confinement or community supervision.
- Dissatisfaction with traditional forms of corrections has spurred the development of community-based facilities and work release and work furlough programs.
- Justice can also be conceived of as a process through which offenders flow.
- The justice process begins with initial contact by a police agency and proceeds through investigation and custody, trial stages, and correctional system processing. At any stage of the process, the offender may be excused because evidence is lacking, the case is trivial, or a decision maker simply decides to discontinue interest in the case.
- Procedures, policies, and practices employed within the criminal justice system are scrutinized by the courts to make sure they do not violate the guidelines in the Bill of Rights, the first 10 amendments to the U.S. Constitution. If a violation occurs, the defendant can appeal the case and seek to overturn the conviction. Among the rights that must be honored are freedom from illegal searches and seizures and treatment with overall fairness and due process.
- Several different philosophies or perspectives dominate the justice process. The crime control model asserts that the goals of justice are protection of the public and incapacitation of known offenders.
- The justice model calls for fair, equal treatment for all offenders.
- The due process model emphasizes liberal principles, such as legal rights and procedural fairness for the offender.
- The rehabilitation model views the justice system as a wise and caring parent.
- The noninterventionist perspective calls for minimal interference in offenders' lives.
- The restorative justice model seeks nonpunitive, humane solutions to the conflict inherent in crime and victimization.

Take a Post-Test. Visit www.thomsonedu.com/criminaljustice/siegel and take the chapter Post-Test to monitor your progress and identify areas for further improvement. In addition to discovering what you've mastered, you'll learn which concepts need your added attention and get specific page references that direct you to the places in the text where you can find more information on them.

Key Terms

criminal justice system 341
discretion 342
community policing 343
problem-oriented policing 343
landmark decision 344
adversary system 345
prosecutor 345
defendant 345
convictability 346
defense attorney 347
right to counsel 347
public defender 347
pro bono 347
probation 348
incarceration 348
jail 348
prison (penitentiary) 348
truth in sentencing 348
parole 349
arrest 349
probable cause 349
booking 350
interrogation 351
indictment 351
grand jury 351
information 351
preliminary hearing 352
arraignment 352
bail 352
recognizance 352
plea bargain 352
hung jury 352
disposition 352
appeal 352
courtroom work group 355
law of criminal procedure 356
Bill of Rights 356
crime control model 357
Miranda rights 357
exclusionary rule 357
justice model 359
determinate sentencing 360
due process model 360
rehabilitation model 361
noninterventionist model 362
restorative justice model 364

Critical Thinking Questions

1. Describe the differences between the formal and informal justice systems. Is it fair to treat some offenders informally?

2. What are the basic elements of each model or perspective on justice? Which best represents your own point of view?

3. How would each perspective on criminal justice consider the use of the death penalty as a sanction for first-degree murder? In your opinion, does the death penalty serve as a deterrent to murder? If not, why not?

4. Discuss the trends that will influence policing during the coming decade.

5. Why does the problem of sentencing disparity exist? Do programs exist that can reduce disparate sentences? If so, what are they?

6. Should all people who commit the same crime receive the same sentence?

Notes

Chapter 1. Crime and Criminology

1. FBI, news release, "Canadian Man Pleads Guilty to Traveling to Georgia to Engage in Sexual Activity with a 10-Year-Old Girl," March 15, 2006, www.usdoj.gov/usao/gan/press/03-15-06.pdf.
2. John Hagan and Alberto Palloni, "Sociological Criminology and the Mythology of Hispanic Immigration and Crime," *Social Problems* 46 (1999): 617–632.
3. Eugene Weber, *A Modern History of Europe* (New York: W. W. Norton, 1971), p. 398.
4. Marvin Wolfgang, *Patterns in Criminal Homicide* (Philadelphia: University of Pennsylvania Press, 1958).
5. Nicole Rafter, "The Murderous Dutch Fiddler: Criminology, History, and the Problem of Phrenology," *Theoretical Criminology* 9 (2005): 65–97.
6. Described in David Lykken, "Psychopathy, Sociopathy, and Crime," *Society* 34 (1996): 29–38.
7. See Peter Scott, "Henry Maudsley," in *Pioneers in Criminology,* ed. Hermann Mannheim (Montclair, NJ: Prentice-Hall, 1981).
8. Nicole Hahn Rafter, "Criminal Anthropology in the United States," *Criminology* 30 (1992): 525–547.
9. Ibid., p. 535.
10. See, generally, Robert Nisbet, *The Sociology of Émile Durkheim* (New York: Oxford University Press, 1974).
11. L. A. J. Quetelet, *A Treatise on Man and the Development of His Faculties* (Gainesville, FL: Scholars' Facsimiles and Reprints, 1969), pp. 82–96.
12. Ibid., p. 85.
13. Émile Durkheim, *Rules of the Sociological Method,* reprint ed., trans. W. D. Halls (New York: Free Press, 1982).
14. Émile Durkheim, *The Division of Labor in Society,* reprint ed. (New York: Free Press, 1997).
15. Robert Park and Ernest Burgess, *The City* (Chicago: University of Chicago Press, 1925).
16. Karl Marx and Friedrich Engels, *Capital: A Critique of Political Economy,* trans. E. Aveling (Chicago: Charles Kern, 1906); Karl Marx, *Selected Writings in Sociology and Social Philosophy,* trans. P. B. Bottomore (New York: McGraw-Hill, 1956). For a general discussion of Marxist thought, see Michael Lynch and W. Byron Groves, *A Primer in Radical Criminology* (New York: Harrow and Heston, 1986), pp. 6–26.
17. Sheldon Glueck and Eleanor Glueck, *Unraveling Juvenile Delinquency* (Cambridge, MA: Harvard University Press, 1950), p. 48.
18. Irvin Wolfgang and Franco Ferracuti, *The Subculture of Violence* (London: Social Science Paperbacks, 1967), p. 20.
19. *Smith et al. v. Doe et al.* 538 U.S. 84 (2003).
20. Marvin Wolfgang, *Patterns in Criminal Homicide.*
21. Edwin Sutherland, *White-Collar Crime: The Uncut Version* (New Haven, CT: Yale University Press, 1983).
22. Samuel Gross, Kristen Jacoby, Daniel Matheson, Nicholas Montgomery, and Sujata Patil, "Exonerations in the United States 1989 Through 2003," *Journal of Criminal Law & Criminology* 95 (2005): 523–559.
23. Hans von Hentig, *The Criminal and His Victim* (New Haven, CT: Yale University Press, 1948); Stephen Schafer, *The Victim and His Criminal* (New York: Random House, 1968).
24. Linda Teplin, Gary McClelland, Karen Abram, and Darinka Mileusnic, "Early Violent Death among Delinquent Youth: A Prospective Longitudinal Study," *Pediatrics* 115 (2005): 1,586–1,593.
25. Charles McCaghy, *Deviant Behavior* (New York: Macmillan, 1976), pp. 2–3.
26. Monitoring the Future, *National Survey Results on Drug Use, 1975–2004*, Vol. I & II, www.monitoringthefuture.org/pubs/monographs/vol1_2004.pdf (accessed October 20, 2005).
27. Edward Brecher, *Licit and Illicit Drugs* (Boston: Little, Brown, 1972), pp. 413–416.
28. Hearings on H.R. 6385 April 27, 28, 29, 30, and May 4, 1937, www.druglibrary.org/schaffer/hemp/taxact/anslng1.htm (accessed July 5, 2006).
29. www.dpf.org/drugwar (accessed July 5, 2006).
30. Federal Communications Commission, In the Matter of Clear Channel Broadcasting, File No. EB-03-IH-0159, Washington, DC, April 7, 2004, www.fcc.gov/eb/Orders/2004/FCC-04-88A1.html.
31. www.howardstern.com/oprah.html (accessed April 7, 2004).
32. Edwin Sutherland and Donald Cressey, *Criminology,* 8th ed. (Philadelphia: J. B. Lippincott, 1960), p. 8.
33. Howard Becker, *Outsiders: Studies in the Sociology of Deviance* (New York: Free Press, 1963), p. 9.
34. Ibid.
35. Oliver Wendell Holmes, *The Common Law*, ed. Mark De Wolf (Boston: Little, Brown, 1881), p. 36.
36. National Institute of Justice, *Project to Develop a Model Anti-Stalking Statute* (Washington, DC: National Institute of Justice, 1994).
37. "Clinton Signs Tougher 'Megan's Law,'" *CNN News Service,* May 17, 1996.
38. Associated Press, "Judge Upholds State's Sexual Predator Law," *Bakersfield Californian,* October 2, 1996.
39. *Lawrence et al. v. Texas,* No. 02-102, June 26, 2003.
40. Joachim Savelsberg, Ryan King, and Lara Cleveland, "Politicized Scholarship? Science on Crime and the State," *Social Problems* 49 (2002): 327–349.
41. See, for example, Michael Hindelang and Travis Hirschi, "Intelligence and Delinquency: A Revisionist Review," *American Sociological Review* 42 (1977): 471–486.
42. Richard Herrnstein and Charles Murray, *The Bell Curve* (New York: Free Press, 1994).
43. Dermot Feenan, "Legal Issues in Acquiring Information about Illegal Behaviour through Criminological Research," *British Journal of Criminology* 42 (2002): 762–781.
44. Anthony Petrosino, Carolyn Turpin-Petrosino, and James Finckenauer, "Well-Meaning Programs Can Have Harmful Effects! Lessons from Experiments of Programs Such as Scared Straight," *Crime and Delinquency* 46 (2000): 354–379.
45. Victor Boruch, Timothy Victor, and Joe Cecil, "Resolving Ethical and Legal Problems in Randomized Experiments," *Crime and Delinquency* 46 (2000): 330–353.

Chapter 2. The Nature and Extent of Crime

1. Information on the Rudolph case can be obtained at www.cnn.com/2003/US/05/31/rudolph.arrest/ and http://crime.about.com/od/current/a/rudolph.htm (both accessed July 5, 2006).
2. Cited on http://en.wikipedia.org/wiki/Eric_Rudolph (accessed August 17, 2005).
3. Federal Bureau of Investigation, *Crime in the United States, 2004* (Washington, DC: U.S. Government Printing Office, 2005).
4. Callie Marie Rennison, *Criminal Victimization 1999: Changes 1998–99 with Trends 1993–98* (Washington, DC: Bureau of Justice Statistics, 2000).

5. Richard Felson, Steven Messner, Anthony Hoskin, and Glenn Deane, "Reasons for Reporting and Not Reporting Domestic Violence to the Police," *Criminology* 40 (2002): 617–648.
6. Bonnie Fisher, Leah Daigle, Francis Cullen, and Michael Turner, "Reporting Sexual Victimization to the Police and Others: Results from a National-Level Study of College Women," *Criminal Justice and Behavior* 30 (2003): 6–39.
7. Duncan Chappell, Gilbert Geis, Stephen Schafer, and Larry Siegel, "Forcible Rape: A Comparative Study of Offenses Known to the Police in Boston and Los Angeles," in *Studies in the Sociology of Sex,* ed. James Henslin (New York: Appleton Century Crofts, 1971), pp. 169–193.
8. Robert O'Brien, "Police Productivity and Crime Rates: 1973–1992," *Criminology* 34 (1996): 183–207.
9. FBI, *UCR Handbook* (Washington, DC: U.S. Government Printing Office, 1998), p. 33.
10. Lynn Addington, "The Effect of NIBRS Reporting on Item Missing Data in Murder Cases," *Homicide Studies* 8 (2004): 193–213.
11. Shannan Catalano, *Criminal Victimization 2005* (Washington, DC: Bureau of Justice Statistics, 2006); Patsy Klaus, *Crime and the Nation's Households, 2004* (Washington, DC: Bureau of Justice Statistics, 2006). Data in this section come from these two reports.
12. L. Edward Wells and Joseph Rankin, "Juvenile Victimization: Convergent Validation of Alternative Measurements," *Journal of Research in Crime and Delinquency* 32 (1995): 287–307.
13. A pioneering effort in self-report research is A. L. Porterfield, *Youth in Trouble* (Fort Worth, TX: Leo Potishman Foundation, 1946); for a review, see Robert Hardt and George Bodine, *Development of Self-Report Instruments in Delinquency Research: A Conference Report* (Syracuse, NY: Syracuse University Youth Development Center, 1965). See also Fred Murphy, Mary Shirley, and Helen Witner, "The Incidence of Hidden Delinquency," *American Journal of Orthopsychology* 16 (1946): 686–696.
14. See John Paul Wright and Francis Cullen, "Juvenile Involvement in Occupational Delinquency," *Criminology* 38 (2000): 863–896.
15. Christiane Brems, Mark Johnson, David Neal, and Melinda Freemon, "Childhood Abuse History and Substance Use among Men and Women Receiving Detoxification Services," *American Journal of Drug & Alcohol Abuse* 30 (2004): 799–821.
16. Leonore Simon, "Validity and Reliability of Violent Juveniles: A Comparison of Juvenile Self-Reports with Adult Self-Reports Incarcerated in Adult Prisons." Paper presented at the annual meeting of the American Society of Criminology, Boston, November 1995, p. 26.
17. Stephen Cernkovich, Peggy Giordano, and Meredith Pugh, "Chronic Offenders: The Missing Cases in Self-Report Delinquency Research," *Journal of Criminal Law and Criminology* 76 (1985): 705–732.
18. Terence Thornberry, Beth Bjerregaard, and William Miles, "The Consequences of Respondent Attrition in Panel Studies: A Simulation Based on the Rochester Youth Development Study," *Journal of Quantitative Criminology* 9 (1993): 127–158.
19. See Spencer Rathus and Larry Siegel, "Crime and Personality Revisited: Effects of MMPI Sets on Self-Report Studies," *Criminology* 18 (1980): 245–251; John Clark and Larry Tifft, "Polygraph and Interview Validation of Self-Reported Deviant Behavior," *American Sociological Review* 31 (1966): 516–523.
20. Mallie Paschall, Miriam Ornstein, and Robert Flewelling, "African-American Male Adolescents' Involvement in the Criminal Justice System: The Criterion Validity of Self-Report Measures in Prospective Study," *Journal of Research in Crime and Delinquency* 38 (2001): 174–187.
21. Lloyd Johnston, Patrick O'Malley, and Jerald Bachman, *Monitoring the Future, 2004* (Ann Arbor, MI: Institute for Social Research, 2005).
22. Jennifer Roberts, Edward Mulvey, Julie Horney, John Lewis, and Michael Arter, "A Test of Two Methods of Recall for Violent Events," *Journal of Quantitative Criminology* 21 (2005): 175–193.
23. Lila Kazemian and David Farrington, "Comparing the Validity of Prospective, Retrospective, and Official Onset for Different Offending Categories," *Journal of Quantitative Criminology* 21 (2005): 127–147.
24. Barbara Warner and Brandi Wilson Coomer, "Neighborhood Drug Arrest Rates: Are They a Meaningful Indicator of Drug Activity? A Research Note," *Journal of Research in Crime and Delinquency* 40 (2003): 123–139.
25. Alfred Blumstein, Jacqueline Cohen, and Richard Rosenfeld, "Trend and Deviation in Crime Rates: A Comparison of UCR and NCVS Data for Burglary and Robbery," *Criminology* 29 (1991): 237–248. See also Michael Hindelang, Travis Hirschi, and Joseph Weis, *Measuring Delinquency* (Beverly Hills, CA: Sage, 1981).
26. Clarence Schrag, *Crime and Justice: American Style* (Washington, DC: U.S. Government Printing Office, 1971), p. 17.
27. James A. Fox, *Trends in Juvenile Violence: A Report to the United States Attorney General on Current and Future Rates of Juvenile Offending* (Boston: Northeastern University, 1996).
28. Steven Levitt, "The Limited Role of Changing Age Structure in Explaining Aggregate Crime Rates," *Criminology* 37 (1999): 581–599.
29. Darrell Steffensmeier and Miles Harer, "Making Sense of Recent U.S. Crime Trends, 1980 to 1996/1998: Age Composition Effects and Other Explanations," *Journal of Research in Crime and Delinquency* 36 (1999): 235–274.
30. Ibid., p. 265.
31. Ellen Cohn, "The Effect of Weather and Temporal Variations on Calls for Police Service," *American Journal of Police* 15 (1996): 23–43.
32. R. A. Baron, "Aggression as a Function of Ambient Temperature and Prior Anger Arousal," *Journal of Personality and Social Psychology* 21 (1972): 183–189.
33. Brad Bushman, Morgan Wang, and Craig Anderson, "Is the Curve Relating Temperature to Aggression Linear or Curvilinear? Assaults and Temperature in Minneapolis Reexamined," *Journal of Personality & Social Psychology* 89 (2005): 62–66.
34. Paul Bell, "Reanalysis and Perspective in the Heat-Aggression Debate," *Journal of Personality & Social Psychology* 89 (2005): 71–73.
35. Ellen Cohn, "The Prediction of Police Calls for Service: The Influence of Weather and Temporal Variables on Rape and Domestic Violence," *Journal of Environmental Psychology* 13 (1993): 71–83.
36. John Simister and Cary Cooper, "Thermal Stress in the U.S.A.: Effects on Violence and on Employee Behaviour," *Stress and Health* 21 (2005): 3–15.
37. Amie Nielsen, Ramiro Martinez, and Richard Rosenfeld, "Firearm Use, Injury, and Lethality in Assaultive Violence: An Examination of Ethnic Differences," *Homicide Studies* 9 (2005): 83–108.
38. See generally Franklin Zimring and Gordon Hawkins, *Crime Is Not the Problem: Lethal Violence in America* (New York: Oxford University Press, 1997).
39. Ibid., p. 36.
40. Gary Kleck and Marc Gertz, "Armed Resistance to Crime: The Prevalence and Nature of Self-Defense with a Gun," *Journal of Criminal Law and Criminology* 86 (1995): 219–249.
41. Robert Nash Parker, "Bringing 'Booze' Back In: The Relationship between Alcohol and Homicide," *Journal of Research in Crime and Delinquency* 32 (1995): 3–38.
42. Victoria Brewer and M. Dwayne Smith, "Gender Inequality and Rates of Female Homicide Victimization across U.S. Cities," *Journal of Research in Crime and Delinquency* 32 (1995): 175–190.

43. Syed Moniruzzaman and Ragnar Andersson, "Age and Sex-specific Analysis of Homicide Mortality as a Function of Economic Development: A Crossnational Comparison." *Scandinavian Journal of Public Health* 33 (2005): 464–471.
44. James Short and F. Ivan Nye, "Extent of Unrecorded Juvenile Delinquency, Tentative Conclusions," *Journal of Criminal Law, Criminology, and Police Science* 49 (1958): 296–302.
45. Ivan Nye, James Short, and Virgil Olsen, "Socio-Economic Status and Delinquent Behavior," *American Journal of Sociology* 63 (1958): 381–389; Robert Dentler and Lawrence Monroe, "Social Correlates of Early Adolescent Theft," *American Sociological Review* 63 (1961): 733–743. See also Terence Thornberry and Margaret Farnworth, "Social Correlates of Criminal Involvement: Further Evidence of the Relationship between Social Status and Criminal Behavior," *American Sociological Review* 47 (1982): 505–518.
46. Charles Tittle, Wayne Villemez, and Douglas Smith, "The Myth of Social Class and Criminality: An Empirical Assessment of the Empirical Evidence," *American Sociological Review* 43 (1978): 643–656.
47. Charles Tittle and Robert Meier, "Specifying the SES/Delinquency Relationship," *Criminology* 28 (1990): 271–301.
48. R. Gregory Dunaway, Francis Cullen, Velmer Burton Jr., and T. David Evans, "The Myth of Social Class and Crime Revisited: An Examination of Class and Adult Criminality," *Criminology* 38 (2000): 589–632.
49. Delbert Elliott and Suzanne Ageton, "Reconciling Race and Class Differences in Self-Reported and Official Estimates of Delinquency," *American Sociological Review* 45 (1980): 95–110.
50. See also Delbert Elliott and David Huizinga, "Social Class and Delinquent Behavior in a National Youth Panel: 1976–1980," *Criminology* 21 (1983): 149–177. For a similar view, see John Braithwaite, "The Myth of Social Class and Criminality Reconsidered," *American Sociological Review* 46 (1981): 35–58; Hindelang, Hirschi, and Weis, *Measuring Delinquency,* p. 196.
51. Judith Blau and Peter Blau, "The Cost of Inequality: Metropolitan Structure and Violent Crime," *American Sociological Review* 147 (1982): 114–129; Richard Block, "Community Environment and Violent Crime," *Criminology* 17 (1979): 46–57; Robert Sampson, "Structural Sources of Variation in Race-Age-Specific Rates of Offending across Major U.S. Cities," *Criminology* 23 (1985): 647–673.
52. Chin-Chi Hsieh and M. D. Pugh, "Poverty, Income Inequality, and Violent Crime: A Meta-Analysis of Recent Aggregate Data Studies," *Criminal Justice Review* 18 (1993): 182–199.
53. Richard Miech, Avshalom Caspi, Terrie Moffitt, Bradley Entner Wright, and Phil Silva, "Low Socioeconomic Status and Mental Disorders: A Longitudinal Study of Selection and Causation during Young Adulthood," *American Journal of Sociology* 104 (1999): 1,096–1,131; Marvin Krohn, Alan Lizotte, and Cynthia Perez, "The Interrelationship between Substance Use and Precocious Transitions to Adult Sexuality," *Journal of Health and Social Behavior* 38 (1997): 87–103, at 88; Richard Jessor, "Risk Behavior in Adolescence: A Psychosocial Framework for Understanding and Action," in *Adolescents at Risk: Medical and Social Perspectives,* eds. D. E. Rogers and E. Ginzburg (Boulder, CO: Westview, 1992).
54. Travis Hirschi and Michael Gottfredson, "Age and the Explanation of Crime," *American Journal of Sociology* 89 (1983): 552–584, at 581.
55. Darrell Steffensmeier and Cathy Streifel, "Age, Gender, and Crime across Three Historical Periods: 1935, 1960 and 1985," *Social Forces* 69 (1991): 869–894.
56. For a comprehensive review of crime and the elderly, see Kyle Kercher, "Causes and Correlates of Crime Committed by the Elderly," in *Critical Issues in Aging Policy,* eds. E. Borgatta and R. Montgomery (Beverly Hills, CA: Sage, 1987), pp. 254–306; Darrell Steffensmeier, "The Invention of the 'New' Senior Citizen Criminal," *Research on Aging* 9 (1987): 281–311.
57. Hirschi and Gottfredson, "Age and the Explanation of Crime."
58. Robert Agnew, "An Integrated Theory of the Adolescent Peak in Offending," *Youth & Society* 34 (2003): 263–302.
59. Margo Wilson and Martin Daly, "Life Expectancy, Economic Inequality, Homicide, and Reproductive Timing in Chicago Neighbourhoods," *British Journal of Medicine* 314 (1997): 1,271–1,274.
60. Edward Mulvey and John LaRosa, "Delinquency Cessation and Adolescent Development: Preliminary Data," *American Journal of Orthopsychiatry* 56 (1986): 212–224.
61. James Q. Wilson and Richard Herrnstein, *Crime and Human Nature* (New York: Simon & Schuster, 1985), pp. 126–147.
62. Ibid., p. 219.
63. Erich Labouvie, "Maturing Out of Substance Use: Selection and Self-Correction," *Journal of Drug Issues* 26 (1996): 457–474.
64. Cesare Lombroso, *The Female Offender* (New York: Appleton, 1920), p. 122.
65. Ibid.
66. Alan Booth and D. Wayne Osgood, "The Influence of Testosterone on Deviance in Adulthood: Assessing and Explaining the Relationship," *Criminology* 31 (1993): 93–118.
67. Jean Bottcher, "Social Practices of Gender: How Gender Relates to Delinquency in the Everyday Lives of High-Risk Youths," *Criminology* 39 (2001): 893–932.
68. Debra Kaysen, Miranda Morris, Shireen Rizvi, and Patricia Resick, "Peritraumatic Responses and Their Relationship to Perceptions of Threat in Female Crime Victims," *Violence Against Women* 11(2005): 1,515–1,535.
69. Freda Adler, *Sisters in Crime* (New York: McGraw-Hill, 1975); Rita James Simon, *The Contemporary Woman and Crime* (Washington, DC: U.S. Government Printing Office, 1975).
70. David Rowe, Alexander Vazsonyi, and Daniel Flannery, "Sex Differences in Crime: Do Mean and Within-Sex Variation Have Similar Causes?" *Journal of Research in Crime and Delinquency* 32 (1995): 84–100; Michael Hindelang, "Age, Sex, and the Versatility of Delinquency Involvements," *Social Forces* 14 (1971): 525–534; Martin Gold, *Delinquent Behavior in an American City* (Belmont, CA: Brooks/Cole, 1970); Gary Jensen and Raymond Eve, "Sex Differences in Delinquency: An Examination of Popular Sociological Explanations," *Criminology* 13 (1976): 427–448.
71. Knut Steen and Steinar Hunskaar, "Gender and Physical Violence," *Social Science & Medicine* 59 (2004): 567–571.
72. Finn-Aage Esbensen and Elizabeth Piper Deschenes, "A Multisite Examination of Youth Gang Membership: Does Gender Matter?" *Criminology* 36 (1998): 799–828.
73. Darrell Steffensmeier, Jennifer Schwartz, Hua Zhong, and Jeff Ackerman, "An Assessment of Recent Trends in Girls' Violence Using Diverse Longitudinal Sources: Is the Gender Gap Closing?" *Criminology* 43 (2005): 355–406.
74. Susan Miller, Carol Gregory, and Leeann Iovanni, "One Size Fits All? A Gender-Neutral Approach to a Gender-Specific Problem: Contrasting Batterer Treatment Programs for Male and Female Offenders," *Criminal Justice Policy Review* 16 (2005): 336–359.
75. Leroy Gould, "Who Defines Delinquency: A Comparison of Self-Report and Officially Reported Indices of Delinquency for Three Racial Groups," *Social Problems* 16 (1969): 325–336; Harwin Voss, "Ethnic Differentials in Delinquency in Honolulu," *Journal of Criminal Law, Criminology, and Police Science* 54 (1963): 322–327; Ronald Akers, Marvin Krohn, Marcia Radosevich, and Lonn Lanza-Kaduce, "Social Characteristics and Self-Reported Delinquency," in *Sociology of Delinquency,* ed. Gary Jensen (Beverly Hills, CA: Sage, 1981), pp. 48–62.
76. Institute for Social Research, *Monitoring the Future* (Ann Arbor, MI: Author, 2001).
77. Paul Tracy, "Race and Class Differences in Official and Self-Reported Delinquency," in *From Boy to Man, from Delinquency*

to Crime, eds. Marvin Wolfgang, Terence Thornberry, and Robert Figlio (Chicago: University of Chicago Press, 1987), p. 120.

78. Miriam Sealock and Sally Simpson, "Unraveling Bias in Arrest Decisions: The Role of Juvenile Offender Type-Scripts," *Justice Quarterly* 15 (1998): 427–457.

79. Phillipe Rushton, "Race and Crime: An International Dilemma," *Society* 32 (1995): 37–42; for a rebuttal, see Jerome Neapolitan, "Cross-National Variation in Homicides: Is Race a Factor?" *Criminology* 36 (1998): 139–156.

80. Robin Shepard Engel and Jennifer Calnon, "Examining the Influence of Drivers' Characteristics during Traffic Stops with Police: Results from a National Survey," *Justice Quarterly* 21 (2004): 49–90.

81. Daniel Georges-Abeyie, "Definitional Issues: Race, Ethnicity and Official Crime/Victimization Rates," in *The Criminal Justice System and Blacks,* ed. D. Georges-Abeyie (New York: Clark Boardman, 1984), p. 12; Robert Sampson, "Race and Criminal Violence: A Demographically Disaggregated Analysis of Urban Homicide," *Crime and Delinquency* 31 (1985): 47–82.

82. James Comer, "Black Violence and Public Policy," in *American Violence and Public Policy,* ed. Lynn Curtis (New Haven, CT: Yale University Press, 1985), pp. 63–86.

83. Michael Leiber and Jayne Stairs, "Race, Contexts and the Use of Intake Diversion," *Journal of Research in Crime and Delinquency* 36 (1999): 56–86; Darrell Steffensmeier, Jeffery Ulmer, and John Kramer, "The Interaction of Race, Gender, and Age in Criminal Sentencing: The Punishment Cost of Being Young, Black, and Male," *Criminology* 36 (1998): 763–798.

84. Hurbert Blalock, Jr., *Toward a Theory of Minority-Group Relations* (New York: Capricorn Books, 1967).

85. Karen Parker, Briam Stults, and Stephen Rice, "Racial Threat, Concentrated Disadvantage and Social Control: Considering the Macro-Level Sources of Variation in Arrests," *Criminology* 43 (2005): 1,111–1,134; Lisa Stolzenberg, J. Stewart D'Alessio, and David Eitle, "A Multilevel Test of Racial Threat Theory," *Criminology* 42 (2004): 673–698.

86. Michael Leiber and Kristan Fox, "Race and the Impact of Detention on Juvenile Justice Decision Making," *Crime and Delinquency* 51 (2005): 470–497; Traci Schlesinger, "Racial and Ethnic Disparity in Pretrial Criminal Processing," *Justice Quarterly* 22 (2005): 170–192.

87. Tracy Nobiling, Cassia Spohn, and Miriam DeLone, "A Tale of Two Counties: Unemployment and Sentence Severity," *Justice Quarterly* 15 (1998): 459–486.

88. Alexander Weiss and Steven Chermak, "The News Value of African-American Victims: An Examination of the Media's Presentation of Homicide," *Journal of Crime and Justice* 21 (1998): 71–84.

89. Jefferson Holcomb, Marian Williams, and Stephen Demuth, "White Female Victims and Death Penalty Disparity Research," *Justice Quarterly* 21 (2004): 877–902.

90. Robert Sampson, Jeffrey Morenoff, and Stephen Raudenbush, "Social Anatomy of Racial and Ethnic Disparities in Violence," *American Journal of Public Health* 95 (2005): 224–233; Joanne Kaufman, "Explaining the Race/Ethnicity–Violence Relationship: Neighborhood Context and Social Psychological Processes," *Justice Quarterly* 22 (2005): 224–251.

91. Karen Parker and Patricia McCall, "Structural Conditions and Racial Homicide Patterns: A Look at the Multiple Disadvantages in Urban Areas," *Criminology* 37 (1999): 447–469.

92. Gary LaFree and Richard Arum, "The Impact of Racially Inclusive Schooling on Adult Incarceration Rates among U.S. Cohorts of African Americans and Whites Since 1930," *Criminology* 44 (2006): 73–103.

93. R. Kelly Raley, "A Shortage of Marriageable Men? A Note on the Role of Cohabitation in Black-White Differences in Marriage Rates," *American Sociological Review* 61 (1996): 973–983.

94. Julie Phillips, "Variation in African-American Homicide Rates: An Assessment of Potential Explanations," *Criminology* 35 (1997): 527–559.

95. Gary LaFree and Richard Arum, "The Impact of Racially Inclusive Schooling on Adult Incarceration Rates among U.S. Cohorts of African Americans and Whites Since 1930"; Robert Sampson, Jeffrey Morenoff, and Stephen Raudenbush, "Social Anatomy of Racial and Ethnic Disparities in Violence."

96. Marvin Wolfgang, Robert Figlio, and Thorsten Sellin, *Delinquency in a Birth Cohort* (Chicago: University of Chicago Press, 1972).

97. See Thorsten Sellin and Marvin Wolfgang, *The Measurement of Delinquency* (New York: Wiley, 1964), p. 120.

98. Paul Tracy and Robert Figlio, "Chronic Recidivism in the 1958 Birth Cohort." Paper presented at the American Society of Criminology meeting, Toronto, October 1982; Marvin Wolfgang, "Delinquency in Two Birth Cohorts," in *Perspective Studies of Crime and Delinquency,* eds. Katherine Teilmann Van Dusen and Sarnoff Mednick (Boston: Kluwer-Nijhoff, 1983), pp. 7–17. The following sections rely heavily on these sources.

99. Lyle Shannon, *Criminal Career Opportunity* (New York: Human Sciences Press, 1988).

100. D. J. West and David P. Farrington, *The Delinquent Way of Life* (London: Heinemann, 1977).

101. Michael Schumacher and Gwen Kurz, *The 8% Solution: Preventing Serious Repeat Juvenile Crime* (Thousand Oaks, CA: Sage, 1999).

102. Peter Jones, Philip Harris, James Fader, and Lori Grubstein, "Identifying Chronic Juvenile Offenders," *Justice Quarterly* 18 (2001): 478–507.

103. Michael Ezell and Amy D'Unger, "Offense Specialization among Serious Youthful Offenders: A Longitudinal Analysis of a California Youth Authority Sample" (Durham, NC: Duke University, 1998, unpublished report).

Chapter 3. Victims and Victimization

1. New England News, "Authorities Develop Case against Bouncer in Grad Student Slaying," March 24, 2006, www1.whdh.com/news/articles/local/BO16577/.

2. Ibid.

3. Children's Safety Network Economics and Insurance Resource Center, "State Costs of Violence Perpetrated by Youth," www.csneirc.org/pubs/tables/youth-viol.htm (accessed July 12, 2000).

4. Ted Miller, Mark Cohen, and Brian Wiersema, *The Extent and Costs of Crime Victimization: A New Look* (Washington, DC: National Institute of Justice, 1996).

5. Ted R. Miller, Mark A. Cohen, and Brian Wiersema, *Victim Costs and Consequences: A New Look* (Washington, DC: National Institute of Justice, 1996), p. 9, table 2.

6. Ross Macmillan, "Adolescent Victimization and Income Deficits in Adulthood: Rethinking the Costs of Criminal Violence from a Life-Course Perspective," *Criminology* 38 (2000): 553–588.

7. James Anderson, Terry Grandison, and Laronistine Dyson, "Victims of Random Violence and the Public Health Implication: A Health Care or Criminal Justice Issue," *Journal of Criminal Justice* 24 (1996): 379–393.

8. Rebecca Campbell and Sheela Raja, "Secondary Victimization of Rape Victims: Insights from Mental Health Professionals Who Treat Survivors of Violence," *Violence and Victims* 14 (1999): 261–274.

9. Peter Finn, *Victims* (Washington, DC: Bureau of Justice Statistics, 1988), p. 1.

10. Angela Scarpa, Sara Chiara Haden, and Jimmy Hurley, "Community Violence Victimization and Symptoms of Posttraumatic Stress Disorder: The Moderating Effects of Coping and Social Support," *Journal of Interpersonal Violence* 21 (2006): 446–469.

11. Catherine Grus, "Child Abuse: Correlations with Hostile Attributions," *Journal of Developmental & Behavioral Pediatrics* 24 (2003): 296–298.

12. Kim Logio, "Gender, Race, Childhood Abuse, and Body Image among Adolescents," *Violence Against Women* 9 (2003): 931–955.
13. Jeanne Kaufman and Cathy Spatz Widom, "Childhood Victimization, Running Away, and Delinquency," *Journal of Research in Crime and Delinquency* 36 (1999): 347–370.
14. N. N. Sarkar and Rina Sarkar, "Sexual Assault on Woman: Its Impact on Her Life and Living in Society," *Sexual & Relationship Therapy* 20 (2005): 407–419.
15. Michael Wiederman, Randy Sansone, and Lori Sansone, "History of Trauma and Attempted Suicide among Women in a Primary Care Setting," *Violence and Victims* 13 (1998): 3–11; Susan Leslie Bryant and Lillian Range, "Suicidality in College Women Who Were Sexually and Physically Abused and Physically Punished by Parents," *Violence and Victims* 10 (1995): 195–215; William Downs and Brenda Miller, "Relationships between Experiences of Parental Violence during Childhood and Women's Self-Esteem," *Violence and Victims* 13 (1998): 63–78; Sally Davies-Netley, Michael Hurlburt, and Richard Hough, "Childhood Abuse as a Precursor to Homelessness for Homeless Women with Severe Mental Illness," *Violence and Victims* 11 (1996): 129–142.
16. Jane Siegel and Linda Williams, "Risk Factors for Sexual Victimization of Women," *Violence Against Women* 9 (2003): 902–930.
17. Michael Miner, Jill Klotz Flitter, and Beatrice Robinson. "Association of Sexual Revictimization with Sexuality and Psychological Function," *Journal of Interpersonal Violence* 21(2006): 503–524.
18. Lana Stermac and Emily Paradis, "Homeless Women and Victimization: Abuse and Mental Health History among Homeless Rape Survivors," *Resources for Feminist Research* 28 (2001): 65–81.
19. Gregory Stuart, Todd M. Moore, Kristina Coop Gordon, Susan Ramsey, and Christopher Kahler, "Psychopathology in Women Arrested for Domestic Violence," *Journal of Interpersonal Violence* 21 (2006): 376–389; Caron Zlotnick, Dawn Johnson, and Robert Kohn, "Intimate Partner Violence and Long-Term Psychosocial Functioning in a National Sample of American Women," *Journal of Interpersonal Violence* 21 (2006): 262–275.
20. K. Daniel O'Leary, "Psychological Abuse: A Variable Deserving Critical Attention in Domestic Violence," *Violence and Victims* 14 (1999): 1–21.
21. Ron Acierno, Alyssa Rheingold, Heidi Resnick, and Dean Kilpatrick, "Predictors of Fear of Crime in Older Adults," *Journal of Anxiety Disorders* 18 (2004): 385–396.
22. Pamela Wilcox Rountree, "A Reexamination of the Crime–Fear Linkage," *Journal of Research in Crime and Delinquency* 35 (1998): 341–372.
23. Ibid.
24. Susan Brison, *Aftermath: Violence and the Remaking of a Self* (Princeton, NJ: Princeton University Press, 2001).
25. Timothy Ireland and Cathy Spatz Widom, *Childhood Victimization and Risk for Alcohol and Drug Arrests* (Washington, DC: National Institute of Justice, 1995).
26. Brigette Erwin, Elana Newman, Robert McMackin, Carlo Morrissey, and Danny Kaloupek, "PTSD, Malevolent Environment, and Criminality among Criminally Involved Male Adolescents," *Criminal Justice and Behavior* 27 (2000): 196–215.
27. Ulrich Orth, Leo Montada, and Andreas Maercker, "Feelings of Revenge, Retaliation Motive, and Posttraumatic Stress Reactions in Crime Victims," *Journal of Interpersonal Violence* 21 (2006): 229–243.
28. Cathy Spatz Widom, *The Cycle of Violence* (Washington, DC: National Institute of Justice, 1992), p. 1.
29. Bureau of Justice Statistics, Criminal Victimization, www.ojp.usdoj.gov/bjs/cvictgen.htm (accessed March 25, 2006).
30. J. DeVoe, K. Peter, M. Noonan, T. Snyder, and K. Baum, *Indicators of School Crime and Safety: 2005* (U.S. Departments of Education and Justice, Washington, DC: U.S. Government Printing Office, 2005).
31. Victoria Titterington, "A Retrospective Investigation of Gender Inequality and Female Homicide Victimization," *Sociological Spectrum* 26 (2006): 205–231.
32. Lamar Jordan, "Law Enforcement and the Elderly: A Concern for the 21st Century," *FBI Law Enforcement Bulletin* 71 (2002): 20–24.
33. Tracy Dietz and James Wright "Age and Gender Differences and Predictors of Victimization of the Older Homeless," *Journal of Elder Abuse & Neglect* 17(2005): 37–59.
34. Karin Wittebrood and Paul Nieuwbeerta, "Criminal Victimization during One's Life Course: The Effects of Previous Victimization and Patterns of Routine Activities," *Journal of Research in Crime and Delinquency* 37 (2000): 91– 122; Janet Lauritsen and Kenna Davis Quinet, "Repeat Victimizations among Adolescents and Young Adults," *Journal of Quantitative Criminology* 11 (1995): 143–163.
35. Denise Osborn, Dan Ellingworth, Tim Hope, and Alan Trickett, "Are Repeatedly Victimized Households Different?" *Journal of Quantitative Criminology* 12 (1996): 223–245.
36. Graham Farrell, "Predicting and Preventing Revictimization," in *Crime and Justice: An Annual Review of Research,* eds. Michael Tonry and David Farrington, vol. 20 (Chicago: University of Chicago Press, 1995), pp. 61–126.
37. Ibid., p. 61.
38. David Finkelhor and Nancy Asigian, "Risk Factors for Youth Victimization: Beyond a Lifestyles/Routine Activities Theory Approach," *Violence and Victimization* 11 (1996): 3–19.
39. Graham Farrell, Coretta Phillips, and Ken Pease, "Like Taking Candy: Why Does Repeat Victimization Occur?" *British Journal of Criminology* 35 (1995): 384–399.
40. Christopher Innes and Lawrence Greenfeld, *Violent State Prisoners and Their Victims* (Washington, DC: Bureau of Justice Statistics, 1990).
41. Hans von Hentig, *The Criminal and His Victim: Studies in the Sociobiology of Crime* (New Haven, CT: Yale University Press, 1948), p. 384.
42. Marvin Wolfgang, *Patterns of Criminal Homicide* (Philadelphia: University of Pennsylvania Press, 1958).
43. Menachem Amir, *Patterns in Forcible Rape* (Chicago: University of Chicago Press, 1971).
44. Susan Estrich, *Real Rape* (Cambridge, MA: Harvard University Press, 1987).
45. Edem Avakame, "Female's Labor Force Participation and Intimate Femicide: An Empirical Assessment of the Backlash Hypothesis," *Violence and Victims* 14 (1999): 277–283.
46. Martin Daly and Margo Wilson, *Homicide* (New York: Aldine de Gruyter, 1988).
47. Lening Zhang, John W. Welte, and William F. Wieczorek, "Deviant Lifestyle and Crime Victimization," *Journal of Criminal Justice* 29 (2001): 133–143.
48. Dan Hoyt, Kimberly Ryan, and Mari Cauce, "Personal Victimization in a High-Risk Environment: Homeless and Runaway Adolescents," *Journal of Research in Crime and Delinquency* 36 (1999): 371–392.
49. See, generally, Gary Gottfredson and Denise Gottfredson, *Victimization in Schools* (New York: Plenum Press, 1985).
50. Gary Jensen and David Brownfield, "Gender, Lifestyles, and Victimization: Beyond Routine Activity Theory," *Violence and Victims* 1 (1986): 85–99.
51. Dana Haynie and Alex Piquero. "Pubertal Development and Physical Victimization in Adolescence," *Journal of Research in Crime and Delinquency* 43 (2006): 3–35.
52. Rolf Loeber, Mary DeLamatre, George Tita, Jacqueline Cohen, Magda Stouthamer-Loeber, and David Farrington, "Gun Injury and Mortality: The Delinquent Backgrounds of Juvenile Offenders," *Violence and Victim* 14 (1999): 339–351.
53. Adam Dobrin, "The Risk of Offending on Homicide Victimization: A Case Control Study," *Journal of Research in Crime and Delinquency* 38 (2001): 154–173.

54. Bonnie Fisher, John Sloan, Francis Cullen, and Chunmeng Lu, "Crime in the Ivory Tower: The Level and Sources of Student Victimization," *Criminology* 36 (1998): 671–710.
55. Bonnie Fisher, Francis Cullen, and Michael Turner, *The Sexual Victimization of College Women* (Washington, DC: National Institute of Justice, 2001).
56. Stephen Farrall and S. Maltby, "The Victimisation of Probationers," *Howard Journal of Criminal Justice* 42 (2003): 32–55.
57. Rolf Loeber, Larry Kalb, and David Huizinga, *Juvenile Delinquency and Serious Injury Victimization* (Washington, DC: Office of Juvenile Justice and Delinquency Prevention, 2001).
58. Maryse Richards, Reed Larson, and Bobbi-Viegas Miller, "Risky and Protective Contexts and Exposure to Violence in Urban African American Young Adolescents" *Journal of Clinical Child and Adolescent Psychology* 33 (2004): 138–148.
59. James Garofalo, "Reassessing the Lifestyle Model of Criminal Victimization," in *Positive Criminology,* eds. Michael Gottfredson and Travis Hirschi (Newbury Park, CA: Sage, 1987), pp. 23–42.
60. Terance Miethe and David McDowall, "Contextual Effects in Models of Criminal Victimization," *Social Forces* 71 (1993): 741–759.
61. Rodney Stark, "Deviant Places: A Theory of the Ecology of Crime," *Criminology* 25 (1987): 893–911.
62. Ibid., p. 902.
63. Pamela Wilcox Rountree, Kenneth Land, and Terance Miethe, "Macro–Micro Integration in the Study of Victimization: A Hierarchical Logistic Model Analysis across Seattle Neighborhoods." Paper presented at the annual meeting of the American Society of Criminology, Phoenix, AZ, November 1993.
64. Lawrence Cohen and Marcus Felson, "Social Change and Crime Rate Trends: A Routine Activities Approach," *American Sociological Review* 44 (1979): 588–608.
65. For a review, see James LeBeau and Thomas Castellano, "The Routine Activities Approach: An Inventory and Critique." Unpublished paper, Center for the Studies of Crime, Delinquency, and Corrections, Southern Illinois University, Carbondale, 1987.
66. Teresa LaGrange, "The Impact of Neighborhoods, Schools, and Malls on the Spatial Distribution of Property Damage," *Journal of Research in Crime and Delinquency* 36 (1999): 393–422.
67. Denise Gottfredson and David Soulé, "The Timing of Property Crime, Violent Crime, and Substance Use among Juveniles," *Journal of Research in Crime & Delinquency* 42 (2005): 110–120.
68. Lawrence Cohen, Marcus Felson, and Kenneth Land, "Property Crime Rates in the United States: A Macrodynamic Analysis, 1947–1977, with Ex-ante Forecasts for the Mid-1980s," *American Journal of Sociology* 86 (1980): 90–118.
69. Steven Messner, Lawrence Raffalovich, and Richard McMillan, "Economic Deprivation and Changes in Homicide Arrest Rates for White and Black Youths, 1967–1998: A National Time Series Analysis," *Criminology* 39 (2001): 591–614.
70. Melanie Wellsmith and Amy Burrell, "The Influence of Purchase Price and Ownership Levels on Theft Targets: The Example of Domestic Burglary," *British Journal of Criminology* 45 (2005): 741–764.
71. Terence Miethe and Robert Meier, *Crime and Its Social Context: Toward an Integrated Theory of Offenders, Victims, and Situations* (Albany, NY: State University of New York Press, 1994).
72. Richard Felson, "Routine Activities and Involvement in Violence as Actor, Witness, or Target," *Violence and Victimization* 12 (1997): 209–223.
73. Georgina Hammock and Deborah Richardson, "Perceptions of Rape: The Influence of Closeness of Relationship, Intoxication, and Sex of Participant," *Violence and Victimization* 12 (1997): 237–247.
74. Wittebrood and Nieuwbeerta, "Criminal Victimization during One's Life Course," pp. 112–113.
75. Patricia Resnick, "Psychological Effects of Victimization: Implications for the Criminal Justice System," *Crime and Delinquency* 33 (1987): 468–478.
76. Dean Kilpatrick, Benjamin Saunders, Lois Veronen, Connie Best, and Judith Von, "Criminal Victimization: Lifetime Prevalence, Reporting to Police, and Psychological Impact," *Crime and Delinquency* 33 (1987): 479–489.
77. U.S. Department of Justice, *Report of the President's Task Force on Victims of Crime* (Washington, DC: U.S. Government Printing Office, 1983).
78. Ibid., pp. 2–10; "Review on Victims: Witnesses of Crime," *Massachusetts Lawyers Weekly,* April 25, 1983, p. 26.
79. Robert Davis, *Crime Victims: Learning How to Help Them* (Washington, DC: National Institute of Justice, 1987).
80. This section leans heavily on Albert Roberts, "Delivery of Services to Crime Victims: A National Survey," *American Journal of Orthopsychiatry* 6 (1991): 128–137. See also Albert Roberts, *Helping Crime Victims: Research, Policy, and Practice* (Newbury Park, CA: Sage, 1990).
81. Randall Schmidt, "Crime Victim Compensation Legislation: A Comparative Study," *Victimology* 5 (1980): 428–437.
82. Ibid.
83. National Association of Crime Victim Compensation Boards, http://nacvcb.org/ (accessed September 24, 2003).
84. Rebecca Campbell, "Rape Survivors' Experiences with the Legal and Medical Systems: Do Rape Victim Advocates Make a Difference?" *Violence Against Women* 12 (2006): 30–45.
85. Ulrich Orth and Andreas Maercker, "Do Trials of Perpetrators Retraumatize Crime Victims?" *Journal of Interpersonal Violence* 19 (2004): 212–228.
86. *Payne v. Tennessee*, 111 S.Ct. 2597, 115 L.Ed.2d 720 (1991).
87. Robert Davis and Barbara Smith, "The Effects of Victim Impact Statements on Sentencing Decisions: A Test in an Urban Setting," *Justice Quarterly* 11 (1994): 453–69; Edna Erez and Pamela Tontodonato, "The Effect of Victim Participation in Sentencing on Sentence Outcome," *Criminology* 28 (1990): 451–474.
88. Douglas E. Beloof, "Constitutional Implications of Crime Victims as Participants," *Cornell Law Review* 88 (2003): 282–305.
89. Pater Jaffe, Marlies Sudermann, Deborah Reitzel, and Steve Killip, "An Evaluation of a Secondary School Primary Prevention Program on Violence in Intimate Relationships," *Violence and Victims* 7 (1992): 129–145.
90. Andrew Karmen, "Victim–Offender Reconciliation Programs: Pro and Con," *Perspectives of the American Probation and Parole Association* 20 (1996): 11–14.
91. National Center for Victims of Crime, www.ncvc.org/policy/issues/rights/ (accessed September 24, 2003).
92. Ibid., pp. 9–10.
93. www.nsopr.gov/ (accessed March 27, 2006).

Chapter 4. Choice Theory: Because They Want To

1. Based on the U.S. Department of Justice press release, "Jury Convicts Hollywood Movie Pirate of Copyright Infringement and Other Federal Charges," June 30, 2005; FBI, "Pirates of Hollywood or the Curse of the Green-Glow Camcorder," July 20, 2005, www.fbi.gov/page2/july05/pirate072005.htm (accessed September 8, 2005).
2. Bob Roshier, *Controlling Crime* (Chicago: Lyceum Books, 1989), p. 10.
3. Gary Becker, "Crime and Punishment: An Economic Approach," *The Journal of Political Economy* 76 (1968): 169–217.
4. James Q. Wilson, *Thinking About Crime,* rev. ed. (New York: Vintage Books, 1983), p. 260.
5. See, generally, Derek Cornish and Ronald Clarke, eds., *The Reasoning Criminal: Rational Choice Perspectives on Offending* (New York: Springer Verlag, 1986); Philip Cook, "The Demand and Supply of Criminal Opportunities," in *Crime and Justice,* vol. 7, eds. Michael Tonry and Norval Morris (Chicago: University of Chicago Press, 1986), pp. 1–28;

Ronald Clarke and Derek Cornish, "Modeling Offenders' Decisions: A Framework for Research and Policy," in *Crime and Justice,* vol. 6, eds. Michael Tonry and Norval Morris (Chicago: University of Chicago Press, 1985), pp. 147–187; Morgan Reynolds, *Crime by Choice: An Economic Analysis* (Dallas, TX: Fisher Institute, 1985).

6. George Rengert and John Wasilchick, *Suburban Burglary: A Time and Place for Everything* (Springfield, IL: Charles C Thomas, 1985).

7. Derek Cornish and Ronald Clarke, "Understanding Crime Displacement: An Application of Rational Choice Theory," *Criminology* 25 (1987): 933–947.

8. Lloyd Phillips and Harold Votey, "The Influence of Police Interventions and Alternative Income Sources on the Dynamic Process of Choosing Crime as a Career," *Journal of Quantitative Criminology* 3 (1987): 251–274.

9. Michael Gottfredson and Travis Hirschi, *A General Theory of Crime* (Stanford, CA: Stanford University Press, 1990).

10. Jeannette Angell, "Confessions of an Ivy League Hooker," *Boston Magazine,* August 2004, pp. 120–134.

11. Christopher Uggen and Melissa Thompson, "The Socioeconomic Determinants of Ill-Gotten Gains: Within-Person Changes in Drug Use and Illegal Earnings," *American Journal of Sociology* 109 (2003): 146–185.

12. Pierre Tremblay and Carlo Morselli, "Patterns in Criminal Achievement: Wilson and Abrahmse Revisited," *Criminology* 38 (2000): 633–660.

13. Steven Levitt and Sudhir Alladi Venkatesh, "An Economic Analysis of a Drug-Selling Gang's Finances," NBER Working Papers 6592 (Cambridge, MA: National Bureau of Economic Research, 1998).

14. Bill McCarthy, "New Economics of Sociological Criminology," *Annual Review of Sociology* (2002): 417–442.

15. Ronald Akers, "Rational Choice, Deterrence and Social Learning Theory in Criminology: The Path Not Taken," *Journal of Criminal Law and Criminology* 81 (1990): 653–676.

16. Neal Shover, *Aging Criminals* (Beverly Hills, CA: Sage, 1985).

17. Robert Agnew, "Determinism, Indeterminism, and Crime: An Empirical Exploration," *Criminology* 33 (1995): 83–109.

18. Ibid., pp. 103–104.

19. Bruce Jacobs and Jody Miller, "Crack Dealing, Gender, and Arrest Avoidance," *Social Problems* 45 (1998): 550–566.

20. Leanne Fiftal Alarid, James Marquart, Velmer Burton Jr., Francis Cullen, and Steven Cuvelier, "Women's Roles in Serious Offenses: A Study of Adult Felons," *Justice Quarterly* 13 (1996): 431–454, at p. 448.

21. Bruce Jacobs, "Crack Dealers' Apprehension Avoidance Techniques: A Case of Restrictive Deterrence," *Justice Quarterly* 13 (1996): 359–381.

22. Ibid., p. 367.

23. Ibid., p. 372.

24. Paul Cromwell, James Olson, and D'Aunn Wester Avary, *Breaking and Entering: An Ethnographic Analysis of Burglary* (Newbury Park, CA: Sage, 1989), p. 24.

25. Ibid., pp. 30–32.

26. George Rengert and John Wasilchick, *Space, Time, and Crime: Ethnographic Insights into Residential Burglary* (Washington, DC: National Institute of Justice, 1989). See also Rengert and Wasilchick, *Suburban Burglary.*

27. Matthew Robinson, "Lifestyles, Routine Activities, and Residential Burglary Victimization," *Journal of Criminal Justice* 22 (1999): 27–52.

28. Patrick Donnelly and Charles Kimble, "Community Organizing, Environmental Change, and Neighborhood Crime," *Crime and Delinquency* 43 (1997): 493–511.

29. Ronald Clarke and Marcus Felson, "Introduction: Criminology, Routine Activity and Rational Choice," in *Routine Activity and Rational Choice* (New Brunswick, NJ: Transaction, 1993), pp. 1–14.

30. Associated Press, "Thrift Hearings Resume Today in Senate," *Boston Globe,* January 2, 1991, p. 10.

31. Ronald Clarke and Patricia Harris, "Auto Theft and Its Prevention," in *Crime and Justice: An Annual Edition,* eds. Michael Tonry and Norval Morris (Chicago: University of Chicago Press, 1992), pp. 1–54, at pp. 20–21.

32. Melanie Wellsmith and Amy Burrell, "The Influence of Purchase Price and Ownership Levels on Theft Targets: The Example of Domestic Burglary," *British Journal of Criminology* 45 (2005): 741–764.

33. Wim Bernasco and Paul Nieuwbeerta, "How Do Residential Burglars Select Target Areas? A New Approach to the Analysis of Criminal Location Choice," *British Journal of Criminology* 45 (2005): 296–315.

34. Gordon Knowles, "Deception, Detection, and Evasion: A Trade Craft Analysis of Honolulu, Hawaii's Street Crack Cocaine Traffickers," *Journal of Criminal Justice* 27 (1999): 443–455.

35. John Petraitis, Brian Flay, and Todd Miller, "Reviewing Theories of Adolescent Substance Use: Organizing Pieces in the Puzzle," *Psychological Bulletin* 117 (1995): 67–86.

36. George Rengert, *The Geography of Illegal Drugs* (Boulder, CO: Westview Press, 1996).

37. Levitt and Venkatesh, "An Economic Analysis of a Drug-Selling Gang's Finances."

38. Richard Felson and Steven Messner, "To Kill or Not to Kill? Lethal Outcomes in Injurious Attacks," *Criminology* 34 (1996): 519–545, at p. 541.

39. Richard Wright and Scott Decker, *Armed Robbers in Action: Stickups and Street Culture* (Boston: Northeastern University Press, 1997).

40. Ibid., p. 52.

41. William Smith, Sharon Glave Frazee, and Elizabeth Davison, "Furthering the Integration of Routine Activity and Social Disorganization Theories: Small Units of Analysis and the Study of Street Robbery as a Diffusion Process," *Criminology* 38 (2000): 489–521.

42. Paul Bellair, "Informal Surveillance and Street Crime: A Complex Relationship," *Criminology* 38 (2000): 137–167.

43. John Gibbs and Peggy Shelly, "Life in the Fast Lane: A Retrospective View by Commercial Thieves," *Journal of Research in Crime and Delinquency* 19 (1982): 229–230.

44. Gary Kleck and Don Kates, *Armed: New Perspectives on Guns* (Amherst, NY: Prometheus Books, 2001).

45. Elizabeth Ehrhardt Mustaine and Richard Tewksbury, "Predicting Risks of Larceny Theft Victimization: A Routine Activity Analysis Using Refined Lifestyle Measures," *Criminology* 36 (1998): 829–858.

46. Bruce A. Jacobs, *Robbing Drug Dealers: Violence Beyond the Law* (Hawthorne, NY: Aldine de Gruyter, 2000).

47. Laura Dugan, Gary LaFree, and Alex Piquero, "Testing a Rational Choice Model of Airline Hijackings," *Criminology* 43 (2005): 1,031–1,065.

48. Andy Hochstetler, "Opportunities and Decisions: Interactional Dynamics in Robbery and Burglary Groups," *Criminology* 39 (2001): 737–763.

49. Peter Wood, Walter Gove, James Wilson, and John Cochran, "Nonsocial Reinforcement and Habitual Criminal Conduct: An Extension of Learning," *Criminology* 35 (1997): 335–366.

50. Jeff Ferrell, "Criminological Verstehen: Inside the Immediacy of Crime," *Justice Quarterly* 14 (1997): 3–23, at p. 12.

51. Jack Katz, *Seductions of Crime* (New York: Basic Books, 1988).

52. Bill McCarthy, "Not Just 'For the Thrill of It': An Instrumentalist Elaboration of Katz's Explanation of Sneaky Thrill Property Crime," *Criminology* 33 (1995): 519–539.

53. Timothy Brezina, "Delinquent Problem-Solving: An Interpretive Framework for Criminological Theory and Research," *Journal of Research in Crime and Delinquency* 37 (2000): 3–30; Andy Hochstetler, "Opportunities and Decisions: Interactional

Dynamics in Robbery and Burglary Groups," *Criminology* 39 (2001): 737–763.

54. Patricia Brantingham, Paul Brantingham, and Wendy Taylor, "Situational Crime Prevention as a Key Component in Embeded Crime Prevention," *Canadian Journal of Criminology & Criminal Justice* 47 (2005): 271–292.

55. Ronald Clarke, *Situational Crime Prevention: Successful Case Studies* (Albany, NY: Harrow and Heston, 1992).

56. Derek Cornish and Ronald Clarke, "Opportunities, Precipitators and Criminal Decisions: A Reply to Wortley's Critique of Situational Crime Prevention," *Crime Prevention Studies* 16 (2003): 41–96; Ronald Clarke and Ross Homel, "A Revised Classification of Situational Prevention Techniques," in *Crime Prevention at a Crossroads*, ed. Steven P. Lab (Cincinnati: Anderson Publishing, 1997).

57. Nancy LaVigne, "Gasoline Drive-Offs: Designing a Less Convenient Environment," in *Crime Prevention Studies,* vol. 2, ed. Ronald Clarke (Monsey, NY: Criminal Justice Press, 1994), pp. 91–114.

58. Barry Webb, "Steering Column Locks and Motor Vehicle Theft: Evaluations for Three Countries," in *Crime Prevention Studies,* vol. 2, ed. Ronald Clarke (Monsey, NY: Criminal Justice Press, 1994), pp. 71–89.

59. Andrew Fulkerson, "Blow and Go: The Breath-Analyzed Ignition Interlock Device as a Technological Response to DWI," *American Journal of Drug and Alcohol Abuse* 29 (2003): 219–235.

60. Marcus Felson, "Those Who Discourage Crime," in *Crime and Place, Crime Prevention Studies,* vol. 4, eds., John Eck and David Weisburd (New York: Criminal Justice Press, 1995), pp. 53–66.

61. John Eck, "Drug Markets and Drug Places: A Case-Control Study of the Spatial Structure of Illicit Drug Dealing." Doctoral dissertation. College Park: MD, Department of Criminology and Criminal Justice, University of Maryland, 1994.

62. William Bratton with Peter Knobler, *Turnaround: How America's Top Cop Reversed the Crime Epidemic* (New York: Random House, 1998).

63. Brandon Welsh and David Farrington, "Effects of Closed-Circuit Television on Crime," *Annals of the American Academy of Political and Social Science* 587 (2003): 110–136.

64. Ronald Clarke, "Deterring Obscene Phone Callers: The New Jersey Experience," in *Situational Crime Prevention,* ed. Ronald Clarke (Albany, NY: Harrow & Heston, 1992), pp. 124–132.

65. Ronald Clarke and David Weisburd, "Diffusion of Crime Control Benefits: Observations of the Reverse of Displacement," in *Crime Prevention Studies,* vol. 2, ed. Ronald Clarke (New York: Criminal Justice Press, 1994).

66. David Weisburd and Lorraine Green, "Policing Drug Hot Spots: The Jersey City Drug Market Analysis Experiment," *Justice Quarterly* 12 (1995): 711–734.

67. Lorraine Green, "Cleaning Up Drug Hot Spots in Oakland, California: The Displacement and Diffusion Effects," *Justice Quarterly* 12 (1995): 737–754.

68. Robert Barr and Ken Pease, "Crime Placement, Displacement, and Deflection," in *Crime and Justice, A Review of Research,* vol. 12, eds. Michael Tonry and Norval Morris (Chicago: University of Chicago Press, 1990), pp. 277–319.

69. Clarke, *Situational Crime Prevention,* p. 27.

70. R. Steven Daniels, Lorin Baumhover, William Formby, and Carolyn Clark-Daniels, "Police Discretion and Elder Mistreatment: A Nested Model of Observation, Reporting, and Satisfaction," *Journal of Criminal Justice* 27 (1999): 209–225.

71. Daniel Nagin and Greg Pogarsky, "Integrating Celerity, Impulsivity, and Extralegal Sanction Threats into a Model of General Deterrence: Theory and Evidence," *Criminology* 39 (2001): 865–892.

72. Daniel Nagin, "Criminal Deterrence Theory at the Outset of the Twenty-First Century," in *Crime and Justice: An Annual Review of Research,* vol. 23, ed. Michael Tonry (Chicago: University of Chicago Press, 1998), pp. 51–92; for an opposing view, see Robert Bursik, Harold Grasmick, and Mitchell Chamlin, "The Effect of Longitudinal Arrest Patterns on the Development of Robbery Trends at the Neighborhood Level," *Criminology* 28 (1990): 431–450.

73. Daniel Nagin and Greg Pogarsky, "An Experimental Investigation of Deterrence: Cheating, Self-Serving Bias and Impulsivity," *Criminology* 41 (2003): 167–195.

74. Michael White, James Fyfe, Suzanne Campbell, and John Goldkamp, "The Police Role in Preventing Homicide: Considering the Impact of Problem-Oriented Policing on the Prevalence of Murder," *Journal of Research in Crime and Delinquency* 40 (2003): 194–226.

75. Tomislav V. Kovandzic and John J. Sloan, "Police Levels and Crime Rates Revisited: A County-Level Analysis from Florida (1980–1998)," *Journal of Criminal Justice 30* (2002): 65–76; Steven Levitt, "Using Electoral Cycles in Police Hiring to Estimate the Effect of Police on Crime," *American Economic Review* 87 (1997): 270–291.

76. Thomas Marvell and Carlisle Moody, "Specification Problems, Police Levels, and Crime Rates," *Criminology* 34 (1996): 609–646; Colin Loftin and David McDowall, "The Police, Crime, and Economic Theory: An Assessment," *American Sociological Review* 47 (1982): 393–401.

77. Richard Timothy Coupe and Laurence Blake, "The Effects of Patrol Workloads and Response Strength on Arrests at Burglary Emergencies," *Journal of Criminal Justice* 33 (2005): 239–255.

78. Greg Pogarsky, "Identifying 'Deterrable' Offenders: Implications for Research on Deterrence," *Justice Quarterly* 19 (2002): 431–453.

79. Ed Stevens and Brian Payne, "Applying Deterrence Theory in the Context of Corporate Wrongdoing: Limitations on Punitive Damages," *Journal of Criminal Justice* 27 (1999): 195–209; Jeffrey Roth, *Firearms and Violence* (Washington, DC: National Institute of Justice, 1994); Thomas Marvell and Carlisle Moody, "The Impact of Enhanced Prison Terms for Felonies Committed with Guns," *Criminology* 33 (1995): 247–281; Gary Green, "General Deterrence and Television Cable Crime: A Field Experiment in Social Crime," *Criminology* 23 (1986): 629–645.

80. Donald Green, "Past Behavior as a Measure of Actual Future Behavior: An Unresolved Issue in Perceptual Deterrence Research," *Journal of Criminal Law and Criminology* 80 (1989): 781–804.

81. Donna Bishop, "Deterrence: A Panel Analysis," *Justice Quarterly* 1 (1984): 311–328; Julie Horney and Ineke Haen Marshall, "Risk Perceptions among Serious Offenders: The Role of Crime and Punishment," *Criminology* 30 (1992): 575–594.

82. Wanda Foglia, "Perceptual Deterrence and the Mediating Effect of Internalized Norms among Inner-City Teenagers," *Journal of Research in Crime and Delinquency* 34 (1997): 414–442; Raymond Paternoster, "Decisions to Participate in and Desist from Four Types of Common Delinquency: Deterrence and the Rational Choice Perspective," *Law and Society Review* 23 (1989): 7–29; Raymond Paternoster, "Examining Three-Wave Deterrence Models: A Question of Temporal Order and Specification," *Journal of Criminal Law and Criminology* 79 (1988): 135–163; Raymond Paternoster, Linda Saltzman, Gordon Waldo, and Theodore Chiricos, "Estimating Perceptual Stability and Deterrent Effects: The Role of Perceived Legal Punishment in the Inhibition of Criminal Involvement," *Journal of Criminal Law and Criminology* 74 (1983): 270–297; M. William Minor and Joseph Harry, "Deterrent and Experiential Effects in Perceptual Deterrence Research: A Replication and Extension," *Journal of Research in Crime and Delinquency* 19 (1982): 190–203; Lonn Lanza-Kaduce, "Perceptual Deterrence and Drinking and Driving among College Students," *Criminology* 26 (1988): 321–341.

83. Steven Klepper and Daniel Nagin, "The Deterrent Effect of Perceived Certainty and Severity of Punishment Revisited," *Criminology* 27 (1989): 721–746; Scott Decker, Richard Wright, and Robert Logie, "Perceptual Deterrence among Active Residential Burglars: A Research Note," *Criminology* 31 (1993): 135–147.
84. Alex Piquero and George Rengert, "Studying Deterrence with Active Residential Burglars," *Justice Quarterly* 16 (1999): 451–462.
85. Ernest Van Den Haag, "The Criminal Law as a Threat System," *Journal of Criminal Law and Criminology* 73 (1982): 709–785.
86. David Lykken, "Psychopathy, Sociopathy, and Crime," *Society* 34 (1996): 30–38.
87. George Lowenstein, Daniel Nagin, and Raymond Paternoster, "The Effect of Sexual Arousal on Expectations of Sexual Forcefulness," *Journal of Research in Crime and Delinquency* 34 (1997): 443–473.
88. Lyn Exum, "The Application and Robustness of the Rational Choice Perspective in the Study of Intoxicated and Angry Intentions to Aggress," *Criminology* 40 (2002): 933–967.
89. David Klinger, "Policing Spousal Assault," *Journal of Research in Crime and Delinquency* 32 (1995): 308–324.
90. James Williams and Daniel Rodeheaver, "Processing of Criminal Homicide Cases in a Large Southern City," *Sociology and Social Research* 75 (1991): 80–88.
91. Greg Pogarsky, "Identifying 'Deterrable' Offenders: Implications for Deterrence Research."
92. Nagin and Pogarsky, "Integrating Celerity, Impulsivity, and Extralegal Sanction Threats into a Model of General Deterrence: Theory and Evidence."
93. James Q. Wilson, *Thinking About Crime* (New York: Basic Books, 1975).
94. James Q. Wilson and Richard Herrnstein, *Crime and Human Nature* (New York: Simon & Schuster, 1985), p. 494.
95. Lawrence Sherman and Richard Berk, "The Specific Deterrent Effects of Arrest for Domestic Assault," *American Sociological Review* 49 (1984): 261–272.
96. J. David Hirschel, Ira Hutchison, and Charles Dean, "The Failure of Arrest to Deter Spouse Abuse," *Journal of Research in Crime and Delinquency* 29 (1992): 7–33; Franklyn Dunford, David Huizinga, and Delbert Elliott, "The Role of Arrest in Domestic Assault: The Omaha Experiment," *Criminology* 28 (1990): 183–206.
97. Lawrence Sherman, Janell Schmidt, Dennis Rogan, Patrick Gartin, Ellen Cohn, Dean Collins, and Anthony Bacich, "From Initial Deterrence to Long-Term Escalation: Short-Custody Arrest for Domestic Violence," *Criminology* 29 (1991): 821.
98. Christina DeJong, "Survival Analysis and Specific Deterrence: Integrating Theoretical and Empirical Models of Recidivism," *Criminology* 35 (1997): 561–576; Paul Tracy and Kimberly Kempf-Leonard, *Continuity and Discontinuity in Criminal Careers* (New York: Plenum Press, 1996).
99. Allen Beck and Bernard Shipley, *Recidivism of Prisoners Released in 1983* (Washington, DC: Bureau of Justice Statistics, 1989).
100. Raymond Paternoster and Alex Piquero, "Reconceptualizing Deterrence: An Empirical Test of Personal and Vicarious Experiences," *Journal of Research in Crime and Delinquency* 32 (1995): 251–258.
101. Cassia Spohn and David Holleran, "The Effect of Imprisonment on Recidivism Rates of Felony Offenders: A Focus on Drug Offenders," *Criminology* 40 (2002): 329–359.
102. Greg Pogarsky and Alex R. Piquero "Can Punishment Encourage Offending? Investigating the 'Resetting' Effect," *Journal of Research in Crime and Delinquency* 40 (2003): 92–117.
103. Doris Layton MacKenzie and Spencer De Li, "The Impact of Formal and Informal Social Controls on the Criminal Activities of Probationers," *Journal of Research in Crime and Delinquency* 39 (2002): 243–276.
104. See, generally, Raymond Paternoster, "Absolute and Restrictive Deterrence in a Panel of Youth: Explaining the Onset, Persistence/Desistance, and Frequency of Delinquent Offending," *Social Problems* 36 (1989): 289–307; Raymond Paternoster, "The Deterrent Effect of Perceived Severity of Punishment: A Review of the Evidence and Issues," *Justice Quarterly* 42 (1987): 173–217.
105. Isaac Ehrlich, "Participation in Illegitimate Activities: An Economic Analysis," *Journal of Political Economy* 81 (1973): 521–567; Lee Bowker, "Crime and the Use of Prisons in the United States: A Time Series Analysis," *Crime and Delinquency* 27 (1981): 206–212.
106. David Greenberg, "The Incapacitative Effects of Imprisonment: Some Estimates," *Law and Society Review* 9 (1975): 541–580.
107. Reuel Shinnar and Shlomo Shinnar, "The Effects of the Criminal Justice System on the Control of Crime: A Quantitative Approach," *Law and Society Review* 9 (1975): 581–611.
108. David Greenberg and Nancy Larkin, "The Incapacitation of Criminal Opiate Users," *Crime and Delinquency* 44 (1998): 205–228.
109. John Wallerstedt, *Returning to Prison: Bureau of Justice Statistics Special Report* (Washington, DC: U.S. Department of Justice, 1984).
110. James Marquart, Victoria Brewer, Janet Mullings, and Ben Crouch, "The Implications of Crime Control Policy on HIV/AIDS-Related Risk among Women Prisoners," *Crime and Delinquency* 45 (1999): 82–98.
111. Jose Canela-Cacho, Alfred Blumstein, and Jacqueline Cohen, "Relationship between the Offending Frequency of Imprisoned and Free Offenders," *Criminology* 35 (1997): 133–171.
112. Kate King and Patricia Bass, "Southern Prisons and Elderly Inmates: Taking a Look Inside." Paper presented at the annual meeting of the American Society of Criminology, San Diego, November 1997.
113. Thomas Marvell and Carlisle Moody, "The Impact of Out-of-State Prison Population on State Homicide Rates: Displacement and Free-Rider Effects," *Criminology* 36 (1998): 513–538; Thomas Marvell and Carlisle Moody, "The Impact of Prison Growth on Homicide," *Homicide Studies* 1 (1997): 205–233.
114. Ilyana Kuziemko and Steven D. Levitt, "An Empirical Analysis of Imprisoning Drug Offenders," NBER Working Papers 8489 (Cambridge, MA: National Bureau of Economic Research, 2001).
115. Marc Mauer, testimony before the U.S. Congress, House Judiciary Committee, on "Three Strikes and You're Out," March 1, 1994.
116. Stephen Markman and Paul Cassell, "Protecting the Innocent: A Response to the Bedeau-Radelet Study," *Stanford Law Review* 41 (1988): 121–170, at p. 153.
117. James Stephan and Tracy Snell, *Capital Punishment, 1994* (Washington, DC: Bureau of Justice Statistics, 1996), p. 8.

Chapter 5. Trait Theory: It's in Their Blood

1. Lee Ellis, "A Discipline in Peril: Sociology's Future Hinges on Curing Biophobia," *American Sociologist* 27 (1996): 21–41.
2. Edmund O. Wilson, *Sociobiology* (Cambridge, MA: Harvard University Press, 1975).
3. Per-Olof Wikstrom and Rolf Loeber, "Do Disadvantaged Neighborhoods Cause Well-Adjusted Children to Become Adolescent Delinquents?" *Criminology* 38 (2000): 1,109–1,142.
4. See, generally, Lee Ellis, *Theories of Rape* (New York: Hemisphere, 1989).
5. Anthony Walsh, "Behavior Genetics and Anomie/Strain Theory," *Criminology* 38 (2000): 1,075–1,108.
6. Dalton Conley and Neil Bennett, "Is Biology Destiny? Birth Weight and Life Chances," *American Sociological Review* 654 (2000): 458–467.
7. Anthony Walsh and Lee Ellis, "Shoring Up the Big Three: Improving Criminological Theories with Biosocial Concepts." Paper presented at the annual meeting of the Society of Criminology, San Diego, November 1997, p. 16.

8. Israel Nachshon, "Neurological Bases of Crime, Psychopathy and Aggression," in *Crime in Biological, Social and Moral Contexts,* eds. Lee Ellis and Harry Hoffman (New York: Praeger, 1990), p. 199.
9. John Cloud, "Harvey Milk: People Told Him No Openly Gay Man Could Win Political Office. Fortunately, He Ignored Them," *Time,* June 14, 1999, www.time.com/time/time100/heroes/profile/milk01.html.
10. G. B. Ramirez, O. Pagulayan, H. Akagi, A. Francisco Rivera, L. V. Lee, A. Berroya, M. C. Vince Cruz, and D. Casintahan, "Tagum Study II: Follow-Up Study at Two Years of Age after Prenatal Exposure to Mercury," *Pediatrics* 111 (2003): 289–295.
11. Eric Konofal, Samuele Cortese, Michel Lecendreux, Isabelle Arnulf, and Marie Christine Mouren, "Effectiveness of Iron Supplementation in a Young Child with Attention-Deficit/Hyperactivity Disorder," *Pediatrics* 116 (2005): 732–734.
12. Alexandra Richardson and Paul Montgomery, "The Oxford-Durham Study: A Randomized Controlled Trial of Dietary Supplementation with Fatty Acids in Children with Developmental Coordination Disorder," *Pediatrics* 115 (2005): 1,360–1,366.
13. Courtney Van de Weyer, "Changing Diets, Changing Minds: How Food Affects Mental Well-Being and Behaviour," Sustain: The Alliance for Better Food and Farming, www.sustainweb.org/pdf/ MHRep_LowRes.pdf (accessed March 26, 2006).
14. Diana Fishbein, "Neuropsychological Function, Drug Abuse, and Violence: A Conceptual Framework," *Criminal Justice and Behavior* 27 (2000): 139–159.
15. E. Podolsky, "The Chemistry of Murder," *Pakistan Medical Journal* 15 (1964): 9–14.
16. J. A. Yaryura-Tobias and F. Neziroglu, "Violent Behavior, Brain Dysrhythmia and Glucose Dysfunction: A New Syndrome," *Journal of Orthopsychiatry* 4 (1975): 182–188.
17. Matti Virkkunen, "Reactive Hypoglycemic Tendency among Habitually Violent Offenders," *Nutrition Reviews Supplement* 44 (1986): 94–103.
18. James Q. Wilson, *The Moral Sense* (New York: Free Press, 1993).
19. Lee Ellis, "Evolutionary and Neurochemical Causes of Sex Differences in Victimizing Behavior: Toward a Unified Theory of Criminal Behavior and Social Stratification," *Social Science Information* 28 (1989): 605–636.
20. Lee Ellis and Phyllis Coontz, "Androgens, Brain Functioning, and Criminality: The Neurohormonal Foundations of Antisociality," in *Crime in Biological, Social and Moral Contexts,* eds. Lee Ellis and Harry Hoffman (New York: Praeger, 1990), pp. 162–193, at p. 181.
21. Stephanie H. M. van Goozen, Walter Matthys, Peggy Cohen-Kettenis, Jos Thijssen, and Herman van Engeland, "Adrenal Androgens and Aggression in Conduct Disorder Prepubertal Boys and Normal Controls," *Biological Psychiatry* 43 (1998): 156–158.
22. Paul Bernhardt, "Influences of Serotonin and Testosterone in Aggression and Dominance: Convergence with Social Psychology," *Current Directions in Psychological Science* 6 (1997): 44–48.
23. Christy Miller Buchanan, Jacquelynne Eccles, and Jill Becker, "Are Adolescents the Victims of Raging Hormones? Evidence for Activational Effects of Hormones on Moods and Behavior at Adolescence," *Psychological Bulletin* 111 (1992): 62–107.
24. Alan Booth and D. Wayne Osgood, "The Influence of Testosterone on Deviance in Adulthood: Assessing and Explaining the Relationship," *Criminology* 31 (1993): 93–117.
25. Albert Reiss Jr. and Jeffrey Roth, eds., *Understanding and Preventing Violence* (Washington, DC: National Academy Press, 1993), p. 118.
26. Anthony Walsh, "Genetic and Cytogenetic Intersex Anomalies: Can They Help Us to Understand Gender Differences in Deviant Behavior?" *International Journal of Offender Therapy and Comparative Criminology* 39 (1995): 151–166.
27. Celina Cohen-Bendahan, Jan Buitelaar, Stephanie van Goozen, Jacob Orlebeke, and Peggy Cohen-Kettenis, "Is There an Effect of Prenatal Testosterone on Aggression and Other Behavioral Traits? A Study Comparing Same-Sex and Opposite-Sex Twin Girls," *Hormones and Behavior,* 47 (2005): 230–237.
28. Walter Gove, "The Effect of Age and Gender on Deviant Behavior: A Biopsychosocial Perspective," in *Gender and the Life Course,* ed. A. S. Rossi (New York: Aldine, 1985), pp. 115–144.
29. For a review of this concept, see Anne E. Figert, "The Three Faces of PMS: The Professional, Gendered, and Scientific Structuring of a Psychiatric Disorder," *Social Problems* 42 (1995): 56–72.
30. Katharina Dalton, *The Premenstrual Syndrome* (Springfield, IL: Charles C. Thomas, 1971).
31. Julie Horney, "Menstrual Cycles and Criminal Responsibility," *Law and Human Nature* 2 (1978): 25–36.
32. Diana Fishbein, "Selected Studies on the Biology of Antisocial Behavior," in *New Perspectives in Criminology,* ed. John Conklin (Needham Heights, MA: Allyn & Bacon, 1996), pp. 26–38.
33. Ibid.; Karen Paige, "Effects of Oral Contraceptives on Affective Fluctuations Associated with the Menstrual Cycle," *Psychosomatic Medicine* 33 (1971): 515–537.
34. Press release, "CDC Releases Most Extensive Assessment Ever of Americans' Exposure to Environmental Chemicals," Atlanta, GA: Centers for Disease Control, January 31, 2003.
35. David C. Bellinger, "Lead," *Pediatrics* 113 (2004): 1,016–1,022; Herbert Needleman, Christine McFarland, Roberta Ness, Stephen Fienberg, and Michael Tobin, "Bone Lead Levels in Adjudicated Delinquents: A Case Control Study," *Neurotoxicology and Teratology* 24 (2002): 711–717.
36. Mark Opler, Alan Brown, Joseph Graziano, Manisha Desai, Wei Zheng, Catherine Schaefer, Pamela Factor-Litvak, and Ezra S. Susser, "Prenatal Lead Exposure, [Delta]-Aminolevulinic Acid, and Schizophrenia," *Environmental Health Perspectives* 112 (2004): 548–553.
37. Jeff Evans, "Asymptomatic, High Lead Levels Tied to Delinquency," *Pediatric News* 37 (2003): 13.
38. Deborah Denno, "Considering Lead Poisoning as a Criminal Defense," *Fordham Urban Law Journal* 20 (1993): 377–400.
39. Jens Walkowiak, Jörg Wiener, Annemarie Fastabend, Birger Heinzow, Ursula Krämer, Eberhard Schmidt, Hans Steingürber, Sabine Wundram, and Gerhard Winneke, "Environmental Exposure to Polychlorinated Biphenyls and Quality of the Home Environment: Effects on Psychodevelopment in Early Childhood," *The Lancet* 358 (2001): 92–93.
40. Terrie Moffitt, "The Neuropsychology of Juvenile Delinquency: A Critical Review," in *Crime and Justice: An Annual Review,* vol. 12, eds. Norval Morris and Michael Tonry (Chicago: University of Chicago Press, 1990), pp. 99–169.
41. Terrie Moffitt, Donald Lynam, and Phil Silva, "Neuropsychological Tests Predicting Persistent Male Delinquency," *Criminology* 32 (1994): 277–300; Elizabeth Kandel and Sarnoff Mednick, "Perinatal Complications Predict Violent Offending," *Criminology* 29 (1991): 519–529; Sarnoff Mednick, Ricardo Machon, Matti Virkkunen, and Douglas Bonett, "Adult Schizophrenia Following Prenatal Exposure to an Influenza Epidemic," *Archives of General Psychiatry* 44 (1987): 35–46; C. A. Fogel, S. A. Mednick, and N. Michelson, "Hyperactive Behavior and Minor Physical Anomalies," *Acta Psychiatrica Scandinavia* 72 (1985): 551–556.
42. Jean Seguin, Robert Pihl, Philip Harden, Richard Tremblay, and Bernard Boulerice, "Cognitive and Neuropsychological Characteristics of Physically Aggressive Boys," *Journal of Abnormal Psychology* 104 (1995): 614–624; Deborah Denno, "Gender, Crime and the Criminal Law Defenses," *Journal of Criminal Law and Criminology* 85 (1994): 80–180.
43. Adrian Raine, Patricia Brennan, Brigitte Mednick, and Sarnoff Mednick, "High Rates of Violence, Crime, Academic Problems,

and Behavioral Problems in Males with Both Early Neuromotor Deficits and Unstable Family Environments," *Archives of General Psychiatry* 53 (1996): 544–549.

44. J. Arturo Silva, Gregory B. Leong, and Michelle M. Ferrari, "A Neuropsychiatric Developmental Model of Serial Homicidal Behavior," *Behavioral Sciences and the Law* 22 (2004): 787–799.
45. Nathaniel Pallone and James Hennessy, "Brain Dysfunction and Criminal Violence," *Society* 35 (1998): 21–27; P. F. Goyer, P. J. Andreason, and W. E. Semple, "Positronic Emission Tomography and Personality Disorders," *Neuropsychopharmacology* 10 (1994): 21–28.
46. Adrian Raine, Monte Buchsbaum, and Lori LaCasse, "Brain Abnormalities in Murderers Indicated by Positron Emission Tomography," *Biological Psychiatry* 42 (1997): 495–508.
47. Laurence Tancredi, *Hardwired Behavior: What Neuroscience Reveals about Morality* (London: Cambridge University Press, 2005).
48. David George, Robert Rawlings, Wendol Williams, Monte Phillips, Grace Fong, Michael Kerich, Reza Momenan, John Umhau, and Daniel Hommer, "A Select Group of Perpetrators of Domestic Violence: Evidence of Decreased Metabolism in the Right Hypothalamus and Reduced Relationships between Cortical/Subcortical Brain Structures in Position Emission Tomography," *Psychiatry Research: Neuroimaging* 130 (2004): 11–25.
49. Yaling Yang, Adrian Raine, Todd Lencz, Susan Bihrle, Lori LaCasse, and Patrick Colletti, "Prefrontal White Matter in Pathological Liars," *British Journal of Psychiatry* 187 (2005): 320–325.
50. Adrian Raine, "The Role of Prefrontal Deficits, Low Autonomic Arousal, and Early Health Factors in the Development of Antisocial and Aggressive Behavior in Children," *Journal of Child Psychology and Psychiatry* 43 (2002): 417–434.
51. Leonore Simon, "Does Criminal Offender Treatment Work?" *Applied and Preventive Psychology* (Summer 1998); Stephen Faraone et al., "Intellectual Performance and School Failure in Children with Attention Deficit Hyperactivity Disorder and in Their Siblings," *Journal of Abnormal Psychology* 102 (1993): 616–623.
52. Simon, "Does Criminal Offender Treatment Work?"
53. Ibid.
54. Terrie Moffitt and Phil Silva, "Self-Reported Delinquency, Neuropsychological Deficit, and History of Attention Deficit Disorder," *Journal of Abnormal Child Psychology* 16 (1988): 553–569.
55. Molina Pelham, Jr., "Childhood Predictors of Adolescent Substance Use in a Longitudinal Study of Children with ADHD," *Journal of Abnormal Psychology* 112 (2003): 497–507; Peter Muris and Cor Meesters, "The Validity of Attention Deficit Hyperactivity and Hyperkinetic Disorder Symptom Domains in Nonclinical Dutch Children," *Journal of Clinical Child & Adolescent Psychology* 32 (2003): 460–466.
56. Elizabeth Hart et al., "Criterion Validity of Informants in the Diagnosis of Disruptive Behavior Disorders in Children: A Preliminary Study," *Journal of Consulting and Clinical Psychology* 62 (1994): 410–414.
57. Russell Barkley, Mariellen Fischer, Lori Smallish, and Kenneth Fletcher, "Young Adult Follow-Up of Hyperactive Children: Antisocial Activities and Drug Use," *Journal of Child Psychology and Psychiatry* 45 (2004): 195–211.
58. Eugene Maguin, Rolf Loeber, and Paul LeMahieu, "Does the Relationship between Poor Reading and Delinquency Hold for Males of Different Ages and Ethnic Groups?" *Journal of Emotional and Behavioral Disorders* 1 (1993): 88–100.
59. Susan Young, Andrew Smolen, Robin Corley, Kenneth Krauter, John De-Fries, Thomas Crowley, and John Hewitt, "Dopamine Transporter Polymorphism Associated with Externalizing Behavior Problems in Children," *American Journal of Medical Genetics* 114 (2002): 144–149.
60. Avshalom Caspi, Joseph McClay, Terrie E. Moffitt, Jonathan Mill, Judy Martin, Ian W. Craig, Alan Taylor, and Richie Poulton, "Role of Genotype in the Cycle of Violence in Maltreated Children," *Science* 297 (2002): 851–854.
61. M. Skondras, M. Markianos, A. Botsis, E. Bistolaki, and G. Christodoulou, "Platelet Monoamine Oxidase Activity and Psychometric Correlates in Male Violent Offenders Imprisoned for Homicide or Other Violent Acts," *European Archives of Psychiatry and Clinical Neuroscience* 254 (2004): 380–386.
62. Lee Ellis, "Monoamine Oxidase and Criminality: Identifying an Apparent Biological Marker for Antisocial Behavior," *Journal of Research in Crime and Delinquency* 28 (1991): 227–251.
63. Matti Virkkunen, David Goldman, and Markku Linnoila, "Serotonin in Alcoholic Violent Offenders," *The Ciba Foundation Symposium: Genetics of Criminal and Antisocial Behavior* (Chichester, England: Wiley, 1995).
64. Lee Ellis, "Left- and Mixed-Handedness and Criminality: Explanations for a Probable Relationship," in *Left-Handedness: Behavioral Implications and Anomalies,* ed. S. Coren (Amsterdam: Elsevier, 1990), pp. 485–507.
65. Lee Ellis, "Arousal Theory and the Religiosity–Criminality Relationship," in *Contemporary Criminological Theory,* eds. Peter Cordella and Larry Siegel (Boston: Northeastern University, 1996), pp. 65–84.
66. Adrian Raine, Peter Venables, and Sarnoff Mednick, "Low Resting Heart Rate at Age 3 Years Predisposes to Aggression at Age 11 Years: Evidence from the Mauritius Child Health Project," *Journal of the American Academy of Adolescent Psychiatry* 36 (1997): 1,457–1,464.
67. David Rowe, "As the Twig Is Bent: The Myth of Child-Rearing Influences on Personality Development," *Journal of Counseling and Development* 68 (1990): 606–611; David Rowe, Joseph Rogers, and Sylvia Meseck-Bushey, "Sibling Delinquency and the Family Environment: Shared and Unshared Influences," *Child Development* 63 (1992): 59–67; Gregory Carey and David DiLalla, "Personality and Psychopathology: Genetic Perspectives," *Journal of Abnormal Psychology* 103 (1994): 32–43.
68. Anita Thapar, Kate Langley, Tom Fowler, Frances Rice, Darko Turic, Naureen Whittinger, John Aggleton, Marianne Van den Bree, Michael Owen, and Michael O'Donovan, "Catechol O-methyltransferase Gene Variant and Birth Weight Predict Early-Onset Antisocial Behavior in Children with Attention-Deficit/Hyperactivity Disorder," *Archives of General Psychiatry* 62 (2005): 1,275–1,278.
69. For an early review, see Barbara Wooton, *Social Science and Social Pathology* (London: Allen & Unwin, 1959); John Laub and Robert Sampson, "Unraveling Families and Delinquency: A Reanalysis of the Gluecks' Data," *Criminology* 26 (1988): 355–380.
70. D. J. West and D. P. Farrington, "Who Becomes Delinquent?" in *The Delinquent Way of Life,* eds. D. J. West and D. P. Farrington (London: Heinemann, 1977), pp. 1–28; D. J. West, *Delinquency: Its Roots, Careers, and Prospects* (Cambridge, MA: Harvard University Press, 1982).
71. West, *Delinquency,* p. 114.
72. David Farrington, "Understanding and Preventing Bullying," in *Crime and Justice,* vol. 17, ed. Michael Tonry (Chicago: University of Chicago Press, 1993), pp. 381–457.
73. Terence Thornberry, Adrienne Freeman-Gallant, Alan Lizotte, Marvin Krohn, and Carolyn Smith, "Linked Lives: The Intergenerational Transmission of Antisocial Behavior," *Journal of Abnormal Child Psychology* 31 (2003): 171–185.
74. David Rowe and David Farrington, "The Familial Transmission of Criminal Convictions," *Criminology* 35 (1997): 177–201.
75. R. J. Cadoret, C. Cain, and R. R. Crowe, "Evidence for a Gene–Environment Interaction in the Development of Adolescent Antisocial Behavior," *Behavior Genetics* 13 (1983): 301–310.

76. Barry Hutchings and Sarnoff A. Mednick, "Criminality in Adoptees and Their Adoptive and Biological Parents: A Pilot Study," in *Biological Bases in Criminal Behavior,* eds. S. A. Mednick and K. O. Christiansen (New York: Gardner Press, 1977).
77. For similar results, see Sarnoff Mednick, Terrie Moffitt, William Gabrielli, and Barry Hutchings, "Genetic Factors in Criminal Behavior: A Review," in *Development of Antisocial and Prosocial Behavior*, eds. Dan Olweus, Jack Block, and Marian Radke-Yarrow (New York: Academic Press, 1986), pp. 3–50; Sarnoff Mednick, William Gabrielli, and Barry Hutchings, "Genetic Influences in Criminal Behavior: Evidence from an Adoption Cohort," in *Perspective Studies of Crime and Delinquency*, eds. Katherine Teilmann Van Dusen and Sarnoff Mednick (Boston: Kluwer-Nijhoff, 1983), pp. 39–57.
78. Michael Lyons, Karestan Koenen, Francisco Buchting, Joanne Meyer, Lindon Eaves, Rosemary Toomey, Seth Eisen, et al., "A Twin Study of Sexual Behavior in Men," *Archives of Sexual Behavior* 33 (2004): 129–136.
79. Sarnoff Mednick and Jan Volavka, "Biology and Crime," in *Crime and Justice,* eds. Norval Morris and Michael Tonry (Chicago: University of Chicago Press, 1980), pp. 85–159 at 94.
80. Edwin J. C. G. van den Oord, Frank Verhulst, and Dorret Boomsma, "A Genetic Study of Maternal and Paternal Ratings of Problem Behaviors in 3-Year-Old Twins," *Journal of Abnormal Psychology* 105 (1996): 349–357.
81. Ping Qin, "The Relationship of Suicide Risk to Family History of Suicide and Psychiatric Disorders," *Psychiatric Times* 20 (2003), www.psychiatrictimes.com/p031262.html.
82. Jane Scourfield, Marianne Van den Bree, Neilson Martin, and Peter McGuffin, "Conduct Problems in Children and Adolescents: A Twin Study," *Archives of General Psychiatry* 61 (2004) 489–496; Jeanette Taylor, Bryan Loney, Leonardo Bobadilla, William Iacono, and Matt McGue, "Genetic and Environmental Influences on Psychopathy Trait Dimensions in a Community Sample of Male Twins," *Journal of Abnormal Child Psychology* 31(2003): 633–645.
83. Ginette Dionne, Richard Tremblay, Michel Boivin, David Laplante, and Daniel Perusse, "Physical Aggression and Expressive Vocabulary in 19-Month-Old Twins," *Developmental Psychology* 39 (2003): 261–273.
84. Sara R. Jaffee, Avshalom Caspi, Terrie Moffitt, Kenneth Dodge, Michael Rutter, Alan Taylor, and Lucy Tully, "Nature x Nurture: Genetic Vulnerabilities Interact with Physical Maltreatment to Promote Conduct Problems," *Development and Psychopathology* 17 (2005): 67–84.
85. Essi Viding, James Blair, Terrie Moffitt, and Robert Plomin, "Evidence for Substantial Genetic Risk for Psychopathy in 7-Year-Olds," *Journal of Child Psychology and Psychiatry* 46 (2005): 592–597.
86. Alice Gregory, Thalia Eley, and Robert Plomin, "Exploring the Association between Anxiety and Conduct Problems in a Large Sample of Twins Aged 2–4," *Journal of Abnormal Child Psychology* 32 (2004): 111–123.
87. Marshall Jones and Donald Jones, "The Contagious Nature of Antisocial Behavior," *Criminology* 38 (2000): 25–46.
88. Lawrence Cohen and Richard Machalek, "A General Theory of Expropriative Crime: An Evolutionary Ecological Approach," *American Journal of Sociology* 94 (1988): 465–501.
89. For a general review, see Martin Daly and Margo Wilson, "Crime and Conflict: Homicide in Evolutionary Psychological Theory," in *Crime and Justice: An Annual Edition*, ed. Michael Tonry (Chicago: University of Chicago Press, 1997), pp. 51–100.
90. Lee Ellis, "The Evolution of Violent Criminal Behavior and Its Nonlegal Equivalent," in *Crime in Biological, Social and Moral Contexts,* eds. Lee Ellis and Harry Hoffman (New York: Praeger, 1990), pp. 63–65.
91. David Rowe, Alexander Vazsonyi, and Aurelio Jose Figuerdo, "Mating-Effort in Adolescence: A Conditional Alternative Strategy," *Personal Individual Differences* 23 (1997): 105–115.
92. Ibid., p. 112.
93. Todd Shackelford, "Risk of Multiple-Offender Rape–Murder Varies with Female Age," *Journal of Criminal Justice* 30 (2002): 135–142.
94. Margo Wilson, Holly Johnson, and Martin Daly, "Lethal and Nonlethal Violence against Wives," *Canadian Journal of Criminology* 37 (1995): 331–361.
95. Lee Ellis and Anthony Walsh, "Gene-Based Evolutionary Theories of Criminology," *Criminology* 35 (1997): 229–276.
96. Byron Roth, "Crime and Child Rearing," *Society* 34 (1996): 39–45.
97. Deborah Denno, "Sociological and Human Developmental Explanations of Crime: Conflict or Consensus," *Criminology* 23 (1985): 711–741.
98. Glenn Walters and Thomas White, "Heredity and Crime: Bad Genes or Bad Research?" *Criminology* 27 (1989): 455–486, at p. 478.
99. Edwin Driver, "Charles Buckman Goring," in *Pioneers in Criminology,* ed. Hermann Mannheim (Montclair, NJ: Patterson Smith, 1970), p. 440.
100. Gabriel Tarde, *Penal Philosophy,* trans. R. Howell (Boston: Little, Brown, 1912).
101. See, generally, Donn Byrne and Kathryn Kelly, *An Introduction to Personality* (Englewood Cliffs, NJ: Prentice-Hall, 1981).
102. See, generally, D. A. Andrews and James Bonta, *The Psychology of Criminal Conduct* (Cincinnati, OH: Anderson, 1994), pp. 72–75.
103. Paige Crosby Ouimette, "Psychopathology and Sexual Aggression in Nonincarcerated Men," *Violence and Victimization* 12 (1997): 389–397.
104. Ellen Kjelsberg, "Gender and Disorder Specific Criminal Career Profiles in Former Adolescent Psychiatric In-Patients," *Journal of Youth & Adolescence* 33 (2004): 261–270.
105. Richard Rowe, Julie Messer, Robert Goodman, Robert Meltzer, and Howard Meltzer, "Conduct Disorder and Oppositional Defiant Disorder in a National Sample: Developmental Epidemiology," *Journal of Child Psychology and Psychiatry* 45 (2004): 609–621.
106. Jennifer Beyers and Rolf Loeber, "Untangling Developmental Relations between Depressed Mood and Delinquency in Male Adolescents," *Journal of Abnormal Child Psychology* 31 (2003): 247–267.
107. Dorothy Espelage, Elizabeth Cauffman, Lisa Broidy, Alex Piquero, Paul Mazerolle, and Hans Steiner, "A Cluster-Analytic Investigation of MMPI Profiles of Serious Male and Female Juvenile Offenders," *Journal of the American Academy of Child & Adolescent Psychiatry* 42 (2003): 770–777.
108. Robert Vermeiren, "Psychopathology and Delinquency in Adolescents: A Descriptive and Developmental Perspective," *Clinical Psychology Review* 23 (2003): 277–318.
109. John Monahan, *Mental Illness and Violent Crime* (Washington, DC: National Institute of Justice, 1996).
110. Eric Silver, "Mental Disorder and Violent Victimization: The Mediating Role of Involvement in Conflicted Social Relationships," *Criminology* 40 (2002): 191–212.
111. Eric Silver, "Extending Social Disorganization Theory: A Multilevel Approach to the Study of Violence among Persons with Mental Illness," *Criminology* 38 (2000): 1,043–1,074.
112. B. Lögdberg, L-L. Nilsson, M. T. Levander, and S. Levander, "Schizophrenia, Neighbourhood, and Crime," *Acta Psychiatrica Scandinavica* 110 (2004): 92–97; Stacy DeCoster and Karen Heimer, "The Relationship between Law Violation and Depression: An Interactionist Analysis," *Criminology* 39 (2001): 799–837.
113. Courtenay Sellers, Christopher Sullivan, Bonita Veysey, and Jon Shane, "Responding to Persons with Mental Illnesses:

Police Perspectives on Specialized and Traditional Practices," *Behavioral Sciences & the Law* 23 (2005): 647–657.

114. This discussion is based on three works by Albert Bandura: *Aggression: A Social Learning Analysis* (Englewood Cliffs, NJ: Prentice-Hall, 1973); *Social Learning Theory* (Englewood Cliffs, NJ: Prentice-Hall, 1977); and "The Social Learning Perspective: Mechanisms of Aggression," in *Psychology of Crime and Criminal Justice,* ed. Hans Toch (New York: Holt, Rinehart & Winston, 1979), pp. 198–236.

115. Amy Street, Lynda King, Daniel King, and David Riges, "The Associations among Male-Perpetrated Partner Violence, Wives' Psychological Distress and Children's Behavior Problems: A Structural Equation Modeling Analysis," *Journal of Comparative Family Studies* 34 (2003): 23–46.

116. David Phillips, "The Impact of Mass Media Violence on U.S. Homicides," *American Sociological Review* 48 (1983): 560–568.

117. Kenneth Dodge, "A Social Information Processing Model of Social Competence in Children," in *Minnesota Symposium in Child Psychology,* vol. 18, ed. M. Perlmutter (Hillsdale, NJ: Erlbaum, 1986), pp. 77–125.

118. Adrian Raine, Peter Venables, and Mark Williams, "Better Autonomic Conditioning and Faster Electrodermal Half-Recovery Time at Age 15 Years as Possible Protective Factors against Crime at Age 29 Years," *Developmental Psychology* 32 (1996): 624–630.

119. Jean Marie McGloin and Travis Pratt, "Cognitive Ability and Delinquent Behavior among Inner-City Youth: A Life-Course Analysis of Main, Mediating, and Interaction Effects," *International Journal of Offender Therapy & Comparative Criminology* 47 (2003): 253–271.

120. Tony Ward and Claire Stewart, "The Relationship between Human Needs and Criminogenic Needs," *Psychology, Crime & Law* 9 (2003): 219–225.

121. David Ward, Mark Stafford, and Louis Gray, "Rational Choice, Deterrence, and Theoretical Integration," *Journal of Applied Social Psychology* 36 (2006): 571–585.

122. L. Huesman and L. Eron, "Individual Differences and the Trait of Aggression," *European Journal of Personality* 3 (1989): 95–106.

123. Rolf Loeber and Dale Hay, "Key Issues in the Development of Aggression and Violence from Childhood to Early Adulthood," *Annual Review of Psychology* 48 (1997): 371–410.

124. Vincent Marziano, Tony Ward, Anthony Beech, Philippa Pattison, "Identification of Five Fundamental Implicit Theories Underlying Cognitive Distortions in Child Abusers: A Preliminary Study," *Psychology, Crime & Law* 12 (2006): 97–105.

125. See, generally, Walter Mischel, *Introduction to Personality,* 4th ed. (New York: Holt, Rinehart & Winston, 1986).

126. Edelyn Verona and Joyce Carbonell, "Female Violence and Personality," *Criminal Justice and Behavior* 27 (2000): 176–195.

127. Gerhard Blickle, Alexander Schlegel, Pantaleon Fassbender, and Uwe Klein, "Some Personality Correlates of Business White-Collar Crime," *Applied Psychology: An International Review* 55 (2006): 220–233.

128. Hans Eysenck and M. W. Eysenck, *Personality and Individual Differences* (New York: Plenum, 1985).

129. Catrien Bijleveld and Jan Hendriks, "Juvenile Sex Offenders: Differences between Group and Solo Offenders," *Psychology, Crime & Law* 9 (2003): 237–246.

130. Laurie Frost, Terrie Moffitt, and Rob McGee, "Neuropsychological Correlates of Psychopathology in an Unselected Cohort of Young Adolescents," *Journal of Abnormal Psychology* 98 (1989): 307–313.

131. David Lykken, "Psychopathy, Sociopathy, and Crime," *Society* 34 (1996): 30–38.

132. Avshalom Caspi, Terrie Moffitt, Phil Silva, Magda Stouthamer-Loeber, Robert Krueger, and Pamela Schmutte, "Are Some People Crime-Prone? Replications of the Personality–Crime Relationship across Countries, Genders, Races and Methods," *Criminology* 32 (1994): 163–195.

133. Lykken, "Psychopathy, Sociopathy, and Crime."

134. Kent Kiehl, Andra Smith, Adrianna Mendrek, Bruce Forster, Robert Hare, and Peter F. Liddle, "Temporal Lobe Abnormalities in Semantic Processing by Criminal Psychopaths as Revealed by Functional Magnetic Resonance Imaging," *Psychiatry Research: Neuroimaging,* 130 (2004): 27–42.

135. Kent Kiehl, Andra Smith, Robert Hare, Adrianna Mendrek, Bruce Forster, Johann Brink, and Peter F. Liddle, "Limbic Abnormalities in Affective Processing by Criminal Psychopaths as Revealed by Functional Magnetic Resonance Imaging," *Biological Psychiatry* 5 (2001): 677–684.

136. Henry Goddard, *Efficiency and Levels of Intelligence* (Princeton, NJ: Princeton University Press, 1920); Edwin Sutherland, "Mental Deficiency and Crime," in *Social Attitudes,* ed. Kimball Young (New York: Henry Holt, 1931), chap. 15.

137. William Healy and Augusta Bronner, *Delinquency and Criminals: Their Making and Unmaking* (New York: Macmillan, 1926).

138. Joseph Lee Rogers, H. Harrington Cleveland, Edwin van den Oord, and David Rowe, "Resolving the Debate over Birth Order, Family Size and Intelligence," *American Psychologist* 55 (2000): 599–612.

139. Sutherland, "Mental Deficiency and Crime."

140. Travis Hirschi and Michael Hindelang, "Intelligence and Delinquency: A Revisionist Review," *American Sociological Review* 42 (1977): 471–586.

141. Anna Elmund, Lennart Melin, Anne-Liis von Knorring, Lemm Proos, and Torsten Tuvemo, "Cognitive and Neuropsychological Functioning in Transnationally Adopted Juvenile Delinquents," *Acta Paediatrica* 93 (2004): 1,507–1,513; Deborah Denno, "Sociological and Human Developmental Explanations of Crime: Conflict or Consensus," *Criminology* 23 (1985): 711–741.

142. James Q. Wilson and Richard Herrnstein, *Crime and Human Nature* (New York: Simon & Schuster, 1985), p. 148.

143. Richard Herrnstein and Charles Murray, *The Bell Curve: Intelligence and Class Structure in American Life* (New York: Free Press, 1994).

144. H. D. Day, J. M. Franklin, and D. D. Marshall, "Predictors of Aggression in Hospitalized Adolescents," *Journal of Psychology* 132 (1998): 427–435; Scott Menard and Barbara Morse, "A Structuralist Critique of the IQ–Delinquency Hypothesis: Theory and Evidence," *American Journal of Sociology* 89 (1984): 1,347–1,378; Denno, "Sociological and Human Developmental Explanations of Crime."

145. Ulric Neisser et al., "Intelligence: Knowns and Unknowns," *American Psychologist* 51 (1996): 77–101, at p. 83.

146. Susan Pease and Craig T. Love, "Optimal Methods and Issues in Nutrition Research in the Correctional Setting," *Nutrition Reviews Supplement* 44 (1986): 122–131.

147. Mark O'Callaghan and Douglas Carroll, "The Role of Psychosurgical Studies in the Control of Antisocial Behavior," in *The Causes of Crime: New Biological Approaches,* eds. Sarnoff Mednick, Terrie Moffitt, and Susan Stack (Cambridge: Cambridge University Press, 1987), pp. 312–328.

148. Reiss Jr. and Roth, *Understanding and Preventing Violence,* p. 389.

149. Kathleen Cirillo, B. E. Pruitt, Brian Colwell, Paul M. Kingery, Robert S. Hurley, and Danny Ballard, "School Violence: Prevalence and Intervention Strategies for At-Risk Adolescents," *Adolescence* 33 (1998): 319–331.

Chapter 6. Social Structure Theory: Because They're Poor

1. Arian Campo-Flores, "The Most Dangerous Gang in the United States," *Newsweek,* March 28, 2006; Ricardo Pollack, "Gang Life Tempts Salvador Teens," BBC news, http://news.bbc.co.uk/1/hi/world/americas/4201183.stm (accessed April 3, 2006).

2. Arlen Egley and Aline Major, *Highlights of the 2002–2003 National Youth Gang Surveys* (Washington, DC: Office of Juvenile Justice and Delinquency Prevention, 2005).

3. Steven Messner and Richard Rosenfeld, *Crime and the American Dream* (Belmont, CA: Wadsworth, 1994), p. 11.
4. Sam Roberts, *Who We Are Now: The Changing Face of America in the Twenty-First Century* (New York: Times Books, Henry Holt, 2004).
5. "High Net Worth Wealth Grows Strongly at Over 8%, Surpassing $30 Trillion in 2004, According to Merrill Lynch and Capgemini," *World Wealth Report*, June 9, 2005, www.us.capgemini.com/worldwealthreport/wwr_pressrelease.asp?ID=489 (accessed June 23, 2006.).
6. Oscar Lewis, "The Culture of Poverty," *Scientific American* 215 (1966): 19–25.
7. Gunnar Myrdal, *The Challenge of World Poverty* (New York: Vintage Books, 1970).
8. Jeanne Brooks-Gunn and Greg Duncan, "The Effects of Poverty on Children," *Future of Children* 7 (1997): 34–39.
9. Greg Duncan, W. Jean Yeung, Jeanne Brooks-Gunn, and Judith Smith, "How Much Does Childhood Poverty Affect the Life Chances of Children?" *American Sociological Review* 63 (1998): 406–423.
10. Ibid., p. 409.
11. Maria Velez, Lauren Krivo, and Ruth Peterson, "Structural Inequality and Homicide: An Assessment of the Black-White Gap in Killings," *Criminology* 41 (2003): 645–672.
12. U.S. Department of Census Data, *Race and Income* (Washington, DC: Census Bureau, 2003).
13. Ronald Mincy, ed., *Black Males Left Behind* (Washington, DC: Urban Institute, 2006); Erik Eckholm, "Plight Deepens for Black Men, Studies Warn," *New York Times*, March 20, 2006.
14. James Ainsworth-Darnell and Douglas Downey, "Assessing the Oppositional Culture Explanation for Racial/Ethnic Differences in School Performances," *American Sociological Review* 63 (1998): 536–553.
15. Julie A. Phillips, "White, Black, and Latino Homicide Rates: Why the Difference?" *Social Problems* 49 (2002): 349–374.
16. Jonathan Crane, "The Epidemic Theory of Ghettos and Neighborhood Effects on Dropping Out and Teenage Childbearing," *American Journal of Sociology* 96 (1991): 1,226–1,259. See also Rodrick Wallace, "Expanding Coupled Shock Fronts of Urban Decay and Criminal Behavior: How U.S. Cities Are Becoming 'Hollowed Out,'" *Journal of Quantitative Criminology* 7 (1991): 333–355.
17. Barbara Warner, "The Role of Attenuated Culture in Social Disorganization Theory," *Criminology* 41 (2003): 73–97.
18. Jeffrey Fagan and Garth Davies, "The Natural History of Neighborhood Violence," *Journal of Contemporary Criminal Justice* 20 (2004): 127–147.
19. Justin Patchin, Beth Huebner, John McCluskey, Sean Varano, and Timothy Bynum, "Exposure to Community Violence and Childhood Delinquency," *Crime & Delinquency* 52 (2006): 307–332.
20. Ibid.
21. See Ruth Kornhauser, *Social Sources of Delinquency* (Chicago: University of Chicago Press, 1978), p. 75.
22. Clifford R. Shaw and Henry D. McKay, *Juvenile Delinquency and Urban Areas,* rev. ed. (Chicago: University of Chicago Press, 1972).
23. Ibid., p. 52.
24. Ibid., p. 171.
25. Claire Valier, "Foreigners, Crime and Changing Mobilities," *British Journal of Criminology* 43 (2003): 1–21.
26. The best known of these critiques is Kornhauser, *Social Sources of Delinquency*.
27. For a general review, see James Byrne and Robert Sampson, eds., *The Social Ecology of Crime* (New York: Springer Verlag, 1985).
28. See, generally, Robert Bursik, "Social Disorganization and Theories of Crime and Delinquency: Problems and Prospects," *Criminology* 26 (1988): 521–539.
29. D. Wayne Osgood and Jeff Chambers, "Social Disorganization Outside the Metropolis: An Analysis of Rural Youth Violence," *Criminology* 38 (2000): 81–117.
30. William Spelman, "Abandoned Buildings: Magnets for Crime?" *Journal of Criminal Justice* 21 (1993): 481–493.
31. Keith Harries and Andrea Powell, "Juvenile Gun Crime and Social Stress: Baltimore, 1980–1990," *Urban Geography* 15 (1994): 45–63.
32. Ellen Kurtz, Barbara Koons, and Ralph Taylor, "Land Use, Physical Deterioration, Resident-Based Control, and Calls for Service on Urban Streetblocks," *Justice Quarterly* 15 (1998): 121–149.
33. Matthew Lee and Terri Earnest, "Perceived Community Cohesion and Perceived Risk of Victimization: A Cross-National Analysis," *Justice Quarterly* 20 (2003): 131–158.
34. Pamela Wilcox, Neil Quisenberry, and Shayne Jones, "The Built Environment and Community Crime Risk Interpretation," *Journal of Research in Crime and Delinquency* 40 (2003): 322–345.
35. Yili Xu, Mora Fiedler, and Karl Flaming, "Discovering the Impact of Community Policing: The Broken Windows Thesis, Collective Efficacy, and Citizens' Judgment," *Journal of Research in Crime and Delinquency* 42 (2005): 147–186.
36. Stephanie Greenberg, "Fear and Its Relationship to Crime, Neighborhood Deterioration, and Informal Social Control," in *The Social Ecology of Crime,* eds. James Byrne and Robert Sampson (New York: Springer Verlag, 1985), pp. 47–62.
37. C. L. Storr, C.-Y. Chen, and J. C. Anthony, "'Unequal Opportunity': Neighborhood Disadvantage and the Chance to Buy Illegal Drugs," *Journal of Epidemiology and Community Health* 58 (2004): 231–238.
38. Pamela Wilcox Rountree and Kenneth Land, "Burglary Victimization, Perceptions of Crime Risk, and Routine Activities: A Multilevel Analysis across Seattle Neighborhoods and Census Tracts," *Journal of Research in Crime and Delinquency* 33 (1996): 147–180.
39. Ted Chiricos, Ranee McEntire, and Marc Gertz, "Social Problems, Perceived Racial and Ethnic Composition of Neighborhood and Perceived Risk of Crime," *Social Problems* 48 (2001): 322–341; Wesley Skogan, "Fear of Crime and Neighborhood Change," in *Communities and Crime,* eds. Albert Reiss Jr. and Michael Tonry (Chicago: University of Chicago Press, 1986), pp. 191–232.
40. Catherine E. Ross, John Mirowsky, and Shana Pribesh, "Powerlessness and the Amplification of Threat: Neighborhood Disadvantage, Disorder, and Mistrust," *American Sociological Review* 66 (2001): 568–580.
41. Jodi Lane and James Meeker, "Social Disorganization Perceptions, Fear of Gang Crime, and Behavioral Precautions among Whites, Latinos, and Vietnamese," *Journal of Criminal Justice,* 32 (2004): 49–62.
42. John Hagan, Carla Shedd, and Monique Payne, "Race, Ethnicity, and Youth Perceptions of Criminal Injustice," *American Sociological Review* 70 (2005): 381–407.
43. William Terrill and Michael Reisig, "Neighborhood Context and Police Use of Force," *Journal of Research in Crime and Delinquency* 40 (2003): 291–321.
44. Finn Aage-Esbensen and David Huizinga, "Community Structure and Drug Use: From a Social Disorganization Perspective," *Justice Quarterly* 7 (1990): 691–709.
45. Karen Parker, Brian Stults, and Stephen Rice, "Racial Threat, Concentrated Disadvantage, and Social Control: Considering the Macro-Level Sources of Variation in Arrests," *Criminology* 43 (2005): 1,111–1,134.
46. Bridget Freisthler, Elizabeth Lascala, Paul Gruenewald, and Andrew Treno, "An Examination of Drug Activity: Effects of Neighborhood Social Organization on the Development of Drug Distribution Systems," *Substance Use & Misuse* 40 (2005): 671–686.

47. Micere Keels, Greg Duncan, Stefanie Deluca, Ruby Mendenhall, and James Rosenbaum, "Fifteen Years Later: Can Residential Mobility Programs Provide a Long-Term Escape from Neighborhood Segregation, Crime, and Poverty?" *Demography* 42 (2005): 51–72.
48. Allen Liska and Paul Bellair, "Violent-Crime Rates and Racial Composition: Convergence Over Time," *American Journal of Sociology* 101 (1995): 578–610.
49. Patricia McCall and Karen Parker, "A Dynamic Model of Racial Competition, Racial Inequality, and Interracial Violence," *Sociological Inquiry* 75 (2005): 273–294.
50. Steven Barkan and Steven Cohn, "Why Whites Favor Spending More Money to Fight Crime: The Role of Racial Prejudice," *Social Problems* 52 (2005): 300–314.
51. Leo Scheurman and Solomon Kobrin, "Community Careers in Crime," in *Communities and Crime,* eds. Albert Reiss Jr. and Michael Tonry (Chicago: University of Chicago Press, 1986), pp. 67–100.
52. Ibid.
53. Paul Stretesky, Amie Schuck, and Michael Hogan, "Space Matters: An Analysis of Poverty, Poverty Clustering, and Violent Crime," *Justice Quarterly* 21 (2004): 817–841.
54. Gregory Squires and Charis Kubrin, "Privileged Places: Race, Uneven Development and the Geography of Opportunity in Urban America," *Urban Studies* 42 (2005): 47–68; Matthew Lee, Michael Maume, and Graham Ousey, "Social Isolation and Lethal Violence across the Metro/Nonmetro Divide: The Effects of Socioeconomic Disadvantage and Poverty Concentration on Homicide," *Rural Sociology* 68 (2003): 107–131.
55. Lee, Maume, and Ousey, "Social Isolation and Lethal Violence across the Metro/Nonmetro Divide"; Charis E. Kubrin, "Structural Covariates of Homicide Rates: Does Type of Homicide Matter?" *Journal of Research in Crime and Delinquency* 40 (2003): 139–170; Darrell Steffensmeier and Dana Haynie, "Gender, Structural Disadvantage, and Urban Crime: Do Macrosocial Variables Also Explain Female Offending Rates?" *Criminology* 38 (2000): 403–438.
56. Jeffrey Morenoff, Robert Sampson, and Stephen Raudenbush, "Neighborhood Inequality, Collective Efficacy, and the Spatial Dynamics of Urban Violence," *Criminology* 39 (2001): 517–560.
57. Scott Menard and Delbert Elliott, "Self-Reported Offending, Maturational Reform, and the Easterlin Hypothesis," *Journal of Quantitative Criminology* 6 (1990): 237–268.
58. Elijah Anderson, *Streetwise: Race, Class and Change in an Urban Community* (Chicago: University of Chicago Press, 1990), pp. 243–244.
59. Jeffrey Michael Cancino, "The Utility of Social Capital and Collective Efficacy: Social Control Policy in Nonmetropolitan Settings," *Criminal Justice Policy Review* 16 (2005): 287–318; Chris Gibson, Jihong Zhao, Nicholas Lovrich, and Michael Gaffney, "Social Integration, Individual Perceptions of Collective Efficacy, and Fear of Crime in Three Cities," *Justice Quarterly* 19 (2002): 537–564; Felton Earls, *Linking Community Factors and Individual Development* (Washington, DC: National Institute of Justice, 1998).
60. Robert J. Sampson and Stephen W. Raudenbush, *Disorder in Urban Neighborhoods: Does It Lead to Crime?* (Washington, DC: National Institute of Justice, 2001).
61. Andrea Altschuler, Carol Somkin, and Nancy Adler, "Local Services and Amenities, Neighborhood Social Capital, and Health," *Social Science and Medicine* 59 (2004): 1,219–1,230.
62. Michael Reisig and Jeffrey Michael Cancino, "Incivilities in Nonmetropolitan Communities: The Effects of Structural Constraints, Social Conditions, and Crime," *Journal of Criminal Justice* 32 (2004): 15–29.
63. Robert Sampson, Jeffrey Morenoff, and Felton Earls, "Beyond Social Capital: Spatial Dynamics of Collective Efficacy for Children," *American Sociological Review* 64 (1999): 633–660.
64. Donald Black, "Social Control as a Dependent Variable," in *Toward a General Theory of Social Control,* ed. D. Black (Orlando, FL: Academic Press, 1990).
65. Jennifer Beyers, John Bates, Gregory Pettit, and Kenneth Dodge, "Neighborhood Structure, Parenting Processes, and the Development of Youths' Externalizing Behaviors: A Multilevel Analysis," *American Journal of Community Psychology* 31 (2003): 35–53.
66. Ronald Simons, Leslie Gordon Simons, Callie Harbin Burt, Gene Brody, and Carolyn Cutrona, "Collective Efficacy, Authoritative Parenting and Delinquency: A Longitudinal Test of a Model Integrating Community and Family-Level Processes," *Criminology* 43 (2005): 989–1,029.
67. April Pattavina, James Byrne, and Luis Garcia, "An Examination of Citizen Involvement in Crime Prevention in High-Risk Versus Low- to Moderate-Risk Neighborhoods," *Crime & Delinquency* 52 (2006): 203–231.
68. Paul Bellair, "Informal Surveillance and Street Crime: A Complex Relationship," *Criminology* 38 (2000): 137–170.
69. Wesley Skogan, *Disorder and Decline: Crime and the Spiral of Decay in American Neighborhoods.* (New York: Free Press, 1990), pp. 15–35.
70. Robert Sampson and W. Byron Groves, "Community Structure and Crime: Testing Social Disorganization Theory," *American Journal of Sociology* 94 (1989): 774–802; Denise Gottfredson, Richard McNeill, and Gary Gottfredson, "Social Area Influences on Delinquency: A Multilevel Analysis," *Journal of Research in Crime and Delinquency* 28 (1991): 197–206.
71. Fred Markowitz, Paul Bellair, Allen Liska, and Jianhong Liu, "Extending Social Disorganization Theory: Modeling the Relationships between Cohesion, Disorder, and Fear," *Criminology* 39 (2001): 293–320.
72. Robert Bursik and Harold Grasmick, "The Multiple Layers of Social Disorganization." Paper presented at the annual meeting of the American Society of Criminology, New Orleans, November 1992.
73. George Capowich, "The Conditioning Effects of Neighborhood Ecology on Burglary Victimization," *Criminal Justice and Behavior* 30 (2003): 39–62.
74. Ruth Perterson, Lauren Krivo, and Mark Harris, "Disadvantage and Neighborhood Violent Crime: Do Local Institutions Matter?" *Journal of Research in Crime and Delinquency* 37 (2000): 31–63.
75. Maria Velez, "The Role of Public Social Control in Urban Neighborhoods: A Multi-Level Analysis of Victimization Risk," *Criminology* 39 (2001): 837–864.
76. David Klinger, "Negotiating Order in Patrol Work: An Ecological Theory of Police Response to Deviance," *Criminology* 35 (1997): 277–306.
77. Rodney Stark, "Deviant Places: A Theory of the Ecology of Crime," *Criminology* 25 (1987): 893–911.
78. Robert Kane, "Compromised Police Legitimacy as a Predictor of Violent Crime in Structurally Disadvantaged Communities," *Criminology* 43 (2005): 469–498.
79. Robert Bursik and Harold Grasmick, "Economic Deprivation and Neighborhood Crime Rates, 1960–1980," *Law and Society Review* 27 (1993): 263–278.
80. Delbert Elliott, William Julius Wilson, David Huizinga, Robert Sampson, Amanda Elliott, and Bruce Rankin, "The Effects of Neighborhood Disadvantage on Adolescent Development," *Journal of Research in Crime and Delinquency* 33 (1996): 389–426.
81. James DeFronzo, "Welfare and Homicide," *Journal of Research in Crime and Delinquency* 34 (1997): 395–406.
82. John Worrall, "Reconsidering the Relationship between Welfare Spending and Serious Crime: A Panel Data Analysis with Implications for Social Support Theory," *Justice Quarterly* 22 (2005): 364–391.

83. Elliott, Wilson, Huizinga, Sampson, Elliott, and Rankin, "The Effects of Neighborhood Disadvantage on Adolescent Development," p. 414.
84. Ruth Peterson, Lauren Krivo, and Mark Harris, "Disadvantage and Neighborhood Violent Crime: Do Local Institutions Matter?" *Journal of Research in Crime and Delinquency* 37 (2000): 31–63.
85. Robert Merton, *Social Theory and Social Structure,* enlarged ed. (New York: Free Press, 1968).
86. Albert Cohen, "The Sociology of the Deviant Act: Anomie Theory and Beyond," *American Sociological Review* 30 (1965): 5–14.
87. Messner and Rosenfeld, *Crime and the American Dream.*
88. Jon Gunnar Bernburg, "Anomie, Social Change and Crime: A Theoretical Examination of Institutional-Anomie Theory," *British Journal of Criminology* 42 (2002): 729–743.
89. John Hagan, Gerd Hefler, Gabriele Classen, Klaus Boehnke, and Hans Merkens, "Subterranean Sources of Subcultural Delinquency Beyond the American Dream," *Criminology* 36 (1998): 309–340.
90. Morenoff, Sampson, and Raudenbush, "Neighborhood Inequality, Collective Efficacy, and the Spatial Dynamics of Urban Violence."
91. John Braithwaite, "Poverty, Power, White-Collar Crime and the Paradoxes of Criminological Theory," *Australian and New Zealand Journal of Criminology* 24 (1991): 40–58.
92. Margo Wilson and Martin Daly, "Life Expectancy, Economic Inequality, Homicide, and Reproductive Timing in Chicago Neighbourhoods," *British Journal of Medicine* 314 (1997): 1,271–1,274.
93. Judith Blau and Peter Blau, "The Cost of Inequality: Metropolitan Structure and Violent Crime," *American Sociological Review* 147 (1982): 114–129.
94. Elliott, Wilson, Huizinga, Sampson, Elliott, and Rankin, "The Effects of Neighborhood disadvantage on Adolescent Development,".
95. Tomislav Kovandzic, Lynne Vieraitis, and Mark Yeisley, "The Structural Covariates of Urban Homicide: Reassessing the Impact of Income Inequality and Poverty in the Post-Reagan Era," *Criminology* 36 (1998): 569–600.
96. Scott South and Steven Messner, "Structural Determinants of Intergroup Association," *American Journal of Sociology* 91 (1986): 1,409–1,430; Steven Messner and Scott South, "Economic Deprivation, Opportunity Structure, and Robbery Victimization," *Social Forces* 64 (1986): 975–991.
97. Richard Fowles and Mary Merva, "Wage Inequality and Criminal Activity: An Extreme Bounds Analysis for the United States 1975–1990," *Criminology* 34 (1996): 163–182.
98. Beverly Stiles, Xiaoru Liu, and Howard Kaplan, "Relative Deprivation and Deviant Adaptations: The Mediating Effects of Negative Self Feelings," *Journal of Research in Crime and Delinquency* 37 (2000): 64–90.
99. Robert Agnew, "Foundation for a General Strain Theory of Crime and Delinquency," *Criminology* 30 (1992): 47–87.
100. Ibid., p. 57.
101. Timothy Brezina, "Adolescent Maltreatment and Delinquency: The Question of Intervening Processes," *Journal of Research in Crime and Delinquency* 35 (1998): 71–99.
102. Paul Mazerolle, Velmer Burton Jr., Francis Cullen, T. David Evans, and Gary Payne, "Strain, Anger, and Delinquent Adaptations Specifying General Strain Theory," *Journal of Criminal Justice* 28 (2000): 89–101; Paul Mazerolle and Alex Piquero, "Violent Responses to Strain: An Examination of Conditioning Influences," *Violence and Victimization* 12 (1997): 323–345.
103. George E. Capowich, Paul Mazerolle, and Alex Piquero, "General Strain Theory, Situational Anger, and Social Networks: An Assessment of Conditioning Influences," *Journal of Criminal Justice* 29 (2001): 445–461.
104. Robert Agnew, Timothy Brezina, John Paul Wright, and Francis T. Cullen, "Strain, Personality Traits, and Delinquency: Extending General Strain Theory," *Criminology* 40 (2002): 43–71.
105. Lee Ann Slocum, Sally Simpson, and Douglas Smith, "Strained Lives and Crime: Examining Intra-Individual Variation in Strain and Offending in a Sample of Incarcerated Women," *Criminology* 43 (2005): 1,067–1,110.
106. Robert Agnew, "Stability and Change in Crime over the Life Course: A Strain Theory Explanation," in *Advances in Criminological Theory: Vol. 7, Developmental Theories of Crime and Delinquency,* ed. Terence Thornberry (New Brunswick, NJ: Transaction Books, 1995), pp. 113–137.
107. Lawrence Wu, "Effects of Family Instability, Income, and Income Instability on the Risk of Premarital Birth," *American Sociological Review* 61 (1996): 386–406.
108. Robert Agnew and Helene Raskin White, "An Empirical Test of General Strain Theory," *Criminology* 30 (1992): 475–499.
109. John Hoffman and Alan Miller, "A Latent Variable Analysis of General Strain Theory," *Journal of Quantitative Criminology* 13 (1997): 111–113; Raymond Paternoster and Paul Mazerolle, "General Strain Theory and Delinquency: A Replication and Extension," *Journal of Research in Crime and Delinquency* 31 (1994): 235–263; G. Roger Jarjoura, "The Conditional Effect of Social Class on the Dropout–Delinquency Relationship," *Journal of Research in Crime and Delinquency* 33 (1996): 232–255.
110. Mazerolle, Burton Jr., Cullen, Evans, and Payne, "Strain, Anger, and Delinquent Adaptations: Specifying General Strain Theory."
111. Timothy Brezina, "Adapting to Strain: An Examination of Delinquent Coping Responses," *Criminology* 34 (1996): 39–61.
112. Stephen Cernkovich, Peggy Giordano, and Jennifer Rudolph, "Race, Crime and the American Dream," *Journal of Research in Crime and Delinquency* 37 (2000): 131–170.
113. Robert Agnew, "Experienced, Vicarious, and Anticipated Strain: An Exploratory Study on Physical Victimization and Delinquency," *Justice Quarterly* 19 (2002): 603–633.
114. Walter Miller, "Lower-Class Culture as a Generating Milieu of Gang Delinquency," *Journal of Social Issues* 14 (1958): 5–19.
115. Ibid., pp. 14–17.
116. Fred Markowitz and Richard Felson, "Social-Demographic Attitudes and Violence," *Criminology* 36 (1998): 117–138.
117. Jeffrey Fagan, *Adolescent Violence: A View from the Street,* NIJ Research Preview (Washington, DC: National Institute of Justice, 1998).
118. Albert Cohen, *Delinquent Boys* (New York: Free Press, 1955).
119. Ibid., p. 25.
120. Ibid., p. 28.
121. Ibid.
122. Ibid., p. 30.
123. Ibid., p. 133.
124. Richard Cloward and Lloyd Ohlin, *Delinquency and Opportunity* (New York: Free Press, 1960).
125. Ibid., p. 171.
126. Ibid., p. 73.
127. James DeFronzo, "Welfare and Burglary," *Crime & Delinquency* 42 (1996): 223–230.

Chapter 7. Social Process Theories: Socialized to Crime

1. Columbine Massacre, http://history1900s.about.com/od/famouscrimesscandals/a/columbine.htm; CNN, Columbine Report, www.cnn.com/SPECIALS/2000/columbine.cd/frameset.exclude.html.
2. Charles Tittle and Robert Meier, "Specifying the SES/Delinquency Relationship," *Criminology* 28 (1990): 271–299, at p. 274.
3. Eric Stewart, Ronald Simons, and Rand Conger, "Assessing Neighborhood and Social Psychological Influences on Childhood Violence in an African-American Sample," *Criminology* 40 (2002): 801–830.
4. Sheldon Glueck and Eleanor Glueck, *Unraveling Juvenile Delinquency* (Cambridge, MA: Harvard University Press, 1950); Ashley Weeks, "Predicting Juvenile Delinquency," *American Sociological Review* 8 (1943): 40–46.

5. Alexander Vazsonyi and Lloyd Pickering, "The Importance of Family and School Domains in Adolescent Deviance: African American and Caucasian Youth," *Journal of Youth and Adolescence* 32 (2003): 115–129; Denise Kandel, "The Parental and Peer Contexts of Adolescent Deviance: An Algebra of Interpersonal Influences," *Journal of Drug Issues* 26 (1996): 289–315; Ann Goetting, "The Parenting–Crime Connection," *Journal of Primary Prevention* 14 (1994): 167–184.
6. John Paul Wright and Francis Cullen, "Parental Efficacy and Delinquent Behavior: Do Control and Support Matter?" *Criminology* 39 (2001): 677–706.
7. Carter Hay, "Parenting, Self-Control, and Delinquency: A Test of Self-Control Theory," *Criminology* 39 (2001): 707–736.
8. Robert Vermeiren, Jef Bogaerts, Vladislav Ruchkin, Dirk Deboutte, and Mary Schwab-Stone, "Subtypes of Self-Esteem and Self-Concept in Adolescent Violent and Property Offenders," *Journal of Child Psychology and Psychiatry* 45 (2004): 405–411.
9. Robert Roberts and Vern Bengston, "Affective Ties to Parents in Early Adulthood and Self-Esteem across 20 Years," *Social Psychology Quarterly* 59 (1996): 96–106.
10. Joseph Rankin and L. Edward Wells, "The Effect of Parental Attachments and Direct Controls on Delinquency," *Journal of Research in Crime and Delinquency* 27 (1990): 140–165.
11. Tiffany Field, "Violence and Touch Deprivation in Adolescents," *Adolescence* 37 (2002): 735–749.
12. Robert Johnson, S. Susan Su, Dean Gerstein, Hee-Choon Shin, and John Hoffman, "Parental Influences on Deviant Behavior in Early Adolescence: A Logistic Response Analysis of Age- and Gender-Differentiated Effects," *Journal of Quantitative Criminology* 11 (1995): 167–192.
13. Thomas Ashby Wills, Donato Vaccaro, Grace McNamara, and A. Elizabeth Hirky, "Escalated Substance Use: A Longitudinal Grouping Analysis from Early to Middle Adolescence," *Journal of Abnormal Psychology* 105 (1996): 166–180.
14. Kristi Holsinger and Alexander Holsinger, " Differential Pathways to Violence and Self-Injurious Behavior: African American and White Girls in the Juvenile Justice System," *Journal of Research in Crime and Delinquency* 42 (2005): 211–242; Carolyn Smith and Terence Thornberry, "The Relationship between Childhood Maltreatment and Adolescent Involvement in Delinquency," *Criminology* 33 (1995): 451–479.
15. Fred Rogosch and Dante Cicchetti, "Child Maltreatment and Emergent Personality Organization: Perspectives from the Five-Factor Model," *Journal of Abnormal Child Psychology* 32 (2004): 123–145.
16. Eric Slade and Lawrence Wissow, "Spanking in Early Childhood and Later Behavior Problems: A Prospective Study of Infants and Young Toddlers," *Pediatrics* 113 (2004): 1,321–1,330; Ronald Simons, Chyi-In Wu, Kuei-Hsiu Lin, Leslie Gordon, and Rand Conger, "A Cross-Cultural Examination of the Link between Corporal Punishment and Adolescent Antisocial Behavior," *Criminology* 38 (2000): 47–79.
17. Murray A. Straus, "Spanking and the Making of a Violent Society: The Short- and Long-Term Consequences of Corporal Punishment," *Pediatrics* 98 (1996): 837–843.
18. *The Forgotten Half: Pathways to Success for America's Youth and Young Families* (Washington, DC: William T. Grant Foundation, 1988); Lee Jussim, "Teacher Expectations: Self-Fulfilling Prophecies, Perceptual Biases, and Accuracy," *Journal of Personality and Social Psychology* 57 (1989): 469–480.
19. Eugene Maguin and Rolf Loeber, "Academic Performance and Delinquency," in *Crime and Justice: A Review of Research*, vol. 20, ed. Michael Tonry (Chicago: University of Chicago Press, 1995), pp. 145–264.
20. Christopher B. Swanson, *Who Graduates? Who Doesn't? A Statistical Portrait of Public High School Graduation, Class of 2001* (Washington, DC: Urban Institute, 2004).
21. G. Roger Jarjoura, "Does Dropping Out of School Enhance Delinquent Involvement? Results from a Large-Scale National Probability Sample," *Criminology* 31 (1993): 149–172; Terence Thornberry, Melanie Moore, and R. L. Christenson, "The Effect of Dropping Out of High School on Subsequent Criminal Behavior," *Criminology* 23 (1985): 3–18.
22. Catherine Dulmus, Matthew Theriot, Karen Sowers, and James Blackburn, "Student Reports of Peer Bullying Victimization in a Rural School," *Stress, Trauma & Crisis: An International Journal* 7 (2004): 1–15.
23. Tonja Nansel, Mary Overpeck, and Ramani Pilla, "Bullying Behaviors among U.S. Youth: Prevalence and Association with Psychosocial Adjustment," *JAMA: Journal of the American Medical Association* 285 (2001): 2,094–3,100.
24. Jill DeVoe, Katharin Peter, Sally Ruddy, Amanda Miller, Mike Planty, Thomas Snyder, and Michael Rand, *Indicators of School Crime and Safety, 2003* (Washington, DC: U.S. Department of Education and Bureau of Justice Statistics, 2004).
25. Ben Brown and William Reed Benedict, "Bullets, Blades, and Being Afraid in Hispanic High Schools: An Exploratory Study of the Presence of Weapons and Fear of Weapon-Associated Victimization among High School Students in a Border Town," *Crime & Delinquency* 50 (2004): 372–395.
26. Irving Janis, *Groupthink: Psychological Studies of Policy Decisions and Fiascoes* (Boston: Houghton Mifflin, 1982).
27. Delbert Elliott, David Huizinga, and Suzanne Ageton, *Explaining Delinquency and Drug Use* (Beverly Hills, CA: Sage, 1985); Helene Raskin White, Robert Padina, and Randy La-Grange, "Longitudinal Predictors of Serious Substance Use and Delinquency," *Criminology* 6 (1987): 715–740.
28. Robert Agnew and Timothy Brezina, "Relational Problems with Peers, Gender and Delinquency," *Youth and Society* 29 (1997): 84–111.
29. Paul Friday, Xin Ren, Elmar Weitekamp, Hans-Jürgen Kerner, and Terrance Taylor, "A Chinese Birth Cohort: Theoretical Implications" *Journal of Research in Crime and Delinquency* 42 (2005): 123–146.
30. Daneen Deptula and Robert Cohen, "Aggressive, Rejected, and Delinquent Children and Adolescents: A Comparison of Their Friendships," *Aggression & Violent Behavior* 9 (2004): 75–104; Stephen W. Baron, "Self-control, Social Consequences, and Criminal Behavior: Street Youth and the General Theory of Crime," *Journal of Research in Crime and Delinquency* 40 (2003): 403–425.
31. Sylive Mrug, Betsy Hoza, and William Bukowski, "Choosing or Being Chosen by Aggressive-Disruptive Peers: Do They Contribute to Children's Externalizing and Internalizing Problems?" *Journal of Abnormal Child Psychology* 32 (2004): 53–66; Terence Thornberry and Marvin Krohn, "Peers, Drug Use and Delinquency," in *Handbook of Antisocial Behavior*, eds. David Stoff, James Breiling, and Jack Maser (New York: Wiley, 1997), pp. 218–233.
32. Mark Warr, "Age, Peers, and Delinquency," *Criminology* 31 (1993): 17–40.
33. David Fergusson, L. John Horwood, and Daniel Nagin, "Offending Trajectories in a New Zealand Birth Cohort," *Criminology* 38 (2000): 525–551.
34. Sara Battin, Karl Hill, Robert Abbott, Richard Catalano, and J. David Hawkins, "The Contribution of Gang Membership to Delinquency Beyond Delinquent Friends," *Criminology* 36 (1998): 93–116.
35. John Paul Wright and Francis Cullen, "Employment, Peers, and Life-Course Transitions," *Justice Quarterly*, 21 (2004): 183–205.
36. Colin Baier and Bradley Wright, "If You Love Me, Keep My Commandments": A Meta-Analysis of the Effect of Religion on Crime," *Journal of Research in Crime and Delinquency* 38 (2001): 3–21; Byron Johnson, Sung Joon Jang, David Larson, and Spencer De Li, "Does Adolescent Religious Commitment

Matter? A Reexamination of the Effects of Religiosity on Delinquency," *Journal of Research in Crime and Delinquency* 38 (2001): 22–44.

37. Sung Joon Jang and Byron Johnson, "Neighborhood Disorder, Individual Religiosity, and Adolescent Use of Illicit Drugs: A Test of Multilevel Hypothesis," *Criminology* 39 (2001): 109–144.

38. T. David Evans, Francis Cullen, R. Gregory Dunaway, and Velmer Burton Jr., "Religion and Crime Reexamined: The Impact of Religion, Secular Controls, and Social Ecology on Adult Criminality," *Criminology* 33 (1995): 195–224.

39. Edwin H. Sutherland, *Principles of Criminology* (Philadelphia: Lippincott, 1939).

40. See, for example, Edwin Sutherland, "White-Collar Criminality," *American Sociological Review* 5 (1940): 2–10.

41. See Edwin Sutherland and Donald Cressey, *Criminology*, 8th ed. (Philadelphia: Lippincott, 1970), pp. 77–79.

42. Carlo Morselli, Pierre Tremblay, and Bill McCarthy, "Mentors and Criminal Achievement," *Criminology* 44 (2006): 17–43.

43. Sandra Brown, Vicki Creamer, and Barbara Stetson, "Adolescent Alcohol Expectancies in Relation to Personal and Parental Drinking Patterns," *Journal of Abnormal Psychology* 96 (1987): 117–121.

44. Terence Thornberry, Adrienne Freeman-Gallant, Alan Lizotte, Marvin Krohn, and Carolyn Smith, "Linked Lives: The Intergenerational Transmission of Antisocial Behavior," *Journal of Abnormal Child Psychology* 31 (2003): 171–184.

45. Paul Vowell and Jieming Chen, "Predicting Academic Misconduct: A Comparative Test of Four Sociological Explanations," *Sociological Inquiry* 74 (2004): 226–249.

46. Andy Hochstetler, Heith Copes, and Matt DeLisi, "Differential Association in Group and Solo Offending," *Journal of Criminal Justice* 30 (2002): 559–566.

47. Dana Haynie, Peggy Giordano, Wendy Manning, and Monica Longmore, "Adolescent Romantic Relationships and Delinquency Involvement," *Criminology* 43 (2005): 177–210.

48. Joel Hektner, Gerald August, and George Realmuto, "Effects of Pairing Aggressive and Nonaggressive Children in Strategic Peer Affiliation," *Journal of Abnormal Child Psychology* 31 (2003): 399–412; Matthew Ploeger, "Youth Employment and Delinquency: Reconsidering a Problematic Relationship," *Criminology* 35 (1997): 659–675; William Skinner and Anne Fream, "A Social Learning Theory Analysis of Computer Crime among College Students," *Journal of Research in Crime and Delinquency* 34 (1997): 495–518; Denise Kandel and Mark Davies, "Friendship Networks, Intimacy, and Illicit Drug Use in Young Adulthood: A Comparison of Two Competing Theories," *Criminology* 29 (1991): 441–467.

49. Warr, "Age, Peers, and Delinquency."

50. Clayton Hartjen and S. Priyadarsini, "Gender, Peers, and Delinquency," *Youth & Society* 34 (2003): 387–414.

51. Craig Reinerman and Jeffrey Fagan, "Social Organization and Differential Association: A Research Note from a Longitudinal Study of Violent Juvenile Offenders," *Crime & Delinquency* 34 (1988): 307–327.

52. Gresham Sykes and David Matza, "Techniques of Neutralization: A Theory of Delinquency," *American Sociological Review* 22 (1957): 664–670; David Matza, *Delinquency and Drift* (New York: John Wiley, 1964).

53. Matza, *Delinquency and Drift*, p. 51.

54. Sykes and Matza, "Techniques of Neutralization." See also David Matza, "Subterranean Traditions of Youths," *The ANNALS of the American Academy of Political and Social Science* 378 (1961): 116.

55. Sykes and Matza, "Techniques of Neutralization."

56. Ibid.

57. Ian Shields and George Whitehall, "Neutralization and Delinquency among Teenagers," *Criminal Justice and Behavior* 21 (1994): 223–235; Robert A. Ball, "An Empirical Exploration of Neutralization Theory," *Criminologica* 4 (1966): 22–32. See also M. William Minor, "The Neutralization of Criminal Offense," *Criminology* 18 (1980): 103–120; Robert Gordon, James Short, Desmond Cartwright, and Fred Strodtbeck, "Values and Gang Delinquency: A Study of Street Corner Groups," *American Journal of Sociology* 69 (1963): 109–128.

58. Michael Hindelang, "The Commitment of Delinquents to Their Misdeeds: Do Delinquents Drift?" *Social Problems* 17 (1970): 500–509; Robert Regoli and Eric Poole, "The Commitment of Delinquents to Their Misdeeds: A Reexamination," *Journal of Criminal Justice* 6 (1978): 261–269.

59. Larry Siegel, Spencer Rathus, and Carol Ruppert, "Values and Delinquent Youth: An Empirical Reexamination of Theories of Delinquency," *British Journal of Criminology* 13 (1973): 237–244.

60. Robert Agnew, "The Techniques of Neutralization and Violence," *Criminology* 32 (1994): 555–580.

61. Jeffrey Fagan, *Adolescent Violence: A View from the Street*, NIJ Research Preview (Washington, DC: National Institute of Justice, 1998).

62. Scott Briar and Irving Piliavin, "Delinquency: Situational Inducements and Commitment to Conformity," *Social Problems* 13 (1965–1966): 35–45.

63. Lawrence Sherman and Douglas Smith, with Janell Schmidt and Dennis Rogan, "Crime, Punishment, and Stake in Conformity: Legal and Informal Control of Domestic Violence," *American Sociological Review* 57 (1992): 680–690.

64. Albert Reiss Jr., "Delinquency as the Failure of Personal and Social Controls," *American Sociological Review* 16 (1951): 196–207.

65. Briar and Piliavin, "Delinquency."

66. Walter Reckless, *The Crime Problem* (New York: Appleton-Century Crofts, 1967), pp. 469–483.

67. Among the many research reports by Reckless and his colleagues are Walter Reckless, Simon Dinitz, and Ellen Murray, "Self-Concept as an Insulator against Delinquency," *American Sociological Review* 21 (1956): 744–746; Walter Reckless, Simon Dinitz, and Barbara Kay, "The Self-Component in Potential Delinquency and Potential Non-Delinquency," *American Sociological Review* 22 (1957): 566–570; Walter Reckless, Simon Dinitz, and Ellen Murray, "The Good Boy in a High Delinquency Area," *Journal of Criminal Law, Criminology, and Police Science* 48 (1957): 12–26; Frank Scarpitti, Ellen Murray, Simon Dinitz, and Walter Reckless, "The Good Boy in a High Delinquency Area: Four Years Later," *American Sociological Review* 23 (1960): 555–558; Walter Reckless and Simon Dinitz, "Pioneering with Self-Concept as a Vulnerability Factor in Delinquency," *Journal of Criminal Law, Criminology, and Police Science* 58 (1967): 515–523.

68. Travis Hirschi, *Causes of Delinquency* (Berkeley: University of California Press, 1969).

69. Ibid., p. 231.

70. Ibid., pp. 66–74.

71. Michael Wiatrowski, David Griswold, and Mary K. Roberts, "Social Control Theory and Delinquency," *American Sociological Review* 46 (1981): 525–541.

72. Helen Garnier and Judith Stein, "An 18-Year Model of Family and Peer Effects on Adolescent Drug Use and Delinquency," *Journal of Youth and Adolescence* 31 (2002): 45–56; Bobbi Jo Anderson, Malcolm Holmes, and Erik Ostresh, "Male and Female Delinquents' Attachments and Effects of Attachments on Severity of Self-Reported Delinquency," *Criminal Justice and Behavior* 26 (1999): 435–452.

73. Teresa LaGrange and Robert Silverman, "Perceived Strain and Delinquency Motivation: An Empirical Evaluation of General Strain Theory." Paper presented at the American Society of Criminology meeting, Boston, November 1995.

74. Patricia Van Voorhis, Francis Cullen, Richard Mathers, and Connie Chenoweth Garner, "The Impact of Family Structure and Quality on Delinquency: A Comparative Assessment of

Structural and Functional Factors," *Criminology* 26 (1988): 235–261.

75. Thomas Vander Ven, Francis Cullen, Mark Carrozza, and John Paul Wright, "Home Alone: The Impact of Maternal Employment on Delinquency," *Social Problems* 48 (2001): 236–257; Patricia Jenkins, "School Delinquency and the School Social Bond," *Journal of Research in Crime and Delinquency* 34 (1997): 337–367; Patricia Jenkins, "School Delinquency and the School Social Bond," *Journal of Research in Crime and Delinquency* 34 (1997): 337–367.

76. Trina Hope, Esther Wilder, and Toni-Terling Watt, "The Relationships among Adolescent Pregnancy, Pregnancy Resolution, and Juvenile Delinquency," *The Sociological Quarterly* 44 (2003): 555–576.

77. John Cochran and Ronald Akers, "An Exploration of the Variable Effects of Religiosity on Adolescent Marijuana and Alcohol Use," *Journal of Research in Crime and Delinquency* 26 (1989): 198–225.

78. Mark Regnerus and Glen Elder Jr., "Religion and Vulnerability among Low-Risk Adolescents," *Social Science Research* 32 (2003): 633–658; Mark Regnerus, "Moral Communities and Adolescent Delinquency: Religious Contexts and Community Social Control," *The Sociological Quarterly* 44 (2003): 523–554.

79. Eugene Maguin and Rolf Loeber, "Academic Performance and Delinquency," pp. 145–264. *Justice Review* 28 (2003): 254–277.

80. Robert Crosnoe, "The Connection between Academic Failure and Adolescent Drinking in Secondary School," *Sociology of Education* 79 (2006): 44–60.

81. Jonathan Zaff, Kristin Moore, Angela Romano Papillo, and Stephanie Williams, "Implications of Extracurricular Activity Participation during Adolescence on Positive Outcomes," *Journal of Adolescent Research* 18 (2003): 599–631; Robert Agnew and David Peterson, "Leisure and Delinquency," *Social Problems* 36 (1989): 332–348.

82. Peggy Giordano, Stephen Cernkovich, and M. D. Pugh, "Friendships and Delinquency," *American Journal of Sociology* 91 (1986): 1,170–1,202.

83. Denise Kandel and Mark Davies, "Friendship Networks, Intimacy, and Illicit Drug Use in Young Adulthood: A Comparison of Two Competing Theories," *Criminology* 29 (1991): 441–467.

84. Stephen Cernkovich, Peggy Giordano, and Jennifer Rudolph, "Race, Crime and the American Dream," *Journal of Research in Crime and Delinquency* 37 (2000): 131–170.

85. Velmer Burton Jr., Francis Cullen, T. David Evans, R. Gregory Dunaway, Sesha Kethineni, and Gary Payne, "The Impact of Parental Controls on Delinquency," *Journal of Criminal Justice* 23 (1995): 111–126.

86. Michael Hindelang, "Causes of Delinquency: A Partial Replication and Extension," *Social Problems* 21 (1973): 471–487.

87. Gary Jensen and David Brownfield, "Parents and Drugs," *Criminology* 21 (1983): 543–554. See also M. Wiatrowski, D. Griswold, and M. Roberts, "Social Control Theory and Delinquency," *American Sociological Review* 46 (1981): 525–541.

88. Leslie Samuelson, Timothy Hartnagel, and Harvey Krahn, "Crime and Social Control among High School Dropouts," *Journal of Crime and Justice* 18 (1990): 129–161.

89. Allen E. Liska and M. D. Reed, "Ties to Conventional Institutions and Delinquency: Estimating Reciprocal Effects," *American Sociological Review* 50 (1985): 547–560.

90. Wiatrowski, Griswold, and Roberts, "Social Control Theory and Delinquency."

91. Linda Jackson, John Hunter, and Carole Hodge, "Physical Attractiveness and Intellectual Competence: A Meta-Analytic Review," *Social Psychology Quarterly* 58 (1995): 108–122.

92. Howard Becker, *Outsiders: Studies in the Sociology of Deviance* (New York: Macmillan, 1963), p. 9.

93. Harold Garfinkle, "Conditions of Successful Degradation Ceremonies," *American Journal of Sociology* 61 (1956): 420–424.

94. Stacy DeCoster and Karen Heimer, "The Relationship between Law Violation and Depression: An Interactionist Analysis," *Criminology* 39 (2001): 799–837.

95. Karen Heimer and Ross Matsueda, "Role-Taking, Role-Commitment and Delinquency: A Theory of Differential Social Control," *American Sociological Review* 59 (1994): 365–390.

96. See, for example, Howard Kaplan and Hiroshi Fukurai, "Negative Social Sanctions, Self-Rejection, and Drug Use," *Youth and Society* 23 (1992): 275–298; Howard Kaplan and Robert Johnson, "Negative Social Sanctions and Juvenile Delinquency: Effects of Labeling in a Model of Deviant Behavior," *Social Science Quarterly* 72 (1991): 98–122; Howard Kaplan, Robert Johnson, and Carol Bailey, "Deviant Peers and Deviant Behavior: Further Elaboration of a Model," *Social Psychology Quarterly* 30 (1987): 277–284.

97. John Lofland, *Deviance and Identity* (Englewood Cliffs, NJ: Prentice-Hall, 1969).

98. Frank Tannenbaum, *Crime and the Community* (New York: Columbia University Press, 1938), pp. 19–20.

99. Edwin Lemert, *Social Pathology* (New York: McGraw-Hill, 1951).

100. Ibid., p. 75.

101. Christy Visher, "Gender, Police Arrest Decision, and Notions of Chivalry," *Criminology* 21 (1983): 5–28.

102. Marjorie Zatz, "Race, Ethnicity and Determinate Sentencing," *Criminology* 22 (1984): 147–171.

103. Christina DeJong and Kenneth Jackson, "Putting Race into Context: Race, Juvenile Justice Processing, and Urbanization," *Justice Quarterly* 15 (1998): 487–504.

104. Joan Petersilia, "Racial Disparities in the Criminal Justice System: A Summary," *Crime & Delinquency* 31 (1985): 15–34.

105. Carl Pope and William Feyerherm, "Minority Status and Juvenile Justice Processing," *Criminal Justice Abstracts* 22 (1990): 327–336. See also Carl Pope, "Race and Crime Revisited," *Crime & Delinquency* 25 (1979): 347–357; National Minority Council on Criminal Justice, *The Inequality of Justice* (Washington, DC: National Minority Advisory Council on Criminal Justice, 1981), p. 200.

106. Howard Kaplan and Robert Johnson, "Negative Social Sanctions and Juvenile Delinquency: Effects of Labeling in a Model of Deviant Behavior," *Social Science Quarterly* 72 (1991): 98–122.

107. Ruth Triplett, "The Conflict Perspective, Symbolic Interactionism, and the Status Characteristics Hypothesis," *Justice Quarterly* 10 (1993): 540–558.

108. Lening Zhang, "Official Offense Status and Self-Esteem among Chinese Youths," *Journal of Criminal Justice* 31 (2003): 99–105.

109. Ross Matsueda, "Reflected Appraisals: Parental Labeling, and Delinquency: Specifying a Symbolic Interactionist Theory," *American Journal of Sociology* 97 (1992): 1,577–1,611.

110. Xiaoru Liu, "The Conditional Effect of Peer Groups on the Relationship between Parental Labeling and Youth Delinquency," *Sociological Perspectives* 43 (2000): 499–515.

111. Suzanne Ageton and Delbert Elliott, *The Effect of Legal Processing on Self-Concept* (Boulder, CO: Institute of Behavioral Science, 1973).

112. Mike Adams, Craig Robertson, Phyllis Gray-Ray, and Melvin Ray, "Labeling and Delinquency," *Adolescence* 38 (2003): 171–186.

113. Jón Gunnar Bernburg, Marvin Krohn, and Craig Rivera, "Official Labeling, Criminal Embeddedness, and Subsequent Delinquency: A Longitudinal Test of Labeling Theory," *Journal of Research in Crime and Delinquency* 43 (2006): 67–88.

114. Christine Bowditch, "Getting Rid of Troublemakers: High School Disciplinary Procedures and the Production of Dropouts," *Social Problems* 40 (1993): 493–507.

115. Melvin Ray and William Downs, "An Empirical Test of Labeling Theory Using Longitudinal Data," *Journal of Research in Crime and Delinquency* 23 (1986): 169–194.

116. Sherman and Smith, with Schmidt and Rogan, "Crime, Punishment, and Stake in Conformity."

117. Lawrence Bench and Terry Allen, "Investigating the Stigma of Prison Classification: An Experimental Design," *Prison Journal* 83 (2003): 367–382.

118. Charles Tittle, "Two Empirical Regularities (Maybe) in Search of an Explanation: Commentary on the Age/Crime Debate," *Criminology* 26 (1988): 75–85.

119. Robert Sampson and John Laub, "A Life-Course Theory of Cumulative Disadvantage and the Stability of Delinquency," in *Developmental Theories of Crime and Delinquency,* ed. Terence Thornberry (New Brunswick, NJ: Transaction Press, 1997), pp. 133–161; Douglas Smith and Robert Brame, "On the Initiation and Continuation of Delinquency," *Criminology* 4 (1994): 607–630.

120. Raymond Paternoster and Leeann Iovanni, "The Labeling Perspective and Delinquency: An Elaboration of the Theory and an Assessment of the Evidence," *Justice Quarterly* 6 (1989): 358–394.

121. Shadd Maruna, Thomas Lebel, Nick Mitchell, and Michelle Maples, "Pygmalion in the Reintegration Process: Desistance from Crime through the Looking Glass," *Psychology, Crime & Law* 10 (2004): 271–281.

Chapter 8. Critical Criminology: It's a Class Thing

1. Peter Ford, "Deep Roots of the Paris Riots," *Christian Science Monitor*, November 4, 2005, www.csmonitor.com/2005/1104/p06s02-woeu.html; BBC News, Riots Erupt in More Paris Suburbs, November 2, 2005, http://news.bbc.co.uk/1/hi/world/europe/4395294.stm.

2. Michael Lynch and W. Byron Groves, *A Primer in Radical Criminology*, 2nd ed. (Albany, NY: Harrow & Heston, 1989), pp. 32–33.

3. Michael Lynch, "Rediscovering Criminology: Lessons from the Marxist Tradition," in *Marxist Sociology: Surveys of Contemporary Theory and Research*, eds. Donald McQuarie and Patrick McGuire (New York: General Hall Press, 1994).

4. Andrew Woolford, "Making Genocide Unthinkable: Three Guidelines for a Critical Criminology of Genocide," *Critical Criminology* 14 (2006): 87–106.

5. Ian Taylor, Paul Walton, and Jock Young, *The New Criminology: For a Social Theory of Deviance* (London: Routledge & Kegan Paul, 1973).

6. Biko Agozino, "Imperialism, Crime and Criminology: Towards the Decolonisation of Criminology," *Crime, Law, and Social Change* 41 (2004): 343–358.

7. William Chambliss and Robert Seidman, *Law, Order, and Power* (Reading, MA: Addison-Wesley, 1971), p. 503.

8. Richard Quinney, *The Social Reality of Crime* (Boston: Little, Brown, 1970).

9. This section borrows heavily from Richard Sparks, "A Critique of Marxist Criminology," in *Crime and Justice*, vol. 2, eds. Norval Morris and Michael Tonry (Chicago: University of Chicago Press, 1980), pp. 159–208.

10. Barbara Sims, "Crime, Punishment, and the American Dream: Toward a Marxist Integration," *Journal of Research in Crime and Delinquency* 34 (1997): 5–24.

11. Gregg Barak, "Revisionist History, Visionary Criminology, and Needs-Based Justice," *Contemporary Justice Review* 6 (2003): 217–225.

12. John Braithwaite, "Retributivism, Punishment, and Privilege," in *Punishment and Privilege,* eds. W. Byron Groves and Graeme Newman (Albany, NY: Harrow & Heston, 1986), pp. 55–66.

13. Agozino, "Imperialism, Crime and Criminology."

14. Barak, "Revisionist History, Visionary Criminology, and Needs-Based Justice."

15. Kitty Kelley Epstein, "The Whitening of the American Teaching Force: A Problem of Recruitment or a Problem of Racism?" *Social Justice* 32 (2005): 89–102.

16. Tony Platt and Cecilia O'Leary, "Patriot Acts," *Social Justice* 30 (2003): 5–21.

17. Garrett Brown, "The Global Threats to Workers' Health and Safety on the Job," *Social Justice* 29 (2002): 12–25.

18. Robert Bohm, "Radical Criminology: Back to the Basics." Paper presented at the annual meeting of the American Society of Criminology, Phoenix, AZ, November 1993, p. 2.

19. Ibid., p. 4.

20. Lynch and Groves, *A Primer in Radical Criminology*, p. 7.

21. Jeffery Reiman, *The Rich Get Richer and the Poor Get Prison* (New York: Wiley, 1984), pp. 43–44.

22. Rob White, "Environmental Harm and the Political Economy of Consumption," *Social Justice* 29 (2002): 82–102.

23. Sims, "Crime, Punishment, and the American Dream."

24. Michael Lynch, "Assessing the State of Radical Criminology: Toward the Year 2000." Paper presented at the annual meeting of the American Society of Criminology, Phoenix, AZ, November 1993.

25. Steven Box, *Recession, Crime, and Unemployment* (London: Macmillan, 1987).

26. David Barlow, Melissa Hickman-Barlow, and W. Wesley Johnson, "The Political Economy of Criminal Justice Policy: A Time-Series Analysis of Economic Conditions, Crime, and Federal Criminal Justice Legislation, 1948–1987," *Justice Quarterly* 13 (1996): 223–241.

27. Mahesh Nalla, Michael Lynch, and Michael Leiber, "Determinants of Police Growth in Phoenix, 1950–1988," *Justice Quarterly* 14 (1997): 144–163.

28. David Friedrichs and Jessica Friedrichs, "The World Bank and Crimes of Globalization: A Case Study," *Social Justice* 29 (2002): 13–36.

29. Gresham Sykes, "The Rise of Critical Criminology," *Journal of Criminal Law and Criminology* 65 (1974): 211–229.

30. David Jacobs, "Corporate Economic Power and the State: A Longitudinal Assessment of Two Explanations," *American Journal of Sociology* 93 (1988): 852–881.

31. Deanna Alexander, "Victims of the L.A. Riots: A Theoretical Consideration." Paper presented at the annual meeting of the American Society of Criminology, Phoenix, AZ, November 1993.

32. Richard Quinney, "Crime Control in Capitalist Society," in *Critical Criminology*, eds. Ian Taylor, Paul Walton, and Jock Young (London: Routledge & Kegan Paul, 1975), p. 199.

33. Ibid.

34. John Hagan, *Structural Criminology* (New Brunswick, NJ: Rutgers University Press, 1989), pp. 110–119.

35. Roy Bhaskar, "Empiricism," in *A Dictionary of Marxist Thought*, ed. T. Bottomore (Cambridge, MA: Harvard University Press, 1983), pp. 149–150.

36. Michael Rustigan, "A Reinterpretation of Criminal Law Reform in Nineteenth-Century England," in *Crime and Capitalism,* ed. D. Greenberg (Palo Alto, CA: Mayfield, 1981), pp. 255–278.

37. Rosalind Petchesky, "At Hard Labor: Penal Confinement and Production in Nineteenth-Century America," in *Crime and Capitalism,* ed. D. Greenberg (Palo Alto, CA: Mayfield, 1981), pp. 341–357; Paul Takagi, "The Walnut Street Jail: A Penal Reform to Centralize the Powers of the State," *Federal Probation* 49 (1975): 18–26.

38. David Jacobs and David Britt, "Inequality and Police Use of Deadly Force: An Empirical Assessment of a Conflict Hypothesis," *Social Problems* 26 (1979): 403–412.

39. Ronald Weitzer and Steven Tuch, "Perceptions of Racial Profiling: Race, Class and Personal Experience," *Criminology* 40 (2002): 435–456.

40. Albert Meehan and Michael Ponder, "Race and Place: The Ecology of Racial Profiling African American Motorists," *Justice Quarterly* 29 (2002): 399–431.

41. Malcolm Homes, "Minority Threat and Police Brutality: Determinants of Civil Rights Criminal Complaints in U.S. Municipalities," *Criminology* 38 (2000): 343–368.

42. Darrell Steffensmeier and Stephen Demuth, "Ethnicity and Judges' Sentencing Decisions: Hispanic-Black-White Comparisons," *Criminology* 39 (2001): 145–178; Alan Lizotte, "Extra-Legal Factors in Chicago's Criminal Courts: Testing the Conflict Model of Criminal Justice," *Social Problems* 25 (1978): 564–580.

43. Terance Miethe and Charles Moore, "Racial Differences in Criminal Processing: The Consequences of Model Selection on Conclusions about Differential Treatment," *Sociological Quarterly* 27 (1987): 217–237.

44. Tracy Nobiling, Cassia Spohn, and Miriam DeLone, "A Tale of Two Counties: Unemployment and Sentence Severity," *Justice Quarterly* 15 (1998): 459–485.

45. Charles Crawford, Ted Chiricos, and Gary Kleck, "Race, Racial Threat, and Sentencing of Habitual Offenders," *Criminology* 36 (1998): 481–511.

46. Michael Lenza, David Keys, and Teresa Guess, "The Prevailing Injustices in the Application of the Missouri Death Penalty (1978 to 1996)," *Social Justice* 32 (2005): 151–166.

47. Thomas Arvanites, "Increasing Imprisonment: A Function of Crime or Socioeconomic Factors?" *American Journal of Criminal Justice* 17 (1992): 19–38.

48. David Greenberg and Valerie West, "State Prison Populations and Their Growth, 1971–1991," *Criminology* 39 (2001): 615–654.

49. Robert Weiss, "Repatriating Low-Wage Work: The Political Economy of Prison Labor Reprivatization in the Postindustrial United States," *Criminology* 39 (2001): 253–292.

50. Jack Gibbs, "An Incorrigible Positivist," *Criminologist* 12 (1987): 2–3.

51. Jackson Toby, "The New Criminology Is the Old Sentimentality," *Criminology* 16 (1979): 513–526.

52. Richard Sparks, "A Critique of Marxist Criminology," in *Crime and Justice,* vol. 2, eds. Norval Morris and Michael Tonry (Chicago: University of Chicago Press, 1980), pp. 159–208.

53. Carl Klockars, "The Contemporary Crises of Marxist Criminology," in *Radical Criminology: The Coming Crisis,* ed. J. Inciardi (Beverly Hills, CA: Sage, 1980), pp. 92–123.

54. Matthew Petrocelli, Alex Piquero, and Michael Smith, "Conflict Theory and Racial Profiling: An Empirical Analysis of Police Traffic Stop Data," *Journal of Criminal Justice* 31 (2003): 1–10.

55. Ibid.

56. Anthony Platt, "Criminology in the 1980s: Progressive Alternatives to 'Law and Order,'" *Crime and Social Justice* 21–22 (1985): 191–199.

57. See, generally, Roger Matthews and Jock Young, eds., *Confronting Crime* (London: Sage, 1986); for a thorough review of left realism, see Martin Schwartz and Walter DeKeseredy, "Left Realist Criminology: Strengths, Weaknesses, and the Feminist Critique," *Crime, Law, and Social Change* 15 (1991): 51–72.

58. John Lea and Jock Young, *What Is to Be Done about Law and Order?* (Harmondsworth, England: Penguin, 1984).

59. Ibid., p. 88.

60. Ian Taylor, *Crime in Context: A Critical Criminology of Market Societies* (Boulder, CO: Westview Press, 1999).

61. Ibid, pp. 30–31.

62. Richard Kinsey, John Lea, and Jock Young, *Losing the Fight against Crime* (London: Blackwell, 1986).

63. Martin Schwartz and Walter DeKeseredy, *Contemporary Criminology* (Belmont, CA: Wadsworth, 1993), p. 249.

64. Schwartz and DeKeseredy, "Left Realist Criminology."

65. For a general review of this issue, see Kathleen Daly and Meda Chesney-Lind, "Feminism and Criminology," *Justice Quarterly* 5 (1988): 497–538; Douglas Smith and Raymond Paternoster, "The Gender Gap in Theories of Deviance: Issues and Evidence," *Journal of Research in Crime and Delinquency* 24 (1987): 140–172; and Pat Carlen, "Women, Crime, Feminism, and Realism," *Social Justice* 17 (1990): 106–123.

66. Herman Schwendinger and Julia Schwendinger, *Rape and Inequality* (Newbury Park, CA: Sage, 1983).

67. Daly and Chesney-Lind, "Feminism and Criminology."

68. Janet Saltzman Chafetz, "Feminist Theory and Sociology: Underutilized Contributions for Mainstream Theory," *Annual Review of Sociology* 23 (1997): 97–121.

69. Ibid.

70. James Messerschmidt, *Capitalism, Patriarchy, and Crime* (Totowa, NJ: Rowman & Littlefield, 1986); for a critique of this work, see Herman Schwendinger and Julia Schwendinger, "The World According to James Messerschmidt," *Social Justice* 15 (1988): 123–145.

71. Kathleen Daly, "Gender and Varieties of White-Collar Crime," *Criminology* 27 (1989): 769–793.

72. Jane Roberts Chapman, "Violence against Women as a Violation of Human Rights," *Social Justice* 17 (1990): 54–71.

73. Carrie Yodanis, "Gender Inequality, Violence against Women, and Fear," *Journal of Interpersonal Violence* 19 (2004): 655–675.

74. Victoria Titterington, "A Retrospective Investigation of Gender Inequality and Female Homicide Victimization," *Sociological Spectrum* 26 (2006): 205–236.

75. James Messerschmidt, *Masculinities and Crime: Critique and Reconceptualization of Theory* (Lanham, MD: Rowman & Littlefield, 1993).

76. Angela P. Harris, "Gender, Violence, Race, and Criminal Justice," *Stanford Law Review* 52 (2000): 777–810.

77. Suzie Dod Thomas and Nancy Stein, "Criminality, Imprisonment, and Women's Rights in the 1990s," *Social Justice* 17 (1990): 1–5.

78. Walter DeKeseredy and Martin Schwartz, "Male Peer Support and Woman Abuse: An Expansion of DeKeseredy's Model," *Sociological Spectrum* 13 (1993): 393–413.

79. Daly and Chesney-Lind, "Feminism and Criminology." See also, Drew Humphries and Susan Caringella-MacDonald, "Murdered Mothers, Missing Wives: Reconsidering Female Victimization," *Social Justice* 17 (1990): 71–78.

80. Hagan, *Structural Criminology*.

81. John Hagan, A. R. Gillis, and John Simpson, "The Class Structure and Delinquency: Toward a Power–Control Theory of Common Delinquent Behavior," *American Journal of Sociology* 90 (1985): 1,151–1,178; John Hagan, John Simpson, and A. R. Gillis, "Class in the Household: A Power–Control Theory of Gender and Delinquency," *American Journal of Sociology* 92 (1987): 788–816.

82. John Hagan, Bill McCarthy, and Holly Foster, "A Gendered Theory of Delinquency and Despair in the Life Course," *Acta Sociologica* 45 (2002): 37–47.

83. Brenda Sims Blackwell, Christine Sellers, and Sheila Schlaupitz, "A Power–Control Theory of Vulnerability to Crime and Adolescent Role Exits—Revisited," *Canadian Review of Sociology and Anthropology* 39 (2002): 199–219.

84. Brenda Sims Blackwell, "Perceived Sanction Threats, Gender, and Crime: A Test and Elaboration of Power–Control Theory," *Criminology* 38 (2000): 439–488.

85. Christopher Uggen, "Class, Gender, and Arrest: An Intergenerational Analysis of Workplace Power and Control," *Criminology* 38 (2001): 835–862.

86. Gary Jensen, "Power–Control versus Social-Control Theory: Identifying Crucial Differences for Future Research." Paper presented at the annual meeting of the American Society of Criminology, Baltimore, MD, November 1990.

87. Gary Jensen and Kevin Thompson, "What's Class Got to Do with It? A Further Examination of Power–Control Theory," *American Journal of Sociology* 95 (1990): 1,009–1,023. For some critical research, see Simon Singer and Murray Levine, "Power–Control Theory, Gender and Delinquency: A Partial Replication with Additional Evidence on the Effects of Peers," *Criminology* 26 (1988): 627–648.

88. Kevin Thompson, "Gender and Adolescent Drinking Problems: The Effects of Occupational Structure," *Social Problems* 36 (1989): 30–38.

89. Kristin Mack and Michael Leiber, "Race, Gender, Single-Mother Households, and Delinquency: A Further Test of Power–Control Theory," *Youth & Society* 37 (2005): 115–144.
90. See, generally, Uggen, "Class, Gender, and Arrest."
91. Brenda Sims Blackwell and Alex Piquero, "On the Relationships between Gender, Power Control, Self-Control, and Crime," *Journal of Criminal Justice* 33 (2005): 1–17.
92. Liz Walz, "One Blood," *Contemporary Justice Review* 6 (2003): 25–36.
93. See, for example, Tifft and Sullivan, *The Struggle to Be Human*; Dennis Sullivan, *The Mask of Love* (Port Washington, NY: Kennikat Press, 1980).
94. Larry Tifft, "Foreword," in Sullivan, *The Mask of Love,* p. 6.
95. Sullivan, *The Mask of Love,* p. 141.
96. Dennis Sullivan and Larry Tifft, *Restorative Justice* (Monsey, NY: Willow Tree Press, 2001).
97. Tomislav Kovandzic and Lynne Vieraitis, "The Effect of County-Level Prison Population Growth on Crime Rates," *Criminology & Public Policy* 5 (2006): 213–244; Robert DeFina and Thomas Arvanites, "The Weak Effect of Imprisonment on Crime: 1971–1998," *Social Science Quarterly* 83 (2002): 635–654.
98. Kathleen Daly and Russ Immarigeon, "The Past, Present and Future of Restorative Justice: Some Critical Reflections," *Contemporary Justice Review* 1 (1998): 21–45.
99. Howard Zehr, *The Little Book of Restorative Justice* (Intercourse, PA: Good Books, 2002): 1–10.
100. Mark Lewis Taylor, *The Executed God: The Way of the Cross in Lockdown America* (Minneapolis, MN: Fortress Press, 2001).
101. Alfred Villaume, "'Life Without Parole' and 'Virtual Life Sentences': Death Sentences by Any Other Name," *Contemporary Justice Review* 8 (2005): 265–277.
102. Gene Stephens, "The Future of Policing: From a War Model to a Peace Model," in *The Past, Present and Future of American Criminal Justice,* eds. Brendan Maguire and Polly Radosh (Dix Hills, NY: General Hall, 1996), pp. 77–93.
103. Rick Shifley, "The Organization of Work as a Factor in Social Well-Being," *Contemporary Justice Review* 6 (2003): 105–126.
104. Kay Pranis, "Peacemaking Circles: Restorative Justice in Practice Allows Victims and Offenders to Begin Repairing the Harm," *Corrections Today* 59 (1997): 74–78.
105. Carol LaPrairie, "The 'New' Justice: Some Implications for Aboriginal Communities," *Canadian Journal of Criminology* 40 (1998): 61–79.
106. Diane Schaefer, "A Disembodied Community Collaborates in a Homicide: Can Empathy Transform a Failing Justice System?" *Contemporary Justice Review* 6 (2003): 133–143.
107. David R. Karp and Beau Breslin, "Restorative Justice in School Communities," *Youth & Society* 33 (2001): 249–272.
108. Paul Jesilow and Deborah Parsons, "Community Policing as Peacemaking," *Policing & Society* 10 (2000): 163–183.
109. Gordon Bazemore and Curt Taylor Griffiths, "Conferences, Circles, Boards, and Mediations: The 'New Wave' of Community Justice Decision Making," *Federal Probation* 61 (1997): 25–37.
110. This section is based on Gordon Bazemore and Mara Schiff, "Paradigm Muddle or Paradigm Paralysis? The Wide and Narrow Roads to Restorative Justice Reform (or, a Little Confusion May Be a Good Thing)," *Contemporary Justice Review* 7 (2004): 37–57.
111. John Braithwaite, "Setting Standards for Restorative Justice," *British Journal of Criminology* 42 (2002): 563–577.
112. David Altschuler, "Community Justice Initiatives: Issues and Challenges in the U.S. Context," *Federal Probation* 65 (2001): 28–33.
113. Lois Presser and Patricia Van Voorhis, "Values and Evaluation: Assessing Processes and Outcomes of Restorative Justice Programs," *Crime & Delinquency* 48 (2002): 162–189.
114. Declan Roche, *Accountability in Restorative Justice (Clarendon Studies in Criminology)* (London: Oxford University Press, 2004).
115. Sharon Levrant, Francis Cullen, Betsy Fulton, and John Wozniak, "Reconsidering Restorative Justice: The Corruption of Benevolence Revisited?" *Crime & Delinquency* 45 (1999): 3–28.
116. Edward Gumz, "American Social Work, Corrections and Restorative Justice: An Appraisal," *International Journal of Offender Therapy & Comparative Criminology* 48 (2004): 449–460.

Chapter 9. Developmental Theories

1. Fox News, "Xbox Slayings Ringleader Has Criminal History," August 11, 2004, www.foxnews.com/story/0,2933,128674, 00.html.
2. See, generally, John Laub and Robert Sampson, "The Sutherland–Glueck Debate: On the Sociology of Criminological Knowledge," *American Journal of Sociology* 96 (1991): 1,402–1,440; John Laub and Robert Sampson, "Unraveling Families and Delinquency: A Reanalysis of the Gluecks' Data," *Criminology* 26 (1988): 355–380.
3. Rolf Loeber and Marc LeBlanc, "Toward a Developmental Criminology," in *Crime and Justice,* vol. 12, eds. Norval Morris and Michael Tonry (Chicago: University of Chicago Press, 1990), pp. 375–473; Rolf Loeber and Marc LeBlanc, "Developmental Criminology Updated," in *Crime and Justice,* vol. 23, ed. Michael Tonry (Chicago: University of Chicago Press, 1998), pp. 115–198.
4. Marvin Krohn, Alan Lizotte, and Cynthia Perez, "The Interrelationship between Substance Use and Precocious Transitions to Adult Sexuality," *Journal of Health and Social Behavior* 38 (1997): 87–103, at 88.
5. Bradley Entner Wright, Avashalom Caspi, Terrie Moffitt, and Phil Silva, "The Effects of Social Ties on Crime Vary by Criminal Propensity: A Life-Course Model of Interdependence," *Criminology* 39 (2001): 321–352.
6. Gerald Patterson, Barbara DeBaryshe, and Elizabeth Ramsey, "A Developmental Perspective on Antisocial Behavior," *American Psychologist* 44 (1989): 329–335.
7. Robert Sampson and John Laub, "Crime and Deviance in the Life Course," *American Review of Sociology* 18 (1992): 63–84.
8. David Farrington, Darrick Jolliffe, Rolf Loeber, Magda Stouthamer-Loeber, and Larry Kalb, "The Concentration of Offenders in Families, and Family Criminality in the Prediction of Boys' Delinquency," *Journal of Adolescence* 24 (2001): 579–596.
9. Raymond Paternoster, Charles Dean, Alex Piquero, Paul Mazerolle, and Robert Brame, "Generality, Continuity, and Change in Offending," *Journal of Quantitative Criminology* 13 (1997): 231–266.
10. Magda Stouthamer-Loeber and Evelyn Wei, "The Precursors of Young Fatherhood and Its Effect on Delinquency of Teenage Males," *Journal of Adolescent Health* 22 (1998): 56–65; Richard Jessor, John Donovan, and Francis Costa, *Beyond Adolescence: Problem Behavior and Young Adult Development* (New York: Cambridge University Press, 1991); Xavier Coll, Fergus Law, Aurelio Tobias, Keith Hawton, and Joseph Tomas, "Abuse and Deliberate Self-Poisoning in Women: A Matched Case-Control Study," *Child Abuse and Neglect* 25 (2001): 1,291–1,293.
11. Richard Miech, Avshalom Caspi, Terrie Moffitt, Bradley Entner Wright, and Phil Silva, "Low Socioeconomic Status and Mental Disorders: A Longitudinal Study of Selection and Causation during Young Adulthood," *American Journal of Sociology* 104 (1999): 1,096–1,131; Krohn, Lizotte, and Perez, "The Interrelationship between Substance Use and Precocious Transitions to Adult Sexuality," p. 88; Richard Jessor, "Risk Behavior in Adolescence: A Psychosocial Framework for Understanding and Action," in *Adolescents at Risk: Medical and Social Perspectives,* eds. D. E. Rogers and E. Ginzburg (Boulder, CO: Westview Press, 1992).
12. Rolf Loeber, Dustin Pardini, D. Lynn Homish, Evelyn Wei, Anne Crawford, David Farrington, Magda Stouthamer-Loeber,

Judith Creemers, Steven Koehler, and Richard Rosenfeld, "The Prediction of Violence and Homicide in Young Men," *Journal of Consulting and Clinical Psychology* 73 (2005): 1,074–1,088.

13. Deborah Capaldi and Gerald Patterson, "Can Violent Offenders Be Distinguished from Frequent Offenders: Prediction from Childhood to Adolescence," *Journal of Research in Crime and Delinquency* 33 (1996): 206–231; D. Wayne Osgood, "The Covariation among Adolescent Problem Behaviors." Paper presented at the annual meeting of the American Society of Criminology, Baltimore, November 1990.
14. For an analysis of more than 30 studies, see Mark Lipsey and James Derzon, "Predictors of Violent or Serious Delinquency in Adolescence and Early Adulthood: A Synthesis of Longitudinal Research," in *Serious and Violent Juvenile Offenders: Risk Factors and Successful Interventions,* eds. Rolf Loeber and David Farrington (Thousand Oaks, CA: Sage, 1998).
15. Gina Wingood, Ralph DiClemente, Rick Crosby, Kathy Harrington, Susan Davies, and Edward Hook, III, "Gang Involvement and the Health of African American Female Adolescents," *Pediatrics* 110 (2002): 57.
16. David Husted, Nathan Shapira, and Martin Lazoritz, "Adolescent Gambling, Substance Use, and Other Delinquent Behavior," *Psychiatric Times* 20 (2003): 52–55.
17. Krohn, Lizotte, and Perez, "The Interrelationship between Substance Use and Precocious Transitions to Adult Sexuality," p. 88; Richard Jessor, "Risk Behavior in Adolescence: A Psychosocial Framework for Understanding and Action," in *Adolescents at Risk: Medical and Social Perspectives,* ed. D. E. Rogers and E. Ginzburg (Boulder, CO: Westview, 1992).
18. Terence Thornberry, Carolyn Smith, and Gregory Howard, "Risk Factors for Teenage Fatherhood," *Journal of Marriage and the Family* 59 (1997): 505–522; Todd Miller, Timothy Smith, Charles Turner, Margarita Guijarro, and Amanda Hallet, "A Meta-Analytic Review of Research on Hostility and Physical Health," *Psychological Bulletin* 119 (1996): 322–348; Marianne Junger, "Accidents and Crime," in *The Generality of Deviance,* eds. T. Hirschi and M. Gottfredson (New Brunswick, NJ: Transaction Books, 1993).
19. James Marquart, Victoria Brewer, Patricia Simon, and Edward Morse, "Lifestyle Factors among Female Prisoners with Histories of Psychiatric Treatment," *Journal of Criminal Justice* 29 (2001): 319–328; Rolf Loeber, David Farrington, Magda Stouthamer-Loeber, Terrie Moffitt, Avshalom Caspi, and Don Lynam, "Male Mental Health Problems, Psychopathy, and Personality Traits: Key Findings from the First 14 Years of the Pittsburgh Youth Study," *Clinical Child and Family Psychology Review* 4 (2002): 273–297.
20. Robert Johnson, S. Susan Su, Dean Gerstein, Hee-Choon Shin, and John Hoffman, "Parental Influences on Deviant Behavior in Early Adolescence: A Logistic Response Analysis of Age and Gender-Differentiated Effects," *Journal of Quantitative Criminology* 11 (1995): 167–192; Judith Brooks, Martin Whiteman, and Patricia Cohen, "Stage of Drug Use, Aggression, and Theft/Vandalism," in *Drugs, Crime and Other Deviant Adaptations: Longitudinal Studies,* ed. Howard Kaplan (New York: Plenum Press, 1995), pp. 83–96.
21. Helene Raskin White, Peter Tice, Rolf Loeber, and Magda Stouthamer-Loeber, "Illegal Acts Committed by Adolescents under the Influence of Alcohol and Drugs," *Journal of Research in Crime and Delinquency* 39 (2002): 131–153; Candace Kruttschnitt, Jane McLeod, and Maude Dornfeld, "The Economic Environment of Child Abuse," *Social Problems* 41 (1994): 299–312.
22. David Fergusson, L. John Horwood, and Elizabeth Ridder, "Show Me the Child at Seven II: Childhood Intelligence and Later Outcomes in Adolescence and Young Adulthood," *Journal of Child Psychology and Psychiatry* 46 (2005): 850–859.
23. Margit Wiesner and Ranier Silbereisen, "Trajectories of Delinquent Behaviour in Adolescence and Their Covariates: Relations with Initial and Time-Averaged Factors," *Journal of Adolescence* 26 (2003): 753–771.
24. Rolf Loeber, Phen Wung, Kate Keenan, Bruce Giroux, Magda Stouthamer-Loeber, Wemoet Van Kammen, and Barbara Maughan, "Developmental Pathways in Disruptive Behavior," *Development and Psychopathology* (1993): 12–48.
25. Sheila Royo Maxwell and Christopher Maxwell, "Examining the 'Criminal Careers' of Prostitutes within the Nexus of Drug Use, Drug Selling, and Other Illicit Activities," *Criminology* 38 (2000): 787–809.
26. Jacqueline Schneider, "The Link Between Shoplifting and Burglary: The Booster Burglar," *British Journal of Criminology* 45 (2005): 395–401.
27. Glenn Deane, Richard Felson, and David Armstrong, "An Examination of Offense Specialization Using Marginal Logit Models," *Criminology* 43 (2005): 955–988.
28. Christopher Sullivan, Jean Marie McGloin, Travis Pratt, and Alex Piquero, "Rethinking the 'Norm' of Offender Generality: Investigating Specialization in the Short-Term," *Criminology* 44 (2006): 199–233.
29. Alex R. Piquero and He Len Chung, "On the Relationships between Gender, Early Onset, and the Seriousness of Offending," *Journal of Criminal Justice* 29 (2001): 189–206.
30. David Nurco, Timothy Kinlock, and Mitchell Balter, "The Severity of Preaddiction Criminal Behavior among Urban, Male Narcotic Addicts and Two Nonaddicted Control Groups," *Journal of Research in Crime and Delinquency* 30 (1993): 293–316.
31. W. Alex Mason, Rick Kosterman, J. David Hawkins, Todd Herrenkohl, Liliana Lengua, and Elizabeth McCauley, "Predicting Depression, Social Phobia, and Violence in Early Adulthood from Childhood Behavior Problems," *Journal of the American Academy of Child & Adolescent Psychiatry* 43 (2004): 307–315; Rolf Loeber and David Farrington, "Young Children Who Commit Crime: Epidemiology, Developmental Origins, Risk Factors, Early Interventions, and Policy Implications," *Development and Psychopathology* 12 (2000): 737–762; Patrick Lussier, Jean Proulx, and Marc LeBlanc, "Criminal Propensity, Deviant Sexual Interests and Criminal Activity of Sexual Aggressors against Women: A Comparison of Explanatory Models," *Criminology* 43 (2005): 249–281.
32. Dawn Jeglum Bartusch, Donald Lynam, Terrie Moffitt, and Phil Silva, "Is Age Important? Testing a General versus a Developmental Theory of Antisocial Behavior," *Criminology* 35 (1997): 13–48.
33. Hanno Petras, Nicholas Alongo, Sharon Lambert, Sandra Barrueco, Cindy Schaeffer, Howard Chilcoat, and Sheppard Kellam, "The Utility of Elementary School TOCA-R Scores in Identifying Later Criminal Court Violence among Adolescent Females," *Journal of the American Academy of Child & Adolescent Psychiatry* 44 (2005): 790–797; Hanno Petras, Howard Chilcoat, Philip Leaf, Nicholas Alongo, and Sheppard Kellam, "Utility of TOCA-R Scores during the Elementary School Years in Identifying Later Violence among Adolescent Males," *Journal of the American Academy of Child & Adolescent Psychiatry* 43 (2004): 88–96.
34. Mason, Kosterman, Hawkins, Herrenkohi, Lengua, and McCauley, "Predicting Depression, Social Phobia, and Violence in Early Adulthood from Childhood Behavior Problems"; Ronald Prinz and Suzanne Kerns, "Early Substance Use by Juvenile Offenders," *Child Psychiatry and Human Development* 33 (2003): 263–268.
35. Glenn Clingempeel and Scott Henggeler, "Aggressive Juvenile Offenders Transitioning into Emerging Adulthood: Factors Discriminating Persistors and Desistors," *American Journal of Orthopsychiatry* 73 (2003): 310–323.
36. David Gadd and Stephen Farrall, "Criminal Careers, Desistance and Subjectivity: Interpreting Men's Narratives of Change," *Theoretical Criminology* 8 (2004): 123–156.

37. Ick-Joong Chung, Karl Hill, J. David Hawkins, Lewayne Gilchrist, and Daniel Nagin, "Childhood Predictors of Offense Trajectories," *Journal of Research in Crime and Delinquency* 39 (2002): 60–91.
38. Amy D'Unger, Kenneth Land, Patricia McCall, and Daniel Nagin, "How Many Latent Classes of Delinquent/Criminal Careers Results from Mixed Poisson Regression Analyses," *American Journal of Sociology* 103 (1998): 1,593–1,630.
39. Alex Piquero and Timothy Brezina, "Testing Moffitt's Account of Adolescent-Limited Delinquency," *Criminology* 39 (2001): 353–370.
40. Terrie Moffitt, "Adolescence-Limited and Life-Course Persistent Antisocial Behavior: A Developmental Taxonomy," *Psychological Review* 100 (1993): 674–701.
41. Terrie Moffitt, "Natural Histories of Delinquency," in *Cross-National Longitudinal Research on Human Development and Criminal Behavior*, eds. Elmar Weitekamp and Hans-Jürgen Kerner (Dordrecht, Netherlands: Kluwer, 1994), pp. 3–65.
42. Andrea Donker, Wilma Smeenk, Peter van der Laan, and Frank Verhulst, "Individual Stability of Antisocial Behavior from Childhood to Adulthood: Testing the Stability Postulate of Moffitt's Developmental Theory," *Criminology* 41 (2003): 593–609.
43. Robert Vermeiren, "Psychopathology and Delinquency in Adolescents: A Descriptive and Developmental Perspective," *Clinical Psychology Review* 23 (2003): 277–318; Paul Mazerolle, Robert Brame, Ray Paternoster, Alex Piquero, and Charles Dean, "Onset Age, Persistence, and Offending Versatility: Comparisons across Sex," *Criminology* 38 (2000): 1,143–1,172.
44. Adrian Raine, Rolf Loeber, Magda Stouthamer-Loeber, Terrie Moffitt, Avshalom Caspi, and Don Lynam, "Neurocognitive Impairments in Boys on the Life-Course Persistent Antisocial Path," *Journal of Abnormal Psychology* 114 (2005): 38–49.
45. Per-Olof Wikstrom and Rolf Loeber, "Do Disadvantaged Neighborhoods Cause Well-Adjusted Children to Become Adolescent Delinquents? A Study of Male Juvenile Serious Offending, Individual Risk and Protective Factors, and Neighborhood Context," *Criminology* 38 (2000): 1,109–1,142.
46. Stephen Farrall and Benjamin Bowling, "Structuration, Human Development, and Desistance from Crime," *British Journal of Criminology* 39 (1999): 253–268.
47. Robert Sampson and John Laub, *Crime in the Making: Pathways and Turning Points through Life* (Cambridge, MA: Harvard University Press, 1993); John Laub and Robert Sampson, "Turning Points in the Life Course: Why Change Matters to the Study of Crime." Paper presented at the annual meeting of the American Society of Criminology, New Orleans, November 1992.
48. Daniel Nagin and Raymond Paternoster, "Personal Capital and Social Control: The Deterrence Implications of a Theory of Criminal Offending," *Criminology* 32 (1994): 581–606.
49. Terri Orbuch, James House, Richard Mero, and Pamela Webster, "Marital Quality over the Life Course," *Social Psychology Quarterly* 59 (1996): 162–171; Lee Lillard and Linda Waite, "'Til Death Do Us Part': Marital Disruption and Mortality," *American Journal of Sociology* 100 (1995): 1,131–1,156.
50. Mark Warr, "Life-Course Transitions and Desistance from Crime," *Criminology* 36 (1998): 183–216.
51. Leonore Simon, "Social Bond and Criminal Record History of Acquaintance and Stranger Violent Offenders," *Journal of Crime and Justice* 22 (1999): 131–146.
52. Raymond Paternoster and Robert Brame, "Multiple Routes to Delinquency? A Test of Developmental and General Theories of Crime," *Criminology* 35 (1997): 49–84.
53. Spencer De Li, "Legal Sanctions and Youths' Status Achievement: A Longitudinal Study," *Justice Quarterly* 16 (1999): 377–401.
54. Shawn Bushway, "The Impact of an Arrest on the Job Stability of Young White American Men," *Journal of Research on Crime and Delinquency* 35 (1999): 454–479.
55. Candace Kruttschnitt, Christopher Uggen, and Kelly Shelton, "Individual Variability in Sex Offending and Its Relationship to Informal and Formal Social Controls." Paper presented at the American Society of Criminology meeting, San Diego, 1997; Mark Collins and Don Weatherburn, "Unemployment and the Dynamics of Offender Populations," *Journal of Quantitative Criminology* 11 (1995): 231–245.
56. Robert Hoge, D. A. Andrews, and Alan Leschied, "An Investigation of Risk and Protective Factors in a Sample of Youthful Offenders," *Journal of Child Psychology and Psychiatry* 37 (1996): 419–424.
57. Richard Arum and Irenee Beattie, "High School Experience and the Risk of Adult Incarceration," *Criminology* 37 (1999): 515–540.
58. Ross Macmillan, Barbara J. McMorris, and Candace Kruttschnitt, "Linked Lives: Stability and Change in Maternal Circumstances and Trajectories of Antisocial Behavior in Children," *Child Development* 75 (2004): 205–220.
59. Avshalom Caspi, Terrie Moffitt, Bradley Entner Wright, and Phil Silva, "Early Failure in the Labor Market: Childhood and Adolescent Predictors of Unemployment in the Transition to Adulthood," *American Sociological Review* 63 (1998): 424–451.
60. Robert Sampson and John Laub, "Socioeconomic Achievement in the Life Course of Disadvantaged Men: Military Service as a Turning Point, circa 1940–1965," *American Sociological Review* 61 (1996): 347–367.
61. Christopher Uggen, "Ex-Offenders and the Conformist Alternative: A Job Quality Model of Work and Crime," *Social Problems* 46 (1999): 127–151.
62. Erich Labouvie, "Maturing Out of Substance Use: Selection and Self-Correction," *Journal of Drug Issues* 26 (1996): 457–474.
63. Mark Warr, "Life-Course Transitions and Desistance from Crime."
64. Doris Layton MacKenzie and Spencer De Li, "The Impact of Formal and Informal Social Controls on the Criminal Activities of Probationers," *Journal of Research in Crime and Delinquency* 39 (2002): 243–278.
65. Pamela Webster, Terri Orbuch, and James House, "Effects of Childhood Family Background on Adult Marital Quality and Perceived Stability," *American Journal of Sociology* 101 (1995): 404–432.
66. Alex Piquero, John MacDonald, and Karen Parker, "Race, Local Life Circumstances, and Criminal Activity over the Life-Course," *Social Science Quarterly* 83 (2002): 654–671.
67. Personal communication with Alex Piquero, September 24, 2002.
68. Ronald Simons, Eric Stewart, Leslie Gordon, Rand Conger, and Glen Elder, Jr., "Test of Life-Course Explanations for Stability and Change in Antisocial Behavior from Adolescence to Young Adulthood," *Criminology* 40 (2002): 401–435.
69. John Paul Wright, David E. Carter, and Francis T. Cullen, "A Life-Course Analysis of Military Service in Vietnam," *Journal of Research in Crime and Delinquency* 42 (2005): 55–83.
70. Eloise Dunlop and Bruce Johnson, "Family and Human Resources in the Development of a Female Crack-Seller Career: Case Study of a Hidden Population," *Journal of Drug Issues* 26 (1996): 175–198.
71. Allison Steele, "4 teenagers arrested in BB gun shootings" *Concord Monitor,* August 9, 2005, p. 1.
72. David Rowe, D. Wayne Osgood, and W. Alan Nicewander, "A Latent Trait Approach to Unifying Criminal Careers," *Criminology* 28 (1990): 237–270.
73. Lee Ellis, "Neurohormonal Bases of Varying Tendencies to Learn Delinquent and Criminal Behavior," in *Behavioral Approaches to Crime and Delinquency,* eds. E. Morris and C. Braukmann (New York: Plenum, 1988), pp. 499–518.
74. David Rowe, Alexander Vazsonyi, and Daniel Flannery, "Sex Differences in Crime: Do Means and Within-Sex Variation Have Similar Causes?" *Journal of Research in Crime and Delinquency* 32 (1995): 84–100.

75. James Q. Wilson and Richard Herrnstein, *Crime and Human Nature* (New York: Simon & Schuster, 1985).
76. Ibid., p. 44.
77. Ibid., p. 171.
78. Michael Gottfredson and Travis Hirschi, *A General Theory of Crime* (Stanford, CA: Stanford University Press, 1990).
79. Ibid., p. 27.
80. Kevin Beaver and John Paul Wright, "Evaluating the Effects of Birth Complications on Low-Control in a Sample of Twins," *International Journal of Offender Therapy & Comparative Criminology* 49 (2005): 450–472.
81. Anthony Walsh and Lee Ellis, "Shoring Up the Big Three: Improving Criminological Theories with Biosocial Concepts." Paper presented at the annual Society of Criminology meeting, San Diego, November 1997, p. 15.
82. Gottfredson and Hirschi, *A General Theory of Crime*, p. 90.
83. Ibid., p. 89.
84. Alex Piquero and Stephen Tibbetts, "Specifying the Direct and Indirect Effects of Low Self-Control and Situational Factors in Offenders' Decision Making: Toward a More Complete Model of Rational Offending," *Justice Quarterly* 13 (1996): 481–508.
85. David Forde and Leslie Kennedy, "Risky Lifestyles, Routine Activities, and the General Theory of Crime," *Justice Quarterly* 14 (1997): 265–294.
86. Gottfredson and Hirschi, *A General Theory of Crime,* p. 112.
87. Ibid.
88. Dennis Giever, "An Empirical Assessment of the Core Elements of Gottfredson and Hirschi's General Theory of Crime." Paper presented at the American Society of Criminology meeting, Boston, November 1995.
89. Robert Agnew, "The Contribution of Social-Psychological Strain Theory to the Explanation of Crime and Delinquency," in *Anomie Theory: Advances in Criminological Theory*, vol. 6, eds. Freda Adler and William Laufer (New Brunswick, NJ: Transaction Books, 1995), pp. 81–96.
90. Travis Hirschi and Michael Gottfredson, "Rethinking the Juvenile Justice System," *Crime & Delinquency* 39 (1993): 262–271.
91. David Brownfield and Ann Marie Sorenson, "Self-Control and Juvenile Delinquency: Theoretical Issues and an Empirical Assessment of Selected Elements of a General Theory of Crime," *Deviant Behavior* 14 (1993): 243–264; Harold Grasmick, Charles Tittle, Robert Bursik, and Bruce Arneklev, "Testing the Core Empirical Implications of Gottfredson and Hirschi's General Theory of Crime," *Journal of Research in Crime and Delinquency* 30 (1993): 5–29; John Cochran, Peter Wood, and Bruce Arneklev, "Is the Religiosity–Delinquency Relationship Spurious? A Test of Arousal and Social Control Theories," *Journal of Research in Crime and Delinquency* 31 (1994): 92–123; Marc LeBlanc, Marc Ouimet, and Richard Tremblay, "An Integrative Control Theory of Delinquent Behavior: A Validation 1976–1985," *Psychiatry* 51 (1988): 164–176.
92. Alexander Vazsonyi, Janice Clifford Wittekind, Lara Belliston, and Timothy Van Loh, "Extending the General Theory of Crime to 'The East': Low Self-Control in Japanese Late Adolescents," *Journal of Quantitative Criminology* 20 (2004): 189–216; Alexander Vazsonyi, Lloyd Pickering, Marianne Junger, and Dick Hessing, "An Empirical Test of a General Theory of Crime: A Four-Nation Comparative Study of Self-Control and the Prediction of Deviance," *Journal of Research in Crime and Delinquency* 38 (2001): 91–131.
93. Michael Benson and Elizabeth Moore, "Are White-Collar and Common Offenders the Same? An Empirical and Theoretical Critique of a Recently Proposed General Theory of Crime," *Journal of Research in Crime and Delinquency* 29 (1992): 251–272.
94. Ronald Akers, "Self-Control as a General Theory of Crime," *Journal of Quantitative Criminology* 7 (1991): 201–211.
95. Gottfredson and Hirschi, *A General Theory of Crime*, p. 88.
96. Moffitt, "Adolescence-Limited and Life-Course Persistent Antisocial Behaviors."
97. Alex Piquero, Robert Brame, Paul Mazerolle, and Rudy Haapanen, "Crime in Emerging Adulthood," *Criminology* 40 (2002): 137–170.
98. Donald Lynam, Alex Piquero, and Terrie Moffitt, "Specialization and the Propensity to Violence: Support from Self-Reports but Not Official Records," *Journal of Contemporary Criminal Justice* 20 (2004): 215–228.
99. Alan Feingold, "Gender Differences in Personality: A Meta Analysis," *Psychological Bulletin* 116 (1994): 429–456.
100. Charles Tittle, David Ward, and Harold Grasmick, "Gender, Age, and Crime/Deviance: A Challenge to Self-Control Theory," *Journal of Research in Crime and Delinquency* 40 (2003): 426–453.
101. Brent Benda, "Gender Differences in Life-Course Theory of Recidivism: A Survival Analysis," *International Journal of Offender Therapy & Comparative Criminology* 49 (2005): 325–342.
102. Gottfredson and Hirschi, *A General Theory of Crime*, p. 153.
103. Ann Marie Sorenson and David Brownfield, "Normative Concepts in Social Control." Paper presented at the annual meeting of the American Society of Criminology, Phoenix, AZ, November 1993.
104. Brent Benda, "An Examination of Reciprocal Relationship between Religiosity and Different Forms of Delinquency within a Theoretical Model," *Journal of Research in Crime and Delinquency* 34 (1997): 163–186.
105. Delbert Elliott and Scott Menard, "Delinquent Friends and Delinquent Behavior: Temporal and Developmental Patterns," in *Crime and Delinquency: Current Theories,* ed. J. David Hawkins (Cambridge: Cambridge University Press, 1996).
106. Graham Ousey and David Aday, "The Interaction Hypothesis: A Test Using Social Control Theory and Social Learning Theory." Paper presented at the American Society of Criminology Meeting, Boston, 1995.
107. Dana Haynie, Peggy Giordano, Wendy Manning, and Monica Longmore, "Adolescent Romantic Relationships and Delinquency Involvement," *Criminology* 43 (2005): 177–210.
108. Julie Horney, D. Wayne Osgood, and Ineke Haen Marshall, "Criminal Careers in the Short-Term: Intra-Individual Variability in Crime and Its Relations to Local Life Circumstances," *American Sociological Review* 60 (1995): 655–673; Martin Daly and Margo Wilson, "Killing the Competition," *Human Nature* 1 (1990): 83–109.
109. Charles R. Tittle and Harold G. Grasmick, "Criminal Behavior and Age: A Test of Three Provocative Hypotheses," *Journal of Criminal Law and Criminology* 88 (1997): 309–342.
110. L. Thomas Winfree, Jr., Terrance Taylor, Ni He, and Finn-Aage Esbensen, "Self-Control and Variability over Time: Multivariate Results Using a 5-Year, Multisite Panel of Youths," *Crime & Delinquency* 2006 (52): 253–286.
111. Ronald Simons, Christine Johnson, Rand Conger, and Glen Elder Jr., "A Test of Latent Trait versus Life-Course Perspectives on the Stability of Adolescent Antisocial Behavior," *Criminology* 36 (1998): 217–244.
112. Carter Hay, "Parenting, Self-Control, and Delinquency: A Test of Self-Control Theory," *Criminology* 39 (2001): 707–736; Douglas Longshore, "Self-Control and Criminal Opportunity: A Prospective Test of the General Theory of Crime," *Social Problems* 45 (1998): 102–114; Finn-Aage Esbensen and Elizabeth Piper Deschenes, "A Multisite Examination of Youth Gang Membership: Does Gender Matter?" *Criminology* 36 (1998): 799–828.
113. Raymond Paternoster and Robert Brame, "The Structural Similarity of Processes Generating Criminal and Analogous Behaviors," *Criminology* 36 (1998): 633–670.
114. Otwin Marenin and Michael Resig, "A General Theory of Crime and Patterns of Crime in Nigeria: An Exploration of

Methodological Assumptions," *Journal of Criminal Justice* 23 (1995): 501–518.

115. Bruce Arneklev, Harold Grasmick, Charles Tittle, and Robert Bursik, "Low Self-Control and Imprudent Behavior," *Journal of Quantitative Criminology* 9 (1993): 225–246.

116. Peter Muris and Cor Meesters, "The Validity of Attention Deficit Hyperactivity and Hyperkinetic Disorder Symptom Domains in Nonclinical Dutch Children," *Journal of Clinical Child & Adolescent Psychology* 32 (2003): 460–466.

117. Francis Cullen, John Paul Wright, and Mitchell Chamlin, "Social Support and Social Reform: A Progressive Crime Control Agenda," *Crime & Delinquency* 45 (1999): 188–207.

118. Alex Piquero, John MacDonald, Adam Dobrin, Leah Daigle, and Francis Cullen, "Self-Control, Violent Offending, and Homicide Victimization: Assessing the General Theory of Crime," *Journal of Quantitative Criminology* 21 (2005): 55–71.

119. Ibid.

120. Richard Wiebe, "Reconciling Psychopathy and Low Self-Control," *Justice Quarterly* 20 (2003): 297–336.

121. Elizabeth Cauffman, Laurence Steinberg, and Alex Piquero, "Psychological, Neuropsychological and Physiological Correlates of Serious Antisocial Behavior in Adolescence: The Role of Self-Control," *Criminology* 43 (2005): 133–176.

122. Donald Lynam and Joshua Miller, "Personality Pathways to Impulsive Behavior and Their Relations to Deviance: Results from Three Samples," *Journal of Quantitative Criminology* 20 (2004): 319–341.

123. Kevin Thompson, "Sexual Harassment and Low Self-Control: An Application of Gottfredson and Hirschi's General Theory of Crime." Paper presented at the annual meeting of the American Society of Criminology, Phoenix, AZ, November 1993.

124. Heather Lonczk, Robert Abbott, J. David Hawkins, Rick Kosterman, and Richard Catalano, "Effects of the Seattle Social Development Project on Sexual Behavior, Pregnancy, Birth, and Sexually Transmitted Disease Outcomes by Age 21 Years," *Archive of Pediatrics and Adolescent Medicine* 156 (2002): 438–447.

125. Kathleen Bodisch Lynch, Susan Rose Geller, and Melinda G. Schmidt, "Multi-Year Evaluation of the Effectiveness of a Resilience-Based Prevention Program for Young Children," *Journal of Primary Prevention* 24 (2004): 335–353.

126. This section leans on Thomas Tatchell, Phillip Waite, Renny Tatchell, Lynne Durrant, and Dale Bond, "Substance Abuse Prevention in Sixth Grade: The Effect of a Prevention Program on Adolescents' Risk and Protective Factors," *American Journal of Health Studies* 19 (2004): 54–61.

127. Nancy Tobler and Howard Stratton, "Effectiveness of School Based Drug Prevention Programs: A Meta-Analysis of the Research," *Journal of Primary Prevention* 18 (1997): 71–128.

Chapter 10. Violent Crime

1. CNN, "Missing Teen's Mother Leaves Aruba," www.cnn.com/2005/LAW/07/31/aruba.missing (accessed September 2, 2005).

2. Robert Nash Parker and Catherine Colony, "Relationships, Homicides, and Weapons: A Detailed Analysis." Paper presented at the annual meeting of the American Society of Criminology, Montreal, November 1987.

3. Rokeya Farrooque, Ronnie Stout, and Frederick Ernst, "Heterosexual Intimate Partner Homicide: Review of Ten Years of Clinical Experience," *Journal of Forensic Sciences* 50 (2005): 648–651; Miltos Livaditis, Gkaro Esagian, Christos Kakoulidis, Maria Samakouri, and Nikos Tzavaras, "Matricide by Person with Bipolar Disorder and Dependent Overcompliant Personality" *Journal of Forensic Sciences* 50 (2005): 658–661.

4. Dorothy Otnow Lewis, Ernest Moy, Lori Jackson, Robert Aaronson, Nicholas Restifo, Susan Serra, and Alexander Simos, "Biopsychosocial Characteristics of Children Who Later Murder," *American Journal of Psychiatry* 142 (1985): 1,161–1,167.

5. Dorothy Otnow Lewis, *Guilty by Reason of Insanity* (New York: Fawcett Columbine, 1998).

6. Richard Rogers, Randall Salekin, Kenneth Sewell, and Keith Cruise, "Prototypical Analysis of Antisocial Personality Disorder," *Criminal Justice and Behavior* 27 (2000): 234–255; Amy Holtzworth-Munroe and Gregory Stuart, "Typologies of Male Batterers: Three Subtypes and the Differences among Them," *Psychological Bulletin* 116 (1994): 476–497.

7. Albert Reiss Jr. and Jeffrey Roth, *Understanding and Preventing Violence* (Washington, DC: National Academy Press, 1993), pp. 112–113.

8. Todd Herrenkhol, Bu Huan, Emiko Tajima, and Stephen Whitney, "Examining the Link between Child Abuse and Youth Violence," *Journal of Interpersonal Violence* 18 (2003): 1,189–1,208; Pamela Lattimore, Christy Visher, and Richard Linster, "Predicting Rearrest for Violence among Serious Youthful Offenders," *Journal of Research in Crime and Delinquency* 32 (1995): 54–83.

9. Rolf Loeber and Dale Hay, "Key Issues in the Development of Aggression and Violence from Childhood to Early Adulthood," *Annual Review of Psychology* 48 (1997): 371–410.

10. Deborah Capaldi and Gerald Patterson, "Can Violent Offenders Be Distinguished from Frequent Offenders: Prediction from Childhood to Adolescence," *Journal of Research in Crime and Delinquency* 33 (1996): 206–231.

11. Adrian Raine, Patricia Brennan, and Sarnoff Mednick, "Interaction between Birth Complications and Early Maternal Rejection in Predisposing Individuals to Adult Violence: Specificity to Serious, Early-Onset Violence," *American Journal of Psychiatry* 154 (1997): 1,265–1,271.

12. Eric Slade and Lawrence Wissow, "Spanking in Early Childhood and Later Behavior Problems: A Prospective Study of Infants and Young Toddlers," *Pediatrics* 113 (2004): 1,321–1,330; Timothy Ireland, Carolyn Smith, and Terence Thornberry, "Developmental Issues in the Impact of Child Maltreatment on Later Delinquency and Drug Use," *Criminology* 40 (2002): 359–401.

13. Richard Reading, "The Enduring Effects of Abuse and Related Adverse Experiences in Childhood: A Convergence of Evidence from Neurobiology and Epidemiology," *Child: Care, Health & Development* 32 (2006): 253–256.

14. Murray Straus, "Discipline and Deviance: Physical Punishment of Children and Violence and Other Crime in Adulthood," *Social Problems* 38 (1991): 133–154.

15. Alan Rosenbaum and Penny Leisring, "Beyond Power and Control: Towards an Understanding of Partner Abusive Men," *Journal of Comparative Family Studies* 34 (2003): 7–26.

16. Sigmund Freud, *Beyond the Pleasure Principle* (London: Inter-Psychoanalytic Press, 1922).

17. Konrad Lorenz, *On Aggression* (New York: Harcourt Brace Jovanovich, 1966).

18. Wade Myers, *Sexual Homicide by Juveniles* (London: Academic Press, 2002).

19. Justin Patchin, Beth Huebner, John McCluskey, Sean Varano, and Timothy Bynum, "Exposure to Community Violence and Childhood Delinquency," *Crime & Delinquency* 2006 (52): 307–332.

20. Jeffrey B. Bingenheimer, Robert T. Brennan, and Felton J. Earls, "Firearm Violence Exposure and Serious Violent Behavior," *Science* 308 (2005): 1,323–1,326; "Witnessing Gun Violence Significantly Increases Likelihood That a Child Will Also Commit Violent Crime; Violence May Be Viewed as Infectious Disease," *AScribe Health News Service,* May 26, 2005.

21. Joanne Kaufman, "Explaining the Race/Ethnicity–Violence Relationship: Neighborhood Context and Social Psychological Processes," *Justice Quarterly* 22 (2005): 224–251; David Farrington, Rolf Loeber, and Madga Stouthamer-Loeber, "How Can the Relationship between Race and Violence by Explained?" in *Violent Crimes: Assessing Race and Ethnic Differences,* ed. Darnell Hawkins (New York: Cambridge University Press, 2003), pp. 213–237.

22. Eric Stewart, Ronald Simons, and Rand Conger, "Assessing Neighborhood and Social Psychological Influences on Childhood Violence in an African-American Sample," *Criminology* 40 (2002): 801–830.

23. David Farrington, Rolf Loeber, and Magda Stouthamer-Loeber, "How Can the Relationship between Race and Violence Be Explained?" in *Violent Crimes: Assessing Race and Ethnic Differences*, ed. Darnell Hawkins (New York: Cambridge University Press, 2003), pp. 213–237.

24. National Survey on Drug Use and Health (NSDUH), Youth Violence and Illicit Drug Use, 2006, www.oas.samhsa.gov/2k6/youthViolence/youthViolence.htm (accessed February 8, 2006).

25. Arnie Nielsen, Ramiro Martinez, and Matthew Lee, "Alcohol, Ethnicity, and Violence: The Role of Alcohol Availability for Latino and Black Aggravated Assaults and Robberies," *Sociological Quarterly* 46 (2005): 479–502; Chris Allen, "The Links between Heroin, Crack Cocaine and Crime: Where Does Street Crime Fit In?" *British Journal of Criminology* 45 (2005): 355–372.

26. Steven Messner, Glenn Deane, Luc Anselin, and Benjamin Pearson-Nelson, "Locating the Vanguard in Rising and Falling Homicide Rates across Cities," *Criminology* 43 (2005): 661–696.

27. Paul Goldstein, Henry Brownstein, and Patrick Ryan, "Drug-Related Homicide in New York: 1984–1988," *Crime & Delinquency* 38 (1992): 459–476.

28. Robert Brewer and Monica Swahn, "Binge Drinking and Violence," *JAMA: Journal of the American Medical Association* 294 (2005): 16–20.

29. Tomika Stevens, Kenneth Ruggiero, Dean Kilpatrick, Heidi Resnick, and Benjamin Saunders, "Variables Differentiating Singly and Multiply Victimized Youth: Results from the National Survey of Adolescents and Implications for Secondary Prevention," *Child Maltreatment* 10 (2005): 211–223; James Collins and Pamela Messerschmidt, "Epidemiology of Alcohol-Related Violence," *Alcohol Health and Research World* 17 (1993): 93–100.

30. Antonia Abbey, Tina Zawacki, Philip Buck, Monique Clinton, and Pam McAuslan, "Sexual Assault and Alcohol Consumption: What Do We Know about Their Relationship and What Types of Research Are Still Needed?" *Aggression and Violent Behavior* 9 (2004): 271–303.

31. Martin Grann and Seena Fazel, "Substance Misuse and Violent Crime: Swedish Population Study," *British Medical Journal* 328 (2004): 1,233–1,234; Susanne Rogne Gjeruldsen, Bjørn Myrvang, and Stein Opjordsmoen, "Criminality in Drug Addicts: A Follow-Up Study over 25 Years," *European Addiction Research* 10 (2004): 49–56; Kenneth Tardiff, Peter Marzuk, Kira Lowell, Laura Portera, and Andrew Leon, "A Study of Drug Abuse and Other Causes of Homicide in New York," *Journal of Criminal Justice* 30 (2002): 317–325.

32. Paul Goldstein, Patricia Bellucci, Barry Spunt, and Thomas Miller, "Volume of Cocaine Use and Violence: A Comparison between Men and Women," *Journal of Drug Issues* 21 (1991): 345–367.

33. Pamela Wilcox and Richard Clayton, "A Multilevel Analysis of School-Based Weapon Possession," *Justice Quarterly* 18 (2001): 509–542.

34. FBI, *Crime in the United States, 2004* (Washington, DC: U.S. Government Printing Office, 2006).

35. David Brent, Joshua Perper, Christopher Allman, Grace Moritz, Mary Wartella, and Janice Zelenak, "The Presence and Accessibility of Firearms in the Home and Adolescent Suicides," *JAMA: Journal of the American Medical Association* 266 (1991): 2,989–2,995.

36. Robert Baller, Luc Anselin, Steven Messner, Glenn Deane, and Darnell Hawkins, "Structural Covariates of U.S. County Homicide Rates Incorporating Spatial Effects," *Criminology* 39 (2001): 561–590.

37. Marvin Wolfgang and Franco Ferracuti, *The Subculture of Violence* (London: Tavistock, 1967).

38. David Luckenbill and Daniel Doyle, "Structural Position and Violence: Developing a Cultural Explanation," *Criminology* 27 (1989): 419–436.

39. Daneen Deptula and Robert Cohen, "Aggressive, Rejected, and Delinquent Children and Adolescents: A Comparison of Their Friendships," *Aggression and Violent Behavior* 9 (2004): 75–104; Beth Bjerregaard and Alan Lizotte, "Gun Ownership and Gang Membership," *Journal of Criminal Law and Criminology* 86 (1995): 37–58.

40. Sylive Mrug, Betsy Hoza, and William Bukowski, "Choosing or Being Chosen by Aggressive-Disruptive Peers: Do They Contribute to Children's Externalizing and Internalizing Problems?" *Journal of Abnormal Child Psychology* 32 (2004): 53–66.

41. Daniel Neller, Robert Denney, Christina Pietz, and R. Paul Thomlinson, "Testing the Trauma Model of Violence," *Journal of Family Violence* 20 (2005): 151–159; James Howell, "Youth Gang Homicides: A Literature Review," *Crime & Delinquency* 45 (1999): 208–241.

42. Rachel Gordon, Benjamin Lahey, Eriko Kawai, Rolf Loeber, Magda Stouthamer-Loeber, and David Farrington, "Antisocial Behavior and Youth Gang Membership," *Criminology* 42 (2004): 55–88.

43. Eric Monkkonen, "Homicide in Los Angeles, 1827–2002," *Journal of Interdisciplinary History* 36 (2005): 167–183.

44. Ibid., 177–178.

45. Charis Kubrin and Ronald Weitzer, "Retaliatory Homicide: Concentrated Disadvantage and Neighborhood Culture," *Social Problems* 50 (2003): 157–180.

46. Robert J. Kane, "Compromised Police Legitimacy as a Predictor of Violent Crime in Structurally Disadvantaged Communities," *Criminology* 43 (2005): 469–499.

47. Jerome Neapolitan, "A Comparative Analysis of Nations with Low and High Levels of Violent Crime," *Journal of Criminal Justice* 27 (1999): 259–274.

48. Ibid., p. 271.

49. Aki Roberts and Gary LaFree, "Explaining Japan's Postwar Violent Crime Trends," *Criminology* 42 (2004): 179–210.

50. William Green, *Rape* (Lexington, MA: Lexington Books, 1988), p. 5.

51. Barbara Krah, Renate Scheinberger-Olwig, and Steffen Bieneck, "Men's Reports of Nonconsensual Sexual Interactions with Women: Prevalence and Impact," *Archives of Sexual Behavior* 32 (2003): 165–176.

52. Siegmund Fred Fuchs, "Male Sexual Assault: Issues of Arousal and Consent," *Cleveland State Law Review* 51 (2004): 93–108.

53. Marlise Simons, "Bosnian Serb Pleads Guilty to Rape Charge before War Crimes Tribunal," *New York Times*, March 10,1998, p. 8.

54. Marc Lacey, "Amnesty Says Sudan Militias Use Rape as Weapon," *New York Times,* July 19, 2004, p. A9.

55. FBI, *Crime in the United States, 2004*, supplemented with preliminary 2005 data. Crime data in this chapter comes from this source.

56. Callie Marie Rennison and Michael Rand, *Criminal Victimization 2002: Changes 2001–2002* (Washington, DC: Bureau of Justice Statistics, 2003), p. 2.

57. Carol Vanzile-Tamsen, Maria Testa, and Jennifer Livingston, "The Impact of Sexual Assault History and Relationship Context on Appraisal of and Responses to Acquaintance Sexual Assault Risk," *Journal of Interpersonal Violence* 20 (2005): 813–822; Arnold Kahn, Jennifer Jackson, Christine Kully, Kelly Badger, and Jessica Halvorsen, "Calling It Rape: Differences in Experiences of Women Who Do or Do Not Label Their Sexual Assault as Rape," *Psychology of Women Quarterly* 27 (2003): 233–242.

58. Amy Buddie and Maria Testa, "Rates and Predictors of Sexual Aggression among Students and Nonstudents," *Journal of Interpersonal Violence* 20 (2005): 713–725.
59. Angela Browne, "Violence against Women: Relevance for Medical Practitioners," *JAMA: Journal of the American Medical Association* 267 (1992): 3,184–3,189.
60. Mark Warr, "Rape, Burglary and Opportunity," *Journal of Quantitative Criminology* 4 (1988): 275–288.
61. A. Nicholas Groth and Jean Birnbaum, *Men Who Rape* (New York: Plenum Press, 1979).
62. For another typology, see Raymond Knight, "Validation of a Typology of Rapists," in *Sex Offender Research and Treatment: State-of-the-Art in North America and Europe*, eds. W. L. Marshall and J. Frenken (Beverly Hills, CA: Sage, 1997), pp. 58–75.
63. R. Lance Shotland, "A Model of the Causes of Date Rape in Developing and Close Relationships," in *Close Relationships*, ed. C. Hendrick (Newbury Park, CA: Sage, 1989), pp. 247–270.
64. Kimberly Tyler, Danny Hoyt, and Les Whitbeck, "Coercive Sexual Strategies," *Violence and Victims* 13 (1998): 47–63.
65. Bonnie Fisher, Leah Daigle, Francis Cullen, and Michael Turner, "Reporting Sexual Victimization to the Police and Others: Results from a National-Level Study of College Women," *Criminal Justice and Behavior* 30 (2003): 6–39.
66. David Finkelhor and Kersti Yllo, *License to Rape: Sexual Abuse of Wives* (New York: Holt, Rinehart and Winston, 1985).
67. Jill Elaine Hasday, "Contest and Consent: A Legal History of Marital Rape," *California Law Review* 88 (2000): 1,373–1,433.
68. Sharon Elstein and Roy Davis, *Sexual Relationships between Adult Males and Young Teen Girls: Exploring the Legal and Social Responses* (Chicago: American Bar Association, 1997).
69. Donald Symons, *The Evolution of Human Sexuality* (Oxford: Oxford University Press, 1979).
70. Lee Ellis and Anthony Walsh, "Gene-Based Evolutionary Theories in Criminology," *Criminology* 35 (1997): 229–276.
71. Suzanne Osman, "Predicting Men's Rape Perceptions Based on the Belief That 'No' Really Means 'Yes,'" *Journal of Applied Social Psychology* 33 (2003): 683–692.
72. Martin Schwartz, Walter DeKeseredy, David Tait, and Shahid Alvi, "Male Peer Support and a Feminist Routine Activities Theory: Understanding Sexual Assault on the College Campus," *Justice Quarterly* 18 (2001): 623–650.
73. Diana Russell and Rebecca M. Bolen, *The Epidemic of Rape and Child Sexual Abuse in the United States* (Thousand Oaks, CA: Sage, 2000).
74. Paul Gebhard, John Gagnon, Wardell Pomeroy, and Cornelia Christenson, *Sex Offenders: An Analysis of Types* (New York: Harper & Row, 1965), pp. 198–205; Richard Rada, ed., *Clinical Aspects of the Rapist* (New York: Grune & Stratton, 1978), pp. 122–130.
75. Stephen Porter, David Fairweather, Jeff Drugge, Huues Herve, Angela Birt, and Douglas Boer, "Profiles of Psychopathy in Incarcerated Sexual Offenders," *Criminal Justice and Behavior* 27 (2000): 216–233.
76. Brad Bushman, Angelica Bonacci, Mirjam van Dijk, and Roy Baumeister, "Narcissism, Sexual Refusal, and Aggression: Testing a Narcissistic Reactance Model of Sexual Coercion," *Journal of Personality and Social Psychology* 84 (2003): 1,027–1,040.
77. Schwartz, DeKeseredy, Tait, and Alvi, "Male Peer Support and a Feminist Routine Activities Theory."
78. Groth and Birnbaum, *Men Who Rape*, p. 101.
79. See, generally, Edward Donnerstein, Daniel Linz, and Steven Penrod, *The Question of Pornography* (New York: Free Press, 1987); Diana Russell, *Sexual Exploitation* (Beverly Hills, CA: Sage, 1985), pp. 115–116.
80. Neil Malamuth and John Briere, "Sexual Violence in the Media: Indirect Effects on Aggression against Women," *Journal of Social Issues* 42 (1986): 75–92.
81. Richard Felson and Marvin Krohn, "Motives for Rape," *Journal of Research in Crime and Delinquency* 27 (1990): 222–242.
82. Laura Monroe, Linda Kinney, Mark Weist, Denise Spriggs Dafeamekpor, Joyce Dantzler, and Matthew Reynolds, "The Experience of Sexual Assault: Findings from a Statewide Victim Needs Assessment," *Journal of Interpersonal Violence* 20 (2005): 767–776.
83. Julie Horney and Cassia Spohn, "The Influence of Blame and Believability Factors on the Processing of Simple versus Aggravated Rape Cases," *Criminology* 34 (1996): 135–163.
84. Patricia Landwehr, Robert Bothwell, Matthew Jeanmard, Luis Luque, Roy Brown III, and Marie-Anne Breaux, "Racism in Rape Trials," *Journal of Social Psychology* 142 (2002): 667–670.
85. Cassia Spohn, Dawn Beichner, and Erika Davis–Frenzel, "Prosecutorial Justifications for Sexual Assault Case Rejection," *Social Problems* 48 (2001): 206–235.
86. "Man Wrongly Convicted of Rape Released 19 Years Later," *The Forensic Examiner* (May–June 2003): 44.
87. Gerald Robin, "Forcible Rape: Institutionalized Sexism in the Criminal Justice System," *Crime & Delinquency* 23 (1977): 136–153.
88. Rodney Kingsworth, Randall MacIntosh, and Jennifer Wentworth, "Sexual Assault: The Role of Prior Relationship and Victim Characteristics in Case Processing," *Justice Quarterly* 16 (1999): 276–302.
89. Susan Estrich, *Real Rape* (Cambridge, MA: Harvard University Press, 1987), pp. 58–59.
90. *Michigan v. Lucas* 90-149 (1991); Comment, "The Rape Shield Paradox: Complainant Protection Amidst Oscillating Trends of State Judicial Interpretation," *Journal of Criminal Law and Criminology* 78 (1987): 644–698.
91. Andrew Karmen, *Crime Victims* (Pacific Grove, CA: Brooks/Cole, 1990), p. 252.
92. "Court Upholds Civil Rights Portion of Violence against Women Act," *Criminal Justice Newsletter* 28 (December 1, 1997), p. 3.
93. Cassia Spohn and David Holleran, "Prosecuting Sexual Assault: A Comparison of Charging Decisions in Sexual Assault Cases Involving Strangers, Acquaintances, and Intimate Partners," *Justice Quarterly* 18 (2001): 651–688; Colleen Fitzpatrick and Philip Reichel, "Conceptions of Rape and Perceptions of Prosecution." Paper presented at the American Society of Criminology meeting, San Diego, 1997.
94. Donald Lunde, *Murder and Madness* (San Francisco: San Francisco Book, 1977), p. 3.
95. Lisa Baertlein, "HIV Ruled Deadly Weapon in Rape Case," *Boston Globe,* March 2, 1994, p. 3.
96. The legal principles here come from Wayne LaFave and Austin Scott Jr., *Criminal Law* (St. Paul, MN: West, 1986; updated 1993). The definitions and discussion of legal principles used in this chapter lean heavily on this work.
97. LaFave and Scott Jr., *Criminal Law*.
98. Evelyn Nieves, "Woman Gets 4-Year Term in Fatal Dog Attack," *New York Times,* July 16, 2002, p. 1.
99. James Alan Fox and Marianne Zawitz, *Homicide Trends in the United States* (Washington, DC: Bureau of Justice Statistics, 2001).
100. Dana Haynie and David Armstrong, "Race and Gender-Disaggregated Homicide Offending Rates: Differences and Similarities by Victim-Offender Relations across Cities," *Homicide Studies* 10 (2006): 3–32.
101. Todd Shackelford, Viviana Weekes-Shackelford, and Shanna Beasley, "An Exploratory Analysis of the Contexts and Circumstances of Filicide-Suicide in Chicago, 1965–1994," *Aggressive Behavior* 31 (2005): 399–406.
102. Ibid.
103. Philip Cook, Jens Ludwig, and Anthony Braga, "Criminal Records of Homicide Offenders," *JAMA: Journal of the American Medical Association* 294 (2005): 598–601.

104. Gabrielle Salfati and Paul Taylor, "Differentiating Sexual Violence: A Comparison of Sexual Homicide and Rape," *Psychology, Crime & Law* 12 (2006): 107–125.

105. Terance Miethe and Wendy Regoeczi with Kriss Drass, *Rethinking Homicide: Exploring the Structure and Process Underlying Deadly Situations* (Cambridge, MA: Cambridge University Press, 2004).

106. Victoria Frye, Vanessa Hosein, Eve Waltermaurer, Shannon Blaney, and Susan Wilt, "Femicide in New York City: 1990 to 1999," *Homicide Studies* 9 (2005): 204–228.

107. Linda Saltzman and James Mercy, "Assaults between Intimates: The Range of Relationships Involved," in *Homicide: The Victim / Offender Connection,* ed. Anna Victoria Wilson (Cincinnati, OH: Anderson Publishing, 1993), pp. 65–74.

108. Angela Browne and Kirk Williams, "Exploring the Effect of Resource Availability and the Likelihood of Female-Perpetrated Homicides," *Law and Society Review* 23 (1989): 75–94.

109. Richard Felson, "Anger, Aggression, and Violence in Love Triangles," *Violence and Victimization* 12 (1997): 345–363.

110. Ibid., p. 361.

111. Scott Decker, "Deviant Homicide: A New Look at the Role of Motives and Victim–Offender Relationships," *Journal of Research in Crime and Delinquency* 33 (1996): 427–449.

112. David Luckenbill, "Criminal Homicide as a Situational Transaction," *Social Problems* 25 (1977): 176–186.

113. Margaret Zahn and Philip Sagi, "Stranger Homicides in Nine American Cities," *Journal of Criminal Law and Criminology* 78 (1987): 377–397.

114. Tomislav Kovandzic, John Sloan, and Lynne Vieraitis, "Unintended Consequences of Politically Popular Sentencing Policy: The Homicide Promoting Effects of 'Three Strikes' in U.S. Cities (1980–1999)," *Criminology and Public Policy* 3 (2002): 399–424.

115. Jill DeVoe, Katharin Peter, Margaret Noonan, Thomas Snyder, Katrina Baum, and Thomas Snyder, *Indicators of School Crime and Safety, 2005* (Washington, DC: U.S. Department of Education and Bureau of Justice Statistics, 2005).

116. Tonja Nansel, Mary Overpeck, and Ramani Pilla, "Bullying Behaviors among US Youth: Prevalence and Association with Psychosocial Adjustment," *JAMA: Journal of the American Medical Association* 285 (2001): 2,094–3,100.

117. Christine Kerres Malecki and Michelle Kilpatrick Demaray, "Carrying a Weapon to School and Perceptions of Social Support in an Urban Middle School," *Journal of Emotional and Behavioral Disorders* 11 (2003): 169–178.

118. Ibid.

119. Pamela Wilcox and Richard Clayton, "A Multilevel Analysis of School-Based Weapon Possession," *Justice Quarterly* 18 (2001): 509–542.

120. Mark Anderson, Joanne Kaufman, Thomas Simon, Lisa Barrios, Len Paulozzi, George Ryan, Rodney Hammond, William Modzeleski, Thomas Feucht, Lloyd Potter, and the School-Associated Violent Deaths Study Group, "School-Associated Violent Deaths in the United States, 1994–1999," *JAMA: Journal of the American Medical Association* 286 (2001): 2,695–2,702.

121. Bryan Vossekuil, Marisa Reddy, Robert Fein, Randy Borum, and William Modzeleski, *Safe School Initiative, An Interim Report on the Prevention of Targeted Violence in Schools* (Washington, DC: United States Secret Service, 2000).

122. Anthony Walsh, "African Americans and Serial Killing in the Media: The Myth and the Reality," *Homicide Studies* 9 (2005): 271–291.

123. Alasdair Goodwill and Laurence Alison, "Sequential Angulation, Spatial Dispersion and Consistency of Distance Attack Patterns from Home in Serial Murder, Rape and Burglary," *Journal of Psychology, Crime & Law* 11 (2005): 161–176.

124. www.crimelibrary.com/serial_killers/weird/swango/pleasure_8.html (accessed September 3, 2005).

125. Aneez Esmail, "Physician as Serial Killer—The Shipman Case," *New England Journal of Medicine* 352 (2005): 1,483–1,844.

126. Christopher Ferguson, Diana White, Stacey Cherry, Marta Lorenz, and Zhara Bhimani, "Defining and Classifying Serial Murder in the Context of Perpetrator Motivation," *Journal of Criminal Justice* 31 (2003): 287–293.

127. James Alan Fox and Jack Levin, "Multiple Homicide: Patterns of Serial and Mass Murder," in *Crime and Justice: An Annual Edition*, vol. 23, ed. Michael Tonry (Chicago: University of Chicago Press, 1998): 407–455. See also James Alan Fox and Jack Levin, *Overkill: Mass Murder and Serial Killing Exposed* (New York: Plenum, 1994); James Alan Fox and Jack Levin, "A Psycho-Social Analysis of Mass Murder," in *Serial and Mass Murder: Theory, Policy, and Research,* eds. Thomas O'Reilly-Fleming and Steven Egger (Toronto: University of Toronto Press, 1993); James Alan Fox and Jack Levin, "Serial Murder: A Survey," in *Serial and Mass Murder*; Jack Levin and James Alan Fox, *Mass Murder* (New York: Plenum Press, 1985).

128. Terry Whitman and Donald Akutagawa, "Riddles in Serial Murder: A Synthesis," *Aggression and Violent Behavior* 9 (2004) 693–703.

129. Belea Keeney and Kathleen Heide, "Gender Differences in Serial Murderers: A Preliminary Analysis," *Journal of Interpersonal Violence* 9 (1994): 37–56.

130. Wade Myers, Erik Gooch, and Reid Meloy, "The Role of Psychopathy and Sexuality in a Female Serial Killer" *Journal of Forensic Sciences* 50 (2005): 652–658.

131. Fox and Levin, "Multiple Homicide: Patterns of Serial and Mass Murder"; Fox and Levin, *Overkill: Mass Murder and Serial Killing Exposed*; James Alan Fox, Jack Levin, and Kenna Quinet, *The Will to Kill: Making Sense of Senseless Murder*, 2nd ed. (Boston: Allyn & Bacon, 2004); Fox and Levin, "A Psycho-Social Analysis of Mass Murder

132. Ibid.

133. Elissa Gootman, "The Hunt for a Sniper: The Victim; 10th Victim Is Recalled as Motivator on Mission," *New York Times*, October 14, 2002, p. A15; Sarah Kershaw, "The Hunt for a Sniper: The Investigation; Endless Frustration but Little Evidence in Search for Sniper," *New York Times*, October 14, 2002, p. A1.

134. "Mugshots, Court TV's Criminal Biography Series Profiles Racist Serial Killer Joseph Paul Franklin," www.courttv.com/archive/press/Franklin.html (accessed September 3, 2005).

135. Francis X. Clines with Christopher Drew, "Prosecutors to Discuss Charges as Rifle Is Tied to Sniper Killings," *New York Times*, October 25, 2002, p. A1.

136. FBI, *Crime in the United States, 2000* (Washington, DC: U.S. Government Printing Office, 2001), p. 34.

137. Salfati Gabrielle and Paul Taylor, "Differentiating Sexual Violence: A Comparison of Sexual Homicide and Rape," *Psychology, Crime and Law* 12 (2006): 107–125; Keith Harries, "Homicide and Assault: A Comparative Analysis of Attributes in Dallas Neighborhoods, 1981–1985," *Professional Geographer* 41 (1989): 29–38.

138. Laurence Zuckerman, "The Air-Rage Rage: Taking a Cold Look at a Hot Topic," *New York Times*, October 4, 1998, p. A3.

139. See, generally, Ruth S. Kempe and C. Henry Kempe, *Child Abuse* (Cambridge, MA: Harvard University Press, 1978).

140. U.S. Department of Health and Human Services, Administration for Children and Families, Children's Bureau, *Child Maltreatment, 2002* (Washington, DC: Author, 2004).

141. National Clearinghouse on Child Abuse and Neglect, *Child Abuse and Neglect Fatalities: Statistics and Interventions, 2004*, http://nccanch.acf.hhs.gov/pubs/factsheets/fatality.cfm (accessed August 8, 2004).

142. Eva Jonzon and Frank Lindblad, "Adult Female Victims of Child Sexual Abuse," *Journal of Interpersonal Violence* 20 (2005): 651–666.

143. Jane Siegel and Linda Williams, "Risk Factors for Sexual Victimization of Women," *Violence against Women* 9 (2003): 902–930.

144. Glenn Wolfner and Richard Gelles, "A Profile of Violence toward Children: A National Study," *Child Abuse and Neglect* 17 (1993): 197–212.
145. Martin Daly and Margo Wilson, "Violence against Step Children," *Current Directions in Psychological Science* 5 (1996): 77–81.
146. Ruth Inglis, *Sins of the Fathers: A Study of the Physical and Emotional Abuse of Children* (New York: St. Martin's Press, 1978), p. 53.
147. Cindy Schaeffer, Pamela Alexander, Kimberly Bethke, and Lisa Kretz, "Predictors of Child Abuse Potential among Military Parents: Comparing Mothers and Fathers," *Journal of Family Violence* 20 (2005): 123–129.
148. Arina Ulman and Murray Straus, "Violence by Children against Mothers in Relation to Violence between Parents and Corporal Punishment by Parents," *Journal of Comparative Family Studies* 34 (2003): 41–63.
149. Richard Gelles and Murray Straus, "Violence in the American Family," *Journal of Social Issues* 35 (1979): 15–39.
150. Miguel Schwartz, Susan O'Leary, and Kimberly Kendziora, "Dating Aggression among High School Students," *Violence and Victimization* 12 (1997): 295–307.
151. Jay Silverman, Anita Raj, Lorelei Mucci, and Jeanne Hathaway, "Dating Violence against Adolescent Girls and Associated Substance Abuse, Unhealthy Weight Control, Sexual Risk Behavior, Pregnancy and Suicidality," *JAMA: Journal of the American Medical Association* 286 (2001): 572–579.
152. Jacquelyn Campbell, Daniel Webster, Jane Koziol-McLain, Carolyn Block, Doris Campbell, Mary Ann Curry, Faye Gary, et al., "Risk Factors for Femicide in Abusive Relationships: Results from a Multisite Case Control Study," *American Journal of Public Health* 93 (2003): 1,089–1,097.
153. FBI, *Crime in the United States, 2000*, p. 29.
154. James Calder and John Bauer, "Convenience Store Robberies: Security Measures and Store Robbery Incidents," *Journal of Criminal Justice* 20 (1992): 553–566.
155. Peter Van Koppen and Robert Jansen, "The Time to Rob: Variations in Time of Number of Commercial Robberies," *Journal of Research in Crime and Delinquency* 36 (1999): 7–29.
156. Richard Wright and Scott Decker, *Armed Robbers in Action, Stickups and Street Culture* (Boston: Northeastern University Press, 1997).
157. Jody Miller, "Up It Up: Gender and the Accomplishment of Street Robbery," *Criminology* 36 (1998): 37–67.
158. Ibid., pp. 54–55.
159. Volkan Topalli, Richard Wright, and Robert Fornango, "Drug Dealers, Robbery and Retaliation: Vulnerability, Deterrence and the Contagion of Violence," *British Journal of Criminology* 42 (2002): 337–351.
160. Richard Felson, Eric Baumer, and Steven Messner, "Acquaintance Robbery," *Journal of Research in Crime and Delinquency* 37 (2000): 284–305.
161. Ibid., p. 287.
162. Ibid.
163. James Brooke, "Gay Student Who Was Kidnapped and Beaten Dies," *New York Times*, October 13, 1998, p. A1.
164. James Garofalo, "Bias and Non-Bias Crimes in New York City: Preliminary Findings." Paper presented at the annual meeting of the American Society of Criminology, Baltimore, MD, November 1990.
165. "Boy Gets 18 Years in Fatal Park Beating of Transient," *Los Angeles Times*, December 24, 1987, p. 9B.
166. Jack McDevitt, Jack Levin, and Susan Bennett, "Hate Crime Offenders: An Expanded Typology," *Journal of Social Issues* 58 (2002): 303–318; Jack Levin and Jack McDevitt, *Hate Crimes: The Rising Tide of Bigotry and Bloodshed* (New York: Plenum, 1993).
167. FBI, Hate Crime Statistics, 2004, www.fbi.gov/ucr/hc2004/section1.htm (accessed April 11, 2006).
168. Gregory Herek, Jeanine Cogan, and Roy Gillis, "Victim Experiences in Hate Crimes Based on Sexual Orientation," *Journal of Social Issues* 58 (2002): 319–340.
169. Brian Levin, "From Slavery to Hate Crime Laws: The Emergence of Race and Status-Based Protection in American Criminal Law," *Journal of Social Issues* 58 (2002): 227–246.
170. Felicia Lee, "Gays Angry Over TV Report on a Murder," *New York Times*, November 26, 2004, A3.
171. Frederick M. Lawrence, *Punishing Hate: Bias Crimes under American Law* (Cambridge, MA: Harvard University Press, 1999).
172. Ibid., p. 3.
173. *Virginia v. Black et al.*, No. 01-1107, 2003.
174. James Alan Fox and Jack Levin, "Firing Back: The Growing Threat of Workplace Homicide," *The ANNALS of the American Academy of Political and Social Science* 536 (1994): 16–30.
175. John King, "Workplace Violence: A Conceptual Framework." Paper presented at the annual meeting of the American Society of Criminology, Phoenix, AZ, November 1993.
176. Robert Simon, *Bad Men Do What Good Men Dream* (Washington, DC: American Psychiatric Press, 1999).
177. Janet R. Copper, "Response to 'Workplace Violence in Health Care: Recognized but Not Regulated' by Kathleen M. McPhaul and Jane A. Lipscomb (September 30, 2004)," *Online Journal of Issues in Nursing* 10 (2005): 53–55.
178. Greg Warchol, *Workplace Violence, 1992–96* (Washington, DC: Bureau of Justice Statistics, 1998).
179. The following sections rely heavily on Patricia Tjaden, *The Crime of Stalking: How Big Is the Problem?* (Washington, DC: National Institute of Justice, 1997). See also Robert M. Emerson, Kerry O. Ferris, and Carol Brooks Gardner, "On Being Stalked," *Social Problems* 45 (1998): 289–298.
180. Patrick Kinkade, Ronald Burns, and Angel Ilarraza Fuentes, "Criminalizing Attractions: Perceptions of Stalking and the Stalker," *Crime & Delinquency* 51 (2005): 3–25.
181. Tjaden, *The Crime of Stalking: How Big Is the Problem?*
182. Bonnie Fisher, Francis Cullen, and Michael Turner, "Being Pursued: Stalking Victimization in a National Study of College Women," *Criminology and Public Policy* 1 (2002): 257–309.
183. Carol Jordan, T. K. Logan, and Robert Walker, "Stalking: An Examination of the Criminal Justice Response," *Journal of Interpersonal Violence* 18 (2003): 148–165.
184. Title 22 of the United States Code section 2656f(d) (1999).
185. Paul Wilkinson, *Terrorism and the Liberal State* (New York: John Wiley, 1977), p. 49.
186. Jack Gibbs, "Conceptualization of Terrorism," *American Sociological Review* 54 (1989): 329–340, at 330.
187. Associated Press, "Malaysia Arrests Five Militants," *New York Times*, October 15, 2002, p. A2.
188. Chung Chien-Peng, "China's War on Terror," *Foreign Affairs* 81 (July–August 2002): 8–13.
189. Jocelyn Parker, "Vehicles Burn at Dealership: SUV Attacks Turn Violent," *Detroit Free Press*, August 23, 2003, p. 1.
190. Fiona Proffitt, "Costs of Animal Rights Terror," *Science* 304 (June 18, 2004): 1,731–1,739.
191. "Brutal Elves in the Woods," *The Economist* 359 (April 14, 2001): 28–30.
192. Jeffrey Kluger, "The Nuke Pipeline: The Trade in Nuclear Contraband Is Approaching Critical Mass. Can We Turn Off the Spigot?" *Time*, December 17, 2001, p. 40.
193. Tamara Makarenko, "The Crime-Terror Continuum: Tracing the Interplay between Transnational Organised Crime and Terrorism." *Global Crime* 6 (2004): 129–145.
194. Chris Dishman, "Terrorism, Crime, and Transformation," *Studies in Conflict & Terrorism* 24 (2001): 43–56.
195. Mark Jurgensmeyer, *Terror in the Mind of God* (Berkeley and Los Angeles: University of California Press, 2000).
196. "Hunting Terrorists Using Confidential Informant Reward Programs," *FBI Law Enforcement Bulletin* 71 (2002): 26–28; Sara

Sun Beale and James Felman, "The Consequences of Enlisting Federal Grand Juries in the War on Terrorism: Assessing the USA Patriot Act's Changes to Grand Jury Secrecy," *Harvard Journal of Law and Public Policy* 25 (2002): 699–721.

197. Graham Allison, *Nuclear Terrorism: The Ultimate Preventable Catastrophe* (New York: Times Books, 2004).

Chapter 11. Property Crimes

1. FBI, "Credit Card Con: Canadian Man Gets 10 Years for $12 Million Telemarketing Scam," www.fbi.gov/page2/nov03/credit112803.htm (accessed April 11, 2006).

2. Andrew McCall, *The Medieval Underworld* (London: Hamish Hamilton, 1979), p. 86.

3. Ibid., p. 104.

4. J. J. Tobias, *Crime and Police in England, 1700–1900* (London: Gill and Macmillan, 1979).

5. Ibid., p. 9.

6. Marilyn Walsh, *The Fence* (Westport, CT: Greenwood Press, 1977), pp. 18–25.

7. John Hepburn, "Occasional Criminals," in *Major Forms of Crime*, ed. Robert Meier (Beverly Hills, CA: Sage, 1984), pp. 73–94.

8. James Inciardi, "Professional Crime," in *Major Forms of Crime*, ed. Robert Meier (Beverly Hills, CA: Sage, 1984), p. 223.

9. This section depends heavily on a classic book: Wayne La Fave and Austin Scott Jr., *Handbook on Criminal Law* (St. Paul, MN: West, 1972).

10. La Fave and Scott Jr., *Handbook on Criminal Law*, p. 622.

11. FBI, *Crime in the United States, 2004* (Washington, DC: U.S. Government Printing Office, 2005). UCR data in this chapter comes from this source.

12. Shannan Catalano, "Criminal Victimization, 2004" (Bureau of Justice Statistics, 2005), www.ojp.usdoj.gov/bjs/abstract/cv04.htm (accessed April 15, 2006).

13. Henrico County Virginia, www.co.henrico.va.us/index.html (accessed April 11, 2006).

14. John Worrall, "The Effect of *Three-Strikes Legislation on Serious Crime in California*," *Journal of Criminal Justice* 32 (2004): 283–296.

15. Margaret Loftus, "Gone: One TV," *U.S. News & World Report*, July 14, 1997, p. 61.

16. Holly Bailey, Pat Wingert, and Steve Tuttle, "Target Practice," *Newsweek*, 147 (March 20, 2006): 32.

17. Mary Owen Cameron, *The Booster and the Snitch* (New York: Free Press, 1964).

18. Ibid., p. 57.

19. Lawrence Cohen and Rodney Stark, "Discriminatory Labeling and the Five-Finger Discount: An Empirical Analysis of Differential Shoplifting Dispositions," *Journal of Research on Crime and Delinquency* 11 (1974): 25–35.

20. Lloyd Klemke, "Does Apprehension for Shoplifting Amplify or Terminate Shoplifting Activity?" *Law and Society Review* 12 (1978): 390–403.

21. Erhard Blankenburg, "The Selectivity of Legal Sanctions: An Empirical Investigation of Shoplifting," *Law and Society Review* 11 (1976): 109–129.

22. George Keckeisen, *Retail Security versus the Shoplifter* (Springfield, IL: Charles C Thomas, 1993), pp. 31–32.

23. "Tesco Trials Electronic Product Tagging," *Computing and Control Engineering* 14 (2003): 3.

24. Jill Jordan Siedfer, "To Catch a Thief, Try This: Peddling High-Tech Solutions to Shoplifting," *U.S. News & World Report*, September 23, 1996, p. 71

25. *Ruditys v. J.C. Penney Co.*, No. 02-4114 (Delaware Co., Pa., Ct. C.P. 2003).

26. Paul Beckett and Jathon Sapsford, "As Credit-Card Theft Grows, a Tussle Over Paying to Stop It," *Wall Street Journal* (Eastern Edition), May 1, 2003, p. A1.

27. Matt Richtell, "Credit Card Theft Is Thriving Online as Global Market," *New York Times*, May 13, 2002, p. A1.

28. La Fave and Scott Jr., *Handbook on Criminal Law*, p. 672.

29. National Insurance Crime Bureau, www.nicb.org/public/newsroom/hotwheels/index.cfm (accessed April 12, 2006).

30. Kim Hazelbaker, "Insurance Industry Analyses and the Prevention of Motor Vehicle Theft," in *Business and Crime Prevention*, eds. Marcus Felson and Ronald Clarke (Monsey, NY: Criminal Justice Press, 1997), pp. 283–293, at p. 287.

31. Charles McCaghy, Peggy Giordano, and Trudy Knicely Henson, "Auto Theft," *Criminology* 15 (1977): 367–381.

32. Donald Gibbons, *Society, Crime and Criminal Careers* (Englewood Cliffs, NJ: Prentice-Hall, 1977), p. 310.

33. Hazelbaker, "Insurance Industry Analyses and the Prevention of Motor Vehicle Theft."

34. "Hot Cars: Parts Crooks Love Best," *BusinessWeek*, September 15, 2003, p. 104.

35. Ian Ayres and Steven D. Levitt, "Measuring Positive Externalities from Unobservable Victim Precaution: An Empirical Analysis of Lojack," *Quarterly Journal of Economics* 113 (1998): 43–78.

36. Hazelbaker, "Insurance Industry Analyses and the Prevention of Motor Vehicle Theft," p. 289.

37. P. Weiss, "Outsmarting the Electronic Gatekeeper: Code Breakers Beat Security Scheme of Car Locks, Gas Pumps," *Science News* 167 (2005): 86.

38. Edwin Lemert, "An Isolation and Closure Theory of Naive Check Forgery," *Journal of Criminal Law, Criminology and Police Science* 44 (1953): 297–298.

39. La Fave and Scott Jr., *Handbook on Criminal Law*, p. 655.

40. 30 Geo. III, C.24 (1975).

41. Susan Gembrowski and Tim Dahlberg, "Over 100 Here Indicted after Telemarketing Fraud Probe around the U.S," *San Diego Daily Transcript Online*, December 8, 1995, www.sddt.com/files/library/95headlines/DN951208/DN95120802.html.

42. Carl Klockars, *The Professional Fence* (New York: Free Press, 1976); Darrell Steffensmeier, *The Fence: In the Shadow of Two Worlds* (Totowa, NJ: Rowman and Littlefield, 1986); Walsh, *The Fence*, pp. 25–28.

43. Simon Fass and Janice Francis, "Where Have All the Hot Goods Gone? The Role of Pawnshops," *Journal of Research in Crime & Delinquency* 41 (2004): 156–179.

44. Walsh, *The Fence*, p. 34.

45. Jerome Hall, *Theft, Law and Society* (Indianapolis, IN: Bobbs-Merrill, 1952), p. 36.

46. La Fave and Scott Jr., *Handbook on Criminal Law*, p. 644.

47. Ibid., p. 649.

48. Dawit Kiros Fantaye, "Fighting Corruption and Embezzlement in Third World Countries," *Journal of Criminal Law* 68 (April 2004): 170.

49. La Fave and Scott Jr., *Handbook on Criminal Law*, p. 708.

50. William Blackstone, *Commentaries on the Laws of England* (London: Clarendon Press, 1769), p. 224.

51. Shannan Catalano, *Criminal Victimization, 2004* (Washington, DC: Bureau of Justice Statistics, 2005).

52. Frank Hoheimer, *The Home Invaders: Confessions of a Cat Burglar* (Chicago: Chicago Review, 1975).

53. Richard Wright, Robert Logie, and Scott Decker, "Criminal Expertise and Offender Decision Making: An Experimental Study of the Target Selection Process in Residential Burglary," *Journal of Research in Crime and Delinquency* 32 (1995): 39–53.

54. Richard Wright and Scott Decker, *Burglars on the Job: Streetlife and Residential Break-ins* (Boston: Northeastern University Press, 1994).

55. Matthew Robinson, "Accessible Targets, but Not Advisable Ones: The Role of 'Accessibility' in Student Apartment Burglary," *Journal of Security Administration* 21 (1998): 28–44.

56. Brent Snook, "Individual Differences in Distance Travelled by Serial Burglars," *Journal of Investigative Psychology & Offender Profiling* 1 (2004): 53–66.

57. Elizabeth Groff and Nancy La Vigne, "Mapping an Opportunity Surface of Residential Burglary," *Journal of Research in Crime and Delinquency* 38 (2001): 257–278.
58. Wim Bernasco and Paul Nieuwbeerta, "How Do Residential Burglars Select Target Areas? A New Approach to the Analysis of Criminal Location Choice," *British Journal of Criminology* 45 (2005): 296–315.
59. Hoheimer, *The Home Invaders: Confessions of a Cat Burglar*.
60. Wright, Logie, and Decker, "Criminal Expertise and Offender Decision Making: An Experimental Study of the Target Selection Process in Residential Burglary."
61. Matthew Robinson, "Accessible Targets, but Not Advisable Ones: The Role of 'Accessibility' in Student Apartment Burglary."
62. Melanie Wellsmith and Amy Burrell, "The Influence of Purchase Price and Ownership Levels on Theft Targets: The Example of Domestic Burglary," *British Journal of Criminology* 45 (2005): 741–764.
63. Matt Hopkins, "Crimes against Businesses: The Way Forward for Future Research," *British Journal of Criminology* 42 (2002): 782–797.
64. Simon Hakim and Yochanan Shachmurove, "Spatial and Temporal Patterns of Commercial Burglaries," *American Journal of Economics and Sociology* 55 (1996): 443–457.
65. Roger Litton, "Crime Prevention and the Insurance Industry," in *Business and Crime Prevention*, eds. Marcus Felson and Ronald Clarke (Monsey, NY: Criminal Justice Press, 1997), p. 162.
66. Graham Farrell, Coretta Phillips, and Ken Pease, "Like Taking Candy: Why Does Repeat Victimization Occur?" *British Journal of Criminology* 35 (1995): 384–399, at p. 391.
67. Ronald Clarke, Elizabeth Perkins, and Donald Smith, "Explaining Repeat Residential Burglaries: An Analysis of Property Stolen," in *Repeat Victimization (Crime Prevention Studies, vol. 12)*, eds. Graham Farrell and Ken Pease (Monsey, NY: Criminal Justice Press, 2001), pp. 119–132.
68. Michael Townsley, Ross Homel, and Janet Chaseling, "Infectious Burglaries," *British Journal of Criminology* 43 (2003): 615–634.
69. See, generally, Neal Shover, "Structures and Careers in Burglary," *Journal of Criminal Law, Criminology and Police Science* 63 (1972): 540–549.
70. Richard Stevenson, Lubica Forsythe, and M. V. Weatherburn, "The Stolen Goods Market in New South Wales, Australia: An Analysis of Disposal Avenues and Tactics," *British Journal of Criminology* 41 (Winter 2001): 101–118.
71. Paul Cromwell, James Olson, and D'Aunn Wester Avary, *Breaking and Entering: An Ethnographic Analysis of Burglary* (Newbury Park, CA: Sage, 1991), pp. 48–51.
72. Scott Decker, Richard Wright, Allison Redfern, and Dietrich Smith, "A Woman's Place Is in the Home: Females and Residential Burglary," *Justice Quarterly* 10 (1993): 143–163.
73. Arson Prevention Bureau of Justice, "Key Facts," www.arsonpreventionbureau.org.uk/News/ (accessed October 15, 2003).
74. Nancy Webb, George Sakheim, Luz Towns-Miranda, and Charles Wagner, "Collaborative Treatment of Juvenile Firestarters: Assessment and Outreach," *American Journal of Orthopsychiatry* 60 (1990): 305–310.
75. Pekka Santtila, Helina Haikkanen, Laurence Alison, and Carrie Whyte, "Juvenile Firesetters: Crime Scene Actions and Offender Characteristics," *Legal and Criminological Psychology* 8 (2003): 1–20.
76. John Taylor, Ian Thorne, Alison Robertson, and Ginny Avery, "Evaluation of a Group Intervention for Convicted Arsonists with Mild and Borderline Intellectual Disabilities," *Criminal Behaviour and Mental Health* 12 (2002): 282–294.
77. Scott Turner, "Funding Sparks Effort to Cut Juvenile Arson Rate," *George Street Journal* 27 (January 31, 2003): 1. Available at www.brown.edu/Administration/George_Street_Journal/vol27/27GSJ16f.html.

Chapter 12. Enterprise Crime: White-Collar Crime, Cyber Crime, and Organized Crime

1. Constance Hays, "ImClone Founder Pleads Guilty to 6 Charges," *New York Times*, October 16, 2002, p. A1.
2. Nikos Passas and David Nelken, "The Thin Line between Legitimate and Criminal Enterprises: Subsidy Frauds in the European Community," *Crime, Law, and Social Change* 19 (1993): 223–243.
3. For a thorough review, see David Friedrichs, *Trusted Criminals* (Belmont, CA: Wadsworth, 1996).
4. Kitty Calavita and Henry Pontell, "Savings and Loan aud as Organized Crime: Toward a Conceptual Typology of Corporate Illegality," *Criminology* 31 (1993): 519–548.
5. Mark Haller, "Illegal Enterprise: A Theoretical and Historical Interpretation," *Criminology* 28 (1990): 207–235.
6. Edwin Sutherland, *White-Collar Crime: The Uncut Version* (New Haven, CT: Yale University Press, 1983).
7. Edwin Sutherland, "White-Collar Criminality," *American Sociological Review* 5 (1940): 2–10.
8. Ronald Kramer and Raymond Michalowski, "State-Corporate Crime." Paper presented at the annual meeting of the American Society of Criminology, Baltimore, MD, November 1990.
9. Natalie Taylor, "Under-Reporting of Crime against Small Business: Attitudes towards Police and Reporting Practices," *Policing and Society* 13 (2003): 79–90.
10. National White Collar Crime Center, www.nw3c.org/index.cfm.
11. The 2005 National Public Survey on White Collar Crime, www.nw3c.org/research/site_files.cfm?mode=p.
12. Marshall Clinard and Richard Quinney, *Criminal Behavior Systems: A Typology* (New York: Holt, Rinehart & Winston, 1973), p. 117.
13. Mark Moore, "Notes toward a National Strategy to Deal with White-Collar Crime," in *A National Strategy for Containing White-Collar Crime,* eds. Herbert Edelhertz and Charles Rogovin (Lexington, MA: Lexington Books, 1980), pp. 32–44.
14. North American Securities Administrators Association (NASAA), "Beware of Oil and Gas Schemes, State Securities Regulators Warn Investors, Con Artists May Seek to Exploit Fears over Mideast, Oil Supply," www.nasaa.org/nasaa/abtnasaa/display_top_ story.asp? stid=348 (accessed August 25, 2004).
15. Earl Gottschalk, "Churchgoers Are the Prey as Scams Rise," *Wall Street Journal*, August 7, 1989, p. C1.
16. Internet Crime Complaint Center, "Fraudulent Sites Capitalizing on Relief Efforts of Hurricane Katrina," www.ifccfbi.gov/strategy/katrina_warning.pdf (accessed June 11, 2006).
17. FBI, Operation Bullpen, www.fbi.gov/hq/cid/fc/ec/sm/smoverview.htm (accessed June 11, 2006).
18. Richard Quinney, "Occupational Structure and Criminal Behavior: Prescription Violation of Retail Pharmacists," *Social Problems* 11 (1963): 179–185. See also John Braithwaite, *Corporate Crime in the Pharmaceutical Industry* (London: Routledge and Kegan Paul, 1984).
19. Pam Belluck, "Prosecutors Say Greed Drove Pharmacist to Dilute Drugs," *New York Times*, August 18, 2001, p. 3.
20. FBI press release, April 22, 2002, Kansas City Division.
21. Anish Vashista, David Johnson, and Muhtashem Choudhury, "Securities Fraud," *American Criminal Law Review* 42 (2005): 877–942.
22. James Armstrong, et al., "Securities Fraud," *American Criminal Law Review* 33 (1995): 973–1,016.
23. Scott McMurray, "Futures Pit Trader Goes to Trial," *Wall Street Journal*, May 8, 1990, p. C1; Scott McMurray, "Chicago Pits' Dazzling Growth Permitted a Free-for-All Mecca," *Wall Street Journal*, August 3, 1989, p. A4.
24. *Carpenter v. United States* 484 U.S. 19 (1987). See also John Boland, "The SEC Trims the First Amendment," *Wall Street Journal*, December 4, 1986, p. 28.

25. Amber Poroznuk and Rena Safaraliyeva, "In Azerbaijan, Advocacy and Legal Advice Centre Reduces Extortion from Prostitutes," April 2006, www.transparency.org/publications/newsletter/2006/april_2006/anti_corruption_work/azerbaijan_alac.
26. Charles V. Bagli, "Kickback Investigation Extends to Middle-Class Buildings in New York," *New York Times*, October 14, 1998, p. A19.
27. United Press International, "Minority Leader in N.Y. Senate Is Charged," *Boston Globe*, September 17, 1987, p. 20.
28. Charles R. Babcock and Jonathan Weisman, "Congressman Admits Taking Bribes, Resigns," *Washington Post*, November 29, 2005, p. 1.
29. Monica Davey and John O'Neil, "Ex-Governor of Illinois Is Convicted on All Charges," *New York Times*, April 18, 2006, p. 1.
30. "DeLay Indicted, Steps Down as Majority Leader," *CNN*, September 29, 2005, www.cnn.com/2005/POLITICS/09/28/delay.indict/index. html (accessed June 11, 2006).
31. Disclosure of Payments to Individuals Connected with Broadcasts, U.S. Criminal Code, Title 47 *Chapter 5 Subchapter V* § 508.
32. Marshall Clinard and Peter Yeager, *Corporate Crime* (New York: Free Press, 1980), p. 67.
33. Ibid.
34. Public Law No. 95-213, 101-104, 91 Stat. 1494.
35. Thomas Burton, "The More Baxter Hides Its Israeli Boycott Role, the More Flak It Gets," *Wall Street Journal*, April 25, 1991, p. 1.
36. Foreign Corrupt Practices Act Update, "Schering-Plough Settles FCPA Case with SEC for Payments to Charity Headed by Government Official," http://wilmer.admin.hubbardone.com/files/tbl_s29Publications%5CFileUpload5665%5C4421%5CFCPA%2006–30–04.pdf (accessed June 30, 2004).
37. Adrian Cho, "Hey Buddy . . . Wanna Buy a Moon Rock?" *Science Now*, July 7, 2002, p. 1.
38. Charles McCaghy, *Deviant Behavior* (New York: Macmillan, 1976), p. 178.
39. "While Stocks Last," *The Economist* 364 (September 21, 2002): 64–67.
40. Highlights from Jack L. Hayes International, Inc.'s, 17th Annual Retail Theft Survey, www.hayesinternational.com/thft_srvys.html (accessed April 16, 2006).
41. J. Sorenson, H. Grove, and T. Sorenson, "Detecting Management Fraud: The Role of the Independent Auditor," in *White-Collar Crime, Theory and Research*, eds. G. Geis and E. Stotland (Beverly Hills, CA: Sage, 1980), pp. 221–251.
42. Kurt Eichenwald, "Hospital Chain Cheated U.S. on Expenses, Documents Show," *New York Times*, December 18, 1997, p. B1.
43. Laura Johannes and Wendy Bounds, "Corning Agrees to Pay $6.8 Million to Settle Medicare Billing Charges," *Wall Street Journal*, February 22, 1996, p. B2.
44. Ibid.
45. 42 USC 1320a-7b(b); 42 USC 1320a-7b(b)(3); 42 CFR 1001.952 (regulatory safe harbors). 42 USC 1395nn (codifying "Stark I" and "Stark II" statutes).
46. *United States v. Bishop,* 412 U.S. 346 (1973).
47. Cited in Nancy Frank and Michael Lynch, *Corporate Crime, Corporate Violence* (Albany, NY: Harrow & Heston, 1992), pp. 12–13.
48. Sutherland, "White-Collar Criminality."
49. Kylie Cooper and Adrienne Dedjinou, "Antitrust Violations," *American Criminal Law Review* 42 (2005): 179–221.
50. 15 U.S.C. section 1 (1994).
51. 15 U.S.C. 1–7 (1976).
52. *Northern Pacific Railways v. United States*, 356 U.S. 1 (1958).
53. Tim Carrington, "Federal Probes of Contractors Rise for Year," *Wall Street Journal*, February 23, 1987, p. 50.
54. *Illinois Ex Rel. Madigan v. Telemarketing Associates, Inc., et al.* Number 01-1806 (2003).
55. Environmental Protection Agency, Criminal Investigation Division, www.epa.gov/compliance/criminal/index.html.
56. Andrew Oliveira, Christopher Schenck, Christopher Cole, and Nicole Janes, "Environmental Crimes (Annual Survey of White Collar Crime)," *American Criminal Law Review* 42 (2005): 347–380.
57. Donald Cressey, *Other People's Money: A Study of the Social Psychology of Embezzlement* (Glencoe, IL: Free Press, 1973), p. 96.
58. Rhonda Evans and Dianne Porche, "The Nature and Frequency of Medicare/Medicaid Fraud and Neutralization Techniques among Speech, Occupational, and Physical Therapists," *Deviant Behavior* 26 (2005): 253–271.
59. John A. Byrne, "At Enron, the Environment Was Ripe for Abuse," *BusinessWeek*, February 25, 2002, p. 14.
60. Travis Hirschi and Michael Gottfredson, "Causes of White-Collar Crime," *Criminology* 25 (1987): 949–974.
61. Michael Gottfredson and Travis Hirschi, *A General Theory of Crime* (Stanford, CA: Stanford University Press, 1990), p. 191.
62. This section relies heavily on Daniel Skoler, "White-Collar Crime and the Criminal Justice System: Problems and Challenges," in *A National Strategy for Containing White-Collar Crime*, eds. Herbert Edelhertz and Charles Rogovin (Lexington, MA: Lexington Books, 1980), pp. 57–76.
63. Theodore Hammett and Joel Epstein, *Prosecuting Environmental Crime: Los Angeles County* (Washington, DC: National Institute of Justice, 1993).
64. Information provided by Los Angeles County District Attorney's Office, April 2003.
65. Ronald Burns, Keith Whitworth, and Carol Thompson, "Assessing Law Enforcement Preparedness to Address Internet Fraud," *Journal of Criminal Justice* 32 (2004): 477–493.
66. Michael Benson, Francis Cullen, and William Maakestad, "Local Prosecutors and Corporate Crime," *Crime & Delinquency* 36 (1990): 356–372.
67. Ibid., pp. 369–370.
68. Michael Lynch, Paul Stretesky, and Ronald Burns, "Slippery Business,"*Journal of Black Studies* 34 (2004): 421–440.
69. This section relies heavily on Albert Reiss, Jr., "Selecting Strategies of Social Control over Organizational Life," in *Enforcing Regulation*, eds. Keith Hawkins and John M. Thomas (Boston: Kluwer Publications, 1984), pp. 25–37.
70. Michael Benson, "Emotions and Adjudication: Status Degradation among White-Collar Criminals," *Justice Quarterly* 7 (1990): 515–528; John Braithwaite, *Crime, Shame, and Reintegration* (Sydney: Cambridge University Press, 1989).
71. John Braithwaite, "The Limits of Economism in Controlling Harmful Corporate Conduct," *Law and Society Review* 16 (1981–1982): 481–504.
72. U.S. Department of Justice, Status Report: Criminal Fines: Criminal Enforcement Division, Anti-Trust Division, June 1, 2002.
73. Christopher M. Brown and Nikhil S. Singhvi, "Antitrust Violations," *American Criminal Law Review* 35 (1998): 467–501.
74. Howard Adler, "Current Trends in Criminal Antitrust Enforcement," *Business Crimes Bulletin* (April 1996): 1.
75. Stephen Taub, "Probation for Adelphia's Michael Rigas," March 6, 2006, www.cfo.com/article.cfm/5598021/c_5591729?f=TodayInFinance_Inside (accessed April 17, 2006).
76. David Weisburd, Elin Waring, and Stanton Wheeler, "Class, Status, and the Punishment of White-Collar Criminals," *Law and Social Inquiry* 15 (1990): 223–243.
77. Sean Rosenmerkel, "Wrongfulness and Harmfulness as Components of Seriousness of White-Collar Offenses," *Journal of Contemporary Criminal Justice* 17 (2001): 308–328.
78. Mark Cohen, "Environmental Crime and Punishment: Legal/Economic Theory and Empirical Evidence on Enforcement of Federal Environmental Statutes," *Journal of Criminal Law and Criminology* 82 (1992): 1,054–1,109.

79. Jonathan Lechter, Daniel Posner, and George Morris, "Antitrust Violations," *American Criminal Law Review* 39 (2002): 225–273.
80. Christopher Palmeri, "For the Feds, White-Collar Crime Pays," *BusinessWeek* 3976 (March 20, 2006): 11.
81. Ed Frauenheim, "IDC: Cyberterror and Other Prophecies," CNET News.com, December 12, 2002, http://news.com.com/2100–1001–977780.html (accessed June 11, 2005).
82. Giles Trendle, "An e-jihad against Government?" *EGOV Monitor*, September 2002.
83. Statement of Michael A. Vatis, Director, National Infrastructure Protection Center, FBI, on cyber crime, before the Senate Judiciary Committee, Criminal Justice Oversight Subcommittee and House Judiciary Committee, Crime Subcommittee, Washington, DC, February 29, 2000, www.cybercrime.gov/vatis.htm (accessed July 12, 2005).
84. Deloitte Touche Tohmatsu, 2005 Global Security Survey, www.deloitte.com/ dtt/research/0,1015,sid=1013&cid=85452,00.html.
85. Andreas Philaretou, "Sexuality and the Internet," *Journal of Sex Research* 42 (2005): 180–181.
86. N2H2 communication, www.n2h2.com/index.php.
87. Jeordan Legon, "Sex Sells, Especially to Web Surfers: Internet Porn a Booming, Billion-dollar Industry," CNN, December 11, 2003, www.cnn.com/2003/TECH/internet/12/10/porn.business/ (accessed June 11, 2006).
88. This section relies heavily on CERT Coordination Center Denial of Service Attacks, www.cert.org/tech_tips/denial_of_service.html (accessed September 8, 2005).
89. The Computer Fraud and Abuse Act (CFAA). 18 U.S.C. §1030 (1998).
90. The Digital Millennium Copyright Act, Public Law 105-304 (1998).
91. Title 18, United States Code, Section 2319.
92. Title 17, United States Code, Section 506.
93. Jim Wolf, "Internet Scams Targeted in Sweep: A 10-Day Crackdown Leads to 62 Arrests and 88 Indictments," *Boston Globe*, May 22, 2001, p. A2.
94. Saul Hansell, "U.S. Tally in Online-Crime Sweep: 150 Charged," *New York Times*, August 27, 2004, www.nytimes.com/2004/08/27/technology/27spam.html?ex=1251432000&en=72e62518f208b407&38;ei=5090&38;partner=rssuserland.
95. Elizabeth Woyke and Dan Beucke,"Many Not-So-Happy Returns," *BusinessWeek*, (August 15, 2005): 10.
96. These sections rely on Phishing Activity Trends Report, June 2005, Anti-Phishing Working Group, www.ncjrs.org/spotlight/identity_theft/publications.html#phishing (accessed August 30, 2005); Special Report of "Phishing," 2004, U.S. Department of Justice, Criminal Division, www.ncjrs.org/spotlight/identity_ theft/publications.html#phishing (accessed August 30, 2005).
97. Public Law 98-473, Title H, Chapter XXI, [sections] 2102(a), 98 Stat. 1837, 2190 (1984).
98. Heather Jacobson and Rebecca Green, "Computer Crime," *American Criminal Law Review* 39 (2002): 273–326; Identity Theft and Assumption Act of 1998 (18 U.S.C. S 1028(a)(7)).
99. Comprehensive Crime Control Act of 1984, PL 98-473, 2101-03, 98 Stat. 1837, 2190 (1984), adding 18 USC 1030 (1984); Counterfeit Active Device and Computer Fraud and Abuse Act Amended by PL 99-474, 100 Stat. 1213 (1986) codified at 18 U.S.C. 1030 (Supp. V 1987); Computer Abuse Amendments Act 18 U.S.C. section 1030 (1994); Copyright Infringement Act 17 U.S.C. section 506(a) 1994; Electronic Communications Privacy Act of 198618 U.S.C. 2510–2520 (1988 and Supp. II 1990).
100. Bruce Swartz, Deputy Assistant General, Criminal Division, Justice Department, "Internet Fraud Testimony before the House Energy and Commerce Committee," May 23, 2001.
101. IC3 Annual Internet Fraud Report, January 1, 2004–December 31, 2004, www.ifccfbi.gov/strategy/2004_IC3Report.pdf.
102. Statement of Mr. Bob Weaver, Deputy Special Agent in Charge, New York Field Office, U.S. Secret Service before the House Financial Services Committee, Subcommittee on Financial Institutions and Consumer Credit and the Subcommittee on Oversight and Investigations, U.S. House of Representatives, April 3, 2003.
103. See, generally, President's Commission on Organized Crime, *Report to the President and the Attorney General, The Impact: Organized Crime Today* (Washington, DC: U.S. Government Printing Office, 1986). Herein cited as *Organized Crime Today*.
104. Frederick Martens and Michele Cunningham-Niederer, "Media Magic, Mafia Mania," *Federal Probation* 49 (1985): 60–68.
105. *Organized Crime Today*, pp. 7–8.
106. Alan Block and William Chambliss, *Organizing Crime* (New York: Elsevier, 1981).
107. Alan Block, *East Side / West Side* (New Brunswick, NJ: Transaction Books, 1983), pp. vii, 10–11.
108. Statement for the record of Thomas V. Fuentes, Chief, Organized Crime Section, Criminal Investigative Division, FBI, "Organized Crime," before the House Subcommittee on Finance and Hazardous Materials, September 13, 2000.
109. Donald Cressey, *Theft of the Nation* (New York: Harper & Row, 1969).
110. Dwight Smith, *The Mafia Mystique* (New York: Basic Books, 1975).
111. *Organized Crime Today*, p. 11.
112. David Binder, "In Europe, Sex Slavery Is Thriving Despite Raids," *New York Times*, October 19, 2002, p. A3.
113. Richard A. Ballezza, "YACS Crime Groups: An FBI Major Crime Initiative," *FBI Law Enforcement Bulletin* 67 (1998): 7–13.
114. Omar Bartos, "Growth of Russian Organized Crime Poses Serious Threat," *CJ International* 11 (1995): 8–9.
115. John Tagliabue, "Russian Racket Linked to New York Bank," *New York Times*, September 28, 1999, p. 1.
116. Robert Kelly and Rufus Schatzberg, "Types of Minority Organized Crime: Some Considerations." Paper presented at the annual meeting of the American Society of Criminology, Montreal, November 1987.
117. George Vold, *Theoretical Criminology*, 2nd ed., rev. Thomas Bernard (New York: Oxford University Press, 1979).
118. 18 U.S.C. 1952 (1976).
119. Public Law 91-452, Title IX, 84 Stat. 922 (1970) (codified at 18 U.S.C. 1961–68, 1976).
120. Richard McFeely, "Enterprise Theory of Investigation," *FBI Law Enforcement Bulletin* 70 (2001): 19–26.
121. National Legal Policy Center, "Bonanno Crime Boss Gets Two Life Terms," August 17, 2005, www.nlpc.org/view.asp?action=viewArticle&aid=975.
122. Selwyn Raab, "A Battered and Ailing Mafia Is Losing Its Grip on America," *New York Times*, October 22, 1990, p. 1.
123. Ibid., p. B7.
124. Rebecca Porter, "Prosecutors, Plaintiffs Aim to Curb Internet Gambling," *Trial* 40 (August 2004): 14.

Chapter 13. Public Order Crimes

1. Bruce Steele and Sean Kennedy, "Hustle and Grow: Texas Gay Candidate Tom Malin Was Undone by the Revelation of His Past as an Escort. Why Do So Many Young Gay Men Turn to Hustling? And Why Does Sex Work Remain the Unforgivable Sin?" *The Advocate* 6 (April 11, 2006): 52.
2. "Ex-Prostitute Candidate Loses District 108 Race," *Dallas Morning News*, March 8, 2006, www.dallasnews.com/s/dws/news/elections/2006/stories/030806dnmetproscand.27b26ab.html.
3. Edwin Schur, *Crimes without Victims* (Englewood Cliffs, NJ: Prentice-Hall, 1965).
4. Andrea Dworkin, quoted in "Where Do We Stand on Pornography?" *Ms* (January–February 1994), p. 34.

5. Russel Falck, Jichuan Wang, and Robert Carlson, "The Epidemiology of Physical Attack and Rape among Crack-Using Women," *Violence and Victims* 16 (2001): 79–89.
6. Morris Cohen, "Moral Aspects of the Criminal Law," *Yale Law Journal* 49 (1940): 1,017.
7. See Joel Feinberg, *Social Philosophy* (Englewood Cliffs, NJ: Prentice-Hall, 1973), chaps. 2, 3.
8. *United States v. 12 200-ft Reels of Super 8mm Film,* 413 U.S. 123 (1973), at p. 137.
9. Irving Kristol, "Liberal Censorship and the Common Culture," *Society* 36 (September 1999): 5.
10. Wayne LaFave and Austin Scott, Jr., *Criminal Law* (St. Paul, MN: West, 1986), p. 12.
11. Ibid.
12. Judith Levine, *Harmful to Minors: The Perils of Protecting Children from Sex* (Minneapolis, MN: University of Minnesota Press, 2002).
13. Howard Becker, *Outsiders* (New York: Macmillan, 1963), pp. 13–14.
14. Andrea Friedman, "Sadists and Sissies: Anti-Pornography Campaigns in Cold War America," *Gender and History* 15 (2003): 201–228.
15. Ronald Weitzer, "Moral Crusade against Prostitution," *Society* 43 (2006): 33–38.
16. Amnesty International, www.amnesty.org/ailib/intcam/femgen/fgm1.htm#a1 (accessed February 1, 2006).
17. *Hillary Goodridge et al. v. Department of Public Health & another*. SJC-08860, November 18, 2003.
18. *Lawrence et al. v. Texas*, No. 02-102, June 26, 2003.
19. *Bowers v. Hardwick,* 106 S.Ct. 2841 (1986); reh. den. 107 S.Ct. 29 (1986).
20. See, generally, Spencer Rathus and Jeffery Nevid, *Abnormal Psychology* (Englewood Cliffs, NJ: Prentice-Hall, 1991), pp. 373–411.
21. W. P. de Silva, "Sexual Variations," *British Medical Journal* 318 (1999): 654–655.
22. See, generally, V. Bullogh, *Sexual Variance in Society and History* (Chicago: University of Chicago Press, 1958), pp. 143–144.
23. Spencer Rathus, *Human Sexuality* (New York: Holt, Rinehart and Winston, 1983), p. 463.
24. Charles McCaghy, *Deviant Behavior* (New York: Macmillan, 1976), pp. 348–349.
25. Marian Pitts, Anthony Smith, Jeffrey Grierson, Mary O'Brien, and Sebastian Misson, "Who Pays for Sex and Why? An Analysis of Social and Motivational Factors Associated with Male Clients of Sex Workers," *Archives of Sexual Behavior* 33 (2004): 353–358.
26. Ibid.
27. Michael Waldholz, "HTLV–I Virus Found in Blood of Prostitutes," *Wall Street Journal*, January 5, 1990, p. B2.
28. Monica Prasad, "The Morality of Market Exchange: Love, Money, and Contractual Justice," *Sociological Perspectives* 42 (1999): 181–187.
29. Elizabeth Bernstein, "The Meaning of the Purchase: Desire, Demand and the Commerce of Sex," *Ethnography* 2 (2001): 389–420.
30. David Enrich, "Trafficking in People," *U.S. News & World Report* 131 (July 23, 2001): 34.
31. Charles Winick and Paul Kinsie, *The Lively Commerce* (Chicago: Quadrangle, 1971), p. 58.
32. Mark-David Janus, Barbara Scanlon, and Virginia Price, "Youth Prostitution," in *Child Pornography and Sex Rings*, ed. Ann Wolbert Burgess (Lexington, MA: Lexington Books, 1989), pp. 127–146.
33. Jennifer James, "Prostitutes and Prostitution," in *Deviants: Voluntary Action in a Hostile World*, eds. E. Sagarin and F. Montanino (New York: Scott, Foresman, 1977), p. 384.
34. Hilary Surratt, James Inciardi, Steven Kurtz, and Marion Kiley, "Sex Work and Drug Use in a Subculture of Violence," *Crime & Delinquency* 50 (2004): 43–60.
35. Teela Sanders, *Sex Work: A Risky Business* (Devon, England: Willan Publishing, 2005).
36. Winick and Kinsie, *The Lively Commerce,* pp. 172–173.
37. Paul Goldstein, "Occupational Mobility in the World of Prostitution: Becoming a Madam," *Deviant Behavior* 4 (1983): 267–279.
38. Ibid.
39. Mireya Navarro, "Group Forced Illegal Aliens into Prostitution, U.S. Says," *New York Times*, April 24, 1998, p. A10.
40. Sarah Bahari, "Online Prostitution a Problem on the Web," *Knight Ridder / Tribune News Service*, August 24, 2004, p. K7343.
41. Lisa Kramer and Ellen Berg, "A Survival Analysis of Timing of Entry into Prostitution: The Differential Impact of Race, Educational Level, and Childhood/Adolescent Risk Factors," *Sociological Inquiry* 73 (2003): 511–529.
42. Alyson Brown and David Barrett, "Knowledge of Evil: Child Prostitution and Child Sexual Abuse in Twentieth Century England" (Devon, England: Willan Publishing, 2002).
43. Jocelyn Brown, Patricia Cohen, Henian Chen, Elizabeth Smailes, and Jeffrey Johnson, "Sexual Trajectories of Abused and Neglected Youths," *Journal of Developmental & Behavioral Pediatrics* 25 (2004): 77–83.
44. Gerald Hotaling and David Finkelhor, *The Sexual Exploitation of Missing Children* (Washington, DC: U.S. Department of Justice, 1988).
45. John Potterat, Richard Rothenberg, Stephen Muth, William Darrow, and Lynanne Phillips-Plummer, "Pathways to Prostitution: The Chronology of Sexual and Drug Abuse Milestones," *Journal of Sex Research* 35 (1998): 333–342.
46. Sheila Royo Maxwell and Christopher Maxwell, "Examining the 'Criminal Careers' of Prostitutes within the Nexus of Drug Use, Drug Selling, and Other Illicit Activities," *Criminology* 38 (2000): 787–809.
47. Michael Miner, Jill Flitter, and Beatrice Robinson, "Association of Sexual Revictimization with Sexuality and Psychological Function," *Journal of Interpersonal Violence* 21 (2006): 503–524.
48. Michael Rekart, "Sex-Work Harm Reduction," *The Lancet* 366 (2005): 2,123–2,134.
49. Nancy Romero-Daza, Margaret Weeks, and Merrill Singer, "'Nobody Gives a Damn if I Live or Die': Violence, Drugs, and Street-Level Prostitution in Inner-City Hartford, Connecticut," *Medical Anthropology* 22 (2003): 233–259.
50. Sarah Lantz, "Students Working in the Melbourne Sex Industry: Education, Human Capital and the Changing Patterns of the Youth Labour Market," *Journal of Youth Studies* 8 (2005): 385–401.
51. Barbara G. Brents and Kathryn Hausbeck, "State-Sanctioned Sex: Negotiating Formal and Informal Regulatory Practices in Nevada Brothels," *Sociological Perspectives* 44 (2001): 307–335.
52. Ibid.
53. Mara Keire, "The Vice Trust: A Reinterpretation of the White Slavery Scare in the United States, 1907–1917," *Journal of Social History* 35 (2001): 5–42.
54. Ronald Weitzer, "The Politics of Prostitution in America," in *Sex for Sale*, ed. R. Weitzer (New York: Routledge, 2000), pp. 159–180.
55. Sherry Plaster Carter, Stanley Carter, and Andrew Dannenberg, "Zoning Out Crime and Improving Community Health in Sarasota, Florida: Crime Prevention through Environmental Design," *American Journal of Public Health* 93 (2003): 1,442–1,445.
56. 18 U.S.C. 2423(b) (2000).
57. The Protect Act, Public Law 108-21 on 4/30/2003.
58. Sara K. Andrews, "U.S. Domestic Prosecution of the American International Sex Tourist: Efforts to Protect Children from Sexual Exploitation," *Journal of Criminal Law and Criminology* 94 (2004): 415–453.

59. Mary Margaret Oliver, "Preventing Sexual Exploitation of Children and Teens," *Journal of Law, Medicine & Ethics* 33 (2005): S38–40.
60. James Joyner, "Loophole Lets Rhode Island Prostitutes Work Indoors, Outside the Beltway," www.outsidethebeltway.com/archives/2005/09/loophole_lets_ri_prostitutes_work_indoors_yahoo_news/ (accessed April 20, 2006).
61. Andrea Dworkin, *Pornography* (New York: Dutton, 1989).
62. Annette Jolin, "On the Backs of Working Prostitutes: Feminist Theory and Prostitution Policy," *Crime & Delinquency* 40 (1994): 60–83, at pp. 76–77.
63. Alexa Albert, *Brothel: Mustang Ranch and Its Women* (New York: Random House, 2001).
64. *Merriam-Webster Dictionary* (New York: Pocket Books, 1974), p. 484.
65. Attorney General's Commission, Report on Pornography, *Final Report* (Washington, DC: U.S. Government Printing Office, 1986), pp. 837–901. Hereafter cited as Pornography Commission.
66. Philip Jenkins, *Beyond Tolerance: Child Pornography Online* (New York: New York University Press, 2001).
67. Christopher Bagley, "Diminishing Incidence of Internet Child Pornographic Images," *Psychological Reports* 93 (2003): 305–306.
68. *Report of the Commission on Obscenity and Pornography* (Washington, DC: U.S. Government Printing Office, 1970).
69. Berl Kutchinsky, "The Effect of Easy Availability of Pornography on the Incidence of Sex Crimes," *Journal of Social Issues* 29 (1973): 95–112.
70. Neil Malamuth, Tamara Addison, and Mary Koss, "Pornography and Sexual Aggression: Are There Reliable Effects and Can We Understand Them?" *Annual Review of Sex Research* 11 (2000): 26–94.
71. See Edward Donnerstein, Daniel Linz, and Steven Penrod, *The Question of Pornography* (New York: Free Press, 1987).
72. Edward Donnerstein, "Pornography and Violence against Women," *Annals of the New York Academy of Science* 347 (1980): 277–288; E. Donnerstein and J. Hallam, "Facilitating Effects of Erotica on Aggression against Women," *Journal of Personality and Social Psychology* 36 (1977): 1,270–1,277; Seymour Fishbach and Neil Malamuth, "Sex and Aggression: Proving the Link," *Psychology Today* 12 (1978): 111–122.
73. Malamuth, Addison, and Koss, "Pornography and Sexual Aggression: Are There Reliable Effects and Can We Understand Them?"
74. 354 U.S. 476; 77 S.Ct. 1304 (1957).
75. 413 U.S. 15 (1973).
76. R. George Wright, "Defining Obscenity: The Criterion of Value," *New England Law Review* 22 (1987): 315–341.
77. *Pope v. Illinois*, 107 S.Ct. 1918 (1987).
78. ACLU news release, "*ACLU v. Reno*, Round 2: Broad Coalition Files Challenge to New Federal Net Censorship Law," October 22, 1998.
79. *Ashcroft, Attorney General, et al. v. Free Speech Coalition et al.*, No. 00-795, April 16, 2002.
80. Anthony Flint, "Skin Trade Spreading across U.S.," *Boston Globe*, December 1, 1996, pp. 1, 36–37.
81. Thomas J. Lueck, "At Sex Shops, Fear That Ruling Means the End Is Near," *New York Times*, February 25, 1998, p. 1.
82. David Rohde, "In Giuliani's Crackdown on Porn Shops, Court Ruling Is a Setback," *New York Times*, August 29, 1998, p. A11.
83. ACLU news release, *Reno v. ACLU*, No. 96-511.
84. Ralph Weisheit, "Studying Drugs in Rural Areas: Notes from the Field," *Journal of Research in Crime and Delinquency* 30 (1993): 213–232.
85. Arnold Trebach, *The Heroin Solution* (New Haven, CT: Yale University Press, 1982).
86. James Inciardi, *The War on Drugs* (Palo Alto, CA: Mayfield, 1986), p. 2.
87. See, generally, David Pittman, "Drug Addiction and Crime," in *Handbook of Criminology*, ed. D. Glazer (Chicago: Rand McNally, 1974), pp. 209–232; Board of Directors, National Council on Crime and Delinquency, "Drug Addiction: A Medical, Not a Law Enforcement Problem," *Crime & Delinquency* 20 (1974): 4–9.
88. Associated Press, "Records Detail Royals' Turn-of-Century Drug Use," *Boston Globe*, August 29, 1993, p. 13.
89. See Edward Brecher, *Licit and Illicit Drugs* (Boston: Little, Brown, 1972).
90. James Inciardi, *Reflections on Crime* (New York: Holt, Rinehart and Winston, 1978), pp. 8–10. See also A. Greeley, William McCready, and Gary Theisen, *Ethnic Drinking Subcultures* (New York: Praeger, 1980).
91. Joseph Gusfield, *Symbolic Crusade* (Urbana, IL: University of Illinois Press, 1963), chap. 3.
92. McCaghy, *Deviant Behavior*, p. 280.
93. Ibid.
94. The annual survey is conducted by Lloyd Johnston, Jerald Bachman, and Patrick O'Malley of the Institute of Social Research, University of Michigan, Ann Arbor.
95. Kristin Finn, "Patterns of Alcohol and Marijuana Use at School," *Journal of Research on Adolescence* 16 (2006): 69–77.
96. National Center on Addiction and Substance Abuse, *Teen Tipplers: America's Underage Drinking Epidemic*, rev. ed. (New York: Author, February 2003).
97. C. Bowden, "Determinants of Initial Use of Opioids," *Comprehensive Psychiatry* 12 (1971): 136–140.
98. Marvin Krohn, Alan Lizotte, Terence Thornberry, Carolyn Smith, and David McDowall, "Reciprocal Causal Relationships among Drug Use, Peers, and Beliefs: A Five-Wave Panel Model," *Journal of Drug Issues* 26 (1996): 205–228.
99. R. Cloward and L. Ohlin, *Delinquency and Opportunity: A Theory of Delinquent Gangs* (Glencoe, IL: Free Press, 1960).
100. Lening Zhang, John Welte, and William Wieczorek, "Youth Gangs, Drug Use and Delinquency," *Journal of Criminal Justice* 27 (1999): 101–109.
101. Peter Giancola, "Constructive Thinking, Antisocial Behavior, and Drug Use in Adolescent Boys with and without a Family History of a Substance Use Disorder," *Personality & Individual Differences* 35 (2003): 1,315–1,331.
102. Irene Elkins, Serena King, Matt McGue, and William Iacono, "Personality Traits and the Development of Nicotine, Alcohol, and Illicit Drug Disorders: Prospective Links from Adolescence to Young Adulthood," *Journal of Abnormal Psychology* 115 (2006): 26–39; Joseph Westermeyer and Paul Thuras, "Association of Antisocial Personality Disorder and Substance Disorder Morbidity in a Clinical Sample," *American Journal of Drug and Alcohol Abuse* 31 (2005): 93–120.
103. Daniel Smith, Joanne Davis, and Adrienne Fricker-Elhai, "How Does Trauma Beget Trauma? Cognitions about Risk in Women with Abuse Histories," *Child Maltreatment* 9 (2004): 292–302.
104. Sean Kidd, "The Walls Were Closing in, and We Were Trapped," *Youth & Society* 36 (2004): 30–55.
105. Substance Abuse and Mental Health Services Administration, Office of Applied Studies, "The Relationship between Mental Health and Substance Abuse among Adolescents," Analytic Series: A-9, 1999.
106. Tracy Hampton, "Genes Harbor Clues to Addiction, Recovery," *JAMA: Journal of the American Medical Association* 292 (2004): 321–323.
107. D. W. Goodwin, "Alcoholism and Genetics," *Archives of General Psychiatry* 42 (1985): 171–174.
108. Martha Vungkhanching, Kenneth Sher, Kristina Jackson, and Gilbert Parra, "Relation of Attachment Style to Family History of Alcoholism and Alcohol Use Disorders in Early Adulthood," *Drug & Alcohol Dependence* 75 (2004): 47–54.
109. For a thorough review of this issue, see John Petraitis, Brian Flay, and Todd Miller, "Reviewing Theories of Adolescent Sub-

stance Use: Organizing Pieces in the Puzzle," *Psychological Bulletin* 117 (1995): 67–86.

110. Judith Brook and Li-Jung Tseng, "Influences of Parental Drug Use, Personality, and Child Rearing on the Toddler's Anger and Negativity," *Genetic, Social and General Psychology Monographs* 122 (1996): 107–128.

111. Thomas Ashby Wills, Donato Vaccaro, Grace McNamara, and A. Elizabeth Hirky, "Escalated Substance Use: A Longitudinal Grouping Analysis from Early to Middle Adolescence," *Journal of Abnormal Psychology* 105 (1996): 166–180.

112. Denise Kandel and Mark Davies, "Friendship Networks, Intimacy, and Illicit Drug Use in Young Adulthood: A Comparison of Two Competing Theories," *Criminology* 29 (1991): 441–471.

113. J. S. Mio, G. Nanjundappa, D. E. Verlur, and M. D. DeRios, "Drug Abuse and the Adolescent Sex Offender: A Preliminary Analysis," *Journal of Psychoactive Drugs* 18 (1986): 65–72.

114. D. Baer and J. Corrado, "Heroin Addict Relationships with Parents during Childhood and Early Adolescent Years," *Journal of Genetic Psychology* 124 (1974): 99–103.

115. The National Center on Addiction and Substance Abuse, press release, "Reducing Teen Smoking Can Cut Marijuana Use Significantly," September 16, 2003.

116. John Wallace and Jerald Bachman, "Explaining Racial/Ethnic Differences in Adolescent Drug Use: The Impact of Background and Lifestyle," *Social Problems* 38 (1991): 333–357.

117. John Donovan, "Problem-Behavior Theory and the Explanation of Adolescent Marijuana Use," *Journal of Drug Issues* 26 (1996): 379–404.

118. Xiaojin Chen, Kimberly Tyler, Les Whitbeck, and Dan Hoyt, "Early Sexual Abuse, Street Adversity, and Drug Use among Female Homeless and Runaway Adolescents in the Midwest," *Journal of Drug Issues* 34 (2004): 1–20; John Donovan, "Problem-Behavior Theory and the Explanation of Adolescent Marijuana Use," *Journal of Drug Issues* 26 (1996): 379–404.

119. A. Christiansen, G. T. Smith, P. V. Roehling, and M. S. Goldman, "Using Alcohol Expectancies to Predict Adolescent Drinking Behavior after One Year," *Journal of Counseling and Clinical Psychology* 57 (1989): 93–99.

120. Icek Ajzen, *Attitudes, Personality and Behavior* (Homewood, IL: Dorsey Press, 1988).

121. Judith Brook, Martin Whiteman, Elinor Balka, and Beatrix Hamburg, "African-American and Puerto Rican Drug Use: Personality, Familial, and Other Environmental Risk Factors," *Genetic, Social, and General Psychology Monographs* 118 (1992): 419–438.

122. Bu Huang, Helene White, Rick Kosterman, Richard Catalano, and J. David Hawkins, "Developmental Associations between Alcohol and Interpersonal Aggression during Adolescence," *Journal of Research in Crime and Delinquency* 38 (2001): 64–83.

123. Andrew Golub and Bruce Johnson, *The Rise of Marijuana as the Drug of Choice among Youthful Adult Arrestees* (Washington, DC: National Institute of Justice, 2001).

124. Marvin Dawkins, "Drug Use and Violent Crime among Adolescents," *Adolescence* 32 (1997): 395–406.

125. Department of Health and Human Services National Survey on Drug Use and Health, National Survey on Youth Violence and Illicit Drug Use, Issue 5 (2006), http://oas.samhsa.gov/2k6/youthViolence/youthViolence.htm.

126. Jeffrey Fagan, *Adolescent Violence: A View from the Street*, NIJ Research Preview (Washington, DC: National Institute of Justice, 1998); Eric Baumer, Janet Lauritsen, Richard Rosenfeld, and Richard Wright, "The Influence of Crack Cocaine on Robbery, Burglary, and Homicide Rates: A Cross-City, Longitudinal Analysis," *Journal of Research in Crime and Delinquency* 35 (1998): 316–340; Carolyn Block and Antigone Christakos, "Intimate Partner Homicide in Chicago over 29 Years," *Crime & Delinquency* 41 (1995): 496–526.

127. National Institute of Justice, 2000 Arrestee Drug Abuse Monitoring (Washington, DC: National Institute of Justice, 2003), www.ncjrs.org/txtfiles1/nij/193013.txt (accessed September 8, 2004).

128. Allen Beck, Darrell Gilliard, Lawrence Greenfeld, Caroline Harlow, Thomas Hester, Lewis Jankowski, Tracy Snell, James Stephen, and Danielle Morton, *Survey of State Prison Inmates, 1991* (Washington, DC: Bureau of Justice Statistics, 1993). The survey of prison inmates is conducted by the Bureau of Justice Statistics every five to seven years.

129. George Speckart and M. Douglas Anglin, "Narcotics Use and Crime: An Overview of Recent Research Advances," *Contemporary Drug Problems* 13 (1986): 741–769.

130. Evelyn Wei, Rolf Loeber, and Helene White, "Teasing Apart the Developmental Associations between Alcohol and Marijuana Use and Violence," *Journal of Contemporary Criminal Justice*, 20 (2004): 166–183.

131. Susan Martin, Christopher Maxwell, Helene White, and Yan Zhang, "Trends in Alcohol Use, Cocaine Use, and Crime," *Journal of Drug Issues* 34 (2004): 333–360.

132. M. Douglas Anglin, Elizabeth Piper Deschenes, and George Speckart, "The Effect of Legal Supervision on Narcotic Addiction and Criminal Behavior." Paper presented at the annual meeting of the American Society of Criminology, Montreal, November 1987, p. 2.

133. Speckart and Anglin, "Narcotics Use and Crime: An Overview of Recent Research Advances," p. 752.

134. See Kenneth Jones, Louis Shainberg, and Carter Byer, *Drugs and Alcohol* (New York: Harper and Row, 1979) pp. 137–146.

135. Controlled Substance Act, 21 U.S.C. 848 (1984).

136. Anti–Drug Abuse Act of 1986, Pub. L. No. 99-570, U.S.C. 841 (1986).

137. Anti–Drug Abuse Act of 1988, Pub. L. No. 100-690; 21 U.S.C. 1501; Subtitle A–Death Penalty, Sec. 7001, Amending the Controlled Substances Abuse Act, 21 U.S.C. 848.

138. Eric Jensen, Jurg Gerber, and Ginna Babcock, "The New War on Drugs: Grass Roots Movement or Political Construction?" *Journal of Drug Issues* 21 (1991): 651–667.

139. Fareed Zakaria, "Warlords, Drugs and Votes: Drugs Have Become the Dominating Feature of Afghanistan's Economy, and Corruption Has Infected Every Aspect of Afghan Political Life," *Newsweek*, August 9, 2004 p. 39.

140. Francisco Gutierrez, "Institutionalizing Global Wars: State Transformations in Colombia, 1978–2002: Colombian Policy Directed at Its Wars, Paradoxically, Narrows the Government's Margin of Maneuver Even as It Tries to Expand It," *Journal of International Affairs* 57 (2003): 135–152.

141. David Hayeslip, "Local-Level Drug Enforcement: New Strategies," *NIJ Reports* (March/April 1989): 1.

142. Mark Moore, *Drug Trafficking* (Washington, DC: National Institute of Justice, 1988).

143. Peter Rossi, Richard Berk, and Alec Campbell, "Just Punishments: Guideline Sentences and Normative Consensus," *Journal of Quantitative Criminology* 13 (1997): 267–283.

144. Robert Davis, Arthur Lurigio, and Dennis Rosenbaum, eds., *Drugs and the Community* (Springfield, IL: Charles C Thomas, 1993), pp. xii–xv.

145. Saul Weingart, "A Typology of Community Responses to Drugs," in *Drugs and the Community,* eds. Robert Davis, Arthur Lurigio, and Dennis Rosenbaum (Springfield, IL: Charles C Thomas, 1993), pp. 85–105.

146. Earl Wyson, Richard Aniskiewicz, and David Wright, "Truth and DARE: Tracking Drug Education to Graduation as Symbolic Politics," *Social Problems* 41 (1994): 448–471.

147. Ibid.

148. Dennis Rosenbaum, Robert Flewelling, Susan Bailey, Chris Ringwalt, and Deanna Wilkinson, "Cops in the Classroom: A Longitudinal Evaluation of Drug Abuse Resistance Education (DARE)," *Journal of Research in Crime and Delinquency* 31 (1994): 3–31.

149. Mareanne Zawitz, *Drugs, Crime, and the Justice System* (Washington, DC: U.S. Government Printing Office, 1992), pp. 115–122.
150. John Goldkamp and Peter Jones, "Pretrial Drug-Testing Experiments in Milwaukee and Prince George's County: The Context of Implementation," *Journal of Research in Crime and Delinquency* 29 (1992): 430–465; Chester Britt, Michael Gottfredson, and John Goldkamp, "Drug Testing and Pretrial Misconduct: An Experiment on the Specific Deterrent Effects of Drug Monitoring Defendants on Pretrial Release," *Journal of Research in Crime and Delinquency* 29 (1992): 62–78. See, generally, Peter Greenwood and Franklin Zimring, *One More Chance* (Santa Monica, CA: Rand Corporation, 1985).
151. See, generally, Greenwood and Zimring, *One More Chance*.
152. Tracy Beswick, David David, Jenny Bearn, Michael Gossop, Michael Sian Rees, and John Strang, "The Effectiveness of Combined Naloxone/Lofexidine in Opiate Detoxification: Results from a Double-Blind Randomized and Placebo-Controlled Trial," *American Journal on Addictions* 12 (2003): 295–306.
153. George De Leon, Stanley Sacks, Graham Staines, and Karen McKendrick, "Modified Therapeutic Community for Homeless Mentally Ill Chemical Abusers: Treatment Outcomes," *American Journal of Drug and Alcohol Abuse* 26 (2000): 461–480.
154. Michael French, H. J. Jeanne Salome, Jody Sindelar, and A. Thomas McLellan, "Benefit–Cost Analysis of Ancillary Social Services in Publicly Supported Addiction Treatment," February 1, 1999, data supplied by the Center for Substance Abuse Research (CESAR), College Park, MD 20740.
155. Jerome Platt, "Vocational Rehabilitation of Drug Abusers," *Psychological Bulletin* 117 (1995): 416–433.
156. Celia Lo, "Sociodemographic Factors, Drug Abuse, and Other Crimes: How They Vary among Male and Female Arrestees," *Journal of Criminal Justice*, 32 (2004): 399–409.
157. The National Center on Addiction and Substance Abuse, *Shoveling Up: The Impact of Substance Abuse on State Budgets* (New York, 2001).
158. Office of National Drug Control Policy, *National Drug Control Strategy: FY 2004 Budget Summary* (Washington, DC, February 2003).
159. Charlie LeDuff, "Cocaine Quietly Reclaims Its Hold as Good Times Return," *New York Times*, August 21, 2000, p. A1.
160. Ethan Nadelmann, "The U.S. Is Addicted to War on Drugs," *Globe and Mail*, May 20, 2003, p. 1; Nadelmann, "America's Drug Problem," *Bulletin of the American Academy of Arts and Sciences* 65 (1991): 24–40.
161. See, generally, Ralph Weisheit, *Drugs, Crime and the Criminal Justice System* (Cincinnati, OH: Anderson, 1990).
162. David Courtwright, "Should We Legalize Drugs? History Answers No," *American Heritage* (February/March 1993): 43–56.
163. Drug Abuse Warning Network, 2003: Interim National Estimates of Drug-Related Emergency Department Visits, http://dawninfo.samhsa.gov/files/DAWN_ED_Interim2003.pdf (accessed April 18, 2006).
164. Kathryn Ann Farr, "Revitalizing the Drug Decriminalization Debate," *Crime & Delinquency* 36 (1990): 223–237.

Chapter 14. The Criminal Justice System

1. For a detailed analysis of this work, see Samuel Walker, "Origins of the Contemporary Criminal Justice Paradigm: The American Bar Foundation Survey, 1953–1969," *Justice Quarterly* 9 (1992): 47–76.
2. President's Commission on Law Enforcement and the Administration of Justice, *The Challenge of Crime in a Free Society* (Washington, DC: U.S. Government Printing Office, 1967).
3. See Public Law 90-351, Title I—Omnibus Crime Control Safe Streets Act of 1968, 90th Congress, June 19, 1968.
4. FBI, *Crime in the United States, 2004* (Washington, DC: Government Printing Office, 2006).
5. Matthew Durose and Patrick Langan, *Felony Sentences in State Courts, 2002* (Washington, DC: Bureau of Justice Statistics, 2004), www.ojp.usdoj.gov/bjs/pub/ascii/fssc02.txt.
6. Bureau of Justice Statistics, www.ojp.usdoj.gov/bjs/sandlle.htm (accessed April 25, 2006).
7. See Albert Reiss Jr., *Police and the Public* (New Haven, CT: Yale University Press, 1972).
8. Matthew Durose, Erica Schmitt, and Patrick A. Langan, *Contacts between Police and the Public: Findings from the 2002 National Survey* (Washington, DC: Bureau of Justice Statistics, 2005), www.ojp.usdoj.gov/bjs/pub/ascii/cpp02.txt (accessed April 25, 2006); Joel Garner, Christopher Maxwell, and Cederick Heraux, "Characteristics Associated with the Prevalence and Severity of Force Used by the Police," *Justice Quarterly* 19 (2002): 705–747; William Terrill and Stephen Mastrofski, "Situational and Officer-Based Determinants of Police Coercion," *Justice Quarterly* 19 (2002): 215–248.
9. Colin Loftin, David McDowall, Brian Wiersema, and Adam Dobrin, "Underreporting of Justifiable Homicides Committed by Police Officers in the United States, 1976–1998," *American Journal of Public Health* 93 (2003): 1,117–1,121; FBI, "Law Enforcement Officers Killed and Assaulted, 2004," www.fbi.gov/ ucr/killed/2004/table1.htm (accessed April 25, 2006).
10. Wesley Skogan, "Asymmetry in the Impact of Encounters with Police," *Policing & Society* 16 (2006): 99–126.
11. James Hawdon and John Ryan, "Police-Resident Interactions and Satisfaction with Police: An Empirical Test of Community Policing Assertions," *Criminal Justice Policy Review* 14 (2003): 55–74.
12. Yili Xu, Mora Fiedler, and Karl Flaming, "Discovering the Impact of Community Policing: The Broken Windows Thesis, Collective Efficacy, and Citizens' Judgment" *Journal of Research in Crime and Delinquency* 42 (2005): 147–186.
13. James Nolan, Norman Conti, and Jack McDevitt, "Situational Policing: Neighbourhood Development and Crime Control," *Policing & Society* 14 (2004): 99–118.
14. Xu, Fiedler, and Flaming, "Discovering the Impact of Community Policing: The Broken Windows Thesis, Collective Efficacy, and Citizens' Judgment."
15. Ling Ren, Liqun Cao, Nicholas Lovrich, and Michael Gaffney, "Linking Confidence in the Police with the Performance of the Police: Community Policing Can Make a Difference," *Journal of Criminal Justice* 33 (January/February 2005): 55–66.
16. Robert Davis, Pedro Mateu-Gelabert, and Joel Miller, "Can Effective Policing Also Be Respectful? Two Examples in the South Bronx," *Police Quarterly* 8 (2005): 229–247.
17. Kevin Ford, Daniel Weissbein, and Kevin Plamondon, "Distinguishing Organizational from Strategy Commitment: Linking Officers' Commitment to Community Policing to Job Behaviors and Satisfaction," *Justice Quarterly* 20 (2003): 159–186.
18. Matthew Durose and Patrick A. Langan, *State Court Sentencing of Convicted Felons, 2002* (Washington, DC: Bureau of Justice Statistics, February 2004).
19. Cassia Spohn, Dawn Beichner, and Erika Davis-Frenzel, "Prosecutorial Justifications for Sexual Assault Case Rejection: Guarding the 'Gateway to Justice'," *Social Problems* 48 (2001): 206–235.
20. *Powell v. Alabama*, 287 U.S. 45, 53 S.Ct. 55, 77 L.Ed. 158 (1932); *Gideon v. Wainwright*, 372 U.S. 335, 83 S.Ct. 792, 9 L.Ed. 2d 799 (1963); *Argersinger v. Hamlin*, 407 U.S. 25, 92 S.Ct. 2006, 32 L.Ed. 2d 530 (1972).
21. *Wiggins v. Smith, Warden*, No. 02-311 [Decided June 26, 2003].
22. Herbert L. Packer, *The Limits of the Criminal Sanction* (Palo Alto, CA: Stanford University Press, 1968), p. 159.
23. Barbara Boland, Catherine Conly, Paul Mahanna, Lynn Warner, and Ronald Sones, *The Prosecution of Felony Arrests, 1987* (Washington, DC: Bureau of Justice Statistics, 1990), p. 3.

24. See Donald Newman, *Conviction: The Determination of Guilt or Innocence without Trial* (Boston: Little, Brown, 1966).
25. Vanessa Barker, "The Politics of Punishing," *Punishment & Society* 8 (2006): 5–32.
26. Richard Timothy Coupe and Laurence Blake, "The Effects of Patrol Workloads and Response Strength on Arrests at Burglary Emergencies," *Journal of Criminal Justice* 33 (2005): 239–255.
27. Paul Cassell, "How Many Criminals Has Miranda Set Free?" *Wall Street Journal*, March 1, 1995, p. A15.
28. Jon Gould and Stephen Mastrofski, "Suspect Searches: Assessing Police Behavior Under the U.S. Constitution," *Criminology & Public Policy* 3 (2004): 315–362.
29. David Garland, *Punishment and Modern Society* (Chicago: University of Chicago Press, 1990).
30. The most often cited of these is Douglas Lipton, Robert Martinson, and Judith Wilks, *The Effectiveness of Correctional Treatment: A Survey of Treatment Evaluation Studies* (New York: Praeger, 1975).
31. "Many State Legislatures Focused on Crime in 1995, Study Finds," *Criminal Justice Newsletter*, January 17, 1996, pp. 1–2.
32. David Fogel, *We Are the Living Proof* (Cincinnati, OH: Anderson, 1975). See also David Fogel, *Justice as Fairness* (Cincinnati: Anderson, 1980).
33. Travis Pratt, "Race and Sentencing: A Meta-Analysis of Conflicting Empirical Research Results," *Journal of Criminal Justice* 26 (1998): 513–525.
34. Packer, *The Limits of the Criminal Sanction.*
35. Eric Lotke, "Hobbling a Generation: Young African-American Men in Washington, D.C.'s Criminal Justice System—Five Years Later," *Crime & Delinquency* 44 (1998): 355–366.
36. Roy Austin and Mark Allen, "Racial Disparity in Arrest Rates as an Explanation of Racial Disparity in Commitment to Pennsylvania's Prisons," *Journal of Research in Crime and Delinquency* 37 (2000): 200–220.
37. Anthony Petrosino and Carolyn Petrosino, "The Public Safety Potential of Megan's Law in Massachusetts: An Assessment from a Sample of Criminal Sexual Psychopaths," *Crime & Delinquency* 43 (1999): 140–158; "New Laws Said to Raise Demands on Justice Information Systems," *Criminal Justice Newsletter,* September 17, 1996, pp. 3–4.
38. Jim Yardley, "Convicted in Murder Case, Man Cleared 7 Years Later," *New York Times*, October 29, 1998, p. 11.
39. Talia Roitberg Harmon and William S. Lofquist, "Too Late for Luck: A Comparison of Post-Furman Exonerations and Executions of the Innocent," *Crime & Delinquency* 51 (2005): 498–520.
40. Richard McCorkle, "Research Note: Punish and Rehabilitate? Public Attitudes Toward Six Common Crimes," *Crime & Delinquency* 39 (1993): 240–252.
41. D. A. Andrews, Ivan Zinger, R. D. Hoge, James Bonta, Paul Gendreau, and Francis Cullen, "Does Correctional Treatment Work? A Clinically-Relevant and Psychologically-Informed Meta-Analysis," *Criminology* 28 (1990): 369–404.
42. John Hepburn, "Recidivism among Drug Offenders Following Exposure to Treatment," *Criminal Justice Policy Review* 16 (2005): 237–259.
43. Denise Gottfredson, "Participation in Drug Treatment Court and Time to Rearrest," *Justice Quarterly* 21 (2004): 637–658.
44. Mark Lipsey and David Wilson, "Effective Intervention for Serious Juvenile Offenders: A Synthesis of Research," in *Serious and Violent Juvenile Offenders: Risk Factors and Successful Interventions,* eds. Rolf Loeber and David Farrington (Thousand Oaks, CA: Sage, 1998), pp. 39–53.
45. Francis Cullen, John Paul Wright, Shayna Brown, Melissa Moon, Michael Blankenship, and Brandon Applegate, "Public Support for Early Intervention Programs: Implications for a Progressive Policy Agenda," *Crime & Delinquency* 44 (1998): 187–204.
46. Shawn Bushway, "The Impact of an Arrest on the Job Stability of Young White American Men," *Journal of Research in Crime and Delinquency* 35 (1998): 454–479.
47. Edwin Lemert, "The Juvenile Court—Quest and Realities," in President's Commission on Law Enforcement and the Administration of Justice, *Task Force Report: Juvenile Delinquency and Youth Crime* (Washington, DC: U.S. Government Printing Office, 1967).
48. Craig Hemmens and Katherine Bennett, "Juvenile Curfews and the Courts: Judicial Response to a Not-So-New Crime Control Strategy," *Crime & Delinquency* 45 (1999): 99–121.
49. James Austin and Barry Krisberg, "The Unmet Promise of Alternatives to Incarceration," *Crime & Delinquency* 28 (1982): 3–19. For an alternative view, see Arnold Binder and Gilbert Geis, "Ad Populum Argumentation in Criminology: Juvenile Diversion as Rhetoric," *Criminology* 30 (1984): 309–333.
50. Herbert Bianchi, *Justice as Sanctuary* (Bloomington, IN: Indiana University Press, 1994); Nils Christie, "Conflicts as Property," *British Journal of Criminology* 17 (1977): 1–15; L. Hulsman, "Critical Criminology and the Concept of Crime," *Contemporary Crises* 10 (1986): 63–80.
51. Larry Tifft, "Foreword," in Dennis Sullivan, *The Mask of Love* (Port Washington, NY: Kennikat Press, 1980), p. 6.
52. Robert Davis, Barbara Smith, and Laura Nickles, "The Deterrent Effect of Prosecuting Domestic Violence Misdemeanors," *Crime & Delinquency* 44 (1998): 434–442.
53. John Braithwaite, "Setting Standards for Restorative Justice," *British Journal of Criminology* 42 (2002): 563–577.
54. Christopher Cooper, "Patrol Police Officer Conflict Resolution Processes," *Journal of Criminal Justice* 25 (1997): 87–101.
55. Robert Coates, Mark Umbreit, and Betty Vos, "Responding to Hate Crimes through Restorative Justice Dialogue," *Contemporary Justice Review* 9 (2006): 7–21; Kathleen Daly and Julie Stubbs, "Feminist Engagement with Restorative Justice," *Theoretical Criminology* 10 (2006): 9–28.
56. Lois Presser and Patricia Van Voorhis, "Values and Evaluation: Assessing Processes and Outcomes of Restorative Justice Programs," *Crime & Delinquency* 48 (2002): 162–189.
57. David Altschuler, "Community Justice Initiatives: Issues and Challenges in the U.S. Context," *Federal Probation* 65 (2001): 28–33.
58. Elliott Currie, *Crime and Punishment in America* (New York: Henry Holt, 1998). See also Elliott Currie, *Confronting Crime: An American Challenge* (New York: Pantheon, 1985); Elliott Currie, *Reckoning: Drugs, the Cities, and the American Future* (New York: Hill and Wang, 1993).

Glossary

acquaintance robbery Robbery in which the victim or victims are people the robber knows.

active precipitation Aggressive or provocative behavior of victims that results in their victimization.

adolescent-limited offender One who follows the most common criminal trajectory, in which antisocial behavior peaks in adolescence and then diminishes.

adversary system U.S. method of criminal adjudication in which prosecution (the state) and defense (the accused) each try to bring forward evidence and arguments, with guilt or innocence ultimately decided by an impartial judge or jury.

aggravated rape Rape involving multiple offenders, weapons, and victim injuries.

aging out The fact that people commit less crime as they mature.

alien conspiracy theory The belief, adhered to by the federal government and many respected criminologists, that organized crime is a direct offshoot of a criminal society that was imported to the United States by Europeans who have a policy of restricting membership to people of their own ethnic background.

American Dream The goal of accumulating material goods and wealth through individual competition; the process of being socialized to pursue material success and to believe it is achievable.

androgens Male sex hormones.

anomie A lack of norms or clear social standards. Because of rapidly shifting moral values, the individual has few guides to what is socially acceptable.

anomie theory View that anomie results when socially defined goals (such as wealth and power) are universally mandated but access to legitimate means (such as education and job opportunities) is stratified by class and status.

antisocial personality Combination of traits, such as hyperactivity, impulsivity, hedonism, and inability to empathize with others, that make a person prone to deviant behavior and violence; also referred to as sociopathic or psychopathic personality.

appeal Taking a criminal case to a higher court on the grounds that the defendant was found guilty because of legal error or violation of constitutional rights; a successful appeal may result in a new trial.

appellate court Court that reviews trial court procedures to determine whether they have complied with accepted rules and constitutional doctrines.

arousal theory The view that people seek to maintain a preferred level of arousal but vary in how they process sensory input. A need for high levels of environmental stimulation may lead to aggressive, violent behavior patterns.

arraignment The step in the criminal justice process when the accused is brought before the trial judge, formal charges are read, defendants are informed of their rights, a plea is entered, bail is considered, and a trial date is set.

arrest The taking into police custody of an individual suspected of a crime.

arson The willful, malicious burning of a home, building, or vehicle.

assault Does not require actual touching but involves either attempted battery or intentionally frightening the victim by word or deed.

attention deficit hyperactivity disorder (ADHD) A developmentally inappropriate lack of attention, along with impulsivity and hyperactivity.

authority conflict pathway Path to a criminal career that begins with early stubborn behavior and defiance of parents.

bail A money bond intended to ensure that the accused will return for trial.

battery Offensive touching, such as slapping, hitting, or punching a victim.

behavior modeling The process of learning behavior (notably, aggression) by observing others. Aggressive models may be parents, criminals in the neighborhood, or characters on television or in movies.

behavior theory The view that all human behavior is learned through a process of social reinforcement (rewards and punishment).

Bill of Rights The first 10 amendments to the U.S. Constitution, including guarantees against unreasonable search and seizure, self-incrimination, and cruel punishment.

biosocial theory Approach to criminology that focuses on the interaction between biological and social factors as they relate to crime.

bipolar disorder An emotional disturbance in which moods alternate between periods of wild elation and deep depression.

booking Fingerprinting, photographing, and recording personal information of a suspect in police custody.

booster Professional shoplifter who steals with the intention of reselling stolen merchandise.

bucketing Skimming customer trading profits by falsifying trade information.

burglary Entering a home by force, threat, or deception with intent to commit a crime.

capable guardians Effective deterrents to crime, such as police or watchful neighbors.

capital punishment The execution of criminal offenders; the death penalty.

cheater theory A theory suggesting that a subpopulation of men has evolved with genes that incline them toward extremely low parental involvement. Sexually aggressive, they use deceit for sexual conquest of as many females as possible.

Chicago School Group of urban sociologists who studied the relationship between environmental conditions and crime.

child abuse Any physical or emotional trauma to a child for which no reasonable explanation, such as an accident or ordinary disciplinary practices, can be found.

child sexual abuse The exploitation of children through rape, incest, and molestation by parents or other adults.

chiseling Using illegal means to cheat an organization, its consumers, or both, on a regular basis.

chronic offenders (career criminals) Small group of persistent offenders who account for a majority of all criminal offenses.

churning Repeated, excessive, and unnecessary buying and selling of a client's stock.

classical criminology The theoretical perspective suggesting that (1) people have free will to choose criminal or conventional behaviors; (2) people choose to commit crime for reasons of greed or personal need; and (3) crime can be controlled only by the fear of criminal sanctions.

cleared crimes Crimes are considered cleared when at least one person is arrested, charged, and turned over to the court for prosecution, or when some element beyond police control, such as the offender leaving the country, precludes the physical arrest of an offender.

Code of Hammurabi The first written criminal code, developed in Babylonia about 2000 BC.

cognitive theory Psychological perspective that focuses on mental processes: how people perceive and mentally represent the world around them and solve problems.

collective efficacy Social control exerted by cohesive communities, based on mutual trust, including intervention in the supervision of children and maintenance of public order.

commitment to conformity A strong personal investment in conventional institutions, individuals, and processes that prevents people from engaging in behavior that might jeopardize their reputation and achievements.

common law Early English law, developed by judges, which became the standardized law of the land in England and eventually formed the basis of the criminal law in the United States.

community policing A style of policing that requires departments to reshape their forces into community change agents in order to work with citizens to reduce crime at the neighborhood level.

compensation Financial aid awarded to crime victims to repay them for their loss and injuries; may cover medical bills, loss of wages, loss of future earnings, and/or counseling.

compensation Financial aid awarded to crime victims to repay them for their loss and injuries; may cover medical bills, loss of wages, loss of future earnings, and/or counseling.

compliance strategies Methods of controlling white-collar crime that rely on the threat of economic sanctions or civil penalties to control potential violators, creating a marketplace incentive to obey the law.

concentration effect As working- and middle-class families flee inner-city poverty areas, the most disadvantaged population is consolidated in urban ghettos.

conduct disorder (CD) A pattern of repetitive behavior in which the rights of others or the social norms are violated.

confidence game A swindle set up to separate victims from their money, many involving a get-rich-quick scheme, often with illegal overtones so that the victim will be afraid or embarrassed to call the police.

conflict theory The view that human behavior is shaped by interpersonal conflict and that those who maintain social power will use it to further their own ends.

conflict view The belief that criminal behavior is defined by those in a position of power to protect and advance their own self-interest.

consensus view The belief that the majority of citizens in a society share common values and agree on what behaviors should be defined as criminal.

consent The victim of rape must prove that she in no way encouraged, enticed, or misled the accused rapist.

constructive possession A legal fiction that applies to situations in which persons voluntarily give up physical custody of their property but still retain legal ownership.

contagion effect People become deviant when they are influenced by others with whom they are in close contact.

convictability Existence of conditions surrounding a criminal case that indicate it has a good chance of a conviction.

corporate (organizational) crime Powerful institutions or their representatives willfully violate the laws that restrain these institutions from doing social harm or require them to do social good.

courtroom work group Prosecution, defense, and judges working together to resolve criminal cases quickly and efficiently through plea bargaining.

covert pathway Path to a criminal career that begins with minor underhanded behavior and progresses to fire starting and theft.

crime An act, deemed socially harmful or dangerous, that is specifically defined, prohibited, and punished under the criminal law.

crime control model View that the overriding purpose of the justice system is to protect the public, deter criminal behavior, and incapacitate known criminals; favors speedy, efficient justice and punishment.

crime discouragers People who serve as guardians of property or people.

criminal justice Referring to the agencies of social control, such as police departments, the courts, and correctional institutions, that handle criminal offenders.

criminal justice system The agencies of government—police, courts, and corrections—responsible for apprehending, adjudicating, sanctioning, and treating criminal offenders.

criminal law The written code that defines crimes and their punishments.

criminology The scientific study of the nature, extent, cause, and control of criminal behavior.

crisis intervention Emergency counseling for crime victims.

critical criminology The view that crime is a product of the capitalist system.

critical feminism Approach that explains both victimization and criminality among women in terms of gender inequality, patriarchy, and the exploitation of women under capitalism.

cultural deviance theory Branch of social structure theory that sees strain and social disorganization together resulting in a unique lower-class culture that conflicts with conventional social norms.

cultural transmission Process whereby values, beliefs, and traditions are handed down from one generation to the next.

culture conflict Result of exposure to opposing norms, attitudes, and definitions of right and wrong, moral and immoral.

culture of poverty A separate lower-class culture, characterized by apathy, cynicism, helplessness, and mistrust of social institutions such as schools, government agencies, and the police that is passed from one generation to the next.

cyber crime Use of the instruments of modern technology for criminal purposes.

cyber theft Use of computer networks for criminal profits. Illegal copyright infringement, identity theft, and Internet securities fraud are examples of cyber theft.

cycle of violence Victims of crime, especially childhood abuse, are more likely to commit crimes themselves.

date rape A rape that involves people who are in some form of courting relationship.

death squads Government-sanctioned covert military or paramilitary groups who carry out assassinations of political opponents and others whom government officials consider undesirable, such as ethnic minority group members.

decriminalized Having criminal penalties reduced rather than eliminated.

defendant In criminal proceedings, the person accused of violating the law.

defense attorney Person responsible for protecting the constitutional rights of the accused and presenting the best possible legal defense; represents a defendant from initial arrest through trial, sentencing, and any appeal.

defensible space The principle that crime can be prevented or displaced by modifying the physical environment to reduce the opportunity individuals have to commit crime.

deliberation Planning a criminal act after careful thought rather than carrying it out on impulse.

delinquent subculture A value system adopted by lower-class youths that is directly opposed to that of the larger society.

demystify To unmask the true purpose of law, justice, or other social institutions.

denial-of-service attack Extorting money from Internet service users by threatening to prevent them from accessing the service.

desist To spontaneously stop committing crime.

determinate sentencing Principle that all offenders who commit the same crime should receive the same sentence.

developmental theory The view that criminality is a dynamic process, influenced by social experiences as well as individual characteristics. Developmental factors include biological, social, and psychological structures and processes.

deviance Behavior that departs from the social norm but is not necessarily criminal.

deviance amplification Process whereby secondary deviance pushes offenders out of mainstream society and locks them into an escalating cycle of deviance, apprehension, labeling, and criminal self-identity.

deviant place theory The view that victimization is primarily a function of where people live.

differential association theory The view that people commit crime when their social learning leads them to perceive more definitions favoring crime than favoring conventional behavior.

differential opportunity The view that lower-class youths, whose legitimate opportunities are limited, join gangs and pursue criminal careers as alternative means to achieve universal success goals.

diffusion An effect that occurs when efforts to prevent one crime unintentionally prevent another.

discouragement An effect that occurs when crime control efforts targeting a particular locale help reduce crime in surrounding areas and populations.

discretion The use of personal decision making by those carrying out police, judicial, and sanctioning functions within the criminal justice system.

disorder Any type of psychological problem (formerly labeled neurotic or psychotic), such as anxiety disorders, mood disorders, and conduct disorders.

displacement An effect that occurs when crime control efforts simply move or redirect offenders to less heavily guarded alternative targets.

disposition Sentencing of a defendant who has been found guilty; usually involves a fine, probation, or incarceration.

diversion programs Programs of rehabilitation that remove offenders from the normal channels of the criminal justice process, thus avoiding the stigma of a criminal label.

dizygotic (DZ) twins Fraternal (nonidentical) twins.

drift Movement in and out of delinquency, shifting between conventional and deviant values.

due process model View that focuses on protecting the civil rights of those accused of crime.

early onset The view that repeat offenders begin their criminal careers at a very young age.

economic compulsive behavior Violence committed by drug users to support their habit.

edgework The excitement or exhilaration of successfully executing illegal activities in dangerous situations.

egalitarian families Husband and wife share similar positions of power at home and in the workplace. Sons and daughters have equal freedom.

ego The part of the personality developed in early childhood that helps control the id and keep people's actions within the boundaries of social convention.

eldercide Murder of a senior citizen.

embezzlement A type of larceny in which someone who is trusted with property fraudulently converts it to his or her own use or for the use of others.

enterprise crime Use of illegal tactics to gain profit in the marketplace. Enterprise crimes can involve both the violation of law in the course of an otherwise legitimate occupation or the sale and distribution of illegal commodities.

enterprise theory of investigation (ETI) A standard investigation tool of the FBI that focuses on criminal enterprise and investigation attacks on the structure of the criminal enterprise rather than on criminal acts viewed as isolated incidents.

equipotentiality The view that all humans are born with equal potential to learn and achieve.

eros The life instinct, which drives people toward self-fulfillment and enjoyment.

e-tailing fraud Using the Internet to illegally buy or sell merchandise on the Internet.

ex post facto law A law applied retroactively to punish acts that were not crimes before its passage, or one that raises the grade of an offense, or that renders an act punishable in a more severe manner than it was when committed.

exclusionary rule The rule that evidence against a defendant may not be presented in court if it was obtained in violation of the defendant's rights.

exploitation (of victims) Forcing victims to pay for services to which they have a clear right.

expressive crimes Offenses committed not for profit or gain but to vent rage, anger, or frustration.

extinction An effect that occurs when crime reduction programs produce a short-term positive effect, but benefits dissipate as criminals adjust to new conditions.

false pretenses (fraud) Misrepresenting a fact in a way that causes a deceived victim to give money or property to the offender.

felony A serious offense that carries a penalty of imprisonment, usually for one year or more, and may entail loss of political rights.

felony murder A killing accompanying a felony, such as robbery or rape.

fence A buyer and seller of stolen merchandise.

filicide Murder of an older child.

first-degree murder Killing a person after premeditation and deliberation.

focal concerns Values, such as toughness and street smarts, that have evolved specifically to fit conditions in lower-class environments.

front running Placing broker's personal orders ahead of a customer's large order to profit from the market effects of the trade.

general deterrence A crime control policy that depends on the fear of criminal penalties, convincing the potential law violator that the pains associated with crime outweigh its benefits.

general strain theory (GST) The view that multiple sources of strain interact with an individual's emotional traits and responses to produce criminality.

General Theory of Crime (GTC) According to Gottfredson and Hirschi, a developmental theory that modifies social control theory by integrating concepts from biosocial, psychological, routine activities, and rational choice theories.

globalization The process of creating transnational markets, politics, and legal systems and forming a global economy.

grand jury A group of citizens chosen to hear testimony in secret and to issue formal criminal accusations (indictments).

grand larceny Theft of money or property of substantial value, punished as a felony.

hate crimes (bias crimes) Violent acts directed toward a particular person or members of a group merely because the targets share a discernible racial, ethnic, religious, or gender characteristic.

hung jury A jury that is unable to agree on a decision, thus leaving the case unresolved and open for a possible retrial.

hypoglycemia A condition that occurs when glucose (sugar) in the blood falls below levels necessary for normal and efficient brain functioning.

id The primitive part of people's mental makeup, present at birth, that represents unconscious biological drives for food, sex, and other life-sustaining necessities. The id seeks instant gratification without concern for the rights of others.

identity theft Using the Internet to steal someone's identity and/or impersonate the victim in order to conduct illicit transactions such as committing fraud using the victim's name and identity.

incapacitation effect The idea that keeping offenders in confinement will eliminate the risk of their committing further offenses.

incarceration Confinement in jail or prison.

index (Part I) crimes The eight most serious offenses included in the UCR: murder, rape, assault, robbery, burglary, arson, larceny, and motor vehicle theft.

indictment A written accusation returned by a grand jury charging an individual with a specified crime, based on the prosecutor's presentation of probable cause.

infanticide Murder of a very young child.

influence peddling Using one's institutional position to grant favors and sell information to which one's co-conspirators are not entitled.

information A filing before an impartial lower-court judge who decides whether the case should go forward (alternative to grand jury).

information technology (IT) All forms of technology used to create, store, retrieve, and exchange data in all its various forms, including electronic, voice, and still image.

information-processing theory Theory that focuses on how people process, store, encode, retrieve, and manipulate information to make decisions and solve problems.

insider trading Illegal buying of stock in a company based on information provided by someone who has a fiduciary interest in the company, such as an employee or an attorney or accountant retained by the firm. Federal laws and the rules of the Securities and Exchange Commission require that all profits from such trading be returned and provide for both fines and a prison sentence.

institutional anomie theory The view that anomie pervades U.S. culture because the drive for material wealth dominates and undermines social and community values.

instrumental crimes Offenses designed to improve the financial or social position of the criminal.

instrumental theory Sees criminal law and the criminal justice system as capitalist instruments for controlling the lower class.

integrated theories Models of crime causation that weave social and individual variables into a complex explanatory chain.

interactionist view The belief that those with social power are able to impose their values on society as a whole, and these values then define criminal behavior.

interdisciplinary Involving two or more academic fields.

international terrorism Terrorism involving citizens or the territory of more than one country.

interrogation The questioning of a suspect in police custody.

involuntary or negligent manslaughter A killing that occurs when a person's acts are negligent and without regard for the harm they may cause others.

jail Institution, usually run by the county, for short-term detention of those convicted of misdemeanors and those awaiting trial or other judicial proceedings.

justice model View that emphasizes fairness and equal treatment in criminal procedures and sentencing.

La Cosa Nostra A national syndicate of 25 or so Italian-dominated crime families who control crime in distinct geographic areas.

landmark decision A ruling by the U.S. Supreme Court that serves as a precedent for similar legal issues; it often influences the everyday operating procedures of police agencies, trial courts, and corrections institutions.

larceny Taking for one's own use the property of another, by means other than force or threats on the victim or forcibly breaking into a person's home or workplace; theft.

latent trait A stable feature, characteristic, property, or condition, present at birth or soon after, that makes some people crime-prone over the life course.

latent trait theories Theoretical views that criminal behavior is controlled by a master trait, present at birth or soon after, that remains stable and unchanging throughout a person's lifetime.

law of criminal procedure Judicial precedents that define and guarantee the rights of criminal defendants and control the various components of the criminal justice system.

left realism Approach that sees crime as a function of relative deprivation under capitalism and favors pragmatic, community-based crime prevention and control.

liberal feminist theory A view of crime that suggests that the social and economic role of women in society controls their crime rates.

life-course persister One of the small group of offenders whose criminal career continues well into adulthood.

life-course theories Theoretical views studying changes in criminal offending patterns over a person's entire life. Are there conditions or events that occur later in life that influence the way people behave, or is behavior predetermined by social or personal conditions at birth?

lifestyle theories Views on how people become crime victims because of lifestyles that increase their exposure to criminal offenders.

Mafia A group that originated in Italy and Sicily and now controls racketeering in major U.S. cities.

mandatory sentences A statutory requirement that a certain penalty shall be carried out in all cases of conviction for a specified offense or series of offenses.

manslaughter Homicide without malice.

marginalization Displacement of workers, pushing them outside the economic and social mainstream.

marital exemption The formerly accepted tradition that a legally married husband could not be charged with raping his wife.

masculinity hypothesis The view that women who commit crimes have biological and psychological traits similar to those of men.

mass murder The killing of four or more victims by one or a few assailants within a single event.

merchant privilege laws Legislation that protects retailers and their employees from lawsuits if they arrest and detain a suspected shoplifter on reasonable grounds.

middle-class measuring rods The standards by which authority figures, such as teachers and employers, evaluate lower-class youngsters and often prejudge them negatively.

Miranda rights Rights of criminal defendants, including the right against self-incrimination and right to counsel, spelled out in the case of *Miranda v. Arizona*.

misdemeanor A minor crime usually punished by a short jail term and/or a fine.

monozygotic (MZ) twins Identical twins.

mood disorder A condition in which the prevailing emotional mood is distorted or inappropriate to the circumstances.

moral entrepreneur A person who creates moral rules that reflect the values of those in power rather than any objective, universal standards of right and wrong.

Mosaic Code The laws of the ancient Israelites, found in the Old Testament of the Judeo-Christian Bible.

motivated offenders People willing and able to commit crimes.

murder The unlawful killing of a human being with malice aforethought.

naive check forgers Amateurs who cash bad checks because of some financial crisis but have little identification with a criminal subculture.

narcissistic personality disorder A pattern of traits and behaviors that indicate infatuation and fixation with one's self to the exclusion of all others and the egotistic and ruthless pursuit of one's gratification, dominance, and ambition.

narcotic A drug that produces sleep and relieves pain, such as heroin, morphine, and opium; a habit-forming drug.

National Crime Victimization Survey (NCVS) The ongoing victimization study conducted jointly by the Justice Department and the U.S. Census Bureau that surveys victims about their experiences with law violation.

National Incident-Based Reporting System (NIBRS) Program that requires local police agencies to provide a brief account of each incident and arrest within 22 crime patterns, including incident, victim, and offender information.

nature theory The view that intelligence is largely determined genetically and that low intelligence is linked to criminal behavior.

negative affective states Anger, frustration, and adverse emotions produced by a variety of sources of strain.

neglect Not providing a child with the care and shelter to which he or she is entitled.

neurophysiology The study of brain activity.

neurotransmitters Chemical compounds that influence or activate brain functions.

neutralization techniques Methods of rationalizing deviant behavior, such as denying responsibility or blaming the victim.

neutralization theory The view that law violators learn to neutralize conventional values and attitudes, enabling them to drift back and forth between criminal and conventional behavior.

noninterventionist model View that arresting and labeling offenders does more harm than good, that youthful offenders in particular should be diverted into informal treatment programs, and that minor offenses should be decriminalized.

nurture theory The view that intelligence is not inherited but is largely a product of environment. Low IQ scores do not cause crime but may result from the same environmental factors.

obscenity Material that violates community standards of morality or decency and has no redeeming social value.

occasional criminals Offenders who do not define themselves by a criminal role or view themselves as committed career criminals.

offender-specific The idea that offenders evaluate their skills, motives, needs, and fears before deciding to commit crime.

offense-specific The idea that offenders react selectively to the characteristics of particular crimes.

oppositional defiant disorder (ODD) A pattern of negativistic, hostile, and defiant behavior lasting at least six months, during which a child often loses temper, often argues with adults, often actively defies or refuses to comply with adults' requests or rules, often deliberately annoys people, often blames others for his or her mistakes or misbehavior, is often touchy or easily annoyed by others, is often angry and resentful, and is often spiteful or vindictive.

organized crime Illegal activities of people and organizations whose acknowledged purpose is profit through illegitimate business enterprise.

overt pathway Path to a criminal career that begins with minor aggression, leads to physical fighting, and eventually escalates to violent crime.

paraphilia Bizarre or abnormal sexual practices that may involve nonhuman objects, humiliation, or children.

parental efficacy Parents who are supportive and effectively control their children in a noncoercive way.

parole Conditional early release from prison, with the offender serving the remainder of the sentence in the community under the supervision of a parole officer.

Part II crimes All crimes, including index crimes.

passive precipitation Personal or social characteristics of victims that make them attractive targets for criminals; such victims may unknowingly either threaten or encourage their attackers.

paternalistic families Father is breadwinner and rule maker; mother has menial job or is homemaker only. Sons are granted greater freedom than daughters.

patriarchal Male-dominated.

payola The practice of record companies paying radio stations to play songs without making listeners aware of the bribes.

peacemaking Approach that considers punitive crime control strategies to be counterproductive and favors the use of humanistic conflict resolution to prevent and control crime.

penology Subarea of criminology that focuses on the correction and control of criminal offenders.

persistence The idea that those who started their delinquent careers early and who committed serious violent crimes throughout adolescence were the most likely to persist as adults.

personality The reasonably stable patterns of behavior, including thoughts and emotions, that distinguish one person from another.

petit (petty) larceny Theft of a small amount of money or property, punished as a misdemeanor.

phishing (carding and spoofing) Illegally acquiring personal information, such as bank passwords and credit card numbers, by masquerading as a trustworthy person or business in what appears to be an official electronic communication, such as an e-mail or instant message. The term phishing is a play on "fishing" for financial information and passwords with increasingly sophisticated lures.

pilferage Systematic theft of company property.

plea bargain Agreement between prosecution and defense in which the accused pleads guilty in return for a reduction of charges, a more lenient sentence, or some other consideration.

population All people who share a particular characteristic, such as all high school students or all police officers.

pornography Sexually explicit books, magazines, films, or tapes intended to provide sexual titillation and excitement for paying customers.

positivism The branch of social science that uses the scientific method of the natural sciences and suggests that human behavior is a product of social, biological, psychological, or economic forces.

post-traumatic stress disorder (PTSD) Psychological reaction to a highly stressful event; symptoms may include depression, anxiety, flashbacks, and recurring nightmares.

power The ability of persons and groups to control behavior of others, to shape public opinion, and to define deviance.

power–control theory The view that gender differences in crime are a function of economic power (class position, one- versus two-earner families) and parental control (paternalistic versus egalitarian families).

precedent A rule derived from previous judicial decisions and applied to future cases; the basis of common law.

preemptive deterrence Efforts to prevent crime through community organization and youth involvement.

preliminary hearing Alternative to a grand jury, in which an impartial lower-court judge decides whether there is probable cause sufficient for a trial.

premeditation Considering the criminal act beforehand, which suggests that it was motivated by more than a simple desire to engage in an act of violence.

premenstrual syndrome (PMS) A condition that involves symptoms including depression, anxiety, fatigue, irritability, headaches, abdominal swelling, and inability to concentrate, which occur in relation to the menstrual cycle and may interfere with a woman's life.

primary deviance A norm violation or crime with little or no long-term influence on the violator.

primary prevention programs Programs, such as substance abuse clinics and mental health associations, that seek to treat personal problems before they manifest themselves as crime.

prison (penitentiary) State or federally operated facility for the incarceration of felony offenders sentenced by the criminal courts.

pro bono Free legal counsel provided to indigent defendants by private attorneys as a service to the profession and the community.

probable cause Evidence of a crime, and of a suspect's involvement in it, sufficient to warrant an arrest.

probation Conditional release of a convicted offender into the community under the supervision of a probation officer and subject to certain conditions.

problem behavior syndrome (PBS) A cluster of antisocial behaviors that may include family dysfunction, substance abuse, smoking, precocious sexuality and early pregnancy, educational underachievement, suicide attempts, sensation seeking, and unemployment, as well as crime.

problem-oriented policing Proactive form of policing: Rather than responding to crime after it occurs, police identify and respond to potential problems before they occur.

professional criminals Offenders who make a significant portion of their income from crime.

Prohibition The period from 1919 until 1933, when the Eighteenth Amendment to the U.S. Constitution outlawed the sale of alcohol; also known as the "noble experiment."

prosecutor Public official who represents the government in criminal proceedings, presenting the case against the accused.

prostitution The granting of nonmarital sexual access for remuneration.

psychodynamic (psychoanalytic) theory Theory originated by Freud that the human personality is controlled by unconscious mental processes developed early in childhood, involving the interaction of id, ego, and superego.

psychopharmacological relationship When violence is the direct consequence of ingesting mood-altering substances.

public defender Attorney employed by the state whose job is to provide free legal counsel to indigent defendants.

public order crime Behavior that is outlawed because it threatens the general well-being of society and challenges its accepted moral principles.

racial threat theory As the size of the black population increases, the perceived threat to the white population increases, resulting in a greater amount of social control imposed against blacks.

Racketeer Influenced and Corrupt Organization Act (RICO) Federal legislation that enables prosecutors to bring additional criminal or civil charges against people engaged in two or more acts prohibited by 24 existing federal and 8 state laws. RICO features monetary penalties that allow the government to confiscate all profits derived from criminal activities. Originally intended to be used against organized criminals, RICO has also been used against white-collar criminals.

rape The carnal knowledge of a female forcibly and against her will.

rational choice theory The view that crime is a function of a decision-making process in which the potential offender weighs the potential costs and benefits of an illegal act.

reaction formation Irrational hostility evidenced by young delinquents, who adopt norms directly opposed to middle-class goals and standards that seem impossible to achieve.

recidivism Repetition of criminal behavior.

recognizance Pledge by the accused to return for trial, which may be accepted in lieu of bail.

reflected appraisal When parents are alienated from their children, their negative labeling reduces their children's self-image and increases delinquency.

rehabilitation Treatment of criminal offenders that is aimed at preventing future criminal behavior.

rehabilitation model View that sees criminals as victims of social injustice, poverty, and racism and suggests that appropriate treatment can change them into productive, law-abiding citizens.

relative deprivation Envy, mistrust, and aggression resulting from perceptions of economic and social inequality.

reliable Producing consistent results from one measurement to another.

replacement An effect that occurs when criminals try new offenses they had previously avoided because situational crime prevention programs neutralized their crime of choice.

restitution Permitting an offender to repay the victim or do useful work in the community rather than face the stigma of a formal trial and a court-ordered sentence.

restorative justice Using humanistic, nonpunitive strategies to right wrongs and restore social harmony.

restorative justice model View that emphasizes the promotion of a peaceful, just society through reconciliation and reintegration of the offender into society.

retrospective reading The reassessment of a person's past to fit a current generalized label.

right to counsel The right of a person accused of crime to the assistance of a defense attorney in all criminal prosecutions.

road rage Violent assault by a motorist who loses control while driving.

robbery Taking or attempting to take anything of value from the care, custody, or control of a person or persons by force or threat of force or violence and/or by putting the victim in fear.

role exit behaviors Strategies such as running away or contemplating suicide used by young girls unhappy with their status in the family.

routine activities theory The view that victimization results from the interaction of three everyday factors: the availability of suitable targets, the absence of capable guardians, and the presence of motivated offenders.

sampling Selecting a limited number of people for study as representative of a larger group.

schizophrenia A severe disorder marked by hearing nonexistent voices, seeing hallucinations, and exhibiting inappropriate responses.

scientific method Using verifiable principles and procedures for the systematic acquisition of knowledge; typically involves formulating a problem, creating a hypothesis, and collecting data through observation and experiment, to verify the hypothesis.

secondary deviance A norm violation or crime that comes to the attention of significant others or social control agents, who apply a negative label with long-term consequences for the violator's self-identity and social interactions.

secondary prevention programs Programs that provide treatment such as psychological counseling to youths and adults after they have violated the law.

second-degree murder A person's wanton disregard for the victim's life and his or her desire to inflict serious bodily harm on the victim, which results in the victim's death.

seductions of crime The situational inducements or immediate benefits that draw offenders into law violations.

self-control A strong moral sense that renders a person incapable of hurting others or violating social norms.

self-control theory According to Gottfredson and Hirschi, the view that the cause of delinquent behavior is an impulsive personality. Kids who are impulsive may find that their bond to society is weak.

self-report survey A research approach that requires subjects to reveal their own participation in delinquent or criminal acts.

sentencing circle A peacemaking technique in which offenders, victims, and other community members are brought together in an effort to formulate a sanction that addresses the needs of all.

serial killer A person who kills three or more persons in three or more separate events.

Sherman Antitrust Act Federal law that subjects to criminal or civil sanctions any person "who shall make any contract or engage in any combination or conspiracy" in restraint of interstate commerce.

shield laws Laws that protect women from being questioned about their sexual history unless it directly bears on the case.

shoplifting The taking of goods from retail stores.

situational crime prevention A method of crime prevention that seeks to eliminate or reduce particular crimes in narrow settings.

situational inducement Short-term influence on a person's behavior, such as financial problems or peer pressure, which increases risk taking.

snitch Amateur shoplifter who does not self-identify as a thief but who systematically steals merchandise for personal use.

social bonds The ties that bind people to society, including relationships with friends, family, neighbors, teachers, and employers. Elements of the social bond include commitment, attachment, involvement, and belief.

social capital Positive relations with individuals and institutions that are life sustaining.

social class Segment of the population whose members are at a relatively similar economic level and who share attitudes, values, norms, and an identifiable lifestyle.

social control theory The view that people commit crime when the forces binding them to society are weakened or broken.

social disorganization theory Branch of social structure theory that focuses on the breakdown of institutions such as the family, school, and employment in inner-city neighborhoods.

social learning theory The view that people learn to be aggressive by observing others acting aggressively to achieve some goal or being rewarded for violent acts.

social process theory The view that criminality is a function of people's interactions with various organizations, institutions, and processes in society.

social reaction (labeling) theory The view that people become criminals when labeled as such and when they accept the label as a personal identity.

social structure theory The view that disadvantaged economic class position is a primary cause of crime.

socialization Process of human development and enculturation. Socialization is influenced by key social processes and institutions.

sociobiology The view that human behavior is motivated by inborn biological urges to survive and preserve the species.

sociological criminology Approach to criminology, based on the work of Quetelet and Durkheim, that focuses on the relationship between social factors and crime.

specific deterrence The view that criminal sanctions should be so powerful that offenders will never repeat their criminal acts.

spree killer A killer of multiple victims whose murders occur over a relatively short span of time and often follow no discernible pattern.

stalking A course of conduct directed at a specific person that involves repeated physical or visual proximity, nonconsensual communication, or verbal, written, or implied threats sufficient to cause fear in a reasonable person.

status frustration A form of culture conflict experienced by lower-class youths because social conditions prevent them from achieving success as defined by the larger society.

statutory crimes Crimes defined by legislative bodies in response to changing social conditions, public opinion, and custom.

statutory rape Sexual relations between an underage minor female and an adult male.

stigmatize To apply negative labeling with enduring effects on a person's self-image and social interactions.

strain The anger, frustration, and resentment experienced by people who believe they cannot achieve their goals through legitimate means.

strain theory Branch of social structure theory that sees crime as a function of the conflict between people's goals and the means available to obtain them.

stratified society People grouped according to economic or social class; characterized by the unequal distribution of wealth, power, and prestige.

structural theory Based on the belief that criminal law and the criminal justice system are means of defending and preserving the capitalist system.

subculture A set of values, beliefs, and traditions unique to a particular social class or group within a larger society.

subculture of violence A segment of society in which violence has become legitimized by the custom and norms of that group.

successful degradation ceremony A course of action or ritual in which someone's identity is publicly redefined and destroyed and they are thereafter viewed as socially unacceptable.

suitable targets Objects of crime (persons or property) that are attractive and readily available.

superego Incorporation within the personality of the moral standards and values of parents, community, and significant others.

surplus value The difference between what workers produce and what they are paid, which goes to business owners as profits.

swindle (sting) A white-collar crime in which people use their institutional or business position to trick others out of their money.

systematic forgers Professionals who make a living by passing bad checks.

systemic link A link between drugs and violence that occurs when drug dealers turn violent in their competition with rival gangs.

target hardening strategy Locking goods into place or using electronic tags and sensing devices as means of preventing shoplifting.

target removal strategy Displaying dummy or disabled goods as a means of preventing shoplifting.

temperance movement The drive to prohibit the sale of alcohol in the United States, culminating in ratification of the Eighteenth Amendment in 1919.

terrorism Premeditated, politically motivated violence perpetrated against noncombatant targets by subnational groups or clandestine agents, usually intended to influence an audience.

terrorist group Any group practicing, or that has significant subgroups that practice, international terrorism.

testosterone The principal male hormone.

thanatos The death instinct, which produces self-destruction.

"three strikes" Laws that require an offender to serve life in prison after being convicted of a third felony.

trait theory The view that criminality is a product of abnormal biological or psychological traits.

transitional neighborhood An area undergoing a shift in population and structure, usually from middle-class residential to lower-class mixed use.

truth in sentencing The requirement that inmates serve a greater percentage of their sentence behind bars before they are eligible for early release mechanisms such as parole.

turning points According to Laub and Sampson, the life events that alter the development of a criminal career.

underclass The lowest social stratum in any country, whose members lack the education and skills needed to function successfully in modern society.

Uniform Crime Report (UCR) Large database, compiled by the FBI, of crimes reported and arrests made each year throughout the United States.

USA Patriot Act (USAPA) An act that gives sweeping new powers to domestic law enforcement and international intelligence agencies in an effort to fight terrorism, to expand the definition of terrorist activities, and to alter sanctions for violent terrorism.

utilitarianism The view that people's behavior is motivated by the pursuit of pleasure and the avoidance of pain.

valid Actually measuring what one intends to measure; relevant.

victim precipitation theory The view that victims may initiate, either actively or passively, the confrontation that leads to their victimization.

victimless crime Public order crime that violates the moral order but has no specific victim other than society as a whole.

victim–offender reconciliation programs (VORPs) Mediated face-to-face encounters between victims and their attackers, designed to produce restitution agreements and, if possible, reconciliation.

victimologists Criminologists who focus on the victims of crime.

victimology The study of the victim's role in criminal events.

victim–witness assistance programs Government programs that help crime victims and witnesses; may include compensation, court services, and/or crisis intervention.

virility mystique The belief that males must separate their sexual feelings from needs for love, respect, and affection.

voluntary or nonnegligent manslaughter A killing committed in the heat of passion or during a sudden quarrel that provoked violence.

warez Refers to efforts of organized groups to download and sell copyrighted software in violation of its license.

white-collar crime Any business-related act that uses deceit, deception, or dishonesty to carry out criminal enterprise.

white-collar crime Illegal acts that capitalize on a person's status in the marketplace. White-collar crimes may include theft, embezzlement, fraud, market manipulation, restraint of trade, and false advertising.

workplace violence Violence such as assault, rape, or murder committed at the workplace.

Name Index

C

L

S

Subject Index

D

T

U

Photo Credits

This page constitutes an extension of the copyright page. We have made every effort to trace the ownership of all copyrighted material and to secure permission from copyright holders. In the event of any question arising as to the use of any material, we will be pleased to make the necessary corrections in future printings. Thanks are due to the following authors, publishers, and agents for permission to use the material indicated.

Inside front cover.

student and teacher: © AP Images/*The News & Advance*/Jill Nance; **tattooed body:** © Elmer Martinez/AFP/Getty Images; **death penalty protest:** © AP Images/Harry Cabluck

Chapter 1.

1: © AP Images/Tina Fineberg; **3:** The Image Works; **9:** Reuters/DOD/HO/Landov; **16:** A. C. Cooper Ltd; by permission of The Inner Temple, London; **19:** © AP Images/Jane Rosenberg

Chapter 2.

23: © Erik S. Lesser/Getty Images; **27:** inset, Marvin Nauman/FEMA photo; **36:** © Simon Taplin/Corbis; **45:** © Fairfax County Police/Handout/Reuters/Corbis; **49:** © AP Images/*The Telegram & Gazette*/Betty Jenewin

Chapter 3.

52: © AP Images/Tina Fineberg; **57:** © AP Images/*Kokomo Tribune*/Tim Bath; **61:** © AP Images/Mike Derer; **62:** inset, © AP Images/Charles Rex Arbogast; **67:** © AP Images/Pool/Brian Ray

Chapter 4.

71: © David McNew/Getty Images; **77:** © AP Images/Los Angeles Police Department; **79:** © National Pictures/Topham/The Image Works; **82:** © Michael Newman/PhotoEdit. All rights reserved; **87:** © AP Images/*Tampa Tribune*/David Kadlubowski

Chapter 5.

92: © J. Redmond/*Ventura County Star*/Corbis Sygma; **100:** Dr. Alan Zametkin/Clinical Brain Imaging, courtesy of Office of Scientific Information, NIMH; **102:** © AP Images/*Jackson Citizen-Patriot*/Bob Keys; **109:** inset, © David J. Phillip/Pool/Reuters/Corbis; **116:** © AP Images/Steven Senne

Chapter 6.

119: © Elmer Martinez/AFP/Getty Images; **128:** © Eric Fowke/PhotoEdit; **131:** © Andrew Lichtenstein/Corbis; **144:** © AP Images/Charlie Riedel

Chapter 7.

146: © AP Images/Ed Andrieski; **148:** © AP Images/*The Jackson Sun*/Helen Comer; **161:** © AP Images/*Independent Mall*/Ken Ruinard; **166:** © AP Images/John Miller; **167:** © AP Images

Chapter 8.

173: © AP Images/Francois Mori; **180:** © Richard Clement/Reuters/Landov; **181:** © AP Images/Jeff Chiu; **182:** inset, © AP Images/Chris Gardner; **185:** © A. Ramey/PhotoEdit; **188:** © AP Images/Harry Cabluck

Chapter 9.

197: © Volusia County Sheriff's Office via Getty Images; **203:** © Photo Courtesy Attorney James Stokes/Getty Images; **207:** © AP Images; **217:** © David McNew/Getty Images; **219:** © AP Images/*The News & Advance*/Jill Nance

Chapter 10.

223: © AP Images/Leslie Mazoch; **227:** © Les Stone/Sygma/Corbis; **229:** © Getty Images; **234:** © AP Images/Roy Dabner; **238:** © AP Images/Kathy Johnson; **239:** © Mark Wilson/Getty Images; **240:** © AP Images/*Morning Telegraph*/Tom Worner; **244:** © Mark Peterson/Corbis; **254:** inset, © Mike Stewart/Corbis Sygma

Chapter 11.

257: © AP Images/Alan Diaz; **259:** Roy 20 CVii f. 41v British Library/Bridgeman Art Library; **262:** inset, © Seth Wenig/Landov; **265:** inset, © Louis Lanzano/*Bloomberg News*/Landov; **271:** © AP Images/Bebeto Matthews; **276:** © AP Images

Chapter 12.

279: © AP Images/Louis Lanzano; **285:** © Chip Somodevilla/Getty Images; **289:** inset, © Peter Morgan/Reuters/Corbis; **296:** © Daniel Berehulak/Getty Images; **304:** © Desmond Boylan/Reuters/Landov

Chapter 13.

310: © AP Images/Charles Dharapak; **315:** © AP Images/Angela Rowlings; **318:** © AP Images/Brad Horn; **329:** © AP Images/Victoria Arocho; **334:** © AP Images/Stephanie S. Cordle

Chapter 14.

339: © Kimberly White/Reuters/Corbis; **345:** top, © AP Images/Louis Lanzano; **345:** bottom, © Seth Wenig/Reuters/Corbis; **348:** © AP Images; **351:** © AP Images/Alan Diaz; **358:** © Shannon Stapleton/Reuters Newmedia/Corbis; **361:** © Scott Olson/Getty Images

TO THE OWNER OF THIS BOOK:

I hope that you have found *Criminology: The Core*, Third Edition useful. So that this book can be improved in a future edition, would you take the time to complete this sheet and return it? Thank you.

School and address: ______________________________

____

Department: ______________________________

Instructor's name: ______________________________

1. What I like most about this book is: ______________________________

____

____

2. What I like least about this book is: ______________________________

____

____

3. My general reaction to this book is: ______________________________

____

____

4. The name of the course in which I used this book is: ______________________________

____

5. Were all of the chapters of the book assigned for you to read? ______________________________

   If not, which ones weren't? ______________________________

6. In the space below, or on a separate sheet of paper, please write specific suggestions for improving this book and anything else you'd care to share about your experience in using this book.

____

____

____

____

____

____

____

DO NOT STAPLE. TAPE HERE. DO NOT STAPLE. TAPE HERE.

FOLD HERE

NO POSTAGE NECESSARY IF MAILED IN THE UNITED STATES

BUSINESS REPLY MAIL
FIRST-CLASS MAIL PERMIT NO. 34 BELMONT CA

POSTAGE WILL BE PAID BY ADDRESSEE

Attn: Chris Caldeira, Criminal Justice Editor

Wadsworth/Thomson Learning
10 Davis Dr
Belmont CA 94002-9801

FOLD HERE

OPTIONAL:

Your name: ______________________________ Date: ____________________

May we quote you, either in promotion for *Criminology: The Core,* Third Edition, or in future publishing ventures?

Yes: __________ No: __________

Sincerely yours,

Larry J. Siegel